THE COMPLETE
Cooking Light
COOKBOOK

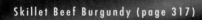
Skillet Beef Burgundy (page 317)

THE COMPLETE

Cooking Light

COOKBOOK

Compiled and Edited by
Cathy A. Wesler

Oxmoor
House

WE'RE HERE FOR YOU!

We at Oxmoor House are dedicated to serving you with reliable information that expands your imagination and enriches your life. We welcome your comments and suggestions. Please write us at:

Oxmoor House, Inc.
Editor, The Complete Cooking Light. Cookbook
2100 Lakeshore Drive
Birmingham, AL 35209

To order additional publications, call 1-205-877-6560.

Cover: Blueberry Pound Cake (page 133) and Vanilla-Buttermilk Ice Cream (page 174)

Back cover: (clockwise from top left) Fruit-and-Honey Spinach Salad (page 396), Greek Feta Burgers (page 426) and Steak Fries (page 499), Scallops and Pasta With Pistachio Pesto (page 235), Banana Pudding (page 169)

Oxmoor House, Inc.

Editor-in-Chief: Nancy Fitzpatrick Wyatt
Senior Foods Editor: Katherine M. Eakin
Senior Editor, Copy and Homes:
    Olivia Kindig Wells
Art Director: James Boone

The Complete Cooking Light Cookbook
Editor: Cathy A. Wesler, R.D.
Copy Editors: Jacqueline B. Giovanelli,
    Catherine Ritter Scholl
Associate Art Director: Cynthia R. Cooper
Senior Designer: Melissa Jones Clark
Editorial Assistant: Heather Averett
Test Kitchens Director: Elizabeth Tyler Luckett
Assistant Test Kitchens Director:
    Julie Christopher
Recipe Editor: Gayle Hays Sadler
Test Kitchens Staff: Rebecca Mohr Boggan;
    Gretchen Feldtman, R.D.; Regan Jones, R.D.;
    Natalie E. King; Jan A. Smith
Senior Photographer: Jim Bathie
Photographer: Brit Huckabay
Senior Photo Stylist: Kay E. Clarke
Photo Stylist: Virginia R. Cravens
Director, Production and Distribution: Phillip Lee
Associate Production Manager: Theresa L. Beste
Production Assistant: Faye Porter Bonner
Publishing Systems Administrator: Rick Tucker

Contributors
Editorial: Susan M. McIntosh, M.S., R.D.
Nutrition: Caroline Grant, M.S., R.D.
Proofreaders: Dolores Hydock, Kathryn Stroud
Indexer: Mary Ann Laurens
Copy Assistant: Jane Lorberau
Test Kitchens: Leigh Mullinax; Kathleen Royal
    Phillips; Kate M. Wheeler, R.D.
Photographer: Howard L. Puckett
Photo Stylists: Cindy Manning Barr,
    Melanie J. Clarke

Cooking Light

Editor: Doug Crichton
Executive Editors: Nathalie Dearing, Rod Davis
Managing Editor: Billy R. Sims
Senior Editors:
    Ellen Templeton Carroll, M.S., R.D.
    (projects); Lisa Delaney (Healthy Living);
    Jill G. Melton, M.S., R.D. (food)
Food Editor: Mary S. Creel, M.S., R.D.
Editorial Coordinator: Carol C. Noe
Associate Editors: Kerri Westenberg
Assistant Editors: Melissa Ewey,
    Krista Ackerbloom Yates, M.S., R.D.
Beauty Editor: Martha Schindler
Art Director: Susan Waldrip Dendy
Assistant Art Director: Lori Bianchi Nichols
Designers: Maya Metz Logue, Paul T. Marince
Photographers: Becky Luigart-Stayner,
    Randy Mayor
Photo Stylists: Lydia E. DeGaris,
    Mary Catherine Muir
Assistant Photo Stylist: Jan Gautro
Test Kitchens Director: Rebecca J. Pate
Food Stylist: Kellie Gerber Kelley
Test Kitchens Staff: Martha Condra,
    Missy Frechette, M. Kathleen Kanen,
    John Kirkpatrick, Julie Walton
Copy Chief: Tim W. Jackson
Copy Editors: Lisa C. Bailey, Ritchey Halphen
Production Editors: Hazel R. Eddins,
    Liz Rhoades
Office Manager: Stacey L. Strawn
Editorial Assistants: Su Reid,
    Joyce McCann Swisdak, Ann Taylor

CONTENTS

WELCOME to *The Complete Cooking Light Cookbook*

Ours was a daunting but delicious task: Select the top 10 percent of the 10,000 recipes *Cooking Light* magazine has published since its launch in 1987. Then create a mega-mall of a cookbook so incredible, so comprehensive, that it's the only one anybody will ever need.

As you thumb through these pages, you'll quickly realize that this is more than just another cookbook. It's about a way of *thinking* about cooking as much as it is about what goes on in your kitchen all week long. Its recipes reflect the magazine's usual high standards of nutrition and ease of preparation, but they're also part of a much larger sense of purpose. This cookbook is a comprehensive road map for an enjoyable lifelong journey along the path of healthy living. Such a life is based on what you eat as much as anything else, and what you eat is the direct result of what makes you happy. And because great taste is the guiding hand behind every recipe we create, this, then, is a book filled with happiness.

Like everything in the award-winning *Cooking Light*—with 6.7 million readers, the most popular kitchen companion with America's home cooks—this cookbook makes good food an easy and pleasant part of your life. We weave ideas about balance, simplicity, healthfulness, and fun into everything from our recipes' ingredient choices to their super-streamlined instructions. Where some cookbooks revel in flights of celebrity ego or novella-length ingredient lists, our goal is to make cooking not only look simple—but actually *be* simple. We've demystified even those more-complicated procedures for all who like to cook but who have a few other things to do, too.

In this one-stop-serves-all cookbook, you'll find that healthy cooking means some of the finest eating you can imagine. In our view, real food comes from the earth more than restaurants revolving atop downtown skyscrapers. It is meant to be savored, and the making of it is but the link from the bounty of nature to the yum in your tummy. To help you make the most of that bounty, we've included menu suggestions throughout this cookbook, along with step-by-step photographs and our trademark nutritional analysis that accompanies every single recipe. You'll also find out more about our guiding principles, such as:

• All foods fit. Our approach to healthy living is about neither sacrifice nor denial; instead, it's about great taste and enjoyment, about moderation, variety, and balance. That's why you'll sometimes find butter, bacon, even heavy cream in our recipes—in modest amounts, of course.

• Spending a few extra cents or dollars to get the very best ingredients—particularly the high-flavor ones such as fresh Parmesan—packs a palpable payoff. Readers always tell us they're glad when they did.

• Selecting the freshest produce each season keeps your meals tasty and varied year-round. I promise that you'll find both fun and wisdom in occasionally adding a farmers' market, local bakery, or fresh-seafood store to your grocery shopping list.

We know you're busy, so we've helped you choose which dishes to make this week by adding preparation and cooking times to every recipe. That way, you can pick super-fast ones for harried weeknights, and save some longer ones to savor during more leisurely weekends. We've made the book's chapters more nimble, too, breaking some big categories into smaller ones and packing them with our top-rated favorites. Desserts, for example, now makes up four chapters: cakes and frostings, cookies, pies and pastries, and just desserts. Even the book's index is built for speed, adding to the recipes all our informative tips on pans, ingredients, cooking methods, and the like.

This is a book you can come to again and again. As you do, you'll not only appreciate our unique approach to cooking, you'll be mastering it more with every bite. So welcome to *The Complete Cooking Light Cookbook.* I hope you enjoy using it as much as we've loved creating it for you. In the meantime, best wishes from all of us at *Cooking Light,* and happy cooking!

—Doug Crichton, Editor
Cooking Light magazine

Our goal is to make cooking not only look simple—but actually *be* simple. We've demystified even those more-complicated procedures for all who like to cook but who have a few other things to do, too.

nutritional analysis

How to use it and why: Glance at the end of any *Cooking Light* recipe, and you'll see how committed we are to helping you make the best of today's light cooking. With four registered dietitians, five test kitchens professionals, three chefs, and a computer system that analyzes every ingredient we use, *Cooking Light* gives you authoritative dietary detail like no other magazine. We go to such lengths so you can see how our recipes fit into your healthful eating plan. If you're trying to lose weight, the calorie and fat figures will help most. But if you're keeping a close eye on the sodium, cholesterol, and saturated fat in your diet, we provide those numbers, too. And because many women don't get enough iron or calcium, we can help there. Finally, there's a fiber analysis for those of us who don't get enough roughage.

What it means and how we get there: We list calories, protein, fat, fiber, iron, and sodium at the end of each recipe, but there are a few things we abbreviate for space.

- *sat* for saturated fat
- *poly* for polyunsaturated fat
- *mono* for monounsaturated fat
- *CARB* for carbohydrates
- *CHOL* for cholesterol
- *CALC* for calcium
- *g* for gram
- *mg* for milligram

We get numbers for those categories based on a few assumptions: When we give a range for an ingredient, we calculate the lesser amount. Some alcohol calories evaporate during heating; we reflect that. And only the amount of marinade absorbed by the food is calculated.

Your Daily Nutrition Guide

	WOMEN AGES 25 TO 50	WOMEN OVER 50	MEN OVER 24
Calories	2,000	2,000 or less	2,700
Protein	50g	50g or less	63g
Fat	67g or less	67g or less	90g or less
Saturated Fat	22g or less	22g or less	30g or less
Carbohydrates	299g	299g	405g
Fiber	25g to 35g	25g to 35g	25g to 35g
Cholesterol	300mg or less	300mg or less	300mg or less
Iron	15mg	10mg	10mg
Sodium	2,400mg or less	2,400mg or less	2,400mg or less
Calcium	1,000mg	1,200mg	1,000mg

Calorie requirements vary according to your size, weight, and level of activity. This chart is a good general guide; additional nutrients are needed during some stages of life. For example, children's calorie and protein needs are based on height and vary greatly as they grow. Compared to adults, teenagers require less protein but more calcium and slightly more iron. Pregnant or breast-feeding women need more protein, calories, and calcium. Also, the need for iron increases during pregnancy but returns to normal after birth.

kitchen basics

2

10 essential kitchen tools No kitchen or cook should be without these tools. They'll make your life far easier.

1. **Whisks** (page 9) Whisks in assorted sizes are ideal for beating eggs and egg whites, blending salad dressings, and dissolving solids in liquids. We consider them essential for making creamy, smooth cooked sauces.

2. **Colanders** A large colander works well for draining pasta, salad greens, and browned ground beef. A small strainer is great for separating fruit juice or pulp from seeds.

3. **High-quality chef's knives** (also called a cook's knife) These knives are ideal for chopping, mincing, or slicing fruits and vegetables. The blade of the knife ranges from 8 to 13 inches. Choose a handle that is shaped so the hand holding the knife doesn't hit the cutting surface.

4. **Heavy 10-inch nonstick skillet** Most of these heavy skillets are made of aluminum, the best heat conductor.

5. **Pepper mill** Give your food just a bite of pungent flavor with a sprinkle of cracked or freshly ground pepper. Pepper is an often-overlooked spice—so keep your pepper mill handy for regular use.

6. **Vegetable peeler** This tool peels the skin from vegetables and fruits. Select one with a comfortable grip.

7. **Stainless-steel box grater** A box-style grater gives you a choice of hole sizes. Use the smaller holes for grating hard cheese or chocolate. For shredding an ingredient like cheddar cheese or carrots, use the largest holes.

8. **Kitchen shears** Keep kitchen shears handy to mince small amounts of herbs, chop canned tomatoes (in the can), trim fat from meat and skin from poultry, make slits in bread dough—plus many more uses.

9. **Oven thermometer** All ovens are equipped with internal thermostats, yet over time, the actual temperature inside the oven may vary. Use an oven thermometer to tell if you need to calibrate your oven thermostat (follow the instructions in your owner's manual or call the manufacturer).

10. **Cutting boards** Whether you choose wood or plastic, you need to wash either thoroughly to avoid food contamination. Use diluted bleach on wooden boards and wash thoroughly. Plastic ones can be sanitized in the dishwasher.

10 things you didn't know you needed

These are those tools and gadgets that may not seem indispensable—until you've used them a couple of times.

1. Pizza stone Also called a baking stone, this heavy round or rectangular stone duplicates the brick floor in pizza and bread ovens and creates a crisp, brown crust. Place on the lowest shelf of the oven before preheating the oven. Then place the dough on the stone, and bake.

2. Heat-resistant spatulas Choose an assortment of wide and narrow spatulas in nylon; they won't scratch nonstick cookware surfaces.

3. Mortar and pestle This pair is used for grinding spices, herbs, and other foods. Press the pestle (the bat-like object) against the food and grind against the mortar (the bowl) until the desired consistency is reached.

4. Ice cream maker There are two types, the manual (like a Donvier or hand crank) and the electric. Some of the manual types fit on a countertop and don't use salt or ice. Instead, they use an aluminum tub you store in your freezer before using. For both types, a clear lid lets you see how well the mixture is freezing.

5. Garlic press Use this tool when a recipe calls for crushed garlic because you'll want both the garlic and its juice.

6. Salad spinner Just a few turns of the handle and you'll remove excess water from freshly washed salad greens.

7. Grill pan A grill pan has gone from being a gourmet item to an everyday must have. It gives the food a grilled appearance and flavor, and it provides a nice browning. Plus, the food in the pan is raised so that you get the tenderness of roasting as well.

8. Heavy-duty stand-up mixer This machine will stand up to all of your baking needs, including stiff doughs or large amounts. It comes with attachments like a balloon whisk (for incorporating air with egg whites), a dough hook (for kneading bread), and a paddle beater (for mixing and combining ingredients).

9. Food processor A full-sized food processor makes quick work out of everyday food preparation. Use the metal blade for chopping and pureeing. The slicing disc and the shredding disc let you slice or shred vegetables in a fraction of the time.

10. Instant-read thermometer Food safety should be a top concern in the kitchen. One key factor is cooking food to the proper temperature. Use an instant-read thermometer to check meringues, meat, and poultry—just be sure not to leave it in the oven. It should be removed from the food after you read the temperature.

7 8
9 10

1

2

3

4

10 must-haves for the pantry

Stock these items, and you'll have the foundation for just about any recipe there is.

1. **Olive oil** Olive oil is one of the most versatile oils for cooking. Just a teaspoon or two is enough to add flavor when sautéing. See page 402 for more info on this oil.

2. **Canned diced tomatoes** Canned tomatoes, in all their forms, provide a consistency of flavor and texture that is sometimes difficult to obtain from their fresh counterparts. You'll find these gems faster to use and perhaps even tastier!

3. **Fresh garlic** This redolent bulb has multiple personalities: pungent and assertive when raw; mellow and sweet when cooked; and nutty and rich when caramelized or cooked at length. The flavor depends on how it's used. Crushed, minced, or finely chopped garlic releases pungent juices and is more potent than garlic that is halved, sliced, or left whole.

4. **Low-sodium soy sauce** This important ingredient in Asian recipes has gone worldwide. Stir it into soups, sauces, and marinades; sprinkle it on meat, fish, chicken, and vegetables; or use it like they do in Asia, as a table condiment.

5. **Basmati rice** You'll enjoy the fresh popcorn aroma as this rice cooks, but its nutty flavor and firm texture will score high ratings on your plate.

6. **Roasted red peppers** When time is short or there are no red peppers in the fridge, pull out a jar of these roasted treasures. Toss with pasta or puree them for sauces for an easy meal.

7. **Chickpeas** Also known as garbanzo beans, these round legumes have a firm texture and a nutlike flavor. They're common in Mediterranean, Indian, and Middle Eastern cuisines, but they're also found in Spanish, Italian, and Mexican dishes. Favorites to toss into salads, soups, and stews, they're packed with protein, a bonus for meatless dishes.

8. **Fat-free, less-sodium chicken broth** Canned chicken broth can be your culinary secret. Use it as the foundation for soups and sauces, and you'll have a dish ready in just minutes. Be sure to read the nutrition label as the sodium and fat contents vary among brands.

9. **Balsamic vinegar** Zip up sautéed vegetables, splash it on salad greens, sprinkle it over grilled chicken or fresh berries. Balsamic vinegar's versatility is endless, and its full-bodied flavor is slightly sweet with a hint of tartness.

10. **Dried pasta** Long, short, curly, twisted, hollow, or flat, pasta's versatility is limited only by your imagination. Substitute similar shapes if you don't have the type specified in a recipe. Be creative and experiment with your favorites!

10 splurge-worthy ingredients

Some ingredients play such a critical role in a dish's flavor that it's important to use the real thing, and not a pale imitation.

1. **Dried mushrooms** Keep dried wild mushrooms—porcini, shiitake, and wood ear to name a few—on hand and you'll enjoy the earthy, woodsy goodness simply by rehydrating them in hot water or broth. They're available whole or in slices or pieces. Store them in a cool, dry place for up to six months.

2. **A fine red wine such as Cabernet Sauvignon, Zinfandel, or Merlot** tempts the palate with its character and complexity—two necessary traits of a fine wine.

3. **Pine nuts** Pine nuts are found inside pine cones, which must be heated so the nuts can be removed. It's this intensive process that makes them so expensive. For more on these buttery-tasting nuts, see page 456.

4. **Good coffee** Brew the best coffee by starting with roasted arabica beans, which are grown at higher elevations and develop a richer flavor and aroma than other coffee beans.

5. **Vanilla beans** Cooking with vanilla beans, as compared to the extract, adds a profound flavor. To use, cut the bean in half lengthwise and scrape out the seeds. Although you can cook with the bean, it should not be eaten.

6. **Parmigiano-Reggiano cheese** Try Italy's luxurious hard grating cheese which typically ages at least two years. Its granular texture melts in your mouth with rich flavor.

7. **Quality extra-virgin olive oil** Primarily used for sautéing and in salad dressings, extra-virgin olive oil offers more flavor. (For a full description, see page 402.) All olive oils are rich in monounsaturated fat, a healthier choice than saturated types. Plus, they outdistance vegetable oils on flavor.

8. **The freshest seafood possible** Inquire at your local fish market about delivery times from the coast. Plan on shopping that day and cooking that night. Fresh-from-the-sea flavor is worth the extra effort.

9. **Gourmet greens** Also called mesclun, gourmet greens are available in most large supermarkets. They're a mixture of tender, young salad greens that can include arugula, dandelion, sorrel, and oakleaf. Gently rinse and spin them in a salad spinner. Store them in a zip-top bag in the refrigerator until ready to use.

10. **Imported olives** Olives imported from Greece, Italy, Spain, and France are so intense in flavor that a little of their flavor goes a long way. Because they are high in monounsaturated fat, they offer the heart-healthy benefits of the Mediterranean diet.

7 8
9 10

1

10 essential herbs
These herbs provide a true spark of flavor for any great dish and can transform even the ordinary into the memorable.

1. **Cilantro** These bright green leaves (also called Chinese parsley) and stems of the coriander plant have a lively, pungent fragrance. Cilantro is widely used in Mexican and Caribbean cooking. It is susceptible to heat, so add it at the end of cooking. It's at its best in cold dishes or added just before serving.

2. **Basil** This popular herb comes in many varieties, from lemon basil (popular in Thai cooking) to opal basil, which is a stunning purple. Fresh basil leaves are large and easy to use. They're a key ingredient in pesto (and Mediterranean cooking in general) and can enhance a variety of tomato dishes.

3. **Parsley** The most popular variety of parsley is curly (a common garnish), but flat-leaf or Italian parsley has a stronger flavor and is preferable for cooking. Parsley gives a kick to almost any dish—especially pasta and soups. For a hurry-up garnish, chop just a bit and sprinkle over food before serving.

4. **Tarragon** This aniselike herb is used in French cooking with chicken, fish, and vegetables and is standard in béarnaise sauce. Tarragon pairs well with dill and parsley, but use it sparingly with other herbs because of its dominant flavor.

5. **Rosemary** Rosemary has long, slender, almost prickly leaves on stalks. Pull the leaves in the opposite direction from which they are growing to remove them from the stems, which are too tough to use. You'll find it's very aromatic and good with chicken, pork, beef, and potatoes.

6. **Mint** Mint can have a strong flavor, so use it sparingly. It provides a refreshing zip to drinks, soups, desserts, and salads.

7. **Dill** Dill is made up of feathery green leaves. Don't confuse it with dill seed, the ingredient in dill pickles. Sensitive to heat, it's best used in chilled or uncooked dishes, especially appetizers and salads.

8. **Sage** A musty mint taste and aroma permeate sage's narrow, oval, gray-green leaves. Sage goes well with poultry and pork; its full flavor develops best when cooked.

9. **Oregano** Often associated with Italian cuisine, oregano goes well with tomato-based dishes. You'll find it to be a wonderful addition to marinades and stews.

10. **Thyme** Thyme is composed of tiny leaves. If the stem is thin, it can be chopped and used along with the leaves. Commonly found in French cuisine, it goes well with many dishes, particularly chicken, fish, and soups.

10 top healthy foods
Healthy eating isn't about what you *can't* eat, but about what you *can* eat. We've used these nutrition-packed foods in many of our recipes.

1. Broccoli Your mother was right when she told you to eat your broccoli. Phytochemicals in broccoli trigger enzyme activity, helping to prevent damage to your cells' DNA.

2. Milk Milk contains a multitude of nutrients: calcium; vitamins A, D, and B_{12}; potassium; phosphorus; protein; niacin; and riboflavin. These nutrients help maintain bone density and may help prevent high blood pressure. And by choosing fat-free milk, you won't be adding any fat.

3. Beans These innocent-looking jewels are rich in the B vitamin folic acid, a nutrient heralded for its potential role in warding off heart disease and some birth defects.

4. Tomatoes While tomatoes are high in vitamin C, they are prized for their lycopene. A powerful antioxidant, lycopene may lower prostate-cancer risk. Cooked and canned tomatoes may have more lycopene activity than uncooked ones.

5. Citrus fruit These treasures from the grove are loaded with vitamin C which helps maintain healthy skin, bones, and muscles and helps keep the immune system strong.

6. Sweet potatoes Beta-carotene, the plant pigment that gives sweet potatoes their bright orange color, is a powerful antioxidant associated with a reduced risk of certain cancers.

7. Garlic Praised for its ability to enhance the flavor of any dish, garlic may also prove healthful by lowering cholesterol and blood pressure.

8. Soy Soy's abundant cancer-fighting phytoestrogens, cholesterol-lowering ability, and suspected ability to help prevent osteoporosis make it a nutritional powerhouse. Soy is available in many different forms including soy milk, tofu, tempeh, and textured vegetable protein such as vegetarian burgers.

9. Carrots Beta-carotene in carrots helps offset damage from environmental pollutants to the cells' DNA.

10. Strawberries This luscious fruit is low in calories, packed with vitamin C, and a good source of fiber and potassium.

appetizers &
beverages

Ratatouille and Goat Cheese
Wrapped in Phyllo (page 36)

APPETIZERS

The great thing about appetizers is their versatility. They welcome friends and neighbors to the occasion. As a first course, they set the tone for the meal. Or offer several choices *as* the meal, combining a variety of flavors and types for a tapas-style menu. Tapas—small portions of multiple foods—have several benefits. They offer your friends a selection of food to mix and match, plus they provide an alternative to preparing a hefty entrée and sides. Just browse through our appetizers and find your favorites to serve.

We've listed the time needed in preparing the recipes so that you can plan your schedule and perhaps even have a moment to yourself before your company arrives.

dips & spreads
Whether you like them cool and creamy or hot and sassy, we've got the dips and spreads to suit your taste.

THREE FRUIT DIP

PREP: 40 MINUTES
CHILL: 2 HOURS 20 MINUTES

½ cup dried apricots, chopped
1 cup orange juice
½ cup applesauce
½ cup vanilla low-fat yogurt
⅛ teaspoon ground cinnamon
Dash of ground ginger

1. Combine apricots and orange juice in a small nonaluminum saucepan. Bring to a boil over medium heat; cook 15 minutes or until apricots are soft and liquid is absorbed, stirring frequently. Remove from heat; cover and cool.
2. Place apricot mixture and remaining ingredients in a food processor; process until smooth. Place in a small bowl; cover and chill. Serve with assorted fresh fruit. Yield: 1⅔ cups (serving size: 2 tablespoons).

CALORIES 39 (5% from fat); FAT 0.2g (sat 0.1g, mono 0g, poly 0g); PROTEIN 0.9g; CARB 9.3g; FIBER 0.9g; CHOL 0mg; IRON 0.4mg; SODIUM 6mg; CALC 21mg

PEANUT BUTTER DIP

PREP: 8 MINUTES   CHILL: 2 HOURS

⅔ cup crumbled firm tofu (about 4 ounces)
⅔ cup 1% low-fat cottage cheese
¼ cup reduced-fat peanut butter
2 teaspoons honey
1 teaspoon vanilla extract
Ground cinnamon (optional)

1. Place all ingredients except cinnamon in a food processor; process until smooth. Cover and chill. Sprinkle with cinnamon, if desired. Serve with sliced apples and pears or graham crackers. Yield: 1⅓ cups (serving size: 2 tablespoons).

CALORIES 61 (36% from fat); FAT 2.9g (sat 0.6g, mono 0.6g, poly 1.3g); PROTEIN 4.4g; CARB 4.2g; FIBER 0.5g; CHOL 1mg; IRON 0.8mg; SODIUM 92mg; CALC 21mg

GUACAMOLE

PREP: 15 MINUTES

1½ cups diced peeled avocado
½ cup diced seeded tomato
¼ cup finely chopped fresh cilantro
¼ cup finely chopped onion
2 tablespoons fresh lime juice
¼ teaspoon salt

1. Combine all ingredients. Serve immediately with baked tortilla chips. Yield: 2¾ cups (serving size: 2 tablespoons).

CALORIES 25 (76% from fat); FAT 2.1g (sat 0.3g, mono 1.3g, poly 0.3g); PROTEIN 0.4g; CARB 1.8g; FIBER 0.8g; CHOL 0mg; IRON 0.2mg; SODIUM 32mg; CALC 3mg

CREAMY GUACAMOLE

PREP: 12 MINUTES   CHILL: 2 HOURS

5 (6-inch) flour tortillas, each cut into 8 wedges
1½ cups cubed peeled avocado
1 cup fat-free ricotta cheese
⅓ cup coarsely chopped onion
2 tablespoons coarsely chopped fresh cilantro
2 tablespoons fresh lime juice
1 tablespoon coarsely chopped seeded jalapeño pepper
½ teaspoon salt

1. Preheat oven to 350°.
2. Place tortilla wedges on a baking sheet; bake at 350° for 10 minutes or until crisp. Set aside.
3. Combine avocado and remaining 6 ingredients in a food processor; process until smooth. Spoon mixture into a bowl; cover and chill. Serve with toasted tortilla wedges. Yield: 20 servings

(serving size: 2 tortilla wedges and 2 tablespoons dip).

CALORIES 55 (39% from fat); FAT 2.4g (sat 0.4g, mono 1.4g, poly 0.5g); PROTEIN 2.7g; CARB 6.6g; FIBER 0.9g; CHOL 1mg; IRON 0.4mg; SODIUM 105mg; CALC 33mg

GARBANZO GUACAMOLE

PREP: 10 MINUTES   CHILL: 30 MINUTES

1 large garlic clove
⅔ cup drained canned chickpeas (garbanzo beans)
1 tablespoon lemon juice
⅓ cup coarsely chopped onion
½ cup cubed peeled avocado
1 tablespoon chopped green chiles
¼ teaspoon salt
¼ teaspoon pepper
¾ cup finely chopped seeded plum tomato
½ cup finely chopped green onions

1. Drop garlic through food chute with food processor on; process until minced. Add beans and lemon juice; process 20 seconds. Add ⅓ cup onion, avocado, green chiles, salt, and pepper; pulse 5 times or until mixture is chunky.
2. Transfer mixture to a bowl. Stir in tomato and green onions; chill. Serve with baked tortilla chips. Yield: 1¾ cups (serving size: 2 tablespoons).

CALORIES 26 (38% from fat); FAT 1.1g (sat 0.2g, mono 0.6g, poly 0.2g); PROTEIN 1g; CARB 3.7g; FIBER 0.8g; CHOL 0mg; IRON 0.4mg; SODIUM 66mg; CALC 8mg

TAHINI

Tahini is a paste made of ground sesame seeds and is used in many Middle Eastern recipes. You can find it in large supermarkets near the other sauces and spreads. Keep it stored in an airtight container in the refrigerator.

TEX-MEX BLACK BEAN DIP

PREP: 20 MINUTES

1 teaspoon vegetable oil
½ cup chopped onion
2 garlic cloves, minced
½ cup diced tomato
⅓ cup bottled picante sauce
½ teaspoon chili powder
½ teaspoon ground cumin
1 (15-ounce) can black beans, drained
¼ cup (1 ounce) shredded reduced-fat Monterey Jack cheese
¼ cup chopped fresh cilantro
1 tablespoon fresh lime juice

1. Heat oil in a medium nonstick skillet over medium heat. Add onion and garlic, and sauté 4 minutes or until tender. Add tomato and next 4 ingredients; cook until thick (about 2 minutes), stirring constantly.
2. Remove from heat; partially mash with a potato masher. Add cheese, cilantro, and lime juice, stirring until cheese melts. Serve immediately with baked tortilla chips. Yield: 1¾ cups (serving size: 2 tablespoons).

CALORIES 39 (21% from fat); FAT 0.9g (sat 0.3g, mono 0.2g, poly 0.2g); PROTEIN 2.4g; CARB 5.7g; FIBER 1.0g; CHOL 1mg; IRON 0.6mg; SODIUM 128mg; CALC 26mg

HUMMUS BI TAHINA

PREP: 6 MINUTES

2 (15-ounce) cans chickpeas (garbanzo beans), undrained
3 small garlic cloves
¼ cup plus 1 tablespoon tahini (sesame-seed paste)
¼ cup fresh lemon juice
3 tablespoons water

1. Drain chickpeas, reserving ¼ cup liquid, and set aside.

2. Drop garlic through food chute with food processor on; process 10 seconds or until minced. Add chickpeas, reserved ¼ cup liquid, tahini, lemon juice, and water; process 3 minutes or until smooth, scraping sides of bowl occasionally.
3. Spoon tahini mixture into a serving bowl. Serve immediately or cover and chill. Serve with pita triangles or raw vegetables. Yield: 3 cups (serving size: 2 tablespoons).

CALORIES 44 (37% from fat); FAT 1.8g (sat 0.3g, mono 0.6g, poly 0.7g); PROTEIN 2.4g; CARB 5.5g; FIBER 1.1g; CHOL 0mg; IRON 0.7mg; SODIUM 74mg; CALC 28mg

SPICY ORANGE HUMMUS

PREP: 9 MINUTES

¼ cup fresh parsley leaves
2 tablespoons chopped onion
1 garlic clove
¼ cup orange juice
2 tablespoons tahini (sesame-seed paste)
2 tablespoons rice vinegar
2 teaspoons low-sodium soy sauce
1 teaspoon Dijon mustard
¼ teaspoon salt
¼ teaspoon ground ginger
¼ teaspoon ground coriander
¼ teaspoon ground turmeric
¼ teaspoon ground cumin
¼ teaspoon paprika
1 (15-ounce) can chickpeas (garbanzo beans), drained

1. Drop parsley, onion, and garlic through food chute with food processor on; process until minced. Add remaining ingredients, and process until smooth. Serve with pita triangles. Yield: 1¾ cups (serving size: 2 tablespoons).

CALORIES 50 (31% from fat); FAT 1.7g (sat 0.2g, mono 0.5g, poly 0.7g); PROTEIN 2.3g; CARB 6.9g; FIBER 1g; CHOL 0mg; IRON 0.9mg; SODIUM 120mg; CALC 23mg

SMOKY BABA GHANOUJ

PREP: 30 MINUTES

CHILL: 2 HOURS

6 (6-inch) pitas
Cooking spray
2 eggplants, cut in half lengthwise
    (about 2 pounds)
1 garlic clove
¼ cup tahini (sesame-seed paste)
3 tablespoons fresh lemon juice
½ teaspoon salt
Dash of paprika

1. Preheat oven to 400°.
2. Split pitas; cut each half into 4 wedges. Place wedges in a single layer on a baking sheet. Bake at 400° for 9 minutes or until crisp and browned. Set aside.
3. Coat a grill rack with cooking spray, and place on grill over medium-hot coals (350° to 400°). Place eggplant halves, cut side up, on rack; grill, covered, 20 minutes or until very tender. Remove from grill, and cool slightly. Peel eggplant, and set aside.
4. Drop garlic through food chute with food processor on; process until minced. Add eggplant, tahini, lemon juice, and salt; process 45 seconds or until smooth,

EASY LOW-FAT DIPPERS

Bagel chips: Cut bagels in half; cut each half into thin slices. Place on a baking sheet; bake at 350° for 5 minutes or until crisp.

Pita chips: Split pita bread; cut each half into 8 wedges. Place on a baking sheet; bake at 400° for 9 minutes or until crisp.

Tortilla chips: Cut each corn or flour tortilla into 8 wedges. Place on a baking sheet; bake at 350° for 10 minutes or until crisp.

scraping sides of bowl once. Transfer to a bowl; cover and chill. Sprinkle with paprika; serve with toasted pita bread wedges. Yield: 24 servings (serving size: 2 tablespoons dip and 2 pita chips).

CALORIES 72 (20% from fat); FAT 1.6g (sat 0.2g, mono 0.5g, poly 0.7g); PROTEIN 2.4g; CARB 12.4g; FIBER 1.6g; CHOL 0mg; IRON 0.8mg; SODIUM 143mg; CALC 28mg

CAPONATA

PREP: 37 MINUTES   CHILL: 2 HOURS

1 (1-pound) eggplant, cut cross-
    wise into ½-inch-thick slices
Cooking spray
2 teaspoons olive oil
1 cup sliced celery
½ cup chopped onion
1 garlic clove, minced
1 cup coarsely chopped tomato
3 tablespoons no-salt-added
    tomato sauce
2 tablespoons red wine vinegar
2 tablespoons chopped ripe olives
1 tablespoon capers
1 teaspoon sugar
⅛ teaspoon salt
¼ teaspoon black pepper
1 tablespoon chopped fresh
    parsley

1. Preheat oven to 500°.
2. Arrange eggplant in a single layer on a baking sheet coated with cooking spray; brush both sides of eggplant with oil. Bake at 500° for 15 minutes, turning after 8 minutes. Dice eggplant; set aside.
3. Coat a large nonstick skillet with cooking spray; place over medium heat. Add celery; sauté 2 minutes. Add onion and garlic; sauté 5 minutes. Add tomato and next 7 ingredients; cook over low heat 10 minutes, stirring occasionally. Remove from heat; stir in eggplant and parsley. Spoon into a bowl; cover and chill 2 hours. Serve with toasted pita

bread wedges or baguette slices. Yield: 3 cups (serving size: 2 tablespoons).

CALORIES 16 (34% from fat); FAT 0.6g (sat 0.1g, mono 0.4g, poly 0.1g); PROTEIN 0.4g; CARB 2.6g; FIBER 0.8g; CHOL 0mg; IRON 0.2mg; SODIUM 56mg; CALC 6mg

LIPTAUER DIP

PREP: 7 MINUTES

Liptauer cheese is a soft, fresh Hungarian cheese that's frequently flavored with herbs, onion, and paprika. Our lower-fat version starts with drained yogurt (see technique photos on opposite page), which is then flavored in the traditional manner.

1 (8-ounce) carton plain low-fat
    yogurt
1 cup (4 ounces) shredded Swiss
    cheese
½ cup coarsely chopped onion
1 tablespoon paprika
¼ teaspoon salt
¼ teaspoon black pepper
2 tablespoons Dijon mustard
½ teaspoon cider vinegar
1 (16-ounce) carton 2% low-fat
    cottage cheese
½ teaspoon caraway seeds

1. Spoon yogurt onto several layers of heavy-duty paper towels; spread to ½-inch thickness. Cover with additional paper towels; let stand 5 minutes.
2. Scrape yogurt into a blender or food processor using a rubber spatula. Add Swiss cheese and next 7 ingredients; process until smooth.
3. Spoon mixture into a bowl; stir in caraway seeds. Serve immediately or cover and chill. Serve dip with pumpernickel bread and raw vegetables. Yield: 3 cups (serving size: 2 tablespoons).

CALORIES 44 (39% from fat); FAT 1.9g (sat 1.2g, mono 0.5g, poly 0.1g); PROTEIN 4.5g; CARB 2g; FIBER 0.1g; CHOL 7mg; IRON 0.1mg; SODIUM 157mg; CALC 77mg

Draining Yogurt

It's easy to transform yogurt into a velvety substitute for high-fat dairy products in recipes. Draining yogurt overnight makes a low-fat, high-calcium alternative to cream cheese and sour cream and can be used in dips and sauces. Yogurt cheese made from plain low-fat yogurt is mildly tart. For a slightly sweet yogurt cheese that is delicious in fruit dips or desserts, use vanilla low-fat yogurt. For successful yogurt cheese:

• Select low-fat yogurt that has no gelatin added. If gelatin is listed in the yogurt's ingredient listing, the liquid will bind to the solids of the yogurt, preventing it from draining off.
• If possible, avoid processing the yogurt cheese in a blender, food processor, or electric mixer.
• Let yogurt cheese come to room temperature before adding it to a hot mixture.

OPTION 1 QUICK DRAIN

One 8-ounce carton of plain low-fat yogurt will yield ¼ cup quick-drained yogurt cheese.

1. Spoon yogurt onto several layers of heavy-duty paper towels; spread to ½-inch thickness.

2. Cover with additional paper towels; let stand 5 minutes.

3. Scrape into a bowl using a rubber spatula; cover and refrigerate.

OPTION 2 OVERNIGHT DRAIN

One 16-ounce carton of plain low-fat yogurt will yield 1 cup overnight-drained yogurt cheese.

1. Place colander in a 2-quart glass measure or medium bowl. Line colander with 4 layers of cheesecloth, allowing cheesecloth to extend over outside edges.

2. Spoon yogurt into colander. Cover loosely with plastic wrap; refrigerate 12 hours.

3. Spoon yogurt cheese into a bowl; discard liquid. Cover and refrigerate.

ROASTED RED PEPPER DIP

3 large red bell peppers
1 small garlic clove
½ cup fat-free sour cream
2 tablespoons chopped fresh basil
¼ teaspoon freshly ground black
   pepper
1 teaspoon anchovy paste
½ teaspoon lemon juice

1. Preheat broiler.
2. Cut bell peppers in half lengthwise; discard seeds and membranes. Place pepper halves, skin sides up, on a foil-lined baking sheet; flatten with hand. Broil 10 minutes or until blackened. Place in a zip-top plastic bag; seal. Let stand 15 minutes. Peel and discard skins.
3. Drop garlic through food chute with food processor on; process 3 seconds or until minced. Add bell pepper, sour cream, and remaining ingredients. Process until smooth. Serve with raw vegetables. Yield: 1½ cups (serving size: 2 tablespoons).

CALORIES 17 (11% from fat); FAT 0.2g (sat 0g, mono 0g, poly 0.1g); PROTEIN 1.1g; CARB 2.6g; FIBER 0.6g; CHOL 0mg; IRON 0.4mg; SODIUM 65mg; CALC 17mg

ROASTED PEPPER-CHEESE DIP

PREP:30 MINUTES

2 large red bell peppers
2 large unpeeled garlic cloves
1 (8-ounce) block ⅓-less-fat cream
   cheese
2 teaspoons balsamic vinegar
¼ teaspoon salt
⅛ to ¼ teaspoon crushed red pepper

1. Preheat broiler.
2. Cut bell peppers in half lengthwise; discard seeds and membranes. Place peppers, skin sides up, on a foil-lined

Roasting Bell Peppers

All bell peppers—green, yellow, and red—can be roasted. Follow the steps below for roasting and peeling bell peppers with ease. Cutting the peppers in half before broiling them simplifies the process. Plus, lining the baking sheet with foil makes cleanup a snap.

1. Cut bell peppers in half lengthwise; discard seeds and membranes.

2. Place pepper halves, skin sides up, on a foil-lined baking sheet; flatten with hand.

3. Broil 3 inches from heat for 10 to 12 minutes or until blackened. Place in zip-top plastic bag; seal and let stand for 15 minutes. (This will loosen the skins and make peeling them much easier.)

4. Peel and discard skins. Store roasted peppers in an airtight container in the refrigerator.

baking sheet; flatten with hand. Add garlic to baking sheet, and broil 4 minutes. Turn garlic over; broil 4 minutes or until blackened. Remove garlic from baking sheet; set aside. Broil peppers an additional 2 minutes or until blackened. Place peppers in a zip-top plastic bag, and seal; let stand 15 minutes. Peel peppers and garlic; discard skins.
3. Place roasted peppers and garlic in food processor; process until smooth, scraping sides of bowl once. Add cheese; process until smooth. Spoon mixture into a bowl, and stir in vinegar, salt, and crushed red pepper. Serve immediately or cover and chill. Serve with raw vegetables. Yield: 1½ cups (serving size: 2 tablespoons).

CALORIES 56 (72% from fat); FAT 4.5g (sat 2.8g, mono 1.3g, poly 0.2g); PROTEIN 2.1g; CARB 2.1g; FIBER 0.4g; CHOL 14mg; IRON 0.4mg; SODIUM 125mg; CALC 17mg

26 appetizers & beverages

BEAN-AND-ROASTED RED PEPPER DIP

PREP: 7 MINUTES   COOK: 5 MINUTES

1   teaspoon extra-virgin olive oil
1   cup chopped onion
2   tablespoons chopped fresh basil
1   (16-ounce) can pinto beans,
    drained
1   (7-ounce) bottle roasted red bell
    peppers, drained and thinly
    sliced

1. Heat oil in a medium nonstick skillet over medium heat. Add onion; sauté 4 minutes or until tender. Add basil and beans; cook over low heat 5 minutes, stirring frequently.
2. Partially mash beans. Stir in roasted red bell pepper. Serve with pita chips or low-fat tortilla chips. Yield: 1¾ cups (serving size: 2 tablespoons).

CALORIES 39 (10% from fat); FAT 0.4g (sat 0.1g, mono 0.3g, poly 0.1g); PROTEIN 1.7g; CARB 6.9g; FIBER 0.9g; CHOL 0mg; IRON 0.7mg; SODIUM 85mg; CALC 12mg

CARAMELIZED ONION DIP

PREP: 35 MINUTES   CHILL: 2 HOURS

1   teaspoon olive oil
1¾   cups chopped onion
1   garlic clove, minced
⅓   cup cider vinegar
3   tablespoons honey
¼   teaspoon white pepper
⅓   cup light mayonnaise
⅓   cup fat-free sour cream
¼   cup plain fat-free yogurt
⅛   teaspoon salt

1. Heat oil in a large skillet over medium heat. Add onion and garlic; cover and cook 8 minutes or until tender, stirring frequently. Stir in vinegar, honey, and white pepper. Bring to a boil over medium-high heat; cook, uncovered, 10 minutes or until onion is golden and liquid evaporates, stirring occasionally.
2. Combine onion mixture, mayonnaise, sour cream, yogurt, and salt in a bowl; cover and chill. Serve with bagel chips. Yield: 1¼ cups (serving size: 2 tablespoons).

CALORIES 65 (40% from fat); FAT 2.9g (sat 0.5g, mono 1g, poly 1.4g); PROTEIN 1.2g; CARB 9.1g; FIBER 0.4g; CHOL 3mg; IRON 0.2mg; SODIUM 87mg; CALC 28mg

ASIAGO DIP WITH CROSTINI

PREP: 10 MINUTES   COOK: 30 MINUTES

1   cup light mayonnaise
½   cup thinly sliced green onions
⅓   cup (about 1½ ounces) grated
      Asiago or Parmesan cheese
¼   cup sliced mushrooms
¼   cup sun-dried tomato sprinkles
1   (8-ounce) carton low-fat sour
      cream
1   tablespoon (¼ ounce) grated
      Asiago or Parmesan cheese
32   (½-inch-thick) slices diagonally
      cut French bread baguette,
      toasted (about 2 baguettes)

1. Preheat oven to 350°.
2. Combine first 6 ingredients in a bowl; spoon into a 1-quart casserole. Sprinkle with 1 tablespoon cheese. Bake at 350° for 30 minutes or until bubbly. Serve with toasted bread. Yield: 32 servings (serving size: 1 tablespoon dip and 1 crostino).

CALORIES 65 (51% from fat); FAT 3.7g (sat 1.1g, mono 1.1g, poly 1.4g); PROTEIN 1.6g; CARB 6.3g; FIBER 0.4g; CHOL 6mg; IRON 0.4mg; SODIUM 137mg; CALC 28mg

Roasted Pepper-
Cheese Dip

PARTY SPINACH DIP

PREP:12 MINUTES   CHILL:3 HOURS

1 (12-ounce) carton 1% low-fat
   cottage cheese
1 (10-ounce) package frozen
   chopped spinach, thawed,
   drained, and squeezed dry
½ cup low-fat sour cream
¼ cup dry vegetable soup mix
2 teaspoons grated fresh onion
1 teaspoon lemon juice
1 (8-ounce) can sliced water
   chestnuts, drained and chopped

1. Place cheese in a food processor, and process until smooth, scraping sides of bowl once. Place in a medium bowl.
2. Stir spinach and remaining ingredients into cheese. Cover and chill. Serve with unsalted crackers, breadsticks, melba toast, or raw vegetables. Yield: 3 cups (serving size: 2 tablespoons).

CALORIES 25 (29% from fat); FAT 0.8g (sat 0.5g , mono 0.2g, poly 0g); PROTEIN 2.4g; CARB 2.3g; FIBER 0.5g; CHOL 3mg; IRON 0.3mg; SODIUM 130mg; CALC 27mg

SPINACH-HAM DIP

PREP:25 MINUTES   COOK:30 MINUTES

2 (1-pound) round loaves unsliced
   French or sourdough bread
½ cup fat-free sour cream
1 (8-ounce) block ⅓-less-fat cream
   cheese, softened
1 (8-ounce) carton plain fat-free yogurt
½ teaspoon garlic powder
1¼ cups diced cooked ham (about 6
   ounces)
1 (10-ounce) package frozen
   chopped spinach, thawed,
   drained, and squeezed dry
1 (2-ounce) jar diced pimento,
   drained
2 tablespoons grated Parmesan
   cheese

Making Bread Bowls

You can hollow out large round loaves of bread to serve dips and spreads, such as Spinach-Ham Dip. Small crusty dinner rolls can be used for individual servings of chili and stews.

1. Slice off top fourth of loaves, using a large serrated knife.

2. Hollow out bottom pieces, leaving 1-inch-thick shells.

3. Cut all reserved bread into bite-size pieces.

4. Place on baking sheet around bread bowls and bake as directed.

1. Preheat oven to 375°.
2. Slice off top fourth of loaves, using a large serrated knife. Hollow out bottom pieces, leaving 1-inch-thick shells; reserve remaining bread. Place bread bowls on a baking sheet. Cut reserved bread into bite-size pieces; place on baking sheet around bread bowls. Bake at 375° for 15 minutes or until dry.
3. Beat sour cream, cream cheese, yogurt, and garlic powder in a bowl at medium speed of a mixer until smooth. Stir in ham, spinach, and pimento. Divide mixture between bread bowls, and sprinkle Parmesan cheese over spinach mixture. Bake filled bowls at 375° for 30 minutes or until thoroughly heated. Serve warm with reserved bread. Yield: 28 servings (serving size: 2 tablespoons dip and about 1 ounce bread).

Note: Dip may be served chilled in bread bowls, if desired. Just fill the bowls with dip, and serve without baking.

CALORIES 123 (24% from fat); FAT 3.3g (sat 1.6g, mono 1.1g, poly 0.3g); PROTEIN 6g; CARB 17.4g; FIBER 0.8g; CHOL 10mg; IRON 1.1mg; SODIUM 314mg; CALC 77mg

HOT CRAB DIP

PREP:22 MINUTES
COOK:30 MINUTES

¾ cup fat-free sour cream
2 tablespoons fresh lemon juice
1 tablespoon grated fresh onion
1 teaspoon Worcestershire sauce
¾ teaspoon dry mustard
¼ teaspoon garlic powder
1 (8-ounce) tub light cream cheese, softened
½ cup (2 ounces) shredded reduced-fat sharp cheddar cheese
1 pound lump crabmeat, drained and shell pieces removed
Cooking spray
Paprika

1. Preheat oven to 325°.
2. Combine first 7 ingredients in a bowl; stir well with a whisk. Stir in cheddar cheese and crabmeat.
3. Spoon crabmeat mixture into a 1½-quart casserole coated with cooking spray, and sprinkle with paprika. Bake at 325° for 30 minutes or until thoroughly heated. Serve warm with crackers or breadsticks. Yield: 3⅔ cups (serving size: 2 tablespoons).

CALORIES 43 (39% from fat); FAT 2.0g (sat 1.0g, mono 0.5g, poly 0.2g); PROTEIN 4.8g; CARB 1.2g; FIBER 0g; CHOL 21mg; IRON 0.2mg; SODIUM 106mg; CALC 52mg

SUN-DRIED TOMATO PESTO SPREAD

PREP:14 MINUTES   CHILL:12 HOURS

For tips on draining yogurt, see "Overnight Drain" photos, page 25.

1 (16-ounce) carton plain fat-free yogurt
1 ounce sun-dried tomatoes, packed without oil (about 13)
¾ cup boiling water
4 garlic cloves
¼ cup grated Parmesan cheese
¼ cup chopped fresh parsley
2 tablespoons slivered almonds, toasted
1 teaspoon dried basil
1 teaspoon vegetable oil

1. Place a colander in a 2-quart glass measure or medium bowl. Line colander with 4 layers of cheesecloth, allowing cheesecloth to extend over outside edges. Spoon yogurt into colander. Cover loosely with plastic wrap, and chill 12 hours. Spoon yogurt cheese into a bowl, discarding cheesecloth and liquid. Cover and chill.
2. Combine tomatoes and water in a bowl; let stand 10 minutes. Drain and set tomatoes aside. Drop garlic through food chute with processor on; process 3 seconds or until minced. Add tomatoes, Parmesan cheese, and remaining 4 ingredients. Process 15 seconds or until minced. Cover and chill.
3. Press yogurt cheese into a mound on a serving platter. Gently press tomato mixture onto mound, completely covering yogurt cheese. Serve with crackers or melba toast. Yield: 1½ cups (serving size: 2 tablespoons).

CALORIES 46 (29% from fat); FAT 1.5g (sat 0.5g, mono 0.6g, poly 0.3g); PROTEIN 3.5g; CARB 4.9g; FIBER 0.5g; CHOL 2mg; IRON 0.4mg; SODIUM 110mg; CALC 108mg

SEAFOOD SALSA WITH CHIPS

PREP:22 MINUTES   CHILL:30 MINUTES

7 (6-inch) corn tortillas
Cooking spray
½ pound bay scallops
½ pound lump crabmeat, drained and shell pieces removed
½ cup fresh lime juice (about 5 limes)
1 teaspoon grated tangerine or orange rind
⅔ cup chopped tangerine or orange
½ cup chopped seeded peeled tomato
2 tablespoons minced red onion
1 tablespoon chopped fresh cilantro
1 tablespoon minced jalapeño pepper
⅛ teaspoon salt
Cilantro leaves (optional)

1. Preheat oven to 350°.
2. Cut each tortilla into 8 wedges; arrange in a single layer on a baking sheet. Bake at 350° for 10 minutes or until crisp; set tortilla chips aside.
3. Coat a large nonstick skillet with cooking spray. Cook scallops in skillet over medium heat 3 minutes or until done; drain. Combine scallops, crabmeat, lime juice, and tangerine rind in a bowl, tossing gently; cover and chill 30 minutes.
4. Combine chopped tangerine and next 5 ingredients in a bowl, tossing gently. Combine scallop mixture and tangerine mixture in a serving bowl; garnish with cilantro leaves, if desired. Serve immediately with tortilla chips. Yield: 28 servings (serving size: 2 tablespoons salsa and 2 tortilla chips).

CALORIES 35 (10% from fat); FAT 0.4g (sat 0.1g, mono 0.1g, poly 0.2g); PROTEIN 3.4g; CARB 4.7g; FIBER 0.5g; CHOL 10mg; IRON 0.2mg; SODIUM 56mg; CALC 24mg

PAPAYA SALSA AND BRIE WITH TORTILLA WEDGES

PREP: 30 MINUTES   COOK: 5 MINUTES

3 cups diced peeled ripe papaya
¾ cup diced peeled kiwifruit
2 tablespoons chopped red bell pepper
1½ tablespoons minced shallot
1½ tablespoons chopped fresh cilantro
1½ tablespoons lime juice
⅛ teaspoon ground allspice
8 (7-inch) flour tortillas
1 (4-ounce) round Brie cheese

1. Combine first 7 ingredients in a bowl; toss well. Cover and chill.

2. Preheat oven to 350°.

3. Cut each tortilla into 8 wedges; place wedges on baking sheet. Bake at 350° for 10 minutes or until crisp; set aside.

4. Place Brie on an ungreased baking sheet. Bake at 350° for 5 minutes or until thoroughly heated. Transfer Brie to a serving platter, and serve immediately with papaya salsa and tortilla wedges. Yield: 16 servings (serving size: ¼ cup salsa, 1 teaspoon Brie, and 4 tortilla wedges).

CALORIES 97 (29% from fat); FAT 3.1g (sat 1.4g, mono 1g, poly 0.5g); PROTEIN 3.2g; CARB 14.6g; FIBER 1.7g; CHOL 7mg; IRON 0.7mg; SODIUM 115mg; CALC 46mg

Papaya Salsa and Brie
With Tortilla Wedges

SAVORY COEUR À LA CRÈME

PREP: 25 MINUTES   CHILL: 36 HOURS

1 (32-ounce) carton plain low-fat yogurt
½ cup port or other sweet red wine
2 tablespoons grated fresh onion
1 (8-ounce) tub fat-free cream cheese, softened
1 (8-ounce) tub reduced-fat cream cheese, softened
1 (1-ounce) package dry ranch dressing mix
1 envelope unflavored gelatin
¼ cup cold water
Herbs, such as chives, oregano, basil, and mint leaves (optional)

1. Place a colander in a 2-quart glass measure or large bowl. Line colander with 4 layers of cheesecloth, allowing cheesecloth to extend over edges. Spoon yogurt into colander. Cover loosely with plastic wrap; refrigerate 12 hours. Spoon drained yogurt into a bowl, discarding cheesecloth and liquid. Moisten another 3 layers of cheesecloth with wine; squeeze excess wine from cheesecloth until barely damp, reserving 2 tablespoons wine. Line a 4-cup gelatin mold or heart-shaped cake pan with dampened cheesecloth, allowing cheesecloth to extend over edges of mold; set aside.

2. Combine reserved 2 tablespoons wine, grated onion, and next 3 ingredients in a large bowl; beat at low speed of a mixer 1 minute or until smooth. Stir in drained yogurt; set aside. Sprinkle gelatin over ¼ cup water in a small saucepan; let stand 1 minute. Cook over low heat, stirring until gelatin dissolves. Remove from heat; cool slightly. Stir 2 tablespoons yogurt mixture into gelatin mixture with a whisk. Stir gelatin mixture into remaining yogurt mixture.

3. Spoon yogurt mixture into prepared mold. Fold cheesecloth over top; cover with plastic wrap and refrigerate up to 24 hours. Unfold cheesecloth, and invert mold onto a serving plate; discard cheesecloth. Garnish with fresh herbs, if desired. Serve with heart-shaped lavosh or plain crackers. Yield: 4 cups (serving size: 2 tablespoons).

CALORIES 55 (25% from fat); FAT 1.5g (sat 1g, mono 0.4g, poly 0.1g); PROTEIN 3.3g; CARB 5.2g; FIBER 0g; CHOL 7mg; IRON 0mg; SODIUM 167mg; CALC 79mg

menu

• Appetizer Open House •

**Roasted Pepper Pesto
Cheesecake Spread**

Potato-and-Caviar Hors d'Oeuvres (page 38)

Three Fruit Dip (page 22)

Fresh fruit tray

ROASTED PEPPER PESTO CHEESECAKE SPREAD

PREP: 12 MINUTES

COOK: 1 HOUR 10 MINUTES

CHILL: 8 HOURS

Cooking spray
2 tablespoons dry breadcrumbs
1 (15-ounce) carton fat-free ricotta cheese
1 (8-ounce) block ⅓-less-fat cream cheese, softened
⅓ cup (1⅓ ounces) grated fresh Parmesan cheese
⅛ teaspoon salt
Dash of ground red pepper
1 large egg
1½ cups Roasted Pepper Pesto (page 456), divided
1 teaspoon all-purpose flour
1 (8-ounce) carton fat-free sour cream
Basil leaves (optional)

60 (¾-ounce) slices diagonally cut French bread baguette, toasted

1. Preheat oven to 325°.
2. Coat a (9-inch) springform pan with cooking spray; sprinkle breadcrumbs evenly over bottom of pan.
3. Beat ricotta and cream cheese in a large bowl at medium speed of a mixer until smooth. Add Parmesan cheese, salt, pepper, and egg; beat until well-blended. Spoon 1½ cups cheese mixture into prepared pan. Spread 1 cup Roasted Pepper Pesto over cheese mixture; top with remaining 1½ cups cheese mixture. Bake at 325° for 1 hour.
4. Combine ½ cup Roasted Pepper Pesto, flour, and sour cream in a bowl. Cover and chill. Spread sour cream mixture over cheesecake; bake an additional 10 minutes. Cool to room temperature; cover and chill at least 8 hours. Garnish with basil leaves, if desired; serve with baguette slices. Yield: 30 servings (serving size: 2 tablespoons cheesecake spread and 2 baguette slices).

CALORIES 177 (23% from fat); FAT 4.5g (sat 1.8g, mono 1.7g, poly 0.7g); PROTEIN 8.3g; CARB 25.8g; FIBER 1.8g; CHOL 15mg; IRON 1.6mg; SODIUM 359mg; CALC 96mg

HAM AND CHEESE BALL

PREP: 15 MINUTES   CHILL: 1 HOUR

1 (8-ounce) block ⅓-less-fat cream cheese, softened
¼ cup plain low-fat yogurt
1 cup (4 ounces) shredded reduced-fat sharp cheddar cheese
¾ cup finely chopped lean cooked ham
2 tablespoons finely chopped green onions
2 teaspoons prepared horseradish
1 teaspoon country-style Dijon mustard
¼ cup chopped fresh parsley

1. Beat cream cheese and yogurt in a large bowl at medium speed of a mixer until smooth. Stir in cheddar cheese, ham, onions, horseradish, and mustard. Cover and chill at least 1 hour.
2. Shape cheese mixture into a ball, and sprinkle with parsley. Press parsley gently into cheese ball. Wrap cheese ball in heavy-duty plastic wrap, and chill. Serve with fat-free crackers. Yield: 2 cups (serving size: 1 tablespoon).

CALORIES 35 (67% from fat); FAT 2.6g (sat 1.5g, mono 0.8g, poly 0.1g); PROTEIN 2.5g; CARB 0.6g; FIBER 0g; CHOL 10mg; IRON 0.1mg; SODIUM 112mg; CALC 41mg

CURRIED TURKEY PÂTÉ

PREP: 8 MINUTES

CHILL: 2 HOURS

2 cups coarsely chopped cooked deli turkey breast (about 10 ounces)
¼ cup sliced green onions
½ cup fat-free sour cream
¼ cup mango chutney
½ to ¾ teaspoon curry powder
1 tablespoon chopped fresh parsley

1. Place first 5 ingredients in a food processor; process until smooth.
2. Line a deep 4-cup bowl with heavy-duty plastic wrap, allowing plastic wrap to extend over edges. Spoon turkey mixture into bowl; cover with plastic wrap, pressing to pack mixture into bowl. Chill 2 hours.
3. Fold back plastic wrap, and invert bowl onto a serving platter. Remove bowl, and carefully remove plastic wrap; sprinkle with parsley. Serve with water crackers or pita chips. Yield: 2 cups (serving size: 2 tablespoons).

CALORIES 41 (9% from fat); FAT 0.4g (sat 0.1g, mono 0.2g, poly 0.1g); PROTEIN 4.0g; CARB 4.3g; FIBER 0.1g; CHOL 5mg; IRON 0.1mg; SODIUM 192mg; CALC 16mg

first-course favorites

These favorites range from bruschetta with Italian flair to Asian-accented saté and pot stickers—around-the-world flavor for your table.

Bruschetta With
Tomatoes

BRUSCHETTA WITH TOMATOES

PREP: 12 MINUTES

  1 large garlic clove, halved
24 (½-inch-thick) slices diagonally cut French bread baguette
1½ cups diced plum tomato (about 4 medium)
  2 tablespoons finely chopped red onion
  1 tablespoon extra-virgin olive oil
24 small basil leaves

1. Preheat oven to 350°.
2. Rub cut sides of garlic over one side of each bread slice; place bread on an ungreased baking sheet. Bake at 350° for 10 minutes or until lightly browned, turning once.
3. Combine tomato, onion, and oil in a bowl. Spoon tomato mixture evenly onto bread slices, and top each with a basil leaf. Yield: 2 dozen (serving size: 1 bruschetta).

CALORIES 36 (23% from fat); FAT 0.9g (sat 0.2g, mono 0.6g, poly 0.1g); PROTEIN 1g; CARB 6g; FIBER 0.5g; CHOL 0mg; IRON 0.3mg; SODIUM 64mg; CALC 9mg

HERBED BRUSCHETTA

PREP: 20 MINUTES

  1 large garlic clove, halved
34 (½-inch-thick) slices diagonally cut French bread baguette
  2 tablespoons extra-virgin olive oil
  1 teaspoon dried rosemary
  1 teaspoon dried thyme
  1 teaspoon dried basil
  ¼ teaspoon coarsely ground black pepper

1. Preheat broiler.
2. Rub cut sides of garlic over one side of each bread slice. Brush with oil; sprinkle with rosemary, thyme, basil, and pepper. Broil 1 minute or until edges are lightly browned. Serve warm or at room temperature. Yield: 34 servings (serving size: 1 bruschetta).

CALORIES 31 (32% from fat); FAT 1.1g (sat 0.2g, mono 0.7g, poly 0.1g); PROTEIN 0.8g; CARB 4.5g; FIBER 0.3g; CHOL 0mg; IRON 0.3mg; SODIUM 52mg; CALC 8mg

MUSHROOM CROSTINI

PREP: 20 MINUTES

Cremini mushrooms resemble button mushrooms but have a darker color and a more robust, earthy flavor. If cremini mushrooms are unavailable, use all button mushrooms instead.

1 teaspoon olive oil
2½ cups sliced cremini mushrooms
1 cup sliced button mushrooms
¼ teaspoon salt
2 teaspoons minced fresh or
½ teaspoon dried thyme
½ teaspoon all-purpose flour
⅛ teaspoon black pepper
1 garlic clove, halved
8 (½-inch-thick) slices Italian bread, toasted (about 4 ounces)

1. Heat oil in a medium nonstick skillet over medium heat. Stir in mushrooms and salt. Cover and cook 5 minutes (do not stir). Increase heat to medium-high; add thyme, flour, and pepper. Cook, uncovered, 1 minute, stirring occasionally.
2. Rub cut sides of garlic over one side of each bread slice. Spoon 2 tablespoons mushroom mixture onto each bread slice. Yield: 8 servings (serving size: 1 crostino).

CALORIES 54 (13% from fat); FAT 0.8g (sat 0.1g, mono 0.5g, poly 0.1g); PROTEIN 2.1g; CARB 9.9g; FIBER 0.9g; CHOL 0mg; IRON 0.8mg; SODIUM 158mg; CALC 5mg

menu

Tomato-and-Feta Crostini

Asparagus Salad With Caesar Vinaigrette (page 398)

Linguine With Two Sauces (page 269)

Hazelnut Biscotti (page 159)

TOMATO-AND-FETA CROSTINI

PREP: 23 MINUTES
COOK: 5 MINUTES

1 cup sun-dried tomatoes, packed without oil
1 teaspoon dried rosemary, crushed
24 (½-inch-thick) slices French bread baguette
Olive oil-flavored cooking spray
½ teaspoon onion powder
½ cup (2 ounces) crumbled feta cheese
1 tablespoon chopped fresh parsley

1. Place tomatoes and rosemary in a 1-quart casserole; add water to cover. Cover with casserole lid, and microwave at HIGH 6 minutes or until water boils. Let stand, covered, 10 minutes. Drain.
2. Preheat oven to 350°.
3. Place tomatoes and rosemary in a food processor or blender. Pulse 10 seconds or until combined. Coat bread slices with cooking spray; sprinkle with onion powder. Spread tomato mixture evenly over bread slices; top each slice with about 1 teaspoon feta cheese.
4. Place crostini in a single layer on a baking sheet. Bake at 350° for 5 minutes or until toasted. Sprinkle with parsley. Serve immediately. Yield: 2 dozen (serving size: 1 crostino).

CALORIES 41 (26% from fat); FAT 1.2g (sat 0.6g, mono 0.3g, poly 0.1g); PROTEIN 1.6g; CARB 6.1g; FIBER 0.6g; CHOL 3mg; IRON 0.5mg; SODIUM 138mg; CALC 27mg

ASPARAGUS WITH HERBED CHEESE ON TOAST

PREP: 30 MINUTES   COOK: 4 MINUTES

18 large fresh asparagus spears (about 1 pound)
1 large Vidalia or other sweet onion (about 1 pound)
1 cup fat-free ricotta cheese
2 tablespoons chopped fresh thyme
2 tablespoons chopped fresh chives
2 tablespoons chopped fresh or
2 teaspoons dried chervil
1 (1-pound) unsliced round loaf pumpernickel bread
2 tablespoons butter, softened
2 teaspoons extra-virgin olive oil
¼ teaspoon salt
¼ teaspoon black pepper

1. Preheat oven to 400°.
2. Snap off tough ends of asparagus. Peel onion, leaving root intact; cut into 6 wedges. Add asparagus and onion to a large saucepan of boiling water; cook 3 minutes. Drain; plunge into ice water. Drain; pat dry with a paper towel. Set aside.
3. Combine ricotta cheese and next 3 ingredients in a bowl; set aside.
4. Cut bread crosswise into 6 (1-inch-thick) slices; reserve remaining bread for another use. Spread butter over 1 side of bread slices. Place bread in a single layer on a baking sheet. Bake at 400° for 5 minutes or until toasted. Cut each bread slice into 6 triangles. Spread cheese mixture over toasted side of triangles.
5. Place oil in a large nonstick skillet over medium-high heat until hot. Add asparagus, onion, salt, and pepper; sauté 4 minutes or until lightly browned. Serve with toast triangles. Yield: 6 servings (serving size: 6 toast triangles, 3 asparagus spears, and 1 onion wedge).

CALORIES 274 (24% from fat); FAT 7.8g (sat 2.9g, mono 2.8g, poly 1.2g); PROTEIN 13.4g; CARB 41g; FIBER 5.9g; CHOL 15mg; IRON 2.5mg; SODIUM 606mg; CALC 138mg

ARTICHOKE-AND-RED PEPPER PIZZA

PREP:20 MINUTES   COOK:10 MINUTES

1   (10-ounce) can refrigerated pizza
      crust
Cooking spray
1   tablespoon olive oil
1   cup red bell pepper strips
1   teaspoon dried basil
1   teaspoon dried oregano
5   garlic cloves, minced
1   (14-ounce) can artichoke hearts,
      drained and coarsely chopped
1   (2.5-ounce) jar sliced
      mushrooms, drained
1½ cups (6 ounces) preshredded
      part-skim mozzarella cheese
Cracked black pepper (optional)

1. Preheat oven to 425°.
2. Unroll pizza dough onto a baking
sheet coated with cooking spray; pat
dough into a 14 x 10-inch rectangle.
Bake at 425° for 6 minutes; set aside.
3. Heat oil in a large nonstick skillet
over medium-high heat. Add red bell
pepper and next 3 ingredients; sauté 5
minutes. Remove from heat; stir in artichokes and mushrooms.
4. Sprinkle half of cheese over prepared
pizza crust, leaving a ½-inch border.
Spread vegetable mixture evenly over
cheese, and top with remaining cheese.
Sprinkle with cracked pepper, if desired.
Bake at 425° for 10 minutes or until crust
is lightly browned. Yield: 16 servings.

CALORIES 94 (32% from fat); FAT 3.3g (sat 1.2g, mono 1.4g,
poly 0.5g); PROTEIN 4.9g; CARB 11.3g; FIBER 0.4g;
CHOL 6mg; IRON 0.8mg; SODIUM 238mg; CALC 81mg

SKEWERED TORTELLINI APPETIZERS

PREP:20 MINUTES

36 fresh cheese tortellini,
      uncooked (about 4 ounces)
¼   cup reduced-calorie Italian dressing
1   tablespoon chopped fresh parsley
36 (¾-inch) squares red bell pepper
      (about 2 large)

1. Cook pasta according to package directions, omitting salt and fat. Drain.
2. Combine pasta and remaining ingredients in a bowl; toss. Thread 3 tortellini
and 3 bell pepper squares alternately
onto each of 12 (6-inch) skewers. Yield:
12 servings (serving size: 1 skewer).

CALORIES 46 (22% from fat); FAT 1.1g (sat 0.3g, mono 0g,
poly 0.1g); PROTEIN 2.1g; CARB 6.7g; FIBER 0.5g;
CHOL 6mg; IRON 0.2mg; SODIUM 118mg; CALC 31mg

Artichoke-and-Red Pepper Pizza

Roasted Pepper and Goat Cheese Strudels

PREP: 56 MINUTES   COOK: 25 MINUTES

- 1 pound red bell peppers (about 2 large)
- 1 pound green bell peppers (about 2 large)
- ¾ cup fresh breadcrumbs
- ¼ cup chopped fresh basil
- 1 teaspoon chopped fresh rosemary
- ½ teaspoon salt
- ¼ teaspoon black pepper
- 1 teaspoon olive oil
- 1 cup diced carrot
- 1 cup finely chopped onion
- 1 garlic clove, minced
- 12 sheets frozen phyllo dough, thawed
- Cooking spray
- ¾ cup (3 ounces) crumbled goat cheese
- 6 tablespoons chopped fresh parsley

1. Preheat broiler.

2. Cut bell peppers in half lengthwise; discard seeds and membranes. Place bell pepper halves, skin sides up, on a foil-lined baking sheet; flatten with hand. Broil 12 minutes or until blackened. Place in a zip-top plastic bag; seal. Let stand 15 minutes. Peel and cut into 1-inch-wide strips. Set aside. Reduce oven temperature to 375°.

3. Combine breadcrumbs, basil, rosemary, salt, and pepper in a small bowl. Set aside.

4. Heat oil in a medium nonstick skillet over medium heat. Add carrot, onion, and garlic; sauté vegetables 8 minutes or until tender and lightly browned. Remove from heat.

5. Place 1 phyllo sheet on a large cutting board or work surface (cover remaining dough to keep from drying); lightly coat with cooking spray. Place another phyllo sheet on top of first sheet; lightly coat with cooking spray. Cut stack in half crosswise, and place 1 half on top of the other half. Sprinkle 2 tablespoons breadcrumb mixture along 1 short edge of phyllo stack, leaving a 2-inch border. Spoon ¼ cup carrot mixture over breadcrumbs; top with one-sixth of red bell pepper strips (about 2 strips), one-sixth of green bell pepper strips (about 2 strips), ½ ounce cheese, and 1 tablespoon parsley. Fold over long edges of phyllo to cover 2 inches of filling. Starting at short edge, roll up jelly-roll fashion (do not roll tightly or strudel may split). Place roll, seam side down, on a baking sheet coated with cooking spray; lightly coat roll with cooking spray. Repeat procedure with remaining sheets of phyllo, breadcrumb mixture, carrot mixture, bell pepper strips, cheese, and parsley.

6. Bake at 375° for 25 minutes or until golden. Serve warm. Yield: 12 servings (serving size: ½ roll).

CALORIES 125 (29% from fat); FAT 4.0g (sat 1.4g, mono 1.1g, poly 1.1g); PROTEIN 3.7g; CARB 20.2g; FIBER 2.2g; CHOL 6mg; IRON 2mg; SODIUM 296mg; CALC 55mg

Deviled Eggs

PREP: 30 MINUTES   CHILL: 1 HOUR

- 8 large eggs
- 1 (8-ounce) carton plain low-fat yogurt
- 2 tablespoons sweet pickle relish, drained
- 1 tablespoon country-style Dijon mustard
- ⅛ teaspoon salt
- ⅛ teaspoon white pepper
- Paprika (optional)

1. Place eggs in a single layer in a saucepan; add water to measure 1 inch over eggs. Cover and bring just to a boil. Remove from heat; let stand, covered, in hot water 15 to 17 minutes. Pour off water. Run cold water over eggs immediately until cool enough to handle. Peel and slice eggs in half lengthwise; carefully remove yolks from 8 egg halves; mash yolks in a bowl. Remove yolks from remaining 8 egg halves, and reserve for another use. Finely chop 4 egg white halves, and add to mashed yolks. Set aside remaining 12 egg white halves.

2. Spoon yogurt onto several layers of heavy-duty paper towels; spread to ½-inch thickness. Cover with additional paper towels; let stand 10 minutes. Scrape into yolk mixture, using a rubber spatula.

3. Spoon relish onto paper towels; squeeze until barely moist. Stir relish and next 3 ingredients into yolk mixture. Spoon about 1 tablespoon yolk mixture into each egg white half. Cover and chill 1 hour. Sprinkle with paprika, if desired. Yield: 12 servings (serving size: 1 filled egg half).

CALORIES 48 (41% from fat); FAT 2.2g (sat 0.7g, mono 0.8g, poly 0.3g); PROTEIN 4.3g; CARB 2.6g; FIBER 0g; CHOL 72mg; IRON 0.2mg; SODIUM 134mg; CALC 44mg

HARD-COOKED EGGS

Place eggs in a single layer in saucepan. Fill pan with water to at least 1 inch above eggs. Cover and bring to a boil; remove from heat. Let stand 15 minutes. (**Don't boil eggs or cook them longer than directed because yolks may become hard and develop an unattractive gray-green ring from overcooking.**) Pour off water, and immediately place eggs under cold running water until cooled. This stops the cooking process and makes the eggs easier to peel. Peel under running water, starting with the large end. Store all eggs in the refrigerator.

RATATOUILLE AND GOAT CHEESE WRAPPED IN PHYLLO

PREP: 22 MINUTES   COOK: 6 MINUTES

(pictured on page 21)

 1 teaspoon olive oil, divided
 2 cups finely diced peeled
     eggplant
 2 cups finely diced zucchini
 1½ cups finely diced yellow squash
 1 cup finely chopped red bell
     pepper
 1 cup finely chopped onion
 2 garlic cloves, minced
 ⅔ cup diced seeded peeled
     tomato
 1½ tablespoons minced fresh basil
 1 teaspoon minced fresh thyme
 ¼ teaspoon salt
 ¼ teaspoon dry mustard
 ¼ teaspoon black pepper
 1 (4-ounce) package crumbled
     goat cheese
 20 sheets frozen phyllo dough,
     thawed
Olive oil-flavored cooking spray
 5 cups gourmet salad greens

1. Heat ¼ teaspoon oil in a large non-stick skillet. Add eggplant, and sauté 2 minutes. Remove eggplant from skillet; set aside.

2. Heat ½ teaspoon oil in skillet; add zucchini, yellow squash, and bell pepper; sauté 2 minutes. Remove zucchini mixture from skillet, and set aside. Heat ¼ teaspoon oil in skillet. Add onion and garlic; sauté 2 minutes. Stir in tomato; cook 3 minutes. Return eggplant and zucchini mixture to skillet, and cook 5 minutes. Remove skillet from heat. Stir in basil and next 5 ingredients.

3. Preheat oven to 450°.

4. Place 1 phyllo sheet on a large cutting board or work surface (cover remaining dough to keep from drying); lightly coat with cooking spray. Place another phyllo sheet on top of first sheet; lightly coat with cooking spray. Repeat with 2 more sheets. Cut stack crosswise into 4 (4½ x 14-inch) strips. Spoon about ¼ cup vegetable mixture onto short end of each stack. Fold left bottom corner of each stack over mixture, forming a triangle; keep folding back and forth into a triangle to end of each strip. Repeat with remaining phyllo and vegetable mixture.

5. Place triangles, seam sides down, on a baking sheet; lightly coat with cooking spray. Bake at 450° for 6 minutes or until golden. Serve warm with gourmet greens. Yield: 10 servings (serving size: 2 turnovers and ½ cup gourmet greens).

CALORIES 178 (28% from fat); FAT 5.5g (sat 2.1g, mono 1.4g, poly 1.5g); PROTEIN 5.8g; CARB 26.7g; FIBER 1.7g; CHOL 10mg; IRON 2mg; SODIUM 375mg; CALC 86mg

PHYLLO DOUGH

Phyllo dough is typically found in the frozen food section in the grocery store, though a specialty market may carry it unfrozen. If the phyllo dough has been frozen, thaw it in the refrigerator for two days.

Handle phyllo sheets slowly and gently. The pastry is very thin and delicate; rough handling will cause breaks or tears. Phyllo dries out easily. Always keep it covered with a damp cloth or plastic wrap when you're not working with it.

STUFFED GRAPE LEAVES

PREP: 22 MINUTES
COOK: 30 MINUTES
CHILL: 1¼ HOURS

Bottled grape leaves can be found in many supermarkets in the international foods section. For information on pine nuts, see "Pine Nuts" on page 456.

 1 cup plain low-fat yogurt
 3 tablespoons chopped fresh mint,
     divided
 1 teaspoon grated lemon rind
 1 teaspoon honey
 30 bottled large grape leaves
 1 tablespoon olive oil
 1¾ cups finely chopped onion
 1 garlic clove, minced
 ¼ cup fresh lemon juice,
     divided
 2 cups hot cooked long-grain rice
 ½ cup dried currants
 ⅓ cup pine nuts, toasted
 1 tablespoon chopped fresh or
     1 teaspoon dried dill
 ½ teaspoon salt
 ¼ teaspoon black pepper
 1 (15-ounce) can chickpeas
     (garbanzo beans), rinsed
     and drained
Cooking spray

1. Combine yogurt, 2 tablespoons fresh mint, 1 teaspoon lemon rind, and 1 teaspoon honey in a small bowl. Cover and chill.

2. Rinse grape leaves with cold water; drain well, and pat dry with paper towels. Remove and discard stems.

3. Heat oil in a large nonstick skillet over medium-high heat. Add chopped onion, and sauté 3 minutes or until tender. Add garlic, and sauté 1 minute. Remove from heat; stir in 1 tablespoon mint, 2 tablespoons lemon juice, rice, and next 6 ingredients.

Stuffing Grape Leaves

1. Rinse grape leaves with cold water, and remove stems.

2. Spoon 1 rounded tablespoon of rice mixture onto center of each grape leaf.

3. Bring one point of leaf to center, and fold over filling.

4. Bring opposite point of leaf to center, and fold over filling.

5. Beginning at 1 short side, roll up leaf tightly, jelly-roll fashion.

6. Place stuffed grape leaves, seam sides down, in a 13 x 9-inch baking dish coated with cooking spray. Drizzle remaining lemon juice over leaves.

4. Preheat oven to 350°.

5. Spoon 1 rounded tablespoon of rice mixture onto center of each grape leaf. Bring 2 opposite points of leaf to center, and fold over filling. Beginning at 1 short side, roll up leaf tightly, jelly-roll fashion.

6. Place stuffed grape leaves, seam sides down, in a 13 x 9-inch baking dish coated with cooking spray. Drizzle 2 tablespoons lemon juice over grape leaves. Cover and bake at 350° for 30 minutes or until stuffed grape leaves are thoroughly heated. Serve grape leaves warm or chilled with yogurt mixture. Yield: 30 servings (serving size: 1 stuffed grape leaf and 1½ teaspoons yogurt mixture).

CALORIES 60 (29% from fat); FAT 1.9g (sat 0.3g, mono 0.8g, poly 0.6g); PROTEIN 1.8g; CARB 9.6g; FIBER 1.6g; CHOL 0mg; IRON 0.5mg; SODIUM 245mg; CALC 25mg

POTATO SKINS WITH CHEESE AND BACON

PREP: 10 MINUTES

COOK: 1 HOUR 13 MINUTES

4 medium baking potatoes (about 2 pounds)
Cooking spray
4 slices turkey bacon
¾ cup (3 ounces) shredded reduced-fat sharp cheddar cheese
¼ cup fat-free sour cream
1 tablespoon minced fresh chives

1. Preheat oven to 425°.
2. Bake potatoes at 425° for 1 hour or until done. Cool slightly. Cut each potato in half lengthwise, and scoop out potato pulp, leaving a ¼-inch-thick shell. Reserve pulp for another use.
3. Place potato shells on a baking sheet. Spray inside of shells with cooking spray. Bake at 425° for 8 minutes or until crisp; set aside.
4. Cook bacon in microwave oven according to package directions; cool slightly. Chop bacon into small pieces.
5. Sprinkle cheese evenly in potato shells. Bake at 425° for 5 minutes or until cheese melts. Sprinkle evenly with bacon. Dollop sour cream on potatoes; sprinkle with chives. Yield: 8 servings (serving size: 1 stuffed potato skin and 1½ teaspoons sour cream).

CALORIES 125 (30% from fat); FAT 4.1g (sat 1.7g, mono 1.4g, poly 0.5g); PROTEIN 6.6g; CARB 14.5g; FIBER 1g; CHOL 16mg; IRON 0.8mg; SODIUM 263mg; CALC 200mg

POTATO-AND-CAVIAR HORS D'OEUVRES

PREP: 44 MINUTES

See page 25 for tips on draining yogurt.

24 (¼-inch-thick) slices red potato (about 6 medium)
⅓ cup plain fat-free yogurt
¼ cup low-fat sour cream
2 tablespoons finely chopped fresh chives
2 tablespoons finely chopped fresh parsley
1 tablespoon red caviar
Freshly ground pepper (optional)

1. Steam potato slices, covered, 12 minutes or just until tender. Drain potato slices, and cool.
2. Combine yogurt and sour cream in a bowl. Spoon mixture onto several layers of heavy-duty paper towels; spread to ½-inch thickness. Cover with additional paper towels; let stand 10 minutes. Scrape mixture into a pastry bag fitted with a fluted tip; set aside.
3. Combine chives and parsley; sprinkle herbs evenly over potato slices. Pipe about ½ teaspoon yogurt mixture onto each potato slice; top each slice with ⅛ teaspoon caviar. Sprinkle with freshly ground pepper, if desired. Serve immediately. Yield: 8 servings (serving size: 3 appetizers).

CALORIES 74 (16% from fat); FAT 1.3g (sat 0.6g, mono 0.4g, poly 0.1g); PROTEIN 2.8g; CARB 13.5g; FIBER 1.4g; CHOL 11mg; IRON 1mg; SODIUM 37mg; CALC 37mg

BEEF TRIANGLES WITH CHUTNEY SAUCE

PREP: 38 MINUTES

COOK: 12 MINUTES

For additional information and tips on working with phyllo, see tip box on page 36. Mango chutney is found with other condiments in the grocery store. It contains mango pulp, vinegar, sugar, and spices. It's usually chunky and can be mild or hot—either are fine for this recipe.

½ cup plain low-fat yogurt
½ cup mango chutney
1 pound ground round
½ cup chopped onion
⅓ cup dried currants
½ teaspoon salt
½ teaspoon ground cumin
¼ teaspoon ground nutmeg
¼ teaspoon ground cinnamon
⅛ teaspoon ground red pepper
⅛ teaspoon black pepper
½ cup water
1 tablespoon cornstarch
15 sheets frozen phyllo dough, thawed
Butter-flavored cooking spray

1. Preheat oven to 400°.
2. Combine yogurt and mango chutney in a bowl; set chutney sauce aside.
3. Cook beef and onion in a large nonstick skillet over medium heat until browned, stirring to crumble. Drain. Wipe drippings from pan with a paper towel.
4. Return beef mixture to skillet. Stir in currants and next 6 ingredients. Combine water and cornstarch; add to beef mixture. Cook over medium heat 2 minutes, stirring constantly. Remove from heat; set aside.
5. Place phyllo sheets on a large cutting board or work surface. Cut sheets

Chives resemble hollow blades of grass and are members of the onion family. Sprinkle them over food just before serving for the freshest flavor.

Beef Triangles

1. Cut sheet lengthwise into 4 (3¼-inch-wide) strips.

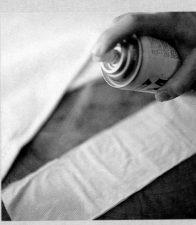

2. Working with 2 strips at a time (cover remaining dough to keep from drying), lightly coat strips with cooking spray.

3. Stack 2 strips, and spoon about 1 tablespoon beef mixture onto one short end of each stack.

4. Fold left bottom corner over mixture, forming a triangle; keep folding back and forth into a triangle to end of strip.

5. Place triangles, seam sides down, on a baking sheet; lightly coat with cooking spray.

6. Remove from oven when golden, and serve warm.

lengthwise into 4 (3¼-inch-wide) strips. Working with 2 strips at a time (cover remaining dough to keep from drying), lightly coat strips with cooking spray. Stack 2 strips of dough, and spoon about 1 tablespoon beef mixture onto one short end of stack. Fold left bottom corner over mixture, forming a triangle, and keep folding back and forth into a triangle to end of strip. Repeat procedure with remaining phyllo strips, cooking spray, and remaining beef mixture.

6. Place beef triangles, seam sides down, on a baking sheet, and lightly coat triangles with cooking spray. Bake at 400° for 12 minutes or until triangles are golden. Serve triangles warm with chutney sauce. Yield: 30 servings (serving size: 1 triangle and 1½ teaspoons sauce).

CALORIES 81 (23% from fat); FAT 2.1g (sat 0.5g, mono 0.8g, poly 0.5g); PROTEIN 4.3g; CARB 10.7g; FIBER 0.1g; CHOL 10mg; IRON 0.7mg; SODIUM 143mg; CALC 15mg

TANDOORI CHICKEN SATÉ

PREP: 42 MINUTES

MARINATE: 2 HOURS

COOK: 10 MINUTES

¼ cup coarsely chopped onion
¼ cup plain low-fat yogurt
1 tablespoon extra-virgin olive oil
½ teaspoon ground coriander
½ teaspoon chopped peeled fresh
   ginger
¼ teaspoon salt
¼ teaspoon ground cumin
¼ teaspoon ground turmeric
¼ teaspoon ground red pepper
¼ teaspoon black pepper
1 garlic clove
1½ pounds skinned, boned chicken
   breast halves, cut into ½-inch-
   wide strips
Cooking spray
Lemon wedges (optional)
Cilantro sprigs (optional)

1. Place first 11 ingredients in a food processor; process until smooth, scraping sides once. Combine yogurt mixture and chicken in a large heavy-duty zip-top plastic bag. Seal and marinate in refrigerator 2 hours, turning bag occasionally.
2. Preheat broiler.
3. Remove chicken from bag, discarding marinade. Thread chicken strips onto 24 (6-inch) skewers. Place skewers on a broiler pan coated with cooking spray; broil 5 minutes on each side or until chicken is done. Arrange skewers on a serving platter, and garnish with lemon wedges and cilantro sprigs, if desired. Yield: 24 servings (serving size: 1 skewer).

CALORIES 39 (23% from fat); FAT 1g (sat 0.3g, mono 0.4g, poly 0.2g); PROTEIN 6.7g; CARB 0.3g; FIBER 0g; CHOL 18mg; IRON 0.2mg; SODIUM 36mg; CALC 7mg

CHICKEN SALAD CREAM PUFFS

PREP: 31 MINUTES   COOK: 19 MINUTES

CHILL: 30 MINUTES

⅓ cup diced celery
¼ cup finely chopped green onions
¼ cup reduced-fat mayonnaise
3 tablespoons chopped fresh
   parsley
2 tablespoons plain fat-free yogurt
1 tablespoon fresh lemon juice
½ teaspoon salt
½ teaspoon dried basil
¼ teaspoon black pepper
1¾ cups chopped cooked chicken
   breast (about ¾ pound)
1 (2-ounce) jar diced pimento,
   drained
1 cup all-purpose flour
2 teaspoons sugar
¼ teaspoon salt
1 cup fat-free milk
2 tablespoons margarine
3 large egg whites
1 large egg yolk
Cooking spray

1. Preheat oven to 425°.
2. Combine first 11 ingredients in a bowl; cover and chill.
3. Lightly spoon flour into a dry measuring cup; level with a knife. Combine flour, sugar, and salt in a bowl; set aside. Combine milk and margarine in a large saucepan; bring to a boil. Reduce heat to low; add flour mixture, stirring well until mixture is smooth and pulls away from sides of pan. Remove from heat; cool 5 minutes.
4. Add egg whites and egg yolk, 1 at a time, beating at low speed of a mixer until smooth. Drop dough by level tablespoonfuls, 2 inches apart, onto baking sheets coated with cooking spray.
5. Bake at 425° for 10 minutes. Reduce oven temperature to 350°, and bake an

additional 9 minutes or until browned and crisp. Remove from oven; pierce the side of each cream puff with the tip of a sharp knife to release steam. Turn oven off; let cream puffs stand in partially-closed oven 5 minutes. Remove from baking sheet to a wire rack, and cool completely.
6. Cut off tops of cream puffs. Fill each cream puff with 1 tablespoon chicken salad; replace tops of cream puffs. Serve immediately. Yield: 28 servings.

CALORIES 55 (34% from fat); FAT 2.1g (sat 0.4g, mono 0.7g, poly 0.7g); PROTEIN 4.3g; CARB 4.4g; FIBER 0.2g; CHOL 17mg; IRON 0.4mg; SODIUM 106mg; CALC 19mg

CHICKEN POT STICKERS

PREP: 33 MINUTES   COOK: 12 MINUTES

You can assemble these pot stickers up to 30 minutes before cooking (assembled too far in advance, the ends of the wrappers will dry out). Cover them tightly, and refrigerate. Then when ready to use, cook as directed.

2 teaspoons vegetable oil
2 cups finely chopped green
   cabbage
½ cup water
½ pound ground chicken or turkey
⅓ cup minced green onions
1 tablespoon minced peeled fresh
   ginger
½ teaspoon salt
½ teaspoon dark sesame oil
1 large egg white, lightly beaten
1 garlic clove, crushed
24 won ton wrappers
2 teaspoons cornstarch
4 teaspoons vegetable oil, divided
1 cup water, divided

1. Heat 2 teaspoons vegetable oil in a large nonstick skillet over medium-high heat. Add cabbage, and cook, stirring

Chicken Pot Stickers

1. Spoon about 1 tablespoon chicken mixture onto center of each won ton wrapper.

2. Moisten edges of dough with water, and bring 2 opposite corners together, pinching points to seal.

3. Place pot stickers on a large baking sheet sprinkled with cornstarch; cover loosely with a towel to keep them from drying out.

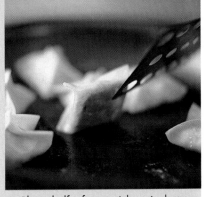

4. Place half of pot stickers in bottom of skillet; cook 3 minutes or until bottoms are lightly browned. Add ½ cup water to skillet; cover and cook 3 minutes or until liquid is absorbed.

HANDLING WON TON WRAPPERS

• Because won ton wrappers dry out very easily, keep them covered with a damp towel while you're working.

• The wrappers come in a variety of shapes and sizes: square, circular, thin, medium, and thick. We used a medium thickness to test our recipes, but don't be afraid to experiment.

• Using a lightly beaten egg white to seal won ton wrappers ensures that they won't open during cooking.

• Egg roll wrappers also work well for these recipes.

• Stuffed won tons can be frozen before cooking. Freeze them on a baking sheet, and then place in a zip-top plastic bag. (If put in the bag before freezing, they'll stick together.) When ready to use, thaw and proceed with cooking instructions.

constantly, 8 minutes or until lightly browned. While cabbage cooks, add ½ cup water, 1 tablespoon at a time, to keep cabbage from sticking to pan. Spoon cabbage into a medium bowl; cool completely.

2. Stir chicken and next 6 ingredients into cabbage.

3. Working with 1 won ton wrapper at a time (cover remaining wrappers with a damp towel to keep them from drying), spoon about 1 tablespoon chicken mixture into center of each wrapper. Moisten edges of dough with water, and bring 2 opposite corners together, pinching points to seal. Bring remaining 2 corners to center, pinching points to seal. Place on a baking sheet sprinkled with cornstarch (cover to keep from drying out).

4. Heat 2 teaspoons vegetable oil in a large nonstick skillet over medium heat. Place half of pot stickers in skillet; cook 3 minutes or until bottoms are lightly browned. Add ½ cup water to skillet; cover and cook 3 minutes or until liquid is absorbed. Transfer to a serving platter; set aside, and keep warm. Wipe skillet with a paper towel. Repeat procedure with 2 teaspoons vegetable oil, remaining pot stickers, and ½ cup water. Yield: 24 servings (serving size: 1 pot sticker).

CALORIES 46 (31% from fat); FAT 1.6g (sat 0.3g, mono 0.5g, poly 0.7g); PROTEIN 3.0g; CARB 4.8g; FIBER 0.2g; CHOL 7mg; IRON 0.4mg; SODIUM 100mg; CALC 8mg

CRAB SPRING ROLLS

PREP: 45 MINUTES   COOK: 5 MINUTES

2 tablespoons sugar
1 cup pink grapefruit juice
2 tablespoons fresh lime juice
⅛ teaspoon freshly ground black
   pepper
Cooking spray
2 cups thinly sliced bok choy
⅔ cup finely chopped green onions
2 tablespoons fresh lime juice
2 teaspoons minced fresh cilantro
½ teaspoon minced pickled ginger or
   minced peeled fresh ginger
⅛ teaspoon salt
⅛ teaspoon freshly ground pepper
6 ounces lump crabmeat, shell
   pieces removed
8 egg roll wrappers
1 egg white
2 tablespoons olive oil
2 cups gourmet salad greens
12 pink grapefruit sections
2 tablespoons slivered almonds,
   toasted

1. Place sugar in a small, heavy saucepan over medium-high heat; cook until sugar dissolves, stirring frequently. Continue cooking 2 minutes or until golden. Remove from heat; carefully stir in grapefruit juice and 2 tablespoons lime juice (caramelized sugar will harden and stick to spoon). Place pan over medium-high heat until caramelized sugar melts. Bring to a boil, and cook until reduced to ½ cup (about 10 minutes). Remove from heat; stir in ⅛ teaspoon pepper. Set aside.
2. Place a nonstick skillet coated with cooking spray over medium-high heat. Add bok choy and onions; sauté until bok choy wilts. Combine bok choy mixture, 2 tablespoons lime juice, and next 5 ingredients in a bowl.
3. Working with 1 egg roll wrapper at a time (cover remaining wrappers to keep

Crab Spring Rolls

PART 1 caramelizing the sugar

1. Place sugar in a small, heavy saucepan over medium-high heat; cook until sugar dissolves, stirring frequently.

2. Continue cooking 2 minutes or until golden.

3. Remove from heat; carefully stir in grapefruit juice and 2 tablespoons lime juice (caramelized sugar will harden and stick to spoon).

4. Cook over medium-high heat 2 minutes or until caramelized sugar dissolves. Bring to a boil, and cook 8 to 10 minutes or until reduced to ½ cup.

from drying), spoon ¼ cup crabmeat mixture into center of each wrapper. Fold lower right corner over crabmeat mixture; fold lower left and top right corners over mixture. Moisten top left corner with egg white; roll up jelly-roll fashion. Repeat procedure with remaining egg roll wrappers, crabmeat mixture, and egg white.
4. Heat oil in skillet over medium-high heat. Add egg rolls, and cook 5 minutes

or until egg rolls are golden, turning frequently.
5. Arrange ½ cup salad greens and 3 grapefruit sections on each of 4 plates; top each with 2 egg rolls. Drizzle 2 tablespoons caramelized sugar mixture over each serving, and sprinkle each with 1½ teaspoons nuts. Yield: 4 servings.

CALORIES 364 (24% from fat); FAT 9.7g (sat 1.2g, mono 6.3g, poly 1.3g); PROTEIN 17.3g; CARB 54.2g; FIBER 3.4g; CHOL 40mg; IRON 2.1mg; SODIUM 250mg; CALC 96mg

1. Working with 1 egg roll wrapper at a time, spoon ¼ cup crabmeat mixture into center of each wrapper (cover remaining wrappers to keep from drying).

2. Fold lower right corner over crabmeat mixture.

3. Fold lower left and top right corners over mixture.

4. Moisten top left corner with egg white; roll up jelly-roll fashion.

5. Roll to end; gently press moistened corner to roll.

MINI POLENTA CAKES WITH SMOKED SALMON

PREP: 20 MINUTES
COOK: 1 HOUR 5 MINUTES

Smoked salmon has a rosy, translucent appearance. You'll find it in your grocer's fresh seafood display. Smoked salmon is perishable and must be refrigerated.

1 cup yellow cornmeal
2 teaspoons stick margarine
1 garlic clove, minced
2⅓ cups fat-free, less-sodium chicken broth
½ cup low-fat buttermilk
¼ cup grated Parmesan cheese
1 cup frozen whole-kernel corn, thawed
⅓ cup coarsely chopped onion
3 large egg whites
1 large egg
¼ teaspoon salt
¼ teaspoon white pepper
¼ teaspoon ground red pepper
Cooking spray
¼ cup fat-free cream cheese, softened
2 tablespoons plain fat-free yogurt
1 teaspoon grated lemon rind
Dash of salt
3 ounces smoked salmon, cut into 30 (2 x ½-inch) strips
Chopped fresh dill (optional)

1. Preheat oven to 400°.
2. Combine first 3 ingredients in a large saucepan. Gradually add broth, stirring constantly with a whisk. Bring to a boil; reduce heat to medium, and cook 4 minutes or until thickened, stirring constantly. Remove from heat; stir in buttermilk and Parmesan cheese, and set aside. Place corn and onion in a food processor, and pulse 2 times or until corn is coarsely chopped. Combine corn mixture, egg whites, and egg in a large bowl. Stir in cornmeal mixture, ¼ teaspoon salt, white pepper, and red

pepper. Pour polenta mixture into an 11 x 7-inch baking dish coated with cooking spray, spreading evenly.
3. Bake polenta at 400° for 50 minutes or until browned. Cool to room temperature. Cut polenta mixture into 30 decorative shapes with a 1½-inch cutter. Remove shapes from baking dish, and arrange on a baking sheet coated with cooking spray; discard remaining polenta. Bake at 400° for 15 minutes.
4. Combine cream cheese, yogurt, lemon rind, and dash of salt in a small bowl, stirring with a whisk. Spoon about ¼ teaspoon cream cheese mixture onto each polenta cake. Top each cake with a salmon strip, and garnish with fresh chopped dill, if desired. Yield: 30 servings (serving size: 1 polenta cake).

CALORIES 48 (24% from fat); FAT 1.3g (sat 0.4g, mono 0.4g, poly 0.3g); PROTEIN 2.8g; CARB 6.6g; FIBER 0.8g; CHOL 10mg; IRON 0.4mg; SODIUM 109mg; CALC 24mg

---

SMOKED SALMON

Smoked salmon is fresh salmon that has undergone one of two types of smoking processes: **hot- or cold-smoking.**

When **hot-smoked,** the salmon is processed for **6 to 12 hours between 120° and 180°** or as needed according to the size of the fish and the flavor desired. **Cold-smoking** takes place at **70° to 90° for 1 day to up to 3 weeks.**

One of the most common types in the U.S. is **kippered salmon,** which has been **soaked in brine and hot-smoked. Lox** is **brine-soaked and cold-smoked salmon,** which is slightly saltier than other smoked salmon.

Smoked salmon in commonly used in paper-thin slices on appetizer trays or to top canapés.

BUFFALO SHRIMP WITH BLUE CHEESE DIP

PREP: 40 MINUTES   CHILL: 30 MINUTES
COOK: 6 MINUTES

48 unpeeled large shrimp (about 2 pounds)
2 tablespoons dark brown sugar
2 tablespoons chopped onion
3 tablespoons cider vinegar
2 tablespoons water
2 tablespoons ketchup
1 tablespoon Worcestershire sauce
2 to 4 teaspoons hot sauce
¼ teaspoon pepper
1 garlic clove, chopped
¾ cup fat-free cottage cheese
3 tablespoons fat-free milk
2 tablespoons crumbled blue cheese
⅛ teaspoon black pepper
Cooking spray

1. Peel shrimp, leaving tails intact. Place shrimp in a shallow dish; cover and chill.
2. Combine sugar and next 8 ingredients in a blender; process until smooth. Pour mixture into a small saucepan. Cook 10 minutes over medium-low heat, stirring occasionally. Cool; pour over shrimp. Cover and marinate in refrigerator 30 minutes, turning shrimp occasionally.
3. Combine cottage cheese and next 3 ingredients in blender; process until smooth. Spoon into a bowl. Cover; chill.
4. Prepare grill or preheat broiler.
5. Remove shrimp from dish, reserving marinade. Arrange shrimp in a single layer on a grill rack or broiler pan coated with cooking spray. Cook 3 minutes; turn shrimp and baste with reserved marinade. Cook 3 minutes or until shrimp is done. Serve with cheese dip. Yield: 8 servings (serving size: 6 shrimp and 2 tablespoons cheese dip).

CALORIES 123 (11% from fat); FAT 1.5g (sat 0.6g, mono 0.3g, poly 0.4g); PROTEIN 21.2g; CARB 5.4g; FIBER 0.1g; CHOL 165mg; IRON 2.8mg; SODIUM 378mg; CALC 68mg

BEVERAGES

All too often, beverages are overlooked as an integral part of a meal. Perhaps you think that it's just easier to serve water or plain iced tea. But let's talk about flavor! You can spritz up a glass of water by starting with carbonated water and adding a twist of citrus; lemon, orange, or lime all can provide a deliciously refreshing accent. Or take the flavor a step further with Cassis-and-Lime Spritzer (page 54) or Cranberry-Raspberry Spritzer (page 57).

For teas, consider the mint options. The leaves of peppermint, spearmint, or lemon mint can be crushed and steeped with the tea. Served hot or iced, it may become your new favorite comfort beverage.

coffee
No longer is a cup of coffee ordinary. Flavored coffees and blends will have you savoring the nuances of coffee.

COFFEE ROYALE

PREP: 10 MINUTES

1¼ cups 1% low-fat milk
1 tablespoon sugar
¼ teaspoon ground cinnamon
2¾ cups hot strong brewed coffee
½ cup amaretto (almond-flavored liqueur)
6 (3-inch) cinnamon sticks (optional)

1. Combine milk, sugar, and ground cinnamon in a medium saucepan. Place over medium heat, and cook 2 minutes or until sugar dissolves, stirring constantly. Remove from heat; stir in coffee and amaretto. Pour into mugs; garnish with cinnamon sticks, if desired. Yield: 6 servings (serving size: ¾ cup).
Note: For a nonalcoholic version, omit amaretto, and increase coffee to 3¼ cups.

CALORIES 96 (6% from fat); FAT 0.6g (sat 0.4g, mono 0.2g, poly 0g); PROTEIN 1.8g; CARB 10.9g; FIBER 0g; CHOL 2mg; IRON 0.5mg; SODIUM 28mg; CALC 66mg

CHILLED ESPRESSO

PREP: 12 MINUTES
CHILL: 2 HOURS

4 cups water
¾ cup finely ground espresso or other dark roast coffee
1 teaspoon grated orange rind
3 tablespoons sugar
2 cups fat-free milk
Orange slices, cut in half (optional)

1. Pour water into percolator; assemble stem and basket in pot. Add espresso and orange rind. Place lid on pot. Plug in coffeepot, and brew until perking stops. Pour espresso into a large pitcher.
2. Stir sugar into espresso. Cover and chill. Stir in milk, and pour into coffee cups. Garnish with orange slices, if desired. Yield: 6 servings (serving size: 1 cup).

CALORIES 56 (2% from fat); FAT 0.1g (sat 0.1g, mono 0g, poly 0g); PROTEIN 2.9g; CARB 10.9g; FIBER 0g; CHOL 2mg; IRON 0.7mg; SODIUM 46mg; CALC 104mg

CAFÉ NOIR

PREP: 7 MINUTES

½ cup finely ground dark roast coffee
2 tablespoons ground roasted chicory
1 quart water

1. Assemble drip coffeemaker according to manufacturer's directions. Place coffee and chicory in the coffee filter or filter basket. Add water to coffeemaker, and brew. Yield: 5 servings (serving size: ¾ cup).

CALORIES 4 (0% from fat); FAT 0g; PROTEIN 0.2g; CARB 0.8g; FIBER 0g; CHOL 0mg; IRON 0.8mg; SODIUM 4mg; CALC 4mg

For the best-tasting coffee, buy roasted whole coffee beans and keep them fresh by storing them in the refrigerator.

Coffee Basics

COFFEE

PREP: 1 MINUTE
COOK: 5 MINUTES

Select the particular grind of coffee that your coffeemaker requires. These amounts are per each ³⁄₄-cup serving.

³⁄₄ cup water
2 tablespoons ground coffee

drip: Assemble drip coffeemaker according to manufacturer's directions. Place ground coffee in the coffee filter or filter basket. Add water to coffeemaker, and brew.

percolator: Pour water into percolator; assemble stem and basket in pot. Add coffee. Place lid on pot. Plug in coffeepot if using an electric percolator, and brew until perking stops. If using a nonelectric model, bring to a boil over high heat; reduce heat, and perk gently 5 to 7 minutes.

vacuum: Bring water to a boil in lower bowl of vacuum pot. Place a filter in the upper bowl, and fill with ground coffee. Reduce heat. The pressure will force the water up through the coffee grounds. Brew 1 to 3 minutes. Remove from heat, and allow coffee to return to lower bowl.

ESPRESSO AU LAIT

PREP: 5 MINUTES   COOK: 5 MINUTES

¼ cup packed brown sugar
¼ cup instant espresso granules
1¾ cups water
1¾ cups 2% reduced-fat milk
Orange rind strips (optional)

1. Combine brown sugar and espresso granules in a 1-quart glass measure. Stir in water and milk. Microwave, uncovered, at HIGH 5 minutes or until heated, stirring every 2 minutes. Pour into mugs; garnish with orange rind strips, if desired. Yield: 4 servings (serving size: 1 cup).

Espresso au Lait for One:
1 tablespoon packed brown sugar
1 tablespoon instant espresso granules
6 tablespoons water
6 tablespoons 2% reduced-fat milk
Orange rind strip (optional)

1. Combine brown sugar and espresso granules in a 1-cup glass measure. Stir in water and milk. Microwave, uncovered, at HIGH 1½ minutes or until heated, stirring after 45 seconds. Garnish with orange rind, if desired. Yield: 1 serving (serving size: 1 cup).

CALORIES 111 (9% from fat); FAT 1.8g (sat 1.1g, mono 0.5g, poly 0.1g); PROTEIN 3.7g; CARB 20g; FIBER 0.1g; CHOL 7mg; IRON 0.5mg; SODIUM 53mg; CALC 131mg

INSTANT ESPRESSO

Instant espresso powder can be found with the instant coffees in large supermarkets and in gourmet-coffee shops. If a recipe calls for 1 teaspoon instant espresso powder, you can substitute 2 teaspoons instant coffee granules.

ALMOND CAPPUCCINO

PREP: 15 MINUTES

To heighten the almond experience, serve this with Almond Biscotti (page 158).

2 cups fat-free milk
1 vanilla bean, split
2 tablespoons instant espresso granules
⅛ teaspoon almond extract
¼ teaspoon unsweetened cocoa

1. Combine milk and vanilla bean in a medium saucepan; cook over low heat until bubbly. Stir in espresso granules, and remove from heat. Discard vanilla bean; stir in almond extract.
2. Pour 1 cup milk mixture into a blender; process until frothy. Pour into a cup, and sprinkle with ⅛ teaspoon cocoa. Repeat with remaining milk mixture and cocoa. Yield: 2 servings (serving size: 1 cup).

CALORIES 96 (5% from fat); FAT 0.5g (sat 0.3g, mono 0.1g, poly 0g); PROTEIN 8.8g; CARB 13.4g; FIBER 0.1g; CHOL 5mg; IRON 0.3mg; SODIUM 129mg; CALC 307mg

FROSTY CAPPUCCINO

PREP: 10 MINUTES
FREEZE: 1 TO 2 HOURS

⅓ cup ground coffee (not instant coffee granules)
2¼ cups water
⅓ cup packed brown sugar
1 cup 2% reduced-fat milk
¼ teaspoon ground cinnamon
2 tablespoons bourbon

1. Assemble drip coffeemaker according to manufacturer's directions. Place coffee in the coffee filter or filter basket. Add water to coffeemaker, and brew. Combine brewed coffee, sugar, milk, and cinnamon in a large bowl. Cool to

room temperature. Pour 2 tablespoons coffee mixture into each of 28 ice cube tray compartments; freeze until firm.

2. Place coffee ice cubes and bourbon in a food processor. Process 4 minutes or until smooth, scraping sides of bowl twice. Serve immediately. Yield: 4 servings (serving size: 1 cup).

CALORIES 120 (10% from fat); FAT 1.2g (sat 0.7g, mono 0.3g, poly 0g); PROTEIN 2.2g; CARB 21.4g; FIBER 0g; CHOL 5mg; IRON 1mg; SODIUM 40mg; CALC 94mg

FLAVORED COFFEE MIX

PREP: 5 MINUTES

6 tablespoons plus 2 teaspoons instant coffee granules
6 tablespoons nonfat dry milk
3 tablespoons plus 1 teaspoon sugar
½ teaspoon ground cinnamon

1. Combine all ingredients; store in an airtight container. For each cup, spoon 1 tablespoon coffee mix into a cup. Stir in ¾ cup boiling water. Yield: 16 servings.

CALORIES 24 (1% from fat); FAT 0g; PROTEIN 1.2g; CARB 4.7g; FIBER 0g; CHOL 1mg; IRON 0.1mg; SODIUM 16mg; CALC 38mg

IRISH MOCHA

PREP: 10 MINUTES   COOK: 5 MINUTES

¼ cup sugar
¼ cup unsweetened cocoa
3½ cups fat-free milk, divided
1 cup hot strong brewed coffee
½ cup Irish whiskey

1. Combine sugar and cocoa in a medium saucepan. Gradually stir in ½ cup milk. Gradually add remaining 3 cups milk, coffee, and whiskey. Place over medium heat; cook 5 minutes or until thoroughly heated, stirring frequently.

2. Pour coffee mixture into a medium bowl; beat at medium speed of a mixer until foamy. Serve immediately. Yield: 5 servings (serving size: 1 cup).

CALORIES 119 (7% from fat); FAT 0.9g (sat 0.6g, mono 0.2g, poly 0g); PROTEIN 7.1g; CARB 20.6g; FIBER 0g; CHOL 4mg; IRON 1mg; SODIUM 92mg; CALC 219mg

HOT MOCHA

PREP: 4 MINUTES   COOK: 4 MINUTES

6 cups hot strong brewed coffee
½ cup sugar
½ cup unsweetened cocoa
6 tablespoons Kahlúa (coffee-flavored liqueur)

1. Combine coffee, sugar, and cocoa in a medium saucepan. Cook coffee mixture over medium heat until hot, stirring frequently. (Do not boil.) Remove coffee mixture from heat; stir in Kahlúa. Yield: 13 servings (serving size: ½ cup).

CALORIES 69 (6% from fat); FAT 0.5g (sat 0.3g, mono 0.2g, poly 0g); PROTEIN 1.1g; CARB 11.8g; FIBER 0g; CHOL 0mg; IRON 1mg; SODIUM 4mg; CALC 7mg

IRISH COFFEE WITH CREAMY TOPPING

PREP: 15 MINUTES   FREEZE: 1 HOUR
CHILL: 30 MINUTES

1 (12-ounce) can evaporated fat-free milk, divided
1 tablespoon cornstarch
2 tablespoons water
1 teaspoon vanilla extract
2 tablespoons powdered sugar
6 cups hot strong brewed coffee
½ cup Irish whiskey
2 tablespoons plus 2 teaspoons granulated sugar

1. Place ½ cup milk in a small saucepan; bring to a simmer over medium heat. Place cornstarch in a bowl; gradually add water, stirring with a wire whisk until blended. Add to simmering milk; bring to a boil, stirring constantly. Cook 1 minute, stirring constantly.

2. Combine cornstarch mixture, 1 cup milk, and vanilla in a large bowl; freeze 1 hour or until a ⅛-inch-thick layer of ice forms on the surface. Beat at high speed of a mixer 5 minutes; gradually add powdered sugar, beating until soft peaks form. Cover and chill.

3. Combine coffee, whiskey, and 2 tablespoons plus 2 teaspoons sugar. Pour ¾ cup coffee into each of 8 mugs; spoon ½ cup topping onto each. Serve immediately. Cover and store remaining topping in refrigerator. Yield: 8 servings.

CALORIES 95 (1% from fat); FAT 0.1g (sat 0.1g, mono 0g, poly 0g); PROTEIN 3.6g; CARB 14.3g; FIBER 0g; CHOL 2mg; IRON 0.9mg; SODIUM 55mg; CALC 133mg

COFFEE-KAHLÚA PUNCH

PREP: 28 MINUTES   CHILL: 2 HOURS

8¼ cups hot strong brewed coffee
⅓ cup sugar
4 cups fat-free milk
1 tablespoon vanilla extract
1¼ cups Kahlúa (coffee-flavored liqueur)
5 cups vanilla fat-free ice cream, softened
1 ounce semisweet chocolate, grated

1. Combine coffee and sugar, stirring until sugar dissolves. Stir in milk and vanilla; cover and chill. Combine chilled coffee mixture and Kahlúa in a punch bowl. Spoon ice cream by tablespoons into coffee mixture; stir until ice cream melts. Sprinkle with chocolate. Yield: 18 servings (serving size: 1 cup).

CALORIES 150 (13% from fat); FAT 2.2g (sat 1.4g, mono 0.7g, poly 0.1g); PROTEIN 3.4g; CARB 21.1g; FIBER 0g; CHOL 6mg; IRON 0.6mg; SODIUM 62mg; CALC 121mg

teas
Not only is a cup of tea comforting, but research is showing that it has important health benefits, too.

Most teas are divided into three types—black, green, or oolong—distinctions based on the way they're processed. **Black tea,** an amber-colored, full-bodied brew, has been fermented. **Oolong tea,** a paler, more delicate drink, has been through a brief fermentation. **Green tea** produces a yellow-to-light green brew and has not been allowed to ferment.

There are over 2,000 varieties of the tea plant. In addition, there are countless herbal blends that contain no tea but are rich in other plants, including hibiscus, jasmine, hawthorn, and chamomile. Each imparts its own characteristic flavor.

Steeping in Flavor

Brewing time depends on the leaf size and the type of tea—green, one to two minutes; full-leaf black, three to five minutes; small-leaf oolong, seven to 10 minutes. Within those limits, teas produce their best flavor. Brewing more than the allotted time, however, may cause many teas to become bitter and astringent. Package directions will recommend a steeping time, but you'll want to experiment a bit to find the perfect point that best suits your taste.

After brewing, remove the tea bag or tea ball immediately. If using tea bags, squeeze them just enough to remove excess water, but not enough to extract bitter tannins. And don't judge the strength of the tea by its color; taste it.

Health Benefits

Research is continuing on the health benefits of tea. It appears that the flavonoids (vitamin-like nutrients) in the leaves make blood cells less prone to clotting, thereby decreasing the risk of a heart attack.

Other studies indicate that the components in green tea may work as an antioxidant, playing a role in the prevention of cancer.

HOT tea COLD tea BASICS

HOT TEA

PREP: 5 MINUTES

1 regular-size tea bag
¾ cup boiling water
Sugar (optional)
Lemon slices (optional)

1. Warm teapot, mug, or cup by rinsing in boiling water. Place tea bag in teapot. Immediately pour ¾ cup boiling water over tea bag. Cover and steep 5 minutes. Remove tea bag; serve with sugar and lemon, if desired. Yield: 1 serving (serving size: ¾ cup).

CALORIES 2 (0% from fat); FAT 0g; PROTEIN 0g; CARB 0.5g; FIBER 0g; CHOL 0mg; IRON 0mg; SODIUM 5mg; CALC 0mg

ICED TEA

PREP: 5 MINUTES

1 tablespoon loose tea, or 3 or
  4 regular-size tea bags, or 1
  family-size tea bag
2 cups boiling water
2 cups water

1. Warm teapot, or glass or ceramic saucepan by rinsing with boiling water. Place loose tea in a tea ball. Place tea ball in teapot. Pour 2 cups boiling water over tea. Cover and steep 3 to 5 minutes. Remove tea ball, and stir in 2 cups water. Serve over ice. Yield: 4 servings (serving size: 1 cup).

CALORIES 3 (0% from fat); FAT 0g; PROTEIN 0g; CARB 0.6g; FIBER 0g; CHOL 0mg; IRON 0mg; SODIUM 0mg; CALC 0mg

MINT LOVERS' TEA

PREP: 35 MINUTES
FREEZE: 2 HOURS

You'll want to prepare Mint Ice Cubes first and freeze them several hours until firm. Store them in the freezer until ready to use. For a flavor twist, you can use flavored mint, such as orange or peppermint, in both the tea and ice cubes.

5 cups boiling water
2 tablespoons loose gunpowder tea
1 cup fresh mint leaves, minced
3 mint-herb tea bags
¼ cup lime juice
¼ cup honey
Mint Ice Cubes
Mint sprigs (optional)

1. Combine first 4 ingredients in a medium bowl; cover and steep 10 minutes. Discard tea bags. Strain mixture through a fine sieve; discard mint and tea leaves. Stir lime juice and honey into tea. Serve over Mint Ice Cubes. Garnish with mint sprigs, if desired. Yield: 9 servings (serving size: ½ cup).

MINT ICE CUBES

  4 cups boiling water
  2 cups mint leaves, crushed

1. Combine water and mint leaves in a medium bowl; cover and let stand 10 minutes. Strain mixture through a fine sieve; discard mint. Pour liquid evenly into 28 ice cube tray compartments; freeze until firm. Yield: 28 ice cubes.

CALORIES 33 (5% from fat); FAT 0g; PROTEIN 0.2g; CARB 9g; FIBER 0g; CHOL 0mg; IRON 0.3mg; SODIUM 4mg; CALC 11mg

LEMON-MINT TEA

PREP: 10 MINUTES

  1 cup boiling water
  1 peppermint tea bag
  1 (3-inch) cinnamon stick
  1 tablespoon sugar
  1 tablespoon lemon juice
Mint sprig (optional)

1. Combine first 3 ingredients in a bowl; cover and steep 5 minutes. Remove and discard tea bag and cinnamon stick. Add sugar and lemon juice, stirring until sugar dissolves. Serve hot or over ice. Garnish with mint sprig, if desired. Yield: 1 serving (serving size: 1 cup).

CALORIES 55 (0% from fat); FAT 0g; PROTEIN 0.1g; CARB 14.5g; FIBER 0.1g; CHOL 0mg; IRON 0.1mg; SODIUM 7mg; CALC 1mg

RUSSIAN TEA

PREP: 9 MINUTES

  ¾ cup boiling water
  1 regular-size English breakfast tea bag
  ¼ cup orange juice
  ¼ teaspoon ground cinnamon
  ⅛ teaspoon ground cloves
Sugar (optional)

1. Combine boiling water and tea bag in a large mug; cover and steep 5 minutes. Discard tea bag. Stir orange juice, cinnamon, and cloves into mug. Serve with sugar, if desired. Yield: 1 serving.

CALORIES 31 (3% from fat); FAT 0.1g (sat 0g, mono 0g, poly 0g); PROTEIN 0.5g; CARB 7.4g; FIBER 0.3g; CHOL 0mg; IRON 0.3mg; SODIUM 1mg; CALC 14mg

cocoa

Once thought of as only a child's wintertime beverage, our cocoa recipes (page 50) offer adult-style flavor year-round.

HOT CHOCOLATE MIX

PREP: 5 MINUTES

5½ cups nonfat dry milk
  1 cup plus 2 tablespoons sugar
  ¾ cup unsweetened cocoa

1. Combine all ingredients; store in an airtight container in a cool, dry place. Yield: 7⅓ cups (serving size: ⅓ cup).

CALORIES 161 (3% from fat); FAT 0.6g (sat 0.4g, mono 0.1g, poly 0g); PROTEIN 11.7g; CARB 27.3g; FIBER 0g; CHOL 6mg; IRON 0.6mg; SODIUM 162mg; CALC 382mg

Hot Chocolate by the Cup

Number of 1-cup servings	Hot Chocolate Mix	Water	Vanilla Extract	Heat in the Microwave on HIGH for
1	⅓ cup	¾ cup	¼ teaspoon	45 to 60 seconds
2	⅔ cup	1½ cups	½ teaspoon	1½ to 2 minutes
4	1⅓ cups	3 cups	1 teaspoon	3 minutes

HOT CHOCOLATE FLOAT

PREP: 4 MINUTES
COOK: 3 MINUTES

1⅓ cups Hot Chocolate Mix
  (page 49)
3¼ cups water
  1 teaspoon vanilla extract
  ¼ cup vanilla fat-free ice cream
Ground cinnamon

1. Place Hot Chocolate Mix in a 1-quart glass measure; stir in water and vanilla. Microwave, uncovered, at HIGH 3 minutes or until heated. Pour 1 cup hot chocolate into each of 4 mugs. Top each with 1 tablespoon ice cream, and sprinkle with cinnamon. Yield: 4 servings.

CALORIES 176 (5% from fat); FAT 1g (sat 0.6g, mono 0.2g, poly 0g); PROTEIN 12g; CARB 29.4g; FIBER 0g; CHOL 7mg; IRON 0.6mg; SODIUM 169mg; CALC 395mg

KAHLÚA MOCHA

PREP: 3 MINUTES
COOK: 3 MINUTES

1⅓ cups Hot Chocolate Mix
  (page 49)
  1 tablespoon plus 1 teaspoon
    instant coffee granules
3¼ cups water
  4 teaspoons Kahlúa (coffee-
    flavored liqueur)

1. Combine Hot Chocolate Mix and coffee granules in a 1-quart glass measure; stir in water and Kahlúa. Microwave, uncovered, at HIGH 3 minutes or until heated. Yield: 4 servings (serving size: 1 cup).

CALORIES 172 (3% from fat); FAT 0.6g (sat 0.1g, mono 0g, poly 0.1g); PROTEIN 11.9g; CARB 29.4g; FIBER 0g; CHOL 6mg; IRON 0.7mg; SODIUM 163mg; CALC 384mg

Hot Chocolate
Float

Hot Chocolate Mix (page 49) and ice cream swirl together in this comforting float. Surprise a friend with a gift jar brimming with the mix—and don't forget to share the accompanying recipes, too!

warm fruit drinks
These fruity favorites will warm you up.

HOT MULLED CRANBERRY-APPLE CIDER

PREP: 8 MINUTES   COOK: 40 MINUTES

- 1 lemon
- 1 orange
- 3½ cups apple cider
- 2½ cups cranberry juice cocktail
- 1 teaspoon whole allspice
- 2 (3-inch) cinnamon sticks
- 6 whole cloves
- 1 (¼-inch) piece peeled fresh ginger, thinly sliced

1. Remove rind from lemon and orange using a vegetable peeler, making sure to avoid the white pith just beneath the rind. Cut rind into 1 x ¼-inch strips. Combine rind strips, cider, and remaining ingredients in a Dutch oven. Bring to a simmer over medium heat; cook until reduced to 4 cups (about 30 minutes). Strain through a sieve into a bowl, discarding solids. Yield: 8 servings (serving size: ½ cup).

CALORIES 98 (1% from fat); FAT 0.1g (sat 0g, mono 0g, poly 0.1g); PROTEIN 0.1g; CARB 24.7g; FIBER 0.2g; CHOL 0mg; IRON 0.5mg; SODIUM 6mg; CALC 10mg

WARM CRANBERRY PUNCH

PREP: 45 MINUTES   COOK: 4 MINUTES

- 2 cups fresh or thawed frozen cranberries
- 2 cups apple juice
- 1 teaspoon ground cinnamon
- 1 teaspoon ground cloves
- ½ cup sugar
- 2 tablespoons orange juice
- 1 quart water

1. Combine first 4 ingredients in a 1-quart glass measure. Cover with wax paper, and microwave at HIGH 8 to 10 minutes, stirring every 4 minutes. Let stand, uncovered, 30 minutes. Press cranberry mixture through a sieve, reserving 2 cups juice; discard solids.
2. Combine reserved juice, sugar, and orange juice in a 2-quart glass measure, stirring until sugar dissolves. Stir in water. Microwave, uncovered, at HIGH 3 to 4 minutes or until heated. Yield: 6 servings (serving size: 1 cup).
Note: To thaw frozen cranberries, place in a 1-quart glass measure. Microwave, uncovered, at HIGH 2 to 3 minutes. Let stand 3 minutes or until thawed.

CALORIES 123 (1% from fat); FAT 0.2g (sat 0g, mono 0g, poly 0.1g); PROTEIN 0.2g; CARB 31.3g; FIBER 0.7g; CHOL 0mg; IRON 0.6mg; SODIUM 4mg; CALC 15mg

MULLED CIDER

PREP: 5 MINUTES   COOK: 15 MINUTES

- 1 teaspoon whole cloves
- 2 (3-inch) cinnamon sticks, broken in half
- 1 quart apple cider
- ¼ cup applejack (apple-flavored brandy)
- Cinnamon sticks (optional)

1. Place cloves and 2 cinnamon sticks on a cheesecloth square. Gather edges of cheesecloth together; tie securely. Combine spice bag and cider in a saucepan. Bring to a boil; reduce heat, and simmer, uncovered, 10 minutes. Stir in applejack, and simmer 5 minutes. Discard cheesecloth spice bag. Serve cider warm with cinnamon sticks, if desired. Yield: 8 servings (serving size: ½ cup).

CALORIES 58 (1% from fat); FAT 0.1g (sat 0g, mono 0g, poly 0g); PROTEIN 0.1g; CARB 14.5g; FIBER 0.2g; CHOL 0mg; IRON 0.5mg; SODIUM 4mg; CALC 9mg

Mulled Cider

1. Place cloves and cinnamon sticks on a cheesecloth square.

2. Bring ends together, and tie securely at top.

3. Simmer cider and spice bag as directed. Discard spice bag before serving.

MULLED FRUIT DRINK

PREP: 17 MINUTES   COOK: 8 MINUTES

  2 cups water
  6 whole cloves
  3 (3-inch) cinnamon sticks
  8 regular-size tea bags
2½ cups pineapple juice
  2 cups apple juice
  ½ cup fresh lemon juice (about 4
       lemons)
  ½ cup sugar

1. Combine first 3 ingredients in a 1-quart glass measure; microwave at HIGH 5 minutes or until boiling. Pour over tea bags in a 2-quart glass measure. Cover and let stand 10 minutes. Discard spices and tea bags. Stir in juices and sugar. Microwave, uncovered, at HIGH 8 minutes or until hot, stirring after 4 minutes. Pour into mugs. Yield: 7 servings (serving size: 1 cup).

CALORIES 143 (1% from fat); FAT 0.1g (sat 0g, mono 0g, poly 0.1g); PROTEIN 0.4g; CARB 36.3g; FIBER 0.3g; CHOL 0mg; IRON 0.5mg; SODIUM 3mg; CALC 21mg

HOT SPICED WINE

PREP: 5 MINUTES   COOK: 20 MINUTES

  2 quarts dry red wine
  2 cups apple juice
  2 cups orange juice
  ⅔ cup sugar
  2 teaspoons whole cloves
  2 (3-inch) cinnamon sticks
  2 oranges, thinly sliced
  2 limes, thinly sliced
     Thin orange slices (optional)

1. Combine first 8 ingredients in a large Dutch oven. Bring to a boil, stirring until sugar dissolves. Reduce heat; simmer, uncovered, 15 minutes.
2. Strain wine mixture, and pour into glasses. Garnish with orange slices, if desired. Yield: 24 servings (serving size: ½ cup).

CALORIES 45 (0% from fat); FAT 0g; PROTEIN 0.3g; CARB 11.3g; FIBER 0.1g; CHOL 0mg; IRON 0.4mg; SODIUM 7mg; CALC 10mg

WASSAIL PUNCH

PREP: 10 MINUTES   COOK: 15 MINUTES

  3 quarts apple cider
  ¼ cup packed brown sugar
  2 unpeeled oranges, cut into ½-inch
       slices
  1 unpeeled lemon, cut into ½-inch
       slices
  2 (3-inch) cinnamon sticks
  8 whole cloves
  6 whole allspice
  6 whole cardamom
  ¾ cup dry white wine

1. Combine all ingredients except wine in a large Dutch oven; bring to a boil. Cover, reduce heat, and simmer 10 minutes. Strain mixture; discard fruit and spices. Add wine; simmer until thoroughly heated. Yield: 12 servings (serving size: 1 cup).
Note: For a nonalcoholic punch, omit wine.

CALORIES 135 (1% from fat); FAT 0.2g (sat 0.1g, mono 0g, poly 0.1g); PROTEIN 0.2g; CARB 33.6g; FIBER 0.5g; CHOL 0mg; IRON 1.1mg; SODIUM 10mg; CALC 22mg

chilled drinks Take a break with these refreshing thirst quenchers.

TOMATO MOCKTAIL

PREP: 12 MINUTES

  2 cups ice cubes
1½ cups no-salt-added tomato juice
  ¼ cup finely chopped celery
  ¼ cup canned tomato puree
  1 tablespoon finely chopped green
       onions
  1 tablespoon fresh lemon juice
  ¼ teaspoon salt
  ¼ teaspoon celery seeds
  ¼ teaspoon hot sauce
     Dash of black pepper
  4 celery stalks with leaves (optional)

1. Combine all ingredients except celery stalks in a blender; process until smooth. Garnish with celery stalks, if desired. Serve immediately. Yield: 4 servings (serving size: ¾ cup).

CALORIES 28 (3% from fat); FAT 0.1g (sat 0g, mono 0g, poly 0g); PROTEIN 1.3g; CARB 6.9g; FIBER 0.6g; CHOL 0mg; IRON 0.8mg; SODIUM 229mg; CALC 18mg

CITRUS COOLER

PREP: 20 MINUTES

1¾ cups water
  1 cup sugar
  ¼ cup chopped fresh orange mint
2¼ cups fresh lemon juice (about 12
       lemons)
  1 (33.8-ounce) bottle club soda,
       chilled
     Mint sprigs (optional)

1. Combine first 3 ingredients in a small saucepan; bring to a boil, stirring until sugar dissolves. Cool completely;

strain and discard mint leaves. Stir in lemon juice and club soda. Pour over ice; garnish with mint sprigs, if desired. Yield: 8 servings (serving size: 1 cup).

CALORIES 113 (0% from fat); FAT 0g; PROTEIN 0.3g; CARB 30.8g; FIBER 0g; CHOL 0mg; IRON 0mg; SODIUM 26mg; CALC 11mg

RASPBERRY LEMONADE

PREP: 8 MINUTES

CHILL: 1 HOUR

3 cups cold water, divided
1 cup fresh raspberries
1 (6-ounce) can thawed
    lemonade concentrate,
    undiluted
Mint sprigs (optional)

1. Combine ¾ cup water and raspberries in a blender; process until smooth. Strain mixture through a sieve, and discard seeds. Combine raspberry liquid, 2¼ cups water, and lemonade concentrate in a pitcher; chill. Garnish with mint, if desired. Yield: 4 servings (serving size: 1 cup).

CALORIES 92 (3% from fat); FAT 0.3g (sat 0g, mono 0g, poly 0.1g); PROTEIN 0.4g; CARB 23.6g; FIBER 2.5g; CHOL 0mg; IRON 0.5mg; SODIUM 2mg; CALC 10mg

WHAT'S IN A LEMON?

Lemons are much easier to squeeze and will yield more juice at room temperature. If they have been refrigerated, heat one at a time in the microwave at HIGH for 20 to 40 seconds or just until warm to the touch. Then roll the lemon firmly on the countertop to soften it.

1 medium lemon: 2 to 3 tablespoons juice

5 to 6 lemons: 1 cup juice

Old-Fashioned Lemonade

OLD-FASHIONED LEMONADE

PREP: 10 MINUTES   CHILL: 1 HOUR

1¼ cups fresh lemon juice (about 8 lemons)
 ¾ cup sugar
4¼ cups cold water
 6 lemon slices

1. Combine lemon juice and sugar in a large pitcher, and stir until sugar dissolves. Stir in water and lemon slices; chill. Pour lemonade with lemon slices over ice. Yield: 6 servings (serving size: 1 cup).

Note: To make decorative lemon ice cubes, place a thin slice of lemon inside each cube of an ice cube tray before freezing.

CALORIES 109 (0% from fat); FAT 0g; PROTEIN 0.2g; CARB 29.4g; FIBER 0g; CHOL 0mg; IRON 0mg; SODIUM 1mg; CALC 4mg

KEY WEST MINTED LIMEADE

PREP: 7 MINUTES

¼ cup sugar
¼ cup fresh lime juice
4 fresh mint leaves
½ cup ice cubes
1 cup ginger ale, chilled
2 lime slices (optional)
Mint sprigs (optional)

1. Combine first 3 ingredients in a blender, and process until smooth. With blender on, add ice cubes, 1 at a time; process until smooth. Stir in ginger ale. Serve over ice; garnish with lime and mint, if desired. Serve immediately. Yield: 2 servings (serving size: 1 cup).

CALORIES 144 (0% from fat); FAT 0g; PROTEIN 0.1g; CARB 38.3g; FIBER 0g; CHOL 0mg; IRON 0mg; SODIUM 7mg; CALC 3mg

CASSIS-AND-LIME SPRITZER

PREP: 5 MINUTES

¼ cup cassis syrup, chilled
¼ cup fresh lime juice, chilled
1½ cups sparkling water, chilled
Lime slices (optional)

1. Combine cassis syrup and lime juice in a pitcher. Add sparkling water; stir gently. Pour over ice; garnish with lime slices, if desired. Yield: 2 servings (serving size: 1 cup).

Note: Look for cassis syrup, made from black currants, in the beverage section of your supermarket.

CALORIES 29 (0% from fat); FAT 0g; PROTEIN 0.1g; CARB 8.4g; FIBER 0g; CHOL 0mg; IRON 0mg; SODIUM 39mg; CALC 3mg

MANGO BELLINI

PREP: 13 MINUTES

1 cup diced peeled mango (about 1 medium)
2½ tablespoons fresh lime juice
6 tablespoons Sugar Syrup, chilled
2 cups extra-dry champagne, chilled
2 teaspoons grenadine

1. Place first 3 ingredients in a food processor, and process until smooth. Strain mango puree through a sieve, and discard pulp. Pour ¼ cup mango puree into each of 4 champagne glasses. Add ½ cup champagne to each glass; slowly pour ½ teaspoon grenadine down into each glass (do not stir before serving). Yield: 4 servings.

SUGAR SYRUP

2 cups sugar
1 cup water

1. Combine sugar and water in a small saucepan. Bring mixture to a boil over medium heat, stirring constantly, and cook 45 seconds or until sugar dissolves. Remove from heat; cool. Store syrup in refrigerator. Yield: 2 cups.

CALORIES 193 (0% from fat); FAT 0.1g (sat 0g, mono 0g, poly 0g); PROTEIN 0.6g; CARB 28.5g; FIBER 0.6g; CHOL 0mg; IRON 0.6mg; SODIUM 6mg; CALC 9mg

Mango Bellini

PASSION POTION

PREP: 18 MINUTES   FREEZE: 1 HOUR

Substitute apricot or papaya nectar if you can't find the passionfruit nectar.

  2 cups cubed peeled ripe mango
  1 cup cubed pineapple
1½ cups orange juice, chilled
  ½ cup passionfruit nectar, chilled

1. Arrange mango cubes and pineapple cubes in a single layer on a baking sheet; freeze until firm (about 1 hour). Remove from freezer; let stand 10 minutes. Combine mango, orange juice, and nectar in a blender, and process until smooth. With blender on, add pineapple; process until smooth. Serve immediately. Yield: 4 servings (serving size: 1 cup).

CALORIES 134 (3% from fat); FAT 0.4g (sat 0.1g, mono 0.1g, poly 0.1g); PROTEIN 1.2g; CARB 33.7g; FIBER 1.9g; CHOL 0mg; IRON 0.4mg; SODIUM 3mg; CALC 19mg

SANGRÍA SLUSH

PREP: 12 MINUTES   FREEZE: 1 HOUR

This is great to serve when entertaining! We prefer making this with a Burgundy wine. For a white Sangría, try Tropical Citrus Sangría (page 56).

  3 cups chopped fresh pineapple
  2 cups orange sections (about 6 oranges)
  6 tablespoons thawed lemonade concentrate
2½ cups dry red wine, chilled and divided
  1 cup club soda, chilled
  8 fresh pineapple chunks

1. Arrange chopped pineapple and orange sections in a single layer on a baking sheet; freeze until firm (about 1 hour).

Coring and Cubing Pineapple

A ripe pineapple should be deep golden-brown in color, have a slightly sweet smell, and be a bit soft to the touch. The leaves should pull out from the top without much effort. Avoid fruit that has dark, mushy spots or a woody-looking or whitish appearance.

1. Cut about 1 inch from each end.

2. Stand pineapple vertically. Using a sharp knife, slice down ½ inch into skin to remove eyes from the pineapple. Keep turning pineapple, slicing 1-inch-wide bands down in a straight line.

3. Cut the pineapple into quarters. While holding each quarter firmly, remove the core. Discard the core.

4. Cut the pineapple wedges in half lengthwise; then cut as needed for your recipe.

2. Place fruit mixture in food processor, and process mixture until chunky. Add lemonade concentrate and 1½ cups wine; process until mixture is smooth. Pour into a large pitcher, and add 1 cup wine and club soda. Stir gently.

3. Pour into individual glasses, and garnish each with a pineapple chunk. Serve immediately. Yield: 8 servings (serving size: 1 cup).

CALORIES 131 (3% from fat); FAT 0.4g (sat 0g, mono 0g, poly 0.1g); PROTEIN 0.9g; CARB 20.8g; FIBER 2.9g; CHOL 0mg; IRON 1mg; SODIUM 15mg; CALC 31mg

TROPICAL CITRUS SANGRÍA

PREP: 7 MINUTES   CHILL: 1 HOUR

- 2 tablespoons sugar
- 2 tablespoons cognac or brandy
- 1¾ cups dry white wine, chilled
- 4 lemon slices
- 4 lime slices
- 4 orange slices
- 1 (10-ounce) bottle club soda, chilled

1. Combine sugar and cognac in a 1-quart glass measure. Microwave at HIGH 1 minute or until sugar dissolves, stirring after 30 seconds. Add wine and fruit slices; stir well. Cover and chill.
2. To serve, add chilled club soda, and stir gently. Yield: 4 servings (serving size: ¾ cup).

CALORIES 110 (0% from fat); FAT 0g; PROTEIN 0.1g; CARB 6.9g; FIBER 0g; CHOL 0mg; IRON 0.5mg; SODIUM 20mg; CALC 13mg

CARIBBEAN STORM

PREP: 12 MINUTES

- 2 cups fresh orange juice (about 6 oranges)
- ¾ cup papaya or mango nectar
- ¼ cup white rum
- ¼ cup blue curaçao liqueur
- ⅛ teaspoon grated whole nutmeg

1. Combine first 3 ingredients in a pitcher; chill. Fill 4 glasses with ice cubes; add ¾ cup orange juice mixture to each glass. Slowly pour 1 tablespoon liqueur into each glass (do not stir before serving). Sprinkle with nutmeg. Yield: 4 servings.

CALORIES 171 (1% from fat); FAT 0.2g (sat 0.1g, mono 0g, poly 0g); PROTEIN 0.8g; CARB 21g; FIBER 0.3g; CHOL 0mg; IRON 0.2mg; SODIUM 2mg; CALC 11mg

TROPICAL WAVE

PREP: 18 MINUTES   FREEZE: 1 HOUR

For an easy way to peel and core pineapple, see page 55.

- 1½ cups sliced ripe banana
- 1 cup cubed fresh pineapple
- 1 cup cubed peeled ripe mango
- 1 cup papaya nectar, chilled
- 2 tablespoons fresh lime juice

1. Arrange banana, pineapple, and mango in a single layer on a baking sheet; freeze until firm (about 1 hour). Remove from freezer, and let stand 10 minutes. Combine fruit, nectar, and juice in a blender; process until smooth. Serve immediately. Yield: 3 servings (serving size: 1 cup).

CALORIES 184 (3% from fat); FAT 0.7g (sat 0.2g, mono 0.1g, poly 0.2g); PROTEIN 1.3g; CARB 47g; FIBER 3.2g; CHOL 0mg; IRON 0.7mg; SODIUM 2mg; CALC 15mg

PEACH MIMOSAS

PREP: 5 MINUTES

- 2 cups peach nectar, chilled
- 1⅓ cups orange juice, chilled
- ⅔ cup grenadine
- 1 (750-milliliter) bottle brut champagne, chilled

1. Combine nectar and orange juice in a pitcher. Spoon 1 tablespoon grenadine syrup into each of 10 champagne glasses. Add ⅓ cup orange juice mixture to each glass; top with champagne. Serve immediately. Yield: 10 servings.

CALORIES 110 (0% from fat); FAT 0.1g (sat 0g, mono 0g, poly 0g); PROTEIN 0.6g; CARB 14.4g; FIBER 0.1g; CHOL 0mg; IRON 0.5mg; SODIUM 9mg; CALC 8mg

PEELING PEACHES

To peel peaches, submerge them in boiling water for 30 seconds; then immediately plunge them into ice water. The loosened skins will slip off easily.

PEACH CHAMPAGNE SLUSH

PREP: 40 MINUTES   FREEZE: 3 HOURS

- 4 cups sliced peeled fresh or frozen peaches (about 2 pounds)
- 1 cup pink champagne
- ⅓ cup sifted powdered sugar

1. Combine all ingredients in a blender, and process until smooth. Pour into a shallow baking dish; cover and freeze 3 hours.
2. Let stand at room temperature 30 minutes or until slushy. Serve immediately. Yield: 10 servings (serving size: ½ cup).

CALORIES 66 (1% from fat); FAT 0.1g (sat 0g, mono 0g, poly 0g); PROTEIN 0.6g; CARB 12.7g; FIBER 1.2g; CHOL 0mg; IRON 0.2mg; SODIUM 1mg; CALC 5mg

PINEAPPLE PLEASURE

PREP: 7 MINUTES

- 1½ cups sliced strawberries, chilled
- 1¼ cups sliced banana
- 1¼ cups pineapple juice, chilled
- 1 cup orange juice, chilled
- 1 cup crushed ice
- 2 tablespoons honey

1. Place all ingredients in a blender, and process until smooth. Serve immediately. Yield: 5 servings (serving size: 1 cup).

CALORIES 131 (3% from fat); FAT 0.4g (sat 0.1g, mono 0.1g, poly 0.1g); PROTEIN 1.2g; CARB 32.9g; FIBER 2.4g; CHOL 0mg; IRON 0.5mg; SODIUM 2mg; CALC 24mg

CRANBERRY-RASPBERRY SPRITZER

PREP: 4 MINUTES

    3 cups raspberry sparkling water,
         chilled
    3 cups cranberry-raspberry drink,
         chilled
    6 tablespoons crème de cassis (black
         currant-flavored liqueur)

1. Combine sparkling water and cranberry-raspberry drink in a pitcher. Spoon 1 tablespoon crème de cassis into each of 6 glasses; add 1 cup juice mixture to each. Yield: 6 servings.
Note: For a nonalcoholic version, omit the crème de cassis—the recipe works fine without it.

CALORIES 82 (0% from fat); FAT 0g; PROTEIN 0.4g; CARB 16.5g; FIBER 0g; CHOL 0mg; IRON 0.2mg; SODIUM 3mg; CALC 3mg

RASPBERRY COOLERS

PREP: 5 MINUTES

    3 tablespoons sugar
    2 tablespoons raspberry vinegar
2¾ cups sparkling water, chilled
    1 (25.4-ounce) bottle Riesling or
         other slightly sweet white wine,
         chilled
  24 fresh raspberries

1. Combine sugar and vinegar in a small bowl; stir until sugar dissolves. Combine sugar mixture, water, and wine in a large pitcher; stir gently. Pour ¾ cup into each of 8 wine glasses; garnish with fresh raspberries. Yield: 8 servings.

CALORIES 145 (0% from fat); FAT 0.1g (sat 0g, mono 0g, poly 0.1g); PROTEIN 0.3g; CARB 10.3g; FIBER 1g; CHOL 0mg; IRON 0.3mg; SODIUM 31mg; CALC 11mg

STRAWBERRY MARGARITAS

PREP: 8 MINUTES

3½ cups fresh or frozen strawberries
2½ cups crushed ice
    ½ cup tequila
    ½ cup fresh lime juice (about 5 limes)
    ¼ cup sugar
    3 tablespoons Cointreau (orange-
         flavored liqueur)
Lime wedges (optional)

1. Combine all ingredients except lime wedges in a blender, and process until smooth. Pour evenly into each of 4 large glasses. Garnish with lime wedges, if desired. Serve immediately. Yield: 4 servings (serving size: 1 cup).

CALORIES 198 (2% from fat); FAT 0.5g (sat 0g, mono 0.1g, poly 0.3g); PROTEIN 0.9g; CARB 27.7g; FIBER 3.4g; CHOL 0mg; IRON 0.5mg; SODIUM 2mg; CALC 21mg

WATERMELON MARGARITAS

PREP: 10 MINUTES

    2 teaspoons sugar
    1 lime wedge
3½ cups cubed seeded watermelon
    ½ cup tequila
    3 tablespoons sugar
    3 tablespoons fresh lime juice
    1 tablespoon triple sec (orange-
         flavored liqueur)
    3 cups crushed ice
Lime wedges (optional)

1. Place 2 teaspoons sugar in a saucer. Rub rims of 6 glasses with lime wedge; spin rim of each glass in sugar to coat. Set prepared glasses aside.
2. Combine watermelon, tequila, 3 tablespoons sugar, lime juice, and liqueur in a blender; process until smooth. Fill each glass with ½ cup crushed ice. Add ½ cup watermelon mixture to each. Garnish each with a lime wedge, if desired.

Serve immediately. Yield: 6 servings.
Note: Add 2 or 3 drops of red food coloring to blender for a deeper color, if desired.

CALORIES 115 (3% from fat); FAT 0.4g (sat 0.2g, mono 0.1g, poly 0g); PROTEIN 0.6g; CARB 15.8g; FIBER 0.5g; CHOL 0mg; IRON 0.2mg; SODIUM 2mg; CALC 8mg

WATERMELON WISDOM

• Look for melons that are firm, symmetrically shaped, and free of dents and cuts.

A melon should feel heavy for its shape and have a nice sheen.

The underside of the melon (the side that grows against the ground) should be pale yellow. Cut watermelon pieces should be deep red in color.

• Slap the side of the melon. A resounding, hollow thump is a good indicator that it's ripe, but not a guarantee.

• Store whole watermelons in the refrigerator; cut pieces should be tightly wrapped and stored in the refrigerator.

WHISKEY SOUR SLUSH

PREP: 6 MINUTES

1½ cups ice cubes
    ½ cup fresh orange juice (about 2
         oranges)
    ¼ cup bourbon
    2 tablespoons sugar
    2 tablespoons fresh lemon juice

1. Combine all ingredients in a blender; process until smooth. Pour into glasses; serve immediately. Yield: 2 servings (serving size: 1 cup).

CALORIES 149 (0% from fat); FAT 0g; PROTEIN 0.5g; CARB 20.5g; FIBER 0.2g; CHOL 0mg; IRON 0.1mg; SODIUM 1mg; CALC 7mg

CHOCOLATE MALT

PREP: 5 MINUTES

1½ cups vanilla fat-free frozen yogurt
1 cup fat-free milk
1 tablespoon malted milk powder
1 tablespoon chocolate syrup
¼ teaspoon vanilla extract
3 ice cubes

1. Combine all ingredients except ice in a blender; process until smooth. Add ice; process until smooth. Serve immediately. Yield: 3 servings (serving size: 1 cup).

CALORIES 133 (3% from fat); FAT 0.5g (sat 0.2g, mono 0.1g, poly 0.1g); PROTEIN 6.5g; CARB 26.5g; FIBER 0g; CHOL 2mg; IRON 0.2mg; SODIUM 115mg; CALC 228mg

CHOCOLATE MOCHA SURPRISE

FREEZE: 2 HOURS
PREP: 8 MINUTES

1 (8-ounce) carton coffee low-fat yogurt
2 teaspoons unsweetened cocoa
4 teaspoons honey
2 cups fat-free milk
¼ cup vanilla low-fat yogurt
Ground nutmeg (optional)

1. Place coffee yogurt in freezer; freeze 2 hours or until almost frozen.
2. Combine cocoa and honey in a small bowl; stir in milk. Gently stir in coffee yogurt. Pour ¾ cup mixture into each of 4 serving glasses. Top each with 1 tablespoon vanilla yogurt, and sprinkle with nutmeg, if desired. Yield: 4 servings.

CALORIES 129 (8% from fat); FAT 1.2g (sat 0.8g, mono 0.3g, poly 0.1g); PROTEIN 7.9g; CARB 22g; FIBER 0g; CHOL 6mg; IRON 0.3mg; SODIUM 111mg; CALC 274mg

MOCHA MUDSLIDE

PREP: 8 MINUTES
FREEZE: 1 HOUR

1 cup fat-free milk
⅔ cup sliced ripe banana
2 tablespoons sugar
1 teaspoon instant coffee granules
¼ cup vanilla low-fat yogurt
Banana slices (optional)

1. Place first 4 ingredients in a blender; process until smooth. Place blender container in freezer; freeze 1 hour or until slightly frozen. Loosen frozen mixture from sides of blender container; add yogurt. Process until smooth, and garnish with banana slices, if desired. Serve immediately. Yield: 2 servings (serving size: 1 cup).

CALORIES 164 (4% from fat); FAT 0.8g (sat 0.5g, mono 0.2g, poly 0.1g); PROTEIN 6.2g; CARB 34.4g; FIBER 1.5g; CHOL 4mg; IRON 0.3mg; SODIUM 83mg; CALC 204mg

CHOCOLATE MOCHA MUDSLIDE:

Use 2% reduced-fat chocolate milk instead of plain fat-free milk, and reduce sugar to 1 tablespoon. Yield: 2 servings (serving size: 1 cup).

CALORIES 186 (15% from fat); FAT 3.1g (sat 1.9g, mono 0.8g, poly 0.1g); PROTEIN 6g; CARB 35g; FIBER 1.3g; CHOL 10mg; IRON 0.5mg; SODIUM 95mg; CALC 195mg

Mocha Mudslide

MORNING SHAKE

PREP: 6 MINUTES

1   cup plain fat-free yogurt
1   cup grapefruit sections (about 1 medium)
1   cup sliced banana
1   tablespoon wheat germ
1   tablespoon honey
1   teaspoon vanilla extract
6   ice cubes

1. Combine all ingredients except ice cubes in a blender; process until smooth. Add ice cubes, 1 at a time, processing at high speed until frothy. Serve immediately. Yield: 3 servings (serving size: 1 cup).

CALORIES 143 (4% from fat); FAT 0.6g (sat 0.2g, mono 0.1g, poly 0.2g); PROTEIN 5.8g; CARB 30g; FIBER 2.2g; CHOL 2mg; IRON 0.4mg; SODIUM 59mg; CALC 163mg

STRAWBERRY-MALTED MILK SHAKE

PREP: 6 MINUTES

2   cups vanilla low-fat ice cream
1½ cups halved strawberries
¼   cup fat-free milk
3   tablespoons malted milk powder
1   tablespoon sugar
Whole strawberries (optional)

1. Place first 5 ingredients in a blender, and process until smooth. Garnish with whole strawberries, if desired. Serve immediately. Yield: 3 servings (serving size: ¾ cup).

CALORIES 254 (21% from fat); FAT 5.9g (sat 3.4g, mono 1.6g, poly 0.6g); PROTEIN 7.2g; CARB 45.6g; FIBER 1.9g; CHOL 13mg; IRON 0.5mg; SODIUM 182mg; CALC 214mg

Berry Refresher

CREAMY STRAWBERRY COOLER

PREP: 8 MINUTES

1½ cups sliced fresh strawberries
1   cup ice cubes
½   cup plain low-fat yogurt
¼   cup fresh orange juice
2   tablespoons no-sugar-added strawberry spread
2   teaspoons sugar
1   teaspoon vanilla extract
⅛   teaspoon almond extract

1. Combine all ingredients in a blender; process until smooth. Yield: 3 servings (serving size: 1 cup).

CALORIES 102 (8% from fat); FAT 0.9g (sat 0.4g, mono 0.2g, poly 0.2g); PROTEIN 2.7g; CARB 20.7g; FIBER 2.1g; CHOL 2mg; IRON 0.4mg; SODIUM 28mg; CALC 84mg

BERRY REFRESHER

PREP: 3 MINUTES

1   cup halved fresh or frozen unsweetened strawberries, thawed
½   cup orange juice
2   tablespoons powdered sugar
1   (8-ounce) carton raspberry low-fat yogurt
10 ice cubes

1. Combine all ingredients in a blender; process until smooth. Serve immediately. Yield: 3 servings (serving size: 1 cup).

CALORIES 128 (8% from fat); FAT 1.1g (sat 0.6g, mono 0.3g, poly 0.1g); PROTEIN 3.6g; CARB 27g; FIBER 1.4g; CHOL 3mg; IRON 0.3mg; SODIUM 41mg; CALC 115mg

PIÑA COLADA

PREP: 5 MINUTES

1½ cups pineapple juice, chilled
¼ cup powdered sugar
1 tablespoon lime juice
¾ teaspoon coconut extract
½ teaspoon rum flavoring
1 (20-ounce) can pineapple chunks in juice, undrained
1 (8-ounce) carton pineapple low-fat yogurt
10 ice cubes

1. Combine all ingredients in a blender; process until smooth. Serve immediately. Yield: 6 servings (serving size: 1 cup).

CALORIES 151 (3% from fat); FAT 0.5g (sat 0.3g, mono 0.1g, poly 0g); PROTEIN 1.8g; CARB 34.8g; FIBER 0.1g; CHOL 2mg; IRON 0.5mg; SODIUM 22mg; CALC 75mg

PIÑA COLADA SLUSH

PREP: 15 MINUTES   FREEZE: 1 HOUR

2 cups cubed fresh pineapple
1½ cups pineapple juice, chilled
¼ cup cream of coconut (such as Coco Lopez)
1 cup ice cubes
1 cup vanilla fat-free frozen yogurt

1. Arrange pineapple in a single layer on a baking sheet; freeze until firm (about 1 hour). Remove from freezer; let stand 10 minutes. Combine juice and cream of coconut in a blender. With blender on, add pineapple and ice cubes, 1 at a time; process until smooth. Add yogurt; process until smooth. Serve immediately. Yield: 4 servings (serving size: 1 cup).

CALORIES 175 (29% from fat); FAT 5.6g (sat 4.6g, mono 0.3g, poly 0.2g); PROTEIN 2.6g; CARB 31.3g; FIBER 1.4g; CHOL 0mg; IRON 0.9mg; SODIUM 28mg; CALC 79mg

GRAPEFRUIT PIÑA COLADA FREEZE

PREP: 8 MINUTES
FREEZE: 1 HOUR

1½ cups grapefruit sections (about 1 large)
2 tablespoons sugar
2 teaspoons honey
¼ teaspoon coconut extract
1 (8-ounce) carton piña colada low-fat yogurt
1 (8-ounce) can crushed pineapple in juice, drained

1. Arrange grapefruit sections in a single layer on a baking sheet lined with aluminum foil; freeze 1 hour.
2. Place frozen grapefruit in a blender; process until finely chopped. Add next 4 ingredients; process until smooth. Add pineapple; pulse 4 times or just until blended. Serve immediately. Yield: 5 servings (serving size: ½ cup).

CALORIES 107 (6% from fat); FAT 0.7g (sat 0.4g, mono 0.2g, poly 0.1g); PROTEIN 2.3g; CARB 24.3g; FIBER 1.1g; CHOL 2mg; IRON 0.2mg; SODIUM 25mg; CALC 72mg

CITRUS SUNSHINE SODAS

PREP: 5 MINUTES

¼ cup thawed orange juice concentrate
1 (8-ounce) can crushed pineapple in juice, undrained
3 cups Citrus Ice Cream (page 175)
4 cups lemon-lime soda (such as Sprite), chilled

1. Combine orange juice concentrate and pineapple in a blender, and process until smooth. Spoon 3 tablespoons orange juice mixture into each of 6 tall glasses. Spoon ½ cup Citrus Ice Cream into each glass. Add ⅔ cup lemon-lime

soda to each glass. Serve immediately. Yield: 6 servings.

CALORIES 212 (2% from fat); FAT 0.4g (sat 0.2g, mono 0.1g, poly 0.1g); PROTEIN 37.1g; CARB 39.7g; FIBER 0.5g; CHOL 2mg; IRON 0.6mg; SODIUM 72mg; CALC 113mg

FUZZY NAVEL SHAKE

PREP: 6 MINUTES

1½ cups vanilla fat-free ice cream
½ cup coarsely chopped peeled peaches
3 tablespoons cranberry juice cocktail
2 tablespoons peach schnapps

1. Combine all ingredients in a blender; process until smooth. Serve immediately. Yield: 2 servings (serving size: 1 cup).

CALORIES 212 (18% from fat); FAT 4.3g (sat 2.6g, mono 1.2g, poly 0.2g); PROTEIN 4.1g; CARB 36.3g; FIBER 0.7g; CHOL 14mg; IRON 0.2mg; SODIUM 84mg; CALC 140mg

HOLIDAY EGGNOG

PREP: 7 MINUTES

2⅓ cups 2% reduced-fat milk
1 (8-ounce) carton frozen egg substitute, partially thawed
¼ cup nonfat dry milk
¼ cup sugar
1 teaspoon vanilla extract
½ teaspoon rum flavoring
⅛ teaspoon ground nutmeg
6 ice cubes
Additional ground nutmeg (optional)

1. Combine first 8 ingredients in a blender; process until smooth. Pour into small glasses; sprinkle with nutmeg, if desired. Serve immediately. Yield: 10 servings (serving size: ½ cup).

CALORIES 72 (14% from fat); FAT 1.1g (sat 0.7g, mono 0.3g, poly 0g); PROTEIN 5.2g; CARB 9.8g; FIBER 0g; CHOL 5mg; IRON 0.5mg; SODIUM 78mg; CALC 114mg

Butternut-Oatmeal Bread
(page 90)

breads

biscuits

The secret to tender, flaky biscuits and scones is handling the dough as little as possible. Overworking the dough will make them tough.

Dropped biscuits and rolled biscuits are the most common types of this popular bread. Dropped biscuits may be less intimidating because the dough is simply dropped by tablespoonfuls onto a baking sheet. They have a higher proportion of liquid to dry ingredients than rolled biscuits, creating a very thick batter rather than a soft dough.

Rolled biscuits take a bit more practice as the dough must be lightly kneaded, rolled out, and cut with a biscuit cutter.

BUTTERMILK BISCUITS

PREP:12 MINUTES   COOK:12 MINUTES

2 cups all-purpose flour
2 teaspoons baking powder
¼ teaspoon baking soda
¼ teaspoon salt
3 tablespoons plus 1 teaspoon
    chilled stick margarine or butter,
    cut into small pieces
¾ cup low-fat or nonfat buttermilk

1. Preheat oven to 450°.
2. Lightly spoon flour into dry measuring cups; level with a knife.
3. Combine flour and next 3 ingredients in a bowl; cut in margarine with a pastry blender or 2 knives until mixture resembles coarse meal. Add buttermilk; stir just until moist.
4. Turn dough out onto a floured surface; knead lightly 4 or 5 times. Roll dough to a ½-inch thickness; cut with a 2½-inch biscuit cutter. Place on a baking sheet. Bake at 450° for 12 minutes or until golden. Yield: 1 dozen (serving size: 1 biscuit).

CALORIES 108 (30% from fat); FAT 3.6g (sat 0.8g, mono 1.5g, poly 1.1g); PROTEIN 2.6g; CARB 16g; FIBER 0.5g; CHOL 0mg; IRON 1.0mg; SODIUM 164mg; CALC 52mg

Buttermilk Biscuits

1. Cut in chilled margarine with a pastry blender until mixture resembles coarse meal.

1a. Or, if you don't have a pastry blender, use 2 knives, pulling them through the margarine until mixture resembles coarse meal.

2. Turn dough out onto a floured surface, and knead lightly 4 or 5 times.

3. Roll dough to a ½-inch thickness. Cut with a 2½-inch biscuit cutter.

A good biscuit dough **will be slightly sticky to the touch** and should be kneaded lightly just a few times.

CINNAMON-RAISIN BISCUITS

PREP:12 MINUTES   COOK:14 MINUTES

For fluffy biscuits, handle dough with a light touch. A good biscuit dough will be slightly sticky to the touch and should be kneaded gently just a few times.

2 cups all-purpose flour
1½ tablespoons granulated sugar
2 teaspoons baking powder
¼ teaspoon salt
½ teaspoon ground cinnamon
¼ cup chilled stick margarine or butter, cut into small pieces
½ cup raisins
¾ cup 1% low-fat milk
1 tablespoon all-purpose flour
Cooking spray
½ cup sifted powdered sugar
1 tablespoon 1% low-fat milk

1. Preheat oven to 400°.
2. Lightly spoon 2 cups flour into dry measuring cups; level with knife. Combine flour, sugar, baking powder, salt, and cinnamon in a bowl; cut in margarine with a pastry blender or 2 knives until mixture resembles coarse meal. Add raisins; toss well. Add ¾ cup milk, stirring just until moist.
3. Sprinkle 1 tablespoon flour evenly over work surface. Turn dough out onto floured surface; knead lightly 4 or 5 times. Roll dough to a ½-inch thickness; cut with a 2½-inch biscuit cutter. Place on a baking sheet coated with cooking spray, with sides slightly touching.
4. Bake at 400° for 13 to 14 minutes or until golden. Combine powdered sugar and 1 tablespoon milk. Drizzle over hot biscuits. Serve immediately. Yield: 1 dozen (serving size: 1 biscuit).

CALORIES 157 (24% from fat); FAT 4.2g (sat 0.9g, mono 1.8g, poly 1.3g); PROTEIN 2.8g; CARB 27.4g; FIBER 0.8g; CHOL 1mg; IRON 1.1mg; SODIUM 156mg; CALC 58mg

GREEN ONION DROP BISCUITS

PREP:6 MINUTES   COOK:15 MINUTES

You may substitute minced fresh or frozen chives for the green onions.

2 cups all-purpose flour
2 teaspoons baking powder
½ teaspoon salt
¼ teaspoon baking soda
3 tablespoons vegetable shortening
¼ cup minced green onions
1 cup low-fat or nonfat buttermilk
Cooking spray

1. Preheat oven to 400°.
2. Lightly spoon flour into dry measuring cups; level with a knife. Combine flour, baking powder, salt, and soda in a large bowl; cut in shortening with a pastry blender or 2 knives until mixture resembles coarse meal. Stir in green onions. Add buttermilk; stir just until moist.
3. Drop batter by heaping tablespoonfuls onto a baking sheet coated with cooking spray. Bake at 400° for 15 minutes or until lightly browned. Yield: 16 servings (serving size: 1 biscuit).

CALORIES 79 (27% from fat); FAT 2.4g (sat 0.8g, mono 1.2g, poly 0.7g); PROTEIN 2.1g; CARB 12g; FIBER 0.5g; CHOL 1mg; IRON 0.8mg; SODIUM 134mg; CALC 45mg

DROP BISCUITS WITH SAUSAGE GRAVY

PREP:19 MINUTES   COOK:11 MINUTES

1 cup all-purpose flour
1½ teaspoons baking powder
⅛ teaspoon salt
½ cup fat-free milk
1 teaspoon stick margarine or butter, melted
Cooking spray
Sausage Gravy (page 441)

Measuring Flour

1. Lightly spoon flour into a dry measuring cup. Do not pack.

2. Level off using the straight edge of a knife.

1. Preheat oven to 450°.
2. Lightly spoon flour into a dry measuring cup; level with a knife. Combine flour, baking powder, and salt in a bowl. Combine milk and margarine; add to flour mixture, stirring just until moist.
3. Drop batter by heaping tablespoonfuls 2 inches apart onto a baking sheet coated with cooking spray. Bake at 450° for 11 minutes or until golden. Split biscuits, and top with Sausage Gravy. Yield: 6 servings (serving size: 1 biscuit and ½ cup gravy).

CALORIES 208 (19% from fat); FAT 4.4g (sat 1g, mono 1.8g, poly 1.1g); PROTEIN 13.6g; CARB 24.2g; FIBER 0.6g; CHOL 26mg; IRON 1.6mg; SODIUM 686mg; CALC 187mg

scones
Best served straight from the oven, this Scottish quick bread presents a delightful alternative to doughnuts and pastries.

Traditionally, scones were triangular, slightly sweet, and baked on griddles. But today's versions can be either sweet or savory, come in all shapes and sizes, and are almost always baked in the oven.

The simplicity of baking scones makes it easy to create new renditions of this teatime classic. Scones work equally well with tea and breakfast fare or as a snack. For best results, use a pastry blender to cut in the margarine until the mixture looks like coarsely ground cornmeal. Add the liquid to the dry ingredients, and stir just until moistened.

DATE SCONES

PREP:20 MINUTES
COOK:17 MINUTES

2 cups all-purpose flour
¼ cup packed brown sugar
1½ teaspoons baking powder
½ teaspoon baking soda
¼ teaspoon salt
⅓ cup chilled stick margarine or
    butter, cut into small pieces
½ cup chopped pitted dates
½ cup 1% low-fat milk
3 tablespoons maple syrup
Cooking spray

1. Preheat oven to 400°.
2. Lightly spoon flour into dry measuring cups; level with a knife. Combine flour and next 4 ingredients in a bowl; cut in margarine with a pastry blender or 2 knives until mixture resembles coarse meal.
3. Add dates; toss well. Combine milk and syrup; add to flour mixture, stirring just until moist (dough will be sticky).
4. Turn dough out onto a lightly floured surface; knead lightly 4 or 5 times with floured hands. Pat dough into an 8-inch circle on a baking sheet coated with cooking spray. Cut into 12 wedges, cutting into but not through dough.
5. Bake at 400° for 17 minutes or until golden. Serve warm. Yield: 1 dozen (serving size: 1 scone).

CALORIES 172 (28% from fat); FAT 5.4g (sat 1.1g, mono 2.3g, poly 1.7g); PROTEIN 2.6g; CARB 28.9g; FIBER 1.1g; CHOL 0mg; IRON 1.2mg; SODIUM 190mg; CALC 49mg

STICKY MAPLE SCONES

PREP:7 MINUTES   COOK:18 MINUTES

2 cups all-purpose flour
2 tablespoons brown sugar
2 teaspoons baking powder
¼ teaspoon salt
¼ cup chilled stick margarine or
    butter, cut into small pieces
6 tablespoons 1% low-fat milk
⅓ cup maple syrup, divided
1 large egg, lightly beaten
Cooking spray

1. Preheat oven to 400°.
2. Lightly spoon flour into dry measuring cups; level with a knife. Combine flour and next 3 ingredients in a bowl; cut in margarine with a pastry blender or 2 knives until mixture resembles coarse meal.
3. Combine milk, 2 tablespoons maple syrup, and egg; stir well with a whisk. Add milk mixture to flour mixture, stirring just until moist (dough will be sticky).
4. Pat dough into an 8-inch round cake pan coated with cooking spray using floured hands. Bake at 400° for 18 minutes or until golden.
5. Pierce top with a fork. Place remaining syrup in a glass measure; microwave at HIGH 30 seconds, and drizzle over top. Cut into 12 wedges, and serve warm. Yield: 1 dozen (serving size: 1 scone).

CALORIES 146 (28% from fat); FAT 4.5g (sat 1g, mono 1.9g, poly 1.3g); PROTEIN 2.8g; CARB 23.5g; FIBER 0.5g; CHOL 18mg; IRON 1.2mg; SODIUM 157mg; CALC 53mg

BUTTERMILK-APRICOT SCONES

PREP:20 MINUTES
COOK:15 MINUTES

2 cups all-purpose flour
1½ teaspoons baking powder
½ teaspoon baking soda
¼ teaspoon salt
¼ cup sugar
¼ cup chilled stick margarine or
    butter, cut into small pieces
⅓ cup chopped dried apricots
1 egg, lightly beaten
¼ cup nonfat or low-fat
    buttermilk
¼ cup apricot nectar
Cooking spray
1 egg white, lightly beaten
1 tablespoon sugar

1. Preheat oven to 400°.
2. Lightly spoon flour into dry measuring cups; level with a knife. Combine flour and next 4 ingredients in a bowl; cut in margarine with a pastry blender or 2 knives until mixture resembles coarse meal.
3. Add apricots; toss well. Combine egg, buttermilk, and nectar; add to dry ingredients, stirring just until moist (dough will be sticky).

Buttermilk-Apricot Scones

1. Combine dry ingredients; cut in chilled margarine with a pastry blender.

2. Add buttermilk mixture, and stir just until dry ingredients are moistened. (Dough will be sticky.)

3. Turn dough out onto a lightly floured surface. With floured hands, gather dough into a ball.

4. Knead lightly 4 or 5 times, and pat dough into an 9-inch circle on a baking sheet coated with cooking spray.

5. Cut dough into 12 wedges, cutting into but not through the dough.

6. Brush with egg white, and sprinkle with sugar.

4. Turn dough out onto a lightly floured surface, and knead 4 or 5 times with floured hands. Pat dough into a 9-inch circle on a baking sheet coated with cooking spray.

5. Cut dough into 12 wedges, cutting into but not through bottom of dough. Brush egg white over surface of dough, and sprinkle with 1 tablespoon sugar. Bake at 400° for 15 minutes or until golden. Serve warm. Yield: 1 dozen (serving size: 1 scone).

CALORIES 148 (27% from fat); FAT 4.5g (sat 0.9g, mono 1.9g, poly 1.3g); PROTEIN 3.2g; CARB 24g; FIBER 1.0g; CHOL 18mg; IRON 1.2mg; SODIUM 184mg; CALC 37mg

TART CHERRY-AND-VANILLA SCONES

PREP: 25 MINUTES   COOK: 18 MINUTES

¾ cup dried tart cherries
¼ cup boiling water
1¾ cups all-purpose flour
⅓ cup sugar
¼ cup yellow cornmeal
2 teaspoons baking powder
¼ teaspoon salt
2 tablespoons chilled stick margarine or butter, cut into small pieces
2 tablespoons vegetable shortening
⅓ cup plain fat-free yogurt
¼ cup evaporated fat-free milk
1 teaspoon vanilla extract
¼ teaspoon butter extract
Cooking spray
1 large egg white, lightly beaten
2 teaspoons sugar

1. Combine cherries and boiling water in a bowl; cover and let stand 10 minutes or until softened. Drain; set aside.
2. Preheat oven to 400°.
3. Lightly spoon flour into dry measuring cups; level with a knife. Combine flour and next 4 ingredients in a large bowl; cut in margarine and shortening with a pastry blender or 2 knives until mixture resembles coarse meal.
4. Combine cherries, yogurt, milk, and extracts; add to flour mixture, stirring just until moist (dough will be sticky). Turn dough out onto a lightly floured surface; knead lightly 4 times with floured hands.
5. Pat dough into an 8-inch circle on a baking sheet coated with cooking spray. Brush egg white over dough, and sprinkle with 2 teaspoons sugar. Cut dough into 8 wedges, cutting into but not through dough.
6. Bake at 400° for 18 minutes or until golden. Serve warm. Yield: 8 servings (serving size: 1 scone).

CALORIES 247 (23% from fat); FAT 6.3g (sat 1.4g, mono 2.9g, poly 2.1g); PROTEIN 4.8g; CARB 43g; FIBER 2g; CHOL 1mg; IRON 2.2mg; SODIUM 211mg; CALC 109mg

CRANBERRY-AND-VANILLA SCONES:

Substitute ¾ cup dried cranberries (such as Craisins) for the tart cherries. Bake as directed, and serve warm. Yield: 8 servings (serving size: 1 scone).

CALORIES 244 (22% from fat); FAT 6g (sat 1.4g, mono 2.8g, poly 2g); PROTEIN 4.7g; CARB 42.1g; FIBER 1.7g; CHOL 1mg; IRON 1.6mg; SODIUM 254mg; CALC 115g

muffins
They're about as satisfying and versatile as a food can be. They harmonize perfectly with coffee and the morning paper, with a salad for a light lunch, or with milk as a snack anytime.

Making muffins could hardly be any easier. All you need are a few utensils and some basic ingredients. We used low-fat dairy products—low-fat buttermilk, fat-free sour cream, and low-fat yogurt—to keep these muffins moist and tender with minimal fat. Here are some tips on baking irresistible, moist, tender muffins that will keep you singing out for more!

• **Preheat the oven first** so that it will be at the correct temperature when the batter is ready.

• **Measure the dry ingredients.** Stir the flour in its storage container, and then lightly spoon it into a measuring cup, leveling it off with a knife. (Do not pack it down.) Place the flour in a large bowl along with the leavening (baking powder and baking soda), salt, and spices; stir the mixture well to combine.

• **If the spices and leavening ingredients are slightly clumpy** when you measure them, put them into a small metal sieve, and sift them into the flour. Otherwise, they may leave yellowish holes and bitter pockets in the baked muffins.

• **Combine wet ingredients** such as juice, oil or melted margarine, milk, yogurt, egg, vanilla, vegetable or fruit.

• **Make a "well"** in the center of the dry ingredients, and add the wet ingredients, stirring just until moistened. Overstirring will produce muffins that

have pointed tops and "air" tunnels throughout. Although this doesn't affect the taste, muffins made from batter that has been stirred until all of the lumps are gone may be tough, rather than tender.

• **We tested these recipes in standard muffin cups** which are 2½ inches in diameter. Using a different size pan will affect the yield and baking time.

• **Bake muffins** in a preheated oven on the middle rack where air circulation is best and the heat is even.

• **Remove muffins** from the pans immediately to keep them from sweating in the pans, which makes muffins soggy on the bottom.

BLUEBERRY-YOGURT MUFFINS

PREP: 12 MINUTES
COOK: 18 MINUTES

2 cups all-purpose flour
⅓ cup sugar
1 teaspoon baking powder
1 teaspoon baking soda
¼ teaspoon salt
¼ cup orange juice
2 tablespoons vegetable oil
1 teaspoon vanilla extract
1 (8-ounce) carton vanilla low-fat yogurt
1 large egg, lightly beaten
1 cup fresh or frozen blueberries, thawed
Cooking spray
1 tablespoon sugar

Muffin Techniques

1. Combine dry ingredients, and stir well. Make a well in center of mixture.

2. Add wet ingredients to dry ingredients. Stir just until dry ingredients are moistened.

3. Gently fold in blueberries.

4. Bake until a wooden pick inserted in center comes out clean.

1. Preheat oven to 400°.

2. Lightly spoon 2 cups flour into dry measuring cups; level with a knife. Combine flour, ⅓ cup sugar, baking powder, baking soda, and salt in a large bowl; make a well in center of mixture. Combine orange juice, oil, vanilla, yogurt, and egg; add to dry ingredients, stirring just until moist. Gently fold in blueberries.

3. Spoon batter into 12 muffin cups coated with cooking spray; sprinkle 1 tablespoon sugar evenly over muffins. Bake muffins at 400° for 18 minutes or until a wooden pick inserted in center comes out clean. Remove muffins from pans immediately, and place muffins on a wire rack. Yield: 1 dozen (serving size: 1 muffin).

CALORIES 150 (20% from fat); FAT 3.4g (sat 0.7g, mono 0.9g, poly 1.3g); PROTEIN 3.5g; CARB 26.4g; FIBER 1.1g; CHOL 19mg; IRON 1mg; SODIUM 161mg; CALC 69mg

BROWN SUGAR-CORNMEAL MUFFINS

PREP: 10 MINUTES   COOK: 20 MINUTES

You'll find tips and techniques for making muffins on pages 66-67.

⅔ cup plus 1 tablespoon packed
      brown sugar, divided
¼ cup plus 2 teaspoons cornmeal,
      divided
2 cups all-purpose flour
1 teaspoon baking soda
1 teaspoon baking powder
¼ teaspoon salt
1 cup vanilla low-fat yogurt
⅔ cup fat-free milk
2 tablespoons stick margarine or
      butter, melted
1 teaspoon vanilla extract
1 large egg, lightly beaten
Cooking spray

1. Preheat oven to 400°.
2. Combine 1 tablespoon brown sugar and 2 teaspoons cornmeal in a small bowl; set aside.
3. Lightly spoon flour into dry measuring cups; level with a knife. Combine flour, ⅔ cup brown sugar, ¼ cup cornmeal, baking soda, baking powder, and salt in a medium bowl; make a well in center of mixture.
4. Combine yogurt and next 4 ingredients; add to flour mixture, stirring just until moist.
5. Spoon batter into 12 muffin cups coated with cooking spray. Sprinkle brown sugar mixture evenly over muffins.
6. Bake at 400° for 20 minutes. Remove muffins from pans immediately; place on a wire rack. Yield: 1 dozen (serving size: 1 muffin).

CALORIES 178 (16% from fat); FAT 3.1g (sat 0.7g, mono 1.1g, poly 0.8g); PROTEIN 4.2g; CARB 33.4g; FIBER 0.8g; CHOL 19mg; IRON 1.4mg; SODIUM 198mg; CALC 81mg

Strawberry-Orange Muffins
Brandied Strawberry Jam
(page 452)

STRAWBERRY-ORANGE MUFFINS

PREP: 10 MINUTES
COOK: 20 MINUTES

Serve these muffins warm with Brandied Strawberry Jam (page 452).

1¼ cups halved strawberries
3 tablespoons butter or stick
      margarine, melted
2 teaspoons grated orange rind
2 large eggs
1½ cups all-purpose flour
1¼ cups sugar
1 teaspoon baking powder
½ teaspoon salt
Cooking spray
2 teaspoons sugar

1. Preheat oven to 400°.
2. Combine first 4 ingredients in a blender, and process just until blended.
3. Lightly spoon flour into dry measuring cups; level with a knife. Combine flour, 1¼ cups sugar, baking powder, and salt in a bowl; make a well in center of mixture. Add strawberry mixture to flour mixture, stirring just until moist.
4. Spoon batter into 12 muffin cups coated with cooking spray. Sprinkle with 2 teaspoons sugar. Bake at 400° for 20 minutes or until muffins spring back when touched lightly in center. Remove from pans immediately; place on a wire rack. Yield: 1 dozen (serving size: 1 muffin).

CALORIES 184 (20% from fat); FAT 4g (sat 2.1g, mono 1.2g, poly 0.3g); PROTEIN 2.8g; CARB 34.8g; FIBER 0.8g; CHOL 45mg; IRON 1mg; SODIUM 179mg; CALC 33mg

APPLE 'N' SPICE MUFFINS

PREP:20 MINUTES
COOK:22 MINUTES

Use a cheese grater's large holes to shred apples. Do not squeeze juice from apples after shredding.

1¼ cups all-purpose flour
½ cup cornmeal
⅓ cup sugar
1 teaspoon baking powder
1 teaspoon ground cinnamon
½ teaspoon baking soda
¼ teaspoon salt
¼ teaspoon ground ginger
1¾ cups shredded Golden
    Delicious apple
¾ cup low-fat or nonfat
    buttermilk
2 tablespoons vegetable oil
1 large egg, lightly beaten
Cooking spray
2 teaspoons sugar
¼ teaspoon ground cinnamon

1. Preheat oven to 400°.
2. Lightly spoon flour into dry measuring cups; level with a knife. Combine flour and next 7 ingredients in a large bowl; make a well in center of mixture. Combine apple, buttermilk, oil, and egg in a bowl. Add to flour mixture, stirring just until moist.
3. Spoon batter into 12 muffin cups coated with cooking spray. Combine 2 teaspoons sugar and ¼ teaspoon cinnamon; sprinkle over muffins. Bake at 400° for 22 minutes or until muffins spring back when touched lightly in center. Remove from pans immediately. Serve warm. Yield: 1 dozen (serving size: 1 muffin).

CALORIES 138 (23% from fat); FAT 3.5g (sat 0.7g, mono 1.1g, poly 1.6g); PROTEIN 2.9g; CARB 24.3g; FIBER 1.3g; CHOL 19mg; IRON 1mg; SODIUM 123mg; CALC 42mg

RASPBERRY-FILLED CINNAMON MUFFINS

PREP:15 MINUTES   COOK:20 MINUTES

1½ cups all-purpose flour
½ cup sugar
2½ teaspoons baking powder
1 teaspoon ground cinnamon
¼ teaspoon salt
⅔ cup low-fat or nonfat
    buttermilk
¼ cup stick margarine or butter,
    melted
1 large egg, lightly beaten
Cooking spray
¼ cup seedless raspberry
    preserves
1 tablespoon sugar
¼ teaspoon ground cinnamon

1. Preheat oven to 400°.
2. Lightly spoon flour into dry measuring cups; level with a knife. Combine flour, ½ cup sugar, baking powder, 1 teaspoon cinnamon, and salt in a medium bowl; make a well in center of mixture. Combine buttermilk, margarine, and egg; add to the flour mixture, stirring just until moist.
3. Spoon about 1 tablespoon batter into 12 muffin cups coated with cooking spray. Spoon 1 teaspoon preserves into center of each muffin cup (do not spread over batter), and top with remaining batter.
4. Combine 1 tablespoon sugar and ¼ teaspoon cinnamon. Sprinkle evenly over muffins. Bake at 400° for 20 minutes or until muffins spring back when touched lightly in center. Remove muffins from pans immediately; place on a wire rack. Yield: 1 dozen (serving size: 1 muffin).

CALORIES 153 (27% from fat); FAT 4.6g (sat 1g, mono 1.9g, poly 1.4g); PROTEIN 2.6g; CARB 25.7g; FIBER 0.5g; CHOL 18mg; IRON 0.9mg; SODIUM 116mg; CALC 63mg

ZUCCHINI-LEMON MUFFINS

PREP:20 MINUTES
COOK:20 MINUTES

2 cups all-purpose flour
½ cup sugar
1 tablespoon baking powder
2 teaspoons grated lemon rind
¼ teaspoon salt
¼ teaspoon ground nutmeg
1 cup shredded zucchini
¾ cup fat-free milk
3 tablespoons vegetable oil
1 large egg, lightly beaten
Cooking spray

1. Preheat oven to 400°.
2. Lightly spoon flour into dry measuring cups; level with a knife. Combine flour and next 5 ingredients in a bowl; make a well in center of mixture.
3. Combine zucchini, milk, oil, and egg; stir well with a whisk. Add to flour mixture, stirring just until moist.
4. Spoon batter into 12 muffin cups coated with cooking spray. Bake at 400° for 20 minutes or until muffins spring back when touched lightly in center.
5. Remove muffins from pans immediately; place on a wire rack. Yield: 1 dozen (serving size: 1 muffin).

CALORIES 148 (26% from fat); FAT 4.3g (sat 0.8g, mono 1.2g, poly 1.8g); PROTEIN 3.1g; CARB 24.3g; FIBER 0.6g; CHOL 18mg; IRON 1.1mg; SODIUM 143mg; CALC 70mg

Linger over a cup of coffee or hot tea as you nibble on a muffin—your day will seem much brighter.

FRESH GINGER-AND-LEMON MUFFINS

PREP:25 MINUTES   COOK:21 MINUTES

   1 cup sugar, divided
  ¼ teaspoon ground ginger
  ¼ teaspoon ground cinnamon
  ¼ cup chopped peeled fresh
       ginger
   1 tablespoon grated lemon rind
   2 cups plus 2 tablespoons
       all-purpose flour
  ¾ teaspoon baking soda
  ¼ teaspoon salt
  ¾ cup low-fat or nonfat buttermilk
  ⅓ cup fat-free fruit puree (such as
       Lighter Bake)
   1 tablespoon vegetable oil
   1 large egg, lightly beaten
   1 large egg white, lightly beaten
      Cooking spray

1. Preheat oven to 375°.
2. Combine 1 tablespoon sugar, ground ginger, and cinnamon, and set aside.
3. Place fresh ginger, ½ cup sugar, and lemon rind in a food processor; process until finely chopped. Set aside.
4. Lightly spoon flour into dry measuring cups; level with a knife. Combine flour, 7 tablespoons sugar, baking soda, and salt in a large bowl; make a well in center of mixture. Combine fresh ginger mixture, buttermilk, and next 4 ingredients; stir with a whisk. Add to flour mixture, stirring just until moist.
5. Spoon batter into 12 muffin cups coated with cooking spray; sprinkle ¼ teaspoon cinnamon mixture over each muffin. Bake at 375° for 21 minutes or until muffins spring back when touched lightly in center. Remove muffins from pans immediately; place on a wire rack. Yield: 1 dozen (serving size: 1 muffin).

CALORIES 168 (12% from fat); FAT 2.2g (sat 0.5g, mono 0.8g, poly 1.1g); PROTEIN 3.5g; CARB 33.5g; FIBER 0.6g; CHOL 19mg; IRON 1.1mg; SODIUM 119mg; CALC 26mg

FIGGY STREUSEL MUFFINS

PREP:14 MINUTES   COOK:22 MINUTES

Fresh figs are available from June until October. Store them in the refrigerator and use within 2 to 3 days.

  ⅓ cup packed brown sugar
  ¼ cup quick-cooking oats
   2 tablespoons finely chopped
       walnuts
   1 tablespoon stick margarine,
       melted
   1 teaspoon vanilla extract
  2½ cups all-purpose flour
  ½ cup granulated sugar
   1 teaspoon baking powder
   1 teaspoon baking soda
  ½ teaspoon salt
  1½ cups chopped fresh figs (about
       ¾ pound)
   1 cup nonfat or low-fat buttermilk
   3 tablespoons vegetable oil
   2 teaspoons vanilla extract
   1 large egg, lightly beaten
      Cooking spray

1. Preheat oven to 400°.
2. Combine first 5 ingredients in a bowl; set aside. Lightly spoon flour into dry measuring cups; level with a knife. Combine flour and next 4 ingredients in a large bowl; make a well in center of mixture.
3. Combine figs, buttermilk, oil, vanilla, and egg. Add to flour mixture, stirring just until moistened.
4. Spoon batter into 18 muffin cups coated with cooking spray; sprinkle oat mixture evenly over muffins. Bake at 400° for 18 to 20 minutes or until a wooden pick inserted in center comes out clean. Remove from pans immediately, and place on a wire rack. Yield: 1½ dozen (serving size: 1 muffin).

CALORIES 157 (25% from fat); FAT 4.4g (sat 0.7g, mono 1.3g, poly 1.9g); PROTEIN 3.1g; CARB 26.3g; FIBER 1.2g; CHOL 12mg; IRON 1mg; SODIUM 156mg; CALC 40mg

Heart-healthy fiber abounds in these luscious bran muffins.

BANANA-BRAN MUFFINS

PREP:16 MINUTES
COOK:16 MINUTES

Each of these muffins packs in almost 5 grams of fiber—that's a significant start to getting the recommended 25 - 35 grams of fiber each day.

  ½ cup low-fat sour cream
  ½ cup mashed ripe banana
  ½ cup fat-free milk
  ⅓ cup sugar
   2 tablespoons vegetable oil
   1 teaspoon vanilla extract
   1 large egg, lightly beaten
  1½ cups morsels of bran cereal (such
       as Bran Buds)
  ¾ cup all-purpose flour
  ½ cup oat bran
   1 teaspoon baking powder
  ¾ teaspoon baking soda
      Cooking spray

1. Combine sour cream, banana, and next 5 ingredients in a bowl; stir well with a whisk. Add cereal; stir well. Let stand 10 minutes.

2. Preheat oven to 400°.

3. Lightly spoon flour into a dry measuring cup. Combine flour, oat bran, baking powder, and baking soda in a large bowl, and make a well in center of flour mixture. Add cereal mixture to flour mixture, stirring just until moist.

4. Spoon batter into 12 muffin cups coated with cooking spray. Bake at 400° for 16 minutes or until muffins spring back when touched lightly in center. Remove from pans immediately; place on a wire rack. Yield: 1 dozen (serving size: 1 muffin).

CALORIES 147 (30% from fat); FAT 4.9g (sat 1.4g, mono 1.3g, poly 1.5g); PROTEIN 4.2g; CARB 25g; FIBER 4.9g; CHOL 22mg; IRON 2.5mg; SODIUM 203mg; CALC 83mg

menu
• Breakfast on the Run •
Raisin-Bran Muffins
Vanilla yogurt topped with
low-fat granola
Fresh strawberries

RAISIN-BRAN MUFFINS

PREP:15 MINUTES
COOK:15 MINUTES

1   cup shreds of wheat bran cereal
    (natural high-fiber cereal such
    as All Bran)
¾   cup fat-free milk
½   cup raisins
¼   cup honey
2   tablespoons vegetable oil
1   large egg, lightly beaten
1   cup all-purpose flour
1½ teaspoons baking powder
¼   teaspoon salt
Cooking spray

1. Preheat oven to 400°.
2. Combine cereal and milk in a bowl;

let stand 5 minutes. Add raisins, honey, oil, and egg; stir well.

3. Lightly spoon flour into a dry measuring cup; level with a knife. Combine flour, baking powder, and salt in a bowl. Add flour mixture to cereal mixture, stirring just until moist.

4. Spoon batter into muffin cups coated with cooking spray, filling two-thirds full. Bake at 400° for 15 minutes or until muffins spring back when touched lightly in center. Serve warm. Yield: 1 dozen (serving size: 1 muffin).

CALORIES 127 (23% from fat); FAT 3.3g (sat 0.6g, mono 0.9g, poly 1.3g); PROTEIN 3.2g; CARB 24g; FIBER 2.9g; CHOL 18mg; IRON 1.8mg; SODIUM 169mg; CALC 71mg

OATMEAL MUFFINS WITH MUSCAT RAISINS

PREP:11 MINUTES
COOK:18 MINUTES

1   cup all-purpose flour
1   cup quick-cooking oats
2   tablespoons sugar
1   teaspoon baking powder
1   teaspoon ground
    cinnamon
½   teaspoon baking soda
⅛   teaspoon salt
¾   cup muscat raisins
½   cup low-fat or nonfat
    buttermilk
¼   cup applesauce
¼   cup molasses
1   tablespoon vegetable oil
1   large egg, lightly beaten
Cooking spray

1. Preheat oven to 400°.
2. Lightly spoon flour into a dry measuring cup; level with a knife. Combine flour and next 6 ingredients in a large bowl; stir in raisins. Make a well in center of mixture. Combine buttermilk, applesauce, molasses, oil, and egg,

and add to flour mixture, stirring just until moist.

3. Spoon batter into 12 muffin cups coated with cooking spray. Bake at 400° for 18 minutes or until a wooden pick inserted in center comes out clean or until muffins spring back when touched lightly in center. Remove muffins from pans immediately, and place on a wire rack. Yield: 1 dozen (serving size: 1 muffin).

CALORIES 137 (18% from fat); FAT 2.4g (sat 0.5g, mono 0.7g, poly 0.9g); PROTEIN 3.3g; CARB 26.5g; FIBER 1.5g; CHOL 18mg; IRON 1.5mg; SODIUM 104mg; CALC 69mg

RAISINS

Dark seedless raisins are the most popular choice for cooking, baking, snacking, salads, and desserts. **They are the most widely used variety of raisin.**

Golden seedless raisins are a light-colored counterpart of dark seedless raisins; both originate from the Thompson seedless grape. Processed to preserve the natural color of the grapes, golden grapes are **ideal for dishes that need a contrast in color or simply a lighter hue.**

Muscat raisins are larger and **offer a more definite fruity flavor** than dark seedless raisins.

Zante currants, small seedless raisins, come from Black Corinth grapes and **have a tart flavor.**

But the bottom line is that most are interchangeable—if you're out of one type, you can substitute one of the others. Just be aware that the flavor will be slightly different.

breakfast breads & coffee cakes Nothing can surpass the

welcoming aroma of a freshly baked coffee cake or pancakes hot off the griddle.

BUTTERMILK PANCAKES

PREP: 5 MINUTES
COOK: 3 MINUTES PER BATCH

These are hearty pancakes that have a lot of body!

 1 cup all-purpose flour
 2 tablespoons sugar
 1 teaspoon baking powder
 ½ teaspoon baking soda
 1 cup low-fat or nonfat buttermilk
 1 tablespoon vegetable oil
 1 large egg, lightly beaten
Maple syrup (optional)

1. Lightly spoon flour into a dry measuring cup; level with a knife. Combine flour, sugar, baking powder, and baking soda in a large bowl. Combine buttermilk, oil, and egg; add to flour mixture, stirring until smooth.
2. Spoon about ¼ cup batter onto a hot nonstick griddle or nonstick skillet. Turn pancakes when tops are covered with bubbles and edges look cooked. Serve with maple syrup, if desired. Yield: 3 servings (serving size: 3 pancakes).

CALORIES 276 (25% from fat); FAT 7.8g (sat 2.4g, mono 2.4g, poly 2.7g); PROTEIN 9g; CARB 42g; FIBER 0.9g; CHOL 75mg; IRON 2.1mg; SODIUM 306mg; CALC 58mg

Buttermilk Pancakes

OATMEAL-BUTTERMILK PANCAKES

PREP: 13 MINUTES
COOK: 3 MINUTES PER BATCH

1¼ cups low-fat or nonfat
  buttermilk
½ cup quick-cooking oats
½ teaspoon vanilla extract
1 tablespoon vegetable oil
1 large egg, lightly beaten
1¼ cups all-purpose flour
2 tablespoons brown sugar
½ teaspoon baking soda
½ teaspoon salt

1. Combine buttermilk, oats, and vanilla; let stand 10 minutes, stirring occasionally. Stir in oil and egg.
2. Lightly spoon flour into dry measuring cups; level with a knife. Combine flour, brown sugar, baking soda, and salt in a large bowl. Add oat mixture to flour mixture, stirring until smooth.
3. Spoon about ⅓ cup batter onto a hot nonstick griddle or nonstick skillet. Turn pancakes when tops are covered with bubbles and edges look cooked. Yield: 4 servings (serving size: 2 pancakes).

CALORIES 287 (22% from fat); FAT 7g (sat 2.1g, mono 1.7g, poly 2.2g); PROTEIN 10.1g; CARB 45g; FIBER 2.1g; CHOL 55mg; IRON 2.5mg; SODIUM 509mg; CALC 116mg

MULTIGRAIN PANCAKES

PREP: 10 MINUTES
COOK: 3 MINUTES PER BATCH

½ cup all-purpose flour
½ cup whole-wheat flour
¼ cup quick-cooking oats
2 tablespoons yellow cornmeal
2 tablespoons brown sugar
1½ teaspoons baking powder
½ teaspoon salt
1 cup 2% reduced-fat milk
¼ cup plain fat-free yogurt
1 tablespoon vegetable oil
1 large egg, lightly beaten

1. Lightly spoon flours into dry measuring cups; level with a knife. Combine flours and next 5 ingredients in a large bowl. Combine milk, yogurt, oil, and egg; add to flour mixture, stirring until smooth.
2. Spoon about ¼ cup batter onto a hot nonstick griddle or nonstick skillet. Turn pancakes when tops are covered with bubbles and edges look cooked. Serve with Cinnamon-Rum Syrup (page 451) or maple syrup and low-fat granola, if desired. Yield: 4 servings (serving size: 3 pancakes).

CALORIES 246 (25% from fat); FAT 6.9g (sat 1.8g, mono 2.1g, poly 2.1g); PROTEIN 9.3g; CARB 38.1g; FIBER 3.3g; CHOL 60mg; IRON 2.1mg; SODIUM 354mg; CALC 225mg

BLUEBERRY WAFFLES

PREP: 5 MINUTES
COOK: 6 MINUTES PER BATCH

1¾ cups all-purpose flour
2 tablespoons sugar
1 tablespoon baking powder
Dash of salt
1⅔ cups fat-free milk
3 tablespoons vegetable oil
2 large egg whites, lightly beaten
1 large egg, lightly beaten
1 cup fresh or frozen blueberries
Cooking spray
Additional blueberries (optional)

1. Lightly spoon flour into dry measuring cups; level with a knife. Combine flour, sugar, baking powder, and salt in a bowl. Combine milk, oil, egg whites, and egg in a small bowl; stir well with a whisk. Add to flour mixture, stirring until smooth. Add blueberries, stirring gently.
2. Coat a waffle iron with cooking spray; preheat. Spoon about ⅓ cup of batter per 4-inch waffle onto hot waffle iron, spreading batter to edges. Cook 5 to 6 minutes or until steaming stops; repeat procedure with remaining batter. Serve with maple syrup. Garnish with additional blueberries, if desired. Yield: 10 servings (serving size: 1 [4-inch] waffle).
Note: If you are using frozen blueberries, do not thaw them before adding to batter.

CALORIES 152 (30% from fat); FAT 5g (sat 1g, mono 1.4g, poly 2.1g); PROTEIN 4.9g; CARB 22g; FIBER 0.9g; CHOL 22mg; IRON 1.1mg; SODIUM 149mg; CALC 110mg

When cooking pancakes, flip them over when the top surface is full of bubbles. The underside will be golden.

BASIC CRÊPES

PREP: 5 MINUTES
COOK: 1 TO 2 MINUTES PER CRÊPE

A ¼-cup dry measure scoops and measures the batter at the same time.

½ cup all-purpose flour
¼ teaspoon salt
¾ cup 1% low-fat milk
2 large egg whites
1 large egg
Cooking spray

1. Lightly spoon flour into a dry measuring cup; level with a knife. Combine flour and salt in a medium bowl. Combine milk, egg whites, and egg in a bowl; stir well with a whisk. Add to flour mixture, stirring with a whisk until almost smooth.

2. Place an 8-inch crêpe pan or nonstick skillet coated with cooking spray over medium-high heat until hot. Remove pan from heat. Pour a scant ¼ cup batter into pan; quickly tilt pan in all directions so batter covers pan with a thin film. Cook about 1 minute.

3. Carefully lift edge of crêpe with a spatula to test for doneness. The crêpe is ready to turn when it can be shaken loose from the pan and the underside is lightly browned. Turn crêpe over, and cook 15 to 30 seconds on other side.

4. Place crêpe on a towel; cool. Repeat procedure until all of the batter is used, stirring batter between crêpes. Stack crêpes between single layers of wax paper or paper towels to prevent sticking. Yield: 10 servings (serving size: 1 crêpe).

CALORIES 41 (18% from fat); FAT 0.8g (sat 0.3g, mono 0.3g, poly 0.1g); PROTEIN 2.6g; CARB 5.8g; FIBER 0.2g; CHOL 23mg; IRON 0.4mg; SODIUM 85mg; CALC 26mg

Basic Crêpes

1. Add the liquids to the flour mixture; whisk just until combined. Don't overstir—this will make the crêpes tough.

2. The ideal crêpe batter should be smooth, not lumpy, and about the consistency of heavy cream.

3. Heat your skillet, then pour in the batter, tilting the pan to cover the bottom. It doesn't matter if your crêpes are perfectly round, but you do want to cover most of the skillet or they'll be too small for the fillings.

4. Crêpes cook very quickly. Check the bottom after about 1 minute. If the crêpe is a speckled light brown, that side is ready. Flip the crêpe over with a spatula, and cook only about 15 to 30 seconds on the other side.

5. Remove the crêpe to a towel or plate to cool. Or stack the crêpes between single layers of wax paper or paper towels. If making ahead, place in a zip-top bag, and freeze for up to 2 months. Crêpes will keep for up to 5 days in the refrigerator.

Fresh Apple Coffee Cake

PREP: 22 MINUTES   COOK: 1 HOUR

    4   cups finely chopped cooking
        apple
    ½   cup orange juice, divided
    1½ teaspoons ground cinnamon
    ½   cup stick margarine or butter,
        softened
    1   cup granulated sugar
    1   (8-ounce) carton egg substitute
    ¼   cup fat-free milk
    3   cups sifted cake flour
    2   teaspoons baking powder
    ¼   teaspoon salt
    2½ teaspoons vanilla extract
        Cooking spray
    2   tablespoons brown sugar

1. Preheat oven to 350°.
2. Combine apple, ¼ cup orange juice, and cinnamon; set aside.
3. Beat margarine at medium speed of a mixer until creamy; gradually add 1 cup sugar, beating until light and fluffy (about 5 minutes). Add egg substitute; beat at medium speed 4 minutes or until well-blended.
4. Combine remaining ¼ cup orange juice and milk. Lightly spoon flour into dry measuring cups; level with a knife.
5. Combine flour, baking powder, and salt; add flour mixture to margarine mixture alternately with milk mixture, beginning and ending with flour mixture. Stir in vanilla.
6. Pour half of batter into a 10-inch tube pan coated with cooking spray; top with half of apple mixture. Pour remaining batter into pan, and top with remaining apple mixture; sprinkle with brown sugar.
7. Bake at 350° for 1 hour or until a wooden pick inserted in center comes out clean. Cool in pan 10 minutes on a wire rack; remove from pan, and cool completely on wire rack. Yield: 18 servings (serving size: 1 slice).

CALORIES 188 (26% from fat); FAT 5.4g (sat 1.1g, mono 2.3g, poly 1.7g); PROTEIN 3.0g; CARB 32.3g; FIBER 1.4g; CHOL 0mg; IRON 1.8mg; SODIUM 168mg; CALC 49mg

Raspberry-Almond Coffee Cake

PREP: 13 MINUTES   COOK: 40 MINUTES

    1   cup fresh raspberries
    3   tablespoons brown sugar
    1   cup all-purpose flour
    ⅓   cup granulated sugar
    ½   teaspoon baking powder
    ¼   teaspoon baking soda
    ⅛   teaspoon salt
    ½   cup plain low-fat yogurt
    2   tablespoons stick margarine or
        butter, melted
    1   teaspoon vanilla extract
    1   large egg, lightly beaten
        Cooking spray
    1   tablespoon sliced almonds
    ¼   cup sifted powdered sugar
    1   teaspoon fat-free milk
    ¼   teaspoon vanilla extract

1. Preheat oven to 350°.
2. Combine raspberries and brown sugar in a bowl. Set aside.
3. Lightly spoon flour into a dry measuring cup; level with a knife. Combine flour and next 4 ingredients in a large bowl. Combine yogurt, margarine, 1 teaspoon vanilla, and egg; add to flour mixture, stirring just until moist.
4. Spoon two-thirds of batter into an 8-inch round cake pan coated with cooking spray. Top with raspberry mixture. Spoon remaining batter over raspberry mixture; top with almonds.
5. Bake at 350° for 40 minutes or until a wooden pick inserted in center comes out clean. Cool 10 minutes on a wire rack. Combine powdered sugar, milk, and ¼ teaspoon vanilla. Drizzle over cake. Serve warm or at room temperature. Yield: 8 servings (serving size: 1 wedge).

CALORIES 176 (23% from fat); FAT 4.5g (sat 1g, mono 1.9g, poly 1.2g); PROTEIN 3.5g; CARB 30.4g; FIBER 1.7g; CHOL 28mg; IRON 1.1mg; SODIUM 131mg; CALC 59mg

Huckleberry Coffee Cake

PREP: 15 MINUTES   COOK: 1 HOUR

    ¼   cup stick margarine or butter,
        softened
    ½   cup (4 ounces) block-style
        fat-free cream cheese
    1   cup sugar
    1   large egg
    1   cup all-purpose flour
    1   teaspoon baking powder
    ¼   teaspoon salt
    1   teaspoon vanilla extract
    2   cups fresh or frozen huckleber-
        ries or blueberries, unthawed
        Cooking spray
    2   tablespoons sugar
    1   teaspoon ground cinnamon

1. Preheat oven to 350°.
2. Beat margarine and cream cheese at medium speed of a mixer until well-blended; gradually add 1 cup sugar, beating well. Add egg; beat well.
3. Lightly spoon flour into a dry measuring cup; level with a knife. Combine flour, baking powder, and salt; stir in margarine mixture. Stir in vanilla; fold in berries. Pour batter into a 9-inch round cake pan coated with cooking spray. Combine 2 tablespoons sugar and cinnamon; sprinkle over batter.
4. Bake at 350° for 1 hour; cool on a wire rack. Yield: 10 servings (serving size: 1 wedge).

CALORIES 218 (23% from fat); FAT 5.6g (sat 1.3g, mono 2.3g, poly 1.6g); PROTEIN 5.3g; CARB 37.1g; FIBER 1.1g; CHOL 23mg; IRON 0.8mg; SODIUM 276mg; CALC 70mg

SOUR CREAM COFFEE CAKE

PREP: 20 MINUTES   COOK: 1 HOUR

Streusel:
- ¼ cup granulated sugar
- ¼ cup coarsely chopped walnuts
- 1 teaspoon ground cinnamon

Cake:
- 2 cups granulated sugar
- 10 tablespoons butter, softened
- ½ cup (4 ounces) block-style fat-free cream cheese
- 2 large egg whites
- 1 large egg
- 2 cups all-purpose flour
- ½ teaspoon baking powder
- ½ teaspoon baking soda
- ¼ teaspoon salt
- 1 cup fat-free sour cream
- ½ teaspoon vanilla extract
- 1 teaspoon powdered sugar

1. Preheat oven to 350°.
2. To prepare streusel, combine first 3 ingredients in a small bowl; set aside.
3. To prepare cake, beat 2 cups sugar, butter, and cheese at medium speed of a mixer until well-blended (about 5 minutes). Add egg whites and egg, 1 at a time; beat well after each addition. Lightly spoon flour into dry measuring cups; level with a knife. Combine flour and next 3 ingredients; stir with a whisk. Add flour mixture to sugar mixture alternately with sour cream, beginning and ending with flour mixture. Stir in vanilla.
4. Spoon half of batter into a 12-cup Bundt pan coated with cooking spray; sprinkle evenly with streusel. Spoon remaining batter over streusel, and spread evenly. Bake at 350° for 1 hour or until a wooden pick inserted in the center comes out clean. Cool in pan 10 minutes on a wire rack; remove from pan. Cool completely on wire rack. Sprinkle with powdered sugar. Yield: 16 servings (serving size: 1 slice).

CALORIES 265 (30% from fat); FAT 8.8g (sat 4.7g, mono 2.5g, poly 1.1g); PROTEIN 5g; CARB 41.9g; FIBER 0.6g; CHOL 34mg; IRON 0.9mg; SODIUM 228mg; CALC 38mg

specialty quick breads These interesting breads will have you bypassing the bakery and heading straight for your kitchen.

SPICED BAKED DOUGHNUTS

PREP: 14 MINUTES
COOK: 10 MINUTES PER BATCH

- 1½ cups all-purpose flour
- ½ cup plus 1 tablespoon granulated sugar
- 1½ teaspoons baking powder
- ¼ teaspoon salt
- 1 teaspoon ground cinnamon
- ½ teaspoon ground nutmeg
- ½ cup 1% low-fat milk
- ¼ cup stick margarine or butter, melted
- ¼ cup egg substitute
- ½ teaspoon vanilla extract
- Cooking spray
- 2 tablespoons powdered sugar

1. Preheat oven to 400°.
2. Lightly spoon flour into dry measuring cups; level with a knife. Combine flour and next 5 ingredients in a large bowl; make a well in center of mixture. Combine milk, margarine, egg substitute, and vanilla, and stir well with a whisk. Add to flour mixture, stirring just until moist.
3. Spoon batter by 2 heaping tablespoonfuls into each cup of a mini-bundtlette pan coated with cooking spray. Smooth tops of batter evenly with a knife.
4. Bake at 400° for 10 minutes or until a wooden pick inserted in center comes out clean. Remove from pan immediately; cool on a wire rack. Repeat procedure with remaining batter. Sift powdered sugar over doughnuts. Serve warm or at room temperature. Yield: 9 servings (serving size: 1 doughnut).

CALORIES 183 (28% from fat); FAT 5.6g (sat 1.2g, mono 2.3g, poly 1.7g); PROTEIN 3.2g; CARB 30g; FIBER 0.6g; CHOL 1mg; IRON 1.2mg; SODIUM 195mg; CALC 57mg

Spiced Baked Doughnuts

We used a minibundtlette pan, which looks like a muffin pan with six individual cups, as a doughnut mold. Spoon the batter into cups, then smooth tops with a knife.

PERFECT POPOVERS

Baking popovers in popover pans produces taller, airier results, but you can use a muffin pan with some minor adjustments.

Whichever pan you use, heat it for about 3 minutes before adding the batter—this ensures a higher volume because the batter crawls up the heated cups.

Baking popovers at 450° for the first 15 minutes creates a crispy crust that traps steam inside. Reducing the heat (without opening the oven door) to 350° allows the insides of the popovers to finish baking.

Use a small sharp knife or scissors to make a slit in the top of each popover. This allows steam to escape and helps prevent the inside of a popover from being gummy.

Popovers should be golden and crispy on the outside and soft on the inside; undercooked ones are pale on the outside and gummy on the inside. **Popovers "deflate" quickly, so serve them immediately.** When done, the interior of a popover should be somewhat hollow and moist.

If using a muffin pan instead of a popover pan, divide the batter evenly among 6 heated cups, filling each cup two-thirds full. (Add water to any empty cups to keep pan from buckling.) Bake at 450° for 15 minutes; then lower the temperature to 350°, and bake 15 additional minutes until popovers are puffed and golden. Slit tops, and bake 2 additional minutes.

EASY POPOVERS

PREP: 7 MINUTES   COOK: 25 MINUTES

Here's a quick fix for the breadtime dilemma—popovers. These miniature "bread balloons"— crusty on the outside and almost hollow on the inside—can be mixed up in about 10 minutes flat! The American cousin of Yorkshire pudding, popovers can accompany everything from soup to hearty meats.

  Cooking spray
¾ cup bread flour
¾ cup 1% low-fat milk
½ cup egg substitute
1 tablespoon sugar
1 tablespoon vegetable oil
¼ teaspoon salt

1. Preheat oven to 450°.
2. Coat 6 popover cups heavily with cooking spray. Heat pans in oven for 2 to 3 minutes or until hot.
3. Lightly spoon flour into a dry measuring cup; level with a knife. Place flour and next 5 ingredients in a food processor. Process until smooth, scraping sides of bowl once.
4. Divide batter evenly among hot cups; bake 15 minutes. Reduce oven temperature to 350° (do not remove popover cups from oven); bake an additional 15 minutes or until golden. Make a slit in top of each popover using a small sharp knife or scissors; bake 2 additional minutes. Serve immediately. Yield: 6 servings (serving size: 1 popover).

CALORIES 105 (26% from fat); FAT 3g (sat 0.6g, mono 0.8g, poly 1.2g); PROTEIN 4.7g; CARB 14.3g; FIBER 0.4g; CHOL 1mg; IRON 1mg; SODIUM 143mg; CALC 46mg

Popovers

1. Process ingredients in a food processor to help achieve high volume.

2. Divide batter evenly among 6 preheated popover cups, filling each cup half full.

3. Bake as directed. Make a slit in top of each popover to let steam escape.

CORNMEAL

Whole-grain cornmeal is often ground the old-fashioned way. The dried corn is crushed between millstones at a gristmill. Cornmeal ground this way (called stone-ground) **has a coarser texture than cornmeal that is ground commercially.**

Because the nutrient-packed germ isn't removed, the oil in whole-grain cornmeal can turn rancid easily. To keep it fresh, store it tightly wrapped in the refrigerator for up to a month or in the freezer for up to two years.

White and yellow cornmeals usually have the outer hull (bran of the dried corn) **removed or degerminated, allowing it to be stored for a longer time.** It's then enriched with B vitamins (niacin, thiamin, and riboflavin) and iron to replace some of the nutrients that have been removed. If covered tightly, this cornmeal will keep for about six months in a cool, dry place or for up to two years in the freezer.

Self-rising cornmeal is **regular white or yellow cornmeal with leavening agents and salt added.**

Blue cornmeal, which is powdery and bluish-gray, **is traditional in the American Southwest and lends a pleasant gritty texture to baked products.** It may be hard to find but you can order it from The Chili Pepper Emporium, 328 San Felipe Road NW, Albuquerque, NM 87104-1470, (505) 242-7538.

PIMENTO-CHEESE SPOON BREAD WITH ROASTED SUMMER SQUASH

PREP: 49 MINUTES COOK: 55 MINUTES

Spoon bread is usually made with cornmeal and baked in a casserole dish. Serve this spicy, savory version as a side dish.

Roasted Summer Squash
1 cup water
½ cup yellow cornmeal
½ cup 1% low-fat milk
½ cup (2 ounces) shredded extra-sharp cheddar cheese
¼ cup grated fresh onion
¼ teaspoon salt
⅛ teaspoon ground red pepper
⅛ teaspoon black pepper
2 garlic cloves, minced
1 (2-ounce) jar diced pimento, drained
3 large egg whites
1 tablespoon sugar
Cooking spray

1. Prepare Roasted Summer Squash; set aside. Reduce oven temperature to 375°.
2. Combine water and cornmeal in a saucepan; bring to a boil, and cook 1 minute, stirring frequently. Remove from heat; stir in milk and next 7 ingredients.
3. Beat egg whites at high speed of a mixer until foamy. Gradually add sugar, beating until stiff peaks form. Gently stir one-fourth of egg white mixture into cornmeal mixture; gently fold in remaining egg white mixture. Fold in Roasted Summer Squash.
4. Spoon mixture into a 1½-quart casserole coated with cooking spray. Bake at 375° for 55 minutes or until set. Let stand 5 minutes before serving. Yield: 4 servings.

CALORIES 191 (30% from fat); FAT 6.4g (sat 3.4g, mono 1.7g, poly 0.7g); PROTEIN 9.8g; CARB 23.9g; FIBER 2.5g; CHOL 16mg; IRON 1.5mg; SODIUM 368mg; CALC 163mg

ROASTED SUMMER SQUASH

2 cups thinly sliced yellow squash (about ¾ pound)
½ teaspoon vegetable oil
¼ teaspoon paprika
⅛ teaspoon salt
⅛ teaspoon garlic powder
⅛ teaspoon ground red pepper
Cooking spray

1. Preheat oven to 450°.
2. Combine first 6 ingredients in a zip-top plastic bag. Seal bag; shake to coat squash. Place squash on a baking sheet coated with cooking spray. Bake at 450° for 20 minutes, turning after 10 minutes. Yield: 2 cups (serving size: ½ cup).

CALORIES 22 (37% from fat); FAT 0.9g (sat 0.1g, mono 0.2g, poly 0.4g); PROTEIN 0.9g; CARB 3.3g; FIBER 1.3g; CHOL 0mg; IRON 0.4mg; SODIUM 75mg; CALC 15mg

GREEN-CHILE CORNSTICKS

PREP: 15 MINUTES
COOK: 20 MINUTES

Cooking spray
¾ cup all-purpose flour
¾ cup yellow cornmeal
¼ cup sugar
2 teaspoons baking powder
½ teaspoon salt
⅔ cup fat-free milk
2 tablespoons vegetable oil
1 large egg, lightly beaten
1 (8¾-ounce) can whole-kernel corn, drained
1 (4.5-ounce) can chopped green chiles, drained

1. Preheat oven to 400°.
2. Coat cast-iron cornstick pans heavily with cooking spray; place in a 400° oven for 10 minutes.
3. Lightly spoon flour into dry measuring cups; level with a knife. Combine

flour and next 4 ingredients in a large bowl; make a well in center of mixture. Combine milk, oil, and egg; add to flour mixture, stirring just until moist. Fold in corn and green chiles.

4. Spoon batter evenly into preheated pans. Bake at 400° for 20 minutes or until lightly browned. Remove cornsticks from pans immediately; serve warm. Yield: 14 servings (serving size: 1 cornstick).

CALORIES 97 (27% from fat); FAT 2.9g (sat 0.5g, mono 0.8g, poly 1.2g); PROTEIN 2.3g; CARB 16g; FIBER 1.1g; CHOL 15mg; IRON 0.7mg; SODIUM 174mg; CALC 43mg

GREEN-CHILE CORN MUFFINS:

1. Prepare muffin pans as for cornsticks. Spoon batter into 12 muffin cups. Bake at 400° for 30 minutes or until a wooden pick inserted in center comes out clean. Remove muffins from pans immediately; place on a wire rack. Yield: 1 dozen (serving size: 1 muffin).

CALORIES 127 (24% from fat); FAT 3.4g (sat 0.6g, mono 0.9g, poly 1.3g); PROTEIN 3.1g; CARB 21.6g; FIBER 1.2g; CHOL 19mg; IRON 1.1mg; SODIUM 255mg; CALC 67mg

JALAPEÑO CORN BREAD

PREP: 12 MINUTES
COOK: 25 MINUTES

(pictured on page 490)

Butter-flavored cooking spray
2 teaspoons vegetable oil
¾ cup all-purpose flour
1 cup yellow cornmeal
1 tablespoon sugar
2 teaspoons baking powder
1 teaspoon salt
1 cup frozen whole-kernel corn, thawed and drained
1 cup low-fat or nonfat buttermilk
⅓ cup fat-free sour cream
¼ cup chopped fresh cilantro

1 tablespoon chopped seeded jalapeño pepper
1 tablespoon vegetable oil
2 large eggs, lightly beaten

1. Preheat oven to 400°.
2. Coat a 9-inch cast-iron skillet with cooking spray; add 2 teaspoons oil, and place in oven for 8 minutes.
3. Lightly spoon flour into a dry measuring cup; level with a knife. Combine flour and next 4 ingredients in a large bowl. Combine corn and next 6 ingredients in a bowl; stir well with a whisk. Add to flour mixture, stirring until moist. Spoon into preheated skillet. Bake at 400° for 25 minutes or until a wooden pick inserted in center comes out clean. Remove from pan; cool completely on a wire rack. Yield: 9 servings (serving size: 1 wedge).

CALORIES 174 (24% from fat); FAT 4.6g (sat 1.1g, mono 1.7g, poly 1.7g); PROTEIN 5.9g; CARB 27.3g; FIBER 1.6g; CHOL 49mg; IRON 1.5mg; SODIUM 367mg; CALC 94mg

quick bread loaves As their name implies, quick breads are easy to make. You can have each of ours into the oven in less than 20 minutes!

MOM'S BANANA BREAD

PREP: 10 MINUTES
COOK: 45 MINUTES

1 cup sugar
¼ cup light butter, softened
1⅔ cups mashed ripe banana (about 3 bananas)
¼ cup fat-free milk
¼ cup low-fat sour cream
2 large egg whites
2 cups all-purpose flour
1 teaspoon baking soda
½ teaspoon salt
Cooking spray

1. Preheat oven to 350°.
2. Beat sugar and butter at medium speed of a mixer until well-blended. Add banana, milk, sour cream, and egg whites; beat well.
3. Lightly spoon flour into dry measuring cups; level with a knife. Combine flour, baking soda, and salt. Add flour mixture to sugar mixture, beating until blended.
4. Spoon batter into 4 (5 x 2½-inch) mini-loaf pans coated with cooking spray. Bake at 350° for 45 minutes or until a wooden pick inserted in center comes out clean. Cool 10 minutes in

pans on a wire rack; remove from pans. Cool completely on wire rack. Yield: 4 loaves, 4 servings per loaf (serving size: 1 slice).

Note: To make one 9-inch loaf, spoon batter into a 9 x 5-inch loaf pan coated with cooking spray; bake at 350° for 1 hour and 10 minutes. Yield: 20 servings (serving size: 1 slice).

CALORIES 147 (14% from fat); FAT 2.2g (sat 1.4g, mono 0.2g, poly 0.1g); PROTEIN 2.5g; CARB 30.2g; FIBER 1.1g; CHOL 7mg; IRON 0.8mg; SODIUM 180mg; CALC 13mg

BANANA-DATE FLAXSEED BREAD

PREP: 15 MINUTES   COOK: 55 MINUTES

Flaxseed has long been popular with European bakers because of its robust, nutty flavor. Flaxseeds can be found at health-food stores and some supermarkets. Store in an airtight container in your refrigerator or freezer.

½ cup flaxseeds
⅔ cup mashed ripe banana
½ cup sugar
¼ cup vegetable oil
2 large eggs
1½ cups all-purpose flour
¼ cup flaxseeds
½ teaspoon baking powder
½ teaspoon baking soda
½ teaspoon salt
½ cup whole pitted dates, chopped
Cooking spray

1. Place ½ cup flaxseeds in a blender; process until ground to measure ¾ cup flaxseed meal. Set aside.
2. Preheat oven to 350°.
3. Beat banana, sugar, oil, and eggs at medium speed of a mixer until well-blended. Lightly spoon flour into dry measuring cups; level with a knife. Combine flour, flaxseed meal, ¼ cup flaxseeds, and next 3 ingredients; gradually add to sugar mixture, beating until well-blended. Stir in dates. Spoon batter into an 8 x 4-inch loaf pan coated with cooking spray. Bake at 350° for 55 minutes or until a wooden pick inserted in center comes out clean. Cool 10 minutes in pan on a wire rack; remove from pan. Cool completely on wire rack. Yield: 16 servings (serving size: 1 slice).

CALORIES 129 (30% from fat); FAT 4.3g (sat 0.9g, mono 1.3g, poly 1.8g); PROTEIN 2.2g; CARB 21g; FIBER 0.9g; CHOL 28mg; IRON 0.7mg; SODIUM 137mg; CALC 16mg

RAISIN-WALNUT WHOLE-WHEAT BREAD

PREP: 12 MINUTES   COOK: 45 MINUTES

2 cups whole-wheat flour
1 teaspoon baking powder
½ teaspoon baking soda
½ teaspoon salt
½ teaspoon ground cinnamon
1 cup low-fat or nonfat buttermilk
¼ cup honey
3 tablespoons vegetable oil
1 large egg, lightly beaten
½ cup raisins
¼ cup chopped walnuts
Cooking spray

1. Preheat oven to 350°.
2. Lightly spoon flour into dry measuring cups; level with a knife. Combine flour and next 4 ingredients in a large bowl; set aside.
3. Combine buttermilk, honey, oil, and egg; stir with a whisk. Make a well in center of flour mixture; add buttermilk mixture, stirring just until moist. Stir in raisins and walnuts.
4. Spoon batter into an 8 x 4-inch loaf pan coated with cooking spray. Bake at 350° for 45 minutes or until a wooden pick inserted in center comes out clean. Cool in pan 10 minutes on a wire rack; remove from pan, and cool completely on wire rack. Yield: 16 servings (serving size: 1 [½-inch] slice).

CALORIES 128 (31% from fat); FAT 4.4g (sat 0.8g, mono 1.4g, poly 2.4g); PROTEIN 3.6g; CARB 20.5g; FIBER 2.2g; CHOL 14mg; IRON 0.9mg; SODIUM 132mg; CALC 41mg

ORANGE MINT TEA BREAD

PREP: 16 MINUTES   COOK: 45 MINUTES

½ cup fat-free milk
3 tablespoons minced fresh orange mint
½ teaspoon grated orange rind
¼ cup water
⅓ cup stick margarine or butter, softened
¼ cup granulated sugar
¼ cup packed brown sugar
2 large eggs
1¾ cups all-purpose flour
1¼ teaspoons baking powder
¼ teaspoon salt
Cooking spray
¼ cup sifted powdered sugar
1 tablespoon thawed orange juice concentrate
⅛ teaspoon lemon juice

1. Preheat oven to 350°.
2. Combine first 3 ingredients in a saucepan. Bring to a boil over medium heat. Remove from heat; stir in water. Cool.
3. Beat margarine at medium speed of a mixer until creamy; gradually add sugars, beating until light and fluffy. Add eggs, one at a time, beating well after each addition.
4. Lightly spoon flour into dry measuring cups; level with a knife. Combine flour, baking powder, and salt; add to butter mixture alternately with milk mixture, beginning and ending with flour mixture. Mix after each addition.
5. Spoon into an 8 x 4-inch loaf pan coated with cooking spray; bake at 350° for 45 minutes or until a wooden pick

inserted in center comes out clean. Cool in pan on a wire rack; remove from pan. Cool completely on wire rack.

6. Combine powdered sugar, juice concentrate, and lemon juice; drizzle over bread. Yield: 16 servings (serving size: 1 [½-inch] slice).

Note: If orange mint isn't available, any fresh mint can be substituted.

CALORIES 126 (33% from fat); FAT 4.6g (sat 1g, mono 1.9g, poly 1.3g); PROTEIN 2.4g; CARB 19g; FIBER 0.3g; CHOL 27mg; IRON 0.8mg; SODIUM 119mg; CALC 34mg

HAZELNUT-PEAR TEA BREAD

PREP: 16 MINUTES

COOK: 55 MINUTES

⅓ cup hazelnuts (about 1¾ ounces)
1¼ cups all-purpose flour
½ cup whole-wheat flour
1 teaspoon baking powder
¾ teaspoon ground cinnamon
½ teaspoon salt
½ teaspoon baking soda
1 cup shredded peeled pear (about 2 medium)
¾ cup sugar
3 tablespoons vegetable oil
½ teaspoon grated lemon rind
½ teaspoon vanilla extract
1 large egg, lightly beaten
1 large egg white, lightly beaten
Cooking spray

1. Preheat oven to 350°.
2. Place hazelnuts on a baking sheet. Bake at 350° for 15 minutes, stirring once. Turn nuts out onto a towel. Roll up towel; rub off skins. Chop nuts, and set aside.
3. Lightly spoon flours into dry measuring cups. Combine flours, nuts, baking powder, cinnamon, salt, and baking soda in a large bowl; make a well in center of mixture. Combine pear and next

6 ingredients in a bowl; add to flour mixture, stirring just until moist.
4. Spoon batter into an 8 x 4-inch loaf pan coated with cooking spray. Bake at 350° for 55 minutes or until a wooden pick inserted in center comes out clean. Cool in pan 10 minutes on a wire rack; remove from pan. Cool completely on wire rack. Yield: 12 servings (serving size: 1 [¾-inch] slice).

CALORIES 188 (34% from fat); FAT 7g (sat 1g, mono 3.4g, poly 2.1g); PROTEIN 3.4g; CARB 29.1g; FIBER 1.6g; CHOL 18mg; IRON 1.1mg; SODIUM 169mg; CALC 33mg

ZUCCHINI BREAD

PREP: 18 MINUTES

COOK: 1 HOUR 10 MINUTES

If your garden is bursting with zucchini, stir up a couple of batches of this recipe. When the loaves have completely cooled, place in zip-top plastic freezer bags and store them in the freezer for up to 3 months.

3 cups shredded zucchini (about 3 medium)
4 cups all-purpose flour
1 cup plus 2 tablespoons granulated sugar, divided
½ cup chopped walnuts, toasted
¼ cup packed brown sugar
5 teaspoons baking powder
1 tablespoon grated lemon rind
1½ teaspoons ground cinnamon
½ teaspoon salt
¼ teaspoon ground nutmeg
1½ cups fat-free milk
6 tablespoons vegetable oil
2 teaspoons vanilla extract
2 large eggs, lightly beaten
Cooking spray

1. Preheat oven to 350°.
2. Press shredded zucchini on several layers of paper towels. Cover with additional paper towels.

3. Lightly spoon flour into dry measuring cups; level with a knife. Combine flour, 1 cup granulated sugar, walnuts, and next 6 ingredients in a large bowl; make a well in center of mixture. Combine milk, oil, vanilla, and eggs; stir in zucchini. Add zucchini mixture to flour mixture, stirring just until moist.
4. Divide batter evenly between 2 (8 x 4-inch) loaf pans coated with cooking spray. Sprinkle each with 1 tablespoon granulated sugar. Bake at 350° for 1 hour and 10 minutes or until a wooden pick inserted in center comes out clean. Cool 5 minutes in pans on a wire rack; remove from pans. Cool completely on wire rack. Yield: 2 loaves, 12 servings per loaf (serving size: 1 slice).

CALORIES 183 (28% from fat); FAT 5.6g (sat 0.8g, mono 3g, poly 1.4g); PROTEIN 4g; CARB 29.6g; FIBER 0.8g; CHOL 19mg; IRON 1.4mg; SODIUM 64mg; CALC 89mg

QUICK KICKS

Try toasting slices of quick breads the day after you make them or once you've taken them out of the freezer. Then top them with a low-fat spread. Here are a few ideas:

- **Soften Gorgonzola or blue cheese** in the microwave oven; stir in plain fat-free yogurt, and cool. Serve with **Raisin-Walnut Whole-Wheat Bread**.

- **Using your mixer, whip together light cream cheese and fat-free milk;** add powdered sugar and vanilla, and spread over **Orange Mint Tea Bread**.

- **Drain plain fat-free yogurt** (see how on page 25), and mix with a little apricot fruit spread for **Hazelnut-Pear Tea Bread**.

- **Spread light cream cheese mixed with** a little honey and vanilla fat-free yogurt on **Banana-Date Flaxseed Bread**.

YEAST BREADS

from yeast to oven: The smell of bread baking is one of those pleasures

1. Proofing the Yeast. Making sure that your yeast is alive, a process known as proofing, is the most crucial step in baking bread. If the yeast is dead, it can't leaven your bread. Live yeast will swell and foam (or activate) a few minutes after it's stirred into the warm liquid.

2. Making the Dough. To make the initial bread dough, add most of the flour to the liquid ingredients all at once, and stir just until the mixture is combined. (Be sure to save some of the flour for kneading.) Then dump the dough onto a floured surface, and you're ready to knead.

3. Kneading the Dough. Knead the dough with authority—punch it out with the heels of your hands; then fold the dough over, give it a quarter-turn, and repeat. Use as little of the remaining flour as possible. After kneading about 10 minutes, the dough should be smooth and elastic but still slightly tacky to the touch.

4. The First Rising. Place the dough in a large bowl during this rising as the dough will double in size. During the rising, cover the bowl with a slightly damp lightweight dishtowel coated with cooking spray.

5. The Touch Test. To tell when the dough has risen enough, simply press 2 fingers into it. If an indentation remains, the dough is ready. If the dough springs back, it needs more rising time.

6. Punching Down. Punch down the dough to deflate it. Then turn the dough out onto a floured surface for rolling.

in life that always appeals to our senses.

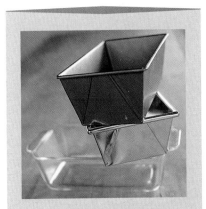

PICKING A PAN

The type of pan you use to bake your bread makes a difference in the final product. We tested all of our recipes in shiny metal loaf pans. If you're using a dark metal pan or a glass dish, lower the oven temperature by 25°.

7. Rolling Out the Dough. To shape the bread, begin by rolling it out. Lift the rolling pin up slightly as you near each end of the rectangular shape.

8. Rolling Up the Dough. Roll up the dough to eliminate air bubbles, giving a better crumb (texture) to the bread. To accomplish this, roll it tightly, pressing firmly as you go.

9. The Second Rising. Once the dough is shaped, it needs to rise a second time. Watch it carefully. If the dough rises too much and starts to fall, your finished bread will be dense and heavy (though still edible). You can avoid this problem—irreversible once it begins—by checking the dough occasionally to make sure it has not begun to deflate. Once it's doubled in size (which will take about 1 hour), the dough is ready to bake.

yeast rolls
Excite the senses with sweet and savory rolls that rise to the occasion.

ANGEL BISCUITS

PREP: 12 MINUTES

CHILL: 1 HOUR

COOK: 13 MINUTES

1 package dry yeast (about 2¼ teaspoons)
½ cup warm water (100° to 110°)
5 cups all-purpose flour
¼ cup sugar
1 teaspoon baking powder
1 teaspoon baking soda
1 teaspoon salt
½ cup vegetable shortening
2 cups low-fat or nonfat buttermilk
Cooking spray
1 tablespoon stick margarine or butter, melted

1. Dissolve yeast in warm water in a small bowl; let stand 5 minutes.
2. Lightly spoon flour into dry measuring cups; level with a knife. Combine flour, sugar, baking powder, baking soda, and salt in a large bowl. Cut in shortening with a pastry blender or 2 knives until mixture resembles coarse meal. Add yeast mixture and buttermilk; stir just until moist. Cover and chill 1 hour.
3. Preheat oven to 450°.
4. Turn dough out onto a heavily floured surface; knead lightly 5 times. Roll dough to a ½-inch thickness; cut with a 3-inch biscuit cutter. Place on a baking sheet coated with cooking spray. Brush melted margarine over biscuit tops. Bake at 450° for 13 minutes or until golden. Yield: 2 dozen (serving size: 1 biscuit).

CALORIES 150 (28% from fat); FAT 4.6g (sat 1.2g, mono 1.5g, poly 1.3g); PROTEIN 3.6g; CARB 23.1g; FIBER 0.8g; CHOL 0mg; IRON 1.3mg; SODIUM 183mg; CALC 41mg

HERBED REFRIGERATOR ROLLS

PREP: 25 MINUTES

CHILL: 24 HOURS   RISE: 1 HOUR

COOK: 10 MINUTES

2 packages dry yeast (about 4½ teaspoons)
1 cup warm water (100° to 110°)
2 tablespoons honey
4 cups all-purpose flour, divided
¼ cup nonfat dry milk
1½ teaspoons salt
1 teaspoon dried tarragon
1 teaspoon dried thyme
1 teaspoon dried dill
2 tablespoons olive oil
1 large egg, lightly beaten
Cooking spray
1 large egg white, lightly beaten
1 tablespoon water

1. Dissolve yeast in warm water in a large bowl. Add honey; let stand 5 minutes. Lightly spoon flour into dry measuring cups; level with a knife. Add 3¾ cups flour and next 7 ingredients, stirring to form a soft dough.
2. Place dough in a large airtight container coated with cooking spray; turn to coat top. Refrigerate up to 24 hours; dough will double in size.
3. Turn out onto a floured surface. Knead until smooth and elastic; add enough of remaining flour, 1 tablespoon at a time, to prevent dough from sticking to hands (dough will feel tacky). Divide dough into 30 equal pieces, shaping each piece into a 6-inch rope. Carefully tie each rope into a knot. Place on a baking sheet coated with cooking spray. Let rise, uncovered, in a warm place (85°), free from drafts, 1 hour or until doubled in size.
4. Preheat oven to 400°.
5. Combine egg white and water, and gently brush over rolls. Bake at 400° for 10 minutes or until golden. Serve rolls warm. Yield: 2½ dozen (serving size: 1 roll).

CALORIES 78 (15% from fat); FAT 1.3g (sat 0.2g, mono 0.8g, poly 0.2g); PROTEIN 2.5g; CARB 13.8g; FIBER 0.6g; CHOL 7mg; IRON 0.9mg; SODIUM 128mg; CALC 18mg

YEAST

Yeast needs a warm environment to be activated, but not too warm or it will die. Water at the right temperature (about **100° to 110°**) should feel warm to the touch, but it should not scald.

Yeast needs "food" to grow, which is why **sugar** is added to the yeast-water mixture in these and most other yeast bread recipes.

Give the yeast mixture **5 minutes to "grow."** You will actually see the yeast **bubble and expand** while it activates. If there's no activity in your mixture, either the yeast was bad (old) or your water was too hot or too cold. Throw out the mixture and start over again.

HOT CROSS BUNS

PREP: 30 MINUTES
RISE: 1 HOUR 5 MINUTES
COOK: 12 MINUTES

5½   cups all-purpose flour, divided
⅓   cup packed brown sugar
¾   teaspoon salt
¾   teaspoon ground cinnamon
¼   teaspoon ground nutmeg
¼   teaspoon ground cloves
1   package dry yeast (about 2¼
      teaspoons)
1½   cups very warm 1% low-fat milk
      (120° to 130°)
2   tablespoons stick margarine or
      butter, melted
1   tablespoon grated lemon rind
1   large egg, lightly beaten
1   large egg white, lightly beaten
½   cup dried currants
Cooking spray
¾   cup sifted powdered sugar
1½   teaspoons fresh lemon juice
1   teaspoon water

Traditionally served on Good Friday, these small buns are typically sweet and feature a glaze drizzled in a cross-shape.

1. Lightly spoon flour into dry measuring cups; level with a knife. Combine 2 cups flour and next 6 ingredients in a large bowl. Combine milk and margarine; add to flour mixture, stirring until well-blended. Add lemon rind, egg, and egg white; beat at medium speed of a mixer 2 minutes or until smooth. Stir in currants. Add 3 cups flour; stir until a soft dough forms.
2. Turn dough out onto a floured surface. Knead until smooth and elastic (about 8 minutes); add enough of remaining flour, 1 tablespoon at a time, to prevent dough from sticking to hands (dough will feel tacky). Place dough in a large bowl coated with cooking spray, turning to coat top. Cover and let rise in a warm place (85°), free from drafts, 45 minutes or until doubled in size. (Press two fingers into dough. If indentation remains, the dough has risen enough.)
3. Punch dough down, and divide into 24 equal portions. Shape each portion into a ball, and place on baking sheets coated with cooking spray. Cover and let rise 20 minutes or until doubled in size.
4. Preheat oven to 400°.
5. Bake at 400° for 12 minutes or until golden. Cool 10 minutes on wire racks. Combine powdered sugar, lemon juice, and water. Drizzle glaze in shape of a cross over top of each bun. Serve warm. Yield: 2 dozen (serving size: 1 bun).

CALORIES 153 (11% from fat); FAT 1.8g (sat 0.4g, mono 0.6g, poly 0.4g); PROTEIN 3.9g; CARB 30.3g; FIBER 0.9g; CHOL 9mg; IRON 1.5mg; SODIUM 100mg; CALC 31mg

yeast bread loaves
All you need to prepare wholesome, homemade yeast bread is a little extra time—and an appetite for the best bread you'll ever slice.

NO-KNEAD BREAD

PREP: 20 MINUTES   RISE: 50 MINUTES
COOK: 40 MINUTES

3   packages dry yeast (about 6¾
      teaspoons)
3¾   cups warm water (100° to 110°)
10   cups all-purpose flour
6   tablespoons sugar
6   tablespoons stick margarine,
      melted
1   tablespoon salt
2   large eggs, lightly beaten
Cooking spray

1. Dissolve yeast in warm water in a large bowl; let stand 5 minutes. Lightly spoon flour into dry measuring cups; level with a knife.
2. Add flour and next 4 ingredients to yeast mixture, stirring until well-blended. Cover and let rise in a warm place (85°), free from drafts, 30 minutes or until doubled in size. (Press two fingers into dough. If indentation remains, the dough has risen enough.) Spoon dough evenly into 3 (9 x 5-inch) loaf pans coated with cooking spray. Let rise 20 minutes or until doubled in size.
3. Preheat oven to 350°.
4. Bake at 350° for 40 minutes or until loaves sound hollow when tapped. Yield: 3 loaves, 16 servings per loaf (serving size: 1 [½-inch] slice).

CALORIES 111 (15% from fat); FAT 1.9g (sat 0.4g, mono 0.7g, poly 0.6g); PROTEIN 2.9g; CARB 20.1g; FIBER 0.8g; CHOL 9mg; IRON 1.2mg; SODIUM 166mg; CALC 6mg

We tested all of our recipes in shiny aluminum pans. If you're using a glass bread dish or a dark metal pan, decrease the oven temperature by 25°, and bake the bread the same length of time.

YEAST PROOF

When you're proofing yeast, the temperature of the liquid is critical—it must be warm enough to activate the yeast, but not so hot that it kills it. To test the temperature, put your finger in the liquid. If you can't keep it there, the liquid is too hot. Or try using an instant-read thermometer; the temperature should be 100° to 110°.

Yeast might not activate for several reasons:

1. The liquid was too cold and didn't activate the yeast;

2. The liquid was too hot and it killed the yeast; or

3. The yeast was very old and therefore **already dead.** (There should be a "use by" date on the package.)

If the yeast doesn't proof, start over.

It's better to waste one package of yeast and water than 4 cups of flour and a lot of time.

Sugar is a food source for yeast and is often added to the liquid to jump-start activation. We have not found quick-rise yeast or bread-machine yeast (it comes in a jar) to perform any differently than regular yeast. Use them interchangeably.

CLASSIC FRENCH BREAD

PREP: 15 MINUTES
RISE: 1 HOUR 15 MINUTES
COOK: 20 MINUTES

This bread is best when eaten the same day it's baked. If you have any left over, do as the French do: Use it to make French toast or a bread pudding.

1 package dry yeast (about 2¼ teaspoons)
1 cup warm water (100° to 110°)
3 cups bread flour
1 teaspoon salt
Cooking spray
1 tablespoon water
1 large egg white, lightly beaten

1. Dissolve yeast in warm water in a small bowl; let stand 5 minutes.
2. Lightly spoon flour into dry measuring cups; level with a knife. Place flour and salt in a food processor, and pulse 2 times or until blended. With processor on, slowly add yeast mixture through food chute; process until dough forms a ball. Process 1 additional minute. Turn dough out onto a lightly floured surface, and knead lightly 4 or 5 times.
3. Place dough in a large bowl coated with cooking spray, turning to coat top. Cover dough, and let rise in a warm place (85°), free from drafts, 45 minutes or until doubled in size. (Press two fingers into dough. If indentation remains, the dough has risen enough.)
4. Punch dough down, and shape into a 6-inch round loaf. Place loaf on a baking sheet coated with cooking spray.

A "CRUSTY" CRUST

The crunchiest crusts are formed by creating steam on the oven. Use an inexpensive plastic bottle such as a plant sprayer to spritz inside the oven several times during baking (being careful not to spray the oven light).

A pizza stone placed on the lower shelf of the oven is about as close as you can get to baking thick-crusted loaves like bakers have been for centuries. Preheat the pizza stone on the bottom of the oven. Simply shape the dough on a baking sheet lined with parchment paper, and let it rise. Then slide the dough, still on the parchment paper, directly onto the pizza stone.

Cover dough and let rise 30 minutes or until doubled in size.
5. Preheat oven to 450°.
6. Uncover dough, and make 3 (¼-inch-deep) diagonal cuts across top of loaf, using a sharp knife. Combine 1 tablespoon water and egg white, and brush mixture over top of loaf. Bake at 450° for 20 minutes or until loaf sounds hollow when tapped. Yield: 12 servings (serving size: 1 slice).
Note: To make a baguette, let the bread dough rise once. Punch dough down, and roll into an 18 x 9-inch rectangle on a lightly floured surface. Roll up dough tightly starting at the long edge, pressing firmly to eliminate air pockets; pinch seam and edges to seal. Cover

dough, let rise, and bake according to recipe instructions.

CALORIES 127 (5% from fat); FAT 0.7g (sat 0.1g, mono 0.1g, poly 0.3g); PROTEIN 4.6g; CARB 25.1g; FIBER 0.2g; CHOL 0mg; IRON 1.6mg; SODIUM 200mg; CALC 6mg

CHEWY ITALIAN BREAD

PREP: 20 MINUTES
RISE: 1 HOUR 15 MINUTES
COOK: 25 MINUTES

6¾ cups all-purpose flour, divided
2 packages dry yeast (about 4½ teaspoons)
2 tablespoons sugar, divided
⅓ cup warm water (100° to 110°)
2 cups fat-free milk
2 tablespoons olive oil
2 teaspoons salt
Cooking spray
1 large egg white, lightly beaten
2 teaspoons water
1 tablespoon poppy seeds or sesame seeds

1. Lightly spoon flour into dry measuring cups; level with a knife.
2. Dissolve yeast and 1 teaspoon sugar in warm water in a large bowl; let stand 5 minutes. Add 4½ cups flour, 5 teaspoons sugar, milk, oil, and salt; beat at medium speed of a mixer until smooth. Stir in 2 cups flour to form a soft dough. Turn dough out onto a floured surface. Knead until smooth and elastic (about 10 minutes); add enough of remaining flour, one tablespoon at a time, to prevent dough from sticking to hands (dough will feel tacky).
3. Place dough in a large bowl coated with cooking spray, turning to coat top. Cover and let rise in a warm place (85°), free from drafts, 45 minutes or until doubled in size. (Press two fingers into dough. If indentation remains, the dough has risen enough.)
4. Punch dough down; cover and let rest 5 minutes. Divide in half. Working with 1 portion at a time (cover remaining dough to keep from drying out), roll each portion into a 14 x 10-inch rectangle on a floured surface. Roll up each rectangle tightly, starting with a long edge, pressing firmly to eliminate air pockets; pinch seam and ends to seal. Place rolls, seam side down, on a large baking sheet coated with cooking spray. Cover and let rise 30 minutes or until doubled in size.
5. Preheat oven to 375°.
6. Uncover dough; using a sharp knife, make 4 (¼-inch-deep) diagonal cuts across tops of loaves using a sharp knife. Combine egg white and 2 teaspoons water; brush over loaves. Sprinkle with poppy seeds. Bake at 375° for 25 minutes or until loaves sound hollow when tapped. Remove from pan immediately; let cool on wire racks. Yield: 2 loaves, 26 servings (serving size: 1 slice).

CALORIES 68 (11% from fat); FAT 0.8g (sat 0.1g, mono 0.4g, poly 0.2g); PROTEIN 2.1g; CARB 12.7g; FIBER 0.5g; CHOL 0mg; IRON 0.8mg; SODIUM 97mg; CALC 18mg

OATMEAL-ONION BATTER BREAD

PREP: 20 MINUTES
RISE: 1 HOUR 15 MINUTES
COOK: 50 MINUTES

1¼ cups warm water (100° to 110°), divided
1 cup plus 1 teaspoon quick-cooking oats, divided
2 tablespoons brown sugar
1 package dry yeast (about 2¼ teaspoons)
3 cups all-purpose flour
¾ cup minced onion
2 tablespoons vegetable oil
1 teaspoon salt
Cooking spray

1. Combine 1 cup warm water, ½ cup oats, and brown sugar in a small bowl.
2. Dissolve yeast in ¼ cup warm water in a large bowl; let stand 5 minutes. Lightly spoon flour into dry measuring cups; level with a knife. Add flour, oat mixture, ½ cup oats, onion, oil, and salt to yeast mixture; stir until well-blended. (Dough will be stiff.)
3. Cover and let rise in a warm place (85°), free from drafts, 45 minutes or until doubled in size. Stir dough well. Spoon into a 9 x 5-inch loaf pan coated with cooking spray. Sprinkle with 1 teaspoon oats. Cover and let rise 30 minutes or until doubled in size.
4. Preheat oven to 375°.
5. Uncover dough; bake at 375° for 50 minutes or until loaf sounds hollow when tapped. Remove bread from pan immediately, and cool on a wire rack. Yield: 16 servings (serving size: 1 slice).

CALORIES 143 (15% from fat); FAT 2.4g (sat 0.4g, mono 0.6g, poly 1.1g); PROTEIN 3.9g; CARB 26.2g; FIBER 1.5g; CHOL 0mg; IRON 1.6mg; SODIUM 148mg; CALC 10mg

The batter for Oatmeal-Onion Batter Bread doesn't require kneading like standard yeast breads. The batter will be stiff enough for a spoon to stand up in.

GRAHAM-CRACKER BREAD

PREP: 22 MINUTES

RISE: 1 HOUR 30 MINUTES

COOK: 30 MINUTES

This bread is also wonderful toasted for breakfast.

1 package dry yeast (about 2¼ teaspoons)
¼ cup warm water (100° to 110°)
2 cups all-purpose flour
½ cup whole-wheat flour
¾ cup low-fat cinnamon crisp graham cracker crumbs (about 5 full cookie sheets)
2 tablespoons honey
½ teaspoon grated orange rind
½ teaspoon salt
2 tablespoons chilled stick margarine or butter, cut into small pieces
⅔ cup warm water (100° to 110°)
2 tablespoons all-purpose flour
Cooking spray

1. Dissolve yeast in ¼ cup warm water in a small bowl, and let stand 5 minutes.
2. Lightly spoon flours into dry measuring cups; level with a knife. Place 2 cups all-purpose flour, whole-wheat flour, cracker crumbs, honey, orange rind, and salt in a food processor; pulse 4 times or until blended. Add margarine; process 10 seconds. With processor on, slowly add yeast mixture and ⅔ cup warm water through food chute; process until combined. With processor on, add 2 tablespoons all-purpose flour through food chute, 1 tablespoon at a time, until dough forms a ball. Process 15 additional seconds.
3. Place dough in a large bowl coated with cooking spray, turning to coat top. Cover and let rise in a warm place (85°), free from drafts, 45 minutes or until doubled in size. (Press two fingers into dough. If indentation remains, the dough has risen enough.)
4. Punch dough down; divide into 3 equal portions. Working with one portion at a time (cover remaining dough to keep from drying), shape each portion into a 12-inch rope. Place ropes lengthwise on a large baking sheet (do not stretch); pinch ends together at one end to seal. Braid ropes; pinch loose ends to seal. Place in an 8 x 4-inch loaf pan coated with cooking spray. Cover and let rise 45 minutes or until doubled in size.
5. Preheat oven to 375°.
6. Bake at 375° for 30 minutes or until loaf sounds hollow when tapped. Remove from pan immediately; cool on a wire rack. Yield: 1 loaf, 16 servings (serving size: 1 slice).

CALORIES 115 (17% from fat); FAT 2.2g (sat 0.4g, mono 0.8g, poly 0.7g); PROTEIN 2.7g; CARB 21.3g; FIBER 1g; CHOL 0mg; IRON 1.2mg; SODIUM 120mg; CALC 7mg

BREAD MACHINE VARIATION:

1. Increase second listing of water from ⅔ cup to 1 cup; follow manufacturer's instructions for placing all dough ingredients in bread pan. Select bake cycle; start bread machine.

Graham-Cracker Bread is well-suited to sweet, fruity sandwich fillings (like PB & J).

BEER-CHEESE BREAD

Beer is a flavor enhancer, as Beer-Cheese Bread demonstrates. But there's no need to put a "not for minors" label on the loaf—most of the beer's alcohol evaporates during the baking, leaving behind only its aroma and flavor imparted by hops.

BEER-CHEESE BREAD

PREP: 35 MINUTES

RISE: 1 HOUR 40 MINUTES

COOK: 40 MINUTES

¾ cup beer
¼ cup stick margarine or butter
3½ cups bread flour, divided
1 tablespoon sugar
½ teaspoon salt
½ teaspoon dry mustard
¼ teaspoon ground red pepper
1 package dry yeast (about 2¼ teaspoons)
1 large egg, lightly beaten
1 cup (4 ounces) shredded reduced-fat sharp cheddar cheese
Cooking spray

1. Combine beer and margarine in a small saucepan; cook over medium-low heat until very warm (120° to 130°).
2. Lightly spoon flour into dry measuring cups; level with a knife. Combine 1½ cups flour, sugar, salt, mustard, pepper, and yeast in a large bowl. Add beer mixture and egg; beat at medium speed of a mixer 2 minutes or until smooth. Stir in cheese and 1½ cups flour to form a soft dough.
3. Turn dough out onto a floured surface. Knead until smooth and elastic

Beer-Cheese Bread

FLOUR AND GRAINS

For whole-grain breads with the volume of traditional high-domed loaves, keep the ratio of specialty grains and flour (which have little or no gluten) small in proportion to wheat and rye flours (which are high in gluten).

The general rule is about 1 cup whole grains or flour per 5 to 6 cups all-purpose or bread flour.

To use oat bran in home-baked breads, grind it to a very fine consistency in a blender or food processor.

While mixing and kneading, leave dough moister than you do when using all-white flour. Whole grains and flour absorb more moisture as they rest and rise. During kneading, add remaining flour one tablespoon at a time and knead until completely absorbed. This ensures moist bread (rather than dry or crumbly bread).

Baked whole-grain breads are best when cooled and reheated, which evaporates excess moisture and sets the crumb.

Store whole grains and flours in tightly covered containers in a cool, dry place. For longer storage, they are best kept in the refrigerator or freezer.

(about 8 minutes); add enough of remaining flour, 1 tablespoon at a time, to prevent dough from sticking to hands (dough will feel tacky).

4. Place dough in a large bowl coated with cooking spray, turning to coat top. Cover and let rise in a warm place (85°), free from drafts, 1 hour or until doubled in size. (Press two fingers into dough. If indentation remains, the dough has risen enough.)

5. Preheat oven to 375°.

6. Punch dough down; cover and let rest 10 minutes. Place in a 1-quart soufflé dish coated with cooking spray. Cover and let rise 40 minutes or until doubled in size. Bake at 375° for 20 minutes. Cover loosely with foil, and bake an additional 20 minutes or until loaf sounds hollow when tapped. Remove from dish; cool on a wire rack. Yield: 1 loaf, 16 servings (serving size: 1 slice).

CALORIES 150 (29% from fat); FAT 4.8g (sat 1.5g, mono 1.8g, poly 1.1g); PROTEIN 5.3g; CARB 20.9g; FIBER 0.8g; CHOL 18mg; IRON 1.3mg; SODIUM 163mg; CALC 70mg

CHEDDAR POTATO BREAD

PREP:50 MINUTES
RISE:1 HOUR 30 MINUTES
COOK:45 MINUTES

2 cups (1-inch) cubed peeled
    baking potato (about ¾ pound)
1 package dry yeast (about 2¼
    teaspoons)
1 teaspoon sugar
3½ cups bread flour, divided
¾ cup (3 ounces) shredded sharp
    cheddar cheese
1 tablespoon olive oil
1½ teaspoons salt
1 teaspoon dry mustard
¼ teaspoon ground red pepper
Cooking spray
½ cup (2 ounces) diced sharp
    cheddar cheese

1. Cook potato in boiling water 10 minutes or until very tender. Drain potato in
a colander over a bowl; reserve 1 cup
cooking liquid. Mash potato until
smooth. Cool cooking liquid to 100° to
110°. Dissolve yeast and sugar in cooled
liquid in a large bowl; let stand 5 minutes. Lightly spoon flour into dry measuring cups; level with a knife. Add 2½
cups flour, potato, ¾ cup shredded
cheese, oil, salt, mustard, and pepper to
yeast mixture; stir until well-blended.
2. Turn dough out onto a floured surface.
Knead until smooth and elastic (about 10
minutes); add ½ cup flour, 1 tablespoon at
a time, to prevent dough from sticking to
hands (dough will feel tacky).
3. Place dough in a large bowl coated
with cooking spray, turning to coat top.
Cover dough, and let rise in a warm
place (85°), free from drafts, 45 minutes
or until doubled in size. (Press two fingers into dough. If indentation remains,
the dough has risen enough.) Punch
dough down; sprinkle with ½ cup diced
cheese. Knead dough until cheese is

well-blended (about 5 minutes); add
enough of remaining flour, 1 tablespoon at a time, to prevent dough from
sticking to hands. Roll into a 14 x 7-
inch rectangle on a lightly floured surface. Roll up rectangle tightly, starting
with a short edge, pressing firmly to
eliminate air pockets; pinch seam and
ends to seal. Place roll, seam side down,
in a 9 x 5-inch loaf pan coated with
cooking spray. Cover and let rise 40
minutes or until doubled in size.
4. Preheat oven to 375°.
5. Uncover dough. Bake at 375° for 45
minutes or until loaf is browned on top
and sounds hollow when tapped. Remove from pan; cool on a wire rack.
Yield: 1 loaf, 16 servings (serving size: 1
slice).

CALORIES 175 (23% from fat); FAT 4.4g (sat 2.1g, mono 1.5g,
poly 0.4g); PROTEIN 6.4g; CARB 26.9g; FIBER 0.5g;
CHOL 9mg; IRON 1.5mg; SODIUM 203mg; CALC 70mg

BUTTERNUT-OATMEAL
BREAD

PREP:20 MINUTES   RISE:1 HOUR
COOK:35 MINUTES

(pictured on page 61)

2 packages dry yeast (about 4½
    teaspoons)
1¼ cups warm water (100° to 110°)
5½ to 5¾ cups bread flour, divided
1¼ cups mashed cooked butternut
    squash (about 1 medium)
¼ cup molasses
2 tablespoons vegetable oil
1½ teaspoons salt
1 cup plus 2 tablespoons quick-
    cooking oats, divided
Cooking spray
1 tablespoon water

1. Dissolve yeast in warm water in a
small bowl; let stand 5 minutes. Lightly
spoon flour into dry measuring cups;

level with a knife. Combine yeast mixture, 3 cups flour, and next 4 ingredients
in a large mixing bowl; beat at medium
speed of a mixer 2 minutes or until
smooth. Stir in 1 cup oats and 2 cups
flour to make a moderately stiff dough.
2. Turn dough out onto a floured surface. Knead until smooth and elastic
(about 10 minutes), adding enough of
remaining flour, ¼ cup at a time, to keep
dough from sticking to hands (dough
will feel tacky). Place dough in a large
bowl coated with cooking spray, turning
to coat top. Cover and let rise in a warm
place (85°), free from drafts, 35 minutes
or until doubled in size.
3. Punch dough down; cover and let rest
5 minutes. Divide in half. Working with
one portion at a time (cover remaining
dough to keep from drying), roll each
portion out onto work surface; knead 4
or 5 times. Roll each into a 14 x 7-inch
rectangle on a lightly floured surface.
Roll up rectangles tightly, starting with a
short edge, pressing to eliminate air pockets; pinch seam and ends to seal. Place
each roll, seam side down, in 8 x 4-inch
loaf pans coated with cooking spray and
sprinkled with 3 teaspoons oats.
4. Brush loaves with 1 tablespoon water;
sprinkle with 1 tablespoon oats. Cover
and let rise 25 minutes or until doubled
in size.
5. Preheat oven to 350°.
6. Bake at 350° for 35 minutes or until
loaves sound hollow when tapped. Remove from pans; cool on wire racks.
Yield: 2 loaves, 16 servings per loaf (serving size: 1 [½-inch] slice).

CALORIES 119 (11% from fat); FAT 1.5g (sat 0.3g, mono 0.4g,
poly 0.7g); PROTEIN 3.6g; CARB 22.7g; FIBER 1.2g;
CHOL 0mg; IRON 1.4mg; SODIUM 112mg; CALC 16mg

BUTTERNUT-OATMEAL ROLLS:

Prepare dough as directed. After first
rising, divide dough in half. Working

with 1 portion at a time (cover remaining portion to keep dough from drying), shape each portion into 15 balls. Place in 2 (9-inch) round cake pans coated with cooking spray. Cover and let rise in a warm place (85°), free from drafts, 25 minutes or until doubled in size. Bake at 350° for 20 to 22 minutes or until browned. Yield: 30 servings (serving size: 1 roll).

CALORIES 127 (12% from fat); FAT 1.6g (sat 0.3g, mono 0.4g, poly 0.7g); PROTEIN 3.9g; CARB 24.2g; FIBER 1.2g; CHOL 0mg; IRON 1.5mg; SODIUM 119mg; CALC 17mg

CHEESE AND CHILE-FILLED BREAD

PREP: 21 MINUTES
RISE: 1 HOUR 20 MINUTES
COOK: 30 MINUTES

2¾ cups bread flour, divided
1 teaspoon sugar
1 teaspoon salt
1 package dry yeast (about 2¼ teaspoons)
1 cup very warm water (120° to 130°)
1 tablespoon extra-virgin olive oil
Cooking spray
¼ cup minced fresh parsley
¼ cup (1 ounce) shredded sharp cheddar cheese
¼ cup (1 ounce) grated fresh Parmesan cheese
3 tablespoons minced jalapeño pepper
3 tablespoons minced green onions
1 tablespoon extra-virgin olive oil
⅛ teaspoon black pepper
4 garlic cloves, minced
1 large egg white, lightly beaten
2 teaspoons water

1. Lightly spoon flour into dry measuring cups; level with a knife.
2. Combine 1 cup flour, sugar, salt, and

Cheese and Chile-Filled Bread

yeast in a large bowl. Add 1 cup very warm water and 1 tablespoon oil; stir until well-blended. Add 1½ cups flour; stir until a soft dough forms.
3. Turn dough out onto a floured surface. Knead until smooth and elastic (about 8 minutes); add enough of remaining flour, 1 tablespoon at a time, to prevent dough from sticking to hands (dough will feel tacky). Place dough in a large bowl coated with cooking spray, turning to coat top. Cover and let rise in a warm place (85°), free from drafts, 45 minutes or until doubled in size. (Press two fingers into dough. If indentation remains, the dough has risen enough.)
4. Punch dough down, and roll into a 15 x 10-inch rectangle on a lightly floured surface. Combine parsley and next 7 ingredients in a bowl. Spread parsley mixture evenly over dough,

leaving a ½-inch border. Roll up rectangle tightly, starting at long side, pressing firmly to eliminate air pockets; pinch seam and ends to seal. Place roll, seam side down, on a large baking sheet coated with cooking spray. Using a sharp knife, make ¼-inch-deep diagonal cuts across top of loaf, using a sharp knife.
5. Cover and let rise 35 minutes or until doubled in size. Combine egg white and 2 teaspoons water, and gently brush over dough.
6. Preheat oven to 375°.
7. Bake at 375° for 25 to 30 minutes or until loaf is golden and sounds hollow when tapped. Cool on a wire rack. Yield: 1 loaf, 16 servings (serving size: 2 [½-inch] slices).

CALORIES 108 (26% from fat); FAT 3.1g (sat 0.9g, mono 1.6g, poly 0.3g); PROTEIN 3.9g; CARB 16.1g; FIBER 0.8g; CHOL 3mg; IRON 1.1mg; SODIUM 183mg; CALC 35mg

PARMESAN-BLACK PEPPER TWISTS

PREP: 40 MINUTES
RISE: 1 HOUR 15 MINUTES
COOK: 25 MINUTES

4½ cups bread flour, divided
1½ cups plus 1 tablespoon
       semolina or pasta flour, divided
¼   cup sugar
2   packages dry yeast (about 4½
       teaspoons)
2   cups warm water (100° to 110°),
       divided
1   cup (4 ounces) grated fresh
       Parmesan cheese
2   teaspoons coarsely ground black
       pepper
1½ teaspoons salt
2   tablespoons extra-virgin
       olive oil
    Cooking spray

1. Lightly spoon flours into dry measuring cups; level with a knife. Combine 1 cup bread flour, sugar, and yeast in a bowl. Add 1 cup warm water; let stand

SLICING BREAD

For slicing bread, an electric knife yields the best results. If you don't have one, a serrated knife will do. Or you can buy a bread-slicing stand, available at department and variety stores.

10 minutes. Combine 3½ cups bread flour, 1½ cups semolina flour, cheese, pepper, and salt in a large bowl; stir. Add yeast mixture, oil, and enough of remaining water to form a soft dough.
2. Turn dough out onto a floured surface, and knead until smooth and elastic (about 8 minutes). Place in a large bowl coated with cooking spray, turning to coat top. Cover and let rise in a warm place (85°), free from drafts, 45 minutes or until doubled in size. (Press two fingers into dough. If indentation remains, the dough has risen enough.)
3. Punch dough down, and knead lightly 4 or 5 times on a floured surface.

Divide dough in half. Working with one portion at a time (cover remaining portion to keep dough from drying), shape each portion into a 36-inch-long rope. Fold each rope in half; pinch ends to seal. Holding sealed ends in one hand and center of rope in the other, twist each rope 3 times, shaping dough into twists.
4. Place loaves 3 inches apart on a baking sheet coated with cooking spray; sprinkle evenly with 1 tablespoon semolina flour. Cover and let rise 30 minutes or until doubled in size.
5. Preheat oven to 400°.
6. Spray dough with water; bake at 400° for 10 minutes. Remove pan from oven; spray loaves with water. Reduce oven temperature to 375°. Rotate baking sheet; bake an additional 15 minutes or until loaves sound hollow when tapped. Remove from pan; cool on wire racks. Yield: 2 loaves, 36 servings per loaf (serving size: 1 slice).

CALORIES 53 (15% from fat); FAT 0.9g (sat 0.3g, mono 0.4g, poly 0.1g); PROTEIN 1.9g; CARB 9.4g; FIBER 0.5g; CHOL 1mg; IRON 0.5mg; SODIUM 67mg; CALC 15mg

Parmesan-Black Pepper Twists

1. Divide the dough in half, shaping each portion into a 36-inch-long rope.

2. Working with 1 rope at a time, fold each rope in half; pinch ends to seal.

3. Holding sealed ends in one hand and center of the rope in the other, twist the dough 3 times, shaping the dough into twists.

Masa Harina-Garlic Loaves

1. Place the loaves, seam side down, on a baking sheet lightly sprinkled with cornmeal.

2. Make 4 (½-inch-deep) cuts across the top of each loaf, using a sharp knife.

3. Lightly spray the loaves with water. This helps produce a crisp crust.

MASA HARINA-GARLIC LOAVES

PREP: 20 MINUTES
RISE: 1 HOUR 20 MINUTES
COOK: 25 MINUTES

Masa harina is a fine-textured corn flour. It was developed in Mexico by treating hominy (a corn product) with lime. The wet hominy is freshly ground to make a meal called masa. When the masa dries, it's referred to as masa harina. You can find it with other flour and cornmeal products in large grocery stores and Mexican-American markets. You may store it in the refrigerator in an airtight container for up to six months.

1   tablespoon vegetable oil
5   garlic cloves, minced
3½ cups bread flour, divided
½   cup masa harina or cornmeal
1   package dry yeast
    (about 2¼ teaspoons)
¾   teaspoon salt
1½ cups very warm water (120° to
    130°)
Cooking spray
2   teaspoons cornmeal, divided

1. Heat oil in a nonstick skillet over medium-high heat until hot. Add garlic; sauté 1 minute or until lightly browned. Strain garlic, reserving garlic and oil; set both aside.

2. Lightly spoon flour into dry measuring cups; level with a knife. Place 3 cups flour, masa harina, yeast, and salt in a food processor; pulse 2 times or until blended. Combine very warm water and reserved oil. With processor on, slowly add water mixture through food chute, and process just until combined; scrape sides of bowl. With processor on, add reserved garlic and remaining ½ cup flour, 1 tablespoon at a time, through food chute; process until dough forms a ball. Process 1 additional minute.

3. Turn dough out onto a lightly floured surface; knead lightly 4 or 5 times. Place in a large bowl coated with cooking spray, turning to coat top. Cover and let rise in a warm place (85°), free from drafts, 45 minutes or until doubled in size. (Press two fingers into dough. If indentation remains, the dough has risen enough.)

4. Punch dough down; cover and let rest 5 minutes. Divide in half. Working with one portion at a time (cover remaining dough to keep from drying), shape each portion into a 15 x 12-inch rectangle on a floured surface. Roll each rectangle tightly, starting with a long edge, pressing firmly to eliminate air pockets. Pinch seams and ends to seal.

5. Place loaves, seam side down, on a baking sheet sprinkled with 1 teaspoon cornmeal. Lightly spray loaves with water, and sprinkle with 1 teaspoon cornmeal. Make 4 (½-inch-deep) cuts across top of each loaf, using a sharp knife. Cover and let rise 35 minutes or until doubled in size.

6. Preheat oven to 400°.

7. Bake at 400° for 15 minutes. Remove pans from oven, and lightly spray loaves with water. Rotate baking sheet a half-turn. Bake an additional 10 minutes or until loaves sound hollow when tapped. Remove from pan, and cool on wire racks. Yield: 2 loaves, 30 servings per loaf (serving size: 1 [½-inch] slice).

CALORIES 32 (11% from fat); FAT 0.4g (sat 0.1g, mono 0.1g, poly 0.2g); PROTEIN 1g; CARB 5.9g; FIBER 0.2g; CHOL 0mg; IRON 0.4mg; SODIUM 30mg; CALC 4mg

PESTO-SWIRLED BREAD

PREP: 16 MINUTES
RISE: 1 HOUR 5 MINUTES
COOK: 30 MINUTES

1 package dry yeast (about 2¼
    teaspoons)
1 teaspoon sugar
2 cups warm water (100° to 110°)
2 cups semolina or pasta flour
3 cups all-purpose flour, divided
2 teaspoons salt
3 tablespoons olive oil
Cooking spray
6 tablespoons commercial pesto
1 large egg, lightly beaten
1 tablespoon water

1. Dissolve yeast and sugar in warm water in a large bowl; let stand 5 minutes. Lightly spoon flours into dry measuring cups; level with a knife. Add semolina, salt, and oil to yeast mixture; beat at medium speed of a mixer until smooth. Stir in 2 cups all-purpose flour to form a soft dough. Turn dough out onto a floured surface. Knead until smooth and elastic (about 10 minutes); add enough of remaining flour, 1 tablespoon at a time, to prevent dough from sticking to hands (dough will feel tacky).

2. Place dough in a large bowl coated with cooking spray, turning to coat top. Cover and let rise in a warm place (85°), free from drafts, 45 minutes or until doubled in size. (Press two fingers into dough. If indentation remains, the dough has risen enough.) Punch dough down; cover and let rest 5 minutes.

3. Divide dough in half. Working with one portion at a time (cover remaining dough to keep from drying), roll each portion into an 11 x 7-inch rectangle on a floured surface. Spread 3 tablespoons of pesto onto each rectangle, leaving a ½-inch margin around edges. Roll up each rectangle tightly, starting with a

long edge, pressing firmly to eliminate air pockets; pinch seam and ends to seal. Place rolls, seam sides down, in a baguette pan coated with cooking spray. Cover and let rise 20 minutes or until doubled in size.

4. Preheat oven to 350°.

5. Uncover dough. Combine egg and 1 tablespoon water; brush over loaves. Bake at 350° for 30 minutes or until loaves are lightly browned and sound hollow when tapped. Remove from pan, and cool on wire racks. Yield: 2 loaves, 16 servings per loaf (serving size: 1 slice).

CALORIES 94 (24% from fat); FAT 2.5g (sat 0.4g, mono 1.5g, poly 0.3g); PROTEIN 2.8g; CARB 15.5g; FIBER 0.9g; CHOL 7mg; IRON 0.9mg; SODIUM 166mg; CALC 14mg

ITALIAN SPINACH-CHEESE SWIRLS

PREP: 50 MINUTES
RISE: 1 HOUR 15 MINUTES
COOK: 27 MINUTES

3 tablespoons olive oil
1 large garlic clove, minced
2 packages dry yeast (about 4½
    teaspoons)
1 tablespoon sugar
2 cups warm water (100° to 110°)
5¼ cups bread flour, divided
1½ teaspoons salt
Cooking spray
1 (10-ounce) package frozen
    chopped spinach, thawed,
    drained, and squeezed dry
½ cup (2 ounces) grated fresh
    Parmesan cheese
1 teaspoon dried Italian seasoning
1 large egg white, lightly beaten
1 tablespoon water

1. Combine oil and garlic in a small bowl. Microwave at HIGH 1 minute; set aside, and cool. Dissolve yeast and sugar in warm water; let stand 5 minutes.

2. Lightly spoon flour into dry measuring cups; level with a knife. Combine 3 cups flour and salt in a large bowl. Add garlic mixture and yeast mixture; stir until well-blended. Add 2 cups flour, stirring until a soft dough forms.

3. Turn dough out onto a floured surface. Knead until smooth and elastic (about 8 minutes); add enough of remaining flour, 1 tablespoon at a time, to prevent dough from sticking to hands (dough will feel tacky).

4. Place dough in a large bowl coated with cooking spray, turning to coat top. Cover and let rise in a warm place (85°), free from drafts, 45 minutes or until doubled in size. (Press two fingers into dough. If indentation remains, the dough has risen enough.)

5. Punch dough down; cover and let rest 5 minutes. Divide in half. Working with one portion at a time (cover remaining dough to keep from drying), roll each portion into a 15 x 10-inch rectangle on a lightly floured surface. Combine chopped spinach, Parmesan cheese, and Italian seasoning. Spread each portion of dough with half of spinach mixture, leaving a ½-inch border. Roll up each rectangle tightly, starting with a long edge, pressing to eliminate air pockets; pinch seam and ends to seal. Place rolls, seam side up, on opposite ends of a large baking sheet coated with cooking spray.

6. Working with one roll at a time, fold roll in half, placing one half directly on top of other half; pinch ends to seal. Using kitchen shears, cut through folded end of roll, cutting through roll to within 1 inch of opposite end. Twist cut halves of dough outward so filling faces up. Repeat procedure with remaining roll. Cover and let rise 30 minutes or until doubled in size.

7. Preheat oven to 350°.

8. Combine egg white and 1 tablespoon water. Uncover dough, and brush egg

Italian Spinach-Cheese Swirls

1. Roll each portion into a 15 x 10-inch rectangle.

2. Arrange spinach mixture evenly over each rectangle, leaving a ½-inch border around edges.

3. Roll up each rectangle, starting with a long edge, pressing to eliminate air pockets.

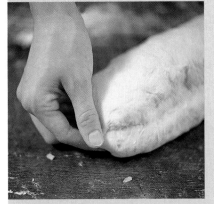

4. Working with one roll at a time, fold roll in half, placing one half directly on top of other half; pinch ends to seal.

5. Using kitchen shears, cut through folded end of roll, cutting through roll to within 1 inch of opposite end.

6. Twist cut halves of dough outward so filling faces up.

white mixture lightly over loaves. Bake at 350° for 27 minutes or until loaves are lightly browned and sound hollow when tapped. Remove loaves from pan, and cool on wire racks. Yield: 2 loaves, 20 servings per loaf (serving size: 1 slice).

CALORIES 74 (19% from fat); FAT 1.6g (sat 0.3g, mono 0.9g, poly 0.2g); PROTEIN 2.6g; CARB 12g; FIBER 0.8g; CHOL 1mg; IRON 0.9mg; SODIUM 111mg; CALC 23mg

To determine if the bread has risen enough, **use the finger test: Press two fingers into the dough.** If the indentation remains, the dough is ready; if it springs back, it needs to rise longer.

specialty yeast breads
Using your imagination to make creative shapes lends another dimension to breadmaking. Shaping the dough into wreaths, buns, and bubble bread adds a new twist to everyday menus.

MAKE-AHEAD OOEY-GOOEY STICKY BUNS

PREP: 40 MINUTES
RISE: 8 HOURS 45 MINUTES
COOK: 23 MINUTES

1 package dry yeast (about 2¼ teaspoons)
1 teaspoon granulated sugar
¼ cup warm water (100° to 110°)
4 cups all-purpose flour, divided
¼ cup granulated sugar
1 teaspoon ground nutmeg
¾ teaspoon salt
1 cup evaporated fat-free milk, divided
¼ cup water
1 large egg, lightly beaten
Cooking spray
1¼ cups packed dark brown sugar, divided
⅓ cup dark corn syrup
2 tablespoons stick margarine or butter
¾ cup chopped pecans
1 tablespoon ground cinnamon

1. Dissolve yeast and 1 teaspoon granulated sugar in ¼ cup warm water in a small bowl; let stand 5 minutes. Lightly spoon flour into dry measuring cups; level with a knife. Place 3¾ cups flour, ¼ cup granulated sugar, nutmeg, and salt in a food processor; pulse 2 times or until blended. Combine ⅔ cup milk, ¼ cup water, and egg. With processor on, slowly add milk mixture and yeast mixture through food chute; process until dough forms a ball. Process 1 additional minute. Turn dough out onto a lightly floured surface; knead until smooth and elastic (about 8 minutes); add enough of remaining flour, 1 tablespoon at a time, to prevent dough from sticking to hands (dough will feel tacky).

2. Place dough in a large bowl coated with cooking spray, turning to coat top. Cover and let rise in a warm place (85°), free from drafts, 45 minutes or until doubled in size. Combine remaining ⅓ cup milk, 1 cup brown sugar, corn syrup, and margarine in a small saucepan; bring to a boil, stirring constantly. Remove from heat. Divide pecans evenly between 2 (9-inch) round cake pans coated with cooking spray. Top each with half of brown sugar mixture.

3. Punch dough down; let rest 5 minutes. Roll into a 24 x 10-inch rectangle on a lightly floured surface; coat dough with cooking spray. Combine remaining ¼ cup brown sugar and cinnamon in a small bowl; sprinkle evenly over dough, leaving a ½-inch border. Beginning with a long side, roll up jelly-roll fashion; pinch seam to seal (do not seal ends of roll). Place a long piece of dental floss or string under the roll; slowly pull ends to cut through the dough. Arrange 12 slices, cut sides up, in each pan. Cover with plastic wrap coated with cooking spray; let rise in refrigerator 8 to 24 hours or until doubled in size.

4. Preheat oven to 375°.

5. Bake rolls at 375° for 23 minutes. Run a knife around outside edges of pans. Place a plate upside down on top of each pan; invert onto plate. Yield: 2 dozen (serving size: 1 bun).

CALORIES 188 (19% from fat); FAT 4g (sat 0.5g, mono 2.1g, poly 1g); PROTEIN 3.7g; CARB 35.1g; FIBER 1g; CHOL 10mg; IRON 1.5mg; SODIUM 110mg; CALC 51mg

BREAD ON THE RISE

A "warm place" as defined by our bread recipes is best to rise your dough, and one option is to use your oven. To warm the oven, turn it on for about 10 seconds, and then turn it off.

You can also place a cup of hot water in the oven. This emits about all the warmth that the dough really requires. Or, you can place the dough anywhere in the house that is warm and free of drafts.

If you set your dough in the oven to rise and it has a crust on it after rising, your oven was too warm. But proceed with the recipe—it will be fine. It's okay if the dough rises, then begins to fall during the first rising. Just proceed according to the recipe, and the bread should turn out fine.

To slice a roll of dough without squishing the slices, **slide a long piece of string or dental floss under the roll of dough.** Cross ends of string over top of roll, and slowly pull ends to cut through the roll.

Make-Ahead Ooey-Gooey Sticky Buns

1. Roll out dough into a rectangle.

2. Use a ruler to make sure rectangle is 24 x 10-inches. Spray dough with cooking spray. This replaces the melted butter that's typically brushed on dough.

3. Sprinkle evenly with brown sugar and cinnamon.

4. Roll up dough beginning with long side.

5. Cut with dental floss, and arrange the rolls in pans.

St. Lucia Saffron Bread

PREP:33 MINUTES

RISE:1 HOUR 5 MINUTES

COOK:30 MINUTES

2 packages dry yeast (about 4½ teaspoons)

2 cups warm water (100° to 110°)

⅓ cup honey

⅛ teaspoon saffron powder

7 to 7½ cups all-purpose flour, divided

½ cup nonfat dry milk

¼ cup golden raisins

1 teaspoon salt

2 large egg whites, lightly beaten

1 large egg, lightly beaten

¼ cup stick margarine or butter, melted

Cooking spray

1 large egg white, lightly beaten

2 tablespoons fat-free milk

2 tablespoons sliced almonds

2 tablespoons coarsely crushed sugar cubes (about 9 cubes)

St. Lucia Saffron Bread

1. Dissolve yeast in warm water in a small bowl; add honey and saffron. Let stand 5 minutes.

2. Lightly spoon flour into dry measuring cups; level with a knife. Place 3 cups flour, yeast mixture, dry milk, raisins, salt, 2 egg whites, and 1 egg in a large heavy-duty stand mixing bowl; beat at medium speed of mixer until smooth. Add margarine, beating just until blended. Stir in 4¼ cups flour to form a soft dough.

3. Turn dough out onto a lightly floured surface. Knead until smooth and elastic (about 10 minutes); add enough remaining flour, 1 teaspoon at a time, to prevent dough from sticking to hands (dough will feel tacky).

4. Place dough in a large bowl coated with cooking spray, turning to coat top. Cover dough, and let rise in a warm place (85°), free from drafts, 50 minutes or until doubled in size. (Press two fingers into dough. If indentation remains, the dough has risen enough.)

5. Punch dough down, and turn out onto a floured surface. Divide dough into 3 equal portions, shaping each portion into a 36-inch rope. Place ropes lengthwise on a baking sheet coated with cooking spray (do not stretch); pinch ends together at one end to seal. Braid ropes; cut 3 inches off one end of braid and set aside. Shape braid into a wreath, pinching ends together to seal. Shape reserved dough into a bow by forming into a rope and tying; place over seam of wreath. Cover dough, and let rise 15 minutes. (Dough will not double in size.)

6. Preheat oven to 375°.

7. Combine 1 egg white and 2 tablespoons milk; brush over dough. Sprinkle with almonds and sugar. Bake at 375° for 30 minutes or until golden. Remove from baking sheet, and cool on a wire rack. Yield: 45 servings (serving size: 1 [1-inch] slice).

Note: Make 2 small wreaths, if desired. Divide dough into 6 equal portions, shaping each portion into an 18-inch rope. Braid 3 ropes for each wreath, and transfer to a baking sheet. Shape into wreaths as directed. Cover and let rise 15 minutes. Brush with milk mixture, and top with almonds and sugar. Bake at 375° for 25 minutes or until golden. Cool on a wire rack.

CALORIES 100 (14% from fat); FAT 1.5g (sat 0.3g, mono 0.6g, poly 0.4g); PROTEIN 3g; CARB 18.6g; FIBER 0.7g; CHOL 5mg; IRON 1mg; SODIUM 77mg; CALC 23mg

St. Lucia Saffron Bread

1. After rolling each portion into a 36-inch rope, braid the 3 ropes together. Cut 3 inches off end of braid. Set aside.

2. Shape braid into a wreath, pinching ends to seal.

3. Shape reserved dough into a rope. Twist rope into a bow, and place on wreath.

HAWAIIAN BUBBLE BREAD

PREP: 50 MINUTES   RISE: 3 HOURS
COOK: 30 MINUTES

You can use any citrus-juice concentrate in this easy-to-make recipe. Forget the knife—just pull it apart to eat.

2 packages dry yeast (about 4½ teaspoons)
1 teaspoon granulated sugar
1 cup warm water (100° to 110°)
1 cup sliced ripe banana
½ cup pineapple-orange-banana juice concentrate
¼ cup honey
2 tablespoons margarine, melted
2 drops yellow food coloring (optional)
5¼ cups bread flour, divided
1 teaspoon salt
Cooking spray
¼ cup cream of coconut
2 tablespoons pineapple-orange-banana juice concentrate
½ cup sifted powdered sugar

1. Dissolve yeast and sugar in warm water; let stand 5 minutes.
2. Combine banana, juice concentrate, honey, margarine, and food coloring, if desired, in a blender; process until smooth.
3. Lightly spoon flour into dry measuring cups; level with a knife. Combine 2 cups flour and salt in a large bowl. Add yeast mixture and banana mixture, stirring until well-blended. Add 2¾ cups flour, stirring to form a soft dough. Turn dough out onto a floured surface; knead until smooth and elastic (about 8 minutes). Add enough of remaining flour, 1 tablespoon at a time, to prevent dough from sticking to hands (dough will feel tacky).
4. Place dough in a large bowl coated with cooking spray, turning to coat top.

Cover dough, and let rise in a warm place (85°), free from drafts, 1½ hours or until doubled in size. (Press two fingers into dough. If indentation remains, the dough has risen enough.) Punch dough down; turn out onto a lightly floured surface, and let rest 5 minutes. Form dough into 1½-inch balls (about 30 balls) on a lightly floured surface. Layer balls in a 10-inch tube pan coated with cooking spray.
5. Combine cream of coconut and 2 tablespoons juice concentrate in a bowl. Pour 3 tablespoons juice mixture over dough, and set remaining juice mixture aside. Cover dough, and let rise 1½ hours or until doubled in size.
6. Preheat oven to 350°.
7. Uncover dough, and bake at 350° for 30 minutes or until loaf sounds hollow when tapped. Cool in pan 20 minutes. Remove from pan; place on a wire rack. Stir powdered sugar into remaining juice mixture; drizzle over top of warm bread. Yield: 26 servings (serving size: 1 slice).

CALORIES 154 (13% from fat); FAT 2.2g (sat 0.9g, mono 0.5g, poly 0.5g); PROTEIN 3.7g; CARB 30g; FIBER 0.3g; CHOL 0mg; IRON 1.4mg; SODIUM 101mg; CALC 9mg

Hawaiian Bubble Bread

Layer the balls of dough in a 10-inch tube pan.

MONKEY BREAD

PREP: 20 MINUTES   RISE: 35 MINUTES
COOK: 25 MINUTES

2   (1-pound) loaves frozen white
      bread dough
1   cup granulated sugar
¼   cup packed brown sugar
¼   cup 1% low-fat milk
1   tablespoon reduced-calorie stick
      margarine
1¼ teaspoons ground cinnamon
¼   cup granulated sugar
½   teaspoon ground cinnamon
Cooking spray

1. Thaw dough in refrigerator 12 hours.
2. Combine 1 cup granulated sugar, brown sugar, milk, margarine, and 1¼ teaspoons cinnamon in a saucepan. Bring to a boil, and cook 1 minute. Remove sugar syrup from heat; cool 10 minutes.
3. Combine ¼ cup granulated sugar and ½ teaspoon cinnamon in a shallow dish. Cut each loaf of dough into 24 equal portions. Roll each portion in dry sugar mixture; layer balls of dough in a 12-cup Bundt pan coated with cooking spray. Pour sugar syrup over dough; cover and let rise in a warm place (85°), free from drafts, 35 minutes or until doubled in size.
3. Preheat oven to 350°.
4. Uncover dough, and bake at 350° for 25 minutes or until lightly browned. Immediately loosen edges of bread with a knife. Place a plate upside down on top of pan; invert onto plate. Remove pan; drizzle any remaining syrup over bread. Yield: 24 servings (serving size: 2 rolls).

CALORIES 201 (10% from fat); FAT 2.2g (sat 0.5g, mono 0.8g, poly 0.8g); PROTEIN 5.2g; CARB 40.1g; FIBER 0g; CHOL 0mg; IRON 1.4mg; SODIUM 302mg; CALC 41mg

---

THAWING FROZEN DOUGH

Remove frozen loaf from package, and wrap in plastic wrap; let thaw in refrigerator 12 hours. Remove plastic wrap, and place on a lightly floured surface; let stand 30 minutes.

Or remove frozen loaf from package, and place on a lightly floured surface. Cover with plastic wrap; let thaw 3 hours.

---

breadsticks

Taking these flavorful creations out of the oven is the cook's reward for all of the twists and turns of breadmaking.

CLASSIC BREADSTICKS

PREP: 17 MINUTES   RISE: 1 HOUR
COOK: 15 MINUTES

3   cups bread flour
¼   cup nonfat dry milk
2   teaspoons olive oil
1   teaspoon salt
1   teaspoon sugar
1   package quick-rise yeast
1   cup plus 2 tablespoons very
      warm water (120° to 130°)
Cooking spray
1   tablespoon cornmeal
1   large egg white, lightly beaten
1   tablespoon water
Sesame seeds, cumin seeds, poppy
      seeds, or fennel seeds
      (optional)

1. Lightly spoon flour into dry measuring cups; level with a knife. Place flour and next 5 ingredients in a food processor; pulse 6 times or until blended. With processor on, slowly add very warm water through food chute, and process until dough forms a ball. Process 1 additional minute. Turn dough out onto a floured surface; knead lightly 4 to 5 times.
2. Place dough in a large bowl coated with cooking spray, turning to coat top. Cover dough, and let rise in a warm place (85°), free from drafts, 40 minutes or until doubled in size. (Press two fingers into dough. If indentation remains, the dough has risen enough.)
3. Coat 2 baking sheets with cooking spray; sprinkle each with 1½ teaspoons cornmeal, and set aside.
4. Punch dough down, and turn out onto a floured surface. Divide dough into 20 equal portions, shaping each portion into a 12-inch rope. Place ropes 2 inches apart on baking sheets. Cover ropes and let rise 20 minutes or until puffy.
5. Preheat oven to 400°.
6. Combine egg white and 1 tablespoon water, and gently brush over breadsticks. Sprinkle breadsticks with seeds, if desired.
7. Bake at 400° for 15 minutes or until lightly browned. Remove from pans; cool on wire racks. Yield: 20 breadsticks (serving size: 1 breadstick).

CALORIES 106 (19% from fat); FAT 2.2g (sat 0.3g, mono 0.8g, poly 0.7g); PROTEIN 3.9g; CARB 17.6g; FIBER 0.8g; CHOL 0mg; IRON 1.4mg; SODIUM 129mg; CALC 47mg

CHEESE BREADSTICKS

PREP: 30 MINUTES

RISE: 1 HOUR   COOK: 12 MINUTES

3¼ cups bread flour
¾ cup grated fresh Romano cheese, divided
¼ cup nonfat dry milk
1 teaspoon salt
1 teaspoon sugar
¼ teaspoon ground red pepper
1 package quick-rise yeast
1 cup plus 2 tablespoons very warm water (120° to 130°)
2 teaspoons olive oil
Cooking spray
2 teaspoons water
1 large egg white, lightly beaten
2 tablespoons cornmeal

1. Lightly spoon flour into dry measuring cups; level with a knife. Place flour, ½ cup cheese, and next 5 ingredients in food processor; pulse 6 times or until blended. With processor on, slowly add very warm water and oil through food chute; process until dough forms a ball.
2. Turn dough out onto a floured surface; knead lightly 5 times. Place dough in a bowl coated with cooking spray, turning to coat top. Cover; let rise in a warm place (85°), free from drafts, 40 minutes or until doubled in size. (Press two fingers into dough. If indentation remains, the dough has risen enough.)
3. Punch dough down; turn out onto a floured surface. Divide in half; roll each portion into a 14 x 10-inch rectangle. Combine 2 teaspoons water and egg white, and brush over rectangles; sprinkle each with 2 tablespoons cheese. Using fingertips, press cheese into dough.
4. Cut each rectangle into 22 (10-inch-long) strips. Gently pick up both ends of each strip, and twist dough. Coat 2 baking sheets with cooking spray; sprinkle each with 1 tablespoon cornmeal.

Place twisted strips of dough 1 inch apart on baking sheets. Cover and let rise 20 minutes or until puffy.
5. Preheat oven to 375°.
6. Bake at 375° for 12 minutes. Remove from pans; cool on wire racks. Yield: 44 servings (serving size: 1 breadstick).

CALORIES 51 (16% from fat); FAT 0.9g (sat 0.4g, mono 0.3g, poly 0.1g); PROTEIN 2.2g; CARB 8.2g; FIBER 0.1g; CHOL 2mg; IRON 0.5mg; SODIUM 82mg; CALC 31mg

CRISP-AND-SPICY CHEESE TWISTS

PREP: 8 MINUTES   COOK: 8 MINUTES

¼ cup grated Parmesan cheese
1 teaspoon paprika
⅛ teaspoon ground red pepper
1 (10-ounce) can refrigerated pizza crust
Butter-flavored cooking spray

1. Preheat oven to 425°.
2. Combine cheese, paprika, and pepper in a small bowl; set aside.
3. Unroll dough; roll into a 12 x 8-inch rectangle. Lightly coat surface of dough with cooking spray, and sprinkle with 2 tablespoons cheese mixture. Fold dough in half to form an 8 x 6-inch rectangle. Roll into a 12 x 8-inch rectangle. Lightly coat surface of dough with cooking spray, and sprinkle dough with remaining cheese mixture. Using fingertips, press cheese mixture into dough.
4. Cut dough into 16 (8-inch-long) strips. Gently pick up both ends of each strip; twist dough. Place twists ½ inch apart on a large baking sheet coated with cooking spray. Bake at 425° for 8 minutes or until lightly browned. Remove from pan; cool on wire racks. Yield: 16 servings (serving size: 1 breadstick).

CALORIES 68 (15% from fat); FAT 1.1g (sat 0.5g, mono 0.1g, poly 0g); PROTEIN 2.7g; CARB 11.9g; FIBER 0.6g; CHOL 1mg; IRON 0.3mg; SODIUM 189mg; CALC 25mg

HERBED BREADSTICKS

PREP: 30 MINUTES   RISE: 20 MINUTES

COOK: 30 MINUTES

3 cups bread flour
1½ tablespoons chopped fresh basil
1½ tablespoons chopped fresh oregano
1½ tablespoons chopped fresh parsley
1 tablespoon sugar
⅛ teaspoon salt
2 packages quick-rise yeast
1 cup very warm water (120° to 130°)
3 tablespoons olive oil
Cooking spray
1 tablespoon water
1 large egg, lightly beaten
1 teaspoon kosher salt

1. Lightly spoon flour into dry measuring cups; level with a knife. Place flour and next 6 ingredients in food processor; pulse 6 times or until blended. With processor on, slowly add very warm water and oil through food chute; process until dough forms a ball.
2. Turn dough out onto a lightly floured surface, and shape into a ball. Divide dough into 16 equal portions; roll each portion into a 15-inch-long rope. Place ropes 1 inch apart on baking sheets coated with cooking spray. Cover and let rise in a warm place (85°), free from drafts, 20 minutes or until puffy.
3. Preheat oven to 350°.
4. Combine 1 tablespoon water and egg, and brush over breadsticks. Sprinkle breadsticks with kosher salt, and bake at 350° for 30 minutes or until lightly browned. Remove from pans, and cool on wire racks. Yield: 16 servings (serving size: 1 breadstick).

CALORIES 112 (27% from fat); FAT 3.3g (sat 0.5g, mono 2g, poly 0.4g); PROTEIN 3.4g; CARB 17.1g; FIBER 0.3g; CHOL 13mg; IRON 1.4mg; SODIUM 169mg; CALC 14mg

GRISSINI ANISE

PREP: 20 MINUTES   RISE: 55 MINUTES
COOK: 10 MINUTES

3¼ cups bread flour
2 tablespoons granulated sugar
1 tablespoon plus 1 teaspoon aniseed
¾ teaspoon salt
1 package quick-rise yeast
1 cup plus 2 tablespoons very warm water (120° to 130°)
1 tablespoon olive oil
1 tablespoon brandy
½ teaspoon vanilla extract
Cooking spray
1 egg white, lightly beaten
1 teaspoon water
2 tablespoons turbinado or granulated sugar

1. Lightly spoon flour into dry measuring cups; level with a knife. Place flour, sugar, aniseed, salt, and yeast in food processor; pulse 6 times or until blended. With processor running, slowly add very warm water, oil, brandy, and vanilla through food chute; process until dough leaves sides of bowl and forms a ball.

2. Turn dough out onto a lightly floured surface; knead lightly 4 to 5 times. Place dough into a large bowl coated with cooking spray, turning to coat top. Cover and let rise in a warm place (85°), free from drafts, 40 minutes or until doubled in size. (Press two fingers into dough. If indentation remains, the dough has risen enough.)

3. Punch dough down; turn out onto a floured surface. Roll into a 24 x 7-inch rectangle, and cut into 24 (1-inch-wide) strips; roll each strip into a 15-inch rope. Place ropes 1 inch apart on baking sheets coated with cooking spray. Cover and let rise 15 minutes or until puffy.

4. Preheat oven to 400°.

5. Combine egg white and 1 teaspoon water, and gently brush over breadsticks; sprinkle with turbinado sugar. Bake at 400° for 10 minutes or until lightly browned. Remove from pans, and cool on wire racks. Yield: 2 dozen (serving size: 1 breadstick).

CALORIES 86 (10% from fat); FAT 1g (sat 0.1g, mono 0.5g, poly 0.2g); PROTEIN 2.6g; CARB 16.4g; FIBER 0.6g; CHOL 0mg; IRON 1mg; SODIUM 76mg; CALC 6mg

LARGE CRYSTALS FOR BIG FLAVOR

You may have noticed that we used kosher salt and turbinado sugar in a couple of these recipes. There's a good reason:

Kosher salt comes in larger crystals, which stick to the bread dough better and lend a nice crunch, similar to the salty crunch of soft pretzels. You can use kosher salt in place of regular salt to top breadsticks.

Turbinado sugar is raw sugar that has been steam-cleaned; it comes in larger crystals than its more common cousin. Turbinado crystals are a **golden caramel color** and are **ideal for sprinkling on breadsticks and cookies.**

pizza crusts A good pizza starts with a good crust. Try any of these crusts—they're sure to deliver great taste.

BASIC PIZZA CRUST

PREP: 14 MINUTES
RISE: 1 HOUR 5 MINUTES

1 package dry yeast (about 2¼ teaspoons)
1 tablespoon sugar
1 cup warm water (100° to 110°)
2¾ cups all-purpose flour, divided
¼ teaspoon salt
1 teaspoon olive oil
Cooking spray
1 tablespoon cornmeal

1. Dissolve yeast and sugar in warm water in a large bowl; let stand 5 minutes. Lightly spoon flour into dry measuring cups; level with a knife. Stir 2½ cups flour, salt, and oil into yeast mixture to form a soft dough.

2. Turn dough out onto a lightly floured surface. Knead until smooth and elastic (about 5 minutes); add enough of remaining flour, 1 tablespoon at a time, to prevent dough from sticking to hands (dough will feel tacky).

3. Place dough in a bowl coated with cooking spray, turning to coat top. Cover; let rise in a warm place (85°), free from drafts, 35 minutes or until doubled in size. (Press two fingers into dough. If indentation remains, the dough has risen enough.)

4. Punch dough down; cover and let rest 5 minutes. Divide dough in half; roll each half into a 12-inch circle on a floured surface. Place dough on two 12-inch pizza pans or baking sheets that are each coated with cooking spray and sprinkled with ½ tablespoon cornmeal.

Crimp edges of dough with fingers to form a rim. Let rise 30 minutes. Top and bake according to recipe directions. Yield: 2 (12-inch) pizza crusts, 4 wedges each (serving size: 1 wedge).

CALORIES 163 (6% from fat); FAT 1.2g (sat 0.2g, mono 0.5g, poly 0.2g); PROTEIN 4.5g; CARB 32.9g; FIBER 1.4g; CHOL 0mg; IRON 2mg; SODIUM 74mg; CALC 7mg

QUICK-AND-EASY PIZZA CRUST

PREP: 35 MINUTES
RISE: 45 MINUTES

2 cups bread flour
½ teaspoon salt
½ teaspoon sugar
1 package quick-rise yeast
¾ cup very warm water (120° to 130°)
1 tablespoon olive oil
Cooking spray
2 tablespoons cornmeal

1. Lightly spoon flour into dry measuring cups; level with a knife. Combine flour, salt, sugar, and yeast in a large bowl. Combine water and oil; add to flour mixture. Stir until mixture forms a ball. Turn dough out onto a floured surface; knead until smooth and elastic (about 10 minutes).
2. Place dough in a large bowl coated with cooking spray, turning to coat top. Cover dough, and let rise in a warm place (85°), free from drafts, 45 minutes or until doubled in size. (Press two fingers into dough. If indentation remains, the dough has risen enough.)
3. Punch dough down; cover and let rest 10 minutes. Divide in half; roll each half into a 10-inch circle on a lightly floured surface. Place dough on baking sheets that are each coated with cooking spray and sprinkled with 1 tablespoon cornmeal. Top and bake according to

recipe directions. Yield: 2 (10-inch) pizza crusts, 3 wedges each (serving size: 1 wedge).

FOOD PROCESSOR VARIATION:

Lightly spoon flour into dry measuring cups; level with a knife. Combine flour, salt, sugar, and yeast in a food processor, and pulse 2 times or until well-blended. With processor on, slowly pour water and oil through food chute; process until dough forms a ball. Process 1 additional minute. Turn dough out onto a floured surface, and knead until dough is smooth and elastic (about 10 minutes). Proceed with step 2 in recipe as directed.

BREAD MACHINE VARIATION:

Lightly spoon flour into dry measuring cups; level with a knife. Follow manufacturer's instructions for placing all ingredients except cooking spray and cornmeal into bread pan. Select dough cycle; start bread machine. Remove dough from machine (do not bake). Proceed with step 2 in recipe as directed.

CALORIES 186 (15% from fat); FAT 3.2g (sat 0.4g, mono 1.8g, poly 0.5g); PROTEIN 5.6g; CARB 33.2g; FIBER 1.2g; CHOL 0mg; IRON 2.1mg; SODIUM 197mg; CALC 7.3mg

WHOLE-WHEAT PIZZA CRUST

PREP: 20 MINUTES
RISE: 1 HOUR 30 MINUTES

1 tablespoon honey
1 package dry yeast (about 2¼ teaspoons)
1 cup warm water (100° to 110°)
2 cups whole-wheat flour, divided
1 cup all-purpose flour
1 teaspoon olive oil
¼ teaspoon salt
Cooking spray
1 tablespoon yellow cornmeal

1. Dissolve honey and yeast in warm water in a large bowl; let stand 5 minutes. Lightly spoon flours into dry measuring cups; level with a knife. Add 1¾ cups whole-wheat flour, 1 cup all-purpose flour, oil, and salt to form a soft dough.
2. Turn dough out onto a floured surface. Knead until smooth and elastic (about 5 minutes), adding enough of remaining whole-wheat flour, 1 tablespoon at a time, to prevent dough from sticking to hands (dough will feel tacky).
3. Place dough in a large bowl coated with cooking spray, turning to coat top. Cover dough, and let rise in a warm place (85°), free from drafts, 1 hour or until doubled in size. (Press two fingers into dough. If indentation remains, the dough has risen enough.)
4. Punch dough down; cover and let rest 5 minutes. Divide dough in half. Roll each half into a 12-inch circle on a floured surface. Place dough on two 12-inch pizza pans or baking sheets that are each coated with cooking spray and sprinkled with ½ tablespoon cornmeal. Crimp edges of dough with fingers to form a rim. Cover and let rise 30 minutes or until puffy. Top and bake according to recipe directions. Yield: 2 (12-inch) pizza crusts, 4 wedges each (serving size: 1 wedge).

CALORIES 183 (8% from fat); FAT 1.6g (sat 0.2g, mono 0.5g, poly 0.5g); PROTEIN 6.2g; CARB 37.5g; FIBER 4.5g; CHOL 0mg; IRON 2.1mg; SODIUM 75mg; CALC 14mg

Note: Each of these recipes makes two crusts. They can be frozen for up to one month, if desired. After dough rises, punch it down, and divide it in half. Dust half with flour; wrap in plastic wrap, and store in a heavy-duty zip-top plastic bag in freezer. To thaw, place dough in refrigerator 12 hours or overnight. Bring to room temperature, and shape as desired.

focaccia

This trendy bread was once only found in Italy. Now you can make it at home with help from the food processor and the microwave.

PLAIN FOCACCIA

PREP: 42 MINUTES
RISE: 25 MINUTES   COOK: 18 MINUTES

  3 cups bread flour
  1 teaspoon sugar
  1 teaspoon salt
  1 package dry yeast (about 2¼
       teaspoons)
  ¾ cup plus 2 tablespoons warm
       water (100° to 110°)
  2 tablespoons plus 1 teaspoon
       olive oil, divided
     Cooking spray
  1 tablespoon cornmeal

1. Lightly spoon flour into dry measuring cups, and level with knife. Place flour, sugar, salt, and yeast in a food processor, and pulse 2 times or until blended. With processor on, slowly add warm water and 2 tablespoons oil through food chute; process until dough forms a ball. Process 1 additional minute.

2. Turn dough out onto a floured surface, and knead lightly 4 or 5 times. Shape dough into a ball. Remove metal blade from processor bowl. Poke a hole through center of dough, and return dough to bowl. Coat top of dough with cooking spray; cover with heavy-duty plastic wrap.

3. Fill a 1-cup glass measure with water, and place in back of microwave. Place processor bowl in center of microwave. Microwave at LOW (10% power) 3 minutes; let stand, covered, in microwave 3 minutes. Repeat procedure 2 times, allowing 6 minutes for the last standing time.

4. Turn dough out onto a floured surface, and knead lightly 4 or 5 times; shape dough into a ball. Coat dough with cooking spray; cover and let rest 10 minutes. Roll dough into a 14-inch circle; place on a baking sheet sprinkled with cornmeal. Brush dough with 1 teaspoon oil. Cover and let rise in a warm place (85°), free from drafts, 25 minutes or until puffy.

5. Preheat oven to 400°.

6. Uncover dough. Make indentations in top of dough using the handle of a wooden spoon or your fingertips. Bake at 400° for 18 minutes or until browned. Cut into wedges; serve warm. Yield: 14 servings (serving size: 1 wedge).

CALORIES 118 (21% from fat); FAT 2.8g (sat 0.4g, mono 1.7g, poly 0.4g); PROTEIN 3.3g; CARB 19.6g; FIBER 0.9g; CHOL 0mg; IRON 1.3mg; SODIUM 169mg; CALC 4mg

Conventional Rising Techniques

1. To let dough rise conventionally, shape dough into a ball. Place dough in a large bowl coated with cooking spray, turning to coat top.

2. Cover and let rise in a warm place (85°), free from drafts, 30 minutes or until doubled in size. (Press two fingers into dough. If indention remains, the dough has risen enough.) **Proceed with step 4 of recipe to shape and bake.**

Micro-Rising Dough

Carefully follow this 3-step procedure for alternating microwaving and standing times to micro-rise dough. We used both a 650-watt and 700-watt microwave oven to test the focaccia recipes. If you have a different wattage, rising time will vary.

Microwave at LOW (10% power):	Let stand in microwave oven:
Step 1. 3 minutes	3 minutes
Step 2. additional 3 minutes	3 minutes
Step 3. additional 3 minutes	6 minutes

Focaccia

1. Place dry ingredients in a food processor. With processor on, slowly add warm water and oil to dry ingredients.

2. Process until dough forms a ball; process 1 additional minute.

3. Turn dough out onto a floured surface, and knead lightly 4 or 5 times; shape dough into a ball.

4. Remove metal blade from processor bowl. Poke a hole through center of dough. Return dough to food processor bowl. Coat top of dough with cooking spray, cover with heavy-duty plastic wrap.

5. Place 1 cup water in back of microwave oven. Place processor bowl in center of microwave oven. Follow micro-rise procedure (see Micro-Rising Dough). After dough has risen, turn out onto a lightly floured surface, and knead lightly 4 or 5 times. Shape into a ball. Cover and let rest 10 minutes.

6. Roll dough into a circle. Place on a baking sheet sprinkled with cornmeal; cover and let rise. Using the handle of a wooden spoon or your fingertips, make indentations in dough. Follow recipe directions for toppings and baking.

This earthy Italian flat bread is best eaten warm. Try it as an appetizer or in place of rolls with a meal.

ROSEMARY-RAISIN FOCACCIA

PREP:51 MINUTES

RISE:25 MINUTES   COOK:18 MINUTES

1½ cups bread flour
 ½ cup whole-wheat flour
 ¼ cup pine nuts, toasted
  1 teaspoon sugar
  1 teaspoon salt, divided
  1 package dry yeast (about 2¼
      teaspoons)
 ¾ cup warm water (100° to 110°)
  1 tablespoon plus 1 teaspoon
      olive oil, divided
Cooking spray
 ⅓ cup raisins
  2 teaspoons minced fresh
      rosemary, divided
  1 tablespoon cornmeal
Rosemary sprigs (optional)

Rosemary-Raisin
Focaccia

1. Lightly spoon flours into dry measuring cups; level with a knife. Place flours, pine nuts, sugar, ¾ teaspoon salt, and yeast in a food processor; pulse 2 times or until blended. With processor on, slowly add warm water and 1 tablespoon oil through food chute; process until dough forms a ball. Process 1 additional minute.

2. Turn dough out onto a floured surface, and knead 4 or 5 times; shape into a ball. Remove metal blade from processor bowl. Poke a hole through center of dough; return dough to bowl. Coat top of dough with cooking spray; cover with heavy-duty plastic wrap.

3. Fill a 1-cup glass measure with water; place in back of microwave. Place processor bowl in center of microwave. Microwave at LOW (10% power) 3 minutes; let stand, covered, in microwave 3 minutes. Repeat procedure 2 times, allowing 6 minutes for last standing time.

4. Turn dough out onto a floured surface, and knead lightly 4 or 5 times. Knead in raisins and 1 teaspoon rosemary; shape into a ball. Coat dough with cooking spray; cover and let rest 10 minutes. Roll dough into a 10-inch circle, and place on a baking sheet sprinkled with cornmeal.

5. Brush dough with 1 teaspoon oil. Cover with heavy-duty plastic wrap, and let rise in a warm place (85°), free from drafts, 25 minutes or until puffy.

6. Preheat oven to 400°. Uncover dough. Make indentations in top of dough using your fingertips. Sprinkle with ¼ teaspoon salt and remaining 1 teaspoon rosemary. Bake at 400° for 18 minutes or until browned. Cut into wedges; serve warm. Garnish with rosemary sprigs, if desired. Yield: 12 servings (serving size: 1 wedge).

CALORIES 132 (33% from fat); FAT 4.9g (sat 0.7g, mono 2.2g, poly 1.5g); PROTEIN 3.5g; CARB 20.1g; FIBER 1.7g; CHOL 0mg; IRON 1.3mg; SODIUM 201mg; CALC 8mg

FOCACCIA

Focaccia is a traditional Italian flat bread that originated as a peasant bread. Cooks dimpled it with their fingers and topped it with whatever they had on hand.

Made with olive oil, what little fat focaccia does contain is monounsaturated. This chewy, yeasty concoction is a bread-lover's dream.

If you buy focaccia at a traditional Italian bakery, the bottom of the loaf may be blackened from baking on a stone.

Focaccia's name comes from the Latin word "focus," which means hearth—the bread was cooked on a hot stone right in the fireplace.

bread-machine recipes

A bread machine allows even the busiest people to enjoy the flavor of homemade bread.

With a bread machine and these recipes, you can have your kitchen smelling like a corner bakery. All it takes is the simple press of a button.

Start by reading the instruction book that comes with your bread machine. Different machines necessitate adding ingredients in varying orders, depending on whether the machine features a yeast dispenser.

Also, various machines make different amounts of bread, ranging from 1- to 2-pound loaves. (The most common loaves are 1½ to 2 pounds.) We've specified the size we achieved in testing; if your machine is smaller, look at the amount of flour called for in your instruction book, and scale the recipes back. (Increase the ingredient amounts for a larger machine.)

We used bread flour in some of our recipes—it's a high-protein flour that stands up to lots of kneading; however, all-purpose flour may be substituted.

As you gain confidence with your bread machine, experiment with new flavor combinations, adding herbs and spices and substituting ingredients. Always include a sweetener, such as honey or sugar, for tenderness. And don't forget the salt; it enhances the flavor of the bread.

Of all of the ingredients that can go into bread, yeast makes the most difference in the final product. Our recipes call for dry yeast—little grains from the familiar packets. Many bread-machine enthusiasts rely on specially formulated, quick-rising bread-machine yeast because they can measure it straight from the jar. You can substitute 2¼ teaspoons of bread-machine yeast for one packet of dry yeast.

Occasionally bread machine yeast causes the bread to rise so much that it touches the top of the machine and burns. If this happens, reduce the amount of yeast by one-fourth, then by one-third, if needed.

Although you can use rapid-rise yeast, we found that bread machine or dry yeast works best.

ANADAMA BREAD

PREP:10 MINUTES
COOK:PER BREAD MACHINE DIRECTIONS

Anadama Bread is an old-fashioned bread, traditionally flavored with molasses and cornmeal.

⅓ cup yellow cornmeal
1½ cups water, divided
1 teaspoon salt
⅓ cup molasses
1½ teaspoons vegetable oil
3 cups all-purpose flour
1 package dry yeast (about 2¼ teaspoons)

1. Combine cornmeal and ½ cup water. Bring 1 cup water and salt to a boil in a small saucepan. Stir in cornmeal mixture, and cook 2 minutes or until thick. Stir in molasses and oil; cool.
2. Lightly spoon flour into dry measuring cups; level with a knife. Follow manufacturer's instructions for placing flour, yeast, and cornmeal mixture into bread pan; select bake cycle. Start bread machine. Yield: 12 servings (serving size: 1 slice).

CALORIES 158 (6% from fat); FAT 1g (sat 0.2g, mono 0.2g, poly 0.4g); PROTEIN 3.8g; CARB 33.2g; FIBER 1.2g; CHOL 0mg; IRON 2.1mg; SODIUM 199mg; CALC 24mg

CHOOSING FLOUR

There isn't much difference between bread made with bread flour or all-purpose flour. **We like using all-purpose flour because that's what most people have on hand.**

Bread flour is a little higher in protein and can, for the most part, be used interchangeably with all-purpose flour for making bread.

Unbleached flour is really a matter of personal preference—it's simply not as white as bleached, but it **performs the same as all-purpose.**

GOOD-FOR-TOAST WHEAT BREAD

PREP:9 MINUTES
COOK:PER BREAD MACHINE DIRECTIONS

1⅔ cups bread flour
1½ cups whole-wheat flour
1 cup water
3 tablespoons sugar
1 tablespoon vegetable oil
1½ teaspoons dry yeast
1¼ teaspoons salt

1. Lightly spoon flours into dry measuring cups; level with a knife. Follow manufacturer's instructions for placing flours and remaining ingredients into bread pan; select bake cycle. Start bread machine. Yield: 12 servings (serving size: 1 slice).

CALORIES 143 (11% from fat); FAT 1.8g (sat 0.3g, mono 0.4g, poly 0.8g); PROTEIN 4.5g; CARB 28g; FIBER 2g; CHOL 0mg; IRON 1.5mg; SODIUM 245mg; CALC 8mg

COUNTRY RYE BREAD

PREP: 6 MINUTES
COOK: PER BREAD MACHINE
DIRECTIONS

2 cups bread flour
1¼ cups rye flour
1 cup water
1 tablespoon caraway seeds
3 tablespoons honey
2 tablespoons vegetable oil
1 teaspoon salt
1 package dry yeast (about 2¼ teaspoons)

1. Lightly spoon flours into dry measuring cups; level with a knife. Follow manufacturer's instructions for placing all ingredients into bread pan; select bake cycle, and start bread machine. Yield: 8 servings (serving size: 1 slice).

CALORIES 214 (18% from fat); FAT 4.2g (sat 0.7g, mono 1.2g, poly 2g); PROTEIN 5.1g; CARB 39.2g; FIBER 2.4g; CHOL 0mg; IRON 1.8mg; SODIUM 294mg; CALC 14mg

PESTO-AND-HERB BREAD

PREP: 9 MINUTES
COOK: PER BREAD MACHINE
DIRECTIONS

3¼ cups bread flour
3 tablespoons sugar
1 tablespoon dried parsley flakes
1½ teaspoons garlic powder
1½ teaspoons bread machine yeast
1 teaspoon dried oregano
1 teaspoon dried basil
¾ teaspoon salt
1 cup plus 2 tablespoons water
2 tablespoons 1% low-fat milk
2 tablespoons commercial pesto
2 teaspoons olive oil

1. Lightly spoon flour into dry measuring cups; level with a knife. Follow

---

FREEZING BREAD

To freeze bread, cool completely, then wrap in plastic wrap and then aluminum foil. Bread will freeze for up to one month. To serve, partially unwrap and let stand at room temperature until thawed.

---

manufacturer's instructions for placing flour and remaining ingredients into bread pan. Select European bake cycle, and start bread machine. Yield: 16 servings (serving size: 1 slice).

CALORIES 129 (15% from fat); FAT 2.1g (sat 0.3g, mono 1.1g, poly 0.4g); PROTEIN 3.9g; CARB 23.5g; FIBER 0.2g; CHOL 0mg; IRON 1.7mg; SODIUM 133mg; CALC 25mg

ROMANO-OREGANO BREAD

PREP: 10 MINUTES
COOK: PER BREAD MACHINE
DIRECTIONS

3 cups bread flour
1 cup water
¾ cup (3 ounces) grated fresh Romano cheese
3 tablespoons sugar
1 tablespoon dried oregano
1½ tablespoons olive oil
1 teaspoon salt
1 package dry yeast (about 2¼ teaspoons)

1. Lightly spoon flour into dry measuring cups; level with a knife. Follow manufacturer's instructions for placing all ingredients into bread pan; select bake cycle, and start bread machine. Yield: 12 servings (serving size: 1 slice).

CALORIES 181 (21% from fat); FAT 4.2g (sat 1.5g, mono 1.8g, poly 0.5g); PROTEIN 6.6g; CARB 28.7g; FIBER 0.2g; CHOL 7mg; IRON 1.8mg; SODIUM 281mg; CALC 87mg

TENDER YEAST ROLLS

PREP: 26 MINUTES
RISE: 20 MINUTES PLUS TIME PER
BREAD MACHINE
COOK: 13 MINUTES

In this recipe, the machine simply mixes the dough and allows it to rise in anticipation of your final shaping and baking.

4 cups bread flour
1 cup water
6 tablespoons sugar
3 tablespoons vegetable oil
1¼ teaspoons salt
1 large egg, lightly beaten
1 package dry yeast (about 2¼ teaspoons)
Cooking spray

1. Lightly spoon flour into dry measuring cups; level with a knife. Follow manufacturer's instructions for placing flour and next 6 ingredients into bread pan; select dough cycle, and start bread machine. Remove dough from machine (do not bake).

2. Turn dough out onto a lightly floured surface, and knead 30 seconds. Cover dough, and let rest 10 minutes.

3. Preheat oven to 400°.

4. Punch dough down, and divide into 18 equal portions. Shape each portion into a ball, and place on baking sheets coated with cooking spray. Cover and let rise in a warm place (85°), free from drafts, 20 minutes. Uncover and bake at 400° for 13 minutes or until browned. Remove rolls from pans, and serve warm or at room temperature. Yield: 1½ dozen (serving size: 1 roll).

CALORIES 152 (18% from fat); FAT 3.1g (sat 0.6g, mono 0.8g, poly 1.4g); PROTEIN 4.1g; CARB 26.4g; FIBER 0.1g; CHOL 12mg; IRON 1.5mg; SODIUM 167mg; CALC 6mg

cakes & frostings

German-Chocolate Cake (page 113)

CAKES

layer cakes
A cake says there's something to celebrate. And with these lightened favorites, there's even more reason to jump for joy.

There's something unpretentious about a layer cake. It's just one, two, or three layers of tender, moist cake covered with a smooth and creamy frosting. They can range from simple to fancy, yet all are good-to-the-last-crumb.

All you need is a heavy-duty mixer (a handheld mixer will also work), a rubber spatula, cake pans, and wax paper. You simply beat the shortening or butter with the sugar and flavorings for a few minutes, beat in the eggs, and then finally mix in the dry ingredients alternately with the liquid for a smooth batter. It's that simple!

LAYER CAKE WITH CARAMEL-PECAN FROSTING

PREP: 25 MINUTES
COOK: 30 MINUTES

Cooking spray
  1 tablespoon all-purpose flour
1⅔ cups sugar
  ½ cup butter or stick margarine, softened
  1 tablespoon vanilla extract
  3 large eggs
2¼ cups all-purpose flour
2¼ teaspoons baking powder
  ½ teaspoon salt
1¼ cups fat-free milk
  Caramel-Pecan Frosting (page 142)

1. Preheat oven to 350°.
2. Coat bottoms of 2 (9-inch) round cake pans with cooking spray (do not coat sides of pans); line bottoms with wax paper. Coat wax paper with cooking spray; dust with 1 tablespoon flour.
3. Beat sugar, butter, and vanilla at medium speed of a mixer until well-blended (about 5 minutes). Add eggs, 1 at a time; beat well after each addition. Lightly spoon 2¼ cups flour into dry measuring cups; level with a knife. Combine flour, baking powder, and salt; stir well with a whisk. Add flour mixture to sugar mixture alternately with milk, beginning and ending with flour mixture.
4. Pour batter into prepared pans. Sharply tap pans once on counter to remove air bubbles. Bake at 350° for 30 minutes or until a wooden pick inserted in center comes out clean. Cool in pans 10 minutes on a wire rack; remove from pans. Remove wax paper. Cool completely on wire rack.
5. Place 1 cake layer on a plate; spread with ½ cup Caramel-Pecan Frosting, and top with remaining layer. Spread remaining frosting over top and sides of cake. Store cake loosely covered in refrigerator. Yield: 18 servings (serving size: 1 slice).

CALORIES 326 (27% from fat); FAT 9.9g (sat 5.1g, mono 3.2g, poly 0.7g); PROTEIN 3.8g; CARB 56g; FIBER 0.5g; CHOL 57mg; IRON 1.1mg; SODIUM 234mg; CALC 83mg

CAKE TIPS

• **We used standard all-purpose flour in most of these recipes.** Unless we specifically called for cake flour, we found that **cake flour in some lower-fat cakes makes the results crumbly and dry.**

• **We used a heavy-duty stand-up mixer** in these recipes, but a handheld mixer will work fine.

• **Sharply tapping the cake pans once on the counter** after the batter is added helps remove air bubbles and makes the cakes rise more evenly.

• **Overbaking is more of a problem with low-fat cakes than with traditional ones.** Always check for doneness 5 to 10 minutes before the stated time in the recipe. How do you know when the cake is done? Lightly press it in the center. If it springs back, it's done. Or you can insert a wooden pick in the center. If it comes out clean, the cake is done.

• **The correct oven temperature is critical for baking.** Be sure to use an oven thermometer—inexpensive metal ones are available at your grocery store. **Tip: Buy the kind you can leave in your oven permanently,** and you'll always know your oven's exact temperature.

Before you begin preparing the cake batter, turn on your oven.
Most ovens take about 10 minutes to preheat.

1. Since we don't heavily grease the pans, lining the cake pans with wax paper will ensure that your cake will not stick to the pan. Coat the inside bottoms of the pans with cooking spray, and then line them with wax paper. Coat the wax paper with cooking spray, and dust with flour.

2. Although we don't call for sifting all-purpose flour, it's still a good idea to stir your flour to make sure there aren't any lumps. And measure flour accurately. Lightly spoon it into a dry measuring cup, and level it with a knife. Don't scoop or pack the flour into the cup—you'll likely get too much, and the cake will be dry.

3. When you beat the shortening (or butter or margarine) and sugar together (a technique called creaming) for a low-fat cake, the mixture will not look creamy and fluffy as in a traditional cake recipe. Instead, the consistency will be more like damp sand—fine-textured, but not cohesive. This is because less fat is used.

4. We've opted for whole eggs (as opposed to whites or substitutes) because the fat from the yolks makes the cake moist and tender. Add them one at a time to the batter, beating each one thoroughly before adding the next.

5. Add the flour mixture alternately with the liquid, as you would with any cake. Beat just until each component is incorporated. Overbeating at this stage can produce a tough cake.

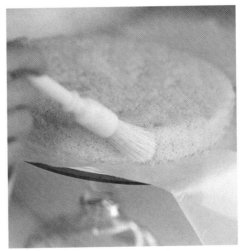

6. When icing the cake, first brush away any loose crumbs with a pastry brush or your hands. Then tear off four strips of wax paper, each 3 inches wide. Place them in a square on the cake plate. Place the cake layers on top of the strips. Ice the cake (a metal spatula is best), and remove the wax paper strips—you'll be left with a clean cake plate.

APPLESAUCE SPICE CAKE WITH CREAM CHEESE FROSTING

PREP: 12 MINUTES   COOK: 35 MINUTES

    3 cups all-purpose flour
    2 teaspoons baking soda
    1 teaspoon ground cinnamon
    ½ teaspoon ground nutmeg
    ¼ teaspoon salt
1½ cups packed brown sugar
    ⅓ cup chilled butter or stick
        margarine
1½ cups chunky applesauce
    ¼ cup apple butter
    2 large egg whites
    1 large egg
    1 cup raisins
Cooking spray
Cream Cheese Frosting (page 140)
    ¼ cup chopped pecans, toasted

1. Preheat oven to 350°.
2. Lightly spoon flour into dry measuring cups; level with a knife. Combine flour, baking soda, cinnamon, nutmeg, and salt, stirring well with a whisk. Beat sugar and butter at medium speed of a mixer until well-blended (about 5 minutes). Add applesauce and next 3 ingredients; beat well. Add flour mixture, beating until blended; stir in raisins.
3. Pour batter into a 13 x 9-inch baking pan coated with cooking spray. Bake at 350° for 35 minutes or until a wooden pick inserted in center comes out clean. Cool completely in pan on a wire rack.
4. Spread Cream Cheese Frosting over cake; sprinkle with pecans. Store cake loosely covered in refrigerator. Yield: 20 servings (serving size: 1 square).

CALORIES 270 (21% from fat); FAT 6.3g (sat 3.2g, mono 2.1g, poly 0.5g); PROTEIN 3.4g; CARB 51.3g; FIBER 1.2g; CHOL 24mg; IRON 1.4mg; SODIUM 185mg; CALC 30mg

ULTIMATE CHOCOLATE LAYER CAKE

PREP: 18 MINUTES   COOK: 35 MINUTES

Cooking spray
    1 tablespoon all-purpose flour
    2 cups sugar
    ½ cup plus 2 tablespoons light
        butter, softened
    ¾ cup egg substitute
    2 cups all-purpose flour
    ½ cup unsweetened cocoa
    ¾ teaspoon baking soda
    ¼ teaspoon salt
    ¾ cup low-fat sour cream
    ¾ cup boiling water
    1 teaspoon vanilla extract
Chocolate Cream Cheese Frosting
        (page 140)

1. Preheat oven to 350°.
2. Coat bottoms of 2 (8-inch) round cake pans with cooking spray (do not coat sides of pans); line bottoms of pans with wax paper. Coat wax paper with cooking spray; dust with 1 tablespoon flour.
3. Beat sugar and butter at medium speed of a mixer until well-blended (about 5 minutes). Gradually add egg substitute; beat well. Lightly spoon 2 cups flour into dry measuring cups; level with a knife. Combine flour, cocoa, baking soda, and salt, stirring well with a whisk. Add flour mixture to sugar mixture alternately with sour cream, beginning and ending with flour mixture. Stir in boiling water and vanilla.
4. Pour into prepared pans. Sharply tap pans once on counter to remove air bubbles. Bake at 350° for 35 minutes or until cake springs back when touched in center. Loosen layers from sides of pans using a narrow metal spatula; turn out onto wire racks. Remove wax paper; cool.
5. Place 1 cake layer on a plate; spread with ½ cup Chocolate Cream Cheese Frosting. Top with remaining cake layer; spread remaining frosting over top and sides of cake. Store cake loosely covered in refrigerator. Yield: 18 servings (serving size: 1 slice).

CALORIES 315 (22% from fat); FAT 7.8g (sat 4.9g, mono 1.3g, poly 0.2g); PROTEIN 4.8g; CARB 58.4g; FIBER 0.4g; CHOL 19mg; IRON 1.7mg; SODIUM 129mg; CALC 46mg

RED VELVET CAKE

PREP: 20 MINUTES   COOK: 28 MINUTES

This cake has half the fat of its traditional namesake.

Cooking spray
1 tablespoon all-purpose flour
1⅔ cups sugar
5 tablespoons vegetable shortening
1 large egg white
1 large egg
3 tablespoons unsweetened cocoa
1 (1-ounce) bottle red food coloring
2¼ cups all-purpose flour
1 teaspoon salt
1 cup low-fat or nonfat buttermilk
1¼ teaspoons vanilla extract
1 tablespoon white vinegar
1 teaspoon baking soda
Cream Cheese Frosting (page 140)

1. Preheat oven to 350°.
2. Coat 2 (9-inch) round cake pans with cooking spray, and dust with 1 tablespoon flour.
3. Beat sugar and shortening at medium speed of a mixer until well-blended (about 5 minutes). Add egg white and egg; beat well. Combine cocoa and food coloring; stir well with a whisk. Add to sugar mixture; mix well.
4. Lightly spoon 2¼ cups flour into dry measuring cups; level with a knife. Combine flour and salt, stirring well with a whisk. Add flour mixture to sugar mixture alternately with buttermilk, beginning and ending with flour mixture. Add vanilla; mix well. Combine vinegar and baking soda in a small bowl; add to batter, mixing well.
5. Pour batter into prepared pans. Sharply tap pans once on counter to remove air bubbles. Bake at 350° for 28 minutes or until a wooden pick inserted in center comes out clean. Cool in pans 10 minutes on wire racks; remove from pans. Cool completely on wire racks.
6. Place 1 cake layer on a plate; spread with ⅓ cup Cream Cheese Frosting, and top with remaining cake layer. Spread remaining frosting over top and sides of cake. Store cake loosely covered in refrigerator. Yield: 16 servings (serving size: 1 slice).

CALORIES 322 (24% from fat); FAT 8.7g (sat 3.3g, mono 1.4g, poly 0.3g); PROTEIN 4.9g; CARB 57.9g; FIBER 0.6g; CHOL 30mg; IRON 1.3mg; SODIUM 310mg; CALC 44mg

menu

Teriyaki Tuna With
Fresh Pineapple (page 227)

Potato-Portobello Salad (page 404)

Crunchy Pea Salad (page 403)

German-Chocolate Cake

GERMAN-CHOCOLATE CAKE

PREP: 22 MINUTES   COOK: 25 MINUTES

(pictured on page 109)

Cooking spray
1 tablespoon cake flour
½ cup unsweetened cocoa
1 ounce sweet baking chocolate
½ cup boiling water
1 cup granulated sugar
¾ cup packed brown sugar
3 tablespoons butter or stick margarine, softened
2 tablespoons vegetable oil
¼ cup plain fat-free yogurt
2½ teaspoons vanilla extract
½ teaspoon coconut extract
2 large egg whites
2¼ cups sifted cake flour
2 teaspoons baking powder
½ teaspoon baking soda
½ teaspoon salt
1 cup low-fat or nonfat buttermilk
Coconut-Pecan Frosting (page 142)

1. Preheat oven to 350°.
2. Coat 3 (8-inch) round cake pans with cooking spray, and dust with 1 tablespoon flour.
3. Combine cocoa and chocolate in a small bowl; add boiling water, stirring until chocolate melts. Set aside.
4. Beat sugars, butter, and oil at medium speed of a mixer until well-blended (about 5 minutes). Add yogurt, extracts, and egg whites, beating well after each addition.
5. Combine 2¼ cups flour, baking powder, baking soda, and salt, stirring well with a whisk. Add flour mixture to sugar mixture alternately with buttermilk, beginning and ending with flour mixture. Beat in cocoa mixture.
6. Pour batter into prepared pans; sharply tap pans once on counter to remove air bubbles. Bake at 350° for 25 minutes or until a wooden pick inserted in center comes out clean. Cool in pans 10 minutes on wire racks, and remove from pans. Cool cake layers completely on wire racks.
7. Place 1 cake layer on a plate; spread with ⅓ cup Coconut-Pecan Frosting, and top with another cake layer. Spread with ⅓ cup frosting, and top with remaining cake layer. Spread remaining frosting over top and sides of cake. Store cake loosely covered in refrigerator. Yield: 18 servings (serving size: 1 slice).

CALORIES 311 (27% from fat); FAT 9.2g (sat 4.2g, mono 2.6g, poly 1.4g); PROTEIN 4.6g; CARB 52.7g; FIBER 0.3g; CHOL 35mg; IRON 2.2mg; SODIUM 186mg; CALC 111mg

MOCHA MINT CAKE

PREP:10 MINUTES
COOK:35 MINUTES

The secret behind this cake's great chocolate flavor? The prunes actually enhance the chocolate flavor.

1¼ cups unsweetened cocoa
1 cup Prune Puree (page 453), divided
½ cup water
¾ teaspoon salt
¼ teaspoon peppermint extract
1 (1-pound) box powdered sugar, sifted
3 large eggs
1½ cups all-purpose flour
1 tablespoon instant coffee granules
1½ teaspoons baking soda
¾ cup boiling water
Cooking spray
2 cups frozen reduced-calorie whipped topping, thawed
Fresh mint sprigs (optional)

1. Preheat oven to 350°.
2. Beat cocoa, ⅔ cup Prune Puree, ½ cup water, salt, extract, and powdered sugar at medium speed of a mixer until mixture is smooth. Reserve ¾ cup cocoa mixture. Add eggs and ⅓ cup Prune Puree to remaining cocoa mixture in bowl. Beat at medium speed until mixture is smooth.
3. Lightly spoon flour into dry measuring cups; level with a knife. Combine flour, coffee granules, and baking soda in a bowl, stirring well with a whisk. Gradually add to cocoa mixture, beating at low speed until blended; stir in boiling water.
4. Pour batter into a 13 x 9-inch baking pan coated with cooking spray. Bake at 350° for 35 minutes or until cake springs back when touched lightly in center.

PRUNE PUREE

The popular use of applesauce to reduce the amount of fat in baked desserts was the starting point. Then we pondered about other fruits.

Could prunes, put through a food processor or blender and added to a batter, do the same?

After experimenting, we found the secret to success: Don't completely do away with a recipe's fats. Instead, cut down on these ingredients, and substitute the prune puree for what's left out.

What is it about prunes that mimics the properties of fat in a baked product?

The answer is pectin and sorbitol, and prunes are very high in both. Like fat, pectin acts as a tenderizing agent by coating the flour particles. Also, like fat, sorbitol adds moisture to baked goods; prunes have the highest sorbitol content of any dried fruit. Just pay careful attention to baking times because a minute or two too long can be the difference between success and failure. Be sure, too, that your oven temperature is accurate.

More good news: Prune puree is quick and easy to make and can be refrigerated for up to two months. You'll find our prune puree recipe on page 453.

Cool cake completely on a wire rack.
5. Fold whipped topping into reserved ¾ cup cocoa mixture; spread over cake. Cover and chill. Garnish with mint sprigs, if desired. Yield: 16 servings (serving size: 1 square).

CALORIES 248 (11% from fat); FAT 3.2g (sat 1.9g, mono 0.7g, poly 0.2g); PROTEIN 4.8g; CARB 51.2g; FIBER 1.1g; CHOL 40mg; IRON 2.1mg; SODIUM 212mg; CALC 29mg

---

MISSISSIPPI MUD CAKE

PREP:25 MINUTES
COOK:16 MINUTES

1 cup sugar
⅓ cup stick margarine or butter, softened
3 large eggs
1 cup all-purpose flour
⅓ cup unsweetened cocoa
½ teaspoon baking powder
¼ teaspoon salt
½ cup chopped pecans
1 teaspoon vanilla extract
Cooking spray
3¼ cups miniature marshmallows
Chocolate Glaze (page 142)

1. Preheat oven to 325°.
2. Beat sugar and margarine at medium speed of a mixer until well-blended (about 5 minutes). Add eggs, 1 at a time, beating well after each addition.
3. Lightly spoon flour into a dry measuring cup; level with a knife. Combine flour, cocoa, baking powder, and salt in a bowl, stirring well with a whisk. Add to sugar mixture, beating at low speed until blended. Stir in pecans and vanilla.
4. Pour batter into a 13 x 9-inch baking pan coated with cooking spray. Bake at 325° for 16 minutes or just until set (do not bake until wooden pick tests clean or cake will be overbaked). Remove cake from oven; top with marshmallows. Bake 2 minutes or until marshmallows are soft. Remove from oven; immediately drizzle with warm Chocolate Glaze. Cool on a wire rack. Yield: 16 servings (serving size: 1 square).

CALORIES 280 (30% from fat); FAT 9.4g (sat 1.9g, mono 4.4g, poly 2.5g); PROTEIN 3.7g; CARB 46.4g; FIBER 0.4g; CHOL 40mg; IRON 1.3mg; SODIUM 130mg; CALC 26mg

CREAMY COCONUT-TOPPED CHOCOLATE CAKE

PREP: 29 MINUTES   COOK: 30 MINUTES

1¼ cups water
¾ cup egg substitute or 4 large egg
      whites
2 tablespoons vegetable oil
1 (18.25-ounce) package chocolate
      cake mix with pudding
Cooking spray
Coconut Filling
Chocolate Frosting (page 141)

1. Preheat oven to 350°.
2. Beat first 4 ingredients in a large bowl at low speed of a mixer until moist. Beat mixture at medium speed 2 minutes; pour into a 13 x 9-inch baking pan coated with cooking spray. Bake at 350° for 30 minutes or until a wooden pick inserted in center comes out clean. Cool completely in pan on a wire rack.
3. Spread warm Coconut Filling evenly over cake; cool.
4. Spread Chocolate Frosting gently over Coconut Filling. Cool until set. Store cake loosely covered in refrigerator. Yield: 18 servings (serving size: 1 square).

CALORIES 290 (32% from fat); FAT 10.2g (sat 5.5g, mono 2.2g, poly 1.9g); PROTEIN 4.6g; CARB 48.4g; FIBER 0.9g; CHOL 0mg; IRON 1mg; SODIUM 246mg; CALC 18mg

COCONUT FILLING

½ cup fat-free milk
½ cup sugar
9 large marshmallows
2 cups flaked sweetened coconut
½ teaspoon cornstarch

1. Combine ½ cup milk, sugar, and marshmallows in a medium saucepan; cook over medium heat 5 minutes or until marshmallows are melted. Stir in coconut and cornstarch; bring to a boil. Cook 1 minute, stirring constantly. Yield: 2 cups.

FUDGY SOUFFLÉ CAKE WITH WARM TURTLE SAUCE

PREP: 20 MINUTES   COOK: 35 MINUTES

Butter-flavored cooking spray
¼ teaspoon sugar
½ cup unsweetened cocoa
6 tablespoons hot water
2 tablespoons stick margarine or
      butter
3 tablespoons all-purpose flour
¾ cup 1% low-fat milk
¼ cup sugar
⅛ teaspoon salt
4 large egg whites
3 tablespoons sugar
Warm Turtle Sauce (page 451)

1. Preheat oven to 375°.
2. Coat a 1½-quart soufflé dish with cooking spray; sprinkle with ¼ teaspoon sugar. Set aside.
3. Combine cocoa and hot water in a bowl. Melt margarine in a small, heavy saucepan over medium heat. Add flour; cook 1 minute, stirring constantly with a whisk. Add milk, ¼ cup sugar, and salt; cook 3 minutes or until thick, stirring constantly. Remove from heat. Add cocoa mixture; stir well. Spoon into a large bowl; cool slightly.
4. Beat egg whites at high speed of a mixer until foamy. Add 3 tablespoons sugar, 1 tablespoon at a time, beating until stiff peaks form. Gently fold 1 cup egg white mixture into cocoa mixture; gently fold in remaining egg white mixture. Spoon mixture into prepared soufflé dish.
5. Bake at 375° for 35 minutes or until puffy and set. Remove from oven; serve warm, at room temperature, or chilled with Warm Turtle Sauce. Yield: 6 servings (serving size: 1 wedge and about 1 tablespoon sauce).

CALORIES 241 (29% from fat); FAT 7.8g (sat 1.7g, mono 3.3g, poly 1.9g); PROTEIN 6.1g; CARB 58.6g; FIBER 0.4g; CHOL 2mg; IRON 1.6mg; SODIUM 182mg; CALC 54mg

Creamy Coconut-Topped
Chocolate Cake

MOCHA PUDDING CAKE

PREP: 15 MINUTES
COOK: 30 MINUTES

This chocolaty dessert forms two layers as it bakes: a creamy pudding on the bottom and a tender cake on the top.

  1 cup all-purpose flour
 ⅔ cup sugar
 ¼ cup unsweetened cocoa
1½ tablespoons instant coffee
     granules
  2 teaspoons baking powder
 ¼ teaspoon salt
 ½ cup 1% low-fat milk
  3 tablespoons vegetable oil
  1 teaspoon vanilla extract
Cooking spray
 ⅓ cup sugar
  2 tablespoons unsweetened
     cocoa
  1 cup boiling water
  1 cup plus 2 tablespoons vanilla
     low-fat or light ice cream

1. Preheat oven to 350°.
2. Lightly spoon flour into a dry measuring cup; level with a knife. Combine flour and next 5 ingredients, stirring well with a whisk. Combine milk, oil, and vanilla; add to flour mixture, and stir well.
3. Spoon batter into an 8-inch square baking pan coated with cooking spray. Combine ⅓ cup sugar and 2 tablespoons cocoa. Sprinkle over batter.
4. Pour 1 cup boiling water over batter. (Do not stir.) Bake at 350° for 30 minutes or until cake springs back when lightly touched in center. Serve warm with ice cream. Yield: 9 servings (serving size: 1 [3 x 3-inch] piece and 2 tablespoons ice cream).

CALORIES 221 (25% from fat); FAT 6.1g (sat 1.7g, mono 1.6g, poly 2.3g); PROTEIN 3.5g; CARB 38.2g; FIBER 0.4g; CHOL 3mg; IRON 1.3mg; SODIUM 154mg; CALC 90mg

Mocha Pudding Cake

DARK-CHOCOLATE SOUFFLÉ CAKE

PREP: 23 MINUTES   COOK: 1 HOUR

Cooking spray
 ½ cup granulated sugar
 ½ cup packed dark brown sugar
 ¾ cup water
  1 tablespoon instant espresso or 2
     tablespoons instant coffee granules
 ⅔ cup Dutch process or
     unsweetened cocoa
 ¼ teaspoon salt
  2 ounces semisweet chocolate, chopped
  2 ounces unsweetened chocolate,
     chopped
  2 tablespoons Kahlúa (coffee-
     flavored liqueur)
  3 large egg yolks
 ⅓ cup sifted cake flour
  6 large egg whites
 ¼ teaspoon cream of tartar
 ⅓ cup granulated sugar
  1 tablespoon powdered sugar

1. Preheat oven to 300°.
2. Coat bottom of a 9-inch springform pan with cooking spray. Set aside.
3. Combine ½ cup granulated sugar and next 3 ingredients in a large saucepan; bring to a boil, stirring until sugar dissolves. Remove sugar mixture from heat; add cocoa, salt, and chocolates, stirring with a whisk until chocolate melts. Stir in Kahlúa and egg yolks. Add flour, stirring until well-blended. Cool to room temperature.
4. Beat egg whites and cream of tartar at high speed of a mixer until foamy. Add ⅓ cup granulated sugar, 1 tablespoon at a time, beating until stiff peaks form. Gently fold one-fourth of egg white mixture into chocolate mixture; fold in remaining egg white mixture, adding one-fourth mixture at a time.
5. Spoon batter into prepared pan. Bake at 300° for 1 hour or until a wooden pick inserted in center comes out almost clean. Run a knife around outside edge. Cool completely on a wire rack. Remove sides from pan; sift powdered sugar over cake. Yield: 12 servings (serving size: 1 wedge).

CALORIES 196 (28% from fat); FAT 6g (sat 3.2g, mono 2g, poly 0.3g); PROTEIN 4.9g; CARB 33.6g; FIBER 0.3g; CHOL 55mg; IRON 1.9mg; SODIUM 84mg; CALC 29mg

GINGERBREAD

PREP: 12 MINUTES   COOK: 25 MINUTES

⅓ cup granulated sugar
¼ cup stick margarine or butter, softened
⅓ cup molasses
1 large egg
1½ cups all-purpose flour
1 teaspoon ground ginger
½ teaspoon baking soda
¼ teaspoon ground nutmeg
⅛ teaspoon salt
⅛ teaspoon ground cloves
⅔ cup 1% low-fat milk
   Cooking spray
2 teaspoons powdered sugar

1. Preheat oven to 350°.
2. Beat granulated sugar and margarine at medium speed of a mixer until well-blended (about 5 minutes). Add molasses and egg; beat well.
3. Lightly spoon flour into dry measuring cups, and level with a knife. Combine flour and next 5 ingredients, stirring well with a whisk. Add flour mixture to sugar mixture alternately with milk, beginning and ending with flour mixture.
4. Pour batter into an 8-inch square baking pan coated with cooking spray; sharply tap pan once on counter to remove air bubbles. Bake at 350° for 25 minutes or until a wooden pick inserted in center comes out clean. Cool in pan on a wire rack. Sift powdered sugar over cake, and serve warm. Yield: 9 servings (serving size: 1 square).

CALORIES 196 (28% from fat); FAT 6.1g (sat 1.3g, mono 2.5g, poly 1.8g); PROTEIN 3.3g; CARB 32.1g; FIBER 0.5g; CHOL 24mg; IRON 1.6mg; SODIUM 158mg; CALC 55mg

PUMPKIN GINGERBREAD WITH CIDER-LEMON SAUCE

PREP: 48 MINUTES   COOK: 50 MINUTES

⅓ cup dried currants
¼ cup chopped pitted dates
2½ tablespoons minced crystallized ginger
2 tablespoons dark rum
1 teaspoon vanilla extract
2 large egg whites
1 large egg
⅔ cup packed brown sugar
⅓ cup molasses
2 cups all-purpose flour
1½ tablespoons ground ginger
1 teaspoon baking soda
¾ teaspoon ground allspice
½ teaspoon salt
½ teaspoon ground nutmeg
¼ teaspoon ground cinnamon
¼ teaspoon ground cloves
⅛ teaspoon pepper
1 cup canned unsweetened pumpkin
⅔ cup low-fat or nonfat buttermilk
2 tablespoons vegetable oil
2 tablespoons stick margarine or butter, melted
   Cooking spray
   Cider-Lemon Sauce (page 450)

1. Preheat oven to 375°.
2. Combine first 5 ingredients in a bowl. Let stand 30 minutes, stirring occasionally.
3. Beat egg whites and egg at medium speed of a mixer until foamy. Gradually add brown sugar, beating until well-blended. Add molasses, and beat well.
4. Lightly spoon flour into dry measuring cups; level with a knife. Combine flour and next 8 ingredients. Combine pumpkin, buttermilk, oil, and margarine. Add flour mixture to egg mixture alternately with pumpkin mixture, beginning and ending with flour mixture; mix well after each addition. Fold in currant mixture.
5. Spoon batter into a 9-inch round cake pan coated with cooking spray. Bake at 375° for 50 minutes or until a wooden pick inserted in center comes out clean. Cool 30 minutes on a wire rack. Serve warm with warm Cider-Lemon Sauce. Yield: 10 servings (serving size: 1 wedge and 2 tablespoons sauce).

CALORIES 337 (17% from fat); FAT 6.5g (sat 1.4g, mono 2.3g, poly 2.6g); PROTEIN 5g; CARB 66.6g; FIBER 2.2g; CHOL 21mg; IRON 4.2mg; SODIUM 300mg; CALC 97mg

CARROT CAKE WITH CREAM CHEESE FROSTING

PREP: 22 MINUTES   COOK: 25 MINUTES

If the thought of shredding carrots steers you away from this recipe, turn to your grocery store's deli for help. Most will shred carrots for free while you wait.

Cooking spray
  1 tablespoon all-purpose flour
2¼ cups all-purpose flour
  2 teaspoons baking powder
1½ teaspoons ground cinnamon
  ½ teaspoon salt
  ¼ teaspoon baking soda
  ¼ teaspoon ground nutmeg
  ⅔ cup granulated sugar
  ⅔ cup packed dark brown sugar
  ½ cup applesauce
  ⅓ cup vegetable oil
  ¼ cup plain fat-free yogurt
2½ teaspoons vanilla extract
  2 large egg whites
  1 large egg
  2 cups finely shredded carrot
Cream Cheese Frosting (page 140)

1. Preheat oven to 375°.
2. Coat 2 (8-inch) round cake pans

Carrot Cake With Cream Cheese Frosting

with cooking spray, and dust with 1 tablespoon flour.

3. Lightly spoon 2¼ cups flour into dry measuring cups; level with a knife. Combine 2¼ cups flour and next 5 ingredients, stirring well with a whisk. Beat granulated sugar and next 7 ingredients at medium speed of a mixer. Add to flour mixture, stirring just until moist. Stir in carrot.

4. Pour batter into prepared pans. Sharply tap pans once on counter to remove air bubbles. Bake at 375° for 25 minutes or until a wooden pick inserted in center comes out clean. Cool in pans 10 minutes on wire racks; remove from pans. Cool completely on wire racks.

5. Place 1 cake layer on a plate; spread with ¾ cup Cream Cheese Frosting, and top with remaining cake layer. Spread remaining frosting over top and sides of cake. Store cake loosely covered in refrigerator. Yield: 16 servings (serving size: 1 slice).

CALORIES 338 (23% from fat); FAT 8.5g (sat 3.1g, mono 2.4g, poly 2.4g); PROTEIN 4.3g; CARB 61.5g; FIBER 1g; CHOL 24mg; IRON 1.3mg; SODIUM 205mg; CALC 59mg

INDIAN PUDDING CAKE WITH MOLASSES CREAM

PREP: 21 MINUTES   COOK: 30 MINUTES

Cooking spray
¾ cup packed brown sugar
⅓ cup vegetable oil
⅓ cup molasses
⅓ cup fat-free sour cream
1 tablespoon dark rum
1 teaspoon vanilla extract
½ cup all-purpose flour
¾ cup yellow cornmeal
1 teaspoon baking powder
1½ teaspoons ground cinnamon
½ teaspoon ground cardamom
¼ teaspoon ground ginger
¼ teaspoon ground nutmeg
¼ teaspoon ground cloves
⅛ teaspoon salt
5 large egg whites
½ teaspoon cream of tartar
2 tablespoons brown sugar
2 teaspoons powdered sugar
Molasses Cream (page 451)

1. Preheat oven to 350°.
2. Coat a 9-inch round cake pan with cooking spray (do not coat side of pan); line bottom of pan with wax paper. Coat wax paper with cooking spray.
3. Combine ¾ cup brown sugar and next 5 ingredients in a large bowl. Lightly spoon flour into a dry measuring cup; level with a knife. Combine flour and next 8 ingredients in a medium bowl, stirring well with wire whisk. Beat egg whites and cream of tartar at high speed of a mixer until foamy. Gradually add 2 tablespoons brown sugar, 1 tablespoon at a time, beating until stiff peaks form. Gently fold egg white mixture and flour mixture alternately into molasses mixture, beginning and ending with egg white mixture.
4. Pour batter into prepared pan. Sharply tap pan once on counter to remove air bubbles. Bake at 350° for 30 minutes or until a wooden pick inserted in center comes out clean; cool in pan for 10 minutes on a wire rack. Remove from pan, and carefully peel off wax paper; cool completely on wire rack. Place cake on a plate; sift powdered sugar over cake. Serve with Molasses Cream. Yield: 8 servings (serving size: 1 cake wedge and 2 tablespoons Molasses Cream).

CALORIES 361 (30% from fat); FAT 12g (sat 3.2g, mono 3.8g, poly 4.6g); PROTEIN 6.7g; CARB 57.1g; FIBER 1.6g; CHOL 8mg; IRON 2.3mg; SODIUM 224mg; CALC 132mg

ITALIAN CREAM CAKE

PREP: 24 MINUTES   COOK: 23 MINUTES

Cream Cheese Frosting
    (page 140)
Cooking spray
1 tablespoon flour
2 cups sugar
½ cup light butter, softened
2 large egg yolks
2 cups all-purpose flour
1 teaspoon baking soda
1 cup low-fat or nonfat
    buttermilk
½ cup chopped pecans
1 teaspoon butter extract
1 teaspoon coconut extract
1 teaspoon vanilla extract
6 large egg whites
Lemon rind (optional)

1. Prepare Cream Cheese Frosting; cover and chill.
2. Preheat oven to 350°.
3. Coat bottoms of 3 (9-inch) round cake pans with cooking spray (do not coat sides of pans); line bottoms of pans with wax paper. Coat wax paper with cooking spray. Dust with 1 tablespoon flour; set aside.
4. Beat sugar and butter at medium speed of a mixer until well-blended (about 5 minutes). Add egg yolks, 1 at a time, beating well after each addition. Lightly spoon 2 cups flour into dry measuring cups; level with a knife. Combine flour and soda, stirring well with a whisk. Add flour mixture to sugar mixture alternately with buttermilk, beginning and ending with flour mixture. Stir in pecans and extracts.
5. Beat egg whites at high speed of a mixer until stiff peaks form (do not overbeat). Fold egg whites into batter; pour batter into prepared pans. Sharply tap once on counter to remove air bubbles. Bake at 350° for 23 minutes. Cool in pans 5 minutes on a wire rack. Loosen cake layers from sides of pans using a narrow metal spatula; turn out onto wire racks. Peel off wax paper; cool completely.
6. Place 1 cake layer on a plate. Spread with ⅔ cup Cream Cheese Frosting; top with another cake layer. Repeat with ⅔ cup frosting and remaining layer. Spread remaining frosting over top and sides of cake. Store cake loosely covered in refrigerator. Garnish with lemon rind, if desired. Yield: 20 servings (serving size: 1 slice).

CALORIES 300 (24% from fat); FAT 8g (sat 3.9g, mono 1.5g, poly 0.6g); PROTEIN 4.5g; CARB 53.8g; FIBER 0.5g; CHOL 39mg; IRON 0.7mg; SODIUM 166mg; CALC 28mg

MAKING SOUR MILK

If you're baking and the recipe calls for buttermilk, don't despair if there's none in your refrigerator. You can make some with these instructions:

For each cup of buttermilk you need, place 1 tablespoon lemon juice or vinegar in a glass measuring cup; then add enough 2% reduced-fat milk to make 1 cup total liquid. Stir the mixture, and let stand 5 minutes before using it in your recipes.

STRAWBERRY SHORTCAKE

PREP: 19 MINUTES   COOK: 25 MINUTES
CHILL: 2 HOURS

We sprinkled turbinado sugar over the cake before baking it. Turbinado sugar crystals are blond-colored and coarser than granulated sugar, which adds a more interesting texture to the cake's crust. If you don't have it, granulated sugar can be substituted.

    4 cups sliced strawberries
    ¼ cup granulated sugar
       Cooking spray
    1 teaspoon all-purpose flour
    ½ cup granulated sugar
    ⅓ cup stick margarine or butter,
          softened
    1¾ cups all-purpose flour
    1½ teaspoons baking powder
    ¼ teaspoon salt
    ¾ cup fat-free milk
    ¼ teaspoon almond extract
    2 large egg whites
    ⅛ teaspoon cream of tartar
    2 tablespoons granulated sugar
    1 tablespoon turbinado or
          granulated sugar
    2 cups frozen reduced-calorie
          whipped topping, thawed and
          divided

1. Preheat oven to 375°.
2. Combine sliced strawberries and ¼ cup granulated sugar in a bowl. Cover and chill 2 hours.
3. Coat a 9-inch round cake pan with cooking spray; line bottom with wax paper. Coat wax paper with cooking spray, and dust with 1 teaspoon flour; set aside.
4. Beat ½ cup sugar and margarine at medium speed of a mixer until well-blended (about 5 minutes). Lightly spoon 1¾ cups flour into dry measuring cups; level with a knife. Combine flour, baking powder, and salt, stirring with a whisk. Add flour mixture to sugar mixture alternately with milk, beginning and ending with flour mixture. Stir in almond extract.
5. Beat egg whites and cream of tartar at high speed of a mixer until foamy. Gradually add 2 tablespoons granulated sugar, 1 tablespoon at a time, beating until stiff peaks form. Gently stir about one-fourth of egg white mixture into batter. Gently fold in remaining egg white mixture.
6. Pour batter into prepared pan. Sprinkle turbinado sugar over cake. Sharply tap pan once on counter to remove air bubbles. Bake at 375° for 25 minutes or until a wooden pick inserted in center comes out clean. Cool in pan 10 minutes on a wire rack; remove from pan, and cool completely on wire rack.
7. Split shortcake in half horizontally, using a serrated knife. Place bottom half, cut side up, on a plate. Drain strawberries, reserving juice; drizzle half of juice over bottom cake layer. Spread 1 cup whipped topping over cake layer, and arrange half of strawberries over whipped topping. Top with remaining cake layer, cut side down, and drizzle with remaining reserved juice. Spread remaining whipped topping over top cake layer; arrange remaining strawberries over whipped topping. Yield: 10 servings (serving size: 1 slice).

CALORIES 254 (29% from fat); FAT 8.2g (sat 3g, mono 2.7g, poly 2.1g); PROTEIN 4.2g; CARB 41.8g; FIBER 1.6g; CHOL 1mg; IRON 1.2mg; SODIUM 208mg; CALC 71mg

WHITE TRIPLE-LAYER CAKE WITH LEMON FILLING

PREP: 25 MINUTES   COOK: 25 MINUTES

You'll need a candy thermometer to make Fluffy White Frosting. Candy thermometers differ from meat thermometers and can be found in many supermarkets.

       Cooking spray
    1 tablespoon cake flour
    3½ cups sifted cake flour
    2 teaspoons baking powder
    ¾ teaspoon salt
    ½ teaspoon baking soda
    1¾ cups sugar
    ¼ cup butter or stick margarine,
          softened
    1½ tablespoons vegetable oil
    2 large egg whites
    1⅔ cups fat-free milk
    ½ cup plain fat-free yogurt
    2½ teaspoons vanilla extract
    ¼ teaspoon butter extract
       Lemon Filling (page 142)
       Fluffy White Frosting (page 141)

1. Preheat oven to 350°.
2. Coat 3 (8-inch) round cake pans with cooking spray, and dust with 1 tablespoon flour.
3. Lightly spoon flour into dry measuring cups; level with a knife. Combine 3½ cups flour, baking powder, salt, and baking soda; stir well with a whisk. Beat sugar, butter, and oil at medium speed of a mixer until well-blended (about 5 minutes). Add egg whites, 1 at a time, beating well after each addition. Combine milk and yogurt. Add flour

mixture to sugar mixture alternately with milk mixture, beginning and ending with flour mixture. Stir in extracts.

4. Pour cake batter into prepared pans. Sharply tap pans once on counter to remove air bubbles. Bake at 350° for 25 minutes or until a wooden pick inserted in center comes out clean. Cool in pans 10 minutes on wire racks; remove from pans. Cool completely on wire racks.

5. Place 1 cake layer on a plate; spread layer with half of Lemon Filling; top with another cake layer. Spread with remaining Lemon Filling, and top with remaining cake layer. Spread Fluffy White Frosting over top and sides of cake. Store cake loosely covered in refrigerator. Yield: 16 servings (serving size: 1 slice).

CALORIES 321 (14% from fat); FAT 5.1g (sat 2.3g, mono 1.5g, poly 0.9g); PROTEIN 4.7g; CARB 64.3g; FIBER 0g; CHOL 36mg; IRON 2mg; SODIUM 186mg; CALC 87mg

COCONUT TRIPLE-LAYER CAKE:

Prepare White Triple-Layer Cake as directed, omitting Lemon Filling and replacing Fluffy White Frosting with Fluffy Coconut Frosting (page 141). To assemble, place cake layer on a plate; spread with ⅔ cup Fluffy Coconut Frosting, and top with another cake layer. Repeat procedure with ⅔ cup frosting and remaining cake layer. Spread remaining frosting over top and sides of cake. Sprinkle ¾ cup flaked sweetened coco-nut over top of cake. Store cake loosely covered in refrigerator. Yield: 16 servings (serving size: 1 slice).

CALORIES 298 (18% from fat); FAT 5.8g (sat 3.3g, mono 1.3g, poly 0.8g); PROTEIN 4.4g; CARB 57.3g; FIBER 0.2g; CHOL 8mg; IRON 2mg; SODIUM 195mg; CALC 83mg

White Triple-Layer Cake With Lemon Filling

crumb cakes

A crumb cake coming out of the oven is sweet and warm—it doesn't get much better than that.

Unlike other cakes, crumb cakes have versatility. They can be served at breakfast, brunch, lunch, for after-school treats, for an after-dinner dessert, or as a late-night snack. Their crumbly topping and homey taste and smell are irresistible.

RASPBERRY-ALMOND CRUMB CAKE

PREP:20 MINUTES

COOK:30 MINUTES

1 cup all-purpose flour
⅓ cup sugar
⅛ teaspoon salt
¼ cup chilled stick margarine or butter, cut into small pieces
½ teaspoon baking powder
¼ teaspoon baking soda
⅓ cup fat-free sour cream
2 tablespoons 1% low-fat milk
1 teaspoon vanilla extract
½ teaspoon almond extract
1 large egg
Cooking spray
⅓ cup (3 ounces) block-style fat-free cream cheese, softened
2 tablespoons sugar
1 large egg white
¼ cup raspberry preserves
⅓ cup fresh raspberries
2 tablespoons sliced almonds

1. Preheat oven to 350°.
2. Lightly spoon flour into a dry measuring cup; level with a knife. Combine flour, ⅓ cup sugar, and salt in a bowl; cut in margarine with a pastry blender or 2 knives until mixture resembles coarse meal. Reserve ½ cup flour mixture for topping; set aside.
3. Combine remaining flour mixture, baking powder, and baking soda. Add sour cream, milk, extracts, and 1 egg. Beat at medium speed of a mixer until blended. Spoon batter into an 8-inch round cake pan coated with cooking spray.
4. Combine cream cheese, 2 tablespoons sugar, and egg white; beat at medium speed until blended. Spread evenly over batter; dot with preserves. Top with raspberries. Combine reserved ½ cup flour mixture and almonds. Sprinkle crumb mixture over raspberries. Bake at 350° for 30 minutes or until cake springs back when touched lightly in center. Cool on a wire rack. Yield: 8 servings (serving size: 1 wedge).

CALORIES 217 (31% from fat); FAT 7.4g (sat 1.4g, mono 3.3g, poly 2.1g); PROTEIN 5.6g; CARB 31.7g; FIBER 0.7g; CHOL 30mg; IRON 1mg; SODIUM 234mg; CALC 66mg

BERRY BEST BERRIES

Look for plump berries with a luscious, bright color. Avoid boxes of berries that show signs of leakage, stains, or mold. Before you store berries, remove those that are mashed and those that show signs of mold. Don't wash the berries until just before you plan to use them. They'll keep one or two days in the refrigerator.

CINNAMON CRUMB CAKE

PREP:15 MINUTES

COOK:30 MINUTES

1¼ cups all-purpose flour
⅔ cup packed brown sugar
¾ teaspoon ground cinnamon
⅛ teaspoon salt
¼ cup chilled stick margarine or butter, cut into small pieces
½ teaspoon baking powder
½ teaspoon baking soda
½ cup low-fat or nonfat buttermilk
1 teaspoon vanilla extract
1 large egg
Cooking spray

1. Preheat oven to 350°.
2. Lightly spoon flour into dry measuring cups; level with a knife. Combine flour, brown sugar, cinnamon, and salt in a bowl; cut in margarine with a pastry blender or 2 knives until mixture resembles coarse meal. Reserve ½ cup flour mixture for topping; set aside.
3. Combine remaining flour mixture, baking powder, and baking soda; add buttermilk, vanilla, and egg to flour mixture. Beat at medium speed of a mixer until blended.
4. Spoon batter into an 8-inch round cake pan coated with cooking spray. Sharply tap pan once on counter to remove air bubbles. Sprinkle reserved ½ cup flour mixture over batter. Bake at 350° for 30 minutes or until cake springs back when touched lightly in center. Cool on a wire rack. Yield: 8 servings (serving size: 1 wedge).

CALORIES 211 (29% from fat); FAT 6.9g (sat 1.5g, mono 2.9g, poly 2g); PROTEIN 3.5g; CARB 33.9g; FIBER 0.6g; CHOL 28mg; IRON 1.5mg; SODIUM 206mg; CALC 62mg

1. Using a large spoon, stir flour gently before measuring, and spoon into a dry measuring cup.

2. Level flour with a knife or small metal spatula. Don't shake the cup—it packs the flour.

Cinnamon Crumb Cake

3. After combining flour, sugar, cinnamon, and salt, cut in chilled stick margarine or butter with a pastry blender or 2 knives until the mixture resembles coarse meal.

4. Reserve ½ cup of crumb mixture, and set aside to use for topping. Combine remaining crumb mixture with remaining ingredients, and beat at medium speed of a mixer until blended.

5. Spoon batter into an 8-inch round cake pan coated with cooking spray. Sprinkle with reserved ½ cup crumb mixture.

GRAHAM CRACKER CRUMB CAKE

PREP: 22 MINUTES
COOK: 35 MINUTES

½ cup granulated sugar
½ cup packed brown sugar
5 tablespoons stick margarine or butter, softened
3 large egg whites
1 teaspoon vanilla extract
½ cup whole-wheat flour
1½ cups graham cracker crumbs
1 teaspoon baking powder
½ teaspoon baking soda
¼ teaspoon salt
1 cup low-fat or nonfat buttermilk
Cooking spray

1. Preheat oven to 350°.
2. Beat sugars and margarine at medium speed of a mixer until well-blended (about five minutes). Add egg whites and vanilla; beat well.
3. Lightly spoon flour into a dry measuring cup; level with a knife. Combine flour, crumbs, baking powder, baking soda, and salt, stirring with a whisk. Add flour mixture to sugar mixture alternately with buttermilk, beginning and ending with flour mixture.
4. Spoon batter into a 9-inch square baking pan coated with cooking spray. Sharply tap once on counter to remove air bubbles. Bake at 350° for 35 minutes or until a wooden pick inserted in center comes out clean. Cool in pan 10 minutes on a wire rack. Yield: 12 servings (serving size: 1 square).

CALORIES 194 (30% from fat); FAT 6.5g (sat 1.5g, mono 2.4g, poly 1.7g); PROTEIN 3.1g; CARB 31.5g; FIBER 1.7g; CHOL 1mg; IRON 0.9mg; SODIUM 272mg; CALC 56mg

PLUM-STREUSEL KUCHEN

PREP: 25 MINUTES   COOK: 45 MINUTES

Any type of plum will work in this recipe.

1⅔ cups all-purpose flour, divided
½ cup sugar
½ teaspoon ground cinnamon
1 tablespoon vegetable oil
2 teaspoons light-colored corn syrup
⅓ cup sugar
1 teaspoon baking powder
¼ teaspoon salt
¼ cup chilled stick margarine or butter, cut into small pieces
½ cup plain fat-free yogurt
2 tablespoons water
1½ teaspoons vanilla extract
¾ teaspoon grated lemon rind
1 large egg
Cooking spray
2 cups sliced plums (about ¾ pound)

1. Preheat oven to 400°.
2. Lightly spoon flour into dry measuring cups; level with a knife. Place ⅓ cup flour, ½ cup sugar, and cinnamon in a food processor; pulse 2 or 3 times. With processor on, slowly add oil and corn syrup through food chute, processing until mixture resembles coarse meal. Remove streusel mixture from food processor, and set aside.
3. Place 1⅓ cups flour, ⅓ cup sugar, baking powder, and salt in food processor, and pulse 2 or 3 times. Add margarine, and process until mixture resembles coarse meal. Place margarine mixture in a large bowl.
4. Combine yogurt, water, vanilla, rind, and egg. Stir yogurt mixture into margarine mixture until well-blended. Spoon batter into a 9-inch round cake pan coated with cooking spray. Sharply tap pan once on counter to remove air bubbles. Sprinkle half of streusel mixture evenly over batter. Top with plums, arranging in a circular pattern. Sprinkle remaining streusel mixture evenly over plums.
5. Bake at 400° for 45 minutes or until a wooden pick inserted in center comes out clean. Cool on a wire rack. Yield: 9 servings (serving size: 1 slice).

CALORIES 258 (27% from fat); FAT 7.7g (sat 1.5g, mono 3.1g, poly 2.5g); PROTEIN 4.2g; CARB 43.6g; FIBER 1.4g; CHOL 25mg; IRON 1.3mg; SODIUM 144mg; CALC 67mg

upside-down cakes

If you have a wooden spoon, a bowl, and measuring utensils, you're just a few minutes away from a moist, warm cake.

The comfort of an upside-down cake lives on in these healthy, full-flavored recipes. We topped these cakes with apples, pineapple, and even fresh rosemary! And we didn't stop there—we created innovative cake batters by adding ginger, yogurt, and sweet potatoes.

Much of the upside-down cake's popularity is due to its ease of preparation. Basically, it's made by covering the bottom of a cake pan with margarine and sugar topped with fruit. During the baking process, the sugar, margarine, and fruit juices combine to create a gooey, caramelized glaze.

UPSIDE-DOWN APPLE GINGERBREAD CAKE

PREP: 19 MINUTES
COOK: 40 MINUTES

 1 tablespoon stick margarine or
     butter, melted
¼ cup packed brown sugar
 2 cups thinly sliced peeled Granny
     Smith apple
1¼ cups all-purpose flour
 1 teaspoon ground ginger
 1 teaspoon ground cinnamon
¾ teaspoon baking soda
¼ teaspoon ground nutmeg
⅛ teaspoon salt
⅛ teaspoon ground cloves
⅓ cup granulated sugar
¼ cup stick margarine or butter,
     softened
⅓ cup molasses
 1 large egg
½ cup plain fat-free yogurt
⅓ cup chopped pitted dates
 3 tablespoons chopped walnuts

1. Preheat oven to 350°.
2. Coat bottom of a 9-inch round cake pan with melted margarine. Sprinkle brown sugar over margarine. Arrange apple spokelike over brown sugar, working from center of pan to edge; set aside.
3. Lightly spoon flour into dry measuring cups; level with a knife. Combine flour and next 6 ingredients; set aside.
4. Beat granulated sugar and ¼ cup margarine at medium speed of a mixer until well-blended (about 5 minutes). Add molasses and egg; beat well. Add flour mixture to sugar mixture alternately with yogurt, beginning and ending with flour mixture; beat well after each addition. Stir in dates and walnuts.
5. Pour batter over apple slices. Sharply tap pan once on counter to remove air bubbles. Bake at 350° for 40 minutes or until a wooden pick inserted in center comes out clean. Cool in pan 5 minutes on a wire rack. Loosen cake from sides of pan using a narrow metal spatula. Place a plate upside down on top of cake pan; invert cake onto plate. Serve warm. Yield: 8 servings (serving size: 1 wedge).

CALORIES 296 (33% from fat); FAT 10.9g (sat 1.9g, mono 4g, poly 4.3g); PROTEIN 4.9g; CARB 46.5g; FIBER 1.6g; CHOL 27mg; IRON 2.1mg; SODIUM 224mg; CALC 80mg

MAKING UPSIDE DOWN BECOME RIGHT SIDE UP

Remove the cake from the pan while it's warm. If it cools in the pan, the sugar-fruit mixture will harden and stick.

When it's first out of the oven, let the cake cool for 5 minutes. Then run a small spatula around the side to loosen it.

Put a serving plate on top of cake pan; wearing an oven mitt, **firmly hold the cake pan, and invert it onto the plate.** Remove the pan.

Upside-down cakes are best served within 2 hours or so after baking. To serve later than that, let the cake cool in the pan; then, just before serving, heat it in a 375° oven for about 4 minutes or until the bottom of the pan is hot. Run a spatula around the sides of the cake to loosen it; then invert.

Upside-down cakes are best served warm. However, they're also fine at room temperature the day they are made.

UPSIDE-DOWN PINEAPPLE-SPICE CAKE

PREP: 13 MINUTES   COOK: 35 MINUTES

    4 teaspoons stick margarine or
        butter
    ⅓ cup orange juice
    ¼ cup packed brown sugar
    6 (½-inch) slices fresh pineapple,
        cut in half
    ½ cup granulated sugar
    ¼ cup stick margarine or butter,
        softened
    ¼ cup honey
    1 large egg
    1¼ cups sifted cake flour
    1 teaspoon baking powder
    ½ teaspoon baking soda
    ½ teaspoon salt
    1½ teaspoons ground cinnamon
    ½ teaspoon ground nutmeg
    ¼ cup fat-free milk
    2 teaspoons grated orange rind
    1¼ teaspoons vanilla extract

1. Preheat oven to 350°.
2. Melt 4 teaspoons margarine in a 10-inch cast-iron or heavy oven-proof skillet. Add orange juice and brown sugar; bring to a boil, stirring constantly. Remove from heat. Arrange pineapple in a single layer over brown sugar mixture, and set aside.
3. Beat granulated sugar and next 3 ingredients at medium speed of a mixer until thick and fluffy. Lightly spoon flour into dry measuring cups; level with a knife. Combine flour and next 5 ingredients, stirring well with a whisk. Add flour mixture to sugar mixture alternately with milk, beginning and ending with flour mixture. Stir in orange rind and vanilla.
4. Pour batter over pineapple slices. Bake at 350° for 35 minutes or until a wooden pick inserted in center comes out clean. Cool in pan 5 minutes on a wire rack. Loosen cake from sides of skillet using a narrow metal spatula. Place a plate upside down on top of skillet; invert cake onto plate. Serve warm. Yield: 10 servings (serving size: 1 wedge).

CALORIES 222 (28% from fat); FAT 6.9g (sat 1.4g, mono 2.9g, poly 2.1g); PROTEIN 2.2g; CARB 39.4g; FIBER 1.1g; CHOL 21mg; IRON 1.5mg; SODIUM 274mg; CALC 46mg

CARAMEL-PINEAPPLE UPSIDE-DOWN CAKE

PREP: 25 MINUTES   COOK: 40 MINUTES

This recipe makes two cakes, so plan on freezing one cake. It will keep for up to three weeks in the freezer.

    1 (20-ounce) can pineapple
        tidbits in juice, undrained
    Cooking spray
    ¼ cup fat-free milk
    1 tablespoon stick margarine or
        butter
    30 small soft caramel candies
    1 cup canned mashed sweet
        potatoes or yams
    ¼ cup vegetable oil
    1 teaspoon ground cinnamon
    ½ teaspoon ground nutmeg
    3 large egg whites
    1 large egg
    1 (18.25-ounce) package light
        yellow cake mix

1. Preheat oven to 350°.
2. Drain pineapple in a colander over a bowl, reserving 1 cup juice. Arrange pineapple tidbits evenly in bottom of 2 (9-inch) round cake pans coated with cooking spray. Combine milk, margarine, and caramels in a small microwave-safe bowl; microwave at HIGH 2½ minutes or until caramels melt, stirring every minute. Pour caramel mixture evenly over pineapple in pans.
3. Beat reserved pineapple juice, sweet potatoes, and remaining ingredients at low speed of a mixer 30 seconds. Beat at medium speed until well-blended (about 2 minutes).
4. Pour batter evenly over caramel layer in pans; bake at 350° for 40 minutes or until a wooden pick inserted in center comes out clean. Cool in pans 5 minutes on a wire rack. Place a plate upside down on each cake pan; invert cakes onto plates. Serve warm. Yield: 2 cakes, 8 servings per cake (serving size: 1 wedge).

CALORIES 262 (20% from fat); FAT 5.9g (sat 1.6g, mono 1.5g, poly 2g); PROTEIN 3.8g; CARB 4.1g; FIBER 0.8g; CHOL 13mg; IRON 0.8mg; SODIUM 276mg; CALC 106mg

PINEAPPLE UPSIDE-DOWN CAKE WITH ROSEMARY

PREP: 15 MINUTES   COOK: 35 MINUTES

    1 tablespoon stick margarine or
        butter, melted
    ⅓ cup packed dark brown sugar
    1 teaspoon chopped fresh rosemary
    6 canned pineapple slices
    1¼ cups all-purpose flour
    1½ teaspoons baking powder
    ⅛ teaspoon salt
    ⅔ cup granulated sugar
    ¼ cup stick margarine or butter,
        softened
    1 teaspoon vanilla extract
    1 large egg
    ½ cup fat-free milk
    Rosemary sprigs (optional)

1. Preheat oven to 350°.
2. Coat bottom of a 9-inch round cake pan with melted margarine. Sprinkle brown sugar and chopped rosemary over margarine. Arrange pineapple slices in a single layer over brown sugar-rosemary mixture; set aside.
3. Lightly spoon flour into dry measuring cups; level with a knife. Combine flour, baking powder, and salt, stirring well with a whisk.

4. Beat granulated sugar and ¼ cup margarine at medium speed of a mixer until well-blended (about 5 minutes). Add vanilla and egg; beat well. Add flour mixture to sugar mixture alternately with milk, beginning and ending with flour mixture.

5. Pour batter over pineapple slices in pan. Bake at 350° for 35 minutes or until a wooden pick inserted in center comes out clean. Cool in pan 5 minutes on a wire rack. Loosen cake from sides of pan using a narrow metal spatula. Place a plate upside down on top of cake pan; invert cake onto plate. Garnish with rosemary sprigs, if desired. Serve warm. Yield: 8 servings (serving size: 1 wedge).

CALORIES 259 (28% from fat); FAT 8.1g (sat 1.7g, mono 3.4g, poly 2.4g); PROTEIN 3.3g; CARB 43.9g; FIBER 0.8g; CHOL 27mg; IRON 1.3mg; SODIUM 200mg; CALC 71mg

cupcakes Cupcakes take minimal effort to make—yet such a little cake will bring big smiles to your family and friends.

CHOCOLATE CUPCAKES

PREP: 20 MINUTES
COOK: 22 MINUTES

For instructions on baking this batter in a 9-inch square baking pan, see page 128.

¾ cup granulated sugar
5 tablespoons butter or stick margarine, softened
1 teaspoon vanilla extract
2 large eggs
1 cup all-purpose flour
¼ cup unsweetened cocoa
½ teaspoon baking soda
¼ teaspoon salt
½ cup fat-free milk
Chocolate Frosting (page 141)

1. Preheat oven to 350°.
2. Beat first 3 ingredients at medium speed of a mixer until well-blended (about 3 minutes). Add eggs, 1 at a time, beating well after each addition. Lightly spoon flour into a dry measuring cup, and level with a knife. Combine flour, cocoa, baking soda, and salt, stirring well with a whisk. Add flour mixture to sugar mixture alternately with ½ cup milk, beginning and ending with flour mixture; mix after each addition.

3. Spoon cupcake batter into 12 muffin cups lined with paper liners. Bake cupcakes at 350° for 22 minutes or until cupcakes spring back easily when touched lightly in the center. Cool cupcakes in muffin pan 10 minutes on a wire rack, and remove cupcakes from pan.

Cool cupcakes completely on wire rack.
4. Spread Chocolate Frosting over cupcakes. Yield: 1 dozen (serving size: 1 cupcake).

CALORIES 261 (28% from fat); FAT 8.2g (sat 4.8g, mono 2.4g, poly 0.4g); PROTEIN 3.5g; CARB 44.5g; FIBER 0.3g; CHOL 53mg; IRON 1.1mg; SODIUM 180mg; CALC 32mg

Chocolate Cupcakes

DOUBLE-MAPLE CUPCAKES

PREP: 20 MINUTES   COOK: 20 MINUTES

½ cup granulated sugar
5 tablespoons butter or stick
   margarine, softened
1 teaspoon vanilla extract
½ teaspoon imitation maple flavoring
2 large eggs
1¼ cups all-purpose flour
1¼ teaspoons baking powder
¼ teaspoon salt
¼ cup 1% low-fat milk
¼ cup maple syrup
Maple Frosting (page 142)

1. Preheat oven to 350°.
2. Beat first 4 ingredients at medium speed of a mixer until well-blended (about 5 minutes). Add eggs, 1 at a time, beating well after each addition. Lightly spoon flour into dry measuring cups; level with a knife. Combine flour, baking powder, and ¼ teaspoon salt in a bowl, stirring well with a whisk. Combine milk and ¼ cup maple syrup. Add flour mixture to sugar mixture alternately with milk mixture, beginning and ending with flour mixture; mix after each addition.

3. Spoon batter into 12 muffin cups lined with paper liners. Bake at 350° for 20 minutes or until a wooden pick inserted in center comes out clean. Cool in pan 10 minutes on a wire rack; remove from pan. Cool completely on wire rack.
4. Spread Maple Frosting over cupcakes. Yield: 1 dozen (serving size: 1 cupcake).

CALORIES 255 (28% from fat); FAT 7.8g (sat 4.5g, mono 2.3g, poly 0.4g); PROTEIN 2.7g; CARB 43.9g; FIBER 0.4g; CHOL 55mg; IRON 1mg; SODIUM 207mg; CALC 50mg

GINGERBREAD CAKES WITH FRUIT AND MOLASSES CREAM

PREP: 15 MINUTES   COOK: 23 MINUTES

1 cup all-purpose flour
¾ teaspoon ground ginger
½ teaspoon baking soda
½ teaspoon salt
½ cup molasses
¼ cup water
3 tablespoons stick margarine or
   butter, melted
1 large egg, lightly beaten
Cooking spray

2 cups sliced peeled peaches
½ pint blueberries or blackberries
6 tablespoons frozen reduced-
   calorie whipped topping, thawed
1 tablespoon molasses

1. Preheat oven to 350°.
2. Lightly spoon flour into a dry measuring cup; level with a knife. Combine flour, ginger, baking soda, and salt, stirring well with a whisk. Add molasses, water, margarine, and egg; beat at medium speed of a mixer 2 minutes.
3. Divide batter evenly among 6 muffin cups coated with cooking spray. Bake at 350° for 23 minutes or until a wooden pick inserted in center comes out clean. Cool in pan 10 minutes on a wire rack; remove from pan, and cool completely.
4. Combine peaches and berries. Combine whipped topping and molasses; stirring gently. Split cupcakes in half, and top each cupcake with ½ cup fruit mixture and 1 tablespoon whipped topping mixture. Yield: 6 servings.

CALORIES 260 (26% from fat); FAT 7.6g (sat 2g, mono 2.9g, poly 2g); PROTEIN 3.7g; CARB 45.5g; FIBER 2.1g; CHOL 35mg; IRON 2.6mg; SODIUM 357mg; CALC 79mg

Gingerbread Cakes With
Fruit and Molasses Cream

tube-pan & bundt cakes

Hefty and moist, these cakes just might start new traditions in your family.

MOTHER'S CHRISTMAS FRUITCAKE

PREP: 35 MINUTES

COOK: 1 HOUR 30 MINUTES

1 (8-ounce) package pitted prunes
2 cups water
¾ cup maraschino cherries, undrained
1¼ cups sugar
¾ cup vegetable shortening
4 large eggs
1 cup chopped walnuts
3 tablespoons whiskey
1 (15¼-ounce) can crushed pineapple, undrained
1 (15-ounce) box raisins (about 2½ cups)
4 cups all-purpose flour
1 tablespoon ground cinnamon
2 teaspoons baking soda
1 teaspoon ground cloves
½ teaspoon salt
Cooking spray

1. Combine prunes and 2 cups water in a medium saucepan; bring to a boil. Cover, reduce heat, and simmer 10 minutes or until tender. Drain, reserving 6 tablespoons cooking liquid. Drain cherries, reserving 3 tablespoons juice. Cut cherries in half.
2. Preheat oven to 350°.
3. Beat sugar, shortening, and eggs at medium speed of a mixer until smooth (about 2 minutes). Stir in prunes, reserved prune cooking liquid, cherries, reserved cherry juice, walnuts, whiskey, pineapple, and raisins. Lightly spoon flour into dry measuring cups; level with a knife. Combine flour, cinnamon, soda, cloves, and salt; add to sugar mixture, stirring well.

A FAVORITE FRUITCAKE

People love to get homemade desserts during the holidays, so why not surprise them with a miniloaf and turn them into fruitcake lovers?

Mini Fruitcakes

• Spoon 1½ cups batter into each of 20 (4 x 2½-inch) miniloaf pans coated with cooking spray. Bake at 350° for 30 minutes.

Small Fruitcakes

• Spoon 1¼ cups batter into each of 8 (5½ x 3-inch) loaf pans coated with cooking spray. Bake at 350° for 50 minutes.

4. Spoon batter into a 10-inch tube pan coated with cooking spray. Sharply tap pan once on counter to remove air bubbles. Bake at 350° for 1 hour 30 minutes or until a wooden pick inserted in center comes out clean. Cool in pan 10 minutes on a wire rack; remove from pan. Cool completely on wire rack. Store tightly wrapped in heavy-duty plastic wrap. Yield: 32 servings (serving size: 1 [¾-inch] slice).
Note: 1 (16-ounce) jar ready-to-serve prunes in heavy syrup, undrained, can be substituted for pitted prunes. (Eliminate the stewing process.) Drain prunes, reserving 6 tablespoons syrup to use in place of the 6 tablespoons reserved cooking liquid.

CALORIES 228 (27% from fat); FAT 6.9g (sat 1.5g, mono 3.0g, poly 2.9g); PROTEIN 3.8g; CARB 39.3g; FIBER 1.8g; CHOL 27mg; IRON 1.4mg; SODIUM 99mg; CALC 22mg

APPLE 'N' SPICE CAKE

PREP: 25 MINUTES

COOK: 1 HOUR 15 MINUTES

2 cups all-purpose flour
1 cup sugar
1 teaspoon baking soda
1 teaspoon ground cinnamon
¼ teaspoon ground nutmeg
⅛ teaspoon salt
½ cup applesauce
1 tablespoon vegetable oil
2 teaspoons vanilla extract
2 large eggs
1 cup golden raisins
1 (20-ounce) can light apple pie filling, coarsely chopped
Cooking spray
¼ cup fat-free caramel sundae syrup

1. Preheat oven to 325°.
2. Lightly spoon flour into dry measuring cups; level with a knife. Combine flour and next 5 ingredients; stir well with a whisk. Combine applesauce, oil, and vanilla.
3. Place eggs in a bowl; stir well with a whisk. Add flour mixture to eggs alternately with applesauce mixture, beginning and ending with flour mixture; stir after each addition until mixture is moist. Fold in raisins and pie filling.
4. Spoon batter into a 10-inch tube pan coated with cooking spray. Sharply tap pan once on counter to remove air bubbles. Bake at 325° for 1 hour and 15 minutes or until a wooden pick inserted in center comes out clean. Cool in pan 10 minutes on a wire rack. Remove from pan; cool completely on wire rack. Drizzle syrup over top of cooled cake. Yield: 12 servings (serving size: 1 slice).

CALORIES 258 (8% from fat); FAT 2.3g (sat 0.5g, mono 0.7g, poly 0.8g); PROTEIN 3.6g; CARB 56.2g; FIBER 1.8g; CHOL 35mg; IRON 1.3mg; SODIUM 130mg; CALC 17mg

ZUCCHINI STREUSEL BUNDT CAKE

PREP: 30 MINUTES   COOK: 1 HOUR

     2   cups shredded zucchini
     ⅓   cup packed brown sugar
     ⅓   cup chopped walnuts
     ⅓   cup currants
     1   tablespoon ground cinnamon
     ½   teaspoon ground allspice
     3   cups all-purpose flour
     1¼   cups granulated sugar
     1½   teaspoons baking powder
     1   teaspoon baking soda
     ½   teaspoon salt
     1⅓   cups plain fat-free yogurt
     ⅓   cup vegetable oil
     1   tablespoon vanilla extract
     2   egg whites, lightly beaten
     1   egg, lightly beaten
          Cooking spray
     1   tablespoon dry breadcrumbs
     ¾   cup sifted powdered sugar
     2   teaspoons fat-free milk
     1   teaspoon vanilla extract

1. Preheat oven to 350°.
2. Place zucchini on several layers of paper towels; cover with additional paper towels. Let stand 5 minutes, pressing down occasionally. Set aside.
3. Combine brown sugar and next 4 ingredients in a bowl; set aside. Lightly spoon flour into dry measuring cups; level with a knife. Combine flour and next 4 ingredients in a large bowl; make a well in center of mixture. Combine yogurt and next 4 ingredients. Add zucchini. Add to flour mixture; stir just until moist.
4. Coat a 12-cup Bundt pan with cooking spray; dust with breadcrumbs. Spoon ⅓ of batter into prepared pan; top with half of brown sugar mixture. Spoon half of remaining batter into pan; top with remaining brown sugar mixture and batter.
5. Bake at 350° for 1 hour or until a wooden pick inserted in center comes out

clean. Cool 10 minutes; remove from pan. Cool on a wire rack. Combine powdered sugar, milk, and vanilla. Drizzle over cake. Yield: 18 servings (serving size: 1 slice).

CALORIES 245 (22% from fat); FAT 6g (sat 1g, mono 1.6g, poly 3g); PROTEIN 4.8g; CARB 43.5g; FIBER 0.9g; CHOL 13mg; IRON 1.5mg; SODIUM 164mg; CALC 80mg

DRIED CRANBERRIES

Dried cranberries resemble raisins and are sweeter than fresh cranberries. Look for them with the specialty-food items or in the aisle with the other dried fruit at your supermarket.

GREAT BIG CAKE WITH FIVE DRIED FRUITS

PREP: 30 MINUTES   COOK: 1 HOUR

          Cooking spray
     3   cups all-purpose flour
     ½   cup cornstarch
     ¼   teaspoon salt
     ½   cup chopped dried peaches
     ½   cup chopped dried dates
     ½   cup chopped dried pears
     ½   cup dried cranberries
     ½   cup dried sour cherries
     2   cups granulated sugar
     ½   cup stick margarine or butter, softened
     1   (8-ounce) block ⅓-less-fat cream cheese, softened
     1   tablespoon grated lemon rind
     1   tablespoon vanilla extract
     4   large eggs
     2   large egg whites
     1   cup fat-free sour cream
     1   teaspoon baking soda
     1   tablespoon powdered sugar

1. Preheat oven to 350°.
2. Coat a 12-cup Bundt pan with cooking spray; set aside.

3. Lightly spoon flour into dry measuring cups; level with a knife. Sift together flour, cornstarch, and salt twice. Combine dried fruits with ¼ cup flour mixture; toss to coat.
4. Beat granulated sugar and next 4 ingredients at medium speed of a mixer until well-blended (about 5 minutes). Add eggs and egg whites, 1 at a time, beating well after each addition. Combine sour cream and baking soda. Add flour mixture to sugar mixture alternately with sour cream mixture, beginning and ending with flour mixture. Mix after each addition. Gently fold in fruit mixture.
5. Pour batter into prepared pan. Sharply tap pan once on counter to remove air bubbles. Bake at 350° for 1 hour or until a wooden pick inserted in center comes out clean. Cool in pan 10 minutes on a wire rack; remove from pan. Cool completely on wire rack. Dust with powdered sugar. Yield: 24 servings (serving size: 1 slice).

CALORIES 259 (25% from fat); FAT 7.1g (sat 2.5g, mono 2.7g, poly 1.5g); PROTEIN 5.1g; CARB 44.4g; FIBER 1.6g; CHOL 44mg; IRON 1.3mg; SODIUM 183mg; CALC 22mg

Easy Chopping

We prefer to chop dried fruit with either scissors or a knife coated with cooking spray. This keeps the fruit from sticking to the utensil, making the process go much quicker.

pound cakes

Enjoy the old-fashioned flavor and simple goodness of a family favorite, pound cake.

While we've captured the texture and richness of traditional pound cakes, we've significantly altered the ingredient list. Pound cake originally got its name because of the ingredients—one pound each of butter, eggs, flour, and sugar. But by taking a light approach to the recipe, the ingredient list has been updated to today's healthy standards. Be sure to follow our step-by-step guidelines—thoroughly beat the sugar and margarine in the first step, and after adding the flour, beat just until blended—to keep the cake from becoming tough.

ALMOND-SPICE POUND CAKE

PREP: 20 MINUTES   COOK: 1 HOUR

⅔ cup sugar
⅔ cup Prune Puree (page 453)
¼ cup stick margarine or butter, softened
½ teaspoon almond extract
½ teaspoon vanilla extract
2 egg whites
1 egg
1¾ cups all-purpose flour
2 teaspoons baking powder
½ teaspoon ground allspice
¼ teaspoon salt
⅓ cup fat-free milk
Cooking spray

1. Preheat oven to 350°.
2. Beat first 5 ingredients at medium speed of a mixer for 2 minutes. Add egg whites and egg; beat 1 minute.
3. Lightly spoon flour into dry measuring cups; level with a knife. Combine flour, baking powder, allspice, and salt; stir well with a whisk. Add flour mixture to prune mixture alternately with milk, beginning and ending with flour mixture.
4. Pour batter into an 8½ x 4½-inch loaf pan coated with cooking spray. Bake at 350° for 1 hour or until a wooden pick inserted in center comes out clean. Cool in pan 15 minutes on a wire rack; remove from pan, and cool on wire rack. Yield: 12 servings (serving size: 1 slice).

CALORIES 183 (22% from fat); FAT 4.5g (sat 0.9g, mono 1.9g, poly 1.3g); PROTEIN 3.3g; CARB 33g; FIBER 1.2g; CHOL 18mg; IRON 1.1mg; SODIUM 115mg; CALC 50mg

RUM-ALLSPICE POUND CAKE WITH AMBROSIA

PREP: 30 MINUTES   COOK: 50 MINUTES

2 cups sugar
⅔ cup stick margarine or butter, softened
2 large eggs
1 large egg white
3 cups all-purpose flour
2 teaspoons baking powder
1 teaspoon baking soda
½ teaspoon ground ginger
½ teaspoon ground allspice
½ teaspoon ground nutmeg
¼ teaspoon salt
1¼ cups low-fat or nonfat buttermilk
¼ cup dark rum
1 tablespoon grated orange rind
1 teaspoon vanilla extract
Cooking spray
Ambrosia

1. Preheat oven to 375°.
2. Beat sugar and margarine at medium speed of a mixer until well-blended (about 5 minutes). Add eggs and egg white, 1 at a time, beating well after each addition. Lightly spoon flour into dry measuring cups; level with a knife. Combine flour and next 6 ingredients. Combine buttermilk, rum, orange rind, and vanilla. Add flour mixture to sugar mixture alternately with buttermilk mixture, beginning and ending with flour mixture.
3. Pour batter into a 10-inch tube pan coated with cooking spray. Sharply tap pan once on counter to remove air bubbles. Bake at 375° for 50 minutes or until a wooden pick inserted in center comes out clean. Cool in pan 10 minutes on a wire rack; remove from pan. Cool completely on wire rack. Serve with Ambrosia. Yield: 18 servings (serving size: 1 slice and ¼ cup Ambrosia).

CALORIES 292 (26% from fat); FAT 8.5g (sat 2.2g, mono 3.4g, poly 2.3g); PROTEIN 4.4g; CARB 48.4g; FIBER 2.5g; CHOL 25mg; IRON 1.3mg; SODIUM 259mg; CALC 79mg

AMBROSIA

3 oranges
2 ruby red or pink grapefruit
2 cups strawberry halves
2 kiwifruit, peeled and cut into wedges
¼ cup flaked sweetened coconut
¼ cup dark rum
3 tablespoons brown sugar

1. Peel and section oranges and grapefruit; extract juices, and pour into a bowl. Add sections to bowl; discard membranes. Stir in strawberries, kiwifruit, coconut, rum, and brown sugar. Cover and chill. Yield: 18 servings (serving size: ¼ cup).

CALORIES 50 (11% from fat); FAT 0.6g (sat 0.4g, mono 0.1g, poly 0.1g); PROTEIN 0.6g; CARB 8.9g; FIBER 1.9g; CHOL 0mg; IRON 0.2mg; SODIUM 4mg; CALC 18mg

SOUR CREAM POUND CAKE

PREP: 26 MINUTES

COOK: 1 HOUR 35 MINUTES

Seven egg whites can be used in place of egg substitute, if desired. Add one egg white at a time to sugar mixture, beating after each addition. This pound cake is excellent toasted.

  3 cups sugar
  ¾ cup stick margarine or butter, softened
1⅓ cups egg substitute
1½ cups low-fat sour cream
  1 teaspoon baking soda
4½ cups sifted cake flour
  ¼ teaspoon salt
  2 teaspoons vanilla extract
Cooking spray

1. Preheat oven to 325°.

2. Beat sugar and margarine at medium speed of a mixer until well-blended (about 5 minutes). Gradually add egg substitute, beating well.

3. Combine sour cream and baking soda in a small bowl. Lightly spoon flour into dry measuring cups; level with a knife. Combine flour and salt. Add flour mixture to sugar mixture alternately with sour cream mixture, beginning and ending with flour mixture. Stir in vanilla.

4. Pour batter into a 9- or 10-inch tube pan coated with cooking spray. Sharply tap pan once on counter to remove air bubbles. Bake at 325° for 1 hour and 35 minutes or until a wooden pick inserted in center comes out clean. Cool in pan 10 minutes on a wire rack; remove from pan. Cool completely on wire rack. Yield: 24 servings (serving size: 1 slice).

CALORIES 241 (28% from fat); FAT 7.6g (sat 2.3g, mono 3.1g, poly 1.9g); PROTEIN 3.3g; CARB 40g; FIBER 0.6g; CHOL 6mg; IRON 1.6mg; SODIUM 152mg; CALC 25mg

Sour Cream Pound Cake

1. Beat sugar and margarine at medium speed of a mixer until well-blended (about 5 minutes).

2. Gradually add egg substitute, beating well.

3. Add one-third of flour mixture to creamed mixture.

4. Add half of sour cream mixture. Add flour mixture and remaining sour cream mixture alternately, ending with flour mixture.

5. Pour batter into a 9- or 10-inch tube pan coated with cooking spray. Sharply tap pan once on counter to remove air bubbles.

FLAVORED POUND CAKES

Use these variations to Sour Cream Pound Cake to cater to your family's tastebuds.

Almond Pound Cake: add 1 teaspoon almond extract, and decrease vanilla extract to 1 teaspoon.

Butter Pound Cake: add 1 teaspoon butter flavoring, and decrease vanilla extract to 1 teaspoon.

Butter Rum Pound Cake: add 1 teaspoon butter rum flavoring, and decrease vanilla extract to 1 teaspoon.

Coconut Pound Cake: add 1 teaspoon coconut flavoring, and decrease vanilla extract to 1 teaspoon.

Lemon Pound Cake: add 1 teaspoon grated lemon rind with vanilla extract.

Blueberry Pound Cake

BLUEBERRY POUND CAKE

PREP: 25 MINUTES
COOK: 1 HOUR 15 MINUTES
(pictured on front cover)

2   cups granulated sugar
⅓   cup butter or stick margarine, softened
½   cup (4 ounces) ⅓-less-fat cream cheese, softened
3   large eggs
1   large egg white
2   teaspoons vanilla extract
3   cups all-purpose flour, divided
2   cups fresh or frozen blueberries
1   teaspoon baking powder
½   teaspoon baking soda
½   teaspoon salt
1   (8-ounce) carton lemon low-fat yogurt
Cooking spray
½   cup sifted powdered sugar
4   teaspoons lemon juice

1. Preheat oven to 350°.

2. Beat granulated sugar, butter, and cream cheese at medium speed of a mixer until well-blended (about 5 minutes). Add eggs and egg white, 1 at a time, beating well after each addition. Beat in vanilla.

3. Lightly spoon flour into dry measuring cups, and level with a knife. Combine 2 tablespoons flour and blueberries in a small bowl; toss to coat. Combine remaining flour, baking powder, baking soda, and salt. Add flour mixture to sugar mixture alternately with yogurt, beginning and ending with flour mixture. Fold in blueberry mixture.

4. Pour batter into a 10-inch tube pan (angel food cake pan) coated with cooking spray. Sharply tap pan once on counter to remove air bubbles. Bake at 350° for 1 hour and 15 minutes or until a wooden pick inserted in center comes out clean.

5. Cool cake in pan 10 minutes on a wire rack; remove cake from sides of pan. Cool 15 additional minutes on wire rack; remove cake from bottom of pan. Combine powdered sugar and lemon juice in a small bowl; drizzle over warm cake. Cut into slices using a serrated knife. Yield: 16 servings (serving size: 1 slice).

CALORIES 288 (22% from fat); FAT 6.9g (sat 3.9g, mono 2g, poly 0.4g); PROTEIN 5g; CARB 52.2g; FIBER 1g; CHOL 56mg; IRON 1.2mg; SODIUM 212mg; CALC 45mg

BLUEBERRIES

Blueberries don't ripen after picking and can deteriorate quickly. Plan to use them within one or two days of purchase. To store for up to two days, arrange unwashed berries in a shallow pan lined with paper towels. Top with more paper towels, and then cover with plastic wrap and refrigerate.

angel food & sponge cakes When beaten egg whites form the structure of a cake, a heavenly dessert is the result.

Angel food cakes

Delicate angel food cake with its sweet taste and tender texture is a favorite treat. Leavened by egg whites and tenderized by sugar, angel food cake is low fat and cholesterol free. You'll want to carefully follow the procedure for beating the egg whites, the key to the cake's volume.

Use an ungreased straight-sided tube pan for baking the cake. Other pans won't suffice—a tube pan allows the cake to bake evenly. The center tube conducts heat to the middle portion of the batter; otherwise the cake would dry out around the edges before the center became done. The ungreased sides of the pan allow the batter to cling and rise to maximum height.

The freshly baked cake will be light and spongy. Cool it upside down to allow its structure to set without collapsing. Some tube pans have metal feet, making it easy to set them upside down on a counter. If your pan doesn't have feet, place it over the neck of a bottle so that air can circulate beneath it.

The weather can influence your results. For maximum volume, prepare an angel food cake during dry weather rather than on a humid or rainy day.

Angel Food Cake

PART 1 beating the egg whites

Beat egg whites and cream of tartar at high speed of mixer until foamy. Gradually add sugar, a tablespoon at a time, beating at high speed of a mixer. At soft-peak stage, the egg white mixture will gently fold over when beaters are pulled away. When glossy peaks form, the egg white mixture is stiff. At this stage it will stand up when the beaters are pulled away.

PART 2 folding in the egg whites

1. Sift flour mixture over egg white mixture, 1/4 cup at a time.

2. Using a rubber spatula, gently fold the flour mixture into the beaten egg whites using an over-and-under stroke.

CALORIES 126 (0% from fat); FAT 0.1g (sat 0g, mono 0g, poly 0g); PROTEIN 3.5g; CARB 27.6g; FIBER 0.3g; CHOL 0mg; IRON 0.6mg; SODIUM 70mg; CALC 3mg

COFFEE ANGEL FOOD CAKE

PREP: 12 MINUTES

COOK: 30 MINUTES

1 tablespoon instant coffee granules
1 tablespoon water
1 (16-ounce) package angel food cake mix
1 teaspoon almond extract
1 teaspoon vanilla extract
2 tablespoons instant coffee granules
1 tablespoon water
6 tablespoons stick margarine, softened
1 (1-pound) box powdered sugar
3 tablespoons fat-free milk

1. Preheat oven to 375°.
2. Combine 1 tablespoon coffee granules and 1 tablespoon water in a small bowl; stir well, and set aside.
3. Prepare angel food cake batter according to package directions. Fold in coffee mixture and extracts. Spoon batter into an ungreased 10-inch tube pan, spreading evenly. Break air pockets by cutting through batter with a knife. Bake at 375° for 30 minutes or until cake springs back when lightly touched. Invert pan; let cool for 40 minutes. Loosen cake from sides of pan using a narrow metal spatula. Invert cake onto a serving plate; set aside.
4. Combine 2 tablespoons coffee granules and 1 tablespoon water in a small bowl; set aside.
5. Beat margarine at high speed of a mixer. Add coffee mixture; beat well. Gradually add powdered sugar, beating

at medium speed until well-blended. Add milk; beat well. Spread frosting over top and sides of cake. Store loosely covered in refrigerator. Yield: 12 servings (serving size: 1 slice).

CALORIES 292 (18% from fat); FAT 5.8g (sat 1.1g, mono 2.5g, poly 1.8g); PROTEIN 2.2g; CARB 58.3g; FIBER 0g; CHOL 0mg; IRON 0.2mg; SODIUM 119mg; CALC 41mg

---

HEAVENLY TREATS

In addition to enjoying a slice of unadorned angel food cake, try these serving suggestions:

• **Cut into cubes** and **layer with pudding and fruit for a trifle.** For extra flavor, brush cake pieces with Grand Marnier or other orange-flavored liqueur.

• **Top with berries or sliced fruit.**

• **Spoon Warm Turtle Sauce** (page 451) or **Chocolate Sauce** (page 450) over slices of cake.

ANGEL FOOD CAKE

PREP: 20 MINUTES

COOK: 40 MINUTES

1 cup sifted cake flour
1¼ cups sugar, divided
10 egg whites
1¼ teaspoons cream of tartar
⅛ teaspoon salt
⅛ teaspoon vanilla extract

1. Preheat oven to 350°.
2. Lightly spoon flour into a dry measuring cup; level with a knife. Sift together flour and ¼ cup sugar; set aside. Beat egg whites until foamy. Add cream of tartar and salt; beat until soft peaks form. Add remaining sugar, 2 tablespoons at a time, beating until stiff peaks form. Sift flour mixture over egg white mixture, ¼ cup at a time; fold in flour mixture. Fold in vanilla.
3. Spoon batter into an ungreased 10-inch tube pan, spreading evenly. Break air pockets by cutting through batter with a knife. Bake at 350° for 40 minutes or until cake springs back when lightly touched. Invert pan; cool for 40 minutes. Loosen cake from sides of pan

---

TIPS FOR BEATING EGG WHITES

• Eggs are easier to separate when cold, but beat up to a greater volume at room temperature. For best results, separate eggs as soon as you take them out of the refrigerator; then gather the rest of the ingredients. This gives the egg whites a few minutes to warm up. Because of egg safety issues, we do not let the egg whites stand at room temperature for more than 30 minutes.

• When the humidity is high, add 1 teaspoon of cornstarch with the sugar when making a meringue. This will help stabilize the egg whites.

• Cream of tartar increases volume and stabilizes egg whites, especially during baking.

• If the egg yolk breaks as you're separating it, you need to make sure that you remove every bit of it from the white. Egg whites that contain even a speck of yolk will not whip up to maximum volume. The best way to remove a bit of yolk is by dabbing it with a small piece of bread; the yolk will usually cling to the bread.

• Always use a clean bowl and clean beaters to beat egg whites. Even the smallest fleck of food or grease will prevent the whites from achieving full volume.

IS IT DONE?

Cakes made from beaten egg whites, such as angel food cakes and sponge cakes, have a different texture than layer cakes. To test for doneness for a foam-type cake, touch the top lightly. The cake is finished baking if the top springs back. When done, remove from the oven and cool, inverted on a bottle or on the feet of the pan.

Sponge cake

While angel food cakes get their structure from beaten egg whites, sponge cakes contain the whites as well as a few beaten egg yolks. Additionally, sponge cakes may contain leavening such as baking powder. Although not quite as airy as an angel food cake, they are somewhat richer in flavor.

Sponge cakes, like angel food cakes, are baked in an ungreased tube pan. This allows the batter to cling to the sides of the pan and rise high. After baking, both types are cooled upside-down in the pan to allow the structure of the cake to set without collapsing.

The springy texture of sponge cake makes it ideal for a variety of uses. You can slice and serve the cake with a fruit topping, or cut it into cubes and layer it with vanilla yogurt or pudding and berries for an easy trifle. Or, split the cake into layers, fill with any flavor of pudding, and frost with our Fluffy White Frosting (page 141).

PREP: 20 MINUTES   COOK: 35 MINUTES

1 cup sifted cake flour
1 teaspoon baking powder
¼ teaspoon salt
3 large eggs, separated
¾ cup sugar
2 teaspoons vanilla extract
¼ cup water
2 large egg whites
¼ cup sugar

1. Preheat oven to 350°.
2. Lightly spoon flour into a dry measuring cup; level with a knife. Combine flour, baking powder, and salt in a medium bowl; stir well with a whisk.
3. Beat 3 egg yolks in a large bowl at high speed of a mixer for 1 minute. Gradually add ¾ cup sugar, beating until egg yolks are thick and pale (about 5 minutes). Add vanilla and ¼ cup water, beating at low speed until blended. Add flour mixture to egg yolk mixture, beating at low speed until blended.
4. Using clean, dry beaters, beat 5 egg whites at high speed until foamy; gradually add ¼ cup sugar, 1 tablespoon at a time, beating until stiff peaks form. Gently stir one-fourth of egg white mixture into batter. Gently fold in remaining egg white mixture.
5. Pour batter into an ungreased 10-inch tube pan. Break air pockets by cutting through batter with a knife. Bake at 350° for 35 minutes or until cake springs back when touched lightly in center. Invert pan; cool 45 minutes. Loosen cake from sides of pan, using a narrow metal spatula.

SPONGE CAKE TIPS

• **Use cake flour** for a tender, fine-textured cake.

• **Sift the flour before measuring;** then lightly spoon into a measuring cup. Level with the edge of a knife or spatula.

• **Double-acting baking powder reacts twice**—on contact with moisture and when placed in a hot oven. (To check for freshness of baking powder, stir a spoonful into ½ cup warm water; if it fizzes, it's fresh.)

• **Carefully separate eggs** to avoid getting any egg yolk into the egg whites. **Yolks contain fat, and even just a trace will prevent the whites from beating to full volume.**

• **Gently fold the meringue** (beaten egg white mixture) into the batter using an over-and-under stroke with a rubber spatula.

Invert cake onto a plate. Yield: 10 servings (serving size: 1 slice).

CALORIES 141 (10% from fat); FAT 1.6g (sat 0.5g, mono 0.6g, poly 0.2g); PROTEIN 3.4g; CARB 28g; FIBER 0g; CHOL 64mg; IRON 0.9mg; SODIUM 119mg; CALC 28mg

COFFEE CHIFFON CAKE:

Prepare Basic Sponge Cake as directed but dissolve 1 teaspoon instant coffee granules in the ¼ cup water listed in the ingredient list. Bake as directed. Yield: 10 serving sizes (serving size: 1 slice).

CALORIES 141 (10% from fat); FAT 1.6g (sat 0.5g, mono 0.6g, poly 0.2g); PROTEIN 3.4g; CARB 28g; FIBER 0g; CHOL 64mg; IRON 0.9mg; SODIUM 119mg; CALC 28mg

The texture of sponge cake is a bit more dense than angel food cake, but using cake flour helps give it a tender, fine crumb.

cheesecakes
We offer a kaleidoscope of flavors and textures, ranging from airy and creamy to dense and rich.

Cheesecake is a classic dessert worthy of its rich reputation. Impressive, indulgent, and able to be made ahead, cheesecake is an ideal choice when serving dessert to company. A springform pan is the only special equipment needed to prepare this cool and silky confection, and our updated recipes are lighter but no less luxurious. So you and your guests can savor each satisfying bite—without guilt.

Cheesecake With Cranberry Glaze

CHEESECAKE WITH CRANBERRY GLAZE

PREP: 30 MINUTES
COOK: 1 HOUR 10 MINUTES
STAND: 1 HOUR   CHILL: 8 HOURS

This cheesecake needs to chill eight hours, so plan on making it a day ahead. The Cranberry Glaze can also be made ahead and chilled.

Crust:
Cooking spray
⅓ cup gingersnap crumbs (about 6 cookies, finely crushed)

Filling:
1 (16-ounce) carton fat-free cottage cheese
1 (8-ounce) block ⅓-less-fat cream cheese, softened
¼ cup all-purpose flour
⅔ cup sugar
1½ teaspoons vanilla extract
½ teaspoon almond extract
2 large eggs
2 large egg whites
1 (8-ounce) carton low-fat sour cream
Cranberry Glaze (page 138)

1. Preheat oven to 300°.
2. To prepare crust, coat bottom of a 9-inch springform pan with cooking spray; sprinkle with cookie crumbs.
3. To prepare filling, place cheeses in a food processor; process 2 minutes or until smooth, scraping sides of bowl once. Lightly spoon flour into a dry measuring cup; level with a knife. Add flour and next 6 ingredients to cheese mixture; process just until mixture is smooth.
4. Pour cheese mixture into prepared pan; bake at 300° for 1 hour and 10 minutes or until almost set. Turn oven off; let cheesecake stand in closed oven 1 hour. Remove cheesecake from oven; run a knife around outside edge. Cool to room temperature. Cover and chill at least 8 hours. Serve with Cranberry Glaze. Yield: 12 servings (serving size: 1 wedge and 2 tablespoons glaze).

CALORIES 226 (29% from fat); FAT 7.4g (sat 4.1g, mono 2.3g, poly 0.5g); PROTEIN 9.8g; CARB 29.6g; FIBER 0.3g; CHOL 61mg; IRON 0.5mg; SODIUM 254mg; CALC 74mg

(continued on page 138)

CRANBERRY GLAZE

½ cup sugar
2 teaspoons cornstarch
2 cups fresh cranberries
⅔ cup water

1. Combine sugar and cornstarch in a medium saucepan; stir in cranberries and water. Bring to a boil over medium-high heat; cook 5 minutes or until cranberries pop. Cool. Yield: 1½ cups. (serving size: 2 tablespoons).

CARAMEL CHEESECAKE

PREP: 22 MINUTES   COOK: 1 HOUR
STAND: 1 HOUR   CHILL: 8 HOURS

Crust:
⅔ cup chocolate graham cracker
    crumbs (about 5 cookie sheets)
Cooking spray

Filling:
2 cups fat-free cottage cheese
1 (8-ounce) block ⅓-less-fat cream
    cheese, softened
¼ cup all-purpose flour
¾ cup packed brown sugar
½ cup granulated sugar
½ cup fat-free sour cream
2 teaspoons vanilla extract
2 large eggs
2 large egg whites
¼ cup fat-free caramel sundae
    syrup, divided
2 (2.07-ounce) chocolate-coated
    caramel-peanut nougat bars (such
    as Snickers), chopped and divided

1. Preheat oven to 300°.

CHEESECAKE CAN-DO

Many cheesecakes end up with a creamy texture if removed from the oven just as they're set. Others require being left in the oven after baking (with the oven turned off). We've specified when this is needed.

To prevent cracks, run a knife or small metal spatula around the edge of the cheesecake immediately after removing it from the oven. This allows the loosened sides to contract freely.

You can freeze cheesecake for up to one month. Remove pan, place cheesecake on a cardboard circle, if desired, and wrap tightly in heavy-duty foil. Thaw in the refrigerator the day before serving.

---

2. To prepare crust, press crumbs into bottom and halfway up sides of a 9-inch springform pan coated with cooking spray.
3. To prepare filling, place cheeses in a food processor; process 2 minutes or until smooth. Lightly spoon flour into a dry measuring cup; level with a knife. Add flour, brown sugar, and next 5 ingredients to cheese mixture; process just until smooth. Pour half of cheese mixture into prepared pan. Drizzle with 2 tablespoons syrup; sprinkle with half of chopped candy bar. Pour remaining cheese mixture into pan; drizzle with 2 tablespoons syrup. Bake at 300° for 50 minutes. Sprinkle with remaining chopped candy bar; bake 10 minutes or until almost set. Turn oven off, and let cheesecake stand in closed oven for 1 hour.
4. Remove cheesecake from oven; cool to

---

room temperature. Cover and chill at least 8 hours. Yield: 12 servings (serving size: 1 wedge).

CALORIES 271 (23% from fat); FAT 6.9g (sat 3.5g, mono 1g, poly 0.5g); PROTEIN 10.9g; CARB 41.8g; FIBER 0.3g; CHOL 49mg; IRON 0.8mg; SODIUM 352mg; CALC 74mg

NEW YORK CHEESECAKE

PREP: 25 MINUTES   COOK: 47 MINUTES
CHILL: 8 HOURS

Crust:
⅔ cup all-purpose flour
2 tablespoons sugar
2 tablespoons chilled stick margarine
    or butter, cut into small pieces
1 tablespoon ice water
Cooking spray

Filling:
3 (8-ounce) blocks fat-free cream
    cheese, softened
2 (8-ounce) blocks ⅓-less-fat
    cream cheese, softened
1¾ cups sugar
3 tablespoons all-purpose flour
1 tablespoon vanilla extract
1½ teaspoons grated orange rind
1 teaspoon grated lemon rind
¼ teaspoon salt
5 large eggs
Lemon zest, orange slices, and lemon
    slices (optional)

1. Preheat oven to 400°.
2. To prepare crust, lightly spoon ⅔ cup flour into dry measuring cups; level with a knife. Place ⅔ cup flour and 2 tablespoons sugar in a food processor; pulse 2 times or until combined. Add chilled margarine; pulse 6 times or until

---

Cheesecakes shrink a little and become firm as they cool, so you can sometimes expect a little cracking around the edges.

mixture resembles coarse meal. With processor on, slowly pour ice water through food chute, processing just until blended (do not allow dough to form a ball). Firmly press mixture into bottom of a 9-inch springform pan coated with cooking spray. Bake at 400° for 10 minutes; cool on a wire rack.

3. Increase oven temperature to 525°.

4. To prepare filling, beat cheeses at high speed of a mixer until smooth. Add 1¾ cups sugar and next 5 ingredients; beat well. Add eggs, 1 at a time, beating well after each addition. Pour cheese mixture into prepared pan; bake at 525° for 7 minutes. Reduce oven temperature to 200° (do not remove cheesecake from oven); bake 40 minutes or until almost set. Remove cheesecake from oven; run a knife around outside edge. Cool to room temperature. Cover and chill at least 8 hours. If desired, garnish with lemon zest, orange slices, and lemon slices. Yield: 16 servings (serving size: 1 wedge).

CALORIES 262 (33% from fat); FAT 9.7g (sat 5g, mono 3.2g, poly 0.9g); PROTEIN 11.4g; CARB 30.8g; FIBER 0.2g; CHOL 95mg; IRON 0.6mg; SODIUM 442mg; CALC 151mg

CREAMY LEMON-LIME TOFU CHEESECAKE

PREP:30 MINUTES
COOK:1 HOUR 28 MINUTES
STAND:50 MINUTES   CHILL:8 HOURS

Crust:
1⅓ cups graham cracker crumbs
    (about 8 cookie sheets)
2 tablespoons brown sugar
1 tablespoon reduced-calorie stick
    margarine, melted
Cooking spray

Filling:
1 cup 2% low-fat cottage cheese
⅔ cup tub-style light cream cheese,
    softened

1 (12.3-ounce) package reduced-
    fat firm tofu, drained
⅓ cup all-purpose flour
1 cup granulated sugar
½ cup bottled fat-free lemon curd
    (such as Crosse & Blackwell)
2 teaspoons grated lime rind
6 tablespoons fresh lime juice
2 large eggs
1 large egg white

Topping:
1¼ cups low-fat sour cream
½ cup granulated sugar
1 teaspoon grated lemon
    rind
½ teaspoon vanilla extract

1. Preheat oven to 325°.

2. To prepare crust, combine first 3 ingredients in a small bowl; toss mixture with a fork until blended. Press mixture into bottom of a 9-inch springform pan coated with cooking spray.

3. To prepare filling, place cheeses and tofu in a food processor, and process until smooth. Lightly spoon flour into a dry measuring cup; level with a knife. Add flour, sugar, and next 5 ingredients to tofu mixture; process until smooth, scraping sides of processor bowl occasionally. Pour filling into prepared pan. Bake at 325° for 1 hour and 20 minutes or until almost set. Remove from oven.

4. To prepare topping, combine sour cream, ½ cup granulated sugar, lemon rind, and vanilla. Spread sour cream mixture over cheesecake, and bake an additional 8 minutes. Turn oven off, and partially open oven door; leave cheesecake in oven 30 minutes. Remove from oven. Cool 20 minutes on a wire rack; cover and chill 8 hours. Yield: 12 servings (serving size: 1 wedge).

CALORIES 308 (25% from fat); FAT 8.4g (sat 4.1g, mono 2g, poly 1g); PROTEIN 9.2g; CARB 49.9g; FIBER 0.1g; CHOL 55mg; IRON 1.1mg; SODIUM 282mg; CALC 80mg

TRIPLE-CHOCOLATE CHEESECAKE

PREP:34 MINUTES   COOK:50 MINUTES
STAND:45 MINUTES   CHILL:8 HOURS

See "Bits about Chocolate" (page 170) for more information on types of chocolate. As a bonus, garnish this cheesecake with chocolate curls made by running a vegetable peeler along a bar of unsweetened chocolate—now you've got four chocolates in this rich dessert!

Crust:
¼ cup sugar
1 tablespoon stick margarine or
    butter
1 tablespoon lightly beaten egg white
1⅓ cups chocolate graham cracker
    crumbs (about 9 cracker sheets)
Cooking spray

Filling:
3 tablespoons dark rum
3 ounces semisweet chocolate
¼ cup chocolate syrup
1 (8-ounce) block fat-free cream
    cheese, softened
1 (8-ounce) block ⅓-less-fat
    cream cheese, softened
1 cup sugar
2 tablespoons unsweetened cocoa
1 teaspoon vanilla extract
¼ teaspoon salt
2 large eggs
½ cup low-fat sour cream
1 tablespoon sugar
2 teaspoons unsweetened cocoa
Chocolate curls (optional)

1. Preheat oven to 350°.

2. To prepare crust, place first 3 ingredients in a bowl; beat at medium speed of a mixer until blended. Add crumbs; stir well. Firmly press crumb mixture into bottom and 1 inch up sides of an
(continued on page 140)

8-inch springform pan coated with cooking spray. Bake at 350° for 10 minutes; cool on a wire rack. Reduce oven temperature to 300°.

3. To prepare filling, combine rum and semisweet chocolate in top of a double boiler; cook over simmering water 2 minutes or until chocolate melts, stirring frequently. Remove from heat; add chocolate syrup, stirring until smooth.

4. Beat cheeses at medium speed until smooth. Add 1 cup sugar, 2 tablespoons cocoa, vanilla, and salt; beat until smooth. Add rum mixture; beat at low speed until well-blended. Add eggs, 1 at a time, beating well after each addition.

5. Pour cheese mixture into prepared pan; bake at 300° for 40 minutes or until almost set. Combine sour cream, 1 tablespoon sugar, and 2 teaspoons cocoa. Turn oven off, and carefully spread sour cream mixture over cheese-cake. Let cheesecake stand in closed oven 45 minutes. Remove cheesecake from oven. Run a knife around outside edge; cool. Cover and chill at least 8 hours. Garnish with chocolate curls, if desired. Yield: 12 servings (serving size: 1 wedge).

CALORIES 289 (35% from fat); FAT 11.1g (sat 5.7g, mono 3.6g, poly 0.7g); PROTEIN 7.9g; CARB 40.7g; FIBER 0.5g; CHOL 57mg; IRON 1.2mg; SODIUM 343mg; CALC 88mg

FROSTINGS

Sometimes the trickiest part of making a cake can be the frosting. Here are some recipes that will help give your cake the perfect finishing touch.

CREAM CHEESE FROSTING

PREP: 10 MINUTES

½ cup (4 ounces) block-style fat-free cream cheese, chilled
¼ cup butter or stick margarine, softened
1 teaspoon grated lemon rind
1 teaspoon vanilla extract
3½ cups powdered sugar

1. Beat first 4 ingredients at medium speed of a mixer until smooth. Gradually add sugar to butter mixture; beat at low speed just until blended (do not overbeat). Yield: 2 cups (serving size: 1 tablespoon).

CALORIES 67 (20% from fat); FAT 1.5g (sat 0.9g, mono 0.4g, poly 0.1g); PROTEIN 0.5g; CARB 13.2g; FIBER 0g; CHOL 5mg; IRON 0mg; SODIUM 36mg; CALC 11mg

CHOCOLATE CREAM CHEESE FROSTING

PREP: 8 MINUTES

½ cup (4 ounces) tub-style light cream cheese, softened
3 tablespoons fat-free milk
3 ounces semisweet chocolate, melted
3 cups sifted powdered sugar
¼ cup unsweetened cocoa
1 teaspoon vanilla extract

1. Beat cheese and milk at high speed of a mixer until smooth. Add melted chocolate, and beat until well-blended.

2. Combine sugar and cocoa; gradually add sugar mixture to cheese mixture, beating at low speed until well-blended. Add vanilla; mix well. Yield: 1¾ cups (serving size: 1 tablespoon).

Note: You don't want to make this frosting ahead of time because it will dry out.

CALORIES 78 (21% from fat); FAT 1.8g (sat 1.1g, mono 0.6g, poly 0.1g); PROTEIN 0.9g; CARB 15.3g; FIBER 0g; CHOL 2mg; IRON 0.3mg; SODIUM 24mg; CALC 10mg

---

STORING CAKES

If a cake has a cream cheese frosting, it should be stored in the refrigerator. Cover the cake with a cake dome, rather than plastic wrap which will stick to the frosting. Don't have a cake dome? A large bowl inverted over the cake works just as well.

CHOCOLATE FROSTING

PREP: 6 MINUTES

COOK: 3 MINUTES

 1 tablespoon butter or stick
    margarine
¼ cup granulated sugar
 3 tablespoons fat-free milk
 1 ounce unsweetened chocolate,
    chopped
1¾ cups powdered sugar
 1 teaspoon vanilla extract

1. Melt butter in a small, heavy saucepan over low heat. Add granulated sugar, milk, and chocolate; cook 3 minutes or until chocolate is melted. Remove from heat, and cool. Stir in powdered sugar and vanilla. Spread frosting over cupcakes. Yield: 1 cup (serving size: 1 tablespoon).

CALORIES 75 (28% from fat); FAT 2.3g (sat 0.8g, mono 0.9g, poly 0.5g); PROTEIN 0.4g; CARB 13.8g; FIBER 0g; CHOL 0mg; IRON 0.2mg; SODIUM 20mg; CALC 5mg

FLUFFY WHITE FROSTING

PREP: 5 MINUTES

COOK: 7 MINUTES

 1 cup sugar
¼ cup water
¼ teaspoon cream of tartar
Dash of salt
 3 large egg whites
 1 teaspoon vanilla extract

1. Combine first 5 ingredients in top of a double boiler. Cook egg white mixture over simmering water, and beat at high speed of a handheld mixer until stiff peaks form and a candy thermometer registers 160°. Add vanilla; beat until blended. Yield: 4 cups (serving size: 1 tablespoon).

CALORIES 13 (0% from fat); FAT 0g; PROTEIN 0.2g; CARB 3.2g; FIBER 0g; CHOL 0mg; IRON 0mg; SODIUM 5mg; CALC 0mg

FLUFFY COCONUT FROSTING

PREP: 5 MINUTES   COOK: 7 MINUTES

 1 cup sugar
¼ cup water
¼ teaspoon cream of tartar
Dash of salt
 3 large egg whites
 1 teaspoon vanilla extract
¼ teaspoon coconut extract

1. Combine first 5 ingredients in top of a double boiler; cook over simmering water. Beat at high speed of a hand-held mixer until stiff peaks form and a candy thermometer registers 160°. Add extracts; beat until well-blended. Yield: 4 cups (serving size: 1 tablespoon).

CALORIES 13 (0% from fat); FAT 0g; PROTEIN 0.2g; CARB 3.2g; FIBER 0g; CHOL 0mg; IRON 0mg; SODIUM 5mg; CALC 0mg

Fluffy White Frosting

This frosting is made by beating egg whites with sugar, water, and other ingredients in a double boiler over barely simmering water. Making sure the candy thermometer reaches 160° ensures that the egg white mixture has cooked to a safe temperature. (Candy thermometers usually have adjustable hooks or clips so they can be attached to the pan.)

1. Attach candy thermometer to side of pan, making sure the end is in the unbeaten egg white mixture but not touching the bottom of the pan.

2. Beat at high speed of a handheld mixer until stiff peaks form and the candy thermometer registers 160°.

Maple Frosting

PREP: 7 MINUTES

3 tablespoons maple syrup
2 tablespoons butter or stick
   margarine, softened
½ teaspoon vanilla extract
½ teaspoon imitation maple flavoring
⅛ teaspoon salt
1¾ cups powdered sugar

1. Beat first 5 ingredients at medium speed of a mixer 1 minute. Gradually add powdered sugar, beating just until blended (do not overbeat). Spread frosting over cupcakes. Yield: 1 cup (serving size: 1 tablespoon).

CALORIES 74 (18% from fat); FAT 1.5g (sat 0.9g, mono 0.9g, poly 0.1g); PROTEIN 0g; CARB 15.6g; FIBER 0g; CHOL 4mg; IRON 0.1mg; SODIUM 33mg; CALC 3mg

Caramel-Pecan Frosting

PREP: 8 MINUTES   COOL: 10 MINUTES
COOK: 7 MINUTES

¼ cup butter or stick margarine
½ cup packed dark brown sugar
6 tablespoons evaporated fat-free milk
2 teaspoons vanilla extract
3 cups sifted powdered sugar
¼ cup chopped pecans

1. Melt butter in a saucepan over medium heat. Add brown sugar. Cook 3 minutes; stir constantly with a whisk. Add milk, 1 tablespoon at a time; cook 3 minutes, stirring constantly. Cool. Stir in vanilla. Combine butter mixture and powdered sugar; beat at high speed of a mixer until smooth. Frost cake as directed; sprinkle with pecans. Yield: 2 cups.
Note: If frosting is too thick, add 1 tablespoon evaporated fat-free milk.

CALORIES: 130 (26% from fat); FAT 3.7g (sat 1.7g, mono 1.4g, poly 0.4g); PROTEIN 0.5g; CARB 24.2g; FIBER 0.1g; CHOL 7mg; IRON 0.2mg; SODIUM 35mg; CALC 20mg

Coconut-Pecan Frosting

PREP: 10 MINUTES   COOK: 6 MINUTES
CHILL: 15 MINUTES

2 tablespoons butter or stick
   margarine
⅓ cup finely chopped pecans
⅔ cup packed brown sugar
2 tablespoons cornstarch
¼ teaspoon salt
1 cup fat-free sweetened
   condensed milk
1 tablespoon light-colored corn syrup
2 large egg yolks
½ cup flaked sweetened coconut,
   toasted
2½ teaspoons vanilla extract
⅛ teaspoon coconut extract

1. Melt butter in a medium saucepan over medium-high heat. Add chopped pecans, and sauté until pecans are browned (about 2½ minutes). Remove from heat, and stir in sugar, cornstarch, and salt. Add milk, syrup, and egg yolks; stir well. Cook over medium-high heat 2 minutes or until thick, stirring constantly. Remove from heat, and stir in flaked coconut and extracts. Pour into a bowl; cover and chill until slightly stiff (about 15 minutes). Yield: 2 cups (serving size: 1 tablespoon).

CALORIES 77 (29% from fat); FAT 2.5g (sat 1.1g, mono 0.9g, poly 0.3g); PROTEIN 1.1g; CARB 12.4g; FIBER 0.2g; CHOL 16mg; IRON 0.2mg; SODIUM 35mg; CALC 31mg

Chocolate Glaze

PREP: 5 MINUTES   COOK: 1 MINUTE

2 cups sifted powdered sugar
6 tablespoons unsweetened cocoa
¼ cup fat-free milk
2 tablespoons stick margarine or
   butter
1 teaspoon vanilla extract

1. Combine sugar and cocoa in a medium bowl. Combine milk and margarine in a 1-cup glass measure. Microwave at HIGH 1 minute. Add milk mixture and vanilla to sugar mixture, stirring with a wire whisk until blended. Yield: 1 cup (serving size: 1 tablespoon).

CALORIES 82 (19% from fat); FAT 1.7g (sat 0.5g, mono 0.7g, poly 0.5g); PROTEIN 0.7g; CARB 16.2g; FIBER 0g; CHOL 0mg; IRON 0.4mg; SODIUM 20mg; CALC 9mg

Lemon Filling

PREP: 5 MINUTES
COOK: 5 MINUTES
CHILL: 1½ HOURS

½ cup sugar
3 tablespoons cornstarch
½ cup warm water
½ cup orange juice
2 teaspoons grated lemon rind
3 tablespoons fresh lemon juice
2 large egg yolks
½ teaspoon vanilla extract

1. Combine sugar and cornstarch in a medium saucepan. Stir in water, orange juice, rind, lemon juice, and egg yolks. Bring to a boil over medium-high heat. Cook until thick (about 2 minutes), stirring constantly. Remove from heat; stir in vanilla. Cover and chill at least 1½ hours or up to 2 days. Stir well before using. Yield: 1 cup (serving size: 1 tablespoon).

CALORIES 42 (15% from fat); FAT 0.7g (sat 0.2g, mono 0.3g, poly 0.1g); PROTEIN 0.4g; CARB 8.8g; FIBER 0g; CHOL 27mg; IRON 0.1mg; SODIUM 1mg; CALC 4mg

cookies

Pinwheels (page 153) and
Chocolate-and-Vanilla Stripes
(page 152)

drop cookies

Cookies don't get much easier than this—just mix and drop the dough onto baking sheets to bake.

These cookies are blissfully easy—they don't contain hard-to-find ingredients, require special equipment, or involve tricky techniques. And as for taste, they're absolutely fabulous.

Several of the recipes call for egg whites instead of whole eggs because the yolks don't contribute much to the taste or texture of the cookies. Others call for a small amount of corn syrup, which adds moistness. All include generous amounts of natural flavorings, such as vanilla extract, spices, citrus rind, and molasses, to provide full flavor without fat.

Not only do these recipes minimize fat, they're very specific about the type of fat to use. Some call for vegetable oil or a combination of vegetable oil and stick margarine or butter. Vegetable oil disperses better than margarine and keeps the cookies moist and tender, while stick margarine prevents the cookies from spreading too much. One key tip: Don't replace stick margarine with the diet or light kind or tub-style spread. These have too much water and too little fat to produce the best results.

ANZAC BISCUITS

Anzac Biscuits, named for the Australia-New Zealand Army Corps, have a chewy, slightly sticky texture that gives them a wonderful richness.

ANZAC BISCUITS

PREP: 20 MINUTES
COOK: 12 MINUTES PER BATCH

1   cup all-purpose flour
1   cup regular oats
1   cup packed brown sugar
½   cup shredded sweetened
      coconut
½   teaspoon baking soda
3   tablespoons water
¼   cup stick margarine or butter,
      melted
2   tablespoons golden cane syrup
      (such as Lyle's Golden Syrup) or
      light-colored corn syrup
Cooking spray

1. Preheat oven to 325°.
2. Lightly spoon flour into a dry measuring cup, and level with a knife.

Combine flour, oats, brown sugar, coconut, and baking soda in a medium bowl. Add water, margarine, and syrup, and stir well.
3. Drop by level tablespoons 3 inches apart onto baking sheets coated with cooking spray (cookies will spread). Bake at 325° for 12 minutes or until almost set. Cool on pans 2 to 3 minutes or until firm. Remove cookies from pans; cool completely on wire racks. Yield: 2 dozen (serving size: 1 cookie).
Note: We found these cookies were much better when made with golden cane syrup. Cane syrup is thicker and sweeter than corn syrup and can be found in supermarkets next to the jellies and syrups or in stores specializing in Caribbean and Creole cookery.

CALORIES 97 (27% from fat); FAT 2.9g (sat 1.1g, mono 0.9g, poly 0.7g); PROTEIN 1.1g; CARB 17.1g; FIBER 0.6g; CHOL 0mg; IRON 0.6mg; SODIUM 51mg; CALC 11mg

Anzac Biscuits

DOUBLE-CHOCOLATE CHEWS

PREP: 18 MINUTES

COOK: 8 MINUTES PER BATCH

1¾ cups all-purpose flour
⅔ cup sifted powdered sugar
⅓ cup unsweetened cocoa
2¼ teaspoons baking powder
⅛ teaspoon salt
 1 cup semisweet chocolate
   mini-morsels, divided
 3 tablespoons vegetable oil
 1 cup packed brown sugar
2½ tablespoons light-colored corn
   syrup
 1 tablespoon water
2½ teaspoons vanilla extract
 3 large egg whites, lightly
   beaten
Cooking spray

1. Preheat oven to 350°.
2. Lightly spoon flour into dry measuring cups; level with a knife. Combine flour, powdered sugar, cocoa, baking powder, and salt in a bowl.
3. Combine ¾ cup chocolate morsels and oil in a small saucepan, and cook over low heat until chocolate melts, stirring constantly. Pour melted chocolate mixture into a large bowl, and cool 5 minutes. Add brown sugar, corn syrup, water, vanilla, and egg whites to chocolate mixture; stir well. Stir in flour mixture and ¼ cup chocolate morsels.
4. Drop dough by level tablespoons 2 inches apart onto baking sheets coated with cooking spray. Bake at 350° for 8 minutes or until almost set. Cool on pans 2 minutes or until firm. Remove cookies from pans; cool on wire racks. Yield: 4 dozen (serving size: 1 cookie).

CALORIES 64 (23% from fat); FAT 1.6g (sat 0.6g, mono 0.5g, poly 0.5g); PROTEIN 0.9g; CARB 11.8g; FIBER 0.1g; CHOL 0mg; IRON 0.5mg; SODIUM 13mg; CALC 19mg

Double-Chocolate Chews and
Easy Peanut Butter Cookies
(page 158)

DATE-SUGAR COOKIES

PREP: 18 MINUTES

COOK: 8 MINUTES PER BATCH

These crunchy cornmeal cookies are shaped like little haystacks. Store cooled cookies in an airtight container to help keep them from drying out.

¾ cup sugar
¼ cup stick margarine or butter,
   softened
 1 large egg
 1 teaspoon vanilla extract
1¼ cups all-purpose flour
¼ cup yellow cornmeal
¾ teaspoon baking soda
⅓ cup finely chopped pecans, toasted
⅓ cup chopped pitted dates
Cooking spray

1. Preheat oven to 350°.
2. Beat sugar and margarine at medium speed of a mixer until well-blended (about 3 minutes). Add egg and vanilla, beating well. Lightly spoon flour into dry measuring cups; level with a knife. Combine flour, cornmeal, and baking soda. Add flour mixture to sugar mixture, stirring well. Stir in chopped pecans and dates.
3. Drop dough by level tablespoons 2 inches apart onto baking sheets coated with cooking spray. Bake at 350° for 8 minutes or until almost set; cool on pans 2 minutes. Remove from pans; cool completely on wire racks. Yield: 2½ dozen (serving size: 1 cookie).

CALORIES 71 (33% from fat); FAT 2.6g (sat 0.4g, mono 1.3g, poly 0.7g); PROTEIN 0.9g; CARB 11.1g; FIBER 0.4g; CHOL 7mg; IRON 0.3mg; SODIUM 41mg; CALC 3mg

LEMON COOKIES

PREP: 18 MINUTES   CHILL: 1 HOUR
COOK: 12 MINUTES PER BATCH

2   cups sifted cake flour
¾   cup granulated sugar
2   teaspoons baking powder
6   tablespoons chilled stick
      margarine or butter, cut into
      small pieces
2   tablespoons grated lemon rind
1   tablespoon lemon juice
1   large egg, lightly beaten
Cooking spray
2   tablespoons powdered sugar

1. Combine first 3 ingredients in a food processor; pulse 2 times. Add margarine and lemon rind; process until mixture resembles coarse meal. Add lemon juice and egg; process until dough leaves sides of bowl and forms a ball. Gently press mixture into a ball; wrap in plastic wrap. Chill 1 hour.
2. Preheat oven to 350°.
3. Drop dough by level teaspoons onto

TIPS FOR GREAT COOKIES

• **If the batter seems dry and you're tempted to add more liquid, don't.** This produces cakelike cookies that spread too much.

• **Don't forget the corn syrup**—it makes the cookies crisp, yet keeps them from drying out. Too much corn syrup, however, will make them soggy.

• **Always use stick margarine or butter** instead of the kind in a tub. Also, be careful not to use low-fat margarine or anything that's labeled "spread."

• **Let the baking sheets cool between batches** so the dough doesn't spread too much.

a baking sheet coated with cooking spray. Bake at 350° for 12 minutes. Remove cookies from pan, and roll in powdered sugar. Cool completely on wire racks. Yield: 3½ dozen (serving size: 1 cookie).

CALORIES 48 (34% from fat); FAT 1.8g (sat 0.4g, mono 0.8g, poly 0.5g); PROTEIN 0.5g; CARB 7.6g; FIBER 0.2g; CHOL 5mg; IRON 0.4mg; SODIUM 36mg; CALC 11mg

OATMEAL-RAISIN HERMITS

PREP: 25 MINUTES
COOK: 12 MINUTES PER BATCH

1½   cups all-purpose flour
¾   teaspoon baking powder
¾   teaspoon baking soda
½   teaspoon ground cinnamon
¼   teaspoon salt
⅛   teaspoon ground nutmeg
1¼   cups packed brown sugar
6   tablespoons stick margarine or
      butter, melted
2   tablespoons light-colored corn
      syrup
1   tablespoon vanilla extract
1   tablespoon water
3   large egg whites
1⅔   cups regular oats
1⅔   cups raisins
⅓   cup chopped pecans, toasted
Cooking spray

1. Preheat oven to 350°.
2. Lightly spoon flour into dry measuring cups; level with a knife. Combine flour and next 5 ingredients in a bowl. Beat brown sugar and next 5 ingredients in a large bowl at medium speed of a mixer until well-blended (about 4 minutes). Stir in oats, raisins, and pecans; let stand 5 minutes. Stir in flour mixture.
3. Drop dough by level tablespoons 2 inches apart onto baking sheets coated with cooking spray. Bake at 350° for 12

minutes or until almost set. Cool on pans 2 minutes or until firm. Remove cookies from pans; cool completely on wire racks. Yield: 51 cookies (serving size: 1 cookie).

CALORIES 78 (24% from fat); FAT 2.1g (sat 0.3g, mono 1g, poly 0.6g); PROTEIN 1.2g; CARB 14.1g; FIBER 0.6g; CHOL 0mg; IRON 0.5mg; SODIUM 51mg; CALC 13mg

Dried-out raisins will absorb moisture from the cookie dough, making the cookies dry.

GIANT OATMEAL-RAISIN COOKIES

PREP: 16 MINUTES
COOK: 14 MINUTES PER BATCH

For moist, old-fashioned cookies use fresh, soft raisins. You can substitute regular raisins for golden ones.

1   cup sugar
¼   cup stick margarine or butter,
      softened
2   large eggs
¾   cup applesauce
1   teaspoon vanilla extract
2   cups all-purpose flour
½   teaspoon baking soda
½   teaspoon pumpkin-pie spice
¼   teaspoon salt
1   cup regular oats
1   cup golden raisins
½   cup chopped pecans
Cooking spray

1. Preheat oven to 375°.
2. Beat sugar and margarine in a large bowl at medium speed of a mixer until

well-blended (about 4 minutes). Add eggs, 1 at a time, beating well after each addition. Add applesauce and vanilla; beat well.

3. Lightly spoon flour into dry measuring cups; level with a knife. Combine flour, baking soda, pumpkin-pie spice, and salt in a bowl. Add to sugar mixture; beat well. Stir in oats, raisins, and pecans.

4. Drop dough into 24 mounds 2 inches apart onto baking sheets coated with cooking spray. Bake at 375° for 14 minutes or until almost set. Remove cookies from pans; cool on wire racks. Yield: 2 dozen (serving size: 1 cookie).

CALORIES 148 (27% from fat); FAT 4.4g (sat 0.7g, mono 2.1g, poly 1.2g); PROTEIN 2.6g; CARB 25.4g; FIBER 1.3g; CHOL 18mg; IRON 0.9mg; SODIUM 80mg; CALC 11mg

POWER CRUNCH COOKIES

PREP: 18 MINUTES
COOK: 7 MINUTES PER BATCH

Whether it's after work, after school, or after exercise, these cookies will help revive your energy!

⅓ cup stick margarine or butter, softened
½ cup packed brown sugar
1 tablespoon water
¾ teaspoon vanilla extract
1 large egg
½ cup all-purpose flour
¼ cup whole-wheat flour
½ teaspoon baking soda
¼ teaspoon salt
1 cup quick-cooking oats
¾ cup wheat bran flakes cereal, lightly crushed
½ cup mixed dried fruit bits
3 tablespoons unsalted sunflower seed kernels, toasted
Cooking spray

1. Preheat oven to 375°.

2. Beat margarine at medium speed of a mixer until light and fluffy; gradually add sugar, beating well. Add water, vanilla, and egg; beat well.

3. Lightly spoon flours into dry measuring cups; level with a knife. Combine flours, baking soda, and salt; add to sugar mixture, beating well. Add oats, cereal, fruit bits, and sunflower seed kernels; stir well.

4. Drop dough by level tablespoons 2 inches apart onto baking sheets coated with cooking spray. Bake at 375° for 7 minutes or until almost set. Remove from pans; cool completely on wire racks. Yield: 28 cookies (serving size: 1 cookie).

CALORIES 78 (36% from fat); FAT 3.1g (sat 0.6g, mono 1.2g, poly 1.1g); PROTEIN 1.4g; CARB 11.5g; FIBER 0.8g; CHOL 8mg; IRON 0.6mg; SODIUM 73mg; CALC 10mg

VANILLA WAFERS

PREP: 18 MINUTES
COOK: 14 MINUTES PER BATCH

Choose a vanilla bean that is pliable rather than brittle. To keep vanilla beans fresh, store them in the freezer—pop one into the microwave for 15 seconds to thaw.

Cooking spray
1 tablespoon all-purpose flour
½ cup sugar
¼ cup cornstarch
2 tablespoons stick margarine or butter, melted
1 large egg
1 (6-inch) piece vanilla bean, split lengthwise
¾ cup all-purpose flour
½ teaspoon baking powder
⅛ teaspoon salt

1. Preheat oven to 350°.

2. Coat 2 large baking sheets with cooking spray; dust with 1 tablespoon flour; set aside.

3. Combine sugar, cornstarch, margarine, and egg in a large bowl; stir well with a whisk. Scrape seeds from vanilla bean; add seeds to sugar mixture, reserving bean for another use. Lightly spoon ¾ cup flour into dry measuring cups, and level with a knife. Combine ¾ cup flour, baking powder, and salt; stir well with a whisk. Add flour mixture to sugar mixture; stir well.

4. Drop dough by rounded teaspoons 2 inches apart onto baking sheets. Bake at 350° for 14 minutes. Remove cookies from pan; cool on wire racks. Yield: 3 dozen (serving size: 1 cookie).

CALORIES 32 (22% from fat); FAT 0.8g (sat 0.2g, mono 0.3g, poly 0.2g); PROTEIN 0.5g; CARB 5.6g; FIBER 0.1g; CHOL 6mg; IRON 0.2mg; SODIUM 22mg; CALC 4mg

BEST BETS FOR BAKING SHEETS

Have you walked into a department store for a baking sheet only to be confused by all of the choices? Here are our opinions on baking sheets.

• **Select light-colored sheets** with no sides (or low sides). If the sheets are dark, they will absorb too much heat and cause the cookies to overbrown.

• **Shiny or Dull?** It depends on what you're baking. **A dull finish helps the cookies to brown evenly,** but for cookies such as sugar cookies where **you don't want the final product to "brown,"** use a shiny sheet.

• **Insulated or not? Insulated sheets are fine for soft cookies,** but if you want the cookie to be crisp, **a non-insulated sheet may produce crispier results.**

bars & squares

Whether you prefer rich, gooey brownies; moist, cakelike bars; or tart lemon squares, you'll find our recipes easy to make.

FUDGY CHOCOLATE BROWNIES

PREP: 19 MINUTES
COOK: 27 MINUTES

    5   tablespoons stick margarine or
        butter
    1   ounce unsweetened chocolate
    ⅔   cup Dutch process or unsweetened
        cocoa
  1½   cups sugar
    3   large egg whites, lightly
        beaten
    1   large egg, lightly beaten
    1   cup all-purpose flour
    ½   teaspoon baking powder
        Cooking spray

1. Preheat oven to 325°.
2. Melt margarine and unsweetened chocolate in a large saucepan over medium heat. Stir in cocoa; cook 1 minute. Stir in sugar, and cook 1 minute. Remove pan from heat, and cool chocolate mixture slightly. Combine beaten egg whites and egg. Gradually add warm chocolate mixture to egg mixture, stirring with a whisk until well-blended.
3. Lightly spoon flour into a dry measuring cup, and level with a knife. Combine flour and baking powder; add flour mixture to chocolate mixture, stirring well.
4. Spoon batter into a 9-inch square baking pan coated with cooking spray. Bake at 325° for 27 minutes (do not overbake). Cool in pan on a wire rack. Yield: 20 servings (serving size: 1 brownie).

CALORIES 131 (30% from fat); FAT 4.3g (sat 1.3g, mono 1.7g, poly 1g); PROTEIN 2.5g; CARB 21.3g; FIBER 0.2g; CHOL 11mg; IRON 0.9mg; SODIUM 54mg; CALC 14mg

BITS ON BARS

• **Cool completely in the pan** before cutting into bars. This will help ensure that you get a nice "clean" cut.

• **Set a timer** for the least amount of bake time given in the recipe. Check at this point to prevent overbaking. Overbaked bar cookies are dry and crumbly.

• **Store bar cookies in the pan** in which they were baked. Seal the pan tightly with plastic wrap to keep cookies fresh.

KAHLÚA-CINNAMON BROWNIES

PREP: 14 MINUTES   COOK: 25 MINUTES

    ¼   cup semisweet chocolate chips
    ¼   cup stick margarine or butter
    ¼   cup Kahlúa (coffee-flavored
        liqueur)
    2   teaspoons vanilla extract
    ¾   cup all-purpose flour
    ¾   teaspoon baking powder
    ¼   cup unsweetened cocoa
    1   teaspoon ground cinnamon
    ¼   teaspoon salt
    ½   cup plus 2 tablespoons packed
        brown sugar
    1   large egg
        Cooking spray
    1   teaspoon granulated sugar

1. Preheat oven to 350°.
2. Combine chocolate chips and margarine in a small saucepan; place over medium-low heat, and cook until chocolate melts. Remove from heat; stir in Kahlúa and vanilla.

3. Lightly spoon ¾ cup flour into dry measuring cups; level with a knife. Combine flour and next 4 ingredients in a medium bowl.
4. Beat brown sugar and egg in a large bowl at low speed of a mixer until blended. Add chocolate mixture; mix well. Add flour mixture, beating until smooth. Pour batter into an 8-inch square baking pan coated with cooking spray. Bake at 350° for 25 minutes or until a wooden pick inserted in center comes out clean. Remove from oven; sprinkle with granulated sugar. Cool in pan on a wire rack. Yield: 16 servings (serving size: 1 brownie).

CALORIES 108 (34% from fat); FAT 4.1g (sat 1.2g, mono 1.7g, poly 1g); PROTEIN 1.5g; CARB 16.5g; FIBER 0.2g; CHOL 13mg; IRON 0.8mg; SODIUM 93mg; CALC 24mg

EASY CHOCOLATE-CARAMEL BROWNIES

PREP: 37 MINUTES   COOK: 39 MINUTES

    ½   cup fat-free sweetened
        condensed milk (not
        evaporated fat-free milk)
    1   (18.25-ounce) package devil's
        food cake mix with pudding
        (such as Pillsbury)
    7   tablespoons reduced-calorie
        stick margarine, melted
    1   large egg white, lightly beaten
        Cooking spray
    2   tablespoons fat-free milk
   27   small soft caramel candies
        (about 8 ounces)
    ½   cup reduced-fat chocolate
        baking chips

1. Preheat oven to 350°.
2. Combine first 4 ingredients in a

Easy Chocolate-Caramel Brownies

bowl; stir well. (Batter will be very stiff.) Coat bottom of a 13 x 9-inch baking pan with cooking spray; lightly dust with flour. Press two-thirds of batter into prepared pan using floured hands; pat evenly. Bake at 350° for 9 minutes.

3. Combine milk and candies in a microwave-safe bowl. Microwave at HIGH 1½ minutes or until mixture is smooth; stir with a whisk after 1 minute.

4. Remove brownies from oven; sprinkle with chips. Drizzle hot caramel mixture over chips; drop remaining batter by spoonfuls over caramel mixture. Bake at 350° for 30 minutes. Cool completely in pan on a wire rack. Yield: 3 dozen (serving size: 1 brownie).

CALORIES 141 (25% from fat); FAT 4g (sat 1.6g, mono 0.3g, poly 0g); PROTEIN 2g; CARB 24.4g; FIBER 0.3g; CHOL 0mg; IRON 0.4mg; SODIUM 160mg; CALC 16mg

CHEWY FIG BARS

PREP: 10 MINUTES   COOK: 25 MINUTES

⅔ cup all-purpose flour
⅔ cup sugar
¼ cup chopped pecans
1 teaspoon ground cinnamon
½ teaspoon baking powder
Dash of salt
1 (8-ounce) package dried Calimyrna figs, finely chopped
2 large eggs, lightly beaten
Cooking spray

1. Preheat oven to 350°.

2. Lightly spoon flour into dry measuring cups; level with a knife. Combine flour and next 6 ingredients in a bowl. Add eggs; stir until blended. (Batter will be very thick.) Spread into a 9-inch

square baking pan coated with cooking spray. Coat hands lightly with cooking spray; press batter into pan with hands. Bake at 350° for 25 minutes or until a wooden pick inserted in center comes out clean. Cool in pan 10 minutes on a wire rack; cut into bars. Yield: 2 dozen (serving size: 1 bar).

CALORIES 74 (18% from fat); FAT 1.5g (sat 0.2g, mono 0.7g, poly 0.3g); PROTEIN 1.3g; CARB 14.9g; FIBER 1.4g; CHOL 18mg; IRON 0.5mg; SODIUM 19mg; CALC 22mg

MAPLE BARS

PREP: 12 MINUTES   COOK: 35 MINUTES

½ cup vegetable shortening
¾ cup sugar
1 cup maple syrup
1 teaspoon vanilla extract
2 large eggs
1 cup all-purpose flour
2 cups regular oats
¼ cup flaked sweetened coconut
1 teaspoon baking powder
½ teaspoon salt
Cooking spray

1. Preheat oven to 350°.

2. Beat shortening and sugar at medium speed of a mixer until light and fluffy (about 3 minutes). Add syrup, vanilla, and eggs, beating well.

3. Lightly spoon flour into a dry measuring cup; level with a knife. Combine flour, oats, coconut, baking powder, and salt. Add flour mixture to sugar mixture; stir just until blended.

4. Pour batter into a 13 x 9-inch baking pan coated with cooking spray. Bake at 350° for 35 minutes or until a wooden pick inserted in center comes out clean. Cool in pan on a wire rack. Yield: 2 dozen (serving size: 1 bar).

CALORIES 145 (30% from fat); FAT 4.9g (sat 1.3g, mono 2.1g, poly 1.2g); PROTEIN 2.1g; CARB 23.8g; FIBER 0.9g; CHOL 18mg; IRON 0.8mg; SODIUM 72mg; CALC 23mg

CRUNCHY OAT-APRICOT BARS

PREP: 7 MINUTES   COOK: 35 MINUTES

Try other fruit preserves in these bars. If you don't have a food processor, margarine can be cut into flour mixture with a pastry blender or 2 knives.

1¾ cups all-purpose flour
2 cups regular oats
1 cup packed brown sugar
⅔ cup reduced-calorie stick margarine
1½ teaspoons vanilla extract
   Cooking spray
1½ cups apricot preserves

1. Preheat oven to 350°.

2. Lightly spoon flour into dry measuring cups; level with a knife. Place flour, oats, brown sugar, margarine, and vanilla in a food processor, and pulse 10 times or until oat mixture resembles coarse meal.

3. Press half of oat mixture into bottom of a 13 x 9-inch baking pan coated with cooking spray. Spread apricot preserves over oat mixture. Sprinkle remaining oat mixture over apricot preserves, and gently press.

4. Bake at 350° for 35 minutes or until bubbly and golden brown. Cool completely in pan on a wire rack. Yield: 3 dozen (serving size: 1 bar).

CALORIES 112 (20% from fat); FAT 2.5g (sat 0.5g, mono 1g, poly 0.2g); PROTEIN 1.3g; CARB 21.9g; FIBER 0.6g; CHOL 0mg; IRON 0.6mg; SODIUM 42mg; CALC 8mg

Crunchy Oat-Apricot Bars

LEMON SQUARES

PREP: 23 MINUTES   COOK: 40 MINUTES

Crust:
¼ cup granulated sugar
3 tablespoons butter or stick margarine, softened
1 cup all-purpose flour

Topping:
3 large eggs
¾ cup granulated sugar
2 teaspoons grated lemon rind
⅓ cup fresh lemon juice
3 tablespoons all-purpose flour
½ teaspoon baking powder
⅛ teaspoon salt
2 teaspoons powdered sugar

1. Preheat oven to 350°.

2. To prepare crust, beat ¼ cup sugar and butter at medium speed of a mixer until light and fluffy. Lightly spoon 1 cup flour into a dry measuring cup, and level with a knife. Gradually add 1 cup flour to sugar mixture, beating at low speed until mixture resembles fine crumbs. Gently press mixture into bottom of an 8-inch square baking pan. Bake at 350° for 15 minutes; cool on a wire rack.

3. To prepare topping, beat eggs at medium speed until foamy. Add ¾ cup sugar and next 5 ingredients; beat until well-blended. Pour egg mixture over partially baked crust. Bake at 350° for 25 minutes or until set. Cool on a wire rack. Sift powdered sugar evenly over top. Yield: 16 servings (serving size: 1 square).

CALORIES 118 (24% from fat); FAT 3.2g (sat 1.7g, mono 1g, poly 0.3g); PROTEIN 2.2g; CARB 20.5g; FIBER 0.3g; CHOL 47mg; IRON 0.6mg; SODIUM 68mg; CALC 16mg

refrigerator cookies

What's great about refrigerator cookies? You make the dough ahead! Then slice and bake whenever you crave fresh, warm cookies.

With these slice-and-bake logs of cookie dough, you can have delicious homemade cookies in no time. Plus, you can make the dough ahead and store it in the refrigerator for up to a week or freeze it for up to 1 month. The logs of dough are similar to the commercial brands sold on supermarket shelves, but our versions are much tastier and far better for you. You probably have the necessary ingredients on hand and can mix them up, form the log, and keep the dough handy in your refrigerator or freezer. At a moment's notice, you can have warm, wholesome cookies in minutes!

BASIC ICEBOX SUGAR COOKIES

PREP:15 MINUTES   FREEZE:3 HOURS
COOK:10 MINUTES PER BATCH

1   cup all-purpose flour
¼   teaspoon baking soda
⅛   teaspoon salt
¼   cup stick margarine or butter, softened
⅔   cup sugar
1   teaspoon vanilla extract
1   large egg white
Cooking spray

1. Lightly spoon flour into a dry measuring cup; level with a knife. Combine flour, baking soda, and salt in a bowl. Beat margarine at medium speed of a mixer until light and fluffy. Gradually add sugar, beating at medium speed of a mixer until well-blended. Add vanilla and egg white, and beat well. Add flour mixture, and stir until well-blended. Turn dough out onto wax paper, and shape into a 6-inch log. Wrap log in wax paper, and freeze for 3 hours or until very firm.

2. Preheat oven to 350°.

3. Cut log into 24 (¼-inch) slices, and place 1 inch apart on a baking sheet coated with cooking spray. Bake at 350° for 8 to 10 minutes. Remove from pan, and cool on wire racks. Yield: 2 dozen (serving size: 1 cookie).

CALORIES 59 (31% from fat); FAT 2g (sat 0.4g, mono 0.8g, poly 0.6g); PROTEIN 0.7g; CARB 9.6g; FIBER 0.1g; CHOL 0mg; IRON 0.2mg; SODIUM 50mg; CALC 2mg

Basic Icebox Sugar Cookies

1. Turn the cookie dough out onto a sheet of wax paper. Working quickly, shape the dough into a 6-inch log.

2. Wrap the dough log in wax paper, and form a compact roll; twist ends of wax paper securely. Freeze the log for 3 hours or until very firm.

3. Immediately after taking the cookie dough from the freezer, unwrap the dough, and cut into ¼-inch slices with dental floss or a very sharp knife.

making chocolate-and-vanilla stripes
First, prepare the doughs for Chocolate Icebox Cookies and Basic Icebox Sugar Cookies (page 151). The striped cookie and the pinwheel variation (at lower right) each make about 4 dozen cookies.

1. Cut each log lengthwise into 4 pieces.

2. Make 2 stacks of dough, alternating chocolate and sugar-cookie dough. Wrap each stack in wax paper, and freeze 3 hours or until firm. Repeat procedure with the remaining chocolate and sugar-cookie dough pieces.

3. Cut the logs into ¼-inch slices with a piece of dental floss or a sharp knife. Place the slices on a baking sheet, and bake at 350° for 10 minutes.

PEANUT BUTTER ICEBOX COOKIES

PREP: 16 MINUTES   FREEZE: 3 HOURS
COOK: 10 MINUTES PER BATCH

1 cup all-purpose flour
¼ teaspoon baking soda
⅛ teaspoon salt
3 tablespoons stick margarine or butter, softened
2 tablespoons chunky peanut butter
½ cup packed brown sugar
¼ cup granulated sugar
1 teaspoon vanilla extract
1 large egg white
Cooking spray

1. Lightly spoon flour into a dry measuring cup; level with a knife. Combine flour, baking soda, and salt in a bowl. Beat margarine and peanut butter at medium speed of a mixer until light and fluffy. Gradually add sugars, beating until well-blended. Add vanilla and egg white; beat well. Add flour mixture; stir well. Turn out onto wax paper; shape into a 6-inch log. Wrap log in wax paper; freeze 3 hours.

2. Preheat oven to 350°.

3. Cut log into 24 (¼-inch) slices, and place 1 inch apart on a baking sheet coated with cooking spray. Bake at 350° for 8 to 10 minutes. Remove from pan, and cool on wire racks. Yield: 2 dozen (serving size: 1 cookie).

CALORIES 69 (31% from fat); FAT 2.4g (sat 0.4g, mono 0.7g, poly 0.5g); PROTEIN 1.2g; CARB 10.8g; FIBER 0.2g; CHOL 9mg; IRON 0.4mg; SODIUM 53mg; CALC 7mg

CHOCOLATE-PEANUT BUTTER ICEBOX COOKIES:

Add 1 ounce of grated semisweet chocolate to flour mixture. Prepare and bake as directed. Yield: 2 dozen (serving size: 1 cookie).

CALORIES 71 (33% from fat); FAT 2.6g (sat 0.6g, mono 1.1g, poly 0.7g); PROTEIN 1.1g; CARB 11.2g; FIBER 0.2g; CHOL 0mg; IRON 0.4mg; SODIUM 48mg; CALC 6mg

Too much flour will make these cookies dry and crumbly. To measure flour correctly, lightly stir the flour, then spoon it into a dry measuring cup, leveling it off with the flat edge of a knife.

CHOCOLATE ICEBOX COOKIES

PREP: 16 MINUTES
FREEZE: 3 HOURS
COOK: 10 MINUTES PER BATCH

Rolling the dough in turbinado sugar gives the cookies a sugary edge. Turbinado sugar is a coarse, blond-colored sugar with a delicate molasses flavor; look for it in your grocery's baking section. This chocolate dough can be used to form both the pinwheels (below) or striped cookies (at left).

¾ cup all-purpose flour
¼ cup unsweetened cocoa
¼ teaspoon baking soda
⅛ teaspoon salt
¼ cup stick margarine or butter, softened
⅔ cup granulated sugar
1 teaspoon vanilla extract
1 large egg white
2 tablespoons turbinado sugar
Cooking spray

Each time you slice off a cookie from the log, roll log one-quarter turn to prevent flattening on one side. If the dough is too soft to shape into designs (such as pinwheels), simply chill until slightly firm.

1. Lightly spoon flour into dry measuring cups; level with a knife. Combine flour, cocoa, baking soda, and salt in a bowl. Beat margarine at medium speed of a mixer until light and fluffy. Gradually add granulated sugar, beating at medium speed until well-blended. Add vanilla and egg white, and beat well. Add flour mixture; stir until well-blended. Turn dough out onto wax paper; shape into a 6-inch log. Wrap log in wax paper; freeze 3 hours or until very firm.
2. Preheat oven to 350°.
3. Roll log in turbinado sugar. Cut log into 24 (¼-inch) slices; place 1 inch apart on a baking sheet coated with cooking spray. Bake at 350° for 8 to 10 minutes. Remove cookies from pan; cool on wire racks. Yield: 2 dozen (serving size: 1 cookie).

CALORIES 61 (31% from fat); FAT 2.1g (sat 0.5g, mono 0.8g, poly 0.6g); PROTEIN 0.8g; CARB 9.8g; FIBER 0.1g; CHOL 0mg; IRON 0.4mg; SODIUM 51mg; CALC 3mg

CHOCOLATE-PEPPERMINT ICEBOX COOKIES:

Substitute 1 teaspoon of peppermint extract for vanilla extract. Prepare and bake as directed. Yield: 2 dozen (serving size: 1 cookie).

CALORIES 62 (30% from fat); FAT 2.1g (sat 0.5g, mono 0.9g, poly 0.6g); PROTEIN 0.8g; CARB 9.8g; FIBER 0.1g; CHOL 0mg; IRON 0.3mg; SODIUM 46mg; CALC 3mg

shaping pinwheels Prepare the doughs for Chocolate Icebox Cookies and Peanut Butter Icebox Cookies.

1. Roll each dough portion between 2 sheets of wax paper to form a 12-inch square (the dough is easier to roll at room temperature). Freeze for 15 minutes.

2. Remove the wax paper, and stack dough portions one on top of the other. Roll together into a log, and wrap in wax paper. Freeze for 3 hours or until firm.

3. Cut the dough log into ¼-inch slices with a piece of dental floss or a sharp knife. Place the slices on a baking sheet, and bake at 350° for 10 minutes.

Logs of dough may be frozen up to 1 month. Slice dough while frozen, and bake as directed.

LEMON-CORNMEAL ICEBOX COOKIES

PREP: 16 MINUTES
FREEZE: 3 HOURS
COOK: 10 MINUTES PER BATCH

¾ cup all-purpose flour
¼ cup yellow cornmeal
¼ teaspoon baking soda
⅛ teaspoon salt
¼ cup stick margarine or butter, softened
¾ cup sugar
2 teaspoons grated lemon rind
1 teaspoon vanilla extract
1 large egg white
Cooking spray

1. Lightly spoon flour into dry measuring cups; level with knife. Combine flour, cornmeal, baking soda, and salt in a bowl. Beat margarine at medium speed of a mixer until light and fluffy. Add sugar; beat until well-blended. Add lemon rind, vanilla, and egg white; beat well. Add flour mixture, and stir until well-blended. Turn dough out onto wax paper; shape into a 6-inch log. Wrap in wax paper; freeze 3 hours.
2. Preheat oven to 350°.
3. Cut log into 24 (¼-inch) slices, and place 1 inch apart on a baking sheet coated with cooking spray. Bake at 350° for 8 to 10 minutes. Remove from pan, and cool on wire racks. Yield: 2 dozen (serving size: 1 cookie).

CALORIES 62 (29% from fat); FAT 2g (sat 0.4g, mono 0.9g, poly 0.6g); PROTEIN 0.7g; CARB 10.4g; FIBER 0.2g; CHOL 0mg; IRON 0.2mg; SODIUM 50mg; CALC 2mg

BROWN SUGAR ICEBOX COOKIES

PREP: 15 MINUTES
FREEZE: 3 HOURS
COOK: 10 MINUTES PER BATCH

1 cup all-purpose flour
¼ teaspoon baking soda
⅛ teaspoon salt
¼ cup stick margarine or butter, softened
⅔ cup packed brown sugar
1 teaspoon vanilla extract
1 large egg white
Cooking spray

1. Lightly spoon flour into a dry measuring cup; level with a knife. Combine flour, baking soda, and salt. Beat margarine at medium speed of a mixer until light and fluffy. Gradually add sugar, beating at medium speed until well-blended. Add vanilla and egg white, and beat well. Add flour mixture, and stir until well-blended. Turn dough out onto wax paper; shape into a 6-inch log. Wrap log in wax paper; freeze 3 hours or until very firm.
2. Preheat oven to 350°.
3. Cut log into 24 (¼-inch) slices, and place 1 inch apart on a baking sheet coated with cooking spray. Bake at 350° for 8 to 10 minutes. Remove from pan; cool on wire racks. Yield: 2 dozen (serving size: 1 cookie).

CALORIES 60 (30% from fat); FAT 2g (sat 0.4g, mono 0.8g, poly 0.6g); PROTEIN 0.7g; CARB 10g; FIBER 0.1g; CHOL 0mg; IRON 0.4mg; SODIUM 52mg; CALC 7mg

BROWN SUGAR-SPICE ICEBOX COOKIES:

Add ½ teaspoon ground cinnamon and ⅛ teaspoon ground cloves to flour mixture. Prepare and bake as directed. Yield: 2 dozen (serving size: 1 cookie).

CALORIES 59 (31% from fat); FAT 2g (sat 0.4g, mono 0.8g, poly 0.6g); PROTEIN 0.7g; CARB 9.7g; FIBER 0.1g; CHOL 0mg; IRON 0.4mg; SODIUM 48mg; CALC 7mg

FRECKLED CHOCOLATE ICEBOX COOKIES:

Add 1 ounce of grated semisweet chocolate to flour mixture. Prepare and bake as directed. Yield: 2 dozen (serving size: 1 cookie).

CALORIES 65 (33% from fat); FAT 2.4g (sat 0.6g, mono 1g, poly 0.6g); PROTEIN 0.7g; CARB 10.4g; FIBER 0.1g; CHOL 0mg; IRON 0.4mg; SODIUM 48mg; CALC 7mg

ESPRESSO MOCHA ICEBOX COOKIES:

Add 2 teaspoons instant espresso granules or 4 teaspoons instant coffee granules to flour mixture. Prepare and bake as directed. Yield: 2 dozen (serving size: 1 cookie).

CALORIES 60 (30% from fat); FAT 2g (sat 0.4g, mono 0.8g, poly 0.6g); PROTEIN 0.7g; CARB 9.7g; FIBER 0.1g; CHOL 0mg; IRON 0.3mg; SODIUM 48mg; CALC 7mg

rolled cookies

There's no limit to the versatility and fun of rolled cookies! With an assortment of cookie cutter shapes, you'll have festive cookies year-round.

Dough for rolled cookies must be firm enough to roll without sticking to the work surface or to the rolling pin. Don't try to rush the chilling process. Chilling the dough makes it easy to handle and helps prevent the cookies from spreading too thin when baked.

BISCOCHITOS

PREP: 26 MINUTES
FREEZE: 1 HOUR
COOK: 10 MINUTES PER BATCH

These Mexican sugar cookies are traditionally enjoyed after church service on Christmas Eve. The aniseed imparts a mild licorice flavor.

    ¾ cup sugar
    5 tablespoons butter or stick
       margarine, softened
    1 large egg
    1 teaspoon vanilla extract
    2 cups sifted cake flour
    2 teaspoons aniseed
    1 teaspoon baking powder
    ⅛ teaspoon salt
    2 teaspoons sugar
    ½ teaspoon ground cinnamon

1. Beat ¾ cup sugar and butter in a large bowl at medium speed of a mixer until well-blended (about 2 minutes). Add egg and vanilla; beat well. Combine flour, aniseed, baking powder, and salt. Add flour mixture to sugar mixture, and beat at low speed until well-blended. Divide dough in half. Shape each half into a ball; wrap in plastic wrap. Freeze 1 hour.
2. Preheat oven to 350°.
3. Working with one half of dough at a time (keep remaining half chilled until ready to use), roll dough to ⅛-inch thickness on a heavily floured surface; cut with a 2-inch round cutter. Place cookies 1 inch apart on baking sheets. Combine 2 teaspoons sugar and cinnamon; sprinkle on top of cookies. Bake at 350° for 8 to 10 minutes or until lightly browned. Remove from pans; cool on wire racks. Yield: 4 dozen (serving size: 1 cookie).

CALORIES 41 (31% from fat); FAT 1.4g (sat 0.8g, mono 0.4g, poly 0.1g); PROTEIN 0.5g; CARB 6.7g; FIBER 0.2g; CHOL 8mg; IRON 0.4mg; SODIUM 26mg; CALC 6mg

LEMON-FROSTED SUGAR COOKIES

PREP: 30 MINUTES
CHILL: 4 HOURS
COOK: 8 MINUTES PER BATCH

You may want to start this recipe early in the day because the dough requires about 4 hours to chill.

Cookies:

    1 cup granulated sugar
    ½ cup stick margarine or butter,
       softened
    1 large egg
    1 large egg white
    1 tablespoon fat-free milk
    1 teaspoon grated lemon rind
    1 teaspoon vanilla extract
    2 cups all-purpose flour
    ¼ cup toasted wheat germ
    1 teaspoon baking powder
    ½ teaspoon baking soda
    ⅛ teaspoon salt

Frosting:

    2 cups sifted powdered sugar
    1 tablespoon fat-free milk
    1 tablespoon fresh lemon juice
    ¼ teaspoon vanilla extract
       Food coloring (optional)
       Assorted sugar sprinkles (optional)

1. To prepare cookies, beat granulated sugar and margarine in a large bowl at medium speed of a mixer until well-blended (about 4 minutes). Add egg, egg white, 1 tablespoon milk, lemon rind, and 1 teaspoon vanilla, beating well. Lightly spoon flour into dry measuring cups; level with a knife. Combine flour, wheat germ, baking powder, baking soda, and salt in a bowl. Add flour mixture to sugar mixture, stirring well. Spoon dough onto plastic wrap; flatten to 1½-inch thickness. Cover tightly with plastic wrap; chill 4 hours or overnight.
2. Preheat oven to 400°.
3. Roll dough to a 15 x 12-inch rectangle on a heavily floured surface. Cut dough into 20 (3-inch) squares using a sharp knife. Place cookies 2 inches apart on ungreased baking sheets. Bake at 400° for 8 minutes or until golden. Immediately remove cookies from pans using a wide spatula; cool on wire racks.
4. To prepare frosting, combine first 4 ingredients. Stir in food coloring, if desired. Spread about 2 teaspoons frosting over each cookie or place frosting in a small zip-top plastic bag. Snip a tiny hole in 1 corner, and drizzle over cookies. Sprinkle with assorted sugar sprinkles, if desired. Yield: 20 cookies (serving size: 1 cookie).

CALORIES 188 (24% from fat); FAT 5.1g (sat 1g, mono 2.1g, poly 1.6g); PROTEIN 2.2g; CARB 33.8g; FIBER 0.6g; CHOL 11mg; IRON 0.8mg; SODIUM 131mg; CALC 21mg

GINGERBREAD PEOPLE COOKIES

PREP: 40 MINUTES   CHILL: 1 HOUR
COOK: 8 MINUTES PER BATCH

2¼   cups all-purpose flour
1½   teaspoons ground ginger
1   teaspoon ground cinnamon
½   teaspoon baking powder
¼   teaspoon baking soda
¼   teaspoon salt
¼   teaspoon ground nutmeg
¼   teaspoon ground cloves
6   tablespoons granulated sugar
¼   cup butter or stick margarine, softened
½   cup molasses
1   large egg white
Cooking spray
2   tablespoons dried currants
1¼   cups sifted powdered sugar
2   tablespoons lemon juice
¼   teaspoon vanilla extract

1. Lightly spoon flour into dry measuring cups; level with a knife. Combine flour and next 7 ingredients in a bowl. Beat granulated sugar and butter in a large bowl at medium speed of a mixer 5 minutes. Add molasses and egg white; beat well. Add flour mixture to sugar mixture; beat at low speed until well-blended. Divide dough in half; shape each half into a ball, and wrap in plastic wrap. Chill 1 hour.

Gingerbread People Cookies

2. Preheat oven to 350°.

3. Working with one half of dough at a time (keep remaining half chilled until ready to use), roll dough to a ⅛-inch thickness on a heavily floured surface; cut with a 2½-inch boy or girl cookie cutter. Place gingerbread cookies 1 inch apart on baking sheets coated with cooking spray. Arrange currants on cookies as buttons and eyes. Bake at 350° for 8 minutes. Remove from pans; cool on wire racks.

4. Combine powdered sugar, lemon juice, and vanilla in a bowl. Spoon into a decorating bag or a heavy-duty zip-top plastic bag with a tiny hole snipped in 1 corner of bag; decorate cookies as desired. Yield: 4 dozen (serving size: 1 cookie).

CALORIES 59 (15% from fat); FAT 1g (sat 0.2g, mono 0.4g, poly 0.3g); PROTEIN 0.7g; CARB 11.9g; FIBER 0.2g; CHOL 0mg; IRON 0.5mg; SODIUM 38mg; CALC 13mg

Piping Icing

For easy clean up, spoon icing into a heavy-duty zip-top plastic bag. Seal bag, and snip a tiny hole in 1 corner.

shaped cookies

Shaping dough into balls is the foundation for these cookies. For uniform baking, roll balls the same size.

ALMOND SUGAR COOKIES

PREP: 20 MINUTES
COOK: 18 MINUTES PER BATCH

3 tablespoons sugar
⅛ teaspoon ground cinnamon
1 cup sugar
7 tablespoons stick margarine, softened
¼ cup fat-free milk
½ teaspoon almond extract
½ teaspoon vanilla extract
1 large egg white
2½ cups all-purpose flour
¼ cup ground almonds
⅛ teaspoon salt
Cooking spray

1. Preheat oven to 325°.
2. Combine 3 tablespoons sugar and cinnamon in a bowl. Set aside.
3. Beat 1 cup sugar and margarine at medium speed of a mixer until light and fluffy. Add milk, extracts, and egg white; beat well. Lightly spoon flour into dry measuring cups; level with a knife. Combine flour, almonds, and salt; add to sugar mixture, beating well.
4. Divide dough in half; cover and chill half of dough. Shape remaining half of dough into 30 (1-inch) balls; roll balls in sugar mixture, coating well. Place balls 2 inches apart on baking sheets coated with cooking spray. Flatten cookies with the bottom of a glass. Bake at 325° for 18 minutes. Remove from pans; cool completely on wire racks. Repeat procedure with remaining dough and cinnamon mixture. Yield: 5 dozen (serving size: 1 cookie).

CALORIES 49 (31% from fat); FAT 1.7g (sat 0.3g, mono 0.7g, poly 0.5g); PROTEIN 0.7g; CARB 7.8g; FIBER 0.2g; CHOL 0mg; IRON 0.3mg; SODIUM 22mg; CALC 4mg

GINGERSNAPS

PREP: 20 MINUTES   CHILL: 1 HOUR
COOK: 12 MINUTES PER BATCH

2½ cups all-purpose flour, divided
1 tablespoon ground ginger
2 teaspoons baking soda
1 teaspoon ground cinnamon
¼ teaspoon black pepper
⅛ teaspoon salt
½ cup stick margarine or butter, softened
½ cup granulated sugar
½ cup packed dark brown sugar
¼ cup molasses
1 large egg
1 large egg white
¼ cup granulated sugar
Cooking spray

1. Lightly spoon flour into dry measuring cups; level with a knife. Combine 2 cups flour and next 5 ingredients. Beat margarine and sugars at medium speed of a mixer until light and fluffy. Add molasses; beat 2 minutes. Add egg and egg white; beat until fluffy. Stir in flour mixture until well-blended. Shape dough into a ball with floured hands; add enough of remaining flour, 1 tablespoon at a time, to prevent dough from sticking. Wrap in plastic wrap; chill 1 hour.
2. Preheat oven to 375°.
3. Shape dough into 30 balls with floured hands. Roll balls in ¼ cup granulated sugar; place 2 inches apart on baking sheets coated with cooking spray. Bake at 375° for 12 minutes. Remove from pans; cool on wire racks. Yield: 2½ dozen (serving size: 1 cookie).

CALORIES 109 (27% from fat); FAT 3.3g (sat 0.7g, mono 1.4g, poly 1g); PROTEIN 1.5g; CARB 18.6g; FIBER 0.3g; CHOL 7mg; IRON 0.8mg; SODIUM 136mg; CALC 13mg

SOFT MOLASSES COOKIES

PREP: 24 MINUTES
COOK: 10 MINUTES PER BATCH

¾ teaspoon baking soda
½ cup molasses
½ cup low-fat or nonfat buttermilk
¼ cup vegetable oil
2 cups all-purpose flour
½ teaspoon ground ginger
¼ teaspoon salt
Cooking spray
½ cup sifted powdered sugar
1 teaspoon water
¼ teaspoon vanilla extract

1. Preheat oven to 375°.
2. Dissolve soda in molasses in a large bowl. Combine buttermilk and oil; stir into molasses mixture. Lightly spoon flour into dry measuring cups; level with a knife. Combine flour, ginger, and salt; gradually add to molasses mixture, stirring well.
3. Coat hands lightly with cooking spray. Shape dough into 48 (1-inch) balls, and place balls 2 inches apart on baking sheets coated with cooking spray. Bake at 375° for 10 minutes. Cool on a wire rack.
4. Combine powdered sugar, water, and vanilla. Spoon into a heavy-duty zip-top plastic bag; seal bag. Snip a tiny hole in 1 corner of bag; drizzle glaze over cookies. Yield: 4 dozen (serving size: 1 cookie).

CALORIES 43 (27% from fat); FAT 1.3g (sat 0.2g, mono 0.4g, poly 0.6g); PROTEIN 0.6g; CARB 7.4g; FIBER 0.1g; CHOL 0mg; IRON 0.4mg; SODIUM 28mg; CALC 11mg

EASY PEANUT BUTTER COOKIES

PREP:25 MINUTES

COOK:7 MINUTES PER BATCH

(pictured on page 145)

1⅔ cups all-purpose flour
1½ tablespoons cornstarch
1¾ teaspoons baking powder
½ teaspoon baking soda
¾ cup packed brown sugar
¼ cup vegetable oil
¼ cup granulated sugar
¼ cup creamy peanut butter

1½ tablespoons light-colored corn syrup
2½ teaspoons vanilla extract
1 large egg
Cooking spray
3 tablespoons granulated sugar

1. Preheat oven to 375°.
2. Lightly spoon flour into dry measuring cups; level with a knife. Combine flour and next 3 ingredients in a bowl. Beat brown sugar and next 3 ingredients at medium speed of a mixer until well-blended. Add corn syrup, vanilla, and egg; beat well. Stir in flour mixture.

3. Coat hands lightly with cooking spray, and shape dough into 48 (1-inch) balls. Roll balls in 3 tablespoons granulated sugar, and place 2 inches apart on baking sheets coated with cooking spray. Flatten cookies with the bottom of a glass.
4. Bake at 375° for 7 minutes or until cookies are lightly browned. Remove from pans, and cool cookies on wire racks. Yield: 4 dozen (serving size: 1 cookie).

CALORIES 59 (31% from fat); FAT 2g (sat 0.4g, mono 0.7g, poly 0.8g); PROTEIN 1g; CARB 9.5g; FIBER 0.2g; CHOL 5mg; IRON 0.3mg; SODIUM 23mg; CALC 14mg

biscotti These twice-baked cookies from Italy are doubly good when dipped in coffee or tea.

Biscotti are Italian biscuits. In Sicily, biscotti replace bread and rolls for breakfast and are served with café latte throughout the day. These twice-baked treats are served alongside espresso in bars and accompany coffee after lunch. Biscotti are also served with afternoon tea and after dinner with a glass of wine.

After being baked in a log shape, biscotti are allowed to cool briefly and then are sliced on a 45° angle. The slices are baked again until they are slightly dry. Double-baking draws off moisture and gives the cookies their hard, crisp texture. It also ensures extended shelf life.

ALMOND BISCOTTI

PREP:15 MINUTES   COOK:50 MINUTES

2 cups all-purpose flour
1 cup sugar
½ cup slivered almonds, chopped and toasted
¾ teaspoon baking soda
¼ teaspoon salt
½ teaspoon vanilla extract
¼ teaspoon almond extract
2 large eggs, lightly beaten
1 large egg white, lightly beaten
Cooking spray

1. Preheat oven to 350°.
2. Lightly spoon flour into dry measuring cups; level with a knife. Combine flour and next 4 ingredients in a large bowl. Combine extracts, eggs, and egg white; add to flour mixture, stirring until blended (dough will be dry).
3. Turn dough out onto a lightly floured surface; knead lightly 7 times. Shape

dough into a 16-inch-long roll. Place roll on a baking sheet coated with cooking spray; flatten to 1-inch thickness.
4. Bake at 350° for 30 minutes. Remove roll from baking sheet; cool 10 minutes on a wire rack.
5. Cut roll diagonally into 30 (½-inch) slices. Place slices, cut sides down, on baking sheet.
6. Reduce oven temperature to 325°. Bake cookies 10 minutes. Turn cookies over; bake an additional 10 minutes (cookies will be slightly soft in center but will harden as they cool). Remove from baking sheet; cool completely on wire rack. Yield: 2½ dozen (serving size: 1 cookie).

CALORIES 72 (18% from fat); FAT 1.4g (sat 0.2g, mono 0.8g, poly 0.3g); PROTEIN 1.7g; CARB 13.1g; FIBER 0.6g; CHOL 14mg; IRON 0.5mg; SODIUM 47mg; CALC 8mg

Almond Biscotti

1. Turn dough out onto a lightly floured surface (dough will be dry). Knead dough lightly 7 times.

2. Shape dough into a 16-inch-long roll; place roll on a baking sheet, and flatten to 1-inch thickness. Bake for 30 minutes.

3. Let cool for 10 minutes on a wire rack; then slice the roll. Bake the slices for 10 minutes on each side.

HAZELNUT BISCOTTI

PREP: 30 MINUTES
COOK: 50 MINUTES

¾ cup hazelnuts (about 4 ounces)
1 cup sugar
¼ cup butter or stick margarine, melted
¼ cup Frangelico (hazelnut-flavored liqueur)
3 large eggs, lightly beaten
3¼ cups all-purpose flour
2 teaspoons baking powder
¼ teaspoon salt
Cooking spray

1. Preheat oven to 350°.
2. Place hazelnuts on a baking sheet. Bake at 350° for 15 minutes, stirring once. Turn nuts out onto a towel. Roll up towel, and rub off skins; chop nuts.
3. Combine chopped nuts, sugar, butter, Frangelico, and eggs in a large bowl. Lightly spoon flour into dry measuring cups; level with a knife. Combine flour, baking powder, and salt; add to nut mixture, stirring until well-blended (dough will be sticky).
4. Turn dough out onto a lightly floured surface, and knead lightly 5 or 6 times. With floured hands, shape dough into a 16-inch-long roll. Place roll on a baking sheet coated with cooking spray; flatten to 1-inch thickness.
5. Bake at 350° for 30 minutes. Remove roll from baking sheet, and cool 10 minutes on a wire rack. Cut roll diagonally into 24 (½-inch) slices. Place slices, cut sides down, on baking sheet. Bake at 350° for 10 minutes; turn cookies over, and bake an additional 10 minutes (cookies will be slightly soft in center but will harden as they cool). Remove from baking sheet; cool completely on wire rack. Yield: 2 dozen (serving size: 1 cookie).

CALORIES 151 (34% from fat); FAT 5.7g (sat 1.6g, mono 3.1g, poly 0.5g); PROTEIN 3.1g; CARB 22.4g; FIBER 0.6g; CHOL 32mg; IRON 1mg; SODIUM 79mg; CALC 30mg

Hazelnut Biscotti

specialty cookies
You'll find that these unusual cookies may become new family favorites.

CHOCOLATE PEPPERMINT STICKS

PREP: 25 MINUTES   COOK: 1 HOUR
DRY: 12 HOURS
FREEZE: 10 MINUTES

2 large egg whites
¼ teaspoon cream of tartar
⅛ teaspoon salt
2½ tablespoons granulated sugar
½ cup sifted powdered sugar
½ teaspoon peppermint extract
Red paste food coloring
1 ounce semisweet chocolate

1. Preheat oven to 200°.
2. Cover a large baking sheet with parchment paper. Draw 30 (4-inch) lines 1 inch apart on paper. Turn paper over; secure with masking tape.
3. Beat egg whites, cream of tartar, and salt at high speed of a mixer until foamy. Gradually add granulated sugar, 1 tablespoon at a time, beating until soft peaks form. Gradually add powdered sugar, 1 tablespoon at a time, beating until stiff peaks form. (Do not underbeat.) Fold in peppermint extract.
4. Fit a large pastry bag with a ½-inch round tip. Using a cotton swab, heavily paint 6 straight lines lengthwise up inside of bag with red paste food coloring. Spoon sugar mixture into bag; pipe mixture onto lines on parchment.
5. Bake at 200° for 1 hour or until dry. Turn oven off; cool meringues in closed oven at least 12 hours. Carefully remove meringues from paper, and arrange in a single layer on a plate.
6. Place chocolate in a heavy-duty zip-top plastic bag; seal bag. Microwave at HIGH 30 seconds or until chocolate melts. Snip a tiny hole in corner of bag; drizzle chocolate over baked meringues. Freeze 10 minutes. Store in an airtight container. Yield: about 2½ dozen (serving size: 1 stick).

CALORIES 18 (15% from fat); FAT 0.3g (sat 0.2g, mono 0.1g, poly 0g); PROTEIN 0.3g; CARB 3.6g; FIBER 0g; CHOL 0mg; IRON 0mg; SODIUM 13mg; CALC 1mg

HAMANTASCHEN

PREP: 40 MINUTES
CHILL: 8 HOURS 30 MINUTES
COOK: 10 MINUTES PER BATCH

Begin preparing these the day ahead so the dough and filling can chill overnight. The pastry's tender, crunchy texture contrasts with the moist, dense filling.

Dough:
⅔ cup sugar
6 tablespoons stick margarine or butter, softened
1 teaspoon vanilla extract
¼ cup (2 ounces) block-style fat-free cream cheese
1 large egg
2 cups all-purpose flour
1½ teaspoons baking powder
¼ teaspoon salt

Filling:
12 ounces dried figs (about 2 cups)
3 tablespoons sugar
3 tablespoons boiling water
1 tablespoon light-colored corn syrup
1 tablespoon lemon juice
Cooking spray

1. To prepare dough, combine first 4 ingredients in a large bowl; beat at medium speed of a mixer 2 minutes or until light and fluffy. Add egg; beat at high speed 1 minute or until very smooth. Lightly spoon flour into dry measuring cups; level with a knife. Combine flour, baking powder, and salt, and add to sugar mixture, beating at low speed just until flour mixture is moist. Divide dough in half, and gently shape each portion into a ball. Wrap dough in plastic wrap, and chill 8 hours or overnight.
2. To prepare filling, place figs in a food processor, and pulse 6 times or until chopped. With processor on, slowly add 3 tablespoons sugar, 3 tablespoons water, corn syrup, and lemon juice through food chute; process until smooth, scraping sides of processor bowl twice. Spoon mixture into a bowl; cover mixture, and chill 8 hours or overnight.
3. Shape each ball of dough into a 10-inch log. Cut each log into 10 (1-inch) slices. Quickly shape slices into 20 balls; place on a tray lined with wax paper. Chill 30 minutes.
4. Preheat oven to 400°.
5. Place each ball of dough between 2 sheets of wax paper, and flatten to a 3½-inch circle. Spoon 1 level tablespoon filling into center of each circle. With floured hands, fold dough over filling to form a triangle, and pinch edges together to seal. Place triangles 2 inches apart on baking sheets coated with cooking spray, and bake at 400° for 10 minutes or until pastries are lightly browned. Remove from pans, and cool on a wire rack. Yield: 20 pastries (serving size: 1 pastry).

CALORIES 163 (22% from fat); FAT 4g (sat 0.8g, mono 1.7g, poly 1.3g); PROTEIN 2.6g; CARB 30.3g; FIBER 3.2g; CHOL 12mg; IRON 1mg; SODIUM 93mg; CALC 57mg

Banana Pudding
(page 169)

desserts

CLASSIC CRÈME CARAMEL

PREP: 14 MINUTES   COOK: 50 MINUTES
CHILL: 4 HOURS

⅓ cup sugar
3 tablespoons water
Cooking spray
3 large eggs
1 large egg white
2 cups 2% reduced-fat milk
1 tablespoon vanilla extract
⅔ cup sugar
⅛ teaspoon salt
Fresh raspberries (optional)

1. Preheat oven to 325°.
2. Combine ⅓ cup sugar and 3 tablespoons water in a small, heavy saucepan; cook over medium-high heat until sugar dissolves. Continue cooking 4 minutes or until golden. Immediately pour into 6 (6-ounce) custard cups coated with cooking spray, tipping quickly until caramelized sugar coats bottom of cups.
3. Beat eggs and egg white in a medium bowl with a whisk. Stir in milk, vanilla, ⅔ cup sugar, and salt. Divide mixture evenly among prepared custard cups. Place cups in a 13 x 9-inch baking pan; add hot water to pan to a depth of 1 inch. Bake at 325° for 50 minutes or until a knife inserted in center comes out clean. Remove cups from pan. Cover and chill at least 4 hours.
4. Loosen edges of custards with a knife or rubber spatula. Place a dessert plate, upside down, on top of each cup; invert onto plates. Drizzle any remaining caramelized syrup over custards. Garnish with raspberries, if desired. Yield: 6 servings.

CALORIES 212 (18% from fat); FAT 4.3g (sat 1.8g, mono 1.5g, poly 0.4g); PROTEIN 6.5g; CARB 37.6g; FIBER 0g; CHOL 117mg; IRON 0.4mg; SODIUM 131mg; CALC 113mg

Making Crème Caramel

Here's our foolproof guide to crème caramel, a classic dessert every cook's repertoire should include. A crème caramel involves two crucial steps: making the caramel syrup and baking the custard atop the syrup. The custard in a crème caramel can be flavored many ways, but how to make the dessert doesn't change. For exact ingredients, quantities, and cooking times, see the individual recipes.

PART 1 making the caramel syrup

1. Combine sugar and water in a heavy saucepan over medium-high heat, stirring until sugar dissolves.

2. Continue to cook without stirring; after about 2 minutes mixture will start to caramelize and turn light brown. After an additional 1 to 2 minutes the mixture will be a deep golden brown.

3. Immediately pour enough caramel into a custard cup or ramekin to cover the bottom of the cup.

4. Tilt the custard cup so that its bottom is completely covered with caramel. Repeat for remaining cups.

ingredients—eggs, milk, and sugar—form the basis for these smooth-as-silk desserts.

PART 2 baking the custard

5. Divide custard mixture (eggs, milk, and flavorings) evenly among prepared cups.

6. Place cups in a 13 x 9-inch baking pan. Carefully add hot tap water to the pan to a depth of 1 inch. Bake at 325° for recommended cooking time.

7. After custards have cooled and chilled, run a thin knife around the edge of each to loosen it from its cup.

8. Place a dessert plate, upside down, on top of each cup. Invert the cup and plate. Lift the cup; the custard should slip out with the caramel syrup on top.

crème caramels   163

ALMOND CRÈME CARAMEL

PREP: 15 MINUTES   COOK: 50 MINUTES
CHILL: 4 HOURS

½ cup sugar
¼ cup water
Cooking spray
2 tablespoons chopped almonds, toasted
⅓ cup sugar
1 tablespoon all-purpose flour
½ cup (4 ounces) ⅓-less-fat cream cheese, softened
2 large egg whites
1 large egg
1½ cups 2% reduced-fat milk
¼ teaspoon almond extract

1. Preheat oven to 325°.
2. Combine ½ cup sugar and water in a small, heavy saucepan; cook over medium-high heat until sugar dissolves, stirring frequently. Continue cooking until golden. Immediately pour into 6 (6-ounce) custard cups coated with cooking spray, tipping each cup quickly until sugar coats bottom of cups. Sprinkle almonds evenly over caramelized sugar; set aside.
3. Combine ⅓ cup sugar and flour. Beat cream cheese at medium speed of a mixer until smooth. Add flour mixture; beat until well-blended. Add egg whites and egg, and beat well. Gradually add milk and almond extract; beat well. Divide evenly among prepared custard cups. Place cups in a 13 x 9-inch baking pan; add hot water to pan to a depth of 1 inch. Bake at 325° for 50 minutes or until a knife inserted in center comes out clean. Remove from pan. Cover and chill at least 4 hours.
4. Loosen edges with a knife or rubber spatula. Place a dessert plate, upside down, on top of each cup; invert. Drizzle any remaining syrup over custards. Yield: 6 servings.

CALORIES 223 (31% from fat); FAT 7.6g (sat 3.9g, mono 2.6g, poly 0.5g); PROTEIN 6.6g; CARB 32.8g; FIBER 0.3g; CHOL 56mg; IRON 0.4mg; SODIUM 135mg; CALC 99mg

PUMPKIN-MAPLE
CRÈME CARAMEL

PREP: 14 MINUTES
COOK: 1 HOUR 10 MINUTES
CHILL: 4 HOURS

½ cup granulated sugar
¼ cup water
Cooking spray
⅓ cup packed dark brown sugar
2 tablespoons maple syrup
3 large eggs
½ cup canned pumpkin
½ cup 2% reduced-fat milk
¼ teaspoon ground nutmeg
½ teaspoon vanilla extract
⅛ teaspoon salt
1 (12-ounce) can evaporated fat-free milk

1. Preheat oven to 325°.
2. Combine granulated sugar and water in a small, heavy saucepan; cook over medium-high heat until sugar dissolves, stirring frequently. Continue cooking until golden. Immediately pour into 6 (6-ounce) custard cups coated with cooking spray, tipping each cup quickly until caramelized sugar coats bottom of cups.
3. Combine brown sugar, syrup, and eggs in a bowl; beat with a whisk. Add pumpkin and next 5 ingredients; stir until well-blended. Divide mixture evenly among prepared custard cups. Place cups in a 13 x 9-inch baking pan; add hot water to pan to a depth of 1 inch. Bake at 325° for 1 hour and 10 minutes or until a knife inserted in center comes out clean. Remove cups from pan. Cover and chill at least 4 hours.
4. Loosen edges with a knife or rubber spatula. Place a dessert plate, upside down, on top of each cup; invert. Drizzle any remaining syrup over custards. Yield: 6 servings.

CALORIES 230 (13% from fat); FAT 3.3g (sat 1.2g, mono 1.2g, poly 0.4g); PROTEIN 8.4g; CARB 42.2g; FIBER 0.8g; CHOL 114mg; IRON 1.1mg; SODIUM 164mg; CALC 222mg

CLASSIC CUSTARD

PREP: 8 MINUTES
COOK: 50 MINUTES

6 large eggs, lightly beaten
½ cup sugar
¼ teaspoon salt
4 cups 1% low-fat milk
1½ teaspoons vanilla extract
½ teaspoon almond extract
Cooking spray

1. Preheat oven to 325°.

2. Combine first 3 ingredients in a large bowl; stir well with a whisk.

3. Heat milk over medium-high heat in a large, heavy saucepan to 180° or until tiny bubbles form around edge (do not boil). Gradually add hot milk to sugar mixture, stirring constantly with a whisk. Stir in vanilla and almond extracts.

4. Pour into a deep 2-quart soufflé dish coated with cooking spray. Place dish in a 13 x 9-inch baking pan, and add hot water to pan to a depth of 1 inch. Bake at 325° for 50 minutes or until a knife inserted in center of custard comes out almost clean. Remove dish from pan; serve custard warm or chilled. Yield: 7 servings (serving size: ¾ cup).

CALORIES 185 (29% from fat); FAT 6g (sat 2.3g, mono 2.1g, poly 0.7g); PROTEIN 10.1g; CARB 21.6g; FIBER 0g; CHOL 195mg; IRON 0.7mg; SODIUM 210mg; CALC 194mg

Classic Custard

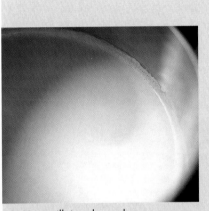

1. Heat milk in a large, heavy saucepan over medium-high heat to 180° or until tiny bubbles form around edge (do not boil).

2. Remove milk from heat, and gradually add to the sugar mixture, stirring constantly with a whisk.

3. Pour into a deep 2-quart soufflé dish coated with cooking spray.

4. Place dish in a 13 x 9-inch baking pan, and add hot water to the pan to a depth of 1 inch. Bake at 325° for 50 minutes or until a knife inserted in center of custard comes out almost clean.

LEMON-ROSEMARY CUSTARD CAKES

PREP: 16 MINUTES   COOK: 35 MINUTES

  3 large egg whites
  ¾ cup granulated sugar, divided
  2 tablespoons stick margarine or
      butter, softened
  ¼ cup all-purpose flour
  1 teaspoon minced fresh rosemary
  1 teaspoon grated lemon rind
  ¼ cup fresh lemon juice
Dash of salt
  3 large egg yolks
1½ cups 1% low-fat milk
Cooking spray
  1 tablespoon powdered sugar
Rosemary sprigs (optional)

1. Preheat oven to 350°.
2. Beat egg whites at high speed of a mixer until foamy. Gradually add ¼ cup granulated sugar, 1 tablespoon at a time, beating until stiff peaks form.
3. Beat ½ cup granulated sugar and margarine at medium speed of a mixer until well-blended (about 3 minutes). Lightly spoon flour into a dry measuring cup; level with a knife. Add flour, rosemary, lemon rind, juice, and salt to sugar mixture, beating well. Add egg yolks and milk, and beat until blended. Gently stir one-fourth of egg white mixture into batter; gently fold in remaining egg white mixture.
4. Spoon into 6 (6-ounce) custard cups coated with cooking spray. Place cups in a 13 x 9-inch baking pan, and add hot water to pan to a depth of 1 inch. Bake cakes at 350° for 35 minutes or until set. Remove cups from pan, and sprinkle with powdered sugar. Garnish with rosemary, if desired. Yield: 6 servings.

CALORIES 222 (30% from fat); FAT 7.3g (sat 2g, mono 2.9g, poly 1.6g); PROTEIN 5.7g; CARB 34.1g; FIBER 0.2g; CHOL 111mg; IRON 0.6mg; SODIUM 131mg; CALC 92mg

BAKED COCONUT CUSTARDS

PREP: 8 MINUTES   COOK: 1½ HOURS
CHILL: 2 HOURS

Try preparing the custards the night before. Just before serving, simply add whipped topping and coconut.

  ½ cup sugar
  2 large eggs
  2 cups 1% low-fat milk
  1 teaspoon coconut extract
  ¼ cup frozen reduced-calorie
      whipped topping, thawed
  ¼ cup flaked sweetened coconut,
      toasted

1. Preheat oven to 325°.
2. Combine sugar and eggs in a bowl; stir well with a whisk.
3. Heat milk over medium-high heat in a large, heavy saucepan to 180° or until tiny bubbles form around edge (do not boil). Gradually add hot milk to sugar mixture, stirring constantly with a whisk. Stir in coconut extract.
4. Pour mixture evenly into 4 (6-ounce) custard cups. Place cups in a 9-inch square baking pan; add hot water to pan to a depth of 1 inch. Bake at 325° for 1 hour 30 minutes or until almost set (center will not be firm, but custard will set up as it chills). Remove cups from pan; cool. Cover and chill. Top each serving with 1 tablespoon whipped topping; sprinkle with 1 tablespoon toasted coconut. Yield: 4 servings.

CALORIES 224 (25% from fat); FAT 6.3g (sat 3.9g, mono 1.4g, poly 0.4g); PROTEIN 7.4g; CARB 34.8g; FIBER 0.3g; CHOL 111mg; IRON 0.5mg; SODIUM 111mg; CALC 166mg

Lemon-Rosemary Custard Cakes

When the custards test done, remove them immediately from the water bath. **Otherwise, they will continue to cook and will become rubbery.**

VIENNESE CARAMEL CUSTARD

PREP: 20 MINUTES   COOK: 45 MINUTES

CHILL: 3 HOURS

1¼ cups sugar, divided
½ teaspoon fresh lemon juice
½ teaspoon water
2½ cups fat-free milk
6 large egg whites
2 large eggs
1 tablespoon vanilla extract
Thin lemon slices (optional)

1. Preheat oven to 300°.
2. Combine ½ cup sugar and lemon juice in a small, heavy saucepan; cook over medium-high heat until sugar dissolves. Continue cooking 4 minutes or until golden. Immediately pour into 6 (4-ounce) ramekins, tipping each cup quickly until caramelized sugar coats bottom of cups.
3. Combine ½ cup sugar and water in a large, heavy saucepan; cook over medium-high heat until sugar dissolves. Continue cooking 4 minutes or until golden, and set aside.
4. Heat ¼ cup sugar and milk over medium-high heat in a small, heavy saucepan to 180° or until bubbles form around edge (do not boil). Gradually add hot milk mixture to sugar mixture in large saucepan, stirring constantly with a whisk. Cook over medium-high heat until sugar melts. Remove from heat.
5. Combine egg whites and eggs in a large bowl, and stir well with a whisk. Gradually add hot milk mixture to eggs, stirring constantly with a whisk. Stir in vanilla extract. Pour into prepared ramekins. Place ramekins in a 13 x 9-inch baking pan, and add hot water to pan to a depth of 1 inch. Bake at 300° for 45 minutes or until a knife inserted in center comes out clean. Remove from pan, and cool completely on a wire rack. Cover and chill at least 3 hours.
6. Loosen edges of custards with a knife or rubber spatula. Place a dessert plate, upside down, on top of each ramekin; invert custards onto plates. Drizzle any remaining syrup over custards; garnish with thin lemon slices, if desired. Yield: 6 servings.

CALORIES 245 (7% from fat); FAT 1.9g (sat 0.7g, mono 0.7g, poly 0.3g); PROTEIN 9g; CARB 47.4g; FIBER 0g; CHOL 76mg; IRON 0.3mg; SODIUM 128mg; CALC 137mg

VANILLA FLOATING ISLAND

PREP: 35 MINUTES

CHILL: 1½ HOURS

COOK: 30 MINUTES

A floating island is a mixture of stiffly beaten sweetened egg whites that are mounded and cooked by poaching. To serve, the "islands" are floated in a custard sauce.

1 (6-inch) vanilla bean, split lengthwise
2½ cups 2% reduced-fat milk
¼ cup sugar
5 tablespoons cornstarch
1 large egg yolk, lightly beaten
Cooking spray
1 teaspoon sugar
4 large egg whites
½ cup sugar
1 teaspoon vanilla extract
½ ounce bittersweet chocolate, grated

1. Scrape seeds from vanilla bean; discard vanilla bean. Combine seeds and milk in a large saucepan; cook over low heat 20 minutes.
2. Combine ¼ cup sugar and cornstarch; add to milk mixture, stirring well. Gradually stir about one-fourth of hot milk mixture into egg yolk; add to remaining hot milk mixture, stirring constantly. Bring to a boil over medium-high heat, stirring constantly. Cook mixture 1 minute, stirring constantly (mixture will not be thick). Pour mixture into a bowl; place plastic wrap on surface. Cool mixture to room temperature. Chill mixture thoroughly (mixture will thicken slightly).
3. Preheat oven to 325°.
4. Coat a 1-quart glass bowl with cooking spray, and sprinkle with 1 teaspoon sugar.
5. Beat egg whites at high speed of a mixer until foamy. Gradually add ½ cup sugar, 1 tablespoon at a time, beating until stiff peaks form. Add vanilla, and beat 10 seconds.
6. Spoon egg white mixture into prepared bowl; gently smooth surface of mixture with a spatula. Place bowl in an 8-inch square baking pan; add hot water to pan to a depth of 1 inch. Bake at 325° for 30 minutes or until a thermometer inserted in center registers 160°. Invert island into a shallow dish. Pour custard sauce around island, and sprinkle with grated chocolate. Serve immediately. Yield: 5 servings (serving size: 1 meringue wedge and ½ cup sauce).

CALORIES 231 (17% from fat); FAT 4.4g (sat 2.3g, mono 1.4g, poly 0.3g); PROTEIN 7.5g; CARB 40.9g; FIBER 0g; CHOL 53mg; IRON 0.3mg; SODIUM 107mg; CALC 156mg

FLAN

PREP: 15 MINUTES
COOK: 1 HOUR
CHILL: 4 HOURS

1⅓ cups sugar, divided
¾ cup egg substitute
¾ teaspoon vanilla extract
2 (12-ounce) cans evaporated
   fat-free milk

1. Preheat oven to 350°.
2. Place 1 cup sugar in a large, heavy skillet, and cook over medium heat 5 minutes or until sugar dissolves (do not stir). Continue cooking until golden, stirring constantly. Immediately pour caramelized sugar into a 9-inch round cake pan, tipping quickly until sugar coats bottom of pan.
3. Combine ⅓ cup sugar, egg substitute, vanilla, and milk. Pour into prepared cake pan; place in a large baking pan. Add hot water to larger pan to a depth of 1 inch. Bake at 350° for 1 hour or until a knife inserted near center comes out clean. Remove cake pan from water; cool completely on a wire rack. Cover and chill 4 hours.
4. Loosen edges of flan with a knife or rubber spatula. Place a serving plate, upside down, on top of cake pan; invert. Drizzle any remaining syrup over flan. Yield: 8 servings (serving size: 1 wedge).

CALORIES 207 (1% from fat); FAT 0.2g (sat 0.1g, mono 0.1g, poly 0g); PROTEIN 8.7g; CARB 43.3g; FIBER 0g; CHOL 3mg; IRON 0.7mg; SODIUM 132mg; CALC 254mg

MAPLE CARAMEL FLAN

PREP: 12 MINUTES
COOK: 1 HOUR 10 MINUTES
CHILL: 2 HOURS

1½ cups maple syrup, divided
   Cooking spray
2 teaspoons all-purpose flour
2 cups 2% reduced-fat milk
1 teaspoon vanilla extract
3 large eggs, lightly beaten

1. Preheat oven to 375°.
2. Cook ½ cup maple syrup in a heavy saucepan over medium-high heat until syrup reaches hard ball stage (260°). Immediately pour into 6 (6-ounce) custard cups coated with cooking spray, tipping each cup quickly until syrup coats bottom of cups.
3. Place flour in a medium bowl; gradually add 1 cup maple syrup, stirring with a whisk until blended. Add milk, vanilla, and eggs; beat at low speed of a mixer until well-blended.
4. Pour milk mixture evenly into prepared cups; place cups in a 13 x 9-inch baking pan. Add hot water to pan to a depth of 1 inch. Bake at 375° for 1 hour and 10 minutes or until a knife inserted in center comes out clean. Remove cups from pan; cool completely on a wire rack. Cover and chill 2 hours.
5. Loosen edges of custards with a knife or rubber spatula. Place a dessert plate, upside down, on top of each cup; invert onto plates. Drizzle any remaining caramelized syrup over custards. Yield: 6 servings.

CALORIES 291 (13% from fat); FAT 4.3g (sat 1.8g, mono 1.4g, poly 0.4g); PROTEIN 5.9g; CARB 58g; FIBER 0g; CHOL 113mg; IRON 1.4mg; SODIUM 79mg; CALC 164mg

puddings
You loved pudding as a child . . . and you will still find these soothing favorites just as comforting.

We're sharing our favorite puddings, which are one of two basic types—stovetop or baked. Those cooked on the stove are thickened by either cornstarch or flour. Baked ones use eggs as a thickener and "set" as they bake.

Unless it's a bread pudding, baked puddings are cooked in a large water-filled pan (called a water bath), which allows for gentle heat to avoid curdling, yielding a creamy, smooth consistency.

VANILLA PUDDING

PREP: 5 MINUTES   COOK: 8 MINUTES

½ cup sugar
3 tablespoons cornstarch
⅛ teaspoon salt
2¼ cups 2% reduced-fat milk
1 large egg, lightly beaten
1 teaspoon vanilla extract

1. Combine first 3 ingredients in a saucepan. Combine milk and egg in a bowl. Gradually add milk mixture to sugar mixture, stirring constantly. Cook over medium heat until thick and bubbly (about 1 minute), stirring constantly.
2. Remove pan from heat; stir in vanilla. Serve warm, or place plastic wrap on surface; cool to room temperature. Chill thoroughly. Yield: 5 servings (serving size: ½ cup).

CALORIES 168 (17% from fat); FAT 3.1g (sat 1.6g, mono 1g, poly 0.2g); PROTEIN 4.9g; CARB 29.9g; FIBER 0g; CHOL 51mg; IRON 0.2mg; SODIUM 127mg; CALC 139mg

BANANA PUDDING

PREP: 28 MINUTES   COOK: 25 MINUTES

(pictured on page 161)

⅓ cup all-purpose flour
Dash of salt
2½ cups 1% low-fat milk
  1 (14-ounce) can fat-free
      sweetened condensed milk
  2 large egg yolks, lightly beaten
  2 teaspoons vanilla extract
  3 cups sliced ripe banana
  45 reduced-calorie vanilla wafers
  4 large egg whites
  ¼ cup sugar

1. Preheat oven to 325°.
2. Lightly spoon flour into a dry measuring cup; level with a knife. Combine flour and salt in a medium saucepan. Gradually stir in milks and egg yolks. Cook over medium heat until thick (about 13 minutes), stirring constantly. Remove from heat; stir in vanilla.
3. Arrange 1 cup banana slices in bottom of a 2-quart baking dish. Spoon one-third of pudding over banana. Arrange 15 wafers on top of pudding. Repeat pudding layer twice and wafer layer once, arranging last 15 wafers around edge of pudding. Push cookies into pudding.
4. Beat egg whites at high speed of a mixer until foamy. Gradually add sugar, 1 tablespoon at a time, beating until stiff peaks form. Spread meringue over pudding, sealing to edge of dish. Bake at 325° for 25 minutes or until meringue is golden. Yield: 10 servings (serving size: ¾ cup).

CALORIES 295 (9% from fat); FAT 3g (sat 0.8g, mono 1g, poly 0.2g); PROTEIN 8.3g; CARB 58g; FIBER 1.1g; CHOL 47mg; IRON 0.9mg; SODIUM 188mg; CALC 199mg

Use bananas that are ripe but firm; they will be sweeter and will have more flavor.

MILE-HIGH MERINGUES

Ever wonder how bakers get those "mile-high meringues" on banana pudding or cream pies? Here are our tips on getting stiff peaks.

• **Egg whites will more than triple in volume when they're at room temperature.** But because eggs are easier to separate right out of the refrigerator, do that first; then set the egg whites aside for about 30 minutes. (For food safety, don't leave at room temperature for longer than this.)

• **Use a copper, stainless steel, or glass bowl.** Plastic won't produce fluffy whites.

• **Make sure the bowl is very clean.** Any fat or grease will interfere with getting maximum volume.

• If you accidentally get some yolk (which contains fat) in the bowl, **touch the yolk with a small piece of bread, and it will cling to the bread** without removing any of the egg white.

• **Start your electric mixer on high speed and beat the whites until they are foamy.** Gradually add the sugar 1 tablespoon at a time to let the sugar dissolve before the egg whites reach their maximum volume.

• **To determine when the peaks are stiff, periodically check them by stopping the mixer** and lifting the beaters out of the egg white mixture. A stiff peak will look shiny and glossy and stand straight up without curling over.

BITTERSWEET CHOCOLATE PUDDING

PREP: 5 MINUTES   COOK: 20 MINUTES

3½ cups fat-free milk, divided
  1 cup Dutch process cocoa
  3 tablespoons cornstarch
  ¼ teaspoon salt
  1 cup sugar
  1 large egg, lightly beaten
  1 large egg yolk, lightly beaten
  2 ounces bittersweet chocolate,
      coarsely chopped
  1 tablespoon vanilla extract

1. Combine 1 cup milk, cocoa, cornstarch, and salt in a large bowl; stir well.
2. Heat 2½ cups milk over medium heat in a large, heavy saucepan to 180° or until tiny bubbles form around edge (do not boil). Remove from heat; add sugar, stirring with a whisk until sugar dissolves. Add cocoa mixture to pan, stirring until blended. Bring to a boil over medium heat, and cook 1 minute, stirring constantly.
3. Combine egg and egg yolk in a medium bowl. Gradually add hot milk-mixture to egg mixture, stirring constantly with a whisk. Return to pan. Cook over medium heat until thick and bubbly (about 2 minutes), stirring constantly. Remove from heat; add bittersweet chocolate and vanilla, stirring until chocolate melts. Serve warm or chilled. Yield: 8 servings (serving size: ½ cup).

CALORIES 249 (18% from fat); FAT 5g (sat 2.7g, mono 1.8g, poly 0.3g); PROTEIN 8.2g; CARB 43g; FIBER 0g; CHOL 56mg; IRON 2.3mg; SODIUM 144mg; CALC 157mg

Many feel that chocolate is the ultimate "feel-good" food when you're down.

MILK-CHOCOLATE PUDDING

PREP: 6 MINUTES   COOK: 11 MINUTES
COOL: 30 MINUTES

½ cup sugar
2 tablespoons cornstarch
2 cups 1% low-fat milk
1½ ounces semisweet chocolate,
    chopped
1 large egg, lightly beaten
1 teaspoon vanilla extract

1. Combine sugar and cornstarch in a saucepan; gradually add milk, stirring with a whisk until well-blended. Stir in chocolate. Bring to a boil over medium heat; cook 7 minutes, stirring constantly.
2. Gradually add hot milk mixture to egg, stirring constantly with a whisk. Return milk mixture to pan, and cook until thick and bubbly (about 30 seconds), stirring constantly. Remove from heat, and stir in vanilla. Spoon mixture into a bowl; place plastic wrap on surface, and cool to room temperature. Yield: 4 servings (serving size: ½ cup).

CALORIES 240 (24% from fat); FAT 6.4g (sat 3.3g, mono 2g, poly 0.3g); PROTEIN 6.1g; CARB 40.8g; FIBER 0.1g; CHOL 60mg; IRON 0.5mg; SODIUM 78mg; CALC 160mg

---

BITS ABOUT CHOCOLATE

Bittersweet or Semisweet Chocolate: **This is the chocolate most often used in cakes and cookies.** "Bittersweet" and "semisweet" are often **used interchangeably,** though bittersweet generally has more chocolate "liquor" (the paste formed from roasted, ground cocoa beans). **Bittersweet and semisweet chocolate have a deep, smooth, intense flavor** that comes from the blend of beans; sugar, vanilla, and cocoa butter are added to the liquor for an even richer taste.

Cocoa Powder: **There are two basic types of cocoa: regular and Dutch process** (sometimes labeled "European process"). **Dutch process cocoa has a slightly stronger flavor and richer color** than regular cocoa: It's been treated with a mild alkali, such as baking soda, which neutralizes its acidity. **Cocoa powder has far less fat and calories** than other chocolate because the cocoa butter has been removed. Cocoa tastes less rich, so when cooking with it, you have to find another way to put the moisture and richness back in.

Milk Chocolate: **The most popular form of eating chocolate** in the United States, milk chocolate has a mild, less robust flavor than sweet or semisweet chocolate.

Sweet Chocolate: Very similar to semisweet chocolate, **sweet chocolate simply has more sugar and less chocolate liquor.** Sweet chocolate can be substituted for semisweet in recipes without a significant change in texture.

Unsweetened Chocolate (baking chocolate): **This chocolate has no added sugar** and **an intense chocolate flavor** that has to be tempered by sugar and other ingredients.

White Chocolate: **White "chocolate" doesn't contain a drop of chocolate.** But it does have cocoa butter, from which it gets its **faintly chocolaty flavor.** The cocoa butter is blended with milk and sugar to form the creamy confection, which is used for both eating and cooking.

MICROWAVE CHOCOLATE PUDDING

PREP: 3 MINUTES   COOK: 5 MINUTES

6 tablespoons sugar
¼ cup unsweetened or Dutch
    process cocoa
2 tablespoons cornstarch
1½ cups 2% reduced-fat milk
½ teaspoon vanilla extract

1. Combine sugar, cocoa, and cornstarch in a 1-quart glass measure; gradually add milk, stirring with a whisk until well-blended. Microwave milk mixture at HIGH 3 minutes, stirring after 1½ minutes.
2. Microwave milk mixture at MEDIUM-HIGH (70% power) 1½ minutes or until thick. Add vanilla; stir well with a whisk. Serve warm or cover and chill thoroughly. Yield: 3 servings (serving size: ½ cup).

CALORIES 212 (14% from fat); FAT 3.3g (sat 2.1g, mono 1.2g, poly 0.1g); PROTEIN 6.2g; CARB 39.3g; FIBER 0g; CHOL 10mg; IRON 1.3mg; SODIUM 65mg; CALC 160mg

BAKED LEMON PUDDING

PREP: 35 MINUTES COOK: 33 MINUTES

2 large egg yolks
1 cup fat-free milk
1 teaspoon grated lemon rind
3 tablespoons fresh lemon juice
1 tablespoon stick margarine or
   butter, melted
⅓ cup granulated sugar
5 tablespoons all-purpose flour
¼ teaspoon baking powder
⅛ teaspoon salt
2 large egg whites
⅓ cup granulated sugar
Cooking spray
1 teaspoon powdered sugar
   (optional)

1. Preheat oven to 375°.
2. Beat egg yolks at high speed of a mixer until thick and pale (about 2 minutes). Gradually add milk, lemon rind, lemon juice, and margarine; beat well. Combine ⅓ cup sugar, flour, baking powder, and salt. Add flour mixture to egg yolk mixture; beat well.
3. Beat egg whites at high speed of a mixer until foamy, using clean, dry beaters. Add ⅓ cup sugar, 1 tablespoon at a time, beating until stiff peaks form. Gently stir one-fourth of egg white mixture into egg yolk mixture; gently fold in remaining egg white mixture.
4. Pour egg mixture into a 1-quart casserole coated with cooking spray. Place in a large baking pan; add hot water to larger pan to a depth of 1 inch. Bake at 375° for 33 minutes or until top is golden and center seems set when touched with a knife. Remove casserole from water. Sift powdered sugar over top, if desired. Serve warm. Yield: 4 servings (serving size: 1 cup).

CALORIES 252 (21% from fat); FAT 5.8g (sat 1.5g, mono 2.3g, poly 1.3g); PROTEIN 6.2g; CARB 44.6g; FIBER 0.3g; CHOL 110mg; IRON 0.8mg; SODIUM 190mg; CALC 103mg

QUEEN OF PUDDINGS

PREP: 25 MINUTES COOK: 1½ HOURS

5 (1-ounce) slices white bread
1 tablespoon sugar
1 tablespoon stick margarine or
   butter, melted
1½ teaspoons grated lemon rind
3 tablespoons sugar
3 cups fat-free milk
2 large egg yolks, lightly beaten
1 teaspoon vanilla extract
Cooking spray
6 tablespoons raspberry preserves
2 large egg whites
3 tablespoons sugar

1. Preheat oven to 400°.
2. Trim and discard crust from bread; cut into ¾-inch cubes; place in a large bowl. Combine 1 tablespoon sugar, margarine, and lemon rind; drizzle over bread cubes, tossing well. Arrange bread cubes in a single layer on a baking sheet. Bake at 400° for 10 minutes or until toasted. Reduce oven temperature to 350°.
3. Combine 3 tablespoons sugar, milk, egg yolks, and vanilla in a saucepan. Cook over medium heat 5 minutes or until warm, stirring constantly (mixture should not thicken).
4. Place ⅓ cup bread cubes into each of 6 (8-ounce) ramekins coated with cooking spray. Add ½ cup milk mixture to each cup. Place cups in a 13 x 9-inch baking pan. Pour hot water into pan to a depth of 1 inch. Bake at 350° for 1 hour 15 minutes or until a knife inserted in center comes out clean.
5. Heat raspberry preserves in a small saucepan over low heat until warm. Spread 1 tablespoon preserves evenly over top of each pudding.
6. Beat egg whites in a small bowl at high speed of a mixer until foamy. Gradually add 3 tablespoons sugar, 1 tablespoon at a time, beating until stiff peaks form.

Spread meringue evenly over puddings. Bake at 350° for 15 minutes or until lightly browned. Remove cups from water; serve warm. Yield: 6 servings.

CALORIES 239 (17% from fat); FAT 4.6g (sat 1.2g, mono 1.8g, poly 0.9g); PROTEIN 8.8g; CARB 41.2g; FIBER 0.6g; CHOL 73mg; IRON 0.8mg; SODIUM 212mg; CALC 181mg

DOUBLE-CHOCOLATE BREAD PUDDING

PREP: 9 MINUTES COOK: 35 MINUTES

Most French bread becomes stale quickly, making it ideal for bread pudding. If it's too hard to cut easily into cubes, break it into small chunks. Soaking it in the milk mixture will soften it.

⅔ cup evaporated fat-free milk
1½ tablespoons sugar
2 teaspoons unsweetened cocoa
½ teaspoon vanilla extract
2 large egg whites, lightly beaten
1¾ cups (½-inch) cubed French bread
Cooking spray
1 tablespoon semisweet chocolate
   minichips

1. Preheat oven to 325°.
2. Combine milk, sugar, and cocoa in a medium bowl. Stir with a whisk until well blended. Add vanilla and egg whites; stir well. Add bread cubes, stirring until moistened.
3. Coat 2 (6-ounce) custard cups with cooking spray. Spoon milk mixture evenly into prepared cups, and top evenly with minichips.
4. Place cups in a 9-inch square baking pan. Add hot water to pan to a depth of 1 inch. Bake at 325° for 35 minutes or until firm. Yield: 2 servings.
Note: This recipe can easily be doubled.

CALORIES 218 (14% from fat); FAT 3.3g (sat 1.4g, mono 1g, poly 0.2g); PROTEIN 12.5g; CARB 34.3g; FIBER 0.7g; CHOL 3mg; IRON 1.2mg; SODIUM 283mg; CALC 270mg

Irish Bread Pudding With Caramel-Whiskey Sauce

PREP: 35 MINUTES   COOK: 35 MINUTES

¼ cup light butter, melted
1 (10-ounce) French bread baguette, cut into 1-inch-thick slices
½ cup raisins
¼ cup Irish whiskey
1¾ cups 1% low-fat milk
1 cup sugar
1 tablespoon vanilla extract
1 (12-ounce) can evaporated fat-free milk
2 large eggs, lightly beaten
Cooking spray
1 tablespoon sugar
1 teaspoon ground cinnamon
Caramel-Whiskey Sauce (page 450)

1. Preheat oven to 350°.
2. Brush melted butter on one side of French bread slices, and place bread, buttered sides up, on a baking sheet. Bake bread at 350° for 10 minutes or until lightly toasted. Cut bread into ½-inch cubes.
3. Combine raisins and whiskey in a small bowl; cover and let stand 10 minutes or until soft (do not drain).
4. Combine 1% low-fat milk and next 4 ingredients in a large bowl; stir well with a whisk. Add bread cubes and raisin mixture, pressing gently to moisten; let stand 15 minutes.
5. Spoon bread mixture into a 13 x 9-inch baking dish coated with cooking spray. Combine 1 tablespoon sugar and cinnamon; sprinkle over pudding. Bake at 350° for 35 minutes or until set. Serve warm with Caramel-Whiskey Sauce. Yield: 12 servings (serving size: 1 [3-inch] square and 2 tablespoons sauce).

CALORIES 362 (17% from fat); FAT 6.7g (sat 4g, mono 2.1g, poly 0.6g); PROTEIN 8.1g; CARB 66.7g; FIBER 0.9g; CHOL 57mg; IRON 1mg; SODIUM 269mg; CALC 155mg

Brown Sugar Bread Pudding With Crème Anglaise

Brown Sugar Bread Pudding With Crème Anglaise

PREP: 30 MINUTES   COOK: 45 MINUTES

1 cup dried mixed fruit, chopped
1 cup pineapple juice
¼ cup packed brown sugar
4 large egg whites
1 large egg
1¼ cups 2% reduced-fat milk
¾ cup evaporated fat-free milk
⅓ cup packed brown sugar
2 teaspoons vanilla extract
¼ teaspoon ground cinnamon
⅛ teaspoon ground nutmeg
12 (1-inch-thick) slices diagonally cut French bread (about 12 ounces)
Cooking spray
4 teaspoons brown sugar
1½ teaspoons butter, cut into pieces
1¾ cups Crème Anglaise, chilled (page 451)

1. Preheat oven to 350°.
2. Combine first 3 ingredients in a small saucepan. Bring to a boil, and cook until reduced to 1 cup (about 8 minutes). Remove from heat.
3. Combine egg whites and egg in a bowl, beating with a whisk until blended. Stir in milks, ⅓ cup brown sugar, vanilla, cinnamon, and nutmeg. Arrange half of bread slices, slightly overlapping, in bottom of an 8-inch square baking pan coated with cooking spray. Spoon fruit mixture evenly over bread. Arrange remaining bread over fruit mixture. Pour egg mixture over bread. Sprinkle top with 4 teaspoons brown sugar and butter. Place pan in a 13 x 9-inch baking pan; add hot water to larger pan to a

depth of 1 inch. Bake at 350° for 45 minutes or until a knife inserted in center comes out clean. Remove 8-inch pan from water. Serve warm with Crème Anglaise. Yield: 10 servings.

CALORIES 319 (15% from fat); FAT 5.4g (sat 2.1g, mono 1.9g, poly 0.7g); PROTEIN 10.3g; CARB 57.5g; FIBER 1.1g; CHOL 116mg; IRON 2.1mg; SODIUM 311mg; CALC 206mg

OLD-FASHIONED VANILLA BREAD PUDDING WITH WINTER FRUIT

PREP: 40 MINUTES   COOK: 50 MINUTES

½ cup boiling water
½ cup chopped dried mixed fruit
¼ cup raisins
1 (6-inch) vanilla bean, split lengthwise
1½ cups 2% reduced-fat milk
10 (½-inch-thick) slices Italian bread
1 tablespoon stick margarine or butter, melted
Cooking spray
1 cup evaporated fat-free milk
½ cup sugar
⅛ teaspoon salt
⅛ teaspoon ground cinnamon
2 large eggs
2 large egg whites

1. Preheat oven to 350°.
2. Combine boiling water, mixed fruit, and raisins in a small bowl; cover and let stand 30 minutes or until softened.
3. Scrape seeds from vanilla bean; place seeds, bean, and 2% reduced-fat milk in a small, heavy saucepan. Heat over medium-heat to 180° or until tiny bubbles form around edge (do not boil). Remove from heat; cool. Discard bean.
4. Place bread on a baking sheet, and brush with margarine. Bake at 350° for 6 minutes or until lightly toasted. Arrange half of bread in an 8-inch square baking dish coated with cooking spray, tearing bread slices to fit dish, if needed. Spoon fruit mixture over bread; top with remaining bread.
5. Combine vanilla-milk mixture, evaporated milk, and next 5 ingredients; stir well with a whisk. Pour over bread; press gently to moisten. Cover dish, and place in a 13 x 9-inch baking pan; add hot water to larger pan to a depth of 1 inch. Bake at 350° for 30 minutes. Uncover and bake an additional 20 minutes or until set. Serve warm. Yield: 8 servings (serving size: 1 square).

CALORIES 228 (15% from fat); FAT 3.9g (sat 1.3g, mono 1.4g, poly 0.7g); PROTEIN 8.4g; CARB 40.5g; FIBER 1.5g; CHOL 58mg; IRON 1.2mg; SODIUM 251mg; CALC 166mg

frozen desserts
We discovered a way to make homemade ice cream that has a smooth, creamy texture without adding cream!

Our secret for making creamy, low-fat ice cream? Make a custard using egg yolks and low-fat milk. (Be careful not to overcook the mixture, or you'll get scrambled eggs. Use a candy thermometer to monitor the temperature.) In some recipes, we used fat-free sweetened condensed skim milk, which adds richness from the milk and concentrated sugar content.

To complete the recipes you can use either a hand-crank or electric ice-cream freezer. Because these vary in time, ice, and type of salt called for (if needed at all), follow the manufacturer's instructions for your model.

STRAWBERRY ICE CREAM

PREP: 1 HOUR   CHILL: 1 HOUR
FREEZE: 2 HOURS

2½ cups 1% low-fat milk, divided
2 large egg yolks
½ cup (4 ounces) ⅓-less-fat cream cheese, cubed and softened
3 cups finely chopped strawberries
1 tablespoon fresh lime juice
1 tablespoon vanilla extract
1 (14-ounce) can fat-free sweetened condensed milk

1. Combine 1¼ cups 1% low-fat milk and egg yolks in a small, heavy saucepan; stir well with a whisk. Heat to 180° or until tiny bubbles form around edge of pan, stirring frequently (do not boil). Remove from heat. Add cream cheese, stirring until smooth. Combine cream cheese mixture, 1¼ cups 1% low-fat milk, strawberries, and remaining ingredients in a large bowl, and stir until well-blended. Cover and chill completely.
2. Pour mixture into the freezer can of an ice-cream freezer, and freeze according to manufacturer's instructions. Spoon ice cream into a freezer-safe container; cover and freeze 2 hours or until firm. Yield: 9½ cups (serving size: ½ cup).

CALORIES 104 (21% from fat); FAT 2.4g (sat 1.3g, mono 0.7g, poly 0.2g); PROTEIN 3.7g; CARB 16.5g; FIBER 0.6g; CHOL 30mg; IRON 0.2mg; SODIUM 62mg; CALC 103mg

Peaches-and-Cream Ice Cream

VANILLA-BUTTERMILK ICE CREAM

PREP: 40 MINUTES
CHILL: 1 HOUR
FREEZE: 1 HOUR

(pictured on front cover)

1   (6-inch) vanilla bean, split
    lengthwise
2   cups 2% reduced-fat milk
¾   cup sugar
1   cup low-fat or nonfat buttermilk
1   (12-ounce) can evaporated
    fat-free milk
Lemon rind (optional)

1. Scrape seeds from vanilla bean; place seeds and bean in a heavy saucepan. Pour 2% reduced-fat milk into pan; heat over medium-high heat to 180° or until tiny bubbles form around edge, stirring frequently (do not boil). Remove from heat; discard vanilla bean.
2. Combine vanilla-milk mixture and sugar in a large bowl, stirring until sugar dissolves. Add buttermilk and evaporated milk, stirring until blended; cover and chill completely.
3. Pour mixture into the freezer can of an ice-cream freezer; freeze according to manufacturer's instructions. Spoon ice cream into a freezer-safe container; cover and freeze 1 hour or until firm. Garnish with lemon rind, if desired. Yield: 16 servings (serving size: ½ cup).

CALORIES 76 (11% from fat); FAT 0.9g (sat 0.6g, mono 0.2g, poly 0g); PROTEIN 3.2g; CARB 14g; FIBER 0g; CHOL 3mg; IRON 0.1mg; SODIUM 48mg; CALC 118mg

PEACHES-AND-CREAM ICE CREAM

PREP: 45 MINUTES   CHILL: 1 HOUR
FREEZE: 1 HOUR

5   cups 1% low-fat milk, divided
4   large egg yolks
4   cups mashed peeled ripe peaches
    (about 8 medium peaches)
2   tablespoons fresh lemon juice
2   tablespoons vanilla extract
½   teaspoon ground ginger
½   teaspoon almond extract
2   (14-ounce) cans fat-free
    sweetened condensed milk
Mint sprigs (optional)

1. Combine 2½ cups 1% low-fat milk and egg yolks in a large, heavy saucepan; stir well with a whisk. Heat to 180° or until thick (about 10 minutes), stirring constantly with a whisk (do not boil). Combine egg yolk mixture, 2½ cups 1% low-fat milk, peaches, lemon juice, and next 4 ingredients in a large bowl; stir until well-blended. Cover and chill completely.
2. Pour mixture into the freezer can of an ice-cream freezer, and freeze according to manufacturer's instructions. Spoon ice cream into a large freezer-safe container; cover and freeze 1 hour or until firm. Garnish with mint sprigs, if desired. Yield: 24 servings (serving size: ½ cup).

CALORIES 140 (9% from fat); FAT 1.4g (sat 0.6g, mono 0.5g, poly 0.2g); PROTEIN 4.9g; CARB 26.2g; FIBER 0.5g; CHOL 40mg; IRON 0.2mg; SODIUM 60mg; CALC 135mg

CITRUS ICE CREAM

PREP: 30 MINUTES   FREEZE: 1 HOUR

This ice cream makes a refreshing soda. Try it in Citrus Sunshine Sodas (page 60).

    ¾ cup sugar
    1 (4-ounce) carton egg substitute
    2 teaspoons grated orange rind
    1 teaspoon grated lemon rind
    1¼ cups orange juice
    ¼ cup fresh lemon juice
    1 cup evaporated fat-free milk
    ½ cup 2% reduced-fat milk

1. Beat sugar and egg substitute in a large bowl at medium speed of a mixer 3 minutes or until sugar dissolves. Add orange and lemon rinds and juices; beat until blended. Stir in milks.

2. Pour mixture into the freezer can of an ice-cream freezer; freeze according to manufacturer's instructions. Spoon into a freezer-safe container; cover and freeze 1 hour or until firm. Yield: 5 cups (serving size: ½ cup).

CALORIES 105 (23% from fat); FAT 0.3g (sat 0.2g, mono 0.1g, poly 0g); PROTEIN 3.7g; CARB 22.7g; FIBER 0.1g; CHOL 2mg; IRON 0.3mg; SODIUM 53mg; CALC 97mg

COFFEE GRANITA

PREP: 8 MINUTES   FREEZE: 3 HOURS

Best when eaten immediately, granita (GRAH-nee-tah) *is Italian for flavored ice and has the texture of coarse snow.*

    1 cup boiling water
    4 teaspoons sugar
    1 tablespoon instant coffee granules
    ½ cup fat-free milk

1. Combine first 3 ingredients in a bowl; stir until coffee granules and sugar dissolve. Add milk, stirring until blended. Pour mixture into an 8-inch square

baking pan; cover and freeze 3 hours or until firm.

2. Remove frozen coffee mixture from freezer, and let stand at room temperature 5 minutes. Break frozen mixture into chunks. Place in a food processor; process until smooth. Serve immediately. Yield: 2 servings (serving size: 1 cup).

CALORIES 58 (2% from fat); FAT 0.1g (sat 0.1g, mono 0g, poly 0g); PROTEIN 2.3g; CARB 11.3g; FIBER 0g; CHOL 1mg; IRON 0.1mg; SODIUM 33mg; CALC 78mg

Refreshing and loaded with vitamin C, Lemon Gelati is a low-fat treat.

LEMON GELATI

PREP: 32 MINUTES   FREEZE: 2 HOURS

    1   cup sugar
    1   tablespoon grated lemon rind
    ⅛   teaspoon salt
    ⅔   cup fresh lemon juice
    1½ cups plain fat-free yogurt
        Mint sprigs (optional)

1. Combine first 4 ingredients in a bowl; stir until sugar dissolves. Add yogurt, and stir well. Pour mixture into the can of an ice-cream freezer, and freeze according to manufacturer's instructions.

2. Spoon gelati into a freezer-safe container; cover and freeze 2 hours or until firm. Garnish with mint, if desired. Yield: 5 servings (serving size: ½ cup).

CALORIES 201 (0% from fat); FAT 0.1g (sat 0.1g, mono 0g, poly 0g); PROTEIN 4g; CARB 48.2g; FIBER 0.1g; CHOL 1mg; IRON 0.1mg; SODIUM 111mg; CALC 140mg

menu
Eggplant Parmesan (page 284)
Three-Grain Summer-Vegetable Salad (page 408)
Banana-Orange Tofu Sherbet

BANANA-ORANGE TOFU SHERBET

PREP: 37 MINUTES   FREEZE: 3 HOURS

The tofu adds creaminess and replaces the milk normally found in a sorbet. It's a vegetarian treat that's completely lactose-free!

    1   (14-ounce) package soft tofu, drained
    ¾   cup sliced ripe banana (about 1 medium)
    ¾   cup light-colored corn syrup
    2   cups fresh orange juice
    1   tablespoon grated orange rind
    1   tablespoon lemon juice
    1   teaspoon vanilla extract

1. Place tofu, banana, and corn syrup in a blender; process 30 seconds. Pour into a medium bowl; add remaining ingredients, stirring well.

2. Pour mixture into the freezer can of an ice-cream freezer. Freeze according to manufacturer's instructions. Spoon sherbet into a freezer-safe container; cover and freeze 3 hours or until firm. Yield: 10 servings (serving size: ½ cup).

CALORIES 128 (8% from fat); FAT 1.1g (sat 0.2g, mono 0.2g, poly 0.6g); PROTEIN 2.9g; CARB 27.1g; FIBER 0.4g; CHOL 0mg; IRON 0.6mg; SODIUM 32mg; CALC 41mg

RUBY-RED GRAPEFRUIT SORBET

PREP: 40 MINUTES   COOL: 45 MINUTES
FREEZE: 2 HOURS

 1 cup sugar
 1 cup water
 Dash of salt
 1 tablespoon grated red
    grapefruit rind
 3 cups fresh red grapefruit juice
 1 cup semisweet sparkling wine

1. Combine first 3 ingredients in a saucepan. Bring to a boil; cook 1 minute or until sugar dissolves, stirring constantly. Remove from heat; pour into a large bowl, and stir in grapefruit rind. Cool to room temperature.
2. Add grapefruit juice and sparkling wine to sugar mixture. Pour mixture into the freezer can of an ice-cream freezer; freeze according to manufacturer's instructions. Spoon sorbet into a freezer-safe container; cover and freeze 2 hours or until firm. Yield: 11 servings (serving size: ½ cup).

CALORIES 122 (0% from fat); FAT 0.1g (sat 0g, mono 0g, poly 0g); PROTEIN 0.4g; CARB 25.2g; FIBER 0g; CHOL 0mg; IRON 1.4mg; SODIUM 16mg; CALC 7mg

FRESH ORANGE SORBET

PREP: 40 MINUTES   COOL: 45 MINUTES
FREEZE: 1 HOUR

 2½ cups water
 1   cup sugar
 Orange rind strips from 2 oranges
 2⅔ cups fresh orange juice
 ⅓   cup fresh lemon juice
 Grated orange rind (optional)

1. Combine water and sugar in a saucepan, and bring to a boil. Add orange rind strips; reduce heat, and simmer 5 minutes. Discard orange rind

strips; remove sugar mixture from heat, and cool completely.
2. Add orange juice and lemon juice to sugar mixture; stir until blended. Pour mixture into the freezer can of an ice-cream freezer. Freeze according to manufacturer's instructions. Spoon sorbet into a freezer-safe container; cover and freeze 1 hour or until firm. Garnish sorbet with grated orange rind, if desired. Yield: 12 servings (serving size: ½ cup).

CALORIES 91 (3% from fat); FAT 0g; PROTEIN 0.4g; CARB 23.2g; FIBER 0.1g; CHOL 0mg;   IRON 0.1mg; SODIUM 1mg; CALC 6mg

CRUNCHY ALMOND CRÈME

PREP: 6 MINUTES

 1 cup vanilla low-fat frozen yogurt
 2 teaspoons amaretto (almond-flavored liqueur)
 2 teaspoons slivered almonds, toasted
 4 amaretti cookies, crushed

1. Spoon yogurt evenly into 2 ice cream dishes. Sprinkle with amaretto, and top with almonds and crushed cookies. Yield: 2 servings (serving size: ½ cup).

CALORIES 160 (24% from fat); FAT 4.3g (sat 1.7g, mono 1g, poly 0.8g); PROTEIN 3.8g; CARB 25.2g; FIBER 0.7g; CHOL 8mg; IRON 0.4mg; SODIUM 28mg; CALC 91mg

ALMOND MOCHA PARFAITS

PREP: 12 MINUTES   FREEZE: 1 HOUR

 3 cups vanilla low-fat ice cream, softened
 2 teaspoons instant espresso granules
 8 teaspoons amaretto (almond-flavored liqueur)
 ½ cup chocolate wafer crumbs (about 8 cookies)
 ¼ cup frozen reduced-calorie whipped topping, thawed

1. Combine ice cream and espresso granules. Spoon ¼ cup ice cream mixture into each of 4 (8-ounce) parfait glasses; top each with 1 teaspoon amaretto and 1 tablespoon cookie crumbs. Repeat layers, ending with ice cream mixture; freeze 1 hour.
2. Top each parfait with 1 tablespoon whipped topping. Serve immediately. Yield: 4 servings.

CALORIES 223 (28% from fat); FAT 7g (sat 3.7g, mono 2g, poly 0.5g); PROTEIN 4.6g; CARB 32.2g; FIBER 0g; CHOL 22mg; IRON 0.4mg; SODIUM 126mg; CALC 152mg

COFFEE-TOFFEE PARFAITS

PREP: 25 MINUTES

Watch toffee closely as it broils—let it bubble, but not burn. You can make your own coffee low-fat ice cream by stirring 1 or 2 teaspoons instant coffee granules into your favorite vanilla low-fat or fat-free ice cream.

 ½ cup packed dark brown sugar
 ¼ cup sliced almonds
 2 teaspoons stick margarine or butter, softened
 Cooking spray
 3 cups coffee low-fat ice cream
 6 tablespoons frozen reduced-calorie whipped topping, thawed

1. Preheat broiler.
2. Combine first 3 ingredients in a food processor; pulse 10 times or until nuts are finely chopped. Press mixture into a 7-inch circle on a baking sheet coated with cooking spray. Broil 2 minutes or until bubbly but not burned.
3. Remove toffee from oven, and let stand 5 minutes. Gently turn toffee over using a wide spatula; broil 1 additional minute. Cool toffee, and break into ½-inch pieces.

4. Spoon ¼ cup ice cream into each of 6 (6-ounce) parfait glasses; top each with 2 tablespoons toffee. Repeat layers; top each parfait with 1 tablespoon whipped topping. Freeze until ready to serve. Yield: 6 servings.

CALORIES 319 (29% from fat); FAT 10.4g (sat 2.8g, mono 5g, poly 1.7g); PROTEIN 7.1g; CARB 45.3g; FIBER 1.1g; CHOL 10mg; IRON 0.7mg; SODIUM 164mg; CALC 191mg

FROZEN MUD PIE SANDWICHES

PREP:18 MINUTES

COOK:7 MINUTES   CHILL:30 MINUTES

FREEZE:1 HOUR

  2 tablespoons sugar
  2 tablespoons light-colored
     corn syrup
1½ tablespoons unsweetened
     cocoa
  1 tablespoon 1% low-fat milk
  1 teaspoon stick margarine or
     butter
  ¼ teaspoon vanilla extract
1¼ cups coffee low-fat frozen
     yogurt, softened
 20 chocolate wafer cookies

1. Combine first 4 ingredients in a small, heavy saucepan; bring to a boil over medium-low heat, stirring frequently with a whisk. Cook 3 minutes or until slightly thickened, stirring frequently. Remove from heat; stir in margarine and vanilla. Cover and chill thoroughly.
2. Spread 2 tablespoons frozen yogurt onto each of 10 cookies; top each with about 1 teaspoon syrup mixture and a cookie, pressing gently. Freeze at least 1 hour. Yield: 10 sandwiches (serving size: 1 sandwich).

CALORIES 95 (29% from fat); FAT 3.1g (sat 1g, mono 1g, poly 0.5g); PROTEIN 1.5g; CARB 15.6g; FIBER 0g; CHOL 10mg; IRON 0.4mg; SODIUM 57mg; CALC 35mg

Frozen Mud Pie Sandwiches

HOT BUSHMILLS SUNDAES

PREP:5 MINUTES   COOK:4 MINUTES

  1 (8-ounce) can unsweetened
     crushed pineapple
  1 tablespoon cornstarch
  1 tablespoon honey
  ¼ cup Bushmills Irish whiskey
  3 cups vanilla fat-free
     frozen yogurt

1. Drain pineapple, reserving juice in a 2-cup glass measure. Add enough water to reserved juice to yield ¾ cup. Add cornstarch and honey; stir with a whisk until smooth.
2. Microwave cornstarch mixture, uncovered, at HIGH 2½ minutes or until thick and bubbly, stirring after 1½ minutes. Stir in whiskey; microwave at HIGH 30 seconds. Stir in pineapple, and microwave at HIGH 30 seconds.
3. Place ½ cup frozen yogurt in each of 6 bowls; top each with ¼ cup sauce. Serve immediately. Yield: 6 servings.

CALORIES 114 (0% from fat); FAT 0g; PROTEIN 3.4g; CARB 26.8g; FIBER 0.3g; CHOL 0mg; IRON 0.1mg; SODIUM 56mg; CALC 125mg

fruit desserts

Fruit desserts capture the jewels of the season—with only a few steps needed to create a mouth-watering treat!

SPARKLING FRUIT SOUP

PREP: 25 MINUTES   COOK: 16 MINUTES
CHILL: 2 HOURS

For tips on selecting fresh, ripe peaches, see page 183.

    2 cups diced plums
    2 cups diced peeled peaches
    2 cups diced cantaloupe
    2 cups apricot nectar
    ¾ cup Moscato D'Asti or other
       sweet sparkling wine
    ¼ cup water
    2 tablespoons honey
    1 (3-inch) cinnamon stick
    1 bay leaf

1. Combine first 3 ingredients in a bowl. Combine nectar and next 5 ingredients in a saucepan; bring to a boil. Reduce heat; simmer 10 minutes. Discard cinnamon stick and bay leaf. Pour nectar mixture over fruit; cover and chill 2 hours. Yield: 7 servings (serving size: 1 cup).

CALORIES 126 (4% from fat); FAT 0.6g (sat 0.1g, mono 0.3g, poly 0.2g); PROTEIN 1.5g; CARB 31.8g; FIBER 2.8g; CHOL 0mg; IRON 0.6mg; SODIUM 9mg; CALC 18mg

RUM-SPIKED WINTER COMPOTE

PREP: 10 MINUTES   COOK: 12 MINUTES

    2   cups fresh cranberries
    1   cup water
    ½   cup white rum
    ½   cup packed brown sugar
    2   (3-inch) cinnamon sticks
    2½ cups tangerine or orange
        sections (about 7 tangerines)
    2½ cups grapefruit sections (about 3
        grapefruit)

1. Combine first 5 ingredients in a medium saucepan; bring to a boil. Reduce heat, and simmer, uncovered, 5 minutes or until cranberries pop. Add fruit sections, stirring gently. Cover and simmer 4 minutes or until thoroughly heated. Discard cinnamon sticks. Serve warm or at room temperature. Yield: 8 servings (serving size: ¾ cup).

CALORIES 117 (2% from fat); FAT 0.2g (sat 0g, mono 0g, poly 0.1g); PROTEIN 1g; CARB 29.8g; FIBER 2.1g; CHOL 0mg; IRON 0.4mg; SODIUM 6mg; CALC 31mg

TOFFEE CANDY APPLES

PREP: 10 MINUTES
COOK: 14 MINUTES

You'll need wooden sticks to make these treats. Also, be sure to use a heavy saucepan to ensure even heating and to help keep from scorching the sugar mixture. Our step-by-step techniques (at right) will guide you to create perfect carnival-style candy apples.

    8   Granny Smith apples
    1½ cups packed dark brown
        sugar
    ⅓   cup water
    ⅓   cup dark corn syrup or
        molasses
    2   tablespoons stick margarine or
        butter
    1   tablespoon white vinegar

1. Wash and dry apples; remove stems. Insert a wooden stick into stem end of each apple; set aside.
2. Line a baking sheet with foil.
3. Combine sugar and remaining 4 ingredients in a heavy saucepan. Bring to a boil over medium heat; cover and

TESTING WITHOUT A CANDY THERMOMETER

Testing for the soft crack stage: Don't despair if you don't have a candy thermometer. You can test the syrup for the candy apples using a glass of cold water. When the syrup for the candy apples is dropped into cold water, the syrup separates into threads that are hard but not brittle. This is known as the soft crack stage.

cook 3 minutes. Uncover and cook 8 minutes, without stirring, until mixture reaches 280°.
4. Remove from heat. Quickly dip apples in sugar mixture; allow excess to drip off. Place apples, stick sides up, on prepared baking sheet; cool completely. Yield: 8 servings.

CALORIES 301 (10% from fat); FAT 3.3g (sat 0.6g, mono 1.3g, poly 1g); PROTEIN 0.3g; CARB 71.8g; FIBER 4.3g; CHOL 0mg; IRON 1mg; SODIUM 66mg; CALC 46mg

Toffee Candy Apples

1. Insert stick into stem end of apple.

2. Bring sugar and remaining ingredients to a boil. Cover and cook 3 minutes.

3. After uncovering, cook to 280° (soft crack stage) (about 8 minutes).

4. Quickly dip apples into sugar mixture, allowing excess to drip off.

5. Place on baking sheet lined with foil.

BRIE STRATA WITH APRICOT-PAPAYA SALSA

PREP: 30 MINUTES   CHILL: 30 MINUTES
COOK: 40 MINUTES

Salsa:
  1 cup apricot nectar
  ¾ cup dried apricots, quartered
  2 cups diced peeled papaya
  1 tablespoon honey
  1 tablespoon fresh lime juice

Strata:
  1 (15-ounce) round Brie cheese
  8 cups (1-inch) cubed French
    bread
  Cooking spray
  2 tablespoons brown sugar
  1 (12-ounce) can evaporated
    fat-free milk
  ¼ teaspoon salt
  3 large egg whites, lightly beaten
  2 large eggs, lightly beaten

1. To prepare salsa, combine nectar and apricots in a microwave-safe bowl. Microwave at HIGH 2 minutes or until mixture boils; cover and let stand 30 minutes or until apricots soften. Drain apricots, reserving 2 tablespoons nectar; discard remaining nectar. Combine apricots, reserved nectar, papaya, honey, and lime juice; stir gently, and set salsa aside.
2. To prepare strata, remove rind from Brie, and discard. Cut Brie into small pieces.
3. Arrange half of bread cubes in a 9-inch square baking dish coated with cooking spray. Top with half of Brie, and sprinkle with half of brown sugar. Repeat procedure with remaining bread, Brie, and brown sugar.
4. Combine milk, salt, egg whites, and eggs; stir well with a wire whisk. Pour over bread; press firmly with back of spoon to moisten all bread cubes. Cover; chill 30 minutes.

5. Preheat oven to 350°.
6. Bake at 350° for 40 minutes or until a knife inserted near center comes out clean. Serve warm with salsa. Yield: 9 servings (serving size: 1 strata square and ⅓ cup salsa).

CALORIES 318 (32% from fat); FAT 11.2g (sat 6.1g, mono 3.4g, poly 0.7g); PROTEIN 15.8g; CARB 39.7g; FIBER 2.3g; CHOL 80mg; IRON 2mg; SODIUM 555mg; CALC 225mg

SWEET PEACH KUGEL

PREP: 8 MINUTES   COOK: 1 HOUR

  1 cup 1% low-fat cottage cheese
  4 (8-ounce) cartons egg substitute
  1 (8-ounce) carton low-fat sour
    cream
  ¾ cup raisins
  ½ cup sugar
  2 tablespoons reduced-calorie stick
    margarine, melted
  1 teaspoon ground cinnamon
  ¼ teaspoon salt
  1 (15-ounce) can unsweetened
    sliced peaches, drained and
    coarsely chopped
  8 cups cooked medium egg
    noodles (about 12 ounces
    uncooked pasta)
  Cooking spray
  ⅓ cup coarsely crushed cornflakes

1. Preheat oven to 325°.
2. Combine first 9 ingredients in a large bowl. Add egg noodles, and toss gently to coat.
3. Spoon mixture into a 13 x 9-inch baking dish coated with cooking spray. Sprinkle cornflakes evenly over noodle mixture; cover and bake at 325° for 45 minutes. Uncover and bake an additional 15 minutes. Yield: 12 servings (serving size: 1 cup).

CALORIES 266 (17% from fat); FAT 5g (sat 2g, mono 1.6g, poly 0.8g); PROTEIN 14.9g; CARB 40.9g; FIBER 1.6g; CHOL 35mg; IRON 3.1mg; SODIUM 287mg; CALC 72mg

CHEESE BLINTZES WITH BLUEBERRIES

PREP: 33 MINUTES   CHILL: 2 HOURS
COOK: 12 MINUTES

  1 cup fat-free cottage cheese
  ½ cup (4 ounces) ⅓-less-fat cream
    cheese, softened
  ¼ cup granulated sugar
  1 teaspoon vanilla extract
  1 cup all-purpose flour
  ¼ teaspoon salt
  1½ cups fat-free milk
  3 large eggs, lightly beaten
  1½ tablespoons vegetable oil
  1½ teaspoons vanilla extract
  Cooking spray
  2 teaspoons powdered sugar
  2 cups blueberries or other fresh
    berries

1. Place cottage cheese in a blender or food processor, and process until smooth, scraping sides of bowl once. Add cream cheese, granulated sugar, and 1 teaspoon vanilla; process until smooth. Pour into a bowl; cover and chill.
2. Lightly spoon flour into a dry measuring cup; level with a knife. Combine flour and salt in a medium bowl. Combine milk, eggs, oil, and 1½ teaspoons vanilla; add to flour mixture, stirring with a whisk until almost smooth. Cover and chill 2 hours.
3. Place a 10-inch crêpe pan or nonstick skillet coated with cooking spray over medium-high heat until hot. Remove pan from heat. Pour a scant ¼ cup batter into pan; quickly tilt pan in all directions so batter covers skillet with a thin film. Cook about 1 minute, or until edges begin to brown. Carefully lift edge of crêpe with a spatula to test for doneness. The crêpe is ready to turn when it can be shaken loose from the pan and the underside is lightly browned. Turn crêpe over; cook 30 seconds on other side.

4. Place crêpe on a towel; cool. Repeat procedure until all of batter is used. Stack crêpes between single layers of wax paper or paper towels to prevent sticking.

5. Spoon 3 tablespoons cheese mixture in center of each crêpe; fold sides and ends of crêpe over, and place, seam side down on a baking sheet lined with plastic wrap. (Blintzes may be covered and chilled at this point.)

6. Place a large nonstick skillet coated with cooking spray over medium heat until hot. Place 4 blintzes, seam sides down, in skillet; cook 2 minutes or until lightly browned. Turn blintzes over; cook 2 minutes. Repeat procedure with remaining blintzes. Sprinkle with powdered sugar and blueberries. Serve warm. Yield: 8 servings (serving size: 1 blintz and ¼ cup blueberries).

CALORIES 225 (33% from fat); FAT 8.2g (sat 3.2g, mono 2.5g, poly 1.7g); PROTEIN 10.8g; CARB 26.6g; FIBER 1.3g; CHOL 93mg; IRON 1.1mg; SODIUM 285mg; CALC 96mg

NEW ENGLAND-STYLE BANANAS FOSTER

PREP: 5 MINUTES   COOK: 8 MINUTES

⅓ cup maple syrup
⅓ cup dark rum
3½ cups diagonally sliced firm ripe banana
⅓ cup chopped walnuts, toasted
3 cups vanilla fat-free frozen yogurt

1. Combine syrup and rum in a large nonstick skillet; bring to a simmer over medium-low heat. Add banana; cook 3 minutes, stirring occasionally. Add walnuts; cook 1 minute. Serve immediately over frozen yogurt. Yield: 6 servings (serving size: ½ cup banana mixture and ½ cup frozen yogurt).

CALORIES 296 (13% from fat); FAT 4.4g (sat 0.4g, mono 0.9g, poly 2.7g); PROTEIN 6.2g; CARB 51.9g; FIBER 3g; CHOL 0mg; IRON 0.7mg; SODIUM 65mg; CALC 156mg

New England-Style Bananas Foster

1. Add bananas to simmering syrup mixture; simmer, uncovered, 3 minutes.

2. Add walnuts to banana mixture; simmer 1 minute.

3. Remove banana mixture from pan immediately after cooking.

POACHING TO PERFECTION

Poaching is one of the gentlest, easiest, healthiest, and tastiest cooking methods. Food is immersed in liquids such as wine (or stock for entrées), then simmered until done. And because poaching preserves the shape and texture of food, dishes prepared this way can be visually stunning, particularly those using fruit.

Poaching isn't difficult—just have all your ingredients ready before you start cooking. Remember, too, that cooked food must be removed immediately from its liquid, or it will continue to cook.

STUFFED FIGS WITH MARSALA

PREP: 5 MINUTES   COOK: 40 MINUTES

Calimyrna figs have yellowish-green skins and milky-white flesh.

  1 cup sweet Marsala
  ¼ cup orange juice
  2 tablespoons sugar
 12 dried Calimyrna figs
  ⅓ cup (3 ounces) ⅓-less-fat cream
     cheese, softened
  ¼ cup grated fresh Parmesan cheese
  1 tablespoon chopped pine nuts
Orange rind curls (optional)
Mint sprigs (optional)
Pine nuts (optional)

1. Combine first 4 ingredients in a small saucepan; bring to a boil. Remove from heat; cover and let stand 15 minutes. Remove figs from pan with a slotted spoon; set aside, and keep warm. Bring Marsala mixture to a boil; cook 10 minutes or until reduced to ¼ cup.
2. Combine cheeses and chopped pine nuts in a small bowl; stir until well-blended. Cut each fig to, but not through, stem end. Stuff about 1½ teaspoons cheese mixture into center of each fig. Spoon 1 tablespoon Marsala sauce onto each dessert plate; arrange 3 stuffed figs on top of sauce. Garnish with orange rind curls, mint sprigs, and pine nuts, if desired. Yield: 4 servings.

CALORIES 288 (28% from fat); FAT 9.1g (sat 4.4g, mono 2.8g, poly 1.4g); PROTEIN 6.3g; CARB 50.1g; FIBER 7.1g; CHOL 20mg; IRON 1.6mg; SODIUM 179mg; CALC 163mg

GINGERED MELON COMPOTE

PREP: 10 MINUTES   COOK: 18 MINUTES

 1½ cups water
  ¾ cup sugar
  2 tablespoons coarsely chopped
     peeled fresh ginger
  6 whole cloves
  6 whole allspice
  2 cups cubed seeded
     watermelon
  1 cup cubed peeled cantaloupe
  1 cup blueberries

1. Combine first 5 ingredients in a small saucepan; bring to a boil. Reduce heat, and simmer 15 minutes or until sugar dissolves, stirring occasionally. Strain sugar syrup through a sieve into a bowl; discard solids. Cover syrup; chill.
2. Divide watermelon, cantaloupe, and blueberries evenly among 6 dessert dishes. Spoon ¼ cup sugar syrup over each serving. Yield: 6 servings (serving size: ⅔ cup fruit and ¼ cup syrup).

CALORIES 137 (3% from fat); FAT 0.4g (sat 0.2g, mono 0.1g, poly 0.1g); PROTEIN 0.7g; CARB 34.4g; FIBER 1.7g; CHOL 0mg; IRON 0.2mg; SODIUM 5mg; CALC 9mg

Stuffed Figs With Marsala

FRESH FRUIT WITH STRAWBERRY SAUCE

PREP: 8 MINUTES

1 cup frozen unsweetened whole strawberries, thawed
2 teaspoons sugar
¼ teaspoon grated orange rind
2 cups orange sections (about 6 oranges)
1 cup cubed peeled kiwifruit (about 3 kiwifruit)

1. Place first 3 ingredients in a blender or food processor, and process until smooth.
2. Spoon ½ cup orange sections and ¼ cup kiwifruit into each of 4 small bowls; top each serving with 3 tablespoons sauce. Yield: 4 servings.

CALORIES 99 (5% from fat); FAT 0.5g (sat 0.1g, mono 0.1g, poly 0.1g); PROTEIN 1.8g; CARB 23.3g; FIBER 6.4g; CHOL 0mg; IRON 0.7mg; SODIUM 1mg; CALC 58mg

PEACH MELBA

PREP: 12 MINUTES
COOK: 8 MINUTES   CHILL: 1 HOUR

½ cup sugar
1 cup water
2 tablespoons lemon juice
5 ripe peaches, peeled, pitted, and halved
2 cups fresh raspberries
¼ cup water
¼ cup sugar
1 teaspoon vanilla extract
½ cup plus 2 tablespoons vanilla low-fat ice cream
Mint sprigs (optional)

1. Combine first 3 ingredients in a large skillet; bring to a boil over medium heat. Place peach halves, cut sides down, in skillet; cover and simmer 3 minutes. Turn peaches over, and cook 3 minutes

or until tender. Drain peaches; cover and chill. Discard cooking liquid.
2. Place raspberries and ¼ cup water in a food processor; process 1 minute or until smooth. Strain and discard seeds.
3. Combine raspberry puree, ¼ cup sugar, and vanilla in a bowl; cover and chill. Place 2 peach halves into each of 5 dessert compotes; top each with 2 tablespoons ice cream and ¼ cup raspberry sauce. Garnish with fresh mint, if desired. Serve immediately. Yield: 5 servings.

CALORIES 181 (5% from fat); FAT 1.1g (sat 0.5g, mono 0.3g, poly 0.2g); PROTEIN 1.9g; CARB 43.6g; FIBER 5.7g; CHOL 2mg; IRON 0.4mg; SODIUM 14mg; CALC 40mg

PEACH MELBA CRISP

PREP: 20 MINUTES   COOK: 45 MINUTES

An easy way to peel peaches is to drop them into boiling water for 30 seconds, and then immediately plunge them into cold water. The skins should slip off easily.

½ cup all-purpose flour
¼ cup granulated sugar
¼ cup packed brown sugar
3 tablespoons chilled stick margarine or butter, cut into small pieces
6 cups sliced peeled peaches (about 3 pounds)
2 teaspoons lemon juice
1 cup raspberries
1 tablespoon granulated sugar
1 tablespoon cornstarch
Cooking spray
1 tablespoon seedless raspberry jam, melted

1. Preheat oven to 375°.
2. Lightly spoon flour into a dry measuring cup; level with a knife. Combine flour, ¼ cup granulated sugar, and brown sugar; cut in margarine with a pastry blender until mixture resembles coarse meal.

3. Combine sliced peaches and lemon juice in a large bowl, and toss gently to coat. Add raspberries, 1 tablespoon granulated sugar, and cornstarch, and toss gently. Spoon fruit mixture into an 8-inch square baking dish coated with cooking spray, and drizzle raspberry jam evenly over fruit mixture. Sprinkle with flour mixture. Bake at 375° for 45 minutes or until brown. Yield: 6 servings (serving size: 1 cup).

CALORIES 258 (22% from fat); FAT 6.2g (sat 1.2g, mono 2.6g, poly 2g); PROTEIN 2.5g; CARB 51.2g; FIBER 4.7g; CHOL 0mg; IRON 1mg; SODIUM 73mg; CALC 25mg

PEACH POINTERS

Juicy, ripe peaches are one of the finest pleasures of summer. To ensure the tastiest peaches possible, heed these pointers.

• **Look for creamy-gold or yellow skin and a strong peachy aroma for true signs of ripeness.** The rosy-red blush is indicative of certain varieties, not ripeness.

• **Peaches with even a touch of green were immature when picked and will never ripen to their characteristic sweet flavor.**

• Peaches are picked when mature but firm for their trip to the market. **To encourage ripening, store peaches in a loosely closed paper bag or ripening bowl.** Trapping the gas the peaches release as they ripen speeds the process. Check daily; refrigerate when ripened.

• **Handle peaches gently, as they bruise easily.** Sort fruit and use the softest fruit first. Bruised fruit spoils quickly and may cause other fruit to deteriorate.

• One pound of peaches (2 large or 3 medium) yields 2 cups sliced peaches or 1⅔ cups chopped peaches.

Vanilla-Poached
Peaches

menu

Parmesan-Crusted Rack of Lamb With
Roasted Garlic Potatoes (page 342)

Steamed asparagus

Whole-wheat rolls

Pears Au Porto With Blue Cheese

PEARS AU PORTO WITH BLUE CHEESE

PREP: **32** MINUTES   COOK: **1** HOUR
CHILL: **8** HOURS

 4 cups water
 2 tablespoons lemon juice
 6 small firm ripe pears (about 2½
    pounds)
2¼ cups ruby port or other sweet red
    wine
 1 (3-inch) cinnamon stick
 ¼ teaspoon black peppercorns
 ½ cup (2 ounces) crumbled blue
    cheese
 ⅓ cup (3 ounces) ⅓-less-fat cream
    cheese, softened

VANILLA-POACHED PEACHES

PREP: **8** MINUTES   COOK: **18** MINUTES
COOL: **30** MINUTES

*You can substitute 1 teaspoon vanilla
extract for the vanilla bean; just stir in
after the mixture is reduced. Six nectarines
can be substituted for the peaches.*

 1 cup water
 ⅓ cup sugar
 1 (3½-inch) piece vanilla bean, split
    lengthwise
 3 large ripe peaches, peeled,
    pitted, and quartered
 2 tablespoons strawberry
    preserves
 4 teaspoons chopped pistachios
Whole strawberries (optional)

1. Combine first 3 ingredients in a
medium nonaluminum saucepan; bring
to a boil. Reduce heat; add peaches, and
simmer 7 minutes or until tender. Remove peaches with a slotted spoon;
place in a shallow dish. Bring cooking
liquid to a boil, and cook until reduced
to ½ cup (about 7 minutes). Discard
vanilla bean; pour syrup over peaches.
Cool to room temperature.
2. Combine strawberry preserves and 4
teaspoons peach syrup; stir with a whisk.
Place 3 peach quarters and 1½ tablespoons
syrup in each of 4 dishes; top each serving
with 2 teaspoons strawberry mixture and 1
teaspoon pistachios. Garnish with strawberries, if desired. Yield: 4 servings.

CALORIES 132 (10% from fat); FAT 1.4g (sat 0.2g, mono 0.9g,
poly 2g); PROTEIN 1.1g; CARB 31g; FIBER 1.5g;
CHOL 0mg; IRON 0.3mg; SODIUM 4mg; CALC 9mg

1. Combine water and juice in a large
bowl. Peel pears; remove cores from
bottom end, leaving stems intact. If
necessary, cut about ¼ inch from base
of each pear so it will sit flat. Add pears
to water mixture.
2. Combine port, cinnamon, and peppercorns in a Dutch oven; bring to a
boil. Reduce heat, and simmer, uncovered, 5 minutes. Add pears and water
mixture. Increase heat to medium-high;
bring to a simmer. Cover and reduce
heat to medium-low; simmer 20 minutes or until pears are tender, turning
pears occasionally. Remove pears with a
slotted spoon; place in a shallow dish.
3. Bring cooking liquid to a boil; cook
until reduced to ¾ cup (about 30 minutes). Strain mixture, reserving liquid;
discard spices. Pour reserved liquid over

pears. Cover and chill 8 hours, turning occasionally. Remove pears with a slotted spoon, reserving liquid.

4. Combine cheeses in a food processor; process until smooth. Spoon cheese mixture into a pastry bag fitted with a small leaf tube. Spoon 2 tablespoons reserved liquid onto each of 6 dessert plates. Cut each pear lengthwise into 3 wedges; arrange on top of sauce. Pipe cheese mixture onto pears. Yield: 6 servings (serving size: 3 wedges).

CALORIES 165 (30% from fat); FAT 5.5g (sat 3.1g, mono 1.5g, poly 0.3g); PROTEIN 4.1g; CARB 27.7g; FIBER 4g; CHOL 14mg; IRON 0.8mg; SODIUM 209mg; CALC 92mg

POACHED PEARS WITH SPICED-WINE SYRUP

PREP: 9 MINUTES   COOK: 20 MINUTES

1½ cups dry red wine
1 cup water
½ cup packed dark brown sugar
1 (3-inch) cinnamon stick
10 black peppercorns
3 tablespoons honey
1 teaspoon vanilla extract
1 tablespoon fresh lemon juice
4 firm Bartlett or Bosc pears
Lemon rind curls (optional)

1. Combine first 8 ingredients in a 3-quart microwave-safe dish; microwave at HIGH 5 minutes or until mixture boils.
2. Peel pears; remove cores from bottom end, leaving stems intact. If necessary, cut about ¼ inch from base of each pear so it will sit flat. Add pears to wine mixture, and cover and microwave at HIGH 10 minutes or until tender. Cool in dish 5 minutes. Remove pears with a slotted spoon.

3. Microwave wine mixture at HIGH 5 minutes or until reduced to 1 cup. Place each pear in a shallow bowl. Spoon ¼ cup wine sauce over each pear. Garnish with lemon rind curls, if desired. Yield: 4 servings.

Note: Look for pears that have long stems for a dramatic presentation. To core a pear, hold it in your left hand. Using a melon baller, make three or four quick cuts into pear from the bottom.

CALORIES 257 (3% from fat); FAT 0.8g (sat 0.1g, mono 0.1g, poly 0.2g); PROTEIN 0.9g; CARB 66g; FIBER 2.7g; CHOL 0mg; IRON 1.4mg; SODIUM 18mg; CALC 50mg

Poached Pears With
Spiced-Wine Syrup

TROPICAL CRISP

PREP: 28 MINUTES   COOK: 35 MINUTES

Ripe papaya can be substituted for the mango, if desired.

½   cup flaked sweetened coconut
2   tablespoons sugar
1   tablespoon all-purpose flour
¼   teaspoon vanilla extract
Dash of salt
1   large egg white
Cooking spray
2   tablespoons graham cracker
    crumbs
2   tablespoons stick margarine or
    butter, melted
1   (15¼-ounce) can crushed
    pineapple, undrained
¼   cup thinly sliced dried apricot
    halves
1   cup chopped peeled mango
2   tablespoons sugar
2   tablespoons cornstarch
2   tablespoons water

1. Preheat oven to 325°.
2. Combine first 6 ingredients in a bowl. Spread coconut mixture evenly onto a baking sheet coated with cooking spray. Bake at 325° for 20 minutes or until edges are lightly browned. Cool completely. Increase oven temperature to 350°.
3. Break coconut mixture into small pieces. Place coconut pieces and cracker crumbs in a food processor, and process until blended. With processor on, slowly add margarine through food chute, and process until blended; set aside.
4. Drain pineapple, reserving ½ cup juice. Combine ¼ cup pineapple juice and apricots in a 1-cup glass measure. Cover with heavy-duty plastic wrap, and vent. Microwave at HIGH 2½ minutes. Let stand, covered, 15 minutes; drain.

5. Combine apricot mixture, remaining ¼ cup pineapple juice, pineapple, mango, 2 tablespoons sugar, cornstarch, and water in a bowl. Spoon fruit mixture into a 1-quart baking dish; sprinkle with coconut mixture. Bake at 350° for 35 minutes or until golden. Yield: 6 servings (serving size: ½ cup).

CALORIES 200 (33% from fat); FAT 7.4g (sat 3.5g, mono 2g, poly 1.4g); PROTEIN 1.7g; CARB 33.8g; FIBER 2.3g; CHOL 0mg; IRON 0.8mg; SODIUM 117mg; CALC 15mg

STRAWBERRIES AND RASPBERRIES IN CUSTARD SAUCE

PREP: 6 MINUTES
COOK: 38 MINUTES
CHILL: 1 HOUR

1½   cups fat-free milk
¼   cup sugar
1   tablespoon all-purpose flour
4   large egg yolks, lightly beaten
¾   teaspoon vanilla extract
1½   cups halved strawberries
1½   cups raspberries

1. Combine first 4 ingredients in the top of a double boiler. Cook over simmering water until mixture thickens (about 38 minutes), stirring constantly. Remove from heat, and stir in vanilla. Place plastic wrap on surface; cool to room temperature. Chill thoroughly.
2. Spoon about ⅓ cup custard sauce into each of 6 stemmed glasses; add ¼ cup strawberries and ¼ cup raspberries to each glass. Yield: 6 servings.

CALORIES 127 (28% from fat); FAT 3.9g (sat 1.2g, mono 1.4g, poly 0.7g); PROTEIN 4.6g; CARB 18.8g; FIBER 3.3g; CHOL 146mg; IRON 0.8mg; SODIUM 37mg; CALC 103mg

COCONUT PAVLOVAS WITH TROPICAL FRUITS AND ICE CREAM

PREP: 30 MINUTES   COOK: 1 HOUR
COOL: 4 HOURS

2   cups (1-inch) cubed fresh
     pineapple
1   cup orange sections
1   cup cubed peeled ripe mango
2   tablespoons sugar
2   tablespoons white rum
⅛   teaspoon ground cinnamon
3   large egg whites
¼   teaspoon cream of tartar
¼   teaspoon almond extract
⅔   cup sugar
½   cup flaked sweetened coconut,
     toasted
⅓   cup dried sweet cherries
1½   cups vanilla low-fat ice cream
Mint sprigs (optional)

1. Preheat oven to 250°.
2. Combine first 6 ingredients in a bowl; cover and chill.
3. Place parchment paper over a baking sheet. Draw 6 (4-inch) circles on paper. Turn paper over; secure with masking tape.
4. Beat egg whites and cream of tartar at high speed of a mixer until foamy; add extract. Gradually add ⅔ cup sugar, 1 tablespoon at a time, beating until stiff peaks form. Fold coconut into egg white mixture.
5. Divide egg white mixture among 6 drawn circles. Shape into nests with 1-inch sides using the back of a spoon. Bake at 250° for 1 hour or until dry. Turn oven off; cool in closed oven at least 4 hours. Carefully remove from paper.
6. Add cherries to fruit mixture. Spoon ¼ cup ice cream into each meringue; top with ⅔ cup fruit mixture. Garnish with mint, if desired. Yield: 6 servings.

CALORIES 301 (14% from fat); FAT 4.8g (sat 3.5g, mono 0.6g, poly 0.2g); PROTEIN 3.9g; CARB 60.4g; FIBER 3.7g; CHOL 5mg; IRON 0.6mg; SODIUM 80mg; CALC 73mg

Coconut Pavlovas With Tropical Fruits and Ice Cream

PART 1 templates

1. Draw 6 (4-inch) circles on parchment paper. Turn parchment paper over, and secure with masking tape.

PART 2 making the meringues

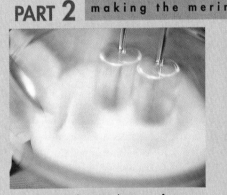

2. Beat egg whites and cream of tartar at high speed of a mixer until foamy.

3. Gradually add ⅔ cup sugar, 1 tablespoon at a time, beating until stiff peaks form.

4. Fold coconut into egg white mixture. Be sure to fold, not stir. Stirring can deflate the beaten egg whites.

5. Divide egg white mixture evenly among the 6 drawn circles. Using the back of spoon, shape meringues into nests with 1-inch sides.

STRAWBERRY DESSERT NACHOS

PREP:14 MINUTES CHILL:30 MINUTES
COOK:7 MINUTES PER BATCH

3 cups sliced strawberries
⅓ cup granulated sugar
¼ cup amaretto (almond-flavored liqueur)
½ cup fat-free sour cream
½ cup frozen reduced-calorie whipped topping, thawed
2 tablespoons granulated sugar
⅛ teaspoon ground cinnamon
6 (7-inch) flour tortillas
Butter-flavored cooking spray
2 teaspoons cinnamon sugar (found in the spice section of the grocery store)
2 tablespoons sliced almonds, toasted
2 teaspoons shaved semisweet chocolate

1. Combine first 3 ingredients in a bowl; cover and chill 30 minutes.
2. Combine sour cream, whipped topping, 2 tablespoons sugar, and cinnamon in a bowl; cover and chill.
3. Preheat oven to 400°.
4. Cut each tortilla into 8 wedges. Arrange tortilla wedges on 2 baking sheets; lightly coat with cooking spray. Sprinkle evenly with cinnamon sugar. Bake at 400° for 7 minutes or until crisp. Cool on a wire rack.
5. Drain strawberry mixture; reserve juice for another use. Place 8 tortilla wedges on each of 6 dessert plates, and top each serving with about ⅓ cup strawberry mixture and 2½ tablespoons sour cream mixture. Divide sliced almonds and shaved semisweet chocolate evenly among nachos. Yield: 6 servings.

CALORIES 263 (20% from fat); FAT 5.7g (sat 1.9g, mono 2.1g, poly 1.6g); PROTEIN 6.1g; CARB 44.7g; FIBER 3.3g; CHOL 0mg; IRON 1.8mg; SODIUM 222mg; CALC 102mg

soufflés A soufflé makes a perfect finale for impressing your friends—just don't tell them how easy it was to make.

MINT CHOCOLATE SOUFFLÉS

PREP:32 MINUTES FREEZE:2 HOURS
COOK:40 MINUTES

Cooking spray
2 teaspoons granulated sugar
⅓ cup granulated sugar
2 cups evaporated fat-free milk, divided
¼ cup mint-chocolate chips
3 tablespoons ⅓-less-fat cream cheese, softened
⅛ teaspoon salt
¼ cup all-purpose flour
1 tablespoon white crème de menthe
1 teaspoon vanilla extract
6 large egg whites
⅛ teaspoon cream of tartar
⅓ cup granulated sugar
1 teaspoon powdered sugar

1. Coat 8 (8-ounce) soufflé dishes with cooking spray; sprinkle each with ¼ teaspoon granulated sugar. Set aside.
2. Combine ⅓ cup granulated sugar, 1½ cups evaporated milk, chocolate chips, cream cheese, and salt in a medium saucepan; cook over medium heat 7 minutes or until chocolate and cheese melt, stirring constantly.
3. Combine ½ cup evaporated milk and flour; stir with a whisk until smooth. Add to chocolate mixture; bring to a boil, stirring constantly. Remove from heat; stir in crème de menthe and vanilla. Pour into a large bowl; cover with plastic wrap, and cool completely.
4. Beat egg whites and cream of tartar in a medium bowl at high speed of a mixer until soft peaks form. Gradually add ⅓ cup granulated sugar, 1 tablespoon at a time, beating until stiff peaks form. Gently fold egg white mixture into chocolate mixture. Spoon evenly into prepared soufflé dishes. Freeze until firm (about 2 hours). Cover with foil until ready to bake.
5. Preheat oven to 350°.
6. Uncover soufflés; place frozen soufflés in 2 (9-inch) square baking pans. Add water to pans to a depth of 1 inch. Bake at 350° for 40 minutes or until puffy and set. Sprinkle with powdered sugar. Serve immediately. Yield: 8 servings.

CALORIES 180 (11% from fat); FAT 2.1g (sat 1.2g, mono 0.6g, poly 0.1g); PROTEIN 8.2g; CARB 31.8g; FIBER 0.1g; CHOL 5mg; IRON 0.8mg; SODIUM 162mg; CALC 191mg

Don't overbeat the egg whites; if beaten for too long, they will separate, turn grainy, and be difficult to fold in.

Mint Chocolate Soufflés

1. Coat each soufflé dish with cooking spray; sprinkle each with ¼ teaspoon sugar.

2. Freeze until firm; wrap soufflés in foil, and keep frozen until ready to bake.

3. Place frozen soufflés in 2 (9-inch) square baking pans. Add water to depth of 1 inch.

Mint Chocolate Soufflés

Here's how to know: **Leave the soufflé undisturbed during baking.** Even if you're tempted to open the oven door and watch it rise, DON'T! You may be watching it fall instead.

(1) Look through your oven window. When the **top appears browned, crusty, and dry,** it's **time to test** the soufflé for doneness.

Do so by **(2) inserting a knife blade into the center.** If it comes out **moist and clean,** the soufflé should be ready.

(3) Otherwise, slide it back into the oven, and **bake it 10 additional minutes.** Repeat the checking procedure.

FRENCH SILK SOUFFLÉS

PREP: 20 MINUTES

FREEZE: 2 HOURS

COOK: 40 MINUTES

Cooking spray
⅓ cup plus 2 teaspoons granulated
     sugar, divided
¼ cup all-purpose flour
¼ cup unsweetened cocoa
 1 teaspoon instant coffee granules
⅛ teaspoon salt
 1 ounce semisweet chocolate, grated
 2 cups evaporated fat-free milk
 1 teaspoon vanilla extract
 6 large egg whites
⅛ teaspoon cream of tartar
⅓ cup granulated sugar
 2 teaspoons powdered sugar

1. Coat 8 (6-ounce) soufflé dishes or custard cups with cooking spray; sprinkle each with ¼ teaspoon granulated sugar. Lightly spoon flour into a dry measuring cup; level with a knife.

Make sure the milk mixture is completely cooled before folding in the egg whites.

2. Combine ⅓ cup sugar, flour, and next 4 ingredients in a medium saucepan. Gradually add milk, stirring with a whisk. Bring to a boil over medium heat, and cook 1 minute, stirring constantly. Remove from heat; stir in vanilla. Pour mixture into a large bowl; cover with plastic wrap. Cool completely.
3. Beat egg whites and cream of tartar at high speed of a mixer until soft peaks form. Gradually add ⅓ cup granulated sugar, 1 tablespoon at a time, beating until stiff peaks form.
4. Gently fold egg white mixture into milk mixture. Spoon evenly into prepared soufflé dishes. Freeze until firm (about 2 hours).
5. Preheat oven to 350°.
6. Place frozen soufflés in 2 (9-inch) square baking pans. Add hot water to pans to a depth of 1 inch. Bake at 350° for 35 to 40 minutes or until puffy and set. Sprinkle with powdered sugar; serve immediately. Yield: 8 servings.

CALORIES 179 (10% from fat); FAT 1.9g (sat 1g, mono 0.6g, poly 0.1g); PROTEIN 8.8g; CARB 32.1g; FIBER 0.1g; CHOL 3mg; IRON 1mg; SODIUM153mg; CALC 194mg

HOT MAPLE SOUFFLÉS

PREP: 25 MINUTES

COOK: 13 MINUTES

 1 tablespoon stick margarine or
     butter, softened
 2 tablespoons granulated sugar
 3 tablespoons maple syrup
 3 tablespoons bourbon
 1 cup maple syrup
 4 large egg whites
⅛ teaspoon salt
 1 teaspoon baking powder
 1 tablespoon sifted powdered sugar

1. Preheat oven to 425°.
2. Coat 6 (10-ounce) ramekins with margarine; sprinkle evenly with granulated sugar. Combine 3 tablespoons maple syrup and bourbon in a small microwave-safe bowl; microwave at HIGH 1½ minutes or until mixture boils. Pour about 1 tablespoon bourbon mixture into each prepared ramekin.
3. Cook 1 cup maple syrup in a medium, heavy saucepan over medium-high heat 8 minutes or until candy thermometer registers 250°. Beat egg whites and salt at medium speed of a mixer until foamy. Pour hot maple syrup in a thin stream over egg whites, beating at medium speed then at high speed until stiff peaks form. Add baking powder; beat well. Spoon evenly into prepared ramekins; place on a jelly-roll pan. Bake at 425° for 13 minutes or until puffy and set. Sprinkle with powdered sugar. Serve immediately. Yield: 6 servings.

CALORIES 212 (8% from fat); FAT 2g (sat 0.4g, mono 0.8g, poly 0.6g); PROTEIN 2.3g; CARB 47.8g; FIBER 0g; CHOL 0mg; IRON 0.8mg; SODIUM 193mg; CALC 89mg

ORANGE SOUFFLÉ

PREP: 20 MINUTES   COOK: 40 MINUTES

Cooking spray
 1 tablespoon granulated sugar
 3 tablespoons all-purpose flour
¾ cup 2% reduced-fat milk
¼ cup granulated sugar
 1 teaspoon grated orange rind
¼ cup fresh orange juice
 5 large egg whites
¼ teaspoon cream of tartar
Dash of salt
 2 tablespoons granulated sugar
 1 teaspoon powdered sugar

1. Preheat oven to 375°.

2. Coat a 1½-quart soufflé dish with cooking spray; sprinkle with 1 table-spoon granulated sugar.

3. Place flour in a small saucepan. Gradually add milk; stir with a whisk until blended. Add ¼ cup granulated sugar and orange rind; stir well. Bring to a boil over medium heat. Cook 1 minute or until thick; stir constantly. Stir in juice.

4. Beat egg whites, ¼ teaspoon cream of tartar, and salt at high speed of a mixer until soft peaks form. Gradually add 2 tablespoons granulated sugar, 1 tablespoon at a time, beating until stiff peaks form. Gently fold one-fourth of egg white mixture into orange mix-ture, and gently fold in remaining egg white mixture. Spoon into prepared soufflé dish.

5. Place soufflé dish in a 9-inch square baking pan, and add hot water to pan to a depth of 1 inch. Bake at 375° for 35 to 40 minutes or until puffy and set. Sprinkle soufflé with powdered sugar. Serve immediately. Yield: 4 servings.

CALORIES 159 (6% from fat); FAT 1.1g (sat 0.6g, mono 0.3g, poly 0.1g); PROTEIN 6.5g; CARB 31.1g; FIBER 0.2g; CHOL 4mg; IRON 0.3mg; SODIUM 128mg; CALC 62mg

chilled desserts
Rich in flavor, these recipes boast of another plus—you make them ahead and simply pull them out of the fridge when you're ready for dessert.

CHOCOLATE-ÉCLAIR ICEBOX DESSERT

PREP: 15 MINUTES
CHILL: 4 HOURS

22½ sheets (about 1 [14-ounce] box) low-fat honey graham crackers, divided
Cooking spray
  3 cups fat-free milk
  2 (3.4-ounce) packages fat-free vanilla instant pudding mix
  1 (8-ounce) tub fat-free cream cheese
  1 (8-ounce) carton frozen reduced-calorie whipped topping, thawed
  ¼ cup fat-free milk
  2 tablespoons stick margarine or butter, softened
  2 tablespoons honey
  2 ounces unsweetened chocolate, melted
  1½ cups sifted powdered sugar

1. Arrange 7½ graham cracker sheets in bottom of a 13 x 9-inch baking dish coated with cooking spray. Combine 3 cups milk, pudding mix, and cream cheese in a large bowl; beat at low speed of a mixer 1 minute or until thick. Fold in whipped topping. Spread half of pudding mixture over graham crackers in dish, and top with 7½ graham cracker sheets. Repeat procedure with remaining half of pudding mixture and 7½ graham cracker sheets.

2. Combine ¼ cup milk, margarine, honey, and chocolate in a medium bowl, and beat well with a mixer. Gradually add powdered sugar to chocolate mixture; beat well. Spread chocolate glaze over graham crackers. Cover dessert, and tent with foil; chill 4 hours. Yield: 18 servings (serving size: 1 [3 x 2-inch] square).

CALORIES 234 (22% from fat); FAT 5.8g (sat 2.7g, mono 1.5g, poly 1.3g); PROTEIN 5.4g; CARB 41.5g; FIBER 0.8g; CHOL 3mg; IRON 1mg; SODIUM 352mg; CALC 105mg

Chocolate-Éclair Icebox Dessert

TIRAMISU

PREP: 25 MINUTES   CHILL: 2 HOURS

⅔ cup sifted powdered sugar
 1 (8-ounce) tub ⅓-less-fat cream
     cheese
1½ cups frozen reduced-calorie
     whipped topping, thawed and
     divided
 ½ cup granulated sugar
 ¼ cup water
 3 large egg whites
 ½ cup hot water
 1 tablespoon granulated sugar
 1 tablespoon instant espresso or 2
     tablespoons instant coffee
     granules
 2 tablespoons Kahlúa (coffee-
     flavored liqueur)
20 ladyfingers
 ½ teaspoon unsweetened cocoa

1. Combine powdered sugar and cream cheese in a bowl; beat at high speed of a mixer until well-blended. Gently fold 1 cup whipped topping into cheese mixture.
2. Combine ½ cup granulated sugar, ¼ cup water, and egg whites in the top of a double boiler; place over simmering water. Beat at high speed of a mixer until stiff peaks form using clean, dry beaters. Gently stir one-fourth of egg white mixture into cheese mixture. Gently fold in remaining egg white mixture.
3. Combine ½ cup hot water, 1 tablespoon granulated sugar, espresso granules, and Kahlúa; stir well. Split ladyfingers in half lengthwise. Arrange 20 ladyfinger halves, cut sides up, in an 8-inch square baking dish. Drizzle half of espresso mixture over ladyfinger halves. Spread half of cheese mixture over ladyfinger halves, and repeat procedure with remaining ladyfinger halves, espresso mixture, and cheese mixture. Spread ½ cup whipped topping evenly over cheese mixture; sprinkle with cocoa.

Tiramisu

4. Place 1 wooden pick in each corner and in center to prevent plastic wrap from sticking to whipped topping; cover with plastic wrap. Chill 2 hours. Yield: 8 servings (serving size: 1 [4 x 2-inch] piece).

CALORIES 226 (28% from fat); FAT 7g (sat 4.1g, mono 2g, poly 0.8g); PROTEIN 4.7g; CARB 30g; FIBER 0g; CHOL 41mg; IRON 0.1mg; SODIUM 199mg; CALC 49mg

CHERRY-CHEESE PARFAITS

PREP: 25 MINUTES   CHILL: 3 HOURS

 1 envelope unflavored gelatin
 ¼ cup cold water
 ⅓ cup sugar
 1 tablespoon fresh lemon juice
 2 teaspoons vanilla extract
 1 (8-ounce) tub light cream cheese
 1 (12-ounce) can evaporated
     fat-free milk
 1 (21-ounce) can cherry pie filling

1. Sprinkle gelatin over cold water in a small saucepan; let stand 1 minute. Cook over low heat, stirring until gelatin dissolves.
2. Combine sugar, lemon juice, vanilla, and cream cheese in a medium bowl; beat at medium speed of a mixer until smooth. Gradually add milk, beating at low speed until smooth. Add gelatin mixture; beat until blended.
3. Spoon 1½ tablespoons pie filling into each of 6 (6-ounce) stemmed glasses, and top with ½ cup cheese mixture. Cover and chill at least 3 hours.
4. Spoon 1½ tablespoons pie filling onto each serving. Yield: 6 servings.

CALORIES 298 (20% from fat); FAT 6.5g (sat 3.9g, mono 1.8g, poly 0.2g); PROTEIN 9.4g; CARB 48.7g; FIBER 0g; CHOL 24mg; IRON 0.2mg; SODIUM 330mg; CALC 223mg

Plum Pinwheel Tart (page 208)

pies & pastries

PIES

CHOCOLATE-CREAM PIE

PREP:15 MINUTES   COOK:15 MINUTES
CHILL:3 HOURS

Graham Cracker Crust (page 214)
2   cups fat-free milk, divided
⅔   cup sugar
⅓   cup unsweetened cocoa
3   tablespoons cornstarch
⅛   teaspoon salt
1   large egg
2   ounces semisweet chocolate,
      chopped
1   teaspoon vanilla extract
1½ cups frozen reduced-calorie
      whipped topping, thawed
¾   teaspoon grated semisweet
      chocolate

1. Prepare Graham Cracker Crust according to directions; set crust aside.
2. Combine ½ cup milk, ⅔ cup sugar, cocoa, cornstarch, salt, and egg in a large bowl, stirring with a whisk.
3. Heat 1½ cups milk over medium-high heat in a heavy saucepan to 180° or until tiny bubbles form around edge (do not boil). Remove from heat. Gradually add hot milk to sugar mixture; stir constantly with a whisk. Return milk mixture to pan. Add chopped chocolate; cook over medium heat until thick and bubbly (about 5 minutes), stirring constantly. Reduce heat to low; cook 2 minutes, stirring constantly. Remove from heat; stir in vanilla.
4. Pour into prepared piecrust; cover surface of filling with plastic wrap. Chill 3 hours or until cold. Remove plastic wrap; spread whipped topping evenly over filling. Sprinkle with grated chocolate. Yield: 10 servings (serving size: 1 wedge).

CALORIES 242 (30% from fat); FAT 8g (sat 4.6g, mono 2.1g, poly 0.8g); PROTEIN 5g; CARB 38.5g; FIBER 0.1g; CHOL 30mg; IRON 1.4mg; SODIUM 189mg; CALC 83mg

Perfect Pie Crusts

A simple mistake in measuring ingredients (too much flour or water, or too little or too much fat) can mean the difference between a perfect pie crust and a baking disaster. Here are some common problems and their causes.

Follow our directions closely and you'll have a pie that will make you proud!

Problem	Common Cause
Tough pastry	Too much water • Too much flour • Too little fat • Overmixing
Crumbly crust	Too little water • Too much fat • Self-rising flour used • Insufficient mixing
Soggy crust	Filling too moist • Oven temperature too low • Too much liquid in pastry
Crust shrinks	Pastry stretched to fit in pan • Dough uneven in thickness • Rolling dough back and forth with rolling pin

BANANA-CREAM PIE

PREP:30 MINUTES   COOK:15 MINUTES
CHILL:4 HOURS

Graham Cracker Crust (page 214)
⅔   cup sugar
⅓   cup cornstarch
2½ cups 2% reduced-fat milk
2   large eggs, lightly beaten
1   large egg yolk, lightly beaten
2   teaspoons vanilla extract
2   drops yellow food coloring
2½ cups sliced ripe banana
1   cup frozen reduced-calorie
      whipped topping, thawed

1. Prepare Graham Cracker Crust according to directions; set crust aside.
2. Combine sugar and cornstarch in a medium saucepan. Gradually add milk, stirring with a whisk. Bring to a boil over medium heat; cook 1 minute, stirring constantly. Combine eggs and egg yolk in a medium bowl. Gradually add hot milk mixture to eggs and egg yolk, stirring constantly with a whisk. Return milk mixture to pan; cook over medium heat until thick (about 4 minutes), stirring constantly. Remove from heat; stir in vanilla and food coloring.
3. Arrange 1¼ cups banana in prepared piecrust; pour half of custard over banana. Top with remaining banana and custard. Cover surface of custard with plastic wrap; chill 4 hours. Remove plastic wrap, and spread whipped topping evenly over filling. Yield: 8 servings (serving size: 1 wedge).

CALORIES 328 (26% from fat); FAT 9.4g (sat 5.4g, mono 2.7g, poly 1.1g); PROTEIN 6.9g; CARB 54.9g; FIBER 1.7g; CHOL 94mg; IRON 1.1mg; SODIUM 203mg; CALC 116mg

APPLE-CIDER PIE

PREP:40 MINUTES   COOK:1 HOUR

Filling:
2   cups apple cider
⅓   cup sugar
3   tablespoons cornstarch
2   tablespoons fresh lemon juice
2   teaspoons vanilla extract

Apple-Cider Pie

1¼ teaspoons pumpkin-pie spice
3 pounds cooking apples (such as Braeburn, Rome, or McIntosh), peeled and quartered

Remaining ingredients:
Double Crust (page 213)
Cooking spray
1 large egg, lightly beaten
1 tablespoon water
1 tablespoon sugar

1. To prepare filling, bring cider to a boil in a large, heavy saucepan over high heat. Cook until reduced to ½ cup (about 20 minutes). Cool completely.
2. Combine cooled cider, ⅓ cup sugar,

cornstarch, lemon juice, vanilla, and pie spice in a large bowl. Cut each apple quarter crosswise into ¼-inch-thick slices. Stir apple slices into cider mixture.
3. Preheat oven to 450°.
4. Remove 1 sheet of plastic wrap from 12-inch circle of Double Crust; fit dough into a 9-inch pie plate coated with cooking spray, allowing dough to extend over edge of plate. Remove top sheet of plastic wrap. Spoon apple mixture into crust, and brush edges of crust lightly with water. Remove 1 sheet of plastic wrap from 11-inch circle; place on top of apple mixture. Remove top sheet of plastic wrap. Press edges of dough together; fold edges under, and flute.

5. Cut 6 (1-inch) slits into top of pastry using a sharp knife. Combine egg and 1 tablespoon water. Brush top and edges of pie with egg mixture; sprinkle with 1 tablespoon sugar. Place pie on a baking sheet; bake at 450° for 15 minutes. Reduce oven temperature to 350° (do not remove pie from oven); bake an additional 45 minutes or until golden. Cool on a wire rack. Yield: 10 servings (serving size: 1 wedge).

CALORIES 302 (28% from fat); FAT 9.5g (sat 2.1g, mono 3.5g, poly 2.9g); PROTEIN 2.9g; CARB 52.6g; FIBER 3.9g; CHOL 0mg; IRON 1.5mg; SODIUM 173mg; CALC 16mg

BLUEBERRY CRUMBLE PIE

PREP: 17 MINUTES   COOK: 40 MINUTES
COOL: 1 HOUR

3 cups fresh or frozen blueberries
1 (6-ounce) reduced-fat graham cracker crust
1 (8-ounce) carton low-fat sour cream
¾ cup packed brown sugar
3 tablespoons all-purpose flour
1½ teaspoons vanilla extract
¼ teaspoon grated lemon rind
¼ cup dry breadcrumbs
1 tablespoon granulated sugar
1 tablespoon stick margarine or butter, melted

1. Preheat oven to 375°.
2. Place blueberries in crust. Combine sour cream, brown sugar, flour, vanilla, and lemon rind. Spread sour cream mixture over blueberries. Combine breadcrumbs, granulated sugar, and margarine; sprinkle over sour cream mixture.
3. Bake at 375° for 40 minutes or until pie is set and crumbs are lightly browned. Remove from oven; cool 1 hour on a wire rack. Yield: 8 servings (serving size: 1 wedge).

CALORIES 290 (25% from fat); FAT 8.2g (sat 3.5g, mono 3g, poly 0.8g); PROTEIN 2.9g; CARB 51g; FIBER 2.1g; CHOL 11mg; IRON 1.1mg; SODIUM 161mg; CALC 59mg

CHERRY PIE

PREP:40 MINUTES   COOK:1 HOUR

Crust:

1½ cups all-purpose flour, divided
7 tablespoons ice water
1 teaspoon lemon juice
¼ teaspoon salt
3 tablespoons chilled butter or stick margarine, cut into small pieces
2 tablespoons vegetable shortening
Cooking spray

Filling:

⅔ cup sugar
2 tablespoons uncooked quick-cooking tapioca
½ teaspoon almond extract
2 (16-ounce) cans pitted tart red cherries in water, drained
2 teaspoons fat-free milk
1 tablespoon sugar

1. To prepare crust, lightly spoon flour into dry measuring cups; level with a knife. Combine ¼ cup flour, ice water, and lemon juice, stirring with a whisk until well-blended. Combine 1¼ cups flour and salt in a bowl; cut in butter and shortening with a pastry blender or 2 knives until mixture resembles coarse meal. Add ice water mixture; toss with a fork until moist. Gently press two-thirds of flour mixture into a 4-inch circle on heavy-duty plastic wrap; cover with additional plastic wrap. Repeat procedure with remaining flour mixture. Roll larger portion of dough, still covered, into an 11-inch circle. Roll smaller portion of dough, still covered, into a 9-inch circle. Place both portions of dough in freezer 10 minutes or until plastic wrap can be easily removed. Working with larger portion of dough, remove 1 sheet of plastic wrap; fit dough, uncovered side down, into a 9-inch pie plate coated with cooking spray. Remove top sheet of plastic wrap.

2. To prepare filling, combine ⅔ cup sugar, tapioca, almond extract, and cherries in a large bowl; let stand 15 minutes, stirring occasionally. Spoon mixture into crust.

3. Preheat oven to 375°.

4. Working with smaller portion of dough, remove 1 sheet of plastic wrap. Cut dough into 6 (1½-inch-wide) strips. Gently remove strips from sheet of plastic wrap; arrange in a lattice design over cherry mixture. Seal strips to edge of crust. Brush lattice with milk; sprinkle with 1 tablespoon sugar.

5. Bake at 375° for 1 hour or until filling is bubbly and crust is browned. Cool on a wire rack. Yield: 8 servings (serving size: 1 wedge).

CALORIES 262 (25% from fat); FAT 7.4g (sat 3.4g, mono 2.5g, poly 1g); PROTEIN 3.2g; CARB 47g; FIBER 1.8g; CHOL 12mg; IRON 2.6mg; SODIUM 127mg; CALC 19mg

PEAR, WALNUT, AND MAPLE SYRUP PIE

PREP:30 MINUTES   COOK:1 HOUR

Pastry:

2 cups all-purpose flour, divided
⅓ cup ice water
½ teaspoon salt
3 tablespoons chilled stick margarine or butter
3 tablespoons vegetable shortening

Filling:

⅓ cup packed brown sugar
⅓ cup chopped walnuts, toasted
3 tablespoons cornstarch
1 tablespoon lemon juice
4 large Comice pears (about 3 pounds), peeled, cored, and cut lengthwise into ½-inch-thick slices
¼ cup maple syrup
1 teaspoon vanilla extract
Cooking spray
2 teaspoons water
1 large egg

Comice pears work best in Pear, Walnut, and Maple Syrup Pie. Toasting the walnuts imparts a deep nutty flavor that contrasts with the maple syrup.

1. Preheat oven to 450°.

2. To prepare pastry, lightly spoon flour into dry measuring cups; level with a knife. Combine ⅓ cup flour and ice water, stirring with a whisk until well-blended. Combine 1⅔ cups flour and salt in a bowl; cut in margarine and shortening with a pastry blender or 2 knives until mixture resembles coarse meal. Add ice water mixture; toss with a fork until moist. Divide mixture in half. Gently press each half of mixture into a 4-inch circle on heavy-duty plastic wrap; cover with additional plastic wrap. Roll one half of dough, still covered, into a 12-inch circle; freeze 10 minutes. Roll other half of dough, still covered, into an 11-inch circle; freeze 10 minutes.

3. To prepare filling, combine brown sugar, walnuts, and cornstarch in a large bowl. Combine lemon juice and pear

slices in a medium bowl; stir in syrup and vanilla. Stir pear mixture into sugar mixture. Remove 1 sheet of plastic wrap from 12-inch circle; fit dough into a 9-inch pie plate coated with cooking spray, allowing dough to extend over edge of plate. Remove top sheet of plastic wrap. Combine 2 teaspoons water and egg in a small bowl; stir well with a whisk. Spoon pear mixture into prepared crust; brush edges of crust lightly with egg mixture. Remove 1 sheet of plastic wrap from 11-inch circle; place on top of pear mixture. Remove top sheet of plastic wrap. Press edges of dough together; fold edges under, and flute.

4. Brush top and edges of pie with egg mixture. Place pie on a baking sheet; cut 5 (1-inch) slits into top of pastry using a sharp knife. Bake at 450° for 15 minutes. Reduce oven temperature to 350° (do not remove pie from oven); bake an additional 45 minutes or until browned. Cool on a wire rack 30 minutes. Serve warm or at room temperature. Yield: 10 servings (serving size: 1 wedge).

CALORIES 290 (31% from fat); FAT 10g (sat 1g, mono 2.3g, poly 2.8g); PROTEIN 4.6g; CARB 46.9g; FIBER 3.1g; CHOL 22mg; IRON 1.8mg; SODIUM 168mg; CALC 30mg

MAPLE, FIG, AND MARSALA PIE

PREP: 18 MINUTES   COOK: 35 MINUTES

  1 (9-inch) Pastry Crust (page 213)
1⅓ cups coarsely chopped dried figs
     (about 8 ounces)
  ⅓ cup sweet Marsala wine or sherry
  2 tablespoons stick margarine or
     butter
  ½ cup packed dark brown sugar
  ¼ teaspoon salt
  ½ cup maple syrup
  1 tablespoon cider vinegar
  2 teaspoons vanilla extract
  3 large eggs

Maple, Fig, and Marsala Pie

1. Prepare and bake Pastry Crust in a 9-inch pie plate according to directions. Cool completely on a wire rack.

2. Combine chopped figs and Marsala in a medium saucepan, and bring to a simmer over medium heat. Cover, reduce heat, and simmer 10 minutes or until liquid is absorbed. Remove fig mixture from heat; place fig mixture in a medium bowl. Cool fig mixture completely.

3. Preheat oven to 350°.

4. Melt margarine in a small, heavy saucepan over low heat. Remove from heat; stir in brown sugar and salt. Stir in maple syrup, vinegar, vanilla, and eggs. Add to fig mixture; stir well. Spoon fig mixture into prepared crust. Bake at 350° for 35 minutes or until filling is set. Cool on a wire rack. Yield: 10 servings (serving size: 1 wedge).

CALORIES 268 (29% from fat); FAT 8.5g (sat 2g, mono 3.6g, poly 2.2g); PROTEIN 3.8g; CARB 45.6g; FIBER 3.1g; CHOL 64mg; IRON 1.7mg; SODIUM 172mg; CALC 63mg

PEAR GALETTE

PREP:30 MINUTES   COOK:45 MINUTES

Pastry:

1½ cups all-purpose flour
1 tablespoon granulated sugar
¼ teaspoon salt
¼ cup chilled stick margarine or
    butter, cut into 4 pieces
3½ to 4 tablespoons ice water
    Cooking spray

Filling:

⅓ cup firmly packed brown sugar
¼ cup cornstarch
⅛ teaspoon ground cloves
6 ripe Bosc pears (about 2½
    pounds), cored, peeled, and cut
    into 1-inch wedges
1 tablespoon granulated sugar

1. Preheat oven to 375°.

2. To prepare pastry, lightly spoon flour into dry measuring cups; level with a knife. Place flour, 1 tablespoon sugar, and salt in a food processor; pulse 2 times or until combined. Add chilled margarine; pulse 4 times or until mixture resembles coarse meal. With processor on, add ice water through food chute, processing just until combined (do not form a ball).

3. Gently press two-thirds of dough into a 4-inch circle on heavy-duty plastic wrap; cover with additional plastic wrap. Repeat procedure with remaining dough.

4. Roll larger portion of dough, still covered, into an 11-inch circle. Place dough in freezer 5 minutes or until plastic wrap can be easily removed. Remove 1 sheet of plastic wrap. Place dough on a baking sheet coated with cooking spray, and remove top sheet of plastic wrap.

5. To prepare filling, combine brown sugar, cornstarch, and cloves in a small bowl. Sprinkle dough with one-third of brown sugar mixture. Arrange half of pear wedges over dough, leaving a 2-inch

border; sprinkle with one-third of brown sugar mixture. Repeat layering procedure with remaining pear wedges and brown sugar mixture.

6. Roll smaller portion of dough, still covered, into a 10-inch circle. Place dough in freezer 5 minutes or until plastic wrap can be easily removed. Remove 1 sheet of plastic wrap. Place dough over pear wedges; remove top sheet of plastic wrap. Bring edges of bottom layer of dough over top layer of dough; pinch edges to seal. Cut 6 slits in top of dough to allow steam to escape. Lightly coat top of dough with cooking spray, and sprinkle with 1 tablespoon sugar. Bake at 375° for 45 minutes or until lightly browned. Cool 20 minutes on a wire rack. Yield: 10 servings (serving size: 1 wedge).

CALORIES 212 (22% from fat); FAT 5.2g (sat 0.9g, mono 2.1g, poly 1.6g); PROTEIN 2.2g; CARB 40.7g; FIBER 3.1g; CHOL 0mg; IRON 1.3mg; SODIUM 115mg; CALC 22mg

PUMPKIN-PRALINE PIE

PREP:16 MINUTES
COOK:55 MINUTES

1 (9-inch) Pastry Crust (page 213)
1 (15-ounce) can pumpkin
1 cup 2% reduced-fat milk
½ cup packed brown sugar
1 tablespoon all-purpose flour
3 tablespoons maple syrup
2 tablespoons bourbon
½ teaspoon salt
1½ teaspoons ground cinnamon
1½ teaspoons vanilla extract
¼ teaspoon ground ginger
¼ teaspoon ground nutmeg
¼ teaspoon ground allspice
2 large egg whites, lightly beaten
1 large egg, lightly beaten
⅓ cup coarsely chopped pecans
¼ cup packed brown sugar
1½ teaspoons dark corn syrup
½ teaspoon vanilla extract

1. Prepare and bake Pastry Crust according to directions; set aside.

2. Preheat oven to 400°.

3. Combine pumpkin and next 13 ingredients in a bowl; stir well with a whisk. Pour into prepared crust; bake at 400° for 35 minutes.

4. Combine pecans, ¼ cup brown sugar, corn syrup, and ½ teaspoon vanilla. Sprinkle pecan mixture over pie; bake an additional 20 minutes or until filling is set. (Shield edges of piecrust with foil, if necessary.) Cool completely on a wire rack. Yield: 8 servings (serving size: 1 wedge).

CALORIES 279 (30% from fat); FAT 9.3g (sat 2.2g, mono 4.4g, poly 2.3g); PROTEIN 5.1g; CARB 44.5g; FIBER 2.9g; CHOL 29mg; IRON 2.3mg; SODIUM 270mg; CALC 87mg

GINGERSNAP-PUMPKIN PIE

PREP:13 MINUTES
COOK:1 HOUR 5 MINUTES

Crust:

1¾ cups gingersnap crumbs (about
    43 cookies, finely crushed)
2½ tablespoons reduced-calorie stick
    margarine, melted
2 tablespoons granulated sugar
    Cooking spray

Filling:

1½ cups fresh or canned pumpkin
    puree
¾ cup packed brown sugar
1 tablespoon cornstarch
1 teaspoon ground cinnamon
1 teaspoon vanilla extract
¼ teaspoon salt
¼ teaspoon ground nutmeg
2 large egg whites, lightly beaten
1 large egg, lightly beaten
1 (12-ounce) can evaporated
    fat-free milk

1. Preheat oven to 325°.

Because pumpkin and sweet potato add body to a pie filling, we were able to use lower-fat milk and no cream. Plus we shaved off an egg yolk or two without sacrificing richness or texture in these pies.

2. To prepare crust, combine first 3 ingredients in a bowl; toss with a fork until moist. Press into bottom and up sides of a 9-inch pie plate coated with cooking spray. Bake at 325° for 5 minutes; cool on a wire rack.

3. To prepare filling, combine pumpkin and remaining ingredients in a bowl. Pour into prepared crust. Bake at 325° for 1 hour or until a knife inserted in center comes out clean. Cool on a wire rack. Yield: 10 servings (serving size: 1 wedge).

CALORIES 295 (25% from fat); FAT 8.2g (sat 2.0g, mono 3.4g, poly 2.1g); PROTEIN 6.6g; CARB 50g; FIBER 0.6g; CHOL 36mg; IRON 3mg; SODIUM 195mg; CALC 189mg

PECAN-CRUSTED SWEET POTATO PIE

PREP:15 MINUTES
COOK:50 MINUTES

 1 (9-inch) unbaked Cream Cheese
    Piecrust (page 213)
1½ cups mashed cooked sweet
    potato (about ¾ pound)
 ⅓ cup packed dark brown sugar
 3 tablespoons evaporated
    fat-free milk
 ¾ teaspoon pumpkin-pie spice
 ¼ teaspoon salt
 1 large egg
 ½ cup packed dark brown sugar
 ½ cup light-colored corn syrup
 2 teaspoons vanilla extract
 ¼ teaspoon ground cinnamon
 ⅛ teaspoon salt
 1 large egg
 ½ cup chopped pecans

1. Prepare Cream Cheese Piecrust; set aside.
2. Preheat oven to 350°.
3. Combine sweet potato and next 5 ingredients in a food processor; process until smooth. Spoon mixture into prepared piecrust. Combine ½ cup brown sugar and next 5 ingredients in a bowl; stir well with a whisk. Stir in pecans. Pour pecan mixture over sweet potato mixture. Bake at 350° for 50 minutes or until set; shield edges of piecrust with foil after 20 minutes. Cool on a wire rack. Yield: 10 servings (serving size: 1 wedge).

CALORIES 322 (00% from fat); FAT 8.9g (sat 2.7g, mono 4g, poly 1.4g); PROTEIN 4.9g; CARB 56.1g; FIBER 2.2g; CHOL 75mg; IRON 1.6mg; SODIUM 248mg; CALC 65mg

PECAN PIE

PREP:13 MINUTES
COOK:45 MINUTES

In order to pack as many pecans in the filling as possible, we kept the fat in the piecrust to a minimum—resulting in a crust that's more bready than short or flaky.

Pastry crust:
 1 cup all-purpose flour
 2 tablespoons granulated sugar
 1 teaspoon baking powder
 ¼ teaspoon salt
 ¼ cup fat-free milk
 1 tablespoon butter or stick
    margarine, melted
 Cooking spray

Filling:
 1 large egg
 4 large egg whites

 1 cup light-colored or dark corn
    syrup
 ⅔ cup packed dark brown sugar
 ¼ teaspoon salt
 1 cup pecan halves
 1 teaspoon vanilla extract

1. To prepare pastry crust, lightly spoon flour into a dry measuring cup; level with a knife. Combine flour, granulated sugar, baking powder, and ¼ teaspoon salt in a bowl. Add milk and butter; toss with a fork until moist.

2. Press mixture gently into a 4-inch circle on heavy-duty plastic wrap; cover with additional plastic wrap. Roll dough, still covered, into an 11-inch circle. Freeze 10 minutes or until plastic wrap can be easily removed.

3. Remove 1 sheet of plastic wrap; fit dough into a 9-inch pie plate coated with cooking spray. Remove top sheet of plastic wrap. Fold edges under; flute.

4. Preheat oven to 350°.

5. To prepare filling, beat egg, egg whites, corn syrup, brown sugar, and ¼ teaspoon salt at medium speed of a mixer until well-blended. Stir in pecans and vanilla. Pour into prepared crust. Bake at 350° for 30 minutes; cover pie with foil. Bake an additional 15 minutes or until a knife inserted 1 inch from edge comes out clean. Cool on a wire rack. Yield: 10 servings (serving size: 1 wedge).

CALORIES 288 (29% from fat); FAT 9.2g (sat 1.5g, mono 5.1g, poly 2g); PROTEIN 4.3g; CARB 48.1g; FIBER 1g; CHOL 25mg; IRON 1.1mg; SODIUM 253mg; CALC 52mg

LEMON-BUTTERMILK CHESS PIE

PREP: 14 MINUTES
COOK: 55 MINUTES

Pastry crust:
    1 cup all-purpose flour
    2 tablespoons sugar
    ⅛ teaspoon salt
    ¼ cup chilled butter or stick
        margarine, cut into small pieces
    3½ tablespoons ice water
    Cooking spray

Filling:
    1 cup sugar
    2 tablespoons all-purpose flour
    2 teaspoons lemon rind
    2 tablespoons fresh lemon juice
    1 teaspoon vanilla extract
    2 large eggs
    2 large egg whites
    1 cup low-fat buttermilk

1. Preheat oven to 425°.
2. To prepare pastry crust, lightly spoon 1 cup flour into a dry measuring cup; level with a knife. Combine 1 cup flour, 2 tablespoons sugar, and salt in a bowl; cut in butter with a pastry blender or 2 knives until mixture resembles coarse meal. Sprinkle surface with ice water, 1 tablespoon at a time; toss with a fork until moist and crumbly (do not form a ball).
3. Press mixture gently into a 4-inch circle on heavy-duty plastic wrap; cover with additional plastic wrap. Roll dough, still covered, into a 12-inch circle. Freeze 10 minutes or until plastic wrap can be easily removed.
4. Remove 1 sheet of plastic wrap; fit dough into a 9-inch pie plate coated with cooking spray. Remove top sheet of plastic wrap. Fold edges under; flute. Line dough with a piece of foil; arrange pie weights (or dried beans) on foil. Bake at 425° for 10 minutes or until edge is lightly browned. Remove pie weights and foil; reduce oven temperature to 350°. Bake piecrust an additional 5 minutes; cool on a wire rack.
5. To prepare filling, combine 1 cup sugar and next 6 ingredients in a bowl; stir with a whisk until well-blended. Gradually stir in buttermilk. Pour egg mixture into prepared crust. Bake at 350° for 40 minutes or until set, shielding piecrust with foil after 30 minutes, if necessary. Cool on a wire rack. Yield: 8 servings (serving size: 1 wedge).

CALORIES 265 (26% from fat); FAT 7.8g (sat 4.3g, mono 2.3g, poly 0.5g); PROTEIN 5.5g; CARB 43.7g; FIBER 0.5g; CHOL 71mg; IRON 1mg; SODIUM 141mg; CALC 50mg

SHOOFLY PIE

PREP: 13 MINUTES
COOK: 40 MINUTES

Thought to be of Pennsylvania Dutch origin, Shoofly Pie is a dark, rich, very sweet molasses pie.

Pastry crust:
    1 cup all-purpose flour
    ¼ teaspoon salt
    ¼ cup vegetable shortening
    3½ tablespoons ice water
    Cooking spray

Filling:
    1 cup flour
    ¼ teaspoon salt
    ½ cup packed brown sugar
    3 tablespoons vegetable shortening
    1 cup boiling water
    1 teaspoon baking soda
    1 cup molasses

1. To prepare pastry crust, lightly spoon flour into a dry measuring cup; level with a knife. Combine 1 cup flour and ¼ teaspoon salt in a bowl; cut in ¼ cup shortening with a pastry blender or 2 knives until mixture resembles coarse meal. Sprinkle surface with ice water, 1 tablespoon at a time; toss with a fork until moist and crumbly (do not form a ball).
2. Press mixture gently into a 4-inch circle on heavy-duty plastic wrap; cover with additional plastic wrap. Roll dough, still covered, into a 12-inch circle. Freeze 10 minutes or until plastic wrap can be easily removed.
3. Remove 1 sheet of plastic wrap; fit dough into a 9-inch pie plate coated with cooking spray. Remove top sheet of plastic wrap. Fold edges under; flute.
4. Preheat oven to 350°.
5. To prepare filling, combine 1 cup flour, ¼ teaspoon salt, and brown sugar in a bowl; cut in 3 tablespoons shortening with a pastry blender or 2 knives until mixture resembles coarse meal. Combine boiling water and baking soda; stir in molasses. Pour molasses mixture into prepared crust; sprinkle flour mixture over molasses mixture. Place pie on a baking sheet; bake at 350° for 40 minutes or until set. Cool on a wire rack. Yield: 10 servings (serving size: 1 wedge).

CALORIES 284 (25% from fat); FAT 7.8g (sat 1.9g, mono 2.5g, poly 2.3g); PROTEIN 2.6g; CARB 51.8g; FIBER 0.7g; CHOL 0mg; IRON 2.9mg; SODIUM 260mg; CALC 79mg

CRUST SWAPPING

You can use a commercial crust (such as Pillsbury refrigerated dough) to save time, but your pie will be slightly higher in fat and calories than if you make our crust. Commercial crusts average 1 to 2 grams more fat per serving.

The nutritional analysis at the end of each of these pie recipes is for one serving and includes the crust and the filling.

KEY LIME PIE

PREP: **30** MINUTES
COOK: **25** MINUTES
CHILL: **4** HOURS

For tips on making a mile-high meringue, see page 169.

Graham Cracker Crust (page 214)
  1 teaspoon unflavored gelatin
  2 tablespoons cold water
  ½ cup fresh lime juice
  2 large egg yolks
  1 (14-ounce) can fat-free
      sweetened condensed milk
  3 large egg whites
  ¼ teaspoon cream of tartar
  ⅛ teaspoon salt
  ⅓ cup sugar
Lime slices (optional)

1. Prepare and bake Graham Cracker Crust according to directions; set crust aside.

2. Sprinkle gelatin over water in a small bowl.

3. Combine lime juice and egg yolks in a small, heavy saucepan; cook over medium-low heat until mixture thickens (about 10 minutes), stirring constantly (do not boil). Add gelatin to lime juice mixture; cook 1 minute, stirring until gelatin dissolves. Remove from heat. Place pan in a large ice-filled bowl for 3 minutes or until mixture comes to room temperature, stirring occasionally (do not allow gelatin mixture to set).

4. Strain gelatin mixture into a medium bowl; discard any solids. Gradually add milk, stirring with a whisk until blended (mixture will be very thick). Spoon mixture into Graham Cracker Crust; spread evenly.

5. Preheat oven to 325°.

6. Beat egg whites, cream of tartar, and salt at high speed of a mixer until foamy.

Key Lime Pie

Gradually add sugar, 1 tablespoon at a time, beating until stiff peaks form. Spread evenly over filling, sealing to edge of crust.

7. Bake at 325° for 25 minutes; cool 1 hour on a wire rack. Chill 3 hours or until set. Cut with a sharp knife dipped in hot water. Garnish with lime slices, if desired. Yield: 8 servings (serving size: 1 wedge).

CALORIES 311 (17% from fat); FAT 6g (sat 2.5g, mono 2g, poly 1g); PROTEIN 7.8g; CARB 56.5g; FIBER 0.5g; CHOL 62mg; IRON 0.8mg; SODIUM 251mg; CALC 138mg

KEY LIMES

To make an official Key lime pie, start with fresh Key limes. (The two main varieties of limes are Persian and Key lime.) Key limes are smaller and rounder than the Persian and are more yellow than green. They can be found in specialty markets and some larger grocery stores. If Key limes are not available, you can substitute juice from Persian limes.

Chocolate Meringue Pie

1. Cook mixture over medium heat, stirring constantly with a whisk, until mixture is thick and bubbly.

2. Spoon hot filling into baked pastry crust.

3. Spread meringue over hot filling, sealing meringue to edge of pastry. Bake as directed.

Chocolate Meringue Pie

CHOCOLATE MERINGUE PIE

PREP: 22 MINUTES   CHILL: 3 HOURS
COOK: 39 MINUTES

1 (9-inch) Pastry Crust (page 213)

Filling:
½ cup sugar
5 tablespoons unsweetened cocoa
3 tablespoons plus 2 teaspoons cornstarch
2 cups 1% low-fat milk
1 large egg, lightly beaten
2 teaspoons vanilla extract

Remaining ingredients:
4 large egg whites
1 teaspoon cornstarch
¼ teaspoon cream of tartar
⅓ cup sugar

1. Prepare and bake Pastry Crust according to directions; set aside.

2. Preheat oven to 325°.

3. To prepare filling, combine ½ cup sugar, cocoa, and 3 tablespoons plus 2 teaspoons cornstarch in a medium saucepan. Gradually add milk, stirring with a whisk until well-blended. Bring to a boil over medium heat, and cook 1 minute, stirring constantly.

4. Gradually stir about one-fourth of hot cocoa mixture into egg, stirring constantly with a whisk; add to remaining hot cocoa mixture, stirring constantly. Cook until thick and bubbly (about 1 minute), stirring constantly. Stir in vanilla. Pour mixture into prepared crust; cover with plastic wrap.

5. To prepare meringue, beat egg whites, 1 teaspoon cornstarch, and cream of tartar at high speed of a mixer until foamy. Gradually add ⅓ cup sugar, 1 tablespoon at a time, beating until stiff peaks form. (Do not overbeat.)

6. Remove plastic wrap from filling; spread meringue evenly over filling, sealing to edge of crust. Bake at 325° for 25 minutes; cool on a wire rack 1 hour. Chill 3 hours or until set. Yield: 8 servings (serving size: 1 wedge).

CALORIES 258 (25% from fat); FAT 7.2g (sat 2.2g, mono 3.1g, poly 1.6g); PROTEIN 7g; CARB 40.5g; FIBER 0.4g; CHOL 29mg; IRON 1.4mg; SODIUM 141mg; CALC 87mg

MOCHA FUDGE PIE

PREP: 18 MINUTES
COOK: 22 MINUTES

Featuring a thick brownie crust, a filling made of creamy mocha pudding, and—for the crowning touch—a coffee-and-Kahlúa whipped topping, this pie is deceptively light.

⅓ cup hot water
4 teaspoons instant coffee granules, divided
½ (20.5-ounce) package low-fat fudge brownie mix (about 2 cups)
2 teaspoons vanilla extract, divided
2 large egg whites
Cooking spray
¾ cup 1% low-fat milk
3 tablespoons Kahlúa (coffee-flavored liqueur), divided
1 (3.9-ounce) package chocolate instant pudding mix or 1 (1.4-ounce) package sugar-free chocolate instant pudding mix
3 cups frozen reduced-calorie whipped topping, thawed and divided
Chocolate curls (optional)

1. Preheat oven to 325°.

2. Combine hot water and 2 teaspoons coffee granules in a bowl. Add brownie mix, 1 teaspoon vanilla, and egg whites; stir until well-blended. Pour mixture into a 9-inch pie plate coated with cooking spray. Bake at 325° for 22 minutes (brownie will be fudgy when tested with a wooden pick). Cool completely on a wire rack.

3. Beat milk, 2 tablespoons Kahlúa, 1 teaspoon coffee granules, 1 teaspoon vanilla, and pudding mix at medium speed of a mixer 30 seconds. Gently fold in 1½ cups whipped topping. Spoon pudding mixture onto brownie crust; spread evenly.

4. Combine 1 teaspoon coffee granules and 1 tablespoon Kahlúa in a bowl; gently fold in 1½ cups whipped topping. Spread whipped topping mixture evenly over pudding mixture. Garnish with chocolate curls, if desired. Serve immediately or store loosely covered in refrigerator. Yield: 8 servings (serving size: 1 wedge).

NONALCOHOLIC VERSION:

When making pudding mixture, substitute 2 tablespoons 1% low-fat milk for Kahlúa. In topping, omit Kahlúa, and dissolve coffee granules in 1 tablespoon water.

Note: Store remaining brownie mix in a zip-top plastic bag in refrigerator. Reserved brownie mix can be used for another pie or to make a small pan of brownies.

To make brownies, combine 2 cups brownie mix, ¼ cup water, and 1 lightly beaten large egg white in a bowl. Stir just until combined. Spread into an 8-inch square pan coated with cooking spray. Bake at 350° for 23 to 25 minutes.

CALORIES 297 (20% from fat); FAT 6.5g (sat 3g, mono 0.1g, poly 1.6g); PROTEIN 4.9g; CARB 51.6g; FIBER 1.2g; CHOL 1mg; IRON 1.4mg; SODIUM 399mg; CALC 50mg

PINEAPPLE-COCONUT-CREAM PIE

PREP: 35 MINUTES   COOK: 8 MINUTES
CHILL: 2 HOURS

½ cup sugar
¼ cup cornstarch
1 large egg, lightly beaten
1½ cups 1% low-fat milk
1 (15¼-ounce) can crushed pineapple in juice, drained
¼ cup flaked sweetened coconut
½ teaspoon grated peeled fresh ginger
1½ cups frozen reduced-calorie whipped topping, thawed
Vanilla Wafer Crust (page 214)
1 tablespoon flaked sweetened coconut, toasted

1. Combine sugar, cornstarch, and egg in a medium bowl, stirring well with a whisk. Heat milk over medium-high heat in a medium, heavy saucepan to 180° or until tiny bubbles form around edge (do not boil). Gradually add hot milk to sugar mixture, stirring constantly with a whisk. Return milk mixture to pan. Cook over medium heat until thick and bubbly (about 3 minutes), stirring constantly. Reduce heat to low, and cook 2 minutes, stirring constantly. Remove from heat; stir in pineapple, ¼ cup coconut, and ginger. Place pan in a large ice-filled bowl for 15 minutes or until milk mixture is chilled; stir mixture occasionally.

2. Remove pan from ice. Fold whipped topping into milk mixture, and spoon mixture into Vanilla Wafer Crust. Sprinkle with toasted coconut. Cover with plastic wrap. Chill 2 hours. Yield: 8 servings (serving size: 1 wedge).

CALORIES 265 (28% from fat); FAT 8.2g (sat 3.8g, mono 2g, poly 1.1g); PROTEIN 3.6g; CARB 45.1g; FIBER 0.5g; CHOL 28mg; IRON 0.7mg; SODIUM 148mg; CALC 79mg

PEACH MELBA PIE

PREP: 20 MINUTES
COOK: 8 MINUTES
FREEZE: 7 HOURS

Vanilla Wafer Crust (page 214)
    4 cups vanilla low-fat frozen yogurt
1½ cups thinly sliced peeled peaches
    3 tablespoons sugar
    2 teaspoons lemon juice
Raspberry Sauce (page 451)

1. Preheat oven to 350°.
2. Prepare Vanilla Wafer Crust as directed. Cool on a wire rack 15 minutes. Freeze piecrust 30 minutes.
3. Place an extra-large bowl in freezer. Remove yogurt from freezer, and let stand at room temperature while crust is cooling.
4. Wipe food processor bowl with a paper towel; add peaches, sugar, and lemon juice. Process until smooth. Spoon yogurt into chilled bowl. Fold in peach mixture until well-blended; freeze 30 minutes or until set but not solid.
5. Spoon yogurt mixture into chilled crust; freeze until set. Cover with plastic wrap; freeze 6 hours or until firm.
6. Place pie in refrigerator 30 minutes before serving to soften. Serve pie with Raspberry Sauce. Yield: 8 servings (serving size: 1 wedge and 3 tablespoons sauce).

CALORIES 301 (21% from fat); FAT 7.2g (sat 2.3g, mono 2.1g, poly 2.2g); PROTEIN 5.1g; CARB 58.1g; FIBER 4.1g; CHOL 9mg; IRON 0.3mg; SODIUM 166mg; CALC 103mg

Peach Melba Pie

FROZEN PIES

Frozen pies can be a little tricky in terms of their texture—**you don't want your pies as hard as a rock, nor do you want "pie soup."** Because low-fat ice creams and frozen yogurts have less butterfat and a higher water content, they melt quickly. Our Test Kitchens staff did numerous tests to achieve the best consistency and found that **these techniques will help you make a pie that's creamy and soft.**

• While the piecrust is cooling, **take the frozen yogurt or ice cream out of the freezer and let it soften.** This makes it easier to fold in the other ingredients for the filling.

• **Freeze the piecrust 30 minutes.** The ice cream or yogurt mixture won't melt as it would if you put it into a piecrust at room temperature.

• **It's best to partially refreeze the filling before putting it into the piecrust.** To do this, combine the slightly softened frozen yogurt or ice cream and other ingredients specified in the recipe in a chilled extra-large bowl. Put the bowl back in the freezer for about 30 to 45 minutes to let it set back up. Don't let the mixture freeze solid, or the consistency will be too hard to spoon into the piecrust.

• **Place the filled piecrust back in the freezer until set;** then cover with plastic wrap.

• Take the pie out of the freezer, and **let it stand in the refrigerator about 30 minutes before serving.** This step will make it easier to cut the pie into wedges.

FROZEN COFFEE-FUDGE PIE

PREP: 12 MINUTES   COOK: 8 MINUTES
FREEZE: 4 1/2 HOURS

Crust:
- 1 cup packaged cream-filled chocolate sandwich cookie crumbs (such as Oreo)
- 1 tablespoon butter or stick margarine, melted
- 1 large egg white, lightly beaten
- Cooking spray

Filling:
- 2 teaspoons instant coffee granules
- 1 tablespoon boiling water
- 3/4 cup fat-free hot fudge topping (such as Smucker's), divided
- 4 cups coffee low-fat ice cream (such as Starbucks Low Fat Latte)

1. Preheat oven to 350°.
2. To prepare crust, combine first 3 ingredients, and toss with a fork until moist. Press into bottom and up sides of a 9-inch pie plate coated with cooking spray. Bake at 350° for 8 minutes. Cool on a wire rack. Place crust in freezer.
3. To prepare filling, place a large bowl in freezer. Combine coffee granules and boiling water in a small bowl; stir until coffee dissolves. Add 3 tablespoons fudge topping; stir well.
4. Spoon ice cream into chilled bowl, and stir in fudge topping mixture. Spoon ice cream mixture into chilled crust; freeze 30 minutes. Cover with plastic wrap; freeze 4 hours or until set. Place pie in refrigerator 20 minutes before serving to soften. Serve pie with 9 tablespoons fudge topping. Yield: 9 servings (serving size: 1 wedge and 1 tablespoon fudge topping).

CALORIES 277 (19% from fat); FAT 5.9g (sat 2g, mono 2.2g, poly 0.6g); PROTEIN 6.1g; CARB 48.6g; FIBER 1g; CHOL 9mg; IRON 0.2mg; SODIUM 225mg; CALC 90mg

tarts We filled these tarts with sweet ingredients that you won't be able to resist.

CHOCOLATE CREAM-RASPBERRY TART

PREP: 30 MINUTES   COOK: 16 MINUTES
CHILL: 2 HOURS

- Graham Cracker Crust (page 214)
- 1 1/2 teaspoons unflavored gelatin
- 1 cup 1% low-fat milk, divided
- 1/2 cup sugar
- 2 1/2 tablespoons cornstarch
- 2 tablespoons unsweetened cocoa
- 1/8 teaspoon salt
- 1/4 cup semisweet chocolate morsels
- 3/4 teaspoon vanilla extract
- 1/4 teaspoon almond extract
- 1 1/2 cups frozen reduced-calorie whipped topping, thawed
- 3 cups fresh raspberries
- 1/4 cup red currant jelly, melted

1. Preheat oven to 350°.
2. Prepare Graham Cracker Crust, pressing mixture into bottom and up sides of a 9-inch round removable-bottom tart pan. Bake at 350° for 10 minutes; cool on a wire rack.
3. Combine gelatin and 1/4 cup milk in a bowl. Combine 1/2 cup sugar, cornstarch, cocoa, and salt in a saucepan. Gradually add 3/4 cup milk, stirring with a whisk. Bring milk mixture to a boil over medium heat (about 5 minutes), stirring constantly; cook 1 minute, stirring constantly. Remove from heat; add chocolate morsels, stirring until melted. Stir in extracts.
4. Add chocolate mixture to gelatin mixture, stirring until gelatin dissolves. Place bowl in a large ice-filled bowl for 3 minutes or until chocolate mixture is cool; remove from ice-filled bowl. Add whipped topping, stirring gently until well-blended. Spoon into tart shell. Arrange raspberries on top of tart. Gently brush raspberries with melted jelly. Chill 2 hours. Yield: 9 servings (serving size: 1 wedge).

CALORIES 258 (26% from fat); FAT 7.5g (sat 5.2g, mono 1.9g, poly 1.4g); PROTEIN 3.9g; CARB 45g; FIBER 3.6g; CHOL 8mg; IRON 1.2mg; SODIUM 190mg; CALC 61mg

Chocolate Cream-Raspberry Tart

BRANDIED SWEET POTATO TART

PREP: 15 MINUTES
COOK: 1 1/2 HOURS

1 (9-inch) Pastry Crust (page 213)
2 cups mashed cooked sweet
    potato (about 1 1/2 pounds)
1/3 cup packed dark brown sugar
1/2 teaspoon pumpkin-pie spice
1/4 teaspoon salt
1/4 cup (2 ounces) 1/3-less-fat cream
    cheese, softened
2 large eggs
3 tablespoons brandy
1 large egg white
3 tablespoons dark brown sugar
3 tablespoons light-colored corn
    syrup
1 teaspoon vanilla extract
Dash of salt
1/4 cup chopped pecans

1. Prepare and bake Pastry Crust according to directions in a 9-inch round
removable-bottom tart pan. Cool crust
completely on a wire rack.
2. Preheat oven to 325°.
3. Beat sweet potato, 1/3 cup brown sugar,
pie spice, 1/4 teaspoon salt, and cream
cheese at medium speed of a mixer until
well-blended. Add eggs and brandy; beat
until well-blended. Spoon filling into
prepared crust.
4. Beat egg white, 3 tablespoons brown
sugar, corn syrup, vanilla, and dash of
salt at medium speed of a mixer for 2
minutes or until light brown. Pour corn
syrup mixture over sweet potato mixture;
sprinkle with pecans. Place on a baking
sheet. Bake at 325° for 1 1/2 hours or until
a knife inserted in center comes out
clean. Cool completely on a wire rack.
Yield: 8 servings (serving size: 1 wedge).

CALORIES 304 (33% from fat); FAT 11.3g (sat 3g, mono 5.1g,
poly 2.5g); PROTEIN 5.5g; CARB 45.6g; FIBER 2.6g;
CHOL 59mg; IRON 1.6mg; SODIUM 239mg; CALC 40mg

menu

Oven-Fried Pork Chops (page 330)

Risotto With Arugula and Toasted Garlic
(page 250)

Poppy Seed-Fruit Salad (page 389)

Apple Frangipane Tart

APPLE FRANGIPANE TART

PREP: 37 MINUTES
COOK: 58 MINUTES

*We lightened the traditional version of
Apple Frangipane Tart by replacing the
butter with light cream cheese and
omitting the egg yolks.*

1/2 cup (4 ounces) block-style 1/3-
    less-fat cream cheese, softened
3/4 cup sugar, divided
1/2 cup ground almonds (2 1/2
    ounces)
1 teaspoon vanilla extract
2 large egg whites
5 sheets frozen phyllo dough,
    thawed
Butter-flavored cooking spray
4 medium Granny Smith apples,
    each peeled, cored and halved
    lengthwise
2 tablespoons warm honey

1. Preheat oven to 350°.
2. Beat cream cheese at medium speed
of a mixer until smooth. Add 1/2 cup
sugar, ground almonds, vanilla, and egg
whites; beat until well-blended.
3. Working with 1 phyllo sheet at a
time, place 1 phyllo sheet on work surface (cover remaining dough to keep
from drying); lightly coat with cooking
spray, and fold in half crosswise, forming a 13 x 8 1/2-inch rectangle. Gently
press folded phyllo sheet into a 10-inch
tart pan, allowing ends to extend over
edges of pan; coat top of phyllo with
cooking spray. Repeat procedure with a
second phyllo sheet, placing it across
first sheet in a crisscross design; coat top
of second phyllo sheet with cooking
spray. Repeat procedure with remaining
3 phyllo sheets. Decoratively crimp
edges of phyllo crust, and pour cheese
mixture into crust.
4. Cut each apple half crosswise into
thin slices, leaving slices stacked together to keep shape of apple half. Place 7
apple halves around edge of tart and 1
in center; sprinkle with 1/4 cup sugar.
Bake at 350° for 58 minutes or until
mixture is puffed and lightly browned
and apples are tender. Brush with
honey. Yield: 8 servings (serving size:
1 wedge).

CALORIES 267 (31% from fat); FAT 9.3g (sat 2.6g, mono 4.2g,
poly 1.6g); PROTEIN 5.5g; CARB 43g; FIBER 2.7g;
CHOL 11mg; IRON 1mg; SODIUM 132mg; CALC 38mg

**Frangipane is an almond-flavored filling made from eggs,
butter, sugar, and ground almonds. When baked, the frangipane
puffs up and sets around the apples.**

Apple Frangipane Tart

PART 1 the crust

1. Working with 1 phyllo sheet at a time, fold in half crosswise, forming a 13 x 8½-inch rectangle.

2. Gently press folded phyllo sheet into a 10-inch tart pan, allowing ends to extend over edges of pan.

3. Place another folded sheet of phyllo across first sheet in a crisscross design.

4. Decoratively crimp edges of phyllo crust.

PART 2 the filling

5. Pour cheese mixture evenly over crust.

6. Cut each apple half crosswise into thin slices, leaving slices stacked together to keep shape of apple half.

7. Place 7 apple halves around edge of tart and 1 in the center. Sprinkle with sugar, and bake as directed.

PLUM PINWHEEL TART

PREP: 23 MINUTES   FREEZE: 2 HOURS

COOK: 25 MINUTES

(pictured on page 193)

Tart dough:

⅔ cup granulated sugar

6 tablespoons stick margarine or butter

1 teaspoon vanilla extract

¼ cup (2 ounces) block-style fat-free cream cheese

1 large egg

2 cups all-purpose flour

¼ teaspoon salt

Cooking spray

Tart filling:

4 cups thinly sliced ripe red-fleshed plums (about 12 medium)

¼ cup red currant jelly

2 tablespoons water

1 large egg

1 teaspoon water

2 tablespoons turbinado or granulated sugar

1. To prepare tart dough, beat first 4 ingredients at medium speed of a mixer for 2 minutes or until light and fluffy. Add egg, and beat at high speed 1 minute or until very smooth.

2. Lightly spoon flour into dry measuring cups; level with a knife. Combine flour and salt; add to sugar mixture, beating at low speed just until flour mixture is moist. Gently shape dough into a ball on heavy-duty plastic wrap; cover with additional plastic wrap. Freeze dough 2 hours.

3. Preheat oven to 400°.

4. Roll dough, still covered, into a 14-inch circle. Remove 1 sheet of plastic wrap. Place dough on a large baking sheet coated with cooking spray, and remove top sheet of plastic wrap.

5. To prepare tart filling, arrange plum slices over dough, leaving a 3-inch

PLUMS AT THEIR PEAK

Ripe plums yield slightly to the touch. But don't squeeze; let the fruit sit in your palm. It should give a little. If you buy firmer fruit, though, don't put it in the refrigerator or the kitchen window—put it in a paper bag in a dark place for a day or two. The paper bag traps ethylene, the gas that naturally ripens fruit, but the bag also lets the fruit breathe. Although plums may taste sweeter when ripened this way, it's actually a trick on your palate. The sugar level remains the same after picking, but the acidity falls, so it only seems sweeter.

border. Combine red currant jelly and 2 tablespoons water in a small microwave-safe dish; microwave at HIGH 30 seconds or until jelly melts. Brush melted jelly mixture over plums. Fold 3-inch border of dough over plums, pressing gently to seal (dough will partially cover plums). Combine egg and 1 teaspoon water. Brush dough with egg mixture; sprinkle with turbinado sugar. Bake at 400° for 25 minutes or until lightly browned. Cool tart on pan 5 minutes. Carefully slide tart onto a platter using a spatula. Yield: 10 servings (serving size: 1 wedge).

CALORIES 293 (26% from fat); FAT 8.6g (sat 1.7g, mono 3.7g, poly 2.5g); PROTEIN 5.3g; CARB 49.6g; FIBER 2.1g; CHOL 45mg; IRON 1.4mg; SODIUM 189mg; CALC 31mg

TROPICAL-FRUIT PIZZA

PREP: 17 MINUTES   COOK: 25 MINUTES

CHILL: 1 HOUR

1 (18-ounce) package refrigerated sugar cookie dough

Cooking spray

⅓ cup sugar

1½ teaspoons grated orange rind

1 teaspoon coconut extract

1 (8-ounce) block fat-free cream cheese, softened

1 cup (1-inch) pieces peeled ripe mango

1 cup sliced banana (about 1 large)

6 (½-inch) slices pineapple, cut in half

2 kiwifruit, each peeled and cut into 8 slices

¼ cup apricot preserves

1 tablespoon triple sec (orange-flavored liqueur) or fresh orange juice

2 tablespoons flaked sweetened coconut, toasted

1. Preheat oven to 350°.

2. Cut cookie dough into 8 slices; firmly press slices into a 12-inch round pizza pan coated with cooking spray (edges of dough slices should touch). Bake at 350° for 25 minutes or until lightly browned. Cool completely on a wire rack.

3. Beat sugar and next 3 ingredients at medium speed of a mixer until blended; spread over cookie crust, leaving a ½-inch border. Arrange mango, banana, pineapple, and kiwifruit on top of cream cheese mixture. Combine preserves and liqueur in a small microwave-safe bowl; microwave at HIGH 30 seconds or until preserves melt. Drizzle over fruit; sprinkle with toasted coconut. Chill 1 hour. Yield: 12 servings (serving size: 1 wedge).

CALORIES 283 (24% from fat); FAT 7.4g (sat 2.4g, mono 0.1g, poly 1g); PROTEIN 4.6g; CARB 48.2g; FIBER 1.7g; CHOL 10mg; IRON 1.3mg; SODIUM 203mg; CALC 63mg

cobblers
Fruit's crowning feature is its innate sweetness, perfect for nestling inside these comforting cobblers.

DRIED-FRUIT COBBLER WITH MOLASSES BISCUITS

PREP: 12 MINUTES   COOK: 50 MINUTES

1½ cups water
 1 cup orange juice
⅓ cup orange marmalade
 2 (8-ounce) packages mixed dried
     fruit, coarsely chopped
 1 cup all-purpose flour
 1 teaspoon baking powder
¼ teaspoon ground cinnamon
⅛ teaspoon baking soda
Dash of ground cloves
⅓ cup chilled stick margarine or
     butter, cut into small
     pieces
 2 tablespoons fat-free milk
 2 tablespoons molasses
 1 tablespoon orange marmalade
 2 teaspoons water

1. Preheat oven to 400°.
2. Combine first 4 ingredients in an 11 x 7-inch baking dish. Bake at 400° for 30 minutes.
3. Lightly spoon flour into a dry measuring cup; level with a knife. Combine flour and next 4 ingredients in a bowl; cut in margarine with a pastry blender or 2 knives until mixture resembles coarse meal. Combine milk and molasses, and add to flour mixture, stirring just until flour mixture is moist.
4. Turn dough out onto a lightly floured surface; knead 5 or 6 times. Roll dough to a ½-inch thickness; cut with a 2-inch biscuit cutter into 10 biscuits. Remove fruit mixture from oven; arrange biscuits over hot fruit mixture. Bake an additional 20 minutes or until biscuits are golden.
5. Combine 1 tablespoon marmalade and 2 teaspoons water; brush over biscuits.

Serve warm. Yield: 10 servings (serving size: ½ cup fruit mixture and 1 biscuit).

CALORIES 275 (20% from fat); FAT 6.2g (sat 1.2g, mono 2.7g, poly 2g); PROTEIN 2.4g; CARB 55.3g; FIBER 6.4g; CHOL 0mg; IRON 2.3mg; SODIUM 133mg; CALC 58mg

FRESH BLUEBERRY COBBLER

PREP: 9 MINUTES   COOK: 35 MINUTES

 4 cups fresh blueberries
 1 teaspoon lemon juice
Cooking spray
 1 cup all-purpose flour
½ cup sugar
 1 teaspoon baking powder
⅛ teaspoon ground nutmeg
Dash of salt
 1 tablespoon vegetable oil
½ teaspoon vanilla extract
 2 large egg whites, lightly beaten
 3 tablespoons sugar
½ teaspoon ground cinnamon

1. Preheat oven to 350°.
2. Combine blueberries and lemon juice in an 8-inch square baking dish coated with cooking spray; stir gently.
3. Lightly spoon flour into a dry measuring cup; level with a knife. Combine flour, ½ cup sugar, baking powder, nutmeg, and salt in a bowl; make a well in center of mixture. Combine oil, vanilla, and egg whites; stir well with a whisk. Add to flour mixture, stirring just until moist. Drop dough by spoonfuls onto blueberry mixture to form 8 dumplings. Combine 3 tablespoons sugar and cinnamon; sprinkle over dumplings.
4. Bake at 350° for 35 minutes or until filling is bubbly and dumplings are lightly browned. Yield: 8 servings.

CALORIES 180 (11% from fat); FAT 2.2g (sat 0.4g, mono 0.6g, poly 1g); PROTEIN 2.8g; CARB 38.6g; FIBER 2.3g; CHOL 0mg; IRON 0.9mg; SODIUM 76mg; CALC 31mg

Fresh Blueberry Cobbler

PEACH COBBLER

PREP: 30 MINUTES   COOK: 45 MINUTES

 2 cups all-purpose flour
 1 tablespoon granulated sugar
 ¼ teaspoon salt
 6 tablespoons chilled stick margarine
   or butter, cut into 6 pieces
 6 tablespoons ice water
   Cooking spray
 6 cups sliced peeled peaches
   (about 3¾ pounds)
 ¾ cup packed brown sugar, divided
 2½ tablespoons all-purpose flour
 1 tablespoon vanilla extract
 1 teaspoon ground cinnamon
 ¼ cup slivered almonds
 1 large egg, lightly beaten
 1 teaspoon water
 1 tablespoon granulated sugar

1. Preheat oven to 375°.
2. Lightly spoon flour into dry measuring cups; level with a knife. Place 2 cups flour, 1 tablespoon sugar, and salt in a food processor; pulse 2 or 3 times. Add chilled margarine, and pulse 10 times or until mixture resembles coarse meal. With processor on, slowly pour ice water through food chute, processing just until combined (do not form a ball).
3. Press flour mixture gently into a 4-inch circle on heavy-duty plastic wrap, and cover with additional plastic wrap. Roll dough, still covered, into a 15 x 13-inch rectangle. Place dough in freezer 5 minutes or until plastic wrap can be easily removed. Remove 1 sheet of plastic wrap. Fit dough into a 2-quart baking dish coated with cooking spray, allowing dough to extend over edges of dish; remove top sheet of plastic wrap.
4. Combine peaches, ½ cup brown sugar, 2½ tablespoons flour, vanilla, and cinnamon in a large bowl; toss gently. Spoon peach mixture into prepared dish; fold edges of dough over peach mixture (it will only partially cover peaches). Sprinkle ¼ cup brown sugar over peach mixture; sprinkle with almonds. Combine egg and 1 teaspoon water. Brush egg mixture over dough; sprinkle with 1 tablespoon sugar. Bake at 375° for 45 minutes or until filling is bubbly and crust is lightly browned. Let stand 30 minutes before serving. Yield: 10 servings.

CALORIES 302 (27% from fat); FAT 9.2g (sat 1.6g, mono 4.3g, poly 2.7g); PROTEIN 4.5g; CARB 51.5g; FIBER 2.8g; CHOL 11mg; IRON 1.9mg; SODIUM 149mg; CALC 39mg

Peach Cobbler

A cobbler is a deep-dish fruit dessert **with a thick biscuit crust which can be a single layer** or individual biscuits that "cobble" when baked.

PEAR COBBLER

PREP: 15 MINUTES   COOK: 45 MINUTES

    6   cups sliced peeled pear (about 3
        pounds)
    ⅓   cup packed brown sugar
    1   tablespoon all-purpose flour
    1   tablespoon lemon juice
    ½   teaspoon apple pie spice
        Cooking spray
    ½   cup all-purpose flour
    ½   cup whole-wheat flour or
        all-purpose flour
    3   tablespoons brown sugar
    1   teaspoon baking powder
    ¼   teaspoon salt
    2   tablespoons chilled stick
        margarine or butter, cut into
        small pieces
    ½   cup fat-free milk
    2   teaspoons stick margarine or
        butter, melted
    1   tablespoon brown sugar

1. Preheat oven to 350°.
2. Combine first 5 ingredients in a large bowl; toss gently to coat. Spoon pear mixture into an 8-inch square baking dish coated with cooking spray.
3. Lightly spoon flours into dry measuring cups; level with a knife. Combine ½ cup all-purpose flour, whole-wheat flour, 3 tablespoons brown sugar, baking powder, and salt in a medium bowl; cut in 2 tablespoons chilled margarine with a pastry blender or 2 knives until mixture resembles coarse meal. Add milk, and toss with a fork until flour mixture is moist.
4. Drop dough by heaping tablespoons onto pear mixture. Brush melted margarine over dough, and sprinkle with brown sugar. Bake at 350° for 45 minutes or until lightly browned and bubbly. Yield: 8 servings.

CALORIES 232 (18% from fat); FAT 4.6g (sat 0.8g, mono 1.8g, poly 1.4g); PROTEIN 3g; CARB 47.7g; FIBER 4.4g; CHOL 0mg; IRON 1.4mg; SODIUM 133mg; CALC 86mg

A pandowdy is like a cobbler but the biscuitlike topping becomes crisp and crumbly when baked. The name "dowdy" may have come from its old-fashioned appearance.

WINTER FRUIT PANDOWDY

PREP: 40 MINUTES
COOK: 50 MINUTES

A pandowdy is so juicy that the crust is pushed down into the fruit to absorb the juice. The technique is called "dowdying."

    2   cups sliced peeled Granny Smith
        apple (about ¾ pound)
    2   cups sliced peeled ripe pear
        (about 1 pound)
    3   tablespoons fresh lemon juice
    ⅓   cup dried cranberries
    ¼   cup sugar
    1   teaspoon ground cinnamon
    ½   teaspoon ground nutmeg
        Cooking spray
    1   cup pear nectar
    ¾   cup all-purpose flour
    ⅛   teaspoon salt
    2½ tablespoons vegetable
        shortening
    2   tablespoons plus 2 teaspoons
        ice water
    ¼   teaspoon fresh lemon juice
    1½ teaspoons fat-free milk
    1   tablespoon sugar
    ¼   teaspoon ground cinnamon

1. Preheat oven to 400°.
2. Combine first 3 ingredients in a bowl. Combine cranberries, ¼ cup sugar, 1 teaspoon cinnamon, and nutmeg; add to apple mixture and toss. Place fruit mixture in an 8-inch square baking dish coated with cooking spray. Pour pear nectar over fruit mixture.

3. Lightly spoon flour into dry measuring cups; level with a knife. Combine flour and salt in a bowl. Cut in shortening with a pastry blender or 2 knives until mixture resembles coarse meal. Combine ice water and ¼ teaspoon lemon juice. Sprinkle surface of flour mixture with ice water mixture, 1 tablespoon at a time, and toss with a fork until moist and crumbly (do not form a ball). Press dough gently into a 4-inch square on heavy-duty plastic wrap; cover with additional plastic wrap.
4. Roll dough, still covered, into an 8¼-inch square. Place dough in freezer 5 minutes or until plastic wrap can be easily removed. Remove 1 sheet of plastic wrap; place dough on top of fruit mixture. Remove top sheet of plastic wrap. Cut slits in top of dough to allow steam to escape. Brush dough with milk. Combine 1 tablespoon sugar and ¼ teaspoon cinnamon, and sprinkle over dough.
5. Bake at 400° for 30 minutes; remove from oven. Score pastry into 1-inch squares, using a sharp knife; gently press crust into fruit mixture with a spoon, allowing juices to moisten top of crust.
6. Bake an additional 20 minutes or until lightly browned and bubbly. Serve pandowdy warm with frozen yogurt, if desired. Yield: 6 servings (serving size: 1 cup).

CALORIES 233 (20% from fat); FAT 5.2g (sat 1.2g, mono 2.3g, poly 1.5g); PROTEIN 2g; CARB 46.7g; FIBER 3.5g; CHOL 0mg; IRON 1.1mg; SODIUM 51mg; CALC 21mg

perfect pastry crusts

1. Make a slurry of ¼ cup flour, ice water, and vinegar, stirring with a whisk until well-blended.

2. Combine ¾ cup flour and salt in a bowl; cut in shortening with a pastry blender until mixture resembles coarse meal.

3. Add slurry, and toss with a fork until flour mixture is moist and crumbly (do not form a ball).

4. Press mixture gently into a 4-inch circle on heavy-duty plastic wrap; cover with additional plastic wrap.

5. Roll dough, still covered, into a 12-inch circle; place dough in freezer 10 minutes or until plastic wrap can be easily removed.

6. Remove 1 sheet of plastic wrap; fit dough into pie plate coated with cooking spray. Remove plastic wrap.

7. Press dough against bottom and up sides of plate. Fold edges under and flute decoratively.

8. Line bottom of dough with foil; arrange pie weights on foil. Bake as directed. Remove pie weights and foil; cool on a wire rack.

Basic Pastry Crusts

PASTRY CRUST

PREP: 23 MINUTES
CHILL: 10 MINUTES
COOK: 20 MINUTES

A slurry is a mixture of flour and liquid (water and vinegar in this recipe). It's the key to this tender low-fat crust. Pie weights can be ordered by mail or found in kitchen shops. You can also use un-cooked dried beans, but save them to reuse as weights. They'll be too hard for cooking.

1 cup all-purpose flour, divided
3 tablespoons ice water
½ teaspoon cider vinegar
¼ teaspoon salt
¼ cup vegetable shortening
Cooking spray

1. Lightly spoon flour into a dry measuring cup; level with a knife. Combine ¼ cup flour, ice water, and vinegar, stirring with a whisk until well-blended.
2. Combine ¾ cup flour and salt in a bowl; cut in shortening with a pastry blender or 2 knives until mixture resembles coarse meal. Add slurry; toss with a fork until flour mixture is moist and crumbly (do not form a ball). Press mixture gently into a 4-inch circle on heavy-duty plastic wrap; cover with additional plastic wrap. Roll dough, still covered, into a 12-inch circle; place dough in freezer 10 minutes or until plastic wrap can be easily removed.
3. Remove 1 sheet of plastic wrap; fit dough into a 9-inch pie plate or a 9-inch round removable-bottom tart pan coated with cooking spray. Remove plastic wrap. Press dough against bottom and up sides of pie plate or pan. Fold edges under and flute decoratively.

For Baked Pastry Crust: Preheat oven to 400°. Line bottom of dough with foil; arrange pie weights on foil. Bake at 400° for 20 minutes or until edge is lightly browned. Remove pie weights and foil; cool on a wire rack. Yield: 1 (9-inch) crust (serving size: ⅛ crust).

CALORIES 100 (50% from fat); FAT 5.5g (sat 1.3g, mono 2.6g, poly 1.5g); PROTEIN 1.5g; CARB 11g; FIBER 0.4g; CHOL 0mg; IRON 0.7mg; SODIUM 74mg; CALC 2mg

DOUBLE CRUST

PREP: 23 MINUTES   CHILL: 10 MINUTES

2 cups all-purpose flour, divided
⅓ cup ice water
½ teaspoon salt
¼ cup chilled stick margarine or butter, cut into small pieces
¼ cup vegetable shortening

1. To prepare crust, lightly spoon flour into dry measuring cups; level with a knife. Combine ⅓ cup flour and ice water, stirring with a whisk until well-blended. Combine 1⅔ cups flour and salt in a bowl; cut in margarine and shortening with a pastry blender or 2 knives until mixture resembles coarse meal. Add ice water mixture; toss with a fork until moist. Divide mixture in half. Gently press each half of mixture into a 4-inch circle on heavy-duty plastic wrap, and cover with additional plastic wrap. Roll one half of dough, still covered, into a 12-inch circle, and chill. Roll other half of dough, still covered, into an 11-inch circle; chill. Yield: 1 (9-inch) double crust (serving size: 1/10 crust).

CALORIES 169 (48% from fat); FAT 9g (sat 2g, mono 4.2g, poly 2.3g); PROTEIN 2.6g; CARB 19.1g; FIBER 0.7g; CHOL 0mg; IRON 1.2mg; SODIUM 171mg; CALC 6mg

CREAM CHEESE PIECRUST

PREP: 17 MINUTES   CHILL: 20 MINUTES

2 tablespoons butter or stick margarine
2 tablespoons (1 ounce) ⅓-less-fat cream cheese
2 tablespoons sugar
1 teaspoon vanilla extract
1 tablespoon 1% low-fat milk
1 large egg yolk
1 cup all-purpose flour
¼ teaspoon baking powder
¼ teaspoon salt
Cooking spray

1. Beat first 4 ingredients at medium speed of a mixer until smooth. Add milk and egg yolk; beat until well-blended. Lightly spoon flour into a dry measuring cup; level with a knife. Add flour, baking powder, and salt, stirring until well-blended.
2. Press mixture gently into a 4-inch circle on heavy-duty plastic wrap; cover with additional plastic wrap. Chill 15 minutes. Roll dough, still covered, into an 11-inch circle. Place dough in freezer 5 minutes or until plastic wrap can be easily removed.
3. Remove 1 sheet of plastic wrap; fit dough into a 9-inch pie plate coated with cooking spray. Remove top sheet of plastic wrap. Press dough against bottom and sides of pie plate. Fold edges under; flute. Fill and bake crust according to recipe directions. Yield: 1 (9-inch) crust (serving size: 1/10 crust).

CALORIES 92 (36% from fat); FAT 3.7g (sat 2.1g, mono 1.1g, poly 0.2g); PROTEIN 1.9g; CARB 12.3g; FIBER 0.3g; CHOL 30mg; IRON 0.7mg; SODIUM 107mg; CALC 16mg

GREEK BAKING POWDER PIECRUST

PREP: 23 MINUTES   CHILL: 20 MINUTES

Not all crusts require a sweet filling. We use this crust for Zucchini, Sweet Onion, and Red Pepper Tart (page 300).

2¼ cups all-purpose flour
2 teaspoons baking powder
½ teaspoon salt
¾ cup water
3 tablespoons olive oil

1. Lightly spoon flour into dry measuring cups; level with a knife. Combine flour, baking powder, and salt in a large bowl; make a well in center of mixture. Add water and oil to flour mixture, stirring until well-blended.
2. Turn dough out onto a lightly floured surface; knead 4 or 5 times. Divide dough in half. Working with one portion at a time, press each half of mixture gently into a 4-inch circle on heavy-duty plastic wrap; cover with additional plastic wrap. Chill for 15 minutes. Place dough in freezer 5 minutes or until plastic wrap can be easily removed. Yield: 2 (10-inch) crusts (serving size: ⅙ crust).

CALORIES 111 (29% from fat); FAT 3.6g (sat 0.5g, mono 2.5g, poly 0.4g); PROTEIN 2.3g; CARB 17.1g; FIBER 0.6g; CHOL 0mg; IRON 1.1mg; SODIUM 151mg; CALC 33mg

GRAHAM CRACKER CRUST

PREP: 5 MINUTES   COOK: 8 MINUTES

40 graham crackers (10 full cookie sheets)
2 tablespoons sugar
2 tablespoons butter or stick margarine, melted
1 large egg white
Cooking spray

1. Preheat oven to 350°.
2. Place crackers in a food processor; process until crumbly. Add 2 tablespoons sugar, butter, and egg white; pulse 6 times or just until moist. Press crumb mixture into bottom and up sides of a 9-inch pie plate coated with cooking spray. Bake at 350° for 8 minutes; cool on a wire rack. Yield: 1 (9-inch) crust (serving size: ⅛ crust).

CALORIES 114 (37% from fat); FAT 4.7g (sat 2.1g, mono 1.5g, poly 0.8g); PROTEIN 1.7g; CARB 16.5g; FIBER 0.5g; CHOL 8mg; IRON 0.7mg; SODIUM 141mg; CALC 5mg

VANILLA WAFER CRUST

PREP: 5 MINUTES   COOK: 8 MINUTES

1½ cups reduced-calorie vanilla wafer crumbs (about 40 cookies)
2 tablespoons butter or stick margarine, melted
1 large egg white, lightly beaten
Cooking spray

1. Preheat oven to 350°.
2. Combine first 3 ingredients; toss with a fork until moist. Press into bottom and up sides of a 9-inch pie plate coated with cooking spray. Bake at 350° for 8 minutes. Cool on a wire rack. Yield: 1 (9-inch) crust (serving size: ⅛ crust).

CALORIES 110 (29% from fat); FAT 3.6g (sat 2.1g, mono 0.8g, poly 0.5g); PROTEIN 1.7g; CARB 15.7g; FIBER 0.3g; CHOL 8mg; IRON 0.4mg; SODIUM 124mg; CALC 1mg

PASTRIES

We've tucked fruit and cream fillings into a variety of pastries—flaky sheets of phyllo, tender biscuit dough, and rich-tasting cream puff pastries.

You'll find make-ahead directions for the cream puffs (which can be filled with our filling or a favorite pudding right before serving) but the other pastries are best when eaten the day they are prepared. You'll want to savor the tenderness of each bite of fresh pastry!

APPLE STRUDEL

PREP: 25 MINUTES   COOK: 35 MINUTES

⅓ cup raisins
3 tablespoons amaretto (almond-flavored liqueur)
3 cups coarsely chopped peeled Granny Smith apple (about 1 pound)
⅓ cup sugar
3 tablespoons all-purpose flour
¼ teaspoon ground cinnamon
8 sheets frozen phyllo dough, thawed
Butter-flavored cooking spray
2 cups vanilla low-fat ice cream

1. Preheat oven to 350°.
2. Combine raisins and amaretto in a bowl. Microwave at HIGH 1½ minutes; drain well.
3. Combine raisins, apple, sugar, flour, and cinnamon in a bowl; toss well.
4. Place 1 phyllo sheet on work surface

(cover remaining dough to keep from drying); lightly coat with cooking spray. Working with 1 phyllo sheet at a time, coat remaining 7 phyllo sheets with cooking spray, placing one on top of the other. Place a sheet of plastic wrap over phyllo, pressing gently to seal sheets together; discard plastic wrap.

5. Spoon apple mixture along 1 long edge of phyllo, leaving 2-inch borders on 1 long edge and 2 short edges. Fold over short edges of phyllo to cover 2 inches of apple mixture on each end.

6. Starting at long edge with 2-inch border, roll up jelly-roll fashion. (Do not roll tightly, or strudel may split.) Place strudel, seam side down, on a jelly-roll pan coated with cooking spray. Cut diagonal slits into top of strudel using a sharp knife. Lightly coat strudel with cooking spray.

7. Bake at 350° for 35 minutes or until golden brown. Serve warm with ice cream. Yield: 8 servings (serving size: 1 slice and ¼ cup ice cream).

CALORIES 211 (16% from fat); FAT 3.9g (sat 1.4g, mono 1.2g, poly 1g); PROTEIN 3.4g; CARB 42.3g; FIBER 1.3g; CHOL 5mg; IRON 1mg; SODIUM 134mg; CALC 55mg

Apple Strudel

1. Working with one phyllo sheet at a time, coat each sheet with cooking spray, and place one on top of the other.

2. Place a sheet of plastic wrap over phyllo, pressing gently to seal sheets together. Discard plastic wrap.

3. After spooning apple mixture along one long edge of phyllo sheet, fold over short edges of phyllo to cover 2 inches of filling on each end.

4. Roll in a jelly-roll fashion. Do not roll too tightly, or the strudel may split.

5. Using a sharp knife, cut several diagonal slits into top.

USING PHYLLO

• **Always prepare the filling mixture first** because phyllo dries out very quickly once it has been unwrapped and exposed to air.

• **Remove only the number of thawed sheets called for** at each step of the recipe, and **place the sheets on a flat surface.**

• **Keep remaining phyllo sheets covered with a damp cotton towel** to keep them from drying out. **The cotton towel shouldn't be too wet** because the phyllo can become too moist, sticky, and hard to handle.

• **Phyllo will stay fresh in the refrigerator for up to one month and can be kept frozen for up to one year.**

• **If frozen, defrost the dough completely in the refrigerator or at room temperature before using.** Defrosting will cause the layers to stick to each other, and working with the phyllo will be very difficult. **Remove phyllo from the refrigerator two hours before using for best handling.** Refreezing thawed phyllo isn't recommended because the dough becomes crumbly, dry, and hard to work with.

Traditionally, a large amount of butter is brushed over each sheet of phyllo to create a crisp, flaky, golden crust. However, **it's possible to decrease the fat in a recipe by coating the phyllo sheets with butter-flavored cooking spray.** The cooking spray creates a golden, flaky crust without the extra fat. Plus, coating the sheets with cooking spray is much faster than brushing them with butter.

ORANGE-PISTACHIO BAKLAVA

PREP: 25 MINUTES   COOK: 30 MINUTES

1¼ cups chopped pistachios
¾ cup wheat saltine cracker crumbs (about 20 crackers)
⅓ cup sugar
½ teaspoon ground cinnamon
12 sheets frozen phyllo dough, thawed
Butter-flavored cooking spray
2 tablespoons stick margarine or butter, melted
¾ cup honey
½ cup thawed orange juice concentrate
⅓ cup water
1 teaspoon ground cinnamon
⅛ teaspoon ground cloves

1. Preheat oven to 350°.
2. Combine first 4 ingredients in a bowl.
3. Working with 1 phyllo sheet at a time (cover remaining dough to keep from drying), lightly coat each sheet with cooking spray. Fold phyllo sheet in half crosswise to form a 13 x 8-inch rectangle; lightly coat both sides of rectangle with cooking spray. Place in bottom of a 13 x 9-inch baking dish coated with cooking spray; sprinkle 3 tablespoons pistachio mixture over phyllo.
4. Repeat layers with 9 sheets of phyllo, cooking spray, and remaining pistachio mixture, ending with pistachio mixture. Lightly coat remaining 2 sheets of phyllo with cooking spray. Fold each phyllo sheet in half crosswise to form a 13 x 8-inch rectangle; lightly coat both sides of each rectangle with cooking spray. Layer each into baking dish.
5. Cut diamond shapes, ¾-inch deep, into layers of phyllo. Drizzle margarine over phyllo using a sharp knife. Bake at 350° for 30 minutes or until golden.
6. Combine honey, juice concentrate,

water, 1 teaspoon cinnamon, and cloves in a small saucepan; bring to a boil. Reduce heat; simmer, uncovered, 5 minutes, stirring frequently. Remove from heat, and drizzle honey mixture over phyllo. Cool completely in pan. Cut into bars. Yield: 1½ dozen (serving size: 1 bar).

CALORIES 198 (35% from fat); FAT 7.7g (sat 1g, mono 4.2g, poly 1.9g); PROTEIN 3.7g; CARB 30.6g; FIBER 1.3g; CHOL 0mg; IRON 1.4mg; SODIUM 114mg; CALC 21mg

DATE-AND-WALNUT SAMBOUSEKS

PREP: 30 MINUTES   COOK: 20 MINUTES

1 cup chopped pitted dates
½ cup orange juice
2 tablespoons finely chopped walnuts
1 teaspoon vanilla extract
½ teaspoon ground cinnamon
1 (7.5-ounce) can refrigerated biscuits
Cooking spray
1 large egg, lightly beaten
1 tablespoon sesame seeds

1. Preheat oven to 350°.
2. Combine chopped dates and orange juice in a medium saucepan. Cover and cook over low heat 15 minutes or until liquid is absorbed. Remove from heat; mash dates with a fork until smooth. Stir in walnuts, vanilla, and cinnamon.
3. Divide dough into 10 biscuits. Working with 1 biscuit at a time, place biscuit between 2 sheets of heavy-duty plastic wrap. Roll biscuit into a 4-inch circle. Remove biscuit from plastic wrap. Spoon about 1 tablespoon date mixture onto half of circle. Moisten edges of dough with water, and fold dough over filling. Press edges of dough together with a fork to seal (dip tines of fork in flour before pressing). Repeat procedure with 9 biscuits and remaining date mixture. Place filled pastries about 2 inches apart on a

baking sheet coated with cooking spray. Brush beaten egg over pastries; sprinkle with sesame seeds.

4. Bake pastries at 350° for 20 minutes or until lightly browned. Remove from pan; cool on a wire rack. Yield: 10 pastries (serving size: 1 pastry).

CALORIES 116 (19% from fat); FAT 2.5g (sat 0.3g, mono 0.7g, poly 1g); PROTEIN 2.8g; CARB 21.7g; FIBER 1.4g; CHOL 21mg; IRON 1mg; SODIUM 196mg; CALC 24mg

PEAR PHYLLO PASTRIES

PREP: 23 MINUTES   COOK: 25 MINUTES

¼ cup dry breadcrumbs
¼ cup packed brown sugar
3 tablespoons stick margarine or
    butter, melted
1 tablespoon vegetable oil
½ cup granulated sugar
½ teaspoon ground cinnamon
¼ teaspoon ground nutmeg
½ teaspoon almond extract
4 cups chopped peeled pear
    (about 4 pears)
½ cup dried cranberries
¼ cup chopped almonds, toasted
12 sheets frozen phyllo dough,
    thawed
Butter-flavored cooking spray

1. Preheat oven to 350°.
2. Combine breadcrumbs and brown sugar in a bowl. Combine melted margarine and oil in a second bowl.
3. Combine granulated sugar, cinnamon, nutmeg, and almond extract in a large bowl. Add pear, cranberries, and almonds; toss gently to coat.
4. Place 1 phyllo sheet on work surface (cover remaining dough to keep from drying); lightly coat with margarine mixture. Working with 1 phyllo sheet at a time, coat 2 additional sheets with margarine mixture, stacking each on top of the first. Place a sheet of plastic wrap over

phyllo; press gently to seal sheets together. Discard plastic wrap. Sprinkle 2 tablespoons breadcrumb mixture over top of stack. Cut stack lengthwise into 3 (4½-inch-wide) strips using a sharp knife or pizza cutter.
5. Spoon about ⅓ cup pear mixture onto 1 end of each phyllo strip. Fold left bottom corner over pear mixture, forming a triangle. Keep folding phyllo back and forth into triangle to end of strip. Repeat procedure with remaining sheets of phyllo, margarine mixture, breadcrumb mixture, and pear mixture.
6. Place triangles, seam sides down, on a baking sheet coated with cooking spray. Coat tops of triangles with cooking spray. Bake at 350° for 25 minutes or until golden. Serve warm or at room temperature. Yield: 12 servings (serving size: 1 pastry).
Note: If dried cranberries are unavailable, substitute dried currants or raisins.

CALORIES 207 (30% from fat); FAT 7g (sat 1.1g, mono 2.7g, poly 2.4g); PROTEIN 2.3g; CARB 34.8g; FIBER 1.6g; CHOL 0mg; IRON 1.1mg; SODIUM 149mg; CALC 24mg

TROPICAL FRUIT NAPOLEONS

PREP: 25 MINUTES   COOK: 12 MINUTES

½ cup fat-free sour cream
⅓ cup sifted powdered sugar
⅓ cup tub-style light cream cheese
¼ cup soft tofu, drained
½ teaspoon grated lemon rind
2 tablespoons dry breadcrumbs
2 tablespoons granulated sugar
¼ teaspoon ground cinnamon
5 sheets frozen phyllo dough, thawed
2 tablespoons reduced-calorie stick
    margarine, melted
Cooking spray
½ cup diced carambola (star fruit)
½ cup diced peeled papaya
½ cup diced banana
1 tablespoon powdered sugar

1. Beat first 5 ingredients at medium speed of a mixer until smooth. Cover and chill.
2. Combine breadcrumbs, granulated sugar, and cinnamon in a bowl.
3. Preheat oven to 375°.
4. Place 1 phyllo sheet on a large cutting board or work surface (cover remaining dough to keep from drying); lightly brush with margarine. Sprinkle with 1 tablespoon breadcrumb mixture. Repeat layers with remaining phyllo, margarine, and breadcrumb mixture, ending with phyllo. Gently press phyllo layers together.
5. Lightly coat top phyllo sheet with cooking spray. Cut 12 (3-inch) circles through phyllo layers using a sharp round cookie cutter. Carefully place layered circles on a baking sheet coated with cooking spray; discard phyllo scraps. Coat the bottom of another baking sheet with cooking spray; place, coated side down, on top of layered phyllo circles. Bake at 375° for 12 minutes or until crisp. Remove top baking sheet; place phyllo stacks on a wire rack. Cool completely.
6. Combine carambola, papaya, and banana; stir gently. Place 1 phyllo stack on each of 4 dessert plates. Spread about 1 tablespoon sour cream mixture on top of each stack; top each with about 3 tablespoons papaya mixture and 1 tablespoon sour cream mixture. Repeat layers with remaining phyllo stacks, sour cream mixture, and papaya mixture, ending with phyllo stacks. Sprinkle powdered sugar over napoleons. Yield: 4 servings (serving size: 1 pastry).

CALORIES 290 (29% from fat); FAT 9.5g (sat 2.8g, mono 3.1g, poly 2.8g); PROTEIN 7.5g; CARB 44.3g; FIBER 1.3g; CHOL 11mg; IRON 1.4mg; SODIUM 326mg; CALC 59mg

COCONUT CREAM PUFFS

PREP: 1 HOUR   CHILL: 4 HOURS
COOK: 20 MINUTES PER BATCH

Filling:
- ½ teaspoon unflavored gelatin
- 1 tablespoon water
- 2 tablespoons granulated sugar
- 1½ tablespoons cornstarch
- 1 large egg, lightly beaten
- ¾ cup fat-free milk
- 1½ teaspoons stick margarine or butter
- 3 tablespoons cream of coconut
- ½ teaspoon coconut extract
- ½ teaspoon vanilla extract
- ¾ cup frozen reduced-calorie whipped topping, thawed

Cream Puffs:
- 1 cup all-purpose flour
- 2 teaspoons granulated sugar
- ¼ teaspoon salt
- 1 cup fat-free milk
- 2 tablespoons stick margarine or butter
- 3 large egg whites
- 1 large egg yolk

Cooking spray
- 2 tablespoons powdered sugar

1. To prepare filling, sprinkle gelatin over water in a small bowl.

2. Combine 2 tablespoons sugar, cornstarch, and egg in a bowl; stir with a whisk. Heat ¾ cup milk over medium-high heat in a heavy saucepan to 180° or until tiny bubbles form around edge (do not boil). Gradually add hot milk to egg mixture, stirring constantly with a whisk. Return milk mixture to pan; add 1½ teaspoons margarine. Bring to a boil over medium heat; cook 1 minute or until thick, stirring constantly with a whisk. Add gelatin to milk mixture; cook over low heat 1 minute, stirring until gelatin dissolves. Remove from heat; stir in cream of coconut, coconut extract, and vanilla.

3. Place pan with gelatin mixture in a large ice-filled bowl for 3 minutes or until mixture reaches room temperature (do not allow gelatin mixture to set), stirring occasionally. Remove pan from ice; add whipped topping to gelatin mixture, stirring gently with a whisk. Cover and chill 4 hours or until thick.

4. To prepare puffs, preheat oven to 425°.

5. Lightly spoon flour into a dry measuring cup; level with a knife. Combine flour, 2 teaspoons sugar, and salt. Combine 1 cup milk and 2 tablespoons margarine in a large saucepan; bring to a boil. Reduce heat to low; add flour mixture, stirring well until mixture is smooth and pulls away from sides of pan. Remove from heat; cool 5 minutes.

6. Add egg whites and egg yolk to dough, 1 at a time, beating vigorously with a wooden spoon until smooth. Drop dough by level tablespoons, 2 inches apart, onto baking sheets coated with cooking spray. Bake at 425° for 10 minutes. Reduce oven temperature to 350° (do not remove puffs from oven); bake an additional 10 minutes or until browned and crisp. Remove from oven; pierce side of each cream puff with tip of a sharp knife. Turn off oven; let cream puffs stand in partially closed oven 5 minutes. Cool completely on a wire rack.

7. Cut tops off cream puffs; fill each with 1 level tablespoon filling. Sprinkle with powdered sugar. Serve immediately. Yield: 32 cream puffs (serving size: 1 cream puff).

Note: To make ahead, place baked and cooled cream puffs in a large heavy-duty zip-top plastic bag; seal and freeze. Cover and chill cooked filling. To reheat cream puffs, remove from bag, and place on a large baking sheet. Bake at 325° for 10 minutes or until crisp. Remove from baking sheet to a wire rack; cool completely. Fill according to recipe directions.

CALORIES 47 (36% from fat); FAT 1.9g (sat 0.7g, mono 0.5g, poly 0.3g); PROTEIN 1.6g; CARB 5.8g; FIBER 0.1g; CHOL 14mg; IRON 0.2mg; SODIUM 45mg; CALC 20mg

Cream Puffs

1. Add flour mixture to milk mixture, stirring well until mixture is smooth and pulls away from sides of pan.

2. Add egg whites and egg yolk, 1 at a time, beating vigorously with a wooden spoon until smooth.

3. After removing cream puffs from oven, pierce the side of each (baked) cream puff with the tip of a sharp knife.

fish & shellfish

Shrimp Scampi (page 241)

FISH

When it comes to making quick, great-tasting entrées that are low in fat, fish is hard to beat. It can take as little as 10 minutes to cook, and it can be prepared in a variety of ways.

Great-quality fish is available both fresh and frozen. Purchase fresh fish from a reputable store that has a quick turnover and that regularly replenishes its stock. One of the best ways to judge freshness is by smell. Fish should have a mild smell, not an offensive, fish odor. Also check for firmness; the flesh should spring back when pressed lightly.

When buying whole fresh fish, look for eyes that are clear, bright, and full or almost bulging, and for shiny skin with firmly attached scales. When you're buying fresh fish steaks and fillets, select ones that are moist and freshly cut; avoid pieces that are yellow or brown around the edges.

Commercially frozen fish has been flash-frozen to capture color, moisture, and flavor. It's an excellent choice if properly thawed. Be sure that frozen fish is wrapped in moisture- and vapor-resistant packaging and is solidly frozen with no discoloration or freezer burns. There should be little or no air within the wrapping. Ice crystals indicate the fish has been thawed and refrozen which can ruin its texture.

To keep fish safe, make the fish counter your last stop when shopping. Fresh fish should go on the bottom shelf or in the meat keeper of your refrigerator, where temperatures are coldest, and should be used within two days of purchase. For frozen seafood, it's best to thaw it in the refrigerator, allowing one day for the food to defrost. Pressed for time? Thaw frozen fish under cold running water or place it in a zip-top plastic bag and immerse in a pan of cold water in the refrigerator for one to two hours per pound of seafood.

CAJUN CATFISH

PREP: 5 MINUTES   COOK: 10 MINUTES

4 (6-ounce) farm-raised catfish
     fillets
1 tablespoon fresh lemon juice
4 teaspoons Cajun Seasoning
     (page 455)
Cooking spray
Lemon wedges (optional)

1. Preheat broiler.
2. Brush both sides of fillets with lemon juice, and sprinkle with Cajun Seasoning. Place fish on a broiler pan coated with cooking spray, and broil 5 minutes on each side or until fish flakes easily when tested with a fork. Serve with lemon wedges, if desired. Yield: 4 servings (serving size: 1 fillet).

CALORIES 204 (33% from fat); FAT 7.5g (sat 1.7g, mono 2.8g, poly 1.9g); PROTEIN 31.2g; CARB 1.5g; FIBER 0.4g; CHOL 99mg; IRON 2.1mg; SODIUM 249mg; CALC 76mg

TUSCAN COD

PREP: 6 MINUTES   COOK: 17 MINUTES

1 teaspoon olive oil
½ cup thinly sliced onion,
     separated into rings
½ cup diced red bell pepper
1 garlic clove, minced
1 cup chopped tomato
1 tablespoon capers
¼ teaspoon ground cumin
⅛ teaspoon crushed red pepper
2 (6-ounce) cod fillets

1. Heat oil in a large nonstick skillet over medium-high heat. Add onion, bell pepper, and garlic; sauté 2 minutes.

Add tomato and next 3 ingredients; cook over medium heat 5 minutes, stirring occasionally. Add fish to skillet, spooning sauce over fish. Cover and cook 10 minutes or until fish flakes easily when tested with a fork. Yield: 2 servings (serving size: 1 fillet and ½ cup sauce).

CALORIES 214 (17% from fat); FAT 4.1g (sat 0.6g, mono 1.9g, poly 0.9g); PROTEIN 32.4g; CARB 11.8g; FIBER 2.7g; CHOL 73mg; IRON 1.9mg; SODIUM 439mg; CALC 49mg

PECAN-CRUSTED FLOUNDER WITH CRAB-PECAN RELISH

PREP: 20 MINUTES   COOK: 4 MINUTES

½ pound fresh lump crabmeat,
     drained and shell pieces removed
¼ cup chopped pecans, toasted
¼ cup chopped green onions
1 tablespoon minced red bell pepper
1 tablespoon fresh lemon juice
¼ teaspoon salt
⅛ teaspoon black pepper
2 tablespoons plus 2 teaspoons
     Creole Seasoning (page 456),
     divided
4 (4-ounce) flounder fillets
¼ cup all-purpose flour
1 large egg, lightly beaten
¼ cup 1% low-fat milk
¼ cup all-purpose flour
3 tablespoons ground pecans
1 tablespoon olive oil
8 lemon wedges

1. Combine first 7 ingredients in a small bowl; set aside.
2. Rub 2 teaspoons Creole Seasoning over fish, and combine ¼ cup flour and 1 tablespoon Creole Seasoning in a

shallow dish. Set aside. Combine egg and milk in a shallow dish. Combine ¼ cup flour, 1 tablespoon Creole Seasoning, and ground pecans in a shallow dish.

3. Dredge each fillet in flour seasoning mixture, dip into milk mixture, and dredge in pecan mixture.

4. Heat oil in a large nonstick skillet over medium-high heat until hot. Add fish; cook 2 minutes on each side or until fish flakes easily when tested with a fork. Serve immediately with crabmeat mixture and lemon wedges. Yield: 4 servings (serving size: 1 fillet, ⅓ cup crabmeat mixture, and 2 lemon wedges).

CALORIES 276 (39% from fat); FAT 16.4g (sat 2.2g, mono 9g, poly 3.6g); PROTEIN 38.4g; CARB 20.7g; FIBER 2.2g; CHOL 165mg; IRON 3.3mg; SODIUM 891mg; CALC 161mg

FISH FAJITAS

PREP: 7 MINUTES   COOK: 8 MINUTES

Grouper not available? Use another lean white fish, such as orange roughy or sea bass, instead.

  12 (6-inch) flour tortillas
  1½ tablespoons vegetable oil
  1½ cups green bell pepper strips
  ¾ cup thinly sliced onion
  1½ pounds grouper fillets, cut into
      ½-inch strips
  ⅓ cup beer
  ¼ teaspoon salt
  ⅛ teaspoon black pepper
  2 cups Tomatillo Guacamole (page 440)
  1½ cups bottled salsa
  6 tablespoons fat-free sour cream

1. Warm tortillas according to package directions; keep warm.

2. Heat oil in a large nonstick skillet over medium-high heat. Add bell pepper, onion, and fish; sauté 3 minutes. Add beer; cook 5 minutes or until almost all liquid evaporates and fish flakes

easily when tested with a fork. Remove from heat; sprinkle with salt and pepper.

3. Divide fish mixture evenly among tortillas, and roll up. Arrange 2 fajitas on each of 6 plates; top each serving with ⅓ cup Tomatillo Guacamole, ¼ cup salsa, and 1 tablespoon sour cream. Yield: 6 servings (serving size: 2 fajitas).

CALORIES 416 (26% from fat); FAT 12.1g (sat 2.1g, mono 4.9g, poly 4.1g); PROTEIN 29.9g; CARB 46.7g; FIBER 6.1g; CHOL 42mg; IRON 5.2mg; SODIUM 959mg; CALC 139mg

GRILLED GROUPER WITH APRICOT-GINGER RELISH

PREP: 20 MINUTES   STAND: 1 HOUR
COOK: 12 MINUTES

If you can't find fresh apricots, substitute peaches. The ginger in this recipe can make this a hot dish!

  2 cups diced fresh apricots (about
      6 medium)
  ½ cup diced red bell pepper
  ⅓ cup rice wine vinegar
  ¼ cup minced green onions
  2 tablespoons sugar
  1 to 2 tablespoons minced peeled
      fresh ginger
  ½ teaspoon freshly ground black
      pepper
  ¼ teaspoon salt
  ¼ teaspoon hot sauce
  1 tablespoon chile paste with garlic
  4 (6-ounce) grouper fillets (½ inch
      thick)
  Cooking spray

1. Combine first 9 ingredients in a small bowl. Cover and let relish stand 1 hour.
2. Prepare grill.
3. Rub chile paste over both sides of fillets.
4. Place fillets on grill rack coated with cooking spray, and grill 6 minutes on each side or until fish flakes easily when

tested with a fork. Serve fish with relish. Yield: 4 servings (serving size: 1 fillet and ½ cup relish).

CALORIES 247 (9% from fat); FAT 2.5g (sat 0.5g, mono 0.5g, poly 0.7g); PROTEIN 36.8g; CARB 17.9g; FIBER 2.6g; CHOL 67mg; IRON 2.5mg; SODIUM 326mg; CALC 48mg

HALIBUT FILLETS WITH TERIYAKI SAUCE

PREP: 5 MINUTES   COOK: 10 MINUTES

Another white fish, such as sea bass, snapper, or monkfish can be substituted for the halibut.

  ½ cup pineapple juice
  3 tablespoons low-sodium teriyaki
      sauce
  1 tablespoon honey
  ¾ teaspoon cornstarch
  ¼ teaspoon garlic powder
  ⅛ teaspoon ground red pepper
  2 tablespoons seasoned
      breadcrumbs
  4 (6-ounce) halibut fillets, skinned
      (about 1 inch thick)
  1 tablespoon vegetable oil

1. Combine first 6 ingredients in a small bowl, stirring well with a whisk. Combine breadcrumbs and fish in a large zip-top plastic bag. Seal and shake to coat.

2. Heat oil in a large nonstick skillet over medium heat. Add fish; cook 4 minutes on each side or until fish flakes easily when tested with a fork. Remove fish from skillet; keep warm.

3. Add teriyaki mixture to skillet. Bring to a boil; cook 1 minute, stirring constantly. Pour over fish. Yield: 4 servings (serving size: 1 fillet and 2 tablespoons sauce).

CALORIES 280 (24% from fat); FAT 7.4g (sat 1.2g, mono 2.1g, poly 3.1g); PROTEIN 36.9g; CARB 14.1g; FIBER 0.1g; CHOL 80mg; IRON 1.9mg; SODIUM 304mg; CALC 96mg

OVEN-POACHED HALIBUT PROVENÇALE

PREP: 38 MINUTES
COOK: 37 MINUTES

Crusty French bread is a great accompaniment to this dish.

    1 cup dry white wine
    6 (6-ounce) halibut steaks
Cooking spray
    6 cups diced tomato
    2 cups finely chopped onion
  ¼ cup chopped fresh or
         4 teaspoons dried basil
  ¼ cup chopped fresh or 4
         teaspoons dried parsley
    2 tablespoons minced kalamata
         olives
    1 tablespoon olive oil
  ½ teaspoon salt
  ½ teaspoon anchovy paste
  ⅛ teaspoon black pepper
    2 garlic cloves, minced
  ¼ cup dry breadcrumbs
    1 tablespoon grated Parmesan
         cheese
    1 teaspoon olive oil

1. Preheat oven to 350°.
2. Place wine and fish in a 13 x 9-inch baking dish coated with cooking spray. Combine tomato and next 9 ingredients in a bowl; spoon over fish. Bake at 350° for 35 minutes or until fish flakes easily when tested with a fork.
3. Preheat broiler.
4. Combine breadcrumbs, cheese, and 1 teaspoon oil in a bowl. Sprinkle breadcrumb mixture over tomato mixture, and broil 1½ minutes or until crumbs are golden. Serve with a slotted spoon. Yield: 6 servings (serving size: 1 halibut steak and 1 cup tomato mixture).

CALORIES 300 (26% from fat); FAT 8.6g (sat 1.3g, mono 3.8g, poly 2.1g); PROTEIN 38.8g; CARB 16.9g; FIBER 3.2g; CHOL 81mg; IRON 3mg; SODIUM 437mg; CALC 131mg

Oven-Poached
Halibut Provençale

GRILLED HALIBUT WITH LEMON SAUCE

PREP: 8 MINUTES
COOK: 12 MINUTES

  ¾ cup fat-free, less-sodium chicken
         broth
  ¼ cup fresh lemon juice
    1 tablespoon cornstarch
    1 tablespoon minced fresh parsley
  ½ teaspoon salt
  ¼ teaspoon dried oregano
  ¼ teaspoon dried rosemary
    8 (6-ounce) halibut fillets
Cooking spray

1. Combine first 3 ingredients in a small saucepan. Bring to a boil; cook 1 minute, stirring constantly. Remove from heat. Stir in parsley, salt, oregano, and rosemary; keep warm.
2. Prepare grill.
3. Place fish on grill rack coated with cooking spray; cover and grill 6 minutes on each side or until fish flakes easily when tested with a fork. Serve with warm sauce. Yield: 8 servings (serving size: 1 fillet and 2 tablespoons sauce).

CALORIES 197 (19% from fat); FAT 4.2g (sat 0.6g, mono 1.1g, poly 1.4g); PROTEIN 35.6g; CARB 1.7g; FIBER 0g; CHOL 80mg; IRON 1.5mg; SODIUM 251mg; CALC 87mg

menu

Lemon-Dill Fish Fillets

California Ranch Slaw (page 400)

Green-Chile Cornsticks (page 78)

Angel food cake with fresh berries

LEMON-DILL FISH FILLETS

PREP:11 MINUTES   COOK:15 MINUTES

½   cup finely crushed plain melba
     snack crackers (about 20
     crackers)
1½ teaspoons paprika
1½ teaspoons grated lemon rind
 1   teaspoon dried dill
½   teaspoon dry mustard
 4   (6-ounce) orange roughy or
     other lean white fish fillets
Cooking spray
¼   teaspoon salt

1. Combine first 5 ingredients in a zip-
top plastic bag; seal bag, and shake well.
2. Preheat oven to 400°.
3. Coat both sides of fish with cooking
spray; sprinkle with salt. Place cracker
mixture in a shallow dish; dredge fish in
cracker mixture. Arrange fish in an 11 x
7-inch baking dish coated with cooking
spray. Bake at 400° for 15 minutes or
until fish flakes easily when tested with
a fork. Yield: 4 servings (serving size: 1
fillet).

CALORIES 174 (14% from fat); FAT 2.7g (sat 0.1g, mono 0.8g,
poly 0.1g); PROTEIN 27g; CARB 9.2g; FIBER 1.2g;
CHOL 34mg; IRON 1mg; SODIUM 367mg; CALC 132mg

Cook fish 10 minutes per inch of thickness, measuring at the thickest point.

GRILLED-FISH SOFT TACOS WITH CITRUS SALSA SLAW

PREP:10 MINUTES   COOK:8 MINUTES

 4   (10-inch) flour tortillas
 1   tablespoon chili powder
 1   tablespoon vegetable oil
 1   tablespoon fresh lime juice
 4   (6-ounce) red snapper or other
     firm white fish fillets
¼   teaspoon salt
⅛   teaspoon black pepper
Cooking spray
 4   cups Citrus Salsa Slaw (page 401)
Cilantro sprigs (optional)

1. Prepare grill.
2. Wrap tortillas in foil; set aside.
3. Combine chili powder, oil, and lime
juice in a small bowl; brush over both
sides of fillets. Sprinkle salt and pepper
over fillets, and arrange in a wire grilling
basket coated with cooking spray.
4. Place tortilla packet and grilling basket on grill rack; grill 4 minutes on each
side or until tortillas are warm and fish
flakes easily when tested with a fork.
Place 1 fillet on each tortilla, and top with
1 cup Citrus Salsa Slaw; fold tortillas in
half. Garnish with cilantro, if desired.
Yield: 4 servings (serving size: 1 taco).

CALORIES 459 (27% from fat); FAT 13.8g (sat 2.4g, mono 4.1g,
poly 5.9g); PROTEIN 43.4g; CARB 39.7g; FIBER 4.9g;
CHOL 67mg; IRON 3mg; SODIUM 658mg; CALC 169mg

Grilled-Fish Soft Tacos With
Citrus Salsa Slaw

MEDITERRANEAN ORANGE ROUGHY

PREP:18 MINUTES   COOK:15 MINUTES

    2 teaspoons olive oil
1⅔ cups vertically sliced onion
    1 cup chopped orange sections
       (about 3 small oranges)
1½ teaspoons chopped fresh or
       ½ teaspoon dried oregano
    ¼ teaspoon salt
    ¼ teaspoon black pepper
    8 pitted ripe olives, halved
    1 garlic clove, minced
    4 (6-ounce) orange roughy or
       other lean white fish fillets
Cooking spray
    ⅓ cup fat-free, less-sodium chicken
       broth
    1 teaspoon grated orange rind

1. Preheat oven to 450°.
2. Heat oil in a large nonstick skillet over medium-high heat. Add onion; cook 5 minutes or until lightly browned, stirring occasionally. Remove from heat. Stir in orange sections, oregano, and next 4 ingredients.
3. Arrange fillets in a single layer in a 13 x 9-inch baking dish coated with cooking spray. Combine broth and orange rind; pour over fish. Spoon onion mixture over fish. Bake at 450° for 15 minutes or until fish flakes easily when tested with a fork. Yield: 4 servings (serving size: 1 fillet and ½ cup onion topping).

CALORIES 210 (20% from fat); FAT 4.6g (sat 0.5g, mono 3.1g, poly 0.4g); PROTEIN 26.6g; CARB 15.5g; FIBER 4.9g; CHOL 34mg; IRON 0.9mg; SODIUM 318mg; CALC 56mg

RED SNAPPER WITH POTATO-LEEK CRUST AND LIMA-AND-WHITE BEAN SUCCOTASH

PREP:55 MINUTES   COOK:20 MINUTES

This fish preparation is delicious with red snapper, orange roughy, or salmon. The secret is not to overcook the fish. You can shoestring the potatoes on a mandoline (a hand-operated slicer) or cut them carefully by hand. For extra color and flavor, add black beans or corn to the succotash.

1½ cups (2-inch) julienne-cut leek
    1 cup fresh flat-leaf parsley leaves
    1 cup shredded baking potato
       (about 1 medium)
    2 tablespoons chopped fresh
       tarragon
    ¼ cup chopped fresh chives
    ¼ teaspoon salt
    ⅛ teaspoon black pepper
    6 (6-ounce) red snapper fillets
    2 tablespoons cornstarch
    3 tablespoons olive oil, divided
Cooking spray
Lima-and-White Bean Succotash
       (page 492)

1. Preheat oven to 450°.
2. Place leek and parsley in a medium saucepan of boiling water; cook 1 minute. Drain and rinse under cold water; drain well. Combine leek mixture, potato, tarragon, and chives in a bowl. Sprinkle salt and pepper over both sides of fillets; pat potato mixture onto one side of each fillet. Sift cornstarch evenly over potato mixture.
3. Heat 1½ tablespoons oil in a large nonstick skillet over medium-high heat. Place 3 fillets, potato sides down, in skillet; cook 4 minutes (do not turn). Remove fillets from skillet; place fillets, potato sides up, on a broiler pan coated with cooking spray. Repeat procedure with 1½ tablespoons oil and remaining 3 fillets. Bake at 450° for 7 minutes or

until fish flakes easily when tested with a fork. Serve with Lima-and-White Bean Succotash. Yield: 6 servings (serving size: 1 fillet and ½ cup succotash).

CALORIES 412 (25% from fat); FAT 11.4g (sat 1.7g, mono 6.6g, poly 1.7g); PROTEIN 44g; CARB 32.1g; FIBER 4.5g; CHOL 63mg; IRON 5.7mg; SODIUM 579mg; CALC 186mg

GRILLED SALMON WITH GINGER-ORANGE MUSTARD GLAZE

PREP: 5 MINUTES

MARINATE: 30 MINUTES

COOK: 10 MINUTES

¼   cup fresh orange juice
¼   cup tamari or soy sauce
¼   cup cream sherry
¼   cup Dijon mustard
2   tablespoons grated peeled fresh ginger
2   tablespoons honey
4   (6-ounce) salmon fillets (about 1 inch thick)
Cooking spray
Green onions and lemon slices (optional)

1. Combine first 6 ingredients in a large zip-top plastic bag. Add fish to bag; seal and marinate in refrigerator 30 minutes. Remove fish from bag; reserve marinade.
2. Prepare grill or broiler.
3. Place fish on grill rack or broiler pan coated with cooking spray. Cook 5 minutes on each side or until fish flakes easily when tested with a fork, basting frequently with reserved marinade.
4. Place remaining marinade in a saucepan; bring to a boil. Serve with fish; garnish with green onions and lemon slices, if desired. Yield: 4 servings (serving size: 1 fillet and 3 tablespoons glaze).

CALORIES 375 (38% from fat); FAT 15.7g (sat 2.6g, mono 7.5g, poly 3.3g); PROTEIN 37.2g; CARB 14.1g; FIBER 0.1g; CHOL 115mg; IRON 1.2mg; SODIUM 1364mg; CALC 15mg

Grilled Salmon With
Ginger-Orange Mustard Glaze

SOY-SALMON WITH CILANTRO-COCONUT CHUTNEY

PREP: 18 MINUTES   MARINATE: 1 HOUR

COOK: 8 MINUTES

¾   cup dark beer
½   cup low-sodium soy sauce
1   tablespoon vegetable oil
1   tablespoon lemon juice
⅛   teaspoon salt
⅛   teaspoon black pepper
1   garlic clove, minced
4   (6-ounce) salmon fillets
Cooking spray
Cilantro-Coconut Chutney (page 453)

1. Combine beer, soy sauce, oil, lemon juice, salt, pepper, and garlic in a large zip-top plastic bag. Add fish to bag; seal. Marinate in refrigerator 1 hour, turning occasionally.
2. Prepare grill.
3. Remove fish from bag, and discard marinade. Place fish on grill rack coated with cooking spray; grill 4 minutes on each side or until fish flakes easily when tested with a fork. Serve with Cilantro-Coconut Chutney. Yield: 4 servings (serving size: 1 fillet and 2½ tablespoons chutney).

CALORIES 340 (47% from fat); FAT 17.8g (sat 4.9g, mono 7.3g, poly 3.4g); PROTEIN 37.1g; CARB 6.2g; FIBER 1.1g; CHOL 115mg; IRON 1.7mg; SODIUM 317mg; CALC 28mg

BROILED SALMON WITH CUCUMBER-DILL MUSTARD SAUCE

PREP: 16 MINUTES
COOK: 12 MINUTES

  1 tablespoon lemon-dill
       mustard
1½ teaspoons water
  4 (6-ounce) salmon steaks (1 inch
       thick)
Cooking spray
  1 cup Cucumber-Dill Mustard
       Sauce (page 444)

1. Combine mustard and water. Brush both sides of fish with mustard mixture; cover and marinate in refrigerator 10 minutes.
2. Preheat broiler.
3. Place fish on a broiler pan coated with cooking spray, and broil 6 minutes on each side or until fish flakes easily when tested with a fork. Serve with Cucumber-Dill Mustard Sauce. Yield: 4 servings (serving size: 1 salmon steak and about ¼ cup sauce).
Note: If you don't have lemon-dill mustard, stir fresh lemon juice and dried dill into Dijon mustard.

CALORIES 339 (43% from fat); FAT 16.1g (sat 3.1g, mono 7.3g, poly 3.2g); PROTEIN 39.4g; CARB 6.2g; FIBER 0.2g; CHOL 119mg; IRON 1mg; SODIUM 399mg; CALC 132mg

PEPPERED SALMON FILLETS WITH MINTED TOMATO SALSA

PREP: 12 MINUTES
COOK: 10 MINUTES

  4 (6-ounce) salmon fillets (about
       1½ inches thick)
Cooking spray
  2 teaspoons Dijon mustard
  1 teaspoon coarsely ground black
       pepper
  2 cups Minted Tomato Salsa (page 439)

1. Preheat broiler.
2. Place fish on a broiler pan coated with cooking spray, and spread each fillet with ½ teaspoon mustard. Sprinkle with black pepper. Broil 5 minutes on each side or until fish flakes easily when tested with a fork. Let stand 2 minutes. Serve with Minted Tomato Salsa. Yield: 4 servings (serving size: 1 fillet and ½ cup salsa).

CALORIES 314 (44% from fat); FAT 15.2g (sat 2.6g, mono 7.1g, poly 3.3g); PROTEIN 37.1g; CARB 5.4g; FIBER 1.4g; CHOL 115mg; IRON 1.3mg; SODIUM 170mg; CALC 18mg

SEA BASS WITH VEGETABLE NAGE

PREP: 49 MINUTES   COOK: 2 HOURS

A nage is a flavorful French stock made from either vegetables or fish and herbs.

  1 whole garlic head
  ½ teaspoon olive oil
  2 cups Vegetable Nage (page 458),
       divided
  1 teaspoon white wine vinegar
  ¼ teaspoon black pepper
Dash of salt
  2 teaspoons olive oil
  ½ cup sliced onion
  ½ cup sliced carrot
  ¼ cup Chardonnay or other dry
       white wine
  1 tablespoon minced shallots
  2 thyme sprigs
  1 bay leaf
  4 (6-ounce) sea bass fillets
  4 teaspoons chopped shallots

1. Preheat oven to 400°.
2. Remove white papery skin from garlic head (do not peel or separate the cloves). Rub ½ teaspoon olive oil over garlic head, and wrap in foil. Bake at 400° for 45 minutes; cool 10 minutes. Separate garlic cloves; peel 4 cloves, and reserve for garnish. Squeeze remaining cloves to extract garlic pulp; discard skins.
3. Combine garlic pulp, 1 cup Vegetable Nage, vinegar, pepper, and salt in a blender; process until smooth. With blender on, add 2 teaspoons olive oil, and process until well-blended. Pour garlic nage mixture into a small saucepan, and cook over low heat until warm. Keep garlic nage mixture warm.
4. Combine 1 cup Vegetable Nage, onion, and next 5 ingredients in a skillet; bring to a simmer. Add fish; cover, reduce heat, and simmer 4 minutes or until fish flakes easily when tested with a fork.

5. Place fillets in individual shallow bowls; discard poaching liquid, vegetables, and herbs. Drizzle ¼ cup warm garlic nage mixture over each fillet; sprinkle each with 1 teaspoon shallots, and garnish with a peeled garlic clove. Yield: 4 servings.

Note: Substitute 1 cup canned vegetable broth and 1 cup Chardonnay or other dry white wine for Vegetable Nage, if desired.

CALORIES 287 (37% from fat); FAT 11.8g (sat 2.1g, mono 6.4g, poly 2.3g); PROTEIN 34g; CARB 10.4g; FIBER 0.7g; CHOL 115mg; IRON 3.7mg; SODIUM 171mg; CALC 194mg

GRILLED SEA-BASS TACOS WITH FRESH-PEACH SALSA

PREP: 6 MINUTES   COOK: 12 MINUTES

    8   taco shells
    1   (1-pound) sea bass fillet (about 2
        inches thick)
Cooking spray
    ¼   teaspoon salt
    ¼   teaspoon black pepper
    2   cups Fresh-Peach Salsa (page 438)
    1   cup shredded green cabbage or
        packaged coleslaw
    ¼   cup minced fresh cilantro

1. Heat taco shells according to package directions; keep warm.
2. Prepare grill.
3. Place fish on grill rack coated with cooking spray; cover and grill 6 minutes on each side or until fish flakes easily when tested with a fork. Sprinkle fish with salt and pepper.
4. Cut fish into 8 pieces, and place 1 piece of fish in each taco shell. Top each taco with ¼ cup Fresh-Peach Salsa, 2 tablespoons cabbage, and 1½ teaspoons cilantro. Serve immediately. Yield: 4 servings (serving size: 2 tacos).

CALORIES 285 (29% from fat); FAT 9.1g (sat 1.6g, mono 1.7g, poly 1.7g); PROTEIN 23.9g; CARB 26.3g; FIBER 2.7g; CHOL 77mg; IRON 2.5mg; SODIUM 396mg; CALC 128mg

Teriyaki Tuna With Fresh Pineapple

TERIYAKI TUNA WITH FRESH PINEAPPLE

PREP: 16 MINUTES   MARINATE: 30 MINUTES
COOK: 8 MINUTES

    1   small pineapple, peeled and cored
    ¼   cup low-sodium soy sauce
    3   tablespoons honey
    3   tablespoons mirin (sweet rice wine)
    2   teaspoons minced peeled fresh ginger
    ½   teaspoon hot sauce
    1   garlic clove, minced
    6   (6-ounce) tuna steaks (about ¾
        inch thick)
Cooking spray
Green onions (optional)

1. Cut pineapple lengthwise into 6 spears. Combine soy sauce and next 5 ingredients in a large zip-top plastic bag. Add pineapple and fish to bag; seal and marinate in refrigerator 30 minutes, turning once. Remove fish and pineapple from bag, reserving marinade.
2. Prepare grill.
3. Place fish and pineapple on grill rack coated with cooking spray; grill 4 minutes on each side or until fish is medium-rare or desired degree of doneness, basting frequently with reserved marinade. Garnish with green onions, if desired. Yield: 6 servings (serving size: 1 tuna steak and 1 pineapple spear).

CALORIES 326 (25% from fat); FAT 9.1g (sat 2.2g, mono 2.8g, poly 2.7g); PROTEIN 40.3g; CARB 20.7g; FIBER 1.8g; CHOL 65mg; IRON 2.4mg; SODIUM 149mg; CALC 11mg

GRILLED TUNA WITH HERBED MAYONNAISE

PREP: 4 MINUTES   COOK: 6 MINUTES

¼ cup fat-free mayonnaise
¼ cup plain fat-free yogurt
1 teaspoon chopped fresh oregano
1 teaspoon chopped fresh tarragon
1 teaspoon lemon juice
¼ teaspoon salt
¼ teaspoon black pepper
4 (6-ounce) tuna steaks (about 1 inch thick)
Cooking spray

1. Combine first 5 ingredients in a small bowl.
2. Prepare grill.
3. Sprinkle salt and pepper over fish. Place fish on grill rack coated with cooking spray; grill 3 minutes on each side or until fish is medium-rare or desired degree of doneness. Serve with mayonnaise mixture. Yield: 4 servings (serving size: 1 tuna steak and 2 tablespoons mayonnaise mixture).

CALORIES 267 (29% from fat); FAT 8.5g (sat 2.2g, mono 2.7g, poly 2.5g); PROTEIN 40.5g; CARB 4.6g; FIBER 0.1g; CHOL 65mg; IRON 1.9mg; SODIUM 414mg; CALC 33mg

GRILLED TROUT WITH WILD RICE

PREP: 19 MINUTES   COOK: 1 HOUR

1 tablespoon olive oil
2 cups thinly sliced leek, divided
1½ cups sliced mushrooms
1 garlic clove, crushed
4 cups water
½ cup uncooked wild rice
⅛ teaspoon salt
⅛ teaspoon black pepper
4 thyme sprigs
Cooking spray
4 (8-ounce) cleaned trout
⅛ teaspoon salt

⅛ teaspoon black pepper
1 tablespoon butter or stick margarine
1 tablespoon chopped fresh parsley
Additional thyme sprigs (optional)

1. Heat oil in a medium saucepan over medium-high heat. Add ¼ cup leek, mushrooms, and garlic; sauté 3 minutes. Add water, rice, ⅛ teaspoon salt, and ⅛ teaspoon pepper; bring to a boil. Cover, reduce heat, and simmer 50 minutes or until rice is tender. Drain rice, reserving 1 cup cooking liquid; set rice aside.
2. Return cooking liquid to pan. Bring to a boil, and cook 8 minutes or until reduced to ½ cup. Remove from heat; keep cooking liquid warm.
3. Place 1 thyme sprig in the center of each of 4 (10-inch) squares of foil coated with cooking spray. Place 1 fish on top of each thyme sprig. Sprinkle ⅛ teaspoon salt and ⅛ teaspoon pepper over inside cavities of fish. Stuff ½ cup rice mixture into cavity of each fish. Wrap fish in foil, twisting ends to seal.
4. Prepare grill.
5. Place foil-wrapped fish on grill rack; grill 10 minutes on each side or until fish flakes easily when tested with a fork. Unwrap fish; remove and discard skin. Keep fish warm.
6. Melt butter in a small saucepan over medium-high heat. Add 1¾ cups leek; sauté 2 minutes or until tender. Divide leek evenly among 4 individual plates; top with fish. Drizzle 2 tablespoons cooking liquid over each fish; sprinkle with parsley. Garnish with thyme sprigs, if desired. Yield: 4 servings (serving size: 1 fish).

CALORIES 397 (39% from fat); FAT 17.3g (sat 4.1g, mono 7.1g, poly 4.2g); PROTEIN 36.1g; CARB 24.3g; FIBER 2.2g; CHOL 96mg; IRON 4.3mg; SODIUM 268mg; CALC 105mg

FIRE UP THE COALS

Grilling seafood is easy if you know which kinds work best. You want fish that has a thick, firm, meaty texture so that it won't fall apart while cooking. The seafood listed below is particularly suitable for the grill.

Grouper: This white-meat fish is sold in fillets and steaks. If you can't find grouper, use sea bass, orange roughy, or mahimahi.

Halibut: The meat of halibut is white and mild-flavored, and comes in steaks and fillets. Although it's a firm fish, it's a tad more delicate than others—so be gentle when turning it on the grill.

Salmon: With a range of flavor from rich to mild, salmon can take on a char and still keep its distinct taste. Salmon comes in steaks and fillets.

Scallops: This bivalve is usually classified into two groups: bay scallops and sea scallops. The larger sea scallops are best for grilling because, like shrimp, they have a meatier texture and can be easily skewered. They cook fast, though, so keep a close eye on them.

Shrimp: Large shrimp are best for grilling. They can be easily skewered, and they cook quickly.

Swordfish: This mild fish has a firm, meaty texture. Its natural oil content keeps it moist while grilling. You can usually find it sold as steaks.

Tuna: If you're new to grilling fish, fresh tuna is a good starter. It cooks like a beef steak, and its deep-red meat almost never sticks to the grill.

SHELLFISH

Because shellfish are highly perishable, purchase them from specialty markets or large supermarkets with a rapid turnover. Whenever possible, buy lobster and crab from markets that keep them live in saltwater tanks.

Mollusks and crustaceans make up the two categories of shellfish. Mollusks include bivalves, such as clams, oysters, and mussels, and have a double-hinged shell with a muscle attached to the inside shell. Crustaceans, such as shrimp, lobster, and crab, have jointed bodies covered with soft shells.

FETTUCCINE WITH FARMERS MARKET CLAM SAUCE

PREP: 19 MINUTES   COOK: 25 MINUTES

- 2 (6½-ounce) cans minced clams, undrained
- 1 tablespoon olive oil
- ½ cup minced fresh onion
- ¾ cup minced carrot
- 6 garlic cloves, minced
- 2 cups chopped tomato
- ¾ cup chopped red bell pepper
- ½ teaspoon salt
- ½ teaspoon black pepper
- ¼ to ½ teaspoon crushed red pepper
- ½ cup chopped fresh parsley
- 5 cups hot cooked fettuccine (about 10 ounces uncooked pasta)

1. Drain clams, reserving 1 cup clam juice.
2. Heat oil in a large nonstick skillet over medium-high heat. Add onion, carrot, and garlic; sauté 3 minutes. Add reserved clam juice, tomato, bell pepper, salt, black pepper, and crushed red pepper; bring to a boil. Reduce heat; simmer 20 minutes or until slightly thick. Remove from heat; stir in clams and parsley. Serve clam sauce over hot cooked fettuccine. Yield: 4 servings (serving size: about ¾ cup sauce and 1¼ cups pasta).

CALORIES 394 (13% from fat); FAT 5.7g (sat 0.8g, mono 2.8g, poly 1.2g); PROTEIN 20.2g; CARB 65.5g; FIBER 4.2g; CHOL 26mg; IRON 14mg; SODIUM 486mg; CALC 82mg

menu
Maryland Crab Cakes

Pasta With Fresh Tomatoes (page 261)

Roasted Peppers (page 497)

Cherry-Cheese Parfaits (page 192)

MARYLAND CRAB CAKES

PREP: 25 MINUTES   COOK: 12 MINUTES

- 1 pound lump crabmeat, shell pieces removed
- 1⅓ cups fresh breadcrumbs
- ⅓ cup minced green onions
- ⅓ cup chopped fresh parsley
- 2 tablespoons lemon juice
- 1 tablespoon 2% reduced-fat milk
- 1 teaspoon hot sauce
- ½ teaspoon salt
- ¼ teaspoon black pepper
- 4 large egg whites, lightly beaten
- 1⅓ cups fresh breadcrumbs
- 2 tablespoons vegetable oil, divided
- Lemon wedges (optional)

1. Combine first 10 ingredients in a bowl. Divide mixture into 8 equal portions; shape each into a ½-inch-thick patty. Place breadcrumbs in a shallow dish; dredge patties in breadcrumbs.
2. Heat 1 tablespoon vegetable oil in a large nonstick skillet over medium-high heat. Add 4 patties, and cook 3 minutes. Carefully turn patties over; cook 3 minutes or until golden. Repeat procedure with 1 tablespoon oil and remaining 4 patties. Serve with lemon wedges, if desired. Yield: 4 servings (serving size: 2 crab cakes).

CALORIES 282 (32% from fat); FAT 10g (sat 1.8g, mono 2.8g, poly 4.4g); PROTEIN 29.4g; CARB 17.2g; FIBER 1g; CHOL 114mg; IRON 2.2mg; SODIUM 830mg; CALC 162mg

THAI CRAB CAKES

PREP: 20 MINUTES   CHILL: 1 HOUR
COOK: 24 MINUTES

- 1¼ cups fresh breadcrumbs
- 1 cup fresh bean sprouts, chopped
- ¼ cup finely chopped green onions
- ¼ cup chopped fresh cilantro
- 2 tablespoons fresh lime juice
- ⅛ teaspoon ground red pepper
- 1 large egg, lightly beaten
- 1 large egg white, lightly beaten
- 1 pound lump crabmeat, shell pieces removed
- 2 teaspoons olive oil, divided
- Cooking spray
- ¾ cup Cilantro-Peanut Sauce (page 444)

1. Combine first 9 ingredients in a bowl; cover and chill 1 hour. Divide mixture into 8 equal portions, shaping each into a ½-inch-thick patty.
2. Heat 1 teaspoon oil in a large nonstick skillet coated with cooking spray over medium heat until hot. Add 4 patties; cook 6 minutes on each side or until lightly browned. Remove patties from skillet; keep warm. Wipe skillet clean with paper towels; recoat with cooking spray. Repeat procedure with 1 teaspoon oil and remaining 4 patties. Serve with Cilantro-Peanut Sauce. Yield: 4 servings (serving size: 2 crab cakes and 3 tablespoons sauce).

CALORIES 297 (31% from fat); FAT 10.1g (sat 1.8g, mono 4.7g, poly 2.4g); PROTEIN 26.9g; CARB 30.5g; FIBER 1.5g; CHOL 150mg; IRON 2.8mg; SODIUM 749mg; CALC 153mg

MEXICALI CRAB CAKES

PREP: 35 MINUTES
COOK: 21 MINUTES

1½ tablespoons stick margarine or
    butter
¼   cup finely chopped celery
¼   cup finely chopped red bell
    pepper
1½ teaspoons chopped seeded
    jalapeño pepper
¼   cup light mayonnaise
1   teaspoon chopped fresh cilantro
    or parsley
1   teaspoon Dijon mustard
½   teaspoon garlic salt
¼   teaspoon black pepper
1   large egg, lightly beaten
¾   cup fresh breadcrumbs (about
    1½ slices bread)
¼   cup chopped green onions
1   pound lump crabmeat, shell
    pieces removed
1   (8¾-ounce) can no-salt-added
    whole-kernel corn, drained
1   cup finely crushed cornflakes
Cooking spray
10 tablespoons cocktail sauce or
    bottled salsa

1. Preheat oven to 450°.
2. Melt margarine in a small nonstick skillet over medium heat. Add celery, bell pepper, and jalapeño; sauté 3 minutes or until tender.
3. Combine mayonnaise and next 5 ingredients in a large bowl. Add celery mixture, breadcrumbs, green onions, crabmeat, and corn; stir well. Divide mixture into 10 equal portions, shaping each into a ½-inch-thick patty. Dredge patties in cornflakes.
4. Place patties on a baking sheet coated with cooking spray. Bake at 450° for 15 minutes; turn patties over, and bake an additional 6 minutes or until golden. Serve crab cakes with cocktail sauce or

Seafood-Stuffed Poblanos With Warm Tomato Salsa

salsa. Yield: 5 servings (serving size: 2 crab cakes and 2 tablespoons sauce).

CALORIES 321 (30% from fat); FAT 10.6g (sat 1.9g, mono 3.4g, poly 4.2g); PROTEIN 22.5g; CARB 35.5g; FIBER 1.5g; CHOL 134mg; IRON 3.3mg; SODIUM 1013mg; CALC 124mg

SEAFOOD-STUFFED POBLANOS WITH WARM TOMATO SALSA

PREP: 20 MINUTES
COOK: 45 MINUTES

3   cups chopped peeled tomato
    (about 1¼ pounds)
2   cups sliced onion
¼   cup water
1   teaspoon white vinegar
¼   teaspoon salt
1   jalapeño pepper, seeded and sliced
1   cup lump crabmeat, shell pieces
    removed
¼   cup (1 ounce) shredded
    reduced-fat sharp cheddar
    cheese
¼   cup (1 ounce) shredded
    Monterey Jack cheese with
    jalapeño peppers
⅛   teaspoon salt
⅛   teaspoon black pepper
2   garlic cloves, minced
2   large poblano chiles, halved and
    seeded
Cooking spray
Cilantro sprigs (optional)

1. Combine first 6 ingredients in a saucepan; bring to a boil over medium-high heat. Cook 15 to 20 minutes or until onion is soft; keep warm.

2. Preheat oven to 350°.

3. Combine crabmeat and next 5 ingredients in a medium bowl. Divide crab mixture evenly among chile halves.

4. Place stuffed chiles in an 11 x 7-inch baking dish coated with cooking spray. Pour warm tomato salsa over stuffed chiles. Cover and bake at 350° for 45 minutes. Garnish with cilantro sprigs, if desired. Yield: 4 servings.

CALORIES 170 (27% from fat); FAT 5.1g (sat 2.3g, mono 1.2g, poly 0.7g); PROTEIN 16.1g; CARB 16.8g; FIBER 3.5g; CHOL 57mg; IRON 1.8mg; SODIUM 457mg; CALC 196mg

LOBSTER TAILS WITH CHUNKY TOMATO SALSA

PREP: 35 MINUTES   COOK: 10 MINUTES

   4 (6- or 7-ounce) lobster tails
   1 tablespoon balsamic vinegar
   1 tablespoon water
  ½ teaspoon olive oil
  ¼ teaspoon dried tarragon
     Chunky Tomato Salsa (page 439)

1. Preheat broiler.

2. Gently loosen lobster meat from top inside of shell. Cut lengthwise through top of shell using kitchen shears; press shell open. Starting at cut end of tail, carefully loosen meat from bottom of shell; keep meat attached at end of tail. Lift meat through top shell opening; place on top of shell. Repeat procedure with remaining tails.

3. Place lobster tails on a rack in a shallow roasting pan. Combine vinegar, water, oil, and tarragon; brush lobster with half of vinegar mixture. Broil 10 minutes or until lobster flesh turns opaque; baste with remaining vinegar mixture after 5 minutes. Serve with Chunky Tomato Salsa. Yield: 4 servings (serving size: 1 lobster tail and ½ cup salsa).

CALORIES 126 (18% from fat); FAT 2.5g (sat 0.4g, mono 1.5g, poly 0.3g); PROTEIN 20.5g; CARB 5g; FIBER 0.9g; CHOL 69mg; IRON 1mg; SODIUM 447mg; CALC 69mg

Lobster Tails

1. Using your index finger, gently loosen lobster meat from top inside of shell.

2. Cut lengthwise through top of lobster shell using kitchen shears.

3. Pull back sides of shell to expose lobster meat.

4. Starting at cut end of tail, carefully loosen lobster meat from bottom of shell, keeping meat attached at end of tail. Lift meat through top shell opening, and place on top of shell.

5. Place lobster tails on a rack in a shallow roasting pan; brush with balsamic vinegar mixture.

Mussels

Scrubbing mussels. Use a stiff brush to scrub mussels; rinse them well.

Debearding mussels. The "beard" is the name given to the strands of tissue attached to the shell. To "debeard," simply pull the strands off. (Some mussels do not have beards when they are harvested.) Mussels spoil quickly after debearding, so prepare them immediately. Fresh mussels are usually cooked in the shell.

Mussels spoil quickly after debearding, so prepare them immediately.

MUSSELS MARINARA

PREP: 20 MINUTES   COOK: 18 MINUTES

- 1 tablespoon olive oil
- 2 cups finely chopped onion
- 6 garlic cloves, minced
- 4 cups chopped tomato
- 1 cup dry white wine
- ⅔ cup chopped fresh flat-leaf parsley
- ¼ cup chopped fresh basil
- 1 teaspoon salt
- 1 teaspoon black pepper
- ½ teaspoon crushed red pepper
- 2 bay leaves
- 5 pounds fresh mussels, scrubbed and debearded (about 120)
- 5 cups hot cooked linguine (about 10 ounces uncooked pasta)

Basil sprigs (optional)

1. Heat oil in an 8-quart stockpot over medium-high heat. Add onion and garlic; sauté 3 minutes. Add tomato and next 7 ingredients; cook over medium heat 10 minutes. Add mussels; cover and cook over medium-high heat 5 minutes or until shells open, stirring after 3 minutes. Remove pot from heat, and discard bay leaves and any unopened shells.

2. Place 1 cup pasta in each of 5 individual shallow bowls. Remove mussels with a slotted spoon, and arrange evenly over pasta. Spoon sauce over mussels. Garnish with basil sprigs, if desired. Yield: 5 servings (serving size: about 24 mussels, 1 cup pasta, and 1 cup sauce).

CALORIES 394 (16% from fat); FAT 6.8g (sat 1.1g, mono 2.8g, poly 1.5g); PROTEIN 23g; CARB 60.6g; FIBER 4.4g; CHOL 31mg; IRON 8.1mg; SODIUM 815mg; CALC 81mg

Mussels Marinara

STEAMED MUSSELS WITH GARLIC, WINE, AND CILANTRO

PREP: 15 MINUTES   COOK: 9 MINUTES

1½ teaspoons olive oil
8 garlic cloves, thinly sliced
1½ cups water
¾ cup dry white wine
4 pounds small mussels, scrubbed and debearded (about 96)
¼ teaspoon freshly ground black pepper
½ cup chopped fresh cilantro

1. Heat oil in a large stockpot over medium-high heat. Add sliced garlic; sauté 3 minutes. Add water and wine; bring to a boil. Add mussels; cover and cook over medium-high heat 6 minutes or until shells open, stirring after 3 minutes. Remove from heat; discard any unopened shells.
2. Sprinkle mussels with pepper and cilantro. Remove mussels with a slotted spoon, and arrange in 8 shallow bowls. Yield: 4 servings (serving size: about 24 mussels).

CALORIES 156 (28% from fat); FAT 4.8g (sat 0.8g, mono 2g, poly 1g); PROTEIN 17.8g; CARB 10.2g; FIBER 0.8g; CHOL 38mg; IRON 6.6mg; SODIUM 398mg; CALC 70mg

PAN-SEARED SCALLOPS WITH GINGER-ORANGE SPINACH

PREP: 29 MINUTES
MARINATE: 30 MINUTES
COOK: 10 MINUTES

1 tablespoon julienne-cut peeled fresh ginger
1 tablespoon sliced green onions
4 garlic cloves, minced
20 sea scallops (about 1½ pounds)
½ cup vodka
¼ cup dry vermouth

When cooked, the pearly white center of a scallop offers a glimpse of the fresh, delicate flavor from the sea.

1 teaspoon stick margarine or butter
1 teaspoon grated orange rind
⅓ cup fresh orange juice
1½ pounds chopped fresh spinach
½ teaspoon salt
⅛ teaspoon black pepper
Cooking spray

1. Combine ginger, green onions, and garlic in a large bowl.
2. Place scallops in a shallow dish. Add vodka, vermouth, and half of ginger mixture; toss gently. Cover and marinate in refrigerator 30 minutes.
3. Melt margarine in a large nonstick skillet over high heat. Add remaining ginger mixture; sauté 30 seconds. Add orange rind and juice; bring to a boil. Stir in spinach, salt, and pepper; cook 2 minutes or until spinach wilts. Remove from skillet; keep warm.
4. Remove scallops from dish, reserving marinade. Coat skillet with cooking spray; place over high heat until hot. Add scallops; cook 2 minutes on each side or until done. Remove from skillet; keep warm. Add reserved marinade to skillet. Bring to a boil; cook until sauce is reduced to ¼ cup (about 3 minutes).
5. Arrange scallops over spinach mixture; drizzle with sauce. Yield: 4 servings (serving size: 5 scallops, ¾ cup spinach mixture, and 1 tablespoon sauce).

CALORIES 247 (19% from fat); FAT 5.3g (sat 1.9g, mono 1.2g, poly 1.1g); PROTEIN 34.2g; CARB 16.7g; FIBER 6.9g; CHOL 56mg; IRON 5.2mg; SODIUM 727mg; CALC 221mg

COQUILLES ST. JACQUES Á LA PROVENÇALE

PREP: 15 MINUTES   COOK: 15 MINUTES

Coquilles St. Jacques *(koh-KEEL sahn-ZHAHK)* is a French specialty made with scallops and a creamy white sauce.

1½ tablespoons stick margarine or butter, divided
⅓ cup minced onion
2 tablespoons minced shallots
1 garlic clove, minced
½ cup all-purpose flour
1¼ pounds sea scallops
⅔ cup dry white wine or fat-free, less-sodium chicken broth
½ teaspoon chopped fresh thyme
⅛ teaspoon salt
½ bay leaf
Dash of white pepper
6 tablespoons (1½ ounces) shredded Swiss cheese

1. Melt 1½ teaspoons margarine in a nonstick skillet over medium heat; add onion. Sauté 3 minutes or until lightly browned. Add shallots and garlic, and sauté 1 minute. Remove from skillet.
2. Place flour in a large, zip-top plastic bag. Add scallops. Seal bag; shake to coat.
3. Preheat broiler.
4. Melt 1 tablespoon margarine in skillet over medium heat. Add scallops; sauté 4 minutes or until scallops are opaque. Return onion mixture to skillet; add wine and next 4 ingredients. Cover, reduce heat, and simmer 4 minutes. Uncover mixture, and bring to a boil; cook 1 minute. Remove and discard bay leaf.
5. Spoon scallop mixture into 6 individual gratin dishes. Top evenly with cheese. Broil 30 seconds or until cheese melts. Serve immediately. Yield: 6 servings.

CALORIES 179 (28% from fat); FAT 5.6g (sat 2g, mono 1.6g, poly 1.2g); PROTEIN 19.2g; CARB 11.7g; FIBER 0.5g; CHOL 38mg; IRON 0.9mg; SODIUM 258mg; CALC 100mg

Bourbon-Bacon Scallops

BOURBON-BACON SCALLOPS

PREP:12 MINUTES   MARINATE:1 HOUR
COOK:8 MINUTES

Serve these scallops over rice with a side of snow peas, bell peppers, and broccoli.

  3 tablespoons minced green onions
  2 tablespoons bourbon
  2 tablespoons maple syrup
  1 tablespoon low-sodium soy sauce
  1 tablespoon Dijon mustard
  ¼ teaspoon black pepper
24 large sea scallops (about 1½ pounds)
  6 low-sodium bacon slices (4 ounces)
Cooking spray
Lemon wedges (optional)

1. Combine first 6 ingredients in a bowl; add scallops, stirring gently to coat. Cover and marinate in refrigerator 1 hour, stirring occasionally.
2. Preheat broiler.
3. Remove scallops from bowl, reserving marinade. Cut each slice of bacon into 4 pieces. Wrap 1 bacon piece around each scallop (bacon may only wrap halfway around scallops). Thread scallops onto 4 (12-inch) skewers, leaving some space between scallops so bacon will cook.
4. Place skewers on a broiler pan coated with cooking spray; broil 8 minutes or until bacon is crisp and scallops are done, basting occasionally with reserved marinade (cooking time will vary with size of scallops). Serve with lemon

wedges, if desired. Yield: 4 servings (serving size: 6 scallops).

CALORIES 245 (26% from fat); FAT 7g (sat 2g, mono 2.5g, poly 1.1g); PROTEIN 32.4g; CARB 11.3g; FIBER 0.1g; CHOL 68mg; IRON 0.7mg; SODIUM 642mg; CALC 51mg

SCALLOPS FLORENTINE

PREP: 16 MINUTES

COOK: 21 MINUTES

1¼ pounds sea scallops
2 (10-ounce) packages fresh spinach
3 garlic cloves
1 tablespoon stick margarine or butter
1½ tablespoons all-purpose flour
¾ cup evaporated fat-free milk
¼ teaspoon salt
⅛ teaspoon ground nutmeg
⅛ teaspoon white pepper
½ cup (2 ounces) shredded reduced-fat, reduced-sodium Swiss cheese (such as Alpine Lace)
3½ cups hot cooked small macaroni shells

1. Cut scallops in half crosswise, and set scallops aside.
2. Remove stems from spinach; set stems aside. Coarsely chop leaves, and set aside.
3. With food processor on, drop garlic through food chute; process 3 seconds or until minced. Add spinach stems through food chute with processor on; process 10 seconds or until minced.
4. Melt margarine in a large Dutch oven over medium-low heat. Add garlic mixture; sauté 5 minutes or until tender. Stir in flour. Gradually add milk, salt, nutmeg, and pepper; bring to a boil. Cook 2 minutes or until thick, stirring constantly. Add cheese; stir until melted. Add chopped spinach leaves; stir. Cook 3 minutes or until spinach wilts, stirring frequently. Add scallops; cook 8 minutes or until scallops are done, stirring frequently. Stir in pasta. Yield: 8 servings (serving size: 1 cup).

CALORIES 208 (20% from fat); FAT 4.6g (sat 1.7g, mono 1g, poly 1.1g); PROTEIN 20.2g; CARB 21.5g; FIBER 3.6g; CHOL 31mg; IRON 2.9mg; SODIUM 291mg; CALC 230mg

SCALLOPS AND PASTA WITH PISTACHIO PESTO

PREP: 18 MINUTES   COOK: 8 MINUTES

1 cup chopped fresh parsley
3 tablespoons coarsely chopped pistachios
1 teaspoon grated lemon rind
¼ teaspoon ground cumin
¼ teaspoon black pepper
⅛ teaspoon salt
⅛ teaspoon paprika
2 tablespoons fresh lemon juice
1¼ teaspoons olive oil
¾ pound sea scallops
¼ cup all-purpose flour
⅛ teaspoon salt
2 teaspoons stick margarine or butter
2 cups hot cooked angel hair pasta (about 4 ounces uncooked pasta)
Freshly ground black pepper

1. Place first 9 ingredients in a food processor, and process until mixture is smooth, scraping sides of bowl occasionally.
2. Combine scallops, flour, and ⅛ teaspoon salt in large zip-top plastic bag; seal and shake to coat.
3. Heat margarine in a nonstick skillet over medium-high heat. Add scallops, and cook 3½ minutes on each side or until done.
4. Combine parsley mixture and pasta in a large bowl, tossing gently. Arrange 1 cup pasta on each plate; divide scallops evenly between plates. Sprinkle with freshly ground pepper. Yield: 2 servings (serving size: 1 cup pasta and about 7 scallops).

CALORIES 556 (25% from fat); FAT 15.2g (sat 2.2g, mono 8.1g, poly 11.5g); PROTEIN 40.6g; CARB 63.5g; FIBER 4.1g; CHOL 56mg; IRON 5.6mg; SODIUM 627mg; CALC 103mg

Scallops and Pasta With Pistachio Pesto

Preparing Shrimp

PART 1 · deveining

Metal deveiner, plastic deveiner

1. To devein shrimp, remove the dark vein, using a deveining tool or a sharp knife.

2. You can then peel back the shell with the deveiner.

PART 2 · peeling

1. To peel shrimp, grasp the tail in one hand and the legs in the other.

2. Then in one motion, pull the legs off.

3. Peel back the shell, and remove.

PART 3 · butterflying

Butterflying—*in cooking terms*—means to split a food down the center, cutting almost through the food. The halves are then opened flat, hence the butterfly shape.

1. To butterfly shrimp, pull a sharp knife along back of shrimp and cut almost through shrimp to split open.

CONFETTI QUESADILLAS

PREP: 12 MINUTES
COOK: 24 MINUTES

- 1 tablespoon stick margarine or butter
- 1 cup chopped onion
- 1 cup fresh corn kernels (about 2 ears)
- 1 garlic clove, minced
- ⅔ cup chopped tomato
- 1½ teaspoons minced seeded jalapeño pepper
- ½ pound medium shrimp, peeled, deveined, and chopped
- 2 tablespoons fresh lemon juice
- 2 tablespoons minced fresh cilantro
- ¼ teaspoon salt
- 8 (8-inch) fat-free flour tortillas
- 1 cup (4 ounces) preshredded part-skim mozzarella cheese
- 1 cup Three-Pepper Salsa (page 439)

1. Heat margarine in a medium non-stick skillet over medium heat. Add onion, corn, and garlic, and sauté 30 seconds. Add tomato and jalapeño; sauté 4 minutes. Stir in shrimp, lemon juice, cilantro, and salt; sauté 3 minutes. Remove corn mixture from skillet; keep warm.

2. Place 1 tortilla in a skillet over medium heat, and top with ¼ cup mozzarella cheese. Spoon ½ cup corn mixture over cheese; top with a tortilla. Cook 3 minutes, pressing down with a spatula until cheese melts. Turn carefully; cook until thoroughly heated (about 1 minute). Repeat procedure with remaining tortillas, cheese, and corn mixture. Cut each quesadilla into quarters. Serve with Three-Pepper Salsa. Yield: 4 servings (serving size: 1 quesadilla and ¼ cup salsa).

CALORIES 430 (19% from fat); FAT 9.2g (sat 3.7g, mono 2.9g, poly 1.7g); PROTEIN 22.5g; CARB 66.9g; FIBER 6.1g; CHOL 81mg; IRON 2.1mg; SODIUM 1125mg; CALC 231mg

Confetti Quesadillas

LEMON-GARLIC SHRIMP

PREP: 10 MINUTES   COOK: 15 MINUTES

Cooking spray
- 1½ pounds medium shrimp, peeled and deveined
- ½ cup dry breadcrumbs
- 3 tablespoons finely chopped fresh parsley
- 1 teaspoon grated lemon rind
- ¼ teaspoon salt
- 3 large garlic cloves, minced
- 2 tablespoons fresh lemon juice
- 4 teaspoons olive oil

1. Preheat oven to 400°.

2. Coat 4 individual gratin dishes with cooking spray. Divide shrimp evenly among dishes.

3. Combine breadcrumbs and next 4 ingredients in a bowl; stir in lemon juice and oil. Sprinkle breadcrumb mixture over shrimp. Place dishes on a baking sheet. Bake at 400° for 15 minutes or until shrimp are done and breadcrumbs are lightly browned. Yield: 4 servings.

CALORIES 234 (30% from fat); FAT 7.8g (sat 1.2g, mono 3.9g, poly 1.4g); PROTEIN 27.7g; CARB 11.8g; FIBER 0.4g; CHOL 194mg; IRON 4mg; SODIUM 444mg; CALC 102mg

CAJUN SHRIMP

PREP: 5 MINUTES

COOK: 5 MINUTES

Try serving these spicy shrimp with easy-to-make cheese grits. Simply stir grated cheese into any kind of cooked grits.

1½	pounds large shrimp, peeled and deveined
1	teaspoon paprika
¾	teaspoon dried thyme
¾	teaspoon dried oregano
¼	teaspoon garlic powder
¼	teaspoon salt
¼	teaspoon black pepper
¼ to ½	teaspoon ground red pepper
1	tablespoon vegetable oil

1. Combine first 8 ingredients in a large zip-top plastic bag; seal bag, and shake to coat.
2. Heat oil in a large nonstick skillet over medium-high heat until hot. Add shrimp mixture; sauté 4 minutes or until shrimp are done. Yield: 4 servings (serving size: 5 ounces).

CALORIES 185 (29% from fat); FAT 6g (sat 1.1g, mono 1.4g, poly 2.7g); PROTEIN 29g; CARB 2.2g; FIBER 0.3g; CHOL 215mg; IRON 4.1mg; SODIUM 357mg; CALC 85mg

Cook shrimp just until they appear opaque and turn pink. Overcooked shrimp will be tough and rubbery.

menu

Shrimp Jambalaya

Classic French Bread (page 86)

Fresh Fruit With Tangy Dressing (page 388)

Flan (page 168)

SHRIMP JAMBALAYA

PREP: 30 MINUTES   COOK: 40 MINUTES

1	tablespoon all-purpose flour
1	tablespoon vegetable oil
1	cup chopped onion
1	cup chopped celery
1	cup chopped green bell pepper
¼	pound diced cooked ham (such as Light and Lean)
2	garlic cloves, minced
2	(10½-ounce) cans low-sodium chicken broth (such as Campbell's)
¼	cup chopped fresh parsley
¾	teaspoon dried thyme
½	teaspoon salt
½	teaspoon dried basil
¼	teaspoon black pepper
⅛	teaspoon ground red pepper
1	(14½-ounce) can no-salt-added whole tomatoes, undrained and chopped
1	cup long-grain rice, uncooked
½	pound medium shrimp, peeled and deveined

Dash of hot sauce (optional)

1. Combine flour and oil in a nonstick skillet. Cook over medium-high heat 2½ minutes or until brown; stir constantly.
2. Add onion, celery, bell pepper, ham, and garlic to flour mixture; sauté 7 minutes or until vegetables are tender. Add broth and next 7 ingredients, stirring well; bring to a boil. Stir in rice. Cover, reduce heat, and simmer 20 minutes or until rice is tender.
3. Add shrimp to rice mixture in skillet; cover and cook 5 minutes or until shrimp are done. Add hot sauce, if desired. Yield: 4 servings (serving size: 1½ cups).

CALORIES 349 (16% from fat); FAT 6.2g (sat 1.4g, mono 1.9g, poly 2.3g); PROTEIN 19.8g; CARB 51.6g; FIBER 3.3g; CHOL 82mg; IRON 4.9mg; SODIUM 805mg; CALC 107mg

SHRIMP AND ARTICHOKES OVER PARMESAN GRITS

PREP: 15 MINUTES   COOK: 18 MINUTES

2	teaspoons olive oil
½	cup chopped onion
1	(9-ounce) package frozen artichoke hearts, thawed
3½	cups fat-free, less-sodium chicken broth, divided
1½	pounds large shrimp, peeled and deveined
2	garlic cloves, minced
1	teaspoon dried oregano
1	teaspoon grated lemon rind
1	teaspoon fresh lemon juice
¼	teaspoon salt
¼	teaspoon black pepper
¾	cup uncooked quick-cooking grits
⅓	cup grated Parmesan cheese

1. Heat oil in a large nonstick skillet over medium-high heat. Add onion and artichokes; sauté 5 minutes. Add 1 cup broth, shrimp, and garlic; sauté 6 minutes. Add oregano, lemon rind, lemon juice, salt, and pepper. Remove from heat; cover and keep warm.
2. Bring 2½ cups broth to a boil in a medium saucepan. Slowly stir in grits; reduce heat to low. Cook 7 minutes or until thick and creamy, stirring occasionally. Stir in cheese. Spoon ½ cup grits into each of 4 bowls, and top each with 1 cup shrimp mixture. Yield: 4 servings.

CALORIES 341 (18% from fat); FAT 7g (sat 2.1g, mono 2.6g, poly 1.2g); PROTEIN 35.9g; CARB 32.5g; FIBER 2.4g; CHOL 199 mg; IRON 4.8mg; SODIUM 912mg; CALC 185mg

SHRIMP-AND-GRITS GRATIN

PREP: 20 MINUTES
MARINATE: 2 HOURS
COOK: 30 MINUTES

Be sure to use instant (not quick-cooking) grits for this dish.

3 tablespoons chopped fresh or 3 teaspoons dried basil
3 tablespoons dry white wine
1 tablespoon olive oil
1 garlic clove, minced
1 pound medium shrimp, peeled and deveined
4 cups boiling water
3 cups uncooked instant grits
¼ cup grated Parmesan cheese, divided
2 tablespoons chopped fresh or 2 teaspoons dried parsley
¼ teaspoon black pepper
Cooking spray
⅛ teaspoon paprika
Basil sprigs (optional)

1. Combine first 4 ingredients in a shallow dish; add shrimp, stirring to coat. Cover and marinate in refrigerator 2 hours, stirring occasionally. Remove shrimp from dish; discard marinade.
2. Preheat oven to 350°.
3. Combine 4 cups boiling water and grits in a large bowl. Add shrimp, 2 tablespoons cheese, parsley, and pepper, stirring well.
4. Spoon grits mixture into a 2-quart casserole coated with cooking spray, and sprinkle with 2 tablespoons Parmesan cheese and ⅛ teaspoon paprika. Bake at 350° for 30 minutes. Garnish with basil sprigs, if desired. Yield: 6 servings (serving size: 1 cup).

CALORIES 183 (17% from fat); FAT 3.5g (sat 1g, mono 1.3g, poly 0.6g); PROTEIN 15.9g; CARB 22.2g; FIBER 1.5g; CHOL 89mg; IRON 13.1mg; SODIUM 677mg; CALC 86mg

SHRIMP-AND-TOMATO TOSTADA

PREP: 35 MINUTES
COOK: 10 MINUTES

Cooking spray
6 (10-inch) flour tortillas
1 (4-ounce) can chopped green chiles, drained
1 (16-ounce) can fat-free refried beans
¾ pound medium shrimp, cooked and peeled
4 cups diced unpeeled tomato (about 2 pounds)
3 cups packed shredded fresh spinach
1 cup diced onion
¼ cup chopped fresh cilantro
¼ cup fresh lime juice
1 tablespoon finely chopped jalapeño pepper
1 tablespoon olive oil
2 teaspoons dried oregano
1 teaspoon ground cumin
¼ teaspoon freshly ground black pepper
1 garlic clove, minced
¾ cup (3 ounces) shredded Monterey Jack cheese with jalapeño peppers
6 tablespoons low-fat sour cream
6 lime wedges (optional)

1. Preheat oven to 400°.
2. Coat outside of 6 (10-ounce) custard cups with cooking spray, and place cups upside-down on baking sheets; place each tortilla over an inverted cup. Bake at 400° for 10 minutes or until crisp. Cool completely on wire racks.
3. Reserve 3 teaspoons chiles; set aside. Combine remaining chiles and refried beans in a small bowl. Combine shrimp and next 11 ingredients in a large bowl; toss gently.
4. Place about ⅓ cup bean mixture in

1. Place each tortilla over an inverted 10-ounce custard cup coated with cooking spray. Bake at 400° for 10 minutes or until crisp.

2. Cool tortilla cups completely on wire racks and fill with shrimp mixture.

each tortilla bowl. Top each with about 1⅔ cups shrimp mixture, 2 tablespoons cheese, and 1 tablespoon sour cream. Top evenly with reserved chiles. Serve with lime wedges, if desired. Serve immediately. Yield: 6 servings.

CALORIES 553 (25% from fat); FAT 15.6g (sat 5.3g, mono 5.9g, poly 3.2g); PROTEIN 32.4g; CARB 72.7g; FIBER 9.4g; CHOL 141mg; IRON 8.4mg; SODIUM 1004mg; CALC 333mg

Tortilla Bowls

SHRIMP ENCHILADO

PREP: 15 MINUTES   COOK: 16 MINUTES

Enchilado *refers to a spicy seafood stew popular throughout the Spanish Caribbean.*

  1 tablespoon olive oil
1½ cups diced onion
  ¾ cup diced red bell pepper
  ¾ cup diced green bell pepper
  ¾ teaspoon dried oregano
  ¾ teaspoon ground cumin
  5 garlic cloves, minced
  1 (6-ounce) can tomato paste
1¾ cups dry white wine
  1 bay leaf
  2 pounds large shrimp, peeled and
      deveined
  ¾ teaspoon salt
  ⅛ teaspoon black pepper
  6 cups hot cooked rice
  3 tablespoons finely chopped fresh
      cilantro

1. Heat oil in a large nonstick skillet over medium heat. Add onion and next 5 ingredients; sauté 5 minutes or until tender.

2. Stir tomato paste into onion mixture, and cook 1 minute. Stir in wine and bay leaf; bring to a boil. Reduce heat; simmer, uncovered, 5 minutes. Add shrimp; stir well.

3. Cover and cook over medium-low heat 5 minutes or until shrimp are done. Remove from heat; discard bay leaf. Stir in salt and pepper. Serve over rice, and sprinkle with cilantro. Yield: 6 servings (serving size: 1 cup shrimp mixture and 1 cup rice).

CALORIES 417 (11% from fat); FAT 5g (sat 0.8g, mono 2.1g, poly 1.2g); PROTEIN 29.3g; CARB 62.7g; FIBER 3.6g; CHOL 172mg; IRON 6.5mg; SODIUM 488mg; CALC 116mg

Greek-Style Scampi

GREEK-STYLE SCAMPI

PREP: 12 MINUTES   COOK: 27 MINUTES

  1 teaspoon olive oil
  5 garlic cloves, minced
  2 (28-ounce) cans whole
      tomatoes, drained and coarsely
      chopped
  ½ cup chopped fresh parsley, divided
1½ pounds large shrimp, peeled and
      deveined
  1 cup (4 ounces) crumbled feta
      cheese
  2 tablespoons fresh lemon juice
  ¼ teaspoon freshly ground black
      pepper

1. Preheat oven to 400°.

2. Heat oil in a large Dutch oven over medium heat. Add garlic; sauté 30 seconds. Add tomatoes and ¼ cup parsley. Reduce heat; simmer 10 minutes. Add shrimp; cook 5 minutes.

3. Pour shrimp mixture into a 13 x 9-inch baking dish; sprinkle with cheese. Bake at 400° for 10 minutes. Sprinkle with ¼ cup parsley, lemon juice, and pepper. Yield: 6 servings.

Note: Serve scampi with rice or pasta, if desired.

CALORIES 203 (36% from fat); FAT 8.1g (sat 4.5g, mono 2g, poly 0.8g); PROTEIN 22.6g; CARB 10g; FIBER 1.2g; CHOL 154mg; IRON 3mg; SODIUM 975mg; CALC 236mg

SHRIMP SCAMPI

PREP: 45 MINUTES
COOK: 8 MINUTES

(pictured on page 219)

See page 236 for tips on peeling and butterflying the shrimp.

2 pounds unpeeled large shrimp (48 shrimp)
3 tablespoons stick margarine or butter
1 cup chopped red bell pepper
8 garlic cloves, crushed
½ cup dry white wine
¼ cup minced fresh parsley
¼ cup fresh lemon juice
½ teaspoon salt
¼ teaspoon black pepper
⅛ teaspoon paprika
6 (2-ounce) slices French bread

1. Peel shrimp, leaving tails intact. Butterfly each shrimp, cutting to, but not through, back of shrimp. Arrange 8 shrimp, cut sides up, in each of 6 gratin dishes; place dishes on a baking sheet and set aside.
2. Preheat broiler.
3. Melt margarine in a medium skillet over medium-high heat. Add bell pepper and garlic; sauté 2 minutes. Remove from heat; stir in wine, parsley, lemon juice, salt, and pepper.
4. Spoon wine mixture evenly over shrimp; sprinkle paprika over shrimp. Broil 6 minutes or until shrimp are done. Serve with crusty French bread. Yield: 6 servings (serving size: 8 shrimp with wine sauce and 1 slice bread).
Note: If you don't have gratin dishes, place shrimp in a 13 x 9-inch baking dish. Pour wine mixture over shrimp, and broil as directed.

CALORIES 342 (26% from fat); FAT 9.5g (sat 1.9g, mono 3.5g, poly 3g); PROTEIN 28.7g; CARB 34.4g; FIBER 2.3g; CHOL 172mg; IRON 4.7mg; SODIUM 779mg; CALC 116mg

BOMBAY CURRIED SHRIMP

PREP: 18 MINUTES   COOK: 10 MINUTES

Curry powder adds the spiciness and the characteristic yellow color to this easy-to-prepare shrimp dish. Since curry loses its pungency fairly quickly, it's best when stored airtight, in a cool dry place for no longer than 2 months. For longer storage, you can keep it in your freezer.

1½ pounds large shrimp, peeled and deveined
1 tablespoon all-purpose flour
2 teaspoons vegetable oil
½ cup minced shallots
1 tablespoon curry powder
1 cup diced red bell pepper
1½ cups diced tomato
½ cup light coconut milk
¼ cup chopped fresh or 4 teaspoons dried basil
1 tablespoon fresh lemon juice
1 teaspoon sugar
½ teaspoon salt
1¼ cups fat-free, less-sodium chicken broth
6 cups hot cooked rice
3 tablespoons flaked sweetened coconut, toasted

1. Combine shrimp and flour; toss well.
2. Heat oil in a large skillet over medium-high heat. Add shallots and curry powder; sauté 1 minute. Add bell pepper; sauté 1 minute. Add tomato and next 6 ingredients; bring to a simmer, and cook 2 minutes. Add shrimp mixture; simmer 4 minutes or until shrimp are done, stirring occasionally. Spoon shrimp mixture over rice, and sprinkle with coconut. Yield: 6 servings (serving size: 1 cup shrimp mixture, 1 cup rice, and 1½ teaspoons coconut).

CALORIES 397 (14% from fat); FAT 6g (sat 2.1g, mono 0.9g, poly 1.5g); PROTEIN 23.2g; CARB 61.2g; FIBER 2.6g; CHOL 129mg; IRON 5.2mg; SODIUM 361mg; CALC 83mg

SHRIMP NEWBURG ON TOAST POINTS

PREP: 6 MINUTES
COOK: 10 MINUTES

The shrimp mixture can also be served over rice or pasta.

2 teaspoons olive oil, divided
¾ pound large shrimp, peeled and deveined
2 cups sliced mushrooms
¾ cup 1% low-fat milk
1 tablespoon all-purpose flour
2 tablespoons dry sherry
1 large egg yolk
¼ teaspoon salt
Dash of ground red pepper
Dash of black pepper
4 (¾-ounce) slices whole-wheat bread, toasted
2 teaspoons chopped fresh chives

1. Heat 1 teaspoon oil in a large nonstick skillet over medium-high heat. Add shrimp; sauté 3 minutes. Remove shrimp from skillet; keep warm.
2. Add 1 teaspoon oil to skillet. Add mushrooms; sauté 5 minutes. Combine milk, flour, sherry, and egg yolk, stirring well with a whisk; add to mushrooms. Bring mixture to a boil; reduce heat, and simmer until thick (about 3 minutes), stirring constantly with a whisk. Return shrimp to skillet, and stir in salt and peppers.
3. Cut each toast slice in half diagonally. Arrange 4 toast triangles on each of 2 plates; top with 1½ cups shrimp mixture, and sprinkle with chives. Yield: 2 servings.

CALORIES 350 (29% from fat); FAT 11.2g (sat 2.7g, mono 5.5g, poly 1.7g); PROTEIN 30.4g; CARB 31.7g; FIBER 3g; CHOL 299mg; IRON 6mg; SODIUM 787mg; CALC 213mg

SWEET-AND-SOUR SHRIMP

PREP: 18 MINUTES

COOK: 5 MINUTES

1 tablespoon cornstarch
¼ teaspoon salt
1 large egg white
1 pound large shrimp, peeled and
    deveined
1 (15¼-ounce) can pineapple
    chunks in juice, undrained
⅓ cup water
3 tablespoons sugar
2 teaspoons cornstarch
¼ teaspoon salt
3 tablespoons ketchup
3 tablespoons cider vinegar
1 teaspoon dark sesame oil
1 tablespoon dry sherry
1 tablespoon dark sesame oil
½ cup diced onion
⅓ cup diced mushrooms
⅓ cup frozen green peas
4 cups hot cooked rice

1. Combine first 3 ingredients in a medium bowl; stir well with a whisk. Add shrimp; stir well. Cover and chill 15 minutes.

2. Drain pineapple, reserving 2 tablespoons juice. Set pineapple aside. Combine reserved juice, ⅓ cup water, and next 7 ingredients; stir well.

3. Remove shrimp from bowl; discard marinade. Heat 1 tablespoon sesame oil in a wok or large nonstick skillet over medium-high heat. Add shrimp; stir-fry 1 minute. Add onion and mushrooms; stir-fry 2 minutes. Add ketchup mixture and peas; stir-fry 1 minute or until thick and bubbly. Remove from heat; stir in pineapple. Serve over rice. Yield: 4 servings (serving size: 1 cup shrimp mixture and 1 cup rice).

CALORIES 465 (13% from fat); FAT 6.7g (sat 1g, mono 2.1g, poly 2.6g); PROTEIN 23g; CARB 78g; FIBER 2.8g; CHOL 129mg; IRON 4.5mg; SODIUM 515mg; CALC 80mg

SPICY SHRIMP WITH UDON NOODLES

PREP: 30 MINUTES

MARINATE: 30 MINUTES

COOK: 6 MINUTES

You can find red curry paste at Asian markets; made primarily from chiles and very concentrated, it imparts a spicy, salty flavor all its own.

1 teaspoon grated lime rind
3 tablespoons fresh lime juice
3 tablespoons low-sodium soy
    sauce
3 tablespoons red curry paste
3 tablespoons brown sugar
1 tablespoon chili oil or
    vegetable oil
2 pounds large shrimp, peeled and
    deveined
2 cups (2 x ¼-inch) julienne-cut
    red bell pepper (about 2
    peppers)
½ cup thinly sliced green onions
⅓ cup minced fresh cilantro
1 cup fresh bean sprouts (about 3
    ounces)
6 cups cooked udon noodles (thick,
    round fresh Japanese wheat noo-
    dles) or spaghetti (about 8
    ounces uncooked)
  Cooking spray
6 tablespoons chopped lightly
    salted, dry-roasted peanuts

1. Combine first 6 ingredients. Combine ⅓ cup lime juice mixture and shrimp in a large zip-top plastic bag; seal bag, and marinate shrimp in refrigerator 30 minutes.

2. Combine remaining lime juice mixture, bell pepper, green onions, cilantro, bean sprouts, and noodles in a large bowl, tossing to coat.

3. Remove shrimp from lime juice mixture; discard marinade. Place a large

nonstick skillet coated with cooking spray over medium-high heat until hot. Add shrimp; sauté 5 minutes or until done. Combine shrimp and pasta mixture, and toss gently. Sprinkle each serving with peanuts. Serve warm or chilled. Yield: 6 servings (serving size: 1½ cups shrimp mixture and 1 tablespoon peanuts).

Note: To save time, you can purchase already peeled and deveined shrimp at the market.

CALORIES 384 (36% from fat); FAT 10.6g (sat 1.6g, mono 3.7g, poly 3.7g); PROTEIN 31.3g; CARB 42g; FIBER 3.5g; CHOL 172mg; IRON 4.5mg; SODIUM 1335mg; CALC 92mg

SHRIMP FRA DIAVOLO WITH FETA

PREP: 11 MINUTES   COOK: 3 MINUTES

Make sure to prepare the pasta and Arrabbiata Sauce before you sauté the shrimp for this devilishly spicy dish.

1 teaspoon olive oil
24 medium shrimp, peeled and
    deveined (about 1 pound)
1 tablespoon lemon juice
4 cups hot cooked linguine (about
    8 ounces uncooked pasta)
3 cups Arrabbiata Sauce (page
    446)
¾ cup (3 ounces) crumbled feta
    cheese

1. Heat oil in a nonstick skillet over medium heat. Add shrimp, and sauté 3 minutes or until done. Drizzle shrimp with lemon juice.

2. Place 1 cup linguine on each of 4 plates; top with ¾ cup Arrabbiata Sauce, 6 shrimp, and 3 tablespoons cheese. Yield: 4 servings.

CALORIES 454 (20% from fat); FAT 9.9g (sat 4g, mono 3.1g, poly 1.5g); PROTEIN 30.3g; CARB 61.7g; FIBER 5.4g; CHOL 148mg; IRON 6.4mg; SODIUM 716mg; CALC 243mg

Pasta Puttanesca (page 262)

grains & pastas

GRAINS

rice
These fluffy, tender grains can go beyond the basics. From flavorful pilafs to creamy risottos, our recipes showcase this simple grain.

With the addition of vegetables and seasonings, rice can star in a variety of recipes. Rice differs in color and size. When harvested, an inedible husk surrounds the kernel. Only the husk is removed from brown rice. Its characteristic color is due to the natural bran layer left on the grain. Cooked brown rice is chewy with a nutty flavor and is high in fiber.

The bran layer, some vitamins and minerals, and most of the fiber are stripped from white rice. Without the bran layer, it cooks in 15 to 20 minutes, whereas brown rice usually takes as long as 40 to 50 minutes. White rice often is enriched with B vitamins and iron to replace some of those lost during milling.

GARLICKY BROWN RICE

PREP: 7 MINUTES
COOK: 55 MINUTES

2 tablespoons olive oil
2 cups uncooked short-grain brown rice
6 garlic cloves, minced
1½ cups water
2 (14.25-ounce) cans fat-free, less-sodium chicken broth
½ teaspoon salt
¼ cup thinly sliced green onions

1. Heat oil in a large skillet over medium-high heat. Add rice, and sauté 1 minute. Add garlic; sauté 2 minutes. Stir in water, broth, and salt; bring to a boil. Cover, reduce heat, and cook over medium-low heat 55 minutes or until

Basic Rice

PREP: 2 MINUTES
COOK: 22 MINUTES

2½ cups water
¼ teaspoon salt
1 cup uncooked long-grain rice

1. Bring water and salt to a boil in a medium saucepan; add rice. Cover, reduce heat, and simmer 20 minutes or until water is absorbed and rice is tender. Yield: 4 servings (serving size: ¾ cup).

CALORIES 169 (2% from fat); FAT 0.3g (sat 0.1g, mono 0.1g, poly 0.1g); PROTEIN 3.3g; CARB 37g; FIBER 0.6g; CHOL 0mg; IRON 2mg; SODIUM 149mg; CALC 13mg

Microwave Directions: Use very hot tap water instead of cool water when microwaving rice. Combine hot water, salt, and rice in a deep 2-quart casserole. Cover tightly with heavy-duty plastic wrap; fold back a small corner to allow steam to escape. Microwave at HIGH 5 minutes. Stir well. Cover and microwave at MEDIUM (50% power) 12 to 14 minutes or until water is absorbed and rice is tender. Let stand 2 minutes. Fluff with a fork.

liquid is absorbed. Spoon into a bowl; fluff with a fork. Top with green onions. Yield: 6 servings (serving size: 1 cup).

CALORIES 288 (20% from fat); FAT 6.3g (sat 1g, mono 4g, poly 1g); PROTEIN 8.7g; CARB 50g; FIBER 2.3g; CHOL 0mg; IRON 1mg; SODIUM 240mg; CALC 22mg

TYPES OF RICE

Arborio rice: An Italian short-grain rice suited for long-cooking creamy risottos.

Basmati rice: A highly aromatic, long-grain rice that has a nutty flavor, and a firm texture. It smells like popcorn when it cooks.

Converted or parboiled rice: Long-grain white or brown rice processed to be extra fluffy. The removal of excess surface starches helps the rice to retain many of its original nutrients. Some parboiled rices take several minutes longer to cook and require additional liquid.

Precooked or instant rice: Cooked partially or completely then dehydrated. Reconstitutes quickly in boiling water.

GREEN RICE

PREP: 13 MINUTES   COOK: 23 MINUTES

6 large tomatillos
2 tablespoons water
⅓ cup minced fresh cilantro
4 teaspoons minced seeded jalapeño pepper
½ teaspoon salt
1 garlic clove, minced
1¼ cups uncooked basmati rice

1. Discard husks and stems from tomatillos. Cook tomatillos in boiling water in a medium saucepan 4 minutes or until soft; drain. Combine tomatillos and

2 tablespoons water in a blender, and process until smooth. Pour tomatillo mixture into a 4-cup glass measure, and add enough water to measure 2½ cups.
2. Combine tomatillo mixture, cilantro, and next 3 ingredients in saucepan; bring to a boil. Add rice; cover, reduce heat, and simmer 20 minutes or until liquid is absorbed. Let stand, covered, 5 minutes. Remove from heat; fluff with a fork. Yield: 6 servings (serving size: ¾ cup).

CALORIES 156 (4% from fat); FAT 0.7g (sat 0.1g, mono 0.2g, poly 0.3g); PROTEIN 3.3g; CARB 33.7g; FIBER 1.4g; CHOL 0mg; IRON 2mg; SODIUM 199mg; CALC 17mg

Spanish Rice

HERBED BASMATI RICE

PREP: 3 MINUTES   COOK: 23 MINUTES

You can use dried herbs in place of fresh; use ½ teaspoon basil and ¼ teaspoon thyme.

- 2 teaspoons stick margarine or butter
- 1 garlic clove, minced
- ½ cup uncooked basmati rice
- 1 cup water
- ¼ teaspoon salt
- 2 tablespoons thinly sliced green onion tops
- 2 tablespoons minced fresh basil
- 1 teaspoon minced fresh thyme
- 2 tablespoons grated fresh Parmesan cheese

1. Melt margarine in a small saucepan over medium heat. Add garlic; sauté 30 seconds. Stir in rice. Add water and salt; bring to a boil. Cover, reduce heat, and simmer 20 minutes or until liquid is absorbed. Stir in green onions, basil, and minced thyme. Sprinkle with cheese. Yield: 4 servings (serving size: ½ cup).

CALORIES 108 (20% from fat); FAT 2.4g (sat 0.6g, mono 1g, poly 0.7g); PROTEIN 2.2g; CARB 19g; FIBER 0.4g; CHOL 1mg; IRON 1.1mg; SODIUM 191mg; CALC 27mg

SPANISH RICE

PREP: 5 MINUTES   COOK: 13 MINUTES

Cooking spray
- 1 cup chopped onion
- ⅔ cup diced green bell pepper
- 1 cup uncooked instant rice
- ½ teaspoon prepared mustard
- ¼ teaspoon black pepper
- 1 (14.5-ounce) can whole tomatoes, undrained and chopped
- 1 (5.5-ounce) can tomato juice

1. Coat a large nonstick skillet with cooking spray; place over medium-high heat until hot. Add onion and bell pepper; sauté 2 minutes or until tender. Add rice, and sauté 5 minutes. Add mustard and remaining ingredients; reduce heat, and simmer, uncovered, 8 minutes or until liquid is absorbed. Yield: 3 servings (serving size: 1 cup).

CALORIES 179 (3% from fat); FAT 0.5g (sat 0.1g, mono 0.1g, poly 0.1g); PROTEIN 4.7g; CARB 39.8g; FIBER 2.7g; CHOL 0mg; IRON 2.7mg; SODIUM 704mg; CALC 66mg

MEXICAN RICE

PREP: 7 MINUTES
COOK: 24 MINUTES

- 1 teaspoon olive oil
- 1 cup chopped onion
- 4 garlic cloves, minced
- 1 cup uncooked long-grain rice
- 1 cup water
- 1 (10-ounce) can diced tomatoes and green chiles, undrained
- ½ cup chopped fresh cilantro

1. Heat oil in a large saucepan over medium-high heat. Add onion and garlic; sauté 4 minutes.
2. Add rice, water, and tomatoes to pan; bring to a boil. Cover, reduce heat, and simmer 20 minutes or until liquid is absorbed. Remove from heat; stir in cilantro. Yield: 4 servings (serving size: 1 cup).

CALORIES 216 (6% from fat); FAT 1.5g (sat 0.3g, mono 0.9g, poly 0.2g); PROTEIN 4g; CARB 43.7g; FIBER 1.9g; CHOL 0mg; IRON 2.3mg; SODIUM 304mg; CALC 30mg

PARMESAN-BASIL RICE PILAF

PREP: 5 MINUTES   COOK: 24 MINUTES

1 teaspoon olive oil
1 teaspoon bottled minced garlic
2 cups uncooked long-grain rice
½ cup water
2 (14.25-ounce) cans fat-free, less-sodium chicken broth
1 cup frozen green peas, thawed
½ cup (2 ounces) preshredded fresh Parmesan cheese
¼ cup chopped green onions
½ teaspoon dried basil
¼ teaspoon black pepper

1. Heat oil in a large saucepan over medium-high heat. Add garlic; sauté 30 seconds or until lightly browned. Add rice; cook 2 minutes, stirring constantly. Stir in water and broth; bring to a boil. Cover, reduce heat, and cook over medium-low heat 20 minutes or until liquid is absorbed. Remove from heat; fluff with a fork. Add peas and remaining ingredients, tossing well. Yield: 7 servings (serving size: 1 cup).

CALORIES 264 (11% from fat); FAT 3.2g (sat 1.5g, mono 1.2g, poly 0.2g); PROTEIN 10.8g; CARB 47.3g; FIBER 1.8g; CHOL 6mg; IRON 2.8mg; SODIUM 198mg; CALC 122mg

GULLAH RICE

PREP: 6 MINUTES   COOK: 25 MINUTES

Gullah is an English-based creole dialect spoken along the coastal regions of the Carolinas, Georgia, and northeastern Florida.

2 teaspoons butter or stick margarine
½ cup chopped celery
½ cup chopped carrot
¼ cup chopped pistachios
2 cups water
½ teaspoon salt
1 cup uncooked long-grain rice
1 tablespoon chopped fresh thyme

1. Melt butter in a medium saucepan over medium heat. Add celery, carrot, and pistachios; sauté 4 minutes or until tender. Add water and salt, and bring to a boil. Add rice and thyme; return to a boil. Cover, reduce heat, and simmer 20 minutes or until most of liquid is absorbed. Let stand, covered, 10 minutes or until liquid is absorbed. Yield: 6 servings (serving size: ¾ cup).

CALORIES 166 (24% from fat); FAT 4.4g (sat 1.2g, mono 2.4g, poly 0.6g); PROTEIN 3.7g; CARB 28g; FIBER 1.7g; CHOL 3mg; IRON 2mg; SODIUM 225mg; CALC 28mg

CAJUN RICE DRESSING

PREP: 30 MINUTES   COOK: 55 MINUTES

2 (4-ounce) turkey Italian sausages
1¼ cups chopped onion
1¼ cups chopped celery
1 cup chopped green bell pepper
4 garlic cloves, minced
2 cups uncooked long-grain rice
1 teaspoon dried oregano
¼ teaspoon salt
¼ teaspoon ground cumin
¼ teaspoon ground red pepper
¼ teaspoon paprika
4 drops of hot sauce
1 bay leaf

Cooking spray
2 (14.25-ounce) cans fat-free, less-sodium chicken broth

1. Preheat oven to 350°.
2. Remove casings from sausage. Cook sausage in a large nonstick skillet over medium heat until browned, stirring to crumble. Drain well. Remove sausage from skillet.
3. Add onion, celery, bell pepper, and garlic to skillet, and sauté 8 to 10 minutes or until tender. Remove from heat; stir in sausage, rice, and next 7 ingredients. Spoon into a 13 x 9-inch baking dish coated with cooking spray.
4. Pour chicken broth over sausage mixture; cover and bake at 350° for 50 to 55 minutes or until liquid is absorbed. Discard bay leaf, and fluff dressing with a fork. Yield: 8 servings (serving size: 1 cup).

Note: For a spicier dressing, use hot turkey sausage. This dish is attractive served as a timbale.

CALORIES 255 (14% from fat); FAT 3.9g (sat 1g, mono 1.5g, poly 0.8g); PROTEIN 10.4g; CARB 42.2g; FIBER 1.7g; CHOL 24mg; IRON 2.8mg; SODIUM 475mg; CALC 34mg

SPINACH-RICE TIMBALES

PREP: 10 MINUTES
COOK: 40 MINUTES

1 (10-ounce) package frozen chopped spinach, thawed and drained
⅔ cup 1% low-fat cottage cheese
½ cup plain fat-free yogurt
¼ cup (1 ounce) crumbled feta cheese
¼ teaspoon salt
¼ teaspoon dried basil
¼ teaspoon coarsely ground black pepper
2 large eggs
2 large egg whites
¾ cup cooked long-grain rice
Cooking spray

1. Preheat oven to 350°.

2. Press spinach between paper towels until barely moist. Combine cottage cheese and next 7 ingredients in a bowl; beat at medium speed of a mixer until blended. Stir in spinach and rice.

3. Divide rice mixture among 6 (6-ounce) custard cups coated with cooking spray. Place cups in a large baking pan, and add hot water to pan to a depth of 1 inch.

4. Bake timbales at 350° for 40 minutes or until a knife inserted near center comes out clean. Remove cups from water; loosen edges of timbales with a knife or rubber spatula. Place a serving plate upside down on top of each cup; invert timbales onto plates. Serve warm. Yield: 6 servings.

CALORIES 89 (30% from fat); FAT 2.9g (sat 1.3g, mono 0.8g, poly 0.3g); PROTEIN 7.7g; CARB 8.2g; FIBER 1.2g; CHOL 59mg; IRON 1.2mg; SODIUM 273mg; CALC 114mg

SUN-DRIED TOMATO-BASIL RICE CAKES

PREP: 20 MINUTES
COOK: 1 HOUR 4 MINUTES

2 cups water
1 cup uncooked jasmine rice or long-grain rice
2 cups boiling water
2 ounces sun-dried tomatoes, packed without oil (about 24)
4 cups diced peeled eggplant
Cooking spray
½ teaspoon salt, divided
½ teaspoon dried Italian seasoning
½ teaspoon olive oil
½ cup finely chopped onion
1 garlic clove, minced
½ cup dry breadcrumbs
¼ cup chopped fresh basil
1 tablespoon capers, chopped
2 large eggs, lightly beaten
2 tablespoons olive oil, divided

Red Pepper Sauce (page 448)
Basil leaves (optional)

1. Bring 2 cups water to a boil in a medium saucepan. Add rice; cover, reduce heat, and simmer 25 minutes or until liquid is absorbed.

2. Combine 2 cups boiling water and tomatoes in a bowl; let stand 30 minutes or until softened. Drain tomatoes, reserving ¼ cup liquid. Chop tomatoes; set aside.

3. Preheat oven to 375°.

4. Place eggplant on a foil-lined baking sheet coated with cooking spray, spreading evenly. Sprinkle ¼ teaspoon salt and Italian seasoning over eggplant. Bake at 375° for 35 minutes or until tender.

5. Heat ½ teaspoon oil in a large nonstick skillet over medium-high heat. Add onion and garlic; sauté 3 minutes.

6. Combine onion mixture, rice, tomatoes, reserved ¼ cup liquid, eggplant, breadcrumbs, ¼ teaspoon salt, chopped basil, capers, and eggs in a large bowl. Divide mixture into 16 equal portions, shaping each into a 3½-inch cake.

7. Heat 1½ teaspoons oil in skillet over medium-high heat. Add 4 cakes, and cook 6 minutes or until golden, turning cakes carefully after 3 minutes. Repeat procedure with remaining oil and cakes. Serve with Red Pepper Sauce, and garnish with basil leaves, if desired. Yield: 8 servings (serving size: 2 cakes and ¼ cup Red Pepper Sauce).

CALORIES 228 (28% from fat); FAT 7.1g (sat 1.2g, mono 3.8g, poly 1.3g); PROTEIN 6.8g; CARB 36.1g; FIBER 3.8g; CHOL 53mg; IRON 3.7mg; SODIUM 567mg; CALC 63mg

FRIED RICE WITH BOK CHOY, HAM, AND EGG

PREP: 30 MINUTES   COOK: 7 MINUTES

½ cup water
½ ounce dried shiitake mushrooms
1 tablespoon vegetable oil, divided
½ cup egg substitute
1 teaspoon minced peeled fresh ginger
2 garlic cloves, minced
2 cups (2-inch) julienne-cut bok choy
¼ pound 33%-less-sodium smoked ham, cut into 1-inch julienne strips
3 cups cold cooked rice
¼ cup fat-free, less-sodium chicken broth
½ teaspoon salt
¼ teaspoon pepper

1. Combine water and mushrooms in a saucepan; bring to a boil. Remove from heat. Cover and let stand 30 minutes. Drain mushrooms, reserving 3 tablespoons cooking liquid. Remove and discard stems. Chop caps, and set aside.

2. Heat 1 teaspoon oil in a nonstick skillet over medium-high heat. Add egg substitute; cook without stirring until mixture sets on bottom. Draw a spatula across bottom of pan to form curds. Continue until egg substitute is thickened, but still moist; do not stir constantly. Break egg into smaller curds. Remove egg from skillet; set aside.

3. Heat 2 teaspoons oil in skillet. Add ginger and garlic; stir-fry 30 seconds. Add mushroom caps, bok choy, and ham; stir-fry 1 minute. Add rice; stir-fry 2 minutes. Add 3 tablespoons reserved cooking liquid, egg, broth, salt, and pepper. Increase heat to high, and stir-fry 2 minutes or until liquid is nearly absorbed. Yield: 5 servings (serving size: 1 cup).

CALORIES 214 (17% from fat); FAT 4.1g (sat 0.9g, mono 1.3g, poly 1.5g); PROTEIN 9.9g; CARB 34g; FIBER 1.4g; CHOL 11mg; IRON 2.1mg; SODIUM 474mg; CALC 68mg

EGG FRIED RICE

PREP: 6 MINUTES   COOK: 12 MINUTES

2 teaspoons dark sesame oil
2 large eggs
2 large egg whites
1 tablespoon vegetable oil
4 cups cold cooked rice
1 cup frozen green peas, thawed
¼ teaspoon black pepper
1½ cups fresh bean sprouts
½ cup chopped green onions
1 tablespoon low-sodium soy sauce

1. Combine first 3 ingredients in a small bowl; stir with a whisk until blended.
2. Heat oil in a nonstick skillet over medium-high heat. Add egg mixture; stir-fry 2 minutes. Add rice; stir-fry 3 minutes. Add green peas and pepper; stir-fry 5 minutes. Add bean sprouts and green onions; stir-fry 2 minutes. Stir in soy sauce. Yield: 7 servings (serving size: 1 cup).

CALORIES 206 (21% from fat); FAT 4.9g (sat 1g, mono 1.7g, poly 1.7g); PROTEIN 7g; CARB 33g; FIBER 1.9g; CHOL 61mg; IRON 1.9mg; SODIUM 129mg; CALC 31mg

SPANISH FRIED RICE

PREP: 8 MINUTES   COOK: 8 MINUTES

1 tablespoon olive oil, divided
4 cups cold cooked rice
Dash of powdered saffron
½ cup chopped onion
¼ cup chopped celery
¼ cup chopped green bell pepper
¼ cup chopped red bell pepper
2 garlic cloves, minced
¼ cup no-salt-added tomato sauce
1 teaspoon chili powder
½ teaspoon sugar
½ teaspoon salt
Dash of ground red pepper
1 (14½-ounce) can no-salt-added whole tomatoes, drained and chopped

1. Heat 1½ teaspoons oil in a large nonstick skillet over medium heat. Add rice and saffron; stir-fry 3 minutes. Remove from skillet.
2. Heat 1½ teaspoons oil in skillet over medium-high heat. Add onion, celery, bell peppers, and garlic; sauté 2 minutes. Add tomato sauce and remaining ingredients; cook 2 minutes, stirring frequently. Return rice mixture to skillet, and stir-fry until thoroughly heated. Yield: 5 servings (serving size: 1 cup).

CALORIES 234 (12% from fat); FAT 3g (sat 0.4g, mono 2g, poly 0.3g); PROTEIN 4.5g; CARB 47g; FIBER 2.1g; CHOL 0mg; IRON 2.1mg; SODIUM 257mg; CALC 47mg

BASIC RISOTTO

PREP: 5 MINUTES   COOK: 25 MINUTES

3 (14½-ounce) cans fat-free, less-sodium chicken broth
1 tablespoon olive oil
⅓ cup finely chopped onion
1½ cups uncooked Arborio rice or other short-grain rice
⅓ cup dry white wine
¼ cup (1 ounce) grated fresh Parmesan cheese

1. Bring broth to a simmer in a medium saucepan (do not boil). Keep warm over low heat.
2. Heat oil in a large Dutch oven over medium-high heat. Add onion; sauté 3 minutes. Add rice; cook 1 minute, stirring constantly. Stir in wine; cook 1 minute or until liquid is nearly absorbed, stirring constantly. Add broth, ½ cup at a time, stirring constantly until each portion of broth is absorbed before adding the next (about 20 minutes total). Remove from heat; stir in cheese. Yield: 4 servings (serving size: 1 cup).

CALORIES 353 (13% from fat); FAT 5.1g (sat 1.4g, mono 3g, poly 0.4g); PROTEIN 7.5g; CARB 63.4g; FIBER 1.3g; CHOL 3mg; IRON 3.3mg; SODIUM 878mg; CALC 66mg

A PEARL OF WISDOM

Risotto gets its classic, creamy texture from plump, starchy rice. Arborio is the most readily available Italian rice that is exported to the United States, but medium- or short-grain American rice can also be used. The big difference is that Italian rice has a core (sometimes called the pearl) that remains firm to the bite, or "al dente," while American-grown rice is a little more tender.

BUTTERNUT RISOTTO

PREP: 20 MINUTES
COOK: 30 MINUTES

3 (14½-ounce) cans fat-free, less-sodium chicken broth
1 tablespoon olive oil
¾ cup thinly sliced leek
1 cup thinly sliced celery
1½ cups uncooked Arborio rice or other short-grain rice
1 tablespoon thinly sliced fresh sage
⅓ cup dry white wine
4 cups (½-inch) cubed peeled butternut squash (about 1¼ pounds)
⅓ cup (1⅓ ounces) grated fresh Parmesan cheese
2 teaspoons lemon juice
¼ teaspoon white pepper

Risotto should be creamy—but not soupy or mushy. As risotto cooks, the grains of rice soften and thicken the liquid to a creamy consistency.

Basic Risotto

1. Heat oil in a large Dutch oven over medium-high heat. Add onion; sauté 3 minutes. Add rice; cook 1 minute, stirring constantly.

2. Add warm broth, ½ cup at a time, stirring constantly until each portion of broth is absorbed before adding the next.

3. The finished product should be tender and creamy with all the liquid absorbed. This should take from 20 to 30 minutes.

---

1. Bring broth to a simmer in a medium saucepan (do not boil). Keep warm over low heat.
2. Heat oil in a large saucepan over medium heat. Add leek and celery; sauté 2 minutes. Add rice and sage; cook 1 minute, stirring constantly. Stir in wine; cook 1 minute or until liquid is nearly absorbed, stirring constantly. Stir in ½ cup broth and squash; cook until liquid is nearly absorbed, stirring constantly. Add remaining broth, ½ cup at a time, stirring constantly until each portion of broth is absorbed before adding the next (about 25 minutes total). Stir in Parmesan cheese, lemon juice, and pepper. Yield: 7 servings (serving size: 1 cup).

CALORIES 245 (12% from fat); FAT 3.2g (sat 1g, mono 1.8g, poly 0.3g); PROTEIN 5.5g; CARB 46.6g; FIBER 1.9g; CHOL 2mg; IRON 2.6mg; SODIUM 530mg; CALC 95mg

FRESH TOMATO-AND-BASIL RISOTTO WITH MOZZARELLA

PREP: 20 MINUTES   COOK: 27 MINUTES

1½ cups diced plum tomato
2 tablespoons chopped fresh basil
1 tablespoon olive oil
½ teaspoon salt
1 garlic clove, crushed
3 (14½-ounce) cans fat-free, less-sodium chicken broth
2 teaspoons olive oil
½ cup finely chopped onion
1½ cups uncooked Arborio rice or other short-grain rice
⅓ cup dry white wine
½ cup (2 ounces) diced part-skim mozzarella cheese
½ teaspoon freshly ground black pepper
2 tablespoons (½ ounce) grated fresh Parmesan cheese

1. Combine first 5 ingredients in a small bowl; set aside.
2. Bring broth to a simmer in a medium saucepan (do not boil). Keep warm over low heat.
3. Heat 2 teaspoons oil in a large saucepan over medium-high heat. Add onion; sauté 3 minutes. Add rice; cook 1 minute, stirring constantly. Add wine; cook 1 minute or until liquid is nearly absorbed, stirring constantly. Add broth, ½ cup at a time, stirring constantly until each portion of broth is absorbed before adding the next (about 25 minutes total). Add tomato mixture; cook 2 minutes, stirring constantly. Remove from heat; stir in mozzarella cheese and pepper. Sprinkle each serving with Parmesan cheese. Yield: 6 servings (serving size: 1 cup).

CALORIES 278 (20% from fat); FAT 6.1g (sat 1.8g, mono 3.4g, poly 0.5g); PROTEIN 7.2g; CARB 45.1g; FIBER 1.4g; CHOL 7mg; IRON 2.5mg; SODIUM 827mg; CALC 93mg

RISOTTO WITH ARUGULA AND TOASTED GARLIC

PREP: 10 MINUTES
COOK: 56 MINUTES

To make this recipe a main dish, stir in 1 pound peeled, uncooked shrimp with the last ½ cup of broth.

2 (14½-ounce) cans fat-free, less-sodium chicken broth
1 tablespoon olive oil
3 garlic cloves, thinly sliced
½ cup chopped onion
1½ cups uncooked Arborio rice or other short-grain rice
½ cup dry white wine
¼ teaspoon black pepper
4 cups trimmed arugula

1. Bring broth to a simmer in a medium saucepan (do not boil). Keep broth warm over low heat.

2. Heat oil in a large saucepan over medium heat. Add garlic; sauté 3 minutes or until lightly browned. Remove garlic with a slotted spoon; set aside. Add onion to pan; sauté over medium-high heat 3 minutes or until tender. Stir in rice; reduce heat to medium, and cook 5 minutes, stirring constantly. Add wine and pepper; cook 1 minute or until wine is nearly absorbed, stirring constantly. Add broth, ½ cup at a time, stirring constantly until each portion of broth is absorbed before adding the next (about 45 minutes total). Remove from heat; stir in garlic and arugula. Yield: 4 servings (serving size: 1 cup).

CALORIES 337 (11% from fat); FAT 4g (sat 0.6g, mono 2.6g, poly 0.4g); PROTEIN 6.5g; CARB 64.9g; FIBER 2.2g; CHOL 0mg; IRON 4.2mg; SODIUM 566mg; CALC 59mg

Risotto With Arugula and Toasted Garlic

SPINACH-AND-SUGAR SNAP RISOTTO

PREP: 18 MINUTES
COOK: 42 MINUTES

2 tablespoons olive oil, divided
1 cup finely chopped onion
¼ teaspoon sugar
3 cups chopped fresh spinach
1¼ cups sugar snap peas, trimmed
2 tablespoons minced fresh or 2 teaspoons dried rubbed sage
¼ teaspoon salt
¼ teaspoon freshly ground black pepper
1 garlic clove, minced
¾ cup water
1 (14½-ounce) can vegetable broth
1 cup uncooked Arborio rice or other short-grain rice
¼ cup dry white wine
6 tablespoons (1½ ounces) grated fresh Parmesan cheese

1. Heat 1 tablespoon oil in a large saucepan over medium-high heat. Add onion and sugar; sauté 30 seconds. Stir in spinach and next 5 ingredients; sauté 30 seconds or until spinach wilts. Remove spinach mixture from pan; set aside.

2. Bring water and broth to a simmer in a small saucepan (do not boil). Keep warm over low heat.

3. Heat 1 tablespoon oil in large saucepan; add rice. Cook 5 minutes, stirring constantly. Stir in wine, and cook until wine is absorbed, stirring constantly.

4. Stir in ½ cup broth mixture; cook 4 minutes or until liquid is nearly absorbed, stirring constantly. Add remaining broth mixture, ½ cup at a time, stirring constantly until each portion of broth mixture is absorbed before adding the next (about 35 minutes total). Stir in spinach mixture and cheese; cook 1 minute or until thoroughly heated. Yield: 5 servings (serving size: 1 cup).

CALORIES 262 (29% from fat); FAT 8.3g (sat 2.2g, mono 4.9g, poly 0.7g); PROTEIN 7.2g; CARB 39.5g; FIBER 2.7g; CHOL 5mg; IRON 3.2mg; SODIUM 630mg; CALC 146mg

FRESH-CORN RISOTTO WITH ROASTED PEPPERS AND SAUSAGE

PREP: 26 MINUTES   COOK: 26 MINUTES

3 yellow bell peppers
5 cups fat-free, less-sodium chicken broth
1 (12-ounce) package 50%-less-fat pork-turkey sausage (such as Louis Rich)
1 teaspoon stick margarine or butter
2 cups fresh corn kernels (about 4 ears) or 2 cups frozen shoepeg corn
2 garlic cloves, minced
1¼ cups uncooked Arborio rice or other short-grain rice
¼ cup (1 ounce) grated fresh Parmesan cheese
2 teaspoons chili powder
¼ teaspoon ground cumin
¼ teaspoon black pepper

1. Preheat broiler.
2. Cut bell peppers in half lengthwise; discard seeds and membranes. Place pepper halves, skin sides up, on a foil-lined baking sheet; flatten with hand. Broil 15 minutes or until blackened. Place in a zip-top plastic bag; seal. Let stand 15 minutes. Peel and cut into strips.
3. Bring broth to a simmer in a medium saucepan (do not boil). Keep warm over low heat.
4. Cook sausage in a Dutch oven over medium-high heat 8 minutes or until browned, stirring to crumble. Drain well;

when cooled, use fingertips to crumble.
5. Melt margarine in Dutch oven over medium heat. Stir in corn and garlic; sauté 8 minutes. Stir in rice; cook 1 minute, stirring constantly. Stir in ½ cup broth, and cook 1 minute or until liquid is nearly absorbed, stirring constantly. Add remaining broth, ½ cup at a time, stirring constantly until each portion of broth is absorbed before adding the next (about 20 minutes total). Stir in roasted bell pepper, sausage, Parmesan cheese, and remaining ingredients. Serve immediately. Yield: 7 cups (serving size: 1 cup).

CALORIES 342 (33% from fat); FAT 12.7g (sat 4.6g, mono 5.2g, poly 1.8g); PROTEIN 14.6g; CARB 40.2g; FIBER 2.8g; CHOL 42mg; IRON 3.2mg; SODIUM 905mg; CALC 63mg

VIDALIA ONION RISOTTO WITH FETA CHEESE

PREP: 5 MINUTES   COOK: 24 MINUTES

2 (14½-ounce) cans vegetable broth
2 teaspoons vegetable oil
2 cups chopped Vidalia or other sweet onion
2 large garlic cloves, minced
1½ cups uncooked Arborio rice or other short-grain rice
½ cup (2 ounces) crumbled feta cheese, divided
⅓ cup chopped fresh flat-leaf parsley
¼ cup grated Parmesan cheese
Freshly ground black pepper

1. Bring broth to a simmer in a medium saucepan (do not boil). Keep warm over low heat.
2. Heat oil in a medium saucepan over medium-high heat. Add onion and garlic; sauté 1 minute. Add rice; cook 1 minute, stirring constantly. Reduce heat to medium. Stir in ½ cup broth; cook until liquid is nearly absorbed, stirring constantly. Add remaining broth, ½ cup at a time, stirring constantly until each

portion of broth is absorbed before adding the next (about 20 minutes total). Remove from heat; stir in ¼ cup feta cheese, parsley, and Parmesan cheese. Spoon rice mixture into a serving bowl; top with ¼ cup feta cheese and pepper. Yield: 5 servings (serving size: 1 cup).

CALORIES 332 (21% from fat); FAT 7.8g (sat 3.7g, mono 2.1g, poly 1.3g); PROTEIN 8.7g; CARB 56g; FIBER 2.1g; CHOL 18mg; IRON 3.2mg; SODIUM 904mg; CALC 158mg

MICROWAVE SUN-DRIED TOMATO RISOTTO

PREP: 23 MINUTES   COOK: 29 MINUTES

½ cup boiling water
¼ cup sun-dried tomato sprinkles
1 tablespoon stick margarine or butter
1 tablespoon olive oil
⅓ cup minced fresh onion
1 cup uncooked Arborio rice or other short-grain rice
3 cups fat-free, less-sodium chicken broth
¼ teaspoon black pepper
1 (4.5-ounce) can chopped green chiles, drained

1. Combine ½ cup boiling water and tomato sprinkles. Cover; let stand 10 minutes. Drain.
2. Combine margarine and oil in an 8-inch square baking dish. Microwave at HIGH 1 minute. Stir in onion; microwave at HIGH 3 minutes. Stir in rice; microwave at HIGH 2 minutes. Stir in broth and pepper; microwave at HIGH 12 minutes. Stir in tomatoes and chiles; microwave at HIGH 11 minutes. Let stand 5 minutes, stirring frequently. Yield: 4 servings (serving size: 1 cup).

CALORIES 309 (21% from fat); FAT 7.1g (sat 1.2g, mono 3.9g, poly 1.5g); PROTEIN 6.7g; CARB 53.9g; FIBER 3.6g; CHOL 0mg; IRON 4.1mg; SODIUM 951mg; CALC 28mg

other grains
These grains may be whole, cracked, or ground to offer a diverse palette of tastes and textures.

BULGUR PILAF

PREP: 10 MINUTES   COOK: 15 MINUTES

Many recipes call for pouring boiling water over bulgur and letting it stand for 30 minutes. This recipe takes the quick route by simmering for 10 minutes. This not only tenderizes the bulgur, but it also plumps the currants and allows the flavors of the vegetables to be absorbed.

Cooking spray
1 cup chopped onion
1 cup shredded carrot
1½ cups plus 2 tablespoons uncooked bulgur or cracked wheat
½ cup currants
½ teaspoon salt
2 cups water
2 tablespoons pine nuts, toasted

1. Place a medium saucepan coated with cooking spray over medium heat until hot. Add onion and carrot; sauté 5 minutes or until tender. Stir in bulgur, currants, and salt. Add water; bring to a boil. Cover, reduce heat, and simmer 10 minutes or until bulgur is tender and liquid is absorbed. Spoon bulgur mixture into a bowl; sprinkle with pine nuts. Yield: 6 servings (serving size: 1 cup).

CALORIES 210 (17% from fat); FAT 3.9g (sat 0.8g, mono 1.2g, poly 1.5g); PROTEIN 6.1g; CARB 42.4g; FIBER 8.3g; CHOL 0mg; IRON 1.6mg; SODIUM 218mg; CALC 35mg

BULGUR BITS

Bulgur is wheat kernels that have been steamed, dried, and crushed. It has a tender, chewy texture, and works best in pilafs and salads, especially tabbouleh. Bulgur cooks in 30 minutes. It's often confused with but not the same as cracked wheat. Cracked wheat can be substituted, if desired.

Cooking Grains

Add interesting flavor to your menus with these grains. If you're not sure how to cook them, follow these simple instructions: Bring water to a boil; stir in grain. Cover, reduce heat, and simmer. Let stand, covered, if indicated.

1 cup Uncooked Grain	Cups of Water	Cooking Time (Minutes)	Standing Time (Minutes)	Cups Yield
Bulgur	1½	*	30	2½
Kasha (buckwheat groats)	2	20	10	3
Millet	2¾	30	15	3
Pearl Barley	3	40	5	3½
Quinoa (rinsed)	2	15	—	3
Rice, brown	2½	45	5	3
Rice, long-grain	2	20	—	3
Rice, wild (rinsed)	3	55	—	3½
Rye berries	2	60	—	2¾
Wheat berries	2	45	—	2½

*Bulgur isn't cooked. Just put the bulgur in a bowl, pour boiling water over it, and let it stand until the water is absorbed.

GORGONZOLA CHEESE GRITS

PREP: 4 MINUTES   COOK: 10 MINUTES

2 (14.25-ounce) cans fat-free, less-sodium chicken broth
¾ cup uncooked quick-cooking grits
1 cup (4 ounces) crumbled Gorgonzola cheese
⅓ cup fat-free sour cream
¼ teaspoon ground nutmeg
¼ teaspoon freshly ground black pepper

1. Bring broth to a boil in a medium saucepan; gradually add grits, stirring constantly. Reduce heat to low; simmer, covered, 5 minutes or until thick, stirring occasionally. Remove from heat; stir in cheese and remaining ingredients. Yield: 4 servings (serving size: 1 cup).

CALORIES 280 (39% from fat); FAT 12.1g (sat 7.7g, mono 3.2g, poly 0.3g); PROTEIN 13.1g; CARB 26.5g; FIBER 1.4g; CHOL 31mg; IRON 1.2mg; SODIUM 592mg; CALC 245mg

BASIC POLENTA

PREP: 3 MINUTES   COOK: 15 MINUTES

1¼ cups yellow cornmeal
½ teaspoon salt
4 cups water

1. Place cornmeal and salt in a large saucepan. Gradually add water, stirring constantly with a whisk. Bring to a boil; reduce heat to medium. Cover and cook 15 minutes, stirring frequently. Yield: 4 servings (serving size: 1 cup).
Note: You can prepare Basic Polenta in the microwave: Place cornmeal and salt in a 3-quart casserole. Gradually add water, stirring until blended. Cover and microwave at HIGH 12 minutes, stirring every 3 minutes. Let stand, covered, 5 minutes. Yield: 4 servings (serving size: 1 cup).

CALORIES 138 (9% from fat); FAT 1.4g (sat 0.2g, mono 0.4g, poly 0.6g); PROTEIN 3.1g; CARB 29.3g; FIBER 4.2g; CHOL 0mg; IRON 1.3mg; SODIUM 306mg; CALC 2mg

PEPPER-SPIKED POLENTA

PREP: 1 MINUTE   COOK: 12 MINUTES

(pictured on page 365)

Cooking spray
4 cups water
1 cup yellow cornmeal
½ teaspoon salt
¼ to ½ teaspoon crushed red pepper
¼ cup grated Parmesan cheese

1. Coat a 2-quart casserole with cooking spray; add water, cornmeal, salt, and pepper. Cover with casserole lid; microwave at HIGH 12 minutes or until thick, stirring after 6 minutes. Stir in cheese. Serve immediately. Yield: 4 servings (serving size: 1 cup).

CALORIES 151 (13% from fat); FAT 2.2g (sat 1g, mono 0.6g, poly 0.3g); PROTEIN 5g; CARB 27g; FIBER 1.8g; CHOL 4mg; IRON 1.5mg; SODIUM 387mg; CALC 71mg

Basic Polenta

1. Place cornmeal and salt in a large saucepan. Gradually add water, stirring constantly with a whisk.

2. Bring to a boil; reduce heat to medium.

3. Cook, covered, 15 minutes, stirring frequently.

POLENTA WITH ROASTED VEGETABLES

PREP: 23 MINUTES
COOK: 43 MINUTES

Carefully turn polenta slices with a spatula—they are soft on the bottom after broiling the first side.

4 cups (1-inch) pieces zucchini (about 2 large)
2½ cups (1-inch) pieces red bell pepper (about 2 peppers)
1 cup (1-inch) pieces red onion
1 tablespoon olive oil
Cooking spray
⅓ cup chopped fresh basil
1½ tablespoons balsamic vinegar
¼ teaspoon black pepper, divided
1 (16-ounce) tube of polenta, cut into 12 slices
¼ teaspoon salt
½ cup (2 ounces) crumbled goat cheese or feta cheese
Basil sprigs (optional)

1. Preheat oven to 475°.
2. Combine first 4 ingredients in a large bowl; arrange in a single layer on a jelly-roll pan coated with cooking spray. Bake at 475° for 25 minutes or until tender, stirring after 15 minutes. Stir in chopped basil, vinegar, and ⅛ teaspoon black pepper.
3. Preheat broiler.
4. Place polenta slices on a large baking sheet; sprinkle with salt and ⅛ teaspoon black pepper. Broil 9 minutes on each side or until lightly browned. Spoon roasted vegetables over polenta; sprinkle with cheese. Garnish with basil sprigs, if desired. Yield: 4 servings (serving size: ¾ cup vegetables, 3 polenta slices, and 2 tablespoons cheese).

CALORIES 212 (36% from fat); FAT 8.5g (sat 3.6g, mono 3.5g, poly 0.7g); PROTEIN 7.1g; CARB 26.7g; FIBER 4.3g; CHOL 18mg; IRON 2.2mg; SODIUM 580mg; CALC 130mg

POLENTA WITH WILD MUSHROOM SAUCE

PREP: 25 MINUTES   CHILL: 2 HOURS
COOK: 25 MINUTES

1⅓ cups yellow cornmeal
½ teaspoon salt
4 cups water
Cooking spray
1 tablespoon olive oil
2 garlic cloves, minced
2 thyme sprigs
1 rosemary sprig
6½ cups thinly sliced shiitake
    mushroom caps (about 1
    pound mushrooms)
1 cup canned crushed tomatoes
⅓ cup dry white wine
3 tablespoons balsamic vinegar
⅛ teaspoon salt
⅛ teaspoon black pepper
2 tablespoons chopped fresh
    parsley
3 tablespoons (¾ ounce) fresh
    grated Parmesan cheese
Thyme sprigs (optional)

1. Place cornmeal and ½ teaspoon salt in a large saucepan. Gradually add water, stirring constantly with a whisk. Bring to a boil; reduce heat to medium, and cook 15 minutes, stirring frequently. Spoon into an 8½ x 4½-inch loaf pan coated with cooking spray, spreading evenly. Press plastic wrap onto surface of polenta; chill 2 hours or until firm.
2. Heat oil in a large nonstick skillet over medium heat. Add garlic, 2 thyme sprigs, and rosemary sprig; cook 3 minutes or just until garlic begins to brown. Stir in mushrooms and next 5 ingredients; bring to a boil. Cover, reduce heat, and simmer 15 minutes, stirring occasionally. Discard thyme and rosemary. Add parsley; cook, uncovered, 5 minutes. Remove from heat; keep warm.
3. Preheat broiler.

Polenta With Wild Mushroom Sauce

Polenta + whatever topping you like— this dish can change from simple, to hearty, to gourmet—it's up to you.

4. Invert polenta onto a cutting board; cut crosswise into 12 slices. Place slices on a baking sheet coated with cooking spray. Broil 7 minutes on each side or until golden brown.
5. Arrange 2 polenta slices on each of 6 individual serving plates. Top each with about ½ cup mushroom sauce and 1½ teaspoons Parmesan cheese. Garnish with thyme sprigs, if desired. Yield: 6 servings (serving size: 2 slices polenta, ½ cup sauce, and 1½ teaspoons cheese).

CALORIES 172 (23% from fat); FAT 4.3g (sat 0.9g, mono 2.2g, poly 0.7g); PROTEIN 4.5g; CARB 31.4g; FIBER 4.3g; CHOL 2mg; IRON 1.6mg; SODIUM 350mg; CALC 50mg

MINNESOTA WILD RICE

PREP: 6 MINUTES
COOK: 1 HOUR 8 MINUTES

Wild rice may look like rice, but it is actually a type of grass valued for its rich, nutty flavor.

1 cup uncooked wild rice
2½ cups water
½ cup beef consommé, undiluted
1 tablespoon stick margarine or
    butter
2 cups sliced fresh mushrooms
¾ cup chopped celery

¾ cup chopped onion
¼ cup dry sherry
¼ teaspoon salt
¼ teaspoon black pepper

1. Combine rice, water, and consommé in a large saucepan; bring to a boil. Cover, reduce heat, and simmer 1 hour or until rice is tender; drain, if necessary.
2. Melt margarine in a medium non-stick skillet over medium-high heat. Add mushrooms, celery, and onion; sauté 6 minutes or until tender. Add mushroom mixture, sherry, salt, and pepper to rice mixture; stir well. Cook over medium heat, uncovered, 8 minutes or until liquid evaporates, stirring frequently. Yield: 5 servings (serving size: 1 cup).

CALORIES 160 (16% from fat); FAT 2.8g (sat 0.5g, mono 1.1g, poly 1g); PROTEIN 6.9g; CARB 28.3g; FIBER 2.7g; CHOL 0mg; IRON 1.4mg; SODIUM 294mg; CALC 23mg

WILD RICE-APPLE PILAF

PREP: 10 MINUTES
COOK: 1 HOUR 18 MINUTES

¼ cup uncooked wild rice
1 teaspoon olive oil
2 tablespoons chopped onion
2¼ cups fat-free, less-sodium chicken broth
1 cup diced peeled Golden Delicious apple (about ¼ pound)
⅔ cup uncooked long-grain brown rice
2 tablespoons chopped dried apple
½ teaspoon salt

1. Wash wild rice in 3 changes of hot water; drain and set aside. Heat oil in a saucepan over medium heat. Add onion; sauté 3 minutes. Add wild rice, broth, and remaining 4 ingredients; stir well. Bring to a boil; cover, reduce heat,

and simmer 1 hour and 10 minutes or until liquid is absorbed. Yield: 4 servings (serving size: ¾ cup).

CALORIES 199 (10% from fat); FAT 2.3g (sat 0.4g, mono 1.2g, poly 0.5g); PROTEIN 4.3g; CARB 39.5g; FIBER 2.5g; CHOL 0mg; IRON 0.7mg; SODIUM 658mg; CALC 12mg

SOUTHWESTERN WHEAT BERRY PILAF

PREP: 30 MINUTES   STAND: 8 HOURS
COOK: 1 HOUR 15 MINUTES

¾ cup uncooked wheat berries
2 (6-inch) Anaheim chiles
1 cup diced red bell pepper
1 cup diced peeled jícama
¾ cup minced red onion
⅓ cup minced fresh cilantro
3 tablespoons fresh lime juice
1½ tablespoons olive oil
½ teaspoon salt
2 garlic cloves, minced
1 (15-ounce) can black beans, rinsed and drained

1. Place wheat berries in a bowl; cover with water to 2 inches above wheat berries. Cover and let stand 8 hours. Drain. Place wheat berries in a medium saucepan; cover with water to 2 inches above wheat berries. Bring to a boil; reduce heat, and simmer, uncovered, 1 hour or until tender. Drain; set aside.
2. Preheat broiler.
3. Cut chiles in half lengthwise; discard seeds and membranes. Place chile halves, skin side up, on a foil-lined baking sheet; flatten with hand. Broil 8 minutes or until blackened. Place in a zip-top plastic bag, and seal; let stand 10 minutes. Peel chiles, and dice.
4. Combine chiles, wheat berries, bell pepper, and remaining 8 ingredients in a large bowl. Serve chilled or at room temperature. Yield: 5 servings (serving size: 1 cup).
Note: You may substitute ¼ cup diced canned green chiles for roasted Anaheims.

CALORIES 232 (20% from fat); FAT 5.2g (sat 0.7g, mono 3g, poly 0.6g); PROTEIN 9.1g; CARB 40.3g; FIBER 8.7g; CHOL 0mg; IRON 2.7mg; SODIUM 375mg; CALC 43mg

Southwestern
Wheat Berry Pilaf

PASTAS

making pastas
A simple mixture of flour and eggs creates a versatile paste that can be shaped, cut, and cooked in a variety of ways.

PART 1 the dough

1. Make a well in center of flour mixture, and add eggs.

2. Stir egg with a fork to gradually incorporate flour and form a dough.

3. Turn dough out onto a lightly floured surface; shape into a ball.

4. Knead until smooth and elastic (about 10 to 15 minutes).

PART 2 the noodles

6. Pass dough through smooth rollers of pasta machine, beginning on widest setting.

7. Pass dough through cutting rollers of machine.

5. Wrap dough in plastic wrap; let rest 10 minutes.

8. Hang pasta on a wooden drying rack.

BASIC PASTA

PREP: 50 MINUTES
COOK: 2 TO 4 MINUTES

1¼ cups plus 1 tablespoon all-purpose flour, divided
½ teaspoon salt
2 large eggs, lightly beaten

1. Lightly spoon flour into dry measuring cups; level with a knife. Combine 1 cup flour and salt in a bowl. Make a well in center of mixture. Add eggs; stir with a fork to gradually incorporate flour and form a dough.
2. Turn dough out onto a lightly floured surface, and shape into a ball. Knead dough until smooth and elastic (about 10 to 15 minutes); add enough of remaining flour, 1 tablespoon at a time, to prevent dough from sticking to hands. Wrap dough in plastic wrap; let rest 10 minutes. Shape and cut dough as directed.

FOOD PROCESSOR METHOD:

1. Place flour and salt in a food processor; pulse 3 times or until combined. With processor on, slowly add eggs through food chute; process until dough forms a ball. Shape and cut dough as directed.

FETTUCCINE:

1. Divide dough into 4 equal portions. Working with 1 portion at a time (cover remaining dough with plastic wrap to keep from drying), pass dough through smooth rollers of pasta machine on widest setting. Continue moving width gauge to narrower settings; pass dough through rollers at each setting, brushing dough lightly with flour if needed to prevent sticking.
2. Roll dough to desired thinness (about ¹⁄₁₆ inch). Pass dough through fettuccine cutting rollers of machine. Hang pasta on a wooden drying rack (dry no longer than 30 minutes). Repeat procedure with remaining portions of dough.
3. Bring 3 quarts water to a rolling boil. Add pasta; cook 2 to 4 minutes or until "al dente." Drain; serve immediately. Yield: 6 servings (serving size: ½ cup).

CALORIES 125 (14% from fat); FAT 1.9g (sat 0.6g, mono 0.7g, poly 0.3g); PROTEIN 4.9g; CARB 21.2g; FIBER 0.7g; CHOL 71mg; IRON 1.5mg; SODIUM 217mg; CALC 12mg

LASAGNA:

1. Divide dough into 2 equal portions. Working with 1 portion at a time (cover remaining dough with plastic wrap to keep from drying), pass dough through smooth rollers of pasta machine on widest setting. Continue moving width gauge to narrower settings; pass dough through rollers at each setting, brushing dough lightly with flour if needed to prevent sticking.
2. Roll dough to setting #6 (second to last). Cut dough sheet into 3 (11 x 2-inch) strips, rerolling scraps once. Hang pasta on a wooden drying rack (dry no longer than 30 minutes). Repeat procedure with remaining portion of dough.
3. Bring 6 quarts water to a rolling boil. Add pasta. Cook 12-15 minutes or until "al dente;" drain. Yield: 6 noodles (serving size: 1 noodle).

CALORIES 125 (14% from fat); FAT 1.9g (sat 0.6g, mono 0.7g, poly 0.3g); PROTEIN 4.9g; CARB 21.2g; FIBER 0.7g; CHOL 71mg; IRON 1.5mg; SODIUM 217mg; CALC 12mg

CANNELLONI:

1. Divide dough into 7 equal portions. Working with 1 portion at a time (cover remaining dough with plastic wrap to keep from drying), pass dough through smooth rollers of pasta machine on widest setting. Continue moving width gauge to narrower settings; pass dough through rollers at each setting, brushing dough lightly with flour if needed to prevent sticking. Turn dough crosswise at settings #2 and #3.
2. Roll dough to desired thinness. Hang pasta on a wooden drying rack (dry no longer than 30 minutes). Repeat procedure with remaining portions of dough.
3. Bring 3 quarts water to a rolling boil. Add pasta. Cook 2 to 4 minutes or until "al dente;" drain. Cut each noodle in half crosswise. Yield: 14 shells (serving size: 1 shell).

CALORIES 54 (13% from fat); FAT 0.8g (sat 0.2g, mono 0.3g, poly 0.2g); PROTEIN 2.1g; CARB 9.1g; FIBER 0.3g; CHOL 30mg; IRON 0.7mg; SODIUM 93mg; CALC 5mg

PASTA IN BROTH:

1. Divide dough into 2 equal portions. Working with 1 portion at a time (cover remaining dough with plastic wrap to keep from drying), pass dough through smooth rollers of pasta machine on widest setting. Continue moving width gauge to narrower settings; pass dough through rollers at each setting, brushing dough lightly with flour if needed to prevent sticking.
2. Roll dough to desired thinness (about ¹⁄₁₆ inch). Place dough sheet on a lightly floured surface. Cut dough into 2 x 1-inch rectangles. Hang pasta on a wooden drying rack (dry no longer than 30 minutes). Repeat procedure with remaining portion of dough.
3. Bring 8 cups fat-free, less-sodium chicken broth to a rolling boil. Add pasta; cook 2 to 4 minutes or until "al dente." Yield: 8 servings (serving size: ⅓ cup pasta and ¾ cup broth).

CALORIES 119 (11% from fat); FAT 1.5g (sat 0.4g, mono 0.5g, poly 0.3g); PROTEIN 4.3g; CARB 18.5g; FIBER 0.6g; CHOL 53mg; IRON 1.2mg; SODIUM 800mg; CALC 10mg

side-dish pastas
Almost everyone likes macaroni and cheese, but pasta's possibilities are almost endless. Be adventurous and give these a try.

Pasta is one of the most versatile and convenient foods available. Dry pasta keeps infinitely when stored in an airtight container in a cool, dry place. Both fresh and dried pasta cook quickly and combine well with other ingredients. Its shapes make meals more interesting, too. Here are a few tips for preparing perfectly cooked pasta.

• **Use a large Dutch oven** or a stockpot to allow room for the pasta to move freely in the boiling water so it will cook evenly.

• **Use 4 to 6 quarts of water to cook spaghetti** and other "long" pastas or to cook 1 pound of shaped pasta.

• **A bundle of long dried pasta** about the diameter of a quarter weighs 4 ounces.

• **It's not necessary to add salt or oil** to the water; we omit them when preparing pasta. For subtle flavor, add the juice of a lemon to the water.

• **Bring the water to a rolling boil** and add the pasta gradually so the water will continue to boil. Once all the pasta has been added, stir and begin timing. Stir frequently—you can't stir too much!

• **Cooking times vary** depending on the shape and thickness of the pasta. Begin checking for doneness after the minimum cooking time. Remove a piece of pasta from the water and bite into it; perfectly cooked pasta will have a firm, tender consistency. This is called "al dente," Italian for "to the tooth."

• **If the pasta is to be used** as part of a dish that requires further cooking, slightly undercook the pasta.

• **Refrigerate leftover pasta** in an airtight container for up to 1 week. Reheat by running hot water over the pasta, or place it in a bowl, cover and microwave at HIGH for 30 seconds to 1 minute.

Pasta Yields Chart

Pasta	Dry Measure	Cooked Amount
Capellini (angel hair)	4 ounces	2 cups
Farfalle (bow tie)	2 cups	2½ cups
Fettuccine	4 ounces	2 cups
Fusilli	2 cups	3 cups
Linguine	4 ounces	2 cups
Mostaccioli	2 cups	4 cups
Penne	2 cups	4 cups
Radiatore	2 cups	3 cups
Rigatoni	2 cups	3 cups
Rotini, rotelle (spirals and twists)	2 cups	2 cups
Shells	2 cups	3 cups
Spaghetti	4 ounces	2 cups
Wagon wheels	2 cups	3 cups
Ziti	2 cups	3 cups

LEMON-VEGETABLE COUSCOUS

PREP: 18 MINUTES   COOK: 5 MINUTES

2¼ cups water
1 (10-ounce) box couscous (about 1½ cups plus 2 tablespoons), uncooked
1⅓ cups chopped seeded tomato (about 1 large)
1 cup coarsely chopped seeded peeled cucumber
1 cup thinly sliced green onions
½ cup finely chopped fresh parsley
¼ cup finely chopped fresh mint
½ cup fresh lemon juice
2 tablespoons water
2 tablespoons olive oil
1 teaspoon salt
1 teaspoon black pepper

1. Bring water to a boil in a medium saucepan; gradually stir in couscous. Remove from heat. Cover and let stand 5 minutes. Fluff with a fork.

2. Combine couscous, tomato, cucumber, onions, parsley, and mint in a large bowl.

3. Combine lemon juice, water, oil, salt, and pepper; stir well with a whisk. Pour over couscous mixture, and toss. Yield: 7 servings (serving size: 1 cup).

CALORIES 186 (21% from fat); FAT 4.4g (sat 0.6g, mono 2.9g, poly 0.4g); PROTEIN 5.6g; CARB 32.8g; FIBER 2.3g; CHOL 0mg; IRON 1.2mg; SODIUM 344mg; CALC 15mg

Pour it from the box and the tiny, round shapes that pile up more closely resemble a grain than any kind of pasta. But couscous (KOOS-koos) is technically classified as a pasta. It's perfect to keep on hand for a quick dish—just add it to boiling water and it practically cooks itself.

Greek Couscous

GREEK COUSCOUS

PREP: 20 MINUTES   COOK: 5 MINUTES

- 1½ cups water
- 1 cup uncooked couscous
- ½ teaspoon dried oregano
- 1½ cups diced plum tomato
- 1 cup diced peeled cucumber
- ⅓ cup (1½ ounces) crumbled feta cheese
- ¼ cup small ripe olives, halved
- 3 tablespoons diced red onion
- 1 (15½-ounce) can chickpeas (garbanzo beans), drained
- ¼ cup water
- 3 tablespoons lemon juice
- 1½ tablespoons extra-virgin olive oil
- ¼ teaspoon salt
- ¼ teaspoon coarsely ground black pepper

1. Bring 1½ cups water to a boil in a medium saucepan; gradually stir in couscous and oregano. Remove from heat; cover and let stand 5 minutes. Fluff with a fork. Combine couscous, tomato, and next 5 ingredients. Combine ¼ cup water and next 4 ingredients; stir with a whisk. Pour dressing over couscous mixture; toss gently to coat. Yield: 7 servings (serving size: 1 cup).

CALORIES 212 (27% from fat); FAT 6.4g (sat 1.8g, mono 3.1g, poly 0.9g); PROTEIN 8.2g; CARB 32.2g; FIBER 3.1g; CHOL 7mg; IRON 2.1mg; SODIUM 292mg; CALC 70mg

LINGUINE WITH GARLIC-AND-RED PEPPER OIL

PREP: 8 MINUTES   COOK: 15 MINUTES

- 4 quarts water
- 1 pound uncooked linguine
- 3 tablespoons olive oil
- ½ teaspoon crushed red pepper
- 4 large garlic cloves, minced
- ½ cup chopped fresh parsley
- 1 teaspoon salt
- ½ teaspoon black pepper

1. Bring water to a rolling boil. Add pasta; cook 10 minutes or until "al dente." Drain; keep warm.

2. Heat oil in a large nonstick skillet over medium-high heat. Add red pepper, and cook 2 minutes. Add garlic; sauté 30 seconds or until lightly browned.

3. Remove skillet from heat; stir in pasta, ½ cup parsley, salt, and black pepper. Yield: 8 servings (serving size: 1 cup).

CALORIES 258 (21% from fat); FAT 6g (sat 0.8g, mono 3.9g, poly 0.8g); PROTEIN 7.4g; CARB 43g; FIBER 1.5g; CHOL 0mg; IRON 2.4mg; SODIUM 298mg; CALC 16mg

MEDITERRANEAN ORZO

PREP: 15 MINUTES

   2 quarts water
   1 cup uncooked orzo (rice-shaped
      pasta)
   1 cup water
  ½ ounce sun-dried tomatoes, packed
      without oil (about 6)
  ¼ cup (1 ounce) crumbled feta
      cheese
  ¼ cup chopped red onion
  ¼ cup chopped yellow bell pepper
  ¼ cup chopped green bell pepper
  ¼ cup chopped red bell pepper
   2 tablespoons chopped fresh parsley
   2 tablespoons sliced ripe olives
  ¼ teaspoon black pepper
   2 tablespoons red wine vinegar
 1½ teaspoons olive oil

1. Bring 2 quarts water to a rolling boil.
Add pasta; cook 6 minutes or until "al
dente." Drain; keep warm.
2. Bring 1 cup water to a boil in a small
saucepan. Add tomatoes; cook 2 minutes or until tender. Drain and chop.
Combine orzo, tomatoes, cheese, and
remaining ingredients; toss well. Yield:
4 servings (serving size: 1 cup).

CALORIES 196 (24% from fat); FAT 5.3g (sat 2g, mono 2.3g,
poly 0.6g); PROTEIN 6.8g; CARB 30.9g; FIBER 2g;
CHOL 9mg; IRON 2.3mg; SODIUM 242mg; CALC 70mg

THAI COCONUT NOODLES

PREP: 10 MINUTES
COOK: 12 MINUTES

*Rice sticks can be found in Asian
specialty food markets or in the Asian section of most supermarkets. For more information on rice sticks, see "Asian
Noodles," page 276.*

   2 cups snow peas, trimmed (about
      8 ounces)
   1 (8-ounce) package rice sticks
      (rice-flour noodles) or
      vermicelli, uncooked
   1 teaspoon dark sesame oil
  ½ cup chopped green onions
 1½ tablespoons minced peeled fresh
      ginger
   3 garlic cloves, minced
  ¾ cup light coconut milk
  ½ cup fat-free, less-sodium chicken
      broth
  ½ cup water
  ¼ cup tomato paste
 1½ teaspoons curry powder
  ¾ teaspoon salt
      Dash of ground red pepper
  ¼ cup minced fresh cilantro

1. Cook snow peas and rice sticks in
boiling water 3 minutes. Drain well.
2. Heat oil in a large nonstick skillet
over medium heat. Add onions, ginger,
and garlic, and sauté 2 minutes. Stir in
coconut milk and next 6 ingredients;
bring to a boil. Reduce heat, and simmer 2 minutes, stirring frequently.
Combine snow peas, rice sticks, and
green onion mixture in a large bowl,
and sprinkle with cilantro. Yield: 4 servings (serving size: 2 cups).

CALORIES 281 (14% from fat); FAT 4.3g (sat 1.6g, mono 0.6g,
poly 0.6g); PROTEIN 8g; CARB 55.6g; FIBER 2.5g;
CHOL 0mg; IRON 2.5mg; SODIUM 417mg; CALC 81mg

RIGATONI WITH BROCCOLI AND CANADIAN BACON

PREP: 8 MINUTES
COOK: 17 MINUTES

   2 quarts water
   4 ounces uncooked rigatoni (short
      tubular pasta)
   4 teaspoons olive oil, divided
   3 cups small broccoli florets
 1⅓ cups (2 x ½-inch) julienne-cut red
      bell pepper
  ½ (6-ounce) package Canadian
      bacon, cut into ¼-inch strips
   2 garlic cloves, minced

1. Bring water to a rolling boil. Add
pasta; cook 10 minutes or until "al
dente." Drain rigatoni, and keep warm.
2. Place a large nonstick skillet over
medium-high heat until hot. Add 1 tablespoon oil. Add broccoli, and cook 8
minutes or until very brown, stirring often. Remove broccoli from skillet.
3. Add 1 teaspoon oil to skillet, and
place over medium-high heat until hot.
Add bell pepper, and cook 5 minutes or
just until bell pepper begins to blacken.
Reduce heat; return broccoli to skillet.
Add Canadian bacon and garlic; cook 2
minutes, stirring occasionally.
4. Combine pasta and broccoli mixture
in a bowl; toss well. Yield: 5 servings
(serving size: 1 cup).

CALORIES 164 (30% from fat); FAT 5.4g (sat 1g, mono 3.3g,
poly 0.7g); PROTEIN 8g; CARB 21.5g; FIBER 2.4g;
CHOL 9mg; IRON 1.8mg; SODIUM 254mg; CALC 30mg

CHILE NOODLES

PREP: 16 MINUTES
COOK: 5 MINUTES

Because of the hot-and-sour dressing, these stir-fried noodles complement grilled meats and seafood.

- 1 (8-ounce) package soba (buckwheat noodles), uncooked
- ½ cup low-sodium soy sauce
- ¼ cup mirin (sweet rice wine)
- 2 tablespoons sugar
- 3 tablespoons Chinese black vinegar or Worcestershire sauce
- 2 teaspoons dark sesame oil
- 1 teaspoon vegetable oil
- 2½ tablespoons minced peeled fresh ginger
- 10 garlic cloves, minced
- ½ teaspoon crushed red pepper
- 2 cups vertically sliced red onion
- 2½ cups julienne-cut zucchini (about 2 medium)
- 2½ cups julienne-cut yellow squash (about 3 small)
- ¼ cup minced fresh parsley

1. Cook soba in boiling water 4 minutes; drain. Rinse with cold water; drain and set aside.
2. Combine soy sauce, mirin, sugar, and black vinegar in a bowl; set aside.
3. Heat oils in a large nonstick skillet or wok over medium-high heat. Add ginger, garlic, and red pepper; stir-fry 15 seconds. Add onion; stir-fry 1 minute. Add zucchini and squash; stir-fry 1½ minutes or until crisp-tender. Remove from heat; add noodles, soy sauce mixture, and parsley, tossing gently to coat. Yield: 6 servings (serving size: 1 cup).

CALORIES 214 (13% from fat); FAT 3g (sat 0.4g, mono 0.9g, poly 1.1g); PROTEIN 6.4g; CARB 36.7g; FIBER 2.3g; CHOL 0mg; IRON 1.4mg; SODIUM 763mg; CALC 47mg

THE ASIAN PANTRY

The following is a list of pantry staples for a taste from Asia. We've allowed East to meet West as we've combined these great Asian flavors with the simplicity of pasta.

Fresh ginger A little ginger goes a long way. It can be stored in the refrigerator for up to one month. For information on grating fresh ginger, see our techniques on page 286.

Garlic If you want to save yourself a lot of chopping, you can buy the preminced garlic in a jar; then simply measure it out.

Mirin Sold in many grocery stores, this sweet rice wine has a lower alcohol content than sake. Mirin balances the salty soy, hoisin, and fish sauce flavors that are used in Asian cooking. It's sold under the Kikkoman label as "sweet cooking seasoning."

Sesame oil The dark variety imparts a rich, nutty flavor to foods.

Soy sauce Soy sauce is in most Asian recipes. We call for the low-sodium version.

JAPANESE NOODLES

PREP: 8 MINUTES
COOK: 14 MINUTES

- 2 quarts water
- 6 ounces uncooked vermicelli or thin lo mein noodles
- 1 tablespoon dark sesame oil
- 2 teaspoons grated peeled fresh ginger
- 1 cup (1½-inch) julienne-cut green onions
- 2½ tablespoons low-sodium soy sauce
- 1 tablespoon seasoned rice vinegar

1. Bring water to a rolling boil. Add pasta; cook 5 minutes or until "al dente." Drain; keep warm.
2. Heat oil in a large nonstick skillet over medium-high heat. Add ginger; sauté 30 seconds. Add vermicelli, tossing to coat with oil. Add green onions; sauté 3 minutes or until tender. Remove from heat. Add soy sauce and vinegar; toss well. Yield: 3 servings (serving size: 1 cup).

CALORIES 264 (19% from fat); FAT 5.5g (sat 0.8g, mono 1.9g, poly 2.3g); PROTEIN 8.2g; CARB 44.8g; FIBER 1.8g; CHOL 0mg; IRON 2.7mg; SODIUM 410mg; CALC 24mg

PASTA WITH FRESH TOMATOES

PREP: 20 MINUTES   COOK: 5 MINUTES

- 3 quarts water
- 12 ounces uncooked vermicelli
- 4 cups diced seeded tomato
- 3 tablespoons chopped fresh oregano
- 3 tablespoons minced green onions
- 3 tablespoons fresh lemon juice
- 1 tablespoon olive oil
- 1 teaspoon coriander seeds, crushed
- ¼ teaspoon salt
- ⅛ teaspoon crushed red pepper
- 2 garlic cloves, minced

1. Bring water to a rolling boil. Add pasta; cook 5 minutes or until "al dente." Drain.
2. Combine tomato and remaining 8 ingredients in a large bowl. Add pasta to tomato mixture; toss well. Serve at room temperature. Yield: 8 servings (serving size: 1 cup).

CALORIES 168 (14% from fat); FAT 2.6g (sat 0.4g, mono 1.4g, poly 0.5g); PROTEIN 5.4g; CARB 31.3g; FIBER 1.9g; CHOL 0mg; IRON 2mg; SODIUM 83mg; CALC 23mg

main-dish pastas
Here's the long and short—from the sheets of lasagna to the spirals of rotini. They each let their nooks and crannies capture the essence of their sauces.

PASTA JAMBALAYA

PREP: 10 MINUTES
COOK: 16 MINUTES

This pasta-based dish combines two regional flavors: Louisianan and Southwestern. It's a spicy entrée that can be served hot or cold.

3   quarts water
2½ cups uncooked penne
       (tube-shaped pasta)
Cooking spray
½ cup diced onion
½ cup diced red bell pepper
1   garlic clove, minced
1   teaspoon Cajun seasoning
1   (15-ounce) can black beans,
       rinsed and drained
1   (10-ounce) can diced tomatoes
       and green chiles, undrained
3   ounces smoked turkey sausage,
       halved lengthwise and thinly
       sliced
½ cup (2 ounces) preshredded
       reduced-fat four-cheese
       Mexican blend cheese (such as
       Sargento)

1. Bring water to a rolling boil. Add pasta; cook 10 minutes or until "al dente." Drain; keep warm.
2. Place a large nonstick skillet coated with cooking spray over medium-high heat until hot. Add onion, bell pepper, and garlic; sauté 5 minutes. Add Cajun seasoning; sauté 1 minute. Stir in beans, tomatoes, and sausage; bring to a boil. Reduce heat; simmer 10 minutes or until thickened.
3. Combine bean mixture and pasta in a large bowl, and top with cheese. Serve immediately. Yield: 8 servings (serving size: 1 cup).

CALORIES 221 (22% from fat); FAT 5.3g (sat 2.5g, mono 1.9g, poly 0.4g); PROTEIN 9.8g; CARB 32.4g; FIBER 3.1g; CHOL 11.5mg; IRON 2.1mg; SODIUM 596mg; CALC 79mg

PASTA PUTTANESCA

PREP: 18 MINUTES
COOK: 16 MINUTES

(pictured on page 243)

2   quarts water
8   ounces uncooked vermicelli
1   tablespoon extra-virgin olive oil
3   garlic cloves, minced
3½ cups diced plum tomato
¼ cup minced fresh flat-leaf parsley
3   tablespoons green olives, coarsely
       chopped
2   tablespoons minced fresh or
       2 teaspoons dried oregano
1½ tablespoons capers
2   teaspoons anchovy paste
⅛ to ¼ teaspoon crushed red
       pepper
Oregano sprigs (optional)

1. Bring water to a rolling boil. Add pasta; cook 5 minutes or until "al dente." Drain; keep warm.
2. Heat oil in a nonstick skillet over medium-low heat. Add garlic; cook 5 minutes. Add tomato and next 6 ingredients. Bring to a boil over medium-high heat; cook 8 minutes or until thick. Combine tomato mixture and pasta; toss well. Garnish with oregano sprigs, if desired. Yield: 4 servings (serving size: 1½ cups).

CALORIES 300 (20% from fat); FAT 6.6g (sat 0.9g, mono 3.7g, poly 1.2g); PROTEIN 9.7g; CARB 51.6g; FIBER 3.6g; CHOL 0mg; IRON 3.7mg; SODIUM 696mg; CALC 47mg

ARTICHOKE MARINARA

PREP: 19 MINUTES
COOK: 15 MINUTES

4   quarts water
16 ounces uncooked angel
       hair pasta
4   (14-ounce) cans artichoke
       hearts, drained
8   large egg whites
4   large eggs
⅔ cup grated Parmesan cheese
½ cup dry breadcrumbs
4   teaspoons dried Italian seasoning
1   teaspoon black pepper
¾ cup all-purpose flour
Cooking spray
4   cups bottled fat-free marinara
       sauce, warmed
½ cup chopped fresh flat-leaf
       parsley

1. Preheat oven to 400°.
2. Bring water to a rolling boil. Add pasta; cook 2 to 3 minutes or until "al dente." Drain; keep warm.
3. Place 24 artichokes in a colander, squeezing each artichoke gently to remove juice from artichokes. (Reserve any remaining artichokes for another use.)
4. Combine egg whites and next 5 ingredients; stir with a whisk. Working with 1 artichoke at a time, dredge artichokes in flour and dip in egg white mixture. Coat a large nonstick skillet with cooking spray; place over medium-high heat until hot. Add 12 artichokes to skillet; cook 3 minutes, turning to brown on all sides. Remove artichokes from skillet; place on a baking sheet coated with cooking spray. Repeat procedure with remaining 12 artichokes, flour, and egg white mixture.

5. Bake artichokes at 400° for 15 minutes. Serve artichokes and warm marinara sauce over pasta. Sprinkle with parsley. Yield: 8 servings (serving size: 3 artichokes, 1 cup pasta, and ½ cup marinara sauce).

CALORIES 466 (18% from fat); FAT 9.2g (sat 2.3g, mono 3.6g, poly 2.1g); PROTEIN 21.2g; CARB 79.5g; FIBER 3.9g; CHOL 73mg; IRON 6.4mg; SODIUM 808mg; CALC 187mg

NOODLE FRITTATA

PREP:12 MINUTES   COOK:22 MINUTES

    2 quarts water
    2 ounces uncooked angel hair pasta
    2 teaspoons vegetable oil
    1 cup chopped broccoli florets
    ½ cup diced carrot
    ½ cup frozen green peas, thawed
    4 large eggs, lightly beaten
    2 large egg whites, lightly beaten
    ⅛ teaspoon salt
    ⅛ teaspoon black pepper
    ½ cup (2 ounces) shredded reduced-fat sharp cheddar cheese
    ½ cup low-fat vegetable primavera spaghetti sauce, warmed

1. Bring water to a rolling boil. Break pasta into fourths; add to water, and cook 3 to 4 minutes or until "al dente." Drain; keep warm.
2. Heat oil in a large nonstick skillet over medium heat. Add broccoli, carrot, and peas; sauté 8 minutes. Stir in pasta; sauté 1 minute. Combine eggs, egg whites, salt, and pepper in a large bowl; stir well with a whisk. Pour over vegetable mixture; cook over medium heat 5 minutes. Top with cheese.
3. Preheat broiler.
4. Wrap handle of skillet with foil; broil frittata 1½ minutes or until cheese melts. Let stand 2 minutes before cutting. Serve with pasta sauce. Yield: 4 servings (serving size: 1 wedge and 2 tablespoons sauce).

CALORIES 278 (36% from fat); FAT 11.1g (sat 3.6g, mono 3.4g, poly 2g); PROTEIN 18.6g; CARB 35.3g; FIBER 3.1g; CHOL 222mg; IRON 4.1mg; SODIUM 959mg; CALC 231mg

CAVATAPPI WITH SPINACH, BEANS, AND ASIAGO CHEESE

PREP:15 MINUTES

    8 cups coarsely chopped spinach leaves
    4 cups hot cooked cavatappi (about 6 ounces uncooked spiral-shaped pasta)
    2 tablespoons olive oil
    ¼ teaspoon salt
    ¼ teaspoon pepper
    1 (19-ounce) can cannellini beans or other white beans, drained
    2 garlic cloves
    ½ cup (2 ounces) shredded Asiago cheese
    Freshly ground black pepper (optional)

1. Combine first 8 ingredients in a large bowl; toss well. Sprinkle with freshly ground black pepper, if desired. Yield: 4 servings (serving size: 2 cups).

CALORIES 401 (27% from fat); FAT 12g (sat 3.4g, mono 6.2g, poly 1.2g); PROTEIN 18.8g; CARB 54.7g; FIBER 6.7g; CHOL 10mg; IRON 6.4mg; SODIUM 464mg; CALC 306mg

Cavatappi With Spinach, Beans, and Asiago Cheese

HOT-AND-HOPPIN' CAVATAPPI

PREP: 30 MINUTES   COOK: 25 MINUTES

Be sure to use the hot pepper sauce that we call for because it contains whole peppers packed in vinegar. Using red-colored hot sauce won't yield good results.

  2 cups water
1½ cups frozen black-eyed peas
  1 teaspoon dried thyme
  2 bay leaves
  ½ cup chopped sun-dried tomatoes, packed without oil
1½ teaspoons hot pepper sauce (such as Cajun Chef)
  2 quarts water
  6 ounces uncooked cavatappi (spiral-shaped pasta)
  ½ cup sliced green onions
  ½ cup chopped fresh parsley
  3 ounces very thinly sliced prosciutto or lean ham, chopped
  ¼ cup hot pepper sauce (such as Cajun Chef)
  1 tablespoon extra-virgin olive oil
  ½ teaspoon dry mustard
  2 tablespoons finely chopped fresh green chile or canned chopped green chiles, drained
  3 garlic cloves, minced

1. Combine first 4 ingredients in a large saucepan; bring to a boil. Cover, reduce heat, and simmer 15 minutes or until peas are tender. Add sun-dried tomatoes and 1½ teaspoons pepper sauce; simmer 5 minutes or until tomatoes are tender. Remove 2 tablespoons cooking liquid from black-eyed pea mixture; set aside. Drain pea mixture; discard bay leaves.
2. Bring 2 quarts water to a rolling boil. Add pasta; cook 8 minutes or until "al dente." Drain.
3. Combine black-eyed pea mixture, pasta, onions, parsley, and prosciutto in a

large bowl. Combine reserved cooking liquid, ¼ cup pepper sauce, and remaining 4 ingredients in a small bowl; stir well with a whisk. Pour chile mixture over pasta mixture; toss well. Serve warm. Yield: 4 servings (serving size: 1½ cups).

CALORIES 349 (19% from fat); FAT 7.4g (sat 1.4g, mono 3.6g, poly 1g); PROTEIN 17.4g; CARB 54g; FIBER 3.5g; CHOL 13mg; IRON 4.7mg; SODIUM 621mg; CALC 55mg

BOW TIE CARBONARA WITH ASPARAGUS

PREP: 14 MINUTES   COOK: 19 MINUTES

  2 quarts water
  8 ounces uncooked farfalle (bow tie pasta)
2½ cups (1-inch) diagonally sliced asparagus
  6 tablespoons (1½ ounces) grated fresh Parmesan cheese, divided
  ¼ cup fat-free milk
  ¼ cup egg substitute
  2 tablespoons chopped fresh chives
  ¼ teaspoon salt
  2 bacon slices
  ¾ cup chopped onion
  2 garlic cloves, minced
Freshly ground black pepper
Chopped fresh chives (optional)

1. Bring 2 quarts water to a rolling boil. Add pasta; cook 11 minutes or until "al dente." Drain; keep warm.
2. Bring water to a boil in a medium saucepan; add asparagus. Cook 5 minutes or until crisp-tender. Drain; set aside.
3. Combine 2 tablespoons cheese, milk, egg substitute, 2 tablespoons chives, and salt in a small bowl; set aside.
4. Cook bacon in a large nonstick skillet over medium-high heat until crisp. Remove bacon, and crumble. Add onion and garlic to bacon drippings in pan; sauté 5 minutes or until tender. Remove from heat; stir in asparagus and bacon.

5. Combine asparagus mixture, pasta, and milk mixture in a large bowl. Divide evenly among 4 shallow bowls; top each serving with 1 tablespoon cheese. Sprinkle with pepper, and top with chives, if desired. Yield: 4 servings (serving size: 1½ cups).

CALORIES 302 (15% from fat); FAT 5g (sat 2.1g, mono 1.6g, poly 0.7g); PROTEIN 15.2g; CARB 49.2g; FIBER 3.3g; CHOL 9mg; IRON 3.3mg; SODIUM 368mg; CALC 150mg

PASTA WITH TOMATOES AND BEANS

PREP: 15 MINUTES
COOK: 6 MINUTES

  2 quarts water
  6 ounces uncooked angel hair pasta
  2 teaspoons olive oil
  2 cups chopped tomato
  2 garlic cloves, minced
  1 (15½-ounce) can chickpeas (garbanzo beans), drained
  ½ cup chopped fresh basil
  ½ teaspoon salt
  ¼ teaspoon black pepper
  ½ cup (2 ounces) grated Asiago cheese
  2 tablespoons balsamic vinegar

1. Bring water to a rolling boil. Add pasta; cook 3 minutes or until "al dente." Drain; keep warm.
2. Heat olive oil in a Dutch oven over medium-high heat. Add tomato and garlic, and sauté 2 minutes. Add pasta, chickpeas, chopped basil, salt, and pepper; cook 2 minutes. Stir in cheese and vinegar. Yield: 4 servings (serving size: 1¼ cups).

CALORIES 359 (21% from fat); FAT 8.5g (sat 2.9g, mono 3.2g, poly 1.5g); PROTEIN 17.1g; CARB 54.9g; FIBER 4.3g; CHOL 9mg; IRON 4mg; SODIUM 658mg; CALC 222mg

FETTUCCINE ALFREDO

PREP:15 MINUTES   COOK:12 MINUTES

Light cream cheese makes this low-fat alfredo sauce taste rich. However, for a smooth sauce it needs to melt separately, and then be added to the white sauce. We did this in the Dutch oven where the pasta was prepared—one less pot to wash.

    2   quarts water
    8   ounces uncooked fettuccine
    1   tablespoon stick margarine or
          butter
    2   garlic cloves, minced
    1   tablespoon all-purpose flour
 1⅓ cups fat-free milk
 1¼ cups (5 ounces) grated fresh
          Parmesan cheese, divided
    2   tablespoons tub-style light cream
          cheese
    2   teaspoons chopped fresh parsley
 Freshly ground black pepper

1. Bring water to a rolling boil in a Dutch oven. Add pasta; cook 10 minutes or until "al dente." Drain.
2. Melt margarine in pan over medium heat. Add garlic; sauté 1 minute. Stir in flour. Gradually add milk, stirring with a whisk until blended; cook until thickened and bubbly (about 8 minutes), stirring constantly. Add 1 cup Parmesan cheese, stirring constantly until it melts.
3. Rinse pasta well with hot water. Set aside. Add cream cheese to pan; cook over low heat, stirring until it melts. Gradually add cheese sauce to melted cream cheese, stirring constantly.
4. Add cooked pasta to sauce mixture, tossing well. Spoon into a serving dish; top with ¼ cup Parmesan cheese, parsley, and pepper. Yield: 4 servings (serving size: 1 cup).

CALORIES 386 (27% from fat); FAT 11.5g (sat 5.6g, mono 3.6g, poly 1.5g); PROTEIN 19.9g; CARB 49.5g; FIBER 1.4g; CHOL 23mg; IRON 2.6mg; SODIUM 517mg; CALC 418mg

THREE-HERB FETTUCCINE WITH VEGETABLES AND SHAVED ASIAGO

PREP:30 MINUTES
COOK:7 MINUTES

Asiago adds a sharp note to this fresh vegetable pasta. If using dried pasta, remember to adjust the cooking time.

    4   quarts water
    1   pound uncooked fresh fettuccine
    2   cups sugar snap peas, trimmed
    1   tablespoon olive oil
    4   garlic cloves, minced
 2½ cups chopped spinach, divided
    ½   cup (½-inch) sliced green onions
    2   zucchini, halved lengthwise and
          thinly sliced (about 3 cups)
    1   cup canned vegetable broth
    2   green tomatoes, peeled, seeded,
          and cut into thin wedges
    ½   cup thinly sliced fresh basil
    2   tablespoons chopped fresh chives
    2   tablespoons chopped fresh oregano
    ½   teaspoon salt
    ½   teaspoon freshly ground black pepper
    4   ounces shaved Asiago cheese

1. Bring water to a rolling boil. Add pasta; cook about 3 minutes or until "al dente." Drain; keep warm.
2. Add peas to a skillet of boiling water; cook 30 seconds. Drain; rinse with cold water.
3. Heat oil in skillet over medium heat. Add garlic; sauté 15 seconds. Add peas, 1¼ cups spinach, green onions, and zucchini; sauté 2 minutes. Add broth and tomatoes; cook 2 minutes, stirring occasionally. Add 1¼ cups spinach, basil, and next 4 ingredients; cook 3 minutes, stirring occasionally.
4. Spoon vegetable mixture over pasta, and top with cheese; toss gently. Yield: 6 servings (serving size: 2 cups).

CALORIES 427 (19% from fat); FAT 8.9g (sat 3.7g, mono 3.3g, poly 1g); PROTEIN 19.6g; CARB 67.7g; FIBER 4.6g; CHOL 13mg; IRON 5.1mg; SODIUM 695mg; CALC 307mg

LAZY LASAGNA

PREP:20 MINUTES
COOK:35 MINUTES

Precooked noodles and prepackaged convenience products make this easy to prepare.

    1   pound ground round
    1   (26-ounce) bottle low-fat
          pasta sauce
    ½   cup water
    2   cups fat-free cottage cheese
    2   tablespoons grated Parmesan cheese
 Cooking spray
    1   (8-ounce) package precooked
          lasagna noodles
    1   cup (4 ounces) preshredded
          reduced-fat mild cheddar cheese
 Chopped fresh parsley (optional)

1. Preheat oven to 350°.
2. Cook beef in a large nonstick skillet over medium-high heat until browned, stirring to crumble. Drain; wipe drippings from pan with paper towels. Return beef to pan. Stir in pasta sauce and water; bring to a boil. Reduce heat, and simmer 5 minutes. Combine cottage and Parmesan cheeses in a bowl.
3. Spread ½ cup beef mixture in bottom of a 13 x 9-inch baking dish coated with cooking spray. Arrange 4 noodles over beef mixture; top with half of cottage cheese mixture, 1 cup beef mixture, and ⅓ cup cheddar cheese. Repeat layers once, ending with noodles. Spread remaining beef mixture over noodles. Cover and bake at 350° for 30 minutes. Uncover; sprinkle with ⅓ cup cheddar cheese, and bake 5 additional minutes or until cheese melts. Let stand 10 minutes before serving. Garnish with parsley, if desired. Yield: 9 servings.

CALORIES 273 (25% from fat); FAT 7.5g (sat 2.8g, mono 2.8g, poly 0.7g); PROTEIN 25.7g; CARB 24.5g; FIBER 2.5g; CHOL 42mg; IRON 2.4mg; SODIUM 536mg; CALC 162mg

HEARTY LASAGNA

PREP: 55 MINUTES
COOK: 1 HOUR 10 MINUTES

¾   pound ground round
Cooking spray
1   cup chopped onion
3   garlic cloves, minced
¼   cup chopped fresh parsley, divided
1   (28-ounce) can whole tomatoes,
      undrained and chopped
1   (14½-ounce) can Italian-style
      stewed tomatoes, undrained and
      chopped
1   (8-ounce) can no-salt-added
      tomato sauce
1   (6-ounce) can tomato paste
2   teaspoons dried oregano
1   teaspoon dried basil
¼   teaspoon black pepper
4   quarts water
12   uncooked lasagna noodles
2   cups fat-free cottage cheese
½   cup (2 ounces) finely grated fresh
      Parmesan cheese
1   (15-ounce) carton fat-free
      ricotta cheese
1   large egg white, lightly beaten
2   cups (8 ounces) shredded
      provolone cheese
Oregano sprigs (optional)

1. Cook beef in a large saucepan over medium heat until browned; stir to crumble. Drain well. Wipe pan with a paper towel.

2. Coat pan with cooking spray; add onion and garlic, and sauté 5 minutes. Return beef to pan. Add 2 tablespoons parsley, chopped whole tomatoes, and next 6 ingredients. Bring to a boil. Cover, reduce heat, and simmer 15 minutes. Uncover; simmer 20 minutes. Remove from heat.

3. Bring 4 quarts water to a rolling boil. Add pasta; cook 12 minutes or until "al dente." Drain and set aside.

Hearty Lasagna

4. Preheat oven to 350°.

5. Combine 2 tablespoons parsley, cottage cheese, Parmesan, ricotta, and egg white in a bowl.

6. Spread ¾ cup tomato mixture in bottom of a 13 x 9-inch baking dish coated with cooking spray. Arrange 4 noodles over tomato mixture; top with half of cottage cheese mixture, 2¼ cups tomato mixture, and ⅔ cup provolone. Repeat layers, ending with noodles. Spread remaining tomato mixture over noodles.

7. Cover dish, and bake at 350° for 1 hour. Sprinkle with ⅔ cup provolone; bake, uncovered, for 10 minutes. Let stand 10 minutes before serving. Garnish with oregano sprigs, if desired. Yield: 9 servings.

CALORIES 380 (25% from fat); FAT 10.5g (sat 5.7g, mono 3g, poly 0.7g); PROTEIN 33.4g; CARB 40.5g; FIBER 2.8g; CHOL 50mg; IRON 3.8mg; SODIUM 703mg; CALC 394mg

FRESH-TOMATO LASAGNA

PREP: 25 MINUTES

COOK: 1 HOUR 35 MINUTES

4½ cups chopped onion (about 3)
 2 garlic cloves, minced
 6 cups chopped seeded peeled
    tomato (about 3½ pounds)
 1 cup chopped fresh parsley
 2 teaspoons dried oregano
 ½ teaspoon salt
 ½ teaspoon dried thyme
 ½ teaspoon dried marjoram
 ½ teaspoon black pepper
 2 (6-ounce) cans Italian-style
    tomato paste
 ½ teaspoon dried basil
 1 (15-ounce) carton fat-free
    ricotta cheese
 1 (12.3-ounce) package reduced-
    fat firm tofu, drained
Cooking spray
12 cooked lasagna noodles
 2 cups (8 ounces) shredded sharp
    provolone cheese
 ½ cup (2 ounces) grated fresh
    Romano or Parmesan cheese

1. Heat a Dutch oven over medium-high heat until hot. Add onion and garlic; cover and cook 5 minutes, stirring occasionally. Add tomato and next 7 ingredients. Bring to a boil; cover, reduce heat, and simmer, 45 minutes, stirring occasionally.
2. Preheat oven to 350°.
3. Combine basil, ricotta, and tofu in a bowl; mash with a potato masher.
4. Spread 2 cups tomato sauce mixture in bottom of a 13 x 9-inch baking dish coated with cooking spray. Arrange 3 noodles over sauce; top with 1 cup tofu mixture, ½ cup provolone cheese, 2 tablespoons Romano, and 1½ cups sauce. Repeat layers twice, ending with noodles. Spread remaining tomato sauce mixture over noodles. Sprinkle with

½ cup provolone cheese and 2 tablespoons Romano. Bake at 350° for 45 minutes. Let stand 10 minutes before serving. Yield: 8 servings.

CALORIES 391 (26% from fat); FAT 11.1g (sat 6.3g, mono 2.9g, poly 1g); PROTEIN 27.7g; CARB 49.5g; FIBER 4.4g; CHOL 33mg; IRON 4.2mg; SODIUM 886mg; CALC 476mg

LASAGNA MARGHERITE

PREP: 15 MINUTES   COOK: 30 MINUTES

Be sure to purchase a package of dried, precooked lasagna noodles; they'll soften in the liquid of the casserole as it bakes.

 1 (26-ounce) bottle fat-free
    tomato-basil pasta sauce
Cooking spray
 1 (15-ounce) carton part-skim
    ricotta cheese
 ⅓ cup chopped fresh basil
 ¼ teaspoon crushed red pepper
 ¼ teaspoon salt
 6 precooked lasagna noodles
 ½ cup (2 ounces) preshredded fresh
    Parmesan cheese
 2 tablespoons chopped fresh basil

1. Preheat oven to 450°.
2. Spread ½ cup pasta sauce in bottom of an 8-inch square baking dish coated with cooking spray. Combine ricotta, ⅓ cup basil, crushed red pepper, and salt. Arrange 2 noodles over sauce; top with 1 cup ricotta mixture and ¾ cup sauce.
3. Repeat layers, ending with noodles. Spread remaining sauce over noodles. Cover and bake at 450° for 25 minutes or until noodles are tender and sauce is bubbly. Uncover lasagna, and top with Parmesan and 2 tablespoons basil. Bake lasagna an additional 5 minutes. Let stand 5 minutes. Yield: 4 servings.

CALORIES 413 (28% from fat); FAT 12.8g (sat 7.6g, mono 3.6g, poly 0.6g); PROTEIN 24.4g; CARB 49.4g; FIBER 2.3g; CHOL 43mg; IRON 4.1mg; SODIUM 899mg; CALC 485mg

LASAGNA-CHICKEN FLORENTINE

PREP: 20 MINUTES   COOK: 30 MINUTES

1½ tablespoons stick margarine or
    butter
 3 tablespoons all-purpose flour
 2 (12-ounce) cans evaporated
    fat-free milk
 ½ teaspoon salt
 ⅛ teaspoon ground nutmeg
Cooking spray
 6 precooked lasagna noodles
1½ cups shredded cooked chicken
    breast (about 7 ounces)
 1 (10-ounce) package frozen
    chopped spinach, thawed,
    drained, and squeezed dry
 ½ teaspoon freshly ground black
    pepper
 ¾ cup (3 ounces) preshredded
    reduced-fat pizza-blend cheese or
    cheddar cheese

1. Preheat oven to 450°.
2. Melt margarine in a medium saucepan over medium heat. Add flour; cook 30 seconds, stirring constantly. Gradually add milk, stirring with a whisk until blended. Stir in salt and nutmeg; cook until thick (about 5 minutes), stirring constantly.
3. Spread ½ cup sauce in bottom of an 8-inch square baking dish coated with cooking spray. Arrange 2 noodles over sauce; top with half of chicken and half of spinach. Sprinkle with ¼ teaspoon pepper; top with ¾ cup sauce. Repeat layers, ending with noodles. Spread remaining sauce over noodles. Cover; bake at 450° for 25 minutes or until noodles are tender and sauce is bubbly. Uncover and top with cheese; bake 5 additional minutes or until cheese melts. Let stand 5 minutes. Yield: 4 servings.

CALORIES 453 (17% from fat); FAT 8.4g (sat 2.4g, mono 3g, poly 2.1g); PROTEIN 41.6g; CARB 54.9g; FIBER 3.5g; CHOL 53mg; IRON 4mg; SODIUM 804mg; CALC 686mg

Cleaning Clams

1. Clams are available fresh shucked, shucked and canned, or unshucked. When purchasing fresh unshucked clams, you'll need to thoroughly rinse them before using. Discard any that are opened or cracked or any heavy ones (they're filled with sand).

2. Scrub clams under cold running water using a stiff brush to remove sand and dirt.

LINGUINE WITH CLAM SAUCE

PREP: 15 MINUTES   COOK: 10 MINUTES

Leaving the clams in their shells adds visual interest to this dish.

    4   quarts water
   16   ounces uncooked linguine
    2   teaspoons olive oil
    3   tablespoons chopped shallots
  1½   cups dry white wine
   ⅓   cup minced fresh flat-leaf parsley
   ½   teaspoon salt
   ¼   to ½ teaspoon crushed red pepper
   ¼   teaspoon black pepper
    8   garlic cloves, minced
   36   small clams in shells (about 2
          pounds), scrubbed
    4   lemon wedges

1. Bring water to a rolling boil. Add pasta; cook 10 minutes or until "al dente." Drain; keep warm.
2. Heat oil in a large nonstick skillet over medium-high heat. Add shallots; sauté 2 minutes. Add wine and next 5 ingredients; bring to a boil. Add clams; cover and cook 5 minutes or until shells open. Remove clams from pan with a slotted spoon. Discard any unopened shells.
3. Place pasta in 4 shallow bowls; spoon wine sauce over pasta, and top with clams. Serve with lemon wedges. Yield: 4 servings (serving size: 2 cups pasta, ½ cup wine sauce, and 9 clams).

CALORIES 520 (8% from fat); FAT 4.9g (sat 0.6g, mono 2g, poly 1.2g); PROTEIN 25.6g; CARB 91.3g; FIBER 3g; CHOL 28mg; IRON 16.4mg; SODIUM 356mg; CALC 82mg

LINGUINE WITH PESTO AND TOMATOES

PREP: 13 MINUTES   COOK: 10 MINUTES

You can substitute feta cheese for goat cheese, if desired.

    3   quarts water
   12   ounces uncooked linguine
   ½   cup Basil Pesto
   ¼   cup water
    2   to 2½ cups sliced plum tomato
          (about 4 medium plum
          tomatoes)
    2   tablespoons chopped fresh basil
   ¼   cup (1 ounce) crumbled goat
          cheese
   ½   teaspoon salt

1. Bring 3 quarts water to a rolling boil. Add pasta; cook 10 minutes or until "al dente." Drain well.
2. Combine Basil Pesto and ¼ cup water in a jar; cover tightly, and shake vigorously.
3. Combine pesto mixture and pasta in a large bowl, and toss well. Add tomato slices, basil, cheese, and salt, tossing gently to coat. Yield: 4 servings (serving size: 1½ cups).

BASIL PESTO

    2   tablespoons pine nuts,
          toasted
    2   large garlic cloves
  2¾   cups loosely packed fresh
          basil leaves (about 1.3 ounces)
    2   tablespoons grated fresh
          Parmesan cheese
    2   teaspoons lemon juice
    3   tablespoons extra-virgin
          olive oil

1. Drop pine nuts and garlic through food chute with food processor on, and process until minced. Add basil, cheese, and lemon juice; process until finely minced. With processor on, slowly pour oil through food chute; process until well-blended. Yield: ½ cup.

CALORIES 495 (33% from fat); FAT 18.1g (sat 4.1g, mono 9.7g, poly 3.1g); PROTEIN 15.7g; CARB 68.7g; FIBER 2.9g; CHOL 11mg; IRON 4.3mg; SODIUM 459mg; CALC 120mg

Linguine With Two Sauces

PREP: 40 MINUTES
COOK: 25 MINUTES

2 teaspoons olive oil
2 garlic cloves, minced
1 tablespoon chopped fresh basil
¼ teaspoon black pepper
¼ teaspoon salt
2 (14.5-ounce) cans Italian-style
  diced tomatoes, undrained
4 quarts water
1 pound uncooked linguine
Cooking spray
4 cups sliced cremini or button
  mushrooms (about 12 ounces)
½ cup all-purpose flour
2 cups 1% low-fat milk
1 cup (4 ounces) shredded reduced-
  fat, reduced-sodium Swiss
  cheese (such as Alpine Lace)
½ cup dry white wine
½ teaspoon black pepper
¼ teaspoon salt
¼ cup (1 ounce) grated fresh
  Parmesan cheese
Oregano sprigs (optional)

1. Preheat oven to 350°.

2. Heat oil in a nonstick skillet over medium heat. Add garlic, and sauté 30 seconds. Add basil, ¼ teaspoon pepper, ¼ teaspoon salt, and tomatoes; cook over low heat 20 minutes, stirring occasionally. Set aside.

3. Bring 4 quarts water to a rolling boil. Add pasta; cook 10 minutes or until "al dente." Drain; keep warm.

4. Place a large saucepan coated with cooking spray over medium-high heat until hot. Add mushrooms, and cook 5 minutes. Remove from pan; set aside. Add flour to saucepan. Gradually add milk, stirring with a whisk until blended. Place flour mixture over medium heat, and cook until thick (about 3 minutes),

Linguine With Two Sauces

stirring constantly. Stir in Swiss cheese, wine, ½ teaspoon pepper, and ¼ teaspoon salt. Cook until cheese melts (about 1 minute), stirring constantly. Remove from heat; stir in mushrooms.

5. Combine linguine and mushroom sauce in a large bowl. Spoon linguine mixture into a 13 x 9-inch baking dish coated with cooking spray. Spread tomato sauce over linguine mixture; sprinkle with Parmesan cheese. Cover and bake at 350° for 20 minutes. Uncover and bake an additional 5 minutes. Garnish with oregano sprigs, if desired. Yield: 8 servings (serving size: 1¼ cups).

CALORIES 349 (19% from fat); FAT 7.2g (sat 3.4g, mono 1.4g, poly 0.6g); PROTEIN 16.3g; CARB 54.8g; FIBER 3.2g; CHOL 15mg; IRON 3.3mg; SODIUM 527mg; CALC 172mg

GREEK MACARONI AND CHEESE

PREP: 23 MINUTES   COOK: 41 MINUTES

3 quarts water
3 cups uncooked medium elbow
   macaroni
⅓ cup all-purpose flour
2¼ cups 1% low-fat milk
¾ cup (3 ounces) shredded fontina
   cheese
⅔ cup (2⅔ ounces) crumbled feta
   cheese
½ cup (2 ounces) grated fresh
   Parmesan cheese
3 ounces light processed cheese
   (such as Velveeta Light), cubed
¼ teaspoon salt
1 (10-ounce) package frozen
   chopped spinach, thawed,
   drained, and squeezed dry
Cooking spray
⅓ cup crushed onion melba snack
   crackers (about 12 crackers)
1 tablespoon reduced-calorie stick
   margarine, softened

1. Preheat oven to 375°.
2. Bring water to a rolling boil. Add pasta; cook 5 minutes or until "al dente." Drain.
3. Place flour in a large saucepan. Gradually add milk, stirring with a whisk until blended. Place over medium heat; cook until thick (about 8 minutes), stirring constantly. Add cheeses; cook 3 minutes or until cheese melts, stirring frequently. Remove from heat; stir in macaroni, salt, and spinach.
4. Spoon macaroni mixture into a 2-quart casserole coated with cooking spray. Combine crushed crackers and margarine. Sprinkle over macaroni mixture. Bake at 375° for 30 minutes or until bubbly. Yield: 8 servings (serving size: 1 cup).

CALORIES 306 (32% from fat); FAT 10.9g (sat 6g, mono 2.9g, poly 1.1g); PROTEIN 17.2g; CARB 34.8g; FIBER 2.6g; CHOL 32mg; IRON 3mg; SODIUM 596mg; CALC 398mg

CREAMY FOUR-CHEESE MACARONI

PREP: 15 MINUTES
COOK: 41 MINUTES

3 quarts water
3 cups uncooked medium elbow
   macaroni
⅓ cup all-purpose flour
2⅔ cups 1% low-fat milk
¾ cup (3 ounces) shredded fontina
   cheese or Swiss cheese
½ cup (2 ounces) grated fresh
   Parmesan cheese
½ cup (2 ounces) shredded
   extra-sharp cheddar cheese
3 ounces light processed cheese
   (such as Velveeta Light), cubed
¼ teaspoon salt
Cooking spray
⅓ cup crushed onion melba snack
   crackers (about 12 crackers)
1 tablespoon reduced-calorie
   margarine, softened

1. Preheat oven to 375°.
2. Bring water to a rolling boil. Add pasta; cook 5 minutes or until "al dente." Drain.
3. Place flour in a large saucepan. Gradually add milk, stirring with a whisk until blended. Place over medium heat; cook until thick (about 8 minutes), stirring constantly. Add cheeses; cook 3 minutes or until cheese melts, stirring frequently. Remove from heat, and stir in macaroni and salt.
4. Spoon macaroni mixture into a 2-quart casserole coated with cooking spray. Combine crushed crackers and margarine in a small bowl; sprinkle over macaroni mixture. Bake at 375° for 30 minutes or until bubbly. Yield: 8 servings (serving size: 1 cup).

CALORIES 350 (29% from fat); FAT 11.2g (sat 6.3g, mono 2.9g, poly 0.9g); PROTEIN 18g; CARB 42.4g; FIBER 2.1g; CHOL 32mg; IRON 1.9mg; SODIUM 497mg; CALC 306mg

PASTA E FAGIOLI

PREP: 16 MINUTES   STAND: 1 HOUR
COOK: 2½ HOURS

Almost any small bean (such as pinto or garbanzo) works in this traditional Italian dish.

1 pound dried navy beans
1 tablespoon olive oil
1 cup chopped onion
½ cup sliced carrot
½ cup chopped celery
2 garlic cloves, crushed
1 (28-ounce) can diced tomatoes,
   undrained
9 cups water
¼ teaspoon crushed red pepper
1 bay leaf
1½ teaspoons salt
1 teaspoon dried oregano
½ teaspoon dried thyme
¼ teaspoon dried rosemary
2 garlic cloves, crushed
¾ cup uncooked medium elbow
   macaroni
½ cup chopped fresh flat-leaf parsley
½ teaspoon black pepper
1 cup (4 ounces) grated fresh
   Parmesan cheese

1. Sort and wash beans, and place in a large Dutch oven. Cover with water to 2 inches above beans; bring to a boil, and cook 2 minutes. Remove from heat; cover and let stand 1 hour. Drain beans.
2. Heat oil in pan over medium heat until hot. Add onion, carrot, and celery; sauté 5 minutes or until tender. Add 2 garlic cloves; sauté 1 minute. Add tomatoes; bring to a boil. Cover, reduce heat, and simmer 10 minutes, stirring occasionally. Add beans, 9 cups water, red pepper, and bay leaf; bring to a boil. Cover, reduce heat, and simmer 1 hour and 50 minutes. Add salt, oregano, thyme, rosemary, and 2 garlic cloves; cover and simmer 25 minutes or

until beans are tender. Discard bay leaf.

3. Place 2 cups bean mixture in a food processor; process until smooth. Return bean puree to pan, and stir well. Add pasta; cook 7 minutes or until pasta is done. Remove from heat; stir in parsley and black pepper. Ladle soup into bowls, and sprinkle with cheese. Yield: 10 servings (serving size: 1½ cups soup and 1½ tablespoons cheese).

CALORIES 265 (15% from fat); FAT 4.4g (sat 1.7g, mono 1.7g, poly 0.6g); PROTEIN 15.6g; CARB 42.4g; FIBER 5.9g; CHOL 5mg; IRON 4.3mg; SODIUM 625mg; CALC 202mg

MOSTACCIOLI-SPINACH BAKE

PREP: 20 MINUTES   COOK: 30 MINUTES

2 quarts water
8 ounces uncooked mostaccioli pasta (tube-shaped pasta)
1 tablespoon stick margarine or butter
1 cup vertically sliced onion
2 teaspoons bottled minced garlic
¼ cup all-purpose flour
2½ cups fat-free milk
1¼ cups (5 ounces) preshredded Parmesan cheese, divided
1½ teaspoons dried Italian seasoning
½ teaspoon black pepper
1 (14.5-ounce) can diced tomatoes with basil, garlic, and oregano
1 (10-ounce) package frozen chopped spinach, thawed and drained
Cooking spray
¼ cup dry breadcrumbs
2 tablespoons (½ ounce) preshredded Parmesan cheese
1 tablespoon stick margarine or butter
Parsley sprigs (optional)

1. Preheat oven to 350°.
2. Bring water to a rolling boil. Add pasta;

Don't be afraid to substitute a pasta different from the one called for in a recipe as long as the size and texture are similar.

cook 10 minutes or until "al dente." Drain.

3. Melt 1 tablespoon margarine in a medium heavy saucepan over medium-high heat. Add onion and garlic; sauté 5 minutes or until tender. Add flour; cook 30 seconds, stirring constantly. Gradually add milk; cook until bubbly (about 4 minutes), stirring constantly. Remove from heat. Stir in ¼ cup cheese, Italian seasoning, and pepper.

4. Combine pasta, cheese sauce, 1 cup cheese, tomatoes, and spinach in a large bowl. Spoon mixture into a 13 x 9-inch baking dish coated with cooking spray.

5. Combine breadcrumbs, 2 tablespoons cheese, and 1 tablespoon margarine; sprinkle over pasta mixture. Bake at 350° for 30 minutes or until golden and bubbly. Garnish with parsley, if desired. Yield: 6 servings (serving size: 1½ cups).

CALORIES 372 (26% from fat); FAT 10.6g (sat 5.1g, mono 3.3g, poly 1.3g); PROTEIN 21g; CARB 49g; FIBER 3.3g; CHOL 20mg; IRON 4mg; SODIUM 832mg; CALC 545mg

TUNA-NOODLE CASSEROLE

PREP: 25 MINUTES
COOK: 15 MINUTES

2 quarts water
5 ounces uncooked egg noodles
1 tablespoon stick margarine or butter
¾ cup diced onion
1 cup 2% reduced-fat milk
1 (10½-ounce) can condensed reduced-fat cream of mushroom soup with cracked pepper and herbs, undiluted
1¼ cups frozen green peas, thawed
1 tablespoon lemon juice
¼ teaspoon salt
¼ teaspoon black pepper
2 (6-ounce) cans low-sodium tuna in water, drained and flaked
1 (2-ounce) jar diced pimento, drained
⅓ cup fresh breadcrumbs
2 tablespoons grated Parmesan cheese

1. Preheat oven to 450°.
2. Bring water to a rolling boil. Add pasta; cook 5 minutes or until "al dente." Drain.
3. Melt margarine in a saucepan over medium-high heat. Add onion; sauté 3 minutes. Add milk and soup. Cook 3 minutes; stir constantly with a whisk.
4. Combine soup mixture, noodles, peas, and next 5 ingredients in a 2-quart casserole. Combine breadcrumbs and cheese; sprinkle over top. Bake at 450° for 15 minutes or until bubbly. Yield: 4 servings (serving size: 1½ cups).

CALORIES 381 (20% from fat); FAT 8.6g (sat 2.9g, mono 2.8g, poly 2.2g); PROTEIN 28.9g; CARB 46.9g; FIBER 2.9g; CHOL 61mg; IRON 3.9mg; SODIUM 672mg; CALC 211mg

PERFECT PASTA AND CHEESE

PREP: 25 MINUTES
COOK: 30 MINUTES

2 quarts water
3½ cups uncooked penne
    (tube-shaped pasta)
    Béchamel Sauce (page 442)
2 cups (8 ounces) shredded
    reduced-fat sharp cheddar
    cheese, divided
2 teaspoons stick margarine or
    butter
½ cup minced shallots
2 cups sliced mushrooms
1½ cups sliced shiitake mushroom
    caps (about 3 ounces)
¼ teaspoon salt
¼ teaspoon black pepper
3 garlic cloves, minced
¼ cup chopped fresh chives,
    divided
¾ cup fresh breadcrumbs

1. Bring water to a rolling boil. Add pasta; cook 10 minutes or until "al dente." Drain; keep warm.
2. Preheat oven to 350°.
3. Combine hot Béchamel Sauce and 1¾ cups cheese; stir until cheese melts. Keep warm.
4. Melt margarine in a large nonstick skillet over medium-high heat. Add shallots; sauté 1 minute. Add mushrooms, salt, pepper, and garlic; sauté 3 minutes or until tender.
5. Combine pasta, cheese sauce, mushroom mixture, and 3 tablespoons chives; spoon into a 2-quart casserole. Combine breadcrumbs, ¼ cup cheese, and 1 tablespoon chives; sprinkle over pasta mixture. Bake at 350° for 30 minutes. Yield: 8 servings (serving size: 1 cup).

CALORIES 322 (30% from fat); FAT 10.9g (sat 5.8g, mono 3.2g, poly 0.9g); PROTEIN 16.8g; CARB 41g; FIBER 1.7g; CHOL 30mg; IRON 2.2mg; SODIUM 464mg; CALC 367mg

ORZO AND PORTOBELLO CASSEROLE

PREP: 30 MINUTES   COOK: 35 MINUTES

For information on portobello mushrooms, see page 404.

¼ cup boiling water
¼ cup sun-dried tomatoes, packed
    without oil
3 quarts water
2 cups uncooked orzo
    (rice-shaped pasta)
1 tablespoon olive oil
2 cups sliced leek
2 cups thinly sliced fennel bulb
    (about 1 large bulb)
2 cups diced portobello
    mushroom caps
1 cup mushrooms, quartered
2 garlic cloves, minced
1 cup tomato juice
2 tablespoons minced fresh or
    2 teaspoons dried basil
2 tablespoons balsamic vinegar
1 teaspoon paprika
⅛ teaspoon black pepper
¼ teaspoon salt
1 cup (4 ounces) shredded sharp
    provolone cheese
¼ cup (1 ounce) grated fresh
    Parmesan cheese

1. Combine ¼ cup boiling water and tomatoes in a small bowl; cover and let stand 10 minutes or until tomatoes are soft. Drain.
2. Bring 3 quarts water to a rolling boil. Add pasta; cook 6 minutes or until "al dente." Drain.
3. Heat oil in a large nonstick skillet over medium-high heat. Add tomatoes, leek, fennel, mushrooms, and garlic; sauté 15 minutes or until vegetables are tender, stirring occasionally. Stir in orzo. Combine tomato juice and next 5 ingredients in a small bowl.

4. Pour juice mixture over orzo mixture. Cover, reduce heat to medium, and simmer 10 minutes or until liquid is almost absorbed, stirring occasionally. Sprinkle cheeses over orzo mixture; cover and cook 10 minutes or until cheese melts. Yield: 6 servings (serving size: 1⅔ cups).

CALORIES 330 (26% from fat); FAT 9.4g (sat 4.2g, mono 3.4g, poly 0.9g); PROTEIN 15.1g; CARB 47.8g; FIBER 3g; CHOL 15mg; IRON 4.6mg; SODIUM 576mg; CALC 252mg

PARMESAN ORZO

PREP: 7 MINUTES
COOK: 10 MINUTES

This recipe can easily be doubled.

1 tablespoon grated Parmesan
    cheese
2 tablespoons (1 ounce) light
    cream cheese with chives and
    onion
2 tablespoons fat-free milk
⅛ teaspoon salt
⅛ teaspoon black pepper
1 (2-ounce) jar diced pimento,
    drained
2 quarts water
⅔ cup uncooked orzo (rice-shaped
    pasta)
⅓ cup sliced green onions

1. Combine first 5 ingredients in a bowl; beat at medium speed of a mixer until smooth. Stir in pimento.
2. Bring 2 quarts water to a rolling boil. Add pasta, and cook 8 minutes. Add green onions, and cook 2 minutes; drain well.
3. Add pasta mixture to cream cheese mixture; stir well. Serve immediately. Yield: 2 servings (serving size: 1 cup).

CALORIES 292 (14% from fat); FAT 4.4g (sat 2.4g, mono 1.1g, poly 0.6g); PROTEIN 11.5g; CARB 50.5g; FIBER 1.8g; CHOL 10mg; IRON 3mg; SODIUM 301mg; CALC 96mg

SPINACH AND CHEESE RAVIOLI

PREP:40 MINUTES   COOK:10 MINUTES

The tomato sauce takes about 40 minutes to prepare and cook. If pressed for time, you can substitute commercial marinara although the fat and sodium content may be higher.

   1 teaspoon olive oil
   1 garlic clove, minced
   1 cup (4 ounces) shredded
        part-skim mozzarella cheese
 ½ cup (2 ounces) shredded Asiago
        cheese
 ½ cup 1% low-fat cottage cheese
 ¼ cup 1% low-fat milk
 ½ teaspoon dried oregano
 ¼ teaspoon ground nutmeg
 ⅛ teaspoon black pepper
   1 (10-ounce) package frozen
        chopped spinach, thawed,
        drained, and squeezed dry
 36 won ton wrappers
   1 large egg white, lightly beaten
   4 quarts water
   3 cups hot Tomato Sauce (page 446)

1. Heat olive oil in a small skillet over medium-high heat. Add garlic, and sauté 1 minute. Place garlic, mozzarella cheese, and next 7 ingredients in a food processor; pulse until well-blended.
2. Working with 1 won ton wrapper at a time (cover remaining wrappers with a damp towel to keep them from drying), spoon about 1 tablespoon spinach mixture into center of each wrapper. Moisten edges of dough with egg white, and bring 2 opposite corners together. Press edges together with a fork to seal, forming a triangle.
3. Bring 4 quarts water to a boil in a large Dutch oven. Add 12 ravioli (cover remaining ravioli with a damp towel to keep them from drying); cook 2 minutes, stirring once. Remove ravioli from water with a slotted spoon; keep warm. Repeat procedure with remaining ravioli. Place ravioli in shallow bowls, and top with Tomato Sauce. Yield: 6 servings (serving size: 6 ravioli and ½ cup Tomato Sauce).

CALORIES 279 (27% from fat); FAT 8.5g (sat 4.1g, mono 3.1g, poly 0.7g); PROTEIN 17.6g; CARB 33.8g; FIBER 2.5g; CHOL 22mg; IRON 3.2mg; SODIUM 683mg; CALC 377mg

PASTA CARBONARA

PREP:5 MINUTES
COOK:15 MINUTES

   3 quarts water
 12 ounces uncooked spaghetti
   6 ounces turkey-bacon slices,
        chopped
   2 garlic cloves, minced
 ¼ cup grated Parmesan cheese
   2 tablespoons minced fresh parsley
 ¼ teaspoon freshly ground black
        pepper
   1 cup 2% reduced-fat milk
   6 tablespoons egg substitute
 Chopped fresh parsley (optional)

1. Bring 3 quarts water to a rolling boil. Add pasta; cook 8 minutes or until "al dente." Drain and keep warm.
2. Cook bacon in a large nonstick skillet over medium-high heat until crisp; stir frequently. Add garlic, and sauté 1 minute or until tender. Reduce heat to low; stir in spaghetti, cheese, minced parsley, and pepper.
3. Combine milk and egg substitute. Stir milk mixture into spaghetti mixture, and cook over low heat 5 minutes or until sauce thickens, stirring constantly. Garnish with chopped parsley, if desired. Serve immediately. Yield: 6 servings (serving size: 1 cup).

CALORIES 362 (24% from fat); FAT 9.8g (sat 3.1g, mono 4.1g, poly 2.2g); PROTEIN 18.7g; CARB 45.2g; FIBER 1.5g; CHOL 41mg; IRON 2.7mg; SODIUM 471mg; CALC 116mg

CHICKEN-LINGUINE PRIMAVERA

PREP:12 MINUTES   COOK:15 MINUTES

   2 quarts water
   4 ounces uncooked linguine
 ½ pound skinned, boned chicken
        breast, cut into bite-size pieces
 ¼ teaspoon salt
 ¼ teaspoon black pepper
 ⅓ cup all-purpose flour
   1 tablespoon olive oil
 Cooking spray
 ⅓ cup diagonally sliced carrot
   1 cup broccoli florets
   1 cup sliced yellow squash
   2 garlic cloves, minced
   2 tablespoons chopped fresh basil
   8 cherry tomatoes, halved
 ½ cup fat-free, less-sodium chicken
        broth
 ⅓ cup dry white wine
 ¼ cup (1 ounce) grated fresh
        Parmesan cheese

1. Bring 2 quarts water to a rolling boil. Add pasta; cook 10 minutes or until "al dente." Drain and keep warm.
2. Sprinkle chicken with salt and pepper; dredge in flour. Heat oil in a large nonstick skillet coated with cooking spray over medium heat until hot. Add carrot; stir-fry 4 minutes. Add chicken; stir-fry 4 minutes. Add broccoli; stir-fry 4 minutes. Add squash and garlic; stir-fry 2 minutes. Stir in basil and tomatoes. Spoon chicken mixture into a large bowl; keep warm.
3. Add broth and wine to skillet, scraping pan to loosen browned bits; bring to a boil. Add broth mixture and pasta to chicken mixture; toss. Sprinkle with cheese. Yield: 3 servings (serving size: 1⅓ cups).

CALORIES 372 (20% from fat); FAT 8.4g (sat 2.1g, mono 4.2g, poly 1.1g); PROTEIN 27.7g; CARB 45.3g; FIBER 3.4g; CHOL 48mg; IRON 3.4mg; SODIUM 480mg; CALC 128mg

Ham Tetrazzini

HAM TETRAZZINI

PREP:21 MINUTES   COOK:10 MINUTES

2 quarts water
5 ounces uncooked wide egg noodles
¼ cup all-purpose flour
1 cup fat-free, less-sodium chicken broth
1 cup 2% reduced-fat milk
¼ teaspoon black pepper
1 tablespoon stick margarine or butter
1 (8-ounce) package presliced mushrooms
½ cup diced green bell pepper
1 cup cubed cooked ham (such as Light and Lean)
⅓ cup grated Parmesan cheese
1 tablespoon dry sherry
Cooking spray
⅓ cup dry breadcrumbs

1. Preheat oven to 450°.
2. Bring 2 quarts water to a rolling boil. Add pasta; cook 5 minutes or until "al dente." Drain.
3. Place flour in a bowl. Add 1 cup broth, milk, and black pepper; stir well with a whisk.
4. Melt margarine in a nonstick skillet over medium-high heat. Add mushrooms and bell pepper; sauté 3 minutes. Add flour mixture. Cook 4 minutes or until thick and bubbly, stirring constantly. Combine sauce, noodles, ham, cheese, and sherry in a 1½-quart casserole or 10-inch round gratin dish coated with cooking spray; sprinkle with breadcrumbs. Bake at 450° for 10 minutes or until bubbly. Yield: 6 servings (serving size: 1 cup).

CALORIES 241 (26% from fat); FAT 7g (sat 2.5g, mono 2.6g, poly 1.2g); PROTEIN 13.9g; CARB 29.9g; FIBER 1.6g; CHOL 42mg; IRON 2.7mg; SODIUM 588mg; CALC 137mg

PAD THAI (THAI FRIED RICE NOODLES)

PREP:25 MINUTES
COOK:14 MINUTES

Vermicelli can be used in place of the rice sticks in this quintessential Thai dish.

½ pound uncooked rice sticks (rice-flour noodles)
4 cups boiling water
3 tablespoons fish sauce
¼ cup ketchup
1½ tablespoons sugar
3 tablespoons water
¼ cup chopped unsalted dry-roasted peanuts
3 tablespoons chopped green onions
2½ tablespoons chopped fresh cilantro
½ teaspoon crushed red pepper
1 tablespoon vegetable oil, divided
1 pound medium shrimp, peeled and deveined
10 garlic cloves, minced
3 large eggs, lightly beaten
2 cups fresh bean sprouts
Lime wedges (optional)

1. Combine rice sticks and boiling water in a bowl; let stand 10 minutes or until soft. Drain.
2. Combine fish sauce, ketchup, sugar, and 3 tablespoons water in a small bowl; set aside.
3. Combine peanuts, green onions, cilantro, and red pepper in a medium bowl; set aside.
4. Heat 1 teaspoon oil in a large nonstick skillet or wok over medium-high heat. Add shrimp, and stir-fry 1½ minutes. Remove shrimp from skillet, and keep warm.
5. Heat 2 teaspoons oil over medium-high heat. Add garlic, and stir-fry 30 seconds. Add eggs; stir-fry 2 minutes. Add rice sticks and fish sauce mixture; stir-fry 3 minutes. Return shrimp to

skillet; add bean sprouts, and stir-fry 30 seconds. Spoon shrimp mixture evenly onto 5 plates; top each with 2 tablespoons peanut mixture. Garnish with lime wedges, if desired. Yield: 5 servings (serving size: 2 cups).

CALORIES 364 (25% from fat); FAT 9.6g (sat 2g, mono 3.5g, poly 2.9g); PROTEIN 21.6g; CARB 49.7g; FIBER 1.3g; CHOL 227mg; IRON 3mg; SODIUM 721mg; CALC 94mg

UDON NOODLES WITH ASIAN VEGETABLES AND PEANUT SAUCE

PREP:32 MINUTES   COOK:8 MINUTES

    2 quarts water
    8 ounces uncooked udon noodles
         (thick, round fresh Japanese
         wheat noodles) or spaghetti
    6 tablespoons water
   ¼ cup reduced-fat peanut butter
    2 tablespoons brown sugar
    2 tablespoons low-sodium soy sauce
    2 tablespoons rice vinegar
1½ teaspoons minced peeled
         fresh ginger
1½ teaspoons dark sesame oil
   ½ teaspoon cornstarch
   ½ teaspoon chile paste with garlic
         (optional)
    2 garlic cloves, minced
    4 cups sliced bok choy
    2 cups snow peas, trimmed and
         halved crosswise
    1 cup shredded carrot

1. Bring 2 quarts water to a rolling boil. Add noodles, and cook 8 minutes; drain.
2. Combine 6 tablespoons water, next 7 ingredients, chili paste, if desired, and garlic in a small saucepan; stir with a whisk until blended. Bring mixture to a boil; cook 1 minute, stirring constantly. Combine noodles, peanut sauce, sliced bok choy, snow peas, and shredded carrot in a large bowl, and toss well to coat.

Yield: 4 servings (serving size: 2 cups).
Note: Chile paste with garlic can be found with other ethnic foods in the supermarket. It can be omitted if you prefer a not-so-hot sauce. If udon noodles are difficult to find, try an Asian market.

CALORIES 366 (21% from fat); FAT 8.6g (sat 1.3g, mono 3.6g, poly 2.8g); PROTEIN 12.4g; CARB 62.5g; FIBER 5.1g; CHOL 0mg; IRON 2.8mg; SODIUM 1064mg; CALC 115mg

BOK CHOY

This vegetable, also known as Chinese white cabbage or pak choy, has crunchy white stalks and full leaves. Use it raw in salads, add it to stir-fries, or serve it cooked as a vegetable side dish. Look for bunches with firm white stalks. The leaves should be crisp and green with no yellowing or wilting.

VERMICELLI STIR-FRY WITH PEANUT SAUCE

PREP:35 MINUTES
COOK:8 MINUTES

You can substitute 1½ teaspoons olive oil and ¼ teaspoon crushed red pepper for the chili oil.

    2 quarts water
    8 ounces uncooked vermicelli
1½ teaspoons dark sesame oil

1½ cups cubed deli, lower-salt turkey
         breast or chopped cooked
         turkey (about ½ pound)
   ⅓ cup thinly sliced green onions
1½ teaspoons chili oil
    2 cups snow peas, diagonally
         halved crosswise
1⅓ cups red bell pepper strips
    3 garlic cloves, minced
   ½ cup fat-free, less-sodium chicken
         broth
    3 tablespoons low-sodium soy sauce
    2 tablespoons reduced-fat peanut
         butter
    2 tablespoons chopped unsalted
         dry-roasted peanuts

1. Bring water to a rolling boil. Add pasta; cook 5 minutes or until "al dente." Drain.
2. Heat sesame oil in a large nonstick skillet over medium heat. Add turkey and green onions; stir-fry 2 minutes. Remove from skillet; keep warm.
3. Heat chili oil in skillet over medium-high heat. Add snow peas, bell pepper, and garlic; sauté 3 minutes. Combine broth, soy sauce, and peanut butter; stir well with a whisk. Add to skillet; cook 2 minutes, stirring frequently. Stir in turkey mixture; remove from heat.
4. Combine pasta and turkey mixture. Divide evenly among 4 shallow bowls; top each serving with 1½ teaspoons chopped peanuts. Yield: 4 servings (serving size: 2 cups).

CALORIES 364 (21% from fat); FAT 8.6g (sat 2.1g, mono 4.7g, poly 4.1g); PROTEIN 19.2g; CARB 50.6g; FIBER 3.7g; CHOL 0mg; IRON 4mg; SODIUM 648mg; CALC 45mg

MUSHROOM-FILLED WON TONS

PREP: 34 MINUTES   CHILL: 20 MINUTES
COOK: 26 MINUTES

These won tons can also be served as an appetizer— just omit the tomato sauce and drizzle with low-sodium soy sauce.

    1   pound mushrooms
    2   teaspoons olive oil
  1/3   cup minced onion
1 1/2   teaspoons minced fresh or
    1/2 teaspoon dried thyme
    1   garlic clove, crushed
    2   tablespoons all-purpose flour,
        divided
    2   teaspoons lemon juice
  3/4   teaspoon salt
   24   won ton wrappers
    2   tablespoons water
Cooking spray
Sherry Tomato Sauce or bottled
        fat-free marinara sauce

1. Place half of mushrooms in a food processor; pulse 8 times or until finely chopped. Spoon into a large bowl. Repeat with remaining mushrooms; set aside.
2. Heat oil in a large nonstick skillet over medium heat. Add onion, thyme, and garlic; sauté 3 minutes. Add mushrooms; cook over high heat 7 minutes or until moisture is almost evaporated, stirring occasionally. Remove from heat. Add 1 tablespoon flour, lemon juice, and salt; stir well. Cool completely.
3. Sprinkle 1 tablespoon flour on a large baking sheet. Working with 1 won ton at a time (cover remaining won tons with a damp towel to keep them from drying), spoon about 1 tablespoon mushroom mixture into center of wrapper. Moisten edges of wrapper with water; bring 2 opposite corners to center, pinching points to seal. Bring remaining 2 corners to center, pinching points to seal. Pinch 4 edges

together to seal; gently twist center point to form a pouch shape. Place on prepared baking sheet; cover loosely with a towel. Repeat procedure with remaining won ton wrappers and mushroom mixture.
4. Arrange pouches in a single layer in a vegetable steamer coated with cooking spray, making sure pouches do not touch. Steam pouches, covered, 5 minutes or until tender. Carefully remove pouches from steamer; keep warm. Repeat procedure with remaining pouches.
5. Preheat broiler.
6. Place won tons on a large baking sheet coated with cooking spray; broil 3 minutes or until lightly browned. Remove from baking sheet; serve hot with Sherry Tomato Sauce. Yield: 3 servings (serving size: 8 won tons and 1/3 cup sauce).

SHERRY TOMATO SAUCE

Cooking spray
    1   tablespoon minced onion
    1   garlic clove, crushed
  3/4   cup 2% reduced-fat milk
    1   tablespoon tomato paste
    2   teaspoons all-purpose flour
  1/8   teaspoon salt
Dash of pepper
    1   tablespoon dry sherry

1. Coat a small saucepan with cooking spray; sauté onion and garlic 1 minute.
2. Combine milk, tomato paste, flour, salt, and pepper in a small bowl; stir with a whisk until well-blended. Add milk mixture to pan; cook over medium heat 5 minutes or until mixture is thick and bubbly, stirring constantly with a whisk. Remove from heat; stir in sherry. Serve warm. Yield: 1 cup (serving size: 1/3 cup).

CALORIES 330 (17% from fat); FAT 6.4g (sat 1.7g, mono 2.8g, poly 1g); PROTEIN 12.6g; CARB 55.6g; FIBER 2.8g; CHOL 10mg; IRON 4.6mg; SODIUM 1090mg; CALC 124mg

ASIAN NOODLES

The range of Asian noodles is extraordinary. But don't worry; it's not necessary to be familiar with every type on the market, just the main varieties. Although most supermarkets stock several kinds of these noodles, a wider selection is available at Asian markets. The following are a few of our favorites. Where possible, we've included substitutions.

Moo shu wrappers These are also called lumpia wrappers or spring roll skins. They are usually sold frozen. In some recipes calling for a steamed wrapper, won ton wrappers or flour tortillas may be substituted.

Rice sticks The most popular of all Asian noodles, rice sticks (as they are labeled) are made from rice flour and water. Although any type of rice-flour noodle may be called rice sticks, we use this term for flat rice noodles, which are sold mainly in three forms. Thin flat rice noodles are used mainly in soups and in some stir-fries. Medium-thick rice sticks (called *pho* in Vietnamese) are all-purpose and may be used in soups, stir-fries, and salads (a slightly wider Thai version is called *jantaboon*). The widest rice sticks (*sha he fen* in Chinese) are found in meat, seafood, and vegetable stir-fries. Vermicelli can be substituted for rice sticks.

Soba Soba noodles from Japan are made with a combination of buckwheat flour, wheat flour, and water.

Somen The most delicate of noodles, they are made with wheat flour, a dash of oil, and water. Somen are served cold with a dipping sauce or hot in soups. The closest substitution would be a very fine pasta such as capellini (angel hair) or vermicelli.

meatless main dishes

Roasted Vegetables and Rice
(page 281)

MEATLESS MAIN DISHES

Studies confirm that a diet containing a sizeable percentage of vegetables, fruits, grains, and soy-based foods provides plant-based natural chemicals called phytochemicals. These power brokers boost the immune system, strengthen the body, and improve overall brain health. And best of all, you don't have to sacrifice flavor and heartiness for all these health benefits! Just flip through this chapter to see the bountiful choices available.

We've arranged the recipes according to the primary protein source—grains, legumes and vegetables, eggs and cheese, and tofu and tempeh. By cooking with a variety of these foods, you'll not only satisfy your family's palate, you'll also feel great knowing you've provided them with perhaps the best nutritional defenses possible. Whether you consider yourself a vegetarian or you're just cutting back on meat, you're sure to find some new favorites.

grains When looking for menu ideas, tempt your family with these hearty, tasty dishes that offer alternatives to meat.

As grains and vegetables move to the center of the American plate, the demand for healthy, alternative vegetarian dishes continues to grow.

These recipes use grains that have become staples in many households. And like rice, these grains couldn't be simpler to cook. In many cases, you just boil water!

MULTI-GRAIN PILAF WITH ROOT VEGETABLES

PREP: 18 MINUTES   COOK: 10 MINUTES

We've called for cooked rice and pearl barley that you may have left over from previous meals. If not, start by cooking them both, allowing about 20 minutes for them to cook.

    4 teaspoons olive oil, divided
    1 cup chopped onion
    1 cup chopped red bell pepper
    1 cup chopped carrot
    ½ cup chopped peeled turnip
    ½ cup chopped peeled celeriac
    2 teaspoons grated peeled fresh
         ginger
    2 cups cooked basmati rice (about
         ⅔ cup uncooked rice)
    2 cups cooked pearl barley
         (about ⅔ cup uncooked barley)
    1 cup drained canned pinto beans
    3 cups torn spinach
    2 tablespoons low-sodium
         soy sauce
    ¼ teaspoon salt

1. Heat 2 teaspoons oil in a large non-stick skillet over medium heat. Add onion and next 5 ingredients; sauté 5 minutes.
2. Stir in rice, barley, and beans; cook 2 minutes. Add 2 teaspoons oil, spinach, soy sauce, and salt; cook 1 minute or just until spinach begins to wilt. Yield: 5 servings (serving size: about 1¾ cups).

CALORIES 323 (13% from fat); FAT 4.5g (sat 0.7g, mono 2.8g, poly 0.7g); PROTEIN 10.4g; CARB 61.5g; FIBER 9.5g; CHOL 0mg; IRON 4.4mg; SODIUM 502mg; CALC 92mg

CELERIAC

This rather unusual vegetable—knobby, hairy, and brown—is known as celeriac or celery root. Trim the ends and peel away the rough exterior, and you'll find creamy, white flesh with a mild flavor. Its intriguing texture combines the crunch of celery with the smoothness of potatoes. Pick small to medium-size roots that are firm and relatively clean.

Almost like a fried rice, this entrée is high in soluble fiber, the type that helps lower blood cholesterol levels.

SPICY WHEAT BERRY ENCHILADAS

PREP: 50 MINUTES   COOK: 30 MINUTES

You can substitute 3 cups cooked brown rice for the cooked wheat berries, if desired.

- 1 cup uncooked wheat berries
- 4 cups water
- 2 teaspoons olive oil
- 2 cups chopped onion
- 1 teaspoon dried oregano
- 1 teaspoon chili powder
- ½ teaspoon ground cumin
- 1 jalapeño pepper, seeded and minced
- 2 cups coarsely chopped spinach
- 2 cups Garden Brown Sauce (page 445)
- ½ cup chopped fresh cilantro
- 1 tablespoon fresh lime juice
- 8 (8-inch) fat-free flour tortillas
- 2 cups bottled salsa, divided
- Cooking spray
- 1 cup (4 ounces) shredded reduced-fat Monterey Jack cheese

1. Bring wheat berries and 4 cups water to a boil in a saucepan. Reduce heat; simmer 50 minutes or until tender. Drain.

2. Preheat oven to 350°.

3. Heat oil in a large nonstick skillet over medium-high heat. Add onion and next 4 ingredients; sauté 2 minutes. Add spinach and next 3 ingredients. Stir in wheat berries; cook 5 minutes (mixture will be thick). Remove from heat.

4. Warm tortillas according to package directions. Spoon ½ cup wheat berry mixture down center of each tortilla; roll up. Spread ½ cup salsa in a 13 x 9-inch baking dish coated with cooking spray. Place tortillas, seam sides down, in dish. Pour 1½ cups salsa over tortillas; top with cheese. Bake at 350° for 30 minutes. Yield: 8 servings (serving size: 1 enchilada).

CALORIES 344 (22% from fat); FAT 8.3g (sat 2.3g, mono 4.3g, poly 0.9g); PROTEIN 13.8g; CARB 55.5g; FIBER 9.3g; CHOL 9mg; IRON 3.1mg; SODIUM 871mg; CALC 178mg

DOUBLE GRAIN-AND-VEGETABLE BURRITOS

PREP: 40 MINUTES
COOK: 40 MINUTES

- 1 tablespoon olive oil
- 1½ cups chopped carrot
- ¾ cup chopped leeks
- ¾ cup chopped onion
- ½ cup chopped red bell pepper
- ½ cup finely chopped mushrooms
- ½ cup chopped celery
- 3 cups canned vegetable broth
- ½ cup uncooked medium-grain rice
- ½ cup uncooked lentils
- ¼ cup uncooked pearl barley
- ¼ cup raisins
- 1½ teaspoons hot chili powder
- 1 teaspoon ground cumin
- ½ teaspoon ground coriander
- ½ teaspoon ground cinnamon
- ⅛ teaspoon salt
- ⅛ teaspoon black pepper
- 1 (15-ounce) can black beans, rinsed and drained
- 2 garlic cloves, minced
- 1 cup chopped tomato
- 5 (10-inch) flour tortillas
- ⅓ cup (1¼ ounces) shredded smoked Gouda cheese
- 1¼ cups shredded leaf lettuce
- ⅓ cup fat-free sour cream
- ⅔ cup peach salsa or other salsa

1. Heat oil in a Dutch oven over medium heat. Add carrot and next 5 ingredients; sauté 5 minutes. Add broth and next 12 ingredients. Bring to a boil; cover, reduce heat, and simmer 30 minutes. Stir in tomato.

2. Warm tortillas according to package directions. Spoon about 1⅓ cups bean mixture down center of each tortilla. Top each with 1 tablespoon cheese and ¼ cup lettuce, and roll up. Cut each burrito in half diagonally, and place 2 burrito halves on each plate. Serve with 1 tablespoon sour cream and 2 tablespoons salsa. Yield: 5 servings.

CALORIES 543 (16% from fat); FAT 9.9g (sat 2.4g, mono 4.3g, poly 2.2g); PROTEIN 21.2g; CARB 95.1g; FIBER 11.1g; CHOL 8mg; IRON 7.1mg; SODIUM 1139mg; CALC 202mg

COUSCOUS-AND-FETA CAKES

PREP: 13 MINUTES
COOK: 36 MINUTES

- 2½ cups water
- 1 cup uncooked couscous
- 4 teaspoons olive oil, divided
- 1 cup minced red onion
- 1 cup minced red bell pepper
- ½ cup minced green bell pepper
- 2 garlic cloves, minced
- 1 cup crumbled feta cheese
- ½ cup all-purpose flour
- ½ cup egg substitute
- 2 tablespoons minced fresh parsley
- ½ teaspoon salt
- ¼ teaspoon white pepper

1. Bring water to a boil in a small saucepan; stir in couscous. Remove from heat; cover and let stand 5 minutes. Fluff with a fork.

2. Place 1 teaspoon oil in an electric skillet; heat to 375°. Add onion and next 3 ingredients; sauté 5 minutes. Combine couscous, onion mixture, cheese, and next 5 ingredients in a large bowl.

3. Place ½ teaspoon oil in skillet; heat to 375°. Spoon couscous mixture by ⅓ cupfuls into skillet (about 4 at a time), shaping each portion into a 3-inch cake in skillet. Cook 3 minutes on each side or until golden brown. Remove cakes, and keep warm. Repeat procedure with remaining oil and couscous mixture. Yield: 7 servings (serving size: 3 cakes).

CALORIES 233 (31% from fat); FAT 8.1g (sat 3.9g, mono 3g, poly 0.5g); PROTEIN 9.9g; CARB 30.8g; FIBER 2g; CHOL 21mg; IRON 1.8mg; SODIUM 460mg; CALC 130mg

COUSCOUS WITH SPRING VEGETABLES AND HARISSA SAUCE

PREP: 34 MINUTES
COOK: 11 MINUTES

1   (5.8-ounce) package roasted-garlic-and-olive-oil couscous (such as Near East) or plain couscous
⅓   cup finely chopped plum tomato
⅛   teaspoon ground allspice
1   tablespoon olive oil
2   cups coarsely chopped leek
1   cup coarsely chopped yellow bell pepper
1   cup sugar snap peas, trimmed
½   cup halved peeled pearl onions
½   cup quartered radishes
6   baby carrots, cut in half lengthwise
3   garlic cloves, minced
2   cups torn spinach
½   cup chopped fresh parsley
½   teaspoon sugar
⅛   teaspoon salt
1   (15-ounce) can chickpeas (garbanzo beans), drained
Harissa Sauce (page 445)

1. Prepare couscous according to package directions, omitting oil. Stir in tomato and allspice; keep warm.
2. Heat oil in a large nonstick skillet over medium-high heat. Add leek and next 6 ingredients; sauté 8 minutes. Add spinach, parsley, sugar, salt, and chickpeas; sauté 2 minutes. Spoon vegetable mixture over couscous mixture, and serve with Harissa Sauce. Yield: 4 servings (serving size: 1¼ cups vegetable mixture, ¾ cup couscous, and 1 tablespoon sauce).

CALORIES 385 (24% from fat); FAT 10.2g (sat 1.2g, mono 5.6g, poly 1.6g); PROTEIN 13.7g; CARB 63.7g; FIBER 6.9g; CHOL 0mg; IRON 5.1mg; SODIUM 716mg; CALC 116mg

Working With Leeks

They may resemble green onions, but versatile leeks have a mellow flavor all their own. Spring and fall are peak times for leeks—when you'll find them small and tender. Other times of the year you'll find larger leeks, which tend to be tough.

1. Cut off root end of leek.

2. Cut off the tough, dark-green leaves, leaving the white and light-green portion.

3. Slice leek in half lengthwise.

4. Wash under cold running water to remove dirt and grit.

5. Slice leek halves horizontally, and then chop.

6. For julienne-cut leeks, cut 2-inch pieces, and then slice lengthwise.

ROASTED VEGETABLES AND RICE

PREP: 20 MINUTES   COOK: 14 MINUTES

(pictured on page 277)

    2   teaspoons olive oil, divided
    1   cup chopped red onion
    1   cup chopped red bell pepper
    1   cup chopped green bell pepper
    2   cups chopped zucchini
1¼ cups chopped yellow squash
    3   cups mushrooms, quartered
    3   garlic cloves, minced
    3   cups cooked long-grain brown rice
    1   tablespoon chopped fresh or
          1 teaspoon dried oregano
  ½   teaspoon black pepper
  ¼   teaspoon salt
  ¼   cup chopped fresh or 1 tablespoon
          dried basil
    1   (4-ounce) package crumbled feta
          cheese

1. Heat 1 teaspoon oil in a large non-stick skillet over medium-high heat. Add onion and bell peppers; cook 3 minutes or until lightly browned (do not stir). Cook 1 minute, stirring constantly. Transfer cooked onion and peppers to a large bowl.
2. Heat ½ teaspoon oil in skillet. Add zucchini and squash; cook 3 minutes or until lightly browned (do not stir). Cook 1 minute, stirring constantly. Remove zucchini and squash from pan; place in bowl.
3. Heat ½ teaspoon oil in skillet. Add mushrooms and garlic; cook 3 minutes or until lightly browned (do not stir). Cook 1 minute, stirring constantly. Return onion, bell peppers, zucchini, and squash to skillet. Stir in rice, oregano, black pepper, and salt; cook just until heated. Remove from heat. Stir in basil and cheese. Yield: 4 servings (serving size: 2 cups).

CALORIES 344 (28% from fat); FAT 10.7g (sat 5g, mono 3.5g, poly 1.3g); PROTEIN 12.5g; CARB 52.6g; FIBER 6.9g; CHOL 25mg; IRON 3.9mg; SODIUM 481mg; CALC 210mg

CARIBBEAN RICE AND BEANS

PREP: 15 MINUTES   COOK: 15 MINUTES

  ⅔   cup water
  ⅔   cup uncooked instant rice
    1   teaspoon vegetable oil
Cooking spray
    1   cup chopped onion
  ½   cup chopped celery
  ½   cup diced green bell pepper
    3   garlic cloves, minced
    1   cup coarsely chopped tomato
  ⅛   teaspoon salt
  ¼   teaspoon crushed red pepper
  ¼   teaspoon ground cumin
  ¼   cup chopped fresh cilantro
    1   (15-ounce) can black beans,
          drained
  ½   cup (2 ounces) preshredded
          part-skim mozzarella cheese

1. Bring water to a boil in a saucepan, and stir in rice. Cover, reduce heat, and simmer 5 minutes or until liquid is absorbed.
2. Heat oil in a large nonstick skillet coated with cooking spray over medium-high heat until hot. Add onion, celery, bell pepper, and garlic; sauté 5 minutes or until tender. Add chopped tomato, salt, crushed red pepper, and cumin; sauté 2 minutes.
3. Stir in cooked rice, cilantro, and black beans; cook 1 minute or until thoroughly heated. Divide bean mixture evenly among 4 plates, and sprinkle with cheese. Yield: 4 servings (serving size: 1 cup bean mixture and 2 tablespoons cheese).

CALORIES 224 (18% from fat); FAT 4.4g (sat 1.8g, mono 1.1g, poly 0.9g); PROTEIN 11.4g; CARB 36.3g; FIBER 4.9g; CHOL 8mg; IRON 2.9mg; SODIUM 326mg; CALC 140mg

Caribbean Rice and Beans

legumes & vegetables

Legumes (beans, peas, and lentils) and vegetables offer power-packed, flavorful meals.

Legumes are available in a multitude of colors, shapes, and flavors. They're shelf stable when stored in airtight containers in a cool, dry place. For convenience, many are sold canned.

A half-cup of dark red kidney beans provides as much iron as 6 ounces of lean red meat, but with only 1 gram of fat—and as much soluble fiber as a bowl of oat bran—plus a multitude of nutrients including thiamin, magnesium phosphorus, potassium, and zinc. Talk about a strong nutrition scorecard!

Add to this the wonderful colors, flavors, and textures of vegetables—and you'll have a rich, delectable, hearty meal. Many of these recipes are one-dish meals; add a simple fruit salad or dessert, and dinner's on the table.

The casseroles serve up a nice surprise, providing comforting flavors in a nourishing meal. Your family may not even notice that their entrée is meatless when you offer some of these family favorites.

BLACK BEAN PATTIES WITH CILANTRO AND LIME

PREP: 35 MINUTES COOK: 12 MINUTES

Canned beans simplify the preparation of this Southwestern-style recipe.

¾ cup yellow cornmeal
2 cups water
1 teaspoon olive oil
1 cup chopped onion
½ cup chopped green bell pepper
½ cup chopped red bell pepper
1 tablespoon minced jalapeño pepper
1 teaspoon chili powder
½ teaspoon dried oregano
½ teaspoon ground cumin
¼ teaspoon salt
2 garlic cloves, minced
1 (15-ounce) can black beans, undrained
1¼ cups dry breadcrumbs
2 tablespoons minced fresh cilantro
1 tablespoon fresh lime juice
¾ cup (3 ounces) shredded Monterey Jack cheese
Cooking spray
¾ cup bottled salsa

1. Place cornmeal in a medium saucepan. Gradually add water, stirring constantly with a whisk. Bring to a boil; reduce heat to medium-low. Cover and cook 5 minutes or until mixture is thick; keep warm.
2. Heat oil in a large nonstick skillet over medium-high heat. Add onion and next 8 ingredients; sauté 10 minutes or until onion is tender. Add beans, and cook 1 minute. Combine bean mixture, cooked cornmeal, breadcrumbs, cilantro, and lime juice in a large bowl.
3. Place 1 cup bean mixture in a food processor; process until smooth. Add pureed bean mixture and cheese to remaining bean mixture; stir well. Divide mixture into 12 equal portions, shaping each into a 3-inch patty.
4. Wipe skillet clean with paper towels. Coat skillet with cooking spray; place over medium-high heat until hot. Add 6 patties; cook 6 minutes or until browned, carefully turning patties after 3 minutes. Repeat procedure with remaining patties. Serve with salsa. Yield: 6 servings (serving size: 2 patties and 2 tablespoons salsa).

CALORIES 317 (22% from fat); FAT 7.8g (sat 3.3g, mono 2.5g, poly 1g); PROTEIN 14.5g; CARB 49.4g; FIBER 6.6g; CHOL 11mg; IRON 4.3mg; SODIUM 688mg; CALC 196mg

SOUTHWESTERN BEAN CASSEROLE

PREP: 30 MINUTES
COOK: 30 MINUTES

1 teaspoon vegetable oil
1 cup chopped onion
2 garlic cloves, minced
1 cup no-salt-added cream-style corn, divided
1 (4.5-ounce) can chopped green chiles, drained and divided
½ cup bottled salsa
½ teaspoon salt
¼ teaspoon ground cumin
¼ teaspoon black pepper
2 (16-ounce) cans pinto beans, drained
1 (14.5-ounce) can no-salt-added stewed tomatoes, undrained
Cooking spray
1 cup (4 ounces) shredded reduced-fat cheddar cheese, divided
¾ cup yellow cornmeal
¼ cup all-purpose flour
1 teaspoon sugar
¼ teaspoon salt
½ cup low-fat or nonfat buttermilk
¼ cup vegetable oil
2 large egg whites, lightly beaten

1. Preheat oven to 375°.
2. Heat 1 teaspoon oil in a saucepan over medium-high heat. Add onion and garlic; sauté 2 minutes. Add ½ cup corn, ¼ cup chiles, and next 6 ingredients; bring to a boil. Reduce heat; simmer 15 minutes. Pour corn mixture into a 13 x 9-inch baking dish coated with cooking spray, and sprinkle with ½ cup cheese.
3. Combine cornmeal, flour, sugar, and ¼ teaspoon salt in a bowl. Combine ½

Hoppin' John Cakes

1. Place 1/3 cup bean mixture onto plate of breadcrumbs.

2. Shape mixture into a 1/2-inch-thick cake, patting breadcrumbs onto bean mixture.

cup corn, remaining chiles, 1/2 cup cheese, buttermilk, 1/4 cup oil, and egg whites; add to cornmeal mixture. Spread over bean mixture. Bake at 375° for 30 minutes. Yield: 6 servings.

CALORIES 461 (30% from fat); FAT 15.2g (sat 4.2g, mono 4.3g, poly 5.5g); PROTEIN 20.6g; CARB 63.4g; FIBER 8g; CHOL 13mg; IRON 4.6mg; SODIUM 920mg; CALC 286mg

HOPPIN' JOHN CAKES WITH TOMATILLO-TOMATO SALSA

PREP:31 MINUTES
COOK:12 MINUTES

1 (15.8-ounce) can black-eyed peas, drained and divided
Cooking spray
3/4 cup diced onion
1 tablespoon diced seeded jalapeño pepper
3 garlic cloves, minced
3 cups fresh breadcrumbs, divided
1 cup cooked basmati or long-grain rice
2 tablespoons all-purpose flour

1 large egg, lightly beaten
1 large egg white, lightly beaten
2 tablespoons vegetable oil, divided
Tomatillo-Tomato Salsa (page 439)

1. Mash 3/4 cup black-eyed peas; set mashed and whole peas aside.
2. Place a large nonstick skillet coated with cooking spray over medium-high heat until hot. Add onion, jalapeño, and garlic; sauté 3 minutes or until onion is lightly browned.
3. Combine mashed peas, whole peas, onion mixture, 1 cup breadcrumbs, rice, flour, egg, and egg white in a bowl. Place 1/3 cup bean mixture onto plate of 2 cups breadcrumbs. Pat breadcrumbs onto bean mixture; shape into a 1/2-inch-thick cake. Repeat with remaining bean mixture and breadcrumbs.
4. Heat 1 tablespoon oil in skillet over medium-high heat. Add 4 cakes; cook 2 to 3 minutes or until lightly browned. Carefully turn cakes over; cook 2 to 3 minutes or until lightly browned. Repeat procedure with 1 tablespoon

oil and remaining cakes. Serve with Tomatillo-Tomato Salsa. Yield: 4 servings (serving size: 2 cakes and 1/2 cup salsa).

CALORIES 404 (24% from fat); FAT 10.7g (sat 2.2g, mono 3.3g, poly 4.1g); PROTEIN 14.7g; CARB 75.3g; FIBER 5.4g; CHOL 54mg; IRON 5.4mg; SODIUM 518mg; CALC 114mg

TUSCAN SKILLET SUPPER

PREP:15 MINUTES
COOK:18 MINUTES

2 teaspoons olive oil
1 1/4 cups chopped zucchini
1/2 cup sliced onion
1/2 cup sliced celery
1/2 cup diced red bell pepper
1 teaspoon dried oregano
2 garlic cloves, minced
1 cup diced tomato
1 (15-ounce) can cannellini beans or other white beans, rinsed and drained
2 rosemary sprigs
1 cup chopped spinach
1/4 teaspoon salt
1/8 teaspoon black pepper
1/2 cup (2 ounces) preshredded part-skim mozzarella cheese

1. Heat oil in a large nonstick skillet over medium-high heat. Add zucchini and next 5 ingredients; sauté 10 minutes. Stir in tomato, beans, and rosemary; cook 5 minutes, stirring frequently.
2. Add spinach, salt, and pepper to zucchini mixture; cook 1 minute or until spinach wilts. Sprinkle with cheese; cover and let stand 1 to 2 minutes or until cheese begins to melt. Remove from heat, and discard rosemary. Yield: 2 servings (serving size: 1 3/4 cups).

CALORIES 318 (29% from fat); FAT 10.4g (sat 3.6g, mono 4.7g, poly 0.8g); PROTEIN 18.3g; CARB 38.2g; FIBER 12.9g; CHOL 16mg; IRON 4.8mg; SODIUM 766mg; CALC 280mg

PARMESAN RISOTTO-STUFFED PORTOBELLOS

PREP: 20 MINUTES   COOK: 1 HOUR

1 (14½-ounce) can vegetable broth
2 cups water
1 tablespoon olive oil, divided
1 cup minced fresh onion
1 cup finely diced celery
1 cup finely diced carrot
1 cup uncooked Arborio rice or
     other short-grain rice
1 cup dry white wine
½ cup grated Parmesan cheese
½ cup minced green onions
4 (5-ounce) portobello mushrooms
     (about 6 inches wide)
¼ cup (1 ounce) preshredded
     part-skim mozzarella cheese
½ cup water
1 tablespoon chopped onion
3 garlic cloves, minced
1 (10-ounce) package fresh
     spinach, trimmed

1. Bring broth and 2 cups water to a simmer in a saucepan (do not boil). Keep warm.
2. Heat 2 teaspoons oil in a large saucepan over medium-high heat. Add 1 cup minced onion, celery, and carrot; sauté 1 minute. Add rice; sauté 5 minutes. Stir in wine; cook 5 minutes or until liquid is nearly absorbed, stirring constantly. Add broth mixture, ½ cup at a time, stirring constantly until each portion of broth is absorbed before adding the next (about 30 minutes total). Remove from heat; stir in Parmesan cheese and green onions.
3. Preheat oven to 375°.
4. Remove stems from mushrooms; discard. Place mushroom caps, gill sides up, in a 13 x 9-inch baking dish. Spoon 1 cup risotto into each cap; top each with 1 tablespoon mozzarella cheese. Pour ½ cup water into dish. Bake at 375° for 30 minutes or until mushroom caps are tender.
5. Heat 1 teaspoon oil in a Dutch oven over medium-high heat until hot. Add chopped onion and garlic; sauté 2 minutes or until tender. Add spinach; sauté 2 minutes or until spinach wilts. Divide spinach mixture evenly on each plate. Remove mushrooms from baking dish; place on spinach mixture. Yield: 4 servings.

CALORIES 364 (23% from fat); FAT 9.1g (sat 3.3g, mono 4g, poly 0.9g); PROTEIN 14.6g; CARB 58.2g; FIBER 7.2g; CHOL 12mg; IRON 6.1mg; SODIUM 789mg; CALC 302mg

PORTOBELLOS

When buying portobellos, look for those with a tight underside and lighter-colored gills. If the gill area appears very dark and spread out, that's a sign of age. And don't discard the thick woody stems; they make excellent stock or broth flavorings.

RATATOUILLE BAKE

PREP: 25 MINUTES   COOK: 40 MINUTES

2 teaspoons olive oil
2 cups diced peeled eggplant
2 cups sliced zucchini
1½ cups diced onion
1 cup diced red bell pepper
½ cup sliced celery
1 tablespoon paprika
2 teaspoons dried oregano
2 teaspoons dried basil
½ teaspoon crushed red pepper
1½ cups uncooked long-grain rice
1 (14½-ounce) can no-salt-added
     whole tomatoes, undrained and
     chopped
1 (14½-ounce) can vegetable broth
1½ cups (6 ounces) crumbled feta
     cheese
1 (15-ounce) can chickpeas
     (garbanzo beans), drained

1. Preheat oven to 375°.
2. Heat oil in a Dutch oven over medium-high heat. Add eggplant and next 8 ingredients; sauté 1 minute.
3. Add rice; sauté 3 minutes. Stir in tomato and broth; bring to a boil. Add cheese and chickpeas; stir well. Spoon rice mixture into a 13 x 9-inch baking dish. Cover and bake at 375° for 40 minutes or until rice is tender. Yield: 6 servings (serving size: 1½ cups).

CALORIES 422 (28% from fat); FAT 13.2g (sat 6.7g, mono 3.6g, poly 1.3g); PROTEIN 15.4g; CARB 63.4g; FIBER 5g; CHOL 37mg; IRON 5.1mg; SODIUM 884mg; CALC 297mg

EGGPLANT PARMESAN

PREP: 30 MINUTES   COOK: 30 MINUTES

½ cup dry white wine
1 tablespoon dried basil
1 tablespoon dried oregano
4 (8-ounce) cans no-salt-added
     tomato sauce
1 (28-ounce) can no-salt-added
     whole tomatoes, undrained
     and chopped
1 (6-ounce) can tomato paste
2 garlic cloves, minced
¼ cup water
¼ teaspoon salt
3 large egg whites, lightly beaten
1¼ cups Italian-seasoned
     breadcrumbs
¼ cup grated Parmesan cheese
2 eggplants (about 1¾ pounds),
     cut crosswise into ¼-inch slices
Cooking spray
3 cups (12 ounces) preshredded
     part-skim mozzarella cheese

1. Combine first 7 ingredients in a large saucepan; bring to a boil. Reduce heat, and simmer, uncovered, 20 minutes.
2. Preheat broiler.
3. Combine ¼ cup water, salt, and egg whites in a shallow bowl. Combine

breadcrumbs and Parmesan cheese. Dip eggplant slices in egg white mixture, and dredge in breadcrumb mixture. Place half of eggplant on a baking sheet coated with cooking spray; broil 5 minutes on each side or until browned. Repeat procedure with remaining eggplant; set aside.

4. Preheat oven to 350°.

5. Spread half of tomato mixture in a 13 x 9-inch baking dish coated with cooking spray. Arrange half of eggplant over tomato mixture; top with half of mozzarella cheese. Repeat layers with remaining tomato mixture, eggplant, and cheese. Bake at 350° for 30 minutes or until bubbly. Let stand 5 minutes before serving. Yield: 8 servings.

CALORIES 303 (26% from fat); FAT 8.6g (sat 5g, mono 2.3g, poly 0.4g); PROTEIN 19.3g; CARB 39.7g; FIBER 6.4g; CHOL 27mg; IRON 3.5mg; SODIUM 892mg; CALC 414mg

CHICKPEA-AND-CORN PATTIES

PREP:26 MINUTES   COOK:18 MINUTES

- 2 teaspoons olive oil, divided
- 1½ cups fresh corn kernels (about 2 ears)
- 1 cup chopped onion
- 1 teaspoon minced fresh or ¼ teaspoon dried thyme
- 1 (19-ounce) can chickpeas (garbanzo beans), rinsed and drained
- ½ cup fresh breadcrumbs
- 2 tablespoons cornmeal
- ½ teaspoon salt
- ¼ teaspoon ground red pepper
- 4 teaspoons cornmeal
- Cooking spray
- ¼ cup fat-free sour cream
- ¼ cup bottled salsa
- Thyme sprigs (optional)

1. Heat 1 teaspoon oil in a large nonstick skillet over medium-high heat. Add corn, onion, and minced thyme; sauté 2 minutes. Place onion mixture, chickpeas, breadcrumbs, 2 tablespoons cornmeal, salt, and red pepper in a food processor. Pulse 8 times or until combined and chunky.

2. Divide chickpea mixture into 8 equal portions, shaping each into a ½-inch-thick patty; dredge patties in 4 teaspoons cornmeal. Heat ½ teaspoon oil in skillet coated with cooking spray over medium-high heat. Add 4 patties; cook 5 minutes.

Carefully turn patties over; cook 4 minutes or until golden. Repeat procedure with ½ teaspoon oil and remaining patties. Serve with fat-free sour cream and salsa. Garnish with thyme sprigs, if desired. Yield: 4 servings (serving size: 2 patties, 1 tablespoon sour cream, and 1 tablespoon salsa).

CALORIES 261 (20% from fat); FAT 5.7g (sat 0.7g, mono 2.5g, poly 1.6g); PROTEIN 11g; CARB 46.7g; FIBER 6.1g; CHOL 0mg; IRON 3.1mg; SODIUM 570mg; CALC 78mg

Chickpea-and-Corn Patties

Ginger

Peel: Use a vegetable peeler or a sharp paring knife.

Slice: Use a sharp French knife. Always slice across the fibers.

Sliver: Thinly slice ginger crosswise. Stack slices, and cut into slivers.

Mince: Line up ginger slivers on a cutting board, then cut crosswise into small pieces.

Julienne: Slice a 1½-inch-long piece from ginger. Peel and slice lengthwise. Stack slices, and cut into thin 1½-inch strips.

Juice: Mound grated ginger into center of a piece of cheesecloth. Bring edges of cheesecloth together at top, and hold securely. Squeeze cheesecloth bag by hand over a small bowl. Juice can be used to flavor sauces and beverages.

Grate: Use a porcelain ginger grater or the finest holes on an all-purpose grater.

LENTIL DAL

PREP: 30 MINUTES   COOK: 42 MINUTES

Lentils are in the legume family and are tiny, typically brownish green, disk-shaped dried seeds. (Other varieties, including yellow and red, are available.) Lentils have a bean-like texture when cooked and offer a mild, nutty flavor. Lentil Dal is a traditional Indian dish with lentils, tomatoes, onions, and spices. The amount of ginger may seem like a lot, but it adds just the right amount of flavor to the volume of lentils and vegetables.

    1 tablespoon olive oil
    1 cup chopped onion
    1 tablespoon minced peeled fresh
         ginger
    1 teaspoon cumin seeds
    1 teaspoon ground turmeric
    ½ teaspoon crushed red pepper
    4 garlic cloves, minced
    2 cups chopped cauliflower florets
    2 cups chopped tomato
 2½ cups water
    1 cup dried lentils
    2 tablespoons fresh lime juice
    1 tablespoon minced fresh cilantro
   ¾ teaspoon salt
    6 cups hot cooked basmati rice or
         long-grain rice

1. Heat oil in a large saucepan over medium-high heat. Add onion and next 5 ingredients; sauté 2 minutes. Add cauliflower and tomato; sauté 1 minute. Stir in water and lentils; bring to a boil. Cover, reduce heat, and simmer 35 minutes or until lentils are tender.
2. Stir lime juice, cilantro, and salt into lentil mixture. Serve over rice. Yield: 6 servings (serving size: 1 cup lentil mixture and 1 cup rice).

CALORIES 385 (7% from fat); FAT 3.2g (sat 0.5g, mono 1.8g, poly 0.5g); PROTEIN 14.7g; CARB 75.3g; FIBER 6.6g; CHOL 0mg; IRON 5.6mg; SODIUM 314mg; CALC 60mg

SELECTING A SPUD

The National Potato Board shares these guidelines for buying potatoes:

• Select potatoes that are firm, smooth, and fairly clean.

• Choose those with regular shapes so there won't be much waste when peeling them.

• Avoid potatoes that are wrinkled or that have wilted skins, soft or dark areas, cut surfaces, or a green appearance.

COWBOY-STYLE MEAT LOAF

PREP: 18 MINUTES
COOK: 40 MINUTES

    2 teaspoons olive oil
    1 cup chopped onion
    ½ cup chopped celery
    ½ cup diced green bell pepper
    ½ cup diced red bell pepper
 1½ teaspoons ground cumin
    2 garlic cloves, minced
    1 jalapeño pepper, seeded and
         minced
    ½ cup barbecue sauce, divided
    2 cups mashed cooked peeled
         baking potato (about 1 pound,
         uncooked)
    1 cup regular oats
   ¼ cup minced fresh cilantro
   ¼ cup ketchup
    1 tablespoon Dijon mustard
    ½ teaspoon salt
    ½ teaspoon black pepper
    1 (16-ounce) can kidney beans,
         drained and mashed
 Cooking spray
   ¾ cup (3 ounces) shredded reduced-
         fat sharp cheddar cheese

1. Preheat oven to 375°.

2. Heat oil in a large skillet over medium-high heat. Add onion and next 6 ingredients; sauté 3 minutes. Stir in ¼ cup barbecue sauce, potato, and next 7 ingredients. Spoon potato mixture into a 9 x 5-inch loaf pan coated with cooking spray. Bake at 375° for 30 minutes.

3. Brush ¼ cup barbecue sauce over loaf, and sprinkle with cheese. Bake an additional 10 minutes or until meat loaf is done. Let stand 10 minutes before slicing. Yield: 6 servings (serving size: 1 slice).

CALORIES 285 (20% from fat); FAT 6.2g (sat 2.1g, mono 2.4g, poly 0.9g); PROTEIN 12.9g; CARB 45.6g; FIBER 5.4g; CHOL 9mg; IRON 3.2mg; SODIUM 781mg; CALC 161mg

SMASHED POTATO-AND-BROCCOLI CASSEROLE

PREP: 25 MINUTES   COOK: 40 MINUTES

2 pounds baking potatoes, halved
1 cup chopped broccoli
½ cup diced onion
½ cup part-skim ricotta cheese
1½ teaspoons chopped fresh or ½ teaspoon dried dill
½ teaspoon salt
⅛ teaspoon ground red pepper
1 (8-ounce) carton fat-free sour cream
Cooking spray
¾ cup (3 ounces) shredded reduced-fat sharp cheddar cheese

1. Preheat oven to 375°.

2. Place potato halves in a saucepan; cover with water. Bring to a boil. Reduce heat; simmer 20 minutes or until tender. Drain in a colander over a bowl, reserving 1 cup cooking liquid. Return potato and 1 cup liquid to pan; mash with a potato masher until slightly chunky.

3. Add broccoli and next 6 ingredients to pan; stir well. Spoon potato mixture

into an 11 x 7-inch baking dish coated with cooking spray; bake at 375° for 35 minutes. Sprinkle with cheddar cheese; bake an additional 5 minutes or until cheese melts. Yield: 6 servings (serving size: 1 cup).

CALORIES 292 (17% from fat); FAT 5.6g (sat 3.2g, mono 1.5g, poly 0.3g); PROTEIN 14.9g; CARB 45.5g; FIBER 3.9g; CHOL 19mg; IRON 2.5mg; SODIUM 405mg; CALC 257mg

CHEESE AND CORN STUFFED POTATOES

PREP: 20 MINUTES
COOK: 1 HOUR 15 MINUTES

4 (8-ounce) baking potatoes
2 teaspoons olive oil
1 cup chopped leek
1 cup chopped onion
2 garlic cloves, minced
¾ cup frozen whole-kernel corn, thawed and drained
½ cup 1% low-fat cottage cheese
½ cup plain fat-free yogurt
½ teaspoon salt
¼ teaspoon ground red pepper
¼ cup (1 ounce) shredded reduced-fat sharp cheddar cheese

1. Preheat oven to 375°.

2. Wrap potatoes in foil; bake at 375° for 1 hour or until tender. Cool slightly.

3. Heat oil in a medium nonstick skillet over medium-high heat. Add leek, onion, and garlic; sauté 8 minutes or until tender.

4. Unwrap potatoes. Cut each potato in half lengthwise; scoop out pulp, leaving ¼-inch-thick shells.

5. Combine potato pulp, onion mixture, corn, cottage cheese, yogurt, salt, and red pepper in a bowl. Spoon potato mixture into shells; sprinkle with cheddar cheese. Place on a baking sheet. Bake at 375° for 15 minutes or until thoroughly heated. Yield: 4 servings.

Note: You can serve one stuffed potato half as a side dish.

CALORIES 287 (14% from fat); FAT 4.5g (sat 1.4g, mono 2.1g, poly 0.4g); PROTEIN 13.3g; CARB 49.9g; FIBER 4.6g; CHOL 7mg; IRON 3.4mg; SODIUM 502mg; CALC 187mg

MOROCCAN STUFFED POTATOES

PREP: 12 MINUTES   COOK: 1 HOUR

¼ cup tahini (sesame-seed paste)
2 tablespoons minced fresh parsley
½ teaspoon salt
1 small garlic clove, minced
1 (8-ounce) carton plain low-fat yogurt
4 (8-ounce) baking potatoes
Olive oil-flavored cooking spray
2 tablespoons lemon juice
1 teaspoon ground cumin
2 teaspoons olive oil
¼ teaspoon ground red pepper
4 cups diced peeled eggplant
1 cup diced onion
1 cup diced red bell pepper

1. Preheat oven to 375°.

2. Combine first 5 ingredients in a small bowl; cover and chill.

3. Coat potatoes with cooking spray. Bake at 375° for 1 hour or until tender.

4. Combine lemon juice and next 3 ingredients in a large bowl. Add eggplant, onion, and bell pepper; toss well. Place eggplant mixture on a jelly-roll pan coated with cooking spray. Bake at 375° for 40 minutes, stirring after 20 minutes.

5. Split open each potato. Spoon 2 tablespoons yogurt mixture into each potato; fluff pulp with a fork. Spoon about ½ cup eggplant mixture into center of each potato; top each with 2 tablespoons yogurt mixture. Yield: 4 servings.

CALORIES 443 (25% from fat); FAT 12.5g (sat 2.1g, mono 4.9g, poly 3.8g); PROTEIN 12.1g; CARB 74.7g; FIBER 8.6g; CHOL 3mg; IRON 5.6mg; SODIUM 374mg; CALC 212mg

ATHENIAN STUFFED POTATOES

PREP: 33 MINUTES   COOK: 1 HOUR

4 (8-ounce) baking potatoes
1 (6-ounce) jar marinated artichoke hearts, undrained
2 teaspoons olive oil
1 onion, diced
1 green bell pepper, diced
1 red bell pepper, diced
1 tomato, diced
2 garlic cloves, minced
1 cup (4 ounces) crumbled feta cheese
2 tablespoons minced kalamata olives
1 teaspoon dried oregano

1. Preheat oven to 375°.
2. Wrap potatoes in foil, and bake at 375° for 1 hour or until tender.
3. Drain artichokes in a colander over a bowl, reserving 1 tablespoon marinade.

Chop artichokes. Heat oil in a large nonstick skillet over medium-high heat. Add onion, peppers, tomato, and garlic; sauté 8 minutes. Add artichokes, reserved marinade, cheese, olives, and oregano; sauté 1 minute or until thoroughly heated.

4. Unwrap potatoes. Cut each potato open; fluff pulp with a fork. Spoon 1 cup vegetable mixture into center of each potato. Yield: 4 servings.

CALORIES 398 (39% from fat); FAT 17.2g (sat 7.4g, mono 5.4g, poly 3.5g); PROTEIN 13.2g; CARB 51.2g; FIBER 5.8g; CHOL 37mg; IRON 4.6mg; SODIUM 668mg; CALC 273mg

DUM SHAK VEGETABLE CASSEROLE

PREP: 1 HOUR 10 MINUTES
COOK: 1 HOUR

1 cup dried yellow split peas
1 cup water
½ teaspoon salt
2 tablespoons vegetable oil
1 tablespoon cumin seeds
3 cups chopped fresh cilantro
2 cups water
2 cups grated fresh coconut or 1 cup flaked unsweetened coconut
3 tablespoons minced serrano chile (about 6 chiles)
2 tablespoons grated peeled fresh ginger
1 teaspoon salt
2 baking potatoes (about 1¼ pounds), peeled and cut into 1-inch cubes
2 sweet potatoes (about 1¼ pounds), peeled and cut into 1-inch cubes
1 large eggplant (about 1¼ pounds), cut into 1-inch cubes
8 garlic cloves, minced

1. Sort and wash peas. Place in an ovenproof Dutch oven; cover with water to 2

Athenian Stuffed Potatoes

inches above peas. Bring to a boil, and cook 2 minutes. Remove from heat; cover and let stand 1 hour. Drain peas, and return to pan.

2. Add 1 cup water and ½ teaspoon salt to pan; bring to a boil. Cover, reduce heat, and simmer 20 minutes or until most of liquid is absorbed. Remove peas from pan. Wipe pan dry with a paper towel.

3. Preheat oven to 400°.

4. Heat 2 tablespoons oil in pan over medium-high heat. Add cumin seeds; sauté 1 minute. Add peas, cilantro, and remaining 9 ingredients, stirring gently. Cover and bake at 400° for 1 hour or until vegetables are tender. Yield: 6 servings (serving size: 2 cups).

CALORIES 456 (36% from fat); FAT 18.3g (sat 12.1g, mono 2.2g, poly 2.7g); PROTEIN 15.4g; CARB 62.8g; FIBER 9.8g; CHOL 0mg; IRON 7.5mg; SODIUM 631mg; CALC 113mg

VEGETABLE MOO SHU

PREP: 30 MINUTES   COOK: 9 MINUTES

You can substitute flour tortillas for the Quick Chinese Pancakes, if desired.

1   (0.5-ounce) package dried wood ear mushrooms
2   cups boiling water
1   teaspoon dark sesame oil
1   teaspoon vegetable oil
1   tablespoon minced peeled fresh ginger
2   garlic cloves, minced
4   cups thinly sliced green cabbage
1   cup thinly sliced red bell pepper
1   cup diagonally sliced green onions
3   tablespoons rice vinegar
2   tablespoons low-sodium soy sauce
2   tablespoons dry sherry
2   tablespoons hoisin sauce
3   large eggs, lightly beaten
Fresh chives (optional)
Quick Chinese Pancakes

1. Combine mushrooms and boiling water in a bowl; cover and let stand 30 minutes or until soft. Drain; slice mushrooms into thin strips.

2. Heat oils in a large nonstick skillet or wok over medium-high heat. Add minced ginger and garlic to pan; stir-fry 1 minute. Add mushrooms, cabbage, and bell pepper; stir-fry 3 minutes. Add onions, vinegar, soy sauce, sherry, and hoisin sauce; stir-fry 2 minutes. Remove vegetables from pan. Add eggs to pan. Cook 2 minutes or until set, stirring constantly. Stir in vegetables. Garnish with fresh chives, if desired. Serve with Quick Chinese Pancakes. Yield: 4 servings (serving size: ½ cup moo shu and 2 pancakes).

CALORIES 358 (30% from fat); FAT 12.1g (sat 2.7g, mono 4.1g, poly 3.5g); PROTEIN 15.6g; CARB 46.8g; FIBER 4.1g; CHOL 215mg; IRON 3.8mg; SODIUM 534mg; CALC 199mg

QUICK CHINESE PANCAKES

1¼ cups all-purpose flour
1½ cups fat-free milk
1   tablespoon stick margarine or butter, melted
1   large egg
1   tablespoon minced fresh chives
¼   teaspoon five-spice powder
Cooking spray

1. Lightly spoon flour into dry measuring cups; level with a knife. Place flour in a medium bowl. Combine milk, margarine, and egg; add milk mixture to flour, stirring with a whisk until almost smooth. Stir in chives and five-spice powder. Cover batter, and chill 1 hour.

2. Place an 8-inch crêpe pan or nonstick skillet coated with cooking spray over medium-high heat until hot. Remove pan from heat. Pour a scant ¼ cup batter into pan; quickly tilt pan in all directions so batter covers pan with a thin film. Cook about 1 minute.

3. Carefully lift edge of pancake with a spatula to test for doneness. The pancake is ready to turn when it can be shaken loose from the pan and the underside is lightly browned. Turn pancake over; cook 30 seconds on other side.

4. Place pancake on a towel; cool. Repeat procedure until all of batter is used. Stack pancakes between single layers of wax paper or paper towels to prevent sticking. Yield: 8 pancakes (serving size: 2 pancakes).

CALORIES 108 (23% from fat); FAT 2.7g (sat 0.6g, mono 0.9g, poly 0.8g); PROTEIN 4.2g; CARB 16.1g; FIBER 0.5g; CHOL 27mg; IRON 1mg; SODIUM 49mg; CALC 64mg

menu

Zucchini Waffles With Pimento Cheese Sauce

Sliced cantaloupe

Citrus Cooler (page 52)

Almond Mocha Parfaits (page 176)

ZUCCHINI WAFFLES WITH PIMENTO CHEESE SAUCE

PREP: 10 MINUTES

COOK: 5 MINUTES PER BATCH

1¼ cups all-purpose flour
1½ teaspoons baking powder
¼ teaspoon dried basil
¼ teaspoon baking soda
¼ teaspoon salt
⅛ teaspoon coarsely ground black pepper
1 cup nonfat or low-fat buttermilk
1 cup shredded zucchini
½ cup no-salt-added cream-style corn
⅓ cup sliced green onions
2 teaspoons vegetable oil
1 large egg, lightly beaten
Cooking spray
Pimento Cheese Sauce (page 444)

1. Lightly spoon flour into dry measuring cups; level with a knife.
2. Combine flour and next 5 ingredients in a large bowl. Combine buttermilk and next 5 ingredients; add to flour mixture, stirring just until moist.
3. Coat a waffle iron with cooking spray; preheat. Spoon about ⅓ cup batter per 4-inch waffle onto hot waffle iron, spreading batter to edges. Cook 5 to 6 minutes or until steaming stops; repeat procedure with remaining batter. Serve warm with Pimento Cheese Sauce. Yield: 4 servings (serving size: 2 waffles and 5 tablespoons sauce).

CALORIES 329 (28% from fat); FAT 10.3g (sat 3.8g, mono 3.2g, poly 2.3g); PROTEIN 15.3g; CARB 44.6g; FIBER 1.7g; CHOL 70mg; IRON 2.8mg; SODIUM 634mg; CALC 367mg

ROASTED VEGETABLE MACARONI AND CHEESE

PREP: 50 MINUTES   COOK: 20 MINUTES

3 cups diced peeled eggplant (about ½ pound)
2 cups sliced mushrooms
1 cup coarsely chopped red bell pepper
1 cup coarsely chopped yellow bell pepper
1 cup coarsely chopped onion
1 small zucchini, quartered lengthwise and sliced (about 1 cup)
4 garlic cloves, minced
Cooking spray
½ cup all-purpose flour
2¾ cups 1% low-fat milk
¾ cup (3 ounces) shredded sharp provolone cheese
¾ cup (3 ounces) grated fresh Parmesan cheese, divided
¼ teaspoon salt
¼ teaspoon freshly ground black pepper
6 cups cooked elbow macaroni (about 12 ounces uncooked pasta)
⅛ teaspoon paprika

1. Preheat oven to 450°.
2. Combine first 7 ingredients in a large shallow roasting pan lined with foil and coated with cooking spray. Bake vegetables at 450° for 30 minutes or until lightly browned, stirring occasionally. Remove pan from oven.
3. Reduce oven temperature to 375°.
4. Place flour in a large saucepan. Gradually add milk, stirring with a whisk until blended. Cook over medium heat 8 minutes or until thick, stirring constantly. Add provolone cheese, ½ cup Parmesan cheese, salt, and black pepper; cook 3 minutes or until cheese melts, stirring frequently.
5. Combine macaroni, roasted vegetables, and cheese sauce in a large bowl. Spoon mixture into a 3-quart casserole coated with cooking spray. Combine ¼ cup Parmesan cheese and paprika, and sprinkle over macaroni mixture. Bake at 375° for 20 minutes or until bubbly. Yield: 10 servings (serving size: 1 cup).

CALORIES 260 (21% from fat); FAT 6g (sat 3.3g, mono 1.5g, poly 0.5g); PROTEIN 13.3g; CARB 38.3g; FIBER 2.3g; CHOL 14mg; IRON 2.3mg; SODIUM 299mg; CALC 258mg

NO-TEAR ONIONS

Why does peeling or chopping onions make us cry?

Cutting into an onion releases a sulfur compound that turns into sulfuric acid when it comes into contact with moisture, such as the natural fluid in our eyes.

Some cooks dilute the irritating sulfur compound by **peeling onions under running water.**

Others slow the release of the sulfur compound by **chilling the onions for at least 1 hour or placing them in a bowl of ice water, mixed with a little lemon juice, for at least 30 minutes before peeling.**

Frozen onions are good only for cooking because freezing changes their texture. But there is good news about the frozen variety: Purchasing them already chopped will keep the tears at bay.

eggs & cheese

From pies and pizzas to soufflés and frittatas, you'll find a variety of egg and cheese recipes to choose from.

Eggs make a simple, satisfying offering for any meal. Before you begin, make sure you have stored the eggs properly. Always store eggs in the refrigerator, away from aromatic foods, because eggs absorb odors. Eggs will keep three to five weeks, and most cartons are stamped with a sell-by date to help you track their age. The USDA does not recommend serving dishes containing raw eggs due to an increased risk of salmonella; all eggs and egg dishes should be cooked to an internal temperature of 160°.

HUEVOS RANCHEROS

PREP: 5 MINUTES

COOK: 19 MINUTES

1 (14.5-ounce) can no-salt-added tomatoes, undrained and chopped
1 (15-ounce) can no-salt-added black beans, drained
1 (4.5-ounce) can chopped green chiles, undrained
2 tablespoons chopped fresh cilantro
2 teaspoons chili powder
½ teaspoon ground cumin
¼ teaspoon salt
⅛ teaspoon black pepper
2 (6-inch) corn tortillas
2 large eggs
2 tablespoons (½ ounce) shredded reduced-fat sharp cheddar cheese
2 tablespoons chopped green onions

1. Combine first 8 ingredients in a nonstick skillet; bring to a boil. Cover, reduce heat to low; simmer 10 minutes.
2. Warm tortillas according to package directions.

3. Break each egg into a custard cup, and slip egg from cup into tomato mixture. Cover and simmer 7 minutes or until eggs are done; remove eggs with a slotted spoon. Place tortillas on individual plates; top with half of tomato

mixture and 1 egg. Sprinkle each with 1 tablespoon cheese and 1 tablespoon green onions. Yield: 2 servings.

CALORIES 312 (23% from fat); FAT 8g (sat 2.6g, mono 2.6g, poly 1.4g); PROTEIN 19.6g; CARB 44g; FIBER 7.9g; CHOL 217mg; IRON 4.9mg; SODIUM 1472mg; CALC 226mg

Huevos Rancheros

1. Combine first 8 ingredients in a large nonstick skillet; bring to a boil. Cover, reduce heat to low, and simmer 10 minutes.

2. Break each egg into a custard cup.

3. Slip eggs from cup into tomato mixture; cover and simmer 7 minutes or until eggs are done.

4. Place tortilla on an individual plate; top with tomato mixture and an egg.

menu

Herbed-Potato Frittata

Fresh Ginger-and-Lemon Muffins (page 70)

*Fresh Fruit With
Strawberry Sauce (page 183)*

HERBED-POTATO FRITTATA

PREP: 25 MINUTES

COOK: 18 MINUTES

2 cups diced red potato
1 tablespoon reduced-calorie stick
    margarine
⅓ cup sliced green onions
1 teaspoon dried basil
½ teaspoon dried marjoram
¼ teaspoon salt
¼ teaspoon black pepper
1 garlic clove, minced
2 (8-ounce) cartons egg substitute
¾ cup (3 ounces) shredded
    reduced-fat sharp cheddar
    cheese

1. Place potato in a saucepan; add water to cover, and bring to a boil. Cover, reduce heat, and simmer 20 minutes or until tender; drain.
2. Melt margarine in a 10-inch nonstick skillet over medium-high heat. Add potato, onions, and next 5 ingredients; sauté 2 minutes. Spread potato mixture evenly in skillet.
3. Pour egg substitute over potato mixture; reduce heat to medium-low. Cook, uncovered, 8 to 10 minutes or until almost set.
4. Preheat broiler.
5. Wrap handle of skillet with foil; broil 3 minutes. Sprinkle with cheese, and broil 30 seconds or until cheese melts. Yield: 4 servings (serving size: 1 wedge).

CALORIES 193 (28% from fat); FAT 5.9g (sat 2.7g, mono 1g, poly 0.7g); PROTEIN 19.5g; CARB 15.5g; FIBER 1.5g; CHOL 14mg; IRON 3.3mg; SODIUM 507mg; CALC 227mg

Pan Handling

If the handle of your skillet isn't ovenproof, wrap it in foil to protect it from heat damage.

SUMMER GARDEN FRITTATA

PREP: 12 MINUTES   COOK: 19 MINUTES

1 cup chopped tomato
2 tablespoons chopped fresh or
    2 teaspoons dried basil
1 tablespoon balsamic vinegar
4 large egg whites, lightly beaten
1 large egg, lightly beaten
½ teaspoon salt
¼ teaspoon black pepper
1 cup cooked seashell pasta (about
    ½ cup uncooked pasta)
2 teaspoons reduced-calorie stick
    margarine
½ cup chopped onion
3 garlic cloves, minced
2 cups diced zucchini
½ cup (2 ounces) preshredded
    part-skim mozzarella cheese
    or reduced-fat Jarlsberg cheese

1. Preheat oven to 450°.
2. Combine first 3 ingredients in a small bowl; set aside. Combine egg whites, egg, salt, and pepper in a medium bowl, stirring with a whisk until well-blended. Stir in pasta.

3. Melt margarine in a 10-inch nonstick skillet over medium heat. Add onion and garlic; sauté 4 minutes or until tender. Add zucchini; sauté 5 minutes. Add egg mixture to skillet, spreading evenly. Cook over medium-low heat 5 minutes or until center is almost set. Sprinkle with cheese.
4. Wrap handle of skillet with foil. Bake at 450° for 5 minutes or until center is set. Serve frittata with tomato mixture. Yield: 2 servings (serving size: ½ frittata and ½ cup tomato mixture).

CALORIES 301 (36% from fat); FAT 12g (sat 5.1g, mono 4g, poly 1.7g); PROTEIN 21g; CARB 28.9g; FIBER 3.2g; CHOL 128mg; IRON 2.4mg; SODIUM 883mg; CALC 210mg

HERBED SPAGHETTI FRITTATA

PREP: 10 MINUTES   COOK: 13 MINUTES

Try your own favorite combination of fresh herbs in this dish.

1 cup cooked spaghetti (about
    3 ounces uncooked pasta)
2 tablespoons chopped fresh
    parsley
1 tablespoon chopped fresh basil
1 teaspoon chopped fresh
    tarragon
½ teaspoon chopped fresh rosemary
2 ounces fat-free cream cheese,
    cut into small pieces
¼ teaspoon pepper
5 large egg whites
1 large egg yolk
Cooking spray
3 garlic cloves, minced
6 (¼-inch-thick) slices plum tomato
¼ cup (1 ounce) grated Asiago
    cheese

1. Preheat oven to 450°.
2. Combine first 9 ingredients in a large bowl, and stir well. Set aside.
3. Coat a 10-inch nonstick skillet with

cooking spray; place over medium heat until hot. Add garlic; sauté 3 minutes. Stir in spaghetti mixture; spread evenly in skillet. Reduce heat to medium-low; cook 5 minutes or until almost set. Arrange tomato slices over spaghetti mixture, and sprinkle with cheese.

4. Wrap handle of skillet with foil; place skillet in oven, and bake at 450° for 5 minutes or until set. Yield: 2 servings (serving size: ½ frittata).

Note: ¾ cup egg substitute may be used instead of the 5 egg whites and 1 yolk.

CALORIES 322 (18% from fat); FAT 6.5g (sat 2.6g, mono 1.9g, poly 0.8g); PROTEIN 24g; CARB 40.3g; FIBER 2.3g; CHOL 120mg; IRON 2.7mg; SODIUM 476mg; CALC 242mg

POTATO-STUFFED OMELETS

PREP:7 MINUTES
COOK:18 MINUTES

For a flavorful topper, serve Chunky Tomato-Basil Sauce (page 448) with this hearty omelet.

    1½ cups cubed potato
    ½   cup chopped onion
    ½   cup chopped red bell
        pepper
    1   garlic clove, minced
    ¼   cup sliced pimento-stuffed
        olives
    1   tablespoon minced fresh
        oregano
    ½   cup (2 ounces) preshredded
        part-skim mozzarella
        cheese
    8   large egg whites
    4   large eggs
    ¼   teaspoon salt
    ⅛   teaspoon black pepper
    ½   teaspoon olive oil, divided
    Cooking spray

1. Place potato in a saucepan, and add water to cover. Bring to a boil; reduce

An omelet is basically a scrambled egg (unscrambled) folded over a flavorful filling. During cooking, loosen the edges gently to let the uncooked eggs flow underneath to cook.

OMELETS FOR ALL

Use your imagination to create your own concoctions. **Sautéed vegetables, salsas, tomato mixtures flavored with herbs, and roasted potatoes flavored with chives or rosemary** all make delectable fillings for omelets.

Spread the filling over half of the cooked omelet, and fold over.

heat, and simmer 10 minutes. Drain and cool.

2. Heat a medium nonstick skillet over medium heat. Add onion, bell pepper, and garlic; sauté 8 minutes. Add potato, olives, and oregano; cook 1 minute or until thoroughly heated. Remove from heat; stir in cheese. Keep warm.

3. Combine egg whites, eggs, salt, and pepper in a bowl; stir well with a whisk.

4. Heat ¼ teaspoon oil in a small non-stick skillet coated with cooking spray over medium-high heat. Add half of egg mixture to skillet. Cook 4 minutes; flip omelet. Spoon 1 cup potato mixture onto half of omelet. Carefully loosen with a spatula; fold in half. Cook 1 minute on each side. Slide onto a plate. Repeat procedure with ¼ teaspoon oil, cooking spray, egg mixture, and potato mixture. Yield: 4 servings (serving size: ½ omelet).

CALORIES 255 (32% from fat); FAT 9.2g (sat 3.2g, mono 3.4g, poly 0.9g); PROTEIN 18.9g; CARB 23.3g; FIBER 2g; CHOL 221mg; IRON 1.8mg; SODIUM 965mg; CALC 148mg

SPINACH, RICE, AND FETA PIE

PREP:15 MINUTES   COOK:35 MINUTES

    2   teaspoons stick margarine
    ¾   cup chopped onion
    2   teaspoons all-purpose flour
    ½   teaspoon salt
    ¼   teaspoon black pepper
    1½ cups 1% low-fat milk
    2   cups cooked long-grain rice
    ¾   cup (3 ounces) crumbled feta cheese
    1   (10-ounce) package frozen
        chopped spinach, thawed,
        drained, and squeezed dry
    1   large egg, lightly beaten
    2   large egg whites, lightly beaten
    Olive oil-flavored cooking spray
    2   tablespoons grated Parmesan cheese

1. Preheat oven to 400°.

2. Melt margarine in a large saucepan over medium heat. Add onion, and sauté 3 minutes. Stir in flour, salt, and pepper. Gradually add milk, stirring with a whisk until well-blended. Bring mixture to a simmer; cook 1 minute or until slightly thick, stirring constantly. Remove saucepan from heat; stir in rice, feta cheese, and spinach. Add egg and egg whites, stirring until well-blended.

3. Pour spinach mixture into a 9-inch pie plate coated with cooking spray. Sprinkle Parmesan cheese over pie. Bake at 400° for 35 minutes or until golden. Yield: 6 servings (serving size: 1 wedge).

CALORIES 212 (34% from fat); FAT 8g (sat 4.3g, mono 2.2g, poly 0.7g); PROTEIN 10.8g; CARB 24.5g; FIBER 2.1g; CHOL 57mg; IRON 2mg; SODIUM 565mg; CALC 268mg

EGGS SARDOU

PREP:18 MINUTES   COOK:10 MINUTES

- 1 tablespoon all-purpose flour
- ¾ cup 1% low-fat milk
- ⅓ cup fat-free sour cream
- 2 tablespoons grated Parmesan cheese
- ¼ teaspoon salt
- ⅛ teaspoon black pepper
- 1 (10-ounce) package frozen chopped spinach, thawed, drained, and squeezed dry
- 2 large eggs
- Cooking spray
- 2 canned artichoke bottoms, thinly sliced crosswise
- 2 teaspoons grated Parmesan cheese

1. Place flour in a saucepan. Gradually add milk, stirring with a whisk until smooth. Add sour cream and next 4 ingredients; stir well. Cook over medium heat 8 minutes, stirring occasionally. Remove from heat; keep warm.

2. Add water to a large skillet, filling two-thirds full. Bring to a boil; reduce heat, and simmer. Break an egg into each of 2 (6-ounce) custard cups coated with cooking spray. Place custard cups in simmering water in pan; cover and cook 6 minutes. Remove cups from water.

3. Preheat broiler.

4. Spoon ½ cup spinach mixture into each of 2 individual gratin dishes; fan sliced artichoke bottoms over spinach mixture. Invert poached eggs onto artichoke, and top each with ¼ cup spinach mixture. Sprinkle each serving with 1 teaspoon Parmesan cheese. Broil 3 minutes or until cheese is lightly browned. Yield: 2 servings.

Note: This recipe can be doubled—just make sure to use a skillet large enough to hold 4 (6-ounce) custard cups.

CALORIES 243 (33% from fat); FAT 9g (sat 3.5g, mono 2.8g, poly 1g); PROTEIN 20.6g; CARB 21.6g; FIBER 4.4g; CHOL 221mg; IRON 4.6mg; SODIUM 775mg; CALC 410mg

Eggs Sardou

1. Break eggs into each of 2 (6-ounce) custard cups coated with cooking spray.

2. Place custard cups in simmering water in a large skillet. Cover and cook 6 minutes.

3. Spoon ½ cup spinach mixture into each gratin dish, and fan sliced artichoke bottoms over spinach mixture.

4. Invert the poached eggs onto artichoke bottom slices.

5. Top with ¼ cup spinach mixture and cheese.

6. Broil 3 minutes or until cheese is lightly browned.

SEVEN-LAYER TORTILLA PIE

PREP: 30 MINUTES   COOK: 40 MINUTES

1 tablespoon olive oil
1 cup chopped red bell pepper
¾ cup chopped green bell pepper
½ cup chopped red onion
½ cup chopped seeded Anaheim
   chile or 1 (4.5-ounce) can
   chopped green chiles, drained
2 tablespoons minced fresh cilantro
1 teaspoon dried oregano
1 teaspoon chili powder
½ teaspoon ground cumin
2 cups no-salt-added tomato juice
2 (15-ounce) cans black beans, drained
2 (15-ounce) cans cannellini beans
   or other white beans, drained
1 cup (4 ounces) shredded reduced-
   fat Monterey Jack cheese
1 cup (4 ounces) shredded reduced-
   fat sharp cheddar cheese
Cooking spray
7 (8-inch) flour tortillas

1. Heat oil in a large nonstick skillet over medium heat. Add bell peppers, onion, and next 5 ingredients; sauté 5 minutes or until tender. Add juice; cook 8 minutes or until reduced to 2½ cups.
2. Combine black beans and half of tomato juice mixture in a bowl. Stir cannellini beans into remaining tomato juice mixture. Combine cheeses in a bowl.
3. Preheat oven to 325°.
4. Line a 9-inch pie plate with foil, allowing 6 inches of foil to extend over opposite edges of pie plate. Repeat procedure, extending foil over remaining edges of pie plate. Coat foil with cooking spray; place 1 tortilla in bottom of dish. Spread 1 cup cannellini bean mixture over tortilla; sprinkle with ¼ cup cheese mixture. Place 1 tortilla over cheese, pressing gently. Spread 1 cup black bean mixture over tortilla; sprinkle with ¼ cup cheese. Place 1 tortilla over cheese,

pressing gently. Repeat layers, ending with black bean mixture and cheese.
5. Bring edges of foil to center; fold to seal. Bake at 325° for 40 minutes. Remove from oven; let stand, covered, 10 minutes. Remove foil packet from dish. Unwrap pie; slide onto a serving plate using a spatula. Cut into wedges. Yield: 8 servings (serving size: 1 wedge).

CALORIES 423 (23% from fat); FAT 11g (sat 4.1g, mono 2.5g, poly 1.9g); PROTEIN 24.5g; CARB 59.3g; FIBER 7.4g; CHOL 18mg; IRON 5mg; SODIUM 758mg; CALC 353mg

SPICY CHEESE PIZZA

PREP: 51 MINUTES   RISE: 1 HOUR 5 MINUTES
COOK: 9 MINUTES

Cooking spray
3 garlic cloves, minced
1 tablespoon chopped fresh or
   1 teaspoon dried oregano
1 tablespoon minced fresh cilantro
¾ teaspoon fennel seeds
¼ teaspoon salt
¼ teaspoon crushed red pepper
1 (8-ounce) can no-salt-added
   tomato sauce
1 recipe Basic Pizza Crust (page 102)
2 teaspoons cornmeal
1½ cups (6 ounces) preshredded part-
   skim mozzarella cheese

1. Place a medium saucepan coated with cooking spray over medium heat until hot. Add garlic; sauté 2 minutes. Add oregano and next 5 ingredients; reduce heat, and simmer, uncovered, 20 minutes or until thick, stirring occasionally.
2. Preheat oven to 450°.
3. Prepare Basic Pizza Crust dough. Punch dough down; let rest 5 minutes. Roll dough into a 12-inch circle on a lightly floured surface. Place on a 12-inch pizza pan coated with cooking spray and sprinkled with 2 teaspoons cornmeal. Crimp edges to form a rim. Let

dough stand, covered, 10 minutes. Spread sauce over crust; sprinkle with cheese. Bake at 450° for 9 minutes or until cheese melts and crust is golden. Yield: 1 pizza, 6 servings (serving size: 1 wedge).

CALORIES 221 (24% from fat); FAT 6g (sat 3g, mono 1.9g, poly 0.4g); PROTEIN 11.2g; CARB 30.2g; FIBER 1.9g; CHOL 16mg; IRON 2.2mg; SODIUM 337mg; CALC 204mg

SPINACH-MUSHROOM PIZZA

PREP: 12 MINUTES   COOK: 15 MINUTES

Cooking spray
2 tablespoons cornmeal
1 (10-ounce) can refrigerated
   pizza crust
1 (10-ounce) package frozen
   chopped spinach, thawed,
   drained, and squeezed dry
¾ cup (3 ounces) preshredded
   part-skim mozzarella cheese
2 teaspoons bottled minced garlic
1 teaspoon dried Italian seasoning
¼ teaspoon black pepper
1 (4.5-ounce) jar sliced mushrooms,
   drained
2 (14½-ounce) cans pasta-style
   tomatoes, drained
½ cup (2 ounces) crumbled feta cheese

1. Preheat oven to 425°.
2. Coat a 15 x 10-inch jelly-roll pan with cooking spray; sprinkle with cornmeal. Unroll dough; press into pan. Bake at 425° for 6 minutes or until crust begins to brown.
3. Combine spinach and next 4 ingredients; spread over crust, leaving a ½-inch border. Top with mushrooms and tomatoes; sprinkle with feta cheese. Bake at 425° for 9 minutes or until crust is lightly browned (feta cheese will not melt). Cut into 6 equal pieces. Yield: 1 pizza, 6 servings (serving size: 1 square).

CALORIES 243 (27% from fat); FAT 7.2g (sat 3.5g, mono 1.3g, poly 0.2g); PROTEIN 12.4g; CARB 32.7g; FIBER 2.8g; CHOL 20mg; IRON 2mg; SODIUM 980mg; CALC 251mg

CHICAGO DEEP-DISH PIZZAS

PREP: 50 MINUTES   RISE: 1 HOUR 10 MINUTES
COOK: 25 MINUTES

1   package dry yeast (about 2¼
    teaspoons)
1   teaspoon sugar
1   cup warm water (100° to 110°)
2½ cups all-purpose flour
½   cup yellow cornmeal
¼   teaspoon salt
1   tablespoon olive oil
Cooking spray
1   tablespoon olive oil
1½ cups chopped green bell pepper
1½ cups chopped onion
1   garlic clove, crushed
2½ cups sliced mushrooms
2   teaspoons dried oregano
¼   teaspoon salt
2   tablespoons yellow cornmeal
1½ cups canned crushed tomatoes
1¼ cups (5 ounces) shredded
       reduced-fat Monterey Jack cheese
¾   cup (3 ounces) shredded
       provolone cheese

1. Dissolve yeast and sugar in warm water in a small bowl; let stand 5 minutes. Lightly spoon flour into dry measuring cups; level with a knife. Place flour, ½ cup cornmeal, and ¼ teaspoon salt in a food processor; pulse 2 times or until blended. With processor on, slowly add yeast mixture and 1 tablespoon oil through food chute; process until dough forms a ball. Process 1 additional minute. Turn dough out onto a lightly floured surface; knead lightly 4 or 5 times. Place dough in a bowl coated with cooking spray, turning to coat top. Cover dough, and let rise in a warm place (85°), free from drafts, 45 minutes or until doubled in size. (Press two fingers into dough. If indentation remains, the dough has risen enough.)

2. Heat 1 tablespoon oil in a large non-stick skillet over medium heat. Add bell pepper, onion, and garlic; sauté 5 minutes. Add mushrooms, oregano, and ¼ teaspoon salt; sauté 3 minutes or until tender. Remove from heat; cool.
3. Preheat oven to 475°.
4. Punch dough down; cover and let rest 5 minutes. Divide dough in half. Roll each half of dough into an 11-inch circle on a lightly floured surface.
5. Place dough in 2 (9-inch) round cake pans coated with cooking spray and each sprinkled with 1 tablespoon cornmeal; press dough up sides of pans. Cover and let rise 20 minutes or until puffy.
6. Spread half of crushed tomatoes over each prepared crust; top each with half of onion mixture. Sprinkle cheeses evenly over pizzas. Bake at 475° for 15 minutes. Reduce oven temperature to 375°; bake an additional 10 minutes. Cut each pizza into 8 wedges. Yield: 2 pizzas, 8 wedges per pizza (serving size: 2 wedges).

CALORIES 336 (29% from fat); FAT 10.7g (sat 4.4g, mono 4.5g, poly 0.8g); PROTEIN 14.5g; CARB 45.6g; FIBER 3.1g; CHOL 19mg; IRON 3.5mg; SODIUM 411mg; CALC 256mg

SICILIAN DEEP-DISH EGGPLANT PIZZAS

PREP: 1 HOUR 5 MINUTES
RISE: 1 HOUR   COOK: 30 MINUTES

1   recipe Basic Pizza Crust (page 102)
Cooking spray
1   tablespoon cornmeal
4   cups diced peeled eggplant
2   tablespoons olive oil
2   teaspoons dried Italian seasoning
¾   teaspoon salt
1   cup drained canned quartered
       artichoke hearts
1   cup (½-inch) cubed seeded tomato
1   cup minced red onion
2   tablespoons capers
1   tablespoon chopped fresh or
       1 teaspoon dried rosemary
2   teaspoons fennel seeds, crushed
4   garlic cloves, minced
2   cups (8 ounces) preshredded
       part-skim mozzarella cheese

1. Prepare Basic Pizza Crust dough; shape into 2 (11-inch) circles. Place in 2 (9-inch) cake pans coated with cooking spray and

Chicago Deep-Dish Pizza

each sprinkled with 1½ teaspoons corn-meal; press dough up sides of pans. Cover; let rise 20 minutes or until puffy.

2. Preheat oven to 375°.

3. Combine eggplant, oil, Italian season-ing, and salt. Place eggplant mixture on a jelly-roll pan, spreading evenly. Bake at 375° for 25 minutes or until tender. Re-move eggplant mixture from oven. In-crease oven temperature to 400°.

4. Combine artichokes and next 6 ingre-dients in a bowl. Divide eggplant mixture and artichoke mixture evenly between pizza crusts, and top each with 1 cup cheese. Bake at 400° for 30 minutes or until crusts are lightly browned. Cut each pizza into 4 wedges. Yield: 2 pizzas, 4 servings per pizza (serving size: 1 wedge).

CALORIES 316 (27% from fat); FAT 9.5g (sat 3.5g, mono 4.3g, poly 0.8g); PROTEIN 13.6g; CARB 44.8g; FIBER 3.2g; CHOL 16mg; IRON 3.4mg; SODIUM 703mg; CALC 228mg

WHITE BEAN HUMMUS-AND-ASIAGO PIZZAS

PREP:1 HOUR   RISE:1 HOUR
COOK:8 MINUTES

2 tablespoons olive oil
7 cups thinly sliced onion,
   separated into rings
2 recipes Quick-and-Easy Pizza
   Crust (page 103)
¾ cup White Bean Hummus (page
   446)
¾ cup grated Asiago cheese
¾ cup crumbled feta cheese
2 cups trimmed arugula, firmly
   packed
1 tablespoon balsamic vinegar
⅓ cup shaved fresh Parmesan cheese

1. Preheat oven to 500°.

2. Heat oil in a large nonstick skillet over medium-high heat. Add onion; cover and cook 15 minutes or until deep golden, stir-ring frequently. Remove from heat.

3. Prepare 2 recipes Quick-and-Easy Pizza Crust dough; shape into 6 (7-inch) circles.

4. Spread 2 tablespoons White Bean Hummus onto each of 6 prepared Quick-and-Easy Pizza Crusts. Top each with about ½ cup onion. Sprinkle evenly with Asiago and feta cheeses. Bake at 500° for 8 minutes or until crusts are crisp.

5. Combine arugula and vinegar; toss. Divide arugula mixture and Parmesan cheese evenly among pizzas. Serve im-mediately. Yield: 6 pizzas, 2 servings per pizza (serving size: ½ pizza).

CALORIES 297 (28% from fat); FAT 9.2g (sat 2.7g, mono 4.4g, poly 1g); PROTEIN 11.2g; CARB 64g; FIBER 3.4g; CHOL 8mg; IRON 2.6mg; SODIUM 437mg; CALC 170mg

VIDALIA-AND-WISCONSIN GORGONZOLA PIZZAS

PREP:2 HOURS   RISE:1 HOUR
COOK:8 MINUTES

6 medium peeled Vidalia or other
   sweet onions (about 3 pounds)
2 tablespoons extra-virgin olive oil
½ teaspoon salt
¼ teaspoon freshly ground black pepper
Cooking spray
4 cups all-purpose flour, divided
1 package dry yeast (about 2¼
   teaspoons)
2 cups water
1 large peeled baking potato (about
   ¾ pound), cut into ½-inch cubes
1 tablespoon honey
1½ teaspoons salt
1 tablespoon olive oil
3 tablespoons cornmeal
½ cup mascarpone cheese, softened
1 cup (4 ounces) crumbled
   Gorgonzola cheese
6 tablespoons coarsely chopped pecans

1. Preheat oven to 350°.

2. Cut each peeled onion into 6 wedges, leaving root end intact. Combine onion,

2 tablespoons oil, ½ teaspoon salt, and pepper in a bowl; toss well. Place in a 13 x 9-inch baking dish coated with cooking spray. Cover; bake at 350° for 45 minutes. Uncover and bake an additional hour or until onions are caramelized; cool.

3. While onion bakes, lightly spoon flour into dry measuring cups, level with a knife. Combine ½ cup flour and yeast in a bowl.

4. Bring 2 cups water to a boil in a saucepan; add potato, and cook 10 min-utes or until tender. Drain, reserving 1 cup cooking liquid. Let liquid cool until very warm (120° to 130°). Mash potato, reserv-ing 1 cup. Combine reserved potato, re-served cooking liquid, and honey; stir into yeast mixture. Let stand 10 minutes.

5. Place 3½ cups flour and 1½ teaspoons salt in a food processor; pulse 2 or 3 times. With processor on, add yeast mixture and 1 tablespoon oil through food chute; process until dough leaves sides of bowl and forms a ball. Process 20 additional sec-onds. Place in a bowl coated with cooking spray, turning to coat top. Cover and let rise in a warm place (85°), free from drafts, 45 minutes or until doubled in size. (Press two fingers into dough. If indentation re-mains, the dough has risen enough.) Punch dough down, and turn out onto a lightly floured surface; knead 3 or 4 times. With floured hands, divide dough into 6 portions; form each into a ball (dough will be sticky). Cover; let rest 15 minutes. Roll each ball into a 9-inch circle; place on bak-ing sheets sprinkled with cornmeal.

6. Preheat oven to 500°.

7. Spread 1 tablespoon mascarpone cheese over each crust; top each evenly with caramelized onions, Gorgonzola cheese, and pecans.

8. Bake at 500° for 8 minutes or until cheese melts. Yield: 6 pizzas, 2 servings per pizza (serving size: ½ pizza).

CALORIES 364 (39% from fat); FAT 15.7g (sat 6.2g, mono 5.7g, poly 2.4g); PROTEIN 10g; CARB 46.6g; FIBER 3.7g; CHOL 24mg; IRON 2.4mg; SODIUM 617mg; CALC 121mg

Fresh Tomato, Basil, and Cheese Pizza

menu

Pizza With Caramelized Onions, Feta, and Olives

Pub Salad (page 391)

Lemon Gelati (page 175)

PIZZA WITH CARAMELIZED ONIONS, FETA, AND OLIVES

PREP: 30 MINUTES

RISE: 1 HOUR

COOK: 18 MINUTES

1 recipe Quick-and-Easy Pizza Crust (page 103)
1 tablespoon cornmeal
2½ cups Caramelized Onions (page 495)
¼ teaspoon salt
¼ teaspoon black pepper
1 garlic clove, minced
1 cup (4 ounces) crumbled feta cheese
¼ cup coarsely chopped pitted kalamata olives

1. Prepare Quick-and-Easy Pizza Crust dough, shaping into a 14-inch circle on a lightly floured surface. Place dough on a 15-inch pizza pan or baking sheet sprinkled with cornmeal.
2. Preheat oven to 450°.
3. Combine Caramelized Onions, ¼ teaspoon salt, pepper, and garlic. Spread onion mixture over dough. Sprinkle feta and olives over onion mixture.
4. Bake at 450° for 18 minutes or until crust is lightly browned. Yield: 1 pizza, 6 servings (serving size: 1 wedge).

CALORIES 306 (29% from fat); FAT 9.8g (sat 4.7g, mono 3.6g, poly 0.8g); PROTEIN 10.2g; CARB 44.7g; FIBER 4g; CHOL 24mg; IRON 3mg; SODIUM 600mg; CALC 178mg

FRESH TOMATO, BASIL, AND CHEESE PIZZA

PREP: 15 MINUTES   COOK: 10 MINUTES

1 (1 pound) Italian cheese-flavored pizza crust (such as Boboli)
2 teaspoons olive oil
½ cup (2 ounces) grated fresh Parmesan cheese, divided
3 tomatoes, cut into ¼-inch slices (about 1½ pounds)
6 garlic cloves, thinly sliced
¼ teaspoon salt
⅛ teaspoon black pepper
¼ cup fresh basil leaves

1. Preheat oven to 450°.
2. Brush crust with olive oil. Sprinkle with ¼ cup Parmesan cheese, leaving a ½-inch border. Arrange tomato slices over cheese, overlapping edges; top with garlic slices, ¼ cup cheese, salt, and pepper.
3. Bake pizza at 450° for 10 to 12 minutes or until crust is golden. Remove pizza to a cutting board, and top with fresh basil leaves. Let stand 5 minutes. Yield: 1 pizza, 6 servings (serving size: 1 wedge).

CALORIES 260 (26% from fat); FAT 7.5g (sat 2.7g, mono 1.8g, poly 0.3g); PROTEIN 11.3g; CARB 38.2g; FIBER 1.6g; CHOL 4mg; IRON 2.1mg; SODIUM 611mg; CALC 224mg

GRILLED PIZZA MARGHERITA

PREP: 8 MINUTES   RISE: 1 HOUR
COOK: 16 MINUTES

1   recipe Quick-and-Easy Pizza
    Crust (page 103)
1   tablespoon cornmeal
2   teaspoons olive oil
⅛   teaspoon salt
⅛   teaspoon black pepper
¼   cup thinly sliced fresh basil
2   tablespoons chopped fresh oregano
Cooking spray
4   plum tomatoes, thinly sliced
    (about ½ pound)
1   cup (4 ounces) preshredded
    part-skim mozzarella cheese

1. Prepare Quick-and-Easy Pizza Crust dough, shaping into 2 (10-inch) circles. Place dough circles on a baking sheet sprinkled with cornmeal.
2. Prepare grill.
3. Combine oil, salt, and pepper. Combine basil and oregano in a small bowl.
4. Place 1 crust, cornmeal side up, on grill rack coated with cooking spray; cover and grill 3 minutes or until puffy and golden. Turn crust; brush with half of oil mixture. Top with half of tomato slices, herb mixture, and mozzarella. Cover; grill 4 to 5 minutes or until cheese melts and crust is lightly browned. Repeat procedure with remaining crust and toppings. Yield: 2 pizzas, 3 servings per pizza (serving size: ⅓ pizza).

CALORIES 261 (28% from fat); FAT 8.1g (sat 2.6g, mono 3.8g, poly 0.9g); PROTEIN 10.8g; CARB 36.3g; FIBER 2.3g; CHOL 11mg; IRON 2.8mg; SODIUM 338mg; CALC 149mg

Grilled Pizza Margherita

With our pizza dough recipe, making your own crust is easier than you might imagine and it's well worth it for the flavor and texture. By following these simple instructions, you'll be ready, able, and grilling in no time.

1. Roll each crust into a 10-inch circle.

2. Place crust on a baking sheet sprinkled with cornmeal.

3. Gently lift crust from the baking sheet to the grill.

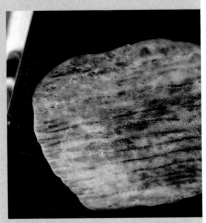

4. Turn crust, grill-mark side up, after about 3 minutes. Arrange toppings over crust, and grill until done.

Because the crusts are thin, it takes only a few minutes to grill the pizzas. This may be one of the best-tasting pizzas your family has ever had—and possibly the first cooked in your own backyard!

ZUCCHINI, SWEET ONION, AND RED PEPPER TART

PREP: 30 MINUTES   COOK: 45 MINUTES

1 (10-inch) Greek Baking
  Powder Piecrust (page 214)
Cooking spray
2 large eggs
2 large egg whites
1 cup chopped Vidalia or other
  sweet onion
2 cups diced red bell pepper
  (about 2 medium)
¾ teaspoon salt, divided
3 cups chopped zucchini (about ¾
  pound)
2 garlic cloves, minced
1 tablespoon water
1 teaspoon chopped fresh or
  ¼ teaspoon dried thyme
½ cup fat-free milk
2 tablespoons nonfat dry milk
¼ cup (1 ounce) finely shredded
  Parmesan cheese
¼ cup (1 ounce) shredded Gruyère
  or Swiss cheese

1. Preheat oven to 375°.
2. Prepare Greek Baking Powder Piecrust, and press into a 10-inch quiche
dish coated with cooking spray. Combine eggs and egg whites in a bowl; beat
well with a whisk. Brush 2 tablespoons
egg mixture over crust; set remaining egg
mixture aside. Bake crust at 375° for 8 to
10 minutes; cool on a wire rack.
3. Place a large nonstick skillet coated
with cooking spray over medium heat
until hot. Add onion, bell pepper, and ½
teaspoon salt; sauté 10 minutes or until
lightly browned. Add zucchini, garlic,
and water; sauté 10 minutes or until vegetables are tender. Stir in thyme. Spoon
zucchini mixture into prepared crust.
4. Add fat-free milk, dry milk, and
¼ teaspoon salt to remaining egg mixture in bowl; beat well. Pour egg mixture

evenly over zucchini mixture; sprinkle
with cheeses. Bake at 375° for 45 minutes or until a knife inserted near center
comes out clean. Yield: 6 servings (serving size: 1 wedge).

CALORIES 218 (33% from fat); FAT 8g (sat 2.5g, mono 3.8g,
poly 0.8g); PROTEIN 11g; CARB 26g; FIBER 2g;
CHOL 78mg; IRON 2.3mg; SODIUM 576mg; CALC 201mg

THREE-PEPPER QUESADILLAS

PREP: 10 MINUTES
COOK: 16 MINUTES

1 cup finely chopped yellow bell
  pepper
1 cup finely chopped red bell
  pepper
½ cup chopped Vidalia or other
  sweet onion
1 tablespoon finely chopped
  seeded jalapeño pepper
½ teaspoon ground cumin
½ teaspoon salt
¼ teaspoon freshly ground black
  pepper
Cooking spray
8 (6-inch) corn tortillas
1 cup (4 ounces) shredded reduced-
  fat Monterey Jack cheese

1. Combine first 7 ingredients in a large
bowl.
2. Place a large skillet coated with cooking spray over medium-high heat until
hot. Add 1 tortilla, and top with ¼ cup
bell pepper mixture. Sprinkle with ¼
cup cheese; top with 1 tortilla. Cook 2
minutes on each side or until golden,
pressing down with a spatula. Repeat
procedure with remaining tortillas, bell
pepper mixture, and cheese. Yield: 4
servings (serving size: 1 quesadilla).

CALORIES 225 (29% from fat); FAT 7.2g (sat 3.4g, mono 1.9g,
poly 0.9g); PROTEIN 12.2g; CARB 30g; FIBER 4.3g;
CHOL 19mg; IRON 2mg; SODIUM 558mg; CALC 327mg

menu

Fat-free refried beans

Low-fat tortilla chips

**Goat Cheese Quesadillas With
Green Chile Salsa**

Strawberry Margaritas (page 57)

GOAT CHEESE QUESADILLAS WITH GREEN CHILE SALSA

PREP: 12 MINUTES
COOK: 25 MINUTES

1 cup (4 ounces) goat cheese
1 cup (4 ounces) shredded
  reduced-fat Monterey Jack
  cheese
¼ cup chopped fresh cilantro
1 tablespoon chili powder
1 (15-ounce) can red beans, rinsed
  and drained
8 (8-inch) fat-free flour
  tortillas
Cooking spray
Green Chile Salsa (page 438)
Cilantro sprigs (optional)

1. Preheat oven to 350°.
2. Combine first 5 ingredients; spread
about ½ cup cheese mixture onto each
of 4 tortillas, leaving a ½-inch border.
Top each with a tortilla, pressing gently
to secure.
3. Place quesadillas on a baking sheet
coated with cooking spray, and cover
with foil. Bake at 350° for 25 minutes or
until cheese melts. Serve with Green
Chile Salsa. Garnish quesadillas with
cilantro sprigs, if desired. Yield: 4 servings (serving size: 1 quesadilla and 1⅓
cups salsa).

CALORIES 537 (25% from fat); FAT 15.1g (sat 9.4g, mono 3.8g,
poly 0.8g); PROTEIN 26.4g; CARB 72g; FIBER 10.1g;
CHOL 55mg; IRON 3.5mg; SODIUM 1334mg; CALC 462mg

CHEESY RICE-AND-BEAN STRATA

PREP: 28 MINUTES   COOK: 35 MINUTES

2 teaspoons olive oil
2 cups minced red onion
1 teaspoon ground cumin
2 garlic cloves, minced
1 (10-ounce) package fresh
   spinach, chopped
2 (19-ounce) cans kidney beans,
   drained
1 (16-ounce) jar picante sauce
Cooking spray
5 cups cooked basmati rice
12 (¼-inch-thick) slices tomato
1 cup (4 ounces) shredded reduced-
   fat sharp cheddar cheese
1 cup (4 ounces) shredded reduced-
   fat Monterey Jack cheese
1 cup Quick Mole Marinara Sauce
   (page 449)
½ cup diagonally sliced green onions
½ cup low-fat sour cream

1. Preheat oven to 350°.
2. Heat oil in a large nonstick skillet over medium-high heat. Add red onion, cumin, and garlic; sauté 2 minutes. Add spinach; sauté 1 minute or until spinach wilts. Remove from heat.
3. Combine beans and picante sauce in a bowl. Spread 2 cups of bean mixture in a 13 x 9-inch baking dish coated with cooking spray. Spread 3 cups rice over bean mixture; top with tomato slices. Layer spinach mixture, 2 cups rice, and remaining bean mixture over tomato slices.
4. Cover; bake at 350° for 30 minutes. Sprinkle with cheeses; bake, uncovered, an additional 5 minutes or until cheese melts. Top each serving with 2 tablespoons marinara sauce, 1 tablespoon green onions, and 1 tablespoon sour cream. Yield: 8 servings.

CALORIES 442 (21% from fat); FAT 10.5g (sat 4.8g, mono 3.9g, poly 1g); PROTEIN 22.3g; CARB 66.7g; FIBER 6.7g; CHOL 25mg; IRON 6.2mg; SODIUM 1226mg; CALC 365mg

SPANAKOPITA STRUDEL

PREP: 30 MINUTES   COOK: 22 MINUTES

Butter-flavored cooking spray
¾ cup chopped onion
2 garlic cloves, minced
2 cups (8 ounces) shredded
   reduced-sodium, reduced-fat
   Jarlsberg cheese
½ teaspoon dried oregano
½ teaspoon black pepper
¼ teaspoon salt
¼ teaspoon dried basil
⅛ teaspoon ground nutmeg
1 (15-ounce) carton fat-free
   ricotta cheese
1 (10-ounce) package frozen
   chopped spinach, thawed,
   drained, and squeezed dry
3 large egg whites, lightly beaten
7 sheets frozen phyllo pastry, thawed
¼ cup dry breadcrumbs

1. Preheat oven to 375°.
2. Place a nonstick skillet coated with cooking spray over medium-high heat until hot. Add onion and garlic; sauté 3 minutes or until tender. Combine onion mixture, Jarlsberg cheese, and next 8 ingredients in a bowl; stir until well-blended.
3. Place 1 phyllo sheet on a slightly damp towel (cover remaining dough to deep from drying), and coat with cooking spray. Sprinkle with 2 teaspoons breadcrumbs. Repeat layers with remaining phyllo sheets, cooking spray, and breadcrumbs, ending with a phyllo sheet. Spoon spinach mixture along 1 long edge of phyllo stack, leaving a 3-inch border; fold border over spinach. Fold over short edges of phyllo stack 1 inch.
4. Starting at long side with border, roll up jelly-roll fashion, folding in short edges while rolling. Place, seam side down, on a 15 x 10-inch jelly-roll pan coated with cooking spray. Score top layer of strudel, using a sharp knife. Lightly coat with cooking spray.

5. Bake strudel at 375° for 22 minutes or until golden. Let stand 10 minutes before serving. Cut into 6 slices. Yield: 6 servings (serving size: 1 slice).

CALORIES 257 (25% from fat); FAT 7.1g (sat 3g, mono 1.8g, poly 1.4g); PROTEIN 27.4g; CARB 23.1g; FIBER 1.9g; CHOL 21mg; IRON 2.4mg; SODIUM 510mg; CALC 460mg

FOUR CORN PUDDING

PREP: 15 MINUTES   COOK: 50 MINUTES

Cooking spray
1 cup chopped onion
2 (8¾-ounce) cans no-salt-added
   whole-kernel corn, drained
1 (14¾-ounce) can no-salt-added
   cream-style corn
1 (15.5-ounce) can white hominy,
   drained
1 (4.5-ounce) can chopped green
   chiles, drained
¼ cup chopped fresh cilantro
¾ cup egg substitute
¾ cup (3 ounces) shredded
   colby-Jack cheese, divided
1 cup cornflakes, finely crushed
¼ cup fat-free sour cream

1. Preheat oven to 375°.
2. Place a small nonstick skillet coated with cooking spray over medium-high heat until hot. Add onion; sauté 5 to 7 minutes or until lightly browned. Combine onion, whole-kernel corn, and next 5 ingredients in a bowl. Stir in ½ cup cheese.
3. Pour corn mixture into a 10-inch deep-dish pie plate coated with cooking spray. Combine ¼ cup cheese and cornflakes; sprinkle over corn mixture.
4. Bake at 375° for 50 minutes or until top is browned and mixture is set. Top each serving with 1 tablespoon sour cream. Yield: 4 servings.

CALORIES 336 (24% from fat); FAT 8.8g (sat 4.5g, mono 2.3g, poly 0.7g); PROTEIN 15.8g; CARB 49.6g; FIBER 3.9g; CHOL 20mg; IRON 2.7mg; SODIUM 741mg; CALC 202mg

Cheese Soufflé With Fresh Corn

PREP: 30 MINUTES   COOK: 35 MINUTES

1½ cups fresh corn kernels (about 2 ears)
½ cup fat-free milk
¼ cup all-purpose flour
½ cup fat-free cottage cheese
½ teaspoon salt
¼ teaspoon ground red pepper
⅛ teaspoon ground nutmeg (optional)
2 large egg yolks, lightly beaten
¾ cup (3 ounces) shredded reduced-fat sharp cheddar cheese
4 large egg whites
½ teaspoon cream of tartar
  Cooking spray
1 teaspoon all-purpose flour

1. Preheat oven to 375°.
2. Place corn, milk, ¼ cup flour, and next 3 ingredients in a food processor; add nutmeg, if desired. Process until blended, scraping sides of processor bowl once. Pour corn mixture into a medium saucepan, and bring to a simmer over medium-high heat. Cook 3 minutes or until mixture is thick; remove from heat. Transfer mixture to a large bowl; cool completely.
3. Add egg yolks and cheddar cheese to corn mixture, stirring with a whisk until thoroughly blended.
4. Beat egg whites and cream of tartar at high speed of a mixer until stiff peaks form. Gently fold one-fourth of egg white mixture into corn mixture; gently fold in remaining egg white mixture. Pour mixture into a 2-quart soufflé dish coated with cooking spray and dusted with 1 teaspoon flour.
5. Bake cheese soufflé at 375° for 35 minutes or until puffy and golden. Yield: 4 servings (serving size: about 1 cup).
Note: When removing corn kernels from the cob, cut them directly into a bowl using a sharp knife.

CALORIES 217 (32% from fat); FAT 7.6g (sat 3.3g, mono 2.3g, poly 0.8g); PROTEIN 18.7g; CARB 19.8g; FIBER 1.9g; CHOL 125mg; IRON 1mg; SODIUM 641mg; CALC 258mg

tofu & tempeh

Tofu and tempeh are starting to appear more frequently on American tables. With their health benefits and versatility, they may be just what you need for dinner tonight.

Spicy Tofu And Noodles With Mushrooms

PREP: 20 MINUTES
COOK: 14 MINUTES

This recipe features three of our top ingredients. See page 16 for dried mushrooms and pine nuts. Health benefits of tofu are listed with soy on page 19.

1 cup boiling water
1 (0.5-ounce) package dried wood ear or shiitake mushrooms
2 quarts water
6 ounces uncooked rice spaghetti-style pasta
1 tablespoon vegetable oil
½ cup finely chopped onion
½ cup finely chopped carrot
½ cup thinly sliced green onions
2 teaspoons minced peeled fresh ginger
1 teaspoon garlic-chili pepper sauce (such as Taste of Thai)
2 garlic cloves, minced
1 tablespoon low-sodium soy sauce
1 tablespoon hoisin sauce
1 teaspoon sugar
2 teaspoons rice vinegar
1 (16-ounce) package firm tofu, drained and cubed (about 3 cups)
18 Bibb lettuce leaves
¼ cup hoisin sauce
¼ cup pine nuts, toasted

1. Combine 1 cup boiling water and mushrooms in a bowl; cover and let stand 15 minutes. Drain and chop mushrooms. Bring 2 quarts water to a rolling boil. Add pasta; cook 6 to 8 minutes or until "al dente." Drain.
2. Heat oil in a large skillet over medium-high heat. Add chopped mushrooms, chopped onion, and next 5 ingredients; sauté 3 minutes. Add soy sauce, 1 tablespoon hoisin sauce, sugar, vinegar, and tofu to skillet. Stir in pasta, and sauté 2 minutes.
3. Place 3 lettuce leaves on each individual serving plate. Spoon ⅓ cup tofu mixture into each lettuce leaf; drizzle 2 teaspoons hoisin sauce over each serving. Sprinkle each serving with 2 teaspoons pine nuts. Yield: 6 servings.

CALORIES 289 (35% from fat); FAT 11.3g (sat 1.8g, mono 3.4g, poly 5.4g); PROTEIN 10.2g; CARB 40.4g; FIBER 3.5g; CHOL 0mg; IRON 6mg; SODIUM 372mg; CALC 140mg

Seasoned Tofu Steaks and Vegetable Stir-Fry With Ginger Sauce

PREP: 16 MINUTES   COOK: 17 MINUTES

1 (12.3-ounce) package
     reduced-fat firm tofu, drained
¼ cup all-purpose flour
2 tablespoons dry breadcrumbs
½ teaspoon dried thyme
¼ teaspoon dried dill
¼ teaspoon salt
¼ teaspoon paprika
¼ teaspoon freshly ground black
     pepper
1 large egg, lightly beaten
2 teaspoons vegetable oil
⅓ cup rice vinegar
⅓ cup sugar
½ cup water
2 tablespoons low-sodium soy sauce
1 tablespoon cornstarch
¼ cup water
1 tablespoon minced peeled fresh
     ginger
1 teaspoon vegetable oil
1 cup yellow bell pepper strips
1 cup snow peas, trimmed
½ cup chopped plum tomato
2 cups hot cooked angel hair pasta
     (about 4 ounces uncooked pasta)

1. Cut tofu lengthwise into 4 (½-inch-thick) slices. Place tofu steaks on several layers of paper towels. Cover steaks with additional paper towels, and let stand 5 minutes.

2. Combine flour and next 6 ingredients. Dredge each tofu steak in flour mixture. Dip in egg; dredge again in flour mixture. Heat 2 teaspoons oil in a large nonstick skillet over medium-high heat. Add tofu steaks; cook 3 minutes on each side. Remove from skillet; cut each tofu steak into 4 squares. Keep warm.

3. Combine vinegar, sugar, ½ cup water, and soy sauce in a small saucepan; bring to a boil over medium-high heat. Reduce heat, and simmer, uncovered, 3 minutes or until sugar is dissolved. Combine cornstarch and ¼ cup water; stir into sugar mixture. Bring to a boil, and cook 1 minute or until thick. Remove from heat; stir in ginger. Keep warm.

4. Heat 1 teaspoon oil in skillet over medium-high heat. Add bell pepper strips and snow peas, and stir-fry 2 minutes. Add tomato; stir-fry 1 minute. Serve over pasta; top with tofu and ginger sauce. Yield: 4 servings (serving size: ½ cup pasta, 4 tofu squares, ½ cup vegetable stir-fry, and ¼ cup ginger sauce).

CALORIES 328 (18% from fat); FAT 6.7g (sat 1.2g, mono 1.9g, poly 2.8g); PROTEIN 12.9g; CARB 54.5g; FIBER 2.5g; CHOL 53mg; IRON 3.9mg; SODIUM 495mg; CALC 61mg

These tofu steaks are also great stacked on a bun with lettuce and a few slices of grilled tomato.

Seasoned Tofu Steaks and Vegetable Stir-Fry With Ginger Sauce

TOFU TIPS

Tofu comes in a variety of textures including **soft, firm, and extra-firm.** Soft tofu can be puréed and added to soups, dips, and spreads. Firm and extra-firm tofu can be marinated, sautéed, or pan-fried. Tofu in aseptic packages tends to be more delicate, regardless of whether it's labeled firm or extra-firm, while water-packed tofu tends to be sturdier.

You can make tofu stronger by heating it, either in simmering water or by "frying" it in a nonstick skillet. This toughens the proteins and, in the case of the skillet method, pulls out excess water while browning it a bit. (This works best with water-packed tofu.)

Another way to get rid of any excess moisture in tofu is to place a weight on the unwrapped tofu for about 30 minutes to force out the liquid. It isn't necessary to do this with Mori-Nu brand.

When marinating tofu, heat firm tofu first, then marinate it. You'll find that it absorbs more marinade this way. Otherwise, the marinade tends to sit on the surface and not penetrate the tofu for full flavor.

THAI-SEARED TOFU

PREP: 20 MINUTES MARINATE: 2 HOURS
COOK: 20 MINUTES

½ cup chopped fresh basil
½ cup chopped fresh cilantro
½ cup low-sodium soy sauce
½ cup fresh lime juice
¼ cup chopped fresh mint
2 tablespoons molasses
1 tablespoon minced peeled fresh ginger
1 tablespoon vegetable oil
2 teaspoons curry powder
¼ to ½ teaspoon crushed red pepper
4 garlic cloves, minced
2 (12.3-ounce) packages firm tofu, drained
Cooking spray
6 cups hot cooked vermicelli (about 12 ounces uncooked pasta)

1. Combine first 11 ingredients in a medium bowl; stir with a whisk until blended. Cut each tofu cake crosswise into 8 slices. Place tofu slices in a 13 x 9-inch baking dish; pour marinade over tofu. Cover and marinate in refrigerator at least 2 hours.
2. Coat a large nonstick skillet with cooking spray; place over medium-high heat until hot. Remove tofu from dish, reserving marinade; pat tofu dry with paper towels. Add 5 tofu slices to skillet; cook 3 minutes on each side or until browned. Remove from skillet; keep warm. Repeat procedure with remaining tofu.
3. Add reserved marinade to skillet; bring to a simmer over medium-high heat, and cook uncovered, 2 minutes. Spoon pasta onto plates; top with tofu. Drizzle warm marinade over tofu and pasta. Yield 4 servings (serving size: 1½ cups pasta, 4 tofu slices, and 3 tablespoons sauce).

CALORIES 550 (23% from fat); FAT 13.9g (sat 2g, mono 3.1g, poly 7.1g); PROTEIN 27.8g; CARB 82.4g; FIBER 4.7g; CHOL 0mg; IRON 14.3mg; SODIUM 993mg; CALC 289mg

ITALIAN VEGETABLE PIE

PREP: 30 MINUTES
COOK: 25 MINUTES

2 teaspoons olive oil
1 cup chopped green bell pepper
1 cup chopped onion
1 cup chopped mushrooms (about 3 ounces)
3 garlic cloves, minced
3 tablespoons tomato paste
1 teaspoon dried Italian seasoning
1 teaspoon fennel seeds
¼ teaspoon crushed red pepper
1 (12.3-ounce) package firm tofu, drained and crumbled
1 (25.5-ounce) bottle fat-free marinara sauce
6 cooked lasagna noodles, cut in half crosswise
Cooking spray
1½ cups (6 ounces) preshredded part-skim mozzarella cheese
¼ cup grated Parmesan cheese

1. Preheat oven to 375°.
2. Heat oil in a large nonstick skillet over medium-high heat. Add bell pepper, onion, mushrooms, and garlic; sauté 3 minutes or until vegetables are tender. Stir in tomato paste and next 5 ingredients; bring mixture to a boil. Reduce heat, and simmer, uncovered, 10 minutes.
3. Arrange lasagna noodles spokelike in the bottom and up sides of a 9-inch deep-dish pie plate coated with cooking spray. Spread 3 cups tofu mixture over noodles. Fold ends of noodles over tofu mixture; top with remaining tofu mixture, covering ends of noodles. Sprinkle with cheeses. Bake at 375° for 20 minutes. Let stand 5 minutes. Yield: 8 servings.

CALORIES 226 (31% from fat); FAT 7.9g (sat 3.2g, mono 2.5g, poly 1.6g); PROTEIN 13.4g; CARB 26.8g; FIBER 1.9g; CHOL 14mg; IRON 4.7mg; SODIUM 344mg; CALC 252mg

Italian Vegetable Pie

1. Arrange the noodles spokelike in the bottom of an 9-inch deep-dish pie plate coated with cooking spray.

2. Spread 3 cups tomato mixture evenly over noodles.

3. Fold ends of noodles over tomato mixture.

4. Top with the remaining tomato mixture, covering ends of noodles. Sprinkle with cheeses.

Tex-Mex Tofu
Burritos

TEX-MEX TOFU BURRITOS

PREP: 20 MINUTES   COOK: 8 MINUTES

1 (10.5-ounce) package extra-firm
    light tofu, drained and cut into
    ½-inch cubes
1 teaspoon ground cumin
1 teaspoon chili powder
½ teaspoon ground cinnamon
2 teaspoons cider vinegar
2 teaspoons vegetable oil
1 cup sliced onion, separated into
    rings
1 cup (3 x ¼-inch) julienne-cut red
    bell pepper
1 cup (3 x ¼-inch) julienne-cut
    zucchini
½ cup corn, black bean, and roasted-
    red pepper salsa (such as Jardine's)
¼ teaspoon salt
5 (8-inch) fat-free flour tortillas
5 tablespoons sliced green onions
5 tablespoons low-fat sour cream
5 tablespoons (1¼ ounces) shredded
    reduced-fat Monterey Jack cheese

Tempeh is a fermented soybean cake that has a texture similar to soft tofu.

1. Place tofu in a shallow dish. Sprinkle with cumin, chili powder, cinnamon, and vinegar. Toss gently to coat.
2. Heat oil in a large nonstick skillet over medium heat. Add onion; sauté 2 minutes. Add bell pepper and zucchini; sauté 4 minutes. Stir in tofu mixture, salsa, and salt; cook 2 minutes, stirring occasionally. Remove from heat.
3. Warm tortillas according to package directions. Spoon about 1 cup tofu mixture down center of each tortilla. Top evenly with green onions, sour cream, and cheese; roll up. Yield: 5 servings (serving size: 1 burrito).
Note: Regular chunky salsa may be substituted for the salsa we call for in this recipe.

CALORIES 221 (25% from fat); FAT 6.2g (sat 2.3g, mono 1.8g, poly 1.6g); PROTEIN 11.8g; CARB 31.6g; FIBER 4.9g; CHOL 10mg; IRON 1.8mg; SODIUM 590mg; CALC 114mg

TEMPEH VEGETABLE STIR-FRY

PREP: 14 MINUTES   COOK: 10 MINUTES

⅓ cup low-sodium soy sauce
4 teaspoons dry sherry
2 teaspoons sugar
½ teaspoon cornstarch
2 teaspoons dark sesame oil
1 (8-ounce) package tempeh, cut
    into ½-inch cubes
1½ cups broccoli florets
1 cup (⅛-inch-thick) diagonally
    sliced carrot
½ cup diced red bell pepper
1 cup thinly sliced shiitake
    mushroom caps (about 3
    ounces mushrooms)
1 teaspoon minced peeled fresh
    ginger
2 garlic cloves, minced
2 cups fresh bean sprouts
½ cup (1-inch) sliced green onions

1. Combine first 4 ingredients in a small bowl; set aside.
2. Heat oil in a large nonstick skillet or wok over medium-high heat until hot. Add tempeh; stir-fry 3 minutes or until light brown. Add broccoli, carrot, and bell pepper; stir-fry 2 minutes. Add mushrooms, ginger, and garlic; stir-fry 1 minute.
3. Stir soy sauce mixture into tempeh mixture; bring to a boil. Stir in sprouts and green onions. Serve over rice. Yield: 4 servings (serving size: 1¼ cups).

CALORIES 207 (31% from fat); FAT 7.2g (sat 1.2g, mono 1.3g, poly 2g); PROTEIN 16.3g; CARB 23.6g; FIBER 7.9g; CHOL 0mg; IRON 2.1mg; SODIUM 664mg; CALC 59mg

meats

Filet Mignon With
Mushroom—Wine Sauce (page 314)

beef

We've added rubs, marinades, and other seasonings that offer around-the-world flavor for these cuts of beef.

We've selected our favorite main dishes made with leaner-than-ever cuts of beef, cooked to perfection. The cut of meat should dictate the cooking method in order to have tender results.

"Tender" cuts come mainly from the rib, loin, and short-loin sections. For these cuts, use dry-heat cooking methods such as roasting, broiling, panbroiling, and sautéing. The less tender cuts, which are leaner, include the chuck, foreshank, brisket, tip, and round and come from the shoulder, leg, breast, and flank. These cuts have more muscle or connective tissue and need a moist-heat cooking method. Braising or stewing will make these cuts fork-tender.

BEEF MEATBALLS

PREP: 12 MINUTES   COOK: 15 MINUTES

Although these are tasty by themselves, these meatballs can be stirred into a pasta sauce (such as Ultimate Quick-and-Easy Pasta Sauce, page 447) and served over spaghetti or spooned onto a warm hoagie roll.

1½ pounds ground round
¼ cup (1 ounce) finely shredded fresh Parmesan cheese
½ cup dry breadcrumbs
⅓ cup chopped fresh parsley
¼ cup tomato sauce
1 teaspoon dry mustard
¾ teaspoon dried Italian seasoning
¼ teaspoon salt
¼ teaspoon crushed red pepper
2 garlic cloves, crushed
Cooking spray

1. Preheat oven to 400°.
2. Combine all ingredients except

cooking spray in a bowl. Shape into 30 (1½-inch) meatballs. Place on a broiler pan coated with cooking spray. Bake at 400° for 15 minutes or until done. Yield: 6 servings (serving size: 5 meatballs).

CALORIES 228 (35% from fat); FAT 8.8g (sat 3.4g, mono 3.5g, poly 0.5g); PROTEIN 27.4g; CARB 8.2g; FIBER 0.8g; CHOL 73mg; IRON 3.4mg; SODIUM 370mg; CALC 95mg

INDONESIAN MEATBALLS WITH PEANUT SAUCE

PREP: 18 MINUTES   COOK: 9 MINUTES

½ pound lean ground pork
½ pound ground round
¼ cup finely chopped green onions
2 tablespoons instant potato flakes (not granules)
2 teaspoons ground cumin
½ teaspoon salt
¼ teaspoon ground allspice
¼ teaspoon ground coriander
⅛ teaspoon black pepper
1 large egg white, lightly beaten
1 (8-ounce) carton plain fat-free yogurt, divided
3 tablespoons water
1 tablespoon creamy peanut butter
2 teaspoons low-sodium soy sauce
2 cups hot cooked basmati rice

1. Combine first 10 ingredients and ¼ cup yogurt in a bowl. Shape mixture into 16 (1½-inch) meatballs. Arrange meatballs in 4 rows on a microwave-safe plastic roasting pan. Microwave at HIGH 4 minutes. Rearrange meatballs on pan, placing 2 center rows on outside and 2 outer rows in center. Microwave at HIGH 4 minutes or until done, and keep warm.
2. Combine water and peanut butter in

Indonesian Meatballs

1. Use a small scoop to form the meatballs, shaping the mixture with your other hand.

2. Arrange meatballs on a microwave-safe roasting rack, and cook as directed.

a 2-cup glass measure; stir well with a whisk. Microwave at HIGH 1 minute. Add remaining ⅔ cup yogurt and soy sauce, stirring well. Microwave at HIGH 15 to 20 seconds or until warm (do not boil). Serve meatballs and sauce over rice. Yield: 4 servings (serving size: 4 meatballs, ¼ cup sauce, and ½ cup rice).

CALORIES 376 (30% from fat); FAT 12.4g (sat 3.9g, mono 5.6g, poly 1.6g); PROTEIN 31.8g; CARB 32.2g; FIBER 1.1g; CHOL 76mg; IRON 3.4mg; SODIUM 514mg; CALC 147mg

Tex-Mex Nachos

HAMBURGER-MUSHROOM PIZZAS

PREP: 15 MINUTES   COOK: 7 MINUTES

1   (16-ounce) loaf Italian bread
½ cup bottled traditional pizza
      sauce
1   small onion, thinly sliced and
      separated into rings
1   cup presliced mushrooms
6   ounces ground sirloin
1   teaspoon dried Italian
      seasoning
½ teaspoon garlic powder
¼ teaspoon crushed red pepper
1½ cups (6 ounces) preshredded
      reduced-fat pizza-blend
      cheese

1. Preheat oven to 500°.
2. Cut bread loaf in half horizontally.
Place both halves of bread, cut sides up,
on a large baking sheet. Spread ¼ cup pizza
sauce over each half. Divide onion rings
and mushrooms evenly between bread
halves. Crumble beef into ½-inch pieces,
and divide evenly between bread halves.
Sprinkle Italian seasoning, garlic powder,
and red pepper evenly over bread halves,
and top each with ¾ cup cheese.
3. Bake pizzas at 500° for 7 minutes or
until beef is done and cheese melts. Cut
each half into 3 equal pieces. Yield: 6
servings (serving size: 1 piece).

CALORIES 387 (26% from fat); FAT 11.3g (sat 5.6g, mono 3.8g,
poly 0.9g); PROTEIN 21.4g; CARB 49.5g; FIBER 3.6g;
CHOL 40mg; IRON 3.8mg; SODIUM 736mg; CALC 279mg

TEX-MEX NACHOS

PREP: 10 MINUTES   COOK: 7 MINUTES

¾ pound ground round
¼ cup sliced green onions
¾ cup taco sauce
¼ teaspoon garlic powder
⅛ teaspoon black pepper
1   (16-ounce) can kidney beans,
      drained
1   (8¾-ounce) can no-salt-added
      whole-kernel corn, drained
2   ounces baked tortilla chips (about
      3 cups or about 42 small chips)
3   cups shredded iceberg lettuce
1   cup chopped tomato
1   cup (4 ounces) shredded
      reduced-fat sharp cheddar cheese
½ cup bottled salsa
½ cup fat-free sour cream

1. Cook beef and green onions in a large
nonstick skillet over medium-high heat
until browned, stirring to crumble.
Drain well; return beef mixture to pan.
Stir in taco sauce, garlic powder, pepper,
beans, and corn; cook until thoroughly
heated. Spoon 1 cup beef mixture over
¾ cup chips; top with ¾ cup lettuce, ¼
cup tomato, ¼ cup cheese, 2 tablespoons
salsa, and 2 tablespoons sour cream. Repeat procedure with remaining ingredients. Yield: 4 servings.

CALORIES 470 (24% from fat); FAT 12.3g (sat 5.1g, mono 3.8g,
poly 0.7g); PROTEIN 35.9g; CARB 52g; FIBER 7.4g;
CHOL 71mg; IRON 3.9mg; SODIUM 1026mg; CALC 370mg

Ground round is the leanest type of ground beef. Sirloin has a bit more fat, and ground chuck contains even more. The fat in ground beef varies, depending on how well the meat was trimmed before it was ground. Check the percentage of fat by weight on the package.

Cheesy Beef-and-Rice Casserole

PREP: 30 MINUTES   COOK: 10 MINUTES

Serve this casserole with either a fruit or green salad and dinner rolls.

- ½ pound ground round
- 1 cup chopped onion
- 1 cup chopped green bell pepper
- ¼ cup water
- 1 tablespoon chili powder
- 2 teaspoons ground cumin
- 1½ teaspoons sugar
- ½ teaspoon dried oregano
- 1 (14.5-ounce) can diced tomatoes, undrained
- 1 (4.5-ounce) can chopped green chiles, drained
- 3 cups cooked long-grain rice
- 1 cup fat-free sour cream
- ½ cup sliced green onions
- ¼ cup fat-free milk
- ¾ cup (3 ounces) shredded reduced-fat sharp cheddar cheese

1. Preheat oven to 375°.
2. Cook first 3 ingredients in a large nonstick skillet over medium-high heat until beef is browned, stirring to crumble. Add water and next 6 ingredients; bring to a boil. Cover, reduce heat, and simmer 10 minutes. Uncover and simmer 2 minutes. Remove from heat.
3. Combine rice, sour cream, green onions, and milk in a bowl; spoon into a 13 x 9-inch baking dish. Top with beef mixture; sprinkle with cheese. Bake at 375° for 10 minutes or until thoroughly heated. Let stand 5 minutes before serving. Yield: 4 servings (serving size: 1¼ cups).
Note: The beef mixture could also be used as a filling for burritos.

CALORIES 442 (26% from fat); FAT 13g (sat 6.8g, mono 3.9g, poly 0.8g); PROTEIN 25.1g; CARB 56.7g; FIBER 3.9g; CHOL 64mg; IRON 5mg; SODIUM 394mg; CALC 290mg

Beef, Bean, and Cornbread Casserole

PREP: 20 MINUTES
COOK: 20 MINUTES

- ¾ pound ground round
- 1 cup chopped onion
- 1 garlic clove, minced
- Cooking spray
- 1 tablespoon chili powder
- 1½ teaspoons ground cumin
- 1 teaspoon sugar
- ½ teaspoon dried oregano
- 2 (8-ounce) cans no-salt-added tomato sauce
- 1 (16-ounce) can pinto beans, drained
- 1 (4.5-ounce) can chopped green chiles, drained
- ¾ cup fat-free milk
- 1 large egg, lightly beaten
- 1⅓ cups self-rising yellow cornmeal mix

1. Cook beef, onion, and garlic in a large saucepan coated with cooking spray over medium-high heat until browned, stirring to crumble beef. Drain beef mixture in a colander.
2. Preheat oven to 400°.
3. Return beef mixture to pan. Add chili powder and next 6 ingredients; cover and cook over medium-low heat 10 minutes. Pour mixture into a 2-quart casserole coated with cooking spray.
4. Combine milk and egg in a bowl; stir in cornmeal mix. Pour cornmeal mixture over beef mixture. Bake at 400° for 20 minutes or until cornbread topping is lightly browned. Yield: 4 servings.

CALORIES 551 (15% from fat); FAT 9.1g (sat 2.7g, mono 3.4g, poly 1.5g); PROTEIN 35.4g; CARB 82.7g; FIBER 9.3g; CHOL 106mg; IRON 8.8mg; SODIUM 1186mg; CALC 320mg

Shepherd's Pie

PREP: 18 MINUTES   COOK: 55 MINUTES

- 1 cup (½-inch) sliced green beans
- ½ pound ground round
- 1 cup chopped onion
- 1 large garlic clove, minced
- 1 teaspoon dried oregano
- 1 teaspoon dried basil
- ¼ teaspoon dried thyme
- 3 cups quartered mushrooms (about 8 ounces)
- ¼ cup all-purpose flour
- ¼ cup dry white wine
- 1 (14.5-ounce) can whole tomatoes, undrained and chopped
- ¼ teaspoon salt
- ⅛ teaspoon pepper
- Cooking spray
- 1½ pounds baking potatoes, peeled and cubed
- ⅓ cup 2% reduced-fat milk
- ¼ teaspoon salt
- ⅛ teaspoon black pepper

1. Steam green beans, covered, 5 to 6 minutes or until crisp-tender.
2. Cook beef, onion, and garlic in a large nonstick skillet over medium-high heat until browned, stirring to crumble. Drain well, and return beef mixture to pan. Stir in oregano, basil, and thyme; cook over medium-high heat 1 minute. Add mushrooms; cook 2 minutes. Stir in flour. Gradually add wine, stirring constantly. Add tomato, ¼ teaspoon salt, and ⅛ teaspoon pepper; cook 2 minutes or until thickened, stirring frequently. Remove from heat; stir in green beans. Spoon beef mixture into a 2½-quart casserole coated with cooking spray.
3. Preheat oven to 375°.
4. Place potato in a large saucepan; cover with water, and bring to a boil. Reduce heat, and simmer, uncovered, 20 minutes or until very tender. Drain

well, and return potato to pan. Add milk, ¼ teaspoon salt, and ⅛ teaspoon pepper; beat at medium speed of a mixer until smooth. Spread mashed potatoes over beef mixture, and bake at 375° for 30 minutes or until thoroughly heated.

5. Preheat broiler.

6. Broil casserole 5 minutes or until potatoes are browned. Yield: 4 servings (serving size: 2 cups).

CALORIES 288 (14% from fat); FAT 4.6g (sat 1.6g, mono 1.6g, poly 0.4g); PROTEIN 19.5g; CARB 44.2g; FIBER 5.3g; CHOL 36mg; IRON 4.6mg; SODIUM 722mg; CALC 110mg

menu

Mama's Meat Loaf

Mashed Potato Casserole (page 497)

Harvard Beets (page 488)

Banana-Cream Pie (page 194)

MAMA'S MEAT LOAF

PREP: 16 MINUTES

COOK: 1 HOUR 10 MINUTES

½ cup finely chopped onion
½ cup finely chopped green bell pepper
3 tablespoons minced fresh parsley
1 teaspoon black pepper
¾ teaspoon salt
2 garlic cloves, minced
1 large egg, lightly beaten
1 (1-ounce) slice white bread, torn into small pieces
1½ pounds ground round
Cooking spray
⅓ cup ketchup

1. Preheat oven to 350°.

2. Combine first 8 ingredients in a large bowl, tossing to moisten bread. Crumble beef over onion mixture; stir just until blended. Shape meat mixture into an 8 x 4-inch loaf on a broiler pan coated with cooking spray. Brush ketchup over meat loaf. Bake at 350° for 1 hour and 10 minutes or until a meat thermometer registers 160°.

3. Let stand 10 minutes before slicing. Yield: 6 servings (serving size: 1 slice).

CALORIES 217 (34% from fat); FAT 8.1g (sat 2.8g, mono 3.3g, poly 0.5g); PROTEIN 26.2g; CARB 8.8g; FIBER 0.9g; CHOL 105mg; IRON 3mg; SODIUM 565mg; CALC 25mg

DOUBLE CHEESE MEAT LOAF

PREP: 15 MINUTES   COOK: 1 HOUR

Cooking spray
1 cup chopped onion
6 tablespoons ketchup, divided
2 tablespoons Dijon mustard, divided
1 cup (4 ounces) preshredded part-skim mozzarella cheese
½ cup Italian-seasoned breadcrumbs
¼ cup chopped fresh parsley
2 tablespoons grated Parmesan cheese
1 teaspoon dried oregano
¼ teaspoon black pepper
1 large egg, lightly beaten
½ pound ground round
½ pound lean ground pork
½ pound lean ground veal

MEAT LOAF PANS

Because our meat loaves are lower in fat than traditional recipes, there are very little fat drippings. But you still can use a draining meat loaf pan. This two-piece pan consists of one pan with holes in the bottom that fits into a slightly larger pan, allowing fat to drain away from the meat loaf into the other pan.

1. Preheat oven to 375°.

2. Place a medium nonstick skillet coated with cooking spray over medium-high heat. Add onion, and sauté 3 minutes. Combine onion, ¼ cup ketchup, 1 tablespoon mustard, mozzarella, and next 6 ingredients in a large bowl. Crumble ground meats over cheese mixture; stir just until blended.

3. Pack meat mixture into an 8 x 4-inch loaf pan coated with cooking spray. Combine 2 tablespoons ketchup and 1 tablespoon mustard; spread over top of loaf. Bake at 375° for 1 hour or until meat thermometer registers 160°. Let stand 10 minutes.

4. Remove meat loaf from pan. Cut into 12 slices. Yield: 6 servings (serving size: 2 slices).

CALORIES 290 (34% from fat); FAT 10.9g (sat 4.5g, mono 3.7g, poly 0.8g); PROTEIN 32.3g; CARB 14g; FIBER 0.8g; CHOL 124mg; IRON 2.3mg; SODIUM 796mg; CALC 182mg

When making meat loaf, place all the ingredients except the ground meat in a large bowl, **and then crumble the meat over the mixture. Use a spoon or your hands to knead the seasonings into the meat.**

Rio Grande Meat Loaf

To crush taco shells or crackers easily, place them in a zip-top bag, and use a rolling pin to crush them.

RIO GRANDE MEAT LOAF

PREP: 15 MINUTES
COOK: 1 HOUR

½ cup chopped onion
½ cup chopped green bell pepper
⅓ cup chopped fresh cilantro
2 tablespoons minced seeded jalapeño pepper
1 teaspoon salt
2 teaspoons ground cumin
2 teaspoons chili powder
½ teaspoon black pepper
4 taco shells, finely crushed (about 1½ ounces)
2 large egg whites, lightly beaten
3 large garlic cloves, minced
1 (15-ounce) can black beans, rinsed and drained
2 pounds ground round
Cooking spray
¾ cup bottled salsa

1. Preheat oven to 375°.
2. Combine first 12 ingredients in a large bowl; crumble beef over vegetable mixture, and stir until well-blended.
3. Pack meat mixture into a 9 x 5-inch

An instant-read thermometer, which quickly registers the temperature of the center of the loaf, is a fail-safe way to check for doneness.

loaf pan coated with cooking spray. Bake at 375° for 1 hour or until a meat thermometer registers 160°. Let stand 10 minutes.
4. Remove meat loaf from pan; top with salsa. Cut loaf into 16 slices. Yield: 8 servings (serving size: 2 slices).
Note: Serve leftover crumbled meat loaf in taco shells; top with lettuce, chopped tomato, and shredded cheese.

CALORIES 237 (25% from fat); FAT 6.5g (sat 3g, mono 2g, poly 0.5g); PROTEIN 30.3g; CARB 13.5g; FIBER 2.6g; CHOL 65mg; IRON 4.1mg; SODIUM 576mg; CALC 40mg

HERBED MEAT LOAF WITH SUN-DRIED TOMATO GRAVY

PREP: 40 MINUTES
COOK: 1 HOUR 10 MINUTES

1 cup sun-dried tomatoes, packed without oil (about 24)
3 cups boiling water
Cooking spray
1 cup finely chopped onion
1 cup finely chopped green bell pepper
2 garlic cloves, crushed
1 (1-ounce) slice whole-wheat bread, torn into small pieces
2 tablespoons 1% low-fat milk
½ cup (2 ounces) shredded sharp provolone cheese
2 teaspoons dried basil
1 teaspoon dried oregano
1 teaspoon black pepper
½ teaspoon salt
½ teaspoon dried thyme
2 large egg whites, lightly beaten
1¾ pounds ground sirloin
Sun-Dried Tomato Gravy

1. Preheat oven to 350°.
2. Combine tomatoes and boiling water in a bowl; cover and let stand 15 minutes or until softened. Drain well, and finely chop; set aside.
3. Coat a medium nonstick skillet with cooking spray, and place over medium-high heat until hot. Add onion, bell pepper, and garlic; sauté 5 minutes or until tender.
4. Place bread in a large bowl, and drizzle with milk; toss to moisten. Add tomatoes, onion mixture, cheese, 2 teaspoons basil, and next 5 ingredients; stir until well-blended. Crumble beef over tomato mixture, and stir just until blended. Pack into a 9 x 5-inch loaf pan coated with cooking spray.
5. Bake at 350° for 1 hour and 10 minutes or until a meat thermometer registers 160°. Let stand 10 minutes; remove from pan, and reserve drippings for Sun-Dried Tomato Gravy. Yield: 8 servings (serving size: 2 slices and about 3 tablespoons gravy).

SUN-DRIED TOMATO GRAVY

¼ cup sun-dried tomatoes, packed without oil (about 6)
1 cup boiling water
2½ tablespoons all-purpose flour
1¼ cups 1% low-fat milk
¼ cup meat loaf pan drippings or beef broth
1 tablespoon finely chopped green onions
¼ teaspoon salt
¼ teaspoon dried basil
⅛ teaspoon black pepper

Herbed Meat Loaf With
Sun-Dried Tomato Gravy

PICADILLO

PREP: 10 MINUTES
COOK: 40 MINUTES

This traditional Latin dish consists of a ground meat-tomato sauce flavored with sweet spices, raisins, olives or capers, and almonds. Serve it with warm flour tortillas.

- 1 teaspoon vegetable oil
- 1½ cups chopped onion
- 1 jalapeño pepper, seeded and finely chopped
- 1 large garlic clove, minced
- 1 pound ground sirloin
- 1½ cups chopped peeled Granny Smith apple (about 1 large)
- ½ cup water
- ¼ cup sliced pimento-stuffed olives
- ¼ cup raisins
- ¾ teaspoon salt
- ¼ teaspoon black pepper
- 2 (3-inch) cinnamon sticks
- 1 (14.5-ounce) can diced tomatoes, undrained
- 3 tablespoons slivered almonds, toasted

1. Heat oil in a large Dutch oven over medium-high heat. Add onion, and sauté 3 minutes. Add jalapeño and garlic, and sauté 1 minute. Add beef, and sauté 3 minutes or until browned, stirring to crumble.

2. Stir apple and next 7 ingredients into beef mixture, and bring to a boil. Reduce heat, and simmer, uncovered, 30 minutes or until sauce is slightly thick. Remove from heat, and discard cinnamon sticks. Stir in toasted almonds. Yield: 5 servings (serving size: about 1 cup).

Let meat loaf stand at room temperature 10 minutes before cutting so the slices won't fall apart.

1. Combine tomatoes and boiling water in a bowl; cover and let stand 15 minutes or until softened. Drain well, and finely chop.

2. Place flour in a small saucepan, and gradually add milk, stirring with a whisk until blended. Stir in tomatoes, pan drippings, green onions, salt, basil, and pepper. Cook over medium heat 5 minutes or until mixture is thickened, stirring constantly with a whisk. Yield: 1½ cups (serving size: about 3 tablespoons).

CALORIES 230 (31% from fat); FAT 7.9g (sat 3.4g, mono 2.9g, poly 0.5g); PROTEIN 27.1g; CARB 12.4g; FIBER 1.8g; CHOL 67mg; IRON 4.2mg; SODIUM 524mg; CALC 142mg

CALORIES 240 (30% from fat); FAT 8.1g (sat 2.2g, mono 3.7g, poly 1.2g); PROTEIN 21.7g; CARB 21.5g; FIBER 4.5g; CHOL 55mg; IRON 3.8mg; SODIUM 580mg; CALC 65mg

FILET MIGNON WITH MUSHROOM-WINE SAUCE

PREP: 25 MINUTES   COOK: 6 MINUTES

(pictured on page 307)

You'll find these steaks are succulent. Accompany them with mashed potatoes, leaving them unpeeled for added color and texture.

1 tablespoon stick margarine or butter, divided
⅓ cup finely chopped shallots
6 ounces fresh shiitake mushroom caps (about 8 ounces whole)
1½ cups dry red wine, divided
1 (10½-ounce) can beef consommé, undiluted and divided
4 (4-ounce) beef tenderloin steaks (1 inch thick)
½ teaspoon cracked black pepper
Cooking spray
1 tablespoon low-sodium soy sauce
2 teaspoons cornstarch
1 teaspoon dried thyme

1. Melt 1½ teaspoons margarine in a nonstick skillet over medium heat. Add shallots and mushroom caps; sauté 4 minutes. Add 1 cup wine and ¾ cup consommé; cook 5 minutes, stirring frequently. Remove mushrooms, and place in a bowl. Cook wine mixture over high heat 5 minutes or until reduced to ½ cup. Add to mushrooms in bowl; wipe skillet with a paper towel.
2. Sprinkle steaks with pepper. Melt 1½ teaspoons margarine in skillet coated with cooking spray over medium heat. Add steaks; cook 3 minutes on each side or until browned. Reduce heat to medium-low; cook 1½ minutes on each side or until done. Place on a platter; keep warm.
3. Combine soy sauce and cornstarch.

Add ½ cup wine and remaining consommé to skillet; scrape skillet to loosen browned bits. Bring to a boil; cook 1 minute. Add mushroom mixture, cornstarch mixture, and thyme; bring to a boil. Cook 1 minute, stirring constantly. Serve mushroom-wine sauce with steaks. Yield: 4 servings (serving size: 3 ounces meat and ½ cup sauce).

CALORIES 254 (37% from fat); FAT 10.4g (sat 3.5g, mono 4.1g, poly 1.3g); PROTEIN 28.3g; CARB 11.5g; FIBER 1g; CHOL 70mg; IRON 4.7mg; SODIUM 630mg; CALC 34mg

PAN-BROILED FILET MIGNONS

PREP: 4 MINUTES   COOK: 18 MINUTES

4 (4-ounce) beef tenderloin steaks (1 inch thick)
3 tablespoons dried green peppercorns
3 tablespoons black peppercorns
½ cup dry vermouth
½ cup beef broth
½ cup brandy

1. Trim fat from steaks. Firmly press green and black peppercorns into steaks. Place a medium nonstick skillet over medium-high heat until hot. Add steaks, and cook 1 minute on each side or until browned. Reduce heat to medium-low; cook 4 minutes on each side or until done. Place steaks on a serving platter; keep warm.
2. Add vermouth and broth to skillet; bring to a boil. Cook 4 minutes or until reduced by half, scraping skillet to loosen browned bits. Add brandy. Bring to a boil, and cook 4 minutes or until reduced by half. Serve steaks with sauce. Yield: 4 servings (serving size: 1 steak and ¼ cup sauce).

CALORIES 182 (37% from fat); FAT 7.4g (sat 3g, mono 2.8g, poly 0.4g); PROTEIN 24.9g; CARB 1.9g; FIBER 0g; CHOL 76mg; IRON 3.3mg; SODIUM 264mg; CALC 9mg

BEEF AND BROCCOLI WITH OYSTER SAUCE

PREP: 16 MINUTES
MARINATE: 15 MINUTES
COOK: 8 MINUTES

1 pound flank steak
1 tablespoon cornstarch
2 tablespoons water
2 tablespoons low-sodium soy sauce
2 teaspoons sugar
3 tablespoons oyster sauce
1 tablespoon low-sodium soy sauce
1 tablespoon dry sherry
1 tablespoon water
2 teaspoons sugar
1 teaspoon cornstarch
1 tablespoon vegetable oil, divided
⅓ cup (½-inch) diagonally sliced green onions
1 tablespoon minced peeled fresh ginger
6 cups broccoli florets (about ¾ pound)
¼ cup water
6 cups hot cooked rice

1. Trim fat from steak. Cut steak diagonally across grain into ¼-inch-thick slices. Combine steak and next 4 ingredients in a large zip-top plastic bag. Seal bag; toss gently to coat steak, and marinate in refrigerator 15 minutes.
2. Combine oyster sauce and next 5 ingredients in a small bowl, stir with a whisk until well-blended. Remove steak from bag; discard marinade.
3. Heat 2 teaspoons oil in a large nonstick skillet or wok over high heat. Add steak mixture; stir-fry 2 minutes. Remove from pan; keep warm. Add 1 teaspoon oil, green onions, and ginger; reduce heat to medium-high, and stir-fry 30 seconds. Stir in broccoli and

¼ cup water; cover and cook 3 minutes. Return steak to pan, and stir in oyster sauce mixture; stir-fry 2 minutes or until thick and bubbly. Serve over rice. Yield: 6 servings (serving size: 1 cup beef mixture and 1 cup rice).

CALORIES 412 (21% from fat); FAT 9.8g (sat 3.5g, mono 3.5g, poly 1.4g); PROTEIN 21.6g; CARB 58.2g; FIBER 1.8g; CHOL 38mg; IRON 3.9mg; SODIUM 410mg; CALC 66mg

BARBECUED FLANK STEAK WITH CHUTNEY-BOURBON GLAZE

PREP: 15 MINUTES

MARINATE: 15 MINUTES   COOK: 16 MINUTES

    1 (1-pound) flank steak
    ⅓ cup peach chutney
    ⅓ cup pineapple juice
    3 tablespoons bourbon or apple
         juice
 1½ tablespoons rice wine vinegar
 1½ tablespoons hot pepper sauce
    ¼ teaspoon salt
    2 garlic cloves, minced
Cooking spray

1. Prepare grill or broiler.
2. Trim fat from steak. Combine steak and next 7 ingredients in a large zip-top plastic bag. Seal bag, and marinate in refrigerator 15 minutes. Remove steak from bag, reserving marinade.
3. Place steak on a grill rack or broiler pan coated with cooking spray. Cook 8 minutes on each side or until desired degree of doneness. Cut steak diagonally across grain into thin slices. Keep warm.
4. Pour reserved marinade into a small saucepan. Bring marinade to a boil; cook 1 minute, stirring occasionally. Serve with steak. Yield: 4 servings (serving size: 3 ounces steak and 2 tablespoons glaze).

CALORIES 254 (39% from fat); FAT 11.1g (sat 4.6g, mono 4.3g, poly 0.4g); PROTEIN 22.8g; CARB 13.9g; FIBER 0.7g; CHOL 57mg; IRON 2.4mg; SODIUM 308mg; CALC 12mg

SIZZLING STEAK FAJITAS

PREP: 15 MINUTES   COOK: 15 MINUTES

    ¾ pound flank steak
    2 teaspoons ground cumin
    2 teaspoons chili powder
    ¼ teaspoon salt
    ⅛ teaspoon garlic powder
    ⅛ teaspoon black pepper
    ⅛ teaspoon ground red pepper
    4 (8-inch) flour tortillas
    1 teaspoon vegetable oil
    2 cups sliced onion
    ⅓ cup green bell pepper strips
    ⅓ cup red bell pepper strips
    ⅓ cup yellow bell pepper strips
    1 tablespoon lime juice
    ¼ cup fat-free sour cream
Green salsa (optional)
Cilantro sprigs (optional)

1. Trim fat from steak. Cut steak diagonally across grain into thin slices. Combine steak and next 6 ingredients in a large zip-top plastic bag. Seal bag; shake to coat.
2. Warm tortillas according to package directions.
3. Heat oil in a large nonstick skillet over medium-high heat. Add steak, onion, and bell peppers; sauté 6 minutes or until steak is done. Remove from heat; stir in lime juice. Divide steak and vegetable mixture evenly among warm tortillas, and roll up. Serve with sour cream. If desired, serve with green salsa and garnish with cilantro sprigs. Yield: 4 servings (serving size: 1 fajita and 1 tablespoon sour cream).

CALORIES 330 (34% from fat); FAT 12.6g (sat 4.2g, mono 4.9g, poly 2.2g); PROTEIN 22.6g; CARB 31g; FIBER 3.3g; CHOL 43mg; IRON 4.3mg; SODIUM 425mg; CALC 81mg

Sizzling Steak Fajitas

You can roll it, skewer it, stuff it, stack it, and score it. Besides being one of the leanest cuts of beef, flank steak is so easy to prepare.

BARBECUED ORIENTAL FLANK STEAK

PREP: 5 MINUTES
MARINATE: 8 HOURS
COOK: 16 MINUTES

1 (1-pound) flank steak
¼ cup dry sherry
¼ cup low-sodium soy sauce
¼ cup honey
2 tablespoons white vinegar
1 tablespoon minced peeled fresh ginger
1 teaspoon dark sesame oil
2 garlic cloves, crushed
Cooking spray

1. Trim fat from steak. Combine sherry and next 6 ingredients in a bowl; stir until honey dissolves. Pour marinade into a large zip-top plastic bag; add steak, and seal bag. Marinate in refrigerator 8 hours, turning bag occasionally.
2. Remove steak from bag; reserve marinade.
3. Prepare grill or broiler.
4. Place steak on grill rack or broiler pan coated with cooking spray, and cook 8 minutes on each side or until desired degree of doneness, basting frequently with reserved marinade. Place remaining marinade in a saucepan; bring to a boil, and remove from heat.
5. Cut steak diagonally across grain into thin slices. Serve with warm marinade. Yield: 4 servings (serving size: 3 ounces steak and 2 tablespoons sauce).

CALORIES 297 (42% from fat); FAT 14g (sat 5.6g, mono 5.8g, poly 0.9g); PROTEIN 22.6g; CARB 20.4g; FIBER 0g; CHOL 60mg; IRON 2.6mg; SODIUM 557mg; CALC 13mg

ASIAN FLANK STEAK

PREP: 25 MINUTES
MARINATE: 8 TO 12 HOURS
COOK: 22 MINUTES

1 (1½-pound) flank steak
⅓ cup fresh lime juice
¼ cup minced fresh mint
¼ cup low-sodium soy sauce
2 tablespoons minced peeled fresh ginger
2 tablespoons minced seeded jalapeño pepper
3 garlic cloves, minced
Cooking spray
1½ pounds green beans, trimmed
1 cup halved cherry tomatoes

1. Trim fat from steak. Combine steak and next 6 ingredients in a large zip-top plastic bag. Seal bag, and marinate in refrigerator 8 to 12 hours, turning bag occasionally. Remove steak from bag, reserving marinade.
2. Prepare grill or broiler.
3. Place steak on grill rack or broiler pan coated with cooking spray; cook 8 minutes on each side or until desired degree of doneness. Cut steak diagonally across grain into thin slices; thread slices onto skewers, if desired. Keep warm.
4. Pour reserved marinade through a sieve into a large saucepan; add 1 tablespoon strained marinade solids back to marinade. Discard remaining solids.

Asian Flank Steak

Bring marinade to a boil over medium-high heat, and cook 1 minute. Add green beans; cook, covered, 5 minutes or until crisp-tender, stirring occasionally. Remove from heat; add tomatoes, and toss gently to coat. Serve with steak. Yield: 6 servings (serving size: 3 ounces steak and 1 cup green bean mixture).

CALORIES 259 (45% from fat); FAT 13g (sat 5.5g, mono 5.4g, poly 0.5g); PROTEIN 24.6g; CARB 11.9g; FIBER 2.8g; CHOL 60mg; IRON 3.7mg; SODIUM 403mg; CALC 54mg

KOREAN-STYLE FLANK STEAK

PREP: 7 MINUTES   MARINATE: 8 HOURS
COOK: 16 MINUTES

    1   (1½-pound) flank steak
    ¼   cup finely chopped green onions
    ¼   cup low-sodium soy sauce
    2   tablespoons sugar
    2   tablespoons dry sherry
    1   tablespoon dark sesame oil
    1   tablespoon water
    ¼   teaspoon coarsely ground pepper
    4   garlic cloves, minced
        Cooking spray

1. Trim fat from steak. Combine steak and next 8 ingredients in a large zip-top plastic bag. Seal bag; marinate in refrigerator 8 hours, turning bag occasionally.
2. Preheat broiler.
3. Remove steak from bag, reserving marinade. Place steak on a broiler pan coated with cooking spray; brush reserved marinade over steak. Broil 8 minutes; turn steak, and brush with marinade. Broil 8 minutes or until desired degree of doneness; discard remaining marinade. Cut steak diagonally across grain into thin slices. Yield: 6 servings (serving size: 3 ounces).

CALORIES 231 (55% from fat); FAT 14g (sat 5.6g, mono 5.8g, poly 0.9g); PROTEIN 22g; CARB 3.1g; FIBER 0.1g; CHOL 60mg; IRON 2.3mg; SODIUM 233mg; CALC 10mg

SKILLET BEEF BURGUNDY

PREP: 17 MINUTES
COOK: 55 MINUTES
(pictured on page 2)

    1½   pounds boned sirloin steak
        Cooking spray
    2   cups (½-inch) sliced carrot
    2   cups quartered mushrooms
        (about 6 ounces)
    ¾   cup coarsely chopped onion
    1   pound small red potatoes, peeled
        and quartered
    ½   teaspoon dried thyme
    ¼   teaspoon salt
    ¼   teaspoon black pepper
    1   (10½-ounce) can beef
        consommé, undiluted
    3   tablespoons all-purpose flour
    ¾   cup dry red wine

1. Trim fat from steak; cut steak into 1-inch cubes. Coat a large nonstick skillet with cooking spray, and place over medium-high heat until hot. Add steak cubes; cook 4 minutes or until steak loses its pink color and is browned on all sides. Remove steak cubes from skillet, and drain well.
2. Recoat skillet with cooking spray; place over medium-high heat until hot. Add carrot, mushrooms, onion, and potato; sauté 5 minutes. Return steak to skillet. Add thyme, salt, pepper, and consommé; stir well. Cover, reduce heat, and simmer 50 minutes or until meat and vegetables are tender, stirring occasionally.
3. Place flour in a small bowl; gradually add wine, blending with a whisk. Add to steak mixture, and cook, uncovered, 5 minutes or until thick and bubbly, stirring occasionally. Yield: 5 servings (serving size: about 1½ cups).

CALORIES 337 (21% from fat); FAT 8g (sat 2.9g, mono 3.2g, poly 0.5g); PROTEIN 37.4g; CARB 27.9g; FIBER 4g; CHOL 91mg; IRON 5.6mg; SODIUM 537mg; CALC 48mg

MUSHROOM PRIMER

Buying: Most mushrooms are prepackaged, which may hamper your ability to scrutinize them. To ensure that you're getting the freshest ones possible, choose those that are firm and unblemished. **They should also have an earthy, fresh smell and a firm, moist flesh.**

Storing: Keep mushrooms cool and dry. Refrigerating them in either plastic or paper containers will help preserve their freshness.

Preparation: For years, the best way to clean mushrooms has been debated. Should they be rinsed with running water, or simply wiped off with a damp paper towel? Either is fine. **If they're particularly dirty, rinse them off. If they're not, go the paper towel route.** Most supermarket mushrooms, including buttons and cremini, don't need trimming. **But if the mushrooms are really dirty, clean them and cut the bottoms of the stems off.** (This is recommended mainly for cremini and buttons, as **the stems of shiitakes and portobellos generally aren't used.)**

Cooking: Mushrooms are mostly water and release a lot of liquid when cooked. Therefore, it's best to cook them over high heat. And **because of their water content, they shrink when cooked a long time, thus providing more flavor than substance. Mushrooms** have a very subtle flavor and **taste best when combined with seasonings such as garlic, onions, and herbs.**

Greek Stuffed Steak

1. Cut horizontally through center of steak, cutting to, but not through, other side; open flat as you would a book.

2. Place steak between 2 sheets of heavy-duty plastic wrap, and flatten to an even thickness, using a meat mallet or rolling pin.

3. Spread spinach mixture over steak, leaving a 1-inch margin around outside edges.

4. Roll up steak, jelly-roll fashion, starting with short side.

5. Secure at 2-inch intervals with heavy string.

GREEK STUFFED STEAK

PREP: 30 MINUTES
COOK: 1 1/2 HOURS

We like to serve this flavorful steak with Feta Mashed Potatoes (page 498).

- 1 (10-ounce) package frozen chopped spinach, thawed, drained, and squeezed dry
- 1/3 cup finely chopped red onion
- 1/3 cup chopped pickled pepperoncini peppers
- 2 tablespoons dry breadcrumbs
- 1/4 teaspoon garlic powder
- 1/4 teaspoon salt
- 1 (1 1/2-pound) flank steak
- Cooking spray
- 1 (14 1/2-ounce) can beef broth
- 1/2 cup dry red wine
- 1/2 cup water
- 1/2 teaspoon dried oregano

1. Combine first 6 ingredients in a bowl; set aside.
2. Trim fat from steak. Cut horizontally through center of steak, cutting to, but not through, other side; open flat as you would a book. Place steak between 2 sheets of heavy-duty plastic wrap; flatten to an even thickness, using a meat mallet or rolling pin.
3. Spread spinach mixture over steak, leaving a 1-inch margin around outside edges. Roll up steak, jelly-roll fashion, starting with short side. Secure roll at 2-inch intervals with heavy string.
4. Coat a large Dutch oven with cooking spray, and place over medium-high heat until hot. Add steak, browning well on all sides. Add broth, wine, water, and oregano to pan; bring to a boil. Cover, reduce heat, and simmer 1 hour and 30 minutes or until tender, turning meat once. Add additional water during cooking, if necessary. Remove string, and cut steak into 8 slices. Serve with

cooking liquid. Yield: 8 servings (serving size: 1 steak slice and about 2 tablespoons cooking liquid).

CALORIES 177 (42% from fat); FAT 8.3g (sat 3.5g, mono 3.3g, poly 0.4g); PROTEIN 20.6g; CARB 4.4g; FIBER 1.3g; CHOL 43mg; IRON 3mg; SODIUM 528mg; CALC 56mg

TANGY FLANK STEAK WITH HORSERADISH CREAM

PREP: 5 MINUTES
MARINATE: 8 TO 12 HOURS
COOK: 14 MINUTES

Scoring the steak allows the marinade to be absorbed more easily. Add even more flavor with Horseradish Cream.

- 1 (1-pound) flank steak
- 1/2 cup cider vinegar
- 1/2 cup thawed apple juice concentrate, undiluted
- 1 tablespoon chopped fresh or 1 teaspoon dried rosemary
- 3 tablespoons prepared horseradish
- 1 tablespoon Worcestershire sauce
- Cooking spray
- Horseradish Cream (page 446)

1. Trim fat from steak. Score a diamond pattern on both sides of steak. Combine steak and next 5 ingredients in a large zip-top plastic bag. Seal bag; marinate in refrigerator 8 to 12 hours, turning bag occasionally. Remove steak from bag; discard marinade.
2. Prepare grill or broiler.
3. Place steak on grill rack or broiler pan coated with cooking spray; cook 7 minutes on each side or until done. Cut diagonally across grain into thin slices. Serve with Horseradish Cream. Yield: 4 servings (serving size: 3 ounces steak and 2 1/2 tablespoons Horseradish Cream).

CALORIES 238 (49% from fat); FAT 13g (sat 5.5g, mono 5.4g, poly 0.4g); PROTEIN 23.7g; CARB 4.5g; FIBER 0.2g; CHOL 60mg; IRON 2.3mg; SODIUM 113mg; CALC 52mg

TENDERLOIN STEAKS WITH PEPPER JELLY SAUCE

PREP: 5 MINUTES
COOK: 15 MINUTES

This recipe uses a dry rub instead of a marinade which gives the steaks a distinct flavor, and the recipe only takes 20 minutes to prepare. Before rubbing the seasonings over the steaks, blot the steaks with paper towels to remove excess moisture. The seasonings will adhere to the meat.

- 4 (4-ounce) beef tenderloin steaks (1 inch thick)
- 3/4 teaspoon chili powder
- 1/2 teaspoon garlic powder
- 1/2 teaspoon coarsely ground black pepper
- 1/4 teaspoon salt
- 1/4 teaspoon dried oregano
- 1/4 teaspoon ground cumin
- 1 teaspoon vegetable oil
- 1/2 cup no-salt-added beef broth
- 1/4 cup balsamic vinegar
- 2 tablespoons red jalapeño pepper jelly

1. Trim fat from steaks. Combine chili powder and next 5 ingredients. Rub chili powder mixture over both sides of steaks.
2. Heat oil in a large nonstick skillet over medium-high heat 2 minutes. Add steaks, and cook 4 minutes on each side or until done. Remove steaks from skillet; keep warm.
3. Add broth, vinegar, and jelly to skillet, and cook 5 minutes or until slightly thickened, stirring frequently. Spoon sauce over steaks. Yield: 4 servings (serving size: 1 steak and 1 tablespoon sauce).

CALORIES 212 (37% from fat); FAT 8.7g (sat 3.2g, mono 3.2g, poly 1.1g); PROTEIN 23.8g; CARB 8.2g; FIBER 0.3g; CHOL 70mg; IRON 3.5mg; SODIUM 215mg; CALC 15mg

TENDERLOIN PUTTANESCA

PREP:10 MINUTES   COOK:13 MINUTES

  2 tablespoons sun-dried tomato
       sprinkles
  ½ cup boiling water
1¾ cups chopped tomato
  ⅓ cup dry red wine
  ¼ cup chopped fresh basil
  ¼ cup chopped ripe olives
  1 garlic clove, crushed
  4 (4-ounce) beef tenderloin steaks
  1 tablespoon Worcestershire sauce
  ¼ teaspoon hickory smoked salt
  ¼ teaspoon black pepper
Cooking spray
  4 ripe olives
Basil sprigs (optional)

1. Combine sun-dried tomato sprinkles
and boiling water in a medium bowl,
and let stand 10 minutes. Drain well.
Add 1¾ cups chopped tomato, wine,
chopped basil, chopped olives, and garlic
to sun-dried tomato; stir well.
2. Trim fat from steaks. Brush Worcestershire sauce over steaks, and sprinkle
with smoked salt and pepper.
3. Coat a large nonstick skillet with
cooking spray; place over medium-high
heat until hot. Add steaks, and cook 1
minute on each side or until browned.
Reduce heat to medium-low, and cook
4 minutes on each side or until done.
Place steaks on a serving platter, and
keep warm.
4. Add tomato mixture to skillet, and
cook over medium-high heat 3 minutes
or until thoroughly heated, stirring occasionally. Spoon tomato mixture over
steaks, and garnish with 4 olives and
basil sprigs, if desired. Yield: 4 servings
(serving size: 3 ounces steak and ½ cup
tomato mixture).

CALORIES 214 (40% from fat); FAT 9.4g (sat 3.3g, mono 4g,
poly 0.8g); PROTEIN 24.9g; CARB 7.2g; FIBER 1.7g;
CHOL 70mg; IRON 4.3mg; SODIUM 419mg; CALC 37mg

BOURBON ROASTED BEEF TENDERLOIN WITH ONION RELISH

PREP:10 MINUTES
MARINATE:30 MINUTES
COOK:55 MINUTES

  1 (5-pound) beef tenderloin
  1 large garlic clove, halved
  ⅓ cup bourbon
  2 tablespoons water
  ¼ teaspoon hot sauce
  ½ teaspoon black pepper, divided
  ½ teaspoon salt
Cooking spray
Onion Relish (page 454)

1. Trim fat from tenderloin; rub tenderloin with cut side of garlic. Combine
bourbon, water, hot sauce, and ¼ teaspoon pepper in a large zip-top plastic
bag. Add tenderloin to bag; seal. Marinate in refrigerator 30 minutes.
2. Preheat oven to 425°.
3. Remove tenderloin from bag, reserving marinade. Sprinkle tenderloin with
salt and ¼ teaspoon pepper. Fold under
3 inches of small end. Place tenderloin
on a broiler pan coated with cooking
spray. Insert meat thermometer into
thickest portion of tenderloin. Bake at
425° for 55 minutes or until thermometer registers 145° (medium-rare) to 160°
(medium), basting frequently with reserved marinade.
4. Place tenderloin on a platter; cover
with foil. Let stand 10 minutes before
slicing. Serve with Onion Relish. Yield:
about 16 servings (serving size: 3 ounces
tenderloin and 2½ tablespoons relish).

CALORIES 192 (36% from fat); FAT 7.6g (sat 2.9g, mono 2.9g,
poly 0.3g); PROTEIN 23.4g; CARB 6.4g; FIBER 1.2g;
CHOL 67mg; IRON 3.1mg; SODIUM 119mg; CALC 20mg

BEEF CARBONNADE

PREP:30 MINUTES   COOK:2 HOURS

  2 bacon slices, diced
  2 pounds boned chuck roast, cut
       into 1-inch cubes
  ½ teaspoon salt
  ½ teaspoon black pepper
  1 garlic clove, minced
  5 cups thinly sliced onion (about
       2 large)
  3 tablespoons all-purpose flour
  1 cup beef broth
  2 teaspoons white wine vinegar
  ½ teaspoon sugar
  ½ teaspoon dried thyme
  1 bay leaf
  1 (12-ounce) can light beer
  1 (12-ounce) package egg
       noodles, cooked
Thyme sprigs (optional)

1. Preheat oven to 325°.
2. Cook bacon in a large Dutch oven
over medium heat until crisp; remove
bacon with a slotted spoon, reserving
drippings in pan. Set bacon aside.
3. Sprinkle beef with salt and pepper.
Cook beef in drippings over medium-
high heat 4 minutes, browning well on
all sides. Add garlic; cook 30 seconds.
Remove beef with a slotted spoon.
4. Add onion to pan; cover and cook
over medium heat 10 minutes, stirring
occasionally. Stir in flour; cook 2 minutes. Add broth and next 5 ingredients;
bring to a boil, scraping pan to loosen
browned bits. Return bacon and beef to
pan. Cover and bake at 325° for 2 hours
or until beef is tender. Discard bay leaf.
Serve over noodles. Garnish with thyme
sprigs, if desired. Yield: 6 servings (serving size: about 1 cup beef mixture and 1
cup noodles).

CALORIES 546 (26% from fat); FAT 15.5g (sat 5.5g, mono 6.2g,
poly 1.8g); PROTEIN 44.5g; CARB 55.2g; FIBER 3.6g;
CHOL 151mg; IRON 7.1mg; SODIUM 593mg; CALC 58mg

Peeling Small Onions

To peel small onions, place them in boiling water for 30 seconds. The skins will then peel off easily.

THREE-MUSHROOM TWO-TOMATO POT ROAST

PREP: 15 MINUTES   COOK: 3 HOURS

- 1 (3-pound) boned beef bottom round roast
- 2 teaspoons vegetable oil
- 1½ cups chopped onion
- 1½ teaspoons dried thyme
- 1 large garlic clove, minced
- 3 bay leaves
- 1 cup low-salt chicken broth
- 1 cup dry red wine
- 1 cup canned whole tomatoes, undrained and chopped
- ½ teaspoon salt
- ¼ teaspoon pepper
- 8 carrots (about 1 pound), peeled and halved
- 8 small boiling onions (about 1¼ pounds), peeled
- 1 ounce sun-dried tomatoes, packed without oil (about 12), chopped
- 4 cups shiitake mushroom caps (about 12 ounces)
- 1 (8-ounce) package button mushrooms, quartered
- 1 (8-ounce) package cremini mushrooms, quartered

1. Preheat oven to 300°.

2. Trim fat from roast. Heat oil in a Dutch oven over medium-high heat until hot. Add roast; brown on all sides. Remove roast. Add chopped onion to pan; sauté 3 minutes. Add thyme, garlic, and bay leaves; sauté 1 minute. Add broth, wine, and canned tomatoes, scraping pan to loosen browned bits. Return roast to pan, and sprinkle with salt and pepper. Cover and bake at 300° for 1 hour.

3. Remove from oven; turn roast over. Add carrots, boiling onions, and sun-dried tomatoes. Cover; bake 1 hour. Add mushrooms. Cover and bake an additional hour or until roast is very tender. Let stand 10 minutes; discard bay leaf. Cut roast across grain into thin slices, and serve with vegetables. Yield: 8 servings (serving size: 3 ounces beef and 1¼ cups mushroom mixture).

CALORIES 282 (23% from fat); FAT 7.2g (sat 2.3g, mono 2.5g, poly 1.1g); PROTEIN 33.7g; CARB 21.9g; FIBER 4.1g; CHOL 73mg; IRON 5mg; SODIUM 380mg; CALC 72mg

CARBONNADES Á LA FLAMANDE

PREP: 40 MINUTES   COOK: 1½ HOURS

While French food has an upscale image, a lot of it is not. Peasant cooking for family meals includes basic hearty dishes. Serve up this one-dish-meal family style from a large platter.

- 1 (1½-pound) rump roast
- 2 medium onions, cut into ½-inch slices
- ¼ teaspoon salt
- ¼ teaspoon black pepper
- 3 garlic cloves, crushed
- 1 (14½-ounce) can no-salt-added beef broth
- 1 (12-ounce) bottle beer
- 1½ tablespoons brown sugar
- ⅛ teaspoon dried thyme
- 1 bay leaf
- 12 small unpeeled round red potatoes, halved (about 1 pound)
- 1 tablespoon chopped fresh parsley
- 2 tablespoons cornstarch
- ¼ teaspoon salt
- 1 tablespoon red wine vinegar

1. Preheat oven to 400°.

2. Trim fat from roast; cut roast into 2 x 1 x ½-inch pieces. Place a large non-stick skillet over medium-high heat until hot. Add beef, and cook until browned on all sides. Remove from pan; set aside.

3. Add onion to pan. Cook over medium heat 10 minutes or until lightly browned, stirring frequently. Remove from heat; stir in ¼ teaspoon salt, pepper, and garlic. Arrange half of beef in bottom of a 3-quart casserole. Top with half of onion mixture. Repeat layers with remaining beef and onion mixture.

4. Combine beef broth, beer, brown sugar, thyme, and bay leaf; pour over beef mixture. Cover and bake at 400° for 1½ hours or until beef is tender.

5. While beef is baking, arrange potato in a vegetable steamer over boiling water. Steam, covered, 20 minutes or until tender; drain. Place potato and parsley in a bowl, and toss well; keep warm.

6. Strain cooking liquid from beef mixture into a saucepan; set beef mixture aside. Discard bay leaf. Combine cornstarch, ¼ teaspoon salt, and vinegar. Add to cooking liquid. Bring to a boil, and cook 2 minutes or until thickened, stirring constantly. Arrange beef mixture and potato halves on a platter; serve with sauce. Yield: 6 servings (serving size: 3 ounces beef, 4 potato halves, and ⅓ cup sauce).

CALORIES 262 (16% from fat); FAT 4.7g (sat 1.7g, mono 1.9g, poly 0.3g); PROTEIN 25.8g; CARB 24.5g; FIBER 2.3g; CHOL 65mg; IRON 3.7mg; SODIUM 222mg; CALC 33mg

PENNSYLVANIA POT ROAST

PREP:15 MINUTES

COOK:3 HOURS 15 MINUTES

We all agree that this old-fashioned pot roast is the very essence of comfort food. Serve with small red potatoes, if desired.

Cooking spray
1 (1½-pound) beef eye-of-round roast
¾ cup beef broth
1 cup chopped onion
½ cup canned crushed tomatoes with added puree, undrained
¼ cup diced carrot
¼ cup diced celery
¼ cup diced turnip
2 tablespoons chopped fresh parsley
¼ teaspoon dried thyme
4 black peppercorns
1 bay leaf

1. Place a large saucepan coated with cooking spray over medium-high heat until hot. Add roast, browning on all sides. Add beef broth and remaining ingredients to pan; bring to a boil. Cover, reduce heat, and simmer 3 hours or until tender.
2. Cut roast across grain into thin slices; place on a serving platter. Set aside; keep warm. Increase heat to medium; cook broth mixture, uncovered, 10 minutes or until reduced to 1⅔ cups. Discard peppercorns and bay leaf. Serve sauce with roast. Yield: 5 servings (serving size: 3 ounces roast and ⅓ cup sauce).

CALORIES 217 (24% from fat); FAT 5.7g (sat 2g, mono 2.2g, poly 0.3g); PROTEIN 33.4g; CARB 6.1g; FIBER 1.2g; CHOL 85mg; IRON 3.4mg; SODIUM 356mg; CALC 28mg

OVEN ROASTING

Be sure your oven is clean. Small bits of debris on oven walls or doors can begin to smoke at high temperatures.

Use the correct pan. The pan should be just large enough to hold the food in a single layer. The side of the pan should be no higher than 2 to 3 inches so that steam is not retained.

Position oven racks correctly. If the food is placed near the bottom of the oven, it's more like sautéing. If the food is placed very close to the top of the oven, it's more like broiling. For roasting, the food should be in the middle of the oven.

EYE-OF-ROUND WITH ROASTED-GARLIC SAUCE

PREP:23 MINUTES   CHILL:1 HOUR

COOK:3 HOURS

3 whole garlic heads
2 cups beef broth, divided
4 teaspoons dried marjoram, divided
1 teaspoon salt, divided
8 garlic cloves, peeled
2 large shallots, peeled
1 (4-pound) beef eye-of-round roast
½ teaspoon black pepper
1 tablespoon brandy

1. Preheat oven to 350°.
2. Remove white papery skin from garlic heads (do not peel or separate the cloves). Place garlic heads in a 1-quart baking dish; add ½ cup broth. Cover and bake at 350° for 1 hour.
3. Combine 3 teaspoons marjoram, ½ teaspoon salt, 8 garlic cloves, and shallots in a food processor; process to a coarse paste.
4. Trim fat from roast; make ¾-inch-deep slits into roast. Spoon ¼ teaspoon marjoram paste into each slit; rub roast with remaining paste. Sprinkle roast with pepper. Cover and chill 1 hour.
5. Cool baked garlic 10 minutes; remove garlic heads, reserving cooking liquid. Separate cloves; squeeze to extract garlic pulp. Discard skins. Place reserved cooking liquid, garlic pulp, 1½ cups broth, 1 teaspoon marjoram, and ½ teaspoon salt in a food processor; process until smooth. Set garlic sauce aside.
6. Preheat oven to 325°.
7. Place roast on a broiler pan; insert meat thermometer into thickest portion of roast. Bake at 325° for 2 hours or until thermometer registers 160° (medium). Place roast on a platter; cover with foil. Let stand 15 minutes.
8. Add brandy and ½ cup garlic sauce to broiler pan, scraping pan to loosen browned bits. Combine brandy mixture and remaining garlic sauce in a saucepan; bring to a boil. Cut roast across grain into very thin slices; serve with garlic sauce. Yield: 16 servings (serving size: 3 ounces beef and 2 tablespoons sauce).

CALORIES 171 (25% from fat); FAT 4.8g (sat 1.8g, mono 2.1g, poly 0.3g); PROTEIN 25.3g; CARB 5.3g; FIBER 0.3g; CHOL 60mg; IRON 2mg; SODIUM 209mg; CALC 33mg

BEEF BRISKET IN BEER

PREP:21 MINUTES

COOK:3 HOURS 20 MINUTES

1 (4-pound) beef brisket
½ teaspoon black pepper
1 cup sliced onion, separated into rings
½ cup chili sauce
3 tablespoons brown sugar
2 garlic cloves, crushed
1 (12-ounce) bottle beer
2½ tablespoons all-purpose flour
¼ teaspoon salt
½ cup plus 2 tablespoons water
Black pepper (optional)

Beef Brisket in Beer

NEW ENGLAND BOILED DINNER

PREP: 20 MINUTES
COOK: 2 HOURS 50 MINUTES

1 (5-pound) cured corned beef brisket
4 quarts water
Cooking spray
½ cup maple syrup
20 small boiling onions, peeled (about 1 pound)
10 carrots, scraped and cut into 2-inch pieces (about 1¼ pounds)
5 baking potatoes, peeled and quartered (about 3½ pounds)
5 turnips, peeled and quartered (about 1¼ pounds)
1 (2-pound) green cabbage, cored and cut into 10 wedges

1. Trim fat from brisket. Place brisket in a large stockpot; add water. Bring to a boil; cover, reduce heat, and simmer 2 hours or until tender.
2. Preheat oven to 400°.
3. Remove brisket from pot; set cooking liquid aside. Place brisket in a large baking dish coated with cooking spray; drizzle with syrup. Bake, uncovered, at 400° for 20 minutes.
4. Add onions, carrot, potato, and turnip to liquid in pot; bring to a boil over high heat. Cover; reduce heat to medium. Cook 25 minutes. Add cabbage; cook 5 minutes or until vegetables are tender. Drain; place on a serving platter.
5. Cut brisket across grain into thin slices, and place on serving platter; drizzle with drippings from baking dish. Yield: 10 servings (serving size: 3 ounces brisket, 2 onions, 4 carrot pieces, 2 potato quarters, 2 turnip quarters, and 1 cabbage wedge).

CALORIES 371 (19% from fat); FAT 7.7g (sat 3.4g, mono 4.3g, poly 0.5g); PROTEIN 23g; CARB 52.2g; FIBER 6.2g; CHOL 64mg; IRON 3.7mg; SODIUM 838mg; CALC 91mg

1. Preheat oven to 350°.
2. Trim fat from brisket; place in a 13 x 9-inch baking dish. Sprinkle top of brisket with ½ teaspoon pepper; arrange onion rings over brisket.
3. Combine chili sauce, brown sugar, garlic, and beer, and pour over brisket. Cover, and bake at 350° for 3 hours. Uncover, and bake an additional 20 minutes or until brisket is tender. Place brisket on a serving platter, reserving cooking liquid. Set brisket aside, and keep warm.
4. Pour 1½ cups cooking liquid into a small saucepan. Place flour and salt in a bowl. Gradually add water, blending with a whisk; add to saucepan. Bring to a boil, and cook 2 minutes or until gravy is thickened, stirring constantly.
5. Serve gravy with brisket. Sprinkle with pepper, if desired. Yield: 11 servings (serving size: 3 ounces brisket and 3 tablespoons gravy).

CALORIES 229 (27% from fat); FAT 6.9g (sat 2.3g, mono 3.1g, poly 0.3g); PROTEIN 30.7g; CARB 9.7g; FIBER 0.5g; CHOL 82mg; IRON 3mg; SODIUM 326mg; CALC 18mg

veal
The mild flavor of veal makes it especially suitable for robust sauces, seasonings, and spicy coatings.

VEAL MEDALLIONS WITH MUSHROOM-WINE SAUCE

PREP:13 MINUTES COOK:22 MINUTES

2 tablespoons all-purpose flour
½ teaspoon salt, divided
¼ teaspoon black pepper, divided
8 (2-ounce) pieces veal tenderloin (about ½ inch thick)
2 teaspoons olive oil, divided
¼ cup minced shallots
1 small garlic clove, minced
1¼ cups diced shiitake mushroom caps (about 3 ounces)
1 cup diced oyster mushroom caps (about 3 ounces)
2 tablespoons finely chopped fresh parsley
¼ teaspoon dried thyme
¼ cup dry white wine
⅔ cup plus 1 tablespoon no-salt-added beef broth, divided
1 teaspoon cornstarch

1. Combine flour, ¼ teaspoon salt, and ⅛ teaspoon pepper; sprinkle over both sides of veal. Heat 1 teaspoon oil in a nonstick skillet over medium-high heat. Add veal; cook 3 minutes on each side or until browned. Remove veal from skillet, and place on a serving platter; keep warm.
2. Heat 1 teaspoon oil in pan over medium heat. Add shallots and garlic; sauté 2 minutes. Add ¼ teaspoon salt, ⅛ teaspoon pepper, mushrooms, parsley, and thyme; sauté 2 minutes. Add wine; sauté 2 minutes. Add ⅔ cup broth; cook 3 minutes. Combine 1 tablespoon broth and cornstarch in a bowl. Add cornstarch mixture to skillet; cook until thick (about 1 minute), stirring constantly. Spoon over veal. Yield: 4 servings (serving size: 4 ounces veal and 5 tablespoons sauce).

CALORIES 201 (28% from fat); FAT 6.3g (sat 1.5g, mono 2.9g, poly 0.7g); PROTEIN 24.6g; CARB 10.7g; FIBER 1.1g; CHOL 91mg; IRON 2.1mg; SODIUM 402mg; CALC 36mg

VEAL BIRDS (BREADED VEAL WITH ARTICHOKES)

PREP:25 MINUTES COOK: 15 MINUTES

½ cup finely chopped onion
Cooking spray
4 (1-ounce) slices white bread, cut into ½-inch cubes
6 tablespoons Riesling or other slightly sweet white wine, divided
2 tablespoons fat-free milk
¼ teaspoon dried thyme
¼ teaspoon dried marjoram
¼ teaspoon dried basil
⅛ teaspoon salt
½ teaspoon coarsely ground pepper
8 (2-ounce) slices veal scaloppine, cut in half crosswise
¼ cup all-purpose flour
2 tablespoons reduced-calorie margarine
1 tablespoon fresh lemon juice
1 (10½-ounce) can low-salt chicken broth
2 cups quartered fresh mushrooms
1 (14-ounce) can artichoke hearts, drained and quartered
2 tablespoons cornstarch
2 tablespoons water
Thin lemon slices (optional)

1. Sauté onion in a skillet coated with cooking spray over medium-high heat 3 minutes or until tender. Stir in bread cubes, 2 tablespoons wine, milk, and next 5 ingredients. Spoon 1 heaping tablespoon bread mixture onto each piece of veal. Roll up jelly-roll fashion, beginning at narrow ends, and secure with wooden picks. Place flour in a shallow bowl. Dredge veal rolls in flour, turning to coat; shake off excess flour.
2. Melt margarine in a large nonstick skillet coated with cooking spray over medium heat. Add veal rolls; cook 3 minutes or until lightly browned, turning frequently. Remove from pan. Wipe drippings from pan with a paper towel.
3. Add lemon juice, broth, and 4 tablespoons wine to pan; bring to a boil. Return veal rolls to pan, and top with mushrooms. Cover, reduce heat, and simmer 10 minutes or until veal is tender. Remove veal rolls from pan; discard wooden picks. Cover and keep warm.
4. Add artichoke hearts to pan. Combine cornstarch and water; add to pan. Bring to a boil; cook 1 minute or until sauce is thickened and bubbly, stirring constantly. Pour sauce over veal rolls, and garnish with lemon slices, if desired. Yield: 8 servings (serving size: 2 veal rolls and 6 tablespoons sauce).

CALORIES 184 (26% from fat); FAT 5.3g (sat 1.2g, mono 1.8g, poly 1.1g); PROTEIN 17g; CARB 16.8g; FIBER 1.1g; CHOL 51mg; IRON1.7mg; SODIUM 287mg; CALC 39mg

GRILLED VEAL SCALOPPINE WITH PORT-WINE SAUCE

PREP:6 MINUTES COOK:3 MINUTES

1 teaspoon olive oil
1 pound veal scaloppine
¼ teaspoon salt
¼ teaspoon pepper
Cooking spray
Port-Wine Sauce (page 448)
Thinly sliced green onions

1. Brush oil over veal, and sprinkle with salt and pepper. Prepare grill or broiler. Place veal on grill rack or broiler pan coated with cooking spray, and cook 1½ minutes on each side or until veal is done. Serve veal with Port-Wine Sauce, and top with green onions. Yield: 4 servings (serving size: 3 ounces veal and 2 tablespoons Port-Wine Sauce).

CALORIES 226 (27% from fat); FAT 6.9g (sat 1.7g, mono 2.8g, poly 0.6g); PROTEIN 27.4g; CARB 8.8g; FIBER 0.1g; CHOL 100mg; IRON 1.6mg; SODIUM 321mg; CALC 32mg

LEMON-CAPER VEAL

PREP:6 MINUTES
COOK:8 MINUTES

4 (2-ounce) veal leg cutlets
½ teaspoon freshly ground black pepper, divided
Cooking spray
½ cup fat-free, less-sodium chicken broth
⅛ teaspoon grated lemon rind
2 tablespoons fresh lemon juice
2 teaspoons capers
1 tablespoon water
½ teaspoon cornstarch

1. Place each cutlet between 2 sheets of heavy-duty plastic wrap; flatten to ⅛-inch thickness, using a meat mallet or rolling pin. Sprinkle ¼ teaspoon pepper over cutlets.
2. Coat a large nonstick skillet with cooking spray; place over medium-high heat. Add cutlets; cook 2 minutes on each side or until done. Remove from pan; keep warm.
3. Add ¼ teaspoon pepper, broth, lemon rind, lemon juice, and capers to pan; cook 2 minutes. Combine water and cornstarch, and add to broth mixture. Bring to a boil, and cook 1 minute, stirring constantly. Serve sauce over

cutlets. Yield: 2 servings (serving size: 3 ounces veal and 2 tablespoons sauce).

CALORIES 139 (16% from fat); FAT 2.4g (sat 0.6g, mono 0.6g, poly 0.2g); PROTEIN 24.5g; CARB 3g; FIBER 0.2g; CHOL 88mg; IRON 1.1mg; SODIUM 462mg; CALC 9mg

OSSO BUCO

PREP:15 MINUTES
COOK:2 HOURS 10 MINUTES

2 tablespoons all-purpose flour
½ teaspoon pepper
¼ teaspoon salt
4 (10-ounce) veal shanks (1½ inches thick)
1 tablespoon olive oil
1 cup minced carrot
1 cup minced celery
1 cup minced onion
1 cup dry white wine
1 large garlic clove, minced
1 (14½-ounce) can plum tomatoes, undrained and chopped
½ cup beef broth
2 teaspoons chopped fresh rosemary
1 bay leaf

1. Preheat oven to 350°.
2. Combine first 3 ingredients in a shallow dish. Dredge veal in flour mixture.
3. Heat oil in a large ovenproof Dutch oven over medium-high heat. Add veal; cook 2½ minutes on each side or until browned. Remove from pan; set aside. Reduce heat to medium; add carrot and next 4 ingredients. Cook 5 minutes, scraping pan to loosen browned bits. Return veal to pan; add tomatoes and next 3 ingredients. Cover and bake at 350° for 2 hours or until veal is tender; discard bay leaf. Serve sauce with veal. Yield: 4 servings.

CALORIES 468 (26% from fat); FAT 13.3g (sat 3.4g, mono 5.6g, poly 1.4g); PROTEIN 60.6g; CARB 15g; FIBER 2.9g; CHOL 233mg; IRON 3.8mg; SODIUM 742mg; CALC 112mg

OSSO BUCO

1. Dredge veal shanks in flour, pepper, and salt. Cook veal on each side until browned; remove from pan.

2. Add carrot, celery, onion, wine, and garlic to pan, stirring to deglaze the pan (to loosen browned bits of food from bottom of pan).

3. Return veal to pan, and add remaining ingredients; cover and bake at 350° for 2 hours.

VEAL OSCAR

PREP: 10 MINUTES   COOK: 7 MINUTES

Traditional Veal Oscar contains about 725 calories and 60 grams of fat, with 74% of calories from fat. Ours contains a fraction of the calories and fat, with 39% of calories from fat. We suggest serving it with ½ cup angel hair pasta to lower each serving to the recommended 30% of calories from fat.

¼   teaspoon salt
¼   teaspoon pepper
12   slices veal scaloppine (about ½ pound)
3   tablespoons all-purpose flour
2   tablespoons reduced-calorie margarine, divided
Cooking spray
½   pound fresh lump crabmeat, drained
1   lemon, halved and seeded
1   pound fresh asparagus, trimmed and steamed
Béarnaise Sauce (page 443)
Fresh tarragon sprigs (optional)

1. Sprinkle salt and pepper over veal. Combine veal and flour in a large zip-top plastic bag; seal bag, and shake to coat veal.
2. Melt 1 tablespoon margarine in a large nonstick skillet over medium heat. Add half of veal, and cook 1 minute on each side or until browned. Remove veal from pan; and keep warm. Repeat with 1 tablespoon margarine and remaining veal. Wipe drippings from pan.
3. Coat pan with cooking spray, and place over medium heat. Add crabmeat, and sauté 1 minute or until warm. Squeeze lemon halves over crabmeat; stir until well-blended. Remove from heat.
4. Place 3 veal slices and one-fourth of steamed asparagus on each of 4 serving plates. Spoon crabmeat evenly over veal, and top each serving with 3 tablespoons Béarnaise Sauce. Garnish with fresh tarragon sprigs, if desired. Serve with angel hair pasta, if desired. Yield: 4 servings.

CALORIES 273 (39% from fat); FAT 11.8g (sat 4.3g, mono 3.6g, poly 2.1g); PROTEIN 28.1g; CARB 15.6g; FIBER 1.3g; CHOL 116mg; IRON 3.2mg; SODIUM 436mg; CALC 188mg

Veal Oscar

pork You'll find a variety of flavorful new pork dishes as well as some old favorites here.

Tenderloin is often considered the choicest cut of pork. Three ounces of roasted, trimmed, pork tenderloin has about the same amount of calories and fat as a roasted skinned chicken breast. Tenderloin is tender and juicy when the meat is still slightly pink in the center and the internal temperature reaches 160°. For the best results, use a meat thermometer to determine if it's done. Pork chops, also a lean cut, need to be cooked just until done. If overcooked, the meat will be dry and tough.

MAPLE SYRUP-BOURBON GLAZED FRESH HAM

PREP: 25 MINUTES   COOK: 2 HOURS

Because fresh ham is an uncured leg of pork, it will be grayish instead of pink-colored. The bone is tricky to remove, so ask your butcher to do it for you.

½ cup maple syrup
2 tablespoons brown sugar
3 tablespoons bourbon
½ teaspoon ground ginger
½ teaspoon ground allspice
1 (6¾-pound) fresh ham, boned
1 garlic clove, minced
2 teaspoons salt, divided
1 teaspoon pepper, divided

1. Combine first 3 ingredients in a saucepan; bring to boil. Reduce heat to low; simmer 5 minutes or until slightly thickened. Remove from heat, and stir in ginger and allspice; cool slightly.
2. Preheat oven to 350°.
3. Unroll ham; trim fat. Spread ⅓ cup syrup mixture and garlic over inside surface of ham; sprinkle with 1 teaspoon salt and ½ teaspoon pepper.

Reroll ham; secure at 2-inch intervals with heavy string. Spread 3 tablespoons syrup mixture over ham, and sprinkle with 1 teaspoon salt and ½ teaspoon pepper.
4. Place ham on a broiler pan; insert meat thermometer into thickest portion of ham. Bake at 350° for 2 hours or until thermometer registers 160°, basting ham with remaining syrup mixture after 1 hour.
5. Place ham on a serving platter; cover with foil, and let stand 15 minutes before slicing. Yield: 15 servings (serving size: 3 ounces).

CALORIES 188 (43% from fat); FAT 9g (sat 2.9g, mono 4.2g, poly 1g); PROTEIN 15g; CARB 11g; FIBER 0.1g; CHOL 48mg; IRON 1mg; SODIUM 1434mg; CALC 18mg

menu

Maple-Glazed Ham With Maple-Mustard Sauce

Corn Custard With Chives (page 491)

Carrot-Parsnip Toss (page 490)

Apple-Cider Pie (page 194)

MAPLE-GLAZED HAM WITH MAPLE-MUSTARD SAUCE

PREP: 25 MINUTES
COOK: 1 HOUR 15 MINUTES

1 (8-pound) 33%-less-sodium smoked, fully cooked ham half
Cooking spray
1¼ cups maple syrup, divided
2 tablespoons Dijon mustard
1 teaspoon grated orange rind
2 tablespoons orange juice
½ cup Dijon mustard
1 (12-ounce) jar orange marmalade

1. Preheat oven to 425°.
2. Trim fat and rind from ham. Score outside of ham in a diamond pattern. Place ham on a broiler pan coated with cooking spray. Insert meat thermometer into thickest portion of ham, making sure not to touch bone.
3. Combine ¼ cup maple syrup, 2 tablespoons mustard, orange rind, and orange juice; brush half of mixture over ham. Set remaining maple syrup mixture aside. Bake at 425° for 5 minutes. Reduce oven temperature to 325°, and bake an additional 1 hour and 10 minutes or until thermometer registers 140°. Baste ham with reserved maple syrup mixture every 30 minutes. Transfer ham to a platter, and let stand 15 minutes before slicing.
4. Combine 1 cup maple syrup, ½ cup mustard, and marmalade in a small saucepan. Cook over medium heat 3 minutes or until thoroughly heated, stirring constantly. Serve with ham. Yield: 20 servings (serving size: 3 ounces ham and 2 tablespoons sauce).

CALORIES 235 (25% from fat); FAT 6.5g (sat 2g, mono 3.1g, poly 0.8g); PROTEIN 21.9g; CARB 23.6g; FIBER 0g; CHOL 60mg; IRON 1.2mg; SODIUM 1147mg; CALC 17mg

Have ham left over? Enjoy grilled ham and cheese sandwiches for lunch tomorrow, or freeze portions in heavy-duty zip-top bags for another meal.

menu

Canadian Bacon-and-Pineapple Pizzas

Tossed Salad With Blackberry Vinaigrette
(page 397)

Chocolate-Éclair Icebox Dessert
(page 191)

CANADIAN BACON-AND-PINEAPPLE PIZZAS

PREP:12 MINUTES
COOK:8 MINUTES

6 English muffins, split
½ cup tub-style light cream cheese
    with pineapple
8 (½-ounce) slices Canadian
    bacon, coarsely chopped
¼ cup sliced green onions
1 (8-ounce) can pineapple
    tidbits, drained
1½ cups (6 ounces) preshredded
    reduced-fat pizza-blend cheese

1. Preheat broiler.
2. Place muffin halves, cut side up, on a large baking sheet. Broil 3 minutes or until lightly toasted.
3. Preheat oven to 425°.
4. Spread about 2 teaspoons cream cheese over each muffin half. Divide Canadian bacon, green onions, and pineapple tidbits evenly among muffin halves; sprinkle each with 2 tablespoons pizza cheese. Bake at 425° for 8 minutes or until pizza cheese melts. Yield: 6 servings (serving size: 2 muffin halves).

CALORIES 374 (35% from fat); FAT 14.4g (sat 7.7g, mono 4.1g, poly 1.1g); PROTEIN 17.4g; CARB 43.2g; FIBER 1.9g; CHOL 44mg; IRON 2.4mg; SODIUM 811mg; CALC 323mg

BREAKFAST QUICHE

PREP:25 MINUTES
COOK:45 MINUTES

Cooking spray
1¾ cups peeled, shredded potato
½ cup chopped green onions
4 ounces lean Canadian-style
    bacon, chopped
½ cup (2 ounces) shredded low-fat
    Jarlsberg cheese
Pastry Crust (page 213)
2 tablespoons all-purpose flour
½ teaspoon dry mustard
¼ teaspoon salt
⅛ teaspoon ground red pepper
1½ cups plus 1 teaspoon fat-free
    milk, divided
1½ cups egg substitute
Green onion fans (optional)
Cherry tomato slices (optional)

1. Coat a large nonstick skillet with cooking spray; place over medium-high heat until hot. Add potato, chopped onions, and bacon; sauté 4 minutes or until potato is lightly browned. Remove from heat; add cheese, tossing well. Spoon into prepared Pastry Crust.
2. Combine all-purpose flour and next 3 ingredients in a medium bowl. Gradually add 1½ cups milk and egg substitute, stirring with a wire whisk until smooth. Pour over potato mixture. Brush remaining 1 teaspoon milk over edges of pastry shell. Bake at 350° for 45 minutes or until set. Let stand 15 minutes. Garnish with green onion fans and cherry tomato slices, if desired. Yield: 6 servings.

CALORIES 282 (33% from fat); FAT 10.2g (sat 2.9g, mono 4.2g, poly 2.2g); PROTEIN 18.5g; CARB 28.1g; FIBER 1.5g; CHOL 14mg; IRON 3.8mg; SODIUM 633mg; CALC 202mg

RUSTIC VEGETABLE QUICHE

PREP:35 MINUTES   COOK:50 MINUTES

Crust:
1 cup all-purpose flour
¼ teaspoon salt
3 tablespoons vegetable shortening
6 tablespoons ice water
Cooking spray

Filling:
2 bacon slices
1 cup chopped red potato
½ cup chopped onion
½ cup (2 ounces) shredded
    reduced-fat Jarlsberg cheese
¼ cup thinly sliced green onions
1½ cups 1% low-fat milk
¼ teaspoon salt
⅛ teaspoon ground red pepper
3 large eggs
¼ teaspoon paprika

1. Preheat oven to 450°.
2. To prepare crust, lightly spoon flour into a dry measuring cup; level with a knife. Combine flour and ¼ teaspoon salt in a bowl; cut in shortening with a pastry blender or 2 knives until mixture resembles coarse meal. Sprinkle surface with ice water, 1 tablespoon at a time, tossing with a fork until moist and crumbly (do not form a ball). Gently press into a 4-inch circle on heavy-duty plastic wrap; cover with additional plastic wrap. Chill for 15 minutes. Roll dough, still covered, into an 11-inch circle. Place in freezer 5 minutes or until plastic wrap can be easily removed.
3. Remove 1 sheet of plastic wrap, and fit dough into a 9-inch pie plate coated with cooking spray. Remove top sheet of plastic wrap. Fold edges of dough under, and flute. Pierce bottom and sides of dough with a fork. Bake at 450° for 10 minutes or until lightly browned. Cool completely on a wire rack.

4. Reduce oven temperature to 375°.

5. To prepare filling, cook bacon in a large nonstick skillet over medium heat until crisp. Remove bacon from skillet; crumble. Add potato and chopped onion to bacon drippings in skillet; sauté 10 minutes or until tender. Remove from heat.

6. Arrange potato mixture, bacon, cheese, and green onions in prepared crust. Combine milk, ¼ teaspoon salt, pepper, and eggs; stir well with a whisk. Pour milk mixture into crust; sprinkle with paprika. Bake at 375° for 40 minutes or until a knife inserted 1 inch from center comes out clean; let stand 10 minutes. Yield: 8 servings (serving size: 1 wedge).

CALORIES 212 (50% from fat); FAT 11.8g (sat 3.9g, mono 5.1g, poly 2.1g); PROTEIN 8.8g; CARB 17.3g; FIBER 0.9g; CHOL 89mg; IRON 1.3mg; SODIUM 279mg; CALC 136mg

MAKE-AHEAD BREAKFAST CASEROLE

PREP: 22 MINUTES   CHILL: 8 HOURS
COOK: 45 MINUTES

Cooking spray
¾ pound lean ground pork breakfast sausage
¾ teaspoon dried Italian seasoning
¼ teaspoon fennel seeds, crushed
2 garlic cloves, minced
1 cup fat-free milk
½ cup (2 ounces) shredded reduced-fat sharp cheddar cheese
¾ teaspoon dry mustard
½ teaspoon salt
¼ teaspoon ground red pepper
3 green onions, chopped
2 (8-ounce) cartons egg substitute
6 (1-ounce) slices white bread, cut into ½-inch cubes
Cherry tomatoes (optional)
Green onion tops (optional)

1. Coat a nonstick skillet with cooking spray; place over medium heat until hot. Add sausage, Italian seasoning, fennel seeds, and garlic; cook until meat is browned, stirring to crumble. Drain well.

2. Combine milk and next 6 ingredients in a bowl. Add pork mixture and bread cubes, stirring just until well-blended. Pour into an 11 x 7-inch baking dish coated with cooking spray. Cover and chill 8 hours.

3. Preheat oven to 350°.

4. Bake casserole, uncovered, at 350° for 45 minutes or until set and lightly browned. If desired, garnish with tomatoes and green onions. Yield: 6 servings.

CALORIES 242 (30% from fat); FAT 8g (sat 2.9g, mono 3.2g, poly 1g); PROTEIN 22.5g; CARB 19.3g; FIBER 1.1g; CHOL 39mg; IRON 3.3mg; SODIUM 843mg; CALC 157mg

SHRIMP-AND-PORK POT STICKERS

PREP: 41 MINUTES   COOK: 18 MINUTES

¼ cup sliced green onions
¼ cup chopped fresh cilantro
2 tablespoons water
2 teaspoons minced peeled fresh ginger
½ teaspoon salt
½ teaspoon dark sesame oil
½ pound medium shrimp, peeled and deveined
½ pound lean ground pork
1 garlic clove, halved
1 large egg white
1 tablespoon all-purpose flour
36 won ton wrappers
1 large egg white, lightly beaten
4 teaspoons vegetable oil, divided
1 cup water, divided
Sesame-Orange Dipping Sauce (page 454)

1. Place first 10 ingredients in a food processor; process until coarsely ground.

2. Sprinkle 1 tablespoon flour over a large baking sheet. Working with 1 won ton wrapper at a time (cover remaining wrappers with a damp towel to keep them from drying), spoon about 1 tablespoon shrimp mixture onto center of each wrapper. Moisten edges of dough with beaten egg white, and bring 2 opposite corners together. Pinch edges together to seal, forming a triangle. Hold each triangle by top point, and tap on counter to flatten bottom of pot sticker. Place pot sticker, flat side down, on prepared baking sheet; cover loosely with a towel to keep them from drying.

3. Heat 2 teaspoons vegetable oil in a large nonstick skillet over medium-high heat. Arrange half of pot stickers, flat side down, in skillet. Cook 2 minutes or until bottoms are lightly browned. Add ½ cup water; cover and cook 3 minutes. Uncover and cook 2 to 3 minutes or until liquid is absorbed. Remove pot stickers, and keep warm. Repeat procedure with 2 teaspoons oil, remaining pot stickers, and ½ cup water. Serve with Sesame-Orange Dipping Sauce. Yield: 6 servings (serving size: 6 pot stickers and 2 tablespoons Sesame-Orange Dipping Sauce).

CALORIES 282 (26% from fat); FAT 8.2g (sat 1.9g, mono 2.8g, poly 2.7g); PROTEIN 19.8g; CARB 30.4g; FIBER 0.3g; CHOL 70mg; IRON 2.9mg; SODIUM 663mg; CALC 49mg

To get lean ground pork for recipes such as Shrimp-and-Pork Pot Stickers, ask your butcher to grind a tenderloin or a piece of the loin.

GRILLED TERIYAKI PORK CHOPS

PREP: 15 MINUTES

MARINATE: 30 MINUTES   COOK: 14 MINUTES

(pictured on page 6)

  4 (6-ounce) center-cut loin pork chops (about ¾ inch thick)
  ¼ cup low-sodium soy sauce
  3 tablespoons minced shallots
  2 tablespoons dry white wine
  2 tablespoons fresh lime juice
  1 tablespoon minced peeled fresh ginger
  1½ teaspoons brown sugar
  2 garlic cloves, minced
Cooking spray

1. Trim fat from pork. Combine pork and next 7 ingredients in a large zip-top plastic bag. Seal and marinate in refrigerator 4 hours, turning bag occasionally. Remove pork from bag, reserving marinade.
2. Prepare grill.
3. Place pork on a grill rack coated with cooking spray; cook 7 minutes on each side or until done, basting frequently with reserved marinade. Yield: 4 servings (serving size: 1 pork chop).

CALORIES 240 (46% from fat); FAT 12.3g (sat 4.2g, mono 5.4g, poly 1.4g); PROTEIN 27.1g; CARB 5g; FIBER 0.1g; CHOL 84mg; IRON 1.5mg; SODIUM 549mg; CALC 27.1mg

OVEN-FRIED PORK CHOPS

PREP: 10 MINUTES   COOK: 40 MINUTES

  4 (5-ounce) boned center-cut loin pork chops (about ½ inch thick)
  1 large egg white, lightly beaten
  2 tablespoons unsweetened pineapple juice
  1 tablespoon low-sodium soy sauce
  ¼ teaspoon ground ginger
  ⅛ teaspoon garlic powder

  5 tablespoons Parmesan-flavored breadcrumbs
  ¼ teaspoon paprika
Cooking spray

1. Preheat oven to 350°.
2. Trim fat from pork. Combine egg white, pineapple juice, soy sauce, ginger, and garlic powder in a shallow bowl; stir with a whisk. Combine breadcrumbs and paprika in a shallow bowl. Dip pork in egg white mixture; dredge in breadcrumb mixture.
3. Place pork on a rack coated with cooking spray; place rack in a shallow roasting pan. Bake at 350° for 20 minutes; turn and bake an additional 20 minutes or until done. Yield: 4 servings (serving size: 1 chop).

CALORIES 273 (36% from fat); FAT 10.8g (sat 3.6g, mono 4.8g, poly 1.2g); PROTEIN 33.6g; CARB 7.6g; FIBER 0.4g; CHOL 89mg; IRON 1.6mg; SODIUM 500mg; CALC 23mg

PORK CHOPS BRAISED IN COUNTRY GRAVY

PREP: 5 MINUTES

COOK: 1 HOUR 25 MINUTES

  4 (4-ounce) boned loin pork chops (about 1 inch thick)
  2 tablespoons all-purpose flour
  ½ teaspoon salt
  ¼ to ½ teaspoon black pepper
  1½ cups 2% reduced-fat milk, divided
  1 teaspoon margarine or butter

1. Trim fat from pork. Combine flour, salt, and pepper in a large zip-top plastic bag. Add pork; seal bag, and shake to coat pork with flour mixture. Remove pork from bag, reserving remaining flour mixture. Place reserved flour mixture in a small bowl. Gradually add ¾ cup milk, stirring with a whisk until blended.
2. Melt margarine in a large skillet over

medium-high heat. Add pork; cook 5 minutes on each side or until browned. Add milk mixture; cover, reduce heat to low, and cook 30 minutes, stirring occasionally. Turn pork. Stir in ¾ cup milk; cover and cook 30 minutes, stirring occasionally.
3. Uncover skillet, and cook pork 15 minutes or until gravy is reduced to ⅔ cup. Spoon gravy over pork. Yield: 4 servings (serving size: 1 chop and 2½ tablespoons gravy).

CALORIES 248 (39% from fat); FAT 10.8g (sat 4.1g, mono 4.6g, poly 1.2g); PROTEIN 28.4g; CARB 7.2g; FIBER 0.1g; CHOL 79mg; IRON 1.2mg; SODIUM 425mg; CALC 119mg

THREE-PEPPER PORK CUTLETS

PREP: 12 MINUTES   COOK: 10 MINUTES

Hungarian paprika is lighter in color than regular paprika, but it's more pungent. You'll find it labeled either sweet (meaning mild) or hot. Look for it in the spice aisle of your supermarket or in specialty food stores.

  1 (1-pound) ultra-lean pork tenderloin (such as Smithfield)
  2 teaspoons Hungarian sweet paprika
  1 teaspoon dried thyme
  1 teaspoon olive oil
  ½ teaspoon dried oregano
  ½ teaspoon dried rosemary, crushed
  ½ teaspoon salt
  ¼ teaspoon white pepper
  ¼ teaspoon freshly ground black pepper
  ⅛ teaspoon ground red pepper
  2 large garlic cloves, minced
Cooking spray

1. Trim fat from pork; cut pork crosswise into 8 pieces. Place between 2 sheets of heavy-duty plastic wrap, and flatten each slice to ¼-inch thickness, using a meat mallet or rolling pin.

2. Preheat broiler.

3. Combine paprika and next 9 ingredients; rub pork with paprika mixture. Place pork on a broiler pan coated with cooking spray. Broil 5 minutes on each side or until pork is done. Yield: 4 servings (serving size: 2 pork cutlets).

CALORIES 160 (31% from fat); FAT 5.5g (sat 1.6g, mono 2.7g, poly 0.7g); PROTEIN 24.8g; CARB 1.8g; FIBER 0.5g; CHOL 79mg; IRON 2.2mg; SODIUM 351mg; CALC 25mg

SWEET-AND-SOUR PORK

PREP: 30 MINUTES   COOK: 10 MINUTES

¼ cup pineapple juice
1 tablespoon cornstarch
2 tablespoons brown sugar
2 tablespoons chopped fresh cilantro
2 tablespoons apple cider vinegar
1 tablespoon low-sodium soy sauce
¼ teaspoon crushed red pepper
½ pound boned pork loin
¼ teaspoon garlic powder
½ teaspoon vegetable oil
¼ cup sliced onion
1 cup sliced red bell pepper
½ cup sliced green bell pepper
½ cup sliced zucchini
1 cup coarsely chopped fresh pineapple
2 cups hot cooked rice

1. Combine first 7 ingredients in a bowl.

2. Trim fat from pork, and cut pork into 1-inch pieces. Sprinkle garlic powder over pork.

3. Heat oil in a wok or large nonstick skillet over medium-high heat until hot. Add pork; cook 3 minutes or until pork loses its pink color. Add onion; stir-fry 1 minute. Add bell peppers and zucchini; stir-fry 3 minutes or until crisp-tender. Stir in pineapple juice mixture and

chopped pineapple; cook 1 minute or until thickened, stirring constantly. Serve over rice. Yield: 2 servings (serving size: 1½ cups pork mixture and 1 cup rice).

CALORIES 549 (18% from fat); FAT 10.7g (sat 3.3g, mono 4.3g, poly 1.8g); PROTEIN 29.6g; CARB 83.4g; FIBER 3.8g; CHOL 68mg; IRON 4.9mg; SODIUM 324mg; CALC 64mg

THREE-ALARM BARBECUE

PREP: 23 MINUTES

MARINATE: 8 HOURS   COOK: 3 TO 4 HOURS

1 (2½-pound) boned pork loin roast
1 cup cider vinegar
1 tablespoon hot sauce
1 teaspoon low-sodium Worcestershire sauce
1 teaspoon cracked black pepper
¾ teaspoon ground red pepper
½ teaspoon salt
4 (3-inch) chunks hickory wood
Cooking spray

1. Trim fat from roast. Combine pork and next 6 ingredients in a large zip-top plastic bag. Seal; marinate in refrigerator 8 hours, turning occasionally. Remove roast from bag, reserving marinade.

2. Prepare charcoal fire in meat smoker; let burn 15 to 20 minutes. Soak hickory wood chunks in water 1 to 24 hours. Drain well. Place hickory chunks on top of coals. Place water pan in smoker; fill with hot tap water.

3. Coat grill rack with cooking spray; place roast on rack in smoker. Insert meat thermometer into thickest portion of roast. Cover with smoker lid; cook 3 to 4 hours or until thermometer registers 160° (slightly pink). Refill water pan with water, and add additional charcoal to fire as needed.

4. Remove roast from smoker, and let stand 10 minutes. Separate roast into bite-sized pieces, using 2 forks. Place

roast pieces in a medium bowl.

5. Place reserved marinade in a small saucepan over medium heat; bring marinade to a boil. Remove from heat. Pour over pork, and toss well. Yield: 6 servings (serving size: 3 ounces).

CALORIES 280 (51% from fat); FAT 15.8g (sat 5.4g, mono 7.1g, poly 1.9g); PROTEIN 30.3g; CARB 2.9g; FIBER 0.2g; CHOL 102mg; IRON 1.7mg; SODIUM 294mg; CALC 15mg

PORK-AND-PINEAPPLE KEBABS

PREP: 20 MINUTES
MARINATE: 1 HOUR
COOK: 14 MINUTES

Canned pineapple can be substituted for fresh. Drain 1 (8-ounce) can unsweetened pineapple chunks, reserving 10 chunks.

1   (¾-pound) pork tenderloin
1½ tablespoons brown sugar
1½ tablespoons low-sodium soy
       sauce
1   tablespoon orange juice
1   tablespoon grated fresh onion
2   teaspoons lemon juice
⅛   teaspoon salt
Dash of black pepper
1   bay leaf
10 (1-inch) cubes fresh pineapple
10 (1-inch) pieces red bell pepper
Cooking spray

1. Trim fat from pork. Cut pork into 10 (1-inch) cubes. Combine brown sugar and next 7 ingredients in a large zip-top plastic bag; add pork. Seal bag, and marinate in refrigerator 1 hour, turning bag occasionally.
2. Remove pork from bag, reserving marinade. Discard bay leaf. Thread 5 pork cubes, 5 pineapple cubes, and 5 bell pepper pieces alternately onto each of 2 (12-inch) skewers.
3. Prepare grill.
4. Place kebabs on grill rack coated with cooking spray, and grill 14 minutes or until done, turning and basting frequently with reserved marinade. Yield: 2 servings (serving size: 1 kebab).

CALORIES 293 (21% from fat); FAT 6.9g (sat 2.2g, mono 2.8g, poly 0.9g); PROTEIN 38g; CARB 18.9g; FIBER 1.6g; CHOL 119mg; IRON 3.1mg; SODIUM 600mg; CALC 29mg

Pork-and-Pineapple Kebabs

SESAME-PORK FAJITAS

PREP: 10 MINUTES
MARINATE: 20 MINUTES
COOK: 6 MINUTES

Moo shu shells are similar to flour tortillas; made with wheat or rice flour, they can be found in Asian markets.

1   (1-pound) pork tenderloin
2   teaspoons dark sesame oil
1   teaspoon grated peeled fresh
       ginger
¼   teaspoon salt
¼   teaspoon ground red pepper
2   garlic cloves, minced
4   moo shu shells
Cooking spray
¼   cup hoisin sauce

1. Trim fat from pork, and cut pork into thin strips. Combine pork and next 5 ingredients in a large zip-top plastic bag; seal bag, and shake well to coat pork strips. Marinate in refrigerator 20 minutes.
2. Warm moo shu shells according to package directions.
3. Coat a medium nonstick skillet with cooking spray; place over medium-high heat until hot. Add pork mixture; stir-fry 5 minutes or until done.
4. Divide pork mixture evenly among moo shu shells. Drizzle hoisin sauce over pork mixture, and roll up. Yield: 4 servings (serving size: 1 fajita).

CALORIES 253 (29% from fat); FAT 8.1g (sat 2g, mono 3.3g, poly 2.1g); PROTEIN 27.1g; CARB 17.7g; FIBER 1.5g; CHOL 80mg; IRON 1.8mg; SODIUM 502mg; CALC 96mg

PORK FAJITAS WITH APPLE-AVOCADO SALSA

PREP: 20 MINUTES
MARINATE: 1 1/2 HOURS
COOK: 20 MINUTES

For a summery flavor, you can use Fresh-Peach Salsa (page 438) in this recipe instead of Apple-Avocado Salsa.

4 dried cascabel chiles
1 cup water
2 tablespoons fresh lime juice
1/4 teaspoon salt
3 large garlic cloves, peeled
1 (1-pound) pork tenderloin
Cooking spray
8 (7-inch) flour tortillas
2 cups Apple-Avocado Salsa
   (page 438)

1. Remove stems and seeds from chiles. Combine chiles and water in a small saucepan, and bring to a boil. Remove from heat; cover and let stand 15 minutes. Drain, reserving 2 tablespoons liquid. Combine chiles, reserved liquid, lime juice, salt, and garlic in a blender. Process until smooth.
2. Trim fat from pork. Place pork in a shallow dish. Pour chile mixture over pork; cover and marinate in refrigerator 1 1/2 hours.
3. Preheat oven to 425°.
4. Remove pork from dish, reserving marinade. Place pork on a broiler pan coated with cooking spray. Insert meat thermometer into thickest portion of pork. Brush reserved marinade over pork. Bake at 425° for 20 minutes or until thermometer registers 160° (slightly pink). Let stand 10 minutes before slicing.
5. Warm tortillas according to package directions.
6. Cut pork diagonally across grain into thin slices. Arrange one-eighth of pork slices and 2 tablespoons Apple-Avocado Salsa in center of each tortilla. Fold bottom half and sides of each tortilla over filling. Top each fajita with 2 tablespoons Apple-Avocado Salsa. Yield: 4 servings (serving size: 2 fajitas).

CALORIES 462 (26% from fat); FAT 13.4g (sat 2.9g, mono 6.3g, poly 3.2g); PROTEIN 32.2g; CARB 52.5g; FIBER 4.6g; CHOL 79mg; IRON 4.4mg; SODIUM 653mg; CALC 120mg

PORK TENDERLOIN WITH ROSEMARY AND GARLIC

PREP: 18 MINUTES
COOK: 20 MINUTES

2 (3/4-pound) pork tenderloins
3 garlic cloves, sliced
1 tablespoon water
1 teaspoon olive oil
1/4 teaspoon salt
1/4 teaspoon pepper
4 rosemary sprigs
Rosemary sprigs (optional)

1. Preheat oven to 400°.
2. Trim fat from pork tenderloins; make 1/2-inch-deep slits on outside of pork, and stuff with garlic slices. Combine water, oil, salt, and pepper in a small bowl. Rub surface of pork evenly with oil mixture.
3. Place tenderloins lengthwise on a double thickness of foil, 15 inches long. Top with 4 rosemary sprigs, and wrap securely. Insert meat thermometer through foil into center of 1 tenderloin.
4. Bake pork at 400° for 20 minutes or until thermometer registers 160° (slightly pink). Discard cooked rosemary sprigs. Garnish with additional rosemary sprigs, if desired. Yield: 6 servings (serving size: 3 ounces).

CALORIES 150 (29% from fat); FAT 4.8g (sat 1.5g, mono 2.4g, poly 0.6g); PROTEIN 24.6g; CARB 0.6g; FIBER 0g; CHOL 79mg; IRON 1.4mg; SODIUM 155mg; CALC 11mg

menu

Cumin Pork Tenderloin With Dried-Apricot Chutney

Herbed Basmati Rice (page 245)

Steamed Brussels sprouts

Indian Pudding Cake With Molasses Cream (page 119)

CUMIN PORK TENDERLOIN WITH DRIED-APRICOT CHUTNEY

PREP: 5 MINUTES
MARINATE: 30 MINUTES
COOK: 25 MINUTES

1 (1-pound) pork tenderloin
2 tablespoons dark brown sugar
1 teaspoon ground cumin
1 teaspoon coarsely ground pepper
2 teaspoons cider vinegar
Dash of salt
Cooking spray
1 cup Dried-Apricot Chutney
   (page 452)

1. Preheat oven to 400°.
2. Trim fat from pork. Combine pork and next 5 ingredients in a large zip-top plastic bag. Seal bag, and marinate in refrigerator 30 minutes, turning bag occasionally. Remove pork from bag, and discard marinade.
3. Place pork on a broiler pan coated with cooking spray. Insert meat thermometer into thickest portion of pork. Bake at 400° for 25 minutes or until thermometer registers 160° (slightly pink). Cut pork into thin slices. Serve with Dried-Apricot Chutney. Yield: 4 servings (serving size: 3 ounces pork and 1/4 cup chutney).

CALORIES 306 (14% from fat); FAT 4.9g (sat 1.5g, mono 2g, poly 0.6g); PROTEIN 26.8g; CARB 42g; FIBER 4.9g; CHOL 79mg; IRON 3.9mg; SODIUM 82mg; CALC 48mg

HONEY-MUSTARD PORK TENDERLOIN

PREP: 4 MINUTES   COOK: 40 MINUTES

 2 (¾-pound) pork tenderloins
 ¼ teaspoon salt
 ⅛ teaspoon black pepper
 1 teaspoon olive oil
Cooking spray
 ¼ cup balsamic vinegar
 1 tablespoon honey
 1 teaspoon Dijon mustard
 1 teaspoon minced fresh rosemary
Rosemary sprigs (optional)

1. Preheat oven to 400°.
2. Trim fat from pork; sprinkle pork with salt and pepper. Heat oil in a large nonstick skillet over medium-high heat. Add pork, and cook 10 minutes.
3. Place pork on a broiler pan coated with cooking spray. Combine vinegar, honey, and mustard in a small bowl; brush over pork. Insert meat thermometer into thickest portion of pork.
4. Bake pork at 400° for 30 minutes or until thermometer registers 160°

WITH MUSTARD, PLEASE

When it comes to zipping up food, nothing can do what mustard can. The basic mustards are as popular as ever, but sharing their space on supermarket shelves are new, upscale concoctions. These varieties are blended with everything from crisp white wines to elegant champagnes, from sharp, crushed peppercorns to smooth, sweet flavors. And because these flavored mustards have herbs and spices, fruits, or wine already packed into the jar, they can conveniently become the primary flavoring element in a whole range of foods.

(slightly pink), basting frequently with vinegar mixture. Place remaining vinegar mixture in a saucepan; bring to a boil. Place pork on a serving platter; sprinkle with minced rosemary. Garnish pork with rosemary sprigs, if desired. Serve with warm vinegar mixture. Yield: 6 servings (serving size: 3 ounces).

CALORIES 161 (28% from fat); FAT 5g (sat 1.5g, mono 2.4g, poly 0.6g); PROTEIN 24.5g; CARB 3.2g; FIBER 0g; CHOL 79mg; IRON 1.4mg; SODIUM 180mg; CALC 9mg

ONION-SMOTHERED PORK TENDERLOIN

PREP: 15 MINUTES
COOK: 45 MINUTES

 2 (¾-pound) pork tenderloins
Cooking spray
 2 teaspoons stick margarine or butter
 2 cups sliced onion
 ½ teaspoon dried thyme
 ½ teaspoon salt
 ¼ teaspoon pepper

1. Preheat oven to 400°.
2. Trim fat from pork; cut a lengthwise slit down center of each tenderloin, cutting about two-thirds of the way through meat. Place on a broiler pan coated with cooking spray. Insert meat thermometer into thickest portion of pork.
3. Melt margarine in a large nonstick skillet over medium-high heat. Add onion, and sauté 5 to 6 minutes or until tender. Add thyme, salt, and pepper. Spread onion mixture evenly into cut tenderloins and over tenderloins. Bake at 400° for 45 minutes or until meat thermometer registers 160° (slightly pink). Yield: 6 servings (serving size: 3 ounces).

CALORIES 168 (29% from fat); FAT 5.5g (sat 2.2g, mono 2.2g, poly 0.6g); PROTEIN 25g; CARB 3.4g; FIBER 0.7g; CHOL 83mg; IRON 1.6mg; SODIUM 267mg; CALC 18mg

Onion-Smothered Pork Tenderloin

To prepare an opening for onion mixture, cut a lengthwise slit down center of each tenderloin, cutting about two-thirds of the way through the meat. Place pork on rack of a broiler pan coated with cooking spray. Top with onion mixture.

PORK WITH POTATOES, APPLES, AND SOUR CREAM-CIDER SAUCE

PREP: 4 MINUTES   COOK: 45 MINUTES

 9 small red potatoes, cut in half (about 1¼ pounds)
Cooking spray
 1 (1½-pound) pork tenderloin
 1 tablespoon olive oil, divided
 1 large onion, cut into 12 wedges
 2 apples, cut into 1-inch cubes
 2 cups apple cider
 1 cup fat-free, less-sodium chicken broth
 ¼ teaspoon salt
 ⅛ teaspoon black pepper
 2 teaspoons all-purpose flour
 ½ cup low-fat sour cream

1. Preheat oven to 400°.
2. Place potato on a 15 x 10-inch jelly-roll pan coated with cooking spray; bake at 400° for 15 minutes.

3. Trim fat from pork. Heat 1 teaspoon oil in a large, ovenproof Dutch oven over medium-high heat. Add pork; cook 8 minutes, browning on all sides. Remove pork from pan.

4. Add 2 teaspoons oil to pan. Add onion; sauté over medium heat 5 minutes. Add pork and potato to pan; insert meat thermometer into thickest portion of pork. Bake, uncovered, at 400° for 15 minutes. Add apple, and bake 20 minutes or until thermometer registers 160° (slightly pink). Remove pork, potato, and onion mixture from pan; keep warm.

5. Add cider, broth, salt, and pepper to pan, scraping pan to loosen browned bits. Bring to a boil over high heat, and cook 10 to 12 minutes or until reduced to 1 cup. Remove from heat. Stir flour into sour cream; add sour cream mixture to cider mixture, stirring with a whisk until well-blended. Reduce heat, and simmer, uncovered, 1 minute. Cut pork into ¼-inch-thick slices. Arrange 3 ounces pork on each of 6 plates; top each with 1 cup potato mixture and about ¼ cup sour cream sauce. Yield: 6 servings.

CALORIES 343 (21% from fat); FAT 8g (sat 2.9g, mono 3.6g, poly 0.7g); PROTEIN 27.3g; CARB 40.1g; FIBER 4.3g; CHOL 81mg; IRON 3.3mg; SODIUM 278mg; CALC 61mg

Maple-Mustard Pork Tenderloin With Apples

MAPLE-MUSTARD PORK TENDERLOIN WITH APPLES

PREP:21 MINUTES   COOK:25 MINUTES

  2 (¾-pound) pork tenderloins
Cooking spray
  3 tablespoons Dijon mustard
  6 tablespoons maple syrup, divided
  1 tablespoon chopped fresh or
       1 teaspoon dried rosemary
  ½ teaspoon salt
  ¼ teaspoon black pepper
  4 Granny Smith apples, peeled and
       thinly sliced (about 2 pounds)
Rosemary sprigs (optional)

1. Preheat oven to 425°.
2. Trim fat from pork. Place pork on a broiler pan coated with cooking spray. Combine mustard, 2 tablespoons syrup, chopped rosemary, salt, and pepper in a small bowl; brush over pork. Insert meat thermometer into thickest part of pork. Bake at 425° for 25 minutes or until thermometer registers 160° (slightly pink).
3. Place a nonstick skillet coated with cooking spray over medium-high heat until hot. Add apple; sauté 5 minutes. Reduce heat to medium-low; add 4 tablespoons maple syrup. Simmer 12 minutes or until apple is tender, stirring occasionally. Cut pork crosswise into slices; spoon apple over pork. Garnish with rosemary sprigs, if desired. Yield: 6 servings (serving size: 3 ounces pork and ½ cup apple).

CALORIES 261 (18% from fat); FAT 5.1g (sat 1.5g, mono 1.9g, poly 0.6g); PROTEIN 24.7g; CARB 28.6g; FIBER 2g; CHOL 79mg; IRON 1.7mg; SODIUM 477mg; CALC 28mg

PORK SATÉ WITH PEANUT SAUCE

PREP: 15 MINUTES   MARINATE: 2 HOURS
COOK: 25 MINUTES

½ cup orange juice
1 tablespoon brown sugar
1 teaspoon ground coriander
¼ teaspoon ground red pepper
3 large garlic cloves, crushed
2 (¾-pound) ultra-lean pork
   tenderloins (such as Smithfield)
1 cup fat-free milk
⅓ cup creamy peanut butter
¼ cup chopped onion
2 teaspoons all-purpose flour
2 tablespoons low-sodium soy
   sauce
1 teaspoon hot sauce
   Cooking spray

Pork Saté With
Peanut Sauce

1. Combine first 5 ingredients in a large zip-top plastic bag; add pork to bag. Seal and marinate in refrigerator 2 hours, turning occasionally.
2. Combine milk and next 5 ingredients in a food processor; process until smooth. Pour sauce into a 2-cup glass measure; cover with plastic wrap, and vent. Microwave at HIGH 3 minutes, stirring with a whisk after 2 minutes; keep warm.
3. Prepare grill.
4. Remove pork from bag, reserving marinade. Place pork on grill rack coated with cooking spray. Insert meat thermometer into thickest portion of pork. Cover and grill 25 minutes or until thermometer registers 160° (slightly pink), turning once and basting occasionally with reserved marinade. Cut pork into ¼-inch-thick slices; serve with peanut sauce. Yield: 6 servings (serving size: 3 ounces pork and ¼ cup sauce).

CALORIES 267 (39% from fat); FAT 11.7g (sat 2.7g, mono 5.4g, poly 2.7g); PROTEIN 30.6g; CARB 10.1g; FIBER 1.1g; CHOL 80mg; IRON 1.8mg; SODIUM 317mg; CALC 72mg

HONEY-BOURBON GRILLED PORK TENDERLOIN

PREP: 5 MINUTES
MARINATE: 30 MINUTES
COOK: 30 MINUTES

The secret to the great flavor is using part of the marinade to make the gravy. The gravy is great on mashed potatoes, too!

3 (¾-pound) pork tenderloins
½ cup diced onion
½ cup lemon juice
½ cup bourbon
½ cup honey
¼ cup low-sodium soy sauce
1 tablespoon minced peeled fresh
   ginger
2 tablespoons olive oil
4 garlic cloves, minced
½ teaspoon salt
¼ teaspoon black pepper
   Cooking spray
3 tablespoons all-purpose flour
1¼ cups water

1. Trim fat from pork. Combine onion and next 7 ingredients in a large zip-top plastic bag. Add pork to bag; seal. Marinate in refrigerator 30 minutes. Remove pork from bag, reserving marinade. Sprinkle salt and pepper over pork.
2. Prepare grill.
3. Place pork on grill rack coated with cooking spray. Insert meat thermometer into thickest portion of pork. Cover and grill 30 minutes or until thermometer registers 160° (slightly pink), turning and basting pork occasionally with ½ cup marinade. Cut pork into ¼-inch-thick slices; keep warm.
4. Place flour in a small saucepan. Gradually add remaining marinade and water, stirring with a whisk until blended. Bring to a boil over medium heat, and cook 3 minutes or until thickened, stirring constantly. Spoon gravy over pork. Yield: 9 servings (serving size: 3 ounces pork and 3½ tablespoons gravy).

CALORIES 218 (30% from fat); FAT 7.2g (sat 1.8g, mono 4.1g, poly 0.8g); PROTEIN 25.3g; CARB 12.5g; FIBER 0.3g; CHOL 79mg; IRON 1.7mg; SODIUM 403mg; CALC 15mg

KUNG PAO PORK

PREP: 16 MINUTES

MARINATE: 15 MINUTES

COOK: 7 MINUTES

1 (1-pound) ultra-lean pork
    tenderloin (such as Smithfield)
1 tablespoon cornstarch
1 tablespoon low-sodium soy
    sauce
1 tablespoon sugar
1 teaspoon cornstarch
¼ teaspoon salt
3 tablespoons water
3 tablespoons low-sodium soy
    sauce
2 tablespoons dry sherry
1 tablespoon white vinegar
1½ teaspoons dark sesame oil
1 tablespoon vegetable oil, divided
8 dried whole hot red chiles
2 cups coarsely chopped green bell
    pepper
¾ cup vertically sliced onion
1 teaspoon minced peeled fresh
    ginger
½ cup unsalted dry-roasted
    peanuts
6 cups hot cooked rice

1. Trim fat from pork; cut pork into 1-inch pieces. Combine 1 tablespoon cornstarch and 1 tablespoon soy sauce in a large zip-top plastic bag; add pork, and seal bag. Toss to coat; marinate in refrigerator 15 minutes.
2. Combine sugar and next 7 ingredients in a small bowl; stir with a whisk until well-blended.
3. Heat 1 teaspoon vegetable oil in a large nonstick skillet or wok over high heat. Add chiles; stir-fry 1 minute or until blackened. (For a milder dish, remove chiles after blackening, and stir in again just before serving.)
4. Add 2 teaspoons vegetable oil and pork mixture to skillet, and stir-fry 2 minutes. Add bell pepper, onion, and ginger; stir-fry 3 minutes or until vegetables are crisp-tender. Add sherry mixture; stir-fry 1 minute or until thick and bubbly. Remove from heat; stir in peanuts. Serve over rice. Yield: 6 servings (serving size: ¾ cup pork mixture and 1 cup rice).

CALORIES 444 (24% from fat); FAT 11.8g (sat 2.1g, mono 5g, poly 3.8g); PROTEIN 24.2g; CARB 59.6g; FIBER 2.9g; CHOL 49mg; IRON 3.7mg; SODIUM 460mg; CALC 44mg

APPLE-FILLED PORK ROAST

PREP: 30 MINUTES

COOK: 1 HOUR 20 MINUTES

Cooking spray
⅓ cup chopped onion
1 cup sliced mushrooms
1 teaspoon dried thyme, divided
½ teaspoon dried rosemary,
    crushed and divided
1 cup diced peeled Rome apple
    (about ⅓ pound)
½ teaspoon salt, divided
⅛ teaspoon black pepper
¼ teaspoon grated lemon rind
1 teaspoon fresh lemon juice
8 large pitted prunes, diced
1 (2-pound) boned pork loin roast
¼ cup apple juice

1. Preheat oven to 325°.
2. Place a large nonstick skillet coated with cooking spray over medium heat until hot. Add onion; sauté 2 minutes. Add mushrooms, ½ teaspoon thyme, and ¼ teaspoon rosemary; sauté 3 minutes. Add apple, ¼ teaspoon salt, pepper, lemon rind, lemon juice, and prunes; sauté 2 minutes or until apple is crisp-tender.
3. Trim fat from pork. Slice pork lengthwise, cutting to, but not through other side. Open the halves, laying pork flat. Slice each half lengthwise cutting to, but not through, other side; open flat. Spread apple mixture down center of pork to within ½ inch of sides. Roll up pork, jelly-roll fashion, starting with long side. Secure pork at 1-inch intervals with heavy string. Sprinkle pork with ½ teaspoon thyme, ¼ teaspoon rosemary, and ¼ teaspoon salt.
4. Place pork on a broiler pan coated with cooking spray. Insert meat thermometer into thickest portion of pork. Bake at 325° for 1 hour and 20 minutes or until thermometer registers 160° (slightly pink), basting frequently with apple juice. Let stand 10 minutes before slicing. Yield: 6 servings.

CALORIES 247 (36% from fat); FAT 9.8g (sat 3.3g, mono 4.3g, poly 1.1g); PROTEIN 26.7g; CARB 12.6g; FIBER 1.7g; CHOL 75mg; IRON 1.9mg; SODIUM 278mg; CALC 25mg

---

A IS FOR APPLE

Sinking your teeth into a crisp juicy apple is the most popular way to enjoy this tree-ripened fruit. But **don't overlook the flavorful possibilities of cooking with apples.** Each variety imparts its own characteristics.

Golden Delicious: **Tender and mildly sweet** makes it an **excellent pick for pies and good for baking.**

Granny Smith: **Tart, crisp, and juicy, making it an excellent choice for cooking or munching.**

Idared: **Tart, firm, and juicy.** Best in salads and fruit cups.

Red Delicious: America's favorite apple. Excellent for snacking, but only fair for baking. Cooks up chunky in sauces.

Rome: Crisp, firm, and slightly tart. Excellent for both pies and baking.

Garlic-Studded
Pork Loin Roast

Garlic-Studded
Pork Loin Roast

1. Use a sharp knife to cut the garlic into thin slices.

2. Make several 1-inch-deep slits in the roast, using a thin boning knife.

3. Insert garlic slices into slits in roast.

GARLIC-STUDDED PORK LOIN ROAST

PREP: 8 MINUTES
COOK: 1 HOUR 40 MINUTES

This is an easy way to infuse pork with garlic. Thinly slice the garlic horizontally. Use a thin boning knife to make 1-inch-deep slits in the roast.

1 (2¼-pound) boned pork loin
   roast
1 tablespoon white vinegar
2 large garlic cloves, thinly sliced
½ teaspoon salt
½ teaspoon cracked black pepper
Cooking spray
Sage, oregano, and rosemary sprigs
   (optional)

1. Preheat oven to 350°.
2. Trim fat from roast. Rub surface of roast with vinegar. Make several 1-inch-deep slits in roast, and stuff with garlic slices. Sprinkle ½ teaspoon salt and ½ teaspoon pepper over roast.
3. Place roast on a broiler pan coated with cooking spray. Insert meat thermometer into thickest portion of roast. Bake at 350° for 1 hour and 40 minutes or until thermometer registers 160° (slightly pink). Garnish roast with herb sprigs, if desired. Yield: 8 servings (serving size: 3 ounces).

CALORIES 185 (52% from fat); FAT 10.6g (sat 3.7g, mono 4.8g, poly 1.3g); PROTEIN 20.4g; CARB 0.4g; FIBER 0g; CHOL 69mg; IRON 0.9mg; SODIUM 199mg; CALC 9mg

Roast Loin of Pork With
Prunes and Apricots

Maple-Sweet Potato Casserole (page 501)

Steamed green beans

Chocolate Cream-Raspberry Tart
(page 205)

ROAST LOIN OF PORK WITH PRUNES AND APRICOTS

PREP: 48 MINUTES

MARINATE: 8 HOURS

COOK: 1 HOUR 20 MINUTES

    1   (3-pound) boned pork loin roast
    7   cups water
    ¼   cup sugar
    1   tablespoon whole allspice
    1   tablespoon dried thyme
    ½   teaspoon salt
    2   bay leaves
    1   cup ruby port or other
        sweet red wine
    ½   cup pitted prunes, halved
    ½   cup dried apricots, halved
    1   tablespoon vegetable oil
Cooking spray
    1   (14½-ounce) can ⅓-less
        sodium chicken broth
    1   cup orange juice
    ½   cup evaporated fat-free milk
    2   teaspoons cornstarch
    ¼   teaspoon salt
    ¼   teaspoon black pepper

1. Preheat oven to 325°.
2. Trim fat from pork. Combine water and next 5 ingredients in a large zip-top plastic bag. Add pork to bag; seal. Marinate in refrigerator 8 hours. Remove pork from bag; discard marinade.
3. Combine port, prunes, and apricots in a bowl; let stand 2 hours. Drain prunes and apricots, reserving port.

4. Using a long, thin knife, cut a 1½-inch-wide horizontal slit through center of pork to form a pocket. Stuff ½ cup prunes and ½ cup apricots into pocket, using the handle of a wooden spoon to push prunes and apricots to center of pork. Secure at 1-inch intervals with heavy string.
5. Heat oil in a large nonstick skillet over medium-high heat. Add pork, and cook until browned on all sides. Place pork on a broiler pan coated with cooking spray. Insert meat thermometer into thickest portion of pork. Bake at 325° for 1 hour and 20 minutes or until thermometer registers 160° (slightly pink). Let stand 10 minutes before slicing.
6. Add reserved port, broth, and orange juice to skillet. Bring to a boil. Cook until reduced to 1¾ cups (about 13 minutes). Combine milk and cornstarch, and add to port mixture. Bring to a boil, and cook 1 minute, stirring constantly. Stir in ¼ teaspoon salt and pepper. Serve with pork. Yield: 12 servings (serving size: 3 ounces pork and about 2½ tablespoons sauce).

CALORIES 264 (43% from fat); FAT 12.6g (sat 4.1g, mono 5.5g, poly 1.9g); PROTEIN 23.3g; CARB 13.2g; FIBER 0.8g; CHOL 74mg; IRON 1.6mg; SODIUM 228mg; CALC 49mg

MAPLE-GLAZED PORK LOIN ROAST

PREP: 6 MINUTES   MARINATE: 8 HOURS
COOK: 3 TO 4 HOURS

    4   (3-inch) chunks hickory wood
    1   (3-pound) boned pork loin
        roast, rolled and tied
    1   cup maple syrup
    ⅔   cup bourbon
    1   teaspoon coarsely ground black
        pepper
    ⅛   teaspoon ground red pepper
    4   sage sprigs
Cooking spray

1. Soak hickory wood chunks in water 1 to 24 hours. Drain well.
2. Trim fat from roast. Combine syrup, bourbon, and peppers in a large zip-top plastic bag. Add roast; seal bag, and marinate in refrigerator 8 hours, turning bag occasionally. Remove roast from bag, reserving marinade.
3. Prepare charcoal fire in meat smoker; let burn 15 to 20 minutes. Place hickory chunks on top of coals. Place water pan in smoker; fill with all but ⅔ cup reserved marinade and sage sprigs. (Refrigerate remaining ⅔ cup marinade.) Add hot tap water to fill pan.
4. Coat grill rack with cooking spray; place roast on rack in smoker. Insert meat thermometer into thickest portion of roast. Cover with smoker lid; cook 3 to 4 hours or until thermometer registers 160° (slightly pink). Refill water pan with water, and add additional charcoal to fire as needed.
5. Remove roast from smoker; let stand 10 minutes. Place remaining ⅔ cup marinade in a small saucepan. Bring to a boil; remove from heat. Cut roast into thin slices; serve with hot marinade. Yield: 12 servings (serving size: 3 ounces).

CALORIES 224 (46% from fat); FAT 11.4g (sat 3.9g, mono 5.1g, poly 1.4g); PROTEIN 21.8g; CARB 7.1g; FIBER 0g; CHOL 74mg; IRON 1.1mg; SODIUM 57mg; CALC 15mg

SMOKING IN FLAVOR

Add even more flavor to marinated meats by smoking them with flavored woods. Smoking woods are available in grocery or hardware stores and stores that sell grills and smokers. For Maple-Glazed Pork Loin Roast (at left), we used hickory. Hickory produces red-hot and long-lasting embers, making it ideal for larger cuts of meat.

lamb Today's lamb is in great shape for your table—it's leaner than ever!

Lamb is leaner than ever. While this is good news for your health, it can mean bad news if you don't watch the cooking time. Most meat thermometers recommend an internal temperature of 180° to 185°, but because most of lamb's fat is on the outside, not the inside, the meat will usually be tough and dry if it's that well-done. For the best flavor and tenderness, cook lamb only until it's pink: medium-rare (145°) or medium (160°).

Lamb pairs well with the bold flavors of many ethnic cuisines, but you'll find it tasty and suitable with simple seasonings, too.

MINTED LAMB CHOPS

PREP: 10 MINUTES

MARINATE: 8 HOURS

COOK: 12 MINUTES

4 (4-ounce) lean lamb loin chops
½ cup dry red wine
1 teaspoon dried rosemary, crushed
1 teaspoon dried mint flakes
½ teaspoon bottled minced fresh garlic
¼ teaspoon salt
¼ cup mint jelly

1. Trim fat from lamb. Combine lamb, wine, rosemary, mint, and garlic in a large zip-top plastic bag. Seal bag; marinate in refrigerator 8 hours, turning bag occasionally.
2. Prepare grill.
3. Remove lamb from bag, reserving marinade. Sprinkle lamb with salt. Place lamb on grill rack; cover and grill 6 minutes on each side or until desired degree of doneness, basting occasionally with reserved marinade. Serve with mint jelly. Yield: 2 servings (serving size: 2 chops and 2 tablespoons jelly).

CALORIES 363 (25% from fat); FAT 10.2g (sat 3.5g, mono 4.2g, poly 0.6g); PROTEIN 30.2g; CARB 28.2g; FIBER 0.3g; CHOL 95mg; IRON 2.5mg; SODIUM 405mg; CALC 41mg

MARINATED LAMB CHOPS WITH HERBS

PREP: 7 MINUTES   MARINATE: 8 HOURS

COOK: 8 MINUTES

These chops are so quick to prepare and so full of flavor!

4 (3-ounce) lamb rib chops
¼ cup dry red wine
2 tablespoons chopped fresh or ½ teaspoon dried mint
2 tablespoons low-sodium soy sauce
1½ teaspoons chopped fresh or ¼ teaspoon dried rosemary
½ teaspoon coarsely ground black pepper
1 garlic clove, crushed

1. Trim fat from lamb. Combine wine and next 5 ingredients in a large zip-top plastic bag. Add lamb, and seal bag. Marinate in refrigerator 8 hours, turning bag occasionally.
2. Preheat broiler.
3. Remove lamb from bag, reserving marinade. Place lamb on a broiler pan; broil 4 minutes on each side or until desired degree of doneness, basting occasionally with reserved marinade. Yield: 2 servings (serving size: 2 chops).

CALORIES 237 (47% from fat); FAT 12.4g (sat 4.4g, mono 5g, poly 1.1g); PROTEIN 27.3g; CARB 2.6g; FIBER 0.2g; CHOL 86mg; IRON 2.8mg; SODIUM 567mg; CALC 28mg

HONEY-ORANGE GLAZED LAMB STEAKS WITH SAGE

PREP: 12 MINUTES   COOK: 8 MINUTES

2 (10-ounce) lean center-cut lamb leg steaks
2 tablespoons honey
2 teaspoons minced fresh sage
½ teaspoon grated orange rind
¼ teaspoon salt
¼ teaspoon coarsely ground black pepper

1. Preheat broiler.
2. Trim fat from steaks; cut each steak in half. Place steaks on a broiler pan.
3. Combine honey, sage, orange rind, salt, and pepper. Brush half of honey mixture over steaks; broil 3 inches from heat 4 minutes. Turn steaks over, and brush with remaining honey mixture; broil 4 minutes or until desired degree of doneness. Yield: 4 servings (serving size: 3 ounces lamb).

CALORIES 206 (35% from fat); FAT 7.9g (sat 2.8g, mono 3.4g, poly 0.5g); PROTEIN 24g; CARB 9g; FIBER 0.1g; CHOL 78mg; IRON 2mg; SODIUM 207mg; CALC 10mg

To give lamb chops great flavor and texture, don't overcook them. To make them tender and juicy, serve them slightly pink, keeping the internal temperature at 145° for medium-rare or 160° for medium.

ROSEMARY-CRUSTED RACK OF LAMB WITH BALSAMIC SAUCE

PREP: 20 MINUTES
MARINATE: 8 HOURS
COOK: 22 MINUTES

Ask your butcher for a French-cut rack of lamb (one that has the bones cleaned down to the loin).

1 (1½-pound) French-cut rack of lamb (about 8 ribs)
3 tablespoons balsamic vinegar
1 tablespoon chopped fresh rosemary, divided
2 garlic cloves, minced
¼ teaspoon salt, divided
⅛ teaspoon black pepper
¼ cup fresh breadcrumbs
½ teaspoon olive oil
¼ cup minced shallots
¼ cup dry white wine
½ cup low-salt chicken broth
2 teaspoons honey
½ teaspoon cornstarch
Rosemary sprigs (optional)

1. Trim fat from lamb. Combine vinegar, 2 teaspoons chopped rosemary, and garlic in a large zip-top plastic bag. Add lamb to bag, and seal. Marinate in refrigerator 8 hours, turning occasionally.
2. Preheat oven to 450°.
3. Remove lamb from bag, reserving marinade. Sprinkle lamb with ⅛ teaspoon salt and pepper. Combine breadcrumbs and 1 teaspoon chopped rosemary, and pat onto meaty side of lamb. Place lamb, meat side up, on a broiler pan. Insert meat thermometer into thickest part of lamb, making sure not to touch bone. Bake lamb at 450° for 20 to 22 minutes or until thermometer registers 145° (medium-rare) or until desired degree of doneness. Let stand 10 minutes before slicing.

4. Heat oil in a large nonstick skillet over medium-high heat; add shallots, and sauté 4 minutes. Add wine and reserved marinade. Bring to a boil; reduce heat, and simmer 8 minutes or until liquid almost evaporates.
5. Add broth and ⅛ teaspoon salt; simmer 5 minutes or until reduced to ⅓ cup. Combine honey and cornstarch; add to broth mixture. Bring to a boil; cook 1 minute or until thickened, stirring constantly.
6. Slice rack into 8 chops. Serve balsamic sauce with lamb. Garnish with rosemary sprigs, if desired. Yield: 4 servings (serving size: 2 lamb chops and 1 tablespoon sauce).

CALORIES 195 (34% from fat); FAT 7.3g (sat 2.4g, mono 3g, poly 1.7g); PROTEIN 23g; CARB 9.4g; FIBER 0.3g; CHOL 70mg; IRON 2.6mg; SODIUM 327mg; CALC 29mg

Rosemary-Crusted Rack of Lamb With Balsamic Sauce

Lamb Chops With Garlic-Peppercorn Crust

PREP:10 MINUTES   COOK:25 MINUTES

Although the blend of black, green, pink, and white peppercorns creates a more interesting flavor, black will do fine.

4 (6-ounce, 2-rib) French-cut lean lamb rib chops
2 tablespoons mixed peppercorns, crushed
3 tablespoons bottled minced roasted garlic
2 tablespoons coarse-grained mustard
½ teaspoon salt
Cooking spray

1. Preheat oven to 375°.
2. Trim fat from lamb chops. Combine peppercorns, garlic, mustard, and salt in a small bowl; stir well. Spread peppercorn mixture over chops. Place chops in an 11 x 7-inch baking dish coated with cooking spray. Bake at 375° for 25 minutes or until desired degree of doneness. Yield: 4 servings (serving size: 1 chop).

CALORIES 170 (42% from fat); FAT 8g (sat 2.7g, mono 3.2g, poly 0.8g); PROTEIN 16.7g; CARB 6.8g; FIBER 0.6g; CHOL 51mg; IRON 2mg; SODIUM 567mg; CALC 45mg

Moroccan Lamb Chops

PREP:18 MINUTES
COOK:25 MINUTES

1 teaspoon ground cumin
1 teaspoon Hungarian sweet paprika
1 teaspoon ground coriander
½ teaspoon salt
¼ teaspoon ground cloves
¼ teaspoon ground red pepper
2 (1½-pound) French-cut racks of lamb, 8 ribs each
Cooking spray
4 cups cooked couscous

1. Preheat oven to 425°.
2. Combine first 6 ingredients in a small bowl. Rub lamb with spice mixture, and let stand 5 minutes.
3. Place lamb on a broiler pan coated with cooking spray. Bake at 425° for 25 minutes or until desired degree of doneness. Let lamb stand 10 minutes before slicing. Serve with couscous. Yield: 8 servings (serving size: 2 rib chops and ½ cup couscous).

CALORIES 267 (33% from fat); FAT 9.8g (sat 3.3g, mono 3.8g, poly 0.9g); PROTEIN 23.4g; CARB 20.5g; FIBER 1.1g; CHOL 65mg; IRON 2.4mg; SODIUM 211mg; CALC 16mg

Parmesan-Crusted Rack Of Lamb With Roasted Garlic Potatoes

PREP:14 MINUTES
COOK:40 MINUTES

1 (1½-pound) French-cut rack of lamb (about 8 ribs)
1 teaspoon water
1 large egg white, lightly beaten
¼ cup fresh breadcrumbs
¼ cup (1 ounce) grated fresh Parmesan cheese
2 teaspoons finely chopped fresh rosemary
1 teaspoon minced fresh parsley
⅛ teaspoon ground red pepper
Roasted Garlic Potatoes (page 498)
Rosemary sprigs (optional)

1. Preheat oven to 425°.
2. Trim fat from lamb; place, meat side up, on a broiler pan. Insert meat thermometer into thickest part of lamb, making sure not to touch bone.
3. Combine water and egg white; brush lamb with egg white mixture. Combine breadcrumbs, cheese, chopped rosemary, parsley, and pepper. Pat breadcrumb mixture into egg white mixture on lamb. Bake at 425° for 40 minutes or until

thermometer registers 145° (medium-rare) to 160° (medium). Cover; let stand 10 minutes. Slice lamb into 8 chops. Serve with Roasted Garlic Potatoes, and garnish with rosemary sprigs, if desired. Yield: 4 servings (serving size: 2 lamb chops and ¾ cup potatoes).

CALORIES 343 (25% from fat); FAT 9.4g (sat 3.3g, mono 3.8g, poly 1.9g); PROTEIN 28.9g; CARB 36.3g; FIBER 3g; CHOL 74mg; IRON 3.6mg; SODIUM 492mg; CALC 98mg

Garlic Roasted Lamb With Oregano Pesto

PREP:25 MINUTES   COOK:1½ HOURS

1 (2-pound) rolled boned leg of lamb
¼ cup Oregano Pesto (page 456), divided
3 garlic cloves, sliced
¼ teaspoon salt
⅛ teaspoon black pepper
1 whole garlic head

1. Preheat oven to 325°.
2. Unroll roast; trim fat. Spread 1 tablespoon Oregano Pesto into folds of roast. Reroll roast, and secure at 1-inch intervals with heavy string. Make several ½-inch-deep slits in surface of roast; stuff garlic slices into slits. Cut 3 additional 1-inch-deep slits into surface of roast; stuff 1 teaspoon pesto into each slit. Spread 2 tablespoons pesto over surface of roast; sprinkle with salt and pepper. Place roast on broiler pan. Insert meat thermometer into thickest portion of roast.
3. Remove white papery skin of garlic head (do not peel or separate cloves). Wrap garlic head in foil; place on broiler pan with roast. Bake roast and garlic at 325° for 1 hour. Remove garlic from oven. Bake roast an additional 30 minutes or until thermometer registers 145° (medium-rare) or until desired degree of doneness. Let roast stand 10 minutes before slicing. Separate garlic head into

Roasting Garlic

Roasting garlic in the oven mellows it into a slightly sweet, nutty spread that has the consistency of butter. Spread it on French bread for an appetizer or add it to dips, spreads, mashed potatoes, sauces, and soups.

1. To roast garlic, remove the white papery skin from the garlic head (do not peel or separate cloves).

2. Wrap each head separately in aluminum foil. Bake at 350° for 45 minutes to 1 hour; let cool 10 minutes.

3. Separate cloves, and squeeze to extract pulp.

cloves; serve with roast. Yield: 7 servings (serving size: 3 ounces lamb).

CALORIES 228 (40% from fat); FAT 10.2g (sat 3.1g, mono 5g, poly 0.9g); PROTEIN 27.8g; CARB 5.6g; FIBER 0.8g; CHOL 83mg; IRON 3.4mg; SODIUM 190mg; CALC 75mg

CROWN ROAST OF LAMB WITH WILD RICE-RISOTTO STUFFING

PREP: 37 MINUTES

COOK: 1 HOUR 57 MINUTES

3½ cups water
1¼ cups uncooked wild rice
2 teaspoons salt, divided
4 teaspoons olive oil, divided
2 cups thinly sliced shiitake mushroom caps
2 teaspoons herbes de Provence
1½ teaspoons black pepper, divided
1 (16-rib) crown roast of lamb
Olive oil-flavored cooking spray
5 cups fat-free, less-sodium chicken broth
1½ cups chopped onion
1 cup diced celery
1 cup uncooked Arborio rice or other short-grain rice
1 cup frozen green peas, thawed
2 teaspoons chopped fresh thyme

1. Bring water to a boil in a medium saucepan. Add wild rice and ½ teaspoon salt; cover, reduce heat, and simmer 50 minutes or until tender. Drain; set aside.
2. Preheat oven to 500°.
3. Heat 2 teaspoons oil in a nonstick skillet over high heat. Add mushrooms; sauté 5 minutes or until browned. Remove from heat; stir in ¼ teaspoon salt.
4. Combine 1 teaspoon salt, herbes de Provence, and ¾ teaspoon pepper. Lightly coat roast with cooking spray; rub herb mixture over roast. Place roast, bone side up, on a broiler pan. Insert meat thermometer into thickest portion of lamb, making sure not to touch bone. Cover bones with foil; place a ball of foil in the center of roast. Place roast in a 500° oven; immediately reduce oven temperature to 400°, and bake 45 minutes or until

thermometer registers 145° (medium-rare) or until desired degree of doneness. Place roast on a large serving platter; cover with foil.
5. Bring broth to a simmer in a saucepan (do not boil). Keep warm over low heat.
6. Heat 2 teaspoons oil in a large saucepan over medium heat. Add onion and celery; sauté 1 minute. Add Arborio rice; cook 1 minute, stirring constantly. Add wild rice and ½ cup warm broth; cook 1 minute or until liquid is nearly absorbed, stirring constantly. Add simmering broth, ½ cup at a time, stirring constantly until each portion of broth is absorbed before adding the next (about 20 minutes total). Stir in ¼ teaspoon salt, ¾ teaspoon pepper, mushrooms, peas, and thyme. Cook risotto until thoroughly heated.
7. Uncover roast; remove ball of foil. Spoon 2 cups risotto into center of roast; spoon remaining risotto around roast. Yield: 8 servings (serving size: 2 rib chops and 1 cup risotto).

CALORIES 467 (28% from fat); FAT 14.7g (sat 4.6g, mono 6.5g, poly 1.5g); PROTEIN 32.6g; CARB 48.5g; FIBER 4.1g; CHOL 82mg; IRON 4.5mg; SODIUM 1126mg; CALC 47mg

venison

Now available in the grocery meat department, these lean cuts of venison offer rich flavor with very little fat.

VENISON MEDALLIONS WITH CHERRY-WINE SAUCE

PREP: 12 MINUTES   COOK: 30 MINUTES

½ cup port or other sweet red wine
½ cup dried tart cherries
½ teaspoon dried thyme
1 (14¼-ounce) can fat-free beef broth
16 whole allspice
½ teaspoon salt, divided
⅛ teaspoon pepper
6 (4-ounce) venison tenderloin steaks (about 1½ inches thick)
2 teaspoons margarine
Cooking spray
½ cup minced shallots
2 garlic cloves, minced
2 teaspoons water
1 teaspoon cornstarch

1. Combine first 4 ingredients in a small saucepan. Bring to a boil. Remove from heat. Cover; set aside.
2. Place allspice in a spice or coffee grinder; process until finely ground. Sprinkle ½ teaspoon ground allspice, ¼ teaspoon salt, and pepper over venison. Melt margarine in a skillet coated with cooking spray over medium-high heat. Add venison; cook 5 minutes on each side or until browned. Reduce heat to medium; cook 3 minutes on each side or until desired degree of doneness. Remove venison from pan; keep warm.
3. Add shallots and garlic to skillet; sauté 2 minutes. Add cherry mixture, 1 teaspoon ground allspice, and ¼ teaspoon salt; bring to a boil. Reduce heat; simmer, uncovered, until reduced to 1 cup (about 3 minutes). Combine water and cornstarch; add to cherry mixture. Bring to a boil; cook 1 minute, stirring constantly. Serve sauce with venison.

Yield: 6 servings (serving size: 3 ounces venison and 2 tablespoons sauce).

CALORIES 201 (18% from fat); FAT 4.1g (sat 1.3g, mono 1.6g, poly 1.1g); PROTEIN 25.6g; CARB 13.4g; FIBER 0.9g; CHOL 0mg; IRON 4.5mg; SODIUM 320mg; CALC 22mg

MARINATED TENDERLOIN OF VENISON

PREP: 15 MINUTES   MARINATE: 24 HOURS
COOK: 20 MINUTES

¾ cup dry red wine
2 tablespoons freshly ground pepper
2 tablespoons chopped fresh rosemary
2 tablespoons chopped fresh thyme
3 tablespoons olive oil
2 tablespoons red wine vinegar
2 tablespoons Dijon mustard
½ teaspoon juniper berries, ground (about 1 teaspoon ground)
1 teaspoon coriander seeds, ground (about 1 teaspoon ground)
½ teaspoon salt
½ teaspoon cardamom pods, ground (about ½ teaspoon ground)
4 garlic cloves, minced
1 star anise, ground (about ½ teaspoon ground)
1 bay leaf
2 pounds venison tenderloin
Cooking spray

1. Combine first 15 ingredients in a large zip-top heavy-duty plastic bag. Seal bag; marinate in refrigerator 24 hours, turning bag occasionally.
2. Preheat broiler.
3. Remove venison from bag; discard marinade. Place venison on a broiler pan coated with cooking spray; broil 10 minutes on each side or until done. Cut venison crosswise into thin slices. Yield:

8 servings (serving size: 3 ounces).

CALORIES 154 (25% from fat); FAT 4.2g (sat 1.2g, mono 1.7g, poly 0.6g); PROTEIN 25.8g; CARB 0.7g; FIBER 0.2g; CHOL 95mg; IRON 4mg; SODIUM 78mg; CALC 12mg

MUSTARD-AND-HERB CRUSTED RACK OF VENISON

PREP: 15 MINUTES   COOK: 30 MINUTES

1 (3-pound) rack of venison (with 8 ribs)
Cooking spray
3 tablespoons Dijon mustard
3 tablespoons honey
2 teaspoons minced fresh thyme
1 teaspoon minced fresh rosemary
¼ teaspoon salt
¼ teaspoon pepper
2 garlic cloves, crushed
1 cup fresh breadcrumbs
1 tablespoon chopped fresh parsley

1. Preheat oven to 400°.
2. Place venison, meat side up, on a broiler pan coated with cooking spray. Insert meat thermometer into thickest portion of venison, making sure not to touch bone. Wrap bones with foil.
3. Combine mustard and next 6 ingredients; spread over venison. Bake at 400° for 20 minutes or until meat thermometer registers 120°.
4. Remove venison from oven. Combine 1 cup breadcrumbs and parsley. Pat breadcrumb mixture into mustard mixture. Bake an additional 10 minutes or until thermometer registers 145° (medium-rare) or 160° (medium). Cut between ribs, forming chops. Yield: 8 servings (serving size: 1 chop).

CALORIES 179 (34% from fat); FAT 6.8g (sat 2.5g, mono 1.8g, poly 1.3g); PROTEIN 28g; CARB 7.9g; FIBER 0.2g; CHOL 77mg; IRON 4.9mg; SODIUM 327mg; CALC 8mg

poultry

Garlic-Rosemary Roasted Chicken
(page 373) and Steak Fries (page 499)

chicken

We've used spicy rubs, herbs, citrus fruits, and fresh flavors to create chicken recipes that are sure to become family favorites.

No more plain chicken with these recipes! We've called for a variety of pieces from skinned, boned breasts to five-pound roasters. A roaster is a bit more flavorful due to its slightly higher fat content, but our low-fat cooking methods keep fat to a minimum.

Food safety is important with any raw meat. Rinse poultry thoroughly before cooking, always use a clean knife and cutting board, and wash your hands immediately after handling raw poultry to prevent cross-contamination with other foods.

CHILES RELLENOS CASSEROLE

PREP: 15 MINUTES
COOK: 1 HOUR 5 MINUTES

½ pound ground chicken
1 cup chopped onion
1¾ teaspoons ground cumin
1½ teaspoons dried oregano
½ teaspoon garlic powder
¼ teaspoon salt
¼ teaspoon black pepper
1 (16-ounce) can fat-free refried beans
2 (4-ounce) cans whole green chiles, drained and cut lengthwise into quarters
1 cup (4 ounces) preshredded colby-Jack cheese
1 cup frozen whole-kernel corn, thawed and drained
⅓ cup all-purpose flour
¼ teaspoon salt
1⅓ cups fat-free milk
⅛ teaspoon hot sauce
2 large eggs, lightly beaten
2 large egg whites, lightly beaten

GROUND POULTRY

Ground chicken is often thigh meat, which is higher in fat than breast meat. You'll probably have to ask a butcher to grind chicken breast for you.

Ground turkey is often a mixture of light and dark meat. Check the label because some products may also have skin ground into the mixture.

Freshly ground turkey breast is all white meat and is very lean. Because it has little fat, cook it just until the pink is gone to avoid overcooking.

1. Preheat oven to 350°.
2. Cook chicken and onion in a non-stick skillet over medium-high heat until browned; stir to crumble. Combine chicken mixture, cumin, and next 5 ingredients in a bowl.
3. Arrange half of green chile strips in an 11 x 7-inch baking dish; top with ½ cup cheese. Spoon mounds of chicken mixture onto cheese; spread gently, leaving a ¼-inch border around edge of dish, and top with corn. Arrange remaining chile strips over corn; top with ½ cup cheese.
4. Combine flour and salt in a bowl; gradually add milk and hot sauce, stirring with a whisk until blended. Stir in eggs and egg whites; pour over casserole. Bake at 350° for 1 hour and 5 minutes or until set; let stand 5 minutes. Yield: 6 servings (serving size: 1 [3½-inch] square).

CALORIES 333 (29% from fat); FAT 10.6g (sat 5g, mono 3.3g, poly 1.2g); PROTEIN 25.5g; CARB 34.1g; FIBER 5.1g; CHOL 113mg; IRON 3.7mg; SODIUM 831mg; CALC 274mg

MALAYSIAN CHICKEN PIZZA

PREP: 30 MINUTES   COOK: 15 MINUTES

¼ cup packed brown sugar
¾ cup rice wine vinegar
¼ cup low-sodium soy sauce
3 tablespoons water
2 tablespoons chunky peanut butter
1 tablespoon peeled minced fresh ginger
½ to ¾ teaspoon crushed red pepper
4 garlic cloves, minced
Cooking spray
½ pound skinned, boned chicken breast, cut into bite-size pieces
½ cup (2 ounces) shredded reduced-fat Swiss cheese
¼ cup (1 ounce) preshredded part-skim mozzarella cheese
1 (12-inch) Basic Pizza Crust (page 102)
¼ cup chopped green onions

1. Preheat oven to 450°.
2. Combine first 8 ingredients in a bowl; stir well with a whisk.
3. Coat a large nonstick skillet with cooking spray; place over medium heat until hot. Add chicken; sauté 2 minutes. Remove from pan.
4. Pour vinegar mixture into pan; bring to a boil over medium-high heat. Cook 5 minutes or until slightly thick. Return chicken to pan, and cook 1 minute or until chicken is done. (Mixture will be consistency of thick syrup.)
5. Sprinkle cheeses over prepared crust, leaving a ½-inch border, and top with chicken mixture. Bake at 450° for 12 to 15 minutes. Sprinkle with green onions.

Remove pizza to a cutting board; let stand 5 minutes. Yield: 6 servings (serving size: 1 wedge).

CALORIES 283 (21% from fat); FAT 6.6g (sat 2.2g, mono 2.4g, poly 1.1g); PROTEIN 18.6g; CARB 36.1g; FIBER 1.2g; CHOL 31mg; IRON 2.3mg; SODIUM 466mg; CALC 167mg

ROASTED CHICKEN-AND-WHITE BEAN PIZZAS

PREP: 20 MINUTES   COOK: 8 MINUTES

These pizza crusts are usually found on a display in front of the dairy section.

  1 (16-ounce) can Great
     Northern beans, drained
  1 teaspoon lemon juice
  ⅛ teaspoon garlic powder
  ⅛ teaspoon black pepper
  2 (4.69-ounce) packages ready-to-eat
     roasted skinned, boned chicken
     breast halves, chopped
  ¼ teaspoon dried rosemary,
     crushed
  1 (12-ounce) package of 3
     (7-inch) pizza crusts (such
     as Mama Mary's)
  1 cup thinly sliced fresh spinach
  ¾ cup (3 ounces) shredded sharp
     provolone cheese

1. Preheat oven to 450°.
2. Place first 4 ingredients in a blender or food processor; process until smooth.
3. Combine chicken and rosemary in a bowl. Spread ⅓ cup bean mixture evenly over each crust, leaving ¼-inch borders. Top each crust with ½ cup chicken mixture, ⅓ cup spinach, and ¼ cup cheese.
4. Place pizzas directly on oven rack; bake at 450° for 8 minutes or until crusts are golden. Yield: 6 servings (serving size: ½ pizza).

CALORIES 391 (24% from fat); FAT 10.6g (sat 4.2g, mono 2.5g, poly 3.8g); PROTEIN 26g; CARB 42.9g; FIBER 4.9g; CHOL 57mg; IRON 2mg; SODIUM 773mg; CALC 197mg

SESAME CHICKEN FINGERS

PREP: 13 MINUTES
COOK: 15 MINUTES

This fast-food favorite goes Asian with the addition of sesame seeds and lime juice; to reduce the fat, it's baked instead of fried. For color contrast, use a mixture of black sesame seeds (available at many Asian markets) and the lighter variety.

  ⅓ cup stone-ground mustard
  ⅓ cup honey
  2 tablespoons lime juice
  ¼ teaspoon salt
  ⅛ teaspoon black pepper
  1 pound skinned, boned chicken
     breast, cut into strips
  ½ cup sesame seeds, toasted
  ½ cup dry breadcrumbs
  2 large egg whites, lightly beaten
Cooking spray

1. Preheat oven to 350°.
2. Combine first 3 ingredients in a shallow bowl.
3. Sprinkle salt and pepper over chicken. Combine sesame seeds and breadcrumbs in a shallow dish. Dip one-fourth of chicken in egg whites, and dredge in sesame seed mixture; repeat procedure with remaining chicken, egg whites, and sesame seed mixture.
4. Arrange chicken in a single layer on a baking sheet coated with cooking spray. Bake at 350° for 15 minutes, turning once. Serve chicken with mustard mixture. Yield: 4 servings (serving size: about 3 ounces chicken and 3 tablespoons mustard mixture).
Note: The tangy mustard mixture makes a great dipping sauce for other Asian appetizers such as spring rolls, won tons, or saté.

CALORIES 398 (29% from fat); FAT 12.9g (sat 1.9g, mono 4.2g, poly 4.5g); PROTEIN 34.2g; CARB 38.7g; FIBER 1.4g; CHOL 66mg; IRON 4.8mg; SODIUM 631mg; CALC 253mg

OVEN-FRIED CHICKEN FINGERS WITH HONEY-MUSTARD DIPPING SAUCE

PREP: 20 MINUTES   COOK: 8 MINUTES

Sauce:
  ¼ cup honey
  ¼ cup spicy brown mustard

Chicken:
  1½ pounds chicken breast tenders
     (about 16 pieces)
  ½ cup low-fat or nonfat buttermilk
  ½ cup coarsely crushed
     cornflakes
  ¼ cup seasoned breadcrumbs
  1 tablespoon instant minced onion
  1 teaspoon paprika
  ¼ teaspoon dried thyme
  ¼ teaspoon black pepper
  1 tablespoon vegetable oil

1. To prepare sauce, combine honey and mustard in a small bowl. Cover and chill sauce.
2. Preheat oven to 400°.
3. To prepare chicken, combine chicken and buttermilk in a shallow dish; cover and chill 15 minutes. Drain chicken, discarding liquid.
4. Combine cornflakes and next 5 ingredients in a large zip-top plastic bag; add 4 chicken pieces to bag. Seal and shake to coat. Repeat procedure with remaining chicken. Spread oil evenly in a jelly-roll pan, and arrange chicken in a single layer in pan. Bake at 400° for 4 minutes on each side or until done. Serve with sauce. Yield: 8 servings (serving size: 2 chicken tenders and 1 tablespoon sauce).

CALORIES 185 (18% from fat); FAT 3.7g (sat 0.8g, mono 1.2g, poly 1.2g); PROTEIN 21.6g; CARB 16g; FIBER 0.3g; CHOL 49mg; IRON 1.3mg; SODIUM 306mg; CALC 46mg

INDIAN CHICKEN CURRY

PREP: 15 MINUTES
COOK: 15 MINUTES

4 cups sliced Swiss chard (about 12 ounces)
4 (4-ounce) skinned, boned chicken breast halves, cut crosswise into thin slices
1 tablespoon cornstarch
1 tablespoon olive oil
1 cup diced onion
1⅓ cups fat-free, less-sodium chicken broth
1 cup sliced baby carrot
½ cup light coconut milk
1 tablespoon tomato paste
2 teaspoons ground cumin
1 teaspoon curry powder
1 teaspoon ground cinnamon
¼ teaspoon salt
¼ to ½ teaspoon ground red pepper
2 cups hot cooked long-grain rice
3 tablespoons chopped unsalted, dry-roasted peanuts

1. Steam Swiss chard, covered, 2 minutes or until crisp tender. Drain.
2. Combine chicken and cornstarch in a small bowl. Heat oil in a large nonstick skillet over medium-high heat until hot. Add onion, and stir-fry 2 minutes. Stir in chicken, and cook 4 minutes or until browned.
3. Stir in broth and next 8 ingredients; reduce heat to medium. Cook 5 minutes, stirring occasionally. Add Swiss chard, and cook 2 minutes. Serve with rice. Sprinkle peanuts over each serving. Yield: 4 servings (serving size: 1 cup chicken mixture, ½ cup rice, and about 2 teaspoons peanuts).

CALORIES 392 (24% from fat); FAT 10.4g (sat 2.9g, mono 4.7g, poly 1.8g); PROTEIN 33.6g; CARB 40.1g; FIBER 4.1g; CHOL 66mg; IRON 4.6mg; SODIUM 576mg; CALC 107mg

CHINESE CHICKEN FRIED RICE

PREP: 20 MINUTES
COOK: 20 MINUTES

⅔ cup egg substitute
½ teaspoon dark sesame oil
¼ teaspoon salt
Cooking spray
2 teaspoons vegetable oil, divided
½ pound skinned, boned chicken breast, cut into strips
2 teaspoons minced peeled fresh ginger
1 garlic clove, minced
1 cup vertically sliced onion
2 ounces cooked ham, cut into julienne strips
3 cups cooked long-grain rice
1 cup frozen green peas, thawed
2 tablespoons low-sodium soy sauce
2 tablespoons dry sherry
¼ teaspoon salt
1 cup thinly sliced romaine lettuce
½ cup sliced green onions

1. Combine first 3 ingredients in a bowl. Place a large nonstick skillet coated with cooking spray over medium-high heat until hot. Add egg substitute mixture; cook, stirring constantly, 1½ minutes or until set. Remove egg mixture from pan; set aside.
2. Wipe pan with a paper towel. Heat 1 teaspoon vegetable oil in pan over high heat. Add chicken, and stir-fry 2 minutes or until done. Remove from pan; keep warm.
3. Heat 1 teaspoon vegetable oil in pan over medium-high heat. Add ginger and garlic; stir-fry 10 seconds. Add 1 cup onion and ham; stir-fry 1 minute. Add rice; stir-fry 2 minutes. Add peas; stir-fry 1 minute. Return egg mixture and chicken to pan. Add soy sauce, sherry, and ¼ teaspoon salt; cook 30 seconds. Remove from heat; stir in lettuce and green onions. Yield: 7 servings (serving size: 1 cup).

CALORIES 196 (13% from fat); FAT 2.8g (sat 0.6g, mono 0.8g, poly 1g); PROTEIN 14.8g; CARB 26.7g; FIBER 1.8g; CHOL 23mg; IRON 2.1mg; SODIUM 483mg; CALC 35mg

ALMOST CHICKEN TEMPURA

PREP: 5 MINUTES
COOK: 20 MINUTES

Sweet-and-sour sauce is an excellent dipping sauce for these crispy chicken strips.

3 tablespoons Thai peanut satay sauce (such as Dynasty)
1 pound skinned, boned chicken breast, cut into 24 (1-inch-wide) strips
¾ cup plus 2 tablespoons chow mein noodles
3 tablespoons sesame seeds
2 tablespoons all-purpose flour
⅛ teaspoon black pepper
Cooking spray

1. Preheat oven to 350°.
2. Place peanut sauce in a shallow dish; add chicken, stirring to coat.
3. Place noodles in a food processor, and process until smooth. Combine noodles, sesame seeds, flour, and pepper in a large zip-top plastic bag.
4. Remove chicken from peanut sauce, discarding sauce. Add chicken to bag. Seal bag, and shake to coat chicken. Place chicken strips on a baking sheet coated with cooking spray. Bake at 350° for 15 to 20 minutes or until chicken is done. Yield: 4 servings (serving size: 6 chicken strips).

CALORIES 265 (34% from fat); FAT 9.9g (sat 1.6g, mono 2.8g, poly 4.3g); PROTEIN 29.5g; CARB 13.6g; FIBER 1.2g; CHOL 66mg; IRON 2.7mg; SODIUM 187mg; CALC 85mg

CREAMY CHICKEN-AND-RICE CASSEROLE

PREP: 30 MINUTES   COOK: 35 MINUTES

    1 (6.9-ounce) package ⅓-less-
        salt chicken-flavored rice-
        and-vermicelli mix (such as
        Rice-A-Roni)
    1 tablespoon stick margarine or
        butter
2¼ cups hot water
    Cooking spray
1½ pounds skinned, boned chicken
        breast, cut into bite-size pieces
    1 cup presliced fresh mushrooms
    ½ teaspoon garlic powder
    ¾ cup fat-free sour cream
    ¼ teaspoon black pepper
    1 (10¾-ounce) can condensed
        reduced-fat, reduced-sodium
        cream of mushroom soup,
        undiluted
    ¼ cup crushed reduced-fat
        multigrain crackers (about 8
        crackers)
    1 tablespoon stick margarine or
        butter, melted
    ½ teaspoon poppy seeds

1. Cook rice mix in a large nonstick skillet according to package directions, using 1 tablespoon margarine and 2¼ cups hot water. Place mixture in a large bowl. Wipe pan with a paper towel.
2. Preheat oven to 350°.
3. Coat skillet with cooking spray; place over high heat until hot. Add chicken, mushrooms, and garlic powder; sauté 4 minutes or until chicken is done. Remove from heat. Add chicken mixture, sour cream, pepper, and soup to rice mixture, stirring until well-blended; spoon into a 2-quart casserole coated with cooking spray. Combine cracker crumbs, margarine, and poppy seeds; sprinkle over chicken mixture. Bake at 350° for 35 minutes or until thoroughly heated. Yield: 6 servings (serving size: about 1 cup).

Make-Ahead Tip: You can assemble the casserole ahead of time, omitting the cracker-crumb mixture; cover and chill in refrigerator or freeze (thaw frozen casserole overnight in refrigerator). Let stand at room temperature 30 minutes; top with cracker-crumb mixture, and bake as directed.

CALORIES 349 (20% from fat); FAT 7.7g (sat 1.6g, mono 2.9g, poly 2.3g); PROTEIN 32.8g; CARB 35.9g; FIBER 1.3g; CHOL 70mg; IRON 1.8mg; SODIUM 779mg; CALC 112mg

CHICKEN WITH ROASTED PEARS AND WILD RICE

PREP: 20 MINUTES   COOK: 30 MINUTES

    2 small firm Bosc pears (about ¾
        pound), cored and cut length-
        wise into ½-inch-thick slices
    Cooking spray
    1 cup apple juice
    ⅔ cup water
1¼ cups uncooked quick-cooking
        wild rice
    1 pound skinned, boned chicken
        breast, cut into 1-inch pieces
    ½ cup dried cranberries or dried
        tart cherries
    2 teaspoons sugar
    ½ teaspoon salt
    ½ teaspoon ground cinnamon

1. Preheat oven to 450°.
2. Arrange pear slices in a single layer on a baking sheet coated with cooking spray. Bake at 450° for 10 minutes or until tender.
3. Reduce oven temperature to 400°.
4. Combine apple juice and water in a medium saucepan; bring to a boil. Add rice; cover, reduce heat, and simmer 5 minutes or until rice is tender. Drain excess water from rice; fluff rice with a fork.
5. Combine rice, chicken, cranberries, sugar, salt, and cinnamon in a medium bowl; spoon mixture into an 11 x 7-inch baking dish. Arrange roasted pear slices over chicken mixture. Cover and bake at 400° for 30 minutes or until chicken is done. Yield: 4 servings (serving size: 1 cup chicken mixture and 3 pear slices).

CALORIES 424 (5% from fat); FAT 2.5g (sat 0.5g, mono 0.5g, poly 0.7g); PROTEIN 33.9g; CARB 67.1g; FIBER 5.3g; CHOL 66mg; IRON 2.3mg; SODIUM 372mg; CALC 39mg

MANGO-MUSTARD GLAZED CHICKEN

PREP: 8 MINUTES   COOK: 25 MINUTES

    1 cup chopped peeled mango
    1 cup pineapple juice
    ½ cup apricot or peach preserves
    ½ cup dry white wine
1½ tablespoons stone-ground
        mustard
    1 tablespoon cornstarch
    1 tablespoon water
    6 (4-ounce) skinned, boned
        chicken breast halves
    ¼ teaspoon salt
    ¼ teaspoon black pepper
    Cooking spray

1. Combine first 7 ingredients in a bowl; stir well with a whisk.
2. Sprinkle chicken with salt and pepper. Heat a large nonstick skillet coated with cooking spray over medium-high heat until hot. Add chicken; cook 3 minutes on each side or until browned. Remove chicken from pan. Add mango mixture; bring to a boil. Return chicken to pan; reduce heat, and simmer 15 minutes or until chicken is done and sauce is thick, stirring occasionally. Yield: 6 servings (serving size: 1 chicken breast half and 3 tablespoons sauce).

CALORIES 241 (7% from fat); FAT 1.9g (sat 0.4g, mono 0.4g, poly 0.4g); PROTEIN 26.9g; CARB 29.3g; FIBER 0.9g; CHOL 66mg; IRON 1.3mg; SODIUM 236mg; CALC 34mg

Chicken Parmesan

on a baking sheet; broil 3 minutes or until cheese melts. Garnish with basil, if desired. Yield: 4 servings.

CALORIES 614 (19% from fat); FAT 12.8g (sat 5g, mono 4.8g, poly 1.5g); PROTEIN 49.1g; CARB 74.8g; FIBER 5.4g; CHOL 86mg; IRON 6.1mg; SODIUM 937mg; CALC 375mg

CHICKEN AND RICE WITH CREAMY GARLIC SAUCE

PREP: 10 MINUTES   COOK: 26 MINUTES

- ¾ cup water
- ¼ cup dry white wine
- 1 teaspoon chicken-flavored bouillon granules
- 4 (4-ounce) skinned, boned chicken breast halves
- 1 tablespoon water
- ½ teaspoon cornstarch
- ⅓ cup tub-style light cream cheese with garlic and spices or light cream cheese with roasted garlic
- 4 cups hot cooked long-grain rice
Chopped fresh parsley

1. Bring first 3 ingredients to a boil in a large skillet; add chicken. Cover, reduce heat, and simmer 15 minutes, turning chicken after 8 minutes. Remove chicken from pan; keep warm.
2. Bring cooking liquid to a boil; cook 4 minutes or until reduced to ⅔ cup. Combine 1 tablespoon water and cornstarch; add to pan. Bring to a boil; cook 1 minute, stirring constantly. Add cream cheese; cook until well-blended, stirring constantly with a whisk. Serve chicken over rice, and spoon garlic sauce over chicken. Sprinkle with parsley. Yield: 4 servings (serving size: 1 chicken breast half, 1 cup rice, and 3½ tablespoons sauce).

CALORIES 396 (12% from fat); FAT 5.3g (sat 2g, mono 1.3g, poly 0.4g); PROTEIN 32g; CARB 52.2g; FIBER 1g; CHOL 81mg; IRON 2.7mg; SODIUM 400mg; CALC 111mg

CHICKEN PARMESAN

PREP: 12 MINUTES
COOK: 13 MINUTES

- 4 (4-ounce) skinned, boned chicken breast halves
- ½ cup seasoned breadcrumbs
- ¼ cup grated Parmesan cheese
- ½ teaspoon dried Italian seasoning
- ⅛ teaspoon black pepper
- ⅓ cup all-purpose flour
- 2 large egg whites, lightly beaten
- 2 teaspoons olive oil
- 4 cups hot cooked spaghetti (about 8 ounces uncooked pasta)
- 3 cups Ultimate Quick-and-Easy Pasta Sauce (page 447)
- 1 cup (4 ounces) preshredded part-skim mozzarella cheese
Chopped fresh basil (optional)

1. Place each chicken breast half between 2 sheets of heavy-duty plastic wrap; flatten to ¼-inch thickness using a meat mallet or rolling pin.
2. Combine breadcrumbs, Parmesan cheese, Italian seasoning, and pepper in a shallow dish. Dredge 1 chicken breast half in flour. Dip in egg whites; dredge in breadcrumb mixture. Repeat procedure with remaining chicken, flour, egg whites, and breadcrumb mixture.
3. Heat oil in a large nonstick skillet over medium-high heat. Add chicken, and cook 5 minutes on each side or until done.
4. Preheat broiler.
5. Place 1 cup spaghetti in each of 4 gratin dishes. Spoon ½ cup Ultimate Quick-and-Easy Pasta Sauce over each serving. Top each with 1 chicken breast half. Spoon ¼ cup sauce over each serving. Sprinkle each serving with ¼ cup mozzarella cheese. Place gratin dishes

SPICY APPLE-GLAZED CHICK 'N' GRITS GORGONZOLA

PREP:10 MINUTES
COOK:20 MINUTES

Flattening a chicken breast allows for more even cooking and helps tenderize the meat.

  4 (4-ounce) skinned, boned
     chicken breast halves
Cooking spray
¼ cup apple butter
¼ cup spicy brown mustard
¼ teaspoon salt
¼ teaspoon ground red pepper
⅛ teaspoon black pepper
Gorgonzola Cheese Grits (page 252)
  2 tablespoons chopped green
     onions
Oregano sprigs (optional)

1. Preheat oven to 350°.
2. Place each chicken breast half between 2 sheets of heavy-duty plastic wrap; flatten to ½-inch thickness using a meat mallet or rolling pin. Place chicken in a baking pan coated with cooking spray.
3. Combine apple butter, mustard, salt, and peppers; brush over chicken. Bake at 350° for 20 minutes.
4. Prepare Gorgonzola Cheese Grits.
5. Cut chicken into ½-inch-thick slices. Spoon Gorgonzola Cheese Grits into 4 shallow serving bowls. Top with chicken; sprinkle with green onions. Garnish with oregano, if desired. Yield: 4 servings (serving size: 1 cup grits, 3 ounces chicken, and 1½ teaspoons green onions).

CALORIES 471 (32% from fat); FAT 16.3g (sat 9.1g, mono 5g, poly 1.5g); PROTEIN 40.5g; CARB 36.2g; FIBER 1.6g; CHOL 103mg; IRON 2.1mg; SODIUM 947mg; CALC 261mg

CUMIN CHICKEN WITH SPICY TOMATO RELISH

PREP:12 MINUTES COOK:14 MINUTES

¾ cup chopped tomato
½ cup chopped peeled cucumber
½ cup chopped green bell pepper
  3 tablespoons chopped red onion
  1 small jalapeño pepper, seeded
     and chopped
  1 garlic clove, minced
¼ teaspoon salt
  2 teaspoons olive oil
  1 tablespoon lime juice
  1 teaspoon chopped cilantro
  1 tablespoon ground cumin
  1 teaspoon black pepper
¼ teaspoon salt
  4 (4-ounce) skinned, boned
     chicken breast halves

1. Combine first 10 ingredients in a small bowl; set aside.
2. Combine cumin, black pepper, and ¼ teaspoon salt; rub chicken breast halves with cumin mixture.
3. Place a large cast-iron skillet over medium-high heat until hot (about 2 minutes). Add chicken, and cook 7 minutes on each side or until done. Cut each chicken breast half diagonally across grain into thin slices, and arrange on individual serving plates. Serve with tomato relish. Yield: 4 servings (serving size: 1 chicken breast half and about ½ cup relish).

CALORIES 191 (28% from fat); FAT 5.9g (sat 1.2g, mono 3g, poly 1g); PROTEIN 27.6g; CARB 6.3g; FIBER 1.5g; CHOL 72mg; IRON 2.5mg; SODIUM 364mg; CALC 41mg

Spicy Apple-Glazed
Chick 'n' Grits Gorgonzola

Chicken With Mole Sauce

PREP: 25 MINUTES   COOK: 15 MINUTES

Mole (MOH-lay) comes from molli, *the Nahuatl word for concoction. It refers to a dark, rich sauce of nuts, seeds, chili peppers, spices, and chocolate that is ground together by hand. The use of a food processor makes this mole very easy to prepare. Try serving this dish with Spanish rice.*

  6 (4-ounce) skinned, boned
    chicken breast halves
½ teaspoon salt, divided
Cooking spray
¼ cup chopped onion
  1 tablespoon minced jalapeño
    pepper
  2 garlic cloves, minced
  1 teaspoon ground cinnamon
¾ teaspoon chili powder
¼ teaspoon ground cumin
⅛ teaspoon ground allspice
⅛ teaspoon ground cloves
  3 tablespoons blanched
    almonds, toasted
  1 (6-inch) day-old corn tortilla,
    broken into pieces
  1 (14.5-ounce) can whole
    tomatoes, undrained
Dash of barbecue smoked
    seasoning (such as Hickory
    Liquid Smoke)
¾ ounce sweet baking chocolate
¼ cup water
  1 tablespoon sesame seeds,
    toasted
Cilantro sprigs (optional)

1. Sprinkle chicken with ¼ teaspoon salt. Coat a large nonstick skillet with cooking spray; place over medium-high heat until hot. Add chicken; cook 6 minutes on each side or until done. Place chicken on a serving platter, and keep warm.

2. Add onion, jalapeño pepper, and garlic to pan; cook 3 minutes or until tender. Add cinnamon, chili powder, cumin, allspice, and cloves. Cook 1 minute.

3. Place almonds and tortilla pieces in a food processor; process until finely ground. Add onion mixture, ¼ teaspoon salt, tomatoes, and smoked seasoning; process until smooth. Pour tomato mixture into pan. Add chocolate; cook over low heat until chocolate melts. Add water; cook until thoroughly heated, stirring frequently.

4. Spoon sauce over chicken; sprinkle with sesame seeds. Garnish with cilantro sprigs, if desired. Yield: 6 servings (serving size: 1 chicken breast half and ¼ cup sauce).

CALORIES 209 (24% from fat); FAT 5.6g (sat 1.4g, mono 2.3g, poly 1.3g); PROTEIN 28.7g; CARB 11.3g; FIBER 1.8g; CHOL 66mg; IRON 2.1mg; SODIUM 398mg; CALC 79mg

Balsamic Chicken With Almond Peppers

PREP: 30 MINUTES   COOK: 14 MINUTES

  2 teaspoons olive oil
  2 red bell peppers, cut into strips
  2 green bell peppers, cut
    into strips
⅓ cup raisins
¼ cup balsamic vinegar
1½ teaspoons sugar
¼ teaspoon salt
⅛ teaspoon black pepper
¼ cup slivered almonds, toasted
  6 (4-ounce) skinned, boned
    chicken breast halves
¼ cup dry breadcrumbs
¼ cup grated Parmesan cheese
¼ cup all-purpose flour
  2 large egg whites, lightly beaten
  2 teaspoons olive oil, divided
  2 tablespoons balsamic vinegar
  2 tablespoons water

1. Heat 2 teaspoons oil in a large nonstick skillet over medium-high heat. Add bell peppers; sauté 8 minutes. Add raisins; sauté 1 minute. Add ¼ cup vinegar, sugar, salt, and black pepper; cook 1 minute. Remove from heat, and stir in almonds; keep warm.

2. Place each chicken breast half between 2 sheets of heavy-duty plastic wrap; flatten to ¼-inch thickness using a meat mallet or rolling pin. Combine breadcrumbs and cheese in a shallow dish. Place flour in a shallow dish; dredge each chicken breast half in flour, and dip in egg whites. Dredge chicken in breadcrumb mixture.

3. Heat 1 teaspoon oil in a large nonstick skillet over medium-high heat. Add half of chicken; cook 3 minutes on each side or until done. Remove from heat. Repeat procedure with 1 teaspoon oil and remaining chicken. Place chicken and bell pepper mixture on a serving platter; keep warm.

4. Add 2 tablespoons vinegar and water to pan; stir with a wooden spoon to loosen browned bits. Spoon vinegar mixture over chicken and bell peppers. Yield: 6 servings (serving size: 1 chicken breast half and ½ cup bell pepper mixture).

CALORIES 291 (27% from fat); FAT 8.7g (sat 1.8g, mono 4.6g, poly 1.6g); PROTEIN 31.9g; CARB 21.6g; FIBER 2.9g; CHOL 68mg; IRON 3.2mg; SODIUM 293mg; CALC 93mg

BALSAMIC VINEGAR

Balsamic vinegar is made from white Trebbiano grapes. This aromatic, flavorful vinegar ages to a dark brown. It has a full-bodied, slightly sweet flavor with a hint of tartness. Use it in small amounts to flavor vinaigrettes, sauces, and berries. You'll find it in large supermarkets and gourmet-food markets.

menu

Raspberry-Balsamic Chicken

Brown rice

Southern Succotash (page 492)

Pear Galette (page 198)

RASPBERRY-BALSAMIC CHICKEN

PREP:15 MINUTES
COOK:17 MINUTES

Other fruit preserves, such as apricot, blackberry, or peach, will also work in this recipe.

    1   teaspoon vegetable oil
  ½   cup chopped red onion
 1½   teaspoons minced fresh or
         ½ teaspoon dried thyme
  ½   teaspoon salt, divided
    4   (4-ounce) skinned, boned
         chicken breast halves
  ⅓   cup seedless raspberry
         preserves
    2   tablespoons balsamic vinegar
  ¼   teaspoon black pepper

1. Heat oil in a large nonstick skillet over medium-high heat until hot. Add onion; sauté 5 minutes. Sprinkle thyme and ¼ teaspoon salt over chicken. Add chicken to pan; sauté 6 minutes on each side or until done. Remove chicken from pan; keep warm.

2. Reduce heat to medium. Add ¼ teaspoon salt, preserves, vinegar, and pepper to pan, stirring constantly until preserves melt. Spoon sauce over chicken, and serve immediately. Yield: 4 servings (serving size: 1 chicken breast half and 2 tablespoons sauce).

CALORIES 213 (11% from fat); FAT 2.6g (sat 0.6g, mono 0.7g, poly 0.9g); PROTEIN 26.5g; CARB 20.1g; FIBER 0.6g; CHOL 66mg; IRON 1.2mg; SODIUM 370mg; CALC 22mg

Raspberry-Balsamic Chicken

CHICKEN MARSALA

PREP:13 MINUTES
COOK:10 MINUTES

  ⅔   cup dry Marsala
  ⅓   cup fat-free beef broth
 1½   teaspoons cornstarch
  ½   teaspoon dried tarragon
  ¼   teaspoon salt
    4   (4-ounce) skinned, boned
         chicken breast halves
  ¼   cup seasoned breadcrumbs
    2   tablespoons grated Parmesan cheese
  ⅛   teaspoon garlic powder
    2   teaspoons olive oil
    2   cups hot cooked angel hair pasta
         (about 4 ounces uncooked pasta)

1. Combine first 5 ingredients in a 1-cup glass measure; stir with a whisk until well-blended. Set aside.

2. Place each chicken breast half between 2 sheets of heavy-duty plastic wrap, and flatten to ¼-inch thickness using a meat mallet or rolling pin. Combine seasoned breadcrumbs, Parmesan cheese, and garlic powder in a shallow dish. Dredge chicken breast halves in breadcrumb mixture.

3. Heat oil in a large nonstick skillet over medium-high heat. Add chicken, and cook 3 minutes on each side or until browned. Reduce heat to low, and add Marsala mixture to pan. Cook 3 to 4 minutes or until chicken is done. Arrange chicken over pasta; spoon sauce over chicken. Yield: 4 servings (serving size: 1 chicken breast half with sauce and ½ cup pasta).

CALORIES 305 (15% from fat); FAT 5.1g (sat 1.3g, mono 2.3g, poly 0.7g); PROTEIN 32.9g; CARB 29.4g; FIBER 0.8g; CHOL 68mg; IRON 2.4mg; SODIUM 577mg; CALC 66mg

LIME GRILLED CHICKEN WITH BLACK BEAN SAUCE

PREP:20 MINUTES   MARINATE:8 HOURS
COOK:20 MINUTES

3 tablespoons fresh lime juice
2 tablespoons vegetable oil
¼ teaspoon ground red pepper
4 garlic cloves, crushed
4 (4-ounce) skinned, boned
   chicken breast halves
Cooking spray
2 cups water
½ cup diced red bell pepper
1 tablespoon chopped red onion
1 cup drained canned black beans
½ cup orange juice
2 tablespoons balsamic vinegar
¼ teaspoon salt
⅛ teaspoon freshly ground black
   pepper
2 garlic cloves, crushed
Cilantro sprigs (optional)

1. Combine first 4 ingredients in a large zip-top plastic bag; add chicken. Seal bag; marinate in refrigerator 8 hours, turning bag occasionally.
2. Prepare grill.
3. Remove chicken from bag, reserving marinade. Place chicken on grill rack coated with cooking spray; grill 10 minutes on each side or until done, basting occasionally with reserved marinade. Keep warm.
4. Bring water to a boil in a small saucepan; add bell pepper and onion. Cook 30 seconds; drain. Plunge into ice water; drain well.
5. Place beans and next 5 ingredients in a food processor; process until smooth. Pour bean mixture into a saucepan; cook over medium heat until thoroughly heated.
6. Spoon 5 tablespoons bean sauce onto each of 4 serving plates. Place 1 chicken breast half on top of sauce; top each with 2 tablespoons bell pepper mixture.

Garnish with cilantro sprigs, if desired. Yield: 4 servings.

CALORIES 278 (29% from fat); FAT 9.1g (sat 1.9g, mono 2.7g, poly 3.5g); PROTEIN 31.1g; CARB 17.6g; FIBER 2.4g; CHOL 72mg; IRON 2.2mg; SODIUM 335mg; CALC 39mg

CHICKEN WITH SHERRIED MUSHROOMS

PREP:12 MINUTES   COOK:43 MINUTES

1 (14½-ounce) can fat-free,
   less-sodium chicken broth
2 tablespoons all-purpose flour
½ teaspoon salt
¼ teaspoon black pepper
4 (4-ounce) skinned, boned
   chicken breast halves
Cooking spray
1 tablespoon butter or stick
   margarine, melted
2 cups presliced mushrooms
2 tablespoons minced shallots
¼ cup dry sherry or Madeira
1 tablespoon chopped fresh parsley

1. Place broth in a small saucepan; bring to a boil over high heat. Cook until reduced to 1 cup (about 7 minutes); set aside.
2. Combine flour, salt, and pepper. Dredge chicken in flour mixture. Place a large skillet coated with cooking spray over medium-high heat until hot. Add chicken; cook 5 minutes on each side or until browned. Remove chicken from pan; set aside. Wipe drippings from pan with a paper towel.
3. Add butter, mushrooms, and shallots to pan; cook over medium-high heat until mushrooms are lightly browned, stirring constantly. Add sherry; bring to a boil. Add 1 cup reduced broth; cook until reduced to 1¼ cups (about 7 minutes).
4. Return chicken to pan; cover, reduce heat, and simmer 12 minutes or until chicken is done. Remove chicken to a

serving platter; keep warm. Bring sauce to a boil; cook 1 minute. Stir in parsley. Serve mushrooms with chicken. Yield: 4 servings (serving size: 1 chicken breast half and 2½ tablespoons mushrooms).

CALORIES 193 (22% from fat); FAT 4.7g (sat 2.2g, mono 1.2g, poly 0.5g); PROTEIN 27.9g; CARB 7.3g; FIBER 0.7g; CHOL 74mg; IRON 1.7mg; SODIUM 678mg; CALC 21mg

CHICKEN PAPRIKASH

PREP:9 MINUTES   COOK:15 MINUTES

Hungarian paprika makes this very hot.
For a milder flavor, use regular paprika.

1 cup green bell pepper strips
½ cup chopped onion
1 garlic clove, minced
½ cup fat-free, less-sodium
   chicken broth
1 tablespoon Hungarian sweet
   paprika
3 tablespoons tomato paste
½ teaspoon salt
¼ teaspoon black pepper
4 (4-ounce) skinned, boned
   chicken breast halves
½ cup low-fat sour cream
3 cups hot cooked egg noodles
   (about 3 cups uncooked)
Coarsely ground black pepper
   (optional)

1. Combine first 3 ingredients in an 8-inch square microwave-safe baking dish. Microwave at HIGH 4 minutes or until tender; stir in broth, paprika, tomato paste, salt, and ¼ teaspoon pepper. Add chicken breast halves, nestling them into vegetable mixture. Cover with heavy-duty plastic wrap; vent. Microwave at HIGH 10 minutes, turning chicken pieces over after 5 minutes.
2. Remove chicken from dish; keep warm. Stir sour cream into vegetable mixture. Microwave at HIGH 30

seconds. Serve chicken and vegetable mixture over noodles. Sprinkle with coarsely ground pepper, if desired. Yield: 4 servings (serving size: 1 chicken breast half, ½ cup vegetable mixture, and ¾ cup noodles).

CALORIES 356 (18% from fat); FAT 7.2g (sat 3.1g, mono 2g, poly 1.2g); PROTEIN 34g; CARB 37.6g; FIBER 4.3g; CHOL 117mg; IRON 3.9mg; SODIUM 480mg; CALC 72mg

menu
Chicken Parmigiana

Spinach-Rice Timbales (page 246)

Creamy Caesar Salad With
Spicy Croutons (page 391)

CHICKEN PARMIGIANA

PREP:15 MINUTES   COOK:35 MINUTES

⅓   cup all-purpose flour
¼   teaspoon garlic powder
¼   teaspoon paprika
¼   teaspoon black pepper
6   (4-ounce) skinned, boned
      chicken breast halves
2   egg whites, lightly beaten
3   cups cornflakes, coarsely crushed
Cooking spray
1   (26-ounce) bottle low-fat
      spaghetti sauce
¾   cup (3 ounces) preshredded
      part-skim mozzarella cheese
2   tablespoons grated Parmesan cheese

1. Preheat oven to 350°.
2. Combine first 4 ingredients in a shallow dish. Dredge 1 chicken breast half in flour mixture. Dip in egg white; dredge in cornflakes. Repeat procedure with remaining chicken, egg white, and cornflakes.
3. Arrange chicken in a 13 x 9-inch baking dish coated with cooking spray. Bake at 350° for 30 minutes or until done.

4. Place spaghetti sauce in a medium saucepan. Cook over medium heat until thoroughly heated. Pour sauce over chicken. Sprinkle with cheeses. Bake an additional 5 minutes or until cheese melts. Yield: 6 servings (serving size: 1 chicken breast half and ½ cup sauce).

CALORIES 312 (16% from fat); FAT 5.9g (sat 2.1g, mono 1.2g, poly 0.7g); PROTEIN 35.3g; CARB 26.8g; FIBER 2.4g; CHOL 75mg; IRON 2.4mg; SODIUM 755mg; CALC 210mg

CHICKEN WITH POLENTA AND BLACK-EYED PEA SALSA

PREP:25 MINUTES   CHILL:2 HOURS
COOK:26 MINUTES

Basic Polenta (page 253)
Cooking spray
1   cup frozen black-eyed peas
1¼ cups diced plum tomato
1   cup frozen whole-kernel corn,
       thawed
¾   cup diced seeded peeled cucumber
¼   cup sliced green onions
2   teaspoons minced jalapeño
       pepper
1   teaspoon dried basil
½   teaspoon sugar
¼   teaspoon salt
⅛   teaspoon black pepper
3   tablespoons white wine vinegar
1   teaspoon extra-virgin olive oil
1   garlic clove, minced
4   (4-ounce) skinned, boned
       chicken breast halves
1   teaspoon ground cumin
⅛   teaspoon black pepper
1   tablespoon stick margarine or
       butter

1. Prepare Basic Polenta. Spread in a 9-inch square baking pan coated with cooking spray. Press heavy-duty plastic wrap on surface of polenta. Chill 2 hours or until firm. Cut into 8 triangles.

2. Place peas in a saucepan; add water to cover. Bring to a boil; cover, reduce heat, and simmer 30 minutes or until peas are tender. Drain and rinse with cold water. Drain well. Combine peas, tomato, and next 11 ingredients in a bowl. Let stand at room temperature, stirring frequently.
3. Sprinkle chicken with cumin and ⅛ teaspoon black pepper. Coat a large nonstick skillet with cooking spray; place over medium-high heat until hot. Add chicken; cook 7 minutes on each side or until done. Remove chicken from skillet; keep warm.
4. Melt margarine in pan; add 4 polenta triangles. Cook 3 minutes on each side or until lightly browned. Remove from pan; keep warm. Repeat procedure with remaining polenta triangles.
5. Cut each chicken breast half across grain into thin slices. Serve with polenta triangles and black-eyed pea salsa. Yield: 4 servings (serving size: 1 chicken breast half, 2 polenta triangles, and ¾ cup black-eyed pea salsa).

CALORIES 417 (16% from fat); FAT 7.2g (sat 1.3g, mono 2.8g, poly 1.9g); PROTEIN 34.6g; CARB 52.9g; FIBER 4.5g; CHOL 66mg; IRON 4.3mg; SODIUM 559mg; CALC 47mg

Seeding a Cucumber

To seed a cucumber, cut in half lengthwise. Scrape out seeds using a spoon.

ROSEMARY CHICKEN WITH TWO-CORN POLENTA

PREP: 17 MINUTES   COOK: 12 MINUTES

See page 253 for tips on cooking polenta.

½ cup yellow cornmeal
½ teaspoon salt
2 cups water
½ cup fresh corn kernels (about 1 ear) or frozen whole-kernel corn, thawed
4 (4-ounce) skinned, boned chicken breast halves
¼ teaspoon salt
⅛ teaspoon black pepper
1 tablespoon chopped fresh rosemary
2 teaspoons extra-virgin olive oil, divided
   Rosemary sprigs (optional)

1. Place cornmeal and ½ teaspoon salt in a large saucepan. Gradually add water, stirring constantly with a whisk. Bring to a boil. Reduce heat to medium; cook 10 minutes, stirring frequently. Stir in corn kernels. Set aside; keep warm.
2. Place each chicken breast half between 2 sheets of heavy-duty plastic wrap; flatten to ¼-inch thickness using a meat mallet or rolling pin. Sprinkle with ¼ teaspoon salt, pepper, and chopped rosemary.
3. Heat 1 teaspoon oil in a large nonstick skillet over medium-high heat. Add half of chicken; sauté 3 minutes on each side or until done. Repeat procedure with 1 teaspoon oil and remaining chicken.
4. Arrange a chicken breast half and ½ cup polenta on each of 4 plates. Garnish with rosemary sprigs, if desired. Yield: 4 servings.

CALORIES 230 (23% from fat); FAT 5.9g (sat 1.3g, mono 2.9g, poly 1.1g); PROTEIN 28.1g; CARB 15.1g; FIBER 2.2g; CHOL 72mg; IRON 1.6mg; SODIUM 509mg; CALC 18mg

UPTOWN CHICKEN AND RED-EYE GRAVY

PREP: 7 MINUTES   COOK: 24 MINUTES

This is great served with grits. For extra flavor, try Gorgonzola Cheese Grits (page 252).

1½ tablespoons all-purpose flour
½ teaspoon paprika
¼ teaspoon salt
⅛ teaspoon black pepper
4 (4-ounce) skinned, boned chicken breast halves
2 teaspoons stick margarine or butter
   Cooking spray
⅓ cup chopped country ham (about 2 ounces)
½ cup strong brewed coffee
¼ cup water
1 tablespoon brown sugar
1 (6-ounce) package presliced portobello mushrooms
1 tablespoon all-purpose flour
1 tablespoon water

1. Combine first 4 ingredients in a large zip-top plastic bag; add chicken. Seal bag, and shake to coat chicken.
2. Melt margarine in a large nonstick skillet coated with cooking spray over medium-high heat. Add chicken; cook 3 minutes on each side or until golden. Combine ham, coffee, ¼ cup water, and sugar; pour over chicken. Bring to a boil; cover, reduce heat, and simmer 3 minutes. Add mushrooms; cover and simmer 7 minutes or until chicken is done and mushrooms are tender. Remove chicken and mushrooms with a slotted spoon, and place on a serving platter; keep warm.
3. Combine 1 tablespoon flour and 1 tablespoon water in a small bowl, stirring with a whisk; add to cooking liquid in pan. Bring to a boil, and cook until

thick (about 1 minute), stirring constantly. Spoon over chicken and mushrooms. Yield: 4 servings (serving size: 1 chicken breast half, about 3 mushroom slices, and 2 tablespoons gravy).

CALORIES 210 (24% from fat); FAT 5.5g (sat 1.4g, mono 2.1g, poly 1.2g); PROTEIN 30.5g; CARB 8.3g; FIBER 0.8g; CHOL 73mg; IRON 1.9mg; SODIUM 442mg; CALC 20mg

ARTICHOKE-AND-GOAT CHEESE-STUFFED CHICKEN BREASTS

PREP: 25 MINUTES   COOK: 34 MINUTES

1 (14-ounce) can artichoke bottoms
½ cup (2 ounces) crumbled goat or feta cheese
¼ cup chopped chives, divided
1½ teaspoons chopped fresh thyme, divided
1½ teaspoons grated lemon rind, divided
8 (4-ounce) skinned, boned chicken breast halves
¼ teaspoon black pepper
2 teaspoons olive oil, divided
1 teaspoon cornstarch
2 tablespoons fresh lemon juice

1. Drain artichokes in a colander over a bowl, reserving liquid. Coarsely chop artichoke bottoms. Combine artichokes, goat cheese, 2 tablespoons chives, 1 teaspoon thyme, and 1 teaspoon lemon rind in a medium bowl.
2. Cut a horizontal slit through thickest portion of each chicken breast half to form a pocket. Stuff about ¼ cup artichoke mixture into pockets. Sprinkle chicken with pepper.
3. Heat 1 teaspoon oil in a large skillet over medium-high heat. Add 4 chicken breast halves; cook 6 to 8 minutes on each side or until chicken is done. Remove chicken from pan; keep warm. Repeat procedure with 1 teaspoon oil

Stuffing Chicken Breast Halves

1. Insert tip of a thin, sharp knife into thickest side of chicken breast half. Make a 2-inch slit. Cut to, but not through, the opposite side.

2. Holding the knife blade parallel to the cutting board, guide the blade around the inside, creating a pocket. Be careful not to cut through sides.

3. Using your fingers, stuff breast half.

and 4 chicken breast halves. Add reserved artichoke liquid, ½ teaspoon thyme, and ½ teaspoon lemon rind to pan. Combine cornstarch and lemon juice; add to pan. Bring to a boil; cook 1 minute, stirring constantly. Return chicken to pan. Cover and simmer 2 minutes or until thoroughly heated. Spoon sauce over chicken. Top with 2 tablespoons chives. Yield: 8 servings (serving size: 1 chicken breast half).

CALORIES 189 (22% from fat); FAT 4.7g (sat 2g, mono 1.6g, poly 0.5g); PROTEIN 29.4g; CARB 6.8g; FIBER 0.1g; CHOL 75mg; IRON 1.6mg; SODIUM 378mg; CALC 86mg

GOUDA-STUFFED CHICKEN WITH APPLES

PREP: 21 MINUTES   COOK: 27 MINUTES

4 (4-ounce) skinned, boned chicken breast halves
3 ounces smoked Gouda cheese, cut into thin slices
2 tablespoons all-purpose flour
2 teaspoons vegetable oil
1 cup fat-free, less-sodium chicken broth
1 cup apple cider
1 garlic clove, minced
1 tablespoon honey
2 Granny Smith or Red Delicious apples (about ¾ pound), each peeled and cut into 12 wedges

1. Cut a horizontal slit through thickest portion of each chicken breast half to form a pocket; divide cheese evenly among pockets. Dredge chicken in flour.
2. Heat oil in a large nonstick skillet over medium-high heat. Add chicken; cook 7 minutes on each side or until done. Remove chicken from pan; keep warm.
3. Add broth, apple cider, and garlic to pan; bring to a boil. Add honey and apple wedges; cook 10 minutes or until apple is tender, stirring occasionally.

Spoon apple wedges and sauce over chicken. Yield: 4 servings (serving size: 1 stuffed chicken breast half and 6 apple wedges).

CALORIES 339 (26% from fat); FAT 9.9g (sat 4.6g, mono 2.7g, poly 1.7g); PROTEIN 32.2g; CARB 29.5g; FIBER 2g; CHOL 90mg; IRON 1.4mg; SODIUM 410mg; CALC 172mg

BRIE-AND-CARAMELIZED ONION-STUFFED CHICKEN BREASTS

PREP: 45 MINUTES   COOK: 25 MINUTES

Although this elegant dish is low in calories, the melted Brie-and-onion combination creates a rich-tasting entrée.

1 teaspoon olive oil, divided
1½ cups sliced onion
4 garlic cloves, thinly sliced
⅔ cup dry white wine, divided
2 ounces Brie cheese, rind removed and cheese cut into small pieces
⅛ teaspoon salt
⅛ teaspoon black pepper
4 (4-ounce) skinned, boned chicken breast halves
2 tablespoons minced onion
1 tablespoon chopped fresh sage
2 garlic cloves, minced
1 (10½-ounce) can low-sodium chicken broth

1. Heat ½ teaspoon oil in a large nonstick skillet over medium heat. Add sliced onion; cook 30 minutes or until golden, stirring often. Add sliced garlic, and sauté 5 minutes. Stir in ⅓ cup wine; cook 5 minutes or until liquid almost evaporates. Spoon onion mixture into a bowl; cool. Stir in Brie, salt, and pepper.
2. Cut a horizontal slit through thickest portion of each chicken breast half to form a pocket. Stuff about 1½ tablespoons onion mixture into pockets.

(continued on page 360)

3. Heat ½ teaspoon oil in pan over medium-high heat. Add chicken; cook 6 minutes on each side or until done. Remove chicken from pan; keep warm.

4. Add ⅓ cup wine, minced onion, chopped sage, and minced garlic to pan. Cook over medium-high heat 2 minutes; stir in broth. Bring to a boil, and cook 7 minutes or until reduced to ¾ cup. Return chicken to pan; cover and simmer 2 minutes or until thoroughly heated. Serve sauce with chicken. Yield: 4 servings (serving size: 1 chicken breast half and 3 tablespoons sauce).

CALORIES 216 (30% from fat); FAT 7.1g (sat 3.1g, mono 2.3g, poly 0.6g); PROTEIN 30.7g; CARB 6.2g; FIBER 0.8g; CHOL 80mg; IRON 1.7mg; SODIUM 267mg; CALC 60mg

SPINACH-STUFFED CHICKEN IN APRICOT SAUCE

PREP: 10 MINUTES

CHILL: 1 HOUR

COOK: 28 MINUTES

1 (10-ounce) package frozen chopped spinach, thawed
½ cup 1% low-fat cottage cheese
⅓ cup dry breadcrumbs
1 tablespoon minced shallot
¼ teaspoon salt
⅛ teaspoon garlic powder
⅛ teaspoon ground nutmeg
1 large egg white, lightly beaten
6 (4-ounce) skinned, boned chicken breast halves
1 tablespoon vegetable oil
1 cup apricot nectar
1 tablespoon tarragon vinegar
2 teaspoons brown sugar
2 teaspoons country-style Dijon mustard
6 unpeeled apricots (about 12 ounces), each cut into 8 wedges

1. Press spinach between paper towels until barely moist. Combine spinach

Spinach-Stuffed Chicken in Apricot Sauce

and next 7 ingredients in a bowl. Cut a horizontal slit through thickest portion of each chicken breast half to form a pocket. Divide spinach mixture evenly among pockets. Cover and chill stuffed chicken breast halves 1 hour.

2. Heat oil in a large nonstick skillet over medium-high heat until hot. Add chicken, and cook 6 minutes on each side or until chicken is done. Remove chicken from pan; keep warm.

3. Combine nectar, tarragon vinegar, brown sugar, and mustard in a saucepan;

bring to a boil. Reduce heat to medium, and cook 7 minutes. Add apricot wedges; cook 5 minutes or until sauce thickens. Serve warm over chicken. Yield: 6 servings (serving size: 1 stuffed chicken breast half and ¼ cup sauce).

Note: Drained canned apricots may be substituted for fresh; use the juice from canned apricots in place of some of the nectar.

CALORIES 253 (17% from fat); FAT 4.7g (sat 1g, mono 1.3g, poly 1.6g); PROTEIN 32.2g; CARB 20.3g; FIBER 3.2g; CHOL 67mg; IRON 2.7mg; SODIUM 392mg; CALC 102mg

STUFFED CHICKEN PARMESAN

PREP: 43 MINUTES
COOK: 25 MINUTES

1 cup boiling water
8 sun-dried tomatoes, packed without oil
1 tablespoon water
2 large egg whites, lightly beaten
⅔ cup Italian-seasoned breadcrumbs
⅓ cup all-purpose flour
¼ cup (1 ounce) grated fresh Parmesan cheese
¼ teaspoon black pepper
4 (4-ounce) skinned, boned chicken breast halves
4 very thin slices fresh Parmesan cheese (about ½ ounce)
2 teaspoons capers
Cooking spray
2 cups hot cooked angel hair (about 4 ounces uncooked pasta)
3 cups Chunky Tomato Sauce (page 447)

1. Combine boiling water and sun-dried tomatoes in a bowl; let stand 30 minutes or until softened. Drain tomatoes, and set aside.
2. Preheat oven to 400°.
3. Combine 1 tablespoon water and egg whites in a shallow bowl; stir well with a whisk. Combine breadcrumbs, flour, grated cheese, and pepper in a shallow dish.
4. Cut a horizontal slit through thickest portion of each chicken breast half to form a pocket. Stuff 2 sun-dried tomatoes, 1 cheese slice, and ½ teaspoon capers into each pocket, and close opening with a wooden pick. Dip each chicken breast half in egg white mixture; dredge in breadcrumb mixture. Place chicken on a baking sheet coated with cooking spray, and lightly coat chicken with cooking spray. Bake at 400° for 15 minutes. Turn chicken over, and lightly coat with cooking

spray. Bake an additional 10 minutes or until done. Discard wooden picks.
5. Place ½ cup pasta on each of 4 plates, and top with stuffed chicken. Spoon ¾ cup Chunky Tomato Sauce over each serving. Yield: 4 servings.

CALORIES 473 (15% from fat); FAT 8g (sat 2.4g, mono 2.7g, poly 1.2g); PROTEIN 41.8g; CARB 59.6g; FIBER 5.2g; CHOL 72mg; IRON 5.4mg; SODIUM 1169mg; CALC 172mg

PAILLARD OF CHICKEN

PREP: 25 MINUTES
COOK: 32 MINUTES

5 (1-ounce) slices whole-wheat bread
2 tablespoons grated Parmesan cheese
2 tablespoons chopped fresh parsley
8 (4-ounce) skinned, boned chicken breast halves
¼ cup fresh lemon juice
⅓ cup whole-wheat flour
1 teaspoon cracked black pepper
1 teaspoon dried thyme
1 teaspoon rubbed sage
¼ teaspoon dried rosemary, crushed
¼ teaspoon salt
3 large egg whites, lightly beaten
2 tablespoons olive oil, divided

1. Place bread in a food processor; process 30 seconds or until crumbs are fine. Combine breadcrumbs, cheese, and parsley; set aside.
2. Place each chicken breast half between 2 sheets of heavy-duty plastic wrap; flatten to ¼-inch thickness using a meat mallet or rolling pin. Brush both sides of chicken with lemon juice. Combine flour and next 4 ingredients in a large zip-top plastic bag. Add chicken, and seal bag; shake to coat.
3. Sprinkle both sides of chicken with salt. Dip chicken in egg white; dredge in breadcrumb mixture.

4. Heat 2 teaspoons oil in a large nonstick skillet over medium heat. Add 3 chicken breast halves; cook 4 minutes on each side or until done. Remove from pan; keep warm. Repeat procedure with 4 teaspoons oil and remaining chicken. Yield: 8 servings (serving size: 1 chicken breast half).

CALORIES 233 (23% from fat); FAT 6g (sat 1.3g, mono 3.3g, poly 0.8g); PROTEIN 30.4g; CARB 13.2g; FIBER 1.6g; CHOL 67mg; IRON 2mg; SODIUM 285mg; CALC 58mg

CHICKEN BREASTS WITH FETA CHEESE SAUCE

PREP: 10 MINUTES   COOK: 23 MINUTES

Cooking spray
6 (6-ounce) skinned chicken breast halves
1 tablespoon butter or stick margarine
4 teaspoons all-purpose flour
1 (12-ounce) can evaporated fat-free milk
1 tablespoon fresh or freeze-dried chives
¾ cup crumbled feta cheese

1. Coat a large nonstick skillet with cooking spray; place over medium-high heat until hot. Add chicken, and cook 9 minutes on each side or until done; keep warm.
2. Melt butter in a saucepan over medium heat; add flour. Cook 1 minute, stirring constantly with a whisk. Gradually add milk, stirring constantly; stir in chives. Reduce heat to medium-low; simmer 3 minutes or until thick, stirring occasionally. Add cheese; stir until cheese melts. Spoon over chicken. Yield: 6 servings (serving size: 1 chicken breast half and ¼ cup sauce).

CALORIES 243 (33% from fat); FAT 9g (sat 5g, mono 2.4g, poly 0.8g); PROTEIN 30.2g; CARB 8.8g; FIBER 0g; CHOL 87mg; IRON 1.1mg; SODIUM 363mg; CALC 281mg

menu

Chicken and Ham Tetrazzini

Crunchy Pea Salad (page 403)

Tossed green salad with
Creamy Tarragon Dressing (page 423)

Fresh Blueberry Cobbler (page 209)

CHICKEN AND HAM TETRAZZINI

PREP: 35 MINUTES   COOK: 20 MINUTES

Leftover chicken (or a store-bought rotisserie chicken) will work just as well in this recipe, particularly if you're in a hurry.

1 (7-ounce) package spaghetti
1 tablespoon reduced-calorie stick margarine
1 cup presliced fresh mushrooms
1 cup chopped onion
1 cup chopped green bell pepper
2 garlic cloves, minced
¼ cup all-purpose flour
½ teaspoon poultry seasoning
½ teaspoon black pepper
1¼ cups 1% low-fat milk
¾ cup (3 ounces) shredded reduced-fat sharp cheddar cheese, divided
1½ cups shredded roasted chicken breast (about 5 ounces)
¾ cup finely chopped cooked ham (about ¼ pound)
⅔ cup grated Parmesan cheese, divided
¼ cup dry sherry
1 (10¾-ounce) can condensed reduced-fat, reduced-sodium cream of mushroom soup, undiluted
1 (4-ounce) jar diced pimento, drained
Cooking spray
1 teaspoon paprika
2 tablespoons sliced almonds

1. Cook spaghetti according to package directions, omitting salt and fat. Drain well; set aside.
2. Preheat oven to 350°.
3. Melt margarine in a large nonstick skillet over medium-high heat. Add mushrooms, onion, green pepper, and garlic; sauté 7 minutes or until tender. Stir in flour, poultry seasoning, and black pepper; cook 30 seconds, stirring constantly. Gradually add milk; cook 1½ minutes or until thick, stirring constantly. Remove from heat, and stir in ¼ cup cheddar cheese; stir until cheese melts. Add chicken, ham, ⅓ cup Parmesan cheese, sherry, soup, and pimento; stir well.
4. Combine spaghetti and chicken mixture in a large bowl; spoon mixture into a 13 x 9-inch baking dish coated with cooking spray.
5. Combine ⅓ cup Parmesan cheese and 1 teaspoon paprika. Sprinkle Parmesan cheese mixture, ½ cup cheddar cheese, and almonds in alternating diagonal rows across top of casserole. Bake uncovered, at 350° for 20 minutes or until bubbly. Yield: 6 servings (serving size: 1½ cups).

CALORIES 387 (27% from fat); FAT 11.5g (sat 5.1g, mono 3.9g, poly 2g); PROTEIN 27g; CARB 41.8g; FIBER 2.1g; CHOL 52mg; IRON 3.1mg; SODIUM 808mg; CALC 381mg

SPANISH RICE WITH CHICKEN AND PEPPERS

PREP: 10 MINUTES
COOK: 33 MINUTES

1 tablespoon vegetable oil
½ pound skinned, boned chicken thighs, cut into ½-inch cubes
1⅓ cups chopped onion
½ cup (1-inch-square) cut green bell pepper (about ½ pepper)
½ cup (1-inch-square) cut red bell pepper (about ½ pepper)
1¼ cups uncooked long-grain rice
½ teaspoon dried oregano
½ teaspoon ground cumin
1 large garlic clove, minced
1 (14½-ounce) can fat-free, less-sodium chicken broth
1 (10-ounce) can whole tomatoes with green chiles, undrained and chopped
¼ teaspoon salt

1. Heat oil in a large skillet over medium-high heat. Add chicken; sauté 3 minutes or until golden. Add onion and bell peppers; sauté 5 minutes. Add rice, oregano, cumin, and garlic; sauté 2 minutes. Add broth, tomatoes, and salt; bring to a boil. Cover, reduce heat, and simmer 20 minutes or until liquid is absorbed. Yield: 4 servings (serving size: about 1¼ cups).

CALORIES 362 (16% from fat); FAT 6.3g (sat 1.3g, mono 1.9g, poly 2.4g); PROTEIN 16.3g; CARB 55g; FIBER 2.2g; CHOL 47mg; IRON 4.3mg; SODIUM 718mg; CALC 58mg

Chicken and Ham Tetrazzini can be assembled (and refrigerated) up to 4 hours ahead of time, omitting the cheese-and-almond topping. **Add the topping just before baking.**

Chicken, Artichoke, and Rice Casserole

PREP: 27 MINUTES

COOK: 50 MINUTES

2   tablespoons olive oil, divided
12 chicken thighs, skinned
3   garlic cloves, minced
3   cups finely chopped onion
2   cups uncooked long-grain rice
3   cups fat-free, less-sodium chicken broth
1   cup dry white wine
1   tablespoon rubbed sage
1   tablespoon dried thyme
1   teaspoon salt
½   teaspoon freshly ground black pepper
1   (10-ounce) package frozen green peas
2   cups diced plum tomato
1   (9-ounce) package frozen artichoke hearts
¾   cup bottled roasted red bell peppers, cut into thin strips

1. Preheat oven to 400°.
2. Heat 1 tablespoon oil in a large non-stick skillet over medium-high heat. Add chicken and garlic; cook 7 minutes on each side or until lightly browned.
3. Heat 1 tablespoon oil in an oven-proof Dutch oven over medium heat. Add onion and rice; cook until rice is lightly browned (about 15 minutes), stirring frequently. Add broth and next 5 ingredients; bring to a boil.
4. Add chicken mixture to Dutch oven; top with peas, tomato, and artichoke hearts. Cover and bake at 400° for 50 minutes. Add roasted peppers; gently fluff mixture with 2 large forks. Yield: 12 servings (serving size: 1 chicken thigh and 1 cup rice mixture).

CALORIES 311 (20% from fat); FAT 6.8g (sat 1.5g, mono 3g, poly 1.4g); PROTEIN 24.7g; CARB 35.8g; FIBER 2.8g; CHOL 84mg; IRON 3.8mg; SODIUM 512mg; CALC 49mg

French Chicken in Vinegar Sauce With Pepper-Spiked Polenta

French Chicken in Vinegar Sauce With Pepper-Spiked Polenta

PREP: 12 MINUTES   COOK: 31 MINUTES

To keep prep time to a minimum, we purchased boned, skinned chicken thighs. Ask your butcher to bone and skin them for you.

Olive oil-flavored cooking spray
2½ cups chopped onion
8   (3-ounce) skinned, boned chicken thighs
½   cup dry white wine
½   cup fat-free, less-sodium chicken broth
3   tablespoons tomato paste
2   tablespoons balsamic vinegar
1   teaspoon minced fresh or ½ teaspoon dried tarragon
½   teaspoon brown sugar
¼   teaspoon salt
¼   teaspoon ground red pepper
Dash of black pepper
Pepper-Spiked Polenta (page 253)

1. Coat a large nonstick skillet with cooking spray; place over medium-high heat until hot. Add onion; cook 5 minutes or until lightly browned. Remove onion from pan. Increase heat to high. Add chicken; cook 3 minutes on each side or until browned.
2. Combine wine and next 8 ingredients in a medium bowl. Add onion and wine mixture to chicken; cover, reduce heat, and simmer 20 minutes. Serve with Pepper-Spiked Polenta. Yield: 4 servings (serving size: 2 thighs, about ½ cup sauce, and 1 cup polenta).

CALORIES 398 (21% from fat); FAT 9.3g (sat 2.8g, mono 2.7g, poly 2g); PROTEIN 39.8g; CARB 36.6g; FIBER 3.7g; CHOL 145mg; IRON 4mg; SODIUM 775mg; CALC 110mg

menu

Spiced Chicken and Barley

Romaine Salad With
Tangy Lemon-Dijon Dressing (page 394)
Lemon-Rosemary Custard Cakes
(page 166)

SPICED CHICKEN AND BARLEY

PREP: 10 MINUTES

COOK: 1 HOUR 5 MINUTES

1 teaspoon ground cumin
¾ teaspoon chili powder
½ teaspoon salt
½ teaspoon ground cinnamon
½ teaspoon dried mint flakes
⅛ teaspoon garlic powder
⅛ teaspoon ground red pepper
6 (4-ounce) chicken thighs, skinned
½ teaspoon vegetable oil
Cooking spray
1½ cups chopped onion
1 cup chopped red bell pepper
1 tablespoon low-sodium soy sauce
2 (14.25-ounce) cans fat-free, less-sodium chicken broth
1¼ cups uncooked pearl barley
1 (14.5-ounce) can diced tomatoes, drained
6 tablespoons chopped green onions

1. Combine first 7 ingredients; rub chicken with half of spice mixture.
2. Heat oil in a large nonstick skillet coated with cooking spray over medium-high heat. Add chicken; cook 3 minutes on each side or until browned. Remove chicken from pan.
3. Add 1½ cups onion and bell pepper to pan; cook over medium-high heat 3 minutes or until vegetables are lightly browned. Stir in soy sauce, broth, barley, tomatoes, and remaining spice mixture.
4. Add chicken to pan, nestling into vegetable mixture. Bring to a boil; cover, reduce heat, and simmer 45 minutes. Uncover; simmer 10 minutes or until liquid almost evaporates. Let stand 15 minutes. Sprinkle with green onions. Yield: 6 servings (serving size: 1 chicken thigh, 1 cup barley mixture, and 1 tablespoon green onions).

CALORIES 304 (14% from fat); FAT 4.8g (sat 1.1g, mono 1.4g, poly 1.5g); PROTEIN 23.4g; CARB 41g; FIBER 9.2g; CHOL 74mg; IRON 3.1mg; SODIUM 737mg; CALC 56mg

Spiced Chicken and Barley

Spiced Chicken and Barley contains almost 10 grams of fiber, which is more than one-third of the recommended daily intake.

CHICKEN CACCIATORE

PREP: 15 MINUTES COOK: 44 MINUTES

Pinot Noir can be quite expensive, especially a decent one from France, but there are some good California and Oregon Pinot Noirs that will pique the flavor of the chicken.

¼ teaspoon black pepper
⅛ teaspoon salt
6 chicken thighs (about 2 pounds), skinned
1 teaspoon olive oil
1 cup sliced mushrooms
½ cup chopped onion
2 garlic cloves, minced
¾ cup Pinot Noir or other dry red wine
1 teaspoon finely chopped fresh or ½ teaspoon dried oregano
¼ teaspoon crushed red pepper
2 (14.5-ounce) cans plum tomatoes, undrained and chopped
6 cups hot cooked vermicelli (about 12 ounces uncooked)

1. Sprinkle black pepper and salt over chicken.
2. Heat oil in a large nonstick skillet over medium-high heat. Add chicken; cook 7 minutes on each side or until browned. Remove chicken from pan; cover and set aside.
3. Add mushrooms, onion, and garlic to pan; sauté over medium-high heat 5 minutes. Add wine, chopped oregano, red pepper, and tomatoes; bring to a boil. Cook 10 minutes or until sauce is slightly thick, stirring occasionally.
4. Return chicken and juices from chicken to pan. Reduce heat to medium; cover and cook 5 minutes. Uncover; turn chicken over, and cook 10 minutes or until chicken is done. Serve over hot vermicelli. Yield: 6 servings (serving size: 1 cup pasta, 1 chicken thigh, and ½ cup sauce).

CALORIES 377 (14% from fat); FAT 6g (sat 1.3g, mono 2g, poly 1.6g); PROTEIN 29g; CARB 50.8g; FIBER 2.8g; CHOL 84mg; IRON 4.5mg; SODIUM 367mg; CALC 66mg

COLLEGE CHICKEN CASSEROLE

PREP: 30 MINUTES COOK: 1 ½ HOURS

6 cups water
½ cup dry white wine
1½ teaspoons dried basil
2 garlic cloves, halved
1 (10½-ounce) can low-sodium chicken broth
6 chicken breast halves (about 2¼ pounds)
4 chicken thighs (about 1 pound)
Cooking spray
4 cups sliced cremini mushrooms (about 8 ounces)
¼ cup all-purpose flour
1 cup 1% low-fat milk
½ teaspoon salt
¼ teaspoon black pepper
2 cups herb-seasoned stuffing mix
3 tablespoons light butter, melted

1. Combine first 5 ingredients in a Dutch oven; bring to a boil. Add chicken; cover, reduce heat, and simmer 30 minutes or until tender. Remove chicken with a slotted spoon; bring broth mixture to a boil. Cook until reduced to 4 cups (about 30 minutes).
2. Place a heavy-duty zip-top plastic bag inside a 4-cup glass measure. Pour reduced broth mixture into bag; let stand 10 minutes (fat will rise to top). Seal bag; carefully snip off 1 bottom corner of bag. Drain 2 cups broth mixture into glass measure, stopping before fat layer reaches opening. Reserve remaining broth mixture for another use. Discard fat.
3. Remove chicken from bones, and discard skin and bones; shred chicken with 2 forks to measure 4½ cups meat. Place in a 13 x 9-inch baking dish coated with cooking spray.
4. Preheat oven to 400°.
5. Place a large skillet coated with cooking spray over medium-high heat. Add mushrooms; sauté 5 minutes. Remove from skillet. Place flour in skillet; gradually add milk, stirring with a whisk until blended. Add 2 cups broth mixture; cook over medium heat until slightly thick (about 12 minutes), stirring constantly with a whisk. Stir in mushrooms, salt, and pepper; pour over chicken.
6. Combine stuffing mix and butter in a bowl; sprinkle over mushroom mixture. Cover and bake at 400° for 20 minutes. Uncover and bake an additional 10 minutes or until bubbly. Yield: 6 servings.

CALORIES 425 (30% from fat); FAT 14.3g (sat 5.2g, mono 4.6g, poly 2.7g); PROTEIN 54.2g; CARB 19.2g; FIBER 1.9g; CHOL 158mg; IRON 4mg; SODIUM 572mg; CALC 108mg

CREMINI MUSHROOMS

Cremini mushrooms are a darker, richer-flavored cousin of the common button mushroom. They have a firm texture that stands up well to cooking. They complement both button and portobello mushrooms, as all three are part of the same family.

HONEY-PECAN CRUSTED CHICKEN

PREP: 16 MINUTES
COOK: 45 MINUTES

You would expect Southern fried chicken to be loaded with calories and fat. Not our version, though—we baked the chicken instead of frying it, and we gave it a crisp, greaseless crust made from crushed cornflakes and chopped pecans. This recipe should please the entire family; there are chicken breasts for the adults, and kids should really enjoy the drumsticks!

- ¼ teaspoon salt
- ¼ teaspoon black pepper
- 4 (6-ounce) skinned chicken breast halves
- 8 (4-ounce) chicken drumsticks, skinned
- ¼ cup honey
- 2 tablespoons Dijon mustard
- ¾ teaspoon paprika
- ⅛ teaspoon garlic powder
- 1¼ cups finely crushed cornflakes
- ½ cup finely chopped pecans
  Cooking spray

1. Preheat oven to 400°.
2. Sprinkle salt and pepper evenly over chicken. Combine honey, mustard, paprika, and garlic powder in a small bowl. Combine cornflakes and pecans in a shallow dish. Brush both sides of chicken with honey mixture; dredge in cornflake mixture.
3. Place chicken on a large baking sheet coated with cooking spray. Lightly coat chicken with cooking spray; bake at 400° for 40 to 45 minutes or until done. Yield: 8 servings.

CALORIES 336 (27% from fat); FAT 10g (sat 1.6g, mono 4.4g, poly 2.5g); PROTEIN 36.5g; CARB 23.5g; FIBER 0.7g; CHOL 109mg; IRON 2.6mg; SODIUM 482mg; CALC 22mg

Honey-Pecan
Crusted Chicken

OVEN-FRIED CHICKEN

PREP: 15 MINUTES   COOK: 50 MINUTES

- 1 cup egg substitute or low-fat buttermilk
- 1½ cups all-purpose flour
- 1 teaspoon garlic powder
- 1 teaspoon paprika
- ½ teaspoon salt
- ½ teaspoon ground thyme
- ¼ teaspoon white pepper
- 3 pounds assorted chicken pieces, skinned
  Cooking spray
- 1 tablespoon stick margarine or butter, melted

1. Preheat oven to 400°.
2. Place egg substitute in a shallow dish. Combine flour and next 5 ingredients

Double dipping gives our Oven-Fried Chicken more crunchy coating.

in a shallow dish. Dip chicken pieces in egg substitute, and dredge in flour mixture. Dip and dredge each piece a second time.
3. Arrange chicken on a jelly-roll pan coated with cooking spray. Drizzle margarine over chicken. Bake at 400° for 50 minutes or until done. Yield: 6 servings.

CALORIES 297 (19% from fat); FAT 6.2g (sat 1.4g, mono 1.9g, poly 1.7g); PROTEIN 34.2g; CARB 23.3g; FIBER 0.9g; CHOL 89mg; IRON 3.4mg; SODIUM 376mg; CALC 37mg

CHICKEN POTPIE

PREP: 40 MINUTES   COOK: 1 1/2 HOURS

- 9 cups water
- 1 tablespoon black peppercorns
- 2½ pounds chicken pieces, skinned
- 3 celery stalks, each cut into 4 pieces
- 1 small onion, quartered
- 1 bay leaf
- 1½ cups diced unpeeled round red potato
- ½ cup chopped celery
- ½ cup chopped red bell pepper
- 1 garlic clove, minced
- ¾ cup thinly sliced carrot
- ½ cup chopped leek (about 1 small)
- 1 cup sliced fresh mushrooms
- ½ cup frozen green peas
- 6 tablespoons all-purpose flour
- 1 teaspoon salt
- 1 teaspoon black pepper
- 1 cup 1% low-fat milk
- Cooking spray
- Biscuit Topping

1. Combine first 6 ingredients in an 8-quart Dutch oven or stock pot; bring to a boil. Reduce heat to medium, and cook, uncovered, 1 hour. Remove from heat.
2. Remove chicken pieces from broth. Place chicken in a large bowl, and chill for 15 minutes. Strain broth through a cheesecloth-lined colander into a bowl; discard solids. Set aside 4½ cups broth; reserve remaining broth for another use.
3. Remove chicken from bones; cut meat into bite-size pieces.
4. Preheat oven to 400°.
5. Bring 4½ cups broth to a boil in a large saucepan over medium-high heat. Add potato, chopped celery, bell pepper, and garlic; cover and cook 5 minutes. Add carrot and leek; cover and cook 3 minutes. Add mushrooms and peas; cover and cook 5 minutes or until vegetables are tender.

6. Combine flour, salt, and black pepper in a medium bowl. Add milk, stirring with a whisk; add to vegetable mixture. Cook over medium heat 3 minutes or until thickened and bubbly, stirring constantly. Remove from heat; add chicken.
7. Spoon into a 13 x 9-inch baking dish coated with cooking spray. Drop Biscuit Topping onto mixture to form 16 biscuits. Bake at 400° for 30 minutes or until golden. Yield: 8 servings (serving size: about 1 cup chicken mixture and 2 biscuits).

CALORIES 327 (18% from fat); FAT 6.6g (sat 1.8g, mono 2.1g, poly 1.7g); PROTEIN 26.5g; CARB 38.8g; FIBER 2.7g; CHOL 64mg; IRON 3.5mg; SODIUM 668mg; CALC 155mg

BISCUIT TOPPING

- 2 cups all-purpose flour
- 2 teaspoons baking powder
- ½ teaspoon salt
- ¼ teaspoon sugar
- ⅛ teaspoon garlic powder
- 1 cup 1% low-fat milk
- 1½ tablespoons stick margarine or butter, melted

1. Lightly spoon flour into dry measuring cups; level with a knife. Combine flour, baking powder, salt, sugar, and garlic powder in a bowl. Stir in milk and margarine just until flour mixture is moistened. Yield: 16 biscuits.

Chicken Potpie

We've adhered to the basic, traditional techniques:
browning the chicken and shallots, and braising them in wine, broth, or both.

Coq au Vin

PREP:12 MINUTES
COOK:1 HOUR 10 MINUTES

¼ cup all-purpose flour
¼ teaspoon black pepper,
     divided
⅛ teaspoon salt
 2 chicken breast halves,
     skinned
 2 chicken thighs, skinned
 2 chicken drumsticks,
     skinned
 1 tablespoon olive oil
 2 tablespoons diced shallots
 1 pound small mushrooms
1¼ cups diced plum tomato
 1 cup diced carrot
 1 cup diced celery
 1 tablespoon chopped fresh
     or 1 teaspoon dried tarragon
 1 bay leaf
⅔ cup dry red wine
½ cup low-salt chicken broth
¼ teaspoon salt
 2 tablespoons finely chopped
     fresh chives

1. Combine flour, ⅛ teaspoon pepper, and ⅛ teaspoon salt in a shallow dish. Dredge chicken in flour mixture.
2. Heat oil in a large Dutch oven over medium-high heat. Add chicken and shallots. Cook 5 minutes, browning on all sides. Remove chicken. Add mushrooms; sauté 3 minutes. Add tomato, carrot, celery, tarragon, and bay leaf. Cook 1 minute, stirring constantly. Stir in wine and broth; scrape pan to loosen browned bits. Return chicken to pan, and bring to a boil. Cover, reduce heat,

Coq au Vin

1. Cook chicken and shallots in a large Dutch oven, browning on all sides. Remove chicken.

2. Add mushrooms; sauté 3 minutes. Add tomato, carrot, celery, tarragon, and bay leaf. Cook 1 minute, stirring constantly.

3. Stir in wine and broth, scraping pan to loosen browned bits.

4. Return chicken to pan; bring to a boil. Cover, reduce heat, and cook as directed.

and simmer 1 hour, stirring occasionally. Stir in ⅛ teaspoon pepper and ¼ teaspoon salt. Discard bay leaf. Garnish with chopped chives. Yield: 4 servings (serving size: 3 ounces chicken and ¼ cup sauce).

CALORIES 326 (26% from fat); FAT 9.4g (sat 2g, mono 4.2g, poly 1.8g); PROTEIN 40.8g; CARB 19.9g; FIBER 4g; CHOL 115mg; IRON 4.2mg; SODIUM 390mg; CALC 62mg

menu

Chicken With 40 Cloves of Garlic

Mediterranean Orzo (page 260)

Steamed asparagus

Coffee Granita (page 175)

CHICKEN WITH 40 CLOVES OF GARLIC

PREP: 20 MINUTES
COOK: 1½ HOURS

This is a classic Provençal-style dish in which the thighs and drumsticks are baked with garlic cloves. The garlic cooks in its own skin, becoming very soft and creamy. Serve it as a spread with French bread. Nothing compares to its rich, aromatic flavor.

2½ cups chopped onion
1 teaspoon dried tarragon
6 parsley sprigs
4 celery stalks, each cut into 3 pieces
8 chicken thighs, skinned (about 3 pounds)
8 chicken drumsticks, skinned (about 2 pounds)
½ cup dry vermouth
1½ teaspoons salt
½ teaspoon pepper
⅛ teaspoon ground nutmeg
40 unpeeled garlic cloves (about 3 heads)
Tarragon sprigs (optional)

1. Preheat oven to 375°.
2. Combine first 4 ingredients in a 4-quart casserole or roasting pan. Arrange chicken over vegetables. Drizzle with vermouth; sprinkle with salt, pepper, and nutmeg. Nestle garlic around chicken. Cover casserole with foil, and bake at 375° for 1½ hours. Garnish with tarragon sprigs, if desired. Yield: 8 servings (serving size: 1 thigh, 1 drumstick, 5 tablespoons vegetable mixture, and 5 garlic cloves).

CALORIES 238 (23% from fat); FAT 6.2g (sat 1.6g, mono 1.9g, poly 1.6g); PROTEIN 34.1g; CARB 10.1g; FIBER 1.4g; CHOL 131mg; IRON 2.2mg; SODIUM 606mg; CALC 65mg

BOSTON BEACH JERK CHICKEN

PREP: 35 MINUTES
MARINATE: 1 TO 4 HOURS
COOK: 45 MINUTES

Jerk is the Jamaican method of barbecue. Add oak, pecan, or hickory wood to a charcoal fire to make your jerk more authentic. Be sure to wear gloves when handling the chiles and packing on the rub; the oil in the chiles will burn your skin.

4 cups (1-inch) pieces green onions
¼ cup fresh thyme leaves
3 tablespoons grated peeled fresh ginger
2 tablespoons fresh lime juice
2 tablespoons vegetable oil
1 tablespoon freshly ground black pepper
1 tablespoon freshly ground coriander seed
2 teaspoons salt
2 teaspoons freshly ground allspice
1 teaspoon freshly ground nutmeg
1 teaspoon ground cinnamon
5 garlic cloves, peeled and halved
3 bay leaves
1 to 2 fresh Scotch bonnet or habañero peppers, halved and seeded
1 (3½-pound) chicken
Cooking spray

1. Place first 14 ingredients in a food processor; process until a thick paste forms, scraping sides of bowl once.
2. Remove and discard giblets and neck from chicken. Rinse chicken with cold water, and pat dry. Remove skin, and trim excess fat; split chicken in half lengthwise. Place chicken in a large shallow dish. Spread 1¼ cups spice mixture over both sides of chicken. Cover and marinate in refrigerator 1 to 4 hours.
3. Prepare grill.
4. Place chicken on grill rack coated with cooking spray; cook 45 minutes or until done, turning frequently and basting with remaining ¼ cup spice mixture. Yield: 6 servings (serving size: 3 ounces chicken).

CALORIES 275 (43% from fat); FAT 13.1g (sat 3.2g, mono 4.3g, poly 4.1g); PROTEIN 32.6g; CARB 6.4g; FIBER 1.6g; CHOL 97mg; IRON 2.8mg; SODIUM 882mg; CALC 69mg

Use an electric coffee bean grinder to grind whole spices. Freshly ground spices impart **much more flavor than bottled ones.**

Reminiscent of French country fare, fricassees are meals meant to warm you up on a cold winter day.

CHICKEN FRICASSEE

PREP:10 MINUTES
COOK:1 HOUR

*A fricassee is a dish in which the meat is browned before it's stewed with vegetables. It gets its name from two French verbs—*frire, *meaning "to fry," and* casser, *meaning "to break."*

¼   cup all-purpose flour
 2   chicken breast halves (about
       1 pound), skinned
 2   chicken drumsticks (about ½
       pound), skinned
 2   chicken thighs (about ½
       pound), skinned
 1   tablespoon olive oil
12   garlic cloves, finely chopped
       (about 2 tablespoons)
1½   cups dry white wine
1½   cups diced plum tomato
 ¼   cup oil-cured olives, pitted
 3   tablespoons chopped fresh or
       1 tablespoon dried basil
 1   tablespoon chopped fresh or
       1 teaspoon dried oregano
 1   tablespoon tomato paste
 ½   teaspoon salt
 ¼   teaspoon black pepper
 1   (16-ounce) tube of polenta,
       cut into 12 slices
Cooking spray
Oregano sprigs (optional)

Chicken Fricassee

1. Place flour in a shallow dish. Dredge chicken in flour.
2. Heat oil in a large Dutch oven over medium-high heat. Add chicken, and cook 5 minutes, browning chicken on all sides. Remove chicken from pan. Add chopped garlic to pan, and sauté 2 minutes or until lightly browned. Stir in wine, scraping pan to loosen browned bits. Add tomato and next 6 ingredients. Return chicken to pan. Cover, reduce heat, and simmer 45 minutes or until chicken is tender.
3. Preheat broiler.
4. Place polenta slices on a baking sheet coated with cooking spray, and broil 5 minutes or until lightly browned. Serve chicken and sauce with polenta. Garnish with oregano sprigs, if desired. Yield: 4 servings (serving size: 3 ounces chicken, ¾ cup tomato sauce, and 3 slices polenta).

CALORIES 386 (23% from fat); FAT 9.9g (sat 2g, mono 4.9g, poly 1.8g); PROTEIN 40.3g; CARB 31g; FIBER 3.8g; CHOL 114mg; IRON 3.9mg; SODIUM 695mg; CALC 64mg

GARLIC-ROSEMARY ROASTED CHICKEN

PREP: 10 MINUTES

COOK: 1 HOUR 45 MINUTES

(pictured on page 345)

For a potato twist, serve this with Steak Fries (page 499) but cut the potatoes lengthwise into thin strips instead of wedges. Season and bake 20 minutes.

1 (5 to 6-pound) roasting chicken
1 tablespoon chopped fresh rosemary
8 garlic cloves, crushed
Cooking spray
2 red onions, quartered
2 whole garlic heads
2 teaspoons olive oil
Rosemary sprigs (optional)

1. Preheat oven to 450°.
2. Remove and discard giblets and neck from chicken. Rinse chicken with cold water; pat dry. Trim excess fat. Starting at neck cavity, loosen skin from breast and drumsticks by inserting fingers, gently pushing fingers between skin and meat. Place chopped rosemary and crushed garlic under loosened skin of breast and drumsticks. Lift wing tips up and over back; tuck under chicken. Place chicken, breast side up, on a broiler pan coated with cooking spray. Insert meat thermometer into meaty part of thigh, making sure not to touch bone. Bake at 450° for 30 minutes.
3. Cut a thin slice from end of each onion quarter. Remove white papery skins from garlic heads (do not peel or separate cloves). Cut tops off garlic heads, leaving root ends intact. Brush onion and garlic with oil; arrange around chicken. Reduce oven temperature to 350°; bake an additional 1 hour and 15 minutes or until meat thermometer registers 180°.
4. Cover chicken loosely with foil; let stand 10 minutes. Discard skin. Squeeze garlic heads to extract pulp; serve with French bread, if desired. Garnish with rosemary sprigs, if desired. Yield: 8 servings (serving size: 3 ounces chicken and 1 onion quarter).

CALORIES 231 (30% from fat); FAT 7.7g (sat 1.9g, mono 3.1g, poly 1.6g); PROTEIN 26.5g; CARB 13.5g; FIBER 2.7g; CHOL 76mg; IRON 1.4mg; SODIUM 78mg; CALC 50mg

GRANDMA'S SIMPLE ROAST CHICKEN

PREP: 10 MINUTES   COOK: 1 HOUR

1 (4 to 5-pound) roasting chicken
½ teaspoon salt
½ teaspoon black pepper
½ teaspoon paprika
1 onion, trimmed and quartered
1 celery stalk, cut into 3-inch pieces
1 carrot, cut into 3-inch pieces
1 garlic clove
1 bay leaf
Cooking spray

1. Preheat oven to 400°.
2. Remove and discard giblets and neck from chicken. Rinse chicken with cold water; pat dry. Trim excess fat.
3. Combine salt, pepper, and paprika. Sprinkle seasoning mixture over breast and drumsticks and into the body cavity. Place onion, celery, carrot, garlic, and bay leaf in body cavity. Tie ends of legs together with cord. Lift wing tips up and over back; tuck under chicken.
4. Place chicken, breast side up, on a broiler pan coated with cooking spray. Insert meat thermometer into meaty part of thigh, making sure not to touch bone. Bake at 400° for 1 hour or until thermometer registers 180°. Cover chicken loosely with foil; let stand 10 minutes. Discard skin, vegetables, and bay leaf. Yield: 8 servings (serving size: 3 ounces chicken).

CALORIES 163 (35% from fat); FAT 6.4g (sat 1.7g, mono 2.3g, poly 1.5g); PROTEIN 24.6g; CARB 0.2g; FIBER 0.1g; CHOL 76mg; IRON 1.1mg; SODIUM 220mg; CALC 14mg

Roasting Chicken

Roasting chicken at a high temperature **(450°) for a short time,** then lowering it to a **moderate temperature (350°)** for the remaining cooking time **seals in the juices,** keeping the chicken moist and tender.

We recommend using a roasting chicken. While you can roast a broiler/fryer with good results, chickens specifically for roasting are labeled "roasting broilers." **These birds generally weigh more and are meatier, moister, and more succulent** (due in part to an added salt solution, which increased our sodium figures only negligibly). However, if you are roasting a broiler/fryer which normally weighs about 3 pounds, decrease the baking time by about 45 minutes.

Always roast the chicken on a rack so that fat can drip off and away from the bird.

Don't fret that all of the flavorings are lost when the skin is removed. **The seasonings that are tucked under the skin** will permeate not only the meat, but **the pan drippings** as well, creating flavorful juices for the gravy and sauce.

Let the roasted chicken stand for about 10 minutes after removing it from the oven. This standing time "sets" the juices and **makes for a moister, more flavorful bird.**

ROAST CHICKEN WITH GARLIC GRAVY

PREP: 30 MINUTES
COOK: 1 HOUR 45 MINUTES

If company is coming during the week, put this recipe at the top of your list. All you have to do is put the chicken in the pan and bake it. Though prepared with 10 garlic cloves, their flavor is really quite mild.

1 (3-pound) chicken
1 teaspoon dried thyme
¼ teaspoon salt
¼ teaspoon black pepper
10 garlic cloves, peeled and divided
½ cup dry white wine
1 (14.25-ounce) can fat-free, less-sodium chicken broth, divided
Cooking spray
1 tablespoon all-purpose flour

1. Preheat oven to 325°.
2. Remove and discard giblets and neck from chicken. Rinse chicken with cold water; pat dry. Trim excess fat. Starting at neck cavity, loosen skin from breast and drumsticks by inserting fingers, gently pushing between skin and meat. Rub thyme, salt, and pepper under loosened skin; place 2 garlic cloves in body cavity. Lift wing tips up and over back; tuck under chicken.
3. Combine 8 garlic cloves, wine, and half of broth in a shallow roasting pan lined with foil. Place chicken on a rack coated with cooking spray; place rack in pan. Insert meat thermometer into meaty part of thigh, making sure not to touch bone.
4. Bake at 325° for 1 hour and 45 minutes or until thermometer registers 180°. Place chicken on a platter, reserving pan drippings. Remove chicken from bones, discarding skin. Place meat on platter; keep warm.
5. Place flour in a small saucepan. Gradually add remaining half of broth, stirring with a whisk until blended. Set aside.
6. Place a zip-top plastic bag inside a 2-cup measure. Pour pan drippings into bag; let stand 10 minutes (fat will rise to the top). Seal bag; snip off 1 bottom corner of bag. Drain drippings into flour mixture in pan, stopping before fat layer reaches opening in bag; discard fat.
7. Bring flour mixture to a boil; cook 1 minute or until thick, stirring constantly with a whisk. Serve gravy with chicken. Yield: 4 servings (serving size: 3 ounces chicken and ¼ cup gravy).

CALORIES 265 (32% from fat); FAT 9.3g (sat 2.5g, mono 3.3g, poly 2.1g); PROTEIN 36.5g; CARB 5.5g; FIBER 0.3g; CHOL 109mg; IRON 2.4mg; SODIUM 453mg; CALC 44mg

cornish hens & duck Quite often cornish hens and duck star only in appearance. Not these—their rich flavors will wow you, too!

CORNISH HENS WITH FRUIT-AND-SAUSAGE STUFFING

PREP: 40 MINUTES   COOK: 55 MINUTES

2 (1½-pound) Cornish hens
½ teaspoon Southern France Spice Mix (page 456)
1 teaspoon olive oil
¼ cup chopped shallots
2 cups cubed French bread (about 2 [1-ounce] slices)
1 cup chopped peeled Rome apple
¼ pound diced smoked turkey sausage
¼ cup sweetened dried cranberries (such as Craisins)
¼ cup coarsely chopped pitted prunes
1 teaspoon Southern France Spice Mix (page 456)
½ teaspoon black pepper
⅛ teaspoon salt
4 (1-inch-thick) slices French bread (4 ounces)
2 tablespoons chopped shallots
6 black peppercorns
1 cup apple juice
1 cup cranberry juice cocktail
2 tablespoons dry red wine
2 teaspoons cornstarch
2 tablespoons sweetened dried cranberries (such as Craisins)
½ teaspoon fresh lemon juice
⅛ teaspoon Southern France Spice Mix (page 456)
Chopped fresh parsley (optional)
Sage sprigs (optional)

1. Preheat oven to 350°.
2. Remove and reserve giblets and necks from hens. Rinse hens with cold water; pat dry. Split hens in half lengthwise; trim excess fat. Loosen skin from breasts and drumsticks by inserting fingers, gently pushing between skin and meat. Rub ½ teaspoon Southern France Spice Mix under loosened skin. Set aside.
3. Heat oil in a nonstick skillet over medium-high heat. Add ¼ cup shallots; sauté 2 minutes. Add bread cubes and

Skinning & Splitting Cornish Hens

1. Loosen and remove skin from hens.

2. Split hens in half lengthwise, using kitchen shears or a butcher knife.

next 7 ingredients; cook 1 minute, stirring until well-blended. Remove from heat.

4. Arrange bread slices in a 13 x 9-inch baking dish. Spoon ¾ cup stuffing mixture onto each slice. Place 1 hen half, skin side up, over each mound of stuffing mixture. Bake at 350° for 55 minutes or until juices run clear; keep warm.

5. Cook giblets, necks, 2 tablespoons shallots, and peppercorns in a large nonstick skillet over medium-high heat until browned. Add apple and cranberry juices; bring to a boil. Reduce heat; simmer, uncovered, 20 minutes or until reduced to 1 cup. Strain through a sieve over a bowl; discard solids. Return liquid to skillet. Combine wine and cornstarch in a bowl. Add cornstarch mixture, 2 tablespoons cranberries, lemon juice, and ⅛ teaspoon Southern France Spice Mix to skillet. Bring to a boil. Cook until thick (about 1 minute), stirring constantly. Serve hens with sauce and stuffing. If desired, garnish with parsley and sage. Yield: 4 servings (serving size: 1 hen half, ¾ cup stuffing, and ¼ cup sauce).

CALORIES 556 (24% from fat); FAT 15.1g (sat 3.7g, mono 5.2g, poly 3.6g); PROTEIN 44.1g; CARB 61.2g; FIBER 4g; CHOL 115mg; IRON 4.2mg; SODIUM 683mg; CALC 109mg

MOROCCAN CORNISH HENS

PREP: 30 MINUTES
MARINATE: 2 HOURS
COOK: 1 HOUR 25 MINUTES

For extra flavor you can marinate the hens up to 24 hours.

¼ cup balsamic vinegar
¼ cup dry Marsala
2 tablespoons honey
2 large oranges, sliced
1 cup whole pitted dates (about 8 ounces)
2 (1½-pound) Cornish hens
¼ cup pimento-stuffed olives
1 cup cilantro sprigs
1 teaspoon ground cumin
¼ teaspoon ground cardamom
⅛ teaspoon ground coriander
6 garlic cloves

1. Combine vinegar, Marsala, and honey; stir with a whisk until well-blended. Cover and refrigerate up to 2 days, if desired.

2. Arrange orange slices in a 13 x 9-inch baking dish, and sprinkle evenly with 1 cup dates.

3. Remove and discard giblets and necks from hens. Rinse hens with cold water; pat dry. Remove skin; trim excess fat. Split hens in half lengthwise. Place hen halves, meaty sides up, on dates. Arrange olives around hens.

4. Place cilantro in a food processor; pulse 6 to 8 times or until coarsely chopped. Add cumin, cardamom, coriander, and garlic; process until finely chopped. Pat cilantro mixture evenly onto hens.

5. Slowly pour vinegar mixture over hens. Cover and marinate in refrigerator 2 to 24 hours, basting once.

6. Preheat oven to 350°.

7. Uncover hens, and bake at 350° for 1 hour and 25 minutes or until juices run clear, basting occasionally with marinade. Shield wings with foil, if needed. Yield: 4 servings.

Note: This recipe makes a great party entrée; it can easily be doubled to make 8 servings.

CALORIES 411 (14% from fat); FAT 6.2g (sat 1.5g, mono 2g, poly 1.4g); PROTEIN 37.2g; CARB 54.9g; FIBER 7.1g; CHOL 114mg; IRON 3.4mg; SODIUM 224mg; CALC 95mg

Cornish hens are small, specially-bred chickens that typically weigh less than 1½ pounds. You'll enjoy them for their delicate, tender meat.

Honey-Apple Glazed
Hens With Rice Pilaf

HONEY-APPLE GLAZED HENS WITH RICE PILAF

PREP:10 MINUTES   COOK:40 MINUTES

2 (1½-pound) Cornish hens
Wild Rice-Apple Pilaf (page 255)
¼ cup honey
2 tablespoons apple juice
1 teaspoon grated lemon rind
1 tablespoon fresh lemon juice
1 teaspoon low-sodium soy sauce
Granny Smith apple slices (optional)
Rosemary sprigs (optional)

1. Preheat oven to 400°.
2. Remove and discard giblets and necks from hens. Rinse hens with cold water; pat dry. Remove skin; trim excess fat. Split hens in half lengthwise.
3. Spoon 4 (¾-cup) mounds of Wild Rice-Apple Pilaf onto a jelly-roll pan lined with foil. Place hens, meaty sides up, over rice mounds. Combine honey, apple juice, lemon rind, lemon juice, and soy sauce in a bowl. Brush over hens. Bake at 400° for 40 minutes or until juices run clear, basting every 10 minutes. Garnish with apple slices and rosemary, if desired. Yield: 4 servings (serving size: 1 hen half and ¾ cup rice pilaf).

CALORIES 467 (14% from fat); FAT 7.3g (sat 1.7g, mono 2.5g, poly 1.8g); PROTEIN 39.4g; CARB 59.5g; FIBER 2.7g; CHOL 114mg; IRON 2.3mg; SODIUM 828mg; CALC 35mg

SEARED DUCK BREAST WITH BULGUR SALAD AND ORANGE DRESSING

PREP:35 MINUTES   COOK:30 MINUTES

1 cup canned vegetable broth
½ cup uncooked bulgur or cracked wheat
2 cups (½-inch) cubed peeled sweet potato
Cooking spray
¼ cup sweetened dried cranberries (such as Craisins)
1 cup boiling water
1 cup coarsely chopped gourmet salad greens
½ teaspoon salt, divided
½ teaspoon black pepper, divided
¼ cup thawed orange juice concentrate
2 teaspoons olive oil
1 teaspoon chopped shallots
1 teaspoon water
4 (6-ounce) boned duck breast halves

1. Preheat oven to 400°.
2. Bring broth to a boil, and add bulgur. Cover and let stand 30 minutes. Fluff with a fork.
3. Place sweet potato on a baking sheet coated with cooking spray. Bake at 400° for 15 minutes or until tender, stirring occasionally.
4. Combine cranberries and 1 cup boiling water in a bowl; cover and let stand 15 minutes. Drain well.
5. Combine bulgur, sweet potato, cranberries, and salad greens in a bowl; sprinkle with ¼ teaspoon salt and ¼ teaspoon pepper, and toss. Cover and chill.
6. Combine juice concentrate, oil, shallots, and 1 teaspoon water in a blender; process until smooth.
7. Wrap handle of a large nonstick skillet with foil; coat skillet with cooking spray. Place pan over medium-high heat

until hot. Sprinkle duck with ¼ teaspoon salt and ¼ teaspoon pepper. Place duck, skin side down, in pan; reduce heat to medium, and cook 20 minutes or until skin is browned (pour off fat frequently).

8. Insert meat thermometer into thickest portion of boned duck breast half. Place pan in oven, and bake at 400° for 10 minutes or until thermometer registers 180°. Discard skin; cut breast meat into ¼-inch-thick strips.

9. Arrange bulgur-sweet potato mixture and duck on 4 serving plates; drizzle with orange dressing. Yield: 4 servings (serving size: 3 ounces duck, about 1 cup bulgur-sweet potato mixture, and 1½ tablespoons dressing).

Note: Substitute pork tenderloin (cooked to 160°) or boned chicken breasts (cooked to 180°) for duck, if desired.

CALORIES 437 (22% from fat); FAT 10.7g (sat 2.6g, mono 3.9g, poly 1.4g); PROTEIN 38g; CARB 46.5g; FIBER 6.7g; CHOL 88mg; IRON 8.8mg; SODIUM 659mg; CALC 38mg

turkey
Turkey's no longer reserved for just holiday meals. You'll see that these favorites offer worldwide, year-round fare.

SAUSAGE, GARLIC, AND MUSHROOM PIZZA

PREP:30 MINUTES   COOK:12 MINUTES

    8 ounces turkey Italian sausage
       Cooking spray
    4 cups finely chopped
       mushrooms (about 12 ounces)
    ½ cup diced onion
    6 garlic cloves, minced
    ¼ cup evaporated fat-free milk
    3 tablespoons chopped fresh parsley
    ½ cup (2 ounces) shredded
       provolone cheese
    1 (12-inch) Whole-Wheat Pizza
       Crust (page 103)
    ¼ cup grated fresh Romano cheese

1. Preheat oven to 500°.
2. Cook sausage in a large nonstick skillet over medium-high heat until browned, stirring to crumble. Drain. Wipe drippings from pan with a paper towel.
3. Coat pan with cooking spray; place over medium-high heat until hot. Add mushrooms, onion, and garlic; sauté 7 minutes or until liquid evaporates. Add milk and parsley; cook 2 minutes.
4. Sprinkle provolone cheese over prepared crust, leaving a ½-inch border. Spread mushroom mixture evenly over cheese, and top with turkey sausage. Sprinkle Romano cheese over pizza. Bake on bottom rack of oven at 500° for 12 minutes. Remove to a cutting board; serve immediately. Yield: 6 servings.

CALORIES 263 (29% from fat); FAT 8.6g (sat 3.5g, mono 2.5g, poly 1.6g); PROTEIN 16.8g; CARB 31.3g; FIBER 3.9g; CHOL 43mg; IRON 2.2mg; SODIUM 467mg; CALC 163mg

TEX-MEX RICE AND BEAN STACK

PREP:12 MINUTES   COOK:17 MINUTES

    5 (5-inch) corn tortillas
       Cooking spray
    ½ pound ground turkey breast
    1 (16-ounce) can pinto beans
    1 (14½-ounce) can no-salt-added
       diced tomatoes
    3 tablespoons no-salt-added
       tomato paste
    1 tablespoon chili powder
    ¾ teaspoon ground cumin
    ¼ teaspoon salt
    2 cups hot cooked long-grain rice
    ½ cup (2 ounces) shredded reduced-
       fat Monterey Jack cheese
    ¼ cup thinly sliced green onions

1. Preheat oven to 400°.
2. Cut each tortilla into 8 wedges; arrange in a single layer on a baking sheet. Bake at 400° for 10 minutes or until crisp.
3. Coat a large nonstick skillet with cooking spray; place over medium-high heat until hot. Add turkey; cook until browned, stirring to crumble. Add beans and next 5 ingredients; bring to a boil. Reduce heat; simmer, uncovered, until thick (about 10 minutes), stirring occasionally.
4. Spoon rice onto a serving platter; top with turkey mixture, cheese, and green onions. Arrange tortilla chips around edge of platter. Yield: 4 servings (serving size: ¾ cup turkey mixture, ½ cup rice, 2 tablespoons cheese, 1 tablespoon green onions, and 10 tortilla chips).

CALORIES 438 (11% from fat); FAT 5.4g (sat 2.1g, mono 1.3g, poly 1g); PROTEIN 29.1g; CARB 69.1g; FIBER 7.1g; CHOL 43mg; IRON 5.1mg; SODIUM 568mg; CALC 280mg

For Tex-Mex Rice and Bean Stack, use chips to scoop up the rice and bean mixture—like eating nachos.

Southern Brunch Soufflé With Chives

PREP:30 MINUTES   COOK:1 HOUR

The "Southern" part of this recipe is the grits. With the addition of turkey sausage, the soufflé makes a filling breakfast or brunch dish.

½ pound turkey breakfast sausage
2 (14.25-ounce) cans fat-free, less-sodium chicken broth
1 cup uncooked quick-cooking grits
2 teaspoons Dijon mustard
½ teaspoon salt
¼ teaspoon black pepper
⅓ cup light Gournay cheese with garlic and fine herbs (such as Boursin)
1 (4-ounce) carton egg substitute
½ cup chopped fresh or freeze-dried chives
5 large egg whites
½ teaspoon cream of tartar
Cooking spray

1. Preheat oven to 400°.
2. Cook sausage in a large saucepan over medium heat until browned, stirring to crumble. Drain. Wipe drippings from pan with a paper towel.
3. Bring broth to a boil in pan; gradually stir in grits. Cover, reduce heat, and simmer 7 minutes, stirring occasionally. Remove from heat; add sausage, mustard, salt, pepper, and cheese, stirring until cheese melts.
4. Place egg substitute in a large bowl. Gradually add hot grits mixture to egg substitute, stirring constantly with a whisk. Stir in chives.
5. Beat egg whites and cream of tartar at high speed of a mixer until stiff peaks form. Gently stir one-fourth of egg white mixture into grits mixture. Gently fold in remaining egg white mixture.

6. Coat bottom of a 2-quart soufflé dish with cooking spray. Pour mixture into dish (mixture will fill dish). Bake at 400° for 10 minutes.
7. Reduce oven temperature to 375° (do not remove dish from oven). Bake an additional 50 minutes or until puffed and golden. Serve immediately. Yield: 6 servings.

CALORIES 237 (31% from fat); FAT 8.1g (sat 2.7g, mono 2.4g, poly 1.9g); PROTEIN 15.7g; CARB 23g; FIBER 1.4g; CHOL 40mg; IRON 1.8mg; SODIUM 722mg; CALC 45mg

Turkey Cutlets With Balsamic-Brown Sugar Sauce

PREP:8 MINUTES   COOK:17 MINUTES

¼ cup all-purpose flour
1 teaspoon salt
1 teaspoon dried thyme
½ teaspoon black pepper
1 pound turkey cutlets
1 tablespoon olive oil
¼ cup minced shallots
⅔ cup dry red wine
⅔ cup fat-free, less-sodium chicken broth
¼ cup balsamic vinegar
2 tablespoons brown sugar
¼ teaspoon salt
Thyme sprigs (optional)

1. Combine first 4 ingredients in a shallow dish; dredge turkey cutlets in flour mixture.
2. Heat oil in a nonstick skillet over medium-high heat. Add cutlets; cook 3 minutes on each side or until done. Remove to a serving platter; keep warm.
3. Add shallots to pan, and sauté 1 minute over medium heat. Add wine and broth; stir with a wooden spoon, scraping bottom of pan to loosen browned bits. Bring to a boil, and cook over medium heat 5 minutes. Add

vinegar, sugar, and ¼ teaspoon salt; bring to a boil. Reduce heat, and simmer 3 minutes. Spoon sauce over cutlets. Garnish with thyme sprigs, if desired. Yield: 4 servings (serving size: 3 ounces turkey and 2 tablespoons sauce).

CALORIES 216 (22% from fat); FAT 5.2g (sat 1.1g, mono 2.8g, poly 0.8g); PROTEIN 27.8g; CARB 12.6g; FIBER 0.4g; CHOL 68mg; IRON 2.8mg; SODIUM 928mg; CALC 35mg

Turkey Cutlets With Apple Chutney

PREP:9 MINUTES   CHILL:20 MINUTES
COOK:50 MINUTES

1¼ cups chopped Granny Smith apple (about 5 ounces)
1 cup diced tomato
¾ cup thinly sliced onion
3 tablespoons brown sugar
2 tablespoons cider vinegar
⅛ teaspoon ground cloves
⅛ teaspoon ground ginger
4 (2-ounce) turkey cutlets
⅛ teaspoon salt
Dash of white pepper
1 teaspoon oil

1. Combine first 7 ingredients in a medium saucepan, and bring to a boil. Cover, reduce heat, and simmer 45 minutes, stirring occasionally. Remove apple mixture from heat, and let stand 10 minutes; cover and chill.
2. Sprinkle turkey with salt and pepper. Heat oil in a large nonstick skillet over medium-high heat. Add turkey to pan; cook 2 minutes on each side or until done. Serve turkey with apple chutney. Yield: 2 servings (serving size: 2 cutlets and ¼ cup chutney).
Note: Refrigerate remaining chutney in an airtight container for up to 2 weeks.

CALORIES 277 (12% from fat); FAT 3.7g (sat 0.7g, mono 0.9g, poly 1.5g); PROTEIN 27.3g; CARB 35.3g; FIBER 4.2g; CHOL 71mg; IRON 2.4mg; SODIUM 207mg; CALC 47mg

GLAZED TURKEY CUTLETS AND BELL PEPPERS

PREP: 6 MINUTES

COOK: 8 MINUTES

Turkey cutlets are slices of breast meat. They're great for quick meals—they cook in just minutes!

¼ cup fat-free, less-sodium
   chicken broth
3 tablespoons balsamic vinegar
2 teaspoons honey
¼ teaspoon salt
¼ teaspoon black pepper
1 pound (¼-inch-thick) turkey
   breast cutlets
2 teaspoons olive oil
2 garlic cloves, minced
1 red bell pepper, seeded and cut
   into strips
1 green bell pepper, seeded and cut
   into strips

1. Combine first 3 ingredients in a bowl.
2. Sprinkle salt and black pepper over both sides of cutlets.
3. Heat oil in a large nonstick skillet over medium-high heat until hot. Add garlic; sauté 30 seconds. Add cutlets, and cook 2 minutes on each side or until done. Remove cutlets from pan, and keep warm.
4. Reduce heat to medium; add bell peppers, and sauté 2 minutes. Add broth mixture to pan, and cook 30 seconds, stirring constantly. Spoon sauce and bell peppers over cutlets. Yield: 4 servings (serving size: 3 ounces turkey and ⅓ cup bell pepper mixture).

CALORIES 180 (22% from fat); FAT 4.3g (sat 0.9g, mono 2g, poly 0.8g); PROTEIN 27.3g; CARB 7g; FIBER 1g; CHOL 68mg; IRON 2.3mg; SODIUM 279mg; CALC 21mg

Glazed Turkey Cutlets and Bell Peppers

TURKEY CUTLETS WITH ORANGE-MUSTARD GLAZE

PREP: 7 MINUTES   COOK: 7 MINUTES

3 tablespoons frozen orange juice
   concentrate
2 teaspoons stone-ground mustard
2 tablespoons water
6 (2-ounce) turkey cutlets
4 garlic cloves, crushed
2 teaspoons stick margarine or
   butter

1. Combine first 3 ingredients in a bowl. Prick both sides of cutlets with a fork; rub crushed garlic onto both sides of cutlets.
2. Melt margarine in a large skillet over medium-high heat. Add cutlets, and cook 2 minutes on each side or until done. Remove from pan; keep warm. Reduce heat to low; add orange juice mixture. Cook until thoroughly heated, stirring constantly. Return cutlets to pan, and spoon sauce over cutlets. Yield: 3 servings (serving size: 2 cutlets and 4 teaspoons sauce).

CALORIES 182 (18% from fat); FAT 3.6g (sat 0.8g, mono 0.9g, poly 1.2g); PROTEIN 27.4g; CARB 8.3g; FIBER 0.2g; CHOL 68mg; IRON 1.5mg; SODIUM 196mg; CALC 27mg

TURKEY PAPRIKASH

PREP: 12 MINUTES
COOK: 13 MINUTES

1 (8-ounce) package medium egg
   noodles, uncooked
2 tablespoons tomato paste
1 (8-ounce) carton plain low-fat
   yogurt
2 teaspoons vegetable oil
1 cup slivered onion
2 garlic cloves, minced
1 pound turkey tenderloin, cut
   into ½-inch pieces
⅓ cup fat-free, less-sodium
   chicken broth
2 tablespoons Hungarian sweet
   paprika
¾ teaspoon salt
¼ teaspoon black pepper

1. Cook egg noodles according to package directions, omitting salt and fat;
drain well. Combine tomato paste and
yogurt.
2. Heat oil in a large nonstick skillet
over medium heat. Add onion, garlic,
and turkey; sauté 5 minutes or until
turkey is no longer pink. Stir in broth,
paprika, salt, and pepper. Cover, reduce
heat, and simmer 5 minutes. Remove
from heat; let stand 1 minute. Stir in
yogurt mixture and egg noodles. Yield:
6 servings (serving size: 1⅓ cups).

CALORIES 293 (16% from fat); FAT 5.2g (sat 1.4g, mono 1.3g,
poly 1.7g); PROTEIN 26g; CARB 34.7g; FIBER 2.3g;
CHOL 84mg; IRON 3.4mg; SODIUM 416mg; CALC 104mg

TURKEY TENDERLOINS WITH PAPAYA SALSA

PREP: 23 MINUTES
MARINATE: 30 MINUTES
COOK: 20 MINUTES

1¼ cups diced peeled papaya
½ cup diced red onion
½ cup coarsely chopped plum
   tomato (about 1 large)
2 tablespoons chopped fresh
   cilantro
1 teaspoon grated lime rind
1½ tablespoons fresh lime
   juice
1 teaspoon grated peeled fresh
   ginger
¼ cup raspberry or white
   wine vinegar
2 tablespoons fresh lime juice
1½ tablespoons Dijon mustard
1 tablespoon chopped fresh or
   1 teaspoon dried rosemary
1 tablespoon minced fresh or
   1 teaspoon dried thyme
2 teaspoons olive oil
2 (½-pound) turkey tenderloins
Cooking spray

1. Combine first 7 ingredients in a
bowl; cover and chill.
2. Preheat broiler.
3. Combine vinegar and next 6 ingredients in a large zip-top plastic bag; seal
bag, and marinate in refrigerator 30
minutes. Remove turkey from bag, reserving marinade.
4. Place turkey on a broiler pan coated
with cooking spray; broil 10 minutes
on each side or until done, basting frequently with marinade. Cut tenderloins into thin slices; serve with papaya
salsa. Yield: 4 servings (serving size:
3 ounces turkey and ½ cup salsa).

CALORIES 204 (26% from fat); FAT 5.8g (sat 1.2g, mono 2.2g,
poly 1g); PROTEIN 26.1g; CARB 10.5g; FIBER 1.8g;
CHOL 59mg; IRON 1.6mg; SODIUM 228mg; CALC 43mg

TURKEY WITH GOLDEN MUSHROOM GRAVY

PREP: 8 MINUTES   COOK: 50 MINUTES

*Dijon mustard rounds out the flavor in
this recipe's rich mushroom gravy.*

2 teaspoons vegetable oil
1 pound turkey tenderloin, cut
   into ½-inch pieces
1 large onion, sliced
   (about 2 cups)
1 (8-ounce) package presliced
   mushrooms
½ cup water
1 tablespoon Dijon mustard
1 (10½-ounce) can beef broth
5 ounces uncooked medium
   egg noodles
½ cup fat-free milk
1 tablespoon all-purpose flour
⅛ teaspoon black pepper
Chopped fresh parsley (optional)

1. Heat oil in a large nonstick skillet
over medium-high heat; add turkey.
Sauté 9 minutes or until lightly
browned. Remove turkey from pan.
2. Add onion to pan; sauté 5 minutes.
Add mushrooms; sauté 5 minutes or
until tender. Stir in water, mustard, and
broth. Return turkey to pan; bring to a
boil. Cover, reduce heat, and simmer 20
minutes.
3. Cook noodles in boiling water 8
minutes or until "al dente;" drain.
4. Combine milk, flour, and pepper,
stirring with a whisk. Add to turkey
mixture. Simmer until slightly thick
(about 5 minutes), stirring constantly.
Serve turkey and gravy over noodles;
garnish with parsley, if desired. Yield: 4
servings (serving size: 1 cup turkey
mixture and 1 cup noodles).

CALORIES 369 (15% from fat); FAT 6.2g (sat 1.4g, mono 1.5g,
poly 2.1g); PROTEIN 38.3g; CARB 38.7g; FIBER 3.2g;
CHOL 102mg; IRON 4.3mg; SODIUM 615mg; CALC 86mg

THYME-AND-GARLIC ROASTED TURKEY BREAST

PREP: 13 MINUTES
COOK: 1 HOUR 15 MINUTES

If you prefer to roast a whole turkey, start with a 12-pound bird. Place herb mixture under skin as directed. Truss according to directions at right. Bake at 350° for 3 hours or until thermometer placed in thigh registers 180°.

  2 teaspoons minced fresh thyme
  1 teaspoon grated lemon rind
 ¼ teaspoon coarsely ground
      black pepper
 ⅛ teaspoon salt
  2 garlic cloves, crushed
  1 (5-pound) turkey breast
Cooking spray
  1 lemon, quartered
  6 thyme sprigs
Additional thyme sprigs (optional)

1. Preheat oven to 400°.
2. Combine first 5 ingredients in a small bowl. Starting at neck edge, loosen skin from turkey breast by inserting fingers, gently pushing between skin and meat. Rub thyme mixture under loosened skin. Gently press skin to secure.
3. Place breast, skin side up, on a broiler pan coated with cooking spray. Place lemon quarters and 6 thyme sprigs in cavity. Insert meat thermometer into meaty part of breast, making sure not to touch bone. Bake at 400° for 1 hour and 15 minutes or until thermometer registers 170°. Let stand 10 minutes. Remove skin, and discard. Cut breast into thin slices; garnish with additional thyme sprigs, if desired. Yield: 6 servings (serving size: 6 ounces).

CALORIES 256 (6% from fat); FAT 1.6g (sat 0.4g, mono 0.2g, poly 0.4g); PROTEIN 56.4g; CARB 0.4g; FIBER 0g; CHOL 156mg; IRON 3mg; SODIUM 146mg; CALC 26mg

trussing and baking
Trussing gives a turkey (or any other bird) a smooth, compact shape so it will cook evenly and retain moisture.

1. Remove outer packaging and the packages containing the giblets and neck from the body and neck cavities (you may need to release the band of skin or the wire or plastic lock from the legs before the neck can be removed). Rinse the body and neck cavities and the outside of the turkey with cold, running water, and pat dry. Trim excess fat.

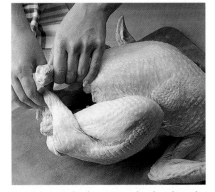

2. Massage the legs to make the skin pliable. When you secure the legs, tuck the excess skin between the breast and the legs so the skin won't split as the turkey cooks. Secure the legs.

3. Lift the tips of the wings up and over the breast to the back, and tuck them under the turkey; secure the excess skin of the neck flap (if necessary, use a wooden pick).
Note: The wishbone can be removed before cooking to make carving the breast meat easier. Pull the neck flap back, and feel along the breast until you locate the wishbone. Using a sharp, narrow-blade knife, cut along both sides of the wishbone and around the top edge. Place your fingers around the wishbone, and pull it loose.

4. Line the bottom of a shallow roasting pan with aluminum foil for easier cleanup. Place turkey on chopped onion, if desired; coat with cooking spray. Insert a meat thermometer in the meaty part of the thigh, making sure it doesn't touch the bone. Check the internal temperature of the turkey at the beginning of the last hour of the cooking time so you don't overcook it. If the turkey is browning too fast, make a tent of aluminum foil to shield the breast. After removing the turkey from the oven, cut a small slit between the thigh and the rib cage to release the juices. Let stand 10 minutes before carving.

Blast Furnace-Roasted Turkey

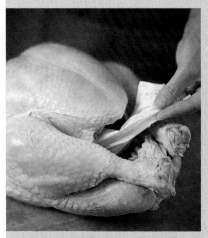

1. Remove and discard giblets and neck from turkey. Rinse turkey with cold water; pat dry.

2. Starting at neck cavity, loosen skin from breast and drumsticks by inserting fingers, gently pushing between skin and meat.

3. Rub herb mixture on breast and drumsticks under loosened skin.

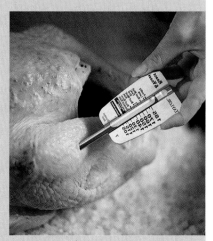

4. Tie ends of legs together with cord.

5. Spread rock salt evenly in bottom of a shallow roasting pan.

6. Insert meat thermometer into meaty part of thigh, making sure not to touch the bone.

The skin of the turkey blackens somewhat, but it is discarded.
Surprisingly, the salt doesn't add any sodium to the Blast Furnace-Roasted Turkey.

BLAST FURNACE-ROASTED TURKEY

PREP: 25 MINUTES
COOK: 1 HOUR 20 MINUTES

1 (12-pound) fresh or frozen turkey, thawed
1 tablespoon salt
3 tablespoons chopped fresh parsley
2 tablespoons minced fresh chives
2 tablespoons minced fresh thyme
2 tablespoons minced fresh sage
2 tablespoons minced shallots
1 teaspoon freshly ground black pepper
8 cups rock salt

1. Preheat oven to 500°.

2. Remove and discard giblets and neck from turkey. Rinse turkey with cold water; pat dry. Trim excess fat. Starting at neck cavity, loosen skin from breast and drumsticks by inserting fingers, gently pushing between skin and meat. Lift wing tips up and over back; tuck under turkey.

3. Combine 1 tablespoon salt and next 6 ingredients; rub herb mixture under loosened skin on breast and drumsticks. Tie ends of legs together with cord.

4. Spread rock salt evenly in bottom of a shallow roasting pan. Place turkey, breast side up, on rock salt. Insert meat thermometer into meaty part of thigh, making sure not to touch bone. Bake at 500° for 1 hour and 20 minutes or until thermometer registers 180° and juices run clear. Cover turkey loosely with foil; let stand 10 minutes. Discard skin. Yield: 12 servings (serving size: 6 ounces).

CALORIES 319 (26% from fat); FAT 9.3g (sat 3.1g, mono 1.9g, poly 2.7g); PROTEIN 54.6g; CARB 0.7g; FIBER 0.2g; CHOL 141mg; IRON 3.6mg; SODIUM 716mg; CALC 57mg

carving a turkey
To make a turkey easier to carve, let it stand for 10 minutes after removing it from the oven. Place a few paper towels on the platter under the turkey to absorb the juices and to keep the bird from sliding as you carve. Use a large, two-tined carving fork and a long, narrow-blade knife with a very sharp edge.

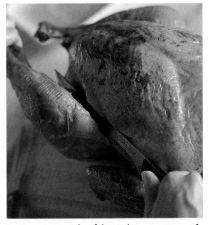

1. Carve one side of the turkey at a time. After cutting and discarding the cord used to tie the legs, grab the end of one of the drumsticks, and pull it away from the body. To free the leg (drumstick plus thigh), follow the knife along the contour of the body, cutting underneath the dark thigh meat.

2. Separate the drumstick and thigh by severing the leg joint. Remove the skin from the thigh, and discard. Cut the thigh meat off the bone, and slice it into pieces. Repeat for the drumstick, or leave the drumstick whole.

3. Remove half of the breast by cutting into the center of the breast meat and slicing downward along the breastbone and rib cage. Remove the skin from the breast half, and discard.

4. Place the breast half on the cutting surface. Holding it steady with the carving fork, slice it evenly against the grain of the meat into serving-size pieces. Repeat process for the other side of the turkey.

To substitute a 5-pound turkey breast for a 12-pound turkey, bake the breast at 350° for 1 hour and 45 minutes **or until a meat thermometer registers 170°.**

FRESH-HERB TURKEY

PREP: 20 MINUTES

COOK: 3 HOURS 15 MINUTES

1   (12-pound) fresh or frozen
      turkey, thawed
2   tablespoons chopped fresh sage
3   teaspoons chopped fresh chives,
      divided
2   teaspoons chopped fresh thyme,
      divided
1   teaspoon chopped fresh
      parsley
   Cooking spray
2¾ cups fat-free, less-sodium
      chicken broth, divided
⅓   cup dry sherry
2   tablespoons all-purpose flour
2   tablespoons chopped fresh
      parsley

1. Preheat oven to 350°.
2. Remove and discard giblets and neck from turkey. Rinse turkey with cold water; pat dry. Trim excess fat. Starting at neck cavity, loosen skin from breast and drumsticks by inserting fingers, gently pushing between skin and meat. Combine sage, 2 teaspoons chives, 1 teaspoon thyme, and 1 teaspoon parsley in a small bowl. Rub sage mixture under loosened skin and into body cavity. Tie ends of legs

SELECTING A TURKEY

Look for a fresh, unbasted turkey. A prebasted bird is usually injected with a mixture of broth, vegetable oil, and seasonings. Reading the label will help you tell if the turkey has been prebasted.

THAWING A TURKEY

The best—and safest—way to thaw a turkey is in the refrigerator. Leave the frozen turkey in its original wrapper and place it **in a large shallow pan to catch any juices.** Keep refrigerated. It will thaw in three to four days. You should allow about 5 hours per pound for it to thaw. Once thawed, a turkey should be cooked immediately.

with cord. Lift wing tips up and over back; tuck under bird.
3. Place turkey on a broiler pan coated with cooking spray. Insert meat thermometer into meaty part of thigh, making sure not to touch bone. Bake at 350° for 3 hours or until thermometer registers 180°. (Cover turkey loosely with foil if it gets too brown.) Remove turkey from oven. Cover loosely with foil; let stand at least 10 minutes.
4. Place a heavy-duty zip-top plastic bag inside a 2-cup glass measure. Pour drippings from pan into bag; let stand 10 minutes (fat will rise to the top). Seal bag; carefully snip off 1 bottom corner of bag. Drain drippings into a medium saucepan, stopping before fat layer reaches opening; discard fat. Stir 2½ cups broth and sherry into drippings in saucepan. Bring to a boil; reduce heat, and simmer 10 minutes.
5. Combine ¼ cup broth and flour in a bowl, stirring well with a whisk. Stir into sherry mixture; bring to a boil, stirring constantly. Stir in 2 tablespoons parsley, 1 teaspoon chives, and 1 teaspoon thyme. Serve sauce with turkey. Yield: 12 servings

(serving size: 6 ounces turkey and ¼ cup sauce).

CALORIES 264 (14% from fat); FAT 4.1g (sat 1.4g, mono 0.9g, poly 1.2g); PROTEIN 51.4g; CARB 1.7g; FIBER 0.1g; CHOL 142mg; IRON 3.1mg; SODIUM 211mg; CALC 35mg

HONEY-APPLE TURKEY WITH GRAVY

PREP: 25 MINUTES   MARINATE: 24 HOURS

COOK: 3 HOURS 25 MINUTES

1   (12-pound) fresh or frozen
      turkey, thawed
½   cup packed brown sugar
½   cup water
4   cups apple juice
¼   cup cider vinegar
½   teaspoon salt
¼   teaspoon black pepper
   Cooking spray
½   cup fat-free, less-sodium
      chicken broth
¼   cup Calvados (apple brandy)
3   tablespoons honey
¼   cup all-purpose flour

1. Remove and discard giblets and neck from turkey. Rinse turkey with cold water; pat dry. Trim excess fat. Tie ends of legs with cord. Lift wing tips up and over back; tuck under turkey.
2. Combine sugar and water in a medium saucepan; cook over medium heat until sugar dissolves (about 5 minutes), stirring frequently. Remove from heat; stir in apple juice, vinegar, salt, and pepper. Pour mixture into a 2-gallon heavy-duty zip-top plastic bag; add turkey. Seal bag, and marinate in refrigerator 24 hours. Remove turkey from bag, reserving 2¾ cups marinade; discard remaining marinade.

3. Preheat oven to 325°.

4. Place turkey on a broiler pan coated with cooking spray. Insert a meat thermometer into meaty part of thigh, making sure not to touch bone. Bake at 325° for 3 hours and 10 minutes or until thermometer registers 180°, basting occasionally with 2 cups reserved marinade. (Cover turkey loosely with foil if it gets too brown.) Remove turkey from oven. Cover turkey loosely with foil; let stand at least 10 minutes before carving. Discard skin.

5. Place a heavy-duty zip-top plastic bag inside a 2-cup glass measure. Pour drippings from pan into bag; let stand 10 minutes (fat will rise to the top). Seal bag; carefully snip off 1 bottom corner of bag. Drain drippings into a medium saucepan, stopping before fat layer reaches opening; discard fat. Add ½ cup reserved marinade, broth, brandy, and honey to pan. Combine ¼ cup reserved marinade and flour in a small bowl, stirring with a whisk; add to gravy mixture in saucepan. Bring to a boil; reduce heat, and simmer 15 minutes, stirring frequently. Serve gravy with turkey. Yield: 12 servings (serving size: 6 ounces turkey and 2 tablespoons gravy).

CALORIES 328 (11% from fat); FAT 4.1g (sat 1.4g, mono 0.9g, poly 1.2g); PROTEIN 50.9g; CARB 19g; FIBER 0.2g; CHOL 142mg; IRON 3.4mg; SODIUM 175mg; CALC 39mg

ORANGE-BOURBON TURKEY

PREP: 15 MINUTES

MARINATE: 4 HOURS

COOK: 3 HOURS 17 MINUTES

The marinade of fresh orange juice, bourbon, and molasses doubles as a tangy sauce.

  1 (12-pound) fresh or frozen turkey, thawed
  2 cups fresh orange juice (about 6 oranges)
  1 cup water
  ¾ cup bourbon, divided
  ⅓ cup molasses
  ¾ teaspoon salt, divided
  4 oranges, peeled
    Cooking spray
  3 tablespoons all-purpose flour
    Orange slices (optional)
    Flat-leaf parsley sprigs (optional)

1. Remove and discard giblets and neck from turkey. Rinse turkey with cold water; pat dry. Trim excess fat. Combine orange juice, water, ½ cup bourbon, and molasses in a 2-gallon heavy-duty zip-top plastic bag; add turkey. Seal bag, and marinate in refrigerator 4 to 24 hours, turning bag occasionally. Remove turkey from bag, reserving marinade.

2. Preheat oven to 350°.

3. Sprinkle ½ teaspoon salt into body cavity. Stuff cavity with oranges. Tie ends of legs with cord. Lift wing tips up and over back, and tuck under turkey. Place turkey on a broiler pan coated with cooking spray. Insert meat thermometer into meaty part of thigh, making sure not to touch bone.

4. Bake at 350° for 3 hours or until thermometer registers 180°. (Cover turkey loosely with foil if it gets too brown.) Remove turkey from oven. Cover turkey loosely with foil, and let stand at least 10 minutes before carving. Discard oranges.

5. Pour reserved marinade into a saucepan; bring to a boil. Skim foam from mixture with a slotted spoon; discard. Reduce heat to medium; cook until reduced to 3½ cups (about 15 minutes).

6. Combine ¼ cup bourbon and flour in a small bowl, stirring well with a whisk. Add to reduced marinade; bring to a boil, and cook 1 minute, stirring constantly. Stir in ¼ teaspoon salt. Serve sauce with turkey. If desired, garnish with orange slices and parsley sprigs. Yield: 12 servings (serving size: 6 ounces turkey and ¼ cup sauce).

CALORIES 305 (12% from fat); FAT 4.1g (sat 1.3g, mono 0.9g, poly 1.2g); PROTEIN 51g; CARB 12.8g; FIBER 0.1g; CHOL 142mg; IRON 3.5mg; SODIUM 251mg; CALC 54mg

GRAVY TIPS

• **Pour pan drippings into a zip-top plastic bag.** Snip one corner of the bag, and pour out just the drippings that will have settled to the bottom of the bag.

(Be alert—the drippings will drain fast.)

• **Before pouring into the bag, let the drippings cool a bit, or they'll melt the bag.**

• **Thoroughly whisk** the flour and drippings to prevent lumps.

If a turkey begins to brown too much before it's done, "tent" or cover it loosely with foil.

This turkey is no run-of-the-mill bird. Fresh citrus and sweet maple syrup offer familiar flavors to a holiday meal. **Keep the skin on while roasting to keep the turkey moist. Pull off the skin when carving.**

ORANGE AND MAPLE ROASTED TURKEY WITH GIBLET GRAVY

PREP: 20 MINUTES
COOK: 3 HOURS

¾ cup orange juice
¼ cup maple syrup
1 (12-pound) fresh or frozen whole turkey, thawed
1 tablespoon poultry seasoning
1 tablespoon grated orange rind
½ teaspoon salt, divided
½ teaspoon black pepper, divided
1 medium orange, quartered
1 medium onion, quartered
Cooking spray
1 teaspoon stick margarine or butter
½ cup water
2 (10.5-ounce) cans low-sodium chicken broth
2 tablespoons fresh orange juice
5 teaspoons cornstarch
1 tablespoon maple syrup
¼ teaspoon grated orange rind
Herb sprigs (optional)
Red grapes (optional)

1. Combine ¾ cup orange juice and ¼ cup maple syrup in a small saucepan, and bring just to a boil. Remove from heat, and set aside.
2. Preheat oven to 375°.
3. Remove giblets, liver, and neck from turkey; set aside. Rinse turkey with cold water; pat dry. Trim excess fat. Tie ends of legs to tail with cord. Lift wing tips up and over back; tuck under turkey. Sprinkle poultry seasoning, 1 tablespoon grated orange rind, ¼ teaspoon salt, and ¼ teaspoon pepper into body cavity and onto turkey. Stuff cavity of turkey with orange quarters and onion quarters. Place turkey on a broiler pan coated with cooking spray; insert meat thermometer into meaty part of thigh, making sure not to touch bone. Bake at 375° for 45 minutes. Baste turkey with orange juice mixture; cover loosely with foil. Bake an additional 2 hours and 15 minutes or until thermometer registers 180°, basting turkey every 30 minutes. Let turkey stand 10 minutes; set pan and drippings aside.
4. While turkey is baking, melt margarine in a saucepan over medium-high heat. Add reserved giblets and neck; cook 5 minutes or until browned on all sides. Add water and broth; bring to a boil. Cover, reduce heat, and simmer 45 minutes. Add liver; simmer 10 minutes. Remove giblets, neck, and liver from broth mixture, reserving broth mixture. Chop giblets and liver. Remove meat from neck bone; discard bone, and chop meat. Strain broth mixture through a sieve over a medium bowl; discard solids.
5. Strain pan drippings through a sieve into bowl with broth mixture; discard solids in sieve. Place a large zip-top plastic bag inside a medium bowl. Pour broth mixture into bag; let stand 10 minutes (fat will rise to the top). Seal bag; carefully snip off 1 bottom corner of bag. Drain liquid into a saucepan, stopping before fat layer reaches opening; discard fat. Add ¼ teaspoon salt, ¼ teaspoon pepper, 2 tablespoons orange juice, cornstarch, 1 tablespoon maple syrup, and ¼ teaspoon orange rind; stir with a whisk until well-blended. Bring to a boil; cook until thick (about 1 minute). Stir in chopped meat from giblets, liver, and neck.
6. Discard skin from turkey. Serve gravy with turkey; if desired, garnish with herb sprigs and grapes. Yield: 12 servings (serving size: 6 ounces turkey and ¼ cup gravy).

CALORIES 373 (25% from fat); FAT 10.3g (sat 3.2g, mono 2.1g, poly 2.8g); PROTEIN 57.1g; CARB 9.4g; FIBER 0.1g; CHOL 168mg; IRON 4.2mg; SODIUM 254mg; CALC 59mg

GARNISHING

When you make your holiday meal grocery list, be sure to include extra items to use for garnishing the turkey platter. A few of our favorites:

fresh herbs
orange slices
flowering kale
small bunches of green or red grapes
fresh cranberries
curly endive
baby carrots with tops
cherry tomatoes
celery leaves
baked acorn squash rings

salads & dressings

Mixed Greens With Pears and Raspberries
(page 394)

SALADS

fruit salads
Fresh fruit is so flavorful that it doesn't need a lot of embellishment—just a drizzle of dressing will make the salad.

The key to a fruit salad is to start with the freshest ingredients possible. This means that proper selection and storage of the fruit is essential. Try to use the fruit within a day or two of purchase, unless it's a "hardy" fruit such as apples or pears.

Look for ripe, plump fruit without blemishes or signs of insect damage. Be sure to check for ripeness. If the fruit is not completely ripe, see page 208 for tips on ripening.

ASPARAGUS-APPLE SALAD

PREP:13 MINUTES   CHILL:3 HOURS

    3 cups (1-inch) diagonally sliced
         asparagus (about 2 pounds)
    4 cups cubed Red Delicious apple
         (about 1¼ pounds)
    2 teaspoons fresh lemon juice
    ¼ cup raisins
    2 tablespoons cider vinegar
    1 tablespoon olive oil
    2 teaspoons honey
    ¼ teaspoon salt
    ¼ teaspoon dried dill
    ⅛ teaspoon black pepper
    7 curly leaf lettuce leaves

1. Bring water to a boil in a large saucepan; add asparagus. Cook 1 minute; drain and plunge into ice water. Drain well.
2. Combine apple and lemon juice in a large bowl, tossing well to coat. Add asparagus and raisins, tossing gently.
3. Combine cider vinegar and next 5 ingredients; stir well with a whisk. Pour vinaigrette over salad; toss gently to coat. Cover and chill 3 to 12 hours. Serve on lettuce leaves. Yield: 7 servings (serving size: 1 cup).

CALORIES 99 (21% from fat); FAT 2.3g (sat 0.3g, mono 1.4g, poly 0.3g); PROTEIN 1.7g; CARB 20.5g; FIBER 2.9g; CHOL 0mg; IRON 0.8mg; SODIUM 88mg; CALC 23mg

CRANBERRY-WALDORF GELATIN SALAD

PREP:16 MINUTES

CHILL:4 HOURS

Make the salad and the cream cheese mixture a day ahead; chill. For an attractive presentation, garnish each serving with apple slices and chopped pecans. This salad is also good without the cream cheese topping. You can substitute two .3-ounce packages sugar-free gelatin for regular gelatin.

    2 (3-ounce) packages cranberry-
         flavored gelatin
 1¾ cups boiling water
    ¾ cup cold water
    ¾ cup diced Red Delicious apple
    ¾ cup diced Golden Delicious
         apple
    ½ cup seedless green grapes,
         quartered
    ¼ cup finely chopped pecans
  Cooking spray
    ½ cup (4 ounces) block-style fat-
         free cream cheese, softened
    ¾ cup low-fat sour cream
    2 tablespoons sugar
    ¼ teaspoon vanilla extract
  Lettuce leaves

1. Combine gelatin and boiling water in a bowl; stir until gelatin dissolves. Stir in cold water. Cover and chill 1½ hours or until the consistency of unbeaten egg white. Fold in apple, grapes, and pecans.
2. Spoon gelatin mixture into a 5-cup gelatin mold coated with cooking spray. Chill until firm.
3. Beat cream cheese at medium speed of a mixer until smooth. Add sour cream, sugar, and vanilla to cream cheese; beat well.
4. Invert salad mold onto a serving plate; cut into 8 pieces. Serve salad on lettuce-lined plates; top each serving with 2 tablespoons cream cheese mixture. Yield: 8 servings.

CALORIES 178 (25% from fat); FAT 4.9g (sat 1.9g, mono 2g, poly 0.6g); PROTEIN 4.7g; CARB 29.2g; FIBER 1.1g; CHOL 11mg; IRON 0.3mg; SODIUM 155mg; CALC 72mg

FRESH FRUIT WITH TANGY DRESSING

PREP:18 MINUTES

    6 tablespoons water
    ⅓ cup sugar
    ⅓ cup lemon juice
    1 tablespoon vegetable oil
    1 teaspoon celery seeds
    1 teaspoon dry mustard
    1 teaspoon paprika
    ½ teaspoon salt
    4 cups cubed cantaloupe
    4 cups sliced banana (about 8
         medium)
    1 avocado, peeled and sliced
  Lettuce leaves

1. Place first 8 ingredients in a blender; process until well-blended.

2. Divide cantaloupe, banana, and avocado evenly among 8 lettuce-lined salad plates. Drizzle 2 tablespoons dressing over each salad. Yield: 8 servings.

CALORIES 186 (25% from fat); FAT 5.2g (sat 1g, mono 2.3g, poly 1.4g); PROTEIN 2.4g; CARB 36.8g; FIBER 3.9g; CHOL 0mg; IRON 1mg; SODIUM 160mg; CALC 29mg

POPPY SEED-FRUIT SALAD

PREP: 23 MINUTES
CHILL: 1 HOUR

⅓ cup apple juice
2 teaspoons cornstarch
⅓ cup fat-free sweet-and-sour dressing
1 tablespoon vegetable oil
½ teaspoon poppy seeds
4 cups whole strawberries, halved
3 cups (1-inch) honeydew melon balls
1½ cups seedless red grapes
1½ cups seedless green grapes
4 peaches, peeled and cut into chunks
2 cups sliced ripe banana

1. Combine apple juice and cornstarch in a small saucepan. Bring to a boil over medium heat, stirring constantly. Reduce heat, and simmer until thick (about 1 minute), stirring constantly. Pour mixture into a small bowl. Add dressing, oil, and poppy seeds, stirring until well-blended. Cool completely.

2. Combine strawberries, melon, grapes, and peach in a large bowl. Add poppy seed mixture; toss gently to coat. Cover and chill. Just before serving, add banana; toss gently. Yield: 15 servings (serving size: 1 cup).

CALORIES 107 (12% from fat); FAT 1.4g (sat 0.3g, mono 0.3g, poly 0.6g); PROTEIN 1.2g; CARB 24.9g; FIBER 2.9g; CHOL 0mg; IRON 0.4mg; SODIUM 89mg; CALC 17mg

JÍCAMA

Jícama is easy to prepare and requires only the removal of its thin skin. This tuber keeps 2 to 3 weeks when stored (whole) unwrapped in the refrigerator. Once cut, cover it tightly and use within a week. Eaten raw, it provides a refreshing crunch to salads and crudités, and it remains crisp when tossed into stir-fries.

FROZEN FRUIT SALAD

PREP: 18 MINUTES   FREEZE: 4 HOURS
STAND: 30 MINUTES

1½ cups seedless red grapes, halved
1½ cups sliced ripe banana (about 3 bananas)
1½ cups grapefruit sections (about 2 large grapefruit)
1½ cups chopped fresh pineapple
1¾ cups pineapple juice
⅓ cup thawed orange juice concentrate

1. Combine all ingredients in a large bowl. Pour into a 13 x 9-inch baking dish. Cover and freeze 4 hours or until firm. Let stand at room temperature 30 minutes or until slightly thawed before serving. Yield: 8 servings (serving size: 1 [4½ x 3¼-inch] piece).

CALORIES 121 (4% from fat); FAT 0.5g (sat 0.1g, mono 0g, poly 0.1g); PROTEIN 1.2g; CARB 30.2g; FIBER 1.8g; CHOL 0mg; IRON 0.5mg; SODIUM 2mg; CALC 25mg

JÍCAMA FRUIT SALAD

PREP: 18 MINUTES

1 teaspoon grated orange rind
¼ cup fresh orange juice
2 tablespoons brown sugar
¾ teaspoon ground cinnamon
⅛ teaspoon ground nutmeg
3 cups julienne-cut peeled jícama
1 red grapefruit, peeled and sectioned
2 oranges, peeled and sliced crosswise
2 kiwifruit, peeled and sliced

1. Combine first 5 ingredients in a medium bowl; stir well with a whisk. Add jícama and remaining ingredients; toss gently to coat. Yield: 5 servings (serving size: 1 cup).

CALORIES 99 (3% from fat); FAT 0.3g (sat 0.1g, mono 0g, poly 0.1g); PROTEIN 1.6g; CARB 24.5g; FIBER 7.3g; CHOL 0mg; IRON 0.8mg; SODIUM 6mg; CALC 51mg

MARINATED ORANGE-STRAWBERRY SALAD

PREP: 20 MINUTES   STAND: 30 MINUTES

2 cups orange sections
1½ cups sliced strawberries
1 tablespoon honey
1 teaspoon olive oil
¼ teaspoon ground cinnamon
¼ teaspoon black pepper
⅛ teaspoon salt
3 cups torn curly leaf lettuce
1 tablespoon pine nuts, toasted

1. Combine first 7 ingredients in a large bowl, tossing gently. Let stand 30 minutes. Add lettuce and pine nuts; toss gently to coat. Yield: 4 servings (serving size: 1½ cups).

CALORIES 107 (27% from fat); FAT 3.2g (sat 0.5g, mono 1.6g, poly 1g); PROTEIN 2.3g; CARB 20.1g; FIBER 5.7g; CHOL 0mg; IRON 0.8mg; SODIUM 76mg; CALC 53mg

MANGO-AVOCADO SALAD

PREP: 20 MINUTES

4 cups gourmet salad greens
1 mango, peeled and sliced
1 small avocado, peeled and sliced
⅓ cup chopped tomato
¼ cup fresh lime juice
2 tablespoons chopped fresh
    cilantro
2 tablespoons chopped fresh basil
1 tablespoon sherry vinegar
1 tablespoon low-sodium soy
    sauce
1 teaspoon minced seeded
    jalapeño pepper
½ teaspoon ground coriander
¼ teaspoon salt
⅛ teaspoon black pepper
2 tablespoons chopped
    dry-roasted cashews

1. Place 1 cup salad greens on each of 4 plates; divide mango and avocado evenly among salads. Combine tomato and next 9 ingredients in a bowl; drizzle about 3 tablespoons dressing over each salad, and top each with 1½ teaspoons cashews. Yield: 4 servings.

CALORIES 106 (53% from fat); FAT 6.3g (sat 1g, mono 3.8g, poly 0.9g); PROTEIN 2g; CARB 12.4g; FIBER 2.8g; CHOL 0mg; IRON 1mg; SODIUM 313mg; CALC 25mg

WARM BLUE CHEESE AND PEAR SALAD

PREP: 10 MINUTES   COOK: 5 MINUTES

¼ cup water
1 tablespoon sugar
1 tablespoon red wine vinegar
½ teaspoon beef-flavored
    bouillon granules
2 cups finely shredded red cabbage
1 cup chopped peeled pear (about
    ½ pound)
4 teaspoons crumbled blue cheese

Cutting a Mango

The mango is originally from India but is now grown in temperate climates around the world, including California and Florida. Look for fruit with unblemished yellow skin, blushed with red. Very fragrant when ripe, mangoes are ready to eat when they become soft to the touch.

1. A mango can be tricky to cut because it has a rather large, flat seed inside. You must therefore cut around it on both sides. Hold the mango vertically on a cutting board.

2. With a sharp knife, slice the fruit lengthwise on each side of the flat pit.

3. Holding the mango half in the palm of your hand, score the pulp. Be sure that you slice to, but not through, the skin.

4. Turn the mango inside out, and cut the chunks from the skin.

1. Combine water, sugar, vinegar, and bouillon granules in a large skillet over high heat. Cover, reduce heat, and simmer 1 minute. Add cabbage to pan, and sauté 2 minutes.
2. Add chopped pear, and sauté 2 minutes or until pear is crisp-tender; remove from heat. Sprinkle salad with crumbled blue cheese, and serve immediately. Yield: 4 servings (serving size: ½ cup).

CALORIES 58 (20% from fat); FAT 1.3g (sat 0.7g, mono 0.3g, poly 0.1g); PROTEIN 1.3g; CARB 11.1g; FIBER 1.6g; CHOL 3mg; IRON 0.3mg; SODIUM 172mg; CALC 39mg

green salads

No need to rely on the same old mound of lettuce—consider the alternatives from Bibb to romaine!

What's the secret to a great salad? Start with fresh, crisp greens. Purchase those with fresh-looking, brightly colored leaves with no sign of wilting, avoiding those with spots and those that are limp. Grocery stores now offer a variety of gourmet greens, but don't overlook a local farmer's market. There you may find freshly-picked greens, only a few hours post-harvest.

To store greens, gently rinse them and shake off excess moisture. Store in your refrigerator crisper drawer in zip-top plastic bags with a paper towel to absorb excess moisture. Use within a day or two for optimum freshness.

CREAMY CAESAR SALAD WITH SPICY CROUTONS

PREP:18 MINUTES   CHILL:1 HOUR

1   large garlic clove, halved
½   cup fat-free mayonnaise
2   tablespoons red wine vinegar
2   teaspoons Dijon mustard
2   teaspoons white wine
      Worcestershire sauce
1   teaspoon anchovy paste
¼   teaspoon black pepper
2   (10-ounce) bags torn romaine
      lettuce (about 18 cups)
⅓   cup (1⅓ ounces) grated fresh
      Parmesan cheese
Spicy Croutons

1. Drop garlic through opening in blender lid with blender on; process until minced. Add mayonnaise and next 5 ingredients; process until well-blended. Cover and chill at least 1 hour.
2. Combine lettuce and dressing in a bowl; toss to coat. Sprinkle with cheese;

top with Spicy Croutons. Yield: 6 servings (serving size: 3 cups salad and ⅓ cup croutons).

CALORIES 140 (23% from fat); FAT 3.6g (sat 1.2g, mono 1.6g, poly 0.3g); PROTEIN 5.9g; CARB 21.4g; FIBER 2.1g; CHOL 3mg; IRON 1.8mg; SODIUM 921mg; CALC 144mg

SPICY CROUTONS

2   teaspoons olive oil
¾   teaspoon Cajun seasoning
1   garlic clove, minced
2   cups (¾-inch) cubed
      sourdough bread

1. Preheat oven to 400°.
2. Combine oil, Cajun seasoning, and minced garlic in a microwave-safe bowl. Microwave at HIGH for 20 seconds. Add bread cubes; toss gently to coat. Spread bread cubes in a single layer on a baking sheet; bake at 400° for 15 minutes or until lightly browned and dry. Yield: 2 cups (serving size: ⅓ cup).

CALORIES 83 (23% from fat); FAT 2.1g (sat 0.5g, mono 1.2g, poly 0.2g); PROTEIN 2.6g; CARB 13.8g; FIBER 0.5g; CHOL 0mg; IRON 0.7mg; SODIUM 386mg; CALC 29mg

PUB SALAD

PREP:9 MINUTES

4   cups torn Boston lettuce (about 2
      small heads)
½   cup pickled sliced beets
½   cup thinly sliced peeled cucumber
1   hard-cooked large egg, sliced
¼   cup diced celery
¼   cup diced onion
Creamy Tarragon Dressing (page 423)
½   cup (2 ounces) shredded
      reduced-fat sharp cheddar
      cheese

1. Arrange 1 cup lettuce on each of 4 salad plates; top with beets, cucumber, egg, celery, and onion. Drizzle 2 tablespoons dressing over each; sprinkle with 2 tablespoons cheese. Yield: 4 servings.

CALORIES 116 (33% from fat); FAT 4.3g (sat 2g, mono 1.3g, poly 0.3g); PROTEIN 7.3g; CARB 12.5g; FIBER 0.7g; CHOL 63mg; IRON 0.4mg; SODIUM 472mg; CALC 188mg

ITALIAN ANTIPASTO SALAD

PREP:20 MINUTES

1   (12-ounce) package European-
      style salad greens
1   (15-ounce) can no-salt-added
      chickpeas (garbanzo beans),
      rinsed and drained
¼   pound thinly sliced ham, cut
      into ½-inch-wide strips
1   (14-ounce) can quartered
      artichoke hearts, drained
1   large red bell pepper, cut into rings
¼   cup balsamic vinegar
2   tablespoons water
1   tablespoon olive oil
2   teaspoons Dijon mustard
1   teaspoon dried oregano
¼   teaspoon black pepper
1   tablespoon grated fat-free
      Parmesan cheese
Chopped fresh parsley (optional)

1. Arrange salad greens on a serving platter, and top with chickpeas, ham, artichokes, and bell pepper rings.
2. Combine vinegar and next 5 ingredients; drizzle over salad. Sprinkle cheese over salad; garnish with chopped parsley, if desired. Yield: 8 servings.

CALORIES 119 (27% from fat); FAT 3.6g (sat 0.6g, mono 1.8g, poly 0.8g); PROTEIN 7.7g; CARB 15.4g; FIBER 2g; CHOL 6mg; IRON 2.2mg; SODIUM 356mg; CALC 54mg

Wilted Greens With
Warm Bacon Dressing

menu

Chunky Gazpacho (page 461)

Grilled Tuna With Herbed Mayonnaise
(page 228)

Orange-and-Avocado Salad

Plain Focaccia (page104)

ORANGE-AND-AVOCADO SALAD

PREP:15 MINUTES

3 large oranges
6 cups torn curly leaf lettuce
¾ cup chopped peeled avocado
2 tablespoons white wine vinegar
1½ teaspoons sugar
½ teaspoon salt
¼ teaspoon black pepper
¼ to ½ teaspoon hot pepper
  sauce

1. Peel and section oranges over a bowl; squeeze membranes to extract juice. Set sections aside; discard membranes. Reserve 3 tablespoons juice.
2. Combine orange sections, lettuce, and avocado in a bowl; toss gently. Combine 3 tablespoons orange juice, vinegar, and remaining 4 ingredients in a small bowl; stir well with a whisk. Pour juice mixture over salad, and toss gently to coat. Yield: 4 servings (serving size: 1½ cups).

CALORIES 95 (37% from fat); FAT 3.9g (sat 0.6g, mono 2.3g, poly 0.6g); PROTEIN 1.8g; CARB 14.9g; FIBER 5.2g; CHOL 0mg; IRON 0.6mg; SODIUM 303mg; CALC 45mg

Shelled green peas give this salad a touch of sweetness. The warm bacon dressing balances the taste with a nice little twang.

WILTED GREENS WITH WARM BACON DRESSING

PREP:22 MINUTES

2 cups water
½ cup shelled green peas
6 cups gourmet salad greens
  (about ¼ pound)
½ cup thinly sliced green onions
4 turkey bacon slices, diced
¼ cup water
2 tablespoons red wine vinegar
2 tablespoons fresh lemon
  juice
Freshly ground black pepper
  (optional)

1. Bring 2 cups water to a boil in a saucepan; add peas. Cover and cook 7 minutes or until crisp-tender. Drain and rinse with cold water; drain well.
2. Combine peas, salad greens, and green onions in a bowl.
3. Cook bacon in a nonstick skillet over medium heat 4 minutes or until crisp. Add ¼ cup water, vinegar, and lemon juice; cook 2 minutes. Immediately pour over salad, and toss gently to coat. Sprinkle each serving with pepper, if desired. Yield: 4 servings (serving size: 1½ cups).

CALORIES 79 (42% from fat); FAT 3.7g (sat 0.9g, mono 1.8g, poly 1g); PROTEIN 5.2g; CARB 5.1g; FIBER 1.4g; CHOL 18mg; IRON 0.8mg; SODIUM 361mg; CALC 27mg

Working With Citrus

1. Gently roll the fruit on a flat surface, using the palm of your hand to soften the pulp inside.

2. Cut the fruit in half crosswise; then use a hand-held reamer, a citrus juicer, or an electric juicer.

Use a hand-held grater to get finely grated rind. Avoid the white pith beneath the skin—it's bitter.

To remove rind easily, use a vegetable peeler.

To julienne, cut a piece of rind (obtained with a vegetable peeler) lengthwise into long, thin slices.

1. First, cut off end of fruit. Stand fruit on end, and cut skin off from top to bottom.

2. Slice fruit between membranes with a sharp paring knife to remove sections, keeping fruit over a bowl to catch the juice. A medium-size orange or grapefruit yields 10 to 12 sections.

CURLY ENDIVE

This lettucelike salad green grows in loose heads with an off-white, compact center and lacy, green-rimmed outer leaves that curl at the tips. It has a prickly texture and slightly bitter taste. Use in salads or stir into soups and bean dishes.

MIXED GREENS WITH PEARS AND RASPBERRIES

PREP:12 MINUTES

(pictured on page 387)

2 cups torn spinach
2 cups torn Boston lettuce
2 cups torn curly endive
2 cups coarsely chopped or sliced pear (about 2 medium)
1 cup fresh raspberries
3 tablespoons raspberry vinegar
2 tablespoons apple juice
1 tablespoon extra-virgin olive oil
1 tablespoon honey
⅛ teaspoon salt
⅛ teaspoon black pepper

1. Combine first 5 ingredients in a large bowl; toss gently.
2. Combine vinegar and remaining 5 ingredients in a small bowl; stir well with a whisk. Divide salad among individual plates; drizzle with dressing. Yield: 6 servings (serving size: 1⅓ cups salad and about ⅓ cup dressing).

CALORIES 76 (31% from fat); FAT 2.6g (sat 0.3g, mono 1.7g, poly 0.3g); PROTEIN 0.9g; CARB 14g; FIBER 3g; CHOL 0mg; IRON 0.6mg; SODIUM 59mg; CALC 24mg

ROMAINE SALAD WITH TANGY LEMON-DIJON DRESSING

PREP:12 MINUTES

¼ cup water
3 tablespoons Dijon mustard
2 tablespoons fresh lemon juice
2 teaspoons olive oil
¼ teaspoon salt
¼ teaspoon black pepper
2 garlic cloves, minced
8 cups torn romaine lettuce
¼ cup finely chopped red onion
6 tablespoons plain croutons
Freshly ground black pepper (optional)

1. Combine first 7 ingredients in a small bowl, and stir well with a whisk. Combine lettuce and onion in a bowl. Drizzle dressing over salad; toss to coat. Top with croutons. Sprinkle with pepper, if desired. Yield: 4 servings (serving size: 1½ cups salad and 1½ tablespoons croutons).

CALORIES 72 (44% from fat); FAT 3.5g (sat 0.6g, mono 1.8g, poly 0.4g); PROTEIN 2.1g; CARB 7.9g; FIBER 1.9g; CHOL 0mg; IRON 1.2mg; SODIUM 541mg; CALC 39mg

OLIVES, ANYONE?

Of the olive varieties available today, the following are the most flavorful and are available in most supermarkets.

Kalamata: This smooth, dark-purple olive comes from Greece. Sometimes spelled "calamata," it has a pleasing aftertaste.

Manzanilla: These are traditional green cocktail olives. They have a crisp flesh and smoky flavor. (Black Mission olives can be substituted in recipes.)

Niçoise: These small, dark-brown or purple olives have a sharp and slightly sour flavor. Because the pits are large for the size of the olive, there isn't much fruit left after they're pitted.

Oil-Cured: Oil-cured olives are jet-black and very wrinkled. They're the most bitter of all.

GREEK SALAD WITH FETA AND OLIVES

PREP:24 MINUTES

8 cups torn romaine lettuce
4 cups torn escarole
1½ cups thinly sliced red onion, separated into rings
1½ cups thinly sliced green bell pepper rings
1½ cups thinly sliced red bell pepper rings
½ cup thinly sliced radishes
¼ cup sliced pitted kalamata olives
2 tomatoes, each cut into 8 wedges
Oregano Vinaigrette
½ cup (2 ounces) crumbled feta cheese

Bartlett, Anjou, and Comice pears are juicy when ripe and an excellent choice for salads.

Greek Salad With Feta and Olives

1. Combine all ingredients in a bowl; stir with a whisk. Cover and chill. Yield: about ⅔ cup.

CALORIES 20 (63% from fat); FAT 1.4g (sat 0.2g, mono 1g, poly 0.1g); PROTEIN 0.1g; CARB 1g; FIBER 0.1g; CHOL 0mg; IRON 0.1mg; SODIUM 59mg; CALC 6mg

SPINACH-STRAWBERRY SALAD WITH GOAT CHEESE BRUSCHETTA

PREP: 20 MINUTES

The bruschetta's pungent flavor contrasts with the sweetness of the strawberries.

¼ cup sugar
2 tablespoons sherry vinegar or white wine vinegar
1½ teaspoons sesame seeds, toasted
1½ teaspoons olive oil
1 teaspoon minced red onion
¾ teaspoon poppy seeds
¼ teaspoon Hungarian sweet paprika
⅛ teaspoon salt
6 cups torn spinach (about 1 pound)
2 cups halved strawberries
2 tablespoons slivered almonds, toasted
1 (3-ounce) log goat cheese, cut into 6 slices
6 (1-ounce) slices French bread, toasted

1. Combine first 8 ingredients in a medium bowl; stir well with a whisk.
2. Combine spinach and strawberries in a bowl. Pour dressing over spinach mixture, tossing gently to coat. Spoon 1 cup salad onto each of 6 plates; sprinkle each with 1 teaspoon almonds. Spread cheese over toast slices; top each salad with 1 bruschetta. Yield: 6 servings.

CALORIES 213 (28% from fat); FAT 6.7g (sat 2.7g, mono 2.6g, poly 1.1g); PROTEIN 7.1g; CARB 31g; FIBER 4.5g; CHOL 13mg; IRON 2.7mg; SODIUM 446mg; CALC 163mg

1. Combine lettuce, escarole, red onion, bell pepper rings, and next 3 ingredients in a large bowl.
2. Pour vinaigrette over salad, and toss gently to coat. Sprinkle cheese over salad. Yield: 9 servings (serving size: 2 cups).

CALORIES 90 (43% from fat); FAT 4.3g (sat 1.7g, mono 1.8g, poly 0.5g); PROTEIN 3.4g; CARB 10.2g; FIBER 2.7g; CHOL 8mg; IRON 1.6mg; SODIUM 210mg; CALC 86mg

OREGANO VINAIGRETTE

¼ cup dry white wine
¼ cup fresh lemon juice
1 tablespoon extra-virgin olive oil
1 tablespoon chopped fresh or 1 teaspoon dried oregano
¼ teaspoon salt
¼ teaspoon black pepper
4 garlic cloves, minced

SPINACH-STRAWBERRY SALAD

PREP: 15 MINUTES

  4 cups torn spinach
  2 cups sliced strawberries
  3 tablespoons fresh orange juice
  2 tablespoons balsamic vinegar
  1 teaspoon olive oil
  1 tablespoon sesame seeds,
     toasted

1. Combine spinach and strawberries in a large bowl.
2. Combine juice, vinegar, and oil in a small bowl; stir well with a whisk. Drizzle vinaigrette over spinach mixture; toss gently to coat. Sprinkle salad with toasted sesame seeds. Yield: 4 servings (serving size: 1½ cups).

CALORIES 54 (43% from fat); FAT 2.6g (sat 0.4g, mono 1.3g, poly 0.8g); PROTEIN 1.7g; CARB 7.3g; FIBER 2.7g; CHOL 0mg; IRON 1.4mg; SODIUM 24mg; CALC 61mg

FRUIT-AND-HONEY SPINACH SALAD

PREP: 15 MINUTES

  8 cups spinach leaves
  2 cups cantaloupe balls
1½ cups halved strawberries
  1 cup fresh blackberries
  ¼ cup seedless raspberry jam
  ¼ cup raspberry vinegar
  2 tablespoons honey
  2 teaspoons olive oil
  ¼ cup chopped macadamia nuts

1. Combine spinach, cantaloupe, strawberries, and blackberries in a large bowl, and toss gently.
2. Combine jam, vinegar, honey, and oil in a small bowl; stir well with a whisk. Drizzle dressing over spinach mixture, and toss gently to coat. Sprinkle spinach mixture with chopped macadamia nuts. Yield: 6 servings (serving size: 2 cups).

CALORIES 138 (36% from fat); FAT 5.6g (sat 0.8g, mono 4g, poly 0.4g); PROTEIN 2.3g; CARB 22.3g; FIBER 4.7g; CHOL 0mg; IRON 1.8mg; SODIUM 43mg; CALC 59mg

Berry Measure

1 pint fresh strawberries equals:

about 3¼ cups whole berries

about 2½ cups sliced berries

1⅔ cups pureed berries

12 very large berries or about 36 small berries

Fruit-and-Honey Spinach Salad

SESAME SPINACH SALAD

PREP: 14 MINUTES

2 tablespoons low-sodium soy
    sauce
1 tablespoon sesame seeds,
    toasted and crushed
1 tablespoon honey
½ pound turnip greens
1 (10-ounce) package fresh spinach
2 quarts water

1. Combine first 3 ingredients in a small bowl.
2. Remove stems from turnip greens and spinach. Bring 2 quarts water to a boil in an 8-quart stockpot or Dutch oven. Add turnip greens; cover and cook 1 minute. Add spinach, and cook until wilted. Drain and rinse greens mixture with cold water; drain and pat dry. Place greens mixture in a large bowl; pour sesame dressing over greens mixture, and toss to coat. Yield: 2 servings (serving size: 2 cups).
Note: Mustard greens can be substituted for turnip greens.

CALORIES 118 (23% from fat); FAT 3g (sat 0.5g, mono 0.9g, poly 1.3g); PROTEIN 5.5g; CARB 19.9g; FIBER 7g; CHOL 0mg; IRON 4.7mg; SODIUM 517mg; CALC 363mg

SPINACH SALAD WITH BEETS AND ORANGES

PREP: 16 MINUTES

2 navel oranges
6 cups torn spinach
3 cups shredded peeled beets
    (about 1 pound)
1 tablespoon olive oil
2 tablespoons minced shallots
¼ cup raspberry vinegar
¼ teaspoon freshly ground black
    pepper
¼ cup minced fresh chives
¼ cup coarsely chopped walnuts

1. Peel oranges, and cut each crosswise into 5 slices.
2. Place spinach on a large platter. Spoon beets onto spinach, and arrange orange slices on beets.
3. Heat oil in a nonstick skillet over medium-high heat. Add shallots, and sauté 1 minute or until tender. Stir in vinegar and pepper; drizzle over salad. Sprinkle salad with chives and walnuts. Yield: 6 servings.

CALORIES 122 (41% from fat); FAT 5.6g (sat 0.6g, mono 2.4g, poly 2.3g); PROTEIN 4.7g; CARB 16.3g; FIBER 5.3g; CHOL 0mg; IRON 2.4mg; SODIUM 104mg; CALC 93mg

menu

Prosciutto-and-Fontina Panini (page 434)
**Tossed Salad With
Blackberry Vinaigrette**
Coffee Chiffon Cake (page 136)

TOSSED SALAD WITH BLACKBERRY VINAIGRETTE

PREP: 22 MINUTES
CHILL: 1 HOUR

1 teaspoon cornstarch
¼ cup water
¼ cup Sweet Blackberry Vinegar
    (page 455)
2 tablespoons fresh lemon juice
¼ teaspoon salt
1 garlic clove, minced
Dash of black pepper
6 cups torn curly leaf lettuce
2 cups torn radicchio (about 1
    large head)
1½ cups blackberries
¾ cup (2-inch) julienne-cut
    yellow bell pepper strips
¼ cup thinly sliced onion,
    separated into rings
¼ cup chopped fresh mint

1. Place cornstarch in a small saucepan.

RADICCHIO

This bitter-flavored member of the chicory family has burgundy-red leaves with white ribs. Most often used in salads, radicchio can also be grilled or roasted. If unavailable, substitute another chicory such as escarole.

Gradually add ¼ cup water, stirring well with a whisk. Stir in Sweet Blackberry Vinegar, lemon juice, salt, garlic, and black pepper. Bring to a boil; cook 1 minute, stirring constantly. Cool; cover and chill.
2. Combine lettuce and remaining 5 ingredients in a large bowl; toss gently. To serve, pour dressing over lettuce mixture, and toss to coat; serve immediately. Yield: 5 servings (serving size: 2 cups).

CALORIES 73 (6% from fat); FAT 0.5g (sat 0.1g, mono 0g, poly 0.3g); PROTEIN 1.6g; CARB 17g; FIBER 4g; CHOL 0mg; IRON 1.1mg; SODIUM 129mg; CALC 39mg

You won't miss the oil in this flavorful, sweet blackberry vinaigrette.

vegetable salads

Vegetables and greens provide spirited inspiration for variety in these side salads. So let your imagination go!

Tossing together a salad is a simple way to enjoy kitchen creativity while livening up meals with bright colors and crunchy textures. Consider yourself an artist and create tasty masterpieces with fresh-from-the-garden produce.

To save on preparation time, stop by your grocer's salad bar. You may find many of these vegetables already cut up. Or put your food processor into action for quick-cutting success.

ASPARAGUS SALAD WITH CAESAR VINAIGRETTE

PREP: 14 MINUTES

See page 486 for tips on purchasing fresh asparagus.

20 asparagus spears (about
        1 pound)
 4 cups gourmet salad greens
 3 tablespoons tarragon vinegar
1½ teaspoons olive oil
 1 teaspoon water
 ½ teaspoon anchovy paste
 ⅛ teaspoon black pepper
 1 garlic clove, minced
 ½ cup garlic-flavored
        croutons
    Chopped fresh parsley
        (optional)

1. Snap off tough ends of asparagus. Steam asparagus, covered, 6 minutes or until crisp-tender. Rinse with cold water; drain well.
2. Arrange 1 cup salad greens on each of 4 plates; top each serving with 5 asparagus spears. Combine vinegar and next 5 ingredients in a bowl; stir well with a whisk. Drizzle 1 tablespoon

vinaigrette over each serving, and top each with 2 tablespoons croutons. Sprinkle salads with fresh parsley, if desired. Yield: 4 servings.

CALORIES 51 (44% from fat); FAT 2.5g (sat 0.3g, mono 1.3g, poly 0.3g); PROTEIN 2.5g; CARB 5.6g; FIBER 1.1g; CHOL 0mg; IRON 0.9mg; SODIUM 205mg; CALC 27mg

ASPARAGUS, VIDALIA, AND BEET SALAD

PREP: 1 HOUR

Assemble this salad right before serving.

 ¾ pound small beets
 ½ cup water
 1 large Vidalia or other sweet
        onion (about ¾ pound),
        peeled
 2 tablespoons water
 2 cups (2-inch) sliced asparagus
        (about ¾ pound)
 2 tablespoons lemon
        juice
 1 tablespoon water
 2 teaspoons olive oil
 1 teaspoon Dijon mustard
 1 teaspoon honey
 ½ teaspoon salt
 ¼ teaspoon black pepper
 1 large shallot, peeled and
        quartered

1. Preheat oven to 375°.
2. Leave roots and 1-inch stems on beets; scrub with a brush. Place beets in an 11 x 7-inch baking dish; add ½ cup water to dish. Cover and bake at 375° for 45 minutes. Drain and cool slightly. Peel and cut each beet into 4 wedges; place in a bowl, and set aside.
3. While beets bake, place onion in a

VIDALIA ONIONS

Vidalia onions, named after the southern Georgia town where they thrive, have a higher natural sugar and water content than other varieties, which makes them bruise easily and difficult to store. Because of this, Vidalias were once available only during harvest season from April to June, but improved storage methods now make them accessible through the fall.

Although there are many different kinds of onions, each with many different uses, there's something special about the sweet onion—and the Vidalia is the sweetest of sweet. They're light golden brown with a white interior, slightly rounded on the bottom, and flat on the stem end.

second 11 x 7-inch baking dish; add 2 tablespoons water to dish.
4. Cover and bake at 375° for 35 minutes. Add asparagus to onion; cover and bake an additional 10 minutes. Drain and cool slightly. Cut onion into 8 wedges. Place onion and asparagus in a bowl; set aside.

5. Place lemon juice and remaining 7 ingredients in a food processor or blender; process until smooth. Pour half of dressing over beets; toss to coat. Pour remaining half of dressing over asparagus mixture; toss to coat.

6. Spoon 1 cup asparagus mixture onto each of 4 salad plates; top each with about ⅓ cup beets. Serve immediately. Yield: 4 servings.

CALORIES 103 (24% from fat); FAT 2.7g (sat 0.4g, mono 1.7g, poly 0.3g); PROTEIN 3.4g; CARB 18.7g; FIBER 3.3g; CHOL 0mg; IRON 1.3mg; SODIUM 379mg; CALC 42mg

GREEN BEAN-AND-YELLOW TOMATO SALAD

PREP: 15 MINUTES

½ pound green beans, trimmed and cut into 2-inch pieces
2 yellow tomatoes, each cut into 8 wedges
⅓ cup vertically sliced red onion
2 tablespoons red wine vinegar
2 teaspoons minced fresh or ½ teaspoon dried thyme
1 teaspoon olive oil
⅛ teaspoon salt
Dash of black pepper
1 garlic clove, minced

1. Steam green beans, covered, 3 minutes or until tender. Rinse with water; drain.
2. Combine beans, tomato wedges, and onion in a bowl. Combine vinegar and remaining 5 ingredients in a bowl; stir well with a whisk. Pour vinegar mixture over bean mixture; toss. Serve at room temperature. Yield: 2 servings (serving size: 1 cup).

CALORIES 118 (24% from fat); FAT 3.2g (sat 0.5g, mono 1.8g, poly 0.6g); PROTEIN 4.4g; CARB 22.2g; FIBER 5.5g; CHOL 0mg; IRON 2.4mg; SODIUM 177mg; CALC 60mg

THREE-BEAN SALAD WITH ROASTED ONION

PREP: 40 MINUTES CHILL: 8 HOURS

1 large red onion, peeled and halved (about ¾ pound)
Cooking spray
¾ pound wax beans, (about 3 cups)
1½ cups frozen black-eyed peas
1½ cups frozen lima beans
¼ cup sherry vinegar
2 tablespoons olive oil
1 teaspoon mustard seeds, crushed
1 teaspoon minced fresh rosemary
½ teaspoon salt
¼ teaspoon black pepper
1 garlic clove, minced

1. Preheat oven to 450°.
2. Place onion halves, cut sides down, in a baking dish coated with cooking spray. Bake, uncovered, at 450° for 30 minutes or until tender. Cool slightly; coarsely chop, and set aside.
3. Trim ends from wax beans, and remove strings. Cook black-eyed peas and lima beans in boiling water 4 minutes. Add wax beans; cook 8 minutes or until tender. Drain.
4. Combine vinegar and remaining 6 ingredients in a large bowl; stir well with a whisk. Add onion, peas, and beans; toss to coat. Cover and marinate in refrigerator at least 8 hours. Yield: 7 servings (serving size: 1 cup).

CALORIES 157 (26% from fat); FAT 4.6g (sat 0.6g, mono 3g, poly 0.5g); PROTEIN 6.6g; CARB 21.9g; FIBER 3.5g; CHOL 0mg; IRON 1.9mg; SODIUM 270mg; CALC 55mg

QUICK AND EASY BEET SALAD

PREP: 18 MINUTES   CHILL: 2 HOURS

1 (16-ounce) can no-salt-added sliced beets, drained and coarsely chopped
2 tablespoons sliced green onions
2 tablespoons fat-free Italian dressing
1 tablespoon chopped fresh parsley
½ cup frozen green peas, thawed
4 curly leaf lettuce leaves
1 hard-cooked large egg, chopped

1. Combine first 4 ingredients in a bowl; toss gently. Cover; chill 2 hours.
2. Add peas to salad; toss just before serving. Serve on lettuce-lined salad plates. Sprinkle with hard-cooked egg. Yield: 4 servings (serving size: ½ cup beet mixture and ¼ egg).

CALORIES 74 (17% from fat); FAT 1.4g (sat 0.4g, mono 0.5g, poly 0.2g); PROTEIN 3.1g; CARB 10.8g; FIBER 1.8g; CHOL 53mg; IRON 0.5mg; SODIUM 157mg; CALC 14mg

APPLE SLAW WITH BLUE CHEESE

PREP: 15 MINUTES   STAND: 1 HOUR

2 large Red Delicious apples, cored and cut into ¼-inch wedges
2 tablespoons lemon juice
6 cups thinly sliced red cabbage
6 cups thinly sliced napa (Chinese) cabbage
¼ cup cider vinegar
¼ cup red wine vinegar
2 tablespoons sugar
1 teaspoon celery seeds
1 teaspoon ground coriander
1 teaspoon olive oil
½ teaspoon salt
½ teaspoon black pepper
½ cup crumbled blue cheese

1. Combine apple and lemon juice in a large bowl; toss to coat. Add cabbages; toss gently.
2. Combine cider vinegar and next 7 ingredients in a bowl. Pour vinaigrette over cabbage mixture, and toss gently to coat. Let stand 1 hour. Add cheese, and toss gently. Serve at room temperature. Yield: 12 servings (serving size: 1 cup).

CALORIES 82 (30% from fat); FAT 2.7g (sat 1.4g, mono 0.9g, poly 0.2g); PROTEIN 2.5g; CARB 13.6g; FIBER 2.4g; CHOL 5mg; IRON 0.7mg; SODIUM 213mg; CALC 89mg

HOT BACON SLAW

PREP: 5 MINUTES
COOK: 7 MINUTES

2 bacon slices
1 (16-ounce) package ready-to-eat coleslaw
¼ cup balsamic vinegar
1½ tablespoons brown sugar
3 tablespoons water
½ teaspoon seasoned salt
¼ teaspoon ground red pepper

The term "coleslaw" originated from the Dutch *kool*, meaning cabbage, and *sla*, meaning salad.

SLAW SAVVY

Cabbage, the staple ingredient of all coleslaws, rivals citrus fruits as a source of vitamin C. Use green, red, Napa, or Chinese (bok choy) cabbages, and mix them with such ingredients as apples, red beans, shrimp, or soy sauce.

Cabbage can be shredded or chopped in a number of ways. To shred with a sharp knife, cut cabbage into quarters, remove core, and then hold firmly and **slice ⅛-inch-wide sections for "fine" and ¼-inch for "coarse" pieces. When chopping,** size depends on personal preference.

Using your food processor to shred or chop cabbage is a timesaver. And, of course, the old fashioned, hand-held shredder is always dependable. Whichever method you choose, **be sure** to cut the **cabbage just before preparing the salad so that you can preserve as much vitamin C as possible.**

1. Cook bacon in a large nonstick skillet over medium-high heat until crisp; remove bacon from pan, reserving drippings in pan. Set bacon aside.
2. Add coleslaw to drippings, and sauté over medium-high heat 3 minutes. Add vinegar, brown sugar, water, salt, and pepper; cook 1 minute, stirring constantly. Remove from heat. Crumble bacon; stir into coleslaw mixture. Serve warm. Yield: 3 servings (serving size: 1 cup).

CALORIES 94 (22% from fat); FAT 2.3g (sat 0.8g, mono 1.1g, poly 0.3g); PROTEIN 3.4g; CARB 16.4g; FIBER 6.7g; CHOL 5mg; IRON 0.3mg; SODIUM 172mg; CALC 5mg

CALIFORNIA RANCH SLAW

PREP: 10 MINUTES

½ cup sliced green onions
2 (10-ounce) packages angel hair slaw
⅔ cup fat-free ranch dressing
2 (11-ounce) cans mandarin oranges in light syrup, well-drained
1 ripe peeled avocado, seeded and chopped

1. Combine green onions and slaw in a large bowl. Add dressing; toss to coat. Add oranges and avocado; toss gently. Serve immediately. Yield: 12 servings (serving size: ⅔ cup).
Note: Unless you plan to serve all of the salad at one time, it's best to make half the recipe. It will become watery if stored in the refrigerator for any length of time.

CALORIES 76 (26% from fat); FAT 2.2g (sat 0.3g, mono 1.3g, poly 0.3g); PROTEIN 1.3g; CARB 13.6g; FIBER 2.3g; CHOL 0mg; IRON 0.5mg; SODIUM 148mg; CALC 26mg

PINEAPPLE SLAW

PREP: 12 MINUTES   CHILL: 1 HOUR

1 (8-ounce) carton vanilla low-fat yogurt or pineapple low-fat yogurt
3 tablespoons light mayonnaise
½ teaspoon lemon juice
5 cups thinly sliced green cabbage or angel hair slaw
1 (8-ounce) can pineapple tidbits in juice, drained

1. Spoon yogurt onto several layers of heavy-duty paper towels; spread to ½-inch thickness. Cover with additional paper towels; let stand 5 minutes. Scrape

into a bowl using a rubber spatula. Stir in mayonnaise and lemon juice.

2. Combine cabbage and pineapple; add yogurt mixture, tossing gently to coat. Cover and chill. Yield: 4 servings (serving size: 1 cup).

CALORIES 98 (15% from fat); FAT 1.6g (sat 0.5g, mono 0.2g, poly 0.5g); PROTEIN 3.9g; CARB 18.2g; FIBER 2.1g; CHOL 3mg; IRON 0.6mg; SODIUM 157mg; CALC 140mg

CITRUS SALSA SLAW

PREP: 27 MINUTES   CHILL: 30 MINUTES

    2 cups thinly sliced green cabbage
    ⅔ cup orange sections
    ½ cup red bell pepper strips
    ⅓ cup vertically sliced red onion
    ¼ cup lemon sections
    ¼ cup lime sections
    ¼ cup thinly sliced fresh basil
    1 tablespoon chopped fresh cilantro
    1 tablespoon vegetable oil
    1 tablespoon seasoned rice vinegar
    ¼ teaspoon salt
    ⅛ teaspoon black pepper

1. Combine all ingredients in a bowl, tossing gently. Cover and chill. Yield: 4 servings (serving size: 1 cup).

CALORIES 64 (52% from fat); FAT 3.7g (sat 0.7g, mono 1g, poly 1.8g); PROTEIN 1.1g; CARB 8.4g; FIBER 2.6g; CHOL 0mg; IRON 0.6mg; SODIUM 154mg; CALC 39mg

SPICY ASIAN SLAW

PREP: 5 MINUTES

    ¼ cup rice vinegar
    2 tablespoons low-sodium soy sauce
    2 teaspoons dark sesame oil
    ¼ teaspoon crushed red pepper
    ¼ cup sliced green onions
    1 (16-ounce) package ready-to-eat coleslaw
    1 tablespoon chopped fresh parsley
    2 teaspoons sesame seeds, toasted

1. Combine first 4 ingredients in a large bowl; add green onions and coleslaw; toss gently to coat. Sprinkle parsley and sesame seeds over slaw mixture. Serve immediately. Yield: 4 servings (serving size: 1 cup).

CALORIES 74 (36% from fat); FAT 3g (sat 0.4g, mono 1.2g, poly 1.3g); PROTEIN 1.7g; CARB 10.5g; FIBER 2.8g; CHOL 0mg; IRON 0.4mg; SODIUM 235mg; CALC 21mg

PAN-FRIED COLESLAW

PREP: 3 MINUTES
COOK: 11 MINUTES

It's better to shred your own cabbage for this recipe. Prepackaged angel hair cabbage gives a lower yield.

    2 slices turkey bacon
    6 cups very thinly sliced green cabbage (about 1 pound)
    3 tablespoons cider vinegar
    2 tablespoons water
    1 tablespoon sugar
    ½ teaspoon salt
    ½ teaspoon celery seeds

1. Cook bacon in a large skillet over medium-high heat until crisp; remove bacon from pan, reserving drippings in pan. Set bacon aside.

2. Cook cabbage in drippings over medium-high heat until browned, stirring frequently. Add vinegar, water, sugar, salt, and celery seeds; cook 1 minute, stirring constantly. Remove from heat; crumble bacon, and stir into cabbage mixture. Serve warm. Yield: 6 servings (serving size: ½ cup).

CALORIES 45 (28% from fat); FAT 1.4g (sat 0.3g, mono 0.6g, poly 0.4g); PROTEIN 2.1g; CARB 6.6g; FIBER 1.8g; CHOL 6mg; IRON 0.5mg; SODIUM 327mg; CALC 39mg

CARROT-RAISIN SALAD

PREP: 9 MINUTES   CHILL: 1 HOUR

Preshredded carrots can be substituted for grating whole carrots.

    1 (8-ounce) can unsweetened crushed pineapple, undrained
    3 tablespoons light mayonnaise
    4 cups shredded carrot (about 9 medium)
    ½ cup raisins

1. Drain pineapple in a sieve over a bowl, reserving juice. Combine reserved juice and mayonnaise, stirring well with a whisk. Combine carrot, raisins, pineapple, and mayonnaise mixture in a bowl; toss well. Cover; chill 1 hour. Yield: 4 servings (serving size: 1 cup).

CALORIES 146 (7% from fat); FAT 1.1g (sat 0.1g, mono 0g, poly 0.6g); PROTEIN 1.7g; CARB 35.5g; FIBER 3.9g; CHOL 0mg; IRON 1mg; SODIUM 137mg; CALC 40mg

KING COLE SALAD

PREP: 25 MINUTES   CHILL: 1 HOUR

    3 cups finely chopped cauliflower florets
    2½ cups finely chopped broccoli florets
    1½ cups finely chopped mushrooms
    1 cup finely chopped broccoli stalk
    1 cup chopped green bell pepper
    1 cup chopped red onion
    1 (8-ounce) bottle fat-free Italian dressing

1. Combine first 6 ingredients in a large bowl. Add dressing, and stir until well-blended. Cover and chill. Stir salad before serving. Yield: 8 servings (serving size: 1 cup).

CALORIES 46 (8% from fat); FAT 0.4g (sat 0.2g, mono 0g, poly 0.2g); PROTEIN 2.5g; CARB 9.7g; FIBER 2.6g; CHOL 0mg; IRON 0.9mg; SODIUM 289mg; CALC 30mg

TUSCAN BREAD SALAD WITH CORN

PREP: 26 MINUTES

1 cup fresh corn kernels (about 2 ears)
½ cup water
2 cups (1-inch) cubed Italian bread
3 garlic cloves, minced
2 tablespoons white wine vinegar
2 tablespoons water
2 tablespoons mango chutney
1 tablespoon olive oil
¼ teaspoon salt
¼ teaspoon coarsely ground black pepper
1 cup chopped seeded peeled cucumber
1 cup chopped seeded tomato
½ cup chopped green onions
½ cup chopped yellow bell pepper

1. Combine corn and water in a small saucepan; bring to a boil. Reduce heat; simmer 10 minutes or until corn is tender. Drain well.
2. Preheat broiler.
3. Combine bread cubes and garlic in a medium bowl; toss to coat. Arrange bread cubes on a jelly-roll pan, and broil 5 minutes or until lightly browned, stirring once.
4. Combine vinegar and next 5 ingredients in a large bowl. Add corn, cucumber, and remaining 3 ingredients. Add bread cubes, and toss gently. Serve immediately. Yield: 6 servings (serving size: 1 cup).

CALORIES 104 (25% from fat); FAT 2.9g (sat 0.4g, mono 1.8g, poly 0.4g); PROTEIN 3g; CARB 17.7g; FIBER 2.2g; CHOL 0mg; IRON 1mg; SODIUM 201mg; CALC 18mg

FRESH CORN-CILANTRO SALAD

PREP: 23 MINUTES   CHILL: 1 HOUR

5 cups fresh corn kernels (about 10 ears)
1½ cups finely chopped onion
1½ cups chopped red bell pepper
1 tablespoon minced peeled fresh ginger
4 garlic cloves, minced
Olive oil-flavored cooking spray
⅔ cup chopped fresh cilantro
¼ cup red wine vinegar
2 tablespoons minced shallots
1 tablespoon minced seeded jalapeño pepper
4 teaspoons extra-virgin olive oil
¼ teaspoon salt
⅛ teaspoon black pepper

1. Combine first 5 ingredients. Heat a large nonstick skillet coated with cooking spray over medium-high heat until hot. Add corn mixture, and sauté 8 minutes or until corn begins to brown.
2. Combine cilantro and remaining 6 ingredients in a small bowl; stir well with a whisk. Combine corn mixture and cilantro mixture; cover and chill. Yield: 8 servings (serving size: ¾ cup).

CALORIES 130 (26% from fat); FAT 3.7g (sat 0.5g, mono 2g, poly 0.8g); PROTEIN 4.1g; CARB 24.3g; FIBER 4.4g; CHOL 0mg; IRON 1.3mg; SODIUM 93mg; CALC 21mg

CUCUMBERS WITH YOGURT AND MINT

PREP: 14 MINUTES   CHILL: 1 HOUR

⅔ cup plain fat-free yogurt
3 tablespoons chopped fresh mint
½ teaspoon salt
½ teaspoon ground cumin
⅛ teaspoon pepper
4 cups sliced seeded peeled cucumber (about 3 medium)

1. Combine first 5 ingredients in a large bowl. Add cucumber to yogurt mixture, and toss gently to coat. Cover and chill 1 hour. Yield: 5 servings (serving size: ¾ cup).

CALORIES 29 (9% from fat); FAT 0.3g (sat 0.1g, mono 0.1g, poly 0.1g); PROTEIN 2.3g; CARB 4.8g; FIBER 0.7g; CHOL 1mg; IRON 0.4mg; SODIUM 260mg; CALC 79mg

When handling hot chiles or fresh jalapeño peppers, wear disposable gloves to avoid burning your skin.

THAI CUCUMBER SALAD

PREP: 23 MINUTES

⅓ cup minced shallots
⅓ cup sliced green onions
4 cucumbers (about 2½ pounds), peeled, halved lengthwise, seeded, and thinly sliced
1 or 2 small hot red chiles, halved lengthwise, seeded, and thinly sliced (about 1 tablespoon)
½ cup rice vinegar
2 tablespoons sugar
½ teaspoon salt
¼ cup chopped fresh cilantro

1. Combine first 4 ingredients in a large bowl. Combine vinegar, sugar, and salt in a small bowl; pour over cucumber mixture, tossing to coat. Stir in cilantro. Yield: 13 servings (serving size: ½ cup).

CALORIES 19 (43% from fat); FAT 0.1g (sat 0g, mono 0g, poly 0g); PROTEIN 0.5g; CARB 4.2g; FIBER 0.5g; CHOL 0mg; IRON 0.2mg; SODIUM 93mg; CALC 11mg

MARINATED CUCUMBER, MUSHROOM, AND ONION SALAD

PREP: 16 MINUTES   CHILL: 2 HOURS

⅓ cup sherry vinegar
2 teaspoons olive oil
2 teaspoons Dijon mustard
½ teaspoon salt
¼ teaspoon dried oregano
⅛ teaspoon pepper
6 cups sliced seeded peeled cucumber
3 cups sliced mushrooms
1 cup vertically sliced red onion

1. Combine first 6 ingredients in a large bowl; stir well with a whisk. Add remaining ingredients; toss gently. Cover and chill 2 hours. Serve with a slotted spoon. Yield: 8 servings (serving size: 1 cup).

CALORIES 49 (26% from fat); FAT 1.4g (sat 0.2g, mono 0.8g, poly 0.2g); PROTEIN 1.4g; CARB 6.4g; FIBER 1.1g; CHOL 0mg; IRON 0.7mg; SODIUM 250mg; CALC 23mg

CRUNCHY PEA SALAD

PREP: 19 MINUTES

2¼ cups frozen green peas, thawed
1¼ cups diced cucumber
½ cup thinly sliced radishes
¼ cup thinly sliced green onions
2 tablespoons rice vinegar
1 tablespoon olive oil
1 tablespoon honey
½ teaspoon coarsely ground black pepper
¼ teaspoon salt

1. Rinse peas with hot water; drain. Combine peas, cucumber, radishes, and green onions in a bowl.
2. Combine vinegar and remaining 4 ingredients in a small bowl; stir well with a whisk. Pour vinegar mixture over vegetable mixture; toss gently to coat.

Yield: 4 servings (serving size: 1 cup).

CALORIES 119 (29% from fat); FAT 3.8g (sat 0.5g, mono 2.5g, poly 0.5g); PROTEIN 4.7g; CARB 17.5g; FIBER 4.3g; CHOL 0mg; IRON 1.6mg; SODIUM 242mg; CALC 32mg

ROASTED EGGPLANT-AND-CANNELLINI BEAN SALAD

PREP: 40 MINUTES

1¾ cups (1-inch) cubed peeled eggplant (about 6 ounces)
1 cup (1-inch) squares red bell pepper
1 cup (1-inch) cubed onion
2 garlic cloves, halved
1 tablespoon olive oil
Cooking spray
1¼ cups (1-inch) cubed tomato
¼ cup coarsely chopped flat-leaf parsley
1 tablespoon chopped fresh oregano
⅛ teaspoon salt
⅛ teaspoon black pepper
1 (16-ounce) can cannellini beans or other white beans, drained
3 tablespoons red wine vinegar
Red leaf lettuce leaves (optional)

1. Preheat oven to 450°.
2. Combine first 4 ingredients in a large bowl. Add oil; toss to coat. Spoon into a 15 x 10-inch jelly-roll pan coated with cooking spray. Bake at 450° for 25 minutes or until tender and browned, stirring every 10 minutes.
3. Add tomato, parsley, oregano, salt, and black pepper. Bake an additional 10 minutes.
4. Combine beans and vinegar in a large bowl, and toss to coat. Add roasted vegetables, tossing gently. Serve on lettuce-lined plates, if desired. Yield: 3 servings (serving size: 1 cup).

CALORIES 192 (26% from fat); FAT 5.6g (sat 0.7g, mono 3.4g, poly 0.7g); PROTEIN 7.3g; CARB 29g; FIBER 7.3g; CHOL 0mg; IRON 3.2mg; SODIUM 290mg; CALC 53mg

SWEET YELLOW PEPPERS AND TOMATOES WITH FETA CHEESE

PREP: 18 MINUTES

3 tablespoons red wine vinegar
1 tablespoon water
1½ teaspoons olive oil
¾ teaspoon dried oregano
½ teaspoon Dijon mustard
⅛ teaspoon salt
1 garlic clove, minced
¾ cup thinly sliced red onion
6 plum tomatoes, cut lengthwise into ⅛-inch-thick slices
2 yellow bell peppers, cut into ⅛-inch-thick rings
¼ cup (1 ounce) crumbled feta cheese
Freshly ground black pepper

1. Combine first 7 ingredients in a small bowl, stirring well with a whisk. Combine 1 tablespoon vinegar mixture and onion in a small bowl, tossing well. Spoon onion mixture evenly onto a serving platter. Arrange tomato around edge of platter; place pepper rings in center of platter on top of onion. Drizzle remaining vinegar mixture over vegetables. Top with cheese; sprinkle with black pepper. Yield: 6 servings.

CALORIES 69 (42% from fat); FAT 3.2g (sat 1.3g, mono 1.2g, poly 0.4g); PROTEIN 2.4g; CARB 9.1g; FIBER 2.2g; CHOL 6mg; IRON 1.2mg; SODIUM 147mg; CALC 49mg

SUGAR SNAP PEAS WITH LIME-AND-BASIL DRESSING

PREP: 22 MINUTES

1½ pounds fresh sugar snap peas
2 small limes
2 tablespoons honey
4 teaspoons minced fresh basil
2 teaspoons olive oil
¼ teaspoon salt
¼ cup vertically sliced red onion

1. Trim ends from peas. Steam peas, covered, 3 minutes or until crisp-tender.
2. Peel and section limes over a bowl, reserving 2 tablespoons juice. Dice lime sections. Combine reserved lime juice, honey, basil, olive oil, and salt; stir with a whisk.
3. Combine peas, lime sections, and onion in a bowl; drizzle lime juice mixture, tossing gently. Serve immediately. Yield: 6 servings (serving size: 1 cup).

CALORIES 90 (18% from fat); FAT 1.8g (sat 0.3g, mono 1.1g, poly 0.3g); PROTEIN 3.3g; CARB 17g; FIBER 3.6g; CHOL 0mg; IRON 2.5mg; SODIUM 103mg; CALC 62mg

OLD-FASHIONED POTATO SALAD

PREP: 25 MINUTES   CHILL: 2 HOURS

9 cups cubed red potato (about 3 pounds)
½ cup diced onion or sliced green onion
½ cup diced celery
3 hard-cooked large eggs, chopped
¾ cup low-fat sour cream
⅓ cup fat-free mayonnaise
¼ cup sweet pickle relish or dill pickle relish, drained
¼ cup chopped fresh parsley
1 teaspoon dry mustard
1 teaspoon salt
¼ teaspoon black pepper
1 garlic clove, minced

1. Place potato in a Dutch oven; cover with water, and bring to a boil. Cook 8 minutes or until tender. Drain; place in a large bowl. Add onion, celery, and egg; toss gently. Combine sour cream and remaining 7 ingredients. Pour sour cream mixture over potato mixture; toss gently. Cover and chill thoroughly. Yield: 10 servings (serving size: 1 cup).

CALORIES 165 (22% from fat); FAT 4g (sat 1.9g, mono 1.3g, poly 0.4g); PROTEIN 5.5g; CARB 27.5g; FIBER 2.6g; CHOL 71mg; IRON 2.1mg; SODIUM 436mg; CALC 61mg

---

PORTOBELLO MUSHROOMS

Surprisingly, these meaty-flavored mushrooms are actually cultivated white or button mushrooms that have been left to grow an extra few days. **Their Italian-sounding name belies the fact that these large** (up to 6 inches in diameter), **dark-brown mushrooms are grown in America.**

When selecting portobellos, look for those with a tight underside and lighter-color gills. If the gill area appears very black and spread out, that's a sign of age.

Never submerge a portobello in water. The gills act like a sponge, absorbing water quickly. This dilutes their flavor and makes it more difficult to brown the mushrooms if they're to be cooked.

While our recipes call for trimming off the stems or using just the caps, **don't discard the thick, woody stems**—they make excellent stock or broth flavorings.

POTATO-PORTOBELLO SALAD

PREP: 25 MINUTES

5 cups (¼-inch-thick) sliced red potato (about 2¼ pounds)
½ cup sliced green onions
¼ cup chopped fresh parsley
3 tablespoons lemon juice
2 tablespoons capers
2 tablespoons extra-virgin olive oil
1 tablespoon balsamic vinegar
½ teaspoon dried basil
½ teaspoon dried oregano
½ teaspoon dried tarragon
¼ teaspoon black pepper
8 garlic cloves, minced
2 portobello mushroom caps, thinly sliced

Potato-Portobello Salad

8 cups (¼-inch-thick) sliced round red potato (about 2 pounds)
2 tablespoons minced fresh parsley
½ teaspoon celery seeds
Cooking spray
4 slices turkey bacon, minced
1 cup chopped onion
2½ tablespoons all-purpose flour
⅓ cup plus 1 tablespoon cider vinegar
1 tablespoon sugar
¼ teaspoon black pepper
1 (10½-ounce) can beef broth

1. Place potato in a Dutch oven; cover with water, and bring to a boil. Cook 8 minutes or until tender. Drain and place in a large bowl. Sprinkle with parsley and celery seeds; set aside.
2. Coat a medium nonstick skillet with cooking spray; place over medium-high heat until hot. Add bacon, and sauté 3 minutes or until crisp. Add onion, and sauté 3 minutes or until tender. Add bacon and onion to potato mixture.
3. Place flour in a small bowl. Gradually add cider vinegar, stirring well with a whisk.
4. Combine sugar, pepper, and broth in pan. Bring to a boil, and cook 2 minutes. Add flour mixture to pan, and cook 3 minutes or until thickened (mixture will reduce to about 1 cup). Pour over potato mixture, and toss gently to coat. Serve warm. Yield: 8 servings (serving size: 1 cup).

CALORIES 144 (13% from fat); FAT 2.1g (sat 0.5g, mono 0.9g, poly 0.5g); PROTEIN 6.5g; CARB 25g; FIBER 2.5g; CHOL 9mg; IRON 2mg; SODIUM 388mg; CALC 25mg

Take Potato-Portobello Salad to your next picnic. The portobello mushrooms give this salad a meaty flavor.

1. Place potato in a large saucepan, and cover with water; bring to a boil. Reduce heat, and simmer 10 minutes or until potato is tender; drain. Cool.
2. Combine green onions, parsley, lemon juice, capers, olive oil, and next 6 ingredients in a large bowl. Add potato and mushrooms, and toss well. Yield: 8 servings (serving size: 1 cup).

CALORIES 119 (27% from fat); FAT 3.6g (sat 0.5g, mono 2.5g, poly 0.4g); PROTEIN 2.8g; CARB 20g; FIBER 2.1g; CHOL 0mg; IRON 1.3mg; SODIUM 177mg; CALC 24mg

Blue Cheese-and-Chive Potato Salad

PREP: 25 MINUTES   CHILL: 2 HOURS

    8 cups cubed red potato (about
       2½ pounds)
    ½ cup diced red onion
    ½ cup diced celery
    ¼ cup chopped fresh chives
    ¾ cup fat-free sour cream
    ⅓ cup low-fat or nonfat buttermilk
  1½ teaspoons cider vinegar
    ½ teaspoon salt
    ½ teaspoon black pepper
    ½ cup (2 ounces) crumbled blue
       cheese

1. Place potato in a Dutch oven; cover with water, and bring to a boil. Cook 8 minutes or until tender. Drain and place in a large bowl. Add onion, celery, and chives; toss gently.
2. Combine sour cream, buttermilk, vinegar, salt, and pepper; stir in cheese. Pour over potato mixture; toss gently to coat. Cover and chill. Yield: 8 servings (serving size: 1 cup).

CALORIES 167 (18% from fat); FAT 3.3g (sat 2.1g, mono 0.9g, poly 0.2g); PROTEIN 7.4g; CARB 27.1g; FIBER 2.9g; CHOL 8mg; IRON 2mg; SODIUM 328mg; CALC 122mg

Caesar Potato Salad

PREP: 40 MINUTES

    2 pounds small red potatoes
    8 unpeeled garlic cloves
    3 tablespoons fresh lemon juice
  1½ tablespoons extra-virgin olive oil
    1 tablespoon water
    2 teaspoons anchovy paste
    ¼ teaspoon salt
    ¼ teaspoon black pepper
    ⅓ cup diced red onion
    ¼ cup chopped fresh parsley
    2 tablespoons grated fresh
       Parmesan cheese

1. Place potatoes and garlic in a Dutch oven; cover with water, and bring to a boil. Cover, reduce heat, and simmer 24 minutes or until potatoes are tender. Drain; cool potatoes and garlic slightly.
2. Peel garlic; place in a large bowl, and mash. Stir in lemon juice and next 5 ingredients. Cut potatoes in quarters; add to garlic mixture. Add onion, parsley, and cheese; toss well. Serve warm, or cover and chill. Yield: 5 servings (serving size: 1 cup).

CALORIES 197 (23% from fat); FAT 5.1g (sat 0.9g, mono 3.1g, poly 0.4g); PROTEIN 5.7g; CARB 33.5g; FIBER 3.6g; CHOL 1mg; IRON 2.6mg; SODIUM 438mg; CALC 60mg

Tuscan Tomato-Bean Salad

PREP: 22 MINUTES   STAND: 1 HOUR

    2 cups diced plum tomato (about
       1 pound)
    ¼ teaspoon salt
    1 tablespoon fresh lemon juice
    2 teaspoons extra-virgin olive oil
    ¼ teaspoon black pepper
    ⅛ teaspoon crushed red pepper
    1 garlic clove, minced
    ¼ cup chopped fresh basil
    ¼ cup finely chopped onion
    2 tablespoons finely chopped
       flat-leaf or curly-leaf parsley
    1 (16-ounce) can cannellini beans
       or other white beans, drained

1. Place plum tomato in a colander; sprinkle with salt, and drain 1 hour.
2. Combine lemon juice, oil, peppers, and garlic in a large bowl, stirring well with a whisk. Add diced tomato, basil, and remaining ingredients, tossing gently to coat. Yield: 4 servings (serving size: 1 cup).

CALORIES 118 (23% from fat); FAT 3g (sat 0.4g, mono 1.7g, poly 0.4g); PROTEIN 5.1g; CARB 18.1g; FIBER 4.2g; CHOL 0mg; IRON 1.9mg; SODIUM 295mg; CALC 29mg

PLUM TOMATOES

Plum tomatoes, also known as Italian plum or Roma tomatoes, are oval-shaped and smaller than regular tomatoes. They hold their shape well and are a natural for sandwiches, salads, and uncooked tomato sauces, especially when regular tomatoes are out of season.

Marinated Tomato-Basil Salad

PREP: 12 MINUTES   CHILL: 2 HOURS

  32 (½-inch-thick) slices red
       tomato (about 8 tomatoes or
       4¼ pounds)
    1 cup thinly sliced red onion,
       separated into rings
    ½ cup chopped fresh basil
    ½ cup rice vinegar
    1 tablespoon olive oil
    1 teaspoon sugar
    ½ teaspoon salt

1. Arrange tomato slices and onion in a 13 x 9-inch dish. Combine basil and remaining 4 ingredients, stirring well with a whisk. Pour over tomato and onion. Cover and chill at least 2 hours. Yield: 8 servings (serving size: 4 tomato slices).

CALORIES 35 (49% from fat); FAT 1.9g (sat 0.3g, mono 1.3g, poly 0.2g); PROTEIN 0.7g; CARB 4.7g; FIBER 1g; CHOL 0mg; IRON 0.4mg; SODIUM 152mg; CALC 10mg

grain, legume & pasta salads

Boasting of being wilt-free, these salads don't have to be eaten immediately to retain their charisma.

These nonleafy salads allow you to make them ahead and are ideal for taking to work or on a picnic. Many of these recipes offer the suggestion for eating right away or chilling for several hours, which will allow the flavors to develop a bit.

BARLEY-AND-BLACK BEAN SALAD

PREP: 55 MINUTES

4 cups water
1 cup uncooked pearl barley
1½ cups frozen whole-kernel corn, thawed
1½ cups diced tomato
1 cup frozen green peas, thawed
1 cup chopped peeled ripe avocado
¼ cup chopped fresh cilantro
1 (15-ounce) can black beans, drained and rinsed
2 tablespoons fresh lemon juice
1 tablespoon grated fresh onion
1 tablespoon vegetable oil
½ teaspoon salt
¼ teaspoon black pepper
2 garlic cloves, minced
9 romaine lettuce leaves
18 (¼-inch-thick) tomato wedges (about 1 medium tomato)
18 (1-inch-thick) lemon wedges

1. Bring 4 cups water to a boil in a large saucepan. Add barley; cover, reduce heat, and simmer 45 minutes. Remove from heat; cover and let stand 5 minutes. Drain and transfer to a large bowl. Add corn and next 5 ingredients, and toss well.
2. Combine lemon juice and next 5 ingredients in a small bowl. Pour over barley mixture, and toss to coat. Serve warm or at room temperature on romaine leaves with tomato and lemon wedges. Yield: 9 servings (serving size: 1 cup salad, 1 lettuce leaf, 2 tomato wedges, and 2 lemon wedges).

CALORIES 207 (21% from fat); FAT 4.8g (sat 0.8g, mono 2.1g, poly 1.4g); PROTEIN 8g; CARB 36.1g; FIBER 7.8g; CHOL 0mg; IRON 2.3mg; SODIUM 262mg; CALC 37mg

PEARL BARLEY SALAD

PREP: 55 MINUTES

Barley's versatility makes it an important part of Med-Rim cooking.

4 cups water
1 cup uncooked pearl barley
3 cups (1-inch) sliced green beans (about ½ pound)
½ cup fresh lemon juice (about 4 lemons)
2 tablespoons extra-virgin olive oil
2 tablespoons anchovy paste
1 tablespoon thinly sliced fresh basil
2 teaspoons herbes de Provence
¼ teaspoon black pepper
4 garlic cloves, minced
2 hard-cooked large egg whites
1 cup finely chopped fennel bulb
½ cup thinly sliced red onion
2 large tomatoes, cut into ¼-inch-thick wedges

1. Bring 4 cups water to a boil in a large saucepan. Add barley; cover, reduce heat, and simmer 45 minutes. Remove from heat; let stand, covered, 5 minutes. Drain barley; spoon into a large bowl.
2. Bring water to a boil in a large saucepan; add green beans, and cook 2 minutes. Drain and rinse with cold water. Add beans to barley.
3. Combine lemon juice and next 6 ingredients in a bowl; stir well with a whisk. Pour over barley mixture; toss gently.
4. Slice egg whites. Add sliced egg white, fennel, onion, and tomato to barley mixture; toss gently. Yield: 6 servings (serving size: 1½ cups).

CALORIES 233 (24% from fat); FAT 6.2g (sat 0.8g, mono 3.4g, poly 0.8g); PROTEIN 8.6g; CARB 39.2g; FIBER 7.9g; CHOL 0mg; IRON 2.7mg; SODIUM 722mg; CALC 74mg

TABBOULEH

PREP: 30 MINUTES   CHILL: 2 HOURS

Tabbouleh is the signature cracked-wheat salad of many Arabic countries.

1¼ cups uncooked bulgur or cracked wheat
1¼ cups boiling water
2 cups diced tomato
1 cup diced seeded peeled cucumber
¾ cup chopped fresh parsley
½ cup diced yellow bell pepper
½ cup sliced green onions
⅓ cup fresh lemon juice
2 tablespoons chopped fresh mint
2 tablespoons olive oil
½ teaspoon salt

1. Combine bulgur and boiling water in a large bowl. Cover and let stand 30 minutes or until liquid is absorbed. Add tomato and remaining ingredients; toss well. Cover and chill. Yield: 7 servings (serving size: 1 cup).

CALORIES 142 (29% from fat); FAT 4.5g (sat 0.6g, mono 2.9g, poly 0.6g); PROTEIN 4g; CARB 24.1g; FIBER 5.8g; CHOL 0mg; IRON 1.3mg; SODIUM 180mg; CALC 26mg

Pomegranate molasses is a thick, piquant liquid made from reduced pomegranate juice, sugar, and lemon. Except for its vivid ruby color and sweet-tart taste, it resembles traditional molasses. Brush it on Cornish hens or chicken, put a splash in champagne or soda water for a refreshing drink, or drizzle over frozen yogurt. You can find it at Middle Eastern markets or order from Dean and Deluca, Inc. at 1-800-221-7714.

MED-RIM TABBOULEH

PREP: 35 MINUTES   CHILL: 2 HOURS

The pomegranate molasses adds a unique taste. You may substitute balsamic vinegar mixed with molasses for pomegranate molasses.

1½ cups uncooked bulgur or cracked wheat
1½ cups boiling water
 1 teaspoon olive oil
1½ cups diced onion
 ¾ cup finely chopped fresh parsley
 ⅓ cup finely chopped fresh cilantro
 ¼ cup slivered almonds, toasted
 3 tablespoons fresh lemon juice
 1 tablespoon ground cumin
 1 tablespoon pomegranate molasses (optional)
 2 teaspoons olive oil
1½ teaspoons dried oregano
 ½ teaspoon salt
 ⅛ teaspoon ground allspice

1. Combine bulgur and boiling water in a large bowl; stir well. Cover and let stand 30 minutes or until liquid is absorbed.
2. Heat 1 teaspoon oil in a small skillet over medium heat. Add onion; sauté 5 minutes or until tender. Add onion to bulgur; stir in parsley and remaining ingredients. Cover and chill. Yield: 5 servings (serving size: 1 cup).

CALORIES 252 (24% from fat); FAT 6.7g (sat 0.8g, mono 4.2g, poly 1.2g); PROTEIN 7.3g; CARB 44.3g; FIBER 9.7g; CHOL 0mg; IRON 3.2mg; SODIUM 250mg; CALC 81mg

TABBOULEH SALAD WITH TOMATOES AND FETA

PREP: 35 MINUTES
CHILL: 8 HOURS

 1 cup uncooked bulgur or cracked wheat
 2 cups boiling water
 ½ teaspoon salt
 ¾ cup (3 ounces) crumbled feta cheese with basil and tomato
 ⅓ cup dried currants or raisins
 ¼ cup minced green onions
 ¼ cup minced fresh mint
 1 tablespoon chopped fresh or 1 teaspoon dried basil
 1 teaspoon grated lemon rind
12 cherry tomatoes, quartered
 2 garlic cloves, minced
 ¼ cup rice vinegar
 2 tablespoons water
 2 teaspoons extra-virgin olive oil
 ½ teaspoon salt
 ½ teaspoon coarsely ground black pepper

1. Combine first 3 ingredients in a large bowl. Cover and let stand 30 minutes. Add cheese and next 7 ingredients.
2. Combine vinegar and remaining 4 ingredients in a small bowl; stir well with a whisk. Pour dressing over salad; toss gently to coat. Cover and chill at least 8 hours. Yield: 10 servings (serving size: ½ cup).

CALORIES 98 (28% from fat); FAT 3.1g (sat 1.4g, mono 1.3g, poly 0.3g); PROTEIN 3.4g; CARB 15.5g; FIBER 2.9g; CHOL 8mg; IRON 0.7mg; SODIUM 336mg; CALC 56mg

THREE-GRAIN SUMMER-VEGETABLE SALAD

PREP: 30 MINUTES

Quinoa (KEEN-wah) is not only high in fiber but also higher in protein than any other grain. Millet, usually found in health-food stores, is a tiny, delicate grain that is also rich in protein.

Cooking spray
 ¼ cup minced fresh onion
 1 cup uncooked basmati rice
 ½ cup uncooked millet
 ½ cup uncooked quinoa
 2 cups water
 1 cup apple juice
 1 (3-inch) cinnamon stick
 1 cup diced peeled Granny Smith apple (about 1 pound)
 ½ cup raisins
 ½ cup sliced green onions
 ½ cup chopped red bell pepper
 ⅓ cup light mayonnaise
 ¼ cup minced fresh cilantro
 2 tablespoons lemon juice
 2 teaspoons curry powder
 ½ teaspoon salt

1. Place a 6-quart pressure cooker coated with cooking spray over medium-high heat until hot. Add onion, and sauté 1 minute. Add rice, millet, and quinoa, and sauté 30 seconds. Stir in water, apple juice, and cinnamon stick. Close lid securely, and bring to high pressure over medium-high heat (about 4 minutes). Adjust heat to low or level needed to maintain high pressure, and cook

5 minutes. Remove from heat, and place pressure cooker under cold running water. Let stand 7 minutes, and remove lid. Discard cinnamon stick; fluff rice mixture with a fork. Spoon mixture into a large bowl; cool 5 minutes.

2. Stir in apple and remaining ingredients. Serve chilled or at room temperature. Yield: 9 servings (serving size: 1 cup).

CALORIES 212 (15% from fat); FAT 3.6g (sat 0.5g, mono 1g, poly 1.7g); PROTEIN 4.2g; CARB 42.5g; FIBER 2.9g; CHOL 3mg; IRON 3mg; SODIUM 207mg; CALC 30mg

SOUTHWESTERN GARBANZO SALAD

PREP: 14 MINUTES

¼ cup sliced green onions
2 tablespoons chopped fresh cilantro
2 tablespoons lemon juice
2 teaspoons olive oil
¾ teaspoon ground cumin
½ teaspoon paprika
¼ teaspoon salt
¼ teaspoon ground coriander
¼ teaspoon black pepper
2 cups chopped seeded plum tomato
2 (19-ounce) cans chickpeas (garbanzo beans), drained

1. Combine first 9 ingredients in a large bowl. Add tomato and chickpeas, tossing gently to coat. Serve at room temperature or chilled. Yield: 6 servings (serving size: 1 cup).

CALORIES 159 (17% from fat); FAT 3g (sat 0.4g, mono 1.5g, poly 0.8g); PROTEIN 6g; CARB 28.1g; FIBER 7.8g; CHOL 0mg; IRON 2mg; SODIUM 431mg; CALC 45mg

Oriental Wild Rice Salad

ORIENTAL WILD RICE SALAD

PREP: 1 HOUR 5 MINUTES   CHILL: 2 HOURS

3 cups water
½ cup uncooked wild rice
1½ cups uncooked long-grain brown rice
1½ cups chopped red bell pepper
1 cup diagonally sliced celery
1 cup frozen green peas, thawed
1 (8-ounce) can water chestnuts, drained and chopped
⅓ cup sliced green onions
⅓ cup thawed orange juice concentrate
¼ cup low-sodium soy sauce
1 tablespoon vegetable oil
1½ teaspoons lemon juice
¼ teaspoon ground ginger
2 garlic cloves, minced
Lettuce leaves (optional)
2 tablespoons chopped unsalted cashews, toasted

1. Bring 3 cups water to a boil in a large saucepan. Add wild rice; cover, reduce heat, and simmer 10 minutes. Add brown rice; cover and simmer 50 minutes or until tender.

2. Drain rice mixture; combine rice mixture, bell pepper, celery, peas, water chestnuts, and onions in a large bowl. Combine orange juice concentrate and next 5 ingredients. Add orange juice mixture to rice mixture; toss well. Cover and chill at least 2 hours. Serve on lettuce leaves, if desired. Sprinkle with cashews before serving. Yield: 8 servings (serving size: about 1 cup).

CALORIES 166 (24% from fat); FAT 4.4g (sat 0.8g, mono 1.9g, poly 1.4g); PROTEIN 4.3g; CARB 28.2g; FIBER 2.5g; CHOL 0mg; IRON 1.5mg; SODIUM 276mg; CALC 27mg

The ingredients in our Macaroni Salad make it the perfect companion to a summertime backyard cookout.

MACARONI SALAD

PREP: 25 MINUTES

CHILL: 2 HOURS

⅔ cup low-fat sour cream
⅓ cup light mayonnaise
2 tablespoons chopped fresh parsley
2 tablespoons sweet pickle relish
1 tablespoon spicy brown mustard
¼ teaspoon white pepper
4 cups cooked elbow macaroni (about 8 ounces uncooked pasta)
1 cup sliced green onions
1 cup frozen green peas, thawed
¾ cup (3 ounces) diced reduced-fat sharp cheddar cheese
½ cup diced carrot
½ cup diced green bell pepper
½ cup sliced celery
½ cup diced lean ham (about 2 ounces)

1. Combine first 6 ingredients in a large bowl. Add macaroni and remaining ingredients; toss well to coat. Cover and chill. Yield: 8 servings (serving size: 1 cup).

CALORIES 239 (32% from fat); FAT 8.6g (sat 3.4g, mono 2.4g, poly 2.2g); PROTEIN 10.5g; CARB 29.8g; FIBER 2.4g; CHOL 22mg; IRON 1.9mg; SODIUM 382mg; CALC 139mg

ITALIAN-MOSTACCIOLI SALAD

PREP: 20 MINUTES   CHILL: 1 HOUR

1½ cups uncooked mostaccioli pasta (tube-shaped pasta)
3 tablespoons white vinegar
2 tablespoons water
1 tablespoon olive oil
¾ teaspoon dried Italian seasoning
¼ teaspoon salt
¼ teaspoon black pepper
2 garlic cloves, crushed
1 cup presliced mushrooms
¾ cup cherry tomatoes, halved
½ cup chopped green bell pepper
½ cup (2 ounces) preshredded part-skim mozzarella cheese
Cherry tomatoes (optional)

1. Cook pasta according to package directions, omitting salt and fat. Drain and rinse with cold water; drain well.
2. Combine vinegar and next 6 ingredients in a medium bowl, stirring well with a whisk. Add pasta, mushrooms, tomato halves, bell pepper, and cheese; toss gently to coat. Cover and chill. Garnish with cherry tomatoes, if desired. Yield: 5 servings (serving size: 1 cup).

CALORIES 160 (29% from fat); FAT 5.1g (sat 1.6g, mono 2.6g, poly 0.6g); PROTEIN 6.7g; CARB 22.3g; FIBER 1.4g; CHOL 7mg; IRON 1.8mg; SODIUM 176mg; CALC 90mg

ORIENTAL PASTA SALAD

PREP: 23 MINUTES   CHILL: 1 HOUR

2 cups broccoli florets
1½ cups cooked spaghetti (about 3 ounces uncooked)
¾ cup thinly sliced red bell pepper
2 tablespoons low-sodium soy sauce
1 tablespoon dark sesame oil
¼ teaspoon crushed red pepper

1. Steam broccoli, covered, 5 minutes or until crisp-tender. Rinse with cold water; drain well.
2. Combine broccoli and remaining ingredients; toss gently. Cover and chill. Yield: 4 servings (serving size: 1 cup).

CALORIES 131 (27% from fat); FAT 4g (sat 0.6g, mono 1.4g, poly 1.7g); PROTEIN 4.5g; CARB 20g; FIBER 2.2g; CHOL 0mg; IRON 1.7mg; SODIUM 255mg; CALC 26mg

BALSAMIC PASTA SALAD

PREP: 19 MINUTES

CHILL: 2 HOURS

¼ cup balsamic vinegar
3 tablespoons water
1½ teaspoons olive oil
¼ teaspoon salt
¼ teaspoon black pepper
1 large garlic clove, minced
½ cup small broccoli florets
½ cup small cauliflower florets
½ cup julienne-cut carrot
½ cup julienne-cut red bell pepper
4 cups cooked farfalle (bow tie pasta) (about 8 ounces uncooked)
2 tablespoons thinly sliced fresh basil
¼ cup (1 ounce) grated Asiago cheese

1. Combine first 6 ingredients in a small bowl.
2. Place broccoli, cauliflower, and carrot in a large saucepan of boiling water; cook 30 seconds. Drain. Rinse with cold water; drain.
3. Combine drained vegetables, bell pepper, pasta, basil, and cheese in a large bowl. Add vinegar mixture, and toss gently to coat. Cover and chill. Yield: 5 servings (serving size: 1 cup).

CALORIES 199 (15% from fat); FAT 3.4g (sat 1.1g, mono 1.4g, poly 0.5g); PROTEIN 7.7g; CARB 34.3g; FIBER 2.9g; CHOL 3mg; IRON 2mg; SODIUM 203mg; CALC 81mg

TORTELLINI SALAD

PREP: 16 MINUTES

1 (9-ounce) package fresh three-cheese tortellini
2 cups (2-inch) julienne-cut zucchini
1 cup cherry tomato halves
½ cup chopped red bell pepper
⅓ cup sliced green onions
⅓ cup fat-free red wine vinaigrette
1 teaspoon chopped fresh dill
¼ teaspoon black pepper
2 tablespoons grated Parmesan cheese

1. Cook tortellini in boiling water 6 minutes. Drain and rinse with cold water; drain well.

2. Combine tortellini, zucchini, tomato halves, bell pepper, and onions in a bowl. Combine vinaigrette, dill, and black pepper; pour over tortellini mixture, and toss gently. Sprinkle with Parmesan cheese before serving. Yield: 6 servings (serving size: 1 cup).

CALORIES 158 (21% from fat); FAT 3.7g (sat 1.9g, mono 1.3g, poly 0.5g); PROTEIN 7.1g; CARB 25.4g; FIBER 1.9g; CHOL 26mg; IRON 1.4mg; SODIUM 472mg; CALC 86mg

main-dish salads Tender young greens and vegetables are tossed with chunks of grilled chicken, seafood, meat, or legumes to create these hearty main attractions.

COUSCOUS-AND-BLACK BEAN SALAD

PREP: 15 MINUTES

1 large orange
⅛ teaspoon salt
⅔ cup uncooked couscous
1 cup canned black beans, rinsed and drained
½ cup chopped red bell pepper
¼ cup chopped green onions
2 tablespoons chopped fresh parsley
1 tablespoon seasoned rice vinegar
1½ teaspoons vegetable oil
¼ teaspoon ground cumin

1. Grate ¼ teaspoon orange rind, and set aside. Squeeze juice from orange over a bowl; reserve ¼ cup juice, and set aside. Add water to remaining juice in bowl to equal 1 cup.

2. Bring 1 cup water mixture and salt to a boil in a medium saucepan; gradually stir in couscous. Remove from heat; cover and let stand 5 minutes. Fluff with a fork. Cool slightly. Stir in ¼ teaspoon orange rind, beans, bell pepper, onions, and parsley.

3. Combine reserved ¼ cup orange juice, vinegar, oil, and cumin. Pour over couscous mixture; toss well. Store in an airtight container in refrigerator. Yield: 2 servings (serving size: 2 cups).

CALORIES 342 (13% from fat); FAT 4.8g (sat 0.8g, mono 1.1g, poly 2g); PROTEIN 14.7g; CARB 62.5g; FIBER 6.6g; CHOL 0mg; IRON 3.9mg; SODIUM 391mg; CALC 46mg

MEXICAN BLACK BEAN-AND-CITRUS SALAD

PREP: 20 MINUTES

Tangelos, a cross between grapefruit and tangerines, add a rich, tart flavor to this bean salad. If you can't find this citrus hybrid, substitute oranges or tangerines. This also can be served as a side salad in ¾-cup portions. As a side, it's great served with chicken, fish, or pork.

1 tablespoon olive oil
1 cup diced onion
1 cup diced red bell pepper
2 teaspoons grated tangelo or orange rind
¼ cup fresh tangelo or orange juice
3 tablespoons fresh lime juice
1 teaspoon sugar
½ teaspoon salt
½ teaspoon ground cumin
¼ teaspoon hot sauce
1½ cups tangelo or orange sections (about 8 tangelos)
¼ cup finely chopped fresh cilantro
2 (15-ounce) cans black beans, rinsed and drained

1. Heat oil in a nonstick skillet over medium-high heat. Add onion and bell pepper; sauté 5 minutes or until vegetables are tender.

2. Combine rind and next 6 ingredients. Combine onion mixture, tangelo sections, cilantro, and beans in a medium bowl. Add juice mixture, and toss gently to coat. Yield: 3 servings (serving size: about 1½ cup).

CALORIES 348 (16% from fat); FAT 6.2g (sat 1g, mono 3.4g, poly 1g); PROTEIN 16.6g; CARB 61.8g; FIBER 13g; CHOL 0mg; IRON 4.8mg; SODIUM 836mg; CALC 112mg

MEXICAN COBB SALAD

PREP: 35 MINUTES

Rather than make several individual servings, arrange this salad on one large platter and let guests serve themselves.

    1   cup fresh corn kernels (about 1
          large ear)
    8   cups mixed greens
    1   cup diced tomato
    1   cup diced red onion
    1   cup diced peeled jícama or
          carrot
    1   cup diced green bell pepper
    1   cup diced peeled avocado
    1   (15-ounce) can black beans,
          rinsed and drained
    1   cup (4 ounces) shredded
          reduced-fat Monterey Jack
          cheese
    1   cup coarsely crushed baked
          tortilla chips
       Lime-Cilantro Vinaigrette (page
          424)

1. Steam corn, covered, 3 minutes or until crisp-tender. Rinse with cold water; set aside to cool.
2. Place 2 cups mixed salad greens on each of 4 plates. Arrange ¼ cup tomato, ¼ cup onion, ¼ cup jícama, ¼ cup bell pepper, ¼ cup corn, ¼ cup avocado, and about ½ cup beans in individual rows over salad greens. Sprinkle ¼ cup cheese and ¼ cup crushed chips over each salad. Drizzle ¼ cup Lime-Cilantro Vinaigrette over each salad. Yield: 4 servings.

CALORIES 373 (33% from fat); FAT 13.8g (sat 4.5g, mono 5.9g, poly 1.7g); PROTEIN 19.3g; CARB 48.5g; FIBER 11g; CHOL 19mg; IRON 3.9mg; SODIUM 678mg; CALC 317mg

Mexican Cobb Salad

WHITE BEAN-VEGETABLE SALAD

PREP: 16 MINUTES

    ¼   cup water
    ¾   cup diced carrot
    3   tablespoons red wine vinegar
    2   tablespoons olive oil
    ¼   teaspoon salt
    ¼   teaspoon dried basil
    ⅛   teaspoon dried thyme
    ⅛   teaspoon crushed red pepper
    ⅛   teaspoon rubbed sage
    ⅛   teaspoon black pepper
    2   garlic cloves, minced
    1   cup diced yellow bell pepper
    ½   cup thinly sliced green onions
   10   cherry tomatoes, quartered
    2   (16-ounce) cans cannellini beans
          or other white beans, rinsed
          and drained
    4   cups torn curly endive

1. Bring water to a boil in a small saucepan; add carrot. Cook 1 minute; drain. Rinse with cold water; drain well.
2. Combine vinegar and next 8 ingredients in a large bowl. Add carrot, bell pepper, green onions, tomato, and beans; toss to coat. Spoon onto individual endive-lined salad plates. Yield: 4 servings (serving size: 1¼ cups bean mixture and 1 cup endive).

CALORIES 316 (30% from fat); FAT 10.5g (sat 1.4g, mono 5.8g, poly 2.3g); PROTEIN 13.4g; CARB 45.5g; FIBER 6.9g; CHOL 0mg; IRON 5mg; SODIUM 439mg; CALC 105mg

DILLED BLACK-EYED PEA SALAD

PREP: 50 MINUTES
CHILL: 8 HOURS

Cooking spray
1 cup chopped onion
3 cups shelled black-eyed peas (about 1 pound unshelled peas)
2¼ cups water
¼ cup chopped cooked ham
¼ teaspoon black pepper
1 (10½-ounce) can low-sodium chicken broth
2 tablespoons white wine vinegar
1 tablespoon olive oil
1 tablespoon lemon juice
1 teaspoon honey
½ teaspoon salt
½ teaspoon dried dill
½ teaspoon dried thyme
¼ teaspoon black pepper
2 garlic cloves, crushed
1 cup halved cherry tomatoes
⅓ cup sliced green onions
Spinach leaves (optional)

1. Coat a large saucepan with cooking spray; place over medium heat until hot. Add onion; sauté 5 minutes or until tender. Stir in peas, water, ham, ¼ teaspoon pepper, and broth; bring to a boil. Cover, reduce heat, and simmer 30 minutes or until peas are tender, stirring occasionally. Drain well.
2. Combine vinegar and next 8 ingredients in a large bowl; stir well with a whisk. Add pea mixture, tomato, and green onions, tossing gently to coat. Cover; marinate in refrigerator 8 hours. Spoon into a spinach-lined bowl, if desired. Yield: 4 servings (serving size: 1 cup).
Note: 3 cups of frozen black-eyed peas can be used as a substitute in this recipe.

CALORIES 232 (23% from fat); FAT 6g (sat 1.2g, mono 3g, poly 0.9g); PROTEIN 13.3g; CARB 33.2g; FIBER 3.3g; CHOL 4mg; IRON 2.5mg; SODIUM 434mg; CALC 54mg

ROTINI-VEGETABLE SALAD WITH PESTO DRESSING

PREP: 18 MINUTES

1 large garlic clove, peeled
1 cup basil leaves
2 tablespoons grated fresh Parmesan cheese
¼ teaspoon salt
¼ teaspoon black pepper
2 tablespoons water
2 tablespoons olive oil
3 cups cooked rotini (about 2 cups uncooked corkscrew pasta)
1½ cups diced zucchini
1½ cups halved cherry tomatoes
1 (16-ounce) can cannellini beans or other white beans, rinsed and drained

1. Drop garlic through food chute with food processor on; process until minced. Add basil, cheese, salt, and pepper; process until finely minced. With food processor on, slowly pour water and oil through food chute; process until well-blended.
2. Combine rotini, zucchini, tomato, and beans in a large bowl. Add pesto mixture, tossing gently to coat. Yield: 4 servings (serving size: 1¾ cups).

CALORIES 365 (26% from fat); FAT 10.6g (sat 1.9g, mono 5.8g, poly 1.9g); PROTEIN 14.7g; CARB 54.9g; FIBER 6.2g; CHOL 2mg; IRON 4.6mg; SODIUM 359mg; CALC 134mg

Rotini-Vegetable Salad With Pesto Dressing

ASIAN CHICKEN-NOODLE SALAD

PREP: 14 MINUTES

4 ounces uncooked angel hair pasta
1 cup (½-inch) diagonally sliced snow peas
2 cups shredded cooked chicken breast
½ cup diced red bell pepper
¼ cup sliced green onions
1 cucumber, peeled, halved lengthwise, and sliced (about ¾ cup)
3 tablespoons low-sodium teriyaki sauce
2 tablespoons rice vinegar
2 teaspoons sesame seeds, toasted
1 teaspoon dark sesame oil
½ teaspoon salt
¼ teaspoon black pepper

1. Break pasta into 5-inch pieces. Cook in boiling water 2 minutes. Add snow peas; cook 1 minute. Drain and rinse with cold water; drain well. Combine pasta mixture, chicken, bell pepper, green onions, and cucumber in a bowl.

2. Combine teriyaki sauce and remaining ingredients in a bowl. Pour over pasta mixture, and toss to coat. Serve at room temperature or chilled. Yield: 4 servings (serving size: 1½ cups).

CALORIES 292 (17% from fat); FAT 5.5g (sat 1.2g, mono 1.9g, poly 1.7g); PROTEIN 31.7g; CARB 26.7g; FIBER 1.9g; CHOL 72mg; IRON 3mg; SODIUM 553mg; CALC 51mg

OLD-FASHIONED CHICKEN SALAD WITH CANTALOUPE

PREP: 17 MINUTES   CHILL: 1 HOUR

¼ cup fat-free mayonnaise
¼ cup plain low-fat yogurt
¼ cup low-fat sour cream
1 teaspoon lemon juice
¼ teaspoon salt
¼ teaspoon black pepper
3 cups chopped cooked chicken breast
1 cup chopped celery
¼ cup sweet pickle relish
3 tablespoons finely chopped onion
1 hard-cooked large egg, chopped
½ cantaloupe, unpeeled

1. Combine first 6 ingredients in a small bowl.

2. Combine chicken, celery, pickle relish, onion, and egg in a bowl. Stir in mayonnaise mixture; cover and chill.

3. Cut cantaloupe lengthwise into 8 slices, and serve with chicken salad. Yield: 4 servings (serving size: 2 slices cantaloupe and 1 cup salad).

CALORIES 294 (23% from fat); FAT 7.5g (sat 2.8g, mono 2.5g, poly 1.2g); PROTEIN 37.1g; CARB 18.9g; FIBER 1.3g; CHOL 151mg; IRON 1.7mg; SODIUM 616mg; CALC 108mg

CURRIED CHICKEN SALAD WITH PEAS

PREP: 20 MINUTES

⅓ cup plain fat-free yogurt
2 tablespoons light mayonnaise
1 teaspoon curry powder
⅛ teaspoon salt
Dash of ground red pepper
8 ounces ready-to-eat roasted skinned, boned chicken breast (such as Tyson), cubed
1½ cups diced Red Delicious apple
1 cup frozen green peas, thawed
½ cup thinly sliced celery
2 cups shredded romaine lettuce
2 tablespoons coarsely chopped dry-roasted peanuts

1. Combine first 5 ingredients in a large bowl. Add chicken, apple, peas, and celery, tossing to coat. Stir in lettuce; sprinkle with peanuts. Yield: 4 servings (serving size: 1¼ cups).

CALORIES 185 (27% from fat); FAT 5.6g (sat 0.9g, mono 2.0g, poly 2.0g); PROTEIN 17.9g; CARB 15.9g; FIBER 2.4g; CHOL 38mg; IRON 1.7mg; SODIUM 488mg; CALC 70mg

CURRIED COUSCOUS-CHICKEN SALAD

PREP: 15 MINUTES

¾ cup water
⅔ cup uncooked couscous
½ teaspoon salt
½ teaspoon curry powder
1 cup cubed cooked chicken breast
½ cup drained canned chickpeas (garbanzo beans)
½ cup chopped red cabbage
¼ cup sliced green onions
¼ cup thinly sliced celery
1 teaspoon grated orange rind
⅓ cup fresh orange juice
2 teaspoons olive oil
¼ teaspoon black pepper

1. Bring water to a boil in a medium saucepan; stir in couscous, salt, and curry powder. Remove from heat. Cover and let stand 5 minutes. Fluff with a fork. Add chicken, chickpeas, cabbage, green onions, and celery.

2. Combine orange rind, orange juice, oil, and pepper, stirring well with a whisk. Pour over couscous mixture, and toss well. Serve immediately, or cover and chill. Yield: 4 servings (serving size: 1 cup).

CALORIES 256 (17% from fat); FAT 4.8g (sat 0.8g, mono 2.4g, poly 0.8g); PROTEIN 20.1g; CARB 33.3g; FIBER 2.7g; CHOL 37mg; IRON 2.1mg; SODIUM 387mg; CALC 37mg

BLACKENED CHICKEN SALAD

PREP:30 MINUTES
COOK:14 MINUTES

3 cups chopped tomato
¾ cup diced yellow or green bell pepper
¼ cup finely chopped red onion
3 tablespoons cider vinegar
1 tablespoon sugar
¼ teaspoon salt
⅛ teaspoon black pepper
¼ cup lemon juice
¼ cup Dijon mustard
3 tablespoons water
1 tablespoon honey
4 (4-ounce) skinned, boned chicken breast halves
3 tablespoons Spicy Seasoning (page 456)
Cooking spray
1 pound sugar snap peas, trimmed
8 cups torn romaine lettuce

1. Combine first 7 ingredients in a bowl; cover and chill.

2. Combine lemon juice, mustard, water, and honey; cover and chill.

Blackened Chicken Salad

3. Rub chicken evenly with Spicy Seasoning. Coat a large heavy skillet with cooking spray, and place over medium-high heat until hot. Add chicken, and cook 7 minutes on each side or until chicken is done. Remove chicken from pan, and cool. Cut chicken across grain into thin slices.

4. Steam peas, covered, 2 minutes. Rinse with cold water, and drain. Combine peas and lettuce in a large bowl; drizzle lemon juice mixture over lettuce mixture, and toss to coat. Place about 2 cups lettuce mixture in each of 4 large salad bowls; top each serving with 1 sliced chicken breast half and about

BLACKENING CHICKEN

We use our Spicy Seasoning (page 456) for blackening chicken. There are commercial mixes you can use, but they are much higher in salt. For a hot spice, try Paul Prudhomme's Magic Seasoning line. If mild is your preference, try McCormick's Cajun Seasoning.

1 cup tomato mixture. Yield: 4 servings.

CALORIES 295 (16% from fat); FAT 5.3g (sat 1g, mono 1.2g, poly 1.3g); PROTEIN 32.2g; CARB 30.4g; FIBER 6.5g; CHOL 72mg; IRON 5.7mg; SODIUM 1172mg; CALC 105mg

FRIED-CHICKEN SALAD

PREP: 20 MINUTES
MARINATE: 30 MINUTES
COOK: 7 MINUTES

See page 185 for descriptions of a variety of blue cheeses.

¼ cup dry breadcrumbs
¼ cup all-purpose flour
1 teaspoon garlic powder
1 teaspoon dried thyme
½ teaspoon salt
½ teaspoon black pepper
¾ pound skinned, boned chicken breast, cut into thin strips
½ cup low-fat or nonfat buttermilk
Cooking spray
1 tablespoon olive oil
4 cups thickly sliced romaine lettuce (cut across rib)
1 (15-ounce) can whole baby beets, drained and halved
½ cup fat-free honey mustard dressing
½ cup (2 ounces) crumbled blue cheese

1. Combine first 6 ingredients in a shallow dish. Combine chicken and buttermilk in a bowl; cover and marinate in refrigerator 30 minutes. Drain chicken; dredge a few strips at a time in breadcrumb mixture.

2. Coat a nonstick skillet with cooking spray. Add oil; place over medium heat until hot. Add chicken to skillet; cook 3 minutes on each side or until done.

3. Arrange 1 cup lettuce on each of 4 plates; divide chicken and beets among plates. Top with 2 tablespoons dressing and 2 tablespoons blue cheese. Yield: 4 servings.

CALORIES 287 (27% from fat); FAT 7.4g (sat 2.2g, mono 3.4g, poly 0.8g); PROTEIN 25.8g; CARB 28.3g; FIBER 2.0g; CHOL 60mg; IRON 2.9mg; SODIUM 710mg; CALC 116mg

Fried-Chicken Salad

Baby beets and blue cheese tingle the taste buds in Fried-Chicken Salad.

CHICKEN CAESAR SALAD

PREP: 20 MINUTES

COOK: 15 MINUTES

 4 (1-ounce) slices French bread,
  cut into 1-inch cubes

Cooking spray

 ½ teaspoon garlic powder

 2 pounds skinned, boned
  chicken breast

 ¼ cup fresh lemon juice

 ¼ cup red wine vinegar

 1 tablespoon olive oil

 1 teaspoon anchovy paste

 ¼ teaspoon freshly ground black
  pepper

 5 garlic cloves, peeled

 9 cups torn romaine lettuce

 ¼ cup (1 ounce) grated fresh
  Parmesan cheese

1. Preheat oven to 350°.
2. Place bread cubes on a baking sheet. Coat bread cubes with cooking spray, and sprinkle with garlic powder; toss to coat. Bake at 350° for 15 minutes or until lightly browned. Set aside.
3. Place a large nonstick skillet coated with cooking spray over medium-high heat until hot. Add chicken; cook 6 to 7 minutes on each side or until done. Remove chicken from pan; cool. Cut chicken diagonally across grain into thin slices.
4. Combine lemon juice and next 5 ingredients in a blender; process until smooth. Add ¼ cup lemon juice mixture to chicken, tossing gently to coat.
5. Place lettuce in a large bowl; drizzle remaining lemon juice mixture over lettuce, and toss to coat. Add chicken mixture and cheese; toss gently. Top with croutons. Yield: 7 servings (serving size: 1½ cups salad and ⅓ cup croutons).

CALORIES 252 (25% from fat); FAT 7.1g (sat 1.8g, mono 3g, poly 1.1g); PROTEIN 33.7g; CARB 11.6g; FIBER 1.4g; CHOL 85mg; IRON 2mg; SODIUM 318mg; CALC 82mg

WALNUT-CHICKEN SALAD

PREP: 25 MINUTES

COOK: 18 MINUTES

 ¼ cup chopped walnuts

 2 tablespoons low-sodium soy
  sauce, divided

Cooking spray

 1 pound skinned, boned chicken
  breast

 1¼ cups water

 1 cup uncooked couscous

 ½ cup shredded carrot

 ⅓ cup sliced green onions

 3 tablespoons minced shallots

 4½ tablespoons rice vinegar

 3 tablespoons water

 1½ tablespoons walnut oil

 1 tablespoon brown sugar

 1½ teaspoons grated lemon rind

 1½ teaspoons grated peeled fresh
  ginger

 ¼ teaspoon salt

 ¼ teaspoon black pepper

 3 garlic cloves, minced

 5 cups fresh spinach leaves

1. Place a large nonstick skillet over medium-high heat until hot; add walnuts. Cook 2 minutes, stirring constantly. Add 1 tablespoon soy sauce, stirring constantly until soy sauce is absorbed. Remove walnuts from pan, and set aside. Wipe browned bits from pan with a paper towel.
2. Coat pan with cooking spray; place over medium-high heat until hot. Add chicken, and cook 6 minutes on each side. Reduce heat to low; cover and cook 5 minutes or until done. Remove from heat. Cut chicken into 1-inch pieces.
3. Bring 1¼ cups water to a boil in a medium saucepan; stir in couscous. Remove from heat. Cover and let stand 5 minutes. Fluff with a fork. Combine couscous, chicken, carrot, and green onions in a large bowl.

4. Combine 1 tablespoon soy sauce, shallots, and next 9 ingredients. Pour over chicken mixture, and toss to coat. Arrange 1 cup spinach leaves on individual serving plates; top with 1 cup chicken mixture. Sprinkle each salad with walnuts. Yield: 5 servings.

CALORIES 344 (27% from fat); FAT 10.4g (sat 1.3g, mono 4.4g, poly 3.4g); PROTEIN 29.1g; CARB 34.1g; FIBER 3.8g; CHOL 58mg; IRON 3.1mg; SODIUM 403mg; CALC 68mg

FIRECRACKER CRAB SALAD

PREP: 13 MINUTES

CHILL: 2 HOURS

 ¾ pound lump crabmeat, drained
  and shell pieces removed

 ⅓ cup thinly sliced celery

 2 tablespoons thinly sliced green
  onions

 ¼ cup light mayonnaise

 1 tablespoon white wine
  vinegar

 ½ teaspoon hot sauce

 ¼ teaspoon cracked black pepper

 ⅛ teaspoon salt

 ⅛ teaspoon white pepper

 1 large garlic clove, minced

 ⅔ cup diced seeded tomato

 4 romaine lettuce leaves

1. Combine first 3 ingredients in a medium bowl, tossing gently. Combine mayonnaise and next 6 ingredients; stir well. Add to crabmeat mixture, tossing to coat. Cover and chill 2 hours; gently stir in tomato. Serve with crackers on lettuce-lined plates. Yield: 4 servings (serving size: ⅔ cup).

CALORIES 113 (20% from fat); FAT 2.5g (sat 0.2g, mono 0.2g, poly 1.1g); PROTEIN 15.6g; CARB 6.6g; FIBER 0.7g; CHOL 74mg; IRON 1mg; SODIUM 437mg; CALC 88mg

DUCK AND WILD RICE SALAD WITH ORANGE DRESSING

PREP: 1 HOUR

If duck breasts aren't available, you can substitute 1 pound of pork tenderloin for the duck.

    1 (6-ounce) package wild rice
       Cooking spray
    4 (4-ounce) skinned, boned duck
       breast halves
    1 cup sliced green onions
    1 cup seedless green grapes, halved
  ¼ cup chopped pecans, toasted
    1 tablespoon grated orange rind
    1 cup fresh orange juice
  ⅓ cup sherry vinegar
  ¼ teaspoon salt
  ⅛ teaspoon black pepper
    7 red leaf lettuce leaves

1. Cook rice according to package directions, omitting salt; drain.
2. Preheat oven to 450°.
3. Place a large nonstick skillet coated with cooking spray over medium-high heat until hot. Add duck; cook 2 minutes on each side or until lightly browned. Place duck in an 11 x 7-inch baking dish coated with cooking spray. Bake at 450° for 20 minutes or until done; cool.
4. Cut duck into ¼-inch-thick strips. Combine duck, rice, green onions, grape halves, and pecans in a large bowl.
5. Combine orange rind, orange juice, vinegar, salt, and pepper in a small bowl; stir well with a whisk. Pour over duck mixture, and toss to coat. Serve salad at room temperature on lettuce-lined plates. Yield: 7 servings (serving size: 1 cup).

CALORIES 250 (23% from fat); FAT 6.5g (sat 1.2g, mono 2.7g, poly 1.4g); PROTEIN 17.7g; CARB 29.3g; FIBER 2.5g; CHOL 50mg; IRON 4.1mg; SODIUM 194mg; CALC 38mg

menu

Chilled Cucumber Soup With
Leeks and Celery (page 460)

Greek Lamb Salad

Classic Breadsticks (page 100)

Strawberries and Raspberries in Custard
Sauce (page 186)

GREEK LAMB SALAD

PREP: 25 MINUTES   MARINATE: 8 HOURS
COOK: 8 MINUTES

You can substitute leftover cooked lamb, beef, or pork in this recipe.

    1 pound lean leg of lamb
  ¼ cup red wine vinegar
  ¼ cup red wine
    2 tablespoons low-sodium soy
       sauce
    1 tablespoon chopped fresh mint
    1 tablespoon minced red onion
    2 teaspoons chopped fresh
       rosemary
    2 teaspoons olive oil
  ½ teaspoon salt
  ½ teaspoon black pepper
    1 garlic clove, crushed
    6 small red potatoes, quartered
       (about ¾ pound)
    3 cups shredded romaine lettuce
  ½ cup chopped celery
  ½ cup cherry tomato halves
  ¼ cup (1 ounce) crumbled feta
       cheese
       Freshly ground black pepper

1. Trim fat from lamb. Combine red wine vinegar and next 9 ingredients in a 1-cup glass measure, stirring well with a whisk. Pour ½ cup marinade into a large heavy-duty zip-top plastic bag; set aside remaining ¼ cup marinade. Add lamb to bag; seal bag. Marinate in refrigerator 8 hours, turning bag

occasionally. Remove lamb from bag, discarding marinade.
2. Prepare grill.
3. Place lamb on grill rack. Grill 4 minutes on each side or until desired degree of doneness. Cut lamb into thin strips.
4. Steam potato, covered, 12 minutes or until tender; cool. Combine lamb, potato, lettuce, celery, tomato halves, and feta cheese in a large bowl. Pour reserved ¼ cup marinade over lamb mixture, tossing to coat. Sprinkle with freshly ground pepper. Yield: 5 servings (serving size: 2 cups).

CALORIES 209 (31% from fat); FAT 7.3g (sat 3g, mono 3g, poly 0.5g); PROTEIN 19.7g; CARB 16.1g; FIBER 2.6g; CHOL 57mg; IRON 3mg; SODIUM 368mg; CALC 81mg

LENTIL SALAD WITH FETA CHEESE

PREP: 30 MINUTES

This lentil salad makes a great filling for whole wheat pitas.

  1¼ cups dried lentils
      3 tablespoons fresh lemon juice
  1½ tablespoons olive oil
    ½ teaspoon dried thyme
    ¼ teaspoon salt
    ⅛ teaspoon coarsely ground black
        pepper
      1 garlic clove, crushed
  1½ cups quartered cherry
        tomatoes
      1 cup diced cucumber
    ½ cup (2 ounces) crumbled feta
        cheese
    ⅓ cup thinly sliced celery
        Romaine lettuce leaves (optional)

1. Place lentils in a large saucepan, and cover with water to 2 inches above lentils. Bring to a boil; cover, reduce heat, and simmer 20 minutes or until tender. Drain well.

2. Combine lemon juice and next 5 ingredients in a medium bowl; stir well with a whisk. Add lentils, tomato, cucumber, cheese, and celery to lemon juice mixture; toss gently to coat. Serve on lettuce-lined plates, if desired. Yield: 6 servings (serving size: 1 cup).

CALORIES 215 (28% from fat); FAT 6.8g (sat 3g, mono 3.2g, poly 0.6g); PROTEIN 13.7g; CARB 26.8g; FIBER 5.4g; CHOL 12mg; IRON 4.1mg; SODIUM 266mg; CALC 100mg

GRECIAN PORK TENDERLOIN SALAD

PREP:17 MINUTES
MARINATE:30 MINUTES
COOK:25 MINUTES

  1   pound pork tenderloin
1½ tablespoons red wine vinegar
1½ teaspoons olive oil
  1   teaspoon chopped fresh
        oregano
  1   garlic clove, crushed
1½ cups sliced peeled cucumber,
        divided
  1   tablespoon chopped fresh dill
  1   (8-ounce) carton plain fat-free
        yogurt
Cooking spray
  4   cups tightly packed torn
        romaine lettuce
½   cup thinly sliced onion,
        separated into rings
½   cup thinly sliced radishes
  2   tablespoons crumbled feta
        cheese
  2   teaspoons chopped fresh mint
  2   tomatoes, each cut into 8
        wedges
  1   green bell pepper, cut crosswise
        into 12 rings
  8   pitted ripe olives

1. Trim fat from pork. Combine vinegar, oil, oregano, and garlic in a large heavy-duty zip-top plastic bag; add pork, turning to coat. Seal bag; marinate in refrigerator 30 minutes, turning bag occasionally.

2. Place ½ cup cucumber, dill, and yogurt in a food processor; process 10 seconds or until smooth, scraping sides of processor bowl once. Set aside.

3. Prepare grill.

4. Remove pork from bag, discarding marinade; place on a grill rack coated with cooking spray. Cover and grill 25 minutes or until meat thermometer registers 160°, turning pork occasionally. Cut pork into thin slices.

5. Divide lettuce among 4 serving plates; top each with one-fourth of remaining cucumber, onion, and remaining 6 ingredients. Divide pork evenly among plates. Top each salad with 6 tablespoons yogurt dressing. Serve immediately. Yield: 4 servings.

CALORIES 256 (28% from fat); FAT 8g (sat 2.3g, mono 3.8g, poly 1.1g); PROTEIN 30.6g; CARB 16g; FIBER 3.3g; CHOL 82mg; IRON 3.4mg; SODIUM 197mg; CALC 186mg

This succulent pork tenderloin also stands alone as an easy 5-ingredient entrée.

Grecian Pork
Tenderloin Salad

PORK AND SUCCOTASH SALAD

PREP:38 MINUTES   COOK:10 MINUTES

      4 ears shucked corn
   1½ cups shelled lima beans
      ½ pound fresh spinach
      1 red bell pepper, finely chopped
      1 small red onion, finely chopped
      ⅛ teaspoon black pepper
   1½ teaspoons ground cumin
      ½ teaspoon garlic powder
      ½ teaspoon chili powder
      ½ pound lean boneless pork, cut
            into thin strips
         Cooking spray
      1 cup orange juice
      1 tablespoon lime juice
      1 tablespoon olive oil

1. Place corn in a Dutch oven, and cover
with water. Bring to a boil, and cook 10
minutes or until tender. Drain and cool.
Cut kernels from ears of corn.
2. Cook beans, uncovered, in boiling
water 15 minutes or until tender; drain.
3. Remove stems from spinach; wash
leaves thoroughly. Tear into bite-size
pieces. Combine corn, beans, spinach, bell
pepper, onion, and black pepper in a bowl.
4. Combine cumin, garlic powder, and
chili powder in a bowl; add pork, tossing
to coat. Coat a large nonaluminum skillet
with cooking spray; place over medium
heat until hot. Add pork to pan; cook 3
minutes or until browned, stirring constantly. Remove pork from pan.
5. Add orange juice to pan, scraping bottom to loosen browned bits. Bring to a
boil; cook until reduced to ½ cup (about 4
minutes). Stir in lime juice and oil. Pour
over spinach mixture. Add pork; toss to
coat. Serve immediately or cover and chill.
Yield: 6 servings (serving size: 1½ cups).

CALORIES 216 (27% from fat); FAT 6.5g (sat 1.5g, mono 3.2g,
poly 1.1g); PROTEIN 13.7g; CARB 28.4g; FIBER 5.9g;
CHOL 23mg; IRON 3.6mg; SODIUM 63mg; CALC 63mg

Pasta Salad With
Shrimp and Basil

Fresh basil makes all the difference in this salad.

PASTA SALAD WITH SHRIMP AND BASIL

PREP:25 MINUTES   CHILL:8 HOURS

      1 pound medium shrimp, cooked
            and peeled
      4 cups cooked seashell pasta
            (about 2 cups uncooked pasta)
      2 cups chopped plum tomato
            (about 1 pound)
      ½ cup chopped green bell pepper
      ⅓ cup fresh lemon juice
      ¼ cup chopped shallots
      ¼ cup chopped fresh or 4
            teaspoons dried basil
      2 tablespoons extra-virgin olive oil
      ½ teaspoon salt
      ½ teaspoon black pepper
      1 garlic clove, minced

1. Combine all ingredients in a large
bowl. Cover and chill at least 8 hours.
Yield: 8 servings (serving size: 1 cup).

CALORIES 197 (21% from fat); FAT 4.5g (sat 0.8g, mono 1.2g,
poly 2.1g); PROTEIN 13.2g; CARB 25.7g; FIBER 1.5g;
CHOL 83mg; IRON 2.8mg; SODIUM 249mg; CALC 30mg

THAI SHRIMP-AND-PASTA SALAD

PREP: 25 MINUTES

Store the shrimp-pasta mixture and the vinaigrette separately in the refrigerator; toss just before serving. Fish sauce is a salty condiment that accounts for the high sodium content of this salad. It comes bottled and is sometimes labeled nampla *in Asian markets or your supermarket's ethnic-food section.*

2   ounces uncooked linguine
½   cup shredded carrot
8   ounces medium shrimp, cooked and peeled
1   cup thinly sliced Boston lettuce leaves
¼   cup fresh cilantro leaves
2   tablespoons chopped unsalted, dry-roasted peanuts
¼   cup fresh lime juice
2   tablespoons fish sauce
2   tablespoons chopped fresh cilantro
1   tablespoon chopped green onions
2½ teaspoons sugar
2   teaspoons vegetable oil
1   teaspoon grated peeled fresh ginger
2   garlic cloves, minced

1. Cook pasta in boiling water 9½ minutes. Add carrot; cook 30 seconds. Drain and cool. Combine pasta mixture, shrimp, lettuce, cilantro leaves, and peanuts in a large bowl.
2. Combine lime juice and remaining 7 ingredients in a small bowl; stir well with a whisk. Pour over pasta mixture, tossing gently to coat. Yield: 2 servings (serving size: 2 cups).

CALORIES 367 (28% from fat); FAT 10.6g (sat 2g, mono 3.8g, poly 4.8g); PROTEIN 26.2g; CARB 37.4g; FIBER 3.2g; CHOL 166mg; IRON 4.9mg; SODIUM 1512mg; CALC 80mg

CARIBBEAN COBB SALAD

PREP: 28 MINUTES

4   cups torn romaine lettuce
1   pound medium shrimp, cooked and peeled
1   cup cubed peeled papaya
1   cup cubed fresh pineapple
½   cup chopped peeled avocado
½   cup chopped red or green bell pepper
1   (15-ounce) can black beans, rinsed and drained
½   cup (2 ounces) shredded reduced-fat Monterey Jack cheese
⅔   cup Orange-Soy Vinaigrette (page 424)
¼   cup chopped unsalted cashews, toasted

1. Arrange lettuce on a serving platter. Spoon shrimp down center of platter; arrange papaya, pineapple, avocado, bell pepper, black beans, and cheese in rows on either side of shrimp. Drizzle Orange-Soy Vinaigrette over salad; sprinkle with cashews. Yield: 4 servings.

CALORIES 383 (35% from fat); FAT 14.7g (sat 3.7g, mono 6.3g, poly 2.7g); PROTEIN 30.6g; CARB 34.6g; FIBER 6.1g; CHOL 175mg; IRON 5.9mg; SODIUM 553mg; CALC 208mg

CURRIED SANTA BARBARA SHRIMP SALAD

PREP: 35 MINUTES

½   cup fat-free mayonnaise
1   tablespoon curry powder
1   tablespoon fresh lime juice
1   teaspoon minced peeled fresh ginger
¾   cup sake (rice wine), divided
½   cup golden raisins
1   pound large shrimp, peeled and deveined
4   cups diced Asian pear or ripe pear
1½ cups diced peeled mango

6   tablespoons slivered almonds, toasted
8   cups gourmet salad greens

1. Combine first 4 ingredients in a small bowl. Cover and chill.
2. Combine ½ cup sake and raisins in a 1-cup glass measure; microwave at HIGH until mixture comes to a boil (about 1 minute). Let stand 30 minutes. Drain.
3. Bring ¼ cup sake to a boil in a nonstick skillet; add shrimp. Cover, reduce heat, and cook 2 minutes or until shrimp are done. Remove from heat; drain.
4. Combine mayonnaise mixture, raisins, shrimp, pear, mango, and almonds. Serve over salad greens. Yield: 4 servings (serving size: 2 cups salad greens and 1½ cups shrimp salad).

CALORIES 393 (17% from fat); FAT 7.5g (sat 0.9g, mono 3.6g, poly 1.9g); PROTEIN 22.8g; CARB 64.8g; FIBER 9.7g; CHOL 129mg; IRON 5.1mg; SODIUM 512mg; CALC 155mg

CREAMY TUNA-PASTA SALAD

PREP: 11 MINUTES

¼   cup water
1   (16-ounce) package frozen broccoli, rotini pasta, peas, and red peppers with Parmesan cheese seasoning (such as Green Giant Pasta Accents Primavera)
⅓   cup fat-free sour cream
1   (6-ounce) can low-sodium tuna in water, drained

1. Combine water and broccoli mixture in a medium saucepan. Bring to a boil; cover, reduce heat to medium, and cook 6 minutes, stirring once.
2. Remove from heat. Add sour cream and tuna to broccoli mixture; toss well. Yield: 3 servings (serving size: 1 cup).

CALORIES 301 (24% from fat); FAT 7.9g (sat 2.1g, mono 4g, poly 0.3g); PROTEIN 23.4g; CARB 32.6g; FIBER 3.3g; CHOL 29.3mg; IRON 1.3mg; SODIUM 488mg; CALC 160mg

SALADE NIÇOISE

PREP: 30 MINUTES   COOK: 8 MINUTES

3 tablespoons fresh lemon juice
2 (8-ounce) tuna steaks
Freshly ground black pepper
Cooking spray
10 small red potatoes (about 1 pound)
½ pound green beans, trimmed
4 cups torn romaine lettuce
4 cups trimmed watercress (about 1 bunch)
3 tomatoes, each cut into 6 wedges
3 hard-cooked large eggs, quartered lengthwise
1 small green bell pepper, cut into strips
½ cup niçoise olives
2 tablespoons capers
6 canned anchovy fillets
Garlic-Basil Vinaigrette (page 424)

1. Drizzle lemon juice over tuna; sprinkle with black pepper. Marinate in refrigerator 15 minutes; discard lemon juice.
2. Prepare grill or broiler.
3. Place tuna on grill rack or broiler pan coated with cooking spray; cook 4 minutes on each side or until medium-well. Break tuna into chunks.
4. Steam potatoes, covered, 3 minutes. Add green beans, and steam, covered, 8 minutes or until vegetables are crisp-tender; cool.
5. Combine lettuce and watercress on a large serving platter. Arrange tuna, potatoes, green beans, tomato, eggs, and bell pepper over greens. Top with olives, capers, and anchovy fillets. Drizzle Garlic-Basil Vinaigrette over salad. Yield: 6 servings.

CALORIES 295 (31% from fat); FAT 10.1g (sat 2.2g, mono 4.4g, poly 2.3g); PROTEIN 30g; CARB 22g; FIBER 4.5g; CHOL 64mg; IRON 4.4mg; SODIUM 458mg; CALC 127mg

MINCED GARLIC

Although we prefer the taste of fresh garlic, you can keep a jar of minced garlic on hand for when you're in a hurry. Look for it in the produce section, and keep it refrigerated once opened. Use it in place of fresh garlic, substituting ½ teaspoon of the bottled for 1 fresh garlic clove.

TUNA AND WHITE BEAN SALAD

PREP: 11 MINUTES

2 tablespoons red wine vinegar
1 tablespoon drained capers
1 tablespoon olive oil
½ teaspoon dried rosemary, crushed
⅛ teaspoon coarsely ground black pepper
1 garlic clove, crushed
1½ cups torn romaine lettuce
1 (16-ounce) can cannellini beans or other white beans, rinsed and drained
1 (6-ounce) can albacore tuna in water, drained
1 (2-ounce) jar diced pimento, drained

1. Combine first 6 ingredients in a small bowl. Combine lettuce, beans, tuna, and pimento in a bowl. Add vinegar mixture; toss gently to coat. Serve at room temperature or chilled. Yield: 3 servings (serving size: 1 cup).

CALORIES 183 (29% from fat); FAT 5.9g (sat 0.9g, mono 3.5g, poly 0.7g); PROTEIN 14.5g; CARB 16.7g; FIBER 3.9g; CHOL 14mg; IRON 2.4mg; SODIUM 533mg; CALC 37mg

Salade Niçoise

SALAD DRESSINGS

BLUE CHEESE-BUTTERMILK DRESSING

PREP: 10 MINUTES

½ cup low-fat or nonfat
    buttermilk
½ cup plain fat-free yogurt
3 tablespoons white wine vinegar
1 teaspoon sugar
½ teaspoon salt
½ teaspoon coarsely ground black
    pepper
½ cup thinly sliced green onions
½ cup (2 ounces) crumbled
    blue cheese

1. Combine first 6 ingredients in a bowl; stir with a whisk until blended. Stir in onions and cheese. Serve over mixed greens. Yield: 1½ cups (serving size: 2 tablespoons).

CALORIES 37 (54% from fat); FAT 2.2g (sat 1.4g, mono 0.6g, poly 0.1g); PROTEIN 2.4g; CARB 2g; FIBER 0.1g; CHOL 6mg; IRON 0.1mg; SODIUM 206mg; CALC 70mg

CREAMY CAESAR DRESSING

PREP: 8 MINUTES
CHILL: 30 MINUTES

⅓ cup plain fat-free yogurt
2 tablespoons fresh lemon juice
1 tablespoon olive oil
2 teaspoons red wine vinegar
2 teaspoons Worcestershire sauce
1 teaspoon anchovy paste
1 teaspoon Dijon mustard
¼ teaspoon salt
¼ teaspoon freshly ground black
    pepper
1 garlic clove, minced

1. Combine all ingredients in a bowl; stir well with a whisk. Cover and chill.

ANCHOVY PASTE

Anchovy paste is a mixture of ground anchovies (tiny salted fish), vinegar, spices, and water. It comes in tubes and should be refrigerated once opened. You can find it in the canned-fish section of the grocery store. Because the flavor is salty and pungent, a little goes a long way in adding a distinct flavor to salad dressings, sauces, and toppings for canapés.

Serve over salad greens. Yield: ½ cup (serving size: 2 tablespoons).

CALORIES 51 (65% from fat); FAT 3.7g (sat 0.5g, mono 2.5g, poly 0.3g); PROTEIN 1.6g; CARB 3.1g; FIBER 0.1g; CHOL 0mg; IRON 0.1mg; SODIUM 394mg; CALC 43mg

CREAMY TARRAGON DRESSING

PREP: 3 MINUTES
CHILL: 30 MINUTES

¼ cup fat-free mayonnaise
¼ cup plain fat-free yogurt
1 tablespoon white wine vinegar
¾ teaspoon Dijon mustard
½ teaspoon dried tarragon

1. Combine all ingredients in a bowl; cover and chill. Serve over salad greens. Yield: ½ cup (serving size: 2 tablespoons).

CALORIES 23 (4% from fat); FAT 0.1g (sat 0g, mono 0g, poly 0g); PROTEIN 0.8g; CARB 4.5g; FIBER 0g; CHOL 0mg; IRON 0mg; SODIUM 248mg; CALC 49mg

CREAMY CUCUMBER DRESSING

PREP: 10 MINUTES
CHILL: 30 MINUTES

1 cup plain low-fat yogurt
½ cup chopped seeded peeled
    cucumber
¼ cup light mayonnaise
2 tablespoons chopped green
    onions
2 tablespoons lemon juice
¼ teaspoon salt
¼ teaspoon dried dill
⅛ teaspoon black pepper

1. Combine all ingredients in a bowl; cover and chill. Serve over mixed salad greens. Yield: 1¾ cups (serving size: 2 tablespoons).

CALORIES 23 (55% from fat); FAT 1.4g (sat 0.3g, mono 0.4g, poly 0.6g); PROTEIN 1g; CARB 1.8g; FIBER 0.1g; CHOL 2mg; IRON 0.1mg; SODIUM 85mg; CALC 32mg

THOUSAND ISLAND DRESSING

PREP: 7 MINUTES
CHILL: 30 MINUTES

½ cup plain low-fat yogurt
½ cup light mayonnaise
¼ cup chili sauce
2 tablespoons sweet pickle relish
1 tablespoon minced fresh onion
1 tablespoon finely chopped celery
1 teaspoon lemon juice
⅛ teaspoon black pepper

1. Combine all ingredients in a bowl; cover and chill. Serve over salad greens. Yield: 1½ cups (serving size: 2 tablespoons).

CALORIES 45 (64% from fat); FAT 3.2g (sat 0.6g, mono 1g, poly 1.7g); PROTEIN 0.7g; CARB 3.6g; FIBER 0.1g; CHOL 4mg; IRON 0.1mg; SODIUM 163mg; CALC 20mg

ZESTY COLESLAW DRESSING

PREP: 6 MINUTES   CHILL: 30 MINUTES

½ cup plain low-fat yogurt
¼ cup fat-free sour cream
1 tablespoon Dijon mustard
1 tablespoon cider vinegar
1 tablespoon lemon juice
1 tablespoon olive oil
1 teaspoon sugar
½ teaspoon celery seeds
½ teaspoon prepared horseradish
¼ teaspoon salt
¼ teaspoon black pepper

1. Combine all ingredients in a bowl; stir well with a whisk until blended. Cover and chill. Serve over shredded cabbage. Yield: 1 cup (serving size: 2 tablespoons).

CALORIES 35 (54% from fat); FAT 2.1g (sat 0.4g, mono 1.3g, poly 0.2g); PROTEIN 1.3g; CARB 2.6g; FIBER 0.1g; CHOL 1mg; IRON 0.1mg; SODIUM 145mg; CALC 39mg

BALSAMIC DRESSING

PREP: 10 MINUTES   CHILL: 30 MINUTES

¼ cup balsamic vinegar
¼ cup minced green onions
2 tablespoons Dijon mustard
1½ tablespoons olive oil
2 tablespoons minced fresh
    or 2 teaspoons dried parsley
1 tablespoon minced fresh or
    1 teaspoon dried tarragon
1 tablespoon water
⅛ teaspoon black pepper
3 garlic cloves, minced

1. Combine all ingredients in a bowl; stir well with a whisk. Cover and chill. Serve over mixed salad greens. Yield: ¾ cup (serving size: 2 tablespoons).

CALORIES 40 (83% from fat); FAT 3.7g (sat 0.5g, mono 2.5g, poly 0.3g); PROTEIN 0.2g; CARB 1.3g; FIBER 0.1g; CHOL 0mg; IRON 0.2mg; SODIUM 150mg; CALC 7mg

HONEY-BASIL DRESSING

PREP: 10 MINUTES
CHILL: 30 MINUTES

This versatile dressing enhances a variety of salads.

⅓ cup fresh lime juice
3 tablespoons chopped fresh basil
3 tablespoons honey
1 tablespoon olive oil
¼ teaspoon salt

1. Combine all ingredients in a medium bowl; stir well with a whisk. Serve over mixed greens, tomatoes, or fruit salad. Yield: about ¾ cup (serving size: about 2 tablespoons).

CALORIES 56 (37% from fat); FAT 2.3g (sat 0.3g, mono 1.7g, poly 0.2g); PROTEIN 0.1g; CARB 10g; FIBER 0g; CHOL 0mg; IRON 0.1mg; SODIUM 98mg; CALC 4mg

GARLIC-BASIL VINAIGRETTE

PREP: 6 MINUTES

⅓ cup low-sodium chicken broth
1½ tablespoons chopped fresh basil
1 tablespoon extra-virgin olive oil
1 tablespoon fresh lemon juice
1 tablespoon red wine vinegar
1 teaspoon Dijon mustard
3 garlic cloves, halved
Freshly ground black pepper

1. Combine all ingredients in a blender; process until smooth. Yield: 6 tablespoons (serving size: 1 tablespoon).

CALORIES 20 (81% from fat); FAT 1.8g (sat 0.2g, mono 1.3g, poly 0.2g); PROTEIN 0.2g; CARB 0.8g; FIBER 0g; CHOL 0mg; IRON 0.1mg; SODIUM 22mg; CALC 3mg

LIME-CILANTRO VINAIGRETTE

PREP: 6 MINUTES
CHILL: 30 MINUTES

¾ cup tomato juice
½ cup cilantro sprigs
¼ cup fresh lime juice
½ teaspoon dried oregano
¼ teaspoon salt
¼ teaspoon ground cumin
1 small jalapeño pepper, halved
    and seeded

1. Place all ingredients in a blender or food processor; process until blended. Cover and chill. Serve over mixed salad greens. Yield: 1 cup (serving size: 2 tablespoons).

CALORIES 7 (6% from fat); FAT 0.1g (sat 0g, mono 0g, poly 0g); PROTEIN 0.3g; CARB 1.9g; FIBER 0.2g; CHOL 0mg; IRON 0.3mg; SODIUM 157mg; CALC 6mg

ORANGE-SOY VINAIGRETTE

PREP: 5 MINUTES
CHILL: 30 MINUTES

½ cup orange juice
½ cup pineapple juice
1 tablespoon minced fresh
    parsley
2 tablespoons fresh lime juice
2 tablespoons low-sodium soy
    sauce
1 tablespoon extra-virgin olive oil
1 tablespoon dark sesame oil
2 teaspoons sugar
1 teaspoon lemon pepper

1. Combine all ingredients in a small bowl; cover and chill. Yield: 1⅓ cups (serving size: 2 tablespoons).

CALORIES 43 (57% from fat); FAT 2.7g (sat 0.4g, mono 1.5g, poly 0.7g); PROTEIN 0.2g; CARB 4.3g; FIBER 0.1g; CHOL 0mg; IRON 0.1mg; SODIUM 79mg; CALC 5mg

sandwiches

Greek Feta Burgers (page 426)
and Steak Fries (page 499)

burgers No more plain burgers—we've packed these full of flavor!

BLUE CHEESE-STUFFED BURGERS

PREP:15 MINUTES
COOK:8 MINUTES

Cooking spray
½ cup finely chopped onion
1 pound ground round
3 tablespoons dry breadcrumbs
2 tablespoons water
1 egg white, lightly beaten
¼ cup (1 ounce) crumbled blue cheese
¼ cup fat-free sour cream
4 English muffins, split and toasted
4 lettuce leaves
4 (¼-inch-thick) slices tomato

1. Coat a small nonstick skillet with cooking spray; place over medium heat until hot. Add onion, and sauté 5 minutes or until tender. Remove from heat; cool slightly. Combine onion, beef, breadcrumbs, water, and egg white in a large bowl. Divide mixture into 8 equal portions, shaping each portion into a ½-inch-thick patty. Spoon 1 tablespoon cheese onto center of each of 4 patties; top with remaining patties. Press edges together to seal.
2. Prepare grill.
3. Place patties on grill rack coated with cooking spray; grill 4 minutes on each side or until done.
4. Spread 1 tablespoon sour cream over cut side of top half of each muffin. Line bottom halves of muffins with lettuce leaves; top each with a tomato slice, a patty, and top half of muffin. Yield: 4 servings.

CALORIES 327 (28% from fat); FAT 10.3g (sat 3.9g, mono 3.7g, poly 0.7g); PROTEIN 31.4g; CARB 25.1g; FIBER 1g; CHOL 75mg; IRON 3.8mg; SODIUM 391mg; CALC 116mg

RANCH BURGERS

PREP:18 MINUTES
COOK:10 MINUTES

Cooking spray
1 cup very thinly sliced green cabbage
½ cup chopped green bell pepper
½ cup chopped onion
¼ cup water
1 teaspoon minced fresh or ¼ teaspoon dried oregano
½ teaspoon minced fresh or ⅛ teaspoon dried rosemary
2 tablespoons dry breadcrumbs
2 tablespoons tomato sauce
¾ teaspoon salt
¼ teaspoon black pepper
1 large egg white, lightly beaten
¾ pound ground round
2 tablespoons light ranch dressing
4 (1½-ounce) hamburger buns, toasted
2 curly leaf lettuce leaves, halved
4 (¼-inch-thick) slices tomato
4 (¼-inch-thick) slices onion

1. Coat a large nonstick skillet with cooking spray; place over medium-high heat until hot. Add cabbage, bell pepper, and onion; sauté 3 minutes. Stir in water, 1 tablespoon at a time, allowing each tablespoon to evaporate before adding the next; cook 5 minutes or until all liquid evaporates and vegetables are golden brown. Remove from heat; stir in oregano and rosemary. Cool slightly.
2. Combine breadcrumbs, tomato sauce, salt, pepper, and egg white in a medium bowl. Add cabbage mixture and beef; stir well. Divide mixture into 4 equal portions, shaping each into a ½-inch-thick patty.
3. Prepare grill.
4. Place patties on grill rack coated with cooking spray; grill 5 minutes on each side or until done.
5. Spread 1½ teaspoons ranch dressing over top half of each bun. Line bottom halves of buns with lettuce leaves; top each with a patty, tomato slice, onion slice, and top half of bun. Yield: 4 servings.

CALORIES 338 (27% from fat); FAT 10.2g (sat 2.7g, mono 3.2g, poly 2.8g); PROTEIN 24.9g; CARB 35.3g; FIBER 3.4g; CHOL 55mg; IRON 4.2mg; SODIUM 924mg; CALC 103mg

GREEK FETA BURGERS

PREP:8 MINUTES
COOK:12 MINUTES
(pictured on page 425)

Substitute ground round for the ground lamb, if desired. We served this with Steak Fries (page 499).

1 (10-ounce) package frozen chopped spinach, thawed, drained, and squeezed dry
1 tablespoon lemon juice
¼ teaspoon black pepper
1 large egg white, lightly beaten
¾ pound lean ground lamb
½ cup (2 ounces) crumbled feta cheese
¼ cup chopped fresh mint or 4 teaspoons dried mint flakes
Cooking spray
4 (2-ounce) hamburger buns with onions
1 cup fresh spinach leaves
½ cup diced tomato
Cucumber-Dill Sauce (page 444)

1. Combine first 4 ingredients; add lamb, cheese, and mint, and stir well. Divide mixture into 4 equal portions, shaping each into a ½-inch-thick patty.

2. Prepare grill.

3. Place patties on grill rack coated with cooking spray; grill, covered, 6 minutes on each side or until done.

4. Line bottom half of each bun with ¼ cup spinach leaves; top each with a patty, 2 tablespoons tomato, 2 tablespoons Cucumber-Dill Sauce, and top half of bun. Yield: 4 servings.

CALORIES 396 (31% from fat); FAT 13.7g (sat 5.9g, mono 3.7g, poly 1.2g); PROTEIN 32.6g; CARB 36.1g; FIBER 4.1g; CHOL 79mg; IRON 4.0mg; SODIUM 655mg; CALC 265mg

PEPPERED TURKEY-WATERCRESS BURGERS

PREP: 13 MINUTES
COOK: 10 MINUTES

      1   pound ground turkey breast
 1½   cups chopped trimmed
            watercress
      ¾   cup plain low-fat yogurt,
            divided
      2   teaspoons cracked black
            pepper, divided
      ½   teaspoon salt
      ½   teaspoon Worcestershire sauce
Cooking spray
      4   (1½-ounce) whole-wheat
            hamburger buns, toasted
      1   cup trimmed watercress
      4   (¼-inch-thick) slices tomato

1. Combine turkey, chopped watercress, ¼ cup yogurt, 1 teaspoon cracked pepper, salt, and Worcestershire sauce in a bowl. Divide mixture into 4 equal portions, shaping each portion into a ½-inch-thick patty. Press remaining 1 teaspoon pepper onto both sides of patties.

2. Prepare grill.

3. Place patties on grill rack coated with cooking spray; grill 5 minutes on each side or until done.

4. Spread 2 tablespoons of remaining ½ cup yogurt over top half of each bun.

Peppered Turkey-
Watercress Burgers

Line bottom half of each bun with ¼ cup trimmed watercress; top each with a patty, a tomato slice, and top half of bun. Yield: 4 servings.

CALORIES 300 (20% from fat); FAT 6.8g (sat 2.2g, mono 1.8g, poly 1.5g); PROTEIN 32.3g; CARB 26.5g; FIBER 2.5g; CHOL 76mg; IRON 2.6mg; SODIUM 656mg; CALC 154mg

Watercress has small, crisp, dark green leaves with a **sharp peppery flavor.**

TURKEY BURGERS

PREP: 15 MINUTES   COOK: 12 MINUTES

½ pound ground turkey
¼ cup Italian-seasoned breadcrumbs
1½ tablespoons finely chopped onion
1 tablespoon finely chopped fresh parsley
½ teaspoon chili powder
¼ teaspoon salt
¼ teaspoon black pepper
⅛ teaspoon dried oregano
Dash of Worcestershire sauce
1 garlic clove, minced
1 large egg white, lightly beaten
2 tablespoons all-purpose flour
Cooking spray
2 (1½-ounce) hamburger buns
2 tomato slices
2 red onion slices

1. Combine first 10 ingredients in a bowl; add egg white, and stir until well-blended. Divide mixture into 2 equal portions, shaping each portion into a ½-inch-thick patty. Dredge patties in flour.
2. Coat a medium nonstick skillet with cooking spray; place over medium heat until hot. Add patties; cook 5 to 6 minutes on each side or until done. Serve patties on hamburger buns with tomato and onion. Yield: 2 servings.

CALORIES 380 (15% from fat); FAT 6.5g (sat 1.8g, mono 1.1g, poly 2.2g); PROTEIN 34g; CARB 44.6g; FIBER 3.1g; CHOL 74mg; IRON 4.4mg; SODIUM 1049mg; CALC 112mg

---

WATCHING SODIUM

The pillars of sandwich making—**bread, lunchmeats, cheese, mustard, and mayonnaise**—really pile on the sodium. Fat-free cheese and reduced-fat condiments help slash fat and calories, but not salt. As a result, these sandwiches are higher in sodium than normal. We've added vegetables to some of them so they can be a "one-dish" meal.

If you're watching your sodium intake, **add low-sodium accompaniments, such as carrot and celery sticks**, rather than chips or pickles.

---

wraps

Doing the wrap? Take a variety of ingredients—from vegetables to meats, cheeses to grains—and create a fresh, filling sandwich for at home or on the run.

CHICKEN-MANGO WRAP

PREP: 42 MINUTES   COOK: 10 MINUTES

1 cup diced plum tomato
1 cup diced peeled mango (about 1 medium)
¼ cup diced red bell pepper
¼ cup diced red onion
¼ cup chopped fresh cilantro
3 tablespoons fresh lime juice
1 tablespoon minced seeded jalapeño pepper
⅛ teaspoon salt
Dash of black pepper
8 (7-inch) fat-free flour tortillas
3 cups shredded cooked chicken breast (about 1½ pounds)
½ teaspoon salt
½ cup low-fat sour cream
2 cups thinly sliced red cabbage

1. Combine first 9 ingredients in a bowl. Let stand at room temperature 30 minutes.
2. Warm tortillas according to package directions.
3. Combine chicken and ½ teaspoon salt. Spread 1 tablespoon sour cream over each tortilla. Divide chicken evenly among tortillas; top each with ¼ cup mango mixture and ¼ cup cabbage. Roll tortillas over mixture, and serve seam side down. Yield: 8 servings.

CALORIES 245 (14% from fat); FAT 3.9g (sat 1.7g, mono 1.2g, poly 0.6g); PROTEIN 20.2g; CARB 32g; FIBER 2.2g; CHOL 50mg; IRON 1.8mg; SODIUM 573mg; CALC 40mg

MEDITERRANEAN WRAP

PREP: 25 MINUTES
COOK: 12 MINUTES

¾ cup chopped tomato
1 tablespoon diced red onion
1 tablespoon chopped fresh cilantro
1 teaspoon lime juice
⅛ teaspoon salt
1 garlic clove, minced
1 cup hot cooked jasmine rice or long-grain rice (about ⅓ cup uncooked rice)

For parties, make an impressive appetizer platter by slicing any of these five wraps into 2-inch-thick pinwheels. Arrange on a platter, cut sides up.

2 tablespoons chopped fresh or
  2 teaspoons dried basil
1 cup chopped red bell pepper
1 cup diced zucchini
1 cup diced yellow squash
¼ cup diced red onion
Cooking spray
2 tablespoons balsamic vinegar
2 teaspoons olive oil
4 (8-inch) fat-free flour tortillas
¼ cup (1 ounce) crumbled feta cheese

1. Preheat broiler.
2. Combine first 6 ingredients in a bowl, and set aside. Combine rice and basil; set aside.
3. Arrange bell pepper, zucchini, yellow squash, and ¼ cup red onion in a single layer on a baking sheet coated with cooking spray. Broil 12 minutes or until vegetables are browned; spoon into a large bowl. Drizzle vinegar and oil over vegetables; toss to coat.
4. Warm tortillas according to package directions. Spoon ¼ cup rice mixture down center of each tortilla. Top each tortilla with about ½ cup vegetables, about 3 tablespoons tomato mixture, and 1 tablespoon feta cheese; roll up. Yield: 4 servings.

CALORIES 250 (18% from fat); FAT 5g (sat 1.9g, mono 2.2g, poly 0.4g); PROTEIN 5.7g; CARB 43.6g; FIBER 4.7g; CHOL 9mg; IRON 1.5mg; SODIUM 424mg; CALC 73mg

HOT PROVENÇALE WRAP

PREP: 34 MINUTES STAND: 20 MINUTES
COOK: 8 MINUTES

Roasted vegetables:
2 tablespoons red wine vinegar
2 tablespoons lemon juice
1 tablespoon extra-virgin olive oil
2 teaspoons dried herbes de Provence
½ (1-pound) eggplant, cut diagonally into ¼-inch-thick slices

2 small yellow squash, cut diagonally into ¼-inch-thick slices (about ½ pound)
1 zucchini, cut diagonally into ¼-inch-thick slices (about ½ pound)
1 cup thinly sliced fennel bulb (about 1 bulb)
Cooking spray

Wrap:
6 (8-inch) fat-free flour tortillas
Herb Hummus (page 445)
6 leaf lettuce leaves
¾ cup sliced bottled roasted red bell peppers
½ cup (2 ounces) shredded provolone cheese

1. To prepare roasted vegetables, combine first 8 ingredients in a large zip-top plastic bag; seal bag, and let stand 20 minutes.
2. Preheat broiler.
3. Remove vegetable mixture from bag; discard marinade. Place vegetable mixture on a jelly-roll pan coated with cooking spray. Broil 18 minutes or until tender, stirring occasionally; set aside.
4. Preheat oven to 350°.
5. To prepare wrap, warm tortillas according to package directions. Spread Herb Hummus evenly over tortillas. Divide lettuce leaves, roasted vegetables, bell peppers, and cheese evenly among tortillas; roll up. Wrap each tortilla in foil; bake at 350° for 8 minutes or until thoroughly heated. Yield: 6 servings.

CALORIES 321 (25% from fat); FAT 8.8g (sat 2.7g, mono 3.2g, poly 2.1g); PROTEIN 14.8g; CARB 47.5g; FIBER 7.4g; CHOL 8mg; IRON 3.9mg; SODIUM 759mg; CALC 209mg

Warm a wrap sandwich by placing it on a baking sheet and heating it at 300° for 5 to 7 minutes. If the wrap has cheese in it, it's especially good warm.

SANTA FE WRAP

PREP: 12 MINUTES

¾ cup canned chickpeas (garbanzo beans), rinsed and drained
¼ cup part-skim ricotta cheese
2 tablespoons tub-style light cream cheese, softened
1 tablespoon fresh lime juice
1 garlic clove
½ cup (2 ounces) crumbled feta cheese
¼ cup canned black beans, rinsed and drained
1 tablespoon minced fresh cilantro
½ teaspoon hot sauce
4 (10-inch) fat-free flour tortillas
1⅓ cups thinly sliced curly leaf lettuce
¾ cup shredded peeled jícama
6 tablespoons (1½ ounces) finely shredded Monterey Jack cheese
3 tablespoons finely diced red onion

1. Place first 5 ingredients in a food processor or blender; process until smooth. Add feta, black beans, cilantro, and hot sauce; pulse 4 or 5 times or until combined.
2. Spread 1½ tablespoons bean mixture over each tortilla; top each with ⅓ cup lettuce. Divide jícama and remaining ingredients evenly among tortillas; roll up tortillas. Cut each wrap in half diagonally. Yield: 4 servings.

CALORIES 324 (26% from fat); FAT 9.5g (sat 5.7g, mono 2.1g, poly 0.7g); PROTEIN 13.8g; CARB 46.7g; FIBER 1.9g; CHOL 30mg; IRON 1.7mg; SODIUM 798mg; CALC 230mg

SIAM STIR-FRY WRAP

PREP: 20 MINUTES
COOK: 6 MINUTES

The sodium content of this wrap is high due to the soy sauce. Pair it with a lower-sodium soup, such as Thai-Style Pumpkin Soup, page 465.

1   tablespoon dark sesame oil
½   cup chopped red bell pepper
1   tablespoon minced peeled fresh ginger
2   teaspoons curry powder
4   garlic cloves, minced
1   (16-ounce) bag cabbage-and-carrot coleslaw
¼   cup low-sodium soy sauce
2   tablespoons minced fresh cilantro
2   tablespoons minced fresh basil
2   tablespoons fresh lime juice
1   (12.3-ounce) package reduced-fat firm tofu, diced
1   (3.75-ounce) package uncooked bean threads (cellophane noodles)
4   curly leaf lettuce leaves
4   (10-inch) fat-free flour tortillas
    Peanut Sauce

1. Heat oil in a large nonstick skillet over medium-high heat. Add bell pepper, ginger, curry powder, garlic, and coleslaw; sauté 4 minutes or until cabbage wilts. Stir in soy sauce, cilantro, basil, lime juice, and tofu; remove from heat.

2. Cook bean threads in boiling water 1 minute; drain well. Place 1 lettuce leaf on each tortilla; divide bean threads evenly over lettuce. Place 1¼ cups tofu mixture over bean threads on each tortilla; spoon 2 tablespoons Peanut Sauce over tofu mixture. Roll up. Cut each wrap in half diagonally. Yield: 4 servings.

CALORIES 415 (24% from fat); FAT 11.1g (sat 1.8g, mono 4.6g, poly 4g); PROTEIN 15.9g; CARB 68g; FIBER 4.3g; CHOL 0mg; IRON 2.5mg; SODIUM 1514mg; CALC 132mg

Siam Stir-Fry Wrap

PEANUT SAUCE

¼   cup fresh lime juice
3   tablespoons creamy peanut butter
3   tablespoons low-sodium soy sauce
3   tablespoons honey
1   tablespoon chile paste with garlic
4   garlic cloves, minced

1. Combine all ingredients in a small bowl. Yield: ½ cup (serving size: 2 tablespoons).

CALORIES 139 (40% from fat); FAT 6.2g (sat 1g, mono 3g, poly 1.9g); PROTEIN 4.4g; CARB 19.4g; FIBER 0.8g; CHOL 0mg; IRON 0.6mg; SODIUM 480mg; CALC 14mg

other sandwiches
Versatility is synonymous with sandwiches. Hot, cold, grilled, broiled, stacked, layered, or open-faced, these sandwiches offer a variety of taste appeal.

Sandwiches have always been a reliable mainstay for quick, casual meals. But our creativity stretches beyond sliced meat between pieces of bread. Here we offer a sandwich smorgasbord.

PHILLY CHEESE SANDWICHES

PREP: 5 MINUTES
COOK: 17 MINUTES

    1   teaspoon olive oil
 1½   cups sliced onion
 1½   cups sliced green bell pepper
    ¼   teaspoon black pepper
 Olive oil-flavored cooking spray
    4   (1-ounce) slices French or
          Italian bread
    8   ounces thinly sliced deli roast
          beef
    4   (1-ounce) slices reduced-fat
          Swiss cheese

1. Heat oil in a nonstick skillet over medium heat. Add onion; cook 10 minutes, stirring frequently. Add bell pepper and black pepper; cook 3 minutes or until bell pepper is crisp-tender.
2. Preheat broiler.
3. Coat top sides of bread with cooking spray. Top each slice with 2 ounces roast beef, ¼ cup onion mixture, and 1 cheese slice.
4. Place sandwiches on a baking sheet coated with cooking spray, and broil 2 minutes or until cheese melts. Yield: 4 servings.

CALORIES 291 (27% from fat); FAT 8.6g (sat 3.7g, mono 3.2g, poly 0.8g); PROTEIN 24.8g; CARB 28.4g; FIBER 2.6g; CHOL 39mg; IRON 3.2mg; SODIUM 819mg; CALC 365mg

THAI BEEF HERO

PREP: 55 MINUTES
MARINATE: 8 HOURS
COOK: 20 MINUTES

    ⅓   cup unsalted dry-roasted
          peanuts
    ⅓   cup packed brown sugar
    ⅓   cup low-sodium soy
          sauce
    ⅓   cup fresh lime juice
    ¼   teaspoon coarsely ground black
          pepper
    4   garlic cloves
    2   small jalapeño peppers,
          seeded
    2   (1-pound) lean, boned sirloin
          steaks
 Cooking spray
    8   (2½-ounce) French bread rolls,
          split
 Thai Slaw
 Tomato-Basil Relish

1. Combine first 7 ingredients in a blender; process until smooth.
2. Trim fat from steaks. Combine steaks and peanut mixture in a large heavy-duty, zip-top plastic bag. Seal bag; marinate in refrigerator 8 hours, turning bag occasionally.
3. Preheat broiler.
4. Remove steaks from bag; discard marinade. Place steaks on a broiler pan coated with cooking spray; broil 10 minutes on each side or to desired degree of doneness. Cut steaks diagonally across grain into thin slices.
5. Place rolls, cut sides up, on a baking sheet; broil 1 minute. Spoon ½ cup Thai Slaw on bottom half of each roll, and top with steak slices and ¼ cup Tomato-Basil Relish. Cover with tops of rolls. Serve sandwiches immediately. Yield: 8 servings.

CALORIES 459 (24% from fat); FAT 12.3g (sat 3.5g, mono 5g, poly 2.3g); PROTEIN 34.8g; CARB 51g; FIBER 3.9g; CHOL 76mg; IRON 5.7mg; SODIUM 725mg; CALC 121mg

THAI SLAW

    3   cups thinly sliced napa cabbage
    1   cup thinly sliced onion,
          separated into rings
    ⅓   cup finely shredded carrot
    2   tablespoons seasoned rice
          vinegar
    1   tablespoon vegetable oil
    ½   teaspoon coarsely ground black
          pepper

1. Combine all ingredients in a bowl; toss well to coat. Cover and chill. Yield: 4 cups (serving size: ½ cup).

CALORIES 28 (58% from fat); FAT 1.8g (sat 0.3g, mono 0.5g, poly 0.9g); PROTEIN 0.6g; CARB 2.6g; FIBER 0.7g; CHOL 0mg; IRON 0.2mg; SODIUM 14mg; CALC 24mg

TOMATO-BASIL RELISH

    ½   cup diced green bell pepper
    ⅓   cup diagonally sliced green
          onions
    ⅓   cup seasoned rice vinegar
    2   tablespoons chopped fresh
          basil
    1   (14.5-ounce) can no-salt-added
          whole tomatoes, drained and
          chopped

1. Combine all ingredients in a bowl; cover and chill. Yield: 2 cups (serving size: ¼ cup).

CALORIES 15 (6% from fat); FAT 0.1g (sat 0g, mono 0g, poly 0g); PROTEIN 0.6g; CARB 3.1g; FIBER 0.6g; CHOL 0mg; IRON 0.4mg; SODIUM 9mg; CALC 21mg

CATFISH AND SLAW SANDWICHES

PREP: 15 MINUTES
COOK: 10 MINUTES

1 cup sliced green cabbage
2 tablespoons minced red onion
2 tablespoons fat-free mayonnaise
1 tablespoon white vinegar
2 teaspoons sugar
½ teaspoon dry mustard
¼ teaspoon salt
¼ teaspoon black pepper
1 teaspoon no-salt-added Creole seasoning
½ teaspoon paprika
¼ teaspoon garlic powder
⅛ teaspoon ground red pepper
⅛ teaspoon black pepper
4 (4-ounce) farm-raised catfish fillets
Cooking spray
4 (2-ounce) Kaiser rolls or hamburger buns, split

1. Preheat broiler.
2. Combine first 8 ingredients in a bowl; set aside.
3. Combine Creole seasoning, paprika, garlic powder, red pepper, and ⅛ teaspoon black pepper; sprinkle over both sides of fillets. Place fillets on a broiler pan coated with cooking spray. Broil 5 minutes; turn fillets, and broil 5 minutes or until fish flakes easily when tested with a fork. Spoon one-fourth of cabbage mixture on each Kaiser roll bottom; top with fillets, and cover with roll tops. Yield: 4 servings (serving size: 1 sandwich).

CALORIES 309 (22% from fat); FAT 7.4g (sat 1.6g, mono 2.8g, poly 1.7g); PROTEIN 22g; CARB 38g; FIBER 1.5g; CHOL 49mg; IRON 3.7mg; SODIUM 685mg; CALC 71mg

EGG-AND-TUNA SALAD SANDWICHES

PREP: 23 MINUTES

4 hard-cooked large eggs, chopped
1 (6-ounce) can chunk light tuna in water, drained
3 tablespoons light mayonnaise
2 tablespoons minced red onion
2 tablespoons Dijon mustard
½ teaspoon freshly ground black pepper
10 (1-ounce) slices whole-wheat bread
5 large red leaf lettuce leaves
5 (¼-inch-thick) slices tomato
1¼ cups alfalfa sprouts

1. Combine first 6 ingredients in a medium bowl. Spread ½ cup egg mixture over each of 5 bread slices. Top each with 1 lettuce leaf, 1 tomato slice, ¼ cup alfalfa sprouts, and 1 bread slice. Yield: 5 sandwiches.

CALORIES 294 (30% from fat); FAT 9.8g (sat 2.3g, mono 2.5g, poly 3.4g); PROTEIN 19.5g; CARB 34.8g; FIBER 4.8g; CHOL 184mg; IRON 4mg; SODIUM 697mg; CALC 176mg

TUNA MELTS

PREP: 15 MINUTES   COOK: 5 MINUTES

⅓ cup chopped celery
3 tablespoons light mayonnaise
2 tablespoons Dijon mustard
2 teaspoons lime juice
½ teaspoon coarsely ground black pepper
1 (12-ounce) can solid white tuna in water, drained
4 English muffins, split and toasted
8 (¼-inch-thick) slices tomato
½ cup (2 ounces) shredded reduced-fat Swiss cheese

1. Preheat broiler.
2. Combine first 6 ingredients. Spread 3 tablespoons tuna mixture onto each muffin half. Top each with 1 tomato slice and 1 tablespoon cheese. Broil 5 minutes or until cheese melts. Yield: 4 servings (serving size: 2 muffin halves).

CALORIES 348 (24% from fat); FAT 9.3g (sat 2.5g, mono 2.4g, poly 3.3g); PROTEIN 26.2g; CARB 38.2g; FIBER 2.2g; CHOL 38mg; IRON 2.6mg; SODIUM 889mg; CALC 282mg

MONTE CRISTO SANDWICHES WITH SWEET MUSTARD SAUCE

PREP: 10 MINUTES   COOK: 12 MINUTES

¼ cup red currant jelly
2 tablespoons Dijon mustard
1 tablespoon orange juice
1 tablespoon water
⅔ cup egg substitute
½ cup fat-free milk
¼ teaspoon salt
¼ teaspoon black pepper
4 (1-ounce) slices cooked turkey breast
4 (1-ounce) slices cooked ham
4 (1-ounce) slices reduced-fat Jarlsberg or Swiss cheese
8 (1-ounce) slices white bread
Cooking spray
1½ teaspoons powdered sugar

1. Combine first 4 ingredients in a saucepan; cook over low heat until jelly melts, stirring well with a whisk.
2. Combine egg substitute, milk, salt, and pepper in a shallow dish.
3. Place one slice each of turkey, ham, and cheese on each of 4 bread slices. Top with remaining bread slices. Dip both sides of each sandwich into egg substitute mixture. Place two sandwiches in a large nonstick skillet coated with cooking spray over medium-high heat. Reduce heat to medium; cook 3 minutes on each side or until golden. Sprinkle with powdered sugar. Repeat procedure

with remaining sandwiches. Serve sandwiches with sauce. Yield: 4 servings (serving size: 1 sandwich and 2 tablespoons sauce).

CALORIES 394 (18% from fat); FAT 7.7g (sat 2.5g, mono 2g, poly 0.9g); PROTEIN 33g; CARB 46.3g; FIBER 1.2g; CHOL 54mg; IRON 2.8mg; SODIUM 1282mg; CALC 348mg

CAROLINA BLOND-BARBECUE SANDWICHES

PREP: 15 MINUTES   COOK: 12 MINUTES

1 (12-ounce) package coleslaw
⅓ cup light coleslaw dressing (such as Marzetti)
¼ teaspoon celery seeds
1 cup no-salt-added ketchup
½ cup water
¼ cup cider vinegar
2 tablespoons instant minced onion
2 tablespoons dark brown sugar
1 tablespoon prepared mustard
1 teaspoon black pepper
1 teaspoon hot sauce
½ teaspoon garlic powder
1½ cups shredded ready-to-eat roasted skinned, boned chicken breasts
4 (2-ounce) slices Texas toast, lightly toasted

1. Combine first 3 ingredients in a bowl; toss well to coat.
2. Combine ketchup and next 8 ingredients in a medium saucepan; bring to a boil. Reduce heat; simmer 5 minutes or until mixture begins to thicken. Stir in chicken; cook 4 minutes or until chicken is thoroughly heated.
3. Top each toasted bread slice with ½ cup chicken and ½ cup coleslaw mixture. Yield: 4 servings.

CALORIES 421 (19% from fat); FAT 8.9g (sat 1.9g, mono 2.3g, poly 3.3g); PROTEIN 26.5g; CARB 64.4g; FIBER 3.5g; CHOL 76mg; IRON 4mg; SODIUM 1075mg; CALC 115mg

Carolina Blond-Barbecue Sandwiches

CORN DOGS

PREP: 14 MINUTES   COOK: 25 MINUTES

¼ cup toasted wheat germ, divided
2 tablespoons seasoned breadcrumbs
1 (11.5-ounce) can refrigerated corn bread twists
1 tablespoon all-purpose flour
8 teaspoons prepared mustard
1 (14-ounce) package fat-free turkey-and-beef hot dogs
2 large egg whites, lightly beaten

1. Preheat oven to 375°.
2. Combine 2 tablespoons wheat germ and breadcrumbs in a shallow dish. Set aside.
3. Unroll dough. Working with 2 dough portions at a time, pinch perforations to seal. Roll dough into a 6 x 3-inch rectangle on a surface sprinkled with 2 tablespoons wheat germ and flour. Spread 1 teaspoon mustard over rectangle. Place 1 hot dog on rectangle. Wrap dough around hot dog; pinch ends to seal. Repeat procedure with remaining dough, mustard, and hot dogs.
4. Dip each corn dog in egg whites; dredge in breadcrumb mixture. Place corn dogs on a baking sheet. Bake at 375° for 25 minutes or until golden brown. Yield: 8 servings (serving size: 1 corn dog).

CALORIES 211 (28% from fat); FAT 6.6g (sat 1.6g, mono 2.6g, poly 2.3g); PROTEIN 11.3g; CARB 25.3g; FIBER 0.6g; CHOL 15mg; IRON 1.9mg; SODIUM 949mg; CALC 8mg

Turkey-Havarti Grinder

1. Preheat broiler.
2. Arrange toast in a 13 x 9-inch baking pan or baking dish. Top each toast slice with 2 ounces turkey and 2 tomato slices; sprinkle with pepper. Spoon Cheddar Cheese Sauce evenly over tomatoes, and sprinkle with bacon and paprika. Broil until lightly browned. Yield: 6 servings.

CALORIES 331 (18% from fat); FAT 6.8g (sat 2.6g, mono 2.3g, poly 1.2g); PROTEIN 28.3g; CARB 37.3g; FIBER 1.8g; CHOL 60mg; IRON 2.8mg; SODIUM 565mg; CALC 210mg

PANINI WITH SAUTÉED SPINACH AND CHICKPEA SPREAD

PREP: 7 MINUTES   COOK: 2 MINUTES

This sandwich can be served on various types of bread such as focaccia, pita bread, and whole grain buns.

   ¾ cup drained canned chickpeas
      (garbanzo beans)
   2 tablespoons lemon juice
   1 tablespoon water
   2 teaspoons capers
   2 teaspoons olive oil
   2 garlic cloves, minced
   4 cups torn spinach
   ¼ teaspoon salt
   ⅛ teaspoon black pepper
   2 (2½-ounce) submarine rolls
   2 large plum tomatoes, sliced
Freshly ground black pepper
      (optional)

1. Place first 4 ingredients in a food processor. Process until smooth; set aside.
2. Heat oil in a large nonstick skillet over medium heat. Add garlic; sauté 1 minute. Add spinach; sauté 1 minute. Remove skillet from heat; stir in salt and pepper.
3. Cut each roll in half horizontally. Spread chickpea mixture over bottom halves of rolls. Top with spinach and

TURKEY-HAVARTI GRINDER

PREP: 10 MINUTES

   ⅓ cup mango chutney
   2 tablespoons chopped unsalted, dry-roasted peanuts
   2 tablespoons light mayonnaise
Dash of ground red pepper
   1 (16-ounce) loaf French bread
   1 pound very thinly sliced deli turkey breast
   6 curly leaf lettuce leaves
   2 ounces thinly sliced reduced-fat Havarti cheese
   6 sandwich-cut bread-and-butter pickles
   1 Red Delicious apple, cored and sliced into rings

1. Combine first 4 ingredients in a bowl. Cut bread loaf in half horizontally, and spread chutney mixture over bottom half of bread; top with turkey, lettuce, cheese, pickles, apple, and top half of bread. Cut loaf into 8 pieces. Yield: 8 servings.

CALORIES 321 (17% from fat); FAT 5.9g (sat 1.3g, mono 1.1g, poly 1g); PROTEIN 19.1g; CARB 45g; FIBER 2.3g; CHOL 8mg; IRON 1.8mg; SODIUM 951mg; CALC 94mg

CLASSIC HOT BROWN

PREP: 12 MINUTES   COOK: 1 MINUTE

   6 (2-ounce) slices Texas toast, lightly toasted
   12 ounces thinly sliced cooked turkey breast
   12 (¼-inch-thick) slices tomato (about 2 tomatoes)
   ¼ teaspoon freshly ground black pepper
Cheddar Cheese Sauce (page 443)
   2 bacon slices, cooked and crumbled
   ¼ teaspoon paprika

tomato slices; garnish with freshly ground pepper, if desired. Cover with top halves of rolls. Yield: 2 servings.

CALORIES 390 (21% from fat); FAT 8.9g (sat 1.4g, mono 4.6g, poly 1.9g); PROTEIN 15.7g; CARB 65g; FIBER 9.2g; CHOL 0mg; IRON 6.6mg; SODIUM 865mg; CALC 184mg

PROSCIUTTO-AND-FONTINA PANINI

PREP:10 MINUTES
COOK:15 MINUTES

Arugula is a bitter green with clusters of dark green leaves that resemble oak leaves. The tangy, peppery flavor lends punch to salads, sandwiches, pasta, pizza, and much more!

    1   (5.25-ounce) package focaccia
        (Italian flatbread) or 1 (8-ounce)
        package Italian cheese-flavored
        pizza crust (such as Boboli)
    ¼   cup (1 ounce) shredded fontina
        cheese
    8   very thin slices prosciutto (about
        2 ounces)
    1   cup trimmed arugula or
        watercress
    2   (⅛-inch-thick) slices red onion,
        separated into rings
    2   teaspoons balsamic vinegar
    ⅛   teaspoon black pepper

1. Preheat oven to 300°.
2. Cut each bread round in half horizontally. Divide fontina cheese between bottom halves of bread, and top each with prosciutto, arugula, and red onion. Drizzle balsamic vinegar over sandwiches, and sprinkle with pepper; cover with top halves of bread. Wrap sandwiches tightly in foil, and bake at 300° for 15 minutes. Yield: 2 servings.

CALORIES 330 (31% from fat); FAT 11.5g (sat 5.6g, mono 2.5g, poly 0.6g); PROTEIN 20.2g; CARB 40.3g; FIBER 4.3g; CHOL 33mg; IRON 0.9mg; SODIUM 846mg; CALC 220mg

CAPRI SANDWICH

PREP:10 MINUTES
COOK:11 MINUTES

    2   teaspoons white wine vinegar
    8   (¼-inch-thick) slices tomato
        (about 2 medium)
    1   (16-ounce) loaf French bread
    1   garlic clove, halved
    1   (1-pound) unpeeled eggplant,
        cut crosswise into ½-inch
        slices
    4   (¼-inch-thick) slices onion
Cooking spray
    2   tablespoons chopped fresh basil
    1   tablespoon chopped kalamata
        olives
    2   (1-ounce) slices provolone
        cheese, halved

1. Drizzle vinegar over tomato slices, and set aside.
2. Preheat broiler.

3. Cut bread in half lengthwise; place, cut sides up, on a baking sheet. Broil 30 seconds or until lightly browned. Rub garlic on cut sides of bread halves; discard garlic.
4. Arrange eggplant and onion slices in a single layer on a baking sheet coated with cooking spray; lightly coat eggplant and onion with cooking spray. Broil eggplant mixture 5 minutes; turn slices over, and broil 5 minutes or until lightly browned.
5. Arrange eggplant and tomato on bottom half of bread. Top with basil and olives. Arrange onion slices and provolone cheese on cut side of top half of bread, and broil 30 seconds or until cheese melts. Invert onto bottom half. To serve, cut loaf into 5 equal pieces. Yield: 5 servings.

CALORIES 349 (19% from fat); FAT 7.2g (sat 2.7g, mono 2.5g, poly 1.1g); PROTEIN 12.9g; CARB 59.3g; FIBER 6.4g CHOL 8mg; IRON 3.3mg; SODIUM 719mg; CALC 177mg

Prosciutto-and-Fontina Panini

FALAFEL SANDWICHES

PREP: 8 MINUTES
COOK: 10 MINUTES

Tahini is a smooth paste made from sesame seeds. It adds flavor to many Middle Eastern dishes.

 1 (15½-ounce) can chickpeas
    (garbanzo beans), drained
 ½ cup chopped onion
 ¼ cup dry breadcrumbs
 1 tablespoon chopped fresh
    parsley
 1 teaspoon ground cumin
 ½ teaspoon ground coriander
 ¼ teaspoon salt
 ⅛ teaspoon black pepper
 ⅛ teaspoon ground red pepper
 2 garlic cloves
Cooking spray
 2 teaspoons olive oil, divided
Tahini Sauce
 2 (6-inch) pitas, cut in half
 4 curly leaf lettuce leaves

1. Place first 10 ingredients in a food processor; process until smooth. Divide mixture into 8 equal portions, shaping each into a 2½-inch patty.
2. Coat a large nonstick skillet with cooking spray; add 1½ teaspoons oil, and place over medium-high heat until hot. Add 4 patties to skillet; cook 2 minutes on each side or until lightly browned. Repeat procedure with ½ teaspoon oil and 4 patties.
3. Spread about 2 tablespoons Tahini Sauce evenly into each pita half; fill each half with 1 lettuce leaf and 2 falafel patties. Yield: 4 servings.

CALORIES 312 (26% from fat); FAT 8.9g (sat 1.2g, mono 3.8g, poly 2.9g); PROTEIN 12.8g; CARB 46.7g; FIBER 4.4g; CHOL 1mg; IRON 4.3mg; SODIUM 536mg; CALC 181mg

TAHINI SAUCE

 ½ cup plain fat-free yogurt
 2 tablespoons tahini (sesame-seed
    paste)
 1 teaspoon lemon juice
Dash of ground red pepper
 1 garlic clove, minced

1. Combine all ingredients in a bowl; stir well with a whisk. Cover and chill. Yield: ½ cup.

ROASTED-VEGETABLE SANDWICH

PREP: 25 MINUTES   COOK: 1 HOUR

The skin of an acorn squash is tough and should be removed.

 1 small whole garlic head
 2 cups sliced portobello
    mushrooms (about 4 ounces)
 1¼ cups diagonally sliced zucchini
 1 cup chopped seeded Anaheim
    chile
 1 small acorn squash, peeled and
    thinly sliced
 ½ cup thinly sliced red
    onion
 2 plum tomatoes, quartered
    lengthwise and seeded
Cooking spray
 1 tablespoon olive oil
 ¼ teaspoon salt
 ¼ teaspoon dried thyme
 ¼ teaspoon black pepper
 4 rosemary sprigs
 1 (8-ounce) carton plain fat-free
    yogurt
 2 tablespoons Dijon mustard
 ½ teaspoon balsamic vinegar
 1 (16-ounce) loaf French bread,
    cut in half lengthwise

1. Preheat oven to 350°.
2. Remove white papery skin from garlic head (do not peel or separate the cloves). Wrap head in foil.
3. Arrange mushrooms and next 5 ingredients on a jelly-roll pan coated with cooking spray. Drizzle with olive oil, and sprinkle with salt, thyme, and pepper; toss well. Nestle rosemary sprigs into vegetables.
4. Bake garlic and vegetables at 350° for 45 minutes, stirring vegetables every 15 minutes. Discard rosemary sprigs. Separate garlic cloves, and squeeze to extract garlic pulp; discard skins.
5. Spoon yogurt onto several layers of heavy-duty paper towels; spread to ½-inch thickness. Cover with additional paper towels; let stand 10 minutes. Scrape yogurt into a bowl, using a rubber spatula. Stir in garlic pulp, mustard, and vinegar.
6. Hollow out top and bottom halves of bread, leaving a 1-inch-thick shell; reserve torn bread for another use. Spread yogurt mixture over top and bottom halves of loaf. Arrange vegetables on bottom half of loaf; replace top half. Wrap loaf in foil; bake at 350° for 15 minutes. Cut into 6 equal portions. Yield: 6 servings.

CALORIES 280 (16% from fat); FAT 5g (sat 0.8g, mono 2.5g, poly 0.8g); PROTEIN 10.2g; CARB 49.9g; FIBER 3.9g; CHOL 1mg; IRON 2.9mg; SODIUM 659mg; CALC 172mg

ROASTED-VEGETABLE SANDWICH WITH HAM AND CHEESE:

Add 2 ounces thinly sliced lean deli ham, 1 tablespoon grated fresh Parmesan cheese, and 1 tablespoon sliced ripe olives per serving.

CALORIES 298 (18% from fat); FAT 6g (sat 0.1g, mono 2.9g, poly 1g); PROTEIN 12.3g; CARB 50g; FIBER 4g; CHOL 7mg; IRON 3.1mg; SODIUM 831mg; CALC 186mg

Crème Anglaise (page 451)

sauces & condiments

salsas & guacamole
These aren't just for chips anymore. We've created north-of-the-border versions that feature fresh, flavorful ingredients.

The word "salsa" is Spanish for sauce, but we've given this south-of-the-border staple a new twist of flavor. What exactly is salsa? In simplest terms, it's an uncooked sauce made with fresh ingredients and usually some form of "fire."

Salsas really heat up when the "fire" is fueled by Anaheim, serrano, or jalapeño peppers. The fresh ingredients can range from crunchy sweet apple to soft-to-the-touch ripe peaches to juicy red tomatoes. Combine these with zesty herbs and pungent seasonings for a powerhouse of flavor.

APPLE-AVOCADO SALSA

PREP: 20 MINUTES

This is a versatile salsa; serve it over any grilled meat, fish, or poultry. We've paired it with Pork Fajitas (page 333).

    1   cup diced Granny Smith apple
    ¼   cup diced red bell pepper
    ¼   cup diced red onion
    1   tablespoon chopped fresh cilantro
    1½ teaspoons minced jalapeño
    ½   teaspoon grated lime rind
    ⅛   teaspoon salt
    1½ tablespoons fresh lime juice
    1   small garlic clove, minced
    Dash of black pepper
    ½   cup diced peeled avocado

1. Combine all ingredients except avocado in a medium bowl. Gently stir in diced avocado. Yield: 2 cups (serving size: ¼ cup).

CALORIES 30 (45% from fat); FAT 1.5g (sat 0.3g, mono 0.9g, poly 0.2g); PROTEIN 0.4g; CARB 4.4g; FIBER 1.1g; CHOL 0mg; IRON 0.2mg; SODIUM 38mg; CALC 5mg

FRESH-PEACH SALSA

PREP: 10 MINUTES   CHILL: 20 MINUTES

(pictured on page 6)

This salsa packs a punch; for a milder version, use less serrano chile, or omit it altogether. You can substitute ripe plums for part of the peaches, if desired.

    1½ cups coarsely chopped peeled
        peaches (about 3 small peaches)
    ½   cup diced red onion
    2   tablespoons fresh lemon juice
    1½ tablespoons minced fresh
        cilantro
    1   tablespoon minced shallot
    ¼   teaspoon chopped seeded
        serrano chile
    ½   teaspoon honey
    ⅛   teaspoon salt

1. Combine all ingredients in a bowl; toss gently. Cover and chill. Serve with grilled chicken, fish, or pork chops. Yield: 2 cups (serving size: ¼ cup).

CALORIES 20 (2% from fat); FAT 0g; PROTEIN 0.4g; CARB 5.2g; FIBER 0.8g; CHOL 0mg; IRON 0mg; SODIUM 32mg; CALC 4mg

---

SECRETS TO SALSA

• Always use fresh, ripe ingredients.
• Use a very sharp knife for a clean dice.
• Be sure to include an ingredient that has a crunchy texture.
• Experiment until you get just the right combination of flavors and colors.
• Always taste the salsa and balance the "fire" before serving.

GREEN CHILE SALSA

PREP: 15 MINUTES

    1⅓ cups diced seeded tomato
    ¼   cup diced sweet onion
    2   teaspoons fresh lime juice
    1   teaspoon minced fresh cilantro
    ¼   teaspoon freshly ground black
        pepper
    1   (4.5-ounce) can chopped green
        chiles, undrained

1. Combine all ingredients in a bowl. Serve with quesadillas, fajitas, tacos, chicken, beef, or grilled fish, or as a dip with pita chips. Yield: 1⅓ cups (serving size: ⅓ cup).

CALORIES 24 (7% from fat); FAT 0.2g (sat 0g, mono 0g, poly 0.1g); PROTEIN 0.9g; CARB 5.5g; FIBER 1.3g; CHOL 0mg; IRON 0.5mg; SODIUM 115mg; CALC 9mg

TOMATO-BASIL SALSA

PREP: 10 MINUTES

    2   cups chopped seeded peeled
        tomato
    ¼   cup chopped fresh basil
    2   tablespoons chopped red onion
    2   tablespoons red wine vinegar
    ¼   teaspoon salt
    ⅛   teaspoon black pepper

1. Combine all ingredients in a bowl. Serve with grilled vegetables, beef, or poultry. Salsa may also be used as a condiment on a grilled-chicken sandwich or toasted bagel with cheese. Yield: 2 cups (serving size: ¼ cup).

CALORIES 11 (16% from fat); FAT 0.2g (sat 0g, mono 0g, poly 0.1g); PROTEIN 0.5g; CARB 2.5g; FIBER 0.6g; CHOL 0mg; IRON 0.2mg; SODIUM 77mg; CALC 5mg

CHUNKY TOMATO SALSA

PREP: 10 MINUTES   CHILL: 1 HOUR

Add a twist to seafood—serve this with
Lobster Tails (page 231).

1½ cups finely chopped seeded
      tomato (about 2 medium)
  2 tablespoons minced green
      onions
  2 tablespoons finely chopped fresh
      parsley
  1 tablespoon balsamic vinegar
  1 teaspoon water
  1 teaspoon olive oil
 ½ teaspoon dried whole tarragon
 ⅛ teaspoon salt
 ⅛ teaspoon black pepper

1. Combine all ingredients in a bowl.
Cover and chill 1 hour. Yield: 2 cups
(serving size: ¼ cup).

CALORIES 12 (60% from fat); FAT 0.8g (sat 0g, mono 0.1g,
poly 0g); PROTEIN 0.4g; CARB 2.0g; FIBER 0.4g;
CHOL 0mg; IRON 0.4mg; SODIUM 40mg; CALC 4mg

Tomatillo-Tomato Salsa

MINTED TOMATO SALSA

PREP: 14 MINUTES

Salsa can be made ahead and refrigerated
for up to one week.

  4 cups chopped tomato
 ¼ cup finely chopped red onion
  2 tablespoons chopped fresh mint
  1 tablespoon chopped fresh basil
  1 tablespoon finely chopped
      seeded jalapeño pepper
  1 tablespoon lemon juice

1. Combine all ingredients in a bowl.
Serve with grilled fish. Yield: 4 cups
(serving size: ½ cup).

CALORIES 23 (12% from fat); FAT 0.3g (sat 0g, mono 0.1g,
poly 0.1g); PROTEIN 0.9g; CARB 5.1g; FIBER 1.1g;
CHOL 0mg; IRON 0.5mg; SODIUM 9mg; CALC 8mg

TOMATILLO-TOMATO SALSA

PREP: 16 MINUTES
STAND: 2 TO 4 HOURS

  1 cup diced tomato
 ¼ cup chopped green onions
  2 tablespoons chopped fresh
      cilantro
  2 tablespoons minced seeded
      jalapeño pepper
 ¼ teaspoon black pepper
  1 (11-ounce) can tomatillos,
      drained and chopped
  1 garlic clove, minced

1. Combine all ingredients in a bowl.
Let stand at room temperature 2 to 4
hours. Serve with grilled fish or as a
dip with pita chips. Yield: 2 cups (serving
size: ½ cup).

CALORIES 46 (4% from fat); FAT 0.2g (sat 0g, mono 0g,
poly 0.1g); PROTEIN 1.1g; CARB 10.2g; FIBER 2.4g;
CHOL 0mg; IRON 2.2mg; SODIUM 256mg; CALC 27mg

THREE-PEPPER SALSA

PREP: 35 MINUTES

1½ cups boiling water
  3 dried ancho chiles or ½ teaspoon
      crushed red pepper
  2 large poblano chiles
  1 large yellow bell pepper
  1 cup diced tomato
 ½ cup diced red onion
 ¼ cup chopped fresh cilantro
  3 tablespoons orange juice
  2 tablespoons lime juice
  2 tablespoons minced seeded
      serrano chile
 ¼ teaspoon salt

1. Combine water and ancho chiles in
a small bowl; cover and let stand 30
minutes or until soft. Drain well. Discard
seeds, and chop ancho chiles.
2. Preheat broiler.

(continued on page 440)

3. Cut poblanos and bell pepper in half lengthwise; discard seeds and membranes. Place poblanos and bell pepper halves, skin sides up, on a foil-lined baking sheet; flatten with hand. Broil 10 minutes or until blackened. Place in a zip-top plastic bag; seal. Let stand 10 minutes. Peel and dice poblanos and bell pepper. Combine anchos, roasted poblanos and bell pepper, tomato, and remaining ingredients; cover and chill. Serve with Confetti Quesadillas (page 237) or with grilled fish. Yield: 9 servings (serving size: ¼ cup).

CALORIES 26 (14% from fat); FAT 0.4g (sat 0.1g, mono 0g, poly 0.2g); PROTEIN 1g; CARB 5.6g; FIBER 1.5g; CHOL 0mg; IRON 0.6mg; SODIUM 79mg; CALC 12mg

TOMATILLO GUACAMOLE

PREP: 8 MINUTES
CHILL: 1 HOUR

1 medium avocado (about ½ pound), peeled and halved
1 (11-ounce) can tomatillos, drained
1 cup chopped onion
2 teaspoons chopped fresh cilantro
2 tablespoons fresh lime juice
1½ teaspoons seeded, minced serrano chile
⅛ teaspoon salt
⅛ teaspoon black pepper

1. Place avocado and tomatillos in a food processor, and process until mixture is smooth.
2. Spoon mixture into a medium bowl; stir in remaining ingredients. Cover and chill 1 hour. Serve with Fish Fajitas (page 221), spread on chicken or turkey sandwiches, dollop on Mexican salads, or serve with chips. Yield: 2 cups (serving size: 2 tablespoons).

CALORIES 25 (47% from fat); FAT 1.3g (sat 0.2g, mono 0.8g, poly 0.2g); PROTEIN 0.4g; CARB 3.3g; FIBER 1.0g; CHOL 0mg; IRON 0.5mg; SODIUM 105mg; CALC 7mg

gravies A gravy is simply the natural juices from cooked meat (or poultry) thickened with flour or cornstarch. But what amazingly rich flavors these simple recipes provide!

Gravy is no longer reserved for holidays and times of indulgence. These low-fat gravies deserve to be used year-round. If you use homemade stock or broth, see our gravy tips on page 385 for skimming the fat from the drippings.

WHITE GRAVY

PREP: 2 MINUTES   COOK: 7 MINUTES

¼ cup all-purpose flour
½ teaspoon salt
¼ to ½ teaspoon black pepper
1 (12-ounce) can evaporated fat-free milk
1 (14½-ounce) can fat-free, less-sodium chicken broth

1. Combine first 3 ingredients in a medium saucepan. Gradually add milk and broth, stirring well with a whisk. Bring mixture to a boil; reduce heat, and simmer until thick (about 3 minutes), stirring constantly with a whisk. Serve with chicken, pork, mashed potatoes, or biscuits. Yield: 3 cups (serving size: ¼ cup).

CALORIES 35 (3% from fat); FAT 0.1g (sat 0g, mono 0g, poly 0g); PROTEIN 2.6g; CARB 5.5g; FIBER 0.1g; CHOL 1mg; IRON 0.2mg; SODIUM 224mg; CALC 87mg

BROWN GRAVY

PREP: 10 MINUTES   COOK: 25 MINUTES

Adding vegetables to the beef broth gives a rich flavor without adding calories or fat.

2 (14½-ounce) cans no-salt-added beef broth
1 cup coarsely chopped onion
½ cup coarsely chopped fresh mushrooms
¼ cup coarsely chopped celery
¼ teaspoon dried thyme
⅛ to ¼ teaspoon black pepper
Cooking spray
2 tablespoons all-purpose flour

1. Combine first 6 ingredients in a medium saucepan. Bring to a boil; cook 15 minutes or until liquid is reduced to 2 cups. Strain broth mixture through a sieve into a bowl; discard solids.
2. Coat a medium skillet with cooking spray; place over medium-high heat until hot. Add flour, and cook 2 minutes or until browned, stirring constantly. Transfer flour to a large bowl, and cool completely. Add ¼ cup reserved broth mixture to flour; stir well with a whisk. Add remaining broth mixture, stirring well with a whisk. Pour mixture into skillet; place over medium-high heat. Bring to a boil; reduce heat, and simmer 3 minutes or until thick, stirring constantly. Serve with mashed potatoes, beef, or pork. Yield: 1¾ cups (serving size: ¼ cup).

CALORIES 20 (5% from fat); FAT 0.1g (sat 0g, mono 0g, poly 0g); PROTEIN 0.5g; CARB 2.6g; FIBER 0.1g; CHOL 0mg; IRON 0.2mg; SODIUM 4mg; CALC 1mg

SAUSAGE GRAVY

PREP: **4** MINUTES

COOK: **12** MINUTES

1 tablespoon stick margarine or butter
1 (10.5 ounce) package 97% fat-free breakfast sausage
3½ tablespoons all-purpose flour
2¼ cups fat-free milk
⅛ teaspoon salt
½ teaspoon black pepper

1. Melt margarine in a saucepan over medium heat; add sausage. Cook until sausage is browned, stirring to crumble. Sprinkle sausage with flour; cook 1 minute, stirring constantly. Gradually add milk; cook over medium heat, until thickened and bubbly, stirring constantly. Remove from heat; stir in salt and pepper. Serve over biscuits. Yield: 3 cups (serving size: ½ cup).

CALORIES 125 (24% from fat); FAT 3.4g (sat 0.8g, mono 1.5g, poly 0.8g); PROTEIN 10.9g; CARB 8.4g; FIBER 0.1g; CHOL 25mg; IRON 0.6mg; SODIUM 539mg; CALC 115mg

The key to smooth, **creamy gravy is** to stir, stir, stir.

Brown Gravy

CREAMY SAGE-GIBLET GRAVY

PREP: **6** MINUTES   COOK: **16** MINUTES

You will have enough gravy to accompany a 14-pound turkey.

1 teaspoon vegetable oil
2½ ounces turkey liver
1 cup degreased turkey drippings
3 tablespoons all-purpose flour
1⅔ cups 2% reduced-fat milk
½ cup evaporated fat-free milk
1½ teaspoons stick margarine or butter
1 teaspoon rubbed sage
1 small garlic clove, minced
2 tablespoons chopped fresh parsley
1 teaspoon spicy brown mustard
½ teaspoon salt

1. Heat oil in a small nonstick skillet over medium heat until hot. Add liver; sauté 5 minutes or until done. Remove liver from skillet. Add drippings to skillet; bring to a boil, stirring with a wooden spoon to loosen browned bits. Remove from heat; set drippings aside. Chop liver, and set aside.
2. Place flour in a bowl. Gradually add milks, stirring well with a whisk.
3. Melt margarine in a saucepan over medium heat. Add sage and garlic; sauté 1 minute. Add milk mixture, stirring constantly. Stir in drippings and liver; bring to a boil, stirring constantly. Reduce heat, and simmer, uncovered, until thick (about 2 minutes). Remove from heat; stir in parsley, mustard, and salt. Serve with turkey and dressing, chicken, mashed potatoes, roasted potatoes, grits, or biscuits. Yield: 3½ cups (serving size: ¼ cup).

CALORIES 42 (32% from fat); FAT 1.5g (sat 0.6g, mono 0.5g, poly 0.3g); PROTEIN 2.8g; CARB 4.1g; FIBER 0.1g; CHOL 25mg; IRON 0.6mg; SODIUM 121mg; CALC 64mg

sauces

Let these sauces dress up your meal. With only a few ingredients and minimal preparation, you'll have the perfect sauce!

Many of these sauces yield an amount for just one meal. When you do have a little left over, remember that tomato-based sauces freeze best. Others may separate or "curdle" upon thawing.

BÉCHAMEL SAUCE

PREP: 2 MINUTES
COOK: 17 MINUTES

Béchamel sauce (pronounced bay-shah-MEHL) is traditionally made by stirring cream into a butter-flour mixture called a roux. This lightened version has rich flavor from steeping the peppercorns, onion, and bay leaf in the milk. This sauce is so versatile you can spoon it over vegetable-filled crêpes, or stir in shredded cheese and serve over pasta.

2½   cups 1% low-fat milk
  8   black peppercorns
  1   onion, cut into ½-inch-thick
        slices
  1   bay leaf
  2   tablespoons butter or stick
        margarine
  ¼   cup all-purpose flour
  ¼   teaspoon salt
  ⅛   teaspoon ground white pepper
Dash of ground nutmeg

1. Combine first 4 ingredients in a heavy saucepan; cook over medium-high heat to 180° or until tiny bubbles form around edge (do not boil). Remove from heat. Cover; let stand 10 minutes. Strain mixture through a sieve into a bowl; discard solids. Set milk mixture aside.
2. Melt 2 tablespoons butter in pan over medium heat. Add flour, stirring

Béchamel Sauce

1. Steep peppercorns, onion, and bay leaf in milk over medium-high heat for about 5 minutes. This flavor combination infuses the milk with sweet, nutty tones.

2. Carefully whisk the flour into the melted butter, and cook 1 minute. Watch carefully, because an overcooked roux will make the white sauce taste burned. A smooth roux is the key to a creamy white sauce.

3. Slowly but vigorously whisk the milk into the roux.

4. Cook over medium heat until thick (about 10 minutes), stirring constantly.

well with a whisk. Cook 1 minute, stirring constantly.
3. Gradually add milk mixture, stirring well with a whisk; cook over medium heat until thick (about 10 minutes). Stir in salt, pepper, and nutmeg. Yield: 2¼ cups (serving size: ¼ cup).

CALORIES 63 (47% from fat); FAT 3.3g (sat 2.1g, mono 1g, poly 0.1g); PROTEIN 2.6g; CARB 5.7g; FIBER 0.1g; CHOL 10mg; IRON 0.2mg; SODIUM 125mg; CALC 85mg

BÉARNAISE SAUCE

PREP: 7 MINUTES
COOK: 2 MINUTES

½ cup thinly sliced shallots (about
   2 ounces)
3 tablespoons dry white wine
2 tablespoons white wine vinegar
1 teaspoon dried tarragon
Dash of salt
Dash of black pepper
⅔ cup low-fat sour cream

1. Combine first 6 ingredients in a small, heavy saucepan; bring to a boil, and cook 1 minute. Strain mixture through a sieve into a bowl; discard solids. Return liquid to saucepan; stir in sour cream. Place over low heat, and cook 1 minute or until warm, stirring frequently. Yield: ¾ cup (serving size: 3 tablespoons).

CALORIES 76 (60% from fat); FAT 5.1g (sat 3g, mono 1.6g, poly 0.2g); PROTEIN 2.4g; CARB 6g; FIBER 0.4g; CHOL 15mg; IRON 1.4mg; SODIUM 21mg; CALC 88mg

CHEDDAR CHEESE SAUCE

PREP: 4 MINUTES
COOK: 10 MINUTES

1 teaspoon stick margarine or
   butter
3 tablespoons all-purpose flour
1½ cups 1% low-fat milk
½ cup (2 ounces) shredded
   reduced-fat sharp cheddar
   cheese
1 tablespoon dry sherry
¼ teaspoon salt
¼ teaspoon ground red pepper
⅛ teaspoon onion powder
1 (2-ounce) jar diced pimento,
   drained

1. Melt margarine in a small, heavy saucepan over medium heat. Add flour, stirring well with a whisk.
2. Gradually add milk, stirring well with a whisk. Cook until thick (about 10 minutes), stirring constantly. Remove from heat; add cheese, stirring until cheese melts. Stir in sherry and remaining ingredients. Yield: 2 cups (serving size: ¼ cup).

CALORIES 57 (38% from fat); FAT 2.4g (sat 1.2g, mono 0.7g, poly 0.2g); PROTEIN 3.9g; CARB 5g; FIBER 0.1g; CHOL 7mg; IRON 0.3mg; SODIUM 154mg; CALC 120mg

Be sure to use a heavy saucepan when making a cheese sauce. The sauce may lump or scorch more easily in a lightweight pan.

Cheddar Cheese Sauce

1. Place flour in a heavy saucepan. Gradually add the milk to the flour, whisking mixture vigorously after each addition. (This is where things can get tricky. If you pour all of the milk into the flour at once, you'll get lumps.)

2. Cook the sauce over medium heat until it is thick, stirring constantly. But don't worry if the sauce hasn't thickened after 10 minutes. Just continue to cook it, stirring constantly. It should coat a spoon when ready.

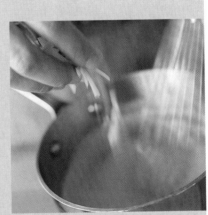

3. Remove the sauce from the heat; add the cheese, stirring until cheese melts. Don't try to save time by cubing the cheese; shredding makes for quick, easy melting.

PIMENTO CHEESE SAUCE

PREP: 3 MINUTES   COOK: 5 MINUTES

2 teaspoons stick margarine or
   butter
5 teaspoons all-purpose flour
⅛ teaspoon salt
⅛ teaspoon dry mustard
Dash of black pepper
1 cup 2% reduced-fat milk
½ cup (2 ounces) shredded
   reduced-fat sharp cheddar
   cheese
1 (2-ounce) jar diced pimento,
   drained

1. Melt margarine in a saucepan over medium heat. Add flour, salt, mustard, and pepper, and cook 1 minute, stirring constantly. Gradually add milk, stirring well with a whisk. Cook until thick and bubbly (2 to 3 minutes), stirring constantly. Remove from heat; add cheese and pimento, stirring until cheese melts. Serve warm with waffles or as a dip with fresh vegetables. Yield: 1¼ cups (serving size: ¼ cup).

CALORIES 84 (50% from fat); FAT 4.7g (sat 2.2g, mono 1.6g, poly 0.6g); PROTEIN 5.3g; CARB 5.2g; FIBER 0.1g; CHOL 12mg; IRON 0.4mg; SODIUM 184mg; CALC 162mg

CUCUMBER-DILL MUSTARD SAUCE

PREP: 20 MINUTES   CHILL: 2 HOURS

½ cup grated seeded peeled
   cucumber
1 cup plain low-fat yogurt
2 tablespoons fat-free
   mayonnaise
1 tablespoon lemon-dill mustard
1 tablespoon apple cider
   vinegar
1 teaspoon dried dill
1 teaspoon grated lemon rind

1. Place cucumber on several layers of heavy-duty paper towels; cover with additional paper towels. Let stand 15 minutes, pressing down occasionally.
2. Spoon yogurt onto several layers of heavy-duty paper towels; spread to ½-inch thickness. Cover with additional paper towels; let stand 5 minutes. Scrape into a bowl using a rubber spatula. Stir in cucumber, mayonnaise, and remaining ingredients. Cover and chill 2 hours. Serve as a dip with fresh vegetables or with grilled fish or Thai lettuce wraps. Yield: 1 cup (serving size: 2 tablespoons).

CALORIES 22 (25% from fat); FAT 0.6g (sat 0.4g, mono 0.2g, poly 0g); PROTEIN 1.4g; CARB 2.8g; FIBER 0g; CHOL 2mg; IRON 0.2mg; SODIUM 54mg; CALC 58mg

CUCUMBER-DILL SAUCE

PREP: 5 MINUTES

¼ cup diced seeded peeled
   cucumber
¼ cup plain low-fat yogurt
½ teaspoon chopped fresh or
   ⅛ teaspoon dried dill
1 small garlic clove, minced

1. Combine all ingredients in a bowl. Serve with grilled trout, salmon, or shellfish or as a dip with fresh vegetables. Yield: ½ cup (serving size: 2 tablespoons).

CALORIES 11 (16% from fat); FAT 0.2g (sat 0.2g, mono 0.1g, poly 0g); PROTEIN 0.9g; CARB 1.5g; FIBER 0.1g; CHOL 1mg; IRON 0.1mg; SODIUM 10mg; CALC 29mg

menu

Chicken fajitas
Cilantro-Peanut Sauce
Orange-and-Avocado Salad
(page 392)
Almond Sugar Cookies (page 157)

CILANTRO-PEANUT SAUCE

PREP: 10 MINUTES
COOK: 4 MINUTES

¼ cup balsamic vinegar
2½ tablespoons granulated sugar
2 tablespoons brown sugar
2 tablespoons low-sodium
   soy sauce
½ teaspoon crushed red pepper
⅛ teaspoon salt
1 garlic clove, minced
2 tablespoons creamy peanut
   butter
½ cup chopped fresh cilantro
2 tablespoons chopped
   fresh mint

1. Combine first 7 ingredients in a small saucepan; bring to a boil, stirring frequently. Remove from heat. Add peanut butter, stirring well with a whisk. Cool; stir in cilantro and mint. Serve with Thai foods (such as lettuce wraps), chicken fajitas, or Asian chicken salad or as a dip with fresh vegetables. Yield: ⅔ cup (serving size: 3 tablespoons).

CALORIES 78 (35% from fat); FAT 4.5g (sat 0.9g, mono 2.7g, poly 1.8g); PROTEIN 3.6g; CARB 17.1g; FIBER 0.9g; CHOL 0mg; IRON 0.9mg; SODIUM 405mg; CALC 18mg

GARDEN BROWN SAUCE

PREP: 13 MINUTES

COOK: 1 HOUR 25 MINUTES

2 tablespoons olive oil
1 cup chopped onion
1 cup chopped carrot
1 cup chopped celery
1 cup sliced mushrooms
4 garlic cloves, halved
¼ cup tomato paste
¼ cup all-purpose flour
1 cup dry red wine
6 cups water
2 tablespoons low-sodium
     soy sauce
2 teaspoons black peppercorns
1 teaspoon dried thyme
½ teaspoon salt
3 bay leaves

1. Heat oil in a saucepan over medium-high heat. Add onion and carrot; sauté 9 minutes or until lightly browned. Add celery, mushrooms, and garlic; cook 10 minutes. Add tomato paste; cook 10 minutes or until browned, stirring constantly. Stir in flour; cook 1 minute, stirring constantly. Stir in wine, scraping pan to loosen browned bits. Add water and remaining ingredients. Bring to a boil; reduce heat, and simmer 45 minutes.
2. Strain mixture through a sieve into a bowl. Discard solids. Store sauce in an airtight container for up to 1 week, or freeze for up to 3 months. Use sauce in Spicy Wheat Berry Enchiladas (page 279) or serve with beef or pork. Yield: 5¼ cups (serving size: ¼ cup).

CALORIES 21 (56% from fat); FAT 1.3g (sat 0.2g, mono 1g, poly 0.1g); PROTEIN 0.4g; CARB 2.2g; FIBER 0.2g; CHOL 0mg; IRON 0.3mg; SODIUM 106mg; CALC 5mg

CRANBERRY JEZEBEL SAUCE

PREP: 3 MINUTES

COOK: 18 MINUTES

CHILL: 1 HOUR

1 cup water
½ cup granulated sugar
½ cup packed brown sugar
1 (12-ounce) bag fresh or frozen
     cranberries
3 tablespoons prepared horseradish
1 tablespoon Dijon mustard
Mint sprigs (optional)

1. Combine first 3 ingredients in a medium saucepan. Bring to a boil over medium heat; add cranberries. Return to a boil, and cook 10 minutes, stirring occasionally. Spoon into a bowl; cool to room temperature.
2. Stir horseradish and mustard into cranberry mixture; cover and chill. Garnish with mint, if desired. Serve with beef, pork, turkey, or shrimp, or over light cream cheese with crackers. Yield: 2½ cups (serving size: ¼ cup).

CALORIES 101 (2% from fat); FAT 0.2g (sat 0g, mono 0g, poly 0.1g); PROTEIN 0.2g; CARB 25.6g; FIBER 0.6g; CHOL 0mg; IRON 0.3mg; SODIUM 63mg; CALC 14mg

HARISSA SAUCE

PREP: 6 MINUTES

Crushed red pepper, garlic, and jalapeño pepper provide the traditional fiery-hot flavor for this sauce.

2 teaspoons caraway seeds
½ teaspoon ground coriander
½ teaspoon ground cumin
½ teaspoon crushed red pepper
½ teaspoon black pepper
1 garlic clove, peeled
1 jalapeño pepper, seeded
2 tablespoons red wine vinegar
1 tablespoon olive oil

1. Place first 7 ingredients in a food processor; process until finely chopped. Add vinegar and oil, and process until smooth. Cover and chill. Serve with couscous, soups, or stews. Yield: ¼ cup (serving size: 1 tablespoon).

CALORIES 10 (83% from fat); FAT 0.9g (sat 0.1g, mono 0.7g, poly 0.1g); PROTEIN 0.1g; CARB 0.4g; FIBER 0.1g; CHOL 0mg; IRON 0.1mg; SODIUM 1mg; CALC 4mg

HERB HUMMUS

PREP: 15 MINUTES

This hummus makes a unique spread on a pizza crust, but it's also great as a dip for pita chips and veggies. Stir it into hot cooked pasta for a meatless main dish.

½ cup fresh parsley leaves
⅓ cup basil leaves
2 tablespoons grated fresh
     Parmesan cheese
1 tablespoon pine nuts
2 tablespoons lemon juice
2 tablespoons tahini (sesame-seed
     paste)
½ teaspoon salt
¼ teaspoon black pepper
1 (15-ounce) can cannellini beans
     or other white beans, drained
2 garlic cloves

1. Place all ingredients in a food processor; process until smooth, scraping sides of processor bowl occasionally. Yield: 1⅔ cups (serving size: 1 tablespoon).

CALORIES 21 (51% from fat); FAT 1.2g (sat 0.2g, mono 0.4g, poly 0.4g); PROTEIN 0.9g; CARB 2.1g; FIBER 0.6g; CHOL 0mg; IRON 0.3mg; SODIUM 83mg; CALC 5mg

WHITE BEAN HUMMUS

PREP: 5 MINUTES

1 (15-ounce) can cannellini beans
    or other white beans, rinsed
    and drained
3 tablespoons fresh lemon juice
1 tablespoon tahini (sesame-seed
    paste)
½ teaspoon ground cumin
½ teaspoon Hungarian sweet paprika
¼ teaspoon salt
2 garlic cloves

1. Place all ingredients in a food processor; process until smooth. Serve with pita chips or White Bean Hummus-and-Asiago Pizzas (page 297). Yield: 1⅓ cups (serving size: 1 tablespoon).

CALORIES 18 (2% from fat); FAT 0.6g (sat 0.1g, mono 0.2g, poly 0.2g); PROTEIN 0.9g; CARB 2.4g; FIBER 0.6g; CHOL 0mg; IRON 0.3mg; SODIUM 66mg; CALC 6mg

HORSERADISH CREAM

PREP: 5 MINUTES   CHILL: 1 HOUR

½ cup fat-free sour cream
2 tablespoons chopped green onions
1 tablespoon prepared horseradish

1. Combine all ingredients; cover and chill. Serve with beef. Yield: 10 tablespoons (serving size: 2½ tablespoons).

CALORIES 22 (0% from fat); FAT 0g; PROTEIN 2.1g; CARB 2.6g; FIBER 0.2g; CHOL 0mg; IRON 0mg; SODIUM 32mg; CALC 44mg

ARRABBIATA SAUCE

PREP: 6 MINUTES   COOK: 25 MINUTES

1 teaspoon olive oil
1 cup chopped onion
4 garlic cloves, minced
½ cup dry red wine or 2 tablespoons
    balsamic vinegar

1 tablespoon sugar
1 tablespoon chopped fresh or
    1 teaspoon dried basil
1 teaspoon crushed red pepper
2 tablespoons tomato paste
1 tablespoon lemon juice
½ teaspoon dried Italian
    seasoning
¼ teaspoon black pepper
2 (14.5-ounce) cans diced
    tomatoes, undrained
2 tablespoons chopped fresh parsley

1. Heat oil in a saucepan or large skillet over medium-high heat. Add onion and garlic; sauté 5 minutes. Stir in wine and next 8 ingredients; bring to a boil. Reduce heat to medium, and cook, uncovered, about 15 minutes. Stir in parsley. Serve with pasta or Shrimp Fra Diavolo With Feta (page 242). Yield: 3 cups (serving size: 1 cup).

CALORIES 133 (17% from fat); FAT 2.5g (sat 0.4g, mono 1.3g, poly 0.5g); PROTEIN 4.4g; CARB 26.7g; FIBER 4.2g; CHOL 0mg; IRON 3mg; SODIUM 468mg; CALC 112mg

TOMATO SAUCE

PREP: 5 MINUTES   COOK: 35 MINUTES

2 teaspoons olive oil
1 cup finely chopped onion
1 teaspoon dried oregano
1 teaspoon dried basil
½ teaspoon crushed red pepper
2 bay leaves
1 garlic clove, minced
½ cup water
½ cup dry white wine
¼ teaspoon salt
¼ teaspoon black pepper
2 (14.5-ounce) cans no-salt-added
    whole tomatoes, undrained
    and chopped

1. Heat oil in a medium saucepan over medium-high heat. Add onion; sauté 4

minutes. Add oregano, basil, red pepper, bay leaves, and garlic; sauté 1 minute. Stir in water and remaining ingredients; bring to a boil. Reduce heat, and simmer 30 minutes. Remove bay leaves. Serve with pasta or spoon over chicken. Yield: 4 cups (serving size: ½ cup).

CALORIES 37 (29% from fat); FAT 1.2g (sat 0.2g, mono 0.8g, poly 0.1g); PROTEIN 1.1g; CARB 6.4g; FIBER 1g; CHOL 0mg; IRON 0.7mg; SODIUM 88mg; CALC 45mg

HERB-TOMATO SAUCE

PREP: 15 MINUTES
COOK: 30 MINUTES

1 tablespoon olive oil
1 large garlic clove, minced
1 (28-ounce) can Italian-style
    tomatoes, undrained and
    chopped
2 tablespoons finely chopped fresh
    oregano
2 tablespoons finely chopped fresh
    thyme
2 tablespoons finely chopped fresh
    flat-leaf parsley
2 tablespoons finely chopped fresh
    basil
¼ teaspoon black pepper

1. Heat oil in a large saucepan over medium heat until hot. Add garlic, and sauté 1 minute. Add tomato and remaining ingredients. Bring to a simmer over medium-high heat; cook 25 minutes or until reduced to 2 cups. Serve over pasta, ravioli, or meat loaf or use as a dipping sauce for breadsticks. Sauce may also be used to prepare pizza. Yield: 2 cups (serving size: ¼ cup).
Note: Sauce can be made ahead, covered, and stored in the refrigerator for up to 4 days.

CALORIES 38 (45% from fat); FAT 1.9g (sat 0.3g, mono 1.3g, poly 0.3g); PROTEIN 1.1g; CARB 4.8g; FIBER 0.9g; CHOL 0mg; IRON 0.9mg; SODIUM 162mg; CALC 36mg

ULTIMATE QUICK-AND-EASY PASTA SAUCE

PREP: 10 MINUTES
COOK: 22 MINUTES

You can substitute crushed or whole tomatoes for the diced. Crushed will give you a smooth, thick sauce; whole adds a nice chunkiness. Serve this sauce with your favorite pasta.

1 teaspoon olive oil
1 cup chopped onion
4 garlic cloves, minced
½ cup dry red wine or
    2 tablespoons balsamic vinegar
1 tablespoon sugar
1 tablespoon chopped fresh or
    2 teaspoons dried basil
2 tablespoons tomato paste
½ teaspoon dried Italian seasoning
¼ teaspoon black pepper
2 (14.5-ounce) cans diced
    tomatoes, undrained
2 tablespoons chopped fresh parsley

1. Heat oil in a saucepan or large skillet over medium-high heat. Add onion and garlic; sauté 5 minutes. Stir in wine and next 6 ingredients, and bring to a boil. Reduce heat to medium, and cook, uncovered, about 15 minutes. Stir in parsley. Yield: 3 cups (serving size: 1 cup).

CALORIES 126 (16% from fat); FAT 2.3g (sat 0.4g, mono 1.3g, poly 0.5g); PROTEIN 4.1g; CARB 25.2g; FIBER 3.7g; CHOL 0mg; IRON 2.8mg; SODIUM 461mg; CALC 110mg

CHUNKY TOMATO SAUCE

PREP: 10 MINUTES   COOK: 20 MINUTES

1 tablespoon olive oil
1 cup chopped onion
2 garlic cloves, minced
6 cups coarsely chopped tomato
    (about 2½ pounds)
⅓ cup tomato paste

Ultimate Quick-and-Easy Pasta Sauce

2 tablespoons balsamic vinegar
1 teaspoon sugar
¼ teaspoon salt
¼ teaspoon black pepper
¼ teaspoon crushed red pepper
¼ cup chopped fresh basil

1. Heat oil in a large nonstick skillet over medium heat. Add onion and garlic; sauté 5 minutes or until tender. Stir in tomato and next 6 ingredients. Reduce heat and simmer, uncovered, 15 minutes. Remove from heat; stir in basil. Serve over pasta or as a dip with fresh vegetables or pita chips. Sauce may also be used to prepare lasagna or pizza. Yield: 5 cups (serving size: 1¼ cups).

Note: Substitute 3 (14.5-ounce) cans diced tomatoes, undrained, for 6 cups chopped tomato, if desired. Omit salt when using canned tomatoes.

CALORIES 118 (34% from fat); FAT 4.5g (sat 0.6g, mono 2.7g, poly 0.7g); PROTEIN 3.4g; CARB 19.8g; FIBER 4.2g; CHOL 0mg; IRON 2mg; SODIUM 185mg; CALC 33mg

One pound of fresh tomatoes **yields approximately two cups of peeled, seeded, and chopped tomatoes.**

CHUNKY TOMATO-BASIL SAUCE

PREP: 10 MINUTES
COOK: 22 MINUTES

2 teaspoons olive oil
1 cup finely chopped onion
3 garlic cloves, thinly sliced
3½ cups finely chopped peeled
    tomato (about 1½ pounds)
¼ cup chopped fresh basil
3 tablespoons tomato paste
1 tablespoon balsamic vinegar
1 teaspoon brown sugar
¼ teaspoon salt
¼ teaspoon crushed red pepper
¼ teaspoon black pepper

1. Heat oil in a large skillet over medium heat. Add onion, and sauté 8 minutes or until lightly browned. Add garlic; sauté 15 seconds. Add remaining ingredients, and bring to a boil. Reduce heat, and simmer 10 minutes or until thick, stirring frequently. Serve over omelets or with a cheese soufflé, chicken, or turkey Parmesan. Yield: 2½ cups (serving size: ½ cup).

CALORIES 55 (36% from fat); FAT 2.2g (sat 0.3g, mono 1.4g, poly 0.3g); PROTEIN 1.5g; CARB 8.9g; FIBER 1.8g; CHOL 0mg; IRON 0.8mg; SODIUM 131mg; CALC 20mg

SUN-DRIED TOMATO SAUCE

PREP: 28 MINUTES

1 cup sun-dried tomatoes, packed
    without oil (about 2 ounces)
2 cups boiling water
1 (5.5-ounce) can low-sodium
    vegetable juice
2 tablespoons olive oil
2 tablespoons balsamic vinegar
½ teaspoon black pepper
¼ teaspoon salt
1 garlic clove

The secret to the flavor in a homemade tomato sauce is vine-ripened tomatoes. To peel them, blanch them briefly in boiling water, and then plunge them into ice water. The skins will then slip off easily in strips.

1. Combine sun-dried tomatoes and 2 cups boiling water; let stand 20 minutes. Drain, reserving 1¼ cups liquid.
2. Place sun-dried tomatoes, vegetable juice, and remaining 5 ingredients in a food processor or blender; process at low speed until smooth. Add reserved liquid; process until blended. Serve with grilled chicken, shrimp, grilled white fish, or flank steak; as a sauce for pasta; over cream cheese with crackers; or as a dip with pita chips. Yield: 2½ cups (serving size: 2 tablespoons).

CALORIES 22 (57% from fat); FAT 1.4g (sat 0.2g, mono 1g, poly 0.2g); PROTEIN 0.5g; CARB 2g; FIBER 0.4g; CHOL 0mg; IRON 0.3mg; SODIUM 93mg; CALC 4mg

RED PEPPER SAUCE

PREP: 4 MINUTES   COOK: 10 MINUTES

2 red bell peppers (about 1 pound)
1 cup tomato juice
1 tablespoon tahini (sesame-seed
    paste)
1 tablespoon tomato paste
1 tablespoon lemon juice
1 teaspoon dried oregano
1 garlic clove, minced

1. Cut bell peppers in half lengthwise; discard seeds and membranes. Place pepper halves, skin sides up, on a foil-lined baking sheet. Flatten with hand. Broil 10 minutes or until blackened. Place in a zip-top plastic bag; seal. Let stand 15 minutes. Peel pepper halves.
2. Place bell pepper and remaining ingredients in a food processor; process until smooth. Serve over Sun-Dried Tomato-Basil Rice Cakes (page 247) or with grilled fish, pork or chicken, or toss with pasta. Yield: 2 cups (serving size: ¼ cup).

CALORIES 34 (34% from fat); FAT 1.3g (sat 0.2g, mono 0.4g, poly 0.6g); PROTEIN 1.2g; CARB 5.5g; FIBER 1.3g; CHOL 0mg; IRON 1.2mg; SODIUM 115mg; CALC 19mg

PORT-WINE SAUCE

PREP: 3 MINUTES   COOK: 35 MINUTES

2 cups port or other sweet red wine
¼ cup sherry vinegar
2 tablespoons sugar

1. Combine all ingredients in a medium saucepan. Bring to a boil; reduce heat, and simmer, uncovered, about 30 minutes or until reduced to ½ cup. Serve with pork, duck, beef, or veal or over dried fruit or fresh plums. Yield: ½ cup (serving size: 2 tablespoons).

CALORIES 47 (0% from fat); FAT 0g; PROTEIN 0.3g; CARB 8.5g; FIBER 0g; CHOL 0mg; IRON 0.5mg; SODIUM 98mg; CALC 10mg

QUICK MOLE MARINARA SAUCE

PREP: 8 MINUTES   COOK: 32 MINUTES

    2   teaspoons olive oil
    1   cup minced red onion
    3   tablespoons minced seeded
          Anaheim chile
    1   teaspoon chili powder
    1   teaspoon dried oregano
    1   teaspoon ground cumin
    1   (28-ounce) jar marinara sauce
          (such as Barilla)
    2   tablespoons unsweetened cocoa
    1   tablespoon minced fresh or
          1 teaspoon dried cilantro

1. Heat oil in a large saucepan over medium-high heat. Add onion, chile, chili powder, oregano, and cumin; sauté 2 minutes. Add marinara sauce; cook over low heat 30 minutes, stirring occasionally. Remove from heat; stir in cocoa and cilantro. Serve with roasted chicken or over Cheesy Rice-and-Bean Strata (page 301). Yield: 3½ cups (serving size: 2 tablespoons).

CALORIES 27 (47% from fat); FAT 1.4g (sat 0.2g, mono 0.8g, poly 0.3g); PROTEIN 0.7g; CARB 3.7g; FIBER 0.3g; CHOL 0mg; IRON 0.4mg; SODIUM 180mg; CALC 9mg

RED BELL PEPPER COULIS

PREP: 5 MINUTES   COOK: 42 MINUTES

    1   teaspoon stick margarine or
          butter
    1   tablespoon chopped shallots
    2   thyme sprigs
    1   garlic clove, crushed
    3   cups fat-free, less-sodium
          chicken broth
  2¼   cups chopped red bell pepper
          (about 2 large)
    ⅛   teaspoon salt
    ⅛   teaspoon black pepper
    1   tablespoon balsamic vinegar

1. Melt margarine in a saucepan over medium heat. Add shallots, thyme, and garlic; sauté 2 minutes. Add broth, bell pepper, salt, and black pepper; bring to a boil, and cook 35 minutes or until reduced to about 1 cup. Discard thyme sprigs.
2. Place bell pepper mixture and vinegar in a blender; process until smooth. Serve with grilled fish, pork, or chicken or as a dip with fresh vegetables. Yield: 1 cup (serving size: 2 tablespoons).

CALORIES 24 (23% from fat); FAT 0.6g (sat 0.1g, mono 0.2g, poly 0.3g); PROTEIN 0.6g; CARB 3.2g; FIBER 0.7g; CHOL 0mg; IRON 0.5mg; SODIUM 283mg; CALC 4mg

MADEIRA-MUSHROOM SAUCE

PREP: 3 MINUTES   COOK: 6 MINUTES

  1½   teaspoons stick margarine or
          butter
    1   cup sliced fresh mushrooms
    ½   teaspoon dried thyme
    ½   cup Madeira
  1¼   cups degreased turkey drippings
    1   teaspoon lemon juice
    ¼   teaspoon salt
    2   tablespoons cornstarch
    2   tablespoons water

1. Melt margarine in a medium saucepan over medium-high heat. Add mushrooms and thyme; sauté 3 minutes or until tender. Add Madeira, turkey drippings, lemon juice, and salt; bring to a boil. Combine cornstarch and water, stirring well with a whisk; add to sauce. Bring to a boil, and cook until slightly thick (about 1 minute), stirring constantly. Serve with beef, pork, chicken, turkey, polenta, grits, or toast points. Yield: 1½ cups (serving size: ¼ cup).

CALORIES 32 (28% from fat); FAT 1g (sat 0.2g, mono 0.4g, poly 0.3g); PROTEIN 0.5g; CARB 4.6g; FIBER 0.3g; CHOL 0mg; IRON 0.4mg; SODIUM 113mg; CALC 5mg

dessert sauces
We don't know an easier way to create a spectacular finale than with one of our low-fat-but-fabulous dessert sauces.

For an easy but delicious dessert, top compotes of fresh berries or fruit, scoops of low-fat ice cream, or slices of angel food cake with any one of these dessert sauces. Many can be completed in less than 10 minutes! Plus, most can be stored for several days in the refrigerator. But with these great flavors, you'll find that they won't be around for long.

APRICOT-WHISKEY SAUCE

PREP: 7 MINUTES   COOK: 3 MINUTES

    2   cups apricot preserves
    ½   cup water
    ⅓   cup whiskey

1. Combine preserves and water in a medium saucepan. Bring to a boil;

cook 1 minute. Strain mixture through a sieve into a bowl. Discard solids. Stir whiskey into strained mixture. Serve over ice cream, pound cake, or angel food cake. Yield: 2¼ cups (serving size: 2 tablespoons).

CALORIES 73 (0% from fat); FAT 0g; PROTEIN 0g; CARB 16.3g; FIBER 0g; CHOL 0mg; IRON 0mg; SODIUM 0mg; CALC 0mg

AMARETTO SAUCE

PREP: 2 MINUTES   COOK: 7 MINUTES

½ cup sugar
½ cup amaretto-flavored liquid
     nondairy creamer
1 cup fat-free milk
2 tablespoons cornstarch

1. Combine sugar and nondairy creamer in a 2-quart glass measure or bowl. Microwave at HIGH 2 minutes or until sugar dissolves, stirring every 30 seconds.
2. Combine milk and cornstarch, and stir well with a whisk. Add cornstarch mixture to creamer mixture; stir well. Microwave at HIGH 5 minutes or until mixture is thick and bubbly, stirring every minute. Serve warm over fresh berries, low-fat pound cake, gingerbread, or bread pudding. Yield: 1½ cups (serving size: 3 tablespoons).

CALORIES 112 (17% from fat); FAT 2.1g (sat 0g, mono 2g, poly 0g); PROTEIN 1g; CARB 22.7g; FIBER 0g; CHOL 1mg; IRON 0mg; SODIUM 25mg; CALC 38mg

CARAMEL-WHISKEY SAUCE

PREP: 5 MINUTES   COOK: 18 MINUTES

1½ cups sugar
⅔ cup water
¼ cup light butter
¼ cup (2 ounces) ⅓-less-fat cream
     cheese
¼ cup Irish whiskey
¼ cup 1% low-fat milk

1. Combine sugar and water in a small, heavy saucepan over medium-high heat; cook until sugar dissolves, stirring constantly. Continue cooking 15 minutes or until golden (do not stir). Remove from heat. Carefully add butter and cream cheese, stirring constantly with a whisk (mixture will be hot and will bubble vigorously). Cool slightly, and stir in

whiskey and milk. Serve with low-fat pound cake, angel food cake, or ice cream. Yield: 1½ cups (serving size: 2 tablespoons).

CALORIES 71 (20% from fat); FAT 1.6g (sat 1g, mono 0.5g, poly 0.6g); PROTEIN 0.4g; CARB 12.9g; FIBER 0g; CHOL 5mg; IRON 0.2mg; SODIUM 23mg; CALC 6mg

CHOCOLATE SAUCE

PREP: 3 MINUTES   COOK: 5 MINUTES

1 cup 1% low-fat milk
3 tablespoons sugar
2 tablespoons unsweetened cocoa
2 teaspoons cornstarch
½ teaspoon vanilla extract

1. Combine first 4 ingredients in a small saucepan, stirring with a whisk until blended. Bring sugar mixture to a boil, and cook 1 minute, stirring constantly. Remove from heat. Stir in vanilla. Cover sauce and chill. Serve over ice cream,

angel food cake, or strawberries. Yield: 1¼ cups (serving size: 2 tablespoons).

CALORIES 32 (11% from fat); FAT 0.4g (sat 0.3g, mono 0.1g, poly 0g); PROTEIN 1.1g; CARB 6g; FIBER 0g; CHOL 1mg; IRON 0.2mg; SODIUM 13mg; CALC 32mg

CIDER-LEMON SAUCE

PREP: 7 MINUTES   COOK: 5 MINUTES

1 cup apple cider
⅓ cup sugar
1 tablespoon cornstarch
⅛ teaspoon salt
1 teaspoon grated lemon rind
¼ cup fresh lemon juice
10 lemon slices (about 2 lemons)

1. Combine first 4 ingredients in a small saucepan; stir with a whisk until blended. Bring to a boil; cook until thick (about 1 minute), stirring constantly. Remove from heat; stir in remaining ingredients.

Chocolate Sauce

To prevent a skin from forming on a dessert sauce, cover the mixture with plastic wrap. Press the wrap directly onto the surface of the sauce to seal completely.

Serve warm over low-fat pound cake, gingerbread, ice cream, warm fruit cobbler, or fresh fruit. Yield: 1½ cups (serving size: 2 tablespoons).

CALORIES 37 (2% from fat); FAT 0.1g (sat 0g, mono 0g, poly 0g); PROTEIN 0.2g; CARB 10.3g; FIBER 0.1g; CHOL 0mg; IRON 0.2mg; SODIUM 26mg; CALC 9mg

MOLASSES CREAM

PREP: 5 MINUTES

½ cup tub-style light cream cheese, softened
½ cup fat-free sour cream
¼ cup sifted powdered sugar
2 tablespoons molasses
½ teaspoon vanilla extract

1. Beat cream cheese at medium speed of a mixer until smooth. Add sour cream, powdered sugar, molasses, and vanilla; beat until well-blended. Serve over gingerbread. Yield: 1 cup (serving size: 2 tablespoons).

CALORIES 70 (31% from fat); FAT 2.4g (sat 1.4g, mono 1g, poly 0g); PROTEIN 2.4g; CARB 5.2g; FIBER 0g; CHOL 8mg; IRON 0.2mg; SODIUM 92mg; CALC 40mg

RASPBERRY SAUCE

PREP: 3 MINUTES   COOK: 4 MINUTES

½ cup seedless raspberry jam
1 tablespoon lemon juice
2½ cups fresh raspberries

1. Melt jam over low heat in a small saucepan; stir in lemon juice. Combine jam mixture and raspberries in a bowl, stirring gently. Serve warm or at room temperature over Peach Melba Pie (page 204) or angel food cake. Yield: 1½ cups (serving size: 3 tablespoons).

CALORIES 62 (3% from fat); FAT 0.2g (sat 0g, mono 0g, poly 0.1g); PROTEIN 0.4g; CARB 35.8g; FIBER 2.6g; CHOL 0mg; IRON 0.2mg; SODIUM 6mg; CALC 9mg

CRÈME ANGLAISE

PREP: 6 MINUTES
COOK: 12 MINUTES
CHILL: 1 HOUR

(pictured on page 437)

You can substitute 2 teaspoons vanilla extract for the vanilla bean, but the flavor will suffer. You can find vanilla beans in your supermarket's spice section.

1¾ cups 1% low-fat milk
1 (3-inch) piece vanilla bean, split lengthwise
⅓ cup sugar
4 large egg yolks

1. Pour milk into a medium saucepan. Scrape seeds from vanilla bean; add seeds and bean to milk. Cook over medium heat 6 minutes (do not boil); discard bean. Remove from heat.
2. Combine sugar and yolks in a bowl, stirring with a whisk until blended. Gradually add milk mixture to bowl, stirring constantly with a whisk. Return mixture to pan. Cook over medium heat 6 minutes or until mixture thinly coats the back of a spoon, stirring constantly with a whisk. Immediately pour mixture into a bowl. Cover and chill (mixture will thicken as it cools). Serve with fresh fruit or cake. Yield: 1¾ cups (serving size: ¼ cup).
Note: Crème Anglaise can be stored in the refrigerator for up to 3 days.

CALORIES 97 (33% from fat); FAT 3.6g (sat 1.3g, mono 1.3g, poly 0.4g); PROTEIN 3.6g; CARB 12.6g; FIBER 0g; CHOL 127mg; IRON 0.4mg; SODIUM 35mg; CALC 88mg

WARM TURTLE SAUCE

PREP: 2 MINUTES   COOK: 30 SECONDS

6 tablespoons fat-free caramel-flavored sundae syrup
3 tablespoons chopped pecans, toasted

1. Place syrup in a bowl; microwave at HIGH 30 seconds or until warm. Stir in pecans. Serve over ice cream, low-fat pound cake, angel food cake, or brownies. Yield: ½ cup (serving size: about 1½ tablespoons).

CALORIES 79 (28% from fat); FAT 2.5g (sat 0.2g, mono 1.5g, poly 0.6g); PROTEIN 0.2g; CARB 35.6g; FIBER 0.2g; CHOL 0mg; IRON 0.1mg; SODIUM 35mg; CALC 1mg

CINNAMON-RUM SYRUP

PREP: 2 MINUTES   COOK: 3 MINUTES

¾ cup light-colored corn syrup
1 teaspoon ground cinnamon
2 teaspoons rum or 1 teaspoon rum extract
1 teaspoon lemon juice

1. Place corn syrup in a small saucepan; cook over low heat until thoroughly heated. Add remaining ingredients; stir well. Serve warm over pancakes, French toast, waffles, or ice cream. Yield: ¾ cup (serving size: 2 tablespoons).

CALORIES 127 (0% from fat); FAT 0g; PROTEIN 0g; CARB 30.4g; FIBER 0.1g; CHOL 0mg; IRON 0.2mg; SODIUM 50mg; CALC 5mg

condiments

Talk about variety—we have condiments for spreading, dipping, or topping in flavors from savory to sweet to sour.

PENNSYLVANIA-DUTCH APPLE BUTTER

PREP: 20 MINUTES
COOK: 1 HOUR 15 MINUTES

6½ cups chopped peeled Granny
    Smith apple (about 2 pounds)
1¼ cups apple cider
¾ cup packed brown sugar
¾ teaspoon ground cinnamon
¼ teaspoon ground allspice
¼ teaspoon ground cloves
¼ teaspoon ground ginger

1. Combine apple and cider in a large saucepan or Dutch oven. Bring to a boil; cover, reduce heat, and simmer 40 minutes or until tender. Place apple mixture in a blender or food processor; process until smooth.
2. Combine pureed apple mixture, sugar, and remaining ingredients in a saucepan; bring to a boil. Reduce heat, and simmer, uncovered, until mixture is thick (about 25 minutes), stirring frequently. Cool. Store apple butter in an airtight container in refrigerator for up to 2 months. Serve with biscuits, French toast, or waffles. Yield: 3 cups (serving size: 1 tablespoon).

CALORIES 25 (4% from fat); FAT 0.1g (sat 0.1g, mono 0g, poly 0g); PROTEIN 0g; CARB 6.4g; FIBER 0.4g; CHOL 0mg; IRON 0.1mg; SODIUM 2mg; CALC 5mg

BRANDIED STRAWBERRY JAM

PREP: 10 MINUTES   COOK: 50 MINUTES

This easy jam doesn't involve canning. It'll keep in the refrigerator for about 2 weeks.

4 cups quartered strawberries
½ cup sugar

Dried-Apricot Chutney

¼ cup brandy, divided
1 teaspoon vanilla extract

1. Combine strawberries, sugar, and 3 tablespoons brandy in a heavy Dutch oven; bring to a boil. Reduce heat; simmer until reduced to 1½ cups (about 45 minutes), stirring occasionally. Remove from heat; stir in 1 tablespoon brandy and vanilla. Spoon into a bowl; cool to room temperature. Cover and chill. Serve with toast, muffins, or biscuits. Yield: 1½ cups (serving size: 1 tablespoon).

CALORIES 26 (3% from fat); FAT 0.1g (sat 0g, mono 0g, poly 0.1g); PROTEIN 0.2g; CARB 6g; FIBER 0.6g; CHOL 0mg; IRON 0.1mg; SODIUM 0mg; CALC 4mg

DRIED-APRICOT CHUTNEY

PREP: 8 MINUTES
COOK: 40 MINUTES

½ cup water
1 cup coarsely chopped dried
    apricot
1 cup coarsely chopped onion
⅓ cup cider vinegar
⅓ cup raisins
1¼ teaspoons pumpkin-pie spice
1 teaspoon dry mustard
⅛ teaspoon crushed red pepper
½ cup water
1 cup coarsely chopped peeled
    Golden Delicious apple

1. Combine first 8 ingredients in a medium saucepan. Bring to a boil; cover, reduce heat, and simmer 20 minutes, stirring occasionally. Add ½ cup water and apple. Cover and cook 15 minutes or until apple is tender. Remove from heat; uncover and let stand 5 minutes before serving. Serve with pork or chicken or with light cream cheese and crackers. Yield: 2½ cups (serving size: ¼ cup).

Note: Store chutney in an airtight container in the refrigerator for up to 1 week.

CALORIES 61 (3% from fat); FAT 0.2g (sat 0g, mono 0g, poly 0g); PROTEIN 0.9g; CARB 15.7g; FIBER 1.9g; CHOL 0mg; IRON 0.9mg; SODIUM 3mg; CALC 14mg

CRANBERRY CHUTNEY

PREP:13 MINUTES
COOK:32 MINUTES

 1 cup chopped peeled Granny
    Smith apple
 1 cup raisins
 1 cup chopped onion
 1 cup sugar
 1 cup white vinegar
 ¾ cup chopped celery
 ¾ cup water
 2 teaspoons ground cinnamon
1½ teaspoons ground ginger
 ¼ teaspoon ground cloves
 1 (12-ounce) package fresh or
    frozen cranberries

1. Combine all ingredients in a large saucepan; bring to a boil. Reduce heat, and simmer, uncovered, 30 minutes or until slightly thick, stirring occasionally. Serve with turkey, chicken, roast pork, or ham or over light cream cheese with gingersnaps or crackers. Chutney may also be used to prepare chicken quesadillas. Yield: 4 cups (serving size: ¼ cup).

CALORIES 98 (2% from fat); FAT 0.2g (sat 0g, mono 0g, poly 0.1g); PROTEIN 0.6g; CARB 25.7g; FIBER 1.2g; CHOL 0mg; IRON 0.4mg; SODIUM 8mg; CALC 15mg

CILANTRO-COCONUT CHUTNEY

PREP:7 MINUTES

 1 cup packed fresh cilantro leaves
 ⅓ cup shredded sweetened coconut
 ¼ cup water
 2 tablespoons fresh lime juice
 1 tablespoon minced seeded
    jalapeño pepper
 1 teaspoon minced peeled fresh ginger
 2 teaspoons curry powder
 ⅛ teaspoon salt
 1 garlic clove, minced

1. Place all ingredients in a food processor; process until well-blended. Serve with fish or shellfish. Yield: ⅔ cup (serving size: 2½ tablespoons).

CALORIES 14 (48% from fat); FAT 0.5g (sat 0.2g, mono 0.1g, poly 0g); PROTEIN 0.5g; CARB 2.6g; FIBER 0.8g; CHOL 0mg; IRON 0.8mg; SODIUM 80mg; CALC 17mg

PRUNE PUREE

PREP:3 MINUTES

 ¼ cup light-colored corn syrup
 2 tablespoons sugar
 1 (12-ounce) package whole
    pitted prunes
 ⅔ cup water

1. Place first 3 ingredients in a food processor; process 10 seconds. With processor running, slowly add water through food chute, and process until mixture is smooth, scraping sides of bowl once. Spoon puree into an airtight container; store in refrigerator for up to 2 months. Use in Mocha Mint Cake (page 114) or in place of commercial prune puree. Yield: 2 cups (serving size: ⅓ cup).

CALORIES 192 (1% from fat); FAT 0.3g (sat 0g, mono 0.2g, poly 0.1g); PROTEIN 1.5g; CARB 49.7g; FIBER 4.0g; CHOL 0mg; IRON 1.4mg; SODIUM 19mg; CALC 29mg

Cranberry Chutney

SESAME-ORANGE DIPPING SAUCE

PREP: 7 MINUTES

⅓ cup thinly sliced green onions
⅓ cup fat-free, less-sodium chicken broth
¼ cup orange juice
1 tablespoon rice vinegar
1 tablespoon low-sodium soy sauce
2 teaspoons grated peeled fresh ginger
1 teaspoon dark sesame oil

1. Combine all ingredients in a small bowl. Serve with chicken strips. Yield: ¾ cup (serving size: 2 tablespoons).

CALORIES 16 (46% from fat); FAT 0.8g (sat 0.1g, mono 0.3g, poly 0.3g); PROTEIN 0.3g; CARB 1.8g; FIBER 0.1g; CHOL 0mg; IRON 0.1mg; SODIUM 94mg; CALC 4mg

CUCUMBER PICKLE SPEARS

PREP: 10 MINUTES   CHILL: 2 HOURS
MARINATE: 5 DAYS TO 6 WEEKS

4 large pickling cucumbers (about 1 pound), each cut lengthwise into 6 spears
2 teaspoons salt
3 large dill sprigs
1 garlic clove, halved
1 cup white vinegar
1 cup water
¼ cup sugar

1. Place cucumber spears in a large bowl. Sprinkle with salt, and toss gently to coat. Cover and chill 2 hours.
2. Drain cucumber spears in a colander. Rinse with cold water; drain well. Pack cucumber spears into a wide-mouth 1-quart jar. Add dill and garlic to jar.
3. Combine vinegar, water, and sugar in a small saucepan; bring to a boil, stirring until sugar dissolves. Pour hot liquid over cucumber spears. Cover jar with metal lid, and screw on band. Cool completely. Marinate in refrigerator 5 days before serving. (Pickles will last up to 6 weeks in refrigerator.) Serve with sandwiches. Yield: 24 spears (serving size: 1 spear).

CALORIES 5 (0% from fat); FAT 0g; PROTEIN 0.2g; CARB 1.3g; FIBER 0.2g; CHOL 0mg; IRON 0.1mg; SODIUM 98mg; CALC 3mg

ONION RELISH

PREP: 10 MINUTES
COOK: 1 HOUR 35 MINUTES

Butter-flavored cooking spray
4 large onions, quartered and thinly sliced (about 2¾ pounds)
¼ cup white wine vinegar
2 tablespoons brown sugar
½ teaspoon black pepper
1 tablespoon chopped fresh thyme

1. Coat a large saucepan with cooking spray, and place over medium heat until hot. Add onion; cover, reduce heat, and simmer 1½ hours, stirring occasionally.
2. Add vinegar and remaining ingredients; cook, uncovered, until slightly thick (about 4 minutes), stirring frequently. Cool; serve at room temperature with sandwiches or beef. Yield: 3½ cups (serving size: ¼ cup).

CALORIES 36 (4% from fat); FAT 0g; PROTEIN 0.8g; CARB 8g; FIBER 1.6g; CHOL 0mg; IRON 0.4mg; SODIUM 4mg; CALC 16mg

SWEET ONION RELISH

PREP: 13 MINUTES
COOK: 1 HOUR 10 MINUTES
CHILL: 8 HOURS

Cooking spray
4¾ cups chopped Vidalia or other sweet onion (about 4 medium)
1 cup thinly sliced Vidalia or other sweet onion
¼ cup minced celery
½ cup sugar
¼ teaspoon salt
¼ to ½ teaspoon celery seeds
⅛ teaspoon black pepper
½ cup cider vinegar
¼ cup water
1 (2-ounce) jar diced pimento, drained

1. Coat a large saucepan with cooking spray; place over medium-high heat until hot. Add onions and celery, and sauté 10 minutes or until tender. Stir in sugar and remaining ingredients; bring to a boil. Reduce heat and simmer, uncovered, 55 minutes or until liquid evaporates and onions are slightly browned, stirring frequently. Cool; spoon into a bowl. Cover and chill 8 hours. Serve cold or at room temperature with sandwiches. Yield: 2½ cups (serving size: ¼ cup).

CALORIES 74 (2% from fat); FAT 0.2g (sat 0g, mono 0g, poly 0.1g); PROTEIN 1g; CARB 18.2g; FIBER 1.6g; CHOL 0mg; IRON 0.4mg; SODIUM 65mg; CALC 20mg

FLAVORED VINEGAR

• **Vinegar can corrode metals** because it's acidic by nature (usually 4% to 6%), so **use glass or nonmetal containers.**

• **Match the vinegar with the ingredients you add to them.** Tart berries or strong-flavored herbs (such as rosemary) can stand up to the boldness of rice vinegar or red wine vinegar, while white wine vinegar is best enhanced with milder fruits and herbs.

• **Keep batches small to keep flavors potent.** Vinegars made with fruit stay at their peak flavor for three to six months. Those with herbs do so for about six months. You can still use these vinegars beyond this (their high acid content keeps them safe indefinitely), they just won't taste as intense.

Sweet Blackberry Vinegar

PREP: 16 MINUTES   STAND: 24 HOURS

3 cups fresh blackberries
2 cups rice vinegar
2 cups sugar

1. Place berries in a food processor; process until smooth. Combine black- berry puree and vinegar in a bowl. Cov- er; let stand at room temperature 24 hours, stirring occasionally. Strain into a large saucepan; discard seeds. Stir in sugar. Bring to a simmer; cook 5 min- utes. Remove from heat; cool to room temperature. Pour vinegar into decora- tive jars; seal with corks or other airtight lids. Use in Tossed Salad With Blackbe- rry Vinaigrette (page 397) or in place of other fruit-flavored vinegars. Yield: 4 cups (serving size: 1 tablespoon).
Note: Store vinegar in airtight containers for up to 3 months.

CALORIES 29 (0% from fat); FAT 0g; PROTEIN 0g; CARB 7.1g; FIBER 0.4g; CHOL 0mg; IRON 0mg; SODIUM 1mg; CALC 2mg

Sweet Blackberry Vinegar

seasonings
The seasoning mixes are dry rubs applied to meats, poultry, and fish before cooking. The pestos feature flavorful herbs and add zest to your favorite Italian dishes.

Shanghai Coastline Spice Mix

PREP: 3 MINUTES

7 tablespoons crushed
   red pepper
2¾ teaspoons ground ginger
2¾ teaspoons anise seeds

1. Combine all ingredients in a spice or coffee grinder; process until finely ground. Store in an airtight container for up to 6 months. Use to season poultry.

Yield: ½ cup (serving size: 1 teaspoon).

CALORIES 4 (19% from fat); FAT 0.1g (sat 0g, mono 0g, poly 0g); PROTEIN 0.1g; CARB 0.7g; FIBER 0.2g; CHOL 0mg; IRON 0.2mg; SODIUM 1mg; CALC 2mg

Cajun Seasoning

PREP: 5 MINUTES

2½ tablespoons paprika
4 teaspoons dried oregano
1 teaspoon salt
1 teaspoon garlic powder
1 teaspoon white pepper
1 teaspoon black pepper
1 teaspoon ground red pepper

1. Combine all ingredients in a zip-top plastic bag; seal bag, and shake well. Store tightly sealed; shake well before each use. Use as a coating mix for fish, poultry, or pork. Yield: 5½ tablespoons (serving size: ½ teaspoon).

CALORIES 3 (30% from fat); FAT 0.1g (sat 0g, mono 0g, poly 0.1g); PROTEIN 0.1g; CARB 0.6g; FIBER 0.2g; CHOL 0mg; IRON 0.2mg; SODIUM 71mg; CALC 4mg

CREOLE SEASONING

PREP: 4 MINUTES

2½ tablespoons paprika
2 tablespoons garlic powder
1 tablespoon salt
1 tablespoon onion powder
1 tablespoon dried oregano
1 tablespoon dried thyme
1 tablespoon ground red pepper
1 tablespoon black pepper

1. Combine all ingredients in a small bowl. Store in an airtight container. Use to season fish or shrimp. Yield: about ⅔ cup (serving size: 1 teaspoon).

CALORIES 6 (19% from fat); FAT 0.1g (sat 0g, mono 0g, poly 0.1g); PROTEIN 0.3g; CARB 1g; FIBER 0.3g; CHOL 0mg; IRON 0.4mg; SODIUM 235mg; CALC 10mg

SOUTHERN FRANCE SPICE MIX

PREP: 3 MINUTES

1 teaspoon dried oregano, crushed
1 teaspoon dried marjoram, crushed
1 teaspoon rubbed sage
½ teaspoon dried rosemary, crushed
½ teaspoon dried basil, crushed
¼ teaspoon ground bay leaf

1. Combine all ingredients; store in an airtight container. Use to season Cornish hens or roasted chicken. Yield: 4 teaspoons (serving size: 1 teaspoon).

CALORIES 3 (28% from fat); FAT 0.1g (sat 0g, mono 0g, poly 0g); PROTEIN 0.1g; CARB 0.7g; FIBER 0.2g; CHOL 0mg; IRON 0.5mg; SODIUM 0mg; CALC 17mg

SPICY SEASONING

PREP: 4 MINUTES

2½ tablespoons paprika
2 tablespoons garlic powder
1 tablespoon salt

1 tablespoon onion powder
1 tablespoon dried thyme
1 tablespoon ground red pepper
1 tablespoon black pepper

1. Combine all ingredients; store in an airtight container. Use to season chicken or fish. Yield: about ⅔ cup (serving size: 1 teaspoon).

CALORIES 5 (18% from fat); FAT 0.1g (sat 0g, mono 0g, poly 0.1g); PROTEIN 0.2g; CARB 1.2g; FIBER 0.3g; CHOL 0mg; IRON 0.4mg; SODIUM 220mg; CALC 6mg

ROASTED PEPPER PESTO

PREP: 15 MINUTES

See our technique for roasting peppers on page 26.

1 cup fresh basil leaves
¼ cup (1 ounce) grated fresh Parmesan cheese
2 tablespoons pine nuts, toasted
1 tablespoon olive oil
¼ teaspoon salt
⅛ teaspoon black pepper
2 pounds red bell peppers (about 4 large), roasted and peeled

1. Place all ingredients in a food processor, and process until smooth, scraping sides of bowl once. Store in an airtight container in refrigerator for up to 1 week. Serve with pasta, chicken, or fish. Yield: 1¾ cups (serving size: 1 tablespoon).

CALORIES 21 (56% from fat); FAT 1.3g (sat 0.3g, mono 0.6g, poly 0.4g); PROTEIN 0.8g; CARB 2g; FIBER 0.6g; CHOL 0mg; IRON 0.5mg; SODIUM 33mg; CALC 13mg

OREGANO PESTO

PREP: 20 MINUTES

2½ cups torn spinach
2 cups fresh oregano leaves
1 cup fresh flat-leaf parsley leaves

PINE NUTS

Pine nuts provide a rich, buttery spark to a number of dishes. Also called **Indian nut, piñon, pignoli,** and **pignolia,** pine nuts are most commonly sold in vacuum-sealed glass jars alongside other nuts in the supermarket.

Because they're rich in fat, they can turn rancid quickly. Store them in an airtight container in the refrigerator for up to one month or in the freezer for up to six months or longer. Chilling and freezing give them a "flabby" texture that can be improved by toasting.

Toast them in a skillet over medium heat until slightly lighter in color than you wish (the natural oil will continue to cook and take the nuts a shade darker). **Or spread them in a single layer in a baking pan.** Bake at 350° for 3 to 5 minutes or until golden, shaking the pan a couple of times. Immediately spread them out on a plate to cool.

2 tablespoons grated fresh Parmesan cheese
2 tablespoons pistachios
4 teaspoons lemon juice
¼ teaspoon salt
2 large garlic cloves
3 tablespoons extra-virgin olive oil

1. Place first 8 ingredients in a food processor, and process until smooth. With processor on, slowly pour oil through food chute; process until well-blended. Cover and chill. Serve with pasta, chicken, fish, or grilled vegetables. Yield: ¾ cup (serving size: 1 tablespoon).

CALORIES 59 (75% from fat); FAT 4.9g (sat 0.8g, mono 3.2g, poly 0.7g); PROTEIN 1.4g; CARB 3.6g; FIBER 1.1g; CHOL 1mg; IRON 2.1mg; SODIUM 68mg; CALC 84mg

Grilled Seafood Cioppino
(page 481)

soups & stews

broths & stocks

Homemade broth and stock offer a rich flavor as a base for soups and stews. Ours can be used in any recipe that calls for the canned variety.

FRESH VEGETABLE BROTH

PREP:15 MINUTES   COOK:4½ HOURS

5 quarts cold water
3 cups chopped onion
2 cups chopped carrot
2 cups chopped celery
2 cups chopped parsnip
1 cup chopped leek
12 black peppercorns
4 unpeeled garlic cloves
3 bay leaves
2 thyme sprigs
1 basil sprig
1 rosemary sprig
1 parsley sprig
1 teaspoon salt

1. Combine all ingredients except salt in an 8-quart stockpot. Bring to a boil. Reduce heat; simmer, uncovered, 4½ hours. Strain through a cheesecloth-lined colander into a bowl; discard solids. Stir in salt. Yield: 7½ cups stock (serving size ½ cup).

CALORIES 10 (4% from fat); FAT 0g; PROTEIN 0.3g; CARB 2.4g; FIBER 0.5g; CHOL 0mg; IRON 0.1mg; SODIUM 162mg; CALC 7mg

VEGETABLE NAGE

PREP:15 MINUTES
COOK:1 HOUR 50 MINUTES

1½ tablespoons olive oil
4 cups sliced leek
2 cups diced onion
1⅓ cups diced fennel bulb
⅓ cup chopped celery
1 whole garlic head, unpeeled and cut in half
2 cups water
15 thyme sprigs
15 parsley sprigs

3 bay leaves
1 (750-milliliter) bottle dry white wine

1. Heat oil in a saucepan over medium heat; add leek and next 4 ingredients. Cover; reduce heat to low. Cook 45 minutes, stirring frequently. Add water and remaining ingredients; bring to a boil. Reduce heat; simmer, uncovered, 1 hour. Strain through a sieve into a bowl; discard solids. Yield: 4 cups stock (serving size: 1 cup).

CALORIES 287 (37% from fat); FAT 11.8g (sat 2.1g, mono 6.4g, poly 2.3g); PROTEIN 34g; CARB 10.4g; FIBER 0.7g; CHOL 115mg; IRON 3.7mg; SODIUM 171mg; CALC 194mg

BEEF BROWN STOCK

PREP:10 MINUTES
COOK:2 HOURS 20 MINUTES   CHILL:8 HOURS

3 pounds beef shank bones, halved
3 large onions, quartered
10 cups water
4 medium carrots, quartered
2 tablespoons black peppercorns
3 garlic cloves, crushed
3 bay leaves
1 bunch fresh parsley

1. Place bones and onions in an 8-quart stockpot; cook over medium-high heat 20 minutes or until very brown, stirring frequently. Add water and remaining ingredients; bring to a boil. Reduce heat; simmer, uncovered, 2 hours. Remove from heat; cool. Strain through a cheesecloth-lined colander; discard solids. Cover; chill 8 hours. Skim solidified fat from surface; discard. Yield: 7 cups stock (serving size: 1 cup).

CALORIES 22 (0% from fat); FAT 0g; PROTEIN 0.5g; CARB 1.9g; FIBER 0g; CHOL 0mg; IRON 0mg; SODIUM 127mg; CALC 0mg

CHICKEN STOCK

PREP:15 MINUTES
COOK:1 HOUR 45 MINUTES
CHILL:8 HOURS

The vinegar lends a kick to the stock, but it may be omitted. A 3½-pound chicken will yield about 4 cups of cooked chicken.

1 (3½-pound) chicken
1 tablespoon black peppercorns
1 teaspoon salt
10 parsley sprigs
6 garlic cloves, sliced
3 bay leaves
2 carrots, cut into 2-inch-thick pieces
1 medium onion, unpeeled and quartered
8 cups water
1 tablespoon cider vinegar (optional)

1. Combine first 8 ingredients in a large Dutch oven; add water. Bring to a boil over medium heat. Reduce heat; simmer, uncovered, 40 minutes or until chicken is done. Remove chicken from cooking liquid; cool. Remove skin from chicken; discard. Remove meat from bones; reserve for another use. Return bones to cooking liquid; stir in vinegar, if desired. Partially cover; simmer 1 hour.
2. Strain stock through a sieve into a large bowl; discard solids. Cover; chill 8 hours. Skim solidified fat from surface; discard. Yield: 6 cups stock (serving size: 1 cup).
Note: Reserved meat from chicken will keep 3 days in an airtight container in refrigerator or 3 months in freezer.

CALORIES 35 (33% from fat); FAT 1.3g (sat 0.4g, mono 0.5g, poly 0.3g); PROTEIN 5.4g; CARB 0.1g; FIBER 0g; CHOL 16mg; IRON 0.2mg; SODIUM 405mg; CALC 3mg

making chicken stock

1. Combine all ingredients except the water in a large Dutch oven or stockpot—one that will accommodate at least 4 quarts.

2. Add water, and bring to a boil.

3. Once the water comes to a boil, reduce heat to a simmer. It is at the right temperature when bubbles barely break the surface. This will keep the chicken tender; boiling will toughen it.

4. After about 45 minutes, carefully lift the chicken out of the stock by inserting a long metal spoon into the cavity and gently lifting. (At this point, the chicken is done, but the stock isn't yet.) Let the chicken cool; then remove the meat from the bones. Remove and discard the skin. Return the bones to the stock; partially cover and simmer 1 hour. This develops and enhances the flavor of the stock.

5. Strain the stock through a sieve into a large bowl. Discard the solids.

6. After the stock has chilled for 8 hours, remove the fat with a spoon.

chilled soups
Serve chilled soups as an appetizer, a side dish, or a dessert.

CHILLED BEET-AND-FENNEL SOUP

PREP:10 MINUTES
COOK:1 HOUR 10 MINUTES
CHILL:1 HOUR

  1 pound small beets
  2 teaspoons fennel seeds
1¾ cups chopped fennel bulb
  1 cup chopped onion
  ¼ cup water
  1 tablespoon olive oil
1½ cups low-fat or nonfat buttermilk
  ½ teaspoon salt
  ¼ teaspoon black pepper

1. Leave root and 1-inch stem on beets; scrub with a brush. Place beets and fennel seeds in a medium saucepan; cover with water. Bring to a boil; cover, reduce heat, and simmer 35 minutes or until tender.
2. Drain beets through a fine sieve over a bowl, reserving fennel seeds and 3 cups cooking liquid. Rinse beets with cold water; drain. Peel beets; cut into ½-inch cubes, reserving ¾ cup for garnish. Combine remaining beets, reserved cooking liquid, and fennel seeds in a bowl; set aside.
3. Combine chopped fennel bulb, onion, ¼ cup water, and oil in a medium nonstick skillet; bring to a boil over medium-high heat. Cover, reduce heat, and simmer 20 minutes or until tender.
4. Place fennel bulb mixture, beet mixture, buttermilk, salt, and pepper in a food processor or blender; process until smooth. Pour soup into a bowl; cover and chill thoroughly.
5. Ladle soup into individual bowls; top each serving with 2 tablespoons reserved beets. Yield: 6 servings (serving size: 1 cup).

CALORIES 90 (36% from fat); FAT 3.6g (sat 0.9g, mono 2g, poly 0.2g); PROTEIN 4.3g; CARB 11.4g; FIBER 1.1g; CHOL 0mg; IRON 1.5mg; SODIUM 266mg; CALC 131mg

CHILLED CUCUMBER SOUP WITH LEEKS AND CELERY

PREP:17 MINUTES   COOK:24 MINUTES
CHILL:1 HOUR

  2 teaspoons butter or stick margarine
  2 cups cubed peeled cucumber
  ¾ cup thinly sliced leek
  ½ cup diced celery
2⅓ cups low-sodium chicken broth
1½ cups diced peeled baking potato
  1 cup water
  ½ teaspoon salt
  ⅛ teaspoon black pepper
  6 tablespoons diced cucumber
  6 tablespoons plain low-fat sour cream

1. Melt butter in a large nonstick skillet over medium heat. Add 2 cups cucumber, leek, and celery; cover, reduce heat to medium-low, and cook 10 minutes or until tender, stirring occasionally. Add broth and next 4 ingredients; bring to a boil. Cover, reduce heat, and simmer 10 minutes or until potato is tender.
2. Place half of cucumber mixture in a blender or food processor, and process until vegetables are finely chopped. Pour processed mixture into a bowl. Repeat procedure with remaining cucumber mixture. Cover and chill thoroughly. Ladle soup into bowls, and top each serving with 1 tablespoon diced cucumber and 1 tablespoon sour cream. Yield: 6 servings (serving size: 1 cup).

CALORIES 92 (36% from fat); FAT 3.7g (sat 1.6g, mono 1.3g, poly 0.7g); PROTEIN 2.9g; CARB 12.7g; FIBER 1.4g; CHOL 7mg; IRON 1.3mg; SODIUM 266mg; CALC 45mg

CHILLED MELON SOUP

PREP:20 MINUTES   CHILL:1 HOUR

  3 cups cubed peeled honeydew melon
  3 cups cubed peeled cantaloupe
  ¼ cup light rum or vodka, divided (optional)
  ¼ cup sugar, divided
  3 tablespoons fresh lime juice, divided
  ¾ cup sliced strawberries

1. Place honeydew in a food processor, and process until smooth; pour into a bowl. Place cantaloupe in food processor, and process until smooth; pour into a second bowl. Add 2 tablespoons rum, 2 tablespoons sugar, and 1 tablespoon lime juice to each bowl; stir well. Cover and chill. Place strawberries in food processor; process until smooth. Pour into a bowl. Add 1 tablespoon lime juice; cover and chill.
2. To serve, pour ½ cup of cantaloupe mixture into each of 4 individual bowls; pour ½ cup honeydew mixture in center of

Fresh Peach Soup and Chilled Melon Soup are ideally suited for mid-summer when peaches and melons are at their peak.

cantaloupe mixture in each bowl. Dollop each serving with 2 tablespoons strawberry mixture; swirl decoratively with a wooden pick. Yield: 4 servings.

CALORIES 180 (3% from fat); FAT 0.5g (sat 0.1g, mono 0g, poly 0.2g); PROTEIN 1.7g; CARB 34.6g; FIBER 2.1g; CHOL 0mg; IRON 0.4mg; SODIUM 22mg; CALC 23mg

FRESH PEACH SOUP

PREP: 15 MINUTES   CHILL: 1 HOUR

3 cups diced honeydew melon
½ cup fresh orange juice
½ cup vanilla low-fat yogurt
2 tablespoons honey
1 teaspoon finely chopped peeled fresh ginger
2 teaspoons fresh lime juice
2 cups diced peeled peaches
1 cup blueberries

1. Place first 6 ingredients in a blender, and process until smooth. Combine melon mixture, peaches, and blueberries in a bowl. Cover and chill. Yield: 5 servings (serving size: 1 cup).

CALORIES 124 (4% from fat); FAT 0.6g (sat 0.3g, mono 0.1g, poly 0.1g); PROTEIN 2.4g; CARB 30g; FIBER 2.4g; CHOL 1mg; IRON 0.3mg; SODIUM 28mg; CALC 55mg

CHUNKY GAZPACHO

PREP: 23 MINUTES   CHILL: 2 HOURS

6 cups coarsely chopped tomato (about 3 pounds)
2 cups coarsely chopped peeled cucumber (about 2)
1½ cups chopped green bell pepper
1¼ cups finely chopped Vidalia or other sweet onion
1 cup finely chopped celery
1 tablespoon olive oil
1 tablespoon balsamic vinegar
1 tablespoon basil vinegar
1 tablespoon rice vinegar

Chunky Gazpacho

Chunky Gazpacho has the vibrant taste of a garden harvest with plump tomatoes, crisp cucumbers, and sweet Vidalia onions.

¾ teaspoon salt
½ teaspoon black pepper
½ teaspoon hot sauce
1 (32-ounce) bottle low-sodium tomato juice
3 garlic cloves, minced

1. Combine all ingredients in a large bowl. Cover and chill. Yield: 8 servings (serving size: 1½ cups).

CALORIES 95 (23% from fat); FAT 2.4g (sat 0.3g, mono 1.3g, poly 0.5g); PROTEIN 3.1g; CARB 17.3g; FIBER 3.7g; CHOL 0mg; IRON 1.3mg; SODIUM 321mg; CALC 29mg

accompaniment soups

Is your sandwich lonely? Need a warm start to any meal? These soups will be your answer to meal-planning dilemmas.

EGG DROP SOUP

PREP:10 MINUTES
STAND:30 MINUTES
COOK:5 MINUTES

¾ cup hot water
¼ ounce dried wood ear mushrooms
2 tablespoons fresh lemon juice
1 tablespoon low-sodium soy sauce
2 teaspoons grated peeled fresh ginger
⅛ teaspoon black pepper
1 garlic clove, halved
3 (14½-ounce) cans fat-free, less-sodium chicken broth
2 large eggs, lightly beaten
3 green onions, thinly sliced

1. Combine water and mushrooms in a small bowl; cover and let stand 30 minutes.
2. Drain mushrooms, reserving ½ cup liquid. Discard mushroom stems. Cut mushroom caps into thin slices. Combine mushroom caps, reserved ½ cup liquid, lemon juice, soy sauce, ginger, pepper, garlic, and broth in a medium saucepan; bring to a boil. Slowly drizzle egg into soup, stirring constantly with a fork. Reduce heat to low, and cook 1 minute, stirring constantly. Remove and discard garlic. Ladle soup into bowls, and sprinkle evenly with green onions. Yield: 6 servings (serving size: 1 cup).

CALORIES 90 (18% from fat); FAT 1.8g (sat 0.6g, mono 0.7g, poly 0.3g); PROTEIN 4.1g; CARB 13.5g; FIBER 1.7g; CHOL 71mg; IRON 0.6mg; SODIUM 659mg; CALC 13mg

MISO-NOODLE SOUP

PREP:18 MINUTES   COOK:7 MINUTES

1 teaspoon dark sesame oil
1 teaspoon minced peeled fresh ginger
2 garlic cloves, minced
2 cups chopped broccoli florets
1¾ cups water
1 cup (⅛-inch-thick) diagonally sliced carrot
1 cup vertically sliced onion
1 teaspoon chile paste
2 (14½-ounce) cans vegetable broth
2 cups cooked Chinese egg noodles (about 4 ounces uncooked)
¼ cup white miso (soybean paste)

1. Heat oil in a large saucepan over medium heat. Add ginger and garlic; sauté 1 minute. Add broccoli and next 5 ingredients; bring to a boil. Reduce heat; simmer, uncovered, 2 minutes. Stir in noodles and miso; cook until miso is blended (about 1 minute), stirring constantly. Yield: 8 servings (serving size: 1 cup).

CALORIES 101 (16% from fat); FAT 1.8g (sat 0.2g, mono 0.6g, poly 0.6g); PROTEIN 2.8g; CARB 18.4g; FIBER 1.6g; CHOL 13mg; IRON 0.9mg; SODIUM 800mg; CALC 20mg

You can find Chinese egg noodles with Asian foods at most grocery stores.

Miso-Noodle Soup

YELLOW-AND-ORANGE PEPPER SOUP WITH RED-CHILE PUREE

PREP: 20 MINUTES   COOK: 1 HOUR

  1 tablespoon olive oil
  2 cups diced orange bell pepper
  2 cups diced yellow bell pepper
  ½ cup diced onion
  ½ cup diced carrot
  3 garlic cloves, minced
  3 cups diced peeled baking potato
       (about 1 pound)
  3 cups water, divided
  ½ teaspoon salt
  ¼ teaspoon black pepper
  1 (14½-ounce) can vegetable broth
  1 large ancho chile (about ¼ ounce)
  ⅛ teaspoon salt
     Chopped fresh cilantro (optional)

1. Heat oil in a Dutch oven over medium-high heat. Add bell peppers, onion, carrot, and garlic; sauté 10 minutes or until lightly browned. Add potato, 2 cups water, ½ teaspoon salt, black pepper, and broth; bring to a boil. Cover, reduce heat, and simmer 30 minutes or until vegetables are tender. Place half of bell pepper mixture in a blender; process until smooth. Pour pureed bell pepper mixture into a large bowl. Repeat procedure with remaining bell pepper mixture; keep warm.

2. Remove stem and seeds from chile. Tear chile into large pieces; place in a small saucepan over medium heat. Cook 3 minutes or until thoroughly heated, turning pieces occasionally (be careful not to burn chile). Add 1 cup water; bring to a simmer. Cover and simmer 5 minutes or until soft. Remove chile from pan with a slotted spoon, reserving 2 tablespoons cooking liquid. Discard remaining cooking liquid. Combine chile, 2 tablespoons cooking liquid, and ⅛ teaspoon salt in a blender; process until smooth. Ladle soup

Yellow-and-Orange Pepper Soup With Red-Chile Puree

into 7 bowls; top with chile puree, and garnish with cilantro, if desired. Yield: 7 servings (serving size: 1 cup soup and 1½ teaspoons puree).

CALORIES 114 (26% from fat); FAT 3.3g (sat 0.7g, mono 1.6g, poly 0.4g); PROTEIN 2.8g; CARB 19.9g; FIBER 3.3g; CHOL 2mg; IRON 1.8mg; SODIUM 483mg; CALC 23mg

QUICK MINESTRONE SOUP

PREP: 9 MINUTES   COOK: 25 MINUTES

  2 cups diced zucchini
  ⅛ teaspoon black pepper
  2 garlic cloves, minced
  2 (16-ounce) cans fat-free,
       less-sodium chicken broth
  1 (14½-ounce) can Italian-style
       stewed tomatoes, undrained
       and coarsely chopped
  1 (16-ounce) can red kidney
       beans, drained
  1 (10-ounce) package frozen peas
       and carrots, thawed
  ½ cup uncooked ditalini (very
       short tube-shaped macaroni)
  ½ cup grated Parmesan
       cheese

1. Combine first 7 ingredients in a large saucepan; bring to a boil. Cover, reduce heat, and simmer 5 minutes.

2. Add pasta to broth mixture, and cook 10 minutes or until pasta is done, stirring occasionally. Stir in Parmesan cheese. Yield: 8 servings (serving size: 1 cup).

CALORIES 162 (12% from fat); FAT 2.1g (sat 1g, mono 0.5g, poly 0.3g); PROTEIN 8.9g; CARB 26.1g; FIBER 3g; CHOL 4mg; IRON 2.3mg; SODIUM 525mg; CALC 113mg

menu

Orecchiette-and-Spinach Soup

Tuna Melts (page 432)

Applesauce Spice Cake With
Cream Cheese Frosting (page 112)

ORECCHIETTE-AND-SPINACH SOUP

PREP: 10 MINUTES   COOK: 22 MINUTES

- 1 cup water
- 3 (10½-ounce) cans low-sodium chicken broth
- 1½ cups uncooked orecchiette ("little ears" pasta)
- 1 (10-ounce) package frozen chopped spinach, thawed
- 1 cup chopped seeded tomato
- 3 tablespoons grated Parmesan cheese
- ½ teaspoon black pepper
- ¼ teaspoon salt
- 1 large egg
- 2 tablespoons grated Parmesan cheese
- Hot sauce (optional)

1. Bring water and broth to a boil in a large Dutch oven. Add pasta and spinach; cover, reduce heat, and simmer 15 minutes or until pasta is tender. Stir in tomato.
2. Combine 3 tablespoons Parmesan cheese, pepper, salt, and egg; stir well with a whisk. Slowly drizzle egg mixture into simmering soup, and cook 2 minutes, stirring constantly. Ladle into soup bowls, and sprinkle each serving with 1 teaspoon Parmesan cheese. Sprinkle with hot sauce, if desired. Serve immediately. Yield: 6 servings (serving size: 1 cup).

CALORIES 129 (25% from fat); FAT 3.6g (sat 1.6g, mono 1.2g, poly 0.5g); PROTEIN 8g; CARB 17.1g; FIBER 2.1g; CHOL 39mg; IRON 2.7mg; SODIUM 276mg; CALC 119mg

Orecchiette-and-Spinach Soup

ROASTED TOMATO-AND-RED PEPPER SOUP

PREP: 30 MINUTES
COOK: 12 MINUTES

- 1½ pounds red bell peppers
- 2 pounds tomatoes, halved and seeded
- 2 tablespoons olive oil
- 1 cup chopped onion
- 4 garlic cloves, minced
- 1½ cups tomato juice
- 1 tablespoon chopped fresh marjoram
- ½ teaspoon salt
- ¼ teaspoon black pepper

1. Preheat broiler.
2. Cut bell peppers in half lengthwise; discard seeds and membranes. Place bell peppers and tomatoes, skin sides up, on a foil-lined baking sheet; flatten peppers with hand. Broil 15 minutes or until vegetables are blackened. Place peppers in a zip-top plastic bag; seal and let stand 10 minutes. Peel peppers and tomato; chop. Place half of chopped peppers and half of chopped tomatoes in a blender; process until smooth.
3. Heat oil in a saucepan over medium-low heat. Add onion and garlic; cover and cook 5 minutes. Add pureed vegetables, remaining chopped bell peppers and tomato, tomato juice, 1 tablespoon marjoram, salt, and black pepper; cook over medium heat until thoroughly heated. Yield: 5 servings (serving size: 1 cup).

CALORIES 126 (25% from fat); FAT 4g (sat 0.6g, mono 2.1g, poly 0g); PROTEIN 3.9g; CARB 22.7g; FIBER 5.6g; CHOL 0mg; IRON 3.4mg; SODIUM 521mg; CALC 42mg

THAI-STYLE PUMPKIN SOUP

PREP:13 MINUTES
COOK:18 MINUTES

2 (14½-ounce) cans fat-free, less-sodium chicken broth
1 (15-ounce) can pumpkin
1 (12-ounce) can mango nectar
¼ cup reduced-fat peanut butter
2 tablespoons rice vinegar
1½ tablespoons minced green onions
1 teaspoon grated peeled fresh ginger
½ teaspoon grated orange rind
¼ teaspoon crushed red pepper
1 garlic clove, crushed
Chopped fresh cilantro (optional)

1. Combine first 3 ingredients in a large saucepan, and bring to a boil. Cover, reduce heat, and simmer 10 minutes. Combine 1 cup pumpkin mixture and peanut butter in a blender or food processor; process until smooth. Add mixture to pan. Stir in vinegar and next 5 ingredients; cook 3 minutes or until thoroughly heated. Ladle into soup bowls. Sprinkle with cilantro, if desired. Yield: 7 servings (serving size: 1 cup).

CALORIES 119 (27% from fat); FAT 3.6g (sat 0.8g, mono 1.6g, poly 1.1g); PROTEIN 3.3g; CARB 17.7g; FIBER 3.4g; CHOL 0mg; IRON 1.1mg; SODIUM 395mg; CALC 18mg

FRESH TOMATO SOUP WITH CILANTRO

PREP:22 MINUTES
COOK:21 MINUTES

1 cup vertically sliced onion
1 teaspoon olive oil
¼ cup thinly sliced celery
1 small garlic clove, minced
1 teaspoon ground cumin
½ teaspoon salt
⅛ to ¼ teaspoon black pepper
4 cups coarsely chopped peeled tomato (about 2½ pounds)
⅓ cup water
1 (16-ounce) can fat-free, less-sodium chicken broth
2 tablespoons chopped fresh cilantro
Cilantro sprigs (optional)

1. Cut onion slices in half. Heat oil in a large saucepan over medium heat. Add onion, celery, and garlic; sauté 4 minutes or until tender. Add cumin, salt, and pepper; cook 2 minutes, stirring constantly. Add tomato, water, and chicken broth; bring to a boil. Reduce heat, and simmer, uncovered, 10 minutes.

2. Place 2½ cups tomato mixture in a blender; process until smooth. Return tomato puree to pan, and stir well. Stir in chopped cilantro. Serve warm or chilled. Garnish with cilantro sprigs, if desired. Yield: 6 cups (serving size: 1 cup).

CALORIES 52 (23% from fat); FAT 1.3g (sat 0.2g, mono 0.7g, poly 0.3g); PROTEIN 1.7g; CARB 9.1g; FIBER 2g; CHOL 0mg; IRON 1mg; SODIUM 352mg; CALC 18mg

CUMIN

Pungent, sharp, and slightly bitter, cumin is a common ingredient in Indian spice blends and Mexican foods. Like other spices, it should be stored in a cool place and away from heat.

creamy soups We've mastered making rich-tasting, creamy soups with only a smidgen of fat!

CREAMY CORN-AND-ZUCCHINI SOUP

PREP:20 MINUTES
COOK:12 MINUTES

6 cups fat-free, less-sodium chicken broth
2 cups diced zucchini (about 2 large)
½ cup chopped onion
6 cups fresh corn kernels (about 12 ears)
¾ teaspoon salt
¼ to ½ teaspoon black pepper
10 tablespoons plain fat-free yogurt
Jalapeño hot sauce (optional)

1. Bring broth to a simmer in a large saucepan. Add zucchini and onion; cover and simmer 2 minutes. Stir in corn, salt, and pepper; cover and simmer 2 minutes. Cool slightly.

2. Place one-third of corn mixture in a blender; process until smooth. Pour pureed mixture into a large bowl. Repeat procedure with remaining corn mixture.

3. Ladle soup into bowls, and top with yogurt. Serve soup with jalapeño hot sauce, if desired. Yield: 10 servings (serving size: 1 cup soup and 1 tablespoon yogurt).

CALORIES 124 (10% from fat); FAT 1.4g (sat 0.2g, mono 0.4g, poly 0.7g); PROTEIN 5.1g; CARB 25g; FIBER 3.9g; CHOL 0mg; IRON 0.7mg; SODIUM 587mg; CALC 37mg

CREAMY CHICKEN, LEEK, AND MUSHROOM SOUP

PREP: 23 MINUTES
COOK: 40 MINUTES

Cooking spray
3 cups chopped leek
2¼ pounds chicken thighs, skinned, boned, and cut into bite-size pieces
3 garlic cloves, minced
4 cups quartered mushrooms (about 12 ounces)
2 (14.25-ounce) cans fat-free, less-sodium chicken broth
⅓ cup dry white wine
½ cup all-purpose flour
2½ cups 2% reduced-fat milk
2 tablespoons medium dry sherry
½ teaspoon salt
¼ teaspoon freshly ground black pepper
Additional freshly ground black pepper (optional)

1. Coat a large Dutch oven with cooking spray; place over medium-high heat until hot. Add leek, chicken, and garlic; sauté 10 minutes. Add mushrooms, and sauté 5 minutes. Add broth and wine; bring to a boil. Reduce heat, and simmer, uncovered, 10 minutes.
2. Place flour in a small bowl. Gradually add milk, stirring well with a whisk; add to soup. Cook over medium heat until thick (about 10 minutes), stirring constantly. Stir in sherry, salt, and ¼ teaspoon pepper. Sprinkle with additional ground pepper, if desired. Yield: 7 servings (serving size: 1½ cups).
Note: Substitute 1¼ pounds skinned, boned chicken thighs for bone-in chicken thighs, if desired.

CALORIES 227 (22% from fat); FAT 5.5g (sat 2g, mono 1.6g, poly 1.1g); PROTEIN 22.6g; CARB 19.9g; FIBER 1.3g; CHOL 79mg; IRON 2.8mg; SODIUM 383mg; CALC 146mg

ROASTED CHESTNUT SOUP

PREP: 14 MINUTES
COOK: 1 HOUR

Start with about 1 pound chestnuts in the shell and roast them according to the instructions at right. We've provided three ways for you to roast the nuts.

1 tablespoon stick margarine or butter
1 cup chopped onion
½ cup chopped celery
½ cup chopped carrot
1 cup cubed peeled baking potato
1 cup roasted chestnuts (about 1 pound in shells)
½ teaspoon salt
¼ teaspoon dried thyme
⅛ to ¼ teaspoon black pepper
5 (10½-ounce) cans low-sodium chicken broth
½ cup 2% reduced-fat milk
2 cups plain croutons
Paprika

1. Melt margarine in a large saucepan over medium heat. Add onion, and sauté 4 minutes. Add chopped celery and chopped carrot; sauté 6 minutes. Add potato and next 5 ingredients. Bring to a boil; reduce heat, and simmer, uncovered, 40 minutes.
2. Place half of chestnut mixture in a food processor; process until smooth. Pour pureed mixture into a large bowl. Repeat procedure with remaining chestnut mixture.
3. Return pureed mixture to pan, and stir in milk. Cook until thoroughly heated. Ladle soup into individual bowls; top each serving with croutons, and sprinkle with paprika. Yield: 8 servings (serving size: 1 cup soup and ¼ cup croutons).

CALORIES 155 (23% from fat); FAT 4g (sat 1.3g, mono 1.7g, poly 1g); PROTEIN 4.8g; CARB 25.6g; FIBER 4g; CHOL 1mg; IRON 1.8mg; SODIUM 260mg; CALC 44mg

Roasting Chestnuts

Soak chestnuts in a bowl of water for about 30 minutes; drain well. Cut a slit in the shell in the rounded side of the chestnut. Make sure the cut goes all the way through the shell; otherwise, the chestnuts can explode.

To bake, arrange chestnuts on a baking sheet. Bake at 400° for 25 minutes.
To microwave, arrange nuts in a single layer in a microwave-safe dish. Microwave at HIGH 2 minutes. Microwave a maximum of 12 nuts at a time so that they cook evenly.
To roast over an open fire, arrange nuts in a single layer in a chestnut pan. Place over an open flame; roast 25 minutes, shaking frequently.

CREAMY POTATO-MUSHROOM SOUP

PREP: 18 MINUTES
COOK: 43 MINUTES

2   bacon slices
2   (8-ounce) packages cremini mushrooms, diced
½   cup diced shallots
3½ cups cubed Yukon gold or baking potato
1   (14½-ounce) can fat-free, less-sodium chicken broth, divided
2   cups 1% low-fat milk
2   tablespoons sherry
½   teaspoon salt
¼   teaspoon black pepper

1. Cook bacon in a Dutch oven over medium heat until crisp. Remove bacon from skillet; crumble and set aside. Add mushrooms and shallots to bacon drippings in pan; sauté 5 minutes or until mushrooms are soft. Remove mushroom mixture from pan.
2. Add potato and broth to pan; bring to a boil. Cover, reduce heat, and simmer 12 minutes or until potato is very tender. Place potato mixture in a food processor; process until smooth. Return to pan. Add mushroom mixture, milk, sherry, salt, and pepper; cook over low

heat 10 minutes or until thoroughly heated. Ladle soup into bowls; top each serving with crumbled bacon. Yield: 7 servings (serving size: 1 cup).

CALORIES 145 (22% from fat); FAT 3.6g (sat 1.5g, mono 1.4g, poly 0.5g); PROTEIN 5.8g; CARB 22.6g; FIBER 2.1g; CHOL 6mg; IRON 1.5mg; SODIUM 400mg; CALC 99mg

ROASTED GARLIC-POTATO SOUP

PREP: 33 MINUTES
COOK: 1 HOUR 10 MINUTES

3   whole garlic heads
2   bacon slices, diced
1   cup diced onion
1   cup diced carrot
2   garlic cloves, minced
6   cups diced baking potato (about 2 pounds)
4   cups fat-free, less-sodium chicken broth
½   teaspoon salt
¼   teaspoon black pepper
1   bay leaf
1   cup 2% reduced-fat milk
¼   cup chopped fresh parsley

1. Preheat oven to 350°.
2. Remove white papery skin from garlic heads (do not peel or separate cloves). Wrap each head separately in foil. Bake at 350° for 1 hour; cool 10 minutes. Separate cloves, and squeeze to extract ¼ cup of garlic pulp; discard skins.
3. Cook bacon in a large saucepan over medium-high heat until crisp. Add onion, carrot, and minced garlic, and sauté 5 minutes. Add potato, broth, salt, pepper, and bay leaf; bring mixture to a boil. Cover, reduce heat, and simmer 20 minutes or until potato is tender; remove bay leaf.
4. Combine ¼ cup garlic pulp and 2 cups potato mixture in a blender or food processor; process until smooth. Return

puree to pan; stir in milk, and cook over low heat until thoroughly heated. Remove from heat; stir in parsley. Yield: 9 servings (serving size: 1 cup).

CALORIES 172 (21% from fat); FAT 4.1g (sat 1.6g, mono 1.7g, poly 0.5g); PROTEIN 5.5g; CARB 28.4g; FIBER 2.7g; CHOL 6mg; IRON 1.7mg; SODIUM 488mg; CALC 95mg

CREAMY LENTIL SOUP

PREP: 22 MINUTES
COOK: 1 HOUR 10 MINUTES

1   tablespoon olive oil
1   cup sliced carrot
1   cup chopped onion
2   cups water
1   cup dried lentils
⅓   cup uncooked long-grain rice
½   teaspoon salt
½   teaspoon ground cumin
½   teaspoon coarsely ground black pepper
2   (14½-ounce) cans fat-free, less-sodium chicken broth
1   (8-ounce) can no-salt-added tomato sauce
2   cups 2% reduced-fat milk

1. Heat oil in a large Dutch oven over medium-high heat until hot. Add carrot and onion; sauté 5 minutes or until tender. Add water and next 7 ingredients, stirring well. Bring to a boil; cover, reduce heat, and simmer 45 minutes or until lentils are tender.
2. Place half of lentil mixture in a food processor; process until smooth. Pour puree into a bowl. Repeat procedure with remaining lentil mixture. Return puree to pan; stir in milk. Cook over low heat until thoroughly heated. Yield: 8 servings (serving size: 1 cup).

CALORIES 191 (15% from fat); FAT 3.2g (sat 1g, mono 1.7g, poly 0.3g); PROTEIN 10.4g; CARB 29.7g; FIBER 4.3g; CHOL 5mg; IRON 3.1mg; SODIUM 341mg; CALC 103mg

main-dish soups

Chock-full of meat and vegetables, these soups make a satisfying meal. Add crusty bread or a salad, and your menu's complete!

Unlike some dishes, most soup recipes don't have to be followed precisely. You can usually add a little more or a little less of an ingredient, or you can make substitutions of similar ingredients. You can even use leftover meat, vegetables, rice, or pasta. All of these things help make soup such a convenient, comforting food.

For a spirited flavor, add wine. Broth can be substituted, but the soup will lack the "punch" that wine provides.

Often soup recipes yield several servings—maybe more than you want to eat over a two- or three-day period. Most soups can be frozen for later use. (Avoid freezing milk-based soups or those that contain cheese; dairy products often curdle when thawed.) Freeze soups in airtight plastic freezer containers or heavy-duty zip-top freezer bags. Use within three to four months for optimum flavor. Thaw soups at room temperature until they're still icy, and then refrigerate them until you're ready to serve. Then just bring to a simmer, serve, and enjoy!

LENTIL SOUP

PREP:14 MINUTES   COOK:52 MINUTES

7½ cups Fresh Vegetable Broth
       (page 458)
1½ cups dried lentils
 1 cup chopped onion
 1 cup chopped carrot
 ½ cup chopped celery
 ½ cup chopped parsnip
 2 tablespoons low-sodium soy
       sauce
 2 teaspoons dried oregano
 ½ teaspoon salt

1. Combine broth and lentils in a 4½-quart Dutch oven; bring to a boil. Cover, reduce heat, and simmer 30 minutes. Add chopped onion and remaining ingredients; cover and simmer 15 minutes. Yield: 8 servings (serving size: 1 cup).

CALORIES 166 (3% from fat); FAT 0.6g (sat 0.1g, mono 0.1g, poly 0.3g); PROTEIN 11.4g; CARB 30.8g; FIBER 6.3g; CHOL 0mg; IRON 4mg; SODIUM 595mg; CALC 56mg

SPICY BLACK BEAN-AND-SAUSAGE SOUP

PREP:10 MINUTES   COOK:15 MINUTES

 2 (15-ounce) cans black beans,
       drained and divided
2½ cups water, divided
 1 tablespoon olive oil
 2 cups diced onion
 1 teaspoon chili powder
 ½ teaspoon ground cumin
 ¼ to ½ teaspoon hot sauce
 ¼ teaspoon black pepper
 1 garlic clove, minced
 6 ounces turkey kielbasa, diced

1. Place 1 cup beans and ½ cup water in a food processor or blender, and process until smooth.
2. Heat oil in a large Dutch oven over medium-high heat. Add onion; sauté 4 minutes or until onion is soft.
3. Add bean puree, remaining beans, 2 cups water, sautéed onion, chili powder, and next 4 ingredients; bring to a boil. Cover, reduce heat, and simmer 5 minutes, stirring occasionally. Stir in kielbasa; cook 1 minute or until thoroughly heated. Yield: 4 servings (serving size: 1½ cups).

CALORIES 291 (26% from fat); FAT 8.3g (sat 2.6g, mono 3.5g, poly 1.5g); PROTEIN 17.8g; CARB 38.9g; FIBER 7g; CHOL 23mg; IRON 7.8mg; SODIUM 789mg; CALC 72mg

SOUTHWESTERN VEGETARIAN BLACK BEAN SOUP

PREP:35 MINUTES   STAND:1 HOUR
COOK:1 HOUR 45 MINUTES

 1 pound dried black beans
 ½ cup water
 ½ ounce dried chipotle chile
 2 tablespoons vegetable oil
1½ cups chopped onion
 ¾ cup chopped carrot
 ¾ cup chopped celery
 ¾ cup chopped green bell pepper
 ¾ cup chopped red bell pepper
 2 garlic cloves, minced
 1 cup dry sherry
 2 tablespoons ground cumin
 1 tablespoon chili powder
 1 tablespoon dried oregano
 2 tablespoons honey
 ½ teaspoon salt
 ½ teaspoon ground cinnamon
 ⅛ teaspoon black pepper
 3 (14½-ounce) cans vegetable
       broth
 2 (14.5-ounce) cans diced
       tomatoes, undrained
 1 bay leaf
10 tablespoons fat-free sour cream
Cilantro sprigs (optional)

1. Sort and wash beans; place in a large Dutch oven. Cover with water to 2 inches above beans; bring to a boil, and cook 2 minutes. Remove from heat; cover and let stand 1 hour.
2. Return beans to a boil; cover, reduce heat, and cook 1 hour or until beans are tender. Drain beans in a colander; set aside.
3. While beans are cooking, combine ½ cup water and chile in a small saucepan; bring to a boil. Remove from heat; cover

and let stand 10 minutes or until chile is softened. Place water and chile in a food processor; process 1 minute or until smooth. Set chile puree aside.

4. Heat oil in a Dutch oven over medium-high heat. Add onion and next 5 ingredients; sauté 7 minutes. Add cooked beans, 2 tablespoons chile puree, sherry, and next 10 ingredients; bring to a boil. Cover, reduce heat, and simmer 30 minutes. Discard bay leaf.

5. Remove 4 cups bean mixture from soup with a slotted spoon. Place half of remaining soup in a blender; process until smooth, and pour into a bowl. Repeat procedure with remaining half of soup. Return pureed soup to pan; stir in reserved 4 cups bean mixture. Cook over medium-low heat until thoroughly heated. Ladle into individual bowls; top with sour cream. Garnish with cilantro, if desired. Serve with remaining chile puree, if desired. Yield: 10 servings (serving size: 1½ cups soup and 1 tablespoon sour cream).

CALORIES 261 (17% from fat); FAT 4.8g (sat 0.8g, mono 1.4g, poly 2g); PROTEIN 12.4g; CARB 45.2g; FIBER 8.3g; CHOL 0mg; IRON 4.5mg; SODIUM 838mg; CALC 129mg

CHUNKY VEGETABLE SOUP

PREP: 15 MINUTES   COOK: 50 MINUTES

Cooking spray
2 teaspoons vegetable oil
1 cup chopped onion
2 garlic cloves, minced
7 cups water
1 tablespoon dried basil
¾ teaspoon salt
½ teaspoon dried marjoram
½ teaspoon black pepper
1 pound red potatoes, cut into 1-inch cubes
½ pound small carrots, cut into ½-inch pieces
1 (16-ounce) can cannellini beans or other white beans, drained

Chunky Vegetable Soup

1 (14.5-ounce) can whole tomatoes, undrained and chopped
1 (10-ounce) package frozen large lima beans
½ cup uncooked orzo (rice-shaped pasta)
½ cup (2 ounces) preshredded part-skim mozzarella cheese

1. Heat oil in a large Dutch oven coated with cooking spray over medium-high heat until hot. Add onion and garlic; sauté 5 minutes or until tender. Add water and next 9 ingredients; bring to a boil. Cover, reduce heat, and simmer 20 minutes. Increase heat to medium-high; simmer, uncovered, 10 minutes. Add orzo; cook, uncovered, 10 minutes. Ladle soup into bowls; sprinkle with cheese. Yield: 8 servings (serving size: 1½ cups soup and 1 tablespoon cheese).
Note: Not recommended for freezing.

CALORIES 259 (10% from fat); FAT 3g (sat 1g, mono 0.7g, poly 0.8g); PROTEIN 11.2g; CARB 47.3g; FIBER 5.5g; CHOL 4mg; IRON 3.8mg; SODIUM 563mg; CALC 116mg

SENATORIAL BEAN SOUP

PREP: 20 MINUTES   STAND: 1 HOUR
COOK: 2 HOURS 45 MINUTES

*For decades this soup has been served in
the cafeteria of our nation's Capitol.*

1   cup dried navy beans
2   tablespoons margarine or butter
2½ cups chopped leek
2   cups sliced carrot
1   cup thinly sliced celery
1   cup diced cooked ham (such as
    Light & Lean)
4   garlic cloves, minced
8   cups water
2   teaspoons chicken-flavored
    bouillon granules
1   teaspoon beef-flavored
    bouillon granules
¼   teaspoon salt
1   teaspoon dried rubbed sage
2   bay leaves

1. Sort and wash beans; place in a large
Dutch oven. Cover with water to 2 inches above beans. Bring to a boil; cook 2
minutes. Remove from heat; cover and
let stand 1 hour. Drain; set aside.
2. Melt margarine in Dutch oven over
medium-high heat. Add leek, carrot,
celery, ham, and garlic; sauté 10 minutes. Add beans, 8 cups water, and remaining ingredients; bring to a boil.
Cover, reduce heat, and simmer 2 hours
or until beans are very tender. Discard
bay leaves.
3. Place half of soup in a blender. Remove lid insert, and cover loosely with a
paper towel; pulse on low speed 8 times
or until smooth. Return pureed mixture
to pan; cook, uncovered, over medium-
low heat 30 minutes. Yield: 10 servings
(serving size: 1 cup).

CALORIES 132 (25% from fat); FAT 3.6g (sat 0.9g, mono 1.4g,
poly 1.1g); PROTEIN 7.9g; CARB 18g; FIBER 3.1g;
CHOL 9mg; IRON 1.9mg; SODIUM 566mg; CALC 57mg

CHICKEN-TORTILLA SOUP

PREP: 14 MINUTES
COOK: 1 HOUR 15 MINUTES

1   teaspoon olive oil
1   cup chopped onion
2   garlic cloves, minced
2   cups shredded cooked chicken
    breast (about 10 ounces)
1   cup frozen whole-kernel corn
¼   cup dry white wine
1   tablespoon chopped seeded
    jalapeño pepper
1   teaspoon ground cumin
1   teaspoon Worcestershire
    sauce
½   teaspoon chili powder
2   (14.25-ounce) cans fat-free,
    less-sodium chicken broth
1   (14.5-ounce) can diced
    tomatoes, undrained
1   (10¾-ounce) can condensed
    reduced-fat, reduced-sodium
    tomato soup (such as
    Campbell's Healthy Request),
    undiluted
1   cup crushed unsalted baked
    tortilla chips (about 20)
½   cup fat-free sour cream
1   lime, cut into 8 wedges
    (optional)

1. Heat oil in a Dutch oven over
medium-high heat. Add onion and garlic; sauté 2 minutes. Stir in chicken and
next 9 ingredients; bring to a boil. Reduce heat, and simmer 1 hour.
2. Ladle soup into bowls; top with tortilla chips and sour cream. Squeeze juice
from one lime wedge into each bowl of
soup before serving, if desired. Yield: 8
servings (serving size: 1 cup soup, 2 tablespoons chips, and 1 tablespoon sour
cream).

CALORIES 179 (15% from fat); FAT 3g (sat 0.4g, mono 0.9g,
poly 0.6g); PROTEIN 13.6g; CARB 23.7g; FIBER 2.7g;
CHOL 26mg; IRON 1.2mg; SODIUM 492mg; CALC 69mg

TEX-MEX CHICKEN SOUP
WITH SPLIT PEAS

PREP: 40 MINUTES
COOK: 1 HOUR

*Split peas can be found with dried beans
in your grocery store. They can be stored
on your pantry shelf in plastic bags.
Although we used the green variety,
yellow split peas can be substituted.*

2   teaspoons chili powder
½   teaspoon ground coriander
⅛   teaspoon salt
⅛   teaspoon garlic powder
⅛   teaspoon ground red pepper
⅛   teaspoon black pepper
1   pound skinned, boned chicken
     breasts
1   teaspoon vegetable oil
Cooking spray
1½   cups vertically sliced onion
⅔   cup thinly sliced yellow bell
     pepper
⅔   cup thinly sliced green bell pepper
⅔   cup thinly sliced red bell pepper
2   cups low-salt chicken broth
2   cups water
½   cup green split peas
¼   teaspoon salt
½   cup bottled salsa
1   tablespoon fresh lime juice
3   (10-inch) flour tortillas, cut into
     ¼-inch-wide strips
¾   cup (3 ounces) shredded
     reduced-fat Monterey Jack
     cheese

1. Combine first 6 ingredients in a shallow dish. Dredge chicken in spice mixture. Heat oil in a large nonstick skillet
coated with cooking spray over medium-
high heat. Add chicken; cook 6 minutes
on each side or until chicken is done.
Remove chicken from pan, and cool.
Cut chicken into ½-inch pieces.
2. Add onion and bell peppers to skillet,

and sauté 3 minutes. Add chicken, broth, water, split peas, and ¼ teaspoon salt; bring to a boil. Partially cover, reduce heat, and simmer 30 minutes or until peas are tender. Add salsa and lime juice, and simmer 10 minutes.

3. Preheat broiler.

4. Spread tortilla strips in a single layer on a baking sheet coated with cooking spray; lightly coat tortilla strips with cooking spray. Broil tortilla strips 4 minutes or until lightly browned, stirring once.

5. Ladle soup into 6 bowls; top with tortilla strips, and sprinkle with cheese. Yield: 6 servings (serving size: 1⅓ cups soup, about ¾ cup tortilla strips, and 2 tablespoons cheese).

CALORIES 322 (22% from fat); FAT 7.8g (sat 2.6g, mono 2.1g, poly 1.8g); PROTEIN 30.2g; CARB 33g; FIBER 3.6g; CHOL 55mg; IRON 3.1mg; SODIUM 526mg; CALC 193mg

CHUNKY-CHICKEN NOODLE SOUP

PREP: 30 MINUTES
COOK: 45 MINUTES

    2 teaspoons olive oil
    1 cup chopped onion
    1 cup diced carrot
    1 cup sliced celery
    1 garlic clove, minced
    3 tablespoons all-purpose flour
    ½ teaspoon dried oregano
    ¼ teaspoon dried thyme
    ¼ teaspoon poultry seasoning
    3 (14½-ounce) cans fat-free,
       less-sodium chicken broth
 2½ cups diced peeled baking potato
    ½ teaspoon salt
    2 cups diced roasted chicken
    1 (12-ounce) can evaporated fat-
       free milk
    2 cups wide egg noodles (4 ounces
       uncooked pasta)
Thyme sprigs (optional)

1. Heat oil in a Dutch oven over medium heat. Add onion, carrot, celery, and garlic; sauté 5 minutes. Sprinkle flour, oregano, dried thyme, and poultry seasoning over vegetables; cook 1 minute.

2. Stir in broth, potato, and salt. Bring to a boil; reduce heat, and simmer, partially covered, 25 minutes or until potato is tender. Add chicken, milk, and noodles, and cook 10 minutes or until noodles are tender. Garnish with thyme sprigs, if desired. Yield: 8 servings (serving size: 1 cup).

CALORIES 240 (17% from fat); FAT 4.5g (sat 1.1g, mono 2g, poly 0.9g); PROTEIN 17.3g; CARB 30.2g; FIBER 2.3g; CHOL 46mg; IRON 2mg; SODIUM 667mg; CALC 161mg

THAI CLAM POT

PREP: 25 MINUTES   COOK: 18 MINUTES

    6 ounces uncooked somen (wheat
       noodles)
    1 teaspoon vegetable oil
    1 teaspoon crushed red pepper
    8 garlic cloves, thinly sliced
    8 green onions, cut into 2-inch
       pieces
 1½ cups water
    ¾ cup mirin (sweet rice wine)
    3 pounds small clams in shells
       (about 48), scrubbed
    1 cup thinly sliced basil
    2 tablespoons fish sauce
                    (continued on page 472)

Chunky-Chicken
Noodle Soup

1. Cook somen in boiling water 5 minutes; drain. Rinse with cold water. Drain; set aside.

2. Heat oil in a large Dutch oven over medium-high heat. Add pepper, garlic, and green onions; stir-fry 30 seconds. Add 1½ cups water and mirin; bring to a boil. Add clams; cover, reduce heat, and simmer 10 minutes or until clams open. Discard any unopened shells. Stir in sliced basil and fish sauce, and cook 1 minute.

3. Divide noodles and clams evenly among 6 bowls; top each with ½ cup cooking liquid. Yield: 6 servings.

CALORIES 150 (8% from fat); FAT 1.4g (sat 0.2g, mono 0.3g, poly 0.6g); PROTEIN 8.9g; CARB 25.1g; FIBER 1.6g; CHOL 13mg; IRON 5.9mg; SODIUM 1011mg; CALC 54mg

MULLIGATAWNY SOUP

PREP: 15 MINUTES   COOK: 35 MINUTES

  1 tablespoon margarine or butter
1½ cups chopped onion
  1 tablespoon curry powder
  2 garlic cloves, minced
  1 pound skinned, boned chicken thighs, chopped
  ½ teaspoon salt
  ⅛ teaspoon black pepper
  2 (10½-ounce) cans low-sodium chicken broth
  ½ cup all-purpose flour
  2 cups 2% reduced-fat milk
  3 cups chopped peeled Golden Delicious apple (about 1 pound)
  ¼ cup chopped parsley

Mulligatawny Soup

1. Melt margarine in a large saucepan over medium heat. Add onion, curry powder, and garlic; sauté 3 minutes. Add chicken; sauté 5 minutes. Add salt, pepper, and broth. Reduce heat to medium-low; simmer 10 minutes.

2. Place flour in a bowl. Add milk; stir until well-blended. Gradually add to soup. Cook until thickened (about 10 minutes), stirring constantly. Add apple; cook 5 minutes. Remove from heat; stir in parsley. Yield: 9 servings (serving size: 1 cup).

CALORIES 155 (28% from fat); FAT 4.8g (sat 1.7g, mono 1.7g, poly 1g); PROTEIN 12.1g; CARB 16.3g; FIBER 1.7g; CHOL 40mg; IRON 1.7mg; SODIUM 236mg; CALC 89mg

OYSTER-ARTICHOKE SOUP

PREP: 15 MINUTES   COOK: 30 MINUTES

  1 (16-ounce) container standard oysters, undrained
  1 teaspoon stick margarine or butter
  ½ cup chopped green onions
  3 (8-ounce) bottles clam juice
  1 tablespoon chopped fresh parsley
  ½ teaspoon dried thyme
  ¼ teaspoon ground red pepper
  6 tablespoons all-purpose flour
  2 cups 2% reduced-fat milk
  1 (14-ounce) can quartered artichoke hearts, drained
  2 tablespoons sliced green onions
Freshly ground black pepper (optional)

1. Drain oysters, reserving ¼ cup juice. Melt margarine in a large saucepan. Add chopped green onions; sauté 3 minutes. Add reserved oyster juice, clam juice, parsley, thyme, and red pepper; bring to a boil. Reduce heat, and simmer, uncovered, 10 minutes.

2. Place flour in a bowl. Gradually add milk, stirring well with a whisk; add to

soup. Cook over medium heat until thick (about 6 minutes), stirring constantly. Stir in oysters and artichokes, and cook 3 minutes or until edges of oysters curl. Ladle soup into bowls; sprinkle sliced green onions over soup, and garnish with black pepper, if desired. Yield: 7 servings (serving size: 1 cup).

CALORIES 123 (25% from fat); FAT 3.4g (sat 1.3g, mono 0.8g, poly 0.7g); PROTEIN 8.6g; CARB 15.2g; FIBER 0.4g; CHOL 38mg; IRON 4.9mg; SODIUM 458mg; CALC 150mg

CORN-AND-SHRIMP SOUP

PREP:22 MINUTES   COOK:22 MINUTES

    3 cups frozen whole-kernel corn,
         thawed and divided
    2 cups fat-free, less-sodium chicken
         broth, divided
    1 tablespoon olive oil
    1 cup chopped onion
    1 cup chopped green bell pepper
    1 cup chopped red bell pepper
    1 cup fat-free milk
  ¾ pound medium shrimp, peeled
  ¼ cup chopped fresh cilantro
  ¼ cup chopped fresh parsley
  ¼ teaspoon salt
  ⅛ teaspoon black pepper

1. Combine 2 cups corn and 1 cup broth in a blender; process until smooth.
2. Heat oil in a large saucepan over medium heat. Add onion and bell peppers; sauté 10 minutes or until tender. Stir in pureed corn mixture, 1 cup broth, and milk. Bring to a boil; cover, reduce heat, and simmer 5 minutes.
3. Add 1 cup corn, shrimp, and remaining ingredients to pan; cover and simmer 5 minutes or until shrimp are done. Yield: 7 servings (serving size: 1 cup).

CALORIES 124 (22% from fat); FAT 3g (sat 0.5g, mono 1.6g, poly 0.6g); PROTEIN 10.5g; CARB 14.4g; FIBER 2g; CHOL 56mg; IRON 1.6mg; SODIUM 343mg; CALC 72mg

WON TON MEE

PREP:45 MINUTES
COOK:35 MINUTES

This is a fun recipe to set on the table and let everyone serve themselves.

  ¾ pound pork tenderloin
    1 teaspoon grated peeled fresh
         ginger
  ½ teaspoon sugar
    1 garlic clove, minced
    1 tablespoon low-sodium soy
         sauce
    2 teaspoons vegetable oil
    1 tablespoon minced water
         chestnuts
    1 tablespoon thinly sliced green
         onions
    1 teaspoon grated peeled fresh
         ginger
    1 teaspoon low-sodium soy sauce
  ¼ teaspoon dark sesame oil
    1 garlic clove, minced
    1 large egg white, lightly beaten
  12 won ton wrappers
    8 cups water
5½ cups low-salt chicken broth
    3 (¼-inch-thick) slices peeled
         fresh ginger
    1 garlic clove, crushed
    2 cups thinly sliced napa (Chinese)
         cabbage
1⅓ cups hot cooked whole-wheat
         spaghetti (about 3 ounces
         uncooked pasta)
  ¼ cup diagonally sliced green onions
    4 teaspoons low-sodium soy sauce
    2 teaspoons oyster sauce
    1 teaspoon dark sesame oil

1. Trim fat from pork. Combine 1 teaspoon ginger, sugar, and 1 minced garlic clove; stir well. Rub pork with ginger mixture. Drizzle 1 tablespoon soy sauce over pork. Heat 2 teaspoons vegetable oil in a nonstick skillet over medium-high heat. Add pork; cook 2 minutes on each side or until browned. Cover; reduce heat to medium-low. Cook 10 minutes; turn and cook 10 minutes or until meat thermometer registers 160° (slightly pink). Remove from skillet, and cool.
2. Finely chop 1½ ounces pork to yield ⅓ cup. Cut remaining pork crosswise into 12 slices; set aside. Combine ⅓ cup chopped pork, water chestnuts, and next 6 ingredients in a small bowl.
3. Working with 1 won ton wrapper at a time (cover remaining wrappers with a damp towel to keep them from drying), spoon 1¼ teaspoons of pork mixture onto center of each wrapper. Moisten edges of dough with water, and bring 2 opposite corners to center, pinching points to seal. Bring remaining 2 corners to center, pinching points to seal. Pinch edges together to seal.
4. Bring 8 cups water to a boil in a large saucepan; add filled won tons. Cook until won tons float to the surface (about 3 minutes); remove with a slotted spoon. Drain; set aside.
5. Combine broth, ginger slices, and crushed garlic clove in a large saucepan, and bring to a boil. Cover, reduce heat, and simmer 20 minutes. Discard ginger slices. Stir in cabbage; cook 1 minute.
6. Ladle 1½ cups broth mixture into each of 4 bowls. Add 3 won tons, 3 slices pork, and ⅓ cup spaghetti to each bowl. Top each serving with 1 tablespoon green onions, 1 teaspoon soy sauce, ½ teaspoon oyster sauce, and ¼ teaspoon sesame oil. Yield: 4 servings.

CALORIES 344 (25% from fat); FAT 9.6g (sat 2.3g, mono 3.5g, poly 2.8g); PROTEIN 28.9g; CARB 36.2g; FIBER 2.9g; CHOL 61mg; IRON 4.5mg; SODIUM 715mg; CALC 56mg

HOT-AND-SOUR SOUP

PREP: 20 MINUTES   COOK: 14 MINUTES

For a vegetarian version, use vegetable broth and replace the pork with a little extra tofu.

10   dried shiitake mushrooms (about
    1 ounce)
1½ cups boiling water
3   (10½-ounce) cans low-sodium
    chicken broth
1   (4-ounce) boned center-cut loin
    pork chop, cut into thin strips
4   ounces firm tofu, cut into
    ½-inch cubes

2   tablespoons cornstarch
3   tablespoons white wine vinegar
3   tablespoons low-sodium soy
    sauce
2   teaspoons fish sauce
¼   teaspoon crushed red pepper
¼   teaspoon black pepper
¼   cup minced green onion tops
1   teaspoon dark sesame oil

1. Combine mushrooms and boiling water in a bowl; cover and let stand 15 minutes. Drain in a colander over a bowl, reserving 1 cup liquid. Discard stems; rinse and cut caps into thin strips.

2. Combine ½ cup reserved mushroom liquid and broth in a large saucepan; bring to a boil. Add mushrooms, pork, and tofu; reduce heat, and simmer 3 minutes. Combine ½ cup reserved mushroom liquid, cornstarch, and next 5 ingredients in a small bowl. Add cornstarch mixture to pan; bring to a boil. Cook 1 minute, stirring constantly. Remove from heat; stir in onion tops and oil. Yield: 4 servings (serving size: 1¼ cups).

CALORIES 162 (34% from fat); FAT 6.1g (sat 1.8g, mono 1.7g, poly 1.5g); PROTEIN 12.9g; CARB 12.6g; FIBER 1.4g; CHOL 22mg; IRON 2.2mg; SODIUM 709mg; CALC 54mg

bisques & chowders When choosing a Dutch oven for these recipes, select one that allows steady simmering with little risk of scorching.

LOBSTER BISQUE

PREP: 15 MINUTES   COOK: 45 MINUTES

Making a quick stock from a lobster shell gives this soup its great taste.

1   (1¼-pound) whole Maine
    lobster, cooked
1¼ cups water
1   (8-ounce) bottle clam juice
2   whole cloves
1   bay leaf
2   teaspoons butter or stick margarine
¼   cup finely chopped onion
¼   cup finely chopped celery
¼   cup all-purpose flour
2½ tablespoons tomato paste
2   cups 2% reduced-fat milk
¼   teaspoon salt
Dash of ground red pepper
1   tablespoon dry sherry

1. Remove meat from cooked lobster tail and claws; chop meat, and set aside.

Place lobster shell in a large, heavy-duty zip-top plastic bag. Coarsely crush shell, using a meat mallet or rolling pin. Place crushed shell in a large saucepan; add water, clam juice, cloves, and bay leaf. Partially cover, and cook over medium-low heat 30 minutes. Strain shell mixture through a sieve into a bowl, reserving stock. Discard solids.

2. Melt butter in a large saucepan over medium heat. Add onion and celery; sauté 5 minutes. Sprinkle flour over onion mixture; cook 1 minute, stirring constantly. Add tomato paste, and cook 1 minute. Gradually add reserved lobster stock, milk, salt, and red pepper, stirring with a whisk. Cook over medium heat until thick (about 8 minutes), stirring constantly. Stir in chopped lobster meat, and cook 1 minute. Remove from heat, and stir in sherry. Yield: 4 servings (serving size: 1 cup).

CALORIES 142 (29% from fat); FAT 4.6g (sat 2.7g, mono 1.3g, poly 0.3g); PROTEIN 10.4g; CARB 14.8g; FIBER 0.9g; CHOL 34mg; IRON 1mg; SODIUM 457mg; CALC 181mg

CARAMELIZED ONION-AND-ROASTED GARLIC BISQUE

PREP: 13 MINUTES
COOK: 1 HOUR 40 MINUTES

1   large whole garlic head
1   tablespoon olive oil
9   cups thinly sliced Vidalia or other
    sweet onion (about 4 large
    onions)
2½ cups sliced leek (about 2 medium)
1   teaspoon salt, divided
1   teaspoon dried thyme
2   tablespoons all-purpose flour
⅓   cup dry white wine
3   (10½-ounce) cans low-sodium
    chicken broth
2   cups 1% low-fat milk

1. Preheat oven to 350°.
2. Remove white papery skin from garlic head (do not peel or separate cloves). Wrap in foil. Bake at 350° for 1 hour; cool 10 minutes. Separate cloves;

squeeze to extract garlic pulp. Discard skins. Set garlic pulp aside.

3. Heat oil in a large Dutch oven over medium heat. Add onion and leek; cook 30 minutes, stirring often. Add ½ teaspoon salt and thyme. Cook 30 minutes or until onion is golden, stirring occasionally. Stir in flour. Add wine and broth; bring to a boil. Reduce heat; simmer 30 minutes. Add garlic pulp, ½ teaspoon salt, and milk; simmer 8 minutes or until thoroughly heated. Place half of onion mixture in a blender; process until smooth. Pour pureed mixture into a large bowl; repeat procedure with remaining onion mixture. Yield: 8 servings (serving size: 1 cup).

CALORIES 143 (22% from fat); FAT 3.5g (sat 1.1g, mono 1.8g, poly 0.5g); PROTEIN 5.9g; CARB 23.8g; FIBER 3.1g; CHOL 2mg; IRON 1.9mg; SODIUM 374mg; CALC 136mg

CURRIED SWEET POTATO BISQUE

PREP: 18 MINUTES   COOK: 40 MINUTES

- 2 teaspoons olive oil
- 1 cup chopped onion
- 2 teaspoons curry powder
- ¼ teaspoon ground allspice
- 5 cups cubed peeled sweet potato (about 3½ pounds)
- 1 cup water
- ½ teaspoon salt
- 3 (10½-ounce) cans low-sodium chicken broth
- 1½ cups plain fat-free yogurt, divided
- Minced fresh chives (optional)
- Cumin seeds (optional)

1. Heat oil in a Dutch oven over medium-high heat. Add onion; sauté 2 minutes. Stir in curry and allspice; cook 1 minute. Add potato, water, salt, and broth. Cook 25 minutes or until potato is tender.
2. Place half of sweet potato mixture in a blender; process until smooth. Pour pureed mixture into a bowl. Repeat procedure

with remaining sweet potato mixture. Return pureed mixture to pan. Bring to a boil; remove from heat. Add 1 cup yogurt, stirring until well-blended. Top each serving with about 1 tablespoon yogurt; garnish with chives and cumin seeds, if desired. Yield: 7 servings (serving size: 1½ cups bisque and about 1 tablespoon yogurt).

CALORIES 258 (10% from fat); FAT 2.9g (sat 0.8g, mono 1g, poly 0.4g); PROTEIN 7.8g; CARB 51.3g; FIBER 6.1g; CHOL 3mg; IRON 1.3mg; SODIUM 289mg; CALC 152mg

SCALLOP BISQUE

PREP: 10 MINUTES   COOK: 25 MINUTES

- 1 teaspoon sugar
- ½ teaspoon dried basil
- 2 (14.5-ounce) cans no-salt-added whole tomatoes, undrained and coarsely chopped
- 2 tablespoons butter or stick margarine
- ¼ cup chopped onion
- 3 tablespoons all-purpose flour
- ½ teaspoon salt
- ⅛ teaspoon black pepper
- 1½ cups 1% low-fat milk
- 1 (8-ounce) bottle clam juice
- 1 pound bay scallops
- 2 tablespoons sherry

1. Combine first 3 ingredients in a large saucepan; cook over medium heat 10 minutes, stirring occasionally. Place mixture in a blender, and process until smooth. Wipe pan with a paper towel.
2. Melt butter in pan over medium heat. Add onion; sauté 5 minutes. Add flour, salt, and pepper; cook 1 minute, stirring constantly with a whisk. Gradually add milk and clam juice, stirring constantly. Cook until thick and bubbly (about 5 minutes), stirring constantly. Add tomato mixture, scallops, and sherry. Cook 3 minutes or until scallops are done. Yield: 8 servings (serving size: 1 cup).

CALORIES 129 (27% from fat); FAT 3.8g (sat 2.2g, mono 1g, poly 0.3g); PROTEIN 12.3g; CARB 11.4g; FIBER 0.9g; CHOL 29mg; IRON 0.9mg; SODIUM 367mg; CALC 112mg

Curried Sweet Potato Bisque

SALMON BISQUE

1 tablespoon vegetable oil
1 cup chopped onion
1 cup chopped celery
4 cups chopped peeled baking
   potato
¼ cup finely chopped parsley
½ teaspoon ground white pepper
½ teaspoon salt
2 (14½-ounce) cans fat-free,
   less-sodium chicken broth
¼ cup dry white wine
2 (12-ounce) cans evaporated
   fat-free milk
1 teaspoon lemon juice
1 (1-pound) salmon fillet, skinned
   and cut into ½-inch pieces
1½ tablespoons chopped fresh dill or
   parsley

1. Heat oil in a Dutch oven over medium heat. Add onion and celery; sauté 10 minutes or until tender. Add potato, parsley, pepper, salt, and broth. Bring to a boil; reduce heat, and simmer 20 minutes or until potato is tender. Place potato mixture in a blender, and process until smooth.

2. Return pureed mixture to pan; stir in wine and milk. Cover and cook over medium-low heat 15 minutes, stirring occasionally. Add lemon juice and fish; cook 10 minutes or until fish flakes easily when tested with a fork, stirring occasionally. Ladle soup into bowls; sprinkle each serving with ½ teaspoon dill. Yield: 9 servings (serving size: 1 cup).

CALORIES 195 (16% from fat); FAT 3.5g (sat 0.7g, mono 1g, poly 1.5g); PROTEIN 17.7g; CARB 21.8g; FIBER 1.4g; CHOL 29mg; IRON 1.3mg; SODIUM 403mg; CALC 246mg

SOUTHWEST ROASTED RED PEPPER BISQUE WITH CILANTRO CREAM

⅓ cup finely chopped fresh cilantro
¼ cup low-fat sour cream
2 teaspoons 2% reduced-fat milk
½ teaspoon salt
2 teaspoons olive oil
2 cups chopped onion
½ cup chopped carrot
1½ pounds red bell peppers (about 3
   large), roasted, peeled, and
   chopped
1 tablespoon tomato paste
½ teaspoon ground cumin
¼ teaspoon chili powder
Dash of ground red pepper
2 garlic cloves, minced
¾ cup cooked long-grain rice
½ cup water
2 (10½-ounce) cans low-sodium
   chicken broth
½ cup 2% reduced-fat milk
¼ teaspoon salt
⅛ teaspoon black pepper

1. Combine first 4 ingredients in a small bowl; set aside.

2. Heat oil in a Dutch oven over medium heat. Add onion and carrot; sauté 8 minutes or until vegetables are lightly browned. Stir in bell pepper, tomato paste, cumin, chili powder, ground red pepper, and garlic; cook 5 minutes, stirring frequently. Stir in rice, water, and broth, scraping skillet to loosen browned bits. Bring to a boil; partially cover, reduce heat, and simmer 15 minutes.

3. Place broth mixture in a food processor; process until smooth. Return puree to pan, and stir in ½ cup milk, ¼ teaspoon salt, and black pepper. Cook over medium heat until thoroughly heated (do not boil). Ladle bisque into bowls; top with sour cream mixture. Yield: 5 servings (serving size: 1 cup bisque and 2 teaspoons sour cream mixture).

CALORIES 167 (29% from fat); FAT 5.4g (sat 1.8g, mono 2.3g, poly 0.8g); PROTEIN 5.5g; CARB 26.1g; FIBER 4.3g; CHOL 7mg; IRON 3.3mg; SODIUM 426mg; CALC 84mg

WISCONSIN CHEESE CHOWDER

Cooking spray
3 cups diced carrot
1 cup sliced celery
¾ cup chopped green onions
4 cups diced peeled red potato
   (about 1½ pounds)
1 (14.25-ounce) can fat-free,
   less-sodium chicken broth
¾ cup Chablis or other dry white
   wine
⅓ cup all-purpose flour
2 cups 2% reduced-fat milk
½ teaspoon salt
¼ teaspoon ground red pepper
¾ cup (3 ounces) shredded sharp
   cheddar cheese
¼ cup (1 ounce) shredded Swiss
   cheese

1. Coat a large Dutch oven with cooking spray; place over medium-high heat until hot. Add carrot, celery, and green onions; sauté 8 minutes. Add potato, broth, and wine; bring to a boil. Cover, reduce heat, and simmer 25 minutes or until potato is tender.

2. Place flour in a bowl. Gradually add milk, stirring well with a whisk; add flour mixture to pan. Stir in salt and red pepper; cook until thick (about 2 minutes). Remove from heat, and add cheeses, stirring until cheeses melt. Ladle chowder into soup bowls. Yield: 6 servings (serving size: 1½ cups).

Note: Substitute ¾ cup low-sodium

chicken broth for the Chablis, if
desired.

CALORIES 291 (25% from fat); FAT 8.1g (sat 4.9g, mono 2.2g,
poly 0.4g); PROTEIN 12.2g; CARB 43.2g; FIBER 6.1g;
CHOL 26mg; IRON 2.2mg; SODIUM 505mg; CALC 305mg

CRAB-AND-CORN CHOWDER

PREP:18 MINUTES   COOK:45 MINUTES

 1   tablespoon olive oil
 ½   cup chopped green onions
 2   cups fresh or frozen corn
       kernels (about 4 ears)
 2   cups diced red potato
 2   cups fat-free milk
 ¼   teaspoon salt
 ¼   teaspoon Worcestershire sauce
 ⅛   teaspoon black pepper
 1   (16-ounce) can fat-free,
       less-sodium chicken broth
 1   thyme sprig
 2   tablespoons cornstarch
 1   (5-ounce) can evaporated
       fat-free milk
 ½   cup chopped chanterelle or other
       fresh wild mushrooms (about 2
       ounces)
 ½   pound lump crabmeat, shell
       pieces removed

1. Heat oil in a Dutch oven over medium heat. Add onions; sauté 2 minutes or
until tender. Add corn and next 7 ingredients; bring to a boil. Reduce heat; simmer
30 minutes or until potato is tender.
2. Combine cornstarch and evaporated
milk in a small bowl; stir well with a
whisk. Add cornstarch mixture to soup;
simmer until thick (about 5 minutes),
stirring occasionally. Add mushrooms
and crab; remove thyme sprig. Ladle
chowder into soup bowls. Yield: 6 servings (serving size: 1 cup).

CALORIES 220 (16% from fat); FAT 3.8g (sat 0.6g, mono 2g,
poly 0.8g); PROTEIN 16.5g; CARB 31.1g; FIBER 2.8g;
CHOL 41mg; IRON 1.1mg; SODIUM 452mg; CALC 233mg

Jalapeño-and-Corn Chowder

JALAPEÑO-AND-CORN CHOWDER

PREP:15 MINUTES   COOK:40 MINUTES

     Cooking spray
 1   cup chopped onion
 1   cup canned vegetable broth
 1   cup chopped cauliflower
 ½   cup sliced carrot
 ½   cup sliced celery
 ½   cup (½-inch) sliced green beans
 1   jalapeño pepper, cut in half
       lengthwise
 ¼   cup all-purpose flour
 3   cups 2% reduced-fat milk
 ¼   teaspoon white pepper
     Dash of ground red pepper
 1   (11-ounce) can whole-kernel
       corn, drained
 ⅔   cup (2⅔ ounces) shredded sharp
       cheddar cheese

1. Coat a large saucepan with cooking
spray; place over medium heat until hot.
Add onion; sauté 5 minutes or until tender. Add broth and next 5 ingredients;
bring to a boil. Cover, reduce heat, and
simmer 20 minutes or until vegetables
are tender.
2. Place flour in a medium bowl. Gradually add milk, stirring well with a
whisk. Add milk mixture, white pepper,
red pepper, and corn to pan; stir well.
Cook over medium heat until thick
(about 7 minutes), stirring constantly.
Discard jalapeño pepper. Ladle chowder
into individual bowls; sprinkle with
cheese. Yield: 5 servings (serving size:
1½ cups chowder and 2 tablespoons
cheese).

CALORIES 233 (33% from fat); FAT 8.6g (sat 5g, mono 2.3g,
poly 0.5g); PROTEIN 11.9g; CARB 29.4g; FIBER 2.5g;
CHOL 28mg; IRON 1.1mg; SODIUM 533mg; CALC 317mg

ROASTED CORN-AND-LOBSTER CHOWDER

PREP: 30 MINUTES

COOK: 1 HOUR 15 MINUTES

The secret to the richness of this soup is the use of the lobster shells in making a stock.

  4 ears corn
  2 (1½-pound) whole Maine
     lobsters, cooked
  2 cups finely chopped leek, divided
  2 cups finely chopped onion, divided
1¾ cups finely chopped celery, divided
1½ cups dry white wine
  4 (14½-ounce) cans fat-free,
     less-sodium chicken broth
  2 thyme sprigs
  1 parsley sprig
  1 bay leaf
  1 tablespoon olive oil
  3 garlic cloves, minced
  3 cups cubed peeled baking potato
¼ cup all-purpose flour
  1 cup fat-free half-and-half
  1 teaspoon salt
⅛ teaspoon ground nutmeg
¼ teaspoon black pepper

1. Prepare grill.
2. Place corn on grill rack; grill 10 minutes or until corn is lightly browned, turning after 5 minutes. Cool. Cut kernels from ears of corn to measure 3 cups, reserving cobs. Set corn kernels aside.
3. Remove meat from lobster tails and claws, reserving shells; coarsely chop meat.
4. Place lobster shells, corn cobs, 1 cup leek, 1 cup onion, 1 cup celery, and wine in a large Dutch oven over medium-high heat. Bring to a boil; cook 10 minutes. Add broth, thyme, parsley, and bay leaf. Bring to a boil; reduce heat. Simmer 40 minutes. Strain lobster stock through a sieve into a bowl; discard solids.
5. Heat oil in a large Dutch oven over medium heat. Add 1 cup leek, 1 cup onion, ¾ cup celery, and garlic; sauté 5 minutes or until tender. Stir in potato and flour. Cook 1 minute, stirring constantly. Gradually add lobster stock to potato mixture, stirring with a whisk until blended. Bring to a boil; simmer, uncovered, 10 minutes. Add corn and half-and-half; simmer 5 minutes. Add lobster, salt, nutmeg, and pepper. Cook until thoroughly heated. Yield: 9 servings (serving size: 1 cup).

CALORIES 196 (13% from fat); FAT 2.5g (sat 0.4g, mono 1.4g, poly 0.5g); PROTEIN 11.3g; CARB 30.4g; FIBER 3.2g; CHOL 24mg; IRON 1.5mg; SODIUM 704mg; CALC 64mg

POTATO CHOWDER

PREP: 13 MINUTES

COOK: 28 MINUTES

  1 tablespoon butter or stick
     margarine
  1 cup chopped onion
½ cup chopped celery
  1 bay leaf
¼ cup all-purpose flour
2½ cups 2% reduced-fat milk
  4 (10½-ounce) cans low-
     sodium chicken broth
  5 cups cubed peeled round red
     potato (about 1¾ pounds)
  1 teaspoon salt
½ teaspoon dried oregano
½ teaspoon freshly ground black
     pepper
Additional freshly ground pepper
     (optional)

1. Melt butter in a large Dutch oven over medium heat; add onion, celery, and bay leaf. Cook until tender (about 5 minutes), stirring occasionally. Stir in flour. Gradually add milk and broth; bring to a boil, stirring constantly.
2. Add potato, salt, oregano, and ½ teaspoon pepper to pan. Reduce heat to low, and simmer, uncovered, 18 minutes or until potato is tender, stirring frequently. Discard bay leaf.
3. Place 2½ cups potato mixture in blender, using a slotted spoon; process until smooth. Return puree to pan; stir well. Serve with additional pepper, if desired. Yield: 10 servings (serving size: 1 cup).

CALORIES 129 (23% from fat); FAT 3.3g (sat 1.9g, mono 1.1g, poly 0.3g); PROTEIN 5.2g; CARB 20.4g; FIBER 1.6g; CHOL 8mg; IRON 1.4mg; SODIUM 328mg; CALC 87mg

NEW ENGLAND FISH CHOWDER

PREP: 10 MINUTES   COOK: 50 MINUTES

  2 tablespoons margarine
  3 tablespoons shredded carrot
  2 tablespoons diced celery
  2 tablespoons minced fresh onion
  2 tablespoons plus 1 teaspoon
     all-purpose flour
3½ cups fat-free milk, divided
  2 cups diced peeled baking potato
½ teaspoon salt
¼ teaspoon black pepper
  1 pound cod or other lean white
     fish fillets, cut into 1-inch
     pieces
Unsalted oyster crackers (optional)

1. Melt margarine in a saucepan over medium heat. Add carrot, celery, and onion; sauté 2 minutes. Stir in flour; gradually add 2½ cups milk, stirring constantly with a whisk. Add potato, salt, and pepper; bring to a boil. Reduce heat. Simmer, uncovered, 30 minutes; stir occasionally.
2. Add fish and 1 cup milk to pan; cook 10 minutes or until fish is done. Serve with oyster crackers, if desired. Yield: 4 servings (serving size: 1½ cups).

CALORIES 299 (21% from fat); FAT 6.9g (sat 1.5g, mono 2.7g, poly 2.1g); PROTEIN 29.6g; CARB 28.3g; FIBER 1.6g; CHOL 53mg; IRON 1.3mg; SODIUM 541mg; CALC 297mg

chili

You're likely to have most of these ingredients on hand, so it's easy to turn a chilly night into a *chili* night.

CROCK-POT® CHILI

PREP: 18 MINUTES
COOK: 4 HOURS

1 pound ground round
1 cup chopped onion
½ cup chopped green bell pepper
¼ cup dry red wine or water
1 tablespoon chili powder
1 teaspoon sugar
1 teaspoon ground cumin
¼ teaspoon salt
1 garlic clove, minced
1 (15-ounce) can kidney beans, undrained
1 (14.5-ounce) can Mexican-style stewed tomatoes with jalapeño peppers and spices, undrained
6 tablespoons (1½ ounces) shredded reduced-fat extra-sharp cheddar cheese

1. Cook beef in a large nonstick skillet over medium-high heat until browned, stirring to crumble. Add onion and next 7 ingredients; cook 7 minutes or until onion is tender.
2. Place meat mixture in an electric slow cooker, and stir in beans and tomatoes. Cover with lid, and cook on low-heat setting for 4 hours. Ladle into bowls; sprinkle with cheese. Yield: 6 servings (serving size: 1¼ cups chili and 1 tablespoon cheese).
Note: The chili can be made on the stovetop if you don't have a slow cooker. After adding beans and tomatoes, bring to a boil. Reduce heat; simmer, partially covered, 1½ hours.

CALORIES 243 (21% from fat); FAT 5.6g (sat 2.3g, mono 1.8g, poly 0.5g); PROTEIN 25.5g; CARB 22.9g; FIBER 3.1g; CHOL 49mg; IRON 4.1mg; SODIUM 637mg; CALC 154mg

CHILI

PREP: 20 MINUTES
COOK: 20 MINUTES

Tired of soup bowls? Use crusty dinner rolls. (See "Making Bread Bowls" on page 28.) Then, just spoon the chili into the individual "bowls," and serve immediately.

Cooking spray
1 pound ground round
1 cup chopped onion
4 garlic cloves, minced
1 tablespoon dried oregano
1½ teaspoons chili powder
1½ teaspoons ground cumin
½ teaspoon salt
¼ to ½ teaspoon ground cinnamon
½ teaspoon black pepper
1 (15-ounce) can no-salt-added kidney beans, undrained
1 (14.5-ounce) can no-salt-added stewed tomatoes, undrained
2 (8-ounce) cans no-salt-added tomato sauce
7 tablespoons fat-free sour cream
Sliced green onions (optional)

1. Coat a large saucepan with cooking spray; place over medium-high heat until hot. Add beef, onion, and garlic; cook until meat is browned, stirring to crumble. Drain well, and return mixture to pan.
2. Add oregano and next 8 ingredients to pan; stir well. Cover, reduce heat, and simmer 20 minutes. Ladle into bowls. Serve with sour cream. Garnish with sliced green onions, if desired. Yield: 7 servings (serving size: 1 cup chili and 1 tablespoon sour cream).

CALORIES 204 (20% from fat); FAT 4.5g (sat 1.5g, mono 1.8g, poly 0.4g); PROTEIN 19.7g; CARB 21.3g; FIBER 3.4g; CHOL 40mg; IRON 4mg; SODIUM 241mg; CALC 83mg

MEXICAN BLACK-BEAN CHILI

PREP: 20 MINUTES
COOK: 30 MINUTES

If you have any of this chili left over, you can serve it on top of cornbread, low-fat tortilla chips, baked potatoes, or taco salad. Or use it to fill a burrito or taco.

1 cup diced onion
1 cup diced green bell pepper
1 pound ground chuck
1½ cups no-salt-added beef broth
1 tablespoon chili powder
1½ teaspoons ground cumin
¾ teaspoon dried oregano
½ teaspoon salt
⅛ teaspoon black pepper
3 garlic cloves, crushed
2 (14.5-ounce) cans no-salt-added diced tomatoes, undrained
2 (15-ounce) cans black beans, drained
¼ cup fat-free sour cream
¼ cup chopped fresh cilantro

1. Place a Dutch oven over medium-high heat until hot. Add first 3 ingredients; cook until beef is browned, stirring to crumble. Drain well; return beef mixture to pan. Add broth and next 8 ingredients; bring to a boil. Reduce heat; simmer 15 minutes or until slightly thick, stirring occasionally.
2. Ladle chili into bowls, and top with sour cream and chopped cilantro. Yield: 4 servings (serving size: 2 cups chili, 1 tablespoon sour cream, and 1 tablespoon cilantro).

CALORIES 493 (32% from fat); FAT 17.3g (sat 6.4g, mono 7.1g, poly 1.2g); PROTEIN 36.1g; CARB 49.5g; FIBER 9.1g; CHOL 66mg; IRON 7mg; SODIUM 762mg; CALC 165mg

CHIPOTLE-BLACK BEAN CHILI

PREP: 6 MINUTES   COOK: 26 MINUTES

    1 teaspoon olive oil
    1 cup finely chopped onion
    6 garlic cloves, minced
    2 tablespoons chili powder
    1 teaspoon minced drained canned
       chipotle chile in adobo sauce
  ¼ teaspoon black pepper
  ⅛ teaspoon salt
    2 (15-ounce) cans black beans,
       drained
    2 (14.5-ounce) cans no-salt-added
       whole tomatoes, undrained
       and chopped
    1 (4.5-ounce) can chopped green
       chiles, drained
Cilantro sprigs (optional)

1. Heat oil in a large saucepan over medium-high heat. Add onion and garlic; sauté 3 minutes or until tender. Add chili powder and next 6 ingredients; bring to a boil. Reduce heat; cover and simmer 15 minutes, stirring occasionally. Ladle chili into individual bowls, and garnish with cilantro sprigs, if desired. Yield: 4 servings (serving size: 1½ cups).

CALORIES 285 (9% from fat); FAT 3g (sat 0.5g, mono 1g, poly 0.8g); PROTEIN 16.4g; CARB 53.2g; FIBER 10.2g; CHOL 0mg; IRON 5mg; SODIUM 634mg; CALC 139mg

Chipotle-Black Bean Chili

WHITE CHILI

PREP: 18 MINUTES   COOK: 37 MINUTES

    1 tablespoon vegetable oil
Cooking spray
    1 pound skinned, boned chicken
       breast, chopped
  ½ cup chopped shallots
    3 garlic cloves, minced
  ½ teaspoon dried oregano
  ½ teaspoon coriander seeds,
       crushed
  ¼ teaspoon ground cumin
    1 (14.5-ounce) can no-salt-added
       whole tomatoes, undrained
       and coarsely chopped
    1 (14.25-ounce) can fat-free,
       less-sodium chicken broth
    1 (11-ounce) can tomatillos,
       drained and coarsely chopped
    1 (4.5-ounce) can chopped green
       chiles, undrained
    2 (16-ounce) cans cannellini beans
       or other white beans, drained
    3 tablespoons lime juice
  ¼ teaspoon black pepper
    9 tablespoons (about 4 ounces)
       shredded reduced-fat sharp
       cheddar cheese

1. Heat oil in a large saucepan coated with cooking spray over medium-high heat until hot. Add chicken; sauté 3 minutes or until done. Remove chicken from pan.

2. Add shallots and garlic to pan; sauté 2 minutes or until tender. Stir in oregano and next 6 ingredients. Bring to a boil; reduce heat, and simmer 20 minutes. Add chicken and beans; cook 5 minutes or until thoroughly heated. Stir in lime juice and pepper. Ladle into bowls; top with cheese. Yield: 9 servings (serving size: 1 cup chili and 1 tablespoon cheese).

CALORIES 247 (23% from fat); FAT 6.2g (sat 2g, mono 1.7g, poly 1.7g); PROTEIN 23.3g; CARB 25.4g; FIBER 3.1g; CHOL 38mg; IRON 2.6mg; SODIUM 593mg; CALC 171mg

stews

These hearty stews are thick enough to be served in a pasta plate. To dress up the plate, sprinkle chopped fresh herbs around the rim.

KENTUCKY BURGOO

PREP: 25 MINUTES
COOK: 2 HOURS 20 MINUTES

Burgoo is a thick stew full of meats and vegetables. Early renditions were more often made with small game such as rabbit and squirrel.

- 1 pound lean boneless chuck steak
- 1½ teaspoons vegetable oil
- 8 cups low-salt beef broth
- 1½ pounds skinned, boned chicken thighs
- 4 cups cubed peeled baking potato (about 1½ pounds)
- 2½ cups chopped carrot
- 1 cup chopped celery
- 1 cup chopped onion
- 1½ teaspoons curry powder
- 1 teaspoon dried thyme
- 1 teaspoon salt
- 1 (14.5-ounce) can whole tomatoes, undrained and coarsely chopped
- 1 garlic clove, minced
- 2 cups frozen whole-kernel corn, thawed
- 1 (10-ounce) package frozen lima beans, thawed

1. Trim fat from steak; cut steak into 1-inch cubes. Heat oil in a large Dutch oven; add steak, and cook until browned on all sides. Add broth; bring to a boil. Cover, reduce heat, and simmer 1 hour.
2. Trim fat from chicken thighs; cut chicken into 1-inch cubes. Add chicken and next 9 ingredients to pan; simmer, uncovered, 1 hour or until vegetables are tender.
3. Add corn and lima beans to pan; cook until beans are tender (about 15 minutes). Yield: 10 servings (serving size: 1½ cups).

CALORIES 247 (13% from fat); FAT 3.5g (sat 0.8g, mono 1g, poly 1.1g); PROTEIN 18g; CARB 34.8g; FIBER 4.5g; CHOL 51mg; IRON 2.8mg; SODIUM 518mg; CALC 60mg

CASSOULET

PREP: 33 MINUTES   COOK: 15 MINUTES

- ¼ pound lean boneless pork loin
- Cooking spray
- 1 cup thinly sliced carrot
- ½ cup thinly sliced leek
- ½ cup chopped onion
- 2 turkey-bacon slices, chopped
- 2 garlic cloves, minced
- 1 (15-ounce) can navy beans, drained
- ½ cup dry red wine
- ⅛ teaspoon black pepper
- 1 bay leaf
- 1 (14.5-ounce) can no-salt-added whole tomatoes, undrained and chopped
- 1 teaspoon chopped fresh thyme
- ¼ cup fresh breadcrumbs
- 2 tablespoons chopped fresh parsley
- 1 garlic clove, minced

1. Preheat oven to 350°.
2. Trim fat from pork; cut pork into ½-inch cubes.
3. Coat a large nonstick skillet with cooking spray; place over medium heat until hot. Add pork, and cook until browned on all sides. Add carrot, leek, onion, bacon, and 2 garlic cloves; sauté 5 minutes or until carrot is tender. Add beans, wine, pepper, bay leaf, and tomato; stir well. Bring to a boil over medium-high heat, and cook, uncovered, 8 to 10 minutes or until mixture thickens and liquid evaporates, stirring occasionally. Discard bay leaf; add thyme.
4. Combine breadcrumbs, parsley, and 1 garlic clove in a bowl. Divide pork mixture between 2 (2-cup) individual casserole dishes or a 1-quart shallow casserole coated with cooking spray; top with breadcrumb mixture. Bake, uncovered, at 350° for 15 minutes or until crumbs are browned. Yield: 2 servings (serving size: 1½ cups).

CALORIES 495 (19% from fat); FAT 10.5g (sat 2.9g, mono 4.4g, poly 2.2g); PROTEIN 33.9g; CARB 69g; FIBER 11.5g; CHOL 59mg; IRON 7mg; SODIUM 840mg; CALC 243mg

GRILLED SEAFOOD CIOPPINO

PREP: 20 MINUTES   COOK: 34 MINUTES
(pictured on page 457)

- 4 teaspoons olive oil, divided
- 1 (8-ounce) sourdough baguette, cut crosswise into 12 slices
- 1½ cups chopped onion
- 3 garlic cloves, minced
- ½ cup dry white wine
- 1 teaspoon dried basil
- 1 teaspoon dried thyme
- ½ teaspoon hot sauce
- ¼ teaspoon salt
- ¼ teaspoon saffron threads
- 2 (14.5-ounce) cans stewed tomatoes, undrained
- 1 (16-ounce) can fat-free, less-sodium chicken broth
- 12 small mussels, scrubbed and debearded
- ¾ pound medium shrimp, peeled
- ¾ pound skinned sea bass, halibut, or snapper fillet, cut into 1-inch pieces
- Cooking spray

1. Brush 2 teaspoons oil over 1 side of bread slices; set aside.

(continued on page 482)

2. Heat 2 teaspoons oil in a large saucepan over medium-high heat. Add onion and garlic; sauté 5 minutes or until tender. Add wine and next 7 ingredients; bring to a boil. Reduce heat, and simmer, uncovered, 20 minutes, stirring occasionally. Add mussels; cover and simmer 2 minutes or until shells open (discard any unopened shells). Remove from heat; keep warm.

3. Prepare grill.

4. Thread shrimp and fish alternately onto each of 6 (9-inch) skewers. Place kebabs and bread slices on grill rack coated with cooking spray; grill 5 to 6 minutes or until seafood is done and bread is toasted, turning both occasionally.

5. Ladle soup into 6 bowls; top with grilled seafood, and serve with toasted bread. Yield: 6 servings (serving size: 1 cup soup, 2 mussels, 3 ounces shrimp and fish, and 2 bread slices).

CALORIES 285 (19% from fat); FAT 6g (sat 0.9g, mono 3g, poly 1g); PROTEIN 24.4g; CARB 32.3g; FIBER 2g; CHOL 80mg; IRON 4mg; SODIUM 915mg; CALC 142mg

Bouillabaisse

BOUILLABAISSE

PREP: 22 MINUTES   COOK: 30 MINUTES

¼ cup fat-free mayonnaise
2 teaspoons tomato paste
⅛ teaspoon ground red pepper
1 small garlic clove, crushed
1 tablespoon olive oil
3 cups thinly sliced fennel bulb (about 1 large bulb)
1 cup chopped onion
1 tablespoon fresh or 1 teaspoon dried thyme
2 garlic cloves, crushed
1½ cups water
¼ teaspoon salt
¼ teaspoon saffron threads (optional)
¼ teaspoon black pepper
¾ pound small red potatoes, quartered
2 (8-ounce) bottles clam juice
1 (10¾-ounce) can tomato puree
1 pound skinned halibut fillets, cut into 2-inch pieces
½ pound bay scallops
½ pound large shrimp, peeled and deveined
Minced fresh parsley (optional)
7 (½-inch-thick) slices French bread, toasted

1. Combine first 4 ingredients in a bowl; cover and chill.

2. Heat oil in a large Dutch oven over medium-high heat. Add fennel, onion, thyme, and 2 garlic cloves; sauté until tender.

3. Add water, salt, saffron, if desired, and next 4 ingredients to fennel mixture; bring to a boil. Cook 15 minutes or until potato is tender. Add halibut, scallops, and shrimp; cover, reduce heat, and simmer 5 minutes or until seafood is done.

4. Ladle soup into individual bowls; garnish with minced parsley, if desired. Serve with toasted French bread topped with mayonnaise mixture. Yield: 7 servings (serving size: 1½ cups soup, 1 toast slice, and about 1 tablespoon mayonnaise mixture).

CALORIES 275 (16% from fat); FAT 4.9g (sat 0.7g, mono 2.1g, poly 1.1g); PROTEIN 29.2g; CARB 29g; FIBER 3.2g; CHOL 80mg; IRON 4.5mg; SODIUM 752mg; CALC 158mg

PORK GOULASH

PREP: 28 MINUTES
COOK: 2½ HOURS

Cooking spray
 1 (3-pound) lean, boned pork
    loin roast, cut into 1-inch
    pieces
 2 bacon slices, chopped
 1 cup diced onion
 ½ cup (½-inch-thick) sliced
    carrot
 ½ cup (½-inch-thick) sliced
    parsnip
 1 cup tomato juice
 1 cup beef broth
 1 tablespoon brown sugar
 2 teaspoons paprika
 1 teaspoon salt
 1 teaspoon dried marjoram
 ½ teaspoon black pepper
 1 (12-ounce) can light beer
 6 cups coarsely chopped Savoy
    cabbage
 3 cups cubed peeled baking
    potato

1. Place a Dutch oven coated with cooking spray over medium-high heat until hot. Add pork; cook 5 minutes, browning on all sides. Drain.

2. Cook bacon in pan over medium heat until crisp. Add onion, carrot, and parsnip to pan; sauté 10 minutes or until tender.

3. Return pork to pan; add tomato juice and next 7 ingredients. Bring to a boil; cover, reduce heat, and simmer 1½ hours or until meat is tender, stirring occasionally. Add chopped cabbage and potato; cover and simmer 30 minutes or until potato is tender, stirring occasionally. Yield: 8 servings (serving size: 1¼ cups).

CALORIES 387 (38% from fat); FAT 16.2g (sat 5.6g, mono 7.2g, poly 1.8g); PROTEIN 38.2g; CARB 21.4g; FIBER 2.3g; CHOL 101mg; IRON 2.7mg; SODIUM 733mg; CALC 51mg

CURRIED LAMB-AND-LENTIL STEW

PREP: 30 MINUTES
COOK: 1 HOUR 15 MINUTES

1½ pounds lean boned leg of lamb
 1 tablespoon olive oil
 ½ cup diced carrot
 ½ cup chopped onion
 ½ cup chopped celery
 2 garlic cloves, minced
 1 tablespoon curry powder
 1 teaspoon ground cumin
 ⅛ teaspoon ground red pepper
 3 cups low-sodium chicken broth
 ¾ cup lentils
3½ cups chopped collard greens or
    spinach (about ¼ pound)
 1 (28-ounce) can crushed
    tomatoes, undrained
 2 tablespoons chopped fresh
    cilantro

1. Trim fat from lamb; cut lamb into 1-inch cubes.

2. Heat oil in a Dutch oven over medium heat until hot. Add lamb; sauté 5 minutes or until browned. Add carrot, onion, celery, and garlic; sauté 5 minutes. Stir in curry, cumin, and ground red pepper.

3. Add broth and lentils; bring to a boil. Cover, reduce heat, and simmer 40 minutes, stirring occasionally. Add greens; cover and simmer 10 minutes or until lamb is tender. Add tomatoes, and simmer 10 minutes. Remove from heat; stir in chopped cilantro. Ladle stew into individual bowls. Yield: 6 servings (serving size: 1½ cups).

CALORIES 274 (25% from fat); FAT 7.7g (sat 1.9g, mono 3.7g, poly 0.9g); PROTEIN 27.8g; CARB 24.8g; FIBER 5.2g; CHOL 54mg; IRON 6.1mg; SODIUM 297mg; CALC 98mg

Curried Lamb-and-Lentil Stew

CAJUN GUMBO

PREP: 30 MINUTES   COOK: 40 MINUTES

Filé, which is made from dried sassafras leaves, is used to thicken and flavor gumbo.

    2 tablespoons all-purpose flour
    1 tablespoon vegetable oil
    1 cup chopped onion
    1 cup chopped celery
    1 cup chopped green bell pepper
    4 garlic cloves, minced
    ¼ cup water
    ¾ teaspoon hot pepper sauce
    1 (14.5-ounce) can no-salt-added
       stewed tomatoes, undrained
    1 (10½-ounce) can low-sodium
       chicken broth
    2 bay leaves
    ½ pound turkey kielbasa, cut into
       ¼-inch-thick slices
    ½ pound medium shrimp, peeled
       and deveined
    1 (10-ounce) package frozen cut
       okra, thawed
    1 tablespoon filé
    3 cups hot cooked rice

1. Place flour in a saucepan. Cook over medium-high heat 7 minutes or until very brown; stir constantly with a whisk. (If flour browns too fast, remove from heat; stir constantly until it cools down.) Place browned flour in a small bowl.
2. Heat oil in pan over medium-high heat. Add onion, celery, bell pepper, and garlic; sauté 8 minutes or until tender. Sprinkle vegetables with browned flour; cook 1 minute, stirring constantly. Stir in water, pepper sauce, tomatoes, broth, and bay leaves. Bring to a boil; reduce heat, and simmer, uncovered, 10 minutes. Add sausage; simmer, uncovered, 5 minutes. Add shrimp and okra; cover and simmer 5 minutes or until shrimp are done. Discard bay leaves. Stir in filé.

Serve over rice. Yield: 6 servings (serving size: 1 cup gumbo and ½ cup rice).

CALORIES 301 (23% from fat); FAT 7.8g (sat 1.8g, mono 2.4g, poly 2.4g); PROTEIN 17.5g; CARB 40.9g; FIBER 2.2g; CHOL 70mg; IRON 3.3mg; SODIUM 445mg; CALC 111mg

HARVEST-VEGETABLE RAGOÛT

PREP: 44 MINUTES   COOK: 52 MINUTES

    5 teaspoons olive oil, divided
    3 cups diced peeled butternut
       squash
    2 cups (½-inch-thick) sliced leek
  1½ cups (½-inch-thick) sliced carrot
  1½ cups (½-inch-thick) sliced parsnip
    1 cup (½-inch-thick) sliced celery
   10 garlic cloves, halved
    2 bay leaves
    2 thyme sprigs
    1 tablespoon tomato paste
    1 tablespoon all-purpose flour
    1 cup dry red wine
    1 cup vegetable broth
    1 (19-ounce) can chickpeas
       (garbanzo beans), drained
    ¾ teaspoon salt, divided
    ½ teaspoon black pepper
    ¼ cup chopped fresh parsley
    6 portobello mushrooms

1. Heat 1 tablespoon oil in a Dutch oven over medium-high heat. Add squash and next 5 ingredients; sauté 8 minutes or until lightly browned. Add bay leaves and thyme sprigs; stir in tomato paste. Stir in flour and wine; reduce heat to medium-low; cook 5 minutes. Stir in broth and chickpeas. Cover; simmer 20 minutes or until vegetables are tender. Stir in ½ teaspoon salt, pepper, and parsley. Discard bay leaves and thyme sprigs.
2. Discard mushroom stems; slice caps. Heat 2 teaspoons oil in a large nonstick skillet over medium-high heat. Add sliced mushrooms; cook 5 minutes, stirring constantly. Sprinkle with ¼ teaspoon salt. Ladle ragoût over mushrooms in individual soup bowls. Yield: 6 servings (serving size: 1 cup ragoût and ½ cup mushrooms).

CALORIES 265 (21% from fat); FAT 6.1g (sat 0.8g, mono 3.3g, poly 1.4g); PROTEIN 9.6g; CARB 47.8g; FIBER 7g; CHOL 0mg; IRON 4.9mg; SODIUM 628mg; CALC 135mg

SPICY FISH STEW

PREP: 20 MINUTES   COOK: 36 MINUTES

  1½ tablespoons olive oil
    2 cups chopped onion
    ¾ cup chopped green bell pepper
    ½ teaspoon crushed red pepper
    3 garlic cloves, minced
    4 cups halved red potato (about
       1¼ pounds)
  1½ cups chopped seeded peeled
       tomato
  1½ cups clam juice
    1 cup dry white wine
    1 tablespoon tomato paste
    ½ teaspoon salt
    ¼ teaspoon black pepper
    1 bay leaf
  1½ pounds cod or other lean white
       fish fillets, cut into 3 x 1-inch
       pieces
    2 tablespoons dry sherry
    2 tablespoons minced fresh parsley

1. Heat oil in a Dutch oven over medium-high heat. Add onion, bell pepper, crushed red pepper, and garlic; sauté 5 minutes. Add potato and next 7 ingredients; bring to a boil. Reduce heat; simmer, uncovered, 20 minutes. Stir in cod and sherry; cook 5 minutes or until fish flakes easily when tested with a fork. Discard bay leaf. Stir in parsley. Yield: 8 servings (serving size: 1 cup).

CALORIES 171 (18% from fat); FAT 3.4g (sat 0.5g, mono 2g, poly 0.5g); PROTEIN 17.8g; CARB 17.5g; FIBER 2.4g; CHOL 38mg; IRON 2mg; SODIUM 302mg; CALC 43mg

vegetable side dishes

Fried Tomatoes With
Lima-Corn Relish (page 506)

VEGETABLE SIDE DISHES

ARTICHOKES WITH ROASTED-GARLIC AÏOLI

PREP: 17 MINUTES   COOK: 45 MINUTES

    3   whole garlic heads
    4   large artichokes
    2   tablespoons lemon juice
    ⅓   cup light mayonnaise
    ⅓   cup plain fat-free yogurt
    ¼   teaspoon black pepper
    ⅛   teaspoon salt

1. Preheat oven to 400°.
2. Remove white papery skin from garlic (do not peel or separate cloves). Wrap each head separately in aluminum foil. Bake at 400° for 45 minutes or until tender; cool.
3. While garlic bakes, cut off stems of artichokes; remove bottom leaves. Trim about ½ inch from tops of artichokes; trim leaves, if desired. Place artichokes, stem ends down, in a large Dutch oven filled two-thirds with water. Add lemon juice; bring to a boil. Cover, reduce heat, and simmer 40 minutes or until a leaf near the center of each artichoke pulls out easily.
4. Separate garlic cloves, and squeeze pulp into a small bowl; discard skins. Mash pulp with a fork. Stir in mayonnaise, yogurt, pepper, and salt. Serve as a dipping sauce with artichokes. Yield: 4 servings (serving size: 1 artichoke and 3 tablespoons aïoli).

CALORIES 201 (30% from fat); FAT 6.6g (sat 1.1g, mono 1.9g, poly 3.6g); PROTEIN 7.3g; CARB 32.5g; FIBER 6.7g; CHOL 8mg; IRON 2.8mg; SODIUM 304mg; CALC 181mg

ASPARAGUS-DILL SOUFFLÉ

PREP: 15 MINUTES   COOK: 55 MINUTES

    Cooking spray
    ¾   pound asparagus

SELECTING ASPARAGUS

When shopping for asparagus, choose firm, pencil-thin spears that are uniform in size with tightly closed bright-green and lavender-tinted tips. (Yellowed or khaki-tinged spears with soggy tips are a sign that the stalks are old, bitter, or stringy.) Uniformity in size and shape is important for even cooking.

    3   tablespoons all-purpose flour
    1½ cups 2% reduced-fat milk
    1   (4-ounce) carton egg substitute
    ¾   cup (3 ounces) grated Gruyère
        cheese
    1   cup mashed potatoes, cooked
        without salt or fat
    2   teaspoons chopped fresh dill
    ¼   teaspoon salt
    ¼ to ½ teaspoon ground red pepper
    5   large egg whites
    ½   teaspoon cream of tartar

1. Cut a piece of foil long enough to fit around a 1½-quart soufflé dish, allowing a 1-inch overlap; fold foil lengthwise

into thirds. Lightly coat one side of foil and bottom of dish with cooking spray. Wrap foil around outside of dish, coated side against dish, allowing it to extend 4 inches above rim to form a collar; secure with string or masking tape.
2. Snap off tough ends of asparagus. Steam asparagus, covered, 3 minutes or until crisp-tender; drain. Cut asparagus spears into thin slices to equal ½ cup; set aside. Cut remaining asparagus spears in half; set aside.
3. Place flour in a medium saucepan. Gradually add milk, stirring well with a whisk. Bring to a boil over medium heat, and cook until thickened (about 3 minutes), stirring constantly.
4. Place egg substitute in a bowl. Gradually add hot milk mixture to egg substitute, stirring constantly with a whisk. Add cheese, stirring until cheese melts.
5. Preheat oven to 400°.
6. Place milk mixture, halved asparagus spears, mashed potatoes, dill, salt, and red pepper in a blender; process until smooth. Return mixture to bowl; stir in sliced asparagus.
7. Beat egg whites and cream of tartar at high speed of a mixer until stiff peaks form. Gently stir one-fourth of egg white mixture into milk mixture. Gently fold in remaining egg white mixture.
8. Pour mixture into prepared soufflé dish. Bake at 400° for 10 minutes. Reduce oven temperature to 350° (do not remove soufflé from oven); bake an additional 45 minutes or until puffy and golden. Carefully remove foil collar; serve immediately. Yield: 6 servings.
Note: A high-quality Swiss cheese can be substituted for Gruyère.

CALORIES 178 (37% from fat); FAT 7.4g (sat 4.3g, mono 2.2g, poly 0.4g); PROTEIN 13.3g; CARB 14.9g; FIBER 1.2g; CHOL 25mg; IRON 1.1mg; SODIUM 257mg; CALC 253mg

Green Beans Amandine

PREP: 10 MINUTES   COOK: 26 MINUTES

- 2 tablespoons butter or stick margarine
- 3 pounds green beans, trimmed
- 3 cups fat-free, less-sodium chicken broth
- ¾ teaspoon freshly ground black pepper
- ½ teaspoon salt
- 2 tablespoons cornstarch
- ¼ cup water
- 2 tablespoons lemon juice
- ¼ cup sliced almonds, toasted

1. Melt butter in a large skillet over medium-high heat. Add beans; sauté 5 minutes. Add broth, pepper, and salt; bring to a boil. Cover, reduce heat, and simmer 15 minutes.

2. Combine cornstarch and water; add to skillet. Bring to a boil, and cook 1 minute, stirring constantly. Stir in lemon juice. Sprinkle with almonds just before serving. Yield: 8 servings (serving size: 1 cup).

CALORIES 137 (51% from fat); FAT 7.8g (sat 3.8g, mono 2.8g, poly 0.7g); PROTEIN 3.9g; CARB 15.3g; FIBER 3.9g; CHOL 16mg; IRON 1.8mg; SODIUM 448mg; CALC 73mg

Green Beans With Bacon-Balsamic Vinaigrette

SHALLOTS

Shallots are small onions which have a cross in flavor between an onion and garlic. Their shape is similar to garlic as they have a head made up of several cloves. Their mild, delicate flavor can be enjoyed raw by chopping for salads, or sautéed and added to vegetables and sauces. Avoid overcooking to prevent a bitter flavor. You can substitute small white onions, although you may miss the unique flavor of the shallot.

Green Beans With Bacon-Balsamic Vinaigrette

PREP: 4 MINUTES   COOK: 10 MINUTES

- 2 pounds green beans, trimmed
- 2 bacon slices
- ¼ cup minced shallots
- 3 tablespoons coarsely chopped almonds
- ¼ cup white balsamic vinegar
- 2 tablespoons brown sugar

1. Cook beans in boiling water 8 minutes or just until crisp-tender. Drain and rinse with cold water. Drain well; set aside.

2. Cook bacon in a small skillet over medium-high heat until crisp. Remove bacon from pan, and crumble. Add shallots to bacon drippings in pan; sauté 1 minute. Add almonds; sauté 1 minute. Remove pan from heat, and cool. Add vinegar and sugar to pan, and stir until sugar dissolves. Add crumbled bacon.

3. Pour vinaigrette over beans, tossing gently to coat. Yield: 8 servings (serving size: ¾ cup).

CALORIES 88 (47% from fat); FAT 4.6g (sat 1.3g, mono 2.3g, poly 0.7g); PROTEIN 2.9g; CARB 10.7g; FIBER 2.5g; CHOL 4mg; IRON 1.3mg; SODIUM 44mg; CALC 49mg

New England Baked Beans

PREP: 15 MINUTES   STAND: 1 HOUR
COOK: 3 HOURS

America's most famous bean dish was invented by the Puritan women of Boston. In addition to molasses and brown sugar, this version gets its sweet tang from barbecue sauce. Rather than salt pork, turkey bacon is used to keep fat to a minimum.

- 3 cups dried Great Northern beans
- 8 cups water
- 1¼ cups chopped onion
- 1 cup barbecue sauce
- ¾ cup packed brown sugar
- ¼ cup molasses
- 1 tablespoon prepared mustard
- ½ teaspoon salt
- ¼ teaspoon black pepper
- ⅛ teaspoon garlic powder
- 4 slices turkey bacon, cut crosswise into ¼-inch strips

1. Sort and wash beans; place in a large ovenproof Dutch oven. Cover with water to 2 inches above beans; bring to a boil, and cook 2 minutes. Remove from heat; cover and let stand 1 hour.
2. Drain beans, and return to pan. Add 8 cups water and onion, and bring to a boil. Cover, reduce heat, and simmer 2 hours or until beans are tender.
3. Preheat oven to 350°.
4. Drain bean mixture, and return to pan. Stir in 1 cup barbecue sauce and remaining ingredients. Cover and bake at 350° for 1 hour. Yield: 16 servings (serving size: ½ cup).

CALORIES 203 (7% from fat); FAT 1.6g (sat 0.4g, mono 0.6g, poly 0.5g); PROTEIN 9.1g; CARB 38.8g; FIBER 7.5g; CHOL 4mg; IRON 2.6mg; SODIUM 313mg; CALC 88mg

Harvard Beets

Harvard Beets

PREP: 11 MINUTES
COOK: 47 MINUTES

- 2½ pounds beets
- ⅔ cup fresh orange juice
- 2 tablespoons cider vinegar
- 2 teaspoons stick margarine or butter
- ¼ cup packed brown sugar
- 1 tablespoon cornstarch
- ¼ teaspoon salt
- ⅛ teaspoon black pepper
- Orange zest (optional)

1. Leave root and 1 inch of stem on beets; scrub with a brush. Place beets in a Dutch oven; cover with water, and bring to a boil. Cover, reduce heat, and simmer 40 minutes or until tender. Drain; peel and cut into ¼-inch-thick slices.
2. Combine juice, vinegar, and margarine in a bowl. Combine sugar, cornstarch, salt, and pepper in a large saucepan. Gradually add juice mixture, stirring well with a whisk. Bring to a boil over medium heat; cook until thick (about 2 minutes), stirring constantly. Add beets, tossing gently to coat. Garnish with orange zest, if desired. Yield: 6 servings (serving size: ¾ cup).

CALORIES 114 (8% from fat); FAT 1g (sat 0.2g, mono 0.4g, poly 0.4g); PROTEIN 2.2g; CARB 25.5g; FIBER 1.1g; CHOL 0mg; IRON 1.3mg; SODIUM 213mg; CALC 31mg

BROCCOLI WITH DIJON VINAIGRETTE

PREP: 15 MINUTES   COOK: 10 MINUTES

2 pounds broccoli spears
4 teaspoons olive oil
¼ cup finely chopped green onions
½ teaspoon dried tarragon
½ teaspoon dry mustard
3 garlic cloves, minced
2 tablespoons red wine vinegar
2 tablespoons water
1 tablespoon Dijon mustard
¼ teaspoon black pepper
⅛ teaspoon salt

1. Steam broccoli, covered, 6 minutes or until crisp-tender. Drain; place in a serving bowl.
2. Heat oil in a small saucepan over medium heat. Add green onions, tarragon, mustard, and garlic; sauté 3 minutes.
3. Remove pan from heat, and add vinegar and remaining 4 ingredients, stirring with a whisk. Drizzle over broccoli, tossing gently to coat. Yield: 8 servings.

CALORIES 55 (45% from fat); FAT 2.8g (sat 0.4g, mono 1.7g, poly 0.4g); PROTEIN 3.2g; CARB 6.3g; FIBER 3.3g; CHOL 0mg; IRON 1mg; SODIUM 120mg; CALC 55mg

BRUSSELS SPROUTS WITH THYME

PREP: 10 MINUTES   COOK: 14 MINUTES

1 teaspoon olive oil
4 cups trimmed Brussels sprouts
2 teaspoons minced fresh or
    ½ teaspoon dried thyme
¾ cup water
¼ teaspoon salt
⅛ teaspoon black pepper
¼ cup chopped fresh flat-leaf parsley

1. Heat oil in a large nonstick skillet over medium heat. Add sprouts and thyme; sauté 5 minutes. Add water, salt,

and pepper; cover and cook 9 minutes or until tender. Remove from heat; stir in parsley. Yield: 8 servings (serving size: ½ cup).

CALORIES 37 (19% from fat); FAT 0.8g (sat 0.1g, mono 0.4g, poly 0.2g); PROTEIN 2.5g; CARB 6.6g; FIBER 3.2g; CHOL 0mg; IRON 1.1mg; SODIUM 92mg; CALC 32mg

SWEET-AND-SOUR BAKED CABBAGE

PREP: 6 MINUTES   COOK: 30 MINUTES

You can use Napa cabbage in place of Savoy, if desired.

7 cups coarsely chopped Savoy cabbage (about ¾ pound)
2 cups coarsely chopped onion
1 tablespoon olive oil
¼ teaspoon salt
⅛ teaspoon black pepper
1 large garlic clove, thinly sliced
3 tablespoons cider vinegar
1 tablespoon honey

1. Preheat oven to 400°.
2. Combine first 6 ingredients in a 13 x 9-inch baking dish; toss to coat. Cover and bake at 400° for 30 minutes or until tender, stirring after 15 minutes. Drizzle vinegar and honey over cabbage mixture; toss well. Yield: 4 servings (serving size: 1 cup).

CALORIES 102 (32% from fat); FAT 3.6g (sat 0.5g, mono 2.5g, poly 0.4g); PROTEIN 2.9g; CARB 17.2g; FIBER 2.1g; CHOL 0mg; IRON 0.7mg; SODIUM 178mg; CALC 52mg

GLAZED JULIENNE CARROTS

PREP: 15 MINUTES   COOK: 15 MINUTES

1 tablespoon stick margarine or butter
¼ cup packed brown sugar
4 cups (2-inch) julienne-cut carrot
¼ teaspoon salt

¼ teaspoon black pepper
1 tablespoon water
¼ cup chopped fresh parsley

1. Melt margarine in a large nonstick skillet over medium-high heat; add sugar, and cook until sugar is melted and bubbly, stirring constantly.
2. Reduce heat to medium; add carrot, salt, pepper, and water. (Sugar will harden slightly, but will dissolve upon heating.) Cook 10 to 11 minutes or until carrot is crisp-tender, stirring occasionally. Remove from heat. Stir in parsley. Yield: 4 servings (serving size: ½ cup).

CALORIES 125 (27% from fat); FAT 3.8g (sat 0.6g, mono 1.5g, poly 1.6g); PROTEIN 1.1g; CARB 23.6g; FIBER 3.3g; CHOL 0mg; IRON 0.9mg; SODIUM 243mg; CALC 42mg

LEMON-DILL CARROTS

PREP: 10 MINUTES   COOK: 12 MINUTES

1 teaspoon olive oil
3 cups diagonally sliced carrot
¼ cup fat-free, less-sodium chicken broth
1 teaspoon grated lemon rind
1 tablespoon fresh lemon juice
½ teaspoon celery salt
¼ teaspoon black pepper
1 tablespoon minced fresh or
    1 teaspoon dried dill

1. Heat oil in a large nonstick skillet over medium-high heat. Add carrot; sauté 2 minutes. Stir in broth, lemon rind, lemon juice, celery salt, and pepper. Cover; reduce heat to medium-low, and cook 10 minutes or until tender, stirring occasionally. Remove from heat; stir in dill. Yield: 4 servings (serving size: ¾ cup).

CALORIES 52 (23% from fat); FAT 1.3g (sat 0.2g, mono 0.9g, poly 0.2g); PROTEIN 1g; CARB 9.9g; FIBER 3g; CHOL 0mg; IRON 0.6mg; SODIUM 335mg; CALC 33mg

CARROT-PARSNIP TOSS

PREP: 20 MINUTES   COOK: 7 MINUTES

A fair-skinned cousin of the carrot, parsnips are a creamy-white root with a pleasantly sweet and nutty flavor. When selecting them, avoid those that are limp, shriveled, or spotted.

1   tablespoon stick margarine or butter
1   tablespoon chopped fresh parsley
½   teaspoon dry mustard
½   teaspoon dried tarragon
¼   teaspoon salt
⅛   teaspoon black pepper
3   cups (2-inch) julienne-cut parsnip
2   cups (2-inch) julienne-cut carrot
¼   cup water

1. Place margarine in a 1-cup glass measure. Microwave at HIGH 15 seconds or until margarine melts. Stir in parsley, mustard, tarragon, salt, and pepper.
2. Combine parsnip, carrot, and ¼ cup water in a 2½-quart casserole; cover with lid. Microwave at HIGH 7 to 8 minutes or until vegetables are tender, stirring after 4 minutes. Let stand, covered, 2 minutes. Drain. Stir in margarine mixture. Yield: 4 servings (serving size: 1 cup).

CALORIES 103 (28% from fat); FAT 3.2g (sat 0.6g, mono 1.4g, poly 1g); PROTEIN 1.5g; CARB 18.3g; FIBER 3.1g; CHOL 0mg; IRON 0.8mg; SODIUM 205mg; CALC 44mg

CREAMY CAULIFLOWER-PEA MEDLEY

PREP: 5 MINUTES
COOK: 7 MINUTES

½   cup water
1   (10-ounce) package frozen cauliflower
1   (10-ounce) package frozen tiny green peas
1   cup peeled, diced cucumber
3   tablespoons light ranch dressing
2   tablespoons fat-free sour cream
¼   teaspoon dried dill

1. Combine first 3 ingredients in a saucepan; bring to a boil. Cover and cook 5 minutes; drain well. Combine cauliflower mixture and remaining ingredients in a bowl; toss well. Serve warm or chilled. Yield: 4 servings (serving size: 1 cup).

CALORIES 112 (25% from fat); FAT 3.1g (sat 0.3g, mono 0.8g, poly 1.9g); PROTEIN 5.8g; CARB 15.8g; FIBER 5.1g; CHOL 4mg; IRON 1.5mg; SODIUM 219mg; CALC 47mg

COLLARD GREENS WITH SMOKED PORK

PREP: 11 MINUTES   COOK: 1 HOUR 5 MINUTES

Pickapeppa sauce is a commercial hot sauce that can be found with the condiments at your grocery store.

3   pounds collard greens
4   cups water
1   cup chopped onion
¼   teaspoon salt
¼   teaspoon black pepper
3   garlic cloves, chopped
2   (16-ounce) cans fat-free, less-sodium chicken broth
2   smoked ham hocks (about 1¼ pounds)
Pickapeppa sauce (optional)

1. Remove stems from greens. Wash and pat dry; coarsely chop to measure 10 cups.
2. Combine water and next 6 ingredients in an 8-quart Dutch oven; bring to a boil. Add greens; cover, reduce heat, and simmer 1 hour or until greens are tender, stirring occasionally. Remove from heat. Remove ham hocks from pan; cool.
3. Remove ham from bones. Finely chop ham, and add to greens mixture; stir well. Cook over medium heat until thoroughly heated. Serve with Pickapeppa sauce, if desired. Yield: 7 servings (serving size: 1 cup).

CALORIES 82 (14% from fat); FAT 1.3g (sat 0.3g, mono 0.3g, poly 0.4g); PROTEIN 6g; CARB 12.6g; FIBER 6.4g; CHOL 4mg; IRON 0.5mg; SODIUM 433mg; CALC 248mg

Collard Greens With Smoked Pork and Jalapeño Corn Bread (page 79)

CORN AND GREEN CHILE SOUFFLÉ

PREP:30 MINUTES   COOK:40 MINUTES

Cooking spray
2 tablespoons dry breadcrumbs
1¼ cups fresh corn kernels (about 2 large ears)
3 tablespoons minced fresh onion
4 teaspoons stick margarine or butter
1 large garlic clove, minced
⅓ cup all-purpose flour
½ teaspoon salt
1⅓ cups fat-free milk
½ teaspoon hot sauce
2 large eggs, separated
1 (4.5-ounce) can chopped green chiles, drained
1 large egg white
¼ teaspoon cream of tartar

1. Preheat oven to 400°.
2. Coat bottom and sides of a 1½-quart soufflé dish with cooking spray; sprinkle evenly with breadcrumbs.
3. Combine corn, onion, margarine, and garlic in a 2-quart glass measure. Microwave, uncovered, at HIGH 4 to 5 minutes or until tender, stirring every 2 minutes.
4. Combine flour and salt; stir flour mixture into corn mixture. Gradually add milk and hot sauce, stirring constantly with a whisk. Microwave, uncovered, at HIGH 5 to 7 minutes or until thick and bubbly, stirring with a whisk after 3 minutes, and then after every minute.
5. Lightly beat egg yolks in a bowl with a whisk. Gradually add one-fourth of hot milk mixture to egg yolks, stirring constantly with a whisk; add to remaining hot mixture, stirring with a whisk. Stir in green chiles. Return milk mixture to pan. Cook over medium heat until thick, stirring constantly.
6. Beat 3 egg whites and cream of tartar at high speed of a mixer until stiff peaks form. Gently fold one-fourth of egg white mixture into corn mixture; gently fold in remaining egg white mixture. Spoon mixture into prepared soufflé dish. Bake at 400° for 15 minutes. Reduce oven temperature to 350° (do not remove soufflé from oven), and bake 25 minutes or until set and golden. Serve immediately. Yield: 6 servings.

CALORIES 135 (33% from fat); FAT 5g (sat 1.2g, mono 1.9g, poly 1.3g); PROTEIN 6.7g; CARB 16.8g; FIBER 1.5g; CHOL 72mg; IRON 1mg; SODIUM 358mg; CALC 86mg

EASY CORN PUDDING

PREP:7 MINUTES
COOK:45 MINUTES

1 (8½-ounce) package corn muffin mix
¼ cup egg substitute
¼ cup reduced-calorie stick margarine, melted
1 (8¾-ounce) can no-salt-added whole-kernel corn, drained
¾ cup no-salt-added cream-style corn
1 (8-ounce) carton plain fat-free yogurt
Cooking spray

1. Preheat oven to 350°.
2. Place muffin mix in a medium bowl; make a well in center of mix.
3. Combine egg substitute, margarine, whole-kernel corn, cream-style corn, and yogurt; add to muffin mix, stirring just until moistened. Spoon into an 8-inch square baking dish coated with cooking spray.
4. Bake at 350° for 45 minutes or until set. Yield: 8 servings.

CALORIES 202 (29% from fat); FAT 6.6g (sat 0.8g, mono 2.1g, poly 2.6g); PROTEIN 5.5g; CARB 31g; FIBER 1g; CHOL 1mg; IRON 0.6mg; SODIUM 320mg; CALC 80mg

menu

Boston Beach Jerk Chicken (page 371)
Corn Custard With Chives
Green Bean-and-Yellow Tomato Salad (page 399)
Plum Pinwheel Tart (page 208)

CORN CUSTARD WITH CHIVES

PREP:7 MINUTES
COOK:1 HOUR 15 MINUTES

¾ cup evaporated fat-free milk
2 tablespoons freeze-dried chives
½ teaspoon salt
⅛ teaspoon black pepper
1 (16-ounce) package frozen whole-kernel corn, thawed
1 (14¾-ounce) can no-salt-added cream-style corn
2 large eggs, lightly beaten
2 large egg whites, lightly beaten
Cooking spray

1. Preheat oven to 325°.
2. Combine all ingredients except cooking spray in a bowl; spoon into an 8-inch square baking dish coated with cooking spray.
3. Place dish in a 13 x 9-inch baking dish; add hot water to larger dish to a depth of 1 inch.
4. Bake at 325° for 1 hour and 15 minutes or until a knife inserted in center comes out clean. Remove custard from water, and let stand 15 minutes. Yield: 6 servings (serving size: ¾ cup).

CALORIES 180 (14% from fat); FAT 2.8g (sat 0.7g, mono 0.9g, poly 0.7g); PROTEIN 9.6g; CARB 33.3g; FIBER 2.7g; CHOL 72mg; IRON 1.4mg; SODIUM 276mg; CALC 126mg

ROASTED SUCCOTASH

PREP: 16 MINUTES   COOK: 12 MINUTES

1½ cups fresh corn kernels (about 3 ears)
  1 cup chopped red bell pepper
  1 cup chopped yellow squash
  ½ cup chopped onion
1½ tablespoons olive oil
  2 garlic cloves, minced
  1 (10-ounce) package frozen baby lima beans, thawed
  ½ cup low-salt chicken broth
  2 tablespoons chopped fresh cilantro
  1 teaspoon ground cumin
  ½ teaspoon salt
  ⅛ teaspoon black pepper
  ⅛ teaspoon hot sauce

1. Place a large nonstick skillet over high heat until hot. Add first 4 ingredients; sauté 6 minutes or until vegetables are slightly blackened. Add oil, garlic, and lima beans; sauté over medium-high heat 1 minute. Stir in broth and remaining ingredients; simmer 5 minutes. Yield: 4 servings (serving size: 1 cup).

CALORIES 193 (28% from fat); FAT 6g (sat 0.8g, mono 4g, poly 0.8g); PROTEIN 7.7g; CARB 29.3g; FIBER 4g; CHOL 0mg; IRON 3.1mg; SODIUM 491mg; CALC 47mg

SOUTHERN SUCCOTASH

PREP: 15 MINUTES   COOK: 35 MINUTES

  1 bacon slice
  ½ cup chopped onion
  1 garlic clove, minced
  4 cups chopped tomato
2½ cups fresh corn kernels
  2 cups sliced okra
  ½ cup water
  ¼ teaspoon salt
  ¾ teaspoon hot pepper sauce
  ⅛ teaspoon black pepper

1. Cook bacon in a large saucepan over

Roasted Succotash

medium-high heat until crisp. Remove bacon from pan, and crumble. Add onion and garlic to bacon drippings in pan; sauté 5 minutes. Add tomato and remaining 6 ingredients, stirring well. Cover, reduce heat, and simmer 25 minutes or until vegetables are tender. Stir in crumbled bacon just before serving. Yield: 6 servings (serving size: 1 cup).
Note: We recommend using young, small pods of okra, which tend to be more tender than the larger pods.

CALORIES 107 (20% from fat); FAT 2.6g (sat 0.7g, mono 0.9g, poly 0.7g); PROTEIN 3.9g; CARB 20.7g; FIBER 3.8g; CHOL 2mg; IRON 1.1mg; SODIUM 140mg; CALC 37mg

LIMA-AND-WHITE BEAN SUCCOTASH

PREP: 10 MINUTES   COOK: 9 MINUTES

  1 (1-pound) fennel bulb with stalks
  2 teaspoons olive oil
  ½ cup sliced green onions
1½ cups cooked baby lima beans
1½ cups drained canned cannellini beans or other white beans
  ½ cup water
  1 tablespoon white wine vinegar
  ¼ teaspoon salt
  ⅛ teaspoon pepper

1. Trim tough outer leaves from fennel; mince feathery fronds to equal 2 tablespoons. Remove and discard stalks. Cut fennel bulb in half lengthwise, and discard core. Finely chop fennel bulb to equal 1 cup. Reserve remaining fennel for another use.

2. Heat oil in a medium saucepan over medium-high heat. Add chopped fennel and green onions; sauté 3 minutes or until tender. Add minced fennel fronds, lima beans, and remaining ingredients. Cover, reduce heat, and simmer 5 minutes or until thoroughly heated. Yield: 6 servings (serving size: ½ cup).

CALORIES 133 (14% from fat); FAT 2.1g (sat 0.2g, mono 1.1g, poly 0.3g); PROTEIN 7.8g; CARB 21.5g; FIBER 3.3g; CHOL 0mg; IRON 3.9mg; SODIUM 263mg; CALC 96mg

ROASTED RATATOUILLE

PREP: 14 MINUTES   COOK: 54 MINUTES

    1 (1-pound) eggplant, cut
           crosswise into ¾-inch slices
    2 teaspoons olive oil, divided
Cooking spray
    3 zucchini, cut crosswise into
           ¾-inch slices (about 1 pound)
1½ cups vertically sliced onion
1½ cups (1-inch-square) cut red bell
           pepper
1½ cups (1-inch-square) cut green
           bell pepper
    2 garlic cloves, crushed
    2 cups chopped seeded unpeeled
           tomato
    2 tablespoons chopped fresh parsley
    ½ teaspoon dried thyme
    ½ teaspoon salt
    ⅛ teaspoon black pepper

1. Preheat broiler.
2. Cut each eggplant slice into 4 wedges;
place in a bowl. Drizzle with 1 teaspoon
oil, and toss well. Arrange eggplant wedges
in a single layer on a baking sheet coated
with cooking spray. Broil 14 minutes or
until browned; place eggplant wedges in a
large bowl, and set aside.
3. Place zucchini in a bowl; drizzle with 1
teaspoon oil, and toss well. Arrange zucchini in a single layer on a baking sheet coated
with cooking spray. Broil 10 minutes or until browned; add to eggplant, and set aside.
4. Coat a large nonstick skillet with cooking spray; place over medium heat until
hot. Add onion, bell peppers, and garlic;
sauté 10 minutes or until tender. Add
tomato; sauté 5 minutes.
5. Stir in eggplant mixture, parsley, and remaining ingredients. Cover, reduce heat,
and simmer 15 minutes. Yield: 5 servings
(serving size: about 1 cup).

CALORIES 98 (28% from fat); FAT 3g (sat 0.4g, mono 1.4g,
poly 0.5g); PROTEIN 3.3g; CARB 17.4g; FIBER 4.9g;
CHOL 0mg; IRON 1.9mg; SODIUM 248mg; CALC 38mg

OVEN-FRIED EGGPLANT

PREP: 11 MINUTES   COOK: 24 MINUTES

    ½ cup fat-free mayonnaise
    1 tablespoon minced fresh onion
  12 (½-inch-thick) slices unpeeled
           eggplant (about 1 pound)
    ⅓ cup dry breadcrumbs
    ⅓ cup grated Parmesan cheese
    ½ teaspoon dried Italian seasoning
Cooking spray

1. Preheat oven to 425°.
2. Combine mayonnaise and onion;
spread evenly over both sides of eggplant
slices. Combine breadcrumbs, cheese,
and Italian seasoning in a shallow bowl;
dredge eggplant in breadcrumb mixture.
3. Place sliced eggplant on a baking sheet
coated with cooking spray. Bake at 425°
for 12 minutes. Turn eggplant over;
bake 12 minutes or until golden. Yield:
4 servings (serving size: 3 slices).

CALORIES 121 (21% from fat); FAT 2.8g (sat 1.4g, mono 0.8g,
poly 0.2g); PROTEIN 5g; CARB 19.8g; FIBER 3g;
CHOL 5mg; IRON 1.1mg; SODIUM 617mg; CALC 164mg

PARMESAN EGGPLANT STACKS

PREP: 10 MINUTES   STAND: 30 MINUTES
COOK: 26 MINUTES

    8 (¾-inch-thick) slices eggplant
           (about 1½ pounds)
    ¾ teaspoon salt, divided
Cooking spray
    ½ teaspoon garlic powder
    ½ teaspoon freshly ground black
           pepper, divided
    8 (½-inch-thick) slices tomato
           (about 1¼ pounds)
    3 tablespoons grated Parmesan
           cheese
    1 tablespoon minced fresh basil

1. Place eggplant slices in a single layer

on paper towels. Sprinkle eggplant with
½ teaspoon salt; let stand 30 minutes.
Pat dry with a paper towel.
2. Preheat oven to 400°.
3. Arrange eggplant in a single layer on
a baking sheet coated with cooking
spray. Coat top of eggplant with cooking spray. Bake at 400° for 12 minutes;
turn eggplant over, and sprinkle with
garlic powder and ¼ teaspoon pepper.
Bake an additional 12 minutes or until
tender. Remove eggplant from oven.
4. Preheat broiler.
5. Top each eggplant slice with a tomato
slice. Combine ¼ teaspoon salt, ¼ teaspoon pepper, Parmesan cheese, and
basil; sprinkle over tomato. Broil 2 minutes or until lightly browned. Yield: 8
servings (serving size: 1 stack).

CALORIES 44 (23% from fat); FAT 1.1g (sat 0.4g, mono 0.2g,
poly 0.2g); PROTEIN 2.1g; CARB 8g; FIBER 2.5g;
CHOL 1mg; IRON 0.6mg; SODIUM 261mg; CALC 33mg

EGGPLANT

Among dozens of varieties—from large
to small, purple to white—the most
common eggplant is the large, dark-
purple American eggplant found in supermarkets throughout the year. Look
for eggplants that have smooth, shiny
skin and are firm but slightly springy.
Store in a cool place, and use within
two days.

Gratin of Leeks

PREP: 30 MINUTES   COOK: 25 MINUTES

The leeks in this dish become soft and mellow-flavored during baking. See page 280 for tips on trimming leeks.

6 cups water
8 leeks (about 3 pounds), trimmed and cut into 2-inch pieces
2 cups 1% low-fat milk
½ teaspoon dried thyme
¼ teaspoon ground nutmeg
4 whole cloves
1 bay leaf
1 garlic clove, minced
¼ cup all-purpose flour
2 tablespoons dry white wine
1 tablespoon stick margarine or butter
½ cup (2 ounces) grated Gruyère or Swiss cheese
¼ teaspoon salt
Cooking spray
2 tablespoons grated Parmesan cheese
⅛ teaspoon ground red pepper

1. Preheat oven to 400°.
2. Bring 6 cups water to a boil in a Dutch oven; add leeks. Cover and cook 8 minutes or until tender; drain well, and pat leeks dry with paper towels.
3. Combine milk and next 5 ingredients in a medium saucepan. Bring to a boil over medium heat; cook 1 minute, stirring constantly. Remove from heat, and cool. Strain milk mixture through a sieve into a bowl; discard solids.
4. Place flour in a medium saucepan. Gradually add strained milk mixture, stirring well with a whisk. Bring to a boil; reduce heat, and simmer until thick (about 2 minutes), stirring constantly. Add wine and margarine; cook 1 minute or until margarine melts, stirring constantly. Remove from heat; add Gruyère cheese and salt, stirring until cheese melts.
5. Arrange leeks in an 11 x 7-inch baking dish coated with cooking spray. Pour milk mixture over leeks; sprinkle with Parmesan cheese and pepper. Bake, uncovered, at 400° for 25 minutes or until lightly browned. Yield: 8 servings (serving size: ½ cup).

CALORIES 160 (29% from fat); FAT 5.2g (sat 2.3g, mono 1.7g, poly 0.8g); PROTEIN 6.8g; CARB 22.7g; FIBER 1.5g; CHOL 11mg; IRON 2.8mg; SODIUM 192mg; CALC 237mg

Stacked Vegetable Portobellos

PREP: 16 MINUTES
MARINATE: 30 MINUTES
COOK: 37 MINUTES

4 (4-inch) portobello mushrooms (about 1 pound)
1 tablespoon minced fresh parsley
1 tablespoon fresh lemon juice
2 teaspoons olive oil
1 teaspoon dried Italian seasoning
¼ teaspoon black pepper
¼ cup dry white wine
1 cup (¼-inch-thick) sliced zucchini
1 cup (¼-inch-thick) sliced yellow squash
½ cup (¼-inch-thick) sliced red onion
2 (¼-inch-thick) slices tomato
¼ cup (1 ounce) crumbled goat cheese

1. Remove stems and brown gills from the undersides of mushrooms using a sharp knife; discard gills. Reserve stems for another use, if desired.
2. Combine mushroom caps, parsley, lemon juice, oil, Italian seasoning, and pepper in a large zip-top plastic bag; seal. Marinate 30 minutes; remove mushrooms, reserving marinade and bag.
3. Preheat oven to 425°.
4. Place mushrooms and wine in a shallow baking dish. Bake at 425° for 15 minutes or until mushrooms are tender.
5. Place zucchini, yellow squash, and onion in reserved plastic bag; shake to coat vegetables with remaining marinade. Place vegetables in a shallow baking dish. Bake at 425° for 10 minutes or until slightly soft.
6. Place 2 mushroom caps, gill sides up, on a baking sheet; arrange baked vegetables evenly on 2 mushroom caps on baking sheet. Top each with a tomato slice, 2 tablespoons cheese, and a mushroom cap. Bake at 425° for 12 minutes or until thoroughly heated. Yield: 2 servings.

CALORIES 190 (47% from fat); FAT 9.9g (sat 3.8g, mono 4.3g, poly 1g); PROTEIN 9g; CARB 21.1g; FIBER 5.2g; CHOL 18mg; IRON 4.2mg; SODIUM 240mg; CALC 167mg

Creamed Onions With Sage

PREP: 15 MINUTES
COOK: 10 MINUTES

¾ pound pearl onions, unpeeled
3 tablespoons all-purpose flour
1 (10½-ounce) can low-sodium chicken broth
¾ cup evaporated fat-free milk
¼ cup water
¼ teaspoon salt
⅛ teaspoon black pepper
1 teaspoon minced fresh sage
½ teaspoon minced fresh thyme
1 tablespoon dry sherry

1. Place onions in a large saucepan of boiling water; return to a boil. Drain and rinse; drain and peel. Return onions to saucepan; add water to cover. Bring to a boil; cover, reduce heat, and simmer 10 minutes or until tender. Drain and set aside.

Caramelizing Onions

1. Slice the onion in half vertically. Place cut side down on cutting board, and slice into thin slivers.

2. Cook over medium-high heat, stirring often. At 10 minutes, the onions begin to soften and release their liquid.

3. Keep stirring. At 15 minutes, the onions begin to take on a golden color, but they're not quite done yet.

4. At 20 minutes, the onions are deep golden brown and done.

2. Place flour in saucepan; gradually add broth, stirring well with a whisk. Stir in milk, water, salt, and pepper. Cook over medium heat 10 minutes or until thick and bubbly, stirring constantly with a whisk. Add onions, and cook until thoroughly heated. Remove from heat; stir in sage, thyme, and sherry. Yield: 6 servings (serving size: ½ cup).

CALORIES 62 (7% from fat); FAT 0.5g (sat 0.1g, mono 0.2g, poly 0.1g); PROTEIN 3.7g; CARB 10.5g; FIBER 0.4g; CHOL 1mg; IRON 0.7mg; SODIUM 156mg; CALC 108mg

CARAMELIZED ONIONS

PREP:7 MINUTES   COOK:20 MINUTES

To caramelize a larger quantity of onions (4 to 8 cups), use a large Dutch oven. You won't need additional olive oil.

1½ teaspoons olive oil
    Cooking spray
  3 cups vertically sliced onion
      (sweet, yellow, white, or red
      onion)

1. Heat oil in a 12-inch nonstick skillet coated with cooking spray over medium-high heat. Add sliced onion and cook 5 minutes, stirring frequently. Continue cooking 15 to 20 minutes or until deep golden brown stirring frequently. Yield: 1 cup.

Note: You'll want to use these onions for Caramelized Onion Custards (below) and Pizza With Caramelized Onions, Feta, and Olives (page 298).

CALORIES 260 (28% from fat); FAT 8.2g (sat 1.1g, mono 5.1g, poly 0.9g); PROTEIN 5.9g; CARB 44g; FIBER 9.4g; CHOL 0mg; IRON 1.1mg; SODIUM 16mg; CALC 102mg

CARAMELIZED-ONION CUSTARDS

PREP:10 MINUTES
COOK:1 HOUR

  1 cup chopped Caramelized
      Onions (recipe at left), cooled
      (about 3 cups uncooked)
  ⅛ teaspoon salt
  ⅛ teaspoon black pepper
  ⅛ teaspoon ground nutmeg
  2 large eggs, lightly beaten
  2 large egg whites, lightly beaten
  1 (12-ounce) can evaporated
      fat-free milk
    Cooking spray

1. Preheat oven to 325°.
2. Combine all ingredients except cooking spray in a large bowl. Spoon onion mixture into 6 (6-ounce) custard cups coated with cooking spray.
3. Place custard cups in a 13 x 9-inch baking pan; add hot water to pan to a depth of 1 inch. Bake at 325° for 1 hour or until a knife inserted in center comes out clean. Yield: 6 servings.

CALORIES 120 (26% from fat); FAT 3.4g (sat 0.8g, mono 1.5g, poly 0.4g); PROTEIN 8.6g; CARB 14.2g; FIBER 1.6g; CHOL 76mg; IRON 0.6mg; SODIUM 156mg; CALC 191mg

ROASTED VIDALIAS

PREP: 6 MINUTES   COOK: 40 MINUTES

    4   Vidalia or other sweet onions,
        each peeled and cut into 8
        wedges (about 2 pounds)
Olive oil-flavored cooking spray
    1   teaspoon dried thyme
  ½   teaspoon salt
  ¼   teaspoon freshly ground black
        pepper
    1   tablespoon balsamic vinegar

1. Preheat oven to 450°.
2. Arrange onion wedges on a jelly-roll
pan coated with cooking spray. Coat
onions with cooking spray; sprinkle
with thyme, salt, and pepper. Bake at
450° for 20 minutes. Turn onion
wedges over; bake an additional 20 minutes or until onions are tender.
3. Spoon onions into a serving dish, and
drizzle with vinegar. Yield: 4 servings
(serving size: ¾ cup).

CALORIES 92 (9% from fat); FAT 0.9g (sat 0.1g, mono 0.1g,
poly 0.1g); PROTEIN 2.7g; CARB 20g; FIBER 4.3g;
CHOL 0mg; IRON 1mg; SODIUM 300mg; CALC 53mg

Roasted Vidalias

GRILLED CAJUN OKRA AND CORN

PREP: 27 MINUTES   MARINATE: 1 HOUR
COOK: 16 MINUTES

  ¼   cup fresh lime juice
    1   tablespoon no-salt-added
        Cajun seasoning
    1   teaspoon grated lime rind
  ½   teaspoon salt
    1   garlic clove, minced
    1   (5.5-ounce) can tomato juice
  ½   pound small okra pods
    3   ears shucked corn, each cut cross-
        wise into 1-inch-thick slices
    1   red bell pepper, cut into 1-inch
        squares
Cooking spray

1. Combine first 6 ingredients in a large
zip-top plastic bag. Add vegetables to
bag, and seal. Marinate in refrigerator 1
hour, turning bag occasionally.
2. Prepare grill.
3. Remove vegetables from bag, reserving marinade. Thread vegetables alternately onto each of 6 (12-inch) skewers.
Place kebabs on grill rack coated with
cooking spray, and grill, covered, 16
minutes or until tender, turning and
basting twice with reserved marinade.
Yield: 6 servings.

CALORIES 62 (10% from fat); FAT 0.7g (sat 0.1g, mono 0.1g,
poly 0.3g); PROTEIN 2.2g; CARB 14.1g; FIBER 2g;
CHOL 0mg; IRON 1mg; SODIUM 302mg; CALC 38mg

MINTED PEAS AND CARROTS

PREP: 10 MINUTES   COOK: 12 MINUTES

    3   cups water
    2   cups shelled green peas (about
        1¾ pounds unshelled)
  ¾   cup diced carrot
    2   teaspoons stick margarine or
        butter
  1½   cups sliced mushrooms
  ¼   cup chopped green onions
    2   tablespoons minced fresh mint
  ¼   teaspoon salt

1. Bring water to a boil in a medium
saucepan. Add peas and carrot; cook 8
minutes or until tender. Drain.

2. Melt margarine in a medium non-stick skillet over medium-high heat. Add mushrooms and green onions; sauté 4 minutes. Add pea mixture, mint, and salt; sauté 2 minutes. Yield: 4 servings (serving size: ¾ cup).

CALORIES 97 (22% from fat); FAT 2.4g (sat 0.5g, mono 0.9g, poly 0.8g); PROTEIN 5.1g; CARB 15.1g; FIBER 3.8g; CHOL 0mg; IRON 1.8mg; SODIUM 182mg; CALC 34mg

SPRING PEAS WITH CARROT AND LETTUCE CONFETTI

PREP: 10 MINUTES   COOK: 30 MINUTES

Sliced lettuce is a crisp addition to the usual peas and carrots.

1 (10½-ounce) can chicken broth
½ cup water
¼ cup sliced green onions
1 garlic clove, sliced
5 whole cloves
1 small bay leaf
2¼ cups shelled green peas (about 1¾ pounds unshelled)
¼ cup diced carrot
1 cup thinly sliced Boston lettuce (about ½ head)

1. Combine first 6 ingredients in a small saucepan. Bring to a boil over medium-high heat; cook until reduced to ½ cup (about 20 minutes). Strain mixture through a sieve into a medium bowl, and discard solids.
2. Return cooking liquid to pan; bring to a boil. Add peas and carrot. Cover, reduce heat, and simmer 3 minutes. Uncover and simmer 7 minutes or until tender. Remove from heat, and stir in lettuce. Yield: 4 servings (½ cup per serving).

CALORIES 96 (8% from fat); FAT 0.9g (sat 0.2g, mono 0.2g, poly 0.3g); PROTEIN 6.9g; CARB 15.9g; FIBER 3.9g; CHOL 0mg; IRON 1.8mg; SODIUM 260mg; CALC 40mg

ROASTED PEPPERS

PREP: 6 MINUTES   COOK: 12 MINUTES
STAND: 15 MINUTES

These peppers can be tossed into a pasta dish or served as a tasty topping for a grilled steak or chicken breast.

3 red bell peppers (about 1¼ pounds)
3 yellow bell peppers (about 1¼ pounds)
2 tablespoons balsamic vinegar
¼ teaspoon salt

1. Preheat broiler.
2. Cut bell peppers in half lengthwise, and discard seeds and membranes. Place pepper halves, skin sides up, on a foil-lined baking sheet, and flatten with hand. Broil 12 minutes or until blackened. Place in a zip-top plastic bag; seal. Let stand 15 minutes.
3. Peel and discard skins. Cut bell peppers into strips.
4. Combine bell pepper strips, vinegar, and salt in a bowl, and toss well. Yield: 3 cups (serving size: ½ cup).

CALORIES 23 (16% from fat); FAT 0.4g (sat 0.1g, mono 0g, poly 0.2g); PROTEIN 0.8g; CARB 4.9g; FIBER 1.5g; CHOL 0mg; IRON 1.2mg; SODIUM 101mg; CALC 6mg

MASHED POTATOES

PREP: 10 MINUTES
COOK: 20 MINUTES

4 cups cubed peeled baking potato (about 1½ pounds)
1 garlic clove, sliced
¾ cup 1% low-fat milk
2 tablespoons grated Parmesan cheese
1 tablespoon butter or stick margarine
½ teaspoon salt
⅛ teaspoon black pepper

1. Place potato and garlic in a medium saucepan; add water to cover. Bring to a boil; cover, reduce heat, and simmer 15 to 17 minutes or until potato is tender. Drain; return potato mixture to pan. Add milk and remaining ingredients; mash with a potato masher. Yield: 4 servings (serving size: ¾ cup).

CALORIES 164 (23% from fat); FAT 4.2g (sat 1.4g, mono 1.6g, poly 1g); PROTEIN 5.4g; CARB 26.8g; FIBER 2.2g; CHOL 4mg; IRON 1.1mg; SODIUM 404mg; CALC 103mg

MASHED POTATO CASSEROLE

PREP: 30 MINUTES   COOK: 30 MINUTES

2 pounds baking potatoes, peeled and cut into 1-inch pieces
1 (8-ounce) tub fat-free cream cheese
1 cup low-fat sour cream
½ teaspoon garlic powder
¼ teaspoon salt
¼ teaspoon black pepper
Cooking spray
1 tablespoon stick margarine or butter, melted
½ teaspoon paprika

1. Preheat oven to 350°.
2. Place potato in a saucepan; add water to cover. Bring to a boil; cover, reduce heat, and simmer 15 minutes or until tender. Drain.
3. Combine potato, cream cheese, and next 4 ingredients in a bowl; beat at medium speed of a mixer 2 minutes or until smooth. Spoon into an 11 x 7-inch baking dish coated with cooking spray; drizzle margarine over potato mixture. Sprinkle with paprika. Bake, uncovered, at 350° for 30 minutes. Yield: 6 servings (serving size: 1 cup).

CALORIES 223 (28% from fat); FAT 7g (sat 3.4g, mono 2.2g, poly 0.9g); PROTEIN 10.1g; CARB 30.7g; FIBER 2.6g; CHOL 22mg; IRON 2mg; SODIUM 329mg; CALC 172mg

HASH BROWN CASSEROLE

PREP: 11 MINUTES COOK: 55 MINUTES

1 cup thinly sliced green onions
⅓ cup evaporated fat-free milk
2 tablespoons stick margarine or
   butter, melted
½ teaspoon black pepper
1 (32-ounce) package frozen
   Southern-style hash brown
   potatoes, thawed
1 (8-ounce) carton fat-free sour
   cream
1 (10¾-ounce) can condensed
   reduced-fat, reduced-sodium
   cream of mushroom soup,
   undiluted
1½ cups (6 ounces) shredded
   reduced-fat sharp cheddar
   cheese, divided
   Cooking spray
½ teaspoon paprika

1. Preheat oven to 350°.
2. Combine first 7 ingredients in a large
bowl; stir in 1 cup cheese. Spoon mixture into a 13 x 9-inch baking dish coated
with cooking spray. Sprinkle with ½
cup cheese and paprika. Bake at 350°
for 55 minutes or until bubbly. Yield: 9
servings (serving size: ¾ cup).

CALORIES 211 (29% from fat); FAT 6.8g (sat 2.9g, mono 2.4g,
poly 1.1g); PROTEIN 9.7g; CARB 26.3g; FIBER 1.4g;
CHOL 15mg; IRON 0.3mg; SODIUM 363mg; CALC 262mg

ROASTED GARLIC POTATOES

PREP: 14 MINUTES COOK: 35 MINUTES

1¾ pounds baking potatoes, peeled
   and cut into 1-inch cubes
3 tablespoons fresh lemon juice
1 teaspoon olive oil
½ teaspoon kosher salt
4 garlic cloves, minced
   Cooking spray

1. Preheat oven to 425°.
2. Combine first 5 ingredients in a
medium bowl; toss well to coat. Let
stand 10 minutes. Spoon potato mixture into an 11 x 7-inch baking dish
coated with cooking spray. Bake at 425°
for 35 minutes or until tender and lightly
browned, stirring occasionally. Yield: 4
servings (serving size: ¾ cup).

CALORIES 153 (9% from fat); FAT 1.5g (sat 0.2g, mono 0.8g,
poly 0.2g); PROTEIN 3.7g; CARB 32.5g; FIBER 2.8g;
CHOL 0mg; IRON 1.3mg; SODIUM 304mg; CALC 18mg

menu

Greek Stuffed Steak (page 319)
Feta Mashed Potatoes
Sugar Snap Peas With Lime-and-Basil
Dressing (page 404)
Pear Phyllo Pastries (page 217)

FETA MASHED POTATOES

PREP: 14 MINUTES COOK: 25 MINUTES

2 pounds baking potatoes, peeled
   and cubed (about 5¼ cups)
¼ cup fat-free milk
3 tablespoons crumbled feta cheese
2 tablespoons fat-free sour cream
½ teaspoon salt
½ teaspoon dried oregano
¼ teaspoon black pepper

1. Place potato in a large saucepan; cover
with water, and bring to a boil. Cover,
reduce heat, and simmer 20 minutes or
until potato is very tender.
2. Drain potato; return to pan. Beat at
high speed of a mixer until smooth. Add
milk, feta cheese, sour cream, salt,
oregano, and pepper; beat well. Yield: 8
servings (serving size: ½ cup).

CALORIES 94 (9% from fat); FAT 0.9g (sat 0.6g, mono 0.2g,
poly 0.1g); PROTEIN 3.1g; CARB 18.7g; FIBER 1.6g;
CHOL 3mg; IRON 0.8mg; SODIUM 200mg; CALC 37mg

TWICE-BAKED SPINACH POTATOES

PREP: 16 MINUTES COOK: 1½ HOURS

*You can also cook the potatoes in the mi-
crowave by piercing them with a fork and
arranging them on paper towels. Microwave at HIGH 16 minutes or until
done, turning and rearranging potatoes
after 8 minutes. Let stand 5 minutes.*

3 large baking potatoes (about 12
   ounces each)
½ cup 1% low-fat milk
½ cup tub-style light cream cheese
1¾ cups (7 ounces) shredded
   reduced-fat sharp cheddar
   cheese, divided
¼ cup finely chopped onion
¼ teaspoon salt
¼ teaspoon black pepper
1 (10-ounce) package frozen
   chopped spinach, thawed,
   drained, and squeezed dry
   Sliced green onions (optional)

1. Preheat oven to 400°.
2. Pierce potatoes with a fork, and bake
at 400° for 1 hour and 15 minutes or
until done; cool slightly. Cut each potato
in half lengthwise; scoop out pulp, leaving a ¼-inch-thick shell. Mash pulp
with a potato masher. Place milk and
cream cheese in a large bowl, and stir
well with a whisk. Stir in potato pulp, 1
cup cheddar cheese, onion, salt, pepper,
and spinach.
3. Spoon potato mixture into shells;
sprinkle each with 2 tablespoons cheddar cheese. Place stuffed potatoes on a
baking sheet; bake at 400° for 15 minutes or until thoroughly heated. Garnish
with green onions, if desired. Yield: 6
servings (serving size: 1 potato half).

CALORIES 349 (26% from fat); FAT 10g (sat 5.8g, mono 1.8g,
poly 0.4g); PROTEIN 17.5g; CARB 49g; FIBER 4.7g;
CHOL 34mg; IRON 3.5mg; SODIUM 501mg; CALC 414mg

The "Works" Stuffed Potatoes

PREP: 15 MINUTES
COOK: 1 HOUR 15 MINUTES

To serve as an entrée, cut a lengthwise slice across the top of each potato instead of cutting potatoes in half. Each main-dish serving would be one stuffed potato.

    4 bacon slices
    Cooking spray
    3 garlic cloves, minced
    4 baking potatoes
        (about 2 pounds)
    1 cup low-fat sour cream
    ½ cup (2 ounces) shredded
        reduced-fat extra-sharp
        cheddar cheese, divided
    ⅓ cup minced green onions,
        divided
    ¼ cup 1% low-fat milk
    ¼ teaspoon salt
    Freshly ground black pepper
        (optional)

1. Preheat oven to 400°.
2. Cook bacon in a medium nonstick skillet over medium heat until crisp. Remove bacon from pan; crumble bacon, and set aside. Wipe pan clean with paper towels.
3. Place pan coated with cooking spray over medium heat until hot. Add garlic; sauté 1 minute. Set aside.
4. Bake potatoes at 400° for 1 hour or until done; cool slightly. Cut each potato in half lengthwise; carefully scoop pulp into a bowl, leaving shells intact. Add half of crumbled bacon, garlic, sour cream, ¼ cup cheese, 3 tablespoons onions, milk, and salt to pulp; mash.
5. Increase oven temperature to 450°.
6. Stuff shells with potato mixture; top with remaining crumbled bacon, ¼ cup cheese, and remaining onions. Place stuffed potatoes on a baking sheet. Bake at 450° for 15 minutes or until thoroughly heated. Sprinkle with pepper, if desired. Yield: 8 servings (serving size: 1 potato half).

CALORIES 213 (30% from fat); FAT 7g (sat 3.4g, mono 2.3g, poly 0.5g); PROTEIN 7.1g; CARB 31.2g; FIBER 2.2g; CHOL 20mg; IRON 1.7mg; SODIUM 233mg; CALC 120mg

Hanukkah Latkes

PREP: 5 MINUTES
COOK: 20 MINUTES

    3 cups cubed peeled baking potato
        (about 1¼ pounds)
    2 tablespoons all-purpose flour
    ½ teaspoon salt
    ¼ teaspoon onion powder
    ¼ teaspoon baking powder
    ¼ teaspoon black pepper
    1 large egg white
    1 large egg
    1 tablespoon vegetable oil,
        divided
    6 tablespoons fat-free sour cream
    Sliced green onions (optional)

1. Place first 8 ingredients in a food processor. Pulse 20 times or until potato is very finely chopped.
2. Heat ½ teaspoon oil in a large nonstick skillet over medium-high heat. For each latke, spoon about 1 heaping tablespoon batter into pan; cook about 2 minutes on each side or until browned. Repeat procedure with remaining oil and batter. Serve latkes with sour cream; garnish with green onions, if desired. Yield: 6 servings (serving size: 4 latkes and 1 tablespoon sour cream).

CALORIES 125 (23% from fat); FAT 3.2g (sat 0.7g, mono 1g, poly 1.3g); PROTEIN 4.3g; CARB 19.7g; FIBER 1.6g; CHOL 35mg; IRON 1mg; SODIUM 239mg; CALC 25mg

Steak Fries

PREP: 8 MINUTES   COOK: 22 MINUTES
(pictured on page 425)

    5 red potatoes (about 1¾ pounds)
    1 tablespoon olive oil
    ½ teaspoon salt
    ¼ teaspoon black pepper
    ⅛ teaspoon ground nutmeg
    1 garlic clove, crushed
    Cooking spray

1. Preheat oven to 450°.
2. Cut each potato lengthwise into 6 wedges. Pat potato dry with paper towels. Combine potato and next 5 ingredients in a bowl; toss well to coat. Arrange potato in a single layer on a baking sheet or roasting pan coated with cooking spray. Bake at 450° for 22 minutes or until crisp and browned, turning once. Yield: 5 servings (serving size: 6 wedges).

CALORIES 136 (20% from fat); FAT 3g (sat 0.4g, mono 2g, poly 0.3g); PROTEIN 3.3g; CARB 24.9g; FIBER 2.7g; CHOL 0mg; IRON 2mg; SODIUM 245mg; CALC 21mg

Faux Potato Chips

PREP: 5 MINUTES   COOK: 35 MINUTES

    1 large baking potato
    Cooking spray
    ¼ teaspoon paprika
    ⅛ teaspoon salt

1. Preheat oven to 400°.
2. Cut potato into thin slices. Arrange slices in a single layer on a baking sheet coated with cooking spray. Coat slices lightly with cooking spray; sprinkle with paprika and salt. Bake at 400° for 35 minutes or until browned, turning once. Yield: 2 servings (serving size: approximately 20 chips).

CALORIES 155 (5% from fat); FAT 0.9g (sat 0.1g, mono 0g, poly 0.1g); PROTEIN 4.4g; CARB 33.3g; FIBER 3.3g; CHOL 0mg; IRON 2.5mg; SODIUM 161mg; CALC 27mg

TWO-POTATO BAKE

PREP: 12 MINUTES
COOK: 1 HOUR

Cooking spray
4 cups thinly sliced peeled sweet
    potato (about 1¼ pounds)
4 cups thinly sliced peeled red
    potato (about 1¼ pounds)
2 tablespoons minced fresh onion
3 tablespoons stick margarine or
    butter, melted
½ teaspoon salt
¼ teaspoon black pepper
¾ cup fat-free milk
2 tablespoons minced fresh
    parsley
2 tablespoons grated fresh
    Parmesan cheese

1. Preheat oven to 425°.

2. Coat an 11 x 7-inch baking dish with cooking spray.

3. Place 2 cups sweet potato in half of dish. Place 2 cups red potato in other half of dish. Sprinkle evenly with onion. Drizzle with 1½ tablespoons margarine. Sprinkle with ¼ teaspoon salt and ⅛ teaspoon pepper. Repeat layers with remaining potato, margarine, salt, and pepper. Bring milk to a boil in a small saucepan; pour over mixture.

4. Cover with aluminum foil; cut 8 (1-inch) slits in foil. Bake at 425° for 50 minutes. Uncover and bake 10 minutes. Remove from oven; sprinkle with parsley and cheese. Let stand 5 minutes before serving. Yield: 8 servings (serving size: ½ cup).

CALORIES 184 (25% from fat); FAT 5.1g (sat 1.2g, mono 2g, poly 1.5g); PROTEIN 4.3g; CARB 31.3g; FIBER 3.6g; CHOL 1mg; IRON 1.6mg; SODIUM 247mg; CALC 75mg

Cranberry-Glazed
Sweet Potatoes

CRANBERRY-GLAZED SWEET POTATOES

PREP: 5 MINUTES   COOK: 23 MINUTES

6 peeled sweet potatoes, cut into
    1-inch pieces (about 3 pounds)
½ cup packed brown sugar
2 tablespoons stick margarine or
    butter
2 tablespoons fresh orange juice
½ teaspoon salt
1 cup whole-berry cranberry sauce
Orange rind (optional)

1. Place sweet potato in a 2-quart casserole. Cover with heavy-duty plastic wrap; microwave at HIGH 10 to 12 minutes or until tender.

2. Combine sugar, margarine, orange juice, and salt in a 2-cup glass measure. Microwave at HIGH 3 minutes, stirring after every minute.

3. Add sugar mixture and cranberry sauce to sweet potato; toss gently. Microwave at HIGH 10 minutes or until thoroughly heated, basting with sauce every 4 minutes. Garnish with orange rind, if desired. Yield: 16 servings (serving size: ½ cup).

CALORIES 121 (12% from fat); FAT 1.6g (sat 0.3g, mono 0.6g, poly 0.5g); PROTEIN 0.9g; CARB 26.5g; FIBER 1.6g; CHOL 0mg; IRON 0.5mg; SODIUM 104mg; CALC 19mg

SWEET POTATO SHOESTRING FRIES

PREP: 12 MINUTES   COOK: 25 MINUTES

3 tablespoons orange juice
1 tablespoon vegetable oil
½ teaspoon ground ginger
¼ teaspoon salt
⅛ teaspoon ground red pepper
2 large sweet potatoes, peeled and
    cut into ⅛-inch strips (about
    1½ pounds)
Cooking spray

Sweet potatoes don't keep as well as white potatoes. Store them in a **cool, dry, dark place for up to one week.**

1. Preheat oven to 450°.
2. Combine first 5 ingredients in a small saucepan. Bring to a boil; boil 2 minutes or until reduced to a syrup. Remove from heat; cool.
3. Combine juice mixture and sweet potato strips in a large bowl; toss well to coat. Arrange strips in a single layer on a baking sheet coated with cooking spray. Bake at 450° for 25 minutes or until browned. Serve immediately. Yield: 4 servings (serving size: ¾ cup).

CALORIES 187 (19% from fat); FAT 4g (sat 0.7g, mono 1g, poly 1.8g); PROTEIN 2.4g; CARB 35.9g; FIBER 4.3g; CHOL 0mg; IRON 0.9mg; SODIUM 165mg; CALC 33mg

GRILLED ASIAN SWEET POTATOES

PREP: 10 MINUTES   COOK: 23 MINUTES

    3 tablespoons low-sodium soy sauce
    2 tablespoons water
    2 tablespoons dry sherry
    2 tablespoons honey
    1 garlic clove, minced
    4 small unpeeled sweet potatoes, each cut lengthwise into 4 wedges (about 2 pounds)
    1 tablespoon dark sesame oil
    Cooking spray

1. Combine first 5 ingredients in a small bowl; set aside.
2. Arrange potato wedges in a single layer on a large microwave-safe platter. Cover with plastic wrap; vent. Microwave at HIGH 13 minutes or until tender, turning one-quarter turn every 3 minutes. Cool slightly.
3. Prepare grill.

4. Brush potato wedges with sesame oil. Arrange potato wedges, cut side down, on grill rack coated with cooking spray. Grill, uncovered, 5 minutes, basting constantly with soy sauce mixture. Turn wedges onto other cut side; repeat cooking and basting procedure. Yield: 8 servings.

CALORIES 155 (12% from fat); FAT 2.1g (sat 0.3g, mono 0.7g, poly 0.9g); PROTEIN 2.2g; CARB 32.6g; FIBER 3.4g; CHOL 0mg; IRON 0.8mg; SODIUM 197mg; CALC 27mg

MAPLE-SWEET POTATO CASSEROLE

PREP: 20 MINUTES   COOK: 50 MINUTES

    ⅓ cup yellow cornmeal
    1½ cups fat-free milk
    2 tablespoons stick margarine or butter
    2 cups mashed cooked sweet potato (about 1¼ pounds)
    ⅓ cup maple syrup
    ½ teaspoon salt
    ½ teaspoon ground cinnamon
    ¼ teaspoon ground allspice
    ¼ teaspoon black pepper
    2 large eggs, lightly beaten
    Cooking spray

1. Preheat oven to 350°.
2. Place ⅓ cup cornmeal in a saucepan. Gradually add milk, stirring well with a whisk. Bring to a boil; reduce heat to medium. Cook, uncovered, 2 minutes, stirring constantly with a whisk. Remove from heat; stir in margarine.
3. Combine sweet potato and next 6 ingredients in a large bowl. Gradually add cornmeal mixture, stirring well. Pour sweet potato mixture into a 1½-quart

casserole coated with cooking spray. Bake at 350° for 50 minutes. Let stand 10 minutes before serving. Yield: 6 servings (serving size: about ½ cup).

CALORIES 242 (23% from fat); FAT 6.2g (sat 1.4g, mono 2.4g, poly 1.7g); PROTEIN 6.2g; CARB 41.1g; FIBER 3.4g; CHOL 72mg; IRON 1.3mg; SODIUM 308mg; CALC 118mg

SWEET POTATO CASSEROLE WITH PRALINE TOPPING

PREP: 38 MINUTES   COOK: 45 MINUTES

    1 cup all-purpose flour
    ⅔ cup packed brown sugar
    ¼ cup chopped pecans, toasted
    ¼ cup stick margarine or butter, melted
    ½ teaspoon ground cinnamon
    4 sweet potatoes, peeled and halved (about 2½ pounds)
    ½ cup granulated sugar
    1½ teaspoons vanilla extract
    1 large egg white
    1 (5-ounce) can evaporated fat-free milk
    Cooking spray

1. Preheat oven to 350°.
2. Lightly spoon flour into a dry measuring cup; level with a knife. Combine flour, brown sugar, pecans, margarine, and cinnamon in a small bowl.
3. Place sweet potato halves in a Dutch oven; add water to cover. Bring to a boil; cover, reduce heat, and simmer 30 minutes or until tender. Drain well; mash in a large bowl. Stir in 1 cup flour mixture, granulated sugar, vanilla, egg white, and milk. Spoon into a 2-quart casserole coated with cooking spray; top with remaining flour mixture. Bake at 350° for 45 minutes. Yield: 8 servings (serving size: ¾ cup).

CALORIES 374 (21% from fat); FAT 8.7g (sat 1.4g, mono 4.1g, poly 2.6g); PROTEIN 5.3g; CARB 69.8g; FIBER 3.8g; CHOL 1mg; IRON 1.8mg; SODIUM 116mg; CALC 100mg

CREAMED SPINACH

PREP:10 MINUTES   COOK:15 MINUTES

The light cream cheese provides a smooth, rich flavor.

  2 (10-ounce) packages fresh spinach
    Cooking spray
  2 tablespoons minced shallots
  2 teaspoons all-purpose flour
  ⅛ teaspoon salt
  ⅛ teaspoon ground nutmeg
  ½ cup fat-free milk
  ½ cup tub-style light cream cheese, softened

1. Remove large stems from spinach; rinse with cold water. Drain. Place a large Dutch oven over medium heat; add spinach. (Spinach will need to be tightly packed into pan to cook all of it in one batch). Cover and cook 7 minutes or until spinach wilts, stirring after 2 minutes. Place spinach in a colander; drain well, pressing spinach with the back of a spoon to remove as much moisture as possible.

2. Coat pan with cooking spray, and place over medium heat until hot. Add shallots; sauté 2 minutes. Combine flour, salt, and nutmeg; add to pan, stirring well. Cook 30 seconds. Add milk and cheese, stirring with a whisk; cook until thick (about 2 minutes), stirring constantly. Add spinach; cook 1 minute or until thoroughly heated. Serve immediately. Yield: 4 servings (serving size: ⅔ cup).

CALORIES 110 (44% from fat); FAT 5.4g (sat 3g, mono 1.4g, poly 0.4g); PROTEIN 8g; CARB 9.4g; FIBER 5.4g; CHOL 17mg; IRON 3.8mg; SODIUM 354mg; CALC 210mg

---

SELECT A SQUASH

All winter squash should be heavy. The stem end should be solid and firm, and the hard shell free from bruises. Store at room temperature for up to one week or in a cool, dark, well-ventilated place for one to two months.

Yield: One butternut squash (about 2½ pounds) yields about 2¼ cups mashed cooked squash. One medium acorn squash (about 1 pound) yields about 1¼ cups mashed cooked squash.

ORANGE-GLAZED ACORN SQUASH

PREP:15 MINUTES
COOK:50 MINUTES

  3 acorn squash (about 1 pound each)
    Cooking spray
  ¼ cup orange marmalade
  1 tablespoon brown sugar
  1 tablespoon lime juice
  2 teaspoons low-sodium soy sauce
  ½ teaspoon vegetable oil
  ¼ teaspoon salt
    Dash of black pepper

For a delicious change, pair Orange-Glazed Acorn Squash **with ham or turkey.**

Orange-Glazed Acorn Squash

1. Preheat oven to 400°.
2. Cut ends off squash, and discard. Cut squash crosswise into 12 (¾-inch-thick) slices, discarding seeds and stringy pulp. Arrange squash slices in a single layer on a large baking sheet coated with cooking spray. Bake squash at 400° for 15 minutes.
3. Combine orange marmalade and remaining 6 ingredients. Brush half of marmalade mixture over squash slices. Bake at 400° for 20 minutes. Brush with remaining marmalade mixture; bake an additional 15 minutes. Yield: 4 servings (serving size: 3 squash slices).

CALORIES 163 (6% from fat); FAT 1g (sat 0.2g, mono 0.2g, poly 0.4g); PROTEIN 2.1g; CARB 41.2g; FIBER 2.9g; CHOL 0mg; IRON 1.6mg; SODIUM 247mg; CALC 90mg

CRANBERRY APPLE-FILLED ACORN SQUASH

PREP:12 MINUTES
COOK:45 MINUTES

3 acorn squash (about 1 pound each)
1 tablespoon stick margarine or butter
1½ cups diced Granny Smith apple
1 (16-ounce) can whole-berry cranberry sauce

1. Preheat oven to 400°.
2. Place squash in a 13 x 9-inch baking dish. Bake at 400° for 45 minutes or until tender.
3. Melt margarine in a medium nonstick skillet over medium heat. Add apple; sauté 5 minutes. Stir in cranberry sauce; cook 2 minutes or until apple is tender, stirring occasionally.
4. Cut squash in half lengthwise; discard seeds and membrane. Spoon ⅓-cup fruit filling into each squash half. Yield: 6 servings.

Microwave Directions: Pierce squash with a fork, and arrange on paper towels in microwave oven. Microwave at HIGH 9 to 10 minutes or until tender. Prepare fruit filling as directed above.

CALORIES 217 (9% from fat); FAT 2.3g (sat 0.4g, mono 0.9g, poly 0.8g); PROTEIN 1.5g; CARB 51.8g; FIBER 3.1g; CHOL 0mg; IRON 1.2mg; SODIUM 49mg; CALC 59mg

BUTTERNUT SQUASH FLANS

PREP:25 MINUTES
COOK:30 MINUTES

3 cups cubed peeled butternut squash
½ cup evaporated fat-free milk
½ teaspoon salt
⅛ teaspoon ground nutmeg
⅛ teaspoon black pepper
2 large eggs
1 large egg white
Cooking spray
Ground nutmeg (optional)

1. Preheat oven to 325°.
2. Place squash in a medium saucepan; cover with water, and bring to a boil. Cover, reduce heat, and simmer 15 minutes or until tender. Drain well.
3. Combine squash and next 6 ingredients in a blender; process until smooth. Divide squash mixture evenly among 6 (6-ounce) custard cups coated with cooking spray. Place cups in a 13 x 9-inch baking pan; add hot water to pan to a depth of 1 inch. Bake at 325° for 30 minutes or until a knife inserted in center comes out clean. Remove cups from water; let stand 5 minutes.
4. Loosen edges of custards with a knife or rubber spatula. Invert custards onto individual plates. Sprinkle with nutmeg, if desired. Yield: 6 servings.

CALORIES 84 (21% from fat); FAT 2g (sat 0.6g, mono 0.7g, poly 0.3g); PROTEIN 5.1g; CARB 12.4g; FIBER 1.1g; CHOL 72mg; IRON 0.8mg; SODIUM 253mg; CALC 110mg

KNOW YOUR SQUASH

Acorn: This standard supermarket squash has orange flesh and is mild and creamy. It's small to medium in size and has ribbed forest-green, marigold, or ivory skin.

Butternut: The flesh of this variety is sweet, fruity, and orange. Look for large ones with evenly tan skin, a small ball end, and a thick neck.

Spaghetti: Yellow, cream, or tan in color, this oblong-shaped medium-sized squash contains mild, crisp, slightly sweet spaghetti-shaped strands and often has more flavor than other squash. Bake, steam, or microwave it.

SIMPLE BAKED SPAGHETTI SQUASH

PREP: 5 MINUTES   COOK: 45 MINUTES

1   (3-pound) spaghetti squash

1. Preheat oven to 350°.
2. Cut squash in half lengthwise, discarding seeds. Place squash halves, cut sides down, in a 13 x 9-inch baking dish; add water to dish to a depth of ½ inch. Bake at 350° for 45 minutes or until squash is tender when pierced with a fork.
3. Remove squash from dish, and cool. Scrape inside of squash with a fork to remove spaghettilike strands. Yield: 5 cups (serving size: 1 cup).

CALORIES 45 (8% from fat); FAT 0.4g (sat 0.1g, mono 0g, poly 0.2g); PROTEIN 1g; CARB 10g; FIBER 2g; CHOL 0mg; IRON 0.5mg; SODIUM 28mg; CALC 33mg

SPAGHETTI SQUASH-AND-VEGETABLE GRATIN

PREP: 20 MINUTES   COOK: 15 MINUTES

1   spaghetti squash (about 2 pounds)
1   teaspoon olive oil
3   cups sliced mushrooms
3   cups diced zucchini
2   garlic cloves, minced
¾   cup (3 ounces) preshredded part-skim mozzarella cheese, divided
¼   cup chopped fresh parsley
½   teaspoon salt
¼   teaspoon black pepper
1   (14.5-ounce) can no-salt-added stewed tomatoes, undrained and chopped
Cooking spray
½   cup fresh breadcrumbs

1. Pierce squash 6 to 8 times with a fork. Place squash on a layer of paper towels in microwave oven. Microwave, uncovered, at HIGH 15 to 18 minutes or until squash is soft to the touch, turning squash over every 5 minutes. Let stand 5 minutes. Cut squash in half lengthwise, and remove seeds. Scrape inside of squash with a fork to remove spaghettilike strands.
2. Preheat oven to 450°.
3. Heat oil in a large nonstick skillet over medium-high heat. Add mushrooms, and sauté 4 minutes. Add zucchini and garlic; sauté 6 minutes or until tender. Remove from heat. Add ¼ cup cheese, parsley, salt, pepper, and chopped tomato.
4. Combine ¼ cup cheese and squash. Arrange squash mixture in a large gratin dish or shallow 1½-quart baking dish coated with cooking spray. Spoon tomato mixture over squash. Combine ¼ cup cheese and breadcrumbs; sprinkle over tomato mixture. Bake at 450° for 15 minutes or until bubbly. Yield: 6 servings (serving size: about 1 cup).

CALORIES 135 (26% from fat); FAT 3.9g (sat 1.7g, mono 1.3g, poly 0.5g); PROTEIN 7.5g; CARB 21.2g; FIBER 3.2g; CHOL 8mg; IRON 2.1mg; SODIUM 325mg; CALC 157mg

Spaghetti Squash

1. Cut squash in half lengthwise with a heavy knife, and scrape out seeds.

2. Place cut sides down in baking dish; add water to depth of ½ inch before cooking.

3. Bake 45 minutes or until squash is tender when pierced with a fork.

4. Scrape out strands of squash using a fork.

GRILLED MARINATED VEGETABLES

PREP: 20 MINUTES
MARINATE: 30 MINUTES
COOK: 16 MINUTES

¾ pound small red potatoes, cut
    into ½-inch pieces
1 cup (½-inch-thick) sliced
    yellow squash
1 cup (½-inch-thick) sliced
    zucchini
1 small onion, cut into 8 wedges
1 large red bell pepper, cut into
    ½-inch-wide strips
⅓ cup rice vinegar
1 tablespoon fresh lemon juice
1 tablespoon Dijon mustard
1½ teaspoons dark sesame oil
⅛ teaspoon salt
⅛ teaspoon black pepper
2 garlic cloves, minced
Cooking spray

1. Place potato in a medium saucepan; cover with water, and bring to a boil. Reduce heat, and simmer, uncovered, 10 to 12 minutes or until tender; drain.
2. Combine potato, squash, and next 10 ingredients in a large zip-top plastic bag. Seal bag, and marinate 30 minutes at room temperature, turning bag occasionally.
3. Prepare grill.
4. Remove vegetables from bag, reserving marinade. Place vegetables in a wire grilling basket coated with cooking spray. Place grilling basket on grill rack, and grill 8 minutes on each side or until tender. Pour reserved marinade over grilled vegetables. Yield: 5 servings (serving size: 1 cup).

CALORIES 99 (19% from fat); FAT 2.1g (sat 0.3g, mono 0.6g, poly 0.7g); PROTEIN 2.8g; CARB 18.1g; FIBER 2.9g; CHOL 0mg; IRON 1.7mg; SODIUM 158mg; CALC 27mg

TOMATOES WITH CHILI-CILANTRO VINAIGRETTE

PREP: 9 MINUTES   MARINATE: 1 HOUR

⅓ cup water
3 tablespoons cider vinegar
1 tablespoon chopped red onion
1½ teaspoons minced fresh cilantro
⅛ teaspoon sugar
⅛ teaspoon dry mustard
⅛ teaspoon paprika
⅛ teaspoon salt
⅛ teaspoon chili powder
⅛ teaspoon garlic powder
2 tomatoes, cut into ¼-inch-thick
    slices (about ¾ pound)

1. Combine first 10 ingredients in a small saucepan. Bring to a boil; remove from heat.
2. Place tomato slices in a single layer in a shallow dish; add vinegar mixture. Cover and marinate in refrigerator 1 hour. Serve with a slotted spoon. Yield: 4 servings.

CALORIES 19 (14% from fat); FAT 0.3g (sat 0g, mono 0g, poly 0.1g); PROTEIN 0.7g; CARB 4.6g; FIBER 0.9g; CHOL 0mg; IRON 0.5mg; SODIUM 81mg; CALC 6mg

QUICK STEWED TOMATOES AND OKRA

PREP: 15 MINUTES
COOK: 6 MINUTES

4 cups water
3 cups frozen cut okra
1 teaspoon vegetable oil
½ cup chopped green bell pepper
¼ cup chopped onion
½ teaspoon salt
¼ teaspoon black pepper
1 (14.5-ounce) can no-salt-added
    diced tomatoes, undrained

1. Combine water and okra in a medium saucepan; bring to a boil. Reduce heat, and simmer, uncovered, 3 minutes. Drain and set aside.
2. Heat oil in pan over medium heat. Add bell pepper and onion; sauté 3 minutes or until tender. Add okra, salt, black pepper, and tomatoes; cook until thoroughly heated. Yield: 7 servings (serving size: ½ cup).

CALORIES 38 (19% from fat); FAT 0.8g (sat 0.2g, mono 0.2g, poly 0.4g); PROTEIN 1.5g; CARB 7.2g; FIBER 1.1g; CHOL 0mg; IRON 0.7mg; SODIUM 177mg; CALC 64mg

Tomatoes With
Chili-Cilantro Vinaigrette

FRIED TOMATOES WITH LIMA-CORN RELISH

PREP: 23 MINUTES

CHILL: 1 HOUR

COOK: 8 MINUTES

(pictured on page 485)

1 cup frozen baby lima beans, cooked
1 cup frozen whole-kernel corn, thawed
½ cup diced red bell pepper
3 tablespoons thinly sliced fresh basil
2 tablespoons hot pepper sauce
1 tablespoon white wine vinegar
1 teaspoon olive oil
2 garlic cloves, crushed
3 tablespoons yellow cornmeal
2 tablespoons grated Parmesan cheese
⅛ teaspoon salt
⅛ teaspoon black pepper
8 (¼-inch-thick) slices green tomato
2 teaspoons olive oil
12 (¼-inch-thick) slices red tomato
Basil sprigs (optional)

1. Combine first 8 ingredients in a bowl; cover and chill 1 hour.
2. Combine cornmeal and cheese in a small zip-top plastic bag. Sprinkle salt and pepper over green tomato slices; place slices, 1 at a time, in cornmeal mixture. Seal bag, and shake to coat.
3. Heat 2 teaspoons oil in a large nonstick skillet over medium-high heat. Add green tomato slices, and cook 3 minutes on each side or until slices are browned.
4. Arrange lima bean mixture, fried green tomato slices, and red tomato slices on a serving platter. Garnish with basil sprigs, if desired. Serve immediately. Yield: 4 servings (serving size: ½ cup

bean mixture, 2 fried green tomato slices, and 3 red tomato slices).

CALORIES 191 (25% from fat); FAT 5.4g (sat 1.1g, mono 2.9g, poly 0.8g); PROTEIN 7.8g; CARB 31.7g; FIBER 4.7g; CHOL 2mg; IRON 2.7mg; SODIUM 256mg; CALC 71mg

STIR-FRIED ASIAN VEGETABLES

PREP: 9 MINUTES

COOK: 6 MINUTES

¾ cup fat-free, less-sodium chicken broth
1 tablespoon cornstarch
3 tablespoons low-sodium soy sauce
½ teaspoon sugar
¼ teaspoon black pepper
1 tablespoon vegetable oil
1 cup diagonally sliced carrot
1 cup diagonally sliced celery
½ cup chopped onion
1½ cups snow peas, trimmed
1 (15-ounce) can whole baby corn, drained
1 (15-ounce) can whole straw mushrooms, drained

1. Combine first 5 ingredients in a small bowl; stir well with a whisk.
2. Heat oil in a wok or large nonstick skillet over high heat. Add carrot, celery, and onion; stir-fry 2 minutes. Add snow peas, corn, and mushrooms; stir-fry 2 minutes. Add broth mixture, and stir-fry 1 minute or until thick and bubbly. Yield: 6 servings (serving size: 1 cup).

CALORIES 75 (29% from fat); FAT 2.4g (sat 0.4g, mono 0.7g, poly 1.2g); PROTEIN 2.8g; CARB 10.3g; FIBER 3.3g; CHOL 0mg; IRON 2.4mg; SODIUM 508mg; CALC 36mg

RUTABAGAS

Rutabagas are a member of the cabbage family. Although sometimes mistaken for turnips, rutabagas are larger, more rounded, denser, and sweeter.

Harvested in autumn and stored during winter, these root vegetables (plants whose underground parts are edible) are typically more robust than spring and summer vegetables. Look for smooth, firm rutabagas that feel heavy for their size; lightweight ones may be woody.

HONEY-BAKED ROOT VEGETABLES

PREP: 15 MINUTES

COOK: 1 HOUR

2 tablespoons honey
1 tablespoon stick margarine or butter, melted
¼ teaspoon salt
1 pound carrots, cut into 4 x ½-inch sticks
1 small rutabaga (about 1 pound), cut into 4 x ½-inch sticks
Cooking spray

1. Preheat oven to 375°.
2. Combine honey, margarine, and salt in a large bowl. Add carrot and rutabaga; toss to coat.
3. Arrange vegetables in a single layer in a jelly-roll pan coated with cooking spray. Bake at 375° for 1 hour or until vegetables are tender, stirring occasionally. Yield: 7 servings (serving size: ½ cup).

CALORIES 76 (22% from fat); FAT 1.9g (sat 0.4g, mono 0.7g, poly 0.6g); PROTEIN 1.2g; CARB 14.8g; FIBER 2.2g; CHOL 0mg; IRON 0.6mg; SODIUM 132mg; CALC 41mg

glossary

We've defined many of the terms and ingredients used throughout the book. You'll find additional terms listed in our Index (beginning on page 512).

Aïoli *(ay-OH-lee)* A garlic-flavored mayonnaise. Usually accompanies fish, meats, and vegetables.

Apple butter A thick preserve made by slowly cooking apples, sugar, spices, and juice or cider together. Used as a spread for breads.

Ancho chile peppers Dried, wrinkled chile peppers that are brick red or mahogany in color. (Fresh ancho peppers are referred to as poblanos.) About 3 inches wide at the stem and 4 inches in length. Have a slightly hot, sweet flavor. Found in the produce section of supermarkets. For most recipes, soak for 30 minutes in hot water to plump before using. Store dried in airtight containers in freezer for up to one year.

Aniseeds Tiny oval seeds that give a sweet licorice flavor to cookies and other desserts as well as some savory dishes. Can be found with spices in grocery stores. Stay pungent for up to one year if stored in a cool, dark, dry place.

Arborio rice A squat, oval-shaped rice with a delightful taste. The classic rice for risotto. Found with other kinds of rice in large supermarkets. May be labeled Italian risotto.

Baking powder A leavening agent comprised of baking soda, cream of tartar, and cornstarch, which when combined with a liquid releases carbon dioxide gas bubbles that cause a dough or batter to rise.

Baking soda A leavening agent, which when combined with an acid such as buttermilk, yogurt, or molasses produces carbon dioxide gas bubbles that cause a dough or batter to rise.

Balsamic vinegar Made from white Trebbiano grapes. Aromatic and ages to a dark brown. Full-bodied, slightly sweet flavor with a hint of tartness. Use it in small amounts in vinaigrettes and sauces. Available in large supermarkets and gourmet-food markets. Store in a cool, dark place for up to six months.

Barbecue smoke seasoning A bottled liquid used during cooking to give food a hickory-smoked flavor. May be labeled "liquid smoke" or "liquid barbecue smoke." Found with condiments in grocery stores.

Basmati rice *(bas-MAH-tee)* A highly aromatic, long-grain rice with the aroma of popcorn when cooking. Has a nutty flavor and firm texture. Less aromatic varieties are grown in the United States, primarily in the Southwest and California. Available in specialty food stores and large supermarkets.

Bean threads or cellophane noodles Made from the starch of green mung beans. Have a different texture from traditional noodles. May be labeled as "transparent" or "shining noodles," "pea-stick noodles," or "mung bean sticks." Only require a quick soak to be rehydrated. Commonly used in spring rolls.

Bok choy A cabbage that has long, pearly-white ribs with dark-green leaves which don't form a head. Also known as "pak choy" or "pak choi." Use in salads and stir-fried dishes. Buy at Chinese markets and large supermarkets. Look for firm ribs and crisp leaves. Store in a plastic bag in refrigerator for up to three days.

Bulgur Wheat kernels that are steamed, dried, and crushed. Has a tender, chewy texture, and works best in salads and pilafs. Main ingredient in tabbouleh.

Capers The dark-green buds, which range from the petite (the nonpareil variety) to the size of a large pearl, are dried in the sun, and then packed in a vinegar brine. Add a unique punch to foods. Cooking intensifies their pungent flavor and saltiness. Used in Italian and Mediterranean cuisines. Can be found with pickles, olives, and other condiments in supermarkets. Choose bottles that have clear liquid and little or no sediment. Refrigerate after opening.

Carambola A deeply ridged, yellow fruit that grows in tropical climates. Sometimes referred to as star fruit because when it's cut in half crosswise, it has a five point star shape. Carambolas don't have to be peeled and can be eaten raw. Flavor ranges from sweet to tart. Vibrant yellow when ripe. Available in large supermarkets with the exotic fruits in the produce section.

Chili sauce A blend of tomatoes, chiles or chili powder, onions, green peppers, vinegar, sugar, and spices that is used as a condiment. Similar in appearance to ketchup.

Cilantro An herb with delicate, lacy green leaves. Resembles parsley in appearance but has a pungent flavor. Sometimes called Chinese parsley. (Marketed as coriander when dried.) Easily confused with flat-leaf parsley in appearance so read the label carefully. Used in Latin American and Asian foods. Choose a bunch with unwilted leaves and a good medium-green color. Found year-round in large supermarkets. (Can be grown from seeds.) Store in refrigerator for several days by putting cut ends in a jar of water and loosely covering leaves with a plastic bag. Change the water every two days.

Coriander Dried seeds and a dry spice. Often used in holiday breads and cookies. Flavor similar to a blend of lemon, sage, and caraway.

Coulis *(koo-LEE)* A thick puree or sauce. Often made from tomatoes or bell peppers.

Couscous *(KOOS-koos)* Wheat that has been moistened with water, lightly coated with flour, and then rolled into tiny, beadlike pellets. Prepared by steaming or combining with boiling liquid and letting it stand until all of the liquid is absorbed. Has its origins in the Middle East and North Africa, where it is typically served with stews. Available in large supermarkets next to the rice.

Cumin seeds Aromatic seeds native to the

Mediterranean area. Used whole or ground in many Middle Eastern dishes.

Deglazing The process of loosening and dissolving solidified particles of food left on the surface of a skillet or pan after browning meat. Use a spatula to gently loosen the particles, and stir in a liquid (such as wine or broth). Heat, stirring to dissolve particles.

Dice To cut food into small ⅛- to ¼-inch cubes.

Dredge To coat food lightly with flour, cornmeal, or breadcrumbs before cooking.

Fennel Has feathery leaves that resemble fresh dill and a fist-sized edible white bulb that resembles the bottom of a celery stalk. Contributes a licorice aroma and taste. Available from fall through spring in produce markets and the produce section of large supermarkets. Look for smooth white bulbs and fresh, unwilted leaves. Refrigerate in a plastic bag for up to four days.

Fennel seeds Small, oval, brown seeds. Give foods a mild licorice flavor. Found with dried spices and herbs in grocery stores. Store in a cool, dark, dry place for up to one year.

Feta cheese Cheese made from goat's or sheep's milk that is soft, dry, and crumbly with a tangy taste. Available in jars (packed in brine) and in shrink-wrap packages in the dairy case in supermarkets and ethnic grocery stores.

Fine rice vermicelli Wide, flat Asian noodles. Similar in shape to fettuccine. Can be found labeled as "rice-stick noodles."

Fish sauce A sauce made from water, anchovies, and salt. Very potent—use sparingly. Common in Asian foods.

Fold To incorporate a light mixture, such as beaten egg whites, into a heavier mixture, such as a custard, using a gentle over-and-under motion.

Hoisin sauce A thick, dark-brown Chinese sauce made from soybeans and chiles. Sugar and salt are added to give the sauce a sweet but biting taste. Available in jars and cans. Can be found in the ethnic-food section of supermarkets and in Asian grocery stores.

Hungarian paprika Comes in sweet or hot. Is considered to be the best paprika, but is interchangeable with regular paprika. Found in the spice section of large supermarkets.

Jícama (HEE-ka-ma) Large, light-brown tuberous root of a tropical plant. Has white, juicy, crunchy flesh with a sweet, nutty flavor. Can be eaten either raw or cooked. Look for it in the produce section of large supermarkets and in Mexican markets; choose roots that have thin skin (thick skin means the jícama is old). Will keep for up to five days in the refrigerator.

Kalamata olives Deep-purple olives imported from Greece. Usually packed in oil in bottles. Found with other olives in supermarkets and specialty-food stores. Will keep for several weeks in the refrigerator. See page 394 for additional information on olive varieties.

Lemon grass An herb with long, reedlike leaves. Use only the bottom 4 inches of the stem. Can be found fresh in the produce section of supermarkets and Asian markets. One teaspoon freshly grated lemon rind can be substituted for 1 teaspoon lemon grass.

Masa harina A corn flour of finer texture than cornmeal. Developed by treating hominy (corn product) with lime again. The wet hominy is freshly ground to make a meal called masa. When masa is dried, it is referred to as masa harina. Can be found along with other flour and cornmeal products in large grocery stores and Mexican-American markets. Store in the refrigerator in air-tight containers for up to six months.

Miso A fermented soybean paste that is the basis of the earthy, salty depth of flavor found in many Japanese dishes. In the U.S., you're most likely to find pungent dark miso, which enhances sturdy broths, and sweet, mild white miso, good for delicate sauces and dressings. Use about 1 tablespoon miso per cup of water, and don't subject it to extremely high temperatures. Stir it in at the end of cooking.

Oyster sauce A sauce made from oysters, brine, and soy sauce. Used to flavor Asian

foods. Bottled and canned versions can be found in Asian grocery stores. Refrigerate after opening; it will keep indefinitely.

Pearl barley Barley with the bran removed. Used in soups and stews. Cooks in 20 to 30 minutes.

Pine nuts (pignolias) Small, oblong, cream-colored nuts gathered from pine trees. Found in the nut section of large supermarkets and in health-food stores. Turn rancid easily, so store in the freezer for up to nine months.

Polenta A cornmeal mush with Italian origins. Often cooked until firm and cut into squares or other shapes, and then baked, broiled, or fried until golden brown and crisp on the outside, soft and creamy on the inside. Often contains cheese and may be topped with a sauce or flavored with herbs.

Quinoa (KEEN-wah) Small, round, and cream-colored seeds (although some varieties are black). Becomes soft when cooked, almost resembling caviar in texture. Contains more protein than any other grain.

Radicchio A slightly bitter Italian chicory. Has firm, deep-red leaves with white ribs. The Verona variety is about the size and shape of Bibb lettuce; the Treviso variety has a long, narrow, tapered head. Can be found in the produce section of large supermarkets and specialty-food stores. Choose a fresh, crisp head with no wilted or bruised leaves. Refrigerate radicchio in a plastic bag for up to four days.

Rice paper An edible, translucent paper similar to phyllo dough in texture. Used to wrap foods to be eaten as is or can be baked. Can be found labeled as "dried pastry flake."

Rice vinegar Vinegar made from either fermented rice or rice wine. Mainly used in Asian cooking. Can be found with other vinegars or in the Asian-food section of supermarkets.

Scaloppine Very thin cuts of meat, most often veal. Usually dredged in flour before cooking.

Turbinado sugar A honey brown sugar with large crystals. Often sprinkled on sweet breads and desserts. Gives a subtle molasses flavor. Found with other sugar products in large supermarkets and gourmet-food stores. Will keep indefinitely in an airtight container. If not available, substitute raw or granulated sugar.

Udon noodles Thick Japanese noodles that are similar to spaghetti. Available as round or square. Typically made from either wheat or corn flour.

Watercress A green that's a member of the mustard family. Flat, dark-green leaves that are peppery and pungent. Sold in bunches in the produce section. Used in salads and sandwiches or stirred into soups or pasta dishes before serving.

Wheat berries Whole, unprocessed wheat kernels used in pilafs and casseroles. Makes an excellent crouton alternative for salad toppings. High in protein and fiber. Must be soaked eight hours; then cooked one hour.

metric equivalents
The recipes that appear in this cookbook use the standard United States method for measuring liquid and dry or solid ingredients (teaspoons, tablespoons, and cups). The information on this chart is provided to help cooks outside the U.S. successfully use these recipes. All equivalents are approximate.

Metric Equivalents for Different Types of Ingredients

A standard cup measure of a dry or solid ingredient will vary in weight depending on the type of ingredient. A standard cup of liquid is the same volume for any type of liquid. Use the following chart when converting standard cup measures to grams (weight) or milliliters (volume).

Standard Cup	Fine Powder (ex. flour)	Grain (ex. rice)	Granular (ex. sugar)	Liquid Solids (ex. butter)	Liquid (ex. milk)
1	140 g	150 g	190 g	200 g	240 ml
¾	105 g	113 g	143 g	150 g	180 ml
⅔	93 g	100 g	125 g	133 g	160 ml
½	70 g	75 g	95 g	100 g	120 ml
⅓	47 g	50 g	63 g	67 g	80 ml
¼	35 g	38 g	48 g	50 g	60 ml
⅛	18 g	19 g	24 g	25 g	30 ml

Useful Equivalents For Liquid Ingredients By Volume

¼ tsp					=	1 ml
½ tsp					=	2 ml
1 tsp					=	5 ml
3 tsp	=	1 tbls		½ fl oz	=	15 ml
		2 tbls	= ⅛ cup	1 fl oz	=	30 ml
		4 tbls	= ¼ cup	2 fl oz	=	60 ml
		5⅓ tbls	= ⅓ cup	3 fl oz	=	80 ml
		8 tbls	= ½ cup	4 fl oz	=	120 ml
		10⅔ tbls	= ⅔ cup	5 fl oz	=	160 ml
		12 tbls	= ¾ cup	6 fl oz	=	180 ml
		16 tbls	= 1 cup	8 fl oz	=	240 ml
		1 pt	= 2 cups	16 fl oz	=	480 ml
		1 qt	= 4 cups	32 fl oz	=	960 ml
				33 fl oz	=	1000 ml = 1 l

Useful Equivalents For Dry Ingredients By Weight

(To convert ounces to grams, multiply the number of ounces by 30.)

1 oz	=	¹⁄₁₆ lb	=	30 g
4 oz	=	¼ lb	=	120 g
8 oz	=	½ lb	=	240 g
12 oz	=	¾ lb	=	360 g
16 oz	=	1 lb	=	480 g

Useful Equivalents For Length

(To convert inches to centimeters, multiply the number of inches by 2.5.)

1 in					=	2.5 cm		
6 in	=	½ ft			=	15 cm		
12 in	=	1 ft			=	30 cm		
36 in	=	3 ft	=	1 yd	=	90 cm		
40 in					=	100 cm	=	1 m

Useful Equivalents For Cooking/Oven Temperatures

	Fahrenheit	Celsius	Gas Mark
Freeze Water	32° F	0° C	
Room Temperature	68° F	20° C	
Boil Water	212° F	100° C	
Bake	325° F	160° C	3
	350° F	180° C	4
	375° F	190° C	5
	400° F	200° C	6
	425° F	220° C	7
	450° F	230° C	8
Broil			Grill

substitution list
If you don't find a particular substitution in this chart, look in our Index (beginning on page 512). If we've written about an ingredient within a recipe chapter, you'll find it listed in the index.

Baking Products

Baking powder, 1 teaspoon
- ½ teaspoon cream of tartar plus ¼ teaspoon baking soda

Chocolate
semisweet, 1 ounce
- 1 ounce unsweetened chocolate plus 1 tablespoon sugar

unsweetened, 1 ounce or square
- 3 tablespoons cocoa plus 1 tablespoon fat

chips, semisweet, 1 ounce
- 1 ounce square semisweet chocolate

chips, semisweet, 6-ounce package, melted
- 2 ounces unsweetened chocolate, 2 tablespoons shortening plus ½ cup sugar

Cocoa, ¼ cup
- 1 ounce unsweetened chocolate (decrease fat in recipe by 1½ teaspoons)

Cornmeal
self-rising, 1 cup
- 1 cup plain yellow cornmeal, 1½ teaspoons baking powder plus ½ teaspoon salt

self-rising cornmeal mix
- Combine 1¼ cups yellow (or white) cornmeal, ¾ cup fat-free milk, 1 tablespoon all-purpose flour, 2 teaspoons baking powder, ½ teaspoon salt, and 1 egg, lightly beaten. Bake as directed.

Cornstarch, 1 tablespoon
- 2 tablespoons all-purpose flour or granular tapioca

Corn syrup, light, ½ cup
- ½ cup sugar plus 2 tablespoons water
- ½ cup honey

Flour
all-purpose, 1 cup sifted
- 1 cup plus 2 tablespoons sifted cake flour
- 1 cup minus 2 tablespoons all-purpose flour (unsifted)
- 1½ cups breadcrumbs
- ⅓ cup cornmeal or soybean flour plus ⅔ cup all-purpose flour
- ¾ cup whole wheat flour or bran flour plus ¼ cup all-purpose flour
- 1 cup rye or rice flour

- ¼ cup soybean flour plus ¾ cup all-purpose flour

Note: *Specialty flours added to yeast bread will result in a reduced volume and a heavier product.*

all-purpose, 1 tablespoon
- 1½ teaspoons cornstarch, potato starch, or rice starch
- 1 tablespoon rice flour or corn flour
- 1½ tablespoons whole wheat flour

cake, 1 cup sifted
- 1 cup minus 2 tablespoons all-purpose flour

self-rising, 1 cup
- 1 cup all-purpose flour, 1 teaspoon baking powder plus ½ teaspoon salt

Sugar
brown, 1 cup packed
- 1 cup granulated white sugar

granulated white, 1 cup
- 1 cup corn syrup (decrease liquid called for in recipe by ¼ cup)
- 1 cup firmly packed brown sugar
- 1 cup honey (decrease liquid called for in recipe by ¼ cup)

powdered, 1 cup
- 1 cup sugar plus 1 tablespoon cornstarch (processed in food processor)

Dairy Products

Butter, ½ cup
- ½ cup margarine (1 stick; do not substitute whipped or low-fat margarine when baking)

Egg
1 large
- ¼ cup egg substitute

2 large
- 3 small eggs

1 egg white (2 tablespoons)
- 2 tablespoons egg substitute
- 2 teaspoons sifted, dry egg white powder plus 2 tablespoons warm water

1 egg yolk (1½ tablespoons)
- 2 tablespoons dry, sifted egg yolk powder plus 2 teaspoons water

Milk
buttermilk, low-fat or fat-free, 1 cup
- 1 tablespoon vinegar or lemon juice plus low-fat or fat-free milk to make 1 cup (let stand 10 minutes)

fat-free, 1 cup
- 4 to 5 tablespoons nonfat dry milk powder plus enough water to make 1 cup
- ½ cup evaporated fat-free milk plus ½ cup water

light coconut milk, 1 cup
- 1 cup low-fat milk plus ¼ teaspoon coconut extract

low-fat sweetened condensed, 1 cup
- Heat the following ingredients until sugar and butter dissolve: ⅓ cup evaporated fat-free milk, ¾ cup sugar, 2 tablespoons butter or margarine.
- Combine 1 cup plus 2 tablespoons nonfat dry milk powder to ½ cup warm water. Stir well. Add ¾ cup sugar; stir until smooth.

Sour Cream, low-fat, 1 cup
- 1 cup plain low-fat or nonfat yogurt plus 1 tablespoon cornstarch (in cooked products)

Fruit & Vegetable Products

Lemon, 1 medium
- 2 to 3 tablespoons juice plus 2 teaspoons grated rind

juice, 1 teaspoon
- ½ teaspoon vinegar

Mushrooms, 1 pound fresh
- 1 (8-ounce) can sliced mushrooms, drained
- 3 ounces dried mushrooms, rehydrated

Onions, chopped, 1 medium
- 1 tablespoon dried minced onion
- 1 teaspoon onion powder

Orange, 1 medium
- ½ cup juice plus 2 tablespoons grated rind

peel, dried, 1 tablespoon
- 1½ teaspoons orange extract

Papaya, 1 cup
- 1 cup mango

Pepper, red or green bell, chopped, 3 tablespoons
- 1 tablespoon dried sweet red or green pepper flakes

red bell, chopped, 3 tablespoons
- 2 tablespoons chopped pimento

Tomatoes, fresh, chopped, 2 cups
• 1 (14.5-ounce) can no-salt-added tomatoes (may need to drain)

Tomato juice, 1 cup
• ½ cup tomato sauce plus ½ cup water

Tomato sauce, 2 cups
• ¾ cup tomato paste plus 1 cup water

Miscellaneous Products

Broth, beef or chicken
canned broth, 1 cup
• 1 bouillon cube or 1 teaspoon bouillon granules dissolved in 1 cup boiling water
bouillon granules, 1 teaspoon
• 1 bouillon cube

Chili sauce, 1 cup
• 1 cup tomato sauce, ¼ cup brown sugar, 2 tablespoons vinegar, ¼ teaspoon cinnamon, dash of ground cloves plus dash of ground allspice

Fish sauce, 1 tablespoon
• 1 tablespoon Worcestershire sauce

Honey, 1 cup
• 1¼ cups sugar plus ¼ cup water

Ketchup, 1 cup
• 1 cup tomato sauce, ½ cup sugar plus 2 tablespoons vinegar (for cooking)

Ladyfingers
• slices of angel food cake or low-fat pound cake

Macaroni, uncooked, 2 cups (4 cups cooked)
• 8 ounces spaghetti, uncooked
• 4 cups fine egg noodles, uncooked

Mayonnaise
low-fat, 1 cup (for salads and dressings)
• ½ cup plain nonfat yogurt plus ½ cup fat-free mayonnaise
• 1 cup fat-free or reduced-fat sour cream

Rice, uncooked, 1 cup regular (3 cups cooked)
• 1 cup uncooked converted rice
• 1 cup uncooked brown rice or wild rice

Vinegar, balsamic, ½ cup
• ½ cup red wine vinegar (some flavor difference)

Seasoning Products

Allspice, ground, 1 teaspoon
• ½ teaspoon ground cinnamon plus ½ teaspoon ground cloves

Apple pie spice, 1 teaspoon
• ½ teaspoon ground cinnamon, ¼ teaspoon ground nutmeg plus ⅛ teaspoon ground cardamom

Bay leaf, 1 whole
• ¼ teaspoon crushed bay leaf

Chives, chopped, 1 tablespoon
• 1 tablespoon chopped green onion tops

Dillweed, fresh or dried, 3 heads
• 1 tablespoon dill seed

Garlic, 1 small clove
• ⅛ teaspoon garlic powder or minced dried garlic

Ginger
crystallized, 1 tablespoon
• ⅛ teaspoon ground ginger
fresh, grated, 1 tablespoon
• ⅛ teaspoon ground ginger
ground, ⅛ teaspoon
• 1 tablespoon grated fresh ginger

Herbs, fresh, chopped, 1 tablespoon
• 1 teaspoon dried herbs or ¼ teaspoon ground herbs

Horseradish, fresh, grated, 1 tablespoon
• 2 tablespoons prepared horseradish

Mustard, dried, 1 teaspoon
• 1 tablespoon prepared mustard

Parsley, dried, 1 teaspoon
• 1 tablespoon fresh parsley, chopped

Pimento, chopped, 2 tablespoons
• rehydrate 1 tablespoon dried sweet red bell pepper
• 2 to 3 tablespoons chopped fresh red bell pepper

Pumpkin pie spice, 1 teaspoon
• ½ teaspoon ground cinnamon, ¼ teaspoon ground ginger, ⅛ teaspoon ground allspice plus ⅛ teaspoon ground nutmeg

Spearmint or peppermint, dried, 1 tablespoon
• 3 tablespoons chopped fresh mint

Vanilla bean, 1 (1 inch)
• 1 teaspoon vanilla extract

Worcestershire sauce, 1 teaspoon
• 1 teaspoon bottled steak sauce

Alcohol Products

Amaretto, 2 tablespoons
• ¼ to ½ teaspoon almond extract*

Bourbon or sherry, 2 tablespoons
• 1 to 2 teaspoons vanilla extract*

Brandy, fruit-flavored liqueur, port wine, rum, or sweet sherry, ¼ cup or more
• Equal amount of unsweetened orange or apple juice plus 1 teaspoon vanilla extract or corresponding flavor

Brandy or rum, 2 tablespoons
• ½ to 1 teaspoon brandy or rum extract*

Grand Marnier or other orange-flavored liqueur, 2 tablespoons
• 2 tablespoons unsweetened orange juice concentrate or 2 tablespoons orange juice plus ½ teaspoon orange extract

Kahlúa, 2 tablespoons
• ½ to 1 teaspoon chocolate extract plus ½ to 1 teaspoon instant coffee dissolved in 2 tablespoons water

Marsala, ¼ cup
• ¼ cup white grape juice or ¼ cup dry white wine plus 1 teaspoon brandy

Wine
red, ¼ cup or more
• Equal measure of red grape juice or cranberry juice
white, ¼ cup or more
• Equal measure of white grape juice or apple juice

Add water, white grape juice, or apple juice to get the specified amount of liquid (when the liquid amount is crucial).

index